Program Consultants

Jeffrey D. Wilhelm, PhD

Douglas Fisher, PhD

Beverly Ann Chin, PhD

Jacqueline Jones Royster, DA

New York, New York   Columbus, Ohio   Chicago, Illinois   Woodland Hills, California

Acknowledgments

Grateful acknowledgment is given authors, publishers, photographers, museums, and agents for permission to reprint the following copyrighted material. Every effort has been made to determine copyright owners. In case of any omissions, the Publisher will be pleased to make suitable acknowledgments in future editions.

Acknowledgments continued on page R102.

 **Glencoe**

The **McGraw·Hill** Companies

Copyright © 2009 by the McGraw-Hill Companies, Inc. All rights reserved. Except as permitted under the United States Copyright Act, no part of this publication may be reproduced or distributed in any form or by any means, or stored in a database or retrieval system, without prior permission of the publisher.

TIME © Time, Inc. TIME and the red border design are trademarks of Time, Inc. used under license.

Send all inquiries to:
Glencoe/McGraw-Hill
8787 Orion Place
Columbus, OH 43240-4027

ISBN-13: (student edition) 978-0-07-845605-3
ISBN-10: (student edition) 0-07-845605-3
ISBN-13: (teacher edition) 978-0-07-845497-4
ISBN-10: (teacher edition) 0-07-845497-2

Printed in the United States of America.

2 3 4 5 6 7 8 9 10 027/055 13 12 11 10 09 08

Consultants

Senior Program Consultants

Jeffrey D. Wilhelm, PhD, a former middle and secondary school English and reading teacher, is currently Professor of Education at Boise State University. He is the author or coauthor of numerous articles and several books on the teaching of reading and literacy, including award-winning titles such as *You Gotta BE the Book* and *Reading Don't Fix No Chevys*. He also works with local schools as part of the Adolescent Literacy Project and recently helped establish the National Writing Project site at Boise State University.

Douglas Fisher, PhD, is Professor of Language and Literacy Education and Director of Professional Development at San Diego State University, where he teaches English language development and literacy. He also serves as Director of City Heights Educational Pilot, which won the Christa McAuliffe Award from the American Association of State Colleges and Universities. He has published numerous articles on reading and literacy, differentiated instruction, and curriculum design. He is coauthor of the book *Improving Adolescent Literacies: Strategies That Work* and coeditor of the book *Inclusive Urban Schools*.

Program Consultants

Beverly Ann Chin, PhD, is Professor of English, Director of the English Teaching Program, former Director of the Montana Writing Project, and former Director of Composition at the University of Montana in Missoula. She currently serves as a Member at Large of the Conference of English Leadership. Dr. Chin is a nationally recognized leader in English language arts standards, curriculum, and assessment. Formerly a high school teacher and an adult education reading teacher, Dr. Chin has taught in English language arts education at several universities and has received awards for her teaching and service.

Jacqueline Jones Royster, DA, is Professor of English and Senior Vice Provost and Executive Dean of the Colleges of Arts and Sciences at The Ohio State University. She is currently on the Writing Advisory Committee of the National Commission on Writing and serves as chair for both the Columbus Literacy Council and the Ohioana Library Association. In addition to the teaching of writing, Dr. Royster's professional interests include the rhetorical history of African American women and the social and cultural implications of literate practices. She has contributed to and helped to edit numerous books, anthologies, and journals.

Advisory Board

Special Consultants

Donald R. Bear, PhD.
Professor, Department of Curriculum and Instruction Director, E. L. Cord Foundation Center for Learning and Literacy at the University of Nevada, Reno. Author of *Words Their Way* and *Words Their Way with English Learners*.

The Writers' Express®
Immediate Impact. Lasting Transformation.   wex.org

Jana Echevarria, PhD.
Professor, Educational Psychology, California State University, Long Beach. Author of *Making Content Comprehensible for English Learners: the SIOP Model*.

FOLDABLES® Dinah Zike, MEd, was a classroom teacher and a consultant for many years before she began to develop Foldables®—a variety of easily created graphic organizers. Zike has written and developed more than 150 supplemental books and materials used in classrooms worldwide. Her *Big Book of Books and Activities* won the Teachers' Choice Award.

Glencoe National Reading and Language Arts Advisory Council

Mary A. Avalos, PhD
Assistant Department Chair, Department of Teaching and Learning
Research Assistant Professor, Department of Teaching and Learning
University of Miami
Coral Gables, Florida

Wanda J. Blanchett, PhD
Associate Dean for Academic Affairs and Associate Professor of Exceptional Education
School of Education
University of Wisconsin–Milwaukee
Milwaukee, Wisconsin

William G. Brozo, PhD
Professor of Literacy
Graduate School of Education
College of Education and Human Development
George Mason University
Fairfax, Virginia

Nancy Drew, EdD
LaPointe Educational Consultants
Corpus Christi, Texas

Susan Florio-Ruane, EdD
Professor
College of Education
Michigan State University
East Lansing, Michigan

Sharon Fontenot O'Neal, PhD
Associate Professor
Texas State University
San Marcos, Texas

Nancy Frey, PhD
Associate Professor of Literacy in Teacher Education
School of Teacher Education
San Diego State University
San Diego, California

Victoria Ridgeway Gillis, PhD
Associate Professor
Reading Education
Clemson University
Clemson, South Carolina

Kimberly Lawless, PhD
Associate Professor
Curriculum, Instruction and Evaluation
College of Education
University of Illinois at Chicago
Chicago, Illinois

William Ray, MA
Lincoln-Sudbury Regional High School
Sudbury, Massachusetts

Janet Saito-Furukawa, MEd
English Language Arts Specialist
District 4
Los Angeles, California

Bonnie Valdes, MEd
Independent Reading Consultant
CRISS Master Trainer
Largo, Florida

Teacher Reviewers

The following teachers contributed to the review of *Glencoe World Literature*.

Bridget M. Agnew
St. Michael School
Chicago, Illinois

Monica Anzaldua Araiza
Dr. Juliet V. Garcia Middle School
Brownsville, Texas

Katherine R. Baer
Howard County Public Schools
Ellicott City, Maryland

Tanya Baxter
Roald Amundsen High School
Chicago, Illinois

Danielle R. Brain
Thomas R. Proctor Senior High
    School
Utica, New York

Yolanda Conder
Owasso Mid-High School
Owasso, Oklahoma

Gwenn de Mauriac
The Wiscasset Schools
Wiscasset, Maine

Courtney Doan
Bloomington High School
Bloomington, Illinois

Susan M. Griffin
Edison Preparatory School
Tulsa, Oklahoma

Cindi Davis Harris
Helix Charter High School
La Mesa, California

Joseph F. Hutchinson
Toledo Public Schools
Toledo, Ohio

Ginger Jordan
Florien High School
Florien, Louisiana

Dianne Konkel
Cypress Lake Middle School
Fort Myers, Florida

Melanie A. LaFleur
Many High School
Many, Louisiana

Patricia Lee
Radnor Middle School
Wayne, Pennsylvania

Linda Copley Lemons
Cleveland High School
Cleveland, Tennessee

Heather S. Lewis
Waverly Middle School
Lansing, Michigan

Sandra C. Lott
Aiken Optional School
Alexandria, Louisiana

Connie M. Malacarne
O'Fallon Township High School
O'Fallon, Illinois

Lori Howton Means
Edward A. Fulton Junior High
    School
O'Fallon, Illinois

Claire C. Meitl
Howard County Public Schools
Ellicott City, Maryland

Patricia P. Mitcham
Mohawk High School
    (Retired)
New Castle, Pennsylvania

Lisa Morefield
South-Western Career Academy
Grove City, Ohio

Kevin M. Morrison
Hazelwood East High School
St. Louis, Missouri

Jenine M. Pokorak
School Without Walls Senior
    High School
Washington, DC

Susan Winslow Putnam
Butler High School
Matthews, North Carolina

Paul C. Putnoki
Torrington Middle School
Torrington, Connecticut

Jane Thompson Rae
Cab Calloway High School of
    the Arts
Wilmington, Delaware

Stephanie L. Robin
N. P. Moss Middle School
Lafayette, Louisiana

Ann C. Ryan
Lindenwold High School
Lindenwold, New Jersey

Pamela Schoen
Hopkins High School
Minnetonka, Minnesota

Megan Schumacher
Friends' Central School
Wynnewood, Pennsylvania

Fareeda J. Shabazz
Paul Revere Elementary School
Chicago, Illinois

Molly Steinlage
Brookpark Middle School
Grove City, Ohio

Barry Stevenson
Garnet Valley Middle School
Glen Mills, Pennsylvania

Paul Stevenson
Edison Preparatory School
Tulsa, Oklahoma

Kathy Thompson
Owasso Mid-High School
Owasso, Oklahoma

Book Overview

Evening Snow on the Asuka Mountain, from 'Eight Views of Environs of Edo', c.1838.
Ando or Utagawa Hiroshige. Woodblock colour print. Brooklyn Museum of Art, New York.

Paisaje (Landscape). Juan Cardenas (Columbian b. 1939). Oil on linen, 50 x 65 cm. Private collection.

Contents

> *"In a great effort he straightened up and was on his feet at one go—but the great bar of iron was twisted and had taken the form of a bow!"*
>
> —Sundiata

"As political prisoners they were
unlike the other prisoners in the
sense that they felt no guilt . . ."

—Bessie Head

UNIT TWO

ANCIENT GREECE AND ROME 1500 B.C.–A.D. 500

PART ONE

ANCIENT GREECE 1500 B.C.–1 B.C.

Epic Hero and Simile, Evaluate Credibility and Cultural Context

"With that he wrenched his bronze spear from the corpse, laid it aside and ripped the bloody armor off the back."

—Homer

Imagery, Paraphrase

PART TWO

ANCIENT ROME   800 B.C.–A.D. 500

"Devouring fire whipped by the winds/ goes churning into the rooftops, flames surging/ over them, scorching blasts raging up the sky."

—Virgil

UNIT THREE

Southwest and South Central Asia 3500 B.C.–Present

PART ONE

Southwest Asia 3500 B.C.–Present

Epic Hero, Visualize

MESOPOTAMIA: **Anonymous:**
from **Gilgamesh**

> *"Do not grieve for what is past;*
> *When a thing is done, vex not yourself about it."*
>
> —*Rumi*

Red Townscape, 1961. Francis Newton Souza. Oil on canvas. Private collection.

"Behind them the interior of the curtained wagon swelled with darkness and from the heart of that darkness shot out the nauseating stench which cut sharper than a sword . . ."

—Khalida Asghar

UNIT FOUR

East Asia and the Pacific
2000 B.C.–Present

PART ONE

East Asia 2000 B.C.–Present

*"In time's assembly line
Night presses against night."*
—Shu Ting

PART TWO

Southeast Asia and the Pacific
500 B.C.–Present

"Do you count me as a friend/ or am I the enemy in your eyes?"
—Nguyen Thi Vinh

Ham Rong Bridge,
1970. Vu Giang Huong.
Woodcut on rice paper,
12 x 16 7/8 in.
Collection of the Artist.

UNIT FIVE

EUROPE A.D. 400–PRESENT

PART ONE

EARLY EUROPE A.D. 400–1650

Description, Summarize

Epic, Evaluate Characters

Suspense,
Monitor Comprehension

"He wept from his
six eyes, and down
three chins/ the tears
ran mixed with bloody
froth and pus."

—Dante Alighieri

MODERN EUROPE 1650–PRESENT

" 'Don't forget that you are in a concentration camp. In this place, it is every man for himself, and you cannot think of others.' "

—Elie Wiesel

Father and Child, 1946. Ben Shahn. Tempera on cardboard, 39 7/8 x 30 in. Gift of James Thrall Soby. The Museum of Modern Art, NY.© VAGA, NY.

THE AMERICAS 3000 B.C.–PRESENT

THE EARLY AMERICAS 3000 B.C.–A.D.1900

"*Broken spears lie in the roads/ we have torn our hair in our grief.*"
—*The Broken Spears*

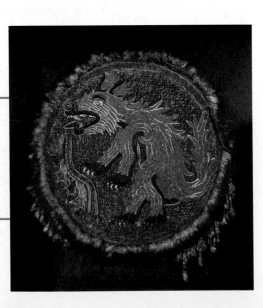

PART TWO

THE MODERN **AMERICAS** 1800–PRESENT

Comparing Literature Across Time and Place

> " . . . *suddenly he saw the red stone, shiny with the blood dripping off it, and the spinning arcs cut by the feet of the victim whom they pulled off . . .*"
>
> —Julio Cortázar

Fire and Destruction, 1985. Juri Palm. Oil on canvas. Art Museum of Estonia, Tallinn.

Reference Section

Selections by Genre

Features

Perspectives

Award-winning nonfiction book excerpts and primary source documents

TIME

High-interest, informative magazine articles

Comparing Literature
Across Time and Place

The Art of Translation

Literary History

Independent Reading

Assessment

Skills Workshops

How to Use *Glencoe World Literature*

Organization

The literature you will read is organized geographically into six units spanning the globe.

Each unit contains the following:

A **PART INTRODUCTION** provides you with the background information to help make your reading experience more meaningful.

- The **TIMELINE** helps you keep track of major literary and historical events.

- **HISTORICAL, SOCIAL, AND CULTURAL FORCES** explain the influences that shape a specific literary period.
- **BIG IDEAS** target three concepts that you can trace as you read the literature.

LITERARY WORKS follow each Part Introduction. The selections are organized as follows.

Why do I need this book?

Glencoe World Literature is more than just a collection of stories, poems, nonfiction articles, and other literary works. Every part is built around **Big Ideas,** concepts that you will want to think about, talk about, and maybe even argue about. Big Ideas help you become part of an important conversation. You can join in lively discussions about who we are, where we have been, and where we are going.

Reading and Thinking

The main literary works in your textbook are arranged in three parts.

- Start with **BEFORE YOU READ**. Learn valuable background information about the literature and preview the skills and strategies that will guide your reading.

MEET THE AUTHOR presents a detailed biography of the writer whose work you will read and analyze.

LITERATURE AND READING PREVIEW lists the basic tools you will use to read and analyze the literary work.

- Next, read the **LITERARY WORK**. As you flip through the selections, you will notice that parts of the text are highlighted in different colors. At the bottom of the page are color-coded questions that relate to the highlighted text. Yellow represents a *Big Idea*, magenta represents a *Literary Element*, and blue represents a *Reading Strategy*. These questions will help you gain a better understanding of the text.

- Wrap up the literature with **AFTER YOU READ**. Explore what you have learned through a wide range of reading, thinking, vocabulary, and writing activities.

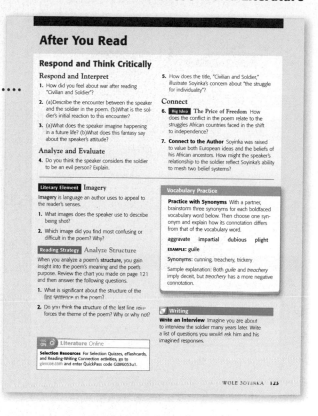

Vocabulary

VOCABULARY WORDS that may be new or difficult are chosen from most selections. They are introduced on the **BEFORE YOU READ** page. Each word is accompanied by its pronunciation, its part of speech, its definition, and the page number on which it appears. The vocabulary word is also used in a sample sentence. Vocabulary words are highlighted in the literary work.

VOCABULARY PRACTICE On the **AFTER YOU READ** pages, you will be able to practice using the vocabulary words in an exercise. This exercise will show you how to apply a vocabulary strategy to understand new or difficult words.

ACADEMIC VOCABULARY Many of the **AFTER YOU READ** pages will also introduce you to a word that is frequently used in academic work. You will be prompted to complete an activity based on that word.

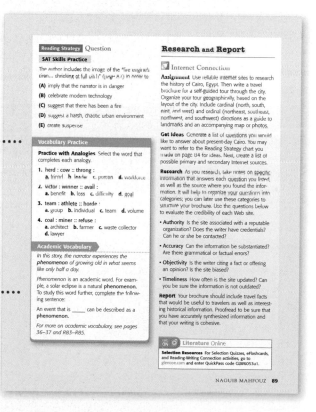

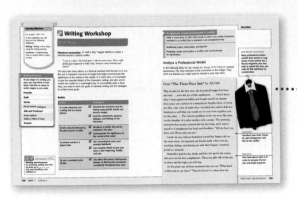

Writing Workshops

Each unit in *Glencoe World Literature* includes a Writing Workshop. The workshop walks you through the writing process as you work on an extended piece of writing related to the unit.

- You will create writing goals and apply strategies to meet them.

- You will pick up tips and polish your critical skills as you analyze professional and workshop models.

- You will focus on mastering specific aspects of writing, including organization, grammar, and vocabulary.

- You will use a rubric to evaluate your own writing.

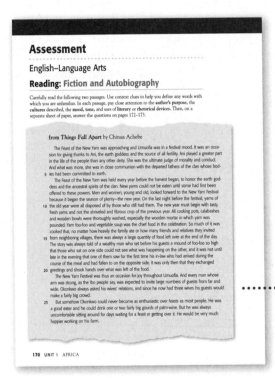

Assessment

English–Language Arts

Reading: Fiction and Autobiography

Carefully read the following two passages. Use context clues to help you define any words with which you are unfamiliar. In each passage, pay close attention to the **author's purpose**, the **cultures** described, the **mood, tone**, and uses of **literary** or **rhetorical devices**. Then, on a separate sheet of paper, answer the questions on pages 172–173.

Assessment

At the end of each unit, you will be tested on the literature, reading, and vocabulary skills you have just learned. Designed to simulate standardized tests, this test will give you the practice you need to succeed while providing an assessment of how you have met the unit objectives.

 BOUND BOOK

Try using this organizer to explore your personal responses to the poetry, play and nonfiction.

Organizing Information

Graphic organizers—such as Foldables®, diagrams, and charts—help you keep your information and ideas organized.

Scavenger Hunt

Glencoe World Literature contains a wealth of information. The trick is to know where to look to access all of that information. If you go through this scavenger hunt, either alone or with teachers or parents, you will quickly learn how the textbook is organized and how to get the most out of your reading and study time.

Let's get started!

1. How many units and parts are there in this book?

2. What is the difference between the Glossary and the Index?

3. Where in the book can you find help for test preparation?

4. In what special feature would you find biographical information about a specific author?

5. If you wanted to find all of the short stories in the book, where would you look?

6. If you wanted to find a definition of the term *allegory*, where would you look?

7. Where can you find the Big Ideas for each part of the book?

8. The Web site for the book is referred to throughout the book. What sort of information does the Web site contain that might help you?

9. Which of the book's main features will provide you with the strategies for developing your writing skills?

After you answer all the questions, meet with a partner or a small group to compare answers.

A Kuban mask of Ngaady aMwaash, Congo. *View the Art* Ngaady aMwaash, a renowned beauty, was the wife of Mwaash aMbooy, the first king of the Kuba, a group living in central Congo. She is often depicted with diagonal lines running beneath her eyes, which represent tears. What emotions does this mask convey?

AFRICA

3100 B.C.—Present

Kwa mwendwo gutiri irima.

On the way to one's beloved there are no hills.

—Kikuyu proverb

A Zebras on a savannah

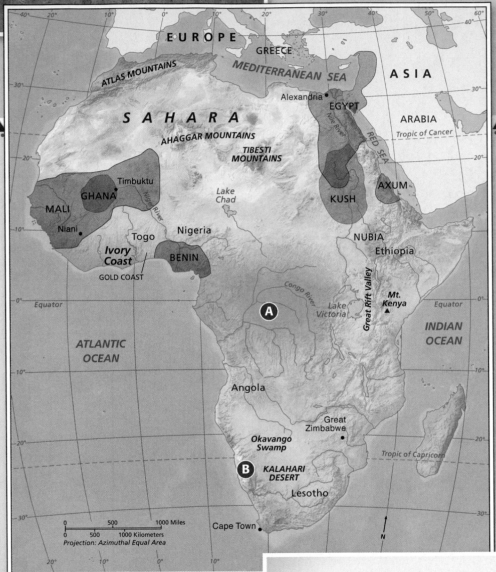

EUROPE
GREECE
MEDITERRANEAN SEA
ASIA
ATLAS MOUNTAINS
Alexandria
EGYPT
ARABIA
Tropic of Cancer
SAHARA
AHAGGAR MOUNTAINS
TIBESTI MOUNTAINS
Nile River
RED SEA
AXUM
Timbuktu
GHANA
KUSH
MALI
Niani
Togo
Nigeria
NUBIA
Ivory Coast
BENIN
Ethiopia
GOLD COAST
Lake Chad
Congo River
Great Rift Valley
Mt. Kenya
Equator
Lake Victoria
Equator
INDIAN OCEAN
ATLANTIC OCEAN
Angola
Great Zimbabwe
Okavango Swamp
Tropic of Capricorn
KALAHARI DESERT
Lesotho
Cape Town
0   500   1000 Miles
0   500   1000 Kilometers
Projection: Azimuthal Equal Area
N

B Sossusvlei Dunes in Namib Desert

LOG ON ▶ **Literature** Online

Literature and Reading For more about the history
and literature of this period, go to glencoe.com and
enter the QuickPass code GLW6053u1.

Early AFRICA

3100 B.C.—A.D. 1800

Male Allegorical Figure in 19th century military dress, possibly representing Gezo, the first ruler of Dahomey.

Being There

The continent of Africa is second only to Asia in size. As many as a thousand languages are spoken by different African ethnic groups, each of which has a distinct history, culture, and set of religious beliefs. Africa's earliest civilizations, Egypt and Kush, developed in the fertile Nile Valley in northeast Africa about 5,000 years ago. Between the eighth and the nineteenth centuries A.D., the trading states of Ghana, Mali, and Benin flourished in West Africa.

Looking Ahead

Ancient Egypt produced a rich written literature, from myths and hymns to love poetry. Across the Sahara in West Africa, oral storytellers known as griots preserved the literary traditions of heroes and kings. Throughout Africa, traditional village-based societies also created a wide variety of oral literature, including myths, folktales, poetry, and proverbs.

Keep the following questions in mind as you read:

▲ What were the most common types of ancient Egyptian literature?

▲ What roles did griots have in West African kingdoms such as Mali?

▲ What are the basic traits of the folklore figure known as the trickster?

TIMELINE 3100 B.C.–A.D. 1800

AFRICAN LITERATURE

3000 B.C.

c. 3000
Earliest surviving
Egyptian writing

16th century
Earliest texts of the Egyptian
Book of the Dead appear
▼

1500 B.C.

c. 1350
Pharaoh Akhenaten
composes hymns to
the sun

c. 1300–1100
Love poetry is composed
during Egypt's New
Kingdom

c. 300
Library of Alexandria,
Egypt, is founded

Funerary mask
of Tutankhamen

AFRICAN EVENTS

3000 B.C.

c. 3100
Menes, the first pharaoh,
unites Egypt

c. 2700
Egypt's Old Kingdom
begins

c. 2540
Pharaoh Khufu builds
Great Pyramid at Giza

c. 2200
Old Kingdom ends

c. 2050
Middle Kingdom begins

1652
Hyksos invade Egypt;
Middle Kingdom ends

1550
New Kingdom begins

1500 B.C.

1450s–1426
Pharaoh Thutmose III
expands Egyptian empire

c. 1085
New Kingdom ends

750
Kingdom of Kush conquers
Egypt

30
Egyptian queen Cleopatra
VII dies; Romans control
Egypt

Hippopotamus from
Thebes, Egypt

WORLD EVENTS

3000 B.C.

c. 3000
Mesopotamians develop
cuneiform writing

c. 2500
Indus Valley civilization
develops

c. 2334
Sargon creates a
Mesopotamian empire

1792
Hammurabi takes power
in Babylon

1500 B.C.

c. 1500
Aryans invade northern
India

c. 509
Roman Republic
is founded

221
Qin Shihuangdi becomes
first Chinese emperor

27
Augustus becomes first
Roman emperor
▼

LOG ON ▶ **Literature** Online

Literature and Reading To explore the Interactive Timeline,
go to glencoe.com and enter QuickPass code GLW6053u1.

A.D. 1

A.D. 1500

A Kaba-blon (shrine) of the
Keita clan whose ancestor is
the semi-mythical Sundiata.

c. 1210
Sundiata, the hero of the
Mali epic, is born

1352
Arab traveler Ibn Battuta
meets griots in Mali

1789 ▶
*The Interesting Narrative
of the Life of Olaudah
Equiano* is published

1799
Rosetta Stone is
discovered

A.D. 1

A.D. 1500

c. 300
Camels are introduced
into Africa

c. 500
Kingdom of Ghana
emerges

641
Arabs conquer Egypt

c. 1100
Timbuktu is founded

c. 1240
Sundiata destroys
Ghanaian city of Kumbi

c. 1450
City of Great Zimbabwe
is abandoned

c. 1490 ▶
Islam spreads through
sub-Saharan Africa

1493
Muhammad Ture seizes
the Songhai Empire

1518
Spanish ship carries
first boatload of slaves to
the Americas

Mosque in
Djenne, Mali.

A.D. 1500

c. 300 ▲
Classic Maya period begins
in Mexico

476
Western Roman Empire falls

800 ▶
Charlemagne is crowned
Holy Roman emperor

1066
Normans conquer England

1521
Spanish conquistador
Hernán Cortés conquers
Aztec Empire

1543
Nicolaus Copernicus
publishes heliocentric
theory

1789
French Revolution begins

Reading Check

Analyze Graphic Information How long was the
Old Kingdom period of Egyptian history?

Learning Objectives

For pages 4–15

In studying this text, you will focus on the following objectives:

Literary Study: Analyzing literary periods.

Reading:
Evaluating historical influences.
Connecting to the literature.

Early AFRICA

3100 B.C.–A.D. 1800

Historical, Social, and Cultural Forces

The Gift of the Nile

The Nile River stretches 4,000 miles through Africa, flowing northward from south of the equator and emptying into the Mediterranean Sea. It is the longest river in the world. The ancient Egyptians called the Nile *Aur*, or "black," a reference to the rich soil left behind by the annual flooding of the river. The Nile was crucial to the formation of ancient Egyptian civilization; the soil left by the floods allowed the Egyptians to farm crops, while the river itself was used to transport people and merchandise. As ancient Greek historian Herodotus observed, Egypt is "the gift of the Nile."

Egypt

The history of Egypt begins in about 3100 B.C., when Menes (mee′nēz) united Upper (southern)

Boat with Sail and Oars,
6th Dynasty. Wall painting.
Tomb of Kaemrhon, Giza.

and Lower (northern) Egypt into a single kingdom. His reign began the first Egyptian dynasty, or family of rule, and the kings after him wore a double crown to mark the unification of their country. Modern historians have divided ancient Egyptian history into three major periods of stable rule, known as the Old Kingdom (2700–2200 B.C.), the Middle Kingdom (2050–1652 B.C.), and the New Kingdom (1550–1085 B.C.). Each of these periods is marked by unique rulers, historical events, and slightly varied cultural values. The periods between the kingdoms were marked by chaos and political instability.

> "Hail to you, O Nile!
> Sprung from Earth,
> Come to nourish Egypt!"
>
> —Egyptian hymn to the Nile

Sacred Writing

Writing in Egypt emerged around 3100 B.C. The Greeks later called this earliest Egyptian writing hieroglyphics (hī′ ər ə glif′iks), meaning "priest carvings" or "sacred writings." Hieroglyphics were used for formal inscriptions in stone. Later, a simplified version of the script was developed for business transactions, record keeping, and the general needs of daily life. This simplified script was written on papyrus (pə pī′rəs), a paper made from the reeds that grew along the Nile. Most of the ancient Egyptian literature that exists was originally written on rolls of papyrus, which survived for thousands of years in the dry climate of Egypt.

Desert Caravans

While the Nile provided one way to traverse the Sahara desert, camel caravans provided an alternative means of transportation. About 1,700 years ago, Africans began using camels to carry people and goods across the desert. As a result, an extensive trade network developed between the people of North Africa and the kingdoms of the sub-Saharan region. Before the trade routes

Asante scorpion ring. African school. Gold. Ghana.

began, people south of the desert lived in villages. The trade routes, however, gave rise to sizable towns, including the desert city of Timbuktu, which flourished as a center of learning as well as a commercial center.

Ghana and Mali

Trade across the Sahara gave rise to a series of West African empires, notably the powerful kingdoms of Ghana and Mali. Ghana, the first great trading empire in West Africa, emerged as early as A.D. 500. Ghana's wealth and power derived from its abundance of gold, which could be traded for salt and other products from North Africa. Ghana flourished for several hundred years until, weakened by various wars, it was defeated by Malian hero-king Sundiata (soōn dyä′tə) around 1240. Sundiata's victory solidified the Mali Empire, which flourished until the sixteenth century.

The Slave Trade

In 1518, a Spanish ship carried the first boatload of enslaved Africans directly from Africa to the Americas. During the next two centuries, the Atlantic trade in African slaves grew dramatically, reaching its peak in the 1700s, when more than six million Africans endured the Middle Passage, the brutal sea voyage from West Africa to the Americas. These slaves frequently died from malnourishment, epidemics, and mutinies while on the boats. Those who arrived in the Americas often died from diseases from which they had little or no immunity.

Visual Arts

Across the continent, early Africans created magnificent visual art for religious, ceremonial, and everyday uses. These artists, like many artists today, used the materials close at hand, such as specific metals or stones, to create their works. The geography of Africa is extremely varied, so traditional African arts were also very diverse. For example, people who lived near forests became accomplished wood-carvers, while those who worked with or near livestock tooled leather.

Music

After about A.D. 700, African people who lived north of the Sahara were influenced by the Arab traditions of music and dance. Musicians and dancers who lived south of the Sahara entertained at royal courts and performed at religious and ceremonial events. Musicians used a wide variety of instruments, including drums, harps, flutes, and xylophones, but the drum was usually considered most important. The West African "talking drum" was designed to change pitch to imitate speech patterns. Traditional African music is polyrhythmic; musicians and dancers created complex and interlocking rhythms by beating drums, striking bells, clapping hands, and stamping feet.

Masked Dogon Funerary dancer at Bandiagara Escarpment, Mali.

◀ Lyre. African school. Wood, beadwork, leather. Horniman Museum, London.

> "We are the men of dance, whose feet regain vigor in striking the hard earth."
>
> —Léopold Sédar Senghor, from "Prayer to the Masks"

Masked Dances

In West Africa and some parts of central Africa, masked dances were a major part of ceremonial life. Important ceremonial events included stages in the agricultural year, such as the first rains and harvesting; rights of passages marking birth, adulthood, marriage, and death; rituals of secret societies; and healing rituals. Masked dances were public, but only members of the masked dance societies were allowed to see the masks outside of performances and to observe dancers putting on their costumes. Dancers were accompanied by musicians and by singing and chanting that were sometimes done in a special language used only on that occasion.

Architecture

The ancient Egyptians were among the world's greatest architects. Egyptians used stone to create great, pillared temples as well as the famous pyramids. The West African kingdoms built great palaces that sometimes covered several acres and were decorated with statues and carvings. Muslim mosques were often built of sun-baked bricks, made according to local custom. In Ethiopia, the Coptic Christians produced churches carved into mountainsides, with interiors richly painted with biblical scenes. In southern Africa, the mysterious ruins called Great Zimbabwe are dominated by the Great Enclosure, an oval space surrounded by a massive wall.

 PREVIEW **Big Ideas** of Early Africa

1 Writing and Immortality	**2** The Magic of Words	**3** Gods and Spirits
Ancient Egyptians highly valued the written word and were also deeply pre-occupied with the afterlife. The convergence of these cultural values gave rise to many works that celebrated the immortality of the gods, the deceased, and the written word itself. **See page 12**	Traditional African society is based on the clan and the village. The histories and cultural values of these social groups have been preserved in both oral and written literature. For example, in West Africa, professional storytellers known as griots serve as oral historians for their communities. **See page 13**	Traditional African religious beliefs are rich and diverse and include many gods, spirits, and tricksters. Trickster tales, which center on cunning, mischievous beings, are often told to reinforce morals about behavior and the nature of wisdom. **See page 14**

The fertility of the Nile Valley provided the Egyptians with a dependable food supply, and the surrounding deserts and mountains usually protected them from invaders. These lucky circumstances gave the civilization of ancient Egypt an optimistic outlook on life.

Dead person drinking the waters at Amenti, west bank of the Nile. Chapter 59 of Book of the Dead. Ragab Papyrus Institute, Cairo.

A Timeless World

The ancient Egyptians believed that their circumstances were the result of blessings bestowed on them by their gods, and religion was a vital part of their daily lives. Among the greatest Egyptian gods were Osiris and his wife, Isis. Osiris was worshipped as the king of the dead, and the myth about his death (see pages 16–22) was the foundation of the Egyptians' elaborate beliefs about the afterlife.

About 1350 B.C., Egyptian ruler Amenhotep IV attempted to replace Egypt's numerous gods with a single deity named Aten, the god of the sun disk. The Aten represented immortality through his return each morning and his life-giving properties. The pharaoh renamed himself Akhenaten ("It is well with Aten") and made his religion mandatory in Egypt. Akhenaten created a new liturgy and even wrote hymns (see pages 24–29). His new religion did not last, however; after his death, Egyptians reverted to their old religious customs.

The Value of Learning

Scribes were masters of the art of hieroglyphics and also its teachers. Training to become a scribe took many years, and boys from the upper classes began school at the age of ten. Discipline was hard, but scribes enjoyed prominent status in society. The writings of the scribes allowed Egyptians to keep official documents and to record myths, songs, and poems. Hieroglyphics were also etched into tombs; the "The Great Hymn to the Aten" survives today because it was etched into the tomb of Akhenaten.

The Afterlife

The ancient Egyptians' optimism extended into the afterlife, which they conceived as a pleasurable continuation of their lives on earth. Ancient Egyptians made careful preparations for the life they expected to enjoy after death. The bodies of royal family members were preserved as mummies and placed in stone tombs. Their burial places contained images of all the things the dead people might need in the afterlife.

Reading Check

Analyze Cause-and-Effect Relationships Why do you think scribes enjoyed a privileged position in ancient Egypt?

When we gather with our friends and families, we often entertain one another through storytelling, which helps us recount our shared past, share this past with others, and hear tales of earlier times. In this way, all of us participate in oral tradition, the passing on of stories, songs, sayings, and other material by word of mouth. In many early African societies, oral tradition served to define and preserve communities.

Family and Clan

Traditional African societies centered on small villages in the countryside. The people in these villages derived their sense of identity from their membership in an extended family and kinship group. The foundation of this group was the extended family, made of up parents, children, grandparents, and other family dependents. These extended families were in turn combined with larger communities, clans, or kinship groups whose members could all claim to be descended from a real or legendary common ancestor.

> *"Without us the names of kings would vanish into oblivion, we are the memory of mankind."*
>
> —Griot Djeli Mamoudou Kouyaté, from the *Sundiata, An Epic of Old Mali*

Oral Tradition and the Griot

Many stories in African literature have been passed on orally from one generation to another for thousands of years. African oral literature includes a variety of literary forms, including histories of ethnic and kinship groups, heroic legends, praise songs for chiefs and kings, trickster stories, animal fables, riddles, and proverbs. As in all oral literatures, the storyteller is free to change or elaborate on the story to suit local audiences. Oral literature has long served as a way to record the past, glorify current leaders, and teach morals and traditions to new generations.

In West Africa, professional oral storytellers called griots (grē′ōz) committed stories and family histories to memory and recited verses while playing a stringed instrument. Griots underwent special training from childhood to enable them to memorize the long, complex oral traditions of their communities. These storytellers were also oral historians who kept alive the past of their peoples. For example, generations of griots preserved much of what survives about the founder of the Mali Empire, Sundiata (see pages 58–64).

Memory Figure Sitting on a Stool. Akan Culture, Ghana. Terracotta. Private collection.

Reading Check

Make Generalizations What role did oral tradition have in early African societies?

Gods and Spirits

As we get older, we realize that many important life events are influenced by random occurrences, comic situations, and other circumstances beyond our control. Traditional African beliefs attributed these puzzling events to gods, ancestors, or mischievous spirits known as tricksters.

Gods

Across early Africa, there were hundreds of religious systems, each with its own gods, shrines, and ceremonies. Most African societies, however, shared some common religious ideas. One of these was a belief in a single creator god, such as the Yoruban god Olorun.

One way to communicate with the gods was through rituals, which were usually carried out by a special class of people called diviners. Diviners were believed to have the power to foretell events, typically by working with supernatural forces. Their ability to contact the gods was thought to guarantee a bountiful harvest or to protect the interests of the community or the kingdom.

Ancestors

Ancestors also played a key role in many early African religions. Each kinship group could trace itself back to a founding ancestor or group of ancestors. These forebears were thought to be closer to the gods, and ritual ceremonies were held in their honor. Their descendants believed the ancestors had the power to influence their lives, for good and for bad; many songs, myths, and stories reflect this belief.

The Trickster

Tricksters, common figures in African and Native American mythologies, are beings who are alternately cunning and foolish, playful and cruel, funny and brutal. They sometimes take animal forms and sometimes appear as humans. One famous African trickster is Anansi the Spider (also spelled Ananse, see pages 39–43), whose stories are told by the Ashanti people of West Africa. The Ashanti, in fact, call all of their folktales *Anansesem*—"Spider stories"—even if Anansi does not appear in them. Another well-known West African trickster is Edju (also spelled Eshu, see pages 52–55), one of the Orishas, the gods of the Yoruba people. As he observes of himself, "Sowing dissension is my chief delight."

"Do they want sacrifice,
do they want blood?
Are they far,
are they near?"

—"The Ancestors," traditional song of the Khoikhoi people of South Africa

Eshu figure, Yoruba Culture, Nigeria. Wood, cowries, and leather. Private collection.

Reading Check

Interpret Why do you think tricksters were popular characters in African oral literature?

Wrap-Up

Legacy of the Period

The civilization of ancient Egypt, which developed at the crossroads of Asia, Africa, and Europe, had a profound influence on other cultures throughout these regions. For example, a simplified form of hieroglyphics contributed to the later development of the Phoenician alphabet, which is the basis for all modern alphabets. Egyptian sculpture deeply influenced the development of classical Greek sculpture.

The horrific slave trade across the Atlantic resulted in misery, human degradation, and the deaths of millions of people. One of its unforeseen results, however, was the spreading of African cultures to the Americas and other parts of the world.

Cultural and Literary Links

▲ The French expedition to Egypt under Napoleon from 1798 to 1801 stimulated a European interest in ancient Egyptian civilization. The results of this fascination can be seen in many works of literature and music, including Percy Shelley's

Chasuble, 1950-1952. Henri Matisse. Collezione d'Arte Religiosa Moderna, Vatican Museums, Vatican State. © ARS, NY.

poem "Ozymandias" and the opera *Aïda* by Italian composer Giuseppe Verdi.

▲ Stories about African tricksters traveled to the Americas with enslaved Africans. Among the Gullah people of the Sea Islands of South Carolina and Georgia, the name *Anansi* became "Aunt Nancy."

▲ Traditional African sculpture influenced the works of Pablo Picasso and Henri Matisse.

 Literature Online

Unit Resources For additional skills practice, go to glencoe.com and enter QuickPass code GLW6053u1.

Activities

 Use what you have learned about the region to do one of these activities.

1. **Follow Up** Go back to the Looking Ahead on page 5 and answer the questions.

2. **Contrast Literary Periods** The belief that spirits and ancestors influence everyday events is present not only in Africa, but in Central and South America as well. A literary movement that reflects this belief is **magic realism**. Research magic realism and write a short essay comparing and contrasting the ideas in the Gods and Spirits Big Idea with the mythical elements of magic realism.

3. **Build Visual Literacy** Collect and display examples of American popular culture (such as movies, advertising, comic books, and video

games) that use elements drawn from the civilization of ancient Egypt. Discuss with your classmates what common assumptions these materials reveal about ancient Egypt.

4. **Take Notes** You might try using this graphic organizer to keep track of the three Big Ideas in this part.

 THREE-TAB BOOK

Big Idea 1 / Big Idea 2 / Big Idea 3

Before You Read

Osiris and Isis

The ancient Egyptians had no word for *religion*. Religious ideas were so deeply interweaved into their lives and their view of the world that *religion* could not be isolated as its own term. The Egyptians worshipped many gods, most of them associated with heavenly bodies and natural forces. Among the most important of the Egyptian gods was Osiris (ō sī′ris), who ruled over the dead.

Egyptian Mythology One of the most famous Egyptian myths tells of the death and resurrection of Osiris. In the myth, Osiris is killed by his evil brother Sêth, who cuts his body into fourteen parts and scatters them. Isis (ī′sis), Osiris's wife, finds and gathers the pieces and brings her husband back to life through her powerful magic. The resurrected Osiris becomes the ruler of the dead and a symbol of eternal resurrection for the Egyptians. By identifying with Osiris, people could hope to gain new life in the afterworld, as the god had done.

The Book of the Dead The ancient Egyptians believed that every deceased soul had to appear before Osiris to be judged in the Hall of the Two Truths. To reach the hall, a soul (which Egyptians called a *ba* [bä]) had to make a dangerous journey through an underworld filled with monsters. The Egyptians placed a collection of prayers and magic spells in tombs to protect souls from these creatures. The final form of these writings, which appeared in the New Kingdom, was known as *The Book of Going Forth by Day*. An Egyptologist renamed it *The Book of the Dead* in 1842.

During judgment, the soul had to recite one of the most important parts of *The Book of the Dead*, called the "Negative Confession," or "Declaration of Innocence." This confession listed misdeeds that the soul claimed it had not committed in life. Afterward, the deceased

person's heart was weighed on a scale against a feather that stood for truth. If the heart was weighed down by sin, it would be heavier than the feather and would tip the scale. The soul would then be devoured by Ammet, a monster with the head of a crocodile, the foreparts of a lion, and the hind parts of a hippopotamus. If the scale balanced, then the soul was led before Osiris, who accepted it into the afterlife.

> *"Hail to you, Great God,*
>   *Lord of the Two Truths!*
> *I have come to you, my Lord,*
> *I was brought to see your beauty."*
>
> —from *The Book of the Dead*

The family of Osiris, 22nd dynasty. Gold, lapis lazuli, and red glass. Louvre, Paris.

Literature and Reading Preview

Connect to the Myth

Have you ever had to sacrifice something to help someone in need? Freewrite for a few minutes about what this person required and why you decided to make that sacrifice.

Build Background

The Egyptians believed that humans had both a physical body and a spiritual body. This spiritual body, or life force, was called the *ka* (kä) and was distinct from the *ba*, or soul. They believed that if the physical body was preserved after death and the tomb furnished with the various objects of daily life, the *ka* could return.

Set Purposes for Reading

Big Idea Writing and Immortality

For the ancient Egyptians, magical writings could be the key to immortality. As you read "Osiris and Isis," ask yourself, How might writings such as this myth have influenced the Egyptians' understanding of immortality?

Literary Element Archetype

An **archetype** (ar′kə tīp′) is a symbol, an image, or a story pattern that recurs in literature and evokes strong responses, often based on subconscious memory. An ancient divine ruler, such as Osiris, who taught his people essential skills is an example of the archetype of the cultural hero. As you read "Osiris and Isis," ask yourself, What archetype does Sêth represent?

Reading Strategy Identify Genre

A **genre** is a category or a type of literature. Examples of genres include poetry, drama, fiction, and nonfiction. Each genre has specific characteristics. As you read this Egyptian myth, ask yourself, What details identify this as a myth?

Tip: List Genre Characteristics Create a chart like the one below, filling in details from "Osiris and Isis" that correspond to the characteristics of the myth genre listed on the left.

Genre Characteristics	Details from "Osiris and Isis"
Gods as characters Good and evil brothers Creation stories Origins of culture Quests	Osiris, Isis, Sêth, and other Egyptian gods

Vocabulary

banquet (bang′kwit) *n.* an elaborate, ceremonial meal; p. 19 *At the end of its successful season, the basketball team held a victory banquet.*

diversified (di vur′sə fīd) *adj.* varied; p. 19 *Because of immigration, the city had a diversified population.*

splendid (splen′did) *adj.* grand; magnificent; p. 19 *The new production of Aïda featured splendid Egyptian costumes.*

lament (lə ment′) *v.* to mourn or express grief for; p. 19 *The whole family lamented the untimely death of their young cousin.*

Tip: Word Usage When you encounter a new word, it might help you to answer a specific question about the word. For example, In what ways is a **banquet** a lavish event?

OSIRIS & ISIS

Retold by
Padraic Colum

Papyrus from the Book of the Dead of Pediamenet, c. 1000 BC. British Museum, London.

When Osiris reigned death was not in the land. Arms were not in men's hands; there were not any wars. From end to end of the land music sounded; men and women spoke so sweetly and out of such depth of feeling that all they said was oratory and poetry.

Osiris taught men and women wisdom and he taught them all the arts. He it was who first planted the vine; he it was who showed men how and when to sow grain, how to plant and tend the fruit-trees; he caused them to rejoice in the flowers also. Osiris made laws for men so that they were able to live together in harmony; he gave them knowledge of the Gods, and he showed them how the Gods might be honored.

And this was what he taught them concerning the Gods: In the beginning was the formless abyss, Nuu. From Nuu came Rê, the Sun. Rê was the first and he was the most divine of all beings. Rê created all forms. From his thought came Shu and Tefênet, the Upper and the Lower Air. From Shu and Tefênet came Qêb and Nut, the Earth and the Sky. The Earth and the Sky had been separated, the one from the other, but once they had been joined together. From the eye of Rê, made out of the essence that is in that eye, came the first man and the first woman.

And from Qêb, the Father, and Nut, the Mother, Osiris was born. When he was born a voice came into the world, crying, "Behold, the Lord of all things is born!"

And with Osiris was born Isis, his sister. Afterwards was born Thout,[1] the Wise One. Then there was born Nephthys. And, last, there was born Sêth. And Sêth tore a hole in his mother's side—Sêth the Violent One. Now Osiris and Isis loved each other as husband and wife, and together they reigned over the land. Thout was with them, and he taught men the arts of

---

Identify Genre *What type of myth does this passage illustrate?*

---

1. *Thout* (also called *Thoth*) was the Egyptian god of wisdom.

writing and of reckoning. Nephthys went with Sêth and was his wife, and Sêth's abode was in the desert.

Sêth, in his desert, was angered against Osiris, for everywhere green things that Sêth hated were growing over the land— vine, and grain, and the flowers. Many times Sêth tried to destroy his brother Osiris, but always his plots were baffled by the watchful care of Isis. One day he took the measurement of Osiris's body—he took the measurement from his shadow— and he made a chest that was the exact size of Osiris.

Soon, at the time before the season of drought, Sêth gave a **banquet**, and to that banquet he invited all the children of Earth and the Sky. To that banquet came Thout, the Wise One, and Nephthys, the wife of Sêth, and Sêth himself, and Isis, and Osiris. And where they sat at banquet they could see the chest that Sêth had made—the chest made of fragrant and **diversified** woods. All admired that chest. Then Sêth, as though he would have them enter into a game, told all of them that he would give the chest to the one whose body fitted most closely in it. The children of Qêb and Nut went and laid themselves in the chest that Sêth had made: Sêth went and laid himself in it, Nephthys went and laid herself in it, Thout went and laid himself in it, Isis went and laid herself in it. All were short; none, laid in the chest, but left a space above his or her head.

Then Osiris took the crown off his head and laid himself in the chest. His form filled it in its length and its breadth. Isis and Nephthys and Thout stood above where he lay, looking down upon Osiris, so resplendent of face, so perfect of limb, and congratulating him upon coming into possession of the **splendid** chest that Sêth had made. Sêth was not beside the chest then. He shouted, and his attendants to the number of seventy-two came into the banquetting hall. They placed the heavy cover upon the chest; they hammered nails into it; they soldered it all over with melted lead. Nor could Isis, nor Thout, nor Nephthys break through the circle that Sêth's attendants made around the chest. And they, having nailed the cover down, and having soldered it, took up the sealed chest, and, with Sêth going before them, they ran with it out of the hall.

Isis and Nephthys and Thout ran after those who bore the chest. But the night was dark, and these three children of Qêb and Nut were separated, one from the other, and from Sêth and his crew. And these came to where the river was, and they flung the sealed chest into the river. Isis, and Thout, and Nephthys, following the tracks that Sêth and his crew had made, came to the riverbank when it was daylight, but by that time the current of the river had brought the chest out into the sea.

Isis followed along the bank of the river, **lamenting** for Osiris. She came to the sea, and she crossed over it, but she did not know where to go to seek for the body of Osiris. She wandered through the world, and where she went bands of children went with her, and they helped her in her search.

Archetype *What character archetype does Sêth represent in this passage?*

Vocabulary

banquet (bang′kwit) *n.* an elaborate, ceremonial meal
diversified (di vur′sə fīd) *adj.* varied

Archetype *What archetypal journey is Isis undertaking here?*

Vocabulary

splendid (splen′did) *adj.* grand; magnificent
lament (lə ment′) *v.* to mourn or express grief for

The Goddess Isis lamenting the death of her husband Osiris.
Painted wood. British Museum, London.

View the Art Isis was often depicted wearing the hieroglyphic sign for "throne" on her head, as she does in this sculpture. What might be the significance of her wearing this headdress as she mourns Osiris?

The chest that held the body of Osiris had drifted in the sea. A flood had cast it upon the land. It had lain in a thicket of young trees. A tree, growing, had lifted it up. The branches of the tree wrapped themselves around it; the bark of the tree spread itself around it; at last the tree grew there, covering the chest with its bark.

The land in which this happened was Byblos.[2] The king and queen of the city, Melquart and Astarte, heard of the wonderful tree, the branches and bark of which gave forth a fragrance. The king had the tree cut down; its branches were trimmed off, and the tree was set up as a column in the king's house. And then Isis, coming to Byblos, was told of the wonderful tree that grew by the sea. She was told of it by a band of children who came to her. She came to the place: she found that the tree had been cut down and that its trunk was now set up as a column in the king's house.

She knew from what she heard about the wonderful fragrance that was in the trunk and branches of the tree that the chest she was seeking was within it. She stayed beside where the tree had been. Many who came to that place saw the queenly figure that, day and night, stood near where the wonderful tree had been. But none who came near was spoken to by her. Then the queen, having heard about the stranger who stood there, came to her. When she came near, Isis put her hand upon her head, and thereupon a fragrance went from Isis and filled the body of the queen.

The queen would have this majestical stranger go with her to her house. Isis went. She nursed the queen's child in the hall in which stood the column that had closed in it the chest which she sought.

She nourished the queen's child by placing her finger in its mouth. At night she would strip wood from the column that had grown as a tree, and throw the wood upon the fire. And in this fire she would lay the queen's child. The fire did not injure it at all; it burned softly around the child. Then Isis, in the form of a swallow, would fly around the column, lamenting.

One night the queen came into the hall where her child was being nursed. She saw no nurse there; she saw her child lying in the fire. She snatched the child up, crying out. Then Isis spoke to the queen from the column on which, in the form of a swallow, she perched. She told the queen that the child would have gained immortality had it been suffered to lie for a night and another

---

2. *Byblos* was a city in the ancient country of Phoenicia, located where Lebanon and Syria are today.

Identify Genre *What mythic element does this passage reflect?*

night longer within the fire made from the wood of the column. Now it would be long-lived, but not immortal. And she revealed her own divinity to the queen, and claimed the column that had been made from the wonderful tree.

The king had the column taken down; it was split open, and the chest which Isis had sought for so long and with so many lamentations was within it. Isis wrapped the chest in linen, and it was carried for her out of the king's house. And then a ship was given to her, and on that ship, Isis, never stirring from beside the chest, sailed back to Egypt.

And coming into Egypt she opened the chest, and took the body of her lord and husband out of it. She breathed into his mouth, and, with the motion of her wings (for Isis, being divine, could assume wings), she brought life back to Osiris. And there, away from men and from all the children of Qêb and Nut, Osiris and Isis lived together.

Visual Vocabulary
Gazelles are antelopes that live in Africa and southwest Asia.

But one night Sêth, as he was hunting gazelles by moonlight, came upon Osiris and Isis sleeping. Fiercely he fell upon his brother; he tore his body into fourteen pieces. Then, taking the pieces that were the body of Osiris, he scattered them over the land.

Death had come into the land from the time Osiris had been closed in the chest through the cunning of Sêth; war was in the land; men always had arms in their hands. No longer did music sound, no longer did men and women talk sweetly and out of the depths of their feelings. Less and less did grain, and fruit trees, and the vine flourish. The green places everywhere were giving way to the desert. Sêth was triumphant; Thout and Nephthys cowered before him.

And all the beauty and all the abundance that had come from Rê would be destroyed if the pieces that had been the body of Osiris were not brought together once more. So Isis sought for them, and Nephthys, her sister, helped her in her seeking. Isis, in a boat that was made of reeds, floated over the marshes, seeking for the pieces. One, and then another, and then another was found. At last she had all the pieces of his torn body. She laid them together on a floating island, and reformed them. And as the body of Osiris was formed once more, the wars that men were waging died down; peace came; grain, and the vine, and the fruit trees grew once more.

And a voice came to Isis and told her that Osiris lived again, but that he lived in the Underworld where he was now the Judge of the Dead, and that through the justice that he meted out, men and women had life immortal. And a child of Osiris was born to Isis: Horus[3] he was named. Nephthys and the wise Thout guarded him on the floating island where he was born. Horus grew up, and he strove against the evil power of Sêth. In battle he overcame him, and in bonds he brought the evil Sêth, the destroyer of his father, before Isis, his mother. Isis would not have Sêth slain: still he lives, but now he is of the lesser Gods, and his power for evil is not so great as it was in the time before Horus grew to be the avenger of his father. ∾

---

3. *Horus* was a falcon-headed Egyptian sky god who succeeded his father Osiris as ruler of Egypt.

Writing and Immortality *Why do you think the Egyptians made Osiris the Judge of the Dead?*

Archetype *In what way is this battle archetypal?*

After You Read

Respond and Think Critically

Respond and Interpret

1. What details in "Osiris and Isis" remind you of other myths and legends you have read?

2. (a)How does Sêth trick Osiris? (b)What do Sêth's actions convey about his character?

3. (a)How does Sêth's rule affect Egyptian civilization? (b)Why might details about Sêth's rule be included in the myth?

4. (a)What does Isis do with the child of Queen Astarte? (b)What does this episode reveal about Isis?

5. (a)What changes does the reformation of Osiris's body produce in the Egyptian landscape? (b)What does this indicate about the nature of Osiris in Egyptian belief?

Analyze and Evaluate

6. (a)How do the roles of Osiris, Isis, and Sêth shift throughout this myth? (b)In your view, which of the three emerges as the most powerful figure, and why?

7. What is your opinion of Isis's decision to spare Sêth?

Connect

8. **Big Idea** **Writing and Immortality** Why do you think the story of Osiris and Isis was central to Egyptian mythology?

9. **Connect to Today** Heroes with extraordinary abilities abound in popular culture. Who are some of these heroes, and why do you think they remain popular?

Literary Element Archetype

Archetypes such as heroes, villains, tricksters, and quests appear frequently in myths and legends.

1. What characteristics associated with Sêth indicate that he is an archetypal figure?

2. Think of another famous archetypal villain. What do this villain and Sêth have in common?

Reading Strategy Identify Genre

A **myth** is a traditional story that may explain a fact about the world, a custom, or a force of nature.

1. "Osiris and Isis" explains the origin of what fact of life?

2. What aspects of Egyptian civilization are explained?

Vocabulary Practice

Practice with Usage Respond to these items to better understand the vocabulary words.

1. Make a list of foods you would like to have served at a **banquet** held in your honor.

2. Identify some pros and cons of having a widely **diversified** set of hobbies.

3. Describe the most **splendid** building you have ever seen.

4. How might you **lament** the death of a pet?

Writing

Write a Movie Scene Choose one scene from "Osiris and Isis" and adapt it into a movie script. Include stage directions and brief descriptions of the set. To get started, use a chart like the one on page 17 to list film conventions, such as dialogue and costumes, and note how you could use these features to illustrate archetypes and themes.

LOG ON ▶ **Literature** Online

Selection Resources For Selection Quizzes, eFlash-cards, and Reading-Writing Connection activities, go to glencoe.com and enter QuickPass code GLW6053u1.

Grammar Workshop

Sentence Fragments

Learning Objectives

In this workshop, you will focus on the following objective:

Grammar: Understanding how to avoid sentence fragments.

Literature Connection A **sentence fragment** is a word or group of words that composes only part of a sentence and does not express a complete thought. Look at this sentence from "Osiris and Isis": "Isis followed along the bank of the river, lamenting for Osiris." Think about the effect if the author had instead written, "Isis followed along the bank of the river. Lamenting for Osiris." "Lamenting for Osiris" is a sentence fragment because it lacks a subject and a verb.

PROBLEM 1 Some sentence fragments lack either a subject or a verb (or both).

> *Tore his body into fourteen pieces.* [lacks a subject]

> *The land in which this happened.* [lacks a verb]

SOLUTION Add the missing subject and/or verb.

> <u>*Sêth*</u> *tore his body into fourteen pieces.*

> *The land in which this happened* <u>*was Byblos.*</u>

PROBLEM 2 Some sentence fragments are really subordinate clauses that have been mistaken for a complete sentence. Although they have a subject and a verb, subordinate clauses do not express a complete thought and cannot stand alone as a sentence.

> *If the pieces that had been the body of Osiris were not brought together once more.*

SOLUTION A Join the subordinate clause to a main clause.

> <u>*Rê would be destroyed*</u> *if the pieces that had been the body of Osiris were not brought together once more.*

SOLUTION B Remove the subordinating conjunction at the beginning of the clause.

> *The pieces that had been the body of Osiris were not brought together once more.*

Revise Use the strategies shown above to correct the sentence fragments in this paragraph.

> *Isis sought the chest. She wrapped the chest in linen. And carried it to the king's house. Given a ship, she sailed back to Egypt. Where she opened the chest. And took out the body of her husband.*

Sentence Fragments

A **sentence fragment** is a word or group of words that composes only part of a sentence and does not express a complete thought.

Tip

One way to eliminate sentence fragments is to join two clauses, or ideas, with a subordinating conjunction. Some common subordinating conjunctions are *after, because, before, if, since, than, though, unless, when, where,* and *while.*

Language Handbook

For more about sentence fragments, see the Language Handbook, p. R40.

LOG ON ▶ **Literature** Online

Grammar For more grammar practice, go to glencoe.com and enter QuickPass code GLW6053u1.

Before You Read

The Great Hymn to the Aten

Meet **Akhenaten**
(ruled 1353 B.C.–1336 B.C.)

Given the overwhelming power of the sun in Egypt, it is not surprising that the sun god Re (rā) was central to the ancient Egyptians' mythology. Re, who was also the creator god, was worshipped as the source of all life and was represented in many forms. The Egyptians depicted him as a sun-shaped disk, a human, a falcon, or a man with a falcon's head. From very early in Egypt's history, the pharaoh took the title "Son of Re," because the ruler was seen as an earthly form of the sun god.

The New Kingdom and Amen-Re Around 1550 B.C., Egyptian princes from the city of Thebes expelled invaders who had ruled Egypt for almost a century. These princes reunited the country and established the New Kingdom, during which Egypt would reach the height of its wealth and power. When Thebes became the capital of Egypt under the New Kingdom pharaohs, the Egyptians combined the worship of the Theban god Amen with that of their sun god Re, calling the new god Amen-Re. Amen-Re became the most important Egyptian god, and his priests eventually gained great power and wealth.

> "How many are your deeds,
> Though hidden from sight,
> O Sole God beside whom there is none!"
>
> —Akhenaten, from
> "The Great Hymn to the Aten"

The Rebel Pharaoh A new ruler named Amenhotep IV (ä′mən hō′tep) came to the throne of Egypt about 1370 B.C. To return power to the pharaohs, Amenhotep closed the great temples of Amen-Re and dismissed the armies of temple workers. His most radical change, however, was the creation of a new religion based on the worship of only a single god, Aten (ät′n), god of the sun disk. The rebel pharaoh changed his own name to Akhenaten (ä′ke nät′n) (also spelled Akhenaton), which means "It is well with Aten." However, only his wife, Nefertiti (nef′ər tē′tē), his family, and his close advisers accepted this new religion.

Akhenaten moved his court from Thebes to a city he built about 250 miles north on the Nile. The pharaoh called his new city Akhetaten, "the Horizon of the Aten" (an archaeological site known today as Tell el-Amarna). Akhenaten and his court created a cultured, pleasant life in Akhetaten. The pharaoh himself composed a beautiful hymn to Aten to be used in temple services there. Found on a tomb wall at Tell el-Amarna, "The Great Hymn to the Aten" is the finest poetry surviving from ancient Egypt.

LOG ON ▶ **Literature** Online

Author Search For more about Akhenaten, go to glencoe.com and enter QuickPass code GLW6053u1.

Literature and Reading Preview

Connect to the Hymn

What about the sun might be impressive enough to inspire worship? Discuss this question with a partner.

Build Background

Before Akhenaten came to power, Egypt had always been tolerant of multiple gods. Many Egyptians viewed Akhenaten's new religion as the destruction of their society. His religious revolution was undone soon after his death, however, by his successor, the boy-pharaoh Tutankhamen (töö´tängk ä´mən), who restored the old gods and the power of the priests.

Set Purposes for Reading

Big Idea Writing and Immortality

In Egyptian mythology, the god Re traveled in his sun-boat each night through the underworld, where monsters attacked him. His reappearance at dawn was a powerful symbol of immortality to the Egyptians. As you read "The Great Hymn to the Aten," ask yourself, How does Akhenaten depict the Aten's immortal role on earth?

Literary Element Tone

Tone is an author's attitude toward his or her subject matter or the audience. Tone is conveyed through elements such as word choice, punctuation, sentence structure, and figures of speech. As you read "The Great Hymn to the Aten," ask yourself, What is the author's attitude toward his subject?

Reading Strategy Analyze Style

Style refers to the expressive qualities that distinguish an author's work, including word choice, the use of figurative language and imagery, and the length and arrangement of sentences. These literary devices work together to evoke emotions in the reader. As you read, ask yourself, How do various literary elements contribute to the author's style?

....

Tip: Make a Style Chart Use a chart like the one below to record lines from the hymn and their effect on style.

Lines from Hymn	Effect on Style
"O living Aten, creator of life!" (line 2)	The starting "O" and the invocation of the god's name contribute to the formal style.

Learning Objectives

For pages 24–29

In studying this text, you will focus on the following objectives:

Literary Study: Analyzing tone.

Reading: Analyzing style.

Writing: Writing a journal entry.

Vocabulary

radiant (rā´dē ənt) *adj.* glowing; beaming; p. 26 *The radiant bonfire illuminated the children's faces.*

hover (huv´ər) *v.* to hang in the air; p. 26 *We watched a hawk hover overhead, looking for prey.*

dispel (dis pel´) *v.* to drive off; p. 27 *The police tried to dispel the onlookers at the scene of the accident.*

....

Tip: Context Clues You can often figure out the meaning of new words by looking at their context, the words and sentences that surround them. For example, in the sentence *We watched a hawk hover overhead, looking for prey,* *hover* must mean "to hang in the air," since the hawk stayed in the air without landing.

You made Hapy in *dat,*°
You bring him when you will,
To nourish the people,
65   For you made them for yourself.
Lord of all who toils for them,
Lord of all lands who shines for them,
Aten of daytime, great in glory!
All distant lands, you make them live,
70   You made a heavenly Hapy descend for them;
He makes waves on the mountains like the sea,
To drench their fields and their towns.
How excellent are your ways, O Lord of eternity!
A Hapy from heaven for foreign peoples,
75   And all lands' creatures that walk on legs,
For Egypt the Hapy who comes from *dat.*

Your rays nurse all fields,
When you shine they live, they grow for you;
You made the seasons to foster all that you made,
80   Winter to cool them, heat that they taste you.
You made the far sky to shine therein,
To behold all that you made;
You alone, shining in your form of living Aten,
Risen, radiant, distant, near.
85   You made millions of forms from yourself alone,
Towns, villages, fields, the river's course;
All eyes observe you upon them,
For you are the Aten of daytime on high. . . .
. . . . . . ‒‒‒. . .

<Those on> earth come from your hand as you made them,
90   When you have dawned they live,
When you set they die;
You yourself are lifetime, one lives by you.
All eyes are on <your> beauty until you set,
All labor ceases when you rest in the west;
95   When you rise you stir [everyone] for the King,
Every leg is on the move since you founded the earth.
You rouse them for your son who came from your body,
The King who lives by Maat,° the Lord of the Two Lands.
Neferkheprure, Sole-one-of-Re,
100   The Son of Re who lives by Maat, the Lord of crowns,
Akhenaten, great in his lifetime;
(And) the great Queen whom he loves, the Lady of the Two
    Lands,
Nefer-nefru-Aten Nefertiti, living forever.

62 Hapy in dat: rain. The Egyptians believed the source of the Nile River (**Hapy**) was in the underworld (**dat**) and that rain was the river descending to earth.

Akhenaten and His Family, ca. 1345 BC. Painted limestone relief, 32.5 x 39 cm. Staatliche Museen zu Berlin, Germany.

View the Art During Akhenaten's reign, Egyptian artists moved away from the formal depictions of royalty that had been popular in earlier dynasties and began to depict the royal family in more natural poses and relaxed settings. This approach is now called the Amarna style. How does this relief exemplify the Amarna style, and what might it reveal about Akhenaten's reign?

98 Maat: the Egyptian goddess who personified truth and justice.

After You Read

Respond and Think Critically

Respond and Interpret

1. How are the author's feelings about the sun in "The Great Hymn to the Aten" like and unlike your own?

2. (a)What events are associated with nightfall in the hymn? (b)What do these events suggest about the Aten's protective role toward humans?

3. (a)What does the poem say in lines 62–76 about the Aten's relationship to the Nile? (b)For the Egyptians, what significance would this relationship give to the Aten?

4. (a)According to the poem, what relationship exists between the Aten and Akhenaten? (b)How would this relationship affect the status of the pharaoh in the eyes of his subjects?

Analyze and Evaluate

5. (a)What kinds of living things are shown responding to the Aten? (b)What do these images reveal about the Aten's power?

6. What characteristics of this hymn might make it effective as an oral presentation?

Connect

7. **Big Idea** **Writing and Immortality** (a)In lines 89–93, what claim does the hymn make about the Aten? (b)How does this claim relate to Egyptian ideas of immortality?

8. **Connect to Today** "The Great Hymn to the Aten" praises the sun. In what ways do people today honor nature?

Literary Element Tone

An author's **tone** might convey a variety of attitudes such as sympathy, objectivity, or humor.

1. How might Akhenaten's chosen subject matter have influenced his tone?

2. What elements help create this tone?

Reading Strategy Analyze Style

Style can reveal an author's **purpose** in writing; for example, a carefree style may reveal that the author is writing to amuse readers.

1. What might be Akhenaten's purposes for writing this hymn?

2. How does the style of "The Great Hymn to the Aten" help convey these purposes?

Vocabulary Practice

Practice with Context Clues Look back at pages 26–28 to find context clues for the vocabulary words below. Record your findings in a chart like the one here.

radiant   hover   dispel

EXAMPLE:

Word: radiant > Textual Clues: The sun "fill[s] every land" with its "rays," so it must be powerfully bright. > Meaning: glowing; beaming

Writing

Write a Journal Entry Imagine that you are one of Akhenaten's subjects. Write a journal entry in which you examine your feelings about his new religion. Imitate the tone Akhenaten used in his poem. Review the chart you made on page 25 for other aspects of his style that you might want to incorporate into your writing.

Before You Read

Egyptian Poetry

Connect to the Poems

In what ways can people be remembered after they're gone? Discuss this question with a partner.

Build Background

"The Immortality of Writers" and "So small are the flowers of Seamu" date from the New Kingdom (around 1550–1085 B.C.), a period in which Egypt reached the height of its power. "The Immortality of Writers" is from a textbook used by boys learning to write hieroglyphs (see pages 34–35). "So small are the flowers of Seamu" is from a collection of love poems.

Set Purposes for Reading

Big Idea Writing and Immortality

The ancient Egyptians were very concerned with life after death. As you read "The Immortality of Writers," ask yourself, What kind of life after death does this poem suggest?

Literary Element Imagery

Imagery is language that appeals to the senses. For example, in "So small are the flowers of Seamu," the poet includes an image of "perfumed flowers". As you read these Egyptian poems, ask yourself, How do they use imagery to evoke readers' emotions?

Reading Strategy Analyze Diction

Authors use language carefully to convey meaning. Their choice of words is called **diction.** As you read, ask yourself, How does diction contribute to the message of these poems?

....

Tip: Chart Diction Make a chart to analyze how the diction differs in these poems. In the left column, list words that contribute to the message of "The Immortality of Writers"; in the right column, list words that contribute to the message of "So small are the flowers of Seamu."

"The Immortality of Writers"	"So small are the flowers of Seamu"
Decays	Flowers

Learning Objectives

For pages 30–33

In studying this text, you will focus on the following objectives:

Literary Study: Analyzing imagery.

Reading: Analyzing diction.

Writing: Writing an essay.

Vocabulary

decay (di kā′) *v.* to rot or decompose; p. 31 *The timbers of the sunken ship will decay over time.*

perish (per′ish) *v.* to die or cease to exist; p. 31 *We must work to save endangered species before they perish.*

tranquil (trang′kwəl) *adj.* calm; peaceful; p. 32 *The family enjoyed the tranquil mornings in the country.*

....

Tip: Word Origins Word origins, also called **etymologies,** are the history and development of words. They are often found in dictionary entries. For example, an entry for the word *tranquil* might include the following information: [ME *tranquill,* fr. *L tranquillus*]. This means that the modern word *tranquil* has a long history; it was derived from the Middle English (ME) word *tranquill,* which in turn was based on the Latin (L) word *tranquillus.*

from
THE **IMMORTALITY** OF WRITERS

Detail of the Book of the Earth, from the burial chamber of the Tomb of Rameses VI. Wall painting. Egypt.

Man **decays**, his corpse is dust,
All his kin have **perished**;
But a book makes him remembered,
Through the mouth of its reciter.
5   Better is a book than a well-built house,
Than tomb-chapels in the West;
Better than a solid mansion,
Than a stela[1] in the temple!

Is there one here like Hardedef?...[2]
10   Is there another like Ptahhotep?...[3]
Death made their names forgotten
But books make them remembered!

---

1. A *stela* (stē′lə) is a carved stone slab or pillar used for commemorative purposes.
2. Hardedef (har′dä def), an Egyptian prince, was buried in an elaborate underground tomb near the Great Pyramid of Khufu.
3. *Ptahhotep* (tä′hō tep′) wrote a work of philosophy dating back to 2800 B.C.

Imagery *What similarities exist between the objects in this line and the objects in lines 6–8?*

Writing and Immortality *What does this observation indicate about the value Egyptians placed on writing?*

Vocabulary

decay (di kā′) *v.* to rot or decompose
perish (per′ish) *v.* to die or cease to exist

Ladies Chat at a Banquet, 18th dynasty. Paint on limestone from tomb of Nebamun. British Museum, London.

View the Art Much of what we know about ancient Egyptian dress comes from artwork, such as this tomb painting from the New Kingdom. What can you infer about Egyptian fashion in the 18th dynasty, based on the outfits of the women in this painting? What can you infer about their lifestyles?

So small are the flowers of Seamu

Translated by Ezra Pound and Noel Stock

So small are the flowers of Seamu
Whoever looks at them feels a giant.

I am first among your loves,
Like a freshly sprinkled garden of grass and perfumed flowers.

5 Pleasant is the channel you have dug
In the freshness of the north wind.

Tranquil our paths
When your hand rests on mine in joy.

Your voice gives life, like nectar.

10 To see you, is more than food or drink.

Analyze Diction *What feelings does the word choice in these lines convey?*

Vocabulary

tranquil (trang′kwəl) *adj.* calm; peaceful

After You Read

Respond and Think Critically

Respond and Interpret

1. What questions would you like to ask the speakers of these poems?

2. (a)How does "The Immortality of Writers" describe death? (b)According to the poem, what is one benefit people can derive from books?

3. (a)What are books compared with in "The Immortality of Writers"? (b)What is unexpected about the fact that a book is compared with these other things?

4. (a)Explain the last two lines in "So small are the flowers of Seamu." (b)What do these lines suggest about the speaker's attitude toward the beloved?

Analyze and Evaluate

5. What might be the significance of the people mentioned in "The Immortality of Writers"?

6. Analyze the rhythm of "So small are the flowers of Seamu." Does the rhythm of the translation seem musical (fluid) or rigid? Explain.

Connect

7. **Big Idea** **Writing and Immortality** What kinds of books help people be remembered?

8. **Connect to Today** Aside from books, what are some ways people today can be remembered after death?

Literary Element Imagery

Strong **imagery** is especially important in poetry, as poets often rely on brief, intense images to convey their message.

1. Select an image from "The Immortality of Writers." How does the image you selected contribute to the meaning of the poem?

2. How does the imagery in this poem differ from that in "So small are the flowers of Seamu"?

Reading Strategy Analyze Diction

Refer to the chart you created on page 30 and answer the following questions.

1. How does the diction in "So small are the flowers of Seamu" help convey the theme of the poem?

2. How does the diction of this poem differ from that of "The Immortality of Writers"?

Vocabulary Practice

Practice with Word Origins Create a word map for each boldfaced vocabulary word. Refer to a dictionary for help.

decay   perish   tranquil

EXAMPLE:

Definition: highest in authority or goodness

Etymology: Latin superus, meaning "upper"

supreme

Sample Sentence: Amen-Re was considered the supreme being of the universe.

Writing

Write an Essay Reflect on the ideas about life and death that these two poems convey. Then write a brief expository essay describing the Egyptian worldview. Use quotations from the poems to support your claims.

Hieroglyphics and the Rosetta Stone

> *"Though I spend the day telling you 'Write,' it seems like a plague to you. Writing is very pleasant!"*
>
> —from an ancient Egyptian exercise book for scribes

Egyptian Writing Systems

The ancient Egyptians developed one of the world's first systems of writing. The earliest surviving examples of this script, known as "hieroglyphics" (from Greek words meaning "priest carvings," or "sacred writings"), date from about 3000 B.C. The complex hieroglyphic script includes pictures that represent words and more abstract forms that represent sounds. Learning and practicing the script took much time and skill. As a result, a highly simplified version of hieroglyphics, known as "hieratic" ("priestly") script, was developed. Hieratic script used the same principles as hieroglyphic writing, but the characters were simplified by using dashes, strokes, and curves rather than the more formal symbols. Much later, a third system, known as "demotic" ("of the people"), was also developed.

Papyrus

Hieroglyphics were used for official inscriptions on temple walls and tombs, which were meant to last for centuries. Hieratic and demotic scripts were used for everyday writing on papyrus, a material produced from the fibers of the papyrus plants that grow along the Nile River. (The English word *paper* comes from *papyrus*.) Papyrus scrolls were made by pressing together moistened layers of papyrus fibers. These sheets were then glued together to form scrolls that were sometimes up to 130 feet in length. In the dry Egyptian climate, papyrus was very durable; the earliest surviving papyrus dates from about 2600 B.C.

The Rosetta Stone, 196 BC. British Museum, London.

Hieroglyphic inscription in the tomb of Sety I, 19th Dynasty. Painted limestone from tomb in the Valley of the Kings at Thebes.

Scribal Schools

Because hieroglyphic script was difficult to master, a highly respected class of scribes came into existence. Scribes functioned as secretaries or clerks and were essential to the Egyptian state—scribes often became important government officials. At the age of ten, boys of the upper classes began attending schools run by scribes. There they learned hieroglyphics by laboriously copying texts, which usually celebrated the virtues of being a scribe. Discipline was strict, and boys were often punished severely.

The Rosetta Stone

Once alphabetical writing came into use in Egypt around the fourth century A.D., the ability to understand hieroglyphics soon faded away. The ancient symbols remained a mystery for hundreds of years. In 1799 in the Egyptian city of Rosetta, however, a French officer serving with Napoleon's expedition to Egypt discovered a large slab of granite covered with writing in three ancient scripts: hieroglyphics, demotic script, and Greek. This slab would prove to be the key to understanding hieroglyphics. The inclusion of Greek on the slab—later named the Rosetta Stone—meant the ancient scripts could be translated and better understood.

The British, who defeated the French in Egypt, seized the Rosetta Stone as a spoil of war. (It was presented to the British Museum in London in 1802 and remains there to this day.) By 1814 British scholar Thomas Young had successfully deciphered the Egyptian demotic inscription using the accompanying Greek text. Building on Young's work, French scholar Jean-François Champollion worked on the hieroglyphic text, which he deciphered by 1824. The Rosetta Stone allowed scholars to unlock the riches of ancient Egyptian civilization by providing the key to reading hieroglyphics. In recent years, Dr. Zawi Hawass, Secretary General of Egypt's Supreme Council of Antiquities, has demanded the return of the Rosetta Stone from Britain, describing it as "the icon of our Egyptian identity."

LOG ON **Literature** Online

Literature and Reading For more about hieroglyphics and the Rosetta Stone, go to glencoe.com and enter QuickPass code GLW6053u1.

Respond and Think Critically

1. What is your opinion on the issue of returning artifacts such as the Rosetta Stone to their country of origin?

2. How did the education of scribes in ancient Egypt differ from contemporary American education?

3. How did the difficulty of hieroglyphics affect the role of scribes in ancient Egypt?

For a complete list of academic vocabulary words, see pages R83–R85.

Test-Taking Tip

These key academic vocabulary words often appear on standardized tests.

Analyze: to systematically and critically examine all parts of an issue or an event

Compare: to show how things are alike

Contrast: to show how things are different

Describe: to present a sketch or an impression

Discuss: to systematically write about all sides of an issue or an event

Evaluate: to make a judgment and support it with evidence

Explain: to clarify or make plain

Vocabulary Workshop

Academic Vocabulary

What Is Academic Vocabulary? Words that are commonly used in academic texts, such as textbooks, directions, and tests, are called **academic vocabulary.** Learning academic vocabulary is important because these words will help you read, write, and research in many academic areas. These words will also help you succeed on standardized tests.

Different Kinds of Words Some words are specific to certain disciplines, or areas of study. For example, the words *onomatopoeia, free verse,* and *simile* pertain to literature. Other words, such as *analysis, definition,* and *estimate,* are used in many areas of study. The charts below show more examples of both kinds of words.

Discipline-Specific Words

Discipline	Words
Math	circumference, percentage, rectangle
Science	chlorophyll, genus, mitosis
Social Studies	antebellum, confederation, federalism

General Academic Vocabulary

area	evident
context	indicate
demonstrator	interpret
evaluate	structure

Academic Words in This Book You will learn about discipline-specific and general academic vocabulary words in this book. Words that are specific to literature and language arts will most often be introduced and explained in Literary Element and Reading Strategy features before and after you read literary works. You will encounter more general academic vocabulary words in features called Academic Vocabulary that appear after literature.

Multiple-Meaning Words Many academic vocabulary words, such as *approach,* have more than one meaning. The first meaning is a literal, more common definition that you may already be familiar with (*approach* means "to come near to"). The second definition is more academic and may be unfamiliar to you (*approach* also means "the method used in setting about a task"). These two definitions are often related, however. In the case of *approach,* the second, academic definition is connected to the common definition because "the method used in setting about a task" allows one to come closer to a goal. The chart below lists additional examples of academic words with more than one meaning.

Words	Definitions	Relationships
chart	*n.* a sheet giving information in tabular form *v.* to make a plan for	Both definitions involve organizing information.
exhibit	*v.* to show or display *n.* something displayed	Both definitions involve displaying
vehicle	*n.* a means of carrying or transporting something *n.* a medium through which something is expressed	Both definitions involve forms of carrying or transmitting

As you encounter academic vocabulary words in this book, you will master the words through various activities. You'll have a chance to practice some of these activities in the exercise below.

Practice Complete the following items.

1. *The Golden Age in Greece was a* **dynamic** *period marked by spectacular cultural and political achievement.*

   Dynamic is an academic word. In more casual conversation, someone might say the best player on a basketball team is a **dynamic** player. Using context clues, try to figure out the meaning of the word in the sentence about Greece above. Check your guess in a dictionary.

2. *"Of all the Socratic dialogues, the most influential was the Republic, which examines the* **nature** *of justice."*
   —from Meet Plato, page 334

   Nature has several meanings. Using context clues, try to figure out the meaning of *nature* in each sentence below and explain the difference between the two meanings.

   a. Brian loved hiking in the mountains; it made him feel connected to **nature.**

   b. The complex **nature** of this research project requires us to work long hours.

Test-Taking Tip

These key academic vocabulary words often appear on standardized tests.

Illustrate: to provide examples or to show with a picture or another graphic

Infer: to read between the lines or to use knowledge or experience to draw conclusions, make generalizations, or form predictions

Justify: to prove or to support a position with specific facts and reasons

Predict: to tell what will happen in the future based on an understanding of prior events and behaviors

State: to briefly and concisely present information

Summarize: to give a brief overview of the main points of an event or an issue

Literature Online

Vocabulary For more vocabulary practice, go to glencoe.com and enter QuickPass code GLW6053u1.

Comparing Literature

Across Time and Place

Compare Literature About Tricksters

Tricksters are mischievous and magical animal-humans who outwit their opponents. The trickster often functions as a hero, a creator, a fool, a destroyer, or a prankster. In the following tales, the trickster is embodied in the form of a spider, a coyote, and a cat.

COMPARE THE `Big Idea` Gods and Spirits

In each of these tales, tricksters use cunning, wit, and supernatural abilities for gains such as a box of stories, the ability to give fire to the world, and wealth. Some of these tricksters defy the gods, while others acquire godlike qualities. As you read, ask yourself, Are these tricksters trying to benefit only themselves or others as well?

COMPARE Trickster Tales

Trickster tales often follow similar narrative patterns, but they may vary in their outcomes. For example, while tricksters are ultimately successful, the result of their trickery may be negative or positive. As you read, ask yourself, Do the end results of the tricksters' actions justify their behavior?

COMPARE Cultures

To understand trickster tales, it is important to know their cultural context. "How Stories Came to Earth" originates from the Ashanti people (also spelled Asante), who live mainly in the villages of Ghana in Africa. "Coyote Steals Fire" comes from the Klamath, a Native American group who lost possession of their ancestral lands. "Master Cat, or Puss in Boots" was written in seventeenth-century France and reflects society under the reign of an absolute monarch. As you read, ask yourself, What aspects of these different cultures are apparent in the stories?

Learning Objectives

For pages 38–51

In studing these texts, you will focus on the following objectives:

Literary Study: Analyzing anthropomorphism.

Reading: Analyzing and comparing cultural contexts. Comparing themes.

Writing: Writing a trickster tale. Comparing trickster tales.

Linguist Staff (Okyeame), 20th century. Ghana (Asante), Guinea Coast. Gold foil, wood, nails, H x W x D: 156.5 x 14.6 x 5.7cm. The Metropolitan Museum of Art, NY.

LOG ON ▶ **Literature** Online

Author Search For more about Charles Perrault, go to glencoe.com and enter QuickPass code GLW6053u1.

Before You Read

How Stories Came to Earth

Connect to the Folktale

Why might trickster tales be passed down from one generation to the next? Discuss this question with a partner.

Build Background

"How Stories Came to Earth" features Anansi the Spider, who is a central trickster in many West African folktales. In these tales, Anansi often opposes the sky god by stealing his stories or by bringing disease into the world. In trickster tales such as these, the trouble caused by the trickster often brings about a necessary change in society.

Stool with curved seat supported by a leopard from the Ashanti tribe of Ghana, Africa. Wood. Private collection.

Set Purposes for Reading

Big Idea **Gods and Spirits**

The traditional religion of the Ashanti is based on an array of gods and spirits, including a distant supreme being. As you read, ask yourself, How does the Ashanti sky-god regard stories?

Literary Element **Anthropomorphism**

Anthropomorphism is the attribution of human characteristics to gods, animals, or inanimate objects. It is often a key element in tales in which animals are the main characters. Storytellers may use anthropomorphism to point out human flaws, such as greed, violence, and selfishness. As you read, ask yourself, How does anthropomorphism function in this story?

Reading Strategy **Analyze Cultural Context**

To **analyze cultural context** means to examine how a literary work reflects a specific culture and how the culture contributes to the meaning of the work. As you read, ask yourself, How does this story reflect the Ashanti culture?

Tip: Take Notes As you read, use a chart to record specific details that reveal something about Ashanti culture.

Cultural Detail	What Detail Reveals
Anansi must find a python, a leopard, and hornets.	The Ashanti deeply respected nature.

Asante mask. Ghana. Gold. Private collection.

How Stories Came to Earth

An Ashanti Legend
Retold by Kaleki

It was long ago in Africa, child, when there was First Spider, Kwaku Anansi. He went everywhere, throughout the world, travelling on his strong web strings—sometimes looking more like a wise old man than a spider.

In that long-ago time, child, there were no stories on Earth for anyone to tell. The sky-god kept all stories to himself, up high in the sky, and locked away in a wooden box.

These the spider wanted, as many creatures had before him, so that he could know the beginnings and endings of things. Yet all who had tried for the stories had returned empty-handed.

Now Anansi climbed up his web to the sky-god, Nyame, to ask for the sky-god's stories.

Child, when the powerful sky-god saw the thin, spidery, old man crawling up to his throne, he laughed at him, "What makes you think that you, of all creatures, can pay the price I ask for my stories?" Spider only wanted to know, "What is the price of the stories?"

"My stories have a great price, four fearsome, elusive creatures: Onini, the python that swallows men whole; Osebo, the leopard with teeth like spears; Mmoboro, the hornets that swarm and sting; and Mmoatia, the fairy who is never seen. Bring these to me."

Bowing, the spider quietly turned and crept back down through the clouds. He meant to capture the four creatures he needed as price for the stories. He first asked his wife, Aso, how he might capture Onini, the python that swallows men whole.

She told him a plan, saying, "Go and cut off a branch of the palm tree and cut some string-creeper as well. Take these to the stream where python lives."

As Anansi went to the swampy stream, carrying these things, he began arguing aloud, "This is longer than he; you lie, no; it is true; this branch is longer and he is shorter, much shorter."

Gods and Spirits *What might this passage reveal about the relationship between gods and stories in Ashanti belief?*

Analyze Cultural Context *Based on Aso's advice to her husband, what can you conclude about the role of women in Ashanti society?*

The python was listening, and asked what spider was talking about, "What are you muttering, Anansi?"

"I tell you that my wife, Aso, is a liar, for she says that you are longer than this palm branch and I say that you are not."

Onini, the python, said, "Come and place the branch next to me and we will see if she is a liar."

And so, Anansi put the palm branch next to the python's body, and saw the large snake stretch himself alongside it. Anansi then bound the python to the branch with the string-creeper and wound it over and over—nwenene! nwenene! nwenene!—until he came to the head. Then the spiderman said to Onini, "Fool, I will now take you to the sky-god."

This Anansi did as he spun a web around the snake to carry him back through the clouds to the sky kingdom.

On seeing the gigantic snake, Nyame merely said, "There remains what still remains."

Spider came back to Earth to find the next creature, Osebo the leopard, with teeth like spears.

His wife, Aso, told him, "Go dig a large hole."

Anansi said, "I understand, say no more."

After following the tracks of the leopard, spider dug a very deep pit. He covered it over with the branches of the trees and came home. Returning in the very early morning, he found a large leopard lying in the pit.

"Leopard, is this how you act? You should not be prowling around at night; look at where you are! Now put your paw here, and here, and I will help you out."

The leopard put his paws up on the sticks that Anansi placed over the pit and began to climb up. Quickly, Anansi hit him over the head with a wooden knife—gao! Leopard fell back into the pit—fom! Anansi quickly spun the leopard to the sticks with his web string.

"Fool, I am taking you to pay for the sky-god's stories."

But the sky-god received the leopard saying, "What remains, still remains."

Next the spiderman went looking for Mmoboro, the hornets that swarm and sting. Spider told his wife, Aso, what he was looking for and she said, "Look for an empty gourd[1] and fill it with water."

This spider did and he went walking through the bush until he saw a swarm of hornets hanging there in a tree. He poured out some of the water and sprinkled it all over their nest. Cutting a leaf from a nearby banana tree, he held it up and covered his head. He then poured the rest of the water from the gourd all over himself. Then while he was dripping he called out to the hornets,

"The rain has come, do you see me standing here with a leaf to cover my head? Fly inside my empty gourd so that the rain will not beat at your wings."

---

1. A *gourd* (gôrd) is the hard-shelled fruit of any of a group of trailing or climbing vines of the gourd family, including the melon, squash, and pumpkin. They can be used as containers.

Anthropomorphism *What human characteristics do the python and Anansi exhibit?*

Anthropomorphism *What actions does Anansi take in this passage? How would you describe his behavior?*

The hornets flew into the gourd, saying, "Thank you—hhhuuummm—Aku; thank you—hhhuuummm—Anansi."

Anansi stopped up the mouth of the gourd, and spinning a thick web around it, said, "Fools, I'm taking you to the sky-god as price for his stories."

The sky-god, Nyame, accepted Mmoboro, the hornets that swarm and sting, and said, "What remains, still remains."

Visual Vocabulary
An *Akua's Child* is a sculpture with a large head and an elongated neck that is sometimes used as a fertility doll in Ghana.

Anansi knew very well what remained—it was the fairy, Mmoatia, who is never seen. When the spider came back to Earth, he asked Aso what to do. And so, he carved an Akua's child, a wooden doll with a black, flat face, and covered it with sticky fluid from a tree.

Walking through the bush, he found the odum tree, where the fairies like to play. He then made eto, pounded yams, and put some in the doll's hand and even more of the yams into a brass basin at her feet—there by the odum tree. Anansi next hid in the bushes, with a vine creeper in his hands that was also tied to the doll's neck.

It wasn't long before the fairies came, two sisters, to play. They saw the doll with the eto and asked if they could have some. Anansi made the doll's head nod, "Yes," by pulling on the string-creeper. Soon the fairies had eaten all the eto and so, thanked the doll, but the doll did not reply. The fairies became angry.

One sister said, "When I thank her, she says nothing."

The other sister replied, "Then slap her in her crying place."

This the fairy did, she slapped it's cheek—"pa!"—but her hand stuck there. She slapped it with her other hand—"pa!"—and that hand stuck, too. She kicked it with both one foot, then the other, and both feet stuck to the sticky wooden doll. Finally, she pushed her stomach to it and that stuck.

Then Anansi came from his hiding place, and said, "Fool, I have got you, and now I will take you to the sky-god to buy his stories once and for all."

Anansi spun a web around the last of the four creatures and brought Mmoatia up to Nyame in the sky kingdom. The sky-god, seeing this last catch, called together all his nobles. He put it before them and told them that the spiderman had done what no one else had been able to do. He said in a loud voice that rang in the sky,

"From now and forever, my sky-god stories belong to you—kose! kose! kose!—my blessing, my blessing, my blessing. We will now call these 'Spider Stories.'"

And so, child, stories came to Earth because of the great cunning of Kwaku Anansi, and his wife, Aso. When Anansi brought the wooden box of stories to his home, he and his wife eagerly learned each one of them. And you can still see today that Aku and Aso tell their stories. Everywhere you look, they spin their webs for all to see. ∽

Analyze Cultural Context *What might this passage reveal about Ashanti views of the supernatural?*

Gods and Spirits *Based on his proclamation, what character traits might be attributed to Nyame?*

After You Read

Respond and Think Critically

Respond and Interpret

1. Do you think Anansi's tricks are justified? Why or why not?

2. (a)What are some of Anansi's physical characteristics? (b)Why might Nyame laugh at Anansi because of these characteristics?

3. (a)What four creatures does the sky-god tell Anansi to capture? (b)What do these creatures have in common?

Analyze and Evaluate

4. (a)What is the significance of Anansi's capture of the other creatures? (b)Why might the tale incorporate both large creatures, such as the leopard, and small creatures, such as fairies?

5. (a)In your opinion, is Anansi a sympathetic character? Explain. (b)Which of his character traits support your opinion?

6. Why might the Ashanti have chosen the image of the web to describe stories?

Connect

7. **Big Idea** **Gods and Spirits** Why might the Ashanti have worshipped a god who they believed kept stories from them, when they value storytelling so highly?

8. **Connect to Today** (a)What famous examples of anthropomorphized animals exist in books or movies today? (b)Why might these types of animals continue to be popular?

Literary Element **Anthropomorphism**

Personification is similar to anthropomorphism but is usually confined to a figure of speech.

1. What are some human characteristics of Anansi?

2. What positive and negative human qualities does Anansi possess?

Reading Strategy Analyze Cultural Context

By reading "How Stories Came to Earth," you can make generalizations about the Ashanti culture.

Partner Activity With a classmate, reread the story, examining the skills and resources Anansi uses to outsmart each creature. Based on what you find, compile a list of the skills and resources most likely valued by the Ashanti people.

LOG ON ▶ **Literature** Online

Selection Resources For Selection Quizzes, eFlashcards, and Reading-Writing Connection activities, go to glencoe.com and enter QuickPass code GLW6053u1.

Academic Vocabulary

*Tricksters deceive people for the **benefit** of society as a whole.*

Benefit is an academic word. Using context clues, try to figure out the meaning of *benefit* in each sentence below.

1. The auction was held as a **benefit** to raise money for the American Red Cross.

2. One **benefit** of switching to public transportation is faster travel time.

For more on academic vocabulary, see pages 36–37 and R83–R85.

Writing

Write a Trickster Tale Using Anansi as a model, write a trickster tale featuring an animal character of your choice. Use the chart you made on page 39 to help you think about the cultural values you want to express in your tale.

Build Background

The trickster assumes many personas in Native American folktales, but Coyote is the most prevalent trickster of all. He is often portrayed as part animal and part human and possesses many human qualities, including greed, strength, weakness, heroism, and cowardice. In various stories, Coyote creates Earth, animals, and humans and brings fire and sunlight to people.

"Coyote Steals Fire" comes from the Native American oral tradition of the Klamath, who now live in south-central Oregon and northern California. Their territorial land is in the southern Cascade mountain range, where they were fishers and hunters. Traditionally, the Klamath lived in villages with leaders, shamans, and medicine men.

Feathered Coyote, c.1500. Aztec. Carved stone. Museo Nacional de Antropologia, Mexico City.

Coyote Steals Fire

Retold by Richard Erdoes and Alfonso Ortiz

There was a time when people had no fire. In winter they could not warm themselves. They had to eat their food raw. Fire was kept inside a huge white rock that belonged to Thunder, who was its caretaker. Thunder was a fearful being. Everybody was afraid of him. Even Bear and Mountain Lion trembled when they heard Thunder's rumbling voice.

Coyote was not afraid of Thunder. He was afraid of nothing. One day, Thunder was in an angry mood and roared and rumbled his loudest, so that the earth trembled and all animals went into hiding. Coyote decided that this was the time to get the fire away from Thunder. Coyote climbed the highest mountain on which Thunder lived. Thunder was at home. "Uncle," said Coyote, "let us play a game of dice. If you win, you can kill me. If I win, you have to give me fire."

"Let us play," said Thunder.

They played with dice made from the gnawing teeth of beavers and woodchucks. The beaver teeth were male dice. The woodchuck teeth were female dice. A design was carved on one side of these teeth. The teeth were thrown on a flat rock. If the male teeth came up with the carved sides, they counted two points. If the female teeth came up with the carved sides, they counted one. If the dice came up uneven, they did not count. There was a bundle of sticks for counting, for keeping track of the points scored.

Now, Coyote is the trickiest fellow alive. He is the master at cheating at all kinds of games. He continuously distracted Thunder so that he could not watch what Coyote was up to. Thunder was no match for Coyote when it came to gambling. Whenever Thunder took his eyes off Coyote's hands, even for just the tiniest part of a moment, Coyote turned his dice up so that they showed the carved sides. He turned Thunder's dice up so that they showed the blank sides. He distracted Thunder and made him blink. Then, quick as a flash, he took a counting stick away from Thunder's pile and added it to his own. In the end, Thunder was completely confused. Coyote had all the counting sticks, Thunder had none. "Uncle, I won," said Coyote. "Hand over the fire." Thunder knew that Coyote had cheated but could not prove it.

Coyote called upon all the animals to come up to the mountaintop to help him carry the big rock that contained the fire. That rock was huge and looked solid, but it was very fragile, as fragile as a seashell. So all the animals prepared to carry the rock away. "Not so fast," growled Thunder. "Coyote won the game and so I give him the fire. But he cheated, and for that I shall take his life. Where is he so that I can kill him?"

Now, Coyote had read Thunder's mind. He had anticipated what Thunder was up to. Coyote could pull the outer part of his body off, as if it were a blanket, so he put his skin, his pelt, his tail, his ears—all of his outside—close by Thunder, and with the inside of his body, his vitals, moved a distance away. Then he changed his voice so that it sounded as if it were coming not from a distance, but like from just a few feet away. "Here I am, Uncle," he cried. "Kill me if you can." Thunder picked up the huge rock containing fire and hurled it at what he thought was Coyote. But he hit only the skin and fur. The rock splintered into numberless pieces. Every animal took a little piece of the fire and put it under its armpit or under its wing, and they hurried all over the world, bringing fire to every tribe on earth. Coyote calmly put on his outer skin and fur again. "Good-bye, Uncle," he said to Thunder. "Don't gamble. It is not what you do best." Then he ran off. ❧

💬 Discussion Starter

"Coyote Steals Fire" is an example of a Native American trickster tale in which the trickster obtains a much-needed item for the inhabitants of Earth. Why does Coyote succeed when others are too afraid to confront Thunder? What might Coyote represent to the Klamath? Discuss these questions with a group.

Build Background

Written in 1697, "Master Cat, or Puss in Boots" first appeared in Charles Perrault's compilation, *Tales of Mother Goose.* It mirrors the French society of Perrault's time, which was fond of pretentious behavior and opulent lifestyles under the reign of Louis XIV. Puss in Boots (Master Cat) gains favor for his manipulation of these values and uses trickery to change his master's social class.

The story applies the trickster motif to the fairy tale genre. Perrault wrote fairy tales to amuse children and added morals at the end of them. However, as in "Puss in Boots," these morals often served as social commentaries, rather than lessons.

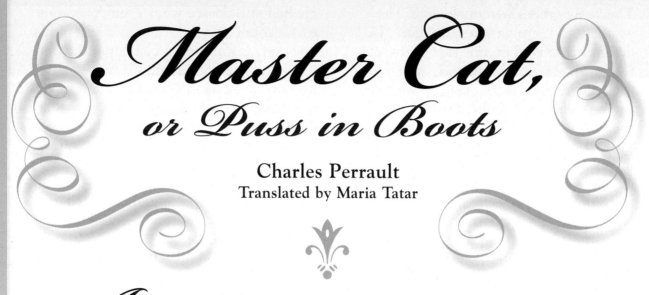

Master Cat,
or Puss in Boots

Charles Perrault
Translated by Maria Tatar

A miller left to his three sons all his worldly possessions: a mill, a donkey, and a cat. The estate was divided up quickly. No one called in a notary[1] or an attorney, for they would have quickly consumed the paltry inheritance. The oldest son got the mill; the second son received the donkey; and the youngest got nothing but the cat.

The youngest son was heartbroken when he saw how little he had inherited. "My brothers can earn an honest living if they decide to join forces," he said. "But as for me, once I've eaten the cat and made a muff[2] from its skin, I will surely starve to death."

The cat listened to this speech but pretended not to hear it and said in a solemn and earnest manner: "Don't be upset, master. Just get me a pouch and have a pair of boots[3] made up so that I can get through the underbrush easily, and you'll see that you really don't have that bad a deal."

Although the cat's master was not encouraged by this declaration, he had noticed that this cat was able to catch rats

---

1. A *notary* is a public officer authorized to administer oaths and certify documents.

2. A *muff* is a fluffy tube often made of fur designed so that one hand can be slipped in at each end for warmth.

3. In seventeenth-century France, a *pair of boots* was a sign of elegance.

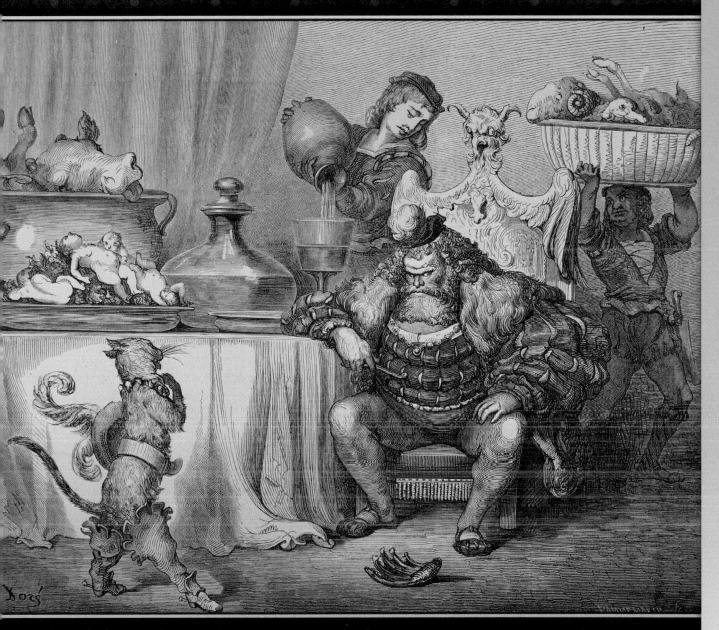

Puss in Boots, 1883. Gustave Dore. Engraving. Private collection.

and mice by playing clever tricks (hanging upside down by his paws or lying down in flour and playing dead), and so he saw a ray of hope in his miserable situation.

As soon as the cat was given what he had asked for, he brashly pulled on his boots, hung the pouch around his neck, held the strings with his forepaws, and raced over to a warren that housed a large number of rabbits. He put a little clover and lettuce into the pouch, lay down next to it, and played dead. Then he waited for one of the little rabbits, one inexperienced in the ways of the world, to crawl into the sack and try to eat what was in it.

Just as he was stretching out, he scented success: a young rabbit, still wet behind the ears, hopped into the sack. Master Cat pulled the strings in a flash, grabbed the bag, and, without feeling the least pity for his prey, killed it.

Proud of his prize, he raced straight to the king's palace and demanded an audience with him. He was ushered into the chambers of His Majesty, and, upon entering, bowed deeply to the king and said: "I am presenting you with a rabbit from my lord, the Marquis de Carabas (that was the name he had bestowed on his master). He has instructed me to present it to you on his behalf."

"Tell your master that I am grateful to him and that he has given me great pleasure."

Some time later, the cat hid in a field of wheat, keeping his pouch open. When two partridges entered it, he pulled the strings and caught both of them. Then he presented them to the king, just as he had done with the rabbits. The king accepted the two partridges gratefully and gave the cat a small token of his appreciation.

For two to three months, the cat continued presenting the king with game of one kind or another, always "shot by his master." One day, he learned that the king was planning to go on an excursion along the riverbank with his daughter, the most beautiful princess in the world. He said to his master: "If you want to make your fortune, then take my advice. Just go over to the river and take a swim at the spot I will show you. Leave the rest to me."

The Marquis de Carabas did as the cat told him, without knowing exactly what good would come of it. While he was in the water, the king drove by, and the cat began to yowl at the top of his lungs: "Help! Help! My lord, the Marquis de Carabas, is drowning!"

Puss in Boots, 1868. Gustave Dore. Engraving. Private collection.

At the sound of the yowling, the king stuck his head out the coach window, and when he recognized the cat that had brought him game so many times, he ordered his guards to hurry to the aid of the Marquis de Carabas.

While the guards were rescuing the poor Marquis de Carabas, the cat went up to the royal coach and told the king that thieves had stolen his master's clothing while he was swimming. He had done everything he could by shouting, "Stop the thieves!" but it was no use. In reality, the scoundrel had hidden the clothes under a rock.

The king ordered the officers of the royal wardrobe to fetch one of his finest suits for the Marquis de Carabas. The king paid him a thousand compliments. Since the fine clothes that the marquis was wearing flattered him (he was both handsome and statuesque), the king's daughter found him much to her liking. All the Marquis de Carabas had to do was to cast two or three respectful and somewhat tender glances in her direction to make her fall head over heels in love with him.

The king insisted that the marquis ride in his carriage and accompany them on their excursion. The cat, delighted to see that his plan was succeeding, ran on ahead. When he came across some peasants who were mowing a field, he said: "Listen to me, my good people. If you do not say that the fields you are mowing belong to the Marquis de Carabas, each and every one of you will be cut into little pieces until you look like chopped meat!"

The king did not fail to ask the mowers whose field they were mowing: "It belongs to our lord, the Marquis de Carabas," they all said in unison, for the cat had frightened them with his threats.

"You have a very substantial inheritance there," the king said to the Marquis de Carabas.

"You can see, Sire, that this field offers an abundant yield every year," the marquis replied.

Master Cat made a point of staying ahead of the coach. When he met some reapers, he said: "Listen to me, my good people. If you do not say that all of this wheat you are reaping belongs to the Marquis de Carabas, you will be cut into little pieces until you look like chopped meat."

The king drove by a moment later and wanted to know who owned the wheat fields in the vicinity. "They belong to the Marquis de Carabas," the mowers all replied, and the king once more expressed his pleasure to the marquis.

Master Cat made a point of staying in front of the coach, and he said the same thing to everyone he met. The king was astonished at the vast amount of property owned by the Marquis de Carabas.

At last Master Cat arrived at a beautiful castle owned by an ogre who was renowned for his wealth.[4] All the lands through which the king had been traveling were in his domain. The cat, who had made a point of finding out who this ogre was and learning the extent of his powers, asked for an audience. He claimed that he could not possibly be so close to his castle without paying his respects.

The ogre received him as politely as an ogre can and asked him to sit down.

"It has been said," the cat stated, "that you have the ability to transform yourself into any animal at all. I'm told that you can, for example, turn yourself into a lion or an elephant."

"It's true," replied the ogre brusquely, "and just to prove it, I will turn into a lion."

---

4. An *ogre who was renowned for his wealth* may refer to a character who symbolizes a feudal lord.

The cat was so terrified at seeing a lion before him that he instantly scurried up to the gutters on the roof, not without some pain and peril, for his boots were not made for walking on tiles.

A little later, when the cat saw that the ogre had turned back to his former state, he scampered back down and admitted that he had been terrified.

"It has also been said," the cat declared, "but I can hardly believe it, that you have the power to take the shape of small animals. I've heard, for example, that you can change into a rat or a mouse. I confess that it seems utterly impossible to me."

"Impossible?" the ogre replied. "Take a look."

At that moment, he transformed himself into a mouse, which ran across the floor. As soon as the cat saw it, he pounced on it and ate it up.

Meanwhile, the king, who could see the beautiful castle of the ogre from his coach, was hoping to enter it. The cat heard the sound of the coach rolling over the drawbridge, ran to meet it, and said to the king: "Your Majesty, welcome to the castle of the Marquis de Carabas!"

"What?" the king shouted. "Does this castle also belong to you, Monsieur Marquis? I have never seen anything as beautiful as this courtyard and the buildings surrounding it. Let's go inside, if you please."

The marquis took the hand of the young princess, and they followed the king, who went up the stairs. When they entered the grand hall, they discovered a magnificent repast[5] prepared by the ogre for his friends, who were supposed to see him that very day, but who did not dare enter, knowing that the king was there.

The king was as charmed by the many qualities of the Marquis de Carabas, as was his daughter, who remained head over heels in love with him. Realizing how much wealth he possessed, the king said to him, after having quaffed[6] five or six glasses of wine: "It's up to you whether you want to become my son-in-law or not, Monsieur Marquis."

The marquis, bowing deeply, accepted the honor conferred on him by the king. That very day he married the princess. The cat became a great lord and never again had to run after mice, except when he wanted to amuse himself.

Moral

However great the benefit
Of inheriting a tidbit
Handed down from father to son.
Young people with industry
Will prefer using ingenuity[7]
Even if the gains are hard-won.

Second Moral

If a miller's son can have success
In winning the heart of a fair
    princess
And drawing tender gazes from her,
Then watch how his manner,
    youth, and dress,
Inspire in her tenderness,
They count for something, you'll
    concur.[8] ❧

---

5. A *repast* is a meal or a snack.

6. *Quaffed* means "to have drunk deeply."
7. *Ingenuity* means "cleverness."
8. *Concur* means "to agree."

✍ Quickwrite

Fairy tales are often intended for children and sometimes contain a lesson. What do you think the intended lesson of "Puss in Boots" was for people in seventeenth-century France? Is this a lesson for children or adults? Explain your answers in a paragraph.

Wrap-Up: Comparing Literature

Across Time and Place

- *How Stories Came to Earth* retold by Kaleki

- *Coyote Steals Fire* retold by Richard Erdoes and Alfonso Ortiz

- *Master Cat, or Puss in Boots* by Charles Perrault

COMPARE THE Big Idea Gods and Spirits

Group Activity Tricksters often use supernatural powers to reach their goals. In "How Stories Came to Earth" and "Coyote Steals Fire," the tricksters use these powers to gain something from a god or a magical being. In "Puss in Boots," the cat uses his wits, rather than supernatural abilities, to gain wealth and status. In a small group, discuss the following questions. Cite evidence from the texts to support your points.

1. Do the tricksters in these three tales use their magical powers for good or bad purposes? Explain.

2. How do the tricksters and others in these tales regard Nyame the sky-god, Thunder, and the ogre?

3. How does "Puss in Boots" differ from the other two tales? Why do you think this story lacks a character that is either a god or a spirit?

COMPARE Trickster Tales

Writing The trickster in each of these tales makes a change that affects the community in which he lives. Some of these changes are for the good of society, while others are more selfish in nature. In a brief essay, compare the strategies each trickster uses to fulfill his goal. Discuss how these strategies are beneficial, destructive, or both. Finally, conclude your essay by discussing whether the outcomes achieved by the tricksters justify the means they used.

COMPARE Cultures

Speaking and Listening To some extent, these trickster tales reflect the cultural beliefs and values of the society from which they were derived or in which they were written. Research the Ashanti, Klamath, and French cultures that shaped these stories. Then give a brief oral presentation to the class about your findings, comparing and contrasting cultural similarities and differences.

Kukujumuku, 1992. John Goba. Painted wood and porcupine quills, 130 x 60 x 65 cm. The Pigozzi Collection, Geneva.

LOG ON ▶ **Literature** Online

Selection Resources For Selection Quizzes, eFlashcards, and Reading-Writing Connection activities, go to glencoe.com and enter QuickPass code GLW6053u1.

Before You Read

Edju and the Two Friends

Connect to the Folktale

Think about a quarrel you once had with a friend. What was the outcome of the argument? Write a journal entry in which you reflect on the quarrel and its outcome.

Build Background

The following trickster tale features Edju (also spelled Eshu), one of the most important gods of the Yoruba people of Nigeria. At first glance, Edju does not seem to deserve much respect—he plays tricks on gods and humans alike and enjoys stirring up mischief. The Yoruba, however, view him as both a creative and a destructive force.

Set Purposes for Reading

Big Idea Gods and Spirits

Traditional African literature often explores the interactions between humans and gods or spirits. As you read the following folktale, ask yourself, What are Edju's motivations for his behavior?

Literary Element Irony

Irony is a contrast between reality and appearance or expectations. **Dramatic irony** occurs when the reader or audience knows something that a character does not know. As you read "Edju and the Two Friends," ask yourself, What are some examples of dramatic irony in this tale?

Reading Strategy Connect to Personal Experience

One way to connect to a literary work is to draw upon your personal background to create meaning. As you read the following folktale, ask yourself, How is the friends' quarrel similar to a quarrel I have had?

....

Tip: Compare Relationships Make a chart like the one below to record similarities and differences between the quarrel described in the story and your own experiences.

"Edju and the Two Friends"	My Own Experience
The two friends always dressed alike.	I bought a shirt that my friend also wanted.

Learning Objectives

For pages 52–55

In studying this text, you will focus on the following objectives:

Literary Study: Analyzing irony.

Reading: Connecting to personal experience.

Writing: Writing an anecdote.

Vocabulary

toil (toil) *n.* fatiguing work or effort; p. 54 *The long day's toil left the laborer exhausted.*

retort (ri tôrt′) *v.* to reply in kind, especially with anger or with a witty or an insulting response; p. 54 *Her comments often cause me to retort sarcastically.*

assailant (ə sā′lənt) *n.* attacker; p. 54 *The police officer captured the young woman's assailant after a foot chase.*

dissension (di sen′shən) *n.* disagreement; discord; p. 54 *The town meeting produced no solution to the problem and only increased dissension.*

....

Tip: Antonyms Antonyms are words that have opposite or nearly opposite meanings and are the same part of speech. For example, the words *toil* and *relaxation* are antonyms.

Edju
& the Two Friends

Translated by Paul Radin

Ayo, 1990. Agbagli Kossi (Togo). Painted wood. Height: 107cm. The Pigozzi Collection, Geneva.

View the Art This sculpture is an Ayo—a servant or an escort for a spirit, according to the Mamy Wata religion. An Ayo usually has three heads. How does this representation of an Ayo reflect the plot of "Edju and the Two Friends"?

Once upon a time, Olorun[1] first created Enja, or mortal man, and, after that, Edju, the god. Once there were a pair of friends. When they went out they were always dressed alike. Everyone said, "These two men are the best of friends." Edju saw them and said, "These men are very dear to each other. I will make them differ and that will be a fine beginning for a very big Idja [lawsuit]." The fields of these friends adjoined. A path ran between and separated them. Edju used to walk on it of a morning and then wore a "filla" or black cap.

Now, when Edju wanted to start this quarrel, he made himself a cap of green, black, red, and white cloth, which showed a different color from whatever side it was looked at. He put it on one morning on his walk abroad. Then he took his tobacco

1. *Olorun* is the original and supreme sky god who created hundreds of other lesser gods according to Yoruban belief.

Connect to Personal Experience *Based on your own experiences with friends, how would you describe the relationship between these two friends?*

pipe and put it, not, as usual, in his mouth, but at the nape[2] of his neck, as if he were smoking at the back of his head. And then he took his staff as usual, but, this time, carried it upside down, that is to say, so that it hung, not over his breast in front, but over his shoulder behind. Both the friends were at work in their fields. They looked up for a second. Edju called out, "Good morning!" They gave him the same and went on with their **toil.**

Then they went home together. One said to the other, "The old man (Edju) went the opposite road through the fields today. I noticed that by his pipe and stick." The other said, "You're wrong. He went the same way as usual, I saw it by the way his feet were going." The first said, "It's a lie; I saw his pipe and his staff much too plainly; and, besides, he had on a white instead of a black cap." The second one **retorted,** "You must be blind or asleep; his cap was red." His friend said, "Then you must have already had some palm-wine this morning, if you could see neither the color of his cap, nor the way he was walking." The other one answered him, "I haven't even seen a drop this morning, but you must be crazed." The other man said, "You are making up lies to annoy me." Then the other one said, "Liar yourself! And not for the first time by a good deal." One of them drew his knife and went for the other who got a wound. He also drew his knife and cut his **assailant.** They both ran away bleeding to the town. The folk saw them and said, "Both these friends have been attacked. There will be war." One of them said, "No, this liar is no friend of mine." And the other one, "Don't believe a single word of his. When he opens his mouth, the lies swarm from it."

Meanwhile, Edju had gone to the King of the town. He said to the King, "Just ask the two friends what is the matter with them! They have cut each other's heads about with knives and are bleeding!" The King said, "What, the two friends, who always wear clothes alike have been quarreling? Let them be summoned!" So it was done. The King asked them, "You are both in sad case. What made you fall out?" They both said, "We could not agree as to what it was that went through our fields this morning." Then the King asked, "How many people went along your footpath?" "It was a man who goes the same way every day. Today he went in another direction, wearing a white cap instead of a black one," said one of the friends. "He lies," shouted the other; "the old man had on a red cap and walked along in the usual direction!" Then the King asked, "Who knows this old man?" Edju said, "It is I. These two fellows quarreled because I so willed it." Edju pulled out his cap and said, "I put on this cap, red on one side, white on the other, green in front, and black behind. I stuck my pipe in my nape. So my steps went one way while I was looking another. The two friends couldn't help quarreling. I made them do it. Sowing **dissension** is my chief delight." ◁

---

2. *Nape* is the back of the neck.

Vocabulary

toil (toil) *n.* fatiguing work or effort
retort (ri tôrt´) *v.* to reply in kind, especially with anger or with a witty or an insulting response
assailant (ə sā´lənt) *n.* attacker

Gods and Spirits *What other figures from world mythology remind you of Edju?*

Vocabulary

dissension (di sen´shən) *n.* disagreement; discord

After You Read

Respond and Think Critically

Respond and Interpret

1. Did you find this story humorous? Why or why not?

2. (a)What does Edju decide to do to the two friends? (b)Why does Edju choose these friends as his victims?

3. (a)What do the two friends see when Edju walks past them? (b)How does Edju's behavior set off a chain of events?

Analyze and Evaluate

4. (a)Why do you think Edju confesses his trickery? (b)What do you think will happen to him after his confession?

5. Do you think the two farmers were truly good friends before their quarrel, or was their friendship superficial? Explain.

6. What do you think is the lesson of "Edju and the Two Friends"?

Connect

7. **Big Idea** **Gods and Spirits** In your opinion, does the tale portray Edju as evil or merely mischievous? Use evidence from the story to support your answer.

8. **Connect to Today** (a)What are some examples of tricksters in film, television, or literature today? (b)Why do you think tricksters have a timeless appeal?

Literary Element Irony

Authors sometimes use dramatic irony for comic effect.

1. Do you think dramatic irony is intended for comedic effect in this story? Explain.

2. What might the dramatic irony of this story teach readers about friendship?

Reading Strategy Connect to Personal Experience

By connecting the events, emotions, and characters in a literary work to your own life, you will be able to better understand the text and to recall information you learned from it.

1. Do you think the account of the two friends' sudden quarrel was realistic? Why or why not?

2. In your experience, what are some of the most frequent causes of quarrels between friends?

LOG ON ▶ **Literature** Online

Selection Resources For Selection Quizzes, eFlashcards, and Reading-Writing Connection activities, go to glencoe.com and enter QuickPass code GLW6053u1.

Vocabulary Practice

Practice with Antonyms With a partner, brainstorm three antonyms for each boldfaced vocabulary word below. Then discuss your choices with your classmates. Be prepared to explain why you chose your words.

toil   retort   assailant   dissension

EXAMPLE: haughty

Antonyms: approachable, humble, modest

Sample explanation: A haughty person behaves coldly toward others, but an approachable person behaves warmly.

Writing

Write an Anecdote "Edju and the Two Friends" employs dramatic irony to describe a quarrel between friends. Think of a comedic or a dramatic event in your life when people around you had more information about the situation than you did. Write an anecdote providing insight into this experience. You may want to use a chart like the one on page 52 to identify examples of dramatic irony in your life.

The Storyteller as Translator

AMONG THE MANDINGO PEOPLE OF WEST AFRICA, THE *SUNDIATA*— the epic of Mali—is a story that lives, grows, and changes. It is an enduring part of people's lives. From childhood on, many West Africans experience the story through the dynamic performances of a griot, a storyteller-musician who chants or sings the verses to music and acts out the dramatic parts.

Griots perform the *Sundiata* at ceremonies and festivals in villages and towns throughout West Africa. Oral versions of the story can be traced to the thirteenth century, but not until the twentieth century did these oral versions start to be preserved through writing. As a result, there are hundreds of variations of the *Sundiata*; each version reflects the unique storytelling of a particular griot.

> *"My guitar, for me, is like a book. Once I start playing, I am inspired and everything comes into my mind."*
>
> —griot Djeli Baba Sissoko

Improvising an Epic

Each time an audience sees a griot perform the *Sundiata*, the experience is a little different. The griot takes the basic story and reworks it to fit the situation and the mood of the audience. For example, the griot may create a song that praises the host or patron or add an ancestor of the patron as a minor character. A griot may modernize the epic by referring to contemporary weapons or clothing, or historical figures. The epic may also be used to explain a village custom. If the audience is enjoying a particular scene, such as a battle, the griot may draw it out to entertain it. If the audience seems bored, the griot may condense a scene. The griot constantly adapts to the audience, who not only claps and sings, but also interjects questions and comments.

Griots relating people's history while looking at fox tracks.

In essence, the griot translates the *Sundiata* by reshaping the basic story to make it relevant to the audience and location of each performance. The version you will read (see pages 58–64) was told by griot Djeli Mamoudou Kouyaté to historian D. T. Niane, who adapted it into prose. As you read, note how Kouyaté's version of Sundiata's first attempt to walk differs from this version by griot Bamba Suso:

> *"When he had grasped the rods, they both broke. They said, 'How will Sunjata [Sundiata] get up?' He himself said to them, 'Call my mother; When a child has fallen down, it is his mother who picks him up.' When his mother came, He laid his hand upon his mother's shoulder, And he arose and stood up."*

Becoming a Living Library

Griots have been called "living libraries" because they store the history, tales, songs, and traditions of the Mandingo people in their minds. They pass on this "library" from one generation to the next by reciting epics and other stories. A griot is both born into this role and trained for it. Mandingo society is organized by occupational castes, or classes, and to become a griot, a person must be born into the griot caste. However, not every child of a griot becomes a storyteller. Only children who show special talent become apprenticed to a master griot within their clan or extended family.

Griots looking at fox tracks in a sand grid to read the future.

In addition to learning the stories, apprentices learn to build, repair, and play musical instruments. Music is just as important to the griot as words. Apprentices study the tunes, rhythms, and words of all the stories in the repertoire of their master. As they practice storytelling, the master coaches them on how to use their voices and incorporate movements and gestures into their performances. Eventually, the apprentice pulls all this training together into the performance of an epic. However, it can take 50 years to become a master. Griots are proud of their knowledge and skill. Kouyaté claimed that the "warmth of the human voice" is superior to books, which cannot speak.

LOG ON ▶ **Literature** Online

Literature and Reading For more about storytellers and the translators in this book, go to glencoe.com and enter QuickPass code GLW6053u1.

Respond and Think Critically

1. Do you agree with Kouyaté's claim, which implies that it is better to hear a story told than to read it in a book? Why or why not?

2. How is each performance of the *Sundiata* a kind of translation?

3. How do birth and training contribute to the development of a griot?

Before You Read

from *Sundiata*

Connect to the Epic

Who are your heroes? What qualities draw you to these men and women? Discuss these questions with a partner.

Build Background

The *Sundiata* (sōōn dyä′tə) is the epic of the Mandingo people, who live in present-day Mali and parts of coastal West Africa. It celebrates the founding of the ancient Mali Empire. A king named Sundiata appears in the epic as a mythical hero. Oral poets known as griots (grē′ōz) have performed the *Sundiata* for more than five centuries and continue to recite it today.

Set Purposes for Reading

Big Idea **The Magic of Words**

As you read, ask yourself, What aspects of Mandingo culture and history are preserved in this oral text?

Literary Element **Epic**

An **epic** is a long narrative poem about a larger-than-life hero who embodies the values of his or her people. Oral epics are passed from generation to generation. As you read, ask yourself, What elements indicate that this text is an epic?

Reading Strategy **Make Inferences About Characters**

To make **inferences about characters** means to come to conclusions based on the evidence about a character's traits, beliefs, or motivations. As you read, ask yourself, What details contribute to my inferences about each character?

....

Tip: Focus on Details Use a chart like the one below to record your inferences about the characters.

Details	Inferences About Characters
"...she kept a little garden in the open ground behind the village. It was there that she passed her brightest moments looking after her onions..."	Sogolon is modest and enjoys the simple things in life.

Learning Objectives

For pages 58–64

In studying this text, you will focus on the following objectives:

Literary Study: Analyzing epic.

Reading: Making inferences about characters.

Writing: Writing a journal entry.

Vocabulary

derisively (di rī′siv lē) *adv.* using ridicule or scorn to show contempt; p. 61 *The old man spoke derisively of his family, which had moved away.*

affront (ə frunt′) *n.* a deliberate insult; p. 61 *The mayor felt that the reporter's question was an affront to his dignity.*

discreetly (dis krēt′lē) *adv.* unnoticeably; p. 61 *The girls discreetly passed out invitations for their friend's surprise birthday party.*

heedless (hēd′lis) *adj.* inconsiderate; thoughtless; p. 62 *We were heedless of our unwashed hands, eager to get to the dinner table.*

....

Tip: Word Parts Recognizing word parts can help you unlock the meaning of an unfamiliar word. For example, heedless is formed from the words *heed,* which means "to pay attention" and *less,* which means "not having."

from The Lion's Awakening from Sundiata

Retold by D. T. Niane
Translated by G. D. Pickett

Characters

MARI DJATA (Also called Sundiata and Sogolon Djata) hero of the epic

SOGOLON KEDJOU Mari Djata's mother

SASSOUMA The Queen Mother

BALLA FASSÉKÉ Mari Djata's griot

FARAKOUROU Master Smith and soothsayer

SOGOLON DJAMAROU Mari Djata's sister

Even before he was born, Sundiata was destined for greatness. Acting on the instructions of a soothsayer, his father, the King of Mali, marries a hideous, hunchbacked woman named Sogolon. As foretold, the couple has a son. It seems, however, that the boy is unlikely to become a great leader as has been predicted. At the age of seven Sundiata is still unable to walk. He and his ugly mother are the object of cruel jokes and jealous abuse by the old king's first wife.

Seated figure. Segou, Mali region. Terracotta.
Musee Barbier-Mueller, Geneva.

View the Art In what way does this figure
remind you of Sundiata?

Sogolon Kedjou and her children lived on the queen mother's leftovers, but she kept a little garden in the open ground behind the village. It was there that she passed her brightest moments looking after her onions and gnougous.[1] One day she happened to be short of condiments and went to the queen mother to beg a little baobab[2] leaf.

"Look you," said the malicious Sassouma, "I have a calabash full. Help yourself, you poor woman. As for me, my son knew how to walk at seven and it was he who went and picked these baobab leaves. Take them then, since your son is unequal to mine." Then she laughed **derisively** with that fierce laughter which cuts through your flesh and penetrates right to the bone.

Sogolon Kedjou was dumbfounded. She had never imagined that hate could be so strong in a human being. With a lump in her throat she left Sassouma's. Outside her hut Mari Djata, sitting on his useless legs, was blandly eating out of a calabash. Unable to contain herself any longer, Sogolon burst into sobs and seizing a piece of wood, hit her son.

Visual Vocabulary
A *calabash* is a gourd whose hard shell is used as a utensil, such as a bottle or a dipper.

1. *Gnougous* (noo′gooz′) are vegetables similar to spinach.
2. A *baobab* (bā′ə bab′) is a tropical tree of the silk-cotton family. Its edible fruit resembles a gourd, and its bark can be used for making paper, cloth, and rope.

Make Inferences About Characters *Why do you think Sassouma focuses her insults on Mari Djata's inability to walk?*

Vocabulary

derisively (di rī′siv lē) *adv.* using ridicule or scorn to show contempt

"Oh son of misfortune, will you never walk? Through your fault I have just suffered the greatest **affront** of my life! What have I done, God, for you to punish me in this way?"

Mari Djata seized the piece of wood and, looking at his mother, said, "Mother, what's the matter?"

"Shut up, nothing can ever wash me clean of this insult."

"But what then?"

"Sassouma has just humiliated me over a matter of a baobab leaf. At your age her own son could walk and used to bring his mother baobab leaves."

"Cheer up, Mother, cheer up."

"No. It's too much. I can't."

"Very well then, I am going to walk today," said Mari Djata. "Go and tell my father's smiths to make me the heaviest possible iron rod. Mother, do you want just the leaves of the baobab or would you rather I brought you the whole tree?"

"Ah, my son, to wipe out this insult I want the tree and its roots at my feet outside my hut."

Balla Fasséké, who was present, ran to the master smith, Farakourou, to order an iron rod.

Sogolon had sat down in front of her hut. She was weeping softly and holding her head between her two hands. Mari Djata went calmly back to his calabash of rice and began eating again as if nothing had happened. From time to time he looked up **discreetly** at his mother who was murmuring in a low voice, "I want the whole tree, in front of my hut, the whole tree."

Make Inferences About Characters *What can you infer about Mari Djata from his offer to bring his mother the whole tree?*

Vocabulary

affront (ə frunt′) *n.* a deliberate insult
discreetly (dis krēt′lē) *adv.* unnoticeably

All of a sudden a voice burst into laughter behind the hut. It was the wicked Sassouma telling one of her serving women about the scene of humiliation and she was laughing loudly so that Sogolon could hear. Sogolon fled into the hut and hid her face under the blankets so as not to have before her eyes this **heedless** boy, who was more preoccupied with eating than with anything else. With her head buried in the bedclothes Sogolon wept and her body shook violently. Her daughter, Sogolon Djamarou, had come and sat down beside her and she said, "Mother, Mother, don't cry. Why are you crying?"

Mari Djata had finished eating and, dragging himself along on his legs, he came and sat under the wall of the hut for the sun was scorching. What was he thinking about? He alone knew.

The royal forges were situated outside the walls and over a hundred smiths worked there. The bows, spears, arrows and shields of Niani's warriors came from there. When Balla Fasséké came to order the iron rod, Farakourou said to him, "The great day has arrived then?"

"Yes. Today is a day like any other, but it will see what no other day has seen."

The master of the forges, Farakourou, was the son of the old Nounfaïri, and he was a soothsayer like his father. In his workshops there was an enormous iron bar wrought by his father Nounfaïri. Everybody wondered what this bar was destined to be used for. Farakourou called six of his apprentices and told them to carry the iron bar to Sogolon's house.

When the smiths put the gigantic iron bar down in front of the hut the noise was so frightening that Sogolon, who was lying down, jumped up with a start. Then Balla

Musician playing a kora. Dogon sculpture. Wood. Brooklyn Museum, NY.

Fasséké, son of Gnankouman Doua, spoke.

"Here is the great day, Mari Djata. I am speaking to you, Maghan, son of Sogolon. The waters of the Niger can efface the stain from the body, but they cannot wipe out an insult. Arise, young lion, roar, and may the bush know that from henceforth it has a master."

The apprentice smiths were still there, Sogolon had come out and everyone was watching Mari Djata. He crept on all fours and came to the iron bar. Supporting himself on his knees and one hand, with the other hand he picked up the iron bar without any effort and stood it up vertically. Now he was resting on nothing but his knees and held the bar with both his hands. A deathly silence had gripped all those present. Sogolon Djata closed his eyes, held tight, the muscles in his arms tensed. With a violent jerk he threw his weight on to it and his knees left the ground. Sogolon Kedjou was all eyes and watched her son's legs which were trembling as though from an electric shock. Djata was sweating and the sweat ran from his brow. In a great effort he straightened up and was on his feet at one go —but the great bar of iron was twisted and had taken the form of a bow!

Then Balla Fasséké sang out the "Hymn to the Bow," striking up with his powerful voice:

"Take your bow, Simbon,
Take your bow and let us go.
Take your bow, Sogolon Djata."

When Sogolon saw her son standing she stood dumb for a moment, then suddenly she sang these words of thanks to God who had given her son the use of his legs:

"Oh day, what a beautiful day,
Oh day, day of joy;
Allah Almighty, you never created a
 finer day.
So my son is going to walk!"

Standing in the position of a soldier at ease, Sogolon Djata, supported by his enormous rod, was sweating great beads of sweat. Balla Fasséké's song had alerted the whole palace and people came running from all over to see what had happened, and each stood bewildered before Sogolon's son. The queen mother had rushed there and when she saw Mari Djata standing up she trembled from head to foot. After recovering his breath Sogolon's son dropped the bar and the crowd stood to one side. His first steps were those of a giant. Balla Fasséké fell into step and pointing his finger at Djata, he cried:

"Room, room, make room!
The lion has walked;
Hide antelopes,
Get out of his way."

Behind Niani there was a young baobab tree and it was there that the children of the town came to pick leaves for their mothers. With all his might the son of Sogolon tore up the tree and put it on his shoulders and went back to his mother. He threw the tree in front of the hut and said, "Mother, here are some baobab leaves for you. From henceforth it will be outside your hut that the women of Niani will come to stock up."

Sogolon Djata walked. From that day forward the queen mother had no more peace of mind. ∾

The Magic of Words *Why might passages such as this be particularly effective when spoken aloud?*

Epic *What do you think is the significance of Balla Fasséké's exclamation and his reference to Djata as a lion?*

After You Read

Respond and Think Critically

Respond and Interpret

1. In a short paragraph, describe your feelings about the main characters.

2. (a)What does Mari Djata declare when he learns about his mother's encounter with Sassouma? (b)How would you describe his attitude on this occasion?

3. (a)Describe how Mari Djata stands up. (b)Why do you think Sassouma trembles when she sees him in this position?

4. (a)What action does Mari Djata perform for his mother? (b)How do you interpret the last statement he makes in this episode?

Analyze and Evaluate

5. (a)Why do you think Sassouma treats Sogolon so unfairly? (b)In your opinion, was Sogolon's reaction to the treatment she received from Sassouma justified? Why or why not?

6. A **symbol** is an object or an action that stands for something else in addition to itself. What does Mari Djata's act of standing up symbolize?

Connect

7. **Big Idea** **The Magic of Words** How is the oral tradition of the griot represented in and by this work?

8. **Connect to Today** Is personal honor as important to people today as it is to the characters in the *Sundiata*? Explain.

Literary Element Epic

The *Sundiata* is called a **folk epic** because it arose through oral storytelling, from the collective experiences of a people.

1. What values do you think were important to the ancient Mandingo people?

2. Why do you think epics are important in many different cultures?

Reading Strategy Make Inferences About Characters

Readers can better understand the theme of a work by making **inferences** about the characters. Review the chart you made on page 58.

1. What inferences did you make about Mari Djata?

2. How did these inferences about Mari Djata help you understand the theme?

LOG ON ▶ **Literature** Online

Selection Resources For Selection Quizzes, eFlash-cards, and Reading-Writing Connection activities, go to glencoe.com and enter QuickPass code GLW6053u1.

Vocabulary Practice

Practice with Word Parts For each boldfaced vocabulary word, identify the word in the right column that shares a part or a root with it. Underline the part they share. Determine the meaning of the related word and explain how it is connected to the vocabulary word.

1. **derisively**   ridiculous

2. **affront**   doubtless

3. **discreetly**   indiscernible

4. **heedless**   confrontation

EXAMPLE: phil<u>anthrop</u>ic, <u>anthrop</u>ology

<u>Philanthropic</u> means "marked by a concern for humankind." <u>Anthropology</u> is the study of human beings. *Philanthropic* and *anthropology* both relate to humans.

Writing

Write a Journal Entry Imagine you are Sassouma. Write a journal entry that describes your feelings about Mari Djata and his sudden ability to walk.

Vocabulary Workshop

Thesaurus Use

Literature Connection

"When the smiths put the gigantic iron bar down in front of the hut the noise was so frightening that Sogolon, who was lying down, jumped up with a start."

In this passage from the *Sundiata*, D. T. Niane could have called the iron bar *big*, instead of *gigantic*. He could also have chosen the word *scary* rather than *frightening*. Niane chose precise words to convey meaning. You can do the same by using **synonyms**, or words with the same or similar meanings. While some synonyms are practically interchangeable, many have subtle differences in meaning or connotation.

Most dictionaries list and explain the differences among synonyms, but for many words you will need a thesaurus. A **thesaurus** is a specialized dictionary of synonyms and antonyms. Thesauruses (or thesauri) are organized either traditionally by concept or in dictionary order.

Traditional Organization Probably the best-known thesaurus is *Roget's Thesaurus,* which organizes large categories of words related to a general concept. To find a synonym for the verb *taste,* for example, browse the alphabetical index of categories until you find the category *senses,* which includes the subentry *taste*. The index will refer you to the page for the subentry, where you will find a list of synonyms.

Dictionary Organization This type of thesaurus presents words in alphabetical order, as a dictionary does.

Here is a sample entry for the word *gigantic.*

gigantic *adj. Russia is a gigantic country, the largest in the world:* ————— part of speech
very large, huge, vast, enormous, immense, giant, colossal, mammoth, ←———— example sentence
massive, tremendous, stupendous; mighty, unwieldy, ponderous, ←——— list of synonyms with the most common ones first
hulking, strapping, bulky, lumpish, lubberly, towering, voluminous,
large-scale, prodigious, gargantuan, Herculean, titanic
Ant. small, little, tiny, miniature, compact; infinitesimal, microscopic; ←——— list of antonyms
feeble, puny, weak; petty, insignificant; dwarfish, pygmy.

Practice Using a thesaurus, find two synonyms for each word below. Then look up the definitions of these synonyms in a dictionary to identify the precise meaning for each one.

    a. laugh   **b.** tenderly   **c.** sorrow   **d.** pity   **e.** mad

Synonyms

Synonyms are words with the same or similar meanings. A **thesaurus** is a reference guide used to find groups of synonyms.

Test-Taking Tip
To decide whether two words are synonyms, first identify the part of speech for each word. Synonyms are always the same part of speech.

LOG ON ▶ **Literature** Online

Vocabulary For more vocabulary practice, go to glencoe.com and enter QuickPass code GLW6053u1.

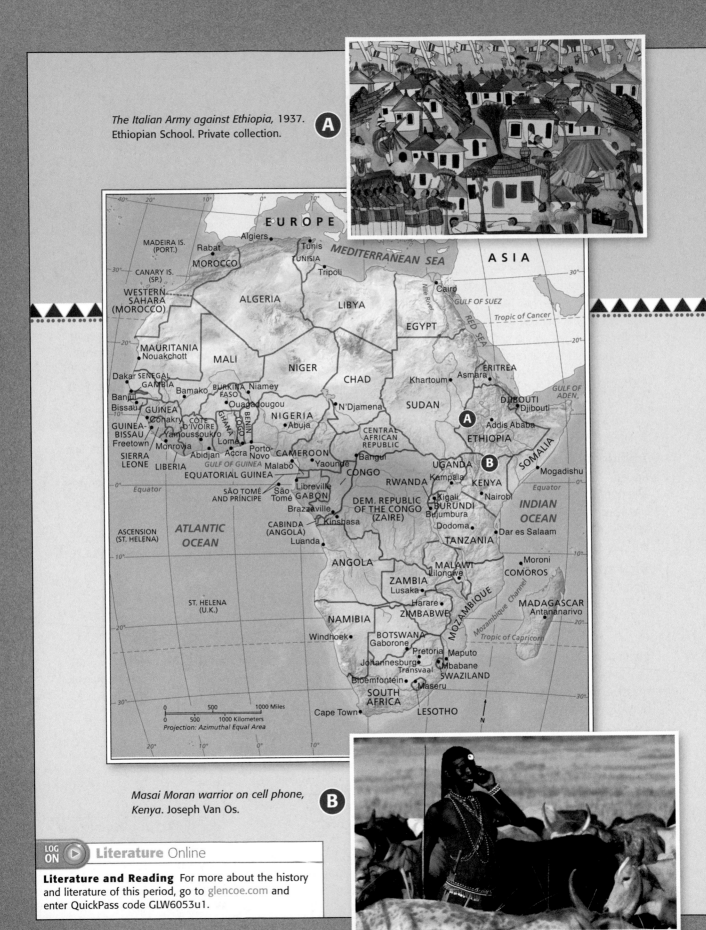

The Italian Army against Ethiopia, 1937. Ethiopian School. Private collection. **A**

Masai Moran warrior on cell phone, Kenya. Joseph Van Os. **B**

LOG ON ▶ **Literature** Online

Literature and Reading For more about the history and literature of this period, go to glencoe.com and enter QuickPass code GLW6053u1.

Modern AFRICA

1800–Present

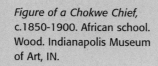

Figure of a Chokwe Chief, c.1850-1900. African school. Wood. Indianapolis Museum of Art, IN.

Being There

Contemporary African nations, like other nations throughout the world, have been deeply affected by political upheavals, rapid technological changes, and globalization. Yet many Africans still value the traditional customs and beliefs of their people. Oral storytellers continue to recount the stories of their ancestors, while tribes such as the Masai continue to wear traditional dress. Throughout the continent, Africans share a common goal: to preserve their heritages while facing the challenges of the modern world.

Looking Ahead

European colonization of Africa in the nineteenth and twentieth centuries left an indelible mark, stripping many African nations of freedom, equality, and traditional values. Modern African literature reflects the struggle of these countries to preserve their cultural values and to build independent nations in the postcolonial era.

Keep the following questions in mind as you read:

▲ How did Africans fight colonialism and racism in the twentieth century?

▲ What are the conflicts between traditional and modern African cultures?

▲ What are the major problems African nations face today?

TIMELINE 1800–Present

AFRICAN LITERATURE

1800

1824
Jean-François Champollion completes translation of the Rosetta Stone

1842
German translator Karl Richard Lepsius publishes first collection of the *Book of the Dead*

1897
Mary Kingsley publishes *Travels in West Africa*

Mary Kingsley

1934
Negritude movement is founded

Figure of Queen Victoria, Yoruba, Nigeria

AFRICAN EVENTS

1800

1816–1828
Shaka establishes and rules the Zulu kingdom

1822
Formerly enslaved people from the United States found Liberia

1837–1901
Queen Victoria reigns

1879
Anglo-Zulu War is fought

1884–1885
European colonialists divide Africa at the Berlin Conference

1900

1910
British and Dutch settlers form the Union of South Africa

1922
Egypt declares independence from Britain

1935
Italy invades Ethiopia

1948
South Africa establishes apartheid

WORLD EVENTS

1800

1807
Britain abolishes the slave trade

1815
Napoleon is defeated at Waterloo

1861
American Civil War begins

1900

◀ **1903**
Wright Brothers make first powered flight

1914 ▶
World War I begins

1917
Russian Revolution begins

1929
Great Depression begins

1939
World War II begins

LOG ON ▶ **Literature** Online

Literature and Reading To explore the Interactive Timeline, go to glencoe.com and enter QuickPass code GLW6053u1.

1950

1956
Naguib Mahfouz publishes
Palace Walk

1958
Chinua Achebe publishes
Things Fall Apart

1960
Wole Soyinka's play
A Dance of the Forests
is produced

1966
Grace Ogot publishes
The Promised Land

1967
Ngugi wa Thiong'o
publishes *A Grain of Wheat*

1968
Bessie Head publishes
When Rain Clouds Gather

1975

1986
Wole Soyinka wins the
Nobel Prize

1986
Mark Mathabane publishes
Kaffir Boy

1988
Naguib Mahfouz wins
the Nobel Prize

1991
Nadine Gordimer wins
the Nobel Prize
▼

1950

1960
Léopold Sédar Senghor
becomes the first president
of Senegal

1962
Nelson Mandela is
arrested and imprisoned
in South Africa

1967
Civil war breaks out
in Nigeria

1975

1979
Idi Amin, ruler of Uganda,
is overthrown
▼

1990
Nelson Mandela is
released from prison;
apartheid begins to
be dismantled

1994
Nelson Mandela is elected
president of South Africa;
Hutu kill 500,000 Tutsi
in Rwanda

1950

1959
Fidel Castro comes to
power in Cuba

1966
Chinese Cultural
Revolution begins

Young Bhopal residents
paint a skull on the
enclosing wall of the
Union Carbide India Ltd

1975

1975
Vietnam War ends

◄ **1984**
Bhopal disaster takes place
in India

1991
Soviet Union collapses,
ending the Cold War

2004
Massive tsunami
devastates southeast Asia

Reading Check

Analyze Graphic Information How long was
Nelson Mandela imprisoned in South Africa?

For pages 66–77

In studying this text, you will focus on the following objectives:

Literary Study: Analyzing literary periods.

Reading: Evaluating historical influences.
Connecting to the literature.

Modern AFRICA

1800–Present

Historical, Social, and Cultural Forces

Leatherwork panel depicting colonial scenes,
Hausa, Northern Nigeria, c.1940.

Colonialism in Africa

Before the nineteenth century, European knowledge of Africa was restricted primarily to the coastal regions. African merchants traded gold, copper, ivory, and timber for imported goods from Europe at trading stations on the coasts; therefore, Europeans did not need to travel to the interior of the continent for goods. Before 1880, Europeans were content to let African rulers and merchants represent European interests. However, between 1880 and 1900, intense rivalries involving nationalism and economics grew among Britain, France, Germany, Belgium, Italy, Spain, and Portugal. These European colonial powers met in Berlin, Germany, in 1884–1885 to settle their competing claims to territory in Africa. No African delegates were present at the Berlin Conference, and as a result, nearly all of Africa was placed under European control.

The age of colonialism lasted only 100 years, yet it had a profound and traumatic effect on the continent. Colonial regimes varied widely in their treatment of African people but were generally characterized by economic exploitation and racism. While some African countries gained independence earlier, many nations did not gain independence until World War II or later.

Rise of African Nationalism

As the twentieth century began, Africans became increasingly resentful of colonial powers. Across the continent, a new class of Africans educated in Europe began to organize political parties and movements seeking the end of foreign rule. Colonial powers often used force to end these efforts, but they also made minor reforms in an attempt to satisfy the demands of native citizens. These small concessions were inadequate, however, and by the 1930s, an increasing number of African leaders were calling for independence. In Kenya, Jomo Kenyatta, who had been educated in Britain, argued that British rule was destroying traditional African culture. Léopold Sédar Senghor, who had studied in France, organized an independence movement in Senegal.

The Transition to Independence

After World War II, Europeans began to realize that colonial rule in Africa was increasingly unnecessary. Many African nations finally won independence when Great Britain and France let go of their colonial empires in the late 1950s and the 1960s. In 1957, the Gold Coast, renamed Ghana, was the first former British colony to gain independence. By 1965, dozens more new African nations had followed. After a series of brutal guerrilla wars, the Portuguese surrendered the colonies of Mozambique and Angola in the 1970s. For many African nations, independence precipitated a new series of problems, including economic stagnation, political corruption, ethnic violence, and overpopulation.

> *"The time for the healing of the wounds has come."*
>
> —Nelson Mandela,
> from his inauguration speech

Demonstrators celebrate the independence of Guinea-Bissau from Portuguese rule.

New Hopes

One of the poisonous legacies of colonialism in South Africa was apartheid, an extreme form of racial segregation. Apartheid faced criticism from around the world, but its most famous critic was Nelson Mandela, who, in 1994, became the first black South African president.

Mandela had been sentenced to life imprisonment in 1962 for his anti-apartheid activities. He served almost 26 years in maximum-security prisons but never wavered from the fight for equality. Worldwide opposition to apartheid finally led the white South African government to dismantle apartheid laws, and Mandela was released in 1990.

Tradition and Innovation

Art often reflects the interests, personal values, and histories of the artists who create it. In modern Africa, traditional art forms are continually reimagined in ways that reflect globalization and contemporary ideals. For example, African musicians such as Ladysmith Black Mambazo and Youssou N'Dour are famous worldwide for their synthesis of traditional African sounds with pop music. Changes in traditional art are also reflected on a regional scale; for example, a hand-blocked West African cloth may have a political slogan, rather than a customary pattern.

> *"Here we stand*
> *infants overblown,*
> *poised between two civilizations…"*
>
> —Mabel Segun, from "Conflict"

Music

The convergence of traditional and modern types of music can be heard across Africa. In Algeria, traditional Arab-influenced songs are accompanied by synthesizers and digital drums. In South Africa, choirs combining Zulu and Christian church choral styles provided anthems for the liberation struggle. Many contemporary African musicians have worked with performers from other cultures. For example, kora (a stringed instrument made from a gourd) players from Mali have recorded with Spanish guitar players and Arab percussionists to produce music that blends a variety of traditions.

Drummer salutes the Kabaka, (Bugandan People's King). Ssentema in Wakiso District, Uganda.

Symbols of the Kings of Abomey. Textile display. Abomey, Benin.

Paintings and Prints

The art of painting has a long history in Africa. The tradition can be seen in prehistoric rock art, traditional ritual body and face painting, and the brightly decorated walls of contemporary African villages. Painting on canvas became increasingly popular throughout the twentieth century. For example, in the early 1970s, Nigerian painters called the Nsukka group began to use Ibo images to express modern themes.

Art in Context

Traditionally, African art was often intended to be seen only when in ceremonial use. Masks were meant to be viewed in motion, made mysterious by shadow and torchlight, rather than admired in an exhibit. However, as African art gained worldwide recognition, museums and galleries began collecting and selling it. African artists have begun to produce masks and other traditional objects as works of art in themselves, rather than for their traditional purposes in rituals.

Ndebele urban mural art. Esther Mahlangu. Mabhoko, South Africa. ▶

 PREVIEW **Big Ideas** of Modern Africa

1 Tradition and Change	**2** The Price of Freedom	**3** Living with Independence
Modern Africa is a study in contrasts. Old and new, native and foreign exist side by side. Modern African authors have responded to these contrasts by exploring the connections between traditional and modern African ways of life. **See page 74**	Imperialism and the efforts of black Africans to gain independence and equal rights have dominated contemporary African history. African authors have explored and documented these issues and their effects on both white and black Africans. **See page 75**	Faced with problems such as ethnic violence and political corruption, many African countries have struggled since gaining independence. African authors have responded to these struggles in works that range from humorous to poignant. **See page 76**

Tradition and Change

The tension between tradition and modern ideas is among the most powerful topics in contemporary African literature and society. This tension often arises when traditional ways of life collide with foreign ideas.

City and Countryside

In Africa, European colonialism was first and most firmly established in the cities. Many cities are direct products of colonial rule, including Dakar, Senegal; Lagos, Nigeria; Cape Town, South Africa; Brazzaville, Republic of the Congo; and Nairobi, Kenya. In rural areas, however, modern influence has had less of an effect. Millions of people throughout Africa live much as their ancestors did, in thatched dwellings without plumbing or electricity. People in rural communities often farm or hunt by traditional methods, wear regional clothing, and adhere to local customs and beliefs. Some people who live in the countryside believe that the cities are corrupting traditional African values and customs.

Man with Bicycle, 20th century. Yoruba people, Nigeria. Wood, Height: 35 3/4 in. Collection of The Newark Museum.

> " ... listen
> *To the deep pulse of Africa beating*
> *in the midst of forgotten villages.*"
>
> —Léopold Sédar Senghor, from
> "Night of Sine"

A Cultural Debate

An early response to colonial influence in African culture was the Negritude movement. Negritude was started in the early 1930s by a group of French-speaking African and Caribbean authors, led by poet Léopold Sédar Senghor (see pages 78–82). They rejected the notion of European superiority and asserted that Africa already had a

vibrant culture of its own. The name *Negritude* was chosen to suggest a common heritage shared by all black people.

English-speaking African authors began to criticize the Negritude movement in the 1950s and 1960s. These authors felt that Negritude idealized Africa and restricted the creative spirit. Authors such as Nigerian novelist Chinua Achebe (see pages 92–101) have explored both the positive and negative aspects of traditional African society. Achebe's fiction illustrates the problems faced by Africans who live amid conflicting cultural values.

Reading Check

Compare and Contrast What is the difference between the outlook of the Negritude movement and that of its critics?

The Price of Freedom

Many black Africans fought in the British and French armies during World War I, hoping that their countries would be rewarded with independence when the war ended. These hopes were not realized.

African Protests

In the years following World War I, Africans became increasingly active in politics and the fight for independence. Soldiers who had fought in the armies of colonial countries had learned new ideas about freedom and nationalism. In Kenya, the Young Kikuyu Association organized a protest against British rule in 1921, resulting in the arrest of the group's leader. When an angry crowd stormed the jail and demanded his release, government authorities fired into the crowd and killed at least twenty people. In the early 1950s, the Kenyan nationalist movement known as Mau Mau began an armed resistance against the British. By the time the Mau Mau rebels were defeated in 1956, more than 11,000 Kikuyu had been killed or put into detention camps. Among the victims were members of the family of Kenyan author Ngugi wa Thiong'o (see pages 133–140). Despite the Mau Mau defeat, the uprising did pave the way to Kenyan independence in 1963. Jomo Kenyatta, who had been jailed as a Mau Mau leader in 1953, became the new nation's first prime minister.

> *"Remember Sharpeville*
> *Remember bullet-in-the-back day"*
>
> —Dennis Brutus, from "Sharpeville"

A protester carries a portrait of Nelson Mandela during funerals for victims of police repression. Cape Town, South Africa.

Fighting Apartheid

In South Africa, black citizens formed the African National Congress (ANC) in 1912. The ANC sought reform, but its efforts met with little success. By the 1950s, South African whites had established apartheid, a system of legalized segregation. In 1960, police in Sharpeville fired on marchers protesting apartheid, killing 69 people. After Nelson Mandela was arrested in 1962, ANC members called for armed resistance. Despite this, after Mandela was elected president of South Africa in 1994, he asked Archbishop Desmond Tutu (see pages 103–106) to lead the Truth and Reconciliation Commission, which sought to review apartheid atrocities without resorting to violent retribution.

Reading Check

Analyze Cause-and-Effect Relationships How did World War I encourage the development of nationalist movements in Africa?

Living with Independence

The hopes and dreams of African nationalists had been directed toward winning independence from Europe. However, for many countries, independence resulted in a number of unexpected economic and social problems.

Political Challenges

African nationalists had hoped that independence would lead to a stable political order based on democracy. Unfortunately, some democratic governments gave way to military regimes and one-party states. Many African authors have been forced to spend long periods in exile because of their criticism of authoritarian governments. Wole Soyinka (see pages 120–123), the first African to be awarded the Nobel Prize in Literature, spent several years in exile after being charged with treason by the military government of Nigeria.

In other countries, warring ethnic groups undermined the concept of nationhood. These conflicts were not surprising, given that European governments had often determined the boundaries of African nations with little regard for the ethnic differences of African people. Ethnic conflicts often resulted in war and bloodshed. During the early 1990s, conflict erupted between the Hutu and Tutsi peoples in the central African states of Burundi and Rwanda. In 1994, a Hutu rampage left some 500,000 Tutsi dead in Rwanda.

Economic and Health Problems

Independence did not bring economic prosperity to Africa. Most African nations still relied on exporting a single crop or natural resource. The efforts to create modern economies were also frustrated by high population growth. Additionally, droughts led to widespread starvation. As a result of these problems, poverty continues to affect many Africans, especially in rural areas.

African cities have grown tremendously and are often surrounded by enormous slums. This growth has overwhelmed sanitation and transportation systems, resulting in pollution and massive traffic jams. Another problem Africa faces is the epidemic of acquired immune deficiency syndrome (AIDS). By the end of the twentieth century, AIDS was the leading cause of death for Africans. The epidemic has resulted in splintered families, devastated communities, and economic hardships across the continent.

With the relaxing of apartheid laws, blacks can ride on white buses in South Africa.

Reading Check

Analyze Cause-and-Effect Relationships How did colonialism create conditions that led to ethnic violence in modern African nations?

Wrap-Up

Legacy of the Period

The impact of European colonialism extends beyond Africa to countries around the world, including many in Asia and the Caribbean. The colonial powers reshaped local religious and cultural traditions while simultaneously stripping native citizens of basic human rights. In Africa, the absence of any African representatives at the Berlin Conference resulted in a continent run almost entirely by colonial rule for decades.

Throughout the twentieth century, African authors, artists, and intellectuals have explored the conflict between traditional ways of life and colonialism in a variety of ways. The works of these artists have given people outside Africa an appreciation of the importance of intercultural understanding and have shown what the influence of globalization may be in years to come.

Cultural and Literary Links

▲ Chinua Achebe's novel *Things Fall Apart* was partially inspired by his desire to refute the

Opportunity Magazine, cover, June 1926. Aaron Douglas. Schomburg Center for Research in Black Culture, The New York Public Library.

primitive impression of Africa given by Joseph Conrad's *Heart of Darkness*.

▲ The Negritude movement drew inspiration from the Harlem Renaissance, the cultural movement among African Americans in the Harlem neighborhood of New York City in the 1920s.

Literature Online

Unit Resources For additional skills practice, go to glencoe.com and enter QuickPass code GLW6053u1.

Activities

Use what you have learned about the period to do one of these activities.

1. Follow Up Go back to Looking Ahead on page 67 and answer the questions.

2. Contrast Literary Periods In the United States, formerly enslaved people, such as Frederick Douglass, wrote slave narratives. Research slave narratives and write an essay comparing the concerns of the authors with those of African postcolonial authors.

3. Speaking/Listening Research the issues involved in the debate between the Negritude movement and the African authors who opposed it. Then hold a panel discussion exploring the relative merits of African tradition and Western culture.

4. Take Notes Use this organizer to explore your responses to the literary works in this part.

 BOUND BOOK

Before You Read

Night of Sine

Senegal

Meet **Léopold Sédar Senghor**
(1906–2001)

Poet, politician, philosopher, and teacher, Léopold Sédar Senghor (seng′hôr) was one of the most brilliant lights of Africa's postcolonial period. In 1960, Senghor became the first president of Senegal, a position he would retain for the next two decades. A leader in the struggle for independence from France, Senghor was also a leader in the effort to modernize and democratize the young country of Senegal, which remains one of the most stable nations in Africa.

> "I leave matter to the engineers. To the Poet belongs the spirit."
>
> —Léopold Sédar Senghor

Africa and the West The son of a wealthy planter and trader, Senghor spent his early years in a traditional Senegalese village in the Sine (sē′nä) region. He was educated in a Roman Catholic seminary with the aim of becoming a priest. By the time he turned twenty, however, Senghor had found that his calling lay elsewhere. After a brief time in Dakar, Senegal's capital, Senghor traveled to Paris, France, in 1928. While there, he completed his studies and began writing poems while working as a teacher. At the start of World War II, Senghor was drafted into the French army. In 1940, he was captured and held in Nazi concentration camps, where he continued to write poetry. After his release two years later, Senghor became active in the underground French Resistance fighting Nazi Germany's occupation.

From Liberation to Retirement As the war came to a close, Senghor became involved in politics, first as a member of the French Constituent Assembly and then as the mayor of Thiès, one of Senegal's largest cities. When Senegal was finally liberated from French rule in 1960, Senghor became the country's first president. Although a coup was attempted only two years into his first term, he remained in power until 1980, when he became the first African president to leave office voluntarily. Senghor's presidency was filled with many advances for Senegal, including the modernization of its agriculture and vast economic and trade reforms. The poet-president also wrote the lyrics to the country's national anthem. After retiring, Senghor returned to France, where he continued to write poetry and completed a memoir. In 1984, Senghor became the first African to be inducted into the French Academy—France's most prestigious, exclusive, and oldest literary organization.

As a poet, Senghor was influenced by black writers from the United States and the Caribbean as well as French poets such as Charles Baudelaire and Arthur Rimbaud.

Literature Online

Author Search For more about Léopold Sédar Senghor, go to glencoe.com and enter QuickPass code GLW6053u1.

Literature and Reading Preview

Connect to the Poem

How do our native country and culture shape us? Write a journal entry in which you reflect on these influences and their effects on your life.

Build Background

In the 1930s, Senghor and other black intellectuals living in Paris formed the Negritude movement. They came together to explore their African heritage and to reclaim it as a source of cultural pride. In Senghor's poetry and the poetry of other Negritude authors, similar topics often recur: the beauty of the African landscape, the dignity of the African people, and the rejection of colonizers' assumptions of superiority.

Set Purposes for Reading

Big Idea Tradition and Change

As you read, ask yourself, What traditions did Africa lose as a result of colonialism?

Literary Element Repetition

Repetition is the recurrence of sounds, words, phrases, lines, or stanzas in a literary work. Repetition may be used to enhance the unity of a work. It can also create a musical or a rhythmic effect or emphasize an idea. As you read, ask yourself, How does repetition affect the meaning of this poem?

Reading Strategy Monitor Comprehension

When you monitor comprehension during reading, you make sure you understand what you are reading. The syntax of this poem can be difficult to follow and may require clarification. As you read, ask yourself, Do I understand this line or stanza? If not, reread it carefully.

Tip: Restate Passages When you encounter passages that are difficult to comprehend, it can be helpful to rewrite them using both language and a sequence that make sense to you. Use a chart like the one below.

Unclear Passage	My Rewrite
"Woman, lay on my forehead your perfumed hands, hands softer than fur."	"Woman, lay your perfumed hands, which are softer than fur, on my forehead."

Learning Objectives

For pages 78–82

In studying this text, you will focus on the following objectives:

Literary Study: Analyzing repetition.

Reading: Monitoring comprehension.

Writing: Writing a monologue.

Vocabulary

rustle (rus′əl) *v.* to make a succession of soft crackling sounds; p. 80 *The student's papers rustle in the light breeze.*

acrid (ak′rid) *adj.* strong, bitter, and often unpleasant in smell or taste; p. 81 *The hikers covered their noses to block out the acrid smell.*

torrent (tôr′ənt) *n.* a powerful flood or outpouring; p. 81 *Every meeting started with a torrent of information.*

Tip: Context Clues Context clues are words and sentences surrounding an unfamiliar term that can help you determine the meaning of the term. For example, in the sentence *The hikers covered their noses to block out the acrid smell,* the fact that the hikers "covered their noses" indicates that the smell was bad, or *acrid.*

Night of Sine

Léopold Sédar Senghor

Translated by John Reed & Clive Wake

Woman, lay on my forehead your perfumed hands, hands
    softer than fur.
Above, the swaying palm trees **rustle** in the high night breeze
Hardly at all. No lullaby even.
The rhythmic silence cradles us.
5 Listen to its song, listen to our dark blood beat, listen
To the deep pulse of Africa beating in the mist of
    forgotten villages.

Baule dancers. African Ivory Coast. Gilded wood. Private collection.

Repetition *In your opinion, what is the effect of the repetition in these lines?*

Vocabulary

rustle (rus′əl) *v.* to make a succession of soft crackling sounds

See the tired moon comes down to her bed on the slack sea
The laughter grows weary, the story-tellers even
Are nodding their heads like a child on the back of its mother

10 The feet of the dancers grow heavy, and heavy the voice of
        the answering choirs.

It is the hour of stars, of Night that dreams
Leaning upon this hill of clouds, wrapped in its long
        milky cloth.
The roofs of the huts gleam tenderly. What do they say so
        secretly to the stars?
Inside the fire goes out among intimate smells that are
        acrid and sweet.

15 Woman, light the clear oil lamp, where the ancestors
        gathered around may talk as parents talk when the children
        are put to bed.
Listen to the voice of the ancients of Elissa.° Exiled like us
They have never wanted to die, to let the **torrent** of their
        seed be lost in the sands.
Let me listen in the smoky hut where there comes a glimpse
        of the friendly spirits
My head on your bosom warm like a *dang*° still steaming
        from the fire.

20 Let me breathe the smell of our Dead, gather and speak out
        again their living voice, learn to
Live before I go down, deeper than diver, into the high
        profundities of sleep.

16 Elissa is a village in Guinea-Bissau, a country directly south of Senegal.

19 Dang is couscous that is cooked in broth.

Tradition and Change *What do the activities in lines 7–10 suggest about the culture's views on tradition?*

Vocabulary

acrid (ak′rid) *adj.* strong, bitter, and often unpleasant in smell or taste
torrent (tôr′ənt) *n.* a powerful flood or outpouring

After You Read

Respond and Think Critically

Respond and Interpret

1. Do the images of night in this poem remind you of any personal memories? If so, which ones?

2. (a)Whom is the speaker addressing in the poem? (b)What is the relationship between the speaker and the person addressed?

3. (a)What does the speaker want to listen to in the hut? (b)Why might listening to this be important to him?

Analyze and Evaluate

4. (a)**Tone** is the attitude a speaker takes toward his or her subject. How would you describe the tone in this poem? (b)Does the tone seem appropriate? Why or why not?

5. (a)To what senses does the imagery in this poem appeal? (b)Do you think the images are effective? Explain.

6. (a)What cultural values does Senghor express in this poem? (b)In what way are these values similar to your own?

Connect

7. **Big Idea** **Tradition and Change** What elements of traditional Africa does this poem present?

8. **Connect to the Author** As the president of Senegal, Senghor tried to ensure that modernization did not destroy Africa's people and ideals. How does this poem reflect his vision?

Literary Element **Repetition**

Alliteration is the repetition of consonant sounds at the beginnings of words.

1. Find an example of alliteration in this poem. What does it add to the poem?

2. What effect does the repetition of the word *listen* have throughout this poem?

Reading Strategy **Monitor Comprehension**

Syntax, or word arrangement, can sometimes make a poem difficult to comprehend.

1. What line or stanza was most difficult for you to understand? Why did you find it confusing?

2. How did you rewrite this portion of the poem to improve your comprehension?

LOG ON ▶ **Literature** Online

Selection Resources For Selection Quizzes, eFlashcards, and Reading-Writing Connection activities, go to glencoe.com and enter QuickPass code GLW6053u1.

Vocabulary Practice

Practice with Context Clues Identify the context clues that help you determine the meaning of each boldfaced vocabulary word in the following sentences.

1. The branches softly **rustled** in the mild breeze.

2. The flowers in the vase no longer smelled mild and sweet; in fact, they were growing **acrid.**

3. A **torrent** of water swept over the town, crushing houses and cars.

Writing

Write a Monologue The poem mentions several voices and speakers, such as the choir, the ancestors, and the roofs of the huts. Write a monologue from the perspective of one of these voices, using repetition to create a rhythmic effect. Refer to the comprehension chart you made on page 79 to clarify the different voices.

Before You Read

Half a Day

Meet **Naguib Mahfouz**
(1911–2006)

When Naguib Mahfouz (nä zhēb′ mä fōōz′) was growing up, the novel had only a minor place in Arabic literature. Mahfouz loved fiction, however, so he learned his craft by focusing on the works of European authors. Mahfouz's major influences included French authors Honoré de Balzac, Gustave Flaubert, and Guy de Maupassant. After studying philosophy at the University of Cairo in Egypt, Mahfouz took a civil service job and wrote fiction in his spare time. He skillfully adapted Western literary techniques to portray Egyptian society and culture.

> "If the urge to write should ever leave me, I want that day to be my last."
>
> —Naguib Mahfouz

Literary Influences Born and raised in Cairo, Mahfouz was influenced by the social, political, and cultural history of his country. Three of his early novels focused on ancient Egypt. However, his novel *New Cairo* was a turning point for his work, and he became "preoccupied, almost without exception, with the present." He claimed that his novel *The Harafish* is partially based on his conversations among his friends in the underclass, about whom he remarked, "nobody had any genuine sympathy for us or understood our situation." The year 1967 marked a new phase in Mahfouz's literary career, and he began writing drama and extended fables. Drawing not only from politics and literature,

Mahfouz found inspiration in world cinema, Arabic music, and Islamic art and architecture.

A Range of Responses Mahfouz's writings earned him both acclaim and criticism. His 1947 novel *Midaq Alley* depicted life in a ghetto in Cairo and established him as a realistic writer. In *The Cairo Trilogy*, his most famous work, Mahfouz chronicles the period from World War I to the military coup that toppled the monarchy of King Farouk in 1952 and the rise of Gamal Abdel Nasser. An early supporter of Nasser's government, Mahfouz eventually expressed distaste for its later reforms. His 1967 novel *Children of Gebelawi*—a narrative about mankind and religion—was originally banned by Islamic fundamentalists, but it is now available in Egypt. Despite the controversy surrounding some of his works, Mahfouz was awarded the Nobel Prize in Literature in 1988, becoming the first Arabic author to win the prestigious award. The Swedish Academy, which grants the prize, hailed Mahfouz as an author who "has formed an Arabian narrative art that applies to all mankind."

LOG ON **Literature** Online

Author Search For more about Naguib Mahfouz, go to glencoe.com and enter QuickPass code GLW6053u1.

Literature and Reading Preview

Connect to the Story

What events have been rites of passage in your life? Write a journal entry about these events and how they affected the way in which you perceive the world.

Build Background

"Half a Day" is set in Cairo, the capital of Egypt. The older sections of Cairo contain medieval mosques and other historic architecture, which stand in contrast to the city's modern downtown. More than a thousand years old, Cairo grew rapidly during the twentieth century, leading to overcrowding and pollution. Mahfouz imaginatively portrays these changes.

Set Purposes for Reading

Big Idea Tradition and Change

As you read, ask yourself, How does the school in the story emphasize Egyptian traditions, and how does the passage of time cause changes in the environment?

Literary Element Plot

Plot is the sequence of events in a story. Most plots develop around a **conflict,** a struggle between opposing forces. A plot begins with **exposition,** which introduces the story's characters, setting, and situation. **Rising action** develops the conflict with complications. **Climax** is the emotional high point of the story. **Falling action** shows what happens after the climax, and the **resolution** shows how the conflict is resolved. As you read "Half a Day," ask yourself, What is the sequence of events in this story?

Reading Strategy Question

Questioning is a step you can take to check your understanding of a literary work or make predictions about what will happen in the text. As you read "Half a Day," ask yourself, What questions can I ask to clarify the events and conflict in this story?

Tip: Answer Your Questions Use a two-column chart to quiz yourself as you read.

Question	Answer
Why does the narrator say he was 'cast' into school?	Cast connotes being discarded. The boy feels he is being abandoned by his parents or punished for some wrongdoing.

Learning Objectives

For pages 83–89

In studying this text, you will focus on the following objectives:

Literary Study: Analyzing plot.

Reading: Questioning.

Researching: Conducting Internet research.

Vocabulary Preview

throng (throng) *n.* a crowd of many people; p. 86 *After the accident, a throng of reporters gathered to observe the situation.*

avail (ə vāl′) *n.* use or advantage; p. 86 *Her efforts to persuade her friend to join the volleyball team were to no avail.*

horde (hôrd) *n.* a teeming crowd or throng; p. 87 *She held her son's hand so she would not lose him in the horde of shoppers.*

refuse (ref′ūs) *n.* trash; garbage; p. 87 *As he cleaned his apartment, he discarded the refuse from each room.*

Tip: Analogies Analogies are comparisons that show similarities between two things that are otherwise dissimilar.

horde : individual :: fleet : ship

The relationship between these words is one of a part to a whole. An individual is part of a horde just as a ship is part of a fleet.

Half a Day

Naguib Mahfouz
Translated by Denys Johnson-Davies

I proceeded alongside my father, clutching his right hand, running to keep up with the long strides he was taking. All my clothes were new: the black shoes, the green school uniform, and the red tarboosh. My delight in my new clothes, however, was not altogether unmarred, for this was no feast day but the day on which I was to be cast into school for the first time.

Visual Vocabulary
A *tarboosh* is a brimless red hat worn by some Muslims.

My mother stood at the window watching our progress, and I would turn toward her from time to time, as though appealing for help. We walked along a street lined with gardens; on both sides were extensive fields planted with crops, prickly pears, henna trees, and a few date palms.

"Why school?" I challenged my father openly. "I shall never do anything to annoy you."

Plot *What conflict is presented here?*

"I'm not punishing you," he said, laughing. "School's not a punishment. It's the factory that makes useful men out of boys. Don't you want to be like your father and brothers?"

I was not convinced. I did not believe there was really any good to be had in tearing me away from the intimacy of my home and throwing me into this building that stood at the end of the road like some huge, high-walled fortress, exceedingly stern and grim.

When we arrived at the gate we could see the courtyard, vast and crammed full of boys and girls. "Go in by yourself," said my father, "and join them. Put a smile on your face and be a good example to others."

I hesitated and clung to his hand, but he gently pushed me from him. "Be a man," he said. "Today you truly begin life. You will find me waiting for you when it's time to leave."

I took a few steps, then stopped and looked but saw nothing. Then the faces of boys and girls came into view. I did not know a single one of them, and none of them knew me. I felt I was a stranger who had lost his way. But glances of curiosity were directed toward me, and one boy approached and asked, "Who brought you?"

"My father," I whispered.

"My father's dead," he said quite simply.

I did not know what to say. The gate was closed, letting out a pitiable screech. Some of the children burst into tears. The bell rang. A lady came along, followed by a group of men. The men began sorting us into ranks. We were formed into an intricate pattern in the great courtyard surrounded on three sides by high buildings of several floors; from each floor we were overlooked by a long balcony roofed in wood.

"This is your new home," said the woman. "Here too there are mothers and fathers. Here there is everything that is enjoyable and beneficial to knowledge and religion. Dry your tears and face life joyfully."

We submitted to the facts, and this submission brought a sort of contentment. Living beings were drawn to other living beings, and from the first moments my heart made friends with such boys as were to be my friends and fell in love with such girls as I was to be in love with, so that it seemed my misgivings had had no basis. I had never imagined school would have this rich variety. We played all sorts of different games: swings, the vaulting horse, ball games. In the music room we chanted our first songs. We also had our first introduction to language. We saw a globe of the Earth, which revolved and showed the various continents and countries. We started learning the numbers. The story of the Creator of the universe was read to us, we were told of His present world and of His

Hereafter, and we heard examples of what He said. We ate delicious food, took a little nap, and woke up to go on with friendship and love, play and learning.

As our path revealed itself to us, however, we did not find it as totally sweet and unclouded as we had presumed. Dust-laden winds and unexpected accidents came about suddenly, so we had to be watchful, at the ready, and very patient. It was not all a matter of playing and fooling around. Rivalries could bring about pain and hatred or give rise to fighting. And while the lady would sometimes smile, she would often scowl and scold. Even more frequently she would resort to physical punishment.

In addition, the time for changing one's mind was over and gone and there was no question of ever returning to the paradise of home. Nothing lay ahead of us but exertion, struggle, and perseverance. Those who were able took advantage of the opportunities for success and happiness that presented themselves amid the worries.

The bell rang announcing the passing of the day and the end of work. The **throngs** of children rushed toward the gate, which was opened again. I bade farewell to friends and sweethearts and passed through the gate. I peered around but found no trace of my father, who had promised to be there. I stepped aside to wait. When I had waited for a long time without **avail**, I decided to return home on my own. After I had taken a few steps, a middle-aged man passed by, and I realized at once that I knew him. He came toward me, smiling, and shook me by

---

Question *What about this sentence suggests that time has passed differently than the reader might assume?*

Vocabulary

throng (throng) *n.* a crowd of many people

avail (ə vāl´) *n.* use or advantage

Plot *Read a little beyond this passage. What is the "rich variety" the narrator speaks of? Why is it important to the rising action of the plot?*

the hand, saying, "It's a long time since we last met—how are you?"

With a nod of my head, I agreed with him and in turn asked, "And you, how are you?"

"As you can see, not all that good, the Almighty be praised!"

Again he shook me by the hand and went off. I proceeded a few steps, then came to a startled halt. Good Lord! Where was the street lined with gardens? Where had it disappeared to? When did all these vehicles invade it? And when did all these **hordes** of humanity come to rest upon its surface? How did these hills of **refuse** come to cover its sides? And where were the fields that bordered it? High buildings had taken over, the street surged with children, and disturbing noises shook the air. At various points stood conjurers[1] showing off their tricks and making snakes appear from baskets. Then there was a band announcing the opening of a circus, with clowns and weight lifters walking in front. A line of trucks carrying central security troops crawled majestically by. The siren of a fire engine shrieked, and it was not clear how the vehicle would cleave its way to reach the blazing fire. A battle raged between a taxi driver and his passenger, while the passenger's wife called out for help and no one answered. Good God! I was in a daze. My head spun. I almost went crazy. How could all this have happened in half a day, between early morning and sunset? I would find the answer at home with my father.

Pedestrians walk down city street in Cairo. Sylvain Grandadam. Robert Harding Picture Library.

But where was my home? I could see only tall buildings and hordes of people. I hastened on to the crossroads between the gardens and Abu Khoda. I had to cross Abu Khoda to reach my house, but the stream of cars would not let up. The fire engine's siren was shrieking at full pitch as it moved at a snail's pace, and I said to myself, "Let the fire take its pleasure in what it consumes." Extremely irritated, I wondered when I would be able to cross. I stood there a long time, until the young lad employed at the ironing shop on the corner came up to me. He stretched out his arm and said gallantly, "Grandpa, let me take you across." ✎

---

1. A *conjurer* is a person who practices magic.

Plot *What is the climax of this story?*

Vocabulary

horde (hôrd) *n.* a teeming crowd or throng
refuse (ref´ūs) *n.* trash; garbage

Tradition and Change *What has changed about the city from the beginning of the story to this point?*

Plot *What is the resolution of the story?*

After You Read

Respond and Think Critically

Respond and Interpret

1. (a)Did the resolution of the story surprise you? Explain. (b)What comment about life might this story be making?

2. (a)What does the middle-aged man say to the narrator when they meet? (b)How does this hint at the passage of time in the story?

3. (a)What events does the narrator witness that illustrate the changes in the city? (b)What does his irritation at these events reveal about the narrator?

Analyze and Evaluate

4. (a)A **symbol** is an object or an action that stands for something else in addition to itself. What do the narrator's day at school and the title of the story symbolize? (b)How does what the narrator learns in school parallel the lessons a person learns throughout his or her life?

5. What might the different descriptions of street life at the beginning and the end of the story reveal about the narrator?

6. A story told from the **first-person point of view** is narrated by one of the characters in the story. Why do you think Mahfouz used a first-person narrator for "Half a Day"?

Connect

7. **Big Idea** **Tradition and Change** How do you think the changes in Cairo, as described in the story, affected its traditional appearance and the traditions of its people? Support your answer with evidence from the story.

8. **Connect to the Author** Mahfouz spent most of his life living in and around Cairo and watched the city change firsthand. Based on this story and what you know about his life, what do you think Mahfouz thought about these changes?

Literary Element Plot

The plot of "Half a Day" has a **surprise ending,** or an unexpected twist at the end of the story. A surprise ending is most effective when it adds to the meaning of a story rather than merely overturning the reader's expectations.

1. Is the ending of "Half a Day" a complete surprise, or did Mahfouz provide clues throughout the story to suggest that years have passed? Explain.

2. (a)Do you think the ending of "Half a Day" is effective? Why or why not? (b)How else might Mahfouz have ended the story?

Review: Imagery

As you learned on page 30, **imagery** is the "word pictures" an author creates to evoke an emotional response. Authors use **sensory details** that appeal

to one or more of the five senses to create effective imagery.

Partner Activity With a partner, review "Half a Day" and discuss imagery that you both feel is particularly strong. In a chart like the one below, list each image, which sense it appeals to, and the details that make the image effective. When you are done, discuss your choices with the class.

Image	Sense	What Makes Image Effective
"…this building that stood…like some huge, high-walled fortress, exceedingly stern and grim"	Sight	Adjectives such as "huge" and "high-walled" describe the building's appearance, while "stern and grim" capture a specific mood.

SAT Skills Practice

The author includes the image of the "fire engine's siren… shrieking at full pitch" (page 87) in order to

(A) imply that the narrator is in danger

(B) celebrate modern technology

(C) suggest that there has been a fire

(D) suggest a harsh, chaotic urban environment

(E) create suspense

Vocabulary Practice

Practice with Analogies Select the word that completes each analogy.

1. **herd : cow :: throng :**
   a. friend   **b.** leader   **c.** person   **d.** workforce

2. **victor : winner :: avail :**
   a. benefit   **b.** loss   **c.** difficulty   **d.** goal

3. **team : athlete :: horde :**
   a. group   **b.** individual   **c.** team   **d.** volume

4. **coal : miner :: refuse :**
   a. architect   **b.** farmer   **c.** waste collector
   d. lawyer

Academic Vocabulary

In this story, the narrator experiences the **phenomenon** *of growing old in what seems like only half a day.*

Phenomenon is an academic word. For example, a solar eclipse is a natural **phenomenon**. To study this word further, complete the following sentence:

An event that is _____ can be described as a **phenomenon.**

For more on academic vocabulary, see pages 36–37 and R83–R85.

Research and Report

 Internet Connection

Assignment Use reliable Internet sites to research the history of Cairo, Egypt. Then write a travel brochure for a self-guided tour through the city. Organize your tour geographically, based on the layout of the city. Include cardinal (north, south, east, and west) and ordinal (northeast, southeast, northwest, and southwest) directions as a guide to landmarks and an accompanying map or photos.

Get Ideas Generate a list of questions you would like to answer about present-day Cairo. You may want to refer to the Reading Strategy chart you made on page 84 for ideas. Next, create a list of possible primary and secondary Internet sources.

Research As you research, take notes on specific information that answers each question you listed, as well as the source where you found the information. It will help to organize your questions into categories; you can later use these categories to structure your brochure. Use the questions below to evaluate the credibility of each Web site.

- **Authority** Is the site associated with a reputable organization? Does the writer have credentials? Can he or she be contacted?

- **Accuracy** Can the information be substantiated? Are there grammatical or factual errors?

- **Objectivity** Is the writer citing a fact or offering an opinion? Is the site biased?

- **Timeliness** How often is the site updated? Can you be sure the information is not outdated?

Report Your brochure should include travel facts that would be useful to travelers as well as interesting historical information. Proofread to be sure that you have accurately synthesized information and that your writing is cohesive.

LOG ON ▶ **Literature** Online

Selection Resources For Selection Quizzes, eFlashcards, and Reading-Writing Connection activities, go to glencoe.com and enter QuickPass code GLW6053u1.

Learning Objectives

For pages 90–91

In this workshop, you will focus on the following objectives:

Grammar: Understanding how to combine sentences.

Understanding how to use prepositional, appositive, and participial phrases.

Understanding how to use coordinating and subordinating conjunctions.

Grammar Workshop

Sentence Combining

Literature Connection In this quotation from "Half a Day," Naguib Mahfouz combines two main clauses, *I hesitated and clung to his hand* and *he gently pushed me from him,* with the coordinating conjunction *but.*

> *"I hesitated and clung to his hand, but he gently pushed me from him."*

Combining sentences can dramatically improve the readability, variety, and style of your writing so that it does not sound choppy and repetitive. There are four general strategies for combining:

- deleting repeated words
- adding connecting words
- rearranging words
- changing the form of words

The example below shows one way of using some of these strategies to combine four choppy sentences.

Mahfouz is a masterful writer~~. He~~ who uses descriptive words~~. He uses~~ and[1] imagery~~.~~ to ~~He~~[2] convey~~s~~[3] important themes.

1. Use connecting words. **2. Delete repeated words.**
3. Change the form of words.

More specific strategies for combining sentences appear below.

Phrases

You can use prepositional, appositive, or participial phrases to combine sentences.

Prepositional phrases clarify relationships, such as those involving space or time. They begin with words such as *in, about,* or *with.*

I read three books. The books were about the colonization of Africa.

I read three books about the colonization of Africa.

Appositive phrases explain unfamiliar nouns. They are often set off from the rest of the sentence by commas, dashes, a colon, or parentheses.

Abu Khoda serves as a key image in the story. Abu Khoda is a busy street.

Abu Khoda, a busy street, serves as a key image in the story.

Drafting Tips

Try these strategies to combine sentences when you write.

- Read sentence variations aloud to yourself to decide which one sounds best.
- Use the context of a paragraph to decide how best to combine sentences.
- Work with a partner to get new ideas and compare sentences.
- Look for stylistic patterns in your writing.
- Take risks—they will help you develop your personal style.

Participial phrases contain verbs that function as adjectives. These verbs, which are also known as **participles,** usually end in *–ing* or *–ed*. Make sure you position participial phrases to correctly modify the right word.

The narrator is searching for his home in Cairo. He is <u>growing confused.</u>

<u>Growing confused,</u> the narrator searches for his home in Cairo.

Conjunctions and Clauses

Try using coordinating or subordinating conjunctions to turn simple sentences into more complex ones.

Coordinating Conjunctions (such as *and, but, or, for,* or *yet*) help combine two sentences that contain equally important ideas. See the quotation from Mahfouz on page 90 for an example of combining sentences using the coordinating conjunction *but.*

Subordinating Conjunctions When two sentences are not equally important, you can add a subordinating conjunction to the beginning of one of the sentences to create an adverb clause or an adjective clause. These clauses typically add supplemental information or describe a relationship based on time, location, or cause and effect.

- **Adverb clauses** modify a verb, an adjective, or another adverb and include subordinating conjunctions such as *after, because,* or *since.*

  The narrator protests. <u>He thinks he is being punished.</u>

  The narrator protests <u>because he thinks he is being punished.</u>

- **Adjective clauses** modify a noun or a pronoun and typically include a subordinating conjunction such as *who, whose,* or *that.*

  Nelson Mandela became president in 1994. He <u>had been imprisoned during apartheid.</u>

  Nelson Mandela, <u>who had been imprisoned during apartheid,</u> became president in 1994.

Revise Apply the strategies described in this workshop to combine each group of sentences below.

1. "Half a Day" is a short story. I wanted to read "Half a Day" tonight. I lost the book.
2. The Sahara desert stretches across most of northern Africa. The Sahara is vast. It consists of sand dunes and oases.
3. British rule of Cairo ended. The number of foreigners living there declined. Cairo is Egypt's capital.

Revising Tips

Evaluate your sentence combining using these criteria.

- ☑ Do I vary long and short sentences?
- ☑ Do I vary sentence openers?
- ☑ Do I use parallel structures of words, phrases, and clauses?
- ☑ Do I create emphasis with commas, colons, semicolons, dashes, and parentheses?
- ☑ Do I use different patterns to emphasize key ideas?

Test-Taking Tip

If you are unsure how to combine two sentences on a test, write down several possible opening words or phrases, and then fill in the rest.

Literature Online

Grammar For more grammar practice, go to glencoe.com and enter QuickPass code GLW6053u1.

Before You Read

The Voter

Meet **Chinua Achebe**
(born 1930)

Chinua Achebe (chēn´wää chā´bā) believes that an author's function, particularly an African author's function, is a social one. In his novels, he criticizes both the dehumanizing effects of British imperialism on the Nigerian population and the destructive influences of Nigerian political corruption that plagued his country after achieving independence. Above all, his novels express his desire to destroy the myth of African inferiority and to inspire a more tolerant society.

> "*The worst thing that can happen to any people is the loss of their dignity and self-respect. The writer's duty is to help them regain it....*"
>
> —Chinua Achebe

Christian and Ibo Roots Born in Ogidi, Nigeria, when Nigeria was still a British colony, Achebe was raised in a Christian family that had converted from the traditional religion of their Ibo (also spelled Igbo) kinsfolk. In his autobiography, he describes his parents as strong in their Christian beliefs but not fanatical. "Their lives were ruled," he says, "as much by reason as by faith; as much by common sense and compassion as by doctrine." Achebe's experiences growing up in two different cultures and his observations of Nigeria under colonial rule and after independence instilled in him a strong belief in the values of objectivity, pragmatism, and tolerance.

Things Fall Apart After graduating from college, Achebe accepted a position as a producer for the Nigerian Broadcasting Corporation. During this period, he published several of the novels that have secured his literary reputation. The first of these, *Things Fall Apart*, is the story of a traditional Ibo community that disintegrates after the arrival of European missionaries. The book earned Achebe international recognition and is regarded by some historians as the most widely read and influential African novel ever written. Achebe's later novels portray Nigerian society during colonial times and following independence.

Award Winner In 2007, Achebe won the prestigious Man Booker International Prize, which is given once every two years to a living author for his or her body of fictional work. One of the judges, South African author Nadine Gordimer, commented that Achebe's "early work made him the father of modern African literature. . . ."

LOG ON ▶ **Literature** Online

Author Search For more about Chinua Achebe, go to glencoe.com and enter QuickPass code GLW6053u1.

Literature and Reading Preview

Connect to the Story

In school elections, how do you decide which candidates to vote for? Freewrite for a few minutes about what qualities you look for in a candidate.

Build Background

Nigeria became an independent nation in 1960, but political corruption and cultural differences among ethnic groups have hampered its efforts to establish a democratic system. Following episodes of violence and a full-scale civil war, Nigeria came under the rule of military regimes at the end of the twentieth century. Achebe's story "The Voter" takes place in an Ibo village shortly after Nigerian independence.

Set Purposes for Reading

Big Idea Living with Independence

As you read, ask yourself, How does this story illustrate the political problems in Nigeria?

Literary Element Motivation

Motivation is the stated or implied reason or cause for a character's actions. As you read "The Voter," think about why the characters behave the way they do toward one another. Ask yourself questions such as, Why does Marcus Ibe host a feast for the villagers in honor of the completion of his new home?

Reading Strategy Activate Prior Knowledge

You can increase your understanding of a work of literature by drawing on knowledge you already have before reading the text. As you read "The Voter," ask yourself, What information do I have that can help me make predictions and better understand the events in this story?"

....

Tip: Use Personal Experience As you read, record details that remind you of your own experiences as well as details that are illuminated by what you have learned about Nigeria from the author biography on page 92 and the Build Background on this page. Use a chart like the one below.

Details Similar to Personal Experience	Details Illuminated by Background Knowledge
Marcus Ibe's feast reminds me of the time Bernie hosted a picnic to encourage us to vote for him.	Marcus Ibe's wealthy lifestyle illustrates the real political corruption in postcolonial Nigeria.

Learning Objectives

For pages 92–101

In studying this text, you will focus on the following objectives:

Literary Study: Analyzing motivation.

Reading: Activating prior knowledge.

Writing: Applying irony.

Vocabulary

gratitude (grat′ə tōōd′) *n.* thankfulness; p. 95 *We expressed heartfelt gratitude for his generosity in our time of need.*

constituency (kən stich′ōō ən sē) *n.* voters in a district; a group of supporters; p. 95 *The crime novel bombed because its ad campaign did not target its core constituency: mystery fans.*

nonentity (non en′tə tē) *n.* a person or a thing of little or no importance; p. 95 *Sam's inexperience with computers made him a nonentity in the eyes of the tech job recruiter.*

defiance (di fī′əns) *n.* a refusal to recognize or obey someone or something; p. 97 *Nadia's refusal to join the conspiracy was apparent by the defiance in her eyes.*

mesmerize (mez′mə rīz′) *v.* to hypnotize; spellbind; p. 97 *The fun-house mirrors started to mesmerize me the more I looked at them.*

Moving on Up, 1999. Francks Deceus. Mixed media on canvas. Private collection.

The Voter

Chinua Achebe

ufus Okeke—Roof for short—was a very popular man in his village. Although the villagers did not explain it in so many words Roof's popularity was a measure of their **gratitude** to an energetic young man who, unlike most of his fellows nowadays had not abandoned the village in order to seek work, any work, in the towns.

And Roof was not a village lout either. Everyone knew how he had spent two years as a bicycle repairer's apprentice in Port Harcourt, and had given up of his own free will a bright future to return to his people and guide them in these difficult times. Not that Umuofia needed a lot of guidance. The village already belonged *en masse* to the People's Alliance Party, and its most illustrious son, Chief the Honorable Marcus Ibe, was Minister of Culture in the outgoing government (which was pretty certain to be the incoming one as well). Nobody doubted that the Honorable Minister would be elected in his **constituency**. Opposition to him was like the proverbial fly trying to move a dunghill. It would have been ridiculous enough without coming, as it did now, from a complete **nonentity**.

As was to be expected Roof was in the service of the Honorable Minister for the coming elections. He had become a real expert in election campaigning at all levels—village, local government or national. He could tell the mood and temper of the electorate at any given time. For instance he had warned the Minister months ago about the radical change that had come into the thinking of Umuofia since the last national election.

The villagers had had five years in which to see how quickly and plentifully politics brought wealth, chieftaincy titles, doctorate degrees and other honors some of which, like the last, had still to be explained satisfactorily to them; for in their naïveté they still expected a doctor to be able to heal the sick. Anyhow, these honors and benefits had come so readily to the man to whom they had given their votes free of charge five years ago that they were now ready to try it a different way.

Their point was that only the other day Marcus Ibe was a not too successful mission school teacher. Then politics had come to their village and he had wisely joined up, some said just in time to avoid imminent dismissal arising from a female teacher's pregnancy. Today he was Chief the Honorable; he had two long cars and had just built himself the biggest house anyone had seen in these parts. But let it be said that none of these successes had gone to Marcus's head as well they might. He remained devoted to his people. Whenever he could he left the good things of the capital and returned to his village which had neither running water nor electricity, although he had lately installed a private plant to supply electricity to his new house. He knew the source of his good fortune, unlike the little bird who ate and drank

---

Motivation *According to the villagers, what was Roof's motivation for leaving a promising career?*

Living with Independence *How does the information in this passage mirror what you have learned about Nigeria after it achieved independence?*

Motivation *Do you think it is devotion to his people or something else that motivates Marcus to visit the village whenever he can? Explain.*

and went out to challenge his personal spirit. Marcus had christened his new house "Umuofia Mansions" in honor of his village, and he had slaughtered five bulls and countless goats to entertain the people on the day it was opened by the Archbishop.

Everyone was full of praise for him. One old man said: "Our son is a good man; he is not like the mortar which as soon as food comes its way turns its back on the ground." But when the feasting was over, the villagers told themselves that they had underrated the power of the ballot paper before and should not do so again. Chief the Honorable Marcus Ibe was not unprepared. He had drawn five months' salary in advance, changed a few hundred pounds into shining shillings and armed his campaign boys with eloquent little jute bags. In the day he made his speeches; at night his stalwarts conducted their whispering campaign. Roof was the most trusted of these campaigners.

Visual Vocabulary
Jute (jōot) is a flexible, glossy fiber made from one of two Asian plants.

"We have a Minister from our village, one of our own sons," he said to a group of elders in the house of Ogbuefi Ezenwa, a man of high traditional title. "What greater honor can a village have? Do you ever stop to ask yourselves why we should be singled out for this honor? I will tell you; it is because we are favored by the leaders of PAP. Whether or not we cast our paper for Marcus, PAP will continue to rule. Think of the pipe-borne water they have promised us . . . "

Besides Roof and his assistant there were five elders in the room. An old hurricane lamp with a cracked, sooty, glass chimney gave out yellowish light in their midst. The elders sat on very low stools. On the floor, directly in front of each of them, lay two shilling pieces. Outside beyond the fastened door, the moon kept a straight face.

"We believe every word you say to be true," said Ezenwa. "We shall, every one of us, drop his paper for Marcus. Who would leave an Ozo feast and go to a poor ritual meal? Tell Marcus he has our papers, and our wives' papers too. But what we do say is that two shillings is shameful." He brought the lamp close and tilted it at the money before him as if to make sure he had not mistaken its value. "Yes, two shillings is too shameful. If Marcus were a poor man—which our ancestors forbid—I should be the first to give him my paper free, as I did before. But today Marcus is a great man and does his things like a great man. We did not ask him for money yesterday; we shall not ask him tomorrow. But today is our day; we have climbed the iroko tree today and would be foolish not to take down all the firewood we need."

Roof had to agree. He had lately been taking down a lot of firewood himself. Only yesterday he had asked Marcus for one of his many rich robes—and had got it. Last Sunday Marcus's wife (the teacher that nearly got him in trouble) had objected (like the woman she was) when Roof pulled out his fifth bottle of beer from the refrigerator; she was roundly and publicly rebuked by her husband. To cap it all Roof had won a land case recently because, among other things, he had been chauffeur-

Activate Prior Knowledge *What does the phrase "whispering campaign" imply about the kind of information campaign workers spread at night? Have you ever overheard a whispering campaign? If so, what was your reaction?*

Motivation *Do you think the elders really believe every word is true? Why or why not? What actually motivates their loyalty to Roof?*

driven to the disputed site. So he understood the elders about the firewood.

"All right," he said in English and then reverted to Ibo. "Let us not quarrel about small things." He stood up, adjusted his robes and plunged his hand once more into the bag. Then he bent down like a priest distributing the host and gave one shilling more to every man; only he did not put it into their palms but on the floor in front of them. The men, who had so far not deigned to touch the things, looked at the floor and shook their heads. Roof got up again and gave each man another shilling.

"I am through," he said with a **defiance** that was no less effective for being transparently faked. The elders too knew how far to go without losing decorum. So when Roof added: "Go cast your paper for the enemy if you like!" they quickly calmed him down with a suitable speech from each of them. By the time the last man had spoken it was possible, without great loss of dignity, to pick up the things from the floor . . .

The enemy Roof had referred to was the Progressive Organization Party (POP) which had been formed by the tribes down the coast to save themselves, as the founders of the party proclaimed, from "total political, cultural, social and religious annihilation." Although it was clear the party had no chance here it had plunged, with typical foolishness, into a straight fight with PAP, providing cars and loudspeakers to a few local rascals and thugs to go around and make a lot of noise. No one knew for certain how much money POP had let loose in Umuofia but it was said to be very considerable. Their local campaigners would end up very rich, no doubt.

Up to last night everything had been "moving according to plan," as Roof would have put it. Then he had received a strange visit from the leader of the POP campaign team. Although he and Roof were well-known to each other, and might even be called friends, his visit was cold and business-like. No words were wasted. He placed five pounds[1] on the floor before Roof and said, "We want your vote." Roof got up from his chair, went to the outside door, closed it carefully and returned to his chair. The brief exercise gave him enough time to weigh the proposition. As he spoke his eyes never left the red notes on the floor. He seemed to be **mesmerized** by the picture of the cocoa farmer harvesting his crops.

"You know I work for Marcus," he said feebly. "It will be very bad . . . "

"Marcus will not be there when you put in your paper. We have plenty of work to do tonight; are you taking this or not?"

"It will not be heard outside this room?" asked Roof.

"We are after votes not gossip."

"All right," said Roof in English.

The man nudged his companion and he brought forward an object covered with a red cloth and proceeded to remove the cover. It was a fearsome little affair contained in a clay pot with feathers stuck into it.

---

1. The *pound* is the basic unit of money in the United Kingdom.

Motivation *Considering the boldness of the campaign rival's offer, why does Roof stall for time instead of immediately turning it down?*

Activate Prior Knowledge *What rationalization do the campaign worker's words imply? What everyday examples of rationalizations can you think of for doing or saying something you know is wrong?*

A Successful Life, 1995. Cheri Samba. Contemporary African Art Collection Limited.

View the Art Samba is known for his realistic brightly colored paintings. How does the lifestyle of the people in this painting compare with that of Marcus?

"The *iyi*[2] comes from Mbanta. You know what that means. Swear that you will vote for Maduka. If you fail to do so, this *iyi* take note."

Roof's heart nearly flew out when he saw the *iyi*; indeed he knew the fame of Mbanta in these things. But he was a man of quick decision. What could a single vote cast in secret for Maduka take away from Marcus's certain victory? Nothing.

"I will cast my paper for Maduka; if not this *iyi* take note."

"Das all," said the man as he rose with his companion who had covered up the object again and was taking it back to their car.

"You know he has no chance against Marcus," said Roof at the door.

"It is enough that he gets a few votes now; next time he will get more. People will hear that he gives out pounds, not shillings, and they will listen."

Election morning. The great day every five years when the people exercise power. Weather-beaten posters on walls of houses, tree trunks and telegraph poles. The few that were still whole called out their message to those who could read. Vote for the People's Alliance Party! Vote for the Progressive Organization Party! Vote for PAP! Vote for POP! The posters that were torn called out as much of the message as they could.

As usual Chief the Honorable Marcus Ibe was doing things in grand style. He had hired a highlife band from Umuru and sta-

2. An *iyi* is a tribal god.

tioned it at such a distance from the voting booths as just managed to be lawful. Many villagers danced to the music, their ballot papers held aloft, before proceeding to the booths. Chief the Honorable Marcus Ibe sat in the "owner's corner" of his enormous green car and smiled and nodded. One enlightened villager came up to the car, shook hands with the great man and said in advance, "Congrats!" This immediately set the pattern. Hundreds of admirers shook Marcus's hand and said "Corngrass!"

Roof and the other organizers were prancing up and down, giving last minute advice to the voters and pouring with sweat.

"Do not forget," he said again to a group of illiterate women who seemed ready to burst with enthusiasm and good humor, "our sign is the motor car . . . "

"Like the one Marcus is sitting inside."

"Thank you, mother," said Roof. "It is the same car. The box with the car shown on its body is the box for you. Don't look at the other with the man's head: it is for those whose heads are not correct."

This was greeted with loud laughter. Roof cast a quick and busy-like glance towards the Minister and received a smile of appreciation.

"Vote for the car," he shouted, all the veins in his neck standing out. "Vote for the car and you will ride in it!"

"Or if we don't, our children will," piped the same sharp, old girl.

The band struck up a new number: "Why walk when you can ride . . . "

In spite of his apparent calm and confidence Chief the Honorable Marcus was a relentless stickler for detail. He knew he would win what the newspapers called "a landslide victory" but he did not wish, even so, to throw away a single vote. So as soon as the first rush of voters was over he promptly asked his campaign boys to go one at a time and put in their ballot papers.

"Roof, you had better go first," he said.

Roof's spirits fell; but he let no one see it. All morning he had masked his deep worry with a surface exertion which was unusual even for him. Now he dashed off in his springy fashion towards the booths. A policeman at the entrance searched him for illegal ballot papers and passed him. Then the electoral officer explained to him about the two boxes. By this time the spring had gone clean out of his walk. He sidled in and was confronted by the car and the head. He brought out his ballot paper from his pocket and looked at it. How could he betray Marcus even in secret? He resolved to go back to the other man and return his five pounds . . . Five pounds! He knew at once it was impossible. He had sworn on that *iyi*. The notes were red; the cocoa farmer busy at work.

At this point he heard the muffled voice of the policeman asking the electoral officer what the man was doing inside. "Abi na pickin im de born?"

Quick as lightning a thought leapt into Roof's mind. He folded the paper, tore it in two along the crease and put one half in each box. He took the precaution of putting the first half into Maduka's box and confirming the action verbally: "I vote for Maduka."

They marked his thumb with indelible purple ink to prevent his return, and he went out of the booth as jauntily as he had gone in. ◞

Living with Independence *Why might Achebe have chosen a car to symbolize the PAP and a head to symbolize the POP?*

Motivation *Why does Roof put the first half of his ballot in Maduka's box and confirm this vote aloud?*

After You Read

Respond and Think Critically

Respond and Interpret

1. In this story, Roof has to make a difficult decision about how to cast his vote. Do you agree with the way he resolves this dilemma? Why or why not?

2. (a)Why is Roof popular in his village? (b)What can you infer about the village's economic situation from the narrator's explanation of Roof's popularity?

3. (a)What do the villagers think of Marcus Ibe? (b)Do you think their opinion of him is deserved? Explain.

4. (a)Why does the leader of the opposition's campaign offer Roof a bribe? (b)Do you think Roof believes he is betraying Marcus Ibe by accepting the bribe? Explain.

5. (a)What decision does Roof make in the voting booth? (b)What do you think will be the result of Roof's vote?

Analyze and Evaluate

6. (a)Apart from offering the villagers bribes, what reasons does Roof give to convince the villagers to vote for Marcus Ibe? (b)Are his reasons sincere or mere campaign rhetoric? Support your answer with evidence from the story.

7. A **theme** is a central message or idea about life in a literary work. What is the main theme in "The Voter"?

8. A **symbol** is an object or an action that stands for something else in addition to itself. What might Roof's torn ballot symbolize?

Connect

9. Big Idea **Living with Independence** How do Roof's actions in this story parallel the problems Nigeria faced after gaining independence?

10. Connect to the Author Achebe is famous for his anti-imperialist views and his appreciation of Ibo culture. Despite this, "The Voter" is a harsh criticism of Nigeria and its politics. Why might Achebe have chosen to criticize his country in this story?

Literary Element Motivation

ACT Skills Practice

The passage "As he spoke… harvesting his crops" (page 97) suggests that Roof accepts the bribe primarily because

A. he knows that Marcus will still win the election

B. he is confident that his vote will be secret

C. he wants the money

D. he is scared of the POP leader

Review: Tone

As you learned on page 25, **tone** is an author's attitude toward his or her subject matter. Tone is conveyed through elements such as word choice, punctuation, sentence structure, and figures of speech.

Partner Activity Meet with a partner to analyze the tone of "The Voter" and answer the following questions.

1. How does Achebe's use of sentence fragments throughout the story contribute to the story's tone?

2. Do you think the tone of the "The Voter" is satiric? Explain your answer, using examples from the text to support your point.

Reading Strategy — Activate Prior Knowledge

Activating prior knowledge includes drawing upon your personal experiences as well as recalling information learned through reading and listening. Review the chart you made on page 93.

1. What character behaviors in the story remind you of behaviors you have displayed or observed in others?

2. What background information pertaining to Nigeria and its problems helped you appreciate the events in the story? How did it help?

Vocabulary Practice

Practice with Word Parts For each bold-faced vocabulary word in the left column, identify the related word with a shared part in the right column. Write each pair and underline the part they have in common. Use a dictionary to look up the meaning of the related word. Then explain how it is related to the vocabulary word.

1. gratitude   nonevent
2. constituency   defile
3. nonentity   mesmeric
4. defiance   gratuitous
5. mesmerize   constitute

Academic Vocabulary

In Achebe's story, the POP does not pose a serious threat to the PAP **regime.**

Regime is an academic word. Nelson Mandela's Government of National Unity, which ruled South Africa in the 1990s, could be called a **regime,** although the word often carries a negative connotation. To further explore the meaning of this word, complete the sentence below.

A political regime that _____ might be characterized as unjust.

For more on academic vocabulary, see pages 36–37 and R83–R85.

Write with Style

 Apply Irony

Assignment Although Roof appears devoted to his political ideals, he is truly motivated by greed. This discrepancy between appearance and reality creates **irony** in the story. Write an expository essay about an ironic situation from the real world that details the motivations of a person or a group.

Get Ideas Brainstorm ironic situations from multiple sources, including your personal experience and background knowledge. For example, you might write about a time when a school group alleged that it supported one idea but behaved in a way that showed support for another idea. Create a three-column chart like the one below to clarify the irony in the situation.

Appearance	Reality	Irony
A group held a vigil to protest the development of a local meadow.	The group was so large that it disturbed wildlife and trampled vegetation.	The group harmed the meadow; its motivation seemed to be publicity instead of environmentalism.

Give It Structure Refer to the chart you made while generating ideas to organize your essay in a logical pattern. Be sure that each section of your essay clearly relates to your thesis and supports the points you want to make.

Look at Language Like short stories, expository essays can benefit from the use of figurative language and proverbs. These additions will give your writing personal style and make it more entertaining. It may be helpful to review Achebe's story for models of figurative language and proverbs.

In this workshop, you will focus on the following objective:

Grammar: Understanding how to use possessive apostrophes.

Grammar Workshop

Possessive Apostrophes

Literature Connection As the following quote from "The Voter" by Chinua Achebe shows, an important use of the apostrophe is to make nouns and some pronouns possessive.

> *"Although the villagers did not explain it in so many words Roof's popularity was a measure of their gratitude . . ."*

To form the possessive, add either an apostrophe or an apostrophe and an -s, as in *Roof's*.

To make the possessive form of a singular noun ending in -s, add an apostrophe and an -s.

Marcus wife was a teacher.
Marcus's wife was a teacher.

If a plural noun ends in -s, make it possessive by adding only an apostrophe.

The man answered the voters questions.
The man answered the voters' questions.

If a plural noun does not end in -s, add an apostrophe and an -s.

The people votes were important to Roof.
The people's votes were important to Roof.

Form the possessive of an indefinite pronoun (for example, *someone* or *everybody*) by adding an apostrophe and an -s. Apostrophes are not used with possessive pronouns, such as *hers* and *theirs*.

Roof used bribes to secure everyones votes.
Roof used bribes to secure everyone's votes.

Possessive Nouns

A **possessive noun** shows possession, ownership, or the relationship between two nouns.

Tip

To decide whether a noun needs an apostrophe only or an apostrophe and an -s, decide what kind of noun it is. Plural nouns ending in -s, such as *countries,* do not take an -s after an apostrophe to make them possessive (*countries',* not *countries's*).

Language Handbook

For more on apostrophes, see Language Handbook, p. R40.

Revise Complete the following items using what you know about possessive apostrophes.

1. On a separate sheet of paper, rewrite the following words as possessive.

   a. ballots   **b.** witness   **c.** someone   **d.** pounds

2. For each sentence below, if the sentence is correct, write *C* on a separate sheet of paper. If the sentence is incorrect, rewrite it correctly.

   a. The childrens' future was at stake.

   b. The village elders knowledge of politics had increased over time.

   c. Roof's mission was to win the election for Marcus Ibe.

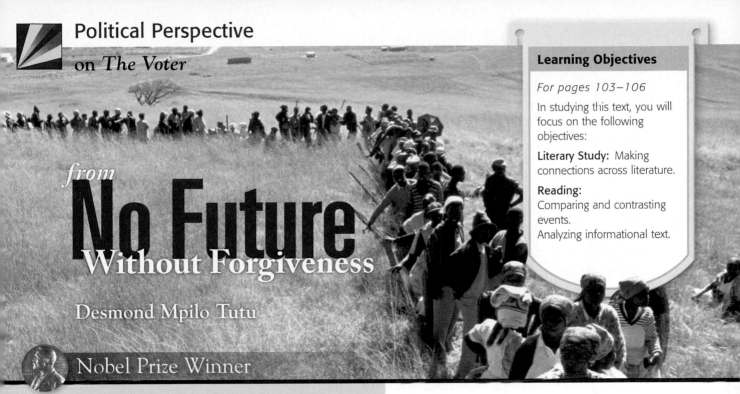

Political Perspective
on *The Voter*

from

No Future
Without Forgiveness

Desmond Mpilo Tutu

Nobel Prize Winner

On the day of South Africa's first post-apartheid election, voters line up for miles waiting to cast their ballot.

Set a Purpose for Reading

Read to learn more about the political process in a newly democratic African nation.

Build Background

Desmond Tutu, the first black archbishop of Cape Town, South Africa, was awarded the Nobel Peace Prize in 1984 for his work to end apartheid, a devastating system of racial segregation. In the following excerpt from his memoir, Tutu describes the experience of voting in South Africa's first multiracial elections in 1994. The elections resulted in a victory for Nelson Mandela, who later appointed Tutu as chair of the Truth and Reconciliation Commission, a group designed to investigate human rights abuses that occurred during apartheid.

Reading Strategy Compare and Contrast Events

To **compare and contrast events** means to look for similarities and differences between events in two or more literary works. As you read, ask yourself, What events in this memoir can I compare and contrast with events in Chinua Achebe's "The Voter"?

I went to vote in Gugulethu, a black township[1] with its typical matchbox-type houses in row after monotonous row. There was a long queue[2] already waiting. People were in good spirits; they were going to need dollops of patience and good humor because they were in for a long wait. My first democratic vote was a media event, and many of our friends from overseas were present, acting as monitors to be able to certify whether the elections were fair and free. But they were doing a great deal more than that. They were really like midwives helping to bring to birth this new delicate infant—free, democratic, nonracial, nonsexist South Africa.

The moment for which I had waited so long came and I folded my ballot paper and cast my vote. Wow! I shouted, "Yippee!" It was giddy stuff. It was like falling in love. The sky looked blue and more beautiful. I

---

1. In South Africa under apartheid, a *township* was a poor urban area reserved for nonwhites.
2. A *queue* is a line.

saw the people in a new light. They were beautiful, they were transfigured.[3] I too was transfigured. It was dreamlike. You were scared someone would rouse you and you would awake to the nightmare that was apartheid's harsh reality. Someone referring to that dreamlike quality had said to his wife, "Darling, don't wake me. I like this dream."

After voting, I went outside and the people cheered and sang and danced. It was like a festival. It was a wonderful vindication for all of those who had borne the burden and the heat of repression, the little people whom apartheid had turned into the anonymous ones, faceless, voiceless, counting for nothing in their motherland, whose noses had been rubbed daily in the dust. They had been created in the image of God but their dignity had been callously trodden underfoot daily by apartheid's minions and those who might have said they were opposed to apartheid but had nonetheless gone on enjoying the privileges and huge benefits that apartheid provided them—just because of an accident of birth, a biological irrelevance, the color of their skin.

I decided to drive around a bit to see what was happening. I was appalled by what I saw. The people had come out in droves, standing in those long lines which have now become world famous. They were so vulnerable. The police and the security forces were probably stretched but they were hardly a conspicuous presence. It would have taken just a few crazy extremists with AK-47s to sow the most awful mayhem and havoc. It did not happen. And virtually everywhere there was a hitch of one sort or the other. Here it was insufficient ballot papers, there it was not enough ink pads, elsewhere the officials had not yet turned up hours after the polls were due to have opened. The people were quite amazing in their patience. It was a comprehensive disaster waiting to happen. And it did not happen.

It was an amazing spectacle. People of all races were standing together in the same queues, perhaps for the very first time in their lives. Professionals, domestic workers, cleaners and their madams—all were standing in those lines that were snaking their way slowly to the polling booth. What should have been a disaster turned out to be a blessing in disguise. Those lines produced a new and peculiarly South African status symbol. Afterward people boasted, "I stood for two hours to vote." "I waited for four hours!"

Those long hours helped us South Africans to find one another. People shared newspapers, sandwiches, umbrellas, and the scales began to fall from their eyes. South Africans found fellow South Africans—they realized what we had been at such pains to tell them, that they shared a common humanity, that race, ethnicity, skin color were really irrelevancies. They discovered not a Colored, a black, an Indian, a white. No, they found fellow human beings. What a profound scientific discovery that blacks, Coloreds (usually people of mixed race), and Indians were in fact human beings, who had the same concerns and anxieties and aspirations. They wanted a decent home, a good job, a safe environment for their families, good schools for their children, and almost none wanted to drive the whites into the sea. They just wanted their place in the sun.

Everywhere else elections are secular political events. Ours was more than this, much, much more. It was a veritable[4] spiritual experience. It was a mountaintop

---

3. *Transfigured* means "changed" or "transformed."

4. *Veritable* means "true."

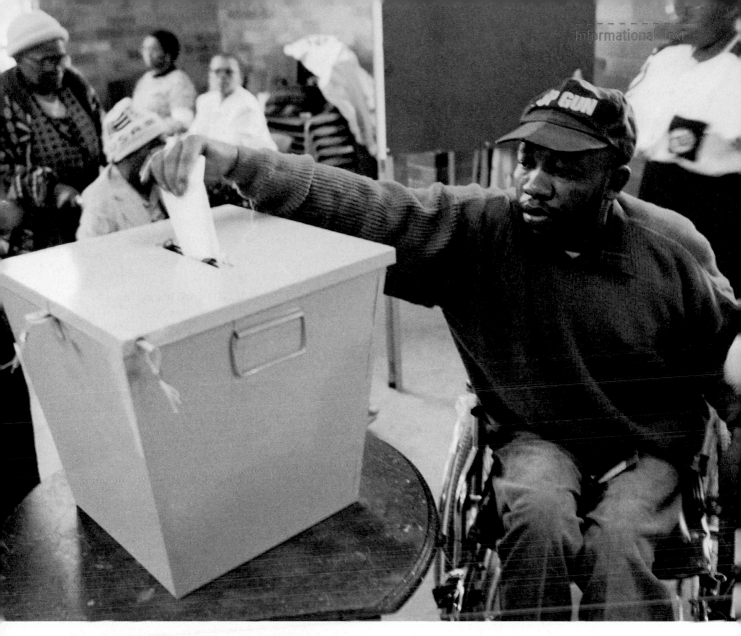

Man casting his ballot in first post-apartheid election.

experience. The black person entered the booth one person and emerged on the other side a new, transfigured person. She entered weighed down by the anguish and burden of oppression, with the memory of being treated like rubbish gnawing away at her very vitals like some corrosive acid. She reappeared as someone new, "I am free," as she walked away with head held high, the shoulders set straighter, and an elastic spring in her step. How do you convey that sense of freedom that tasted like sweet nec-

tar for the first time? How do you explain it to someone who was born into freedom? It is impossible to convey.

The white person entered the voting booth burdened by the load of guilt for having enjoyed the fruits of oppression and injustice. He emerged as somebody new. He too cried out, "The burden has been lifted from my shoulders, I am free, transfigured, made into a new person." He walked tall, with head held high and shoulders set square and straight.

White people found that freedom was indeed indivisible.[5] We had kept saying in the dark days of apartheid's oppression that white South Africans would never be truly free until we blacks were free as well. Many thought it was just another Tutu slogan, irresponsible as all his others had been. Today they were experiencing it as a reality. I used to refer to an intriguing old film *The Defiant Ones*, in which Sidney Poitier was one of the stars. Two convicts escape from a chain gang. They are manacled[6] together, the one white, the other black. They fall into a ditch with slippery sides. The one convict claws his way nearly to the top and out of the ditch but cannot make it because he is bound to his mate, who has been left at the bottom in the ditch. The only way they can make it is together as they strive up and up and up together and eventually make their way over the side wall and out.

So too I would say we South Africans will survive and prevail only together, black and white bound together by circumstance and history as we strive to claw our way out of the morass[7] that was apartheid racism. Up and out together, black and white together. Neither group on its own could or would make it. God had bound us, manacled us, together. In a way it was to live out what Martin Luther King, Jr., had said, "Unless we learn to live together as brothers [and sisters] we will die together as fools." ∾

---

5. *Indivisible* means "unable to be separated."
6. *Manacled* means "shackled together, as with handcuffs."

7. In this context, *morass* means "a difficult or an overwhelming situation."

Respond and Think Critically

Respond and Interpret

1. Write a brief summary of the main ideas in this excerpt before you answer the following questions. For help on writing a summary, see page 1147.

2. Were you surprised by the way Tutu describes the experience of voting? Explain.

3. (a)How do the people behave while waiting in line to vote? (b)According to Tutu, what effect does waiting to vote have on the population?

Analyze and Evaluate

4. (a)At the end of the excerpt, to what does Tutu compare the situation of black and white South Africans? (b)What is this comparison meant to illustrate? Is it effective? Explain.

5. (a)According to Tutu, voting "transfigures" both black and white voters. What images does Tutu use to describe this change? (b)Given what you know about the history of South Africa, why might voting have this effect?

Connect

6. (a)Contrast Tutu's experience of voting with the experience of voting described in Chinua Achebe's "The Voter." (b)Considering the histories of South Africa and Nigeria, why might these two authors portray voting differently?

Before You Read

The Rain Came

Meet **Grace Ogot**
(born 1930)

Banana Fields, Kenya, 2001. John Newcomb. Watercolor.
Private collection.

Grace Ogot (ō´gōt) was born in western Kenya's Nyanza district, which lies along the shores of Lake Victoria. She is a member of the Luo people, an African ethnic group that resides in parts of Kenya, Tanzania, and Uganda. Much of Ogot's fiction is set against the background of the Lake Victoria region and is based on the customs, legends, and history of the Luo. Their ancestors were nomadic herders who moved southward hundreds of years ago from Sudan to the areas they occupy today. One of the largest ethnic groups in Kenya, the Luo participated actively in the struggle for Kenyan independence from Great Britain in the 1950s and early 1960s. Ogot came of age as an author during this time, and she has often written about conflicts between the Luo and the British.

A Diverse Career Ogot's fascination with storytelling stems from her childhood, when she would eagerly listen to her grandmother recite folktales. Later, Ogot would loosely base many of her short stories on the Luo tales she heard from her grandmother. As a young woman, Ogot trained as a nurse and a midwife in both Uganda and England. Ogot's work as a nurse later allowed her to write about the conflict between traditional healing methods and modern Western medicine. While training as a midwife, she met and married Professor Bethwell Allan Ogot, a Luo and a prominent African historian. In addition to writing fiction, Grace Ogot has served as a member of Kenya's parliament, held positions in broadcasting and public relations, and represented her country at the United Nations and at UNESCO (United Nations Educational, Scientific, and Cultural Organization).

> *"There are more tragic incidents in life than there are comic ones."*
>
> —Grace Ogot

Themes of Sacrifice Grace Ogot began publishing her fiction in the late 1960s. When she submitted her first manuscript to a Kenyan publisher, the manager complained that her stories were not very uplifting. Still, Ogot persisted in writing about the subjects that interested her, including sacrifice, one of her major topics. She often portrays characters who are willing to give up personal happiness for the sake of family or community. Ogot has become perhaps the best-known woman writer in Kenya, publishing works in both English and Luo.

 Literature Online

Author Search For more about Grace Ogot, go to glencoe.com and enter QuickPass code GLW6053u1.

Literature and Reading Preview

Connect to the Story

What is the greatest sacrifice you have ever made? List the reasons you made the sacrifice and how this sacrifice benefited others.

Build Background

Ancestor worship is common in traditional African societies. People worship the spirits of the dead through prayer, sacrifice, and celebrations involving storytelling and dance. Usually the worshippers view their ancestors as beneficial spirits who can stop illness or drought, encourage the fertility of crops, help couples have children, and intervene with the gods on behalf of their descendants.

Set Purposes for Reading

Big Idea Tradition and Change

As you read, ask yourself, Why might the village in the story continue to follow traditional Luo values?

Literary Element Setting

Setting is the time and place in which the events of a literary work occur. The elements of setting may include geographical location, historical period, season of the year, time of day, and the beliefs and customs of a society. "The Rain Came" is set in a Luo village in Kenya during a drought. As you read, ask yourself, How are the seasonal circumstances integral to this story's plot?

Reading Strategy Analyze Cultural Context

To **analyze cultural context** means to examine the values, ideas, and traditions that are apparent in a text to better understand the culture in which that text was written. As you read "The Rain Came," ask yourself, What details illustrate the cultural context that shapes this story?

Tip: Take Notes As you read, use a chart like the one below to record details from the story and what they indicate about Luo culture.

Detail	Cultural Context
p. 110, "A young woman whispered to her co-wife . . ."	In Luo society, a man can have more than one wife.

Learning Objectives

For pages 107–119

In studying this text, you will focus on the following objectives:

Literary Study: Analyzing setting.

Reading: Analyzing cultural context.

Vocabulary

consecrate (kon′sə krāt′) *v.* to elevate into a sacred position through a religious rite; p. 110 *The bishop came to consecrate several new priests.*

rebuke (ri būk′) *v.* to criticize sharply; p. 110 *The librarian rebuked the noisy children.*

coax (kōks) *v.* to persuade by means of gentle urging or flattery; p. 112 *My sister tried to coax me into attending her rehearsal by telling me she wanted my opinion of her acting.*

denizen (den′ə zən) *n.* an inhabitant; p. 114 *The denizens of the swamp included alligators, opossums, and turtles.*

retaliation (ri tal′ē ā′shən) *n.* revenge; p. 116 *His witty retaliation for his friends' Halloween prank made everyone laugh.*

The *Rain* Came

Grace Ogot

Girl in Red, 1992. Tilly Willis. Oil on canvas. Private collection.

The chief was still far from the gate when his daughter Oganda saw him. She ran to meet him. Breathlessly she asked her father, "What is the news, great Chief? Everyone in the village is anxiously waiting to hear when it will rain." Labong'o held out his hands for his daughter but he did not say a word. Puzzled by her father's cold attitude Oganda ran back to the village to warn the others that the chief was back.

The atmosphere in the village was tense and confused. Everyone moved aimlessly and fussed in the yard without actually doing any work. A young woman whispered to her co-wife, "If they have not solved this rain business today, the chief will crack." They had watched him getting thinner and thinner as the people kept on pestering him. "Our cattle lie dying in the fields," they reported. "Soon it will be our children and then ourselves. Tell us what to do to save our lives, oh great Chief." So the chief had daily prayed with the Almighty through the ancestors to deliver them from their distress.

Instead of calling the family together and giving them the news immediately, Labong'o went to his own hut, a sign that he was not to be disturbed. Having replaced the shutter, he sat in the dimly lit hut to contemplate.

It was no longer a question of being the chief of hunger-stricken people that weighed Labong'o's heart. It was the life of his only daughter that was at stake. At the time when Oganda came to meet him, he saw the glittering chain shining around her waist. The prophecy was complete. "It is Oganda, Oganda, my only daughter, who must die so young." Labong'o burst into tears before finishing the sentence.

The chief must not weep. Society had declared him the bravest of men. But Labong'o did not care any more. He assumed the position of a simple father and wept bitterly.

He loved his people, the Luo, but what were the Luo for him without Oganda? Her life had brought a new life in Labong'o's world and he ruled better than he could remember. How would the spirit of the village survive his beautiful daughter? "There are so many homes and so many parents who have daughters. Why choose this one? She is all I have." Labong'o spoke as if the ancestors were there in the hut and he could see them face to face. Perhaps they were there, warning him to remember his promise on the day he was enthroned when he said aloud, before the elders, "I will lay down life, if necessary, and the life of my household, to save this tribe from the hands of the enemy." "Deny! Deny!" he could hear the voice of his forefathers mocking him.

When Labong'o was **consecrated** chief he was only a young man. Unlike his father, he ruled for many years with only one wife. But people **rebuked** him because his only wife did not bear him a daughter. He married a second, a third, and a fourth wife, but they all gave birth to male children. When Labong'o married a fifth wife she bore him a daughter. They called her Oganda, meaning "beans," because her skin was very fair. Out of Labong'o's twenty children, Oganda was the only girl. Though she was the chief's favorite, her mother's co-wives swallowed their jealous feelings

---

Analyze Cultural Context *Based on this passage, what qualities must a chief in Luo society have?*

Vocabulary

consecrate (kon′sə krāt′) *v.* to elevate into a sacred position through a religious rite
rebuke (ri būk′) *v.* to criticize sharply

Analyze Cultural Context *What does this passage reveal about the role of ancestors in Luo religion?*

and showered her with love. After all, they said, Oganda was a female child whose days in the royal family were numbered. She would soon marry at a tender age and leave the enviable position to someone else.

Never in his life had he been faced with such an impossible decision. Refusing to yield to the rainmaker's request would mean sacrificing the whole tribe, putting the interests of the individual above those of the society. More than that. It would mean disobeying the ancestors, and most probably wiping the Luo people from the surface of the earth. On the other hand, to let Oganda die as a ransom for the people would permanently cripple Labong'o spiritually. He knew he would never be the same chief again.

The words of Ndithi, the medicine man, still echoed in his ears. "Podho, the ancestor of the Luo, appeared to me in a dream last night, and he asked me to speak to the chief and the people," Ndithi had said to the gathering of tribesmen. "A young woman who has not known a man must die so that the country may have rain. While Podho was still talking to me, I saw a young woman standing at the lakeside, her hands raised, above her head. Her skin was as fair as the skin of young deer in the wilderness. Her tall slender figure stood like a lonely reed at the river bank. Her sleepy eyes wore a sad look like that of a bereaved mother. She wore a gold ring on her left ear, and a glittering brass chain around her waist. As I still marveled at the beauty of this young woman, Podho told me, 'Out of all the women in this land, we have chosen this one. Let her offer herself as a sacrifice to the lake monster! And on that day, the rain will come down in torrents. Let everyone stay at home on that day, lest he be carried away by the floods.'"

Outside there was a strange stillness, except for the thirsty birds that sang lazily on the dying trees. The blinding mid-day heat had forced the people to retire to their huts. Not far away from the chief's hut, two guards were snoring away quietly. Labong'o removed his crown and the large eagle-head that hung loosely on his shoulders. He left the hut, and instead of asking Nyabog'o the messenger to beat the drum, he went straight and beat it himself. In no time the whole household had assembled under the siala tree where he usually addressed them. He told Oganda to wait a while in her grandmother's hut.

When Labong'o stood to address his household, his voice was hoarse and the tears choked him. He started to speak, but words refused to leave his lips. His wives and sons knew there was great danger. Perhaps their enemies had declared war on them. Labong'o's eyes were red, and they could see he had been weeping. At last he told them. "One whom we love and treasure must be taken away from us. Oganda is to die." Labong'o's voice was so faint, that he could not hear it himself. But he continued, "The ancestors have chosen her to be offered as a sacrifice to the lake monster in order that we may have rain."

They were completely stunned. As a confused murmur broke out, Oganda's mother fainted and was carried off to her own hut. But the other people rejoiced. They danced around singing and chanting, "Oganda is the lucky one to die for the people. If it is to save the people, let Oganda go."

In her grandmother's hut Oganda wondered what the whole family were discussing about her that she could not hear. Her grandmother's hut was well away from the

---

Tradition and Change *How might a decision to ignore the rainmaker's request affect Luo tradition?*

Setting *What elements of the setting highlight the problem the Luo face?*

chief's court and, much as she strained her ears, she could not hear what was said. "It must be marriage," she concluded. It was an accepted custom for the family to discuss their daughter's future marriage behind her back. A faint smile played on Oganda's lips as she thought of the several young men who swallowed saliva at the mere mention of her name.

There was Kech, the son of a neighboring clan elder. Kech was very handsome. He had sweet, meek eyes and a roaring laughter. He would make a wonderful father, Oganda thought. But they would not be a good match. Kech was a bit too short to be her husband. It would humiliate her to have to look down at Kech each time she spoke to him. Then she thought of Dimo, the tall young man who had already distinguished himself as a brave warrior and an outstanding wrestler. Dimo adored Oganda, but Oganda thought he would make a cruel husband, always quarreling and ready to fight. No, she did not like him. Oganda fingered the glittering chain on her waist as she thought of Osinda. A long time ago when she was quite young Osinda had given her that chain, and instead of wearing it around her neck several times, she wore it round her waist where it could stay permanently. She heard her heart pounding so loudly as she thought of him. She whispered, "Let it be you they are discussing, Osinda, the lovely one. Come now and take me away . . . "

The lean figure in the doorway startled Oganda, who was rapt in thought about the man she loved. "You have frightened me, Grandma," said Oganda laughing. "Tell me, is it my marriage you are discussing? You can take it from me that I won't marry any of

them." A smile played on her lips again. She was **coaxing** the old lady to tell her quickly, to tell her they were pleased with Osinda.

In the open space outside the excited relatives were dancing and singing. They were coming to the hut now, each carrying a gift to put at Oganda's feet. As their singing got nearer Oganda was able to hear what they were saying: "If it is to save the people, if it is to give us rain, let Oganda go. Let Oganda die for her people, and for her ancestors." Was she mad to think that they were singing about her? How could she die? She found the lean figure of her grandmother barring the door. She could not get out. The look on her grandmother's face warned her that there was danger around the corner. "Mother, it is not marriage then?" Oganda asked urgently. She suddenly felt panicky like a mouse cornered by a hungry cat. Forgetting that there was only one door in the hut Oganda fought desperately to find another exit. She must fight for her life. But there was none.

She closed her eyes, leapt like a wild tiger through the door, knocking her grandmother flat to the ground. There outside in mourning garments Labong'o stood motionless, his hands folded at the back. He held his daughter's hand and led her away from the excited crowd to the little red-painted hut where her mother was resting. Here he broke the news officially to his daughter.

For a long time the three souls who loved one another dearly sat in darkness. It was no good speaking. And even if they tried, the

---

Analyze Cultural Context *In the paragraph that follows, what does Oganda's assessment of possible husbands indicate about Luo marriage customs?*

Setting *How might the setting here symbolize Oganda's dilemma?*

Vocabulary

coax (kōks) v. to persuade by means of gentle urging or flattery

words could not have come out. In the past they had been like three cooking stones, sharing their burdens. Taking Oganda away from them would leave two useless stones which would not hold a cooking-pot.

Visual Vocabulary
Cooking stones are rocks that support a cooking pot.

News that the beautiful daughter of the chief was to be sacrificed to give the people rain spread across the country like wind. At sunset the chief's village was full of relatives and friends who had come to congratulate Oganda. Many more were on their way coming, carrying their gifts. They would dance till morning to keep her company. And in the morning they would prepare her a big farewell feast. All these relatives thought it a great honor to be selected by the spirits to die, in order that the society may live. "Oganda's name will always remain a living name among us," they boasted.

But was it maternal love that prevented Minya from rejoicing with the other women? Was it the memory of the agony and pain of childbirth that made her feel so sorrowful? Or was it the deep warmth and understanding that passes between a suckling babe and her mother that made Oganda part of her life, her flesh? Of course it was an honor, a great honor, for her daughter to be

chosen to die for the country. But what could she gain once her daughter was blown away by the wind? There were so many other women in the land, why choose her daughter, her only child! Had human life any meaning at all—other women had houses full of children while she, Minya, had to lose her only child!

In the cloudless sky the moon shone brightly, and the numerous stars glittered with a bewitching beauty. The dancers of all age-groups assembled to dance before Oganda, who sat close to her mother, sobbing quietly. All these years she had been with her people she thought she understood them. But now she discovered that she was a stranger among them. If they loved her as they had always professed why were they not making any attempt to save her? Did her people really understand what it felt like to die young? Unable to restrain her emotions any longer, she sobbed loudly as her age-group got up to dance. They were young and beautiful and very soon they would marry and have their own children. They would have husbands to love and little huts for themselves. They would have reached maturity. Oganda touched the chain around her waist as she thought of Osinda. She wished Osinda was there too, among her friends. "Perhaps he is ill," she thought gravely. The chain comforted

Analyze Cultural Context *How will Oganda's relatives benefit from her death?*

Tradition and Change *In this passage, how do the traditions of her people affect Oganda's perception of her community?*

Oganda—she would die with it around her waist and wear it in the underground world.

In the morning a big feast was prepared for Oganda. The women prepared many different tasty dishes so that she could pick and choose. "People don't eat after death," they said. Delicious though the food looked, Oganda touched none of it. Let the happy people eat. She contented herself with sips of water from a little calabash. The time for her departure was drawing near, and each minute was precious. It was a day's journey to the lake. She was to walk all night, passing through the great forest. But nothing could touch her, not even the **denizens** of the forest. She was already anointed with sacred oil. From the time Oganda received the sad news she had expected Osinda to appear any moment. But he was not there. A relative told her that Osinda was away on a private visit. Oganda realized that she would never see her beloved again.

In the afternoon the whole village stood at the gate to say good-bye and to see her for the last time. Her mother wept on her neck for a long time. The great chief in a mourning skin came to the gate barefooted, and mingled with the people—a simple father in grief. He took off his wrist bracelet and put it on his daughter's wrist saying, "You will always live among us. The spirit of our forefathers is with you."

Tongue-tied and unbelieving Oganda stood there before the people. She had nothing to say. She looked at her home once more. She could hear her heart beating so painfully within her. All her childhood plans were coming to an end. She felt like a flower nipped in the bud never to enjoy the morning dew again. She looked at her weeping mother, and whispered, "Whenever you want to see me, always look at the sunset. I will be there."

Oganda turned southwards to start her trek to the lake. Her parents, relatives, friends and admirers stood at the gate and watched her go.

Her beautiful slender figure grew smaller and smaller till she mingled with the thin dry trees in the forest. As Oganda walked the lonely path that wound its way in the wilderness, she sang a song, and her own voice kept her company.

The ancestors have said Oganda must die
The daughter of the chief must be sacrificed,
When the lake monster feeds on my flesh.
The people will have rain.
Yes, the rain will come down in torrents.
And the floods will wash away the sandy beaches
When the daughter of the chief dies in the lake.
My age-group has consented
My parents have consented
So have my friends and relatives.
Let Oganda die to give us rain.
My age-group are young and ripe,
Ripe for womanhood and motherhood
But Oganda must die young,
Oganda must sleep with the ancestors.
Yes, rain will come down in torrents.

The red rays of the setting sun embraced Oganda, and she looked like a burning candle in the wilderness.

Analyze Cultural Context *What Luo custom is noted in this passage, and what seems to be its significance?*

Vocabulary

denizen (den' ə zən) n. an inhabitant

Setting *What characteristics of the setting stand out as Oganda leaves the village?*

Analyze Cultural Context *What role does the "age-group" seem to have in Luo society?*

The people who came to hear her sad song were touched by her beauty. But they all said the same thing: "If it is to save the people, if it is to give us rain, then be not afraid. Your name will forever live among us."

At midnight Oganda was tired and weary. She could walk no more. She sat under a big tree, and having sipped water from her calabash, she rested her head on the tree trunk and slept.

When Oganda woke up in the morning the sun was high in the sky. After walking for many hours, she reached the *tong'*, a strip of land that separated the inhabited part of the country from the sacred place (*kar lamo*). No layman could enter this place and come out alive—only those who had direct contact with the spirits and the Almighty were allowed to enter this holy of holies. But Oganda had to pass through this sacred land on her way to the lake, which she had to reach at sunset.

A large crowd gathered to see her for the last time. Her voice was now hoarse and painful, but there was no need to worry any more. Soon she would not have to sing. The crowd looked at Oganda sympathetically, mumbling words she could not hear. But none of them pleaded for life. As Oganda opened the gate, a child, a young child, broke loose from the crowd, and ran towards her. The child took a small earring from her sweaty hands and gave it to Oganda saying, "When you reach the world of the dead, give this earring to my sister. She died last week. She forgot this ring." Oganda, taken aback by the strange request, took the little ring, and handed her precious water and food to the child. She did not need them now. Oganda did not know whether to laugh or cry. She had heard mourners sending their love to their sweethearts, long dead, but this idea of sending gifts was new to her.

Nighttime Landscape 1. Wendy L. Goldberg-Hammon. Getty collection.

Oganda held her breath as she crossed the barrier to enter the sacred land. She looked appealingly at the crowd, but there was no response. Their minds were too preoccupied with their own survival. Rain was the precious medicine they were longing for, and the sooner Oganda could get to her destination the better.

A strange feeling possessed Oganda as she picked her way in the sacred land. There were strange noises that often startled her, and her first reaction was to take to her heels. But she remembered that she had to fulfill the wish of her people. She was exhausted, but the path was still winding. Then suddenly the path ended on sandy land. The water had retreated miles away from the shore leaving a wide stretch of sand. Beyond this was the vast expanse of water.

Oganda felt afraid. She wanted to picture the size and shape of the monster, but fear would not let her. The society did not talk about it, nor did the crying children who were silenced by the mention of its name. The sun was still up, but it was no longer hot. For a long time Oganda walked ankle-deep in the sand. She was exhausted and longed desperately for her calabash of water. As she moved on, she had a strange feeling that something was following her. Was it the monster? Her hair stood erect, and a cold paralyzing feeling ran along her spine. She looked behind, sideways and in front, but there was nothing, except a cloud of dust.

Oganda pulled up and hurried but the feeling did not leave her, and her whole body became saturated with perspiration.

The sun was going down fast and the lake shore seemed to move along with it.

Oganda started to run. She must be at the lake before sunset. As she ran she heard a noise from behind. She looked back sharply, and something resembling a moving bush was frantically running after her. It was about to catch up with her.

Oganda ran with all her strength. She was now determined to throw herself into the water even before sunset. She did not look back, but the creature was upon her. She made an effort to cry out, as in a nightmare, but she could not hear her own voice. The creature caught up with Oganda. In the utter confusion, as Oganda came face to face with the unidentified creature, a strong hand grabbed her. But she fell flat on the sand and fainted.

When the lake breeze brought her back to consciousness, a man was bending over her. ". . . . . !" Oganda opened her mouth to speak, but she had lost her voice. She swallowed a mouthful of water poured into her mouth by the stranger.

"Osinda, Osinda! Please let me die. Let me run, the sun is going down. Let me die, let them have rain." Osinda fondled the glittering chain around Oganda's waist and wiped the tears from her face.

"We must escape quickly to the unknown land," Osinda said urgently. "We must run away from the wrath of the ancestors and the **retaliation** of the monster."

"But the curse is upon me, Osinda, I am no good to you any more. And moreover the eyes of the ancestors will follow us everywhere and bad luck will befall us. Nor can we escape from the monster."

Oganda broke loose, afraid to escape, but Osinda grabbed her hands again.

"Listen to me, Oganda! Listen! Here are two coats!" He then covered the whole of Oganda's body, except her eyes, with a leafy attire made from the twigs of *Bwombwe*. "These will protect us from the eyes of the ancestors and the wrath of the monster. Now let us run out of here." He held Oganda's hand and they ran from the sacred land, avoiding the path that Oganda had followed.

The bush was thick, and the long grass entangled their feet as they ran. Halfway through the sacred land they stopped and looked back. The sun was almost touching the surface of the water. They were frightened. They continued to run, now faster, to avoid the sinking sun.

"Have faith, Oganda—that thing will not reach us."

When they reached the barrier and looked behind them trembling, only a tip of the sun could be seen above the water's surface.

"It is gone! It is gone!" Oganda wept, hiding her face in her hands.

"Weep not, daughter of the chief. Let us run, let us escape."

There was a bright lightning. They looked up, frightened. Above them black furious clouds started to gather. They began to run. Then the thunder roared, and the rain came down in torrents. ∾

Tradition and Change *How might Oganda's possible death have changed the way Osinda views tradition?*

Vocabulary

retaliation (ri tal′ē ā′shən) *n.* revenge

After You Read

Respond and Think Critically

Respond and Interpret

1. What was your reaction to the outcome of the story?

2. (a)According to the medicine man's prophecy, what is the only way to end the drought in Oganda's village? (b)Why does Labong'o obey the prophecy?

3. (a)How do the villagers react when Labong'o tells them about the prophecy? (b)Why does Oganda feel like a stranger among her people during the feast held in her honor?

4. (a)How does Oganda react when she realizes what is planned for her? (b)Do you think Oganda's feelings about her fate change as the story unfolds? Explain.

Analyze and Evaluate

5. (a)An **internal conflict** is a struggle within a character's mind. Describe one internal conflict in "The Rain Came." (b)Is this conflict resolved convincingly? Explain.

6. (a)A **symbol** is an object or an action that stands for something else in addition to itself. What does the brass chain around Oganda's waist symbolize? (b)Do you think this is an effective symbol? Explain.

Connect

7. **Big Idea** **Tradition and Change** What view of Luo tradition does "The Rain Came" offer the reader? Explain.

8. **Connect to Today** What kinds of sacrifices do people today make for the good of their communities?

Daily Life & Culture

Proverbs from Kenya

The oral traditions of African peoples are rich in **proverbs.** These short, vivid sayings express a truth about life or contain a bit of popular wisdom. The following proverbs are from the Luo and Kikuyu peoples, two of the largest ethnic groups in Kenya.

Luo Proverbs

A cowardly hyena lives for many years.

An eye that you treat is the one that turns against you.

The fierce white ants cause the death of the kind and harmless ants.

Kikuyu Proverbs

To get the warmth of fire one must stir the embers.

Darkness caused to dance even him who cannot.

Group Activity Discuss the following questions with your classmates. Refer to the proverbs.

1. The Luo proverb about the ants refers to two species that live together: destructive termites and a species the Luo value as food. What do you think the proverb means?

2. What proverbs do you know that are similar to any of the ones here?

ACT Skills Practice

1. The setting of Ogot's "The Rain Came" evokes a mood of
   A. boredom and frustration.
   B. joviality and freedom.
   C. urgency and conflict.
   D. exhilaration and chaos.

2. As members of Luo society, the chief and his daughter
   F. must adhere to its customs.
   G. find hope in its desolation.
   H. must convert outsiders to its culture.
   J. trick people to gain social status.

Review: Situational Irony

As you learned on page 52, **irony** is a discrepancy between reality and appearance or expectations. **Situational irony** occurs when the outcome of a situation is the opposite of what is expected.

Partner Activity With a partner, identify and explain the situational irony in this story. Use a diagram like the one below to record your information.

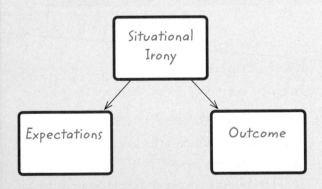

Literature Online

Selection Resources For Selection Quizzes, eFlashcards, and Reading-Writing Connection activities, go to glencoe.com and enter QuickPass code GLW6053u1.

Reading Strategy Analyze Cultural Context

The traditional beliefs and customs of the Luo people shape the narrative of "The Rain Came." Review your chart on cultural context on page 108 and answer the following questions.

1. How would you describe traditional Luo religious beliefs?

2. What is the relationship between the individual and the community in traditional Luo society?

Vocabulary Practice

Practice with Analogies Choose the word that best completes each analogy. Use a dictionary if you need help.

1. consecrate : holy :: sanitize :
   a. lovely   b. clean   c. small

2. rebuke : commend :: gratify :
   a. disappoint   b. tease   c. warn

3. coax : force :: offer :
   a. deserve   b. metal   c. steal

4. denizen : outsider :: enemy :
   a. war   b. innocent   c. ally

5. retaliation : revenge :: quarantine :
   a. isolation   b. freedom   c. loneliness

Academic Vocabulary

*Oganda's people believe that sacrificing her to the monster will **guarantee** the end of the drought.*

Guarantee is an academic word. In a commercial setting, a salesperson might say that she will **guarantee** your satisfaction with a product. To further explore the meaning of this word, answer the following question: What are some enterprises in which success is difficult to **guarantee**, and why?

For more on academic vocabulary, see pages 36–37 and R83–R85.

Respond Through Writing

Research Report

Learning Objectives

In this assignment, you will focus on the following objectives:

Writing: Writing a research report.

Grammar: Using parentheses and brackets

Investigate Setting A severe drought plays a key role in "The Rain Came." Using this setting as a springboard, research the agriculture, geography, and climate of Kenya and how these factors affect the Luo people. Prepare a research report of 1,500 words or more exploring this topic, using primary and secondary sources for reference.

Understand the Task **Primary sources** are firsthand accounts, such as diaries or eyewitness news articles. **Secondary sources** are materials written by people who did not influence or experience an event but have studied it.

Prewrite Plan carefully before you begin to research by writing four or five questions about the topic. Then gather the information you need to answer those questions from primary and secondary sources. To help structure your report, make an outline similar to the one below.

I. Lake Victoria and Kenya

   A. Part of the arid and flat East African Rift System

   B. Setting of many of Ogot's stories

II. The Luo people

   A. Agricultural heritage

   B. Participated in Kenya's struggle for independence

Draft Gather evidence to support your thesis from the questions and answers you wrote, making sure to convey information accurately and coherently. Also, be sure to use technical terms such as "East African Rift System" correctly. You should anticipate readers' potential misunderstandings of these terms by including brief explanations.

Revise As you incorporate the information from your notes, evaluate whether the information is relevant. Exchange your paper with a partner and create a checklist to review organization, clarity, and use of language.

Edit and Proofread Proofread your paper, correcting any errors in spelling, grammar, and punctuation. Review the Grammar Tip in the side column for information on how to use parentheses and brackets.

Grammar Tip

Parentheses and Brackets

Parentheses are used to distinguish in-text citations in research papers. They are also used to mark supplemental information in a sentence, as in the following example.

The Owen Falls Dam (now called the Nalubaale Dam) was completed in 1954.

Brackets can be used to provide clarifying information within a quotation, as in the sentence below.

Ogot writes, "He loved his people, the Luo [an ethnic group in western Kenya], but what were the Luo for him without Oganda?"

Before You Read

Civilian and Soldier

Meet **Wole Soyinka**
(born 1934)

Wole Soyinka (wō′lā shoi ān′kä) has earned an international reputation as a distinguished and powerful voice for social change and human rights. His plays, poetry, novels, and essays have not only brought the beautiful traditions and folklore of Africa to the world, but they have also exposed Nigeria's struggles with colonial rule, dictatorship, modernization, civil war, oppression, and injustice.

Between Tradition and Modernization
Born in Nigeria when it was under British rule, Soyinka is the son of educators who supported colonial ideas. Early in his childhood, he recognized the conflicting cultures that surrounded him: African tradition versus British modernization. When Soyinka's father recommended that he attend a government school, Soyinka's grandfather intervened. He believed that his grandson should live by the Yoruban traditions and customs of his people, so he taught his grandson about the Yoruba gods and folklore. These lessons greatly influenced Soyinka's life and writing.

The Voice of Truth At the start of the Nigerian civil war in 1967, Soyinka was falsely imprisoned for two years, spending most of that time in solitary confinement. To preserve his sanity, Soyinka manufactured his own ink and began a diary using anything he could find to write on—toilet paper, cigarette packages, and book pages. These notes were later published in *The Man Died: Prison Notes of Wole Soyinka*, which is considered one of the most significant works ever written about the Biafran war. Soyinka was released in 1969. Nearly three decades later, Soyinka, living in self-imposed exile, was charged with treason and sentenced to death for criticizing the Nigerian government. He was later granted amnesty by a new Nigerian government. In 1986, Soyinka became the first African to receive the Nobel Prize in Literature.

> "My writing grows more and more preoccupied with the theme of the oppressive boot, the irrelevance of the color of the foot that wears it and the struggle for individuality."
>
> —Wole Soyinka

Literature and Reading Preview

Connect to the Poem

What does freedom mean to you? With a partner, discuss which aspects of freedom you believe to be crucial.

Build Background

Since gaining independence from Britain in 1960, Nigeria has experienced ethnic and religious conflict. Thousands of Ibo living in the north were massacred in 1966 during a military revolt against the civilian government. In 1967, the Ibo declared their traditional homeland in the eastern region to be the independent Republic of Biafra, and Nigeria plunged into civil war. "Civilian and Soldier" belongs to a group of six poems Soyinka wrote during the buildup to the war.

Set Purposes for Reading

Big Idea Living with Independence

As you read, ask yourself, How does the relationship between the civilian and the soldier highlight the struggles African countries faced in the shift to independence?

Literary Element Imagery

Imagery refers to the "word pictures" that authors create to evoke emotional responses. In creating effective images, authors use **sensory details,** or descriptions that appeal to one or more of the five senses. As you read Soyinka's poem, ask yourself, How does the imagery depict the civilian and the soldier?

Reading Strategy Analyze Structure

To **analyze structure** means to focus on the form of a poem and determine how this form relates to the poem's effect and meaning. Structure can include rhythm, rhyme, line breaks, and punctuation. As you read, ask yourself, How does the structure of this poem contribute to its effect?

Tip: Take Notes Create diagrams like the one below to analyze the structure of "Civilian and Soldier."

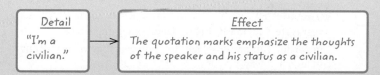

Detail		Effect
"I'm a civilian."	→	The quotation marks emphasize the thoughts of the speaker and his status as a civilian.

Vocabulary

aggravate (ag′rə vāt′) *v.* to make something worse; p. 122 *Eating sugar will only aggravate your cavities.*

impartial (im pär′shəl) *adj.* treating everyone or everything in an equal way; p. 122 *The jury should act as an impartial observer when hearing the facts of a case.*

dubious (dōō′bē əs) *adj.* of a questionable nature; p. 122 *His dubious plan to sneak out after dark would only get him in trouble.*

plight (plīt) *n.* a situation that is hard to manage or resolve; p. 122 *Many passengers faced the plight of being stranded at the airport.*

Tip: Synonyms Synonyms are words that have nearly the same meaning. For example, the words *impartial* and *fair* are synonyms that describe someone who is unbiased. Synonyms are always the same part of speech.

Civilian and Soldier

Wole Soyinka

Civil war. Mural, Length: 95m. Mozambique, Maputo, Africa.

My apparition rose from the fall of lead,
Declared, "I'm a civilian." It only served
To **aggravate** your fright. For how could I
Have risen, a being of this world, in that hour
5   Of **impartial** death! And I thought also: nor is
Your quarrel of this world.

You stood still
For both eternities, and oh I heard the lesson
Of your training sessions, cautioning—
Scorch earth behind you, do not leave
10   A **dubious** neutral to the rear. Reiteration
Of my civilian quandary, burrowing earth
From the lead festival of your more eager friends
Worked the worse on your confusion, and when
You brought the gun to bear on me, and death
15   Twitched me gently in the eye, your **plight**
And all of you came clear to me.

I hope some day
Intent upon my trade of living, to be checked
In stride by *your* apparition in a trench,
Signaling, I am a soldier. No hesitation then
20   But I shall shoot you clean and fair
With meat and bread, a gourd of wine
A bunch of breasts from either arm, and that
Lone question—do you friend, even now, know
What it is all about?

Analyze Structure *What is the effect of this line's indentation?*

Imagery *What is the meaning of the imagery Soyinka uses in these lines?*

Vocabulary

aggravate (ag´rə vāt´) *v.* to make something worse
impartial (im pär´shəl) *adj.* treating everyone or everything in an equal way
dubious (dōō´bē əs) *adj.* of a questionable nature
plight (plīt) *n.* a situation that is hard to manage or resolve

After You Read

Respond and Think Critically

Respond and Interpret

1. How did you feel about war after reading "Civilian and Soldier"?

2. (a)Describe the encounter between the speaker and the soldier in the poem. (b)What is the soldier's initial reaction to this encounter?

3. (a)What does the speaker imagine happening in a future life? (b)What does this fantasy say about the speaker's attitude?

Analyze and Evaluate

4. Do you think the speaker considers the soldier to be an evil person? Explain.

5. How does the title, "Civilian and Soldier," illustrate Soyinka's concern about "the struggle for individuality"?

Connect

6. **Big Idea** **The Price of Freedom** How does the conflict in the poem relate to the struggles African countries faced in the shift to independence?

7. **Connect to the Author** Soyinka was raised to value both European ideas and the beliefs of his African ancestors. How might the speaker's relationship to the soldier reflect Soyinka's ability to mesh two belief systems?

Literary Element Imagery

Imagery is language an author uses to appeal to the reader's senses.

1. What images does the speaker use to describe being shot?

2. Which image did you find most confusing or difficult in the poem? Why?

Reading Strategy Analyze Structure

When you analyze a poem's **structure**, you gain insight into the poem's meaning and the poet's purpose. Review the chart you made on page 121 and then answer the following questions.

1. What is significant about the structure of the first sentence in the poem?

2. Do you think the structure of the last line reinforces the theme of the poem? Why or why not?

Vocabulary Practice

Practice with Synonyms With a partner, brainstorm three synonyms for each boldfaced vocabulary word below. Then choose one synonym and explain how its connotation, or implied meaning, differs from that of the vocabulary word.

aggravate   impartial   dubious   plight

EXAMPLE: guile

Synonyms: cunning, treachery, trickery

Sample explanation: Both *guile* and *treachery* imply deceit, but *treachery* has a more negative connotation.

Writing

Write an Interview Imagine you are about to interview the soldier many years later. Write a list of questions you would ask him and his imagined responses.

LOG ON **Literature** Online

Selection Resources For Selection Quizzes, eFlashcards, and Reading-Writing Connection activities, go to glencoe.com and enter QuickPass code GLW6053u1.

The Prisoner Who Wore Glasses

Meet **Bessie Head**

(1937–1986)

From her own troubled life, Bessie Head discovered a means of conveying racial oppression and sexist discrimination in a way that was deeply personal rather than overtly political. In fact, her themes extend past the borders of South Africa and Botswana to become enduring, universal messages about freedom and equality, alienation, the individual's responsibility to society, and the abuse of power and authority. Head noted that "Every story or book starts with something just for myself. Then from that small me it becomes a panorama—the big view that has something for everyone."

"We black Africans did not know who or what we were, apart from objects of abuse and exploitation."

—Bessie Head

A Difficult Beginning Head was born in a South African mental hospital to an upper-class white woman who had been declared "insane" because of her relationship with Head's father, a black servant. Their relationship was illegal under apartheid, a system designed to maintain white dominance by segregating the black community, which was three-quarters of South Africa's population. As a result, Head grew up in a foster family and later in an orphanage, where she was trained to be a teacher. She disliked teaching, however, and became a journalist for the African magazine *Drum*. In 1964, she decided she could no longer live under the oppression of apartheid, and she and her infant son moved north to Botswana, where they were declared political refugees. She eventually found a sense of peace in the refugee community, despite living in poverty and feeling alienated.

A Life's Work Head used African oral traditions, folklore, and aspects of village life for inspiration. While examining apartheid and exile in her work, Head also considered the power of love and the potential for good in the face of evil. She believed "that love is really good . . . and . . . that it is important to be an ordinary person. More than anything else I want to be noble."

In her short life, Head wrote three novels and numerous short stories, articles, and essays, culminating in a personal glimpse into South African apartheid and African life.

Literature and Reading Preview

Connect to the Story

Have you ever seen someone treat others unfairly? Freewrite for a few minutes about this injustice.

Build Background

In the 1600s, a Dutch colony was established in what is now South Africa. Dutch descendants known as Afrikaners instituted the forced segregation policy of apartheid, which lasted until 1990. "The Prisoner Who Wore Glasses" takes place during apartheid and is based on a true story Head heard from a South African refugee.

Set Purposes for Reading

Big Idea The Price of Freedom

As you read, ask yourself, How do the prisoners uphold their beliefs against a racist, unjust government?

Literary Element Character

Literary **characters** can be classified as round or flat, and as dynamic or static. A **round character** shows varied and sometimes contradictory traits, whereas a **flat character** reveals only one personality trait. A **dynamic character** changes during a story, but a **static character** remains basically the same. As you read, ask yourself, What types of characters are Brille and Hannetjie?

Reading Strategy Identify Assumptions

When you **identify assumptions,** you recognize the beliefs held by the author or characters and how those beliefs impact the story. As you read, ask yourself, What assumptions does Head make about the relationship between prisoners and guards, and what assumptions do Brille and Hannetjie make about each other?

Tip: Track Assumptions Use a chart like the one below to track assumptions and evaluate their validity and importance.

Assumption	Validity	Importance
Hannetjie assumes that guards can easily intimidate prisoners.	The guards intimidated most prisoners.	Brille will not let the guards intimidate him.

Learning Objectives

For pages 124–132

In studying this text, you will focus on the following objectives:

Literary Study: Analyzing character.

Reading: Identifying assumptions.

Listening and Speaking: Conducting a debate.

Vocabulary

obscure (əb skyoor′) *v.* to hide from view; p. 126 *The high rows of hedges obscure the house.*

assertive (ə sur′tiv) *adj.* bold; forceful in a confident way; p. 127 *She was so assertive that she could approach anyone without feeling shy.*

bedlam (bed′ləm) *n.* a state of uproar or confusion; p. 128 *With six children, the bedlam in the house never ceased.*

cunningly (kun′ing lē) *adv.* cleverly; sneakily; p. 130 *John cunningly tricked Ted into thinking he wasn't late by telling him his watch was fast.*

Tip: Word Origins Understanding a word's origin can help you learn the meaning of a new word or phrase. For example, *cunningly* comes from the base word *cunning,* which derives from the Middle English word *connen,* meaning "to know."

The Prisoner Who Wore Glasses

Bessie Head

Scarcely a breath of wind disturbed the stillness of the day and the long rows of cabbages were bright green in the sunlight. Large white clouds drifted slowly across the deep blue sky. Now and then they **obscured** the sun and caused a chill on the backs of the prisoners who had to work all day long in the cabbage field. This trick the clouds were playing with the sun eventually caused one of the prisoners who wore glasses to stop work, straighten up and peer shortsightedly at them. He was a thin little fellow with a hollowed out chest and comic knobbly knees. He also had a lot of fanciful ideas because he smiled at the clouds.

"Perhaps they want me to send a message to the children," he thought, tenderly, noting that the clouds were drifting in the direction of his home some hundred miles away. But before he could frame the message, the warder[1] in charge of his work span shouted: "Hey, what do you think you're doing, Brille?"

The prisoner swung round, blinking rapidly, yet at the same time sizing up the enemy. He was a new warder, named Jacobus Stephanus Hannetjie. His eyes were the color of the sky but they were

Vocabulary

obscure (əb skyoor′) v. to hide from view

1. A *warder* is a prison guard.

frightening. A simple, primitive, brutal soul gazed out of them. The prisoner bent down quickly and a message was quietly passed down the line: "We're in for trouble this time, comrades."

"Why?" rippled back up the line.

"Because he's not human," the reply rippled down and yet only the crunching of the spades as they turned over the earth disturbed the stillness.

This particular work span was known as Span One. It was composed of ten men and they were all political prisoners. They were grouped together for convenience as it was one of the prison regulations that no black warder should be in charge of a political prisoner lest this prisoner convert him to his view. It never seemed to occur to the authorities that this very reasoning was the strength of Span One and a clue to the strange terror they aroused in the warders. As political prisoners they were unlike the other prisoners in the sense that they felt no guilt nor were they outcasts of society. All guilty men instinctively cower, which was why it was the kind of prison where men got knocked out cold with a blow at the back of the head from an iron bar. Up until the arrival of Warder Hannetjie, no warder had dared beat any member of Span One and no warder had lasted more than a week with them. The battle was entirely psychological. Span One was **assertive** and it was beyond the scope of white warders to handle assertive black men. Thus, Span One had got out of control. They were the best thieves and liars in the camp. They

lived all day on raw cabbages. They chatted and smoked tobacco. And since they moved, thought and acted as one, they had perfected every technique of group concealment.

Trouble began that very day between Span One and Warder Hannetjie. It was because of the shortsightedness of Brille. That was the nickname he was given in prison and is the Afrikaans[2] word for someone who wears glasses. Brille could never judge the approach of the prison gates and on several occasions he had munched on cabbages and dropped them almost at the feet of the warder and all previous warders had overlooked this. Not so Warder Hannetjie.

"Who dropped that cabbage?" he thundered.

Brille stepped out of line.

"I did," he said meekly.

"All right," said Hannetjie. "The whole Span goes three meals off."

"But I told you I did it," Brille protested.

The blood rushed to Warder Hannetjie's face.

"Look 'ere," he said. "I don't take orders from a kaffir.[3] I don't know what kind of kaffir you think you are. Why don't you say Baas.[4] I'm your Baas. Why don't you say Baas, hey?"

Brille blinked his eyes rapidly but by contrast his voice was strangely calm.

"I'm twenty years older than you," he said. It was the first thing that came to mind but the comrades seemed to think it a huge joke. A titter swept up the line. The

---

Identify Assumptions *What assumptions does Head make about political prisoners?*

Vocabulary

assertive (ə sur′tiv) *adj.* bold; forceful in a confident way

2. *Afrikaans* is a language derived from Dutch that is spoken by Afrikaners. It is one of the official languages of South Africa.
3. Usually used disparagingly, *kaffir* (kaf′ər) is a term for a black South African.
4. *Baas* is a form of address meaning "master" or "boss."

Visual Vocabulary
A *knobkerrie* is a short, wooden club with a heavy round knob at one end. It is used as a weapon in South Africa, particularly by the Zulu people.

next thing Warder Hannetjie whipped out a knobkerrie and gave Brille several blows about the head. What surprised his comrades was the speed with which Brille had removed his glasses or else they would have been smashed to pieces on the ground.

That evening in the cell Brille was very apologetic.

"I'm sorry, comrades," he said. "I've put you into a hell of a mess."

"Never mind, brother," they said. "What happens to one of us, happens to all."

"I'll try to make up for it, comrades," he said. "I'll steal something so that you don't go hungry."

Privately, Brille was very philosophical about his head wounds. It was the first time an act of violence had been perpetrated against him but he had long been a witness of extreme, almost unbelievable human brutality. He had twelve children and his mind traveled back that evening through the sixteen years of **bedlam** in which he had lived. It had all happened in a small drab little three-bedroomed house in a small drab little street in the Eastern Cape, and the children kept coming year after year because neither he nor Martha ever managed the contraceptives the right way, and a teacher's salary never allowed moving to a bigger house, and he was always taking exams to improve his salary only to have it all eaten up by hungry mouths. Everything was pretty horrible, especially the way the children fought. They'd get hold of each other's heads and give them a good bashing against the wall. Martha gave up somewhere along the line so they worked out a thing between them. The bashings, biting and blood were to operate in full swing until he came home. He was to be the bogeyman[5] and when it worked he never failed to have a sense of godhead at the way in which his presence could change savages into fairly reasonable human beings.

Yet somehow it was this chaos and mismanagement at the center of his life that drove him into politics. It was really an ordered beautiful world with just a few basic slogans to learn along with the rights of mankind. At one stage, before things became very bad, there were conferences to attend, all very far away from home.

"Let's face it," he thought ruefully. "I'm only learning right now what it means to be a politician. All this while I've been running away from Martha and the kids."

And the pain in his head brought a hard lump to his throat. That was what the children did to each other daily and Martha wasn't managing and if Warder Hannetjie had not interrupted him that morning he would have sent the following message: "Be good comrades, my children. Cooperate, then life will run smoothly."

---

5. A *bogeyman* is a terrifying or dreaded person.

The Price of Freedom *What have the members of Span One accepted about their choices and their fate?*

Vocabulary

bedlam (bed´ləm) *n.* a state of uproar or confusion

Character *Why do you think Head describes Brille's life before he was a prisoner?*

The Price of Freedom *What reason might Brille have for wanting to send this message to his children?*

The next day Warder Hannetjie caught this old man of twelve children stealing grapes from the farm shed. They were an enormous quantity of grapes in a ten gallon tin and for this misdeed the old man spent a week in the isolation cell. In fact, Span One as a whole was in constant trouble. Warder Hannetjie seemed to have eyes at the back of his head. He uncovered the trick about the cabbages, how they were split in two with the spade and immediately covered with earth and then unearthed again and eaten with split-second timing. He found out how tobacco smoke was beaten into the ground and he found out how conversations were whispered down the wind.

For about two weeks Span One lived in acute misery. The cabbages, tobacco and conversations had been the pivot of jail life to them. Then one evening they noticed that their good old comrade who wore the glasses was looking rather pleased with himself. He pulled out a four ounce packet of tobacco by way of explanation and the comrades fell upon it with great greed. Brille merely smiled. After all, he was the father of many children. But when the last shred had disappeared, it occurred to the comrades that they ought to be puzzled. Someone said: "I say, brother. We're watched like hawks these days. Where did you get the tobacco?"

"Hannetjie gave it to me," said Brille.

There was a long silence. Into it dropped a quiet bombshell.

"I saw Hannetjie in the shed today," and the failing eyesight blinked rapidly. "I caught him in the act of stealing five bags of fertilizer and he bribed me to keep my mouth shut."

There was another long silence.

Dogon pendant of a seated prisoner. Mali. Bronze. Private collection.

"Prison is an evil life," Brille continued, apparently discussing some irrelevant matter. "It makes a man contemplate all kinds of evil deeds."

He held out his hand and closed it.

"You know, comrades," he said. "I've got Hannetjie. I'll betray him tomorrow."

Everyone began talking at once.

"Forget it, brother. You'll get shot."

Brille laughed.

"I won't," he said. "That is what I mean about evil. I am a father of children and I saw today that Hannetjie is just a child and stupidly truthful. I'm going to punish him severely because we need a good warder."

The Price of Freedom *Do you think Brille is justified in going back on his word to Hannetjie? Why or why not?*

The following day, with Brille as witness, Hannetjie confessed to the theft of the fertilizer and was fined a large sum of money. From then on Span One did very much as they pleased while Warder Hannetjie stood by and said nothing. But it was Brille who carried this to extremes. One day, at the close of work Warder Hannetjie said: "Brille, pick up my jacket and carry it back to the camp."

"But nothing in the regulations says I'm your servant, Hannetjie," Brille replied coolly.

"I've told you not to call me Hannetjie. You must say Baas," but Warder Hannetjie's voice lacked conviction. In turn, Brille squinted up at him.

"I'll tell you something about this Baas business, Hannetjie," he said. "One of these days we are going to run the country. You are going to clean my car. Now, I have a fifteen year old son and I'd die of shame if you had to tell him that I ever called you Baas."

Warder Hannetjie went red in the face and picked up his coat.

On another occasion Brille was seen to be walking about the prison yard, openly smoking tobacco. On being taken before the prison commander he claimed to have received the tobacco from Warder Hannetjie. Throughout the tirade from his chief, Warder Hannetjie failed to defend himself but his nerve broke completely. He called Brille to one side.

"Brille," he said. "This thing between you and me must end. You may not know it but I have a wife and children and you're driving me to suicide."

"Why don't you like your own medicine, Hannetjie?" Brille asked quietly.

"I can give you anything you want," Warder Hannetjie said in desperation.

"It's not only me but the whole of Span One," said Brille, **cunningly**. "The whole of Span One wants something from you."

Warder Hannetjie brightened with relief.

"I think I can manage if it's tobacco you want," he said.

Brille looked at him, for the first time struck with pity, and guilt.

He wondered if he had carried the whole business too far. The man was really a child.

"It's not tobacco we want, but you," he said. "We want you on our side. We want a good warder, because without a good warder we won't be able to manage the long stretch ahead."

Warder Hannetjie interpreted this request in his own fashion and his interpretation of what was good and human often left the prisoners of Span One speechless with surprise. He had a way of slipping off his revolver and picking up a spade and digging alongside Span One. He had a way of producing unheard of luxuries like boiled eggs from his farm nearby and things like cigarettes, and Span One responded nobly and got the reputation of being the best work span in the camp. And it wasn't only take from their side. They were awfully good at stealing certain commodities like fertilizer which were needed on the farm of Warder Hannetjie. ❧

Character *What causes Hannetjie's final transformation into a good person? What type of character is he?*

Vocabulary

cunningly (kun´ing lē) *adv.* cleverly; sneakily

After You Read

Respond and Think Critically

Respond and Interpret

1. What new insights into human nature did Brille's actions give you?

2. (a)How were political prisoners treated differently from other prisoners before Warder Hannetjie's arrival at the camp? (b)How did the political prisoners view themselves?

3. (a)What violence had Brille witnessed at home before he became a prisoner? (b)How do his memories of this violence and his home life give him insight into Warder Hannetjie's character?

4. (a)What deal do the prisoners of Span One strike with Warder Hannetjie? (b)Why might Hannetjie's interpretation of their deal surprise the prisoners of Span One?

Analyze and Evaluate

5. (a)Why are the warders intimidated by the political prisoners? (b)Why don't the members of Span One relent and become submissive when Hannetjie arrives at camp and treats them brutally?

6. **Irony** is a contrast between what is expected and what actually exists or occurs. What is ironic about Brille's eyesight?

7. **Foreshadowing** occurs when an author provides hints about what will happen in a story. How does the story foreshadow Brille's transformation of Warder Hannetjie into a "good warder"?

8. Early in the story, Brille says that Hannetjie is not human. Do you think Brille changes his mind by the end of the story? Explain.

Connect

9. **Big Idea** **The Price of Freedom** Do you think the story expresses optimism or pessimism about the future of South Africa? Explain.

10. **Connect to the Author** Head left South Africa in 1964 and became a political refugee in Botswana. What similarities might there be between her exile and the imprisonment of the political prisoners in this story?

Literary Element Character

A **round character** displays a variety of personality traits, while a **flat character** is dominated by a single personality trait. A **dynamic character** changes significantly in a story, whereas a **static** character undergoes very little change.

1. (a)Is Brille a round or a flat character? (b)What character traits does he display?

2. Would you classify Warder Hannetjie as a static or a dynamic character? Explain.

Review: Motivation

As you learned on page 93, **motivation** is the stated or implied reason or cause for a character's actions. A character's motivation affects how he or she interacts with other characters, how the story unfolds, and how conflicts are resolved.

Partner Activity With a partner, review the text and look for specific passages that reveal Brille's and Hannetjie's motivations.

1. (a)What do both men want emotionally? (b)What do they want materially?

2. (a)How do their motivations initially affect their choices and actions? (b)How do these motivations affect the resolution of the story?

SAT Skills Practice

Hannetjie's assumptions about the prisoners of Span One are most strongly refuted by

(A) Brille's imaginative nature

(B) Brille's refusal to submit to Hannetjie

(C) Brille's discovery that Hannetjie has been stealing

(D) the prisoners' bad behavior

(E) the regulations that govern this prison

Vocabulary Practice

Practice with Word Origins Create a word map like the one below to study the word origins for each of the boldfaced vocabulary words. Use a dictionary for help.

obscure   assertive   bedlam   cunningly

EXAMPLE:

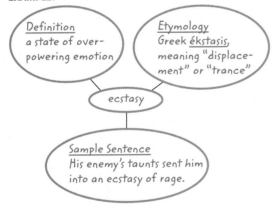

Academic Vocabulary

The political prisoners of Span One fight for ***legal*** *rights, including equality and freedom.*

Legal is an academic word. The **legal** system interprets laws. To further explore the meaning of this word, answer the following question. What **legal** rights were denied to black South Africans under apartheid?

For more on academic vocabulary, see pages 36–37 and R83–R85.

Listening and Speaking

Debate

Assignment Do Hannetjie and the prisoners come to like and trust one another by the end of the story, or do they cooperate only because it is in their best interest? Divide into two teams to conduct a debate on whether Hannetjie and the prisoners become allies or remain adversaries.

Prepare Look at the chart you made on page 125 to review the characters' assumptions and behavior. Write a list of clear arguments that support your team's thesis. Organize your arguments and evidence in a chart to make sure you include all the important points.

Argument	Evidence
Hannetjie begins to treat the prisoners humanely.	He helps with the work and brings the prisoners boiled eggs.

Then research the cultural attitudes and practices of the apartheid era to find information to strengthen and support your arguments.

Debate In the debate, use logical, emotional, and ethical appeals to argue your side and to convince the audience. These appeals should be supported with specific evidence from the text and from your research.

Evaluate Create a pro-and-con chart to evaluate the strengths and weaknesses of your peers' performances in the debate. Consider the content of their appeals, the evidence they used to support them, and their use of oral delivery techniques.

Before You Read

The Return

Meet **Ngugi wa Thiong'o**
(born 1938)

Ngugi wa Thiong'o (ng o͞o′gē wä tē ōn′ gō) is one of East Africa's most important novelists. His political outlook and literary ambitions were greatly influenced by his poverty-stricken childhood and his experiences growing up under the brutal British colonial government.

Colonialism and Resistance Ngugi is a member of the Kikuyu (or Gikuyu) people, Kenya's largest ethnic group. The Kikuyu began fighting for Kenyan independence as early as the 1920s. This resistance sparked a violent backlash from the British authorities, which led to the deaths of more than 11,000 people.

Ngugi earned two bachelor's degrees, first at Makerere University in Uganda and then later at the University of Leeds in England. Around this time, Ngugi's family was swept up in the anticolonial movement known as the Mau Mau (mou′mou′) rebellion. During the conflict, his stepbrother was killed and his mother was tortured. Ngugi's first novel, *Weep Not, Child*, published in 1964, is set during the rebellion. Two later novels, *The River Between* (1965) and *A Grain of Wheat* (1967), also explore issues of independence, colonialism, and cultural conflict.

Radicalism, Arrest, and Exile In the 1970s, Ngugi became increasingly pro-African and anticolonial. He began composing novels and plays in his native Kikuyu language.

After the performance of a radical, politically charged play he coauthored, *I Will Marry When I Want*, Ngugi was held for a year by the Kenyan government in a maximum-security prison. During his imprisonment, Ngugi wrote

> "I belong to Kenyan people, African people, Third World people, all peoples struggling against economic exploitation and social oppression, those in the world struggling for human dignity."
>
> —Ngugi wa Thiong'o

Devil on the Cross, the first modern novel composed in Kikuyu.

After his release, he left Kenya and eventually moved to the United States. In 2004, Ngugi returned to Kenya to promote *Wizard of the Crow*, his latest novel. His prolific and observant writings have both documented and examined life in modern Kenya.

LOG ON ▶ **Literature** Online

Author Search For more about Ngugi wa Thiong'o, go to glencoe.com and enter QuickPass code GLW6053u1.

Literature and Reading Preview

Connect to the Story

In general, why do people resist change? Why is the future sometimes frightening? Discuss these questions with a partner.

Build Background

"The Return" is set in Kenya in the 1950s during the Mau Mau rebellion. The Kikuyu people, who led the uprising, were angry because British colonists had taken large tracts of their land. The Mau Mau advocated the violent overthrow of the British authorities. In 1950, the organization was banned, and in 1952, the British imprisoned tens of thousands of Kikuyu. Although the Mau Mau rebellion failed, it helped convince the British government to grant independence to Kenya in 1963.

Set Purposes for Reading

Big Idea The Price of Freedom

As you read, ask yourself, What details in this story hint at the struggle Kenyans faced in the rebellion?

Literary Element Personification

Personification is a figure of speech in which an animal, an object, a force of nature, or an idea is given human qualities. As you read, ask yourself, What are examples of personification in this story?

Reading Strategy Make and Verify Predictions

When you **make a prediction,** you make an educated guess about what will happen. As you read, ask yourself, What predictions can I make about the outcome of this story?

....

Tip: Take Notes Use a graphic organizer like the one below to make, verify, and adjust your predictions.

> Prediction: Kamau will be greeted like a returning hero.

↓

> Verifying Evidence: "Again they looked at him. They stared at him with cold, hard looks; like everything else, they seemed to be deliberately refusing to know or own him."

↓

> Actual Outcome: Things have changed a great deal in the village since Kamau's departure.

Vocabulary

animosity (an′ə mos′ə tē) *n.* ill will or resentment; p. 135 *The students expressed animosity toward their unfair teacher.*

desist (di zist′) *v.* to cease; to stop; p. 136 *It has been made clear that personal calls during work hours must desist.*

flout (flout) *v.* to treat with disdain or contempt; scoff at; p. 137 *It is not a good idea to flout the authorities in this situation.*

incessant (in ses′ənt) *adj.* continuing without interruption; p. 139 *The birds' chirping was incessant throughout the morning.*

....

Tip: Antonyms Antonyms are words that have opposite or nearly opposite meanings. They are always the same part of speech. For example, *animosity* and *affection* are antonyms.

THE RETURN

Ngugi wa Thiong'o

El-Molo young woman from Lake Turkana, Kenya.

The road was long. Whenever he took a step forward, little clouds of dust rose, whirled angrily behind him, and then slowly settled again. But a thin train of dust was left in the air, moving like smoke. He walked on, however, unmindful of the dust and ground under his feet. Yet with every step he seemed more and more conscious of the hardness and apparent **animosity** of the road. Not that he looked down; on the contrary, he looked straight ahead as if he would, any time now, see a familiar object that would hail him as a friend and tell him that he was near home. But the road stretched on.

He made quick, springing steps, his left hand dangling freely by the side of his once white coat, now torn and worn out. His right hand, bent at the elbow, held onto a string tied to a small bundle on his slightly drooping back. The bundle, well wrapped with a cotton cloth that had once been printed with red flowers now faded out, swung from side to side in harmony with the rhythm of his steps. The bundle held the bitterness and hardships of the years spent in detention camps. Now and then he looked at the sun on its homeward journey. Sometimes he darted quick side-

---

Personification *What is being personified in this sentence? Is this an effective use of personification? Explain.*

Vocabulary

animosity (an'ə mos'ə tē) *n.* ill will or resentment

glances at the small hedged strips of land which, with their sickly-looking crops, maize,[1] beans, and peas, appeared much as everything else did—unfriendly. The whole country was dull and seemed weary. To Kamau, this was nothing new. He remembered that, even before the Mau Mau emergency, the overtilled Gikuyu[2] holdings wore haggard looks in contrast to the sprawling green fields in the settled area.

A path branched to the left. He hesitated for a moment and then made up his mind. For the first time, his eyes brightened a little as he went along the path that would take him down the valley and then to the village. At last home was near and, with that realization, the faraway look of a weary traveler seemed to desert him for a while. The valley and the vegetation along it were in deep contrast to the surrounding country. For here green bush and trees thrived. This could only mean one thing: Honia River still flowed. He quickened his steps as if he could scarcely believe this to be true till he had actually set his eyes on the river. It was there; it still flowed. Honia, where so often he had taken a bath, plunging stark naked into its cool living water, warmed his heart as he watched its serpentine movement around the rocks and heard its slight murmurs. A painful exhilaration passed all over him, and for a moment he longed for those days. He sighed. Perhaps the river would not recognize in his hardened features that same boy to whom the riverside world had meant everything. Yet as he approached Honia,

he felt more akin to it than he had felt to anything else since his release.

A group of women were drawing water. He was excited, for he could recognize one or two from his ridge. There was the middle-aged Wanjiku, whose deaf son had been killed by the Security Forces just before he himself was arrested. She had always been a darling of the village, having a smile for everyone and food for all. Would they receive him? Would they give him a "hero's welcome"? He thought so. Had he not always been a favorite all along the ridge? And had he not fought for the land? He wanted to run and shout: "Here I am. I have come back to you." But he **desisted**. He was a man.

"Is it well with you?" A few voices responded. The other women, with tired and worn features, looked at him mutely as if his greeting was of no consequence. Why! Had he been so long in the camp?[3] His spirits were damped as he feebly asked: "Do you not remember me?" Again they looked at him. They stared at him with cold, hard looks; like everything else, they seemed to be deliberately refusing to know or own him. It was Wanjiku who at last recognized him. But there was neither warmth nor enthusiasm in her voice as she said, "Oh, is it you, Kamau? We thought you—" She did not continue. Only now he noticed something else—surprise? fear? He could not tell. He saw their quick glances dart at him and he knew for certain that a secret from which he was excluded bound them together.

---

1. Here, *maize* is a grain.
2. *Gikuyu* (gē kōō′yōō), more commonly Kikuyu, are the most numerous ethnic group in Kenya.

Make and Verify Predictions *Based on this passage, what prediction can you make about the reception Kamau will receive at home?*

---

3. *Camp* refers to "Operation Anvil," the colonial government's final effort to end the Mau Mau rebellion in 1954. The government screened the entire Kikuyu population and forced thousands of Kikuyu into detention camps.

Vocabulary

desist (di zist′) *v.* to cease; to stop

"Perhaps I am no longer one of them!" he bitterly reflected. But they told him of the new village. The old village of scattered huts spread thinly over the ridge was no more.

He left them, feeling embittered and cheated. The old village had not even waited for him. And suddenly he felt a strong nostalgia for his old home, friends and surroundings. He thought of his father, mother and—and—he dared not think about her. But for all that, Muthoni, just as she had been in the old days, came back to his mind. His heart beat faster. He felt desire and a warmth thrilled through him. He quickened his step. He forgot the village women as he remembered his wife. He had stayed with her for a mere two weeks; then he had been swept away by the colonial forces. Like many others, he had been hurriedly screened and then taken to detention without trial. And all that time he had thought of nothing but the village and his beautiful woman.

The others had been like him. They had talked of nothing but their homes. One day he was working next to another detainee from Muranga. Suddenly the detainee, Njoroge, stopped breaking stones. He sighed heavily. His worn-out eyes had a faraway look.

"What's wrong, man? What's the matter with you?" Kamau asked.

"It is my wife. I left her expecting a baby. I have no idea what has happened to her."

Another detainee put in: "For me, I left my woman with a baby. She had just been delivered. We were all happy. But on the same day, I was arrested . . ."

And so they went on. All of them longed for one day—the day of their return home. Then life would begin anew.

Kamau himself had left his wife without a child. He had not even finished paying the bride price.[4] But now he would go, seek work in Nairobi, and pay off the remainder to Muthoni's parents. Life would indeed begin anew. They would have a son and bring him up in their own home. With these prospects before his eyes, he quickened his steps. He wanted to run—no, fly to hasten his return. He was now nearing the top of the hill. He wished he could suddenly meet his brothers and sisters. Would they ask him questions? He would, at any rate, not tell them all: the beating, the screening and the work on roads and in quarries with an askari always nearby ready to kick him if he relaxed. Yes. He had suffered many humiliations, and he had not resisted. Was there any need? But his soul and all the vigor of his manhood had rebelled and bled with rage and bitterness. One day these wazungu[5] would go!

Visual Vocabulary
An *askari* is an indigenous soldier who serves in the troops of a colonial power.

One day his people would be free! Then, then—he did not know what he would do. However, he bitterly assured himself no one would ever **flout** his manhood again.

---

4. A *bride price* can be either money or material assets that a prospective husband pays to the bride's parents for allowing the marriage.
5. A *wazungu* (wä zōō′ngōō) is a white person.

The Price of Freedom *What does Kamau's anger here reveal about the toll that oppression has taken on him?*

Vocabulary

flout (flout) *v.* to treat with disdain or contempt; scoff at

He mounted the hill and then stopped. The whole plain lay below. The new village was before him—rows and rows of compact mud huts, crouching on the plain under the fast-vanishing sun. Dark blue smoke curled upward from various huts, to form a dark mist that hovered over the village. Beyond, the deep, blood-red sinking sun sent out fingerlike streaks of light that thinned outward and mingled with the gray mist shrouding the distant hills.

In the village, he moved from street to street, meeting new faces. He inquired. He found his home. He stopped at the entrance to the yard and breathed hard and full. This was the moment of his return home. His father sat huddled up on a three-legged stool. He was now very aged and Kamau pitied the old man. But he had been spared—yes, spared to see his son's return—

"Father!"

The old man did not answer. He just looked at Kamau with strange vacant eyes. Kamau was impatient. He felt annoyed and irritated. Did he not see him? Would he behave like the women Kamau had met by the river?

In the street, naked and half-naked children were playing, throwing dust at one another. The sun had already set and it looked as if there would be moonlight.

"Father, don't you remember me?" Hope was sinking in him. He felt tired. Then he saw his father suddenly start and tremble like a leaf. He saw him stare with unbelieving eyes. Fear was discernible in those eyes. His mother came, and his brothers too. They crowded around him. His aged mother clung to him and sobbed hard.

Mji Ni Watu Si Mji Na Sisi Hapa Tulipo Ni Watu Kama Wewe (A Town Is Composed of People. Without People It Is No Longer a Town. We Are Here as People Just Like You.), 1992. George Lilanga D. Nyama. Acrylic on Plywood, 242 x 122 c.m. The Pigozzi Collection, Geneva.

View the Art This painting, which is filled with bodies in motion, offers a powerful vision of the spiritual cohesiveness of traditional communities. How does this painting reflect its title?

"I knew my son would come. I knew he was not dead."

"Why, who told you I was dead?"

"That Karanja, son of Njogu."

And then Kamau understood. He understood his trembling father. He understood

Personification *What is being personified in this sentence? How does this personification mirror the occupants of the village?*

the women at the river. But one thing puzzled him: he had never been in the same detention camp with Karanja. Anyway he had come back. He wanted now to see Muthoni. Why had she not come out? He wanted to shout, "I have come, Muthoni; I am here." He looked around. His mother understood him. She quickly darted a glance at her man and then simply said:

"Muthoni went away."

Kamau felt something cold settle in his stomach. He looked at the village huts and the dullness of the land. He wanted to ask many questions but he dared not. He could not yet believe that Muthoni had gone. But he knew by the look of the women at the river, by the look of his parents, that she was gone.

"She was a good daughter to us," his mother was explaining. "She waited for you and patiently bore all the ills of the land. Then Karanja came and said that you were dead. Your father believed him. She believed him too and keened[6] for a month. Karanja constantly paid us visits. He was of your Rika,[7] you know. Then she got a child. We could have kept her. But where is the land? Where is the food? Ever since land consolidation, our last security was taken away. We let Karanja go with her. Other women have done worse—gone to town. Only the infirm and the old have been left here."

He was not listening; the coldness in his stomach slowly changed to bitterness. He felt bitter against all, all the people including his father and mother. They had betrayed him. They had leagued against him, and Karanja had always been his rival.

Five years was admittedly not a short time. But why did she go? Why did they allow her to go? He wanted to speak. Yes, speak and denounce everything—the women by the river, the village and the people who dwelled there. But he could not. This bitter thing was choking him.

"You—you gave my own away?" he whispered.

"Listen, child, child . . . "

The big yellow moon dominated the horizon. He hurried away bitter and blind, and only stopped when he came to the Honia River.

And standing at the bank, he saw not the river, but his hopes dashed on the ground instead. The river moved swiftly, making ceaseless monotonous murmurs. In the forest the crickets and other insects kept up an **incessant** buzz. And above, the moon shone bright. He tried to remove his coat, and the small bundle he had held on to so firmly fell. It rolled down the bank and before Kamau knew what was happening, it was floating swiftly down the river. For a time he was shocked and wanted to retrieve it. What would he show his—Oh, had he forgotten so soon? His wife had gone. And the little things that had so strangely reminded him of her and that he had guarded all those years, had gone! He did not know why, but somehow he felt relieved. Thoughts of drowning himself dispersed. He began to put on his coat, murmuring to himself, "Why should she have waited for me? Why should all the changes have waited for my return?" ∿

---

6. To *keen* is "to lament or mourn loudly."
7. *Rika* (re ka′) is Swahili for age group or generation.

Make and Verify Predictions *Why do you think Karanja lied about Kamau's death?*

Personification *How does personification here contribute to the story's mood?*

Vocabulary

incessant (in ses′ənt) *adj.* continuing without interruption

After You Read

Respond and Think Critically

Respond and Interpret

1. What emotions did you experience at the end of the story?

2. (a)Why has Kamau been away from the village? (b)How would you describe his feelings as he approaches the village?

3. (a)What does Kamau learn from the women at the river? (b)How would you describe his emotions after learning this information?

Analyze and Evaluate

4. (a)A **symbol** is an object or an action that stands for something else in addition to itself. What might Kamau's bundle symbolize? (b)Do you think it is an effective symbol? Why or why not?

5. Consider the conversation between the detainees regarding their families. How might the prisoners feel about the people and villages they left behind?

Connect

6. **Big Idea** **The Price of Freedom** What details in this story suggest why Kamau and other Kikuyu men revolted against colonial rule?

7. **Connect to the Author** Ngugi witnessed the great injustice perpetrated on the Kikuyu. Why might he have chosen to write about a returning protester, rather than the villagers who stayed behind?

Literary Element Personification

Authors often use **personification** to reinforce the mood of a literary work and to suggest the unspoken feelings of their characters.

1. In the first paragraph, what does Kamau hope to see, and how does he personify it?

2. What does this personification reveal about Kamau's emotions as he approaches home?

Reading Strategy Make and Verify Predictions

As you read, you **make predictions** about what will happen next. Review the chart you made on page 134 and answer these questions.

1. What details helped you predict the ending of "The Return"?

2. Which turn in the plot most surprised you?

LOG ON ▶ **Literature** Online

Selection Resources For Selection Quizzes, eFlashcards, and Reading-Writing Connection activities, go to glencoe.com and enter QuickPass code GLW6053u1.

Vocabulary Practice

Practice with Antonyms With a partner, match each boldfaced vocabulary word below with its antonym. Use a thesaurus or a dictionary to check your answers. You will not use all the answer choices.

1. animosity   a. unpleasant   e. continue
2. desist   b. goodwill   f. obey
3. flout   c. intermittent
4. incessant   d. celebrate

Writing

Write a Dialogue Imagine that Kamau and Muthoni run into each other at a later time. Write a brief description of where they meet, using personification. Then, write a dialogue, imagining the conversation they have.

Before You Read

Bones

Meet **Sadru Kassam**
(born 1941)

Like many fellow African writers and artists, Sadru Kassam (sä drōō′ kä säm′) has developed an art form that is both inspired and complicated by the changes Africa has faced in modern times. Kassam, who wrote and performed for the Free Travelling Theatre, uses modern group theater to help Africans from a variety of cultures, regions, and languages better understand the common problems they will encounter as Africa continues to embrace independence.

> "[W]ith the Free Travelling Theatre, performance in the open air would give birth to a huge 'cast' of three hundred, four hundred, and more people because all the villagers used to join in. . . ."
>
> —Micere Githae Mũgo,
> Kenyan playwright and poet

Theater and Satire Kassam was born in Mombasa, the second-largest city in Kenya. He became involved with the Free Travelling Theatre while studying English at Makerere University in Uganda. Professors and students formed the Free Travelling Theatre to bring theater to rural villages and towns, and it served as an important testing ground for new African drama.

Kassam originally wrote *Bones* in Swahili, one of Kenya's two official languages (along with English). He performed the lead role of the butcher with exaggerated comic gestures.

Magie-de-Nuit, 1992. Francks Deceus. Oil on canvas. Private collection.

According to one of the founders of the Free Travelling Theatre, the play was "unfailingly a tumultuous success." Audiences from different cultures identified with the social problems that Kassam satirized in his play.

Spotlight on Swahili Swahili (also called *kiSwahili* or *Kiswahili*) is a Bantu language spoken mainly on the east coast of Africa, from Kenya to southern Tanzania. Although the people of this region speak a variety of languages and dialects, Swahili is common among many of them. Swahili was greatly influenced by Arabic. In fact, the name *Swahili* comes from the Arabic word *sawahili*, meaning "of the coast." The Arabic influence resulted from centuries of trading between Arabians and the inhabitants of Africa's east coast. As a result of the Arab influence, Swahili became the common language among several close Bantu-speaking tribal groups along the coast. The spread of Arab ivory and slave caravans into Congo and Uganda during the nineteenth century furthered the spread of Swahili westward. While the oldest preserved Swahili literature is written in Arabic script, Swahili is now written in the Roman alphabet.

Literature and Reading Preview

Connect to the Play

When might it be acceptable to use your position, influence, or wealth to make a change? When would it be inappropriate? Discuss these questions with a partner.

Build Background

In Kenya, as in most African countries, a number of languages are spoken. Thus, the actors in the Free Travelling Theatre, which was popular nationwide, had to learn to perform in several languages, including Runyoro, Luganda, English, and Swahili.

Set Purposes for Reading

Big Idea Living with Independence

As you read *Bones,* ask yourself, How do these characters respond to the complexities of independence?

Literary Element Satire

A **satire** ridicules human flaws, ideas, social customs, or institutions in order to effect change in society. The ultimate purpose of satire is to persuade, although satires can be effective only if they also entertain. As you read, ask yourself, What details in this drama indicate that it is a satire?

Reading Strategy Visualize

To **visualize** means to picture an author's ideas or descriptions in your mind's eye. Visualizing can help you "see," "hear," and interpret the action of a play in your mind. As you read, ask yourself, How can I visualize this scene to help me better understand how it might be staged?

....

Tip: Interpret Characters As you read, use a chart like the one below to record the characters' actions you visualize, and interpret what each action reveals about him or her.

Character:	Character's Action:	Interpretation:
Butcher	The butcher drops a meat joint and then just brushes it off instead of throwing it away.	The butcher is unconcerned with cleanliness.

Vocabulary

vigorously (vig′ər əs lē) *adv.* energetically; p. 143 *Tom vigorously shook the blanket to get the dust out.*

endorse (en dôrs′) *v.* to inscribe with one's signature to show legal or official approval; p. 145 *She didn't want to endorse the check because she knew it might bounce.*

pester (pes′tər) *v.* to harass or annoy with petty irritations; p. 145 *If Paul bought candy, his younger brothers would pester him until he gave them some.*

fumble (fum′bəl) *v.* to grope or handle clumsily; p. 147 *Eagle High School had a winning baseball season thanks in part to its star shortstop, who would never fumble the ball.*

Bones

Sadru Kassam
Translated by the Author

CHARACTERS ◆◆◆◆◆◆◆◆◆◆◆◆◆◆◆◆◆◆◆◆◆◆◆◆◆◆◆◆◆◆◆◆

THE BUTCHER

DONGO: a health inspector

KANUBHAI: a Hindu trader

A WOMAN
A GIRL
} customers

SCENE: *A butcher's shop. A sign reads: "SALEH BIN AWADH, The Big Butcher, P. O. MAJI MOTO, Coast Region." On one wall is a painting of a bull, and on another a picture of the BUTCHER slaughtering another bull. There are notices reading: "FRASH MEAT" and "WEL-COME."*

NOTE: *It is intended that each scene shall open with an extended mime by the BUTCHER, which can be developed from the outlines in the stage directions.*

SCENE 1 ◆◆◆◆◆◆◆◆◆◆◆◆◆◆◆◆◆◆◆◆◆◆◆◆◆◆◆◆◆◆◆◆

*[The shop is tolerably clean and tidy. The BUTCHER wears an almost white coat and his hair is combed. He sings as he arranges his meat to conceal its shortcomings. A joint tumbles to the ground: he looks to see if anyone is around, then picks it up and brushes it before replacing it, clean side upwards. He spits and scratches himself **vigorously**. He starts dividing some meat into smaller sections with a large knife, swinging the blade dangerously.*

Vocabulary

vigorously (vig′ər əs lē) *adv.* energetically

SADRU KASSAM **143**

At length he cuts himself, shrieks, prances around, tends his bleeding finger, wipes the blood off on a piece of meat and sucks the wound. The WOMAN *is heard singing as she approaches. She enters, wearing a khanga.*[1]]

WOMAN. Eee, banakuba![2] How are you?

BUTCHER. Me? Very well, mama, very well. You want meat?

WOMAN. Yes, banakuba, I want meat. How's your meat? Is it good?

BUTCHER. Very good, mama. Good and fresh. Can't you see me in the picture there slaughtering a bull?

WOMAN. From what part will you give me?

BUTCHER. Any part you want, mama. Whatever you ask for, I'm here to serve you.

[*He sharpens his knife on his file.*]

WOMAN. I want some of that. I hope it's fresh.

BUTCHER. Completely fresh, mama: numberi[3] one. How much do you want?

WOMAN. Aaaah! A shilling's worth only—unless you want to give me more on credit.

BUTCHER. No, no, no, not today.

[*The* BUTCHER *cuts a small piece from the meat the* WOMAN *has chosen, and then begins to cut larger pieces from another joint.*]

WOMAN. A-a-a-a, I want off that only.

BUTCHER. Yes, but you want good and fresh meat, isn't it? This is very good. See . . . excellent! Numberi one! I tell you.

WOMAN. [Violently.] I don't want it.

BUTCHER. O.K. . . . your wish. Was it this one you wanted?

WOMAN. That's it. Now you know it.

[*He puts some meat on the scales, and is about to add several bones.*]

WOMAN. What's that you're doing there? I didn't ask for stones. I don't want them. Remove them at once.

BUTCHER. Mama, they aren't stones. They are very good bones with plenty of meat on them. See . . . excellent! Grade one!

WOMAN. And what am I to do with bones? I'm not a dog.

[*He finishes weighing the meat and wraps it. The* WOMAN *takes out a small pouch and offers money which she draws back as the* BUTCHER *tries to snatch it, so that he pitches across his counter before she gives it to him.*]

BUTCHER. Here it is, mama, your meat.

WOMAN. And here's your money . . . unless you don't want it.

BUTCHER. Eh, why not? Thank you, mama, thank you very much. God help you.

WOMAN. O.K., banakuba, good-bye.

---

1. A *khanga* (KHän′gä) is a loincloth worn by women in East Africa. Khangas are usually decorated and are often inscribed with slogans or proverbs.
2. *Eee, banakuba* (ē bä nä kōō′bä) is a Swahili slang term of respect meaning "hey, big man."
3. *Numberi* (nōōm bä′rē) means "number."

Visualize *How do the stage directions help you envision the butcher before he says a word?*

Living with Independence *What do the butcher's actions suggest about life after independence?*

[A GIRL *enters, dressed in a dirty, tattered* frock[4] *and carrying a kikapu.*[5]]

GIRL. Get me half a pound of meat, please. Nice—like you!

[*As the* WOMAN *is going out she bumps into* DONGO *as he enters.*]

DONGO. Good morning, mama.

WOMAN. Good morning, brother.

DONGO. What's the quarrel with the butcher?

WOMAN. Aaaa, nothing.

DONGO. Weren't you complaining of ill-treatment? I heard you shouting.

WOMAN. No, no, no. I was just joking with him. That butcher is a very nice man, you know.

DONGO. I see. O.K. Good-bye.

WOMAN. Good-bye. [*Exit.*]

GIRL. Give me very good meat, and no bones, please.

BUTCHER. No, no, no. No bones. Just a little one for your father.

GIRL. No. My father has no teeth.

BUTCHER. Oh, I see. [DONGO *has been clearing his throat loudly to attract the* BUTCHER'S *attention.*] Dongo, Mr. Dongo! Just come over here, please. I'm delighted to see you. How are you?

DONGO. Excellent, thank you. And you?

BUTCHER. Aaaa, not well at all, because you know you still haven't **endorsed** my trading license. Please do it just now. Only a week is left before the closing date.

[DONGO *stands as if ready to receive a gift. He looks away, pauses, then looks back at his hand as if surprised to see it empty.*]

DONGO. Your trading license? Hasn't anyone taught you how to get it? [*The* BUTCHER *shakes his head.*] Just look at your shop! [DONGO *sweeps a pile of scraps from the counter onto the floor.*] See, the whole floor is littered with scraps and bones. When did you last sweep it? [DONGO *wipes his hands, now covered in blood from the meat, on the* BUTCHER's *apron.*] And why is your apron so dirty? Where is your file? [DONGO *takes the file and breaks it in two.*] Why is it broken? [*He runs his hands through the* BUTCHER's *hair, ruffling it.*] And why have you not combed your hair? Who made you a big butcher? Look, you must get things in order before **pestering** me to endorse your license. Do you understand that?

Visualize *What does this stage direction suggest about Dongo and his job?*

Satire *How is Dongo's response to the butcher satirical? What is Kassam satirizing here?*

---

4. A *frock* is a woman's dress.
5. A *kikapu* (kē kä′ poo) is a basket.

Vocabulary

endorse (en dôrs′) *v.* to inscribe with one's signature to show legal or official approval

Vocabulary

pester (pes′tər) *v.* to harass or annoy with petty irritations

BUTCHER. I . . . I . . . I'm sorry. I didn't know about these things. If . . . if you return next week, I promise everything will be in order. But please, I must have the license endorsed by next Monday.

DONGO. That's your business. I'm warning you, if everything is not ready by next week, you won't get your license, is that clear?

BUTCHER. Yes, yes. Everything will be in order next week. I promise.

DONGO. Your business. [*Exit.*]

GIRL. Come on, where's my meat?

BUTCHER. Oh, dear, yes. I'm sorry. I won't be a minute. Here it is. [*She exits. The* BUTCHER *surveys his shop in despair.*] What's to be done? And that girl, she didn't pay me. Which way did she go? Too late: she's made off. [*Enter* KANUBHAI, *a Hindu trader, in dhoti and cap. He holds his nose in disgust as he passes the* BUTCHER's *shop.*] Kanubhai! Oh, Kanubhai! Just come over here please, quick.

Visual Vocabulary
A *dhoti* (thō′ te) is a loincloth worn by Hindu men.

KANUBHAI. Come near your stinking meat? No, no, no, never!

BUTCHER. Ah, this old man! [*He comes from his shop and crosses to* KANUBHAI.] Kanubhai, please help me. You know that health inspector, he's refusing to endorse my trading license. I whitewashed[6] my shop and I bought a new apron, but still he comes and asks me why my shop's dirty, and why my hair is not stylishly done, and what not. What am I to do?

KANUBHAI. That man! I know him. He's a dog. He's hungry.

BUTCHER. Hungry?

KANUBHAI. Yes, hungry. He wants some bones. [*He pretends to snarl.*]

BUTCHER. Bones?

KANUBHAI. Yes, bones. You still don't understand? [*He takes out some coins, jingles them, and pretends to eat them, snarling as he does so.*] He wants bones, bones!

BUTCHER. Oh, bones, bones! Yes, I see, he wants some bones.

[*As* KANUBHAI *exits, the* BUTCHER *leaps joyfully into the air, claps his hands, and returns purposefully to his shop.*]

SCENE 2 ◆◆◆◆◆◆◆◆◆◆◆◆◆

[*The same scene a week later. The floor is littered with rubbish. The* BUTCHER's *apron is filthy. Rusty knives and broken implements lie around.*]

ANNOUNCER. The same scene. One week later.

[*The* BUTCHER *stretches, yawns, scratches himself, spits on the floor, kicks at the rubbish. Enter* DONGO; *he coughs. The* BUTCHER *works at his counter, pretending not to have seen* DONGO, *who strolls with exaggerated casualness up to the shop. The* BUTCHER *looks up, pretending surprise.*]

BUTCHER. Oh, Dongo! Good morning. How are you?

DONGO. Mmm! Not so well.

BUTCHER. Not well? I'm very sorry. Anyway, I hope you've come to endorse my license.

DONGO. Endorse your license? Just like that? With such a dirty shop?

BUTCHER. Oh, by the way, Mr. Dongo, I

---

6. *Whitewashed* means "applied a mixture of lime and water to whiten a surface."

Visualize *Why does Kanubhai take out coins, pretend to eat them, and snarl? What is he trying to show?*

almost forgot: I have something for you. I thought you might like a few bones to take home.

[*The butcher hands dongo a small package.*]

DONGO. Bones? Bones? What should I want with bones? [*As he* **fumbles** *with the package, a couple of coins fall out. He chases after them, and then slips the package in his pocket.*] Oh, bones, bones! That's very thoughtful of you. They will come in very handy. [*He smiles broadly.*] Mr. Awadh, your shop looks really clean today. See, no cobwebs, a clean scale, a new broom, a dustbin outside. It's the way we want it. Don't you worry about your hair. Come on, give me those forms. [*The* BUTCHER *hands him the forms.* DONGO *takes out a pen, goes to sign, but finds the nib[7] is broken.*] Just lend me your pen, please. Something's gone wrong with mine.

BUTCHER. Certainly, certainly. I'm at your service.

[*The* BUTCHER *hands over his pen, which* DONGO *examines admiringly.*]

DONGO. Eh, you've bought a new pen. [*He finishes signing and slips the pen into his own pocket.*] Well that's done. Now you'll be all right. O.K., Mr. Awadh, kwaheri.[8]

BUTCHER. Thank you. Kwaheri, kwaheri.

DONGO. Kwaheri.

BUTCHER. Kwaheri.

[*DONGO goes out and then returns for his hat, which he had put on the counter while signing.*]

DONGO. Ah, my hat, there it is. Kwaheri, kwaheri.

BUTCHER. Kwaheri. [*DONGO goes out. The BUTCHER returns to his work. Enter the WOMAN. She surveys the shop, screws up her face, holds her nose, and walks past with her head in the air.*] Hello, mama! Good morning. [*She eyes him sourly.*] Aren't you coming to buy meat today?

WOMAN. Just look at your shop! And at yourself! Dirty and stinking! I'm not going to buy meat from you anymore. I'm going to the next butcher, to a cleaner shop. [*Exit.*]

BUTCHER. But mama, mama, I have my license. Listen. [*He reads.*] "Certified clean and fit to sell meat for human consumption." Mama! Mama! ✎

Curtain.

---

7. A *nib* is a pen point.
8. *Kwaheri* (kwä hä′ rē) is Swahili for "good-bye."

Living with Independence *Why is Dongo's action surprising here? What does the action suggest about life in an independent society?*

Vocabulary

fumble (fum′bəl) *v.* to grope or handle clumsily

Satire *Why is the woman's sudden refusal to buy the butcher's meat satirical?*

After You Read

Respond and Think Critically

Respond and Interpret

1. Which character in the play did you find the most amusing? Explain.

2. (a)A **metaphor** is a comparison between two seemingly unlike things. What metaphor does Kanubhai use to explain to the butcher how to get a license? (b)Is the metaphor appropriate? Explain.

3. (a)How does the cleanliness of the butcher shop in scene 2 compare to that in scene 1? (b)What might be the reason for this change?

Analyze and Evaluate

4. (a)What are some of the butcher's positive and negative traits? (b)Are any of his negative traits justifiable? Explain.

5. Who do you think is more dishonest in the play, Dongo or the butcher? Explain.

6. **Irony** is a contrast between what is expected and what actually exists or occurs. Identify an example of irony in the play.

Connect

7. **Big Idea** **Living with Independence**
A country's newfound independence is generally considered beneficial to all its citizens. (a)Based on the play, what flaws are there in this reasoning? (b)Do all citizens benefit equally from independence?

8. **Connect to Today** Do you think a shop such as the butcher's would be allowed to remain open in your community? Explain.

Literary Element Satire

Authors use **satire** to expose human flaws and questionable social customs and institutions in an entertaining way.

1. (a)What does Kassam satirize in *Bones*? (b)What literary devices does he use?

2. How would you describe the tone of Kassam's satire? Support your response with evidence from the text.

Reading Strategy Visualize

Review the chart you made on page 142.

1. How do the stage directions in *Bones* contribute to your visualization of the butcher?

2. From an actor's perspective, what might be the benefit of having no stage directions?

LOG ON ▶ **Literature** Online

Selection Resources For Selection Quizzes, eFlashcards, and Reading-Writing Connection activities, go to glencoe.com and enter QuickPass code GLW6053u1.

Vocabulary Practice

Practice with Usage Respond to these statements to help you explore the meanings of vocabulary words from the play.

1. Describe a time when you worked **vigorously** to achieve one of your goals.

2. List some documents that one might need to **endorse**.

3. Give an example of a time when you were **pestered** by a family member or a friend.

4. List some things that might cause someone to **fumble**.

Writing

Write an Editorial Imagine that the butcher and his shop are in your town and you have just learned about his bribery. Write a brief editorial in which you address the problem of corrupt businesses in your community.

Before You Read

A House for Us

Meet **Etidal Osman**
(born 1942)

Etidal Osman (e ti´däl ōōs´män) belongs to a group of contemporary women authors from Cairo, Egypt, who experiment with language and literary techniques. Although Osman wrote extensively as a teenager, she did not begin publishing her work until she was more than 40 years old. Since then, she has published collections of stories and critical essays. Before moving to the United Arab Emirates, Osman was the managing editor of *Sutoor,* an Egyptian cultural magazine.

> *"Etidal Osman is interested in making language itself the main character of her stories."*
>
> —Marilyn Booth, from *My Grandmother's Cactus: Stories by Egyptian Women*

North African Women Authors In many North African countries, women find it difficult to pursue writing careers because of cultural and religious restrictions. Egyptian women authors face similar obstacles, but they have established a strong literary tradition that dates to the late nineteenth century. Women from earlier generations usually wrote in a realistic style and focused on issues such as gender discrimination in education, employment, and politics. Osman's writing is more experimental and somewhat more abstract, yet it still successfully explores the region's history and the social and political issues critical to the future of North Africa and the Middle East. Her belief in the value of creative freedom is underscored by her

Cairo Night, 1996. Lucy Willis. Watercolor on paper. Private collection.

membership in International PEN, an organization that "stands for the principle of unhampered transmission of thought within each nation and between all nations."

Spotlight on Egypt Egypt is in the northeast corner of Africa. Since Egypt's emergence as a republic in 1953, its government has demonstrated both dictatorial and democratic tendencies. In many ways, its political life has been a steady reaction to regional conditions and international conflicts. Clashes with Israel, pan-Arabism (a movement to unite Arab people and countries and reject colonialism), the Cold War, socialism, and Islamic extremism have all played a role in Egypt's development. Osman's short story "A House for Us" highlights some of the political and religious conflicts of the region.

Osman is now an instructor of Arabic language and literature at Zayed University in Dubai, although she remains a member of the Supreme Council of Culture in Egypt. Her works include *Sun Tattoo, Short Stories* (1992) and *Illuminating the Text, Readings in Modern Arabic Poetry* (1988).

LOG ON **Literature** Online

Author Search For more about Etidal Osman, go to glencoe.com and enter QuickPass code GLW6053u1.

Literature and Reading Preview

Connect to the Story

Can friendships survive major differences of opinion? Write a journal entry about this question.

Build Background

Possession of the city of Bethlehem—a sacred place for Christians, Jews, and Muslims—has been a controversial issue. In 1967, Israel gained control of the West Bank, where Bethlehem is situated, and ordered the demolition of many Palestinian homes, claiming they had been built illegally. Palestinians believed that Israel had made it nearly impossible for them to obtain legal building permits. Egypt and Israel went to war several times over this and other issues before signing a peace agreement in 1979. In 1995, Israel placed Bethlehem and other areas under Palestinian self-rule, but problems continue. One of the characters in Osman's story is a member of the Christian Palestinian minority, a refugee from Bethlehem.

Set Purposes for Reading

Big Idea | Living with Independence

As you read, ask yourself, How do the characters in the story cope with the political difficulties and religious differences faced by their newly independent countries?

Literary Element | Description

Description is writing that creates a clear image of a feeling, an action, or a scene in the reader's mind. The use of figurative language and precise verbs, adjectives, and adverbs can also help make description vivid. As you read, ask yourself, What are some effective descriptive details in this story?

Reading Strategy | Make Inferences About Theme

When you **make inferences about theme,** you make a reasonable guess about the message of a literary work. As you read "A House for Us," ask yourself, What inferences can I make to determine the story's theme?

Tip: Take Notes Use a chart like the one below to record inferences you make from the details in the story.

Detail	Inference

Learning Objectives

For pages 149–154

In studying this text, you will focus on the following objectives:

Literary Study: Analyzing description.

Reading: Making inferences about theme.

Writing: Writing a description.

Vocabulary

coincide (kō′in sīd′) *v.* to occupy the same place in space or time; p. 151 *The lunar eclipse will coincide with the start of winter.*

taut (tôt) *adj.* having no give or slack; tightly drawn; p. 152 *The taut kite line loosened as the wind died down.*

stifled (stī′fəld) *adj.* muffled or repressed; p. 153 *She could hear the young girls hiding behind the curtain, despite their stifled laughter.*

submerge (səb murj′) *v.* to go under water; p. 153 *The old, decayed fishing boat eventually submerged in the lake.*

Tip: Synonyms Synonyms are words that have the same or similar meanings. They are always the same part of speech. For example, *submerge* and *immerse* have about the same meaning.

A House for Us

Etidal Osman · Translated by Marilyn Booth

Stormy Day, Aqaba, 1984. Nicholas Egon. Watercolour and pastel on handmade paper. Collection of HM King Hussein of Jordan.

Rami and me, me and Rami . . . always together, except on Sunday mornings and Christian holidays, which fall at times other than our Lesser and Greater Feasts and never even **coincide** with the Prophet's Birthday.

Together, we feel our love for the sea when it is right there at our balcony and when its white birds circle overhead. They come from afar, from Rami's country which lies beyond the sea.

When the sun grows hot we play in the shade of my room. We divide up the colored crystal marbles: the blue ones, the color of the sea, are for you; the green ones, green as the plants around us, are mine.

Vocabulary

coincide (kō´ in sīd´) v. to occupy the same place in space or time

---

Description *What literary elements in this passage make the description effective?*

Every time, we fight over a lone, lead-toned marble, its grayness a lustrous, silvery gleam. Your little hand always takes that marble first, folding over it tightly, clasping it forcefully. For a moment you gaze at something before you, something I cannot see. You speak to someone other than me, when there is no one but us in the room: "I know this lead."

I feel the wings of a white bird fluttering in my heart, and I'm content to let you be the first to take aim. And always . . . always, the marbles run into your row. No matter what I do, I lose every round. I change the position from which I will shoot; I come closer or move further away, or I veer into a corner. I look carefully, consider everything minutely, and adjust the position of my hand until it is just right. I incline my body as far as I possibly can until I am nearly prostrate[1] on the camel-wool rug; or else I crouch down on my knees and hold my breath before the lead-gray marble shoots off from between my fingers and misses the other marbles. You win, getting the larger share.

I'm so angry that I practically burst into tears. As I sit on the floor facing the wall, fuming and waiting, you come to my side, the marbles cupped in your palms, and you put them in my lap.

"They're all for you."

In the late afternoons we open books, lots of them, bright with pictures. We travel together to the land of marvels. You read to me, I read to you: about Sindbad who rode the high seas and came back with a bird in a cage, its feathers of silver and gold. And about Sitt el-Husn and el-Shatir Hasan, the seas between them, and the haunted house with the thousand windows and thousand rooms, all of them open but one. And about the djinni[2] who guards that room and has not slept for a thousand thousand years.

You are reading. Suddenly you stop and say, "In Bethlehem there's a house that belongs to us."

The words take me by surprise—as if I have forgotten that you, like the seabirds, come from far away. You go on, as if to assure me with further words.

"Bethlehem is our city, and it's the city of the Lord's House, and of grapevine trellises and olive trees."

I was sitting next to you on the large sofa that is draped in a heavy cotton weave of tiny, interwined stars and circles. Between us was a heavy cushion, flattened, the cushion-cover **taut**, on which we rested the book. I found that the patterns in the weaving were becoming blurred. My head was growing hot and my cheeks started to burn. I

Visual Vocabulary
A *trellis* (trel´ is) is a latticework frame used to support climbing plants.

---

1. *Prostrate* means "lying flat."

2. A *djinni* (jē´ nē) is one of a class of supernatural spirits that, according to Muslim belief, can take different forms and wield various powers. A *genie* in a lamp is an example of these spirits.

Description *How does the description of the narrator's reaction advance the plot of the story?*

Vocabulary

taut (tôt) *adj.* having no give or slack; tightly drawn

heard a **stifled** voice, not mine, coming from between my lips: "God is in the heavens, and everywhere. He doesn't have a house."

You gazed at me, astonished, seeking to understand. Your almond-shaped eyes, wide in silent distress yet tearless, gave off a brownish flash. It vanished only to return with a stubbornness that pierced my chest. My heart no longer fluttered on a pair of wings.

I was afraid of my own confusion and anger, and of the darkness that now attacked us, and of the stubborn light radiating outwards to **submerge** itself in the sea. You spoke in a calm but insistent masculine voice years older than yourself.

"Our house was made of white stones. It was built on a small hill and it had a little set of stairs outside, five steps. The last one was split on one edge, the crack would be on my left when I was going down the steps to the narrow flagstone path that led to the beginning of the street . . . to the city of the Lord's House . . . I saw our house turn into a heap of rubble, and my father was underneath it, still holding his Mauser rifle. There were four leads in it, I counted them with him, and there's a fifth one with me . . . in my pocket, it never leaves me . . . here it is, look, just like the leaden marble except it's pointed."

I didn't look. I remained silent, afraid, my face towards the wall, the cushion between us. I wasn't expecting that Rami would push the cushion away to put something in my lap.

The next moment his mother's voice was calling from beneath the balcony. "Rami, Rami . . . it's nearly evening . . . come on down now."

Rami went. And for many days thereafter I felt angry with the balcony and the sea and refused to go near them, and I forgot Rami. I withdrew into a corner of my room, with my many-colored books and lots of blank, white paper on which I drew a hill and a house made of large stones; a house that had five steps. And the sun was getting ready to begin its journey, taking from the flowers along the house's flagstone path a dark purplish hue that shone on crystal windows, all of them closed but one. From that one open window a single eye gazed out: an eye lit up with brown rays, shining forth, stubborn like the eye of a haunted lighthouse guarding the sea, ever sleepless.

I drew and drew but I didn't know, and I still don't know, how to draw a calm masculine voice, coming from the depths, the voice of a youth who never grew old. And I don't know how to draw the house of the Lord which I will never see. Yet I do draw, often, a house for us. ✎

Living with Independence *How might Rami's experience reflect the experiences of others living in this region?*

Make Inferences About Theme *What can you infer about the theme from the story's final sentences?*

Vocabulary

stifled (stī′fəld) *adj.* muffled or repressed
submerge (səb murj′) *v.* to go under water

After You Read

Respond and Think Critically

Respond and Interpret

1. Did the narrator's reaction to Rami's story surprise you? Explain.

2. (a)How would you describe the relationship between the children before Rami tells the narrator his story? (b)What factors create conflict between Rami and the narrator?

3. (a)What happened to Rami's house in Bethlehem? (b)Why do you think he tells this story to the narrator?

4. (a)How does the narrator react to Rami's story? (b)Why do you think the narrator reacts this way?

Analyze and Evaluate

5. (a)A **symbol** is an object or an action that stands for something else in addition to itself. What symbols appear in the story? (b)Do you think these symbols are effective? Why or why not?

6. (a)Why do you think the author shifts from the present tense to the past tense midway through the story? (b)What does this shift contribute to the story?

Connect

7. **Big Idea** **Living with Independence** How does the children's conflict reflect some of the issues related to countries that are newly independent?

8. **Connect to the Author** Osman's country, Egypt, fought Israel over the destruction of Palestinian homes. How might Egypt's struggle have affected the way Osman wrote this story?

Literary Element Description

Effective **description** can make a scene more believable and make characters more vivid.

1. Why is the description of Rami's house in Bethlehem crucial to the plot?

2. Which words in Osman's description of the marble game help you picture the children's movements?

Reading Strategy Make Inferences About Theme

Refer to the chart you made on page 150.

1. (a)Is the theme of "A House for Us" directly stated or implied? (b)How can you tell?

2. What is this story's theme? Support your claim with evidence from the text.

LOG ON ▶ **Literature** Online

Selection Resources For Selection Quizzes, eFlashcards, and Reading-Writing Connection activities, go to glencoe.com and enter QuickPass code GLW6053u1.

Vocabulary Practice

Practice with Synonyms With a partner match each boldfaced vocabulary word below with its synonym. Use a thesaurus or dictionary to check your answers. You will not use all the answer choices.

1. coincide   **a.** sink   **e.** smothered

2. taut   **b.** tight   **f.** correspond

3. stifled   **c.** loose

4. submerge   **d.** released

Writing

Write a Description Write a description of a confrontation you once had with another person, narrating from that person's perspective. What might that person have wanted you to understand about his or her perspective? What larger issues were at stake? Use figurative language to describe the misunderstanding.

Set a Purpose for Reading

Read to learn how one man journeyed from imprisonment to a career as an AIDS health-care worker. Consider how his story relates to the challenges facing Africans living with independence.

Preview the Article

"Heroes Among Us" profiles the life of Patrick Chamusso, whose imprisonment during apartheid in South Africa inspired him to help children with AIDS.

1. Examine the photograph and caption on page 156. What do they reveal?

2. Read the sentence below the title. What do you think is the focus of this article?

Reading Strategy Analyze Text Structure

When you analyze text structure, you recognize the pattern of organization. As you read, ask yourself, What are some causes and effects detailed in the article? Use a graphic organizer like this one to keep track of your answers.

Cause	Effect
Chamusso is arrested at oil refinery.	Chamusso becomes a freedom fighter.

TIME

HEROES Among Us

A former freedom fighter makes a home for kids orphaned by AIDS.

By SUSAN SCHINDEHETTE

ON A COOL AUTUMN AFTERNOON IN NEW YORK CITY, Patrick Chamusso gently traces a finger over photographs of his wife and children—not just his son and two daughters but also the dozens of AIDS orphans he considers his own. "It's too cold here," he says softly. "I am so homesick. I miss South Africa. Oh my, I miss you people."

That faraway country is the only real home Chamusso has ever known, from the poverty-stricken rural streets where he grew up to the threatening walls of the infamous Robben Island prison. Along with men like former South Africa President Nelson Mandela, Chamusso was imprisoned at Robben Island and held for a decade as an enemy of the apartheid government. (Under apartheid, a variety of laws allowed South Africa's ruling white minority to segregate people of African, Asian, and mixed race, denying them basic human and political rights for decades.)

Even 14 years after his release, as he traveled to promote *Catch a Fire*, the movie that tells the remarkable story of his life, it was still difficult for him to recall those days of unspeakable horror. "Whenever I start talking about it, I go right back to the room where they tortured me," he said. "They did awful, unbelievable things that I cannot begin to tell you about. It is like opening a wound on my heart."

Yet even more inspiring than the tale of Chamusso's survival is the story of what he has done with his hard-won freedom since. Released from Robben Island in 1992 during the fall of apartheid,

Khali Mazraawi–AFP/GETTY

ALL HIS CHILDREN "I was worried what would happen to me, and Patrick saved me," says Sandile Ndlovu (front row, in beige T-shirt, with Chamusso, Conney, and some of the children at the Two Sisters shelter in 2005).

Chamusso soon learned about a new affliction in his homeland: AIDS. "We had fought so hard for freedom," he says. "And now there was this sickness that was making so many of us prisoners of disease."

Spurred to action by that crisis, in 1999 Chamusso founded Two Sisters, a modest shelter for orphans in the village of Mganduzweni. There, with small donations and his $260 monthly pension, he and his wife, Conney Thibedi, struggle to provide shelter, food, care, and love to a group of children who have been affected by the disease. Named for two HIV-positive girls the couple took in who later died, Two Sisters is a full-time home for 15 children who have lost one or both parents to AIDS. It's a second home for about 110 more who live with relatives or foster families in the village and come to Two Sisters during the day to eat, bathe, play, and be taken to school or a nearby medical clinic for treatment. "These are all my children," says Chamusso. "I love them as much as if I was their real father. I love each one as my own."

In an area hit hard by poverty and the AIDS epidemic, the four-room shelter is a rare safety net. Sincedile Malatji began coming after her father died of AIDS. "There was no food at home," says Malatji, whose mother worked harvesting bark from trees. Chamusso and Conney "gave me clothes to wear and made it a welcoming place," she says. It can also be a sad one. Some of the children have HIV or AIDS themselves. "Whenever a child dies, Patrick measures the child, and because coffins are so expensive to buy, makes one from planks and then buries them," says Conney. "It breaks his heart every time."

More than 40 years ago, Chamusso was himself a poor teenager struggling to make ends meet. After his father abandoned him, he was trained as a boilermaker and a housepainter and in 1976 won a highly valued job as a foreman in the Secunda oil refinery. Then, in 1980, members of the anti-apartheid African National Congress (ANC) staged a bombing at Secunda in an attempt to disrupt the country's economy. Though innocent, Chamusso was arrested and tortured. "They smashed my teeth and pulled out my fingernails. They tied my hands behind my back and used a machine to lift me off the ground.

Day after day they said, 'Confess, confess!' But I didn't know the truth," he says quietly. "I didn't know anything."

Months later, Chamusso was released—a changed man: "I thought, if they can beat an innocent man like this, they can do anything to anyone." His experience inspired Chamusso to work for revolutionary change, and he trained to become an ANC freedom fighter. "Now, I thought, even if I am arrested and killed, I would have suffered and died for a reason," he says. In 1982, after planting several bombs at the Secunda refinery, he was found guilty of terrorism and sentenced to 24 years in prison. "I dreamed of vengeance," he says. "But the older prisoners said, 'No, we must show them that we are not what they think we are.' Forgiveness was the biggest lesson I learned on Robben Island." Ten years later, Chamusso was released: "Being on that boat leaving the island was the most beautiful day of my life."

His joy faded when he first learned about the little-understood disease that was sweeping his country. Determined to make a difference, Chamusso took a course in health care. He educated himself about how AIDS is treated and how the virus that causes the disease spreads and began providing home-based care for the sick. "So many people were being shunned and left in the street to die," he says. "There were orphans everywhere. No one would help the children whose parents had died."

> **These are all my children. I love them as much as if I was their real father. I love each one as my own.**
>
> —Patrick Chamusso

Chamusso did. Battling ignorance and fear, he built the house that now serves as Two Sisters. Today, even as he struggles to raise the money needed "for so many things: fresh eggs for the children, medicine, schoolbooks," he seems a man focused on forgiveness—and the future. His grand dream is to build a soccer field for his kids in a country where that sport is almost a religion. "Sometimes, I ask the children, 'Do you want to play as well as [David] Beckham [the world-famous professional soccer player]?'" he says. "And they reply, 'No, we want to play better than him. We want to be the best players in the world.'"

Chamusso is inspired by his kids' goals. He thinks that "Black kids in South Africa dreaming of being the best in the world at something—and not being afraid to say it out loud" is a sort of miracle. "For me, that is true victory. It is everything I fought for."

—Reported by Steve Erwin/ New York City; Pete Norman/ Mganduzweni

Respond and Think Critically

Respond and Interpret

1. Write a brief summary of the main ideas in this article before you answer the following questions. For help on writing a summary, see page 1147.

2. In your opinion, what is one of Chamusso's most striking character traits?

3. (a)What happened to Chamusso during his boyhood? (b)How did this influence his adult life?

4. (a)When was Chamusso first arrested? (b)How did this lead him to fight against apartheid?

Analyze and Evaluate

5. (a)How might apartheid have contributed to the spread of AIDS in South Africa? (b)What parallel does Chamusso see between apartheid and the spread of AIDS?

6. In what ways might the name of Chamusso's orphanage be significant?

7. (a)What lesson did Chamusso learn on Robben Island, and how did he learn it? (b)Why do you think this lesson is important in his life now?

Connect

8. How does Chamusso's life reflect the realities that people face in postcolonial Africa?

Writing Workshop

Short Story

Literature Connection In "Half a Day," Naguib Mahfouz creates a narrative around a central conflict.

> *"I was in a daze. My head spun. I almost went crazy. How could all this have happened in half a day, between early morning and sunset?"*

This story, like many others, is a fictional narrative that focuses on a conflict and a character's moment of insight that helps communicate the significance of the events to the reader. In a short story, it is important to give the essential details of the characters, setting, and plot, and to resolve the conflict in a meaningful way. To successfully write a short story, you need to learn the goals of narrative writing and the strategies to achieve those goals.

Writing Process

At any stage of a writing process, you may think of new ideas. Feel free to return to earlier stages as you write.

Prewrite

Draft

Revise

Focus Lesson: Dialogue

Edit and Proofread

Focus Lesson:
Shifts in Point of View

Present

Rubric

Goals	Strategies
To create characters and a setting that are clearly defined	☑ Describe the characters and the setting using specific details and sensory images ☑ Describe movements, gestures, dialogue, and feelings of the characters
To tell a story by developing the plot around a conflict	☑ Introduce a conflict that will be resolved in the story ☑ Communicate the significance of the events to the reader
To present events in a logical order	☑ Use chronological order (and possibly flashback) ☑ Use narrative details to give your story a clear beginning, middle, and end
To use a consistent point of view	☑ Use either first person, third-person limited, or third-person omniscient consistently throughout your story

Assignment: Create and Resolve a Conflict

Write a short story of 400–500 words in which you create characters involved in a conflict that is resolved in an unexpected way.

Audience: peers, classmates, and teacher

Purpose: create and resolve a conflict and communicate its significance

Analyze a Professional Model

In the following story, Ali Deb reveals the danger of focusing on outward appearance. Pay close attention to the comments in the margin. They point out features you might want to include in your own story.

From *"The Three-Piece Suit"* by Ali Deb

This month, for the first time, the household budget has been met and . . . even left me a little supplement. . . . I don't know why, I went against my habits and bought myself an elegant three-piece suit, tailored in a magnificent English fabric of lovely sky-blue—the color of sunlit days—in which the tailor's skill was displayed so well that one would say we were born together, one for the other . . . The buttons sparkling in the sun were like stars on the shoulder of a sailor swollen with courage. The spinning sensation that its price aroused did not last long, and I said to myself as I straightened my head and shoulders, "Tell me how you dress, and I'll say who you are."

I made my way without hesitation toward the largest café on the main street. As expected, my friends made a fuss over me, touching, feeling, and dusting me with their fingers. I strutted, proud as a peacock . . .

Naturally I paid for the drinks and left a fat tip for the waiter, who gave me his best compliments. There was glib talk of the rise in prices and the high cost of living.

At this point one of them murmured into my ear, "What kind of shirt and tie are these?" Then he led me to a shop that was

Exposition

Introduce your main character, give background, and hint at the conflict.

Suspense

Give hints about what is to come to increase the tension and build suspense.

Narrative Details

Give precise details and use transitions to explain what happens when.

celebrated for the high quality of its merchandise and for its voraciousness. His good taste and affability were such that my pockets were emptied, and it was only with great difficulty that I managed to pay the ticket home.

For one whole week, I concentrated on straightening out my accounts and forced myself to exactitude and strict austerity. I was thus obliged to forgo luxury and excess such as eggs and butter. I also reduced by half my consumption of meat . . . and pretended to lack the time for entertainment with my friends. . . . I managed somehow or other to put my accounts back in order, while still not forgetting to trim my mustache, smooth my face with a close shave, and spray myself with aftershave.

There I was, strolling about, puffed up with pride, on the main street, taking care to pass by the women's soaks since their tastes are more refined and assured and their eyes are sharper. . . . I heard as though a murmur in my ear, "The flaw is in your shoes." I turned and noticed a light blush on the face of a young girl. I counted the age of my shoes on my fingers. Goodness, how quickly the months had flown by. "Only a pair of shoes stands between me and perfection!" I chose a pair on Liberty Avenue, then returned to my friends. They directed their entire repertoire of flattering expressions my way, and I was literally overcome by a delicious peace that was troubled only by the price of a cup of coffee. I almost proposed another spot in which to drink it but gave up; this café was better suited to my attire. My only recourse was a long, discreet sigh.

On the way home, the weather took a sudden turn, and fine little drops fell on my oh-so-proud-nose. "Abominable sky," and I bought an umbrella that saved me, in spite of its poor quality.

On Barcelona Square, I was accosted by young beggars. Their sullen faces, extended hands, and supplications surrounded me to the point of suffocation. There were three of them, I handed fifty millimes to each one and, rid of their harassment, I gave a sigh of relief, but their leader came after me, repeating, "You're worth much more," showing the coin to all the passersby. I bought his silence for double the amount . . .

I walked prudently, taking the sidewalk, avoiding the dust on carts and jostling pedestrians. I fled the crowd and buses and never forgot to polish my shoes and iron my shirts carefully, often using the fire to dry them faster. The January cold suddenly came to mind, and I anticipated the need to buy a coat and change my suit when winter had passed. Should I hold out my hand for a loan or draw directly form the company's cash box? Finally, I got on the train. I breathed in the fetid breath of the passengers. I leaned on the armrest of a seat; a lady grumbled and said to her neighbor, "They're even contesting our second-class seats." So I slipped into the first class where a seat and a supplementary fee of some consequence awaited me. I went into the local supermarket. It had been quite some time since I had taken care of my shopping. Upon seeing me, a neighbor literally shrieked for joy, shook my hand and then, raising his flat voice, asked me for a loan that I would have naturally refused him if I had not been wearing my suit.

I bought several items and held them in my arms against my chest. The salesgirl greeted me and unhooked a suitable basket. I had no other alternative but to deposit my purchases inside, and since the proper sort of people, my sort, buy without consideration for the price, I did not even bother to look at the cash register total. When I had returned home, my blood pressure was at its peak, my head was literally boiling, my tongue was twisted, and my chest heaving. I no longer saw where I walked or where I threw my jacket, vest, and trousers. I clenched my teeth and gritted them as I cursed the traps of this century and the folly of fools. I finally went back to being my old self, and since that day no one has troubled me anymore.

Narration

Dialogue

Use dialogue to reveal characters' personalities and background.

Sensory Details

Describe sights, sounds, smells, tastes, and textures vividly.

Setting

Give details about the setting that help emphasize the conflict or the theme.

Resolution

Present the final outcome or consequences of the conflict. Make the significance of the events clear to the reader.

Prewrite

Gather Ideas You might try thinking about people, places, and experiences in your own life to help you generate story ideas. Use your imagination to add details and develop a unique and engaging narrative.

Imagine Characters Whom is your story about? Choose your main character and the necessary minor characters. Consider what the characters will look like, how they will speak, move, and behave, and what they will try to achieve.

Create Setting Where and when does your story take place? Use vivid details to establish your setting.

Develop Plot Once you think of a possible character or situation, consider some *what ifs* to help you formulate the plot: What if your character got lost? What if your character is not the person everyone thinks he or she is? Keep the plot simple and focus on a conflict the main character faces. The conflict can be **external** (between a character and an outside force) or **internal** (inside a character's head). Before you begin writing, fill out a plot diagram like the one below to plan your short story.

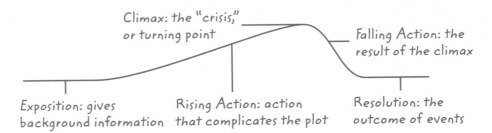

Climax: the "crisis," or turning point

Falling Action: the result of the climax

Exposition: gives background information

Rising Action: action that complicates the plot

Resolution: the outcome of events

Choose a Point of View Point of view is the perspective from which a story is told. You can use **first-person point of view** if you want to tell the story from the narrator's standpoint using *I* and *me*. Or, you can use **third-person point of view** to tell the story through the eyes of a narrator who stands outside the action.

Show Your Style Use figurative language, irony, symbols, and imagery to help develop your characters, setting, and themes.

Reading-Writing Connection Think about the writing techniques you just encountered and try them out in the short story you write.

Draft

Get Going As you draft, use your plot diagram as a guide, but if you find yourself getting stuck, try altering some aspects of the plot. You can add or delete details when you revise later.

Analyze a Workshop Model

Here is a final draft of a short story. Read the story and answer the questions in the margin. Use the answers to these questions to guide you as you write.

Rush

"Hey, Pop," I said as I rushed in through the back door of our restaurant. My father hardly shifted his gaze from the stove.

"Here, slice these," he said, handing me two onions. "*Thin* slices. Not those big chunks." I grabbed a cutting board. "Are you taking the test soon?" he asked. He meant my driver's test. I had had my learner's permit since May, but I had practiced driving only once. I nodded, trying not to look at him. My father threw three plates of fettuccini on the counter, yelling, "Order up!" Just then my brother Stanley slid into the kitchen. He loaded his tray, swung it over his shoulder, and waltzed out. Stanley never got frazzled at work. But none of this translated to the road.

When I got my learner's permit in May, Stanley took me driving. During our first lesson, he panicked every time I got near another car. I was horrified. As the test got closer, my stomach was in knots. So, I called the DMV and canceled.

After Stanley took the fettuccini out, my father checked the calendar. "The test was today!" he cried. "How did it go?" I was caught off guard. "Fine," I lied, finishing the onions.

The next night my brother went home sick. Then during the dinner rush, we ran out of bread. "Here," said my father throwing me his keys. "Go get some." I stood there, staring at the car keys.

"Hey, Pop," I muttered. "I can't." My father slowly turned toward me. The kitchen seemed to stop. I saw his forehead beaded with sweat and creases line his brow. He looked so old. "I never took the test," I said, handing him back the keys.

That night after we closed up, my father let me drive on the back roads in the country. "It's worth it, isn't it?" he asked. "For this alone it's worth it." "It is," I said. It was.

Narration

Writing Frames

As you read the workshop model, think about the writer's use of the following dialogue frames.

- "_____," I said as I _____.
- "_____," he said, _____.

Exposition

How does this story's opening make the exposition more interesting?

Dialogue

How does the dialogue in this conversation help distinguish the characters?

Descriptive Details

How do descriptive details in this paragraph reveal Stanley's character?

Flashback

How does this flashback help advance the plot?

Point of View

Is this paragraph told from a consistent point of view? Explain.

Rising Action

What makes this part of the story the rising action?

Climax

How does the writer create suspense during the climax?

Resolution

How does the writer reveal the significance of events?

Revise

Peer Review When you finish your draft, meet with a partner to exchange papers and discuss ways to improve your story. Make sure the story includes a conflict that is resolved in a meaningful way. Use the checklist below to evaluate and strengthen your story.

Checklist

☑ Do you use descriptive details to create a setting and characters that are clearly defined?

☑ Do you introduce and resolve a conflict and communicate its significance?

☑ Do you use narrative details and present events in chronological order?

☑ Do you maintain a consistent point of view?

Focus Lesson

Dialogue

Dialogue, or the conversation between characters, brings characters in a story to life. Use dialogue to advance the plot, help establish conflict, or reveal character.

Draft:

"Hello Dad," I said as I rushed in through the back door of our restaurant. . . .

"Hello, son. Here are some onions to slice," he said, handing me two onions. "Cut thin slices instead of big chunks."

Revision:

"<u>Hey, Pop</u>,"[1] I said as I rushed in through the back door of our restaurant. . . .

"<u>Here, slice these</u>,"[2] he said, handing me two onions. "<u>Thin slices. Not those big chunks.</u>"[3]

1: <u>**Write dialogue that reflects a character's age and background.**</u>

2: <u>**Mimic the disconnected flow of real speech.**</u>

3: <u>**Use fragments and emphasis to make dialogue sound natural.**</u>

Edit and Proofread

Get It Right When you have completed the final draft of your story, proofread it for errors in grammar, usage, mechanics, and spelling. Refer to the Language Handbook, pages R40–R59, as a guide.

> **Focus Lesson**

Shifts in Point of View

After revising your draft, make sure the point of view is consistent. Use the pronoun *I* for first-person narrators and *he, she, it,* or *they* for third person.

Original: The narrative switches from first-person to third-person point of view.

When I got my learner's permit in May, Stanley took him driving.

Improved: Pronoun shifts to maintain a consistent point of view.

When I got my learner's permit in May, Stanley took me driving.

Original: The first-person narrator gives details about the father's actions and feelings that he or she could not know.

My father slowly turned toward me. The kitchen seemed to stop. I saw his forehead beaded with sweat and creases line his brow. He felt much older than he was.

Improved: Edit so that the first-person narrator tells only what he or she could know and experience.

My father slowly turned toward me. The kitchen seemed to stop. I saw his forehead beaded with sweat and creases line his brow. He looked so old.

Present/Publish

The Final Touch Before you turn in your story, make sure it is free of errors and is 400–500 words. If you typed your story on a computer, make sure the margins, tabs, and spacing are set correctly. If you wrote your story by hand, make sure it is neat and legible.

Peer Review Tips

If you review a classmate's story, take notes as you read so you can give constructive feedback. Use the following questions as a guide.

- Are the characters and conflict clearly presented?

- Is the sequence of events easy to follow?

- Is the setting clearly described?

- Does the story have a satisfying ending?

Word-Processing Tip

If you are typing your story on a computer, make sure you use an appropriate font and size. Choose a font that is easy to read and not too ornate or distracting. Many word processing programs automatically default to a 12-point size, which is usually adequate.

Writer's Portfolio
Place a clean copy of your short story in your portfolio to review later.

Speaking, Listening, and Viewing Workshop

Oral Response to Literature

Literature Connection Many people interpret literature in their own ways. Wole Soyinka said, "My father used to tell me stories before I fell asleep. When the children would gather, at a certain point, I had a tendency to make up my own elementary variations on stories I had heard, or to invent totally new ones."

After reading a short story, it is helpful to discuss your thoughts and interpretations with a group. When you deliver an oral interpretation of literature, you share your responses to the story with others, making connections between your ideas and the text.

> **Assignment** **Discuss a Short Story** In groups, discuss and respond to the major themes present in a short story from Unit One.

Know Your Audience

Keep in mind that your audience consists of people who have already read the story. Therefore, you do not need to summarize the plot when delivering your interpretation. Instead, focus on making connections between your ideas and elements from the story.

Prepare

Assign roles, such as facilitator and recorder, to members in your group. Each group member is to be equally responsible for discussion. This rubric will help you understand these roles.

Leader/Facilitator	Group Participants (All)	Recorder
☑ Introduces the discussion topic	☑ Form ideas and questions about the literature before the discussion	☑ Helps the group leader form conclusions based on the discussion
☑ Invites each participant to speak	☑ Contribute throughout the discussion	☑ Keeps track of the most important points
☑ Keeps the discussion focused and interactive	☑ Support any opinions with facts	☑ Helps summarize the discussion
☑ Keeps track of the time	☑ Listen carefully to other group members	
☑ Helps participants arrive at a consensus	☑ Avoid repeating what has been said earlier	
	☑ Evaluate and respect the opinions of others	

Gather Evidence

When delivering an oral interpretation of literature, you are making a series of judgments about a story. For others to understand your views, you need to support your ideas with evidence from the text. You must first ask yourself what point you want to make about the story. Then, you must connect your ideas to quotations, facts, and other information pulled directly from the story.

Listen Effectively

You can gain valuable insights about a text from listening to the opinions of other group members. When you listen well, you understand, evaluate, and remember what you hear so that you are better able to respond to a speaker's message. Use the techniques below to improve your listening skills.

- Prepare to listen. Clear you mind of other thoughts and focus on the speaker, keeping eye contact. Do not glance around the room, look through papers, or let your mind wander.

- Note the topic and recall what you already know about it. It is easier to understand and remember information about a subject with which you are familiar. Connect the subject to information you have read about or discussed previously.

- Ask questions, aloud or silently. If you don't understand a point a speaker is trying to make, ask questions. Even when you do understand, ask yourself silent questions to evaluate what you hear.

Speaking Frames

As you discuss interpretations, think about using some of the following frames to get started.

- The author implies _____ by saying _____.

- The author uses details such as _____ and _____ to create _____.

- I really like the point _____ made about _____, because _____.

LOG ON ▶ **Literature** Online

Speaking, Listening, and Viewing For project ideas, templates, and presentation tips, go to glencoe.com and enter QuickPass code GLW6053u1.

Techniques for Delivering an Oral Interpretation of a Short Story

Verbal Techniques	Nonverbal Techniques
☑ **Pace** Allow each group member enough time to voice his or her opinion before moving on.	☑ **Listen** Remain quiet until it is your turn to speak.
☑ **Discuss** Try to ask questions that have no right or wrong answer to promote discussion.	☑ **Poise** Maintain eye contact and upright posture to show that you are listening and understand what the speaker is saying.
☑ **Volume** Speak loudly and clearly so that the rest of the group can hear what you are saying. However, do not distract any nearby discussion groups.	☑ **Gestures** Avoid nervous habits and other movements that may distract the speaker.

Independent Reading

Literature of the Region

ONE OF THE MOST ENDURING CULTURAL LEGACIES OF AFRICA'S COLONIAL past is the European languages—usually English or French—spoken by many Africans today. Modern African authors must often decide in what language to write. This is not a simple decision; to some authors, writing in a European language implies an endorsement of colonialism. Writing in an African language, however, may significantly limit an author's audience. To enable their works to reach an international audience, as well as a broad African one, many authors in Africa today write in Arabic or in a European language. Recently, some African authors have begun publishing first in their own African languages and then translating the work for a larger audience.

The Dark Child

Camara Laye

Born into the Malinke people in what was then the colony of French Guinea, Camara Laye left his homeland when he was eighteen for further schooling in France. He was working in a factory in Paris when he wrote his first book, *L'Enfant Noir (The Dark Child)*, an autobiographical novel describing his childhood and youth. A lyrical, nostalgic lament for the passing of a traditional way of life, *The Dark Child* (1953) presents one of Laye's pivotal topics, the contrast between a village upbringing and a modern education.

Burger's Daughter

Nadine Gordimer

Nobel Prize–winning author Nadine Gordimer grew up in South Africa when apartheid was its official policy of racial segregation. Her stories and novels explore the negative consequences of the system. In *Burger's Daughter* (1979), Rosa Burger must come to terms with her anti-apartheid family history after the death of her parents. Under the watchful eye of the government, Rosa realizes how the political environment of South Africa affects her daily life and has made her who she is.

Things Fall Apart

Chinua Achebe

One of the most influential African novels ever written, *Things Fall Apart* is set at the beginning of the twentieth century as Britain's imperial ambitions extend deeper into Africa. The traditional Ibo village where the novel takes place succumbs to the influence of missionaries who ignore local customs, causing a centuries-old way of life to vanish. Tension with the villagers escalates into violence, and Okonkwo, the larger-than-life protagonist, meets his moving, tragic end.

An honest account of what happens when cultures clash, the novel explores a variety of topics, including the role of women in society, human dignity, the nature of racism, and justification for violence.

 Write a Review

Read one of the books listed on these pages and write a review of it for your classmates. Be sure to summarize the characters, plot, and major themes and explain why other students might enjoy the book. Present your review to the class.

CRITICS' CORNER

"Using his African background, [Soyinka] explores the human condition. . . . He makes the fullest use of Yoruba mythology, the Nigerian landscape—mountain, stream and forest—as well as its steel bridges, power stations, night clubs, and tenement houses. The local pantheon of deities, the shrines in which they were and are worshiped, the animals, the plants, the rocks, all form the environment against which Soyinka treats his essential subject, homo sapiens, in his constant struggle of adjustment to the changing environment."

—Eldred D. Jones, from *Introduction to Nigerian Literature*

Aké: The Years of Childhood

Wole Soyinka

Nobel Prize–winning playwright and poet Wole Soyinka was born in Nigeria when it was a British colony. Yoruban culture has been an important element in his writing, but Soyinka has been an outspoken opponent of the Afrocentrist cultural movement known as Negritude. In his memoir *Aké: The Years of Childhood*, Soyinka vividly recalls the village where he grew up, his parents, and his education in Yoruban traditions.

Assessment

English–Language Arts

Reading: Fiction and Autobiography

Carefully read the following two passages. Use context clues to help you define any words with which you are unfamiliar. In each passage, pay close attention to the **author's purpose,** the **cultures** described, the **mood, tone,** and uses of **literary** or **rhetorical devices.** Then, on a separate sheet of paper, answer the questions on pages 172–173.

from *Things Fall Apart* by Chinua Achebe

The Feast of the New Yam was approaching and Umuofia was in a festival mood. It was an occasion for giving thanks to Ani, the earth goddess and the source of all fertility. Ani played a greater part in the life of the people than any other deity. She was the ultimate judge of morality and conduct. And what was more, she was in close communion with the departed fathers of the clan whose bod-
5 ies had been committed to earth.

The Feast of the New Yam was held every year before the harvest began, to honor the earth goddess and the ancestral spirits of the clan. New yams could not be eaten until some had first been offered to these powers. Men and women, young and old, looked forward to the New Yam Festival because it began the season of plenty—the new year. On the last night before the festival, yams of
10 the old year were all disposed of by those who still had them. The new year must begin with tasty, fresh yams and not the shriveled and fibrous crop of the previous year. All cooking pots, calabashes and wooden bowls were thoroughly washed, especially the wooden mortar in which yam was pounded. Yam foo-foo and vegetable soup was the chief food in the celebration. So much of it was cooked that, no matter how heavily the family ate or how many friends and relatives they invited
15 from neighboring villages, there was always a large quantity of food left over at the end of the day. The story was always told of a wealthy man who set before his guests a mound of foo-foo so high that those who sat on one side could not see what was happening on the other, and it was not until late in the evening that one of them saw for the first time his in-law who had arrived during the course of the meal and had fallen to on the opposite side. It was only then that they exchanged
20 greetings and shook hands over what was left of the food.

The New Yam Festival was thus an occasion for joy throughout Umuofia. And every man whose arm was strong, as the Ibo people say, was expected to invite large numbers of guests from far and wide. Okonkwo always asked his wives' relations, and since he now had three wives his guests would make a fairly big crowd.
25 But somehow Okonkwo could never become as enthusiastic over feasts as most people. He was a good eater and he could drink one or two fairly big gourds of palm-wine. But he was always uncomfortable sitting around for days waiting for a feast or getting over it. He would be very much happier working on his farm.

The festival was now only three days away. Okonkwo's wives had scrubbed the walls and the
30 huts with red earth until they reflected light. They had then drawn patterns on them in white, yellow
and dark green. They then set about painting themselves with cam wood and drawing beautiful black
patterns on their stomachs and on their backs. The children were also decorated, especially their hair,
which was shaved in beautiful patterns. The three women talked excitedly about the relations who
had been invited, and the children reveled in the thought of being spoiled by these visitors from
35 the motherland.

from *Aké: The Years of Childhood* by Wole Soyinka

They were all strangers. I had seen none of the faces before. I wondered if they were passers-by who
had climbed the steps leading up to the gate for an even clearer view. I thought they looked at me in
some rather uncertain way, but, they made way for me to come to the front and we ignored each
other's presence at the sight of the police band, the cause of the excitement. They had on bright
5 sashes, bright red fez caps with dangling tassels and what looked like embroidered waistcoats. The
drum which was strapped to the man in front was unbelievable in its size; at every step I expected
him to topple over, but he pounded its white skin with complete mastery, his gaze set rigidly to the
front. His arms made flourishes in the air, giving the heavy-ended drumsticks a twirl, then dashing
them against the sides. The man in the lead juggled an enormous mace, threw it in the air, spun
10 around and caught it as it descended. Once, he even caught it backwards, earning a roar from the
crowd. A gleaming brass funnel rose between the players; the face which blew into it looked
as if it would burst. It gave off notes which were nearly as deep as the big drum but the strain on the
player's face far exceeded that of the drummers.

I had a strange sensation. Each time the big drum was hit, it seemed that the vibrations entered
15 my stomach, echoed around its walls, then went out again to re-join the drum. I listened and *felt*
each time the *boom* came and I was left in no doubt about it; obviously it was the way of the big
drum, I had no doubt that it affected everyone the same way. I noticed little boys following the band,
some walked directly behind, imitating the march of the policemen, others walked alongside, at the
extreme edges of the road. They seemed not much bigger than I, and I soon joined them. Unlike the
20 strangers at the gate, none of them seemed to notice me. I stayed with the group at the back, taking
care however not to mimic the swagger of the others. It did not seem a decorous thing to do and
the policemen looked stern enough to take offence.

Use the passage from *Things Fall Apart* (pages 170–171) to help you answer questions 1–5.

1. The statement in lines 2–3 ("Ani played... deity") suggests that
   (A) the people of Umuofia worship only one god
   (B) the people of Umuofia worship more than one god
   (C) all the deities worshipped in Umuofia are male
   (D) all the deities worshipped in Umuofia are female
   (E) all the deities worshipped in Umuofia take human forms

2. In line 8, *powers* most nearly means
   (A) the harvest
   (B) all the people of Umuofia
   (C) the Feast of the New Yam
   (D) Ani and the clan's ancestors
   (E) the earth goddess

3. Which answer best represents the community of Umuofia as it is presented in lines 6–11?
   (A) Umuofia is primarily an agricultural community.
   (B) Umuofia is primarily an urban community.
   (C) Festivals are unimportant to people in Umuofia.

   (D) Yams are the sole source of food for people in Umuofia.
   (E) Beef and pork are the chief foods in the Umuofia festival.

4. The primary purpose of the first two paragraphs is to
   (A) explain the traditions associated with the New Yam Festival
   (B) highlight why Okonkwo is apathetic toward the New Yam Festival
   (C) persuade the reader to visit the New Yam Festival
   (D) suggest that the New Yam Festival is outdated
   (E) justify the existence of the New Yam Festival

5. The information about domestic life in Umuofia in lines 23–24 ("Okonkwo always... crowd") suggests that
   (A) religion plays an important role in daily life
   (B) families are very small
   (C) families are very large
   (D) women are free to divorce their husbands
   (E) men may have more than one spouse

Use the passage from *Aké: The Years of Childhood* (page 171) to help you answer questions 6–10.

6. The narrator's observation in lines 2–4 ("I thought...excitement") is made in a tone of
   (A) personal triumph
   (B) utter confusion
   (C) joking nonchalance
   (D) dark cynicism
   (E) mild uncertainty

7. Soyinka uses descriptive language in lines 4–5 ("They had...waistcoats") primarily to
   (A) highlight the comedy of the situation
   (B) de-emphasize the narrator's unease
   (C) show that the people were strangers
   (D) offer a vivid picture of the police band
   (E) underscore the confidence of the band

8. In line 8, *dashing* most nearly means
   (A) spirited
   (B) running
   (C) striking
   (D) spinning
   (E) touching

9. The "gleaming brass funnel" (line 11) refers to
(A) the twirling drumsticks
(B) a brass instrument
(C) the mace
(D) the tassels on the police band hats
(E) a metal bandstand

10. From line 19 ("They seemed...them"), it can be inferred that the speaker is
(A) generally very unhappy
(B) elderly
(C) a child
(D) an orphan
(E) wealthy

Use the passages from *Things Fall Apart* and *Aké: The Years of Childhood* to help you answer questions 11 and 12.

11. Which statement best characterizes the overall relationship between the two passages?
(A) Passage 2 is a first-person account of the events of Passage 1.
(B) Passage 1 and Passage 2 both tell about some kind of festival.
(C) Passage 1 has a decidedly darker tone than Passage 2.
(D) Passage 1 has no discernible relationship to Passage 2.
(E) Passage 1 and Passage 2 both tell the story of a young African boy.

12. Based on these two passages, with which statement would both Achebe and Soyinka agree?
(A) Festivals are unimportant distractions.
(B) Nothing is more important than community festivals.
(C) Unpleasant commotion fills African village life.
(D) African village life is lively and complex.
(E) Food is an integral part of any festival.

Essay

Think carefully about the following quotation and assignment.

> The role of community is of key importance in our modern world. It relates to...the need for a sense of connection and meaning within our lives.
>
> —F. David Peat, physicist and writer

Assignment: Do you agree with F. David Peat about the importance of community in the modern world? On a separate sheet of paper, write a brief essay in which you discuss whether you think a sense of community and community celebrations are important. Support your opinion with reasons and examples from literature or your own life.

As you write, keep in mind that your essay will be checked for **ideas, organization, voice, word choice, sentence fluency, conventions,** and **presentation.**

Vocabulary Skills: Sentence Completion

For each item in the Vocabulary Skills section, choose the word or words that best complete the sentence. Write your answers on a separate sheet of paper.

1. The _____ of workers who were constructing the Great Pyramid at Giza disrupted the _____ ambience of the desert.
   (A) throngs...acrid
   (B) bedlam...radiant
   (C) constituency...splendid
   (D) hordes...tranquil
   (E) torrents...stifled

2. The international community has repeatedly _____ President Mugabe of Zimbabwe for his country's poor human rights record.
   (A) rebuked
   (B) obscured
   (C) pestered
   (D) availed
   (E) submerged

3. If poachers continue to _____ the law, the African elephant may well _____ in the coming decades.
   (A) hover...decay
   (B) desist...coincide
   (C) rustle...dispel
   (D) flout...perish
   (E) fumble...flout

4. Many politicians, activists, and celebrities have campaigned _____ to end hunger and poverty in sub-Saharan Africa.
   (A) cunningly
   (B) discreetly
   (C) vigorously
   (D) derisively
   (E) tautly

5. The government could not _____ the documents until a lawyer had reviewed them.
   (A) consecrate
   (B) endorse
   (C) lament
   (D) coax
   (E) retort

6. The Mbuti people, _____ of the Ituri rain forest in the Democratic Republic of the Congo, _____ the destruction of their homeland by logging companies, settlers, and poachers.
   (A) assailants...aggravate
   (B) affronts...mesmerize
   (C) banquets...dispel
   (D) torrent...retort
   (E) denizens...lament

7. As more African nations create _____ economies, the African continent will play a greater role in the global marketplace.
   (A) stifled
   (B) heedless
   (C) diversified
   (D) impartial
   (E) acrid

8. In 2001, the Nobel Foundation showed its _____ for United Nations Secretary-General Kofi Annan, awarding him the Nobel Peace Prize for, among other things, his effort to address the _____ of poor Africans infected by HIV/AIDS.
   (A) toil...refuse
   (B) defiance...denizen
   (C) gratitude...plight
   (D) dissension... animosity
   (E) nonentity...bedlam

Grammar and Writing Skills:
Sentence Improvement

Read the following sentences carefully. Then, on a separate sheet of paper, write the letter of the answer that correctly fixes each underlined portion.

1. Global warming has become such a hot-button <u>issue, but politicians</u> have had to reconsider their positions on it.
   (A) issue, but
   (B) issue that
   (C) issue, that
   (D) issue, also
   (E) issue when

2. Because many cargo ships are too large to pass through the Panama Canal, <u>the Panamanian government planning to widen the waterway.</u>
   (A) the Panamanian government planning to widen the waterway
   (B) the Panamanian government plans to widen the waterway
   (C) the waterway is widened by the Panamanian government
   (D) the Panamanian government is plans to widen the waterway
   (E) the Panama Canal has widen

3. Among the most beautiful cities in the United States, <u>San Francisco benefits from its location on a peninsula and its hilly terrain.</u>
   (A) San Francisco benefits from its location on a peninsula and its hilly terrain
   (B) San Francisco benefits as a hilly peninsula
   (C) the hilly terrain and peninsula location benefit San Francisco
   (D) the benefit of San Francisco is its hilly peninsula
   (E) as San Francisco benefits from its location on a peninsula and its hilly terrain

4. Cultures that lack written language often have strong oral traditions <u>which stories are passed down by word of mouth.</u>
   (A) which stories are passed down by word of mouth

   (B) by which word-of-mouth is passed down in stories
   (C) that stories are passed down by word of mouth
   (D) however, stories are passed down by word of mouth
   (E) in which stories are passed down by word of mouth

5. <u>The Tale of Genji often considered the world's first novel, was written</u> in the early eleventh century.
   (A) The Tale of Genji often considered the world's first novel, was written
   (B) The Tale of Genji often considered the world's first novel was written
   (C) The Tale of Genji, often considered the world's first novel, was written
   (D) Considered the world's first novel The Tale of Genji was written
   (E) The Tale of Genji—often considered the world's first novel, was written

6. Many jobs require long hours in front of a computer, <u>or many workers have developed carpal tunnel syndrome.</u>
   (A) or many workers have developed carpal tunnel syndrome
   (B) because many workers have carpal tunnel syndrome
   (C) however many workers have developed carpal tunnel syndrome
   (D) and many workers have developed carpal tunnel syndrome
   (E) so develops carpal tunnel syndrome

LOG ON ▶ **Literature** Online

Assessment For additional test practice, go to glencoe.com and enter QuickPass code GLW6053u1.

Poseidon, Apollo, and Artemis (detail). Phidias. Parthenon frieze. Acropolis Museum, Athens.

View the Art The sculptor Phidias supervised, or created himself, the statues of the Parthenon. What do these figures suggest about ancient Greece?

ANCIENT GREECE AND ROME

1500 B.C.–A.D. 500

Μνάσεσθαί τινά φαμι καὶ ὕστερον ἀμμέων

Someone, I tell you, will remember us.

—Sappho, Fragment 138

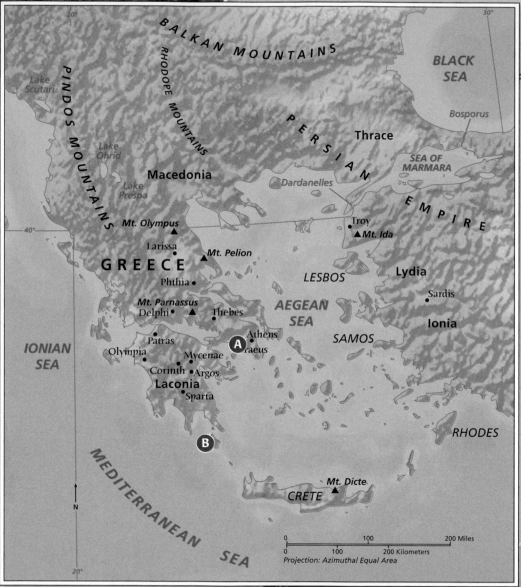

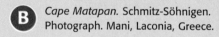

A *The Acropolis.* Reed Kaestner.
Athens, Greece.

B *Cape Matapan.* Schmitz-Söhnigen.
Photograph. Mani, Laconia, Greece.

LOG ON ▶ **Literature** Online

Literature and Reading For more about the history
and literature of this period, go to glencoe.com and
enter QuickPass code GLW6053u2.

PART ONE

ANCIENT GREECE

1500 B.C.–1 B.C.

Running girl, 520-500 BC. Greek.
Bronze figure. British Museum, London.

Being There

Ancient Greek civilization developed on a rugged peninsula and many islands scattered throughout the surrounding sea. Much of Greece consists of small plains and river valleys surrounded by high mountain ranges. Separated by natural barriers, the Greeks developed small, fiercely independent communities, or city-states. The area's challenging landscape was matched by its history. Early centuries were marked by waves of destructive invasions. Later, the Greeks were threatened by their mighty neighbor, the Persian Empire.

Looking Ahead

History and geography combined to form the Greek character. Greek civilization valued the individual human being. In art, history, and philosophy, Greeks focused on the human body and mind. Ancient Greek literature explored an ideal of heroism, a concept of the good life, and a tragic sense of human destiny.

Keep the following questions in mind as you read:

📓 What was the ancient Greek ideal of heroism?

📓 How did the Greeks explore concepts of the good life?

📓 What social and cultural functions did drama serve in ancient Athens?

TIMELINE 1500 B.C. – 1 B.C.

GREEK LITERATURE

1500

Vessel depicting scene from Homer's *Iliad*

800

◄ **c. ninth century**
Homer composes the *Iliad* and the *Odyssey*

c. 610–570
Lyric poet Sappho flourishes

The Charioteer of Delphi

GREEK EVENTS

1500

1450
Minoan civilization on Crete begins to collapse

▲ **1300**
Mycenaean civilization flourishes

c. early 12th century
The Trojan War begins (according to ancient Greek tradition)

800

eighth century
Apollo's oracle is established at Delphi

776
First Olympic Games are held

c. 700
Athens becomes unified city-state

WORLD EVENTS

1500

1479–1426
Egyptian Empire flourishes under Thutmose III

c. 1350
Akhenaten institutes sun worship in Egypt

970
Solomon becomes King of Israel

800

▲ **586**
Jews are exiled to Babylon

559
Cyrus the Great founds the Persian Empire

◄ **551**
Chinese philosopher Confucius is born

LOG ON ▶ **Literature** Online

Literature and Reading To explore the Interactive Timeline, go to glencoe.com and enter QuickPass code GLW6053u2.

500 **100**

Bust of Socrates

468
Sophocles wins his
first victory in dramatic
competition

c. 430
Pericles delivers his
funeral oration

399
Socrates is executed
in Athens

411
Thucydides leaves
his *Peloponnesian War*
incomplete

c. 387
Plato founds his Academy
in Athens

Votive relief of Athena
from the Acropolis

100

445
Athenian Empire expands

405
Athenian Empire
is destroyed

432
Parthenon is completed

326
Alexander the Great
reaches India

c. 500
Golden Age of
Athens begins

431–404
Peloponnesian War between
Athens and Sparta

490
Greeks defeat Persians
at Marathon

500 **100**

480
Siddhārtha Gautama,
founder of Buddhism, dies

▼

100
Europe and China
are linked through the
Silk Road

▲
c. 400
Olmec civilization
declines in Mexico

▲
c. 220
Construction of the Great
Wall of China is begun

c. 274
Asoka becomes ruler
of India

Reading Check

Analyze Graphic Information About how many
years passed between the Golden Age of Athens
and its collapse?

Learning Objectives

For pages 178–189

In studying this text, you
will focus on the following
objectives:

Literary Study: Analyzing
literary periods.

Reading: Evaluating historical
influences.
Connecting to the literature.

ANCIENT GREECE

1500 B.C.–1 B.C.

Historical, Social, and Cultural Forces

The Greek World

Greece is a land of islands, mountains, and peninsulas. Rocky hilltops separate parts of the territory from each other and make the soil difficult to farm. White limestone cliffs drop off into the blue and ever-present sea. Most parts of Greece are within 50 miles of saltwater, and this rugged, maritime landscape has affected Greece's history from its beginning. The rough terrain meant settlements were isolated and self-sufficient, and

Hoplites and cavaliers. Princeton Painter. Attic black figure amphora. Louvre, Paris.

the proximity to the sea encouraged trade and provided access to other cultures. The Greeks eventually developed a type of community they called a *polis*, or city-state. (*Polis* is the root of such English words as *politics* and *political*.) The polis was a city, a town, or even a village that controlled the surrounding countryside. The most powerful of the ancient Greek city-states were Athens and Sparta. Although they were fiercely independent, these city-states shared a common language, religion, and social organization.

Athens

Athens grew over the centuries from a small city-state to become the center of one of the most successful and cultured societies in the history of the world. By the fifth century B.C., history's first democratic government had taken hold there. Free Athenian men spent much of their time in public outdoor spaces, discussing philosophy and politics. Wealth from nearby silver mines, from other cities paying tribute, and from trade allowed Athenians ample time to pursue learning. While citizens enjoyed freedom and opportunity, however, most people in Athens were not citizens. Scholars estimate at least forty percent of the Athenian population was enslaved. Although enslaved people could often buy their freedom, they could never gain full rights as citizens. Free women could not participate openly in politics and were expected to spend their time at home.

Sparta

While Athens was known for its democratic government and flourishing culture, Sparta was known for its military strength. The Spartan government believed the lives of its citizens should center on the military. For this reason, young boys were taken away from their parents and housed in dormitories while they underwent rigorous physical training. Girls were trained in all-female groups. From the age of twenty until the age of 60, men belonged to the army. Although they were allowed to marry, only after 30 could they live with their wives.

> "'Our love of what is beautiful does not lead to extravagance; our love of the things of the mind does not make us soft.'"
>
> —Thucydides, *The Peloponnesian War*

The Challenge of Persia

As the Greek city-states developed, they came into conflict with the vast and powerful Persian Empire to the east. In 490 B.C., an invading Persian force landed on the Plain of Marathon, only 26 miles from Athens. Badly outnumbered, the Athenians decisively defeated the Persian army. According to legend, a messenger from Marathon raced to Athens with news of the Persian defeat and uttered only the word *Nike* ("victory") before dropping dead of exhaustion.

Ten years later, 300 Spartan soldiers delayed a second and even larger Persian invasion, holding back 180,000 Persian troops at the pass of Thermopylae while fighting to the last man. The onslaught of the enemy forces threatened the Athenians; they abandoned their city, which the Persians burned. In a sea battle off the island of Salamis, however, the Greek fleet, though out-numbered, outmaneuvered the Persian fleet and defeated it. The defeat of Persia allowed Athens to assume the leadership of Greece and reach the height of political power and cultural brilliance.

Bust of Pericles, 2nd century BC. Roman. Marble. British Museum, London.

The Age of Pericles

Under Pericles (per′ə klēz′), the leader who dominated Athenian politics from 461 to 429 B.C., Athens became the center of Greek culture. The Persians had destroyed much of the city during the Persian Wars, but Pericles set in motion a vast rebuilding program. New temples and statues soon symbolized the greatness of Athens. Art, architecture, and philosophy flourished. The greatest symbol of Periclean Athens is the Parthenon (pär′thə nän′), the beautiful temple of the city's patroness Athena, goddess of wisdom. This temple displays grace and harmony, the ideals of classical art.

Sculpture

Greek sculptors usually presented human forms. They used symmetry and proportion to create a new kind of beauty. Initially, Greek sculptures showed figures with their weight balanced equally on both legs. However, Greek sculptors soon began experimenting with a more natural, asymmetrical style in which the weight of the figure rests primarily on one leg. Sculptors studied how muscles and bones work together, and their realistic sculptures reflected this new knowledge.

The Olympics

Athletics was highly valued in ancient Greece. The best athletes trained for years to participate in the Olympic Games, the premier competition of the time. Held every four years in the Greek city of Olympia, the games were elaborate festivals that focused on religion, poetry, and music as well as on sports. The first Olympics featured only one event, a foot race across the distance of the stadium. In later years more races and other events were added. Only men could compete in the Olympics, and usually only wealthy men had time to train, practice, and travel to Olympia. While there were no official cash prizes, cities often rewarded their champions with large sums.

Sophocles, c. 340-30 BC. Museo Gregoriano Profano, Vatican Museums, Vatican State.

Running hoplite, 520-510 BC. Skythos Painter. Interior of a red-figured cup from Tanagra. Louvre, Paris.

> *"Beauty of style and harmony and grace and good rhythm depend on simplicity."*
>
> —Plato, from *The Republic*

Architecture

Although Greek people lived in humble houses, they constructed magnificent public buildings. Each city-state had an acropolis, or a fortified area at the highest point in the city, where temples were built. The Acropolis of Athens includes the Parthenon, the temple of the goddess Athena that symbolizes classical Greek architecture. The Athenian Acropolis contains examples of the three main styles, or "orders," of Greek architecture.

- The Doric order, which is plain, severe, and dignified, was the earliest style. The Parthenon exemplifies the Doric order.

- The Ionic order, which is more light, delicate, and complex, came into wide use about a century after the Doric order.

- The Corinthian order was the last and most elaborate style, featuring decorations of leaves and scrolls.

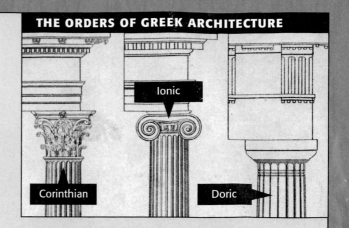

THE ORDERS OF GREEK ARCHITECTURE

Ionic

Corinthian

Doric

Facade of the Parthenon, 447-432 BC.
Callicrates and Ictinus. Acropolis, Athens. ▶

PREVIEW **Big Ideas** of Ancient Greece

1 The Heroic Ideal

Although Greece was organized into small, fiercely independent city-states, the Greeks shared a cultural heritage. One of the key elements of this heritage was the literature of Homer. His epic poems provided models of heroic behavior.

See page 186

2 The Good Life

Greek civilization sought to discover what constitutes the good life. Introducing personal values into literature, Greek lyric poets such as Sappho explored what mattered personally to them. Greek philosophers such as Socrates questioned traditional values in an attempt to determine how individuals should behave.

See page 187

3 The Tragic Vision

The Greeks of Athens invented drama, which they used to explore vital social and religious questions. Athenian dramatists such as Sophocles created powerful, darkly beautiful visions of human destiny, as well as tragic heroes, whose character flaws partly contribute to their downfall.

See page 188

The Good Life

W hat can humans do to create better lives for themselves? Is happiness found in family life, in passion, in the natural world, or in the pursuit of wisdom or art? The ancient Greeks sought to discover what constitutes the good life.

Greek Lyric Poetry

The Homeric epics are objective and impersonal in that the poet seldom introduces personal feelings into the narrative. Later Greek poets such as Sappho (sa′fō) (see pages 241–247), however, created a different kind of poetry which dealt with the concerns of individuals and everyday life. Sappho's lyric poetry celebrates the beauty of the world, the pleasures (and pains) of love, the joys of family life, and the power of art to transcend death.

Greek Philosophy

The Greek emphasis on the human experience gave rise to systematic questioning and observation of the world at large. As a result, the Greeks made great advances in science, medicine, and philosophy. Philosophy is the methodical use of reason to discover the truth. The term derives from a Greek word meaning "love of wisdom."

The Sophists were an influential group of ancient Greek philosophers who taught that there was no absolute right or wrong. Many Greeks viewed the Sophists as dangerous, especially to young people, because of their moral relativism.

> "The unexamined life is not worth living."
>
> —Plato, the *Apology*

Seated Girl with Dove, 2nd half 4th century BC. Late Classical Greek. Terracotta, height:. 21.4 cm. Antikensammlung, Staatliche Museen zu Berlin, Germany.

Among the critics of the Sophists was the philosopher Socrates (sok′rə tēz). Because he left no writings, we know about him primarily through the works of his pupil, Plato (plā′tō). Socrates' teaching approach, known as the Socratic method, used a question-and-answer format to lead pupils to discover the truth. Socrates believed individuals could discover the truth within themselves through rational inquiry.

Besides Socrates and Plato, other notable Greek thinkers include

- Hippocrates (hi pok′rə tēz), who trained doctors to look into the causes of disease.
- Aristotle (ar′is tot′əl), who systematized the study of science.
- Herodotus (hə rod′ə təs), who established the idea that history could be studied as a collection of true facts, rather than a series of legends.

Reading Check

Compare and Contrast How did Socrates differ from the Sophists?

Big Idea 3
The Tragic Vision

What contributes most to human unhappiness? Do evil deeds bring about suffering, or is misery primarily the result of an error in judgment? The ancient Greek dramatists pondered these questions.

Athenian Drama

One of the great Greek achievements was drama, created by the Athenians. In Athens, tragedies were performed at religious festivals and often explored the relationship between humans and the gods. In the process, they raised important questions about life. The first Greek tragedies were presented in a trilogy, or a set of three plays, that explored a common theme. For example, Aeschylus (es′kə ləs) composed the *Oresteia*, a trilogy that relates the fate of Agamemnon and his family after his return from the Trojan War. In these plays, evil breeds more evil and greater suffering. Yet in the end, reason triumphs over the forces of blood-guilt and revenge.

> "*Count no man happy till he dies, free of pain at last.*"
>
> —Sophocles, *Oedipus the King*

Sophocles (sof′ə klēz) (see pages 250–318), another Athenian playwright, composed *Oedipus the King*. In this timeless tragedy, a plague sent by the gods ravages the people of Thebes. Oedipus, the king of Thebes, diligently tries to relieve his people of the plague but in the process discovers a horrifying truth about himself.

The Nature of Tragedy

Central to Greek tragedy is the fall of a great man (or woman, though in ancient Greece her part would have been acted by a man)—the tragic hero, whose fate is partly brought about by a flaw within his or her own character. The tragic hero's aim was to inspire audiences to examine their own lives, to define their beliefs, and to cleanse their emotions of pity and terror through compassion for the character. Greek tragedies were so insightful and complex that they continue to be relevant today. They have profoundly influenced the Western literary tradition.

Oedipus visiting the Sphinx, 5th century BC. Attic red figure kylix (drinking cup). Museo Gregoriano Etrusco, Vatican Museums, Vatican State.

Reading Check

Analyze Cause-and-Effect Relationships How did the experience of drama help the ancient Greeks deal with their problems?

WRAP-UP

Kelly Holmes celebrates as she crosses the finish line to win the Olympics women's 1500 metres, 2004. Mike Blake. Athens.

Legacy of the Period

The ancient Greeks laid the intellectual and cultural foundations of Western civilization. They debated basic questions about the nature of the universe, the purpose of life, and the meaning of truth. The Greeks not only strove to answer these questions but also created a logical method for exploring them—philosophy.

The Greeks were the first to use reason to explain natural phenomena. In other words, they were the first scientists. The Greek philosopher Aristotle wrote on a number of scientific subjects, including astronomy, geology, biology, and physics. Until the seventeenth century, science in the Western world remained largely based on Aristotle's ideas.

In general, the Greeks established one of the bedrock values of Western civilization—the importance of the individual. Athenians founded democracy, proclaiming the right of ordinary individuals to govern themselves.

Cultural and Literary Links

- Greek mythology has provided a rich treasury of narratives and characters for Western art and literature. Even some scientific concepts, such as the Oedipus complex and the Gaia hypothesis, are named after Greek myths.

- Homer remains one of the most influential authors in world literature. His epic poems have inspired countless works, from the *Aeneid* by the Roman poet Virgil to *Omeros* by the Caribbean Nobel Prize laureate Derek Walcott.

- In A.D. 393, the Romans banned the ancient Olympic Games. In the summer of 1896, however, the first modern Olympics took place in Athens.

LOG ON ▶ **Literature** Online

Unit Resources For additional skills practice, go to glencoe.com and enter QuickPass code GLW6053u2.

Activities

Use what you have learned about the period to do one of these activities.

1. **Follow Up** Go back to Looking Ahead on page 179 and answer the questions.

2. **Contrast Literary Periods** Working with other students, hold a panel discussion about how one of this period's Big Ideas still influences American culture today. You can use examples from literature, fine art, music, movies, or other kinds of artistic expression.

3. **Build Visual Literacy** Create a display of images of modern buildings that reflect the influence of Greek architecture.

4. **Take Notes** You might try using this graphic organizer to keep track of the three Big Ideas in this part.

 FOLDABLES Study Organizer **THREE-POCKET BOOK**

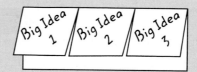

The Homeric Epics

> *"Well let me die—*
> *but not without struggle, not without glory, no,*
> *in some great clash of arms that even men to come*
> *will hear of down the years!"*
>
> —Homer, from the *Iliad*

DOOMED BY THE GODS, THE TROJAN HERO Hector speaks these words in the *Iliad*. He imagines his deeds will live on, perhaps in the immortal lines of a poet. The oral poets of ancient Greece composed narratives of heroic deeds, chanting them to musical accompaniment. The greatest of these oral poets was Homer. The Greeks attributed to him two of the earliest surviving epic poems—the *Iliad* and its sequel, the *Odyssey*—which celebrated the heroes of the Trojan War.

The Art of the Bard

How did an oral poet such as Homer compose his poems? In some ways, he was like a musician who starts with a well-known tune and plays variations on it every time he performs. Just as a musician plays to a steady rhythm, so Homer established a steady rhythm in his words. The long and short syllables alternate in a regular pattern.

Composing poetry in front of an audience without "drawing a blank" may seem like an arduous task, but the fact that Homer performed to a rhythm simplified the job. It meant certain phrases worked better than others because they fit rhythmically into a line of poetry. Homer used those phrases again and again. For example, he repeatedly referred to the goddess Athena as "gray-eyed Athena" and to Dawn's "fingertips of rose." He also recycled longer passages that described routine actions, such as a character's way of entering a room, donning armor, or saying good-bye.

Marble seated harp player, Ca. 2800-2700 BC. Marble, H. with harp 11 1/2 in. The Metropolitan Museum of Art, NY.

This use of repetition helped Homer and pleased his audience. The poet did not have to memorize or make up every word. Though the story may have been somewhat different in each retelling, the repeated phrases remained like handles for the poet to grip. Homer's audience looked forward to these repetitions, as listeners today look forward to the chorus of a song.

Attic red-figure hydria, c. 440-420 BC. Greek. Ceramic. Ashmolean Museum, University of Oxford, UK.

Epic Poetry

Homer's *Iliad* and *Odyssey* have been read for centuries as **epic poems**. Since Homer's time, epic poetry has been considered a subgenre, or type, of literature. An epic poem has the following characteristics:

- It is a long narrative poem built around heroic adventures.

- The setting is vast. It may include the sea, a palace, and the abode of the gods.

- The main character is a legendary hero who usually embodies the goals and virtues of an entire culture.

- The action includes extraordinary or superhuman deeds. Typically, the epic hero struggles with natural and supernatural obstacles and antagonists, which test his bravery, wits, and physical prowess.

- Gods or supernatural beings take part in the action, protecting, advising, and sometimes punishing epic heroes.

- The purpose is not only to entertain, but to teach values and ideals, inspiring the audience with models of heroic behavior.

Epic Narration

An epic poem is narrated in predictable ways.

- In an invocation, the poet-narrator states the subject and prays for inspiration to a muse, a goddess of poetry.

- The narrator begins the tale in the "middle of things," describing what is happening after certain important events have already occurred.

- The narrative includes speeches by the principal characters—including gods and antagonists of the epic hero—which reveal their personalities.

- The language is elevated, and the style is formal rather than conversational.

- The use of figurative language makes the narrative vivid and exciting, maintaining a dignified tone. Figurative language includes epic similes, which are longer and more elaborate than ordinary similes.

The *Iliad*, the epic you are about to read, is a monumental artistic achievement. It presents the climactic events of a long, brutal war. Because of Homer's superb depiction of both the glory and the horror of battle, the *Iliad* still moves readers today, nearly 3,000 years after its creation.

LOG ON ▶ **Literature** Online

Literature and Reading For more about the Homeric epics, go to glencoe.com and enter QuickPass code GLW6053u2.

Respond and Think Critically

1. Why do you think Homer's epics are still enjoyed today?

2. How did the composition method of ancient Greek oral poets resemble that of a musician?

3. What purposes did Homer's epics serve for the ancient Greeks?

FROM THE ILIAD

from Book I:

THE RAGE OF ACHILLES

Homer

Translated by Robert Fagles

Achilles battling Agamemnon, c. 1757. Giovanni Battista Tiepolo. Italy Wall painting Hall of the Iliad, Villa Valmarana, Vicenza, Italy.

Rage—Goddess, sing the rage of Peleus' son Achilles,
murderous, doomed, that cost the Achaeans countless losses,
hurling down to the House of Death so many sturdy souls,
great fighters' souls, but made their bodies carrion,
5   feasts for the dogs and birds,
and the will of Zeus was moving toward its end.
Begin, Muse, when the two first broke and clashed,
Agamemnon lord of men and brilliant Achilles.

     What god drove them to fight with such a fury?
10 Apollo the son of Zeus and Leto. Incensed at the king
he swept a fatal plague through the army—men were dying
and all because Agamemnon spurned Apollo's priest.
Yes, Chryses approached the Achaeans' fast ships
to win his daughter back, bringing a priceless ransom
15 and bearing high in hand, wound on a golden staff,
the wreaths of the god, the distant deadly Archer.°
He begged the whole Achaean army but most of all
the two supreme commanders, Atreus' two sons,
"Agamemnon, Menelaus—all Argives° geared for war!
20 May the gods who hold the halls of Olympus° give you
Priam's city to plunder, then safe passage home.
Just set my daughter free, my dear one . . . here,
accept these gifts, this ransom. Honor the god
who strikes from worlds away—the son of Zeus, Apollo!"

10–16 Incensed at the king . . . deadly Archer (Apollo): In a raid on Thebes, a Trojan ally, the Greeks captured Chryseis, daughter of Chryses, Apollo's high priest. Agamemnon claimed her as his share of the plunder.

19 Argives: natives of the city-state of Argos; Greeks.

20 Olympus: highest mountain in Greece; in mythology, the home of the deities.

Evaluate Credibility *Is Chryses sincere in this speech? Do you think Agamemnon believes him? Explain.*

25   And all ranks of Achaeans cried out their assent:
       "Respect the priest, accept the shining ransom!"
       But it brought no joy to the heart of Agamemnon.
       The king dismissed the priest with a brutal order
       ringing in his ears: "Never again, old man,
30   let me catch sight of you by the hollow ships!°
       Not loitering now, not slinking back tomorrow.
       The staff and the wreaths of god will never save you then.
       The girl—I won't give up the girl. Long before that,
       old age will overtake her in *my* house, in Argos,
35   far from her fatherland, slaving back and forth
       at the loom, forced to share my bed!
                                           Now go,
       don't tempt my wrath—and you may depart alive."

       The old man was terrified. He obeyed the order,
       turning, trailing away in silence down the shore
40   where the battle lines of breakers crash and drag.
       And moving off to a safe distance, over and over
       the old priest prayed to the son of sleek-haired Leto,
       lord Apollo, "Hear me, Apollo! God of the silver bow
       who strides the walls of Chryse and Cilla sacrosanct—
45   lord in power of Tenedos—Smintheus,° god of the plague!
       If I ever roofed a shrine to please your heart,
       ever burned the long rich bones of bulls and goats
       on your holy altar, now, now bring my prayer to pass.
       Pay the Danaans back—your arrows for my tears!"

50   His prayer went up and Phoebus° Apollo heard him.
       Down he strode from Olympus' peaks, storming at heart
       with his bow and hooded quiver slung across his shoulders.
       The arrows clanged at his back as the god quaked with rage,
       the god himself on the march and down he came like night.
55   Over against the ships he dropped to a knee, let fly a shaft
       and a terrifying clash rang out from the great silver bow.
       First he went for the mules and circling dogs but then,
       launching a piercing shaft at the men themselves,
       he cut them down in **droves**—
60   and the corpse-fires burned on, night and day, no end in sight.

30 ships: The Greek camp was on the beaches before the city of Troy. The 1,000-ship navy that carried them there lay at anchor offshore.

44–45 Chryse, Cilla, Tenedos: places near Troy that **Smintheus** (another name for Apollo) considers sacrosanct, or sacred.

50 Phoebus: literally means "bright"; a reference to Apollo's role as the sun god.

The Heroic Ideal *What does this response suggest about Agamemnon?*

Vocabulary

droves (drōvz) *n.* large numbers of animals or people, moving along together; crowd

Nine days the arrows of god swept through the army.°
On the tenth Achilles called all ranks to muster—
the impulse seized him, sent by white-armed Hera
grieving to see Achaean fighters drop and die.
65 Once they'd gathered, crowding the meeting grounds,
the swift runner Achilles rose and spoke among them:
"Son of Atreus, now we are beaten back, I fear,
the long campaign is lost. So home we sail . . .
if we can escape our death—if war and plague
70 are joining forces now to crush the Argives.
But wait: let us question a holy man,
a prophet, even a man skilled with dreams—
dreams as well can come our way from Zeus—
come, someone to tell us why Apollo rages so,
75 whether he blames us for a vow we failed, or sacrifice.
If only the god would share the smoky savor of lambs
and full-grown goats, Apollo might be willing, still,
somehow, to save us from this plague."

                                                    So he proposed
and down he sat again as Calchas rose among them,
80 Thestor's son, the clearest by far of all the seers°
who scan the flight of birds.° He knew all things that are,
all things that are past and all that are to come,
the seer who had led the Argive ships to Troy
with the second sight° that god Apollo gave him.
85 For the armies' good the seer began to speak:
"Achilles, dear to Zeus . . .
you order me to explain Apollo's anger,
the distant deadly Archer? I will tell it all.
But strike a pact with me, swear you will defend me
90 with all your heart, with words and strength of hand.
For there is a man I will enrage—I see it now—
a powerful man who lords it over all the Argives,
one the Achaeans must obey . . . A mighty king,
raging against an inferior, is too strong.
95 Even if he can swallow down his wrath today,
still he will nurse the burning in his chest
until, sooner or later, he sends it bursting forth.
Consider it closely, Achilles. Will you save me?"

        And the matchless runner reassured him: "Courage!
100 Out with it now, Calchas. Reveal the will of god,
whatever you may know. And I swear by Apollo

The Heroic Ideal *What do Achilles' first words in the poem reveal about him?*

51–61 Down he strode . . . swept through the army: Apollo causes a plague to break out in the Greek camp. Homer uses imagery (Apollo as "deadly archer") to convey the effect of the disease.

80 seers: individuals with extraordinary moral and spiritual insight. The Greeks believed that seers had mystical powers given to them by the gods.

81 scan the flight of birds: The examination of animal behavior and their internal organs helped seers make predictions or interpret the will of the deities.

84 second sight: the ability to see remote or future objects or events.

dear to Zeus, the power you pray to, Calchas,
when you reveal god's will to the Argives—
    no one,
not while I am alive and see the light on earth,
    no one

105 will lay his heavy hands on you by the
        hollow ships.
None among all the armies. Not even if you
    mean
Agamemnon here who now claims to be, by far,
the best of the Achaeans."
                            The seer took heart
and this time he spoke out, bravely: "Beware—

110 he casts no blame for a vow we failed, a sacrifice.
The god's enraged because Agamemnon spurned
    his priest,
he refused to free his daughter, he refused the
    ransom.
That's why the Archer sends us pains and he will
    send us more
and never drive this shameful destruction from the
    Argives,

115 not till we give back the girl with sparkling eyes
to her loving father—no price, no ransom paid—
and carry a sacred hundred bulls to Chryse town.°
Then we can calm the god, and only then **appease** him."

So he declared and sat down. But among them rose

120 the fighting son of Atreus, lord of the far-flung kingdoms,
Agamemnon—furious, his dark heart filled to the brim,
blazing with anger now, his eyes like searing fire.
With a sudden, killing look he wheeled on Calchas first:
"Seer of misery! Never a word that works to my advantage!

125 Always misery warms your heart, your prophecies—
never a word of profit said or brought to pass.
Now, again, you divine° god's will for the armies,
bruit° it about, as fact, why the deadly Archer

Achilles. Attic red figure amphora. Museo Gregoriano Etrusco, Vatican Museums, Vatican State.

117 **carry a sacred hundred bulls to Chryse town:** sacrifice a hundred bulls on the altar to Apollo at Chryse.

127 **divine:** to discover hidden knowledge; here, to interpret the will of a god.

128 **bruit** (br<u>oo</u>t): to make known loudly and publicly.

The Epic Hero *What values does Achilles reflect in these lines?*

Evaluate Credibility *Why might the Greeks view Calchas as a credible informant?*

Vocabulary

appease (ə pēz´) *v.* to satisfy insistent demands

multiplies our pains: because I, I refused
130 that glittering price for the young girl Chryseis.
     Indeed, I prefer *her* by far, the girl herself,
     I want her mine in my own house! I rank her higher
     than Clytemnestra, my wedded wife—she's nothing less
     in build or breeding, in mind or works of hand.
135 But I am willing to give her back, even so,
     if that is best for all. What I really want
     is to keep my people safe, not see them dying.
     But fetch me another prize, and straight off too,
     else I alone of the Argives go without my honor.
140 That would be a disgrace. You are all witness,
     look—*my* prize is snatched away!"
                                          But the swift runner
     Achilles answered him at once, "Just how, Agamemnon,
     great field marshal . . . most grasping man alive,
     how can the generous Argives give you prizes now?
145 I know of no troves of treasure, piled, lying idle,
     anywhere. Whatever we dragged from towns we plundered,
     all's been portioned out. But collect it, call it back
     from the rank and file? *That* would be the disgrace.
     So return the girl to the god, at least for now.
150 We Achaeans will pay you back, three, four times over,
     if Zeus will grant us the gift, somehow, someday,
     to raze° Troy's massive ramparts to the ground."

     But King Agamemnon countered, "Not so quickly,
     brave as you are, godlike Achilles—trying to cheat *me*.
155 Oh no, you won't get past me, take me in that way!
     What do you want? To cling to your own prize°
     while I sit calmly by—empty-handed here?
     Is that why you order me to give her back?
     No—if our generous Argives *will* give me a prize,
160 a match for my desires, equal to what I've lost,
     well and good. But if they give me nothing
     I will take a prize myself—your own, or Ajax'°
     or Odysseus' prize—I'll **commandeer** her myself

152 raze: to destroy completely.

156 To cling to your own prize:
After a raid on the city of Lyrnessos,
Achilles had chosen, as his share of
the plunder, the young woman
named Briseis.

162 Ajax: The Greek army had two
great warriors named Ajax. Ajax, the
son of Telamon, was considered
second only to Achilles in skill and
courage.

The Heroic Ideal *The ancient Greeks believed acquiring a war prize was an
honor for a warrior, and losing one was a disgrace. How does this help explain
Agamemnon's response?*

Evaluate Credibility *Is Achilles' advice reasonable? Is his promise sincere? Explain.*

Vocabulary

commandeer (kom′ ən dēr′) *v.* to take arbitrary or forceful possession of

The Abduction of Helen. Zenone Veronese. Oil on canvas, 44 x 112 in.
Private collection.

View the Art The abduction of Helen of Troy by the Trojan prince Paris triggered the Trojan War. In this painting, the artist portrays Paris carrying Helen to the ships waiting to set sail for Troy. How would you describe the way the artist presents Helen's departure from Sparta?

and let that man I go to visit choke with rage!
165 Enough. We'll deal with all this later, in due time.
Now come, we haul a black ship down to the bright sea,
gather a decent number of oarsmen along her locks
and put aboard a sacrifice, and Chryseis herself,
in all her beauty . . . we embark her too.
170 Let one of the leading captains take command.
Ajax, Idomeneus, trusty Odysseus or you, Achilles,
you—the most violent man alive—so you can perform
the rites for us and calm the god yourself."
                                        A dark glance
and the headstrong runner answered him in kind:
    "Shameless—
175 armored in shamelessness—always shrewd with greed!
How could any Argive soldier obey your orders,
freely and gladly do your sailing for you
or fight your enemies, full force? Not I, no.
It wasn't Trojan spearmen who brought me here to fight.
180 The Trojans never did *me* damage, not in the least,
they never stole my cattle or my horses, never
in Phthia° where the rich soil breeds strong men
did they lay waste my crops. How could they?
Look at the endless miles that lie between us . . .
185 shadowy mountain ranges, seas that surge and thunder.
No, you colossal, shameless—we all followed you,
to please you, to fight for you, to win your honor

182 **Phthia** (thē′ə): a small kingdom in Greece ruled by Peleus, the father of Achilles.

back from the Trojans—Menelaus and you, you dog-face!
What do *you* care? Nothing. You don't look right or left.°
190 And now you threaten to strip me of my prize in person—
the one I fought for long and hard, and sons of Achaea
handed her to me.
　　　　　　　My honors never equal yours,
whenever we sack some wealthy Trojan stronghold—
my arms bear the brunt of the raw, savage fighting,
195 true, but when it comes to dividing up the plunder
the lion's share is yours, and back I go to my ships,
clutching some scrap, some pittance that I love,
when I have fought to exhaustion.
　　　　　　　　　　　No more now—
back I go to Phthia. Better that way by far,
200 to journey home in the beaked ships° of war.
I have no mind to linger here disgraced,
brimming your cup and piling up your plunder."

But the lord of men Agamemnon shot back,
"*Desert,* by all means—if the spirit drives you home!
205 I will never beg you to stay, not on *my* account.
Never—others will take my side and do me honor,
Zeus above all, whose wisdom rules the world.
You—I hate you most of all the warlords
loved by the gods. Always dear to your heart,
210 strife, yes, and battles, the bloody grind of war.
What if you are a great soldier? That's just a gift of god.
Go home with your ships and comrades, lord it over your
　　　Myrmidons!°
You *are* nothing to me—you and your overweening° anger!
But let this be my warning on your way:
215 since Apollo insists on taking my Chryseis,
I'll send her back in my own ships with *my* crew.
But I, I will be there in person at your tents
to take Briseis in all her beauty, your own prize—
so you can learn just how much greater I am than you
220 and the next man up may shrink from matching words
　　　with me,
from hoping to rival Agamemnon strength for strength!"

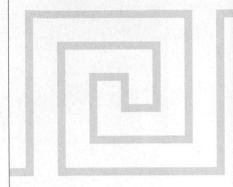

189 **You don't look right or left:**
You are completely self-centered.

200 **beaked ships:** ships with a
metal-pointed beam that projected
from the bow, or front, of an ancient
ship. The beak was used to pierce an
enemy ship's hull.

212 **Myrmidons:** warriors who
followed Achilles to Troy.

213 **overweening:** arrogant;
presumptuous; overstepping proper
bounds.

The Epic Hero *What does Homer reveal about Achilles in these lines? Does his behavior seem heroic? Explain.*

The Heroic Ideal *What is ironic about Agamemnon's admission that he hates Achilles for being "a great soldier"?*

He broke off and anguish gripped Achilles.
The heart in his rugged chest was pounding, torn . . .
Should he draw the long sharp sword slung at his hip,
225   thrust through the ranks° and kill Agamemnon now?—
or check his rage and beat his fury down?
As his racing spirit veered back and forth,
just as he drew his huge blade from its sheath,
down from the vaulting heavens swept Athena,
230   the white-armed goddess Hera sped her down:
Hera loved both men and cared for both alike.
Rearing behind him Pallas seized his fiery hair—
only Achilles saw her, none of the other fighters—
struck with wonder he spun around, he knew her at once,
235   Pallas Athena! the terrible blazing of those eyes,
and his winged words went flying: "Why, why now?
Child of Zeus with the shield of thunder,° why come now?
To witness the outrage Agamemnon just committed?
I tell you this, and so help me it's the truth—
240   he'll soon pay for his arrogance with his life!"

    Her gray eyes clear, the goddess Athena answered,
"Down from the skies I come to check your rage
if only you will yield.
The white-armed goddess Hera sped me down:
245   she loves you both, she cares for you both alike.
Stop this fighting, now. Don't lay hand to sword.
Lash him with threats of the price that he will face.°
And I tell you this—and I *know* it is the truth—
one day glittering gifts will lie before you,
250   three times over to pay for all his outrage.
Hold back now. Obey us both."
                So she urged
and the swift runner complied at once: "I must —
when the two of you hand down commands, Goddess,
a man submits though his heart breaks with fury.
255   Better for him by far. If a man obeys the gods
they're quick to hear his prayers."
                And with that
Achilles stayed his burly hand on the silver hilt
and slid the huge blade back in its sheath.
He would not fight the orders of Athena.

---

225 thrust through the ranks: push past Agamemnon's bodyguards.

237 shield of thunder: Zeus is the god of thunder and lightning. He often hurled thunderbolts as an expression of his anger.

247 Lash him with threats of the price that he will face: Warn Agamemnon that his arrogance will cost him your support and that Achilles and the Myrmidons will withdraw from the war.

The Epic Hero *How might Achilles' impulse to attack Agamemnon be viewed as both heroic and unheroic?*

260 Soaring home to Olympus, she rejoined the gods
aloft in the halls of Zeus whose shield is thunder.

But Achilles rounded on Agamemnon once again,
lashing out at him, not relaxing his anger for a moment:
"Staggering drunk, with your dog's eyes, your fawn's heart!°
265 Never once did you arm with the troops and go to battle
or risk an ambush packed with Achaea's picked men—
you lack the courage, you can see death coming.
Safer by far, you find, to foray° all through camp,
commandeering the prize of any man who speaks against you.
270 King who devours his people! Worthless husks, the men you
     rule—
if not, Atrides, this outrage would have been your last.
I tell you this, and I swear a mighty oath upon it . . .
by this, this scepter,° look,
that never again will put forth crown and branches,
275 now it's left its stump on the mountain ridge forever,
nor will it sprout new green again, now the brazen° ax
has stripped its bark and leaves,° and now the sons of Achaea
pass it back and forth as they hand their judgments down,
upholding the honored customs whenever Zeus commands—
280 This scepter will be the mighty force behind my oath:
someday, I swear, a yearning for Achilles will strike
Achaea's sons and all your armies! But then, Atrides,
harrowed° as you will be, *nothing* you do can save you—
not when your hordes of fighters drop and die,
285 cut down by the hands of man-killing Hector! Then—
then you will tear your heart out, desperate, raging
that you disgraced the best of the Achaeans!"

                                    Down on the ground
he dashed the scepter studded bright with golden nails,
then took his seat again. The son of Atreus smoldered,
290 glaring across at him, but Nestor rose between them,
the man of winning words, the clear speaker of Pylos . . .
Sweeter than honey from his tongue the voice flowed on
     and on.
Two generations of mortal men he had seen go down by now,
those who were born and bred with him in the old days,
295 in Pylos' holy realm, and now he ruled the third.
He pleaded with both kings, with clear good will,
"No more—or enormous sorrow comes to all Achaea!

264 your dog's eyes, your fawn's heart: expressions meant to suggest that Agamemnon is a coward.

268 foray: to plunder.

273 scepter (sep′tər): a staff borne by a ruler as an emblem or symbol of authority.

274–277 that never again . . . stripped its bark and leaves: having been cut and carved from a living tree, the staff is dead wood.

276 brazen: Here, the adjective has a double meaning: figuratively— bold, defiant; literally—the blade of the ax may have been made from brass.

283 harrowed: under constant attack.

The Heroic Ideal *Based on this portrayal of Agamemnon, do you think he fulfills the heroic ideal? Explain.*

How they would exult, Priam and Priam's sons
and all the Trojans. Oh they'd leap for joy

300 to hear the two of you battling on this way,
you who excel us all, first in Achaean councils,
first in the ways of war.
                              Stop. Please.
Listen to Nestor. You are both younger than I,
and in my time I struck up with better men than you,

305 even you, but never once did they make light of me.
I've never seen such men, I never will again . . .
men like Pirithous, Dryas, that fine captain,
Caeneus and Exadius, and Polyphemus, royal prince,
and Theseus,° Aegeus' boy, a match for the immortals.°

310 They were the strongest mortals ever bred on earth,
the strongest, and they fought against the strongest too,
shaggy Centaurs,° wild brutes of the mountains—
they hacked them down, terrible, deadly work.
And I was in their ranks, fresh out of Pylos,

315 far away from home—they **enlisted** me themselves
and I fought on my own, a free lance, single-handed.
And none of the men who walk the earth these days
could battle with those fighters, none, but they,
they took to heart my counsels, marked my words.

320 So now you listen too. Yielding is far better . . .
Don't seize the girl, Agamemnon, powerful as you are—
leave her, just as the sons of Achaea gave her,
his prize from the very first.°
And you, Achilles, never hope to fight it out

325 with your king, pitting force against his force:
no one can match the honors dealt a king, you know,
a sceptered king to whom great Zeus gives glory.°
Strong as you are—a goddess was your mother—
he has more power because he rules more men.

330 Atrides, end your anger—look, it's Nestor!
I beg you, cool your fury against Achilles.
Here the man stands over all Achaea's armies,
our rugged bulwark° braced for shocks of war."

307–309 **Pirithous . . . Theseus:**
The individuals named are all
heroes of Nestor's generation.

309 **Aegeus' boy, a match for the
immortals:** Theseus of Athens is the
hero of many adventure tales.

312 **Centaurs:** a race of savage
creatures, fabled to be half man and
half horse, who lived in the
mountains of Greece.

322–323 **leave her . . . his prize
from the very first:** Let her remain
with Achilles, since the Greek army
agreed that she should be his
reward for valor in battle.

326–327 **no one can match . . .
great Zeus gives glory:** No one has
the right to defy a king who rules by
the will of the gods.

333 **bulwark** (bool′wərk): a
solid wall-like structure raised for
defense; a strong support or
protection. Here, it refers to Achilles'
position of strength among the
Greek army.

Evaluate Credibility *What argument does Nestor use to try to persuade Agamemnon
and Achilles to stop quarreling? Is his argument based on sound reasoning? Explain.*

The Epic Hero *Read the side note about the word* bulwark. *What do Nestor's lines
suggest about Achilles?*

Vocabulary

enlist (en list′) *v.* to join or give help; convince (someone) to join or to give help

The surrender of Briseis.
Roman fresco. Museo
Archeologico Nazionale,
Naples, Italy.

Patroclus obeyed his great friend's command.
He led Briseis in all her beauty from the lodge
410 and handed her over to the men to take away.
And the two walked back along the Argive ships
while she trailed on behind, reluctant, every
  step.
But Achilles wept, and slipping away from his
  companions,
far apart, sat down on the beach of the heaving
  gray sea
415 and scanned the endless ocean. Reaching out his
  arms,
again and again he prayed to his dear mother:
  "Mother!
You gave me life, short as that life will be°
so at least Olympian Zeus, thundering up on high,
should give me honor—but now he gives me nothing.
420 Atreus' son Agamemnon, for all his far-flung kingdoms—
the man disgraces me, seizes and keeps my prize,
he tears her away himself!"
                    So he wept and prayed
and his noble mother heard him, seated near her father,
the Old Man of the Sea° in the salt green depths.
425 Suddenly up she rose from the churning surf
like mist and settling down beside him as he wept,
stroked Achilles gently, whispering his name, "My child—
why in tears? What sorrow has touched your heart?
Tell me, please. Don't harbor it deep inside you.
We must share it all."
430   And now from his depths
the proud runner groaned: "You know, you know,
why labor through it all? You know it all so well . . .
We raided Thebe once, Eetion's° sacred citadel,
we ravaged° the place, hauled all the plunder here
435 and the armies passed it round, share and share alike,
and they chose the beauty Chryseis for Agamemnon.
But soon her father, the holy priest of Apollo
the distant deadly Archer, Chryses approached
the fast trim ships of the Argives armed in bronze
440 to win his daughter back, bringing a priceless ransom
and bearing high in hand, wound on a golden staff,
the wreaths of the god who strikes from worlds away.°

417 short as that life will be: The
Fates, goddesses who determine
human affairs, prophesied that
Achilles would die in the war if he
joined the expedition against Troy.

424 the Old Man of the Sea:
Nereus, a sea god.

433 Eetion: king of Thebes, slain
by Achilles.

434 ravaged: devastated
destructively and violently.

**442 the god who strikes from
worlds away:** Apollo, god of
archery, whose arrows are deadly.

The Epic Hero *Does Achilles' knowledge of his early death enhance his stature as
an epic hero? Why or why not?*

He begged the whole Achaean army but most of all
the two supreme commanders, Atreus' two sons,
445 and all ranks of Achaeans cried out their assent,
'Respect the priest, accept the shining ransom!'
But it brought no joy to the heart of Agamemnon,
our high and mighty king dismissed the priest
with a brutal order ringing in his ears.
450 And shattered with anger, the old man withdrew
but Apollo heard his prayer—he loved him, deeply—
he loosed his shaft° at the Argives, withering plague,
and now the troops began to drop and die in droves,
the arrows of god went showering left and right,
455 whipping through the Achaeans' vast encampment.
But the old seer who knew the cause full well
revealed the will of the archer god Apollo.
And I was the first, mother, I urged them all,
'Appease the god at once!' That's when the fury
460 gripped the son of Atreus. Agamemnon leapt to his feet
and hurled his threat—his threat's been driven home.
One girl, Chryseis, the fiery-eyed Achaeans
ferry out in a fast trim ship to Chryse Island,
laden with presents for the god. The other girl,
465 just now the heralds came and led her away from camp,
Briseus' daughter, the prize the armies gave me.
But you, mother, if you have any power at all,
protect your son! Go to Olympus, plead with Zeus,
if you ever warmed his heart with a word or any action . . .

470   Time and again I heard your claims in father's halls,
boasting how you and you alone of all the immortals
rescued Zeus, the lord of the dark storm cloud,
from ignominious, stark defeat . . .
That day the Olympians tried to chain him down,
475 Hera, Poseidon lord of the sea, and Pallas Athena—
you rushed to Zeus, dear Goddess, broke those chains,
quickly ordered the hundred-hander° to steep Olympus,
that monster whom the immortals call Briareus
but every mortal calls the Sea-god's son, Aegaeon,
480 though he's stronger than his father. Down he sat,
flanking Cronus' son,° gargantuan in the glory of it all,

452 **loosed his shaft:** shot his arrow.

477 **hundred-hander:** Briareus, a monster with one hundred hands who warred with the gods until he was banished to the infernal regions.

481 **Cronus' son:** Zeus.

Evaluate Credibility *Review lines 437–466. Has Achilles given his mother a credible account of the quarrel with Agamemnon? Explain.*

Before You Read

Book XXII: The Death of Hector from the *Iliad*

Build Background

After Achilles and the Myrmidons withdraw from the war, the Trojan army drives the Greeks back to the edge of the sea. Patroclus, Achilles' best friend, cannot endure the slaughter of his comrades. He wears Achilles' armor, leading the Myrmidons into combat, but is slain by Hector. The death of Patroclus enrages Achilles, who returns to the battlefield in search of Hector. The Trojan army flees into the city, leaving Hector alone to await his rival.

Set Purposes for Reading

Big Idea **The Heroic Ideal**

As you read, ask yourself, What actions in Book XXII either reflect or violate the heroic ideal?

Literary Element **Epic Simile**

An **epic simile** (sometimes called a Homeric simile) extends a comparison with elaborate descriptive details that can fill several lines of verse. As you read, ask yourself, How does Homer's use of epic similes evoke readers' emotions?

Reading Strategy **Analyze Cultural Context**

When you **analyze cultural context,** you think about how the values of the people living in a particular time and place might have influenced a literary work. The ancient Greeks believed the universe consisted of mortals and gods who sometimes intervened in human affairs. As you read, ask yourself, How does the *Iliad* reflect this belief?

.....

Tip: Determine Influences As you read, list examples of the gods' influence on events.

God or Goddess	Action
Apollo	Lines 9–21: tricks Achilles into chasing him, allowing the Trojans to escape.

Vocabulary

bereft (bi reft´) *adj.* deprived or robbed; p. 213 *After losing her husband, the widow was bereft of her best friend.*

glistening (glis´ən´ing) *adj.* glittering; twinkling; p. 216 *Glistening in the rain, the street seemed strangely beautiful.*

barbaric (bär bar´ik) *adj.* crude; wild in taste, style, or manner; p. 222 *He shoveled food into his mouth with his hands in a barbaric manner.*

gloat (glōt) *v.* to regard with malignant satisfaction; p. 224 *Terry's opponent sneered and gloated over his error.*

.....

Tip: Denotation and Connotation
The **denotation** of a word is its literal meaning; the **connotation** of a word is its implied meanings. For example, the word *gloat* evokes negative feelings.

The Fury of Achilles. Charles-Antoine Coypel. Hermitage, St. Petersburg, Russia.

FROM THE ILIAD

from Book XXII: The Death of

HECTOR

Homer

Translated by Robert Fagles

So all through Troy the men who had fled like panicked fawns
were wiping off their sweat, drinking away their thirst,
leaning along the city's massive ramparts now
while Achaean troops, sloping shields to shoulders,
5 closed against the walls. But there stood Hector,
shackled fast by his deadly fate,° holding his ground,
exposed in front of Troy and the Scaean Gates.°
And now Apollo turned to taunt Achilles:
"Why are you chasing *me*?° Why waste your speed?—
10 son of Peleus, you a mortal and I a deathless god.
You still don't know that I am immortal, do you?—
straining to catch me in your fury! Have you forgotten?
There's a war to fight with the Trojans you stampeded,
look, they're packed inside their city walls, but you,
15 you've slipped away out here. You can't kill *me*—
I can never die—it's not my fate!"

　　　　　　　　　Enraged at that,
Achilles shouted in mid-stride, "You've blocked my way,
you distant, deadly Archer, deadliest god of all—
you made me swerve away from the rampart there.

6 by his deadly fate: Hector had told his wife, Andromache, that he knew in his heart he would die in the war and Troy would fall.

7 Scaean (skē´ən) Gates: one of the main gates in the wall around Troy.

9 "Why are you chasing me?": Apollo had disguised himself as a Trojan leader, tempting Achilles into pursuing him. This gave the Trojan army time to flee.

The Heroic Ideal *What traits set Hector apart from the other Trojans?*

20   Else what a mighty Trojan army had gnawed the dust
      before they could ever straggle through their gates!
      Now you've robbed me of great glory, saved their lives
      with all your deathless ease. Nothing for you to fear,
      no punishment to come. Oh I'd pay you back
25   if I only had the power at my command!"

      No more words—he dashed toward the city,
      heart racing for some great exploit, rushing on
      like a champion stallion drawing a chariot full tilt,
      sweeping across the plain in easy, tearing strides—
30   so Achilles hurtled on, driving legs and knees.

      And old King Priam was first to see him coming,
      surging over the plain, blazing like the star
      that rears at harvest,° flaming up in its brilliance,—
      far outshining the countless stars in the night sky,
35   that star they call Orion's° Dog—brightest of all
      but a fatal sign emblazoned on the heavens,
      it brings such killing fever down on wretched men.
      So the bronze flared on his chest as on he raced—
      and the old man moaned, flinging both hands high,
40   beating his head and groaning deep he called,
      begging his dear son who stood before the gates,
      unshakable, furious to fight Achilles to the death.
      The old man cried, pitifully, hands reaching out to him,
      "Oh Hector! Don't just stand there, don't, dear child,
45   waiting that man's attack—alone, cut off from friends!
      You'll meet your doom at once, beaten down by Achilles,
      so much stronger than you—that hard, headlong man.
      Oh if only the gods loved him as much as I do . . .°
      dogs and vultures would eat his fallen corpse at once!—
50   with what a load of misery lifted from my spirit.
      That man who robbed me of many sons, brave boys,
      cutting them down or selling them off as slaves,
      shipped to islands half the world away . . .
      Even now there are two, Lycaon and Polydorus—°
55   I cannot find them among the soldiers crowding Troy,
      those sons Laothoë° bore me, Laothoë queen of women.
      But if they are still alive in the enemy's camp,
      then we'll ransom them back with bronze and gold.

32–33 the star that rears at harvest: Sirius, the dog star, which first appears in the fall and was thought to bring disease.

35 Orion: a mighty hunter who was placed among the stars as a constellation by Artemis, goddess of the hunt.

48 if only the gods loved him as much as I do: an example of irony—the real meaning of the statement is the opposite of the surface meaning. Priam then explains his hatred for Achilles.

54 Lycaon and Polydorus: sons of Priam slain by Achilles in battle.

56 Laothoë: one of Priam's wives; daughter of Altes, a wealthy king.

Analyze Cultural Context *What prevents Achilles from taking revenge on Apollo?*

Epic Simile *To what does Homer compare Achilles in these lines? What aspects of Achilles' character does this emphasize?*

We have hoards inside the walls, the rich dowry
60   old and famous Altes presented with his daughter.
But if they're dead already, gone to the House of Death,
what grief to their mother's heart and mine—
      we gave them life.
For the rest of Troy, though, just a moment's grief
unless you too are battered down by Achilles.
65   Back, come back! Inside the walls, my boy!
Rescue the men of Troy and the Trojan women—
don't hand the great glory to Peleus' son,
bereft of your own sweet life yourself.
                              Pity me too!—
still in my senses, true, but a harrowed, broken man
70   marked out by doom—past the threshold of old age . . .
and Father Zeus will waste me with a hideous fate,
and after I've lived to look on so much horror!
My sons laid low,° my daughters dragged away
and the treasure-chambers looted, helpless babies
75   hurled to the earth in the red barbarity of war . . .
my sons' wives hauled off by the Argives' bloody hands!
And I, I last of all—the dogs before my doors
will eat me raw, once some enemy brings me down
with his sharp bronze sword or spits° me with a spear,
80   wrenching the life out of my body, yes, the very dogs
I bred in my own halls to share my table, guard my gates—
mad, rabid at heart° they'll lap their master's blood
and loll before my doors.
                              Ah for a young man
all looks fine and noble if he goes down in war,
85   hacked to pieces under a slashing bronze blade—
he lies there dead . . . but whatever death lays bare,
all wounds are marks of glory. When an old man's killed
and the dogs go at the gray head and the gray beard
and mutilate the genitals—that is the cruelest sight
90   in all our wretched lives!"
                              So the old man groaned
and seizing his gray hair tore it out by the roots
but he could not shake the fixed resolve of Hector.
And his mother wailed now, standing beside Priam,
weeping freely, loosing her robes with one hand

73 **laid low:** slain.

79 **spits:** here, pierces with something pointed; impales.

82 **rabid at heart:** extremely violent; exhibiting the behavior of an animal suffering from rabies.

The Heroic Ideal *What aspect of the heroic ideal does Priam reference in these lines?*

95   and holding out her bare breast with the other,
her words pouring forth in a flight of grief and tears:
"Hector, my child! Look—have some respect for *this*!
Pity your mother too, if I ever gave you the breast
to soothe your troubles, remember it now, dear boy—

100   beat back that savage man from safe inside the walls!
Don't go forth, a champion pitted against him—
merciless, brutal man. If he kills you now,
how can I ever mourn you on your deathbed?—
dear branch in bloom, dear child I brought to birth!—

105   Neither I nor your wife, that warm, generous woman . . .
Now far beyond our reach, now by the Argive ships
the rushing dogs will tear you, bolt your flesh!"

    So they wept, the two of them crying out
to their dear son, both pleading time and again

110   but they could not shake the fixed resolve of Hector.
No, he waited Achilles, coming on, gigantic in power.
As a snake in the hills, guarding his hole, awaits a man—
bloated with poison, deadly hatred seething inside him,
glances flashing fire as he coils round his lair . . .

115   so Hector, nursing his quenchless fury, gave no ground,
leaning his burnished shield against a jutting wall,
but harried still, he probed his own brave heart:
"No way out. If I slip inside the gates and walls,
Polydamas° will be first to heap disgrace on me—

120   he was the one who urged me to lead our Trojans
back to Ilium° just last night, the disastrous night
Achilles rose in arms like a god. But did I give way?
Not at all. And how much better it would have been!
Now my army's ruined, thanks to my own reckless pride,

125   I would die of shame to face the men of Troy
and the Trojan women trailing their long robes . . .
Someone less of a man than I will say, 'Our Hector—
staking all on his own strength, he destroyed his army!'
So they will mutter. So now, better by far for me

130   to stand up to Achilles, kill him, come home alive
or die at his hands in glory out before the walls.
But wait—what if I put down my studded shield
and heavy helmet, prop my spear on the rampart
and go forth, just as I am, to meet Achilles,

Greek warrior with a shield in hand. Hellenistic reliefs from frieze on the tomb of a Lycian prince. Kunsthistorisches Museum, Vienna, Austria

119 Polydamas: a cautious Trojan leader; a rival who often opposes Hector's military strategy.

121 Ilium: another name for the city of Troy.

Epic Simile *What does this comparison convey about Hector?*

135 noble Prince Achilles . . .
     why, I could promise to give back Helen, yes,
     and all her treasures with her, all those riches
     Paris once hauled home to Troy in the hollow ships—
     and they were the cause of all our endless fighting—
140 Yes, yes, return it all to the sons of Atreus now
     to haul away, and then, at the same time, divide
     the rest with all the Argives, all the city holds,
     and then I'd take an oath for the Trojan royal
         council
     that we will hide nothing! Share and share alike the hoards
145 our handsome citadel stores within its depths and—
     Why debate, my friend? Why thrash things out?
     I must not go and implore him. He'll show no mercy,
     no respect for me, my rights—he'll cut me down
     straight off—stripped of defenses like a woman
150 once I have loosed the armor off my body.
     No way to parley° with that man—not now—
     not from behind some oak or rock to whisper,
     like a boy and a young girl, lovers' secrets
     a boy and girl might whisper to each other . . .
155 Better to clash in battle, now, at once—
     see which fighter Zeus awards the glory!"

                                        So he wavered,
     waiting there, but Achilles was closing on him now
     like the god of war, the fighter's helmet flashing,
     over his right shoulder shaking the Pelian ash spear,°
160 that terror, and the bronze around his body° flared
     like a raging fire or the rising, blazing sun.
     Hector looked up, saw him, started to tremble,
     nerve gone, he could hold his ground no longer,
     he left the gates behind and away he fled in fear—
165 and Achilles went for him, fast, sure of his speed
     as the wild mountain hawk, the quickest thing on wings,
     launching smoothly, swooping down on a cringing dove
     and the dove flits out from under, the hawk screaming
     over the quarry, plunging over and over, his fury

151 **parley:** to discuss terms.

159 **Pelian ash spear:** Achilles' spear was carved from an ash tree on Mount Pelion. Chiron, wisest of the Centaurs, gave it to him and taught him to use it.

160 **the bronze around his body:** his armor.

The Heroic Ideal *What do these lines suggest about Hector?*

Analyze Cultural Context *According to Hector, what role will the gods play in this conflict?*

Epic Simile *To what birds does Homer compare Achilles and Hector? What might these birds represent?*

170   driving him down to beak and tear his kill—
so Achilles flew at him, breakneck on in fury
with Hector fleeing along the walls of Troy,
fast as his legs would go. On and on they raced,
passing the lookout point, passing the wild fig tree

175   tossed by the wind, always out from under the ramparts
down the wagon trail they careered° until they reached
the clear running springs where whirling Scamander°
rises up from its double wellsprings bubbling strong—
and one runs hot and the steam goes up around it,

180   drifting thick as if fire burned at its core
but the other even in summer gushes cold
as hail or freezing snow or water chilled to ice . . .
And here, close to the springs, lie washing-pools
scooped out in the hollow rocks and broad and smooth

185   where the wives of Troy and all their lovely daughters
would wash their **glistening** robes in the old days,
the days of peace before the sons of Achaea came . . .
Past these they raced, one escaping, one in pursuit
and the one who fled was great but the one pursuing

190   greater, even greater—their pace mounting in speed
since both men strove, not for a sacrificial beast
or oxhide trophy, prizes runners fight for, no,
they raced for the life of Hector breaker of horses.°
Like powerful stallions sweeping round the post for trophies,

195   galloping full stretch with some fine prize at stake,
a tripod, say, or woman offered up at funeral games
for some brave hero fallen—so the two of them
whirled three times around the city of Priam,
sprinting at top speed while all the gods gazed down,

200   and the father of men and gods broke forth among them now:
"Unbearable—a man I love, hunted round his own city walls
and right before my eyes. My heart grieves for Hector.
Hector who burned so many oxen in my honor, rich cuts,
now on the rugged crests of Ida, now on Ilium's heights.°

205   But now, look, brilliant Achilles courses him round
the city of Priam in all his savage, lethal speed.
Come, you immortals, think this through. Decide.
Either we pluck the man from death and save his life
or strike him down at last, here at Achilles' hands—

210   for all his fighting heart."
                       But immortal Athena,

176 careered: went at top speed, especially in a headlong manner.

177 Scamander (skə man′ dər): chief river near the city of Troy.

193 breaker of horses: Hector was famed for his ability to tame horses.

203–204 Hector who burned . . . heights: Hector sacrificed oxen to Zeus on Mount Ida, overlooking Troy.

Vocabulary

glistening (glis′ ən′ ing) *adj.* glittering; twinkling

her gray eyes wide, protested strongly: "Father!
Lord of the lightning, king of the black cloud,
what are you saying? A man, a mere mortal,
his doom sealed long ago?° You'd set him free
215　from all the pains of death?
　　　　　　　　　　　　　　Do as you please—
but none of the deathless gods will ever praise you."

　　And Zeus who marshals the thunderheads replied,
"Courage, Athena, third-born of the gods, dear child.
Nothing I said was meant in earnest, trust me,
220　I mean you all the good will in the world. Go.
Do as your own impulse bids you. Hold back no more."

　　So he launched Athena already poised for action—
down the goddess swept from Olympus' craggy peaks.

　　And swift Achilles kept on coursing Hector, nonstop
225　as a hound in the mountains starts a fawn from its lair,
hunting him down the gorges, down the narrow glens
and the fawn goes to ground,° hiding deep in brush
but the hound comes racing fast, nosing him out
until he lands his kill. So Hector could never throw
230　Achilles off his trail, the swift racer Achilles—
time and again he'd make a dash for the Dardan Gates,
trying to rush beneath the rock-built ramparts, hoping
men on the heights might save him, somehow, raining spears
but time and again Achilles would intercept him quickly,
235　heading him off, forcing him out across the plain
and always sprinting along the city side himself—
endless as in a dream . . .
when a man can't catch another fleeing on ahead
and he can never escape nor his rival overtake him—
240　so the one could never run the other down in his speed
nor the other spring away. And how could Hector have fled
the fates of death so long? How unless one last time,
one final time Apollo had swept in close beside him,
driving strength in his legs and knees to race the wind?

214 his doom sealed long ago: his fate: all humans are mortal and doomed to die from birth.

227 goes to ground: tries to avoid notice by remaining motionless.

Analyze Cultural Context *What apparent contradiction regarding the ancient Greeks' attitude toward fate is illustrated in Athena's remarks?*

Epic Simile *How does this simile echo the one in lines 165–167?*

245   And brilliant Achilles shook his head at the armies,
      never letting them hurl their sharp spears at Hector—
      someone might snatch the glory, Achilles come in second.
      But once they reached the springs for the fourth time,
      then Father Zeus held out his sacred golden scales:
250   in them he placed two fates of death that lays men low—
      one for Achilles, one for Hector breaker of horses—
      and gripping the beam mid-haft° the Father raised it high
      and down went Hector's day of doom, dragging him down
      to the strong House of Death—and god Apollo left him.°
255   Athena rushed to Achilles, her bright eyes gleaming,
      standing shoulder-to-shoulder, winging orders now:
      "At last our hopes run high, my brilliant Achilles—
      Father Zeus must love you—
      we'll sweep great glory back to Achaea's fleet,
260   we'll kill this Hector, mad as he is for battle!
      No way for him to escape us now, no longer—
      not even if Phoebus the distant deadly Archer
      goes through torments, pleading for Hector's life,
      groveling over and over before our storming Father Zeus.
265   But you, you hold your ground and catch your breath
      while I run Hector down and persuade the man
      to fight you face-to-face."
                                  So Athena commanded
      and he obeyed, rejoicing at heart—Achilles stopped,
      leaning against his ashen spearshaft barbed in bronze.
270   And Athena left him there, caught up with Hector at once,
      and taking the build and vibrant voice of Deiphobus
      stood shoulder-to-shoulder with him, winging orders:
      "Dear brother, how brutally swift Achilles hunts you—
      coursing you round the city of Priam in all his lethal speed!
275   Come, let us stand our ground together—beat him back."

         "Deiphobus!"—Hector, his helmet flashing, called
             out to her—
      "dearest of all my brothers, all these warring years,
      of all the sons that Priam and Hecuba produced!
      Now I'm determined to praise you all the more,

> **249–254 Zeus held out . . .
> Apollo left him:** Fate determined
> that Hector would lose this battle.
> Apollo, realizing that further help
> was futile, returned to Olympus.
>
> **252 gripping the beam mid-haft:**
> holding the scales impartially so as
> not to favor one side or the other.

Analyze Cultural Context *What does this passage suggest about the gods and fate?*

The Heroic Ideal *Why doesn't Athena kill Hector herself, thus sparing Achilles the effort?*

280 you who dared—seeing me in these straits—
to venture out from the walls, all for *my* sake,
while the others stay inside and cling to safety."

The goddess answered quickly, her eyes blazing,
"True, dear brother—how your father and mother both
285 implored me, time and again, clutching my knees,
and the comrades round me begging me to stay!
Such was the fear that broke them, man for man,
but the heart within me broke with grief for you.
Now headlong on and fight! No letup, no lance spared!
290 So now, now we'll *see* if Achilles kills us both
and hauls our bloody armor back to the beaked ships
or *he* goes down in pain beneath your spear."

Athena luring him on with all her immortal cunning—
and now, at last, as the two came closing for the kill
295 it was tall Hector, helmet flashing, who led off:
"No more running from you in fear, Achilles!
Not as before. Three times I fled around
the great city of Priam—I lacked courage then
to stand your onslaught. Now my spirit stirs me
300 to meet you face-to-face. Now kill or be killed!
Come, we'll swear to the gods, the highest witnesses—
the gods will oversee our binding pacts. I swear
I will never mutilate you—merciless as you are—
if Zeus allows me to last it out and tear your life away.
305 But once I've stripped your glorious armor, Achilles,
I will give your body back to your loyal comrades.
Swear you'll do the same."
                                    A swift dark glance
and the headstrong runner answered, "Hector,
    stop!
You unforgivable, you . . . don't talk to me of
    pacts.
310 There are no binding oaths between men and
    lions—
wolves and lambs can enjoy no meeting of the
    minds—
they are all bent on hating each other to the death.

Statue of Athena. Ancient Greece The National Museum, Athens.

he drew the whetted° sword that hung at his side,
tempered,° massive, and gathering all his force
365   he swooped like a soaring eagle
launching down from the dark clouds to earth
to snatch some helpless lamb or trembling hare.
So Hector swooped now, swinging his whetted sword
and Achilles charged too, bursting with rage, **barbaric**,°
370   guarding his chest with the well-wrought blazoned° shield,
head tossing his gleaming helmet, four horns strong
and the golden plumes shook that the god of fire°
drove in bristling thick along its ridge.
Bright as that star amid the stars in the night sky,
375   star of the evening, brightest star that rides the heavens,
so fire flared from the sharp point of the spear Achilles
brandished high in his right hand, bent on Hector's death,
scanning his splendid body—where to pierce it best?
The rest of his flesh seemed all encased in armor,
380   burnished, brazen—*Achilles'* armor that Hector stripped
from strong Patroclus when he killed him—true,
but one spot lay exposed,
where collarbones lift the neckbone off the shoulders,°
the open throat, where the end of life comes quickest—*there*
385   as Hector charged in fury brilliant Achilles drove his spear
and the point went stabbing clean through the tender neck
but the heavy bronze weapon failed to slash the windpipe—
Hector could still gasp out some words, some last reply . . .
he crashed in the dust—

godlike Achilles gloried over him:
390   "Hector—surely you thought when you stripped
    Patroclus' armor
that you, you would be safe! Never a fear of me—
far from the fighting as I was—you fool!
Left behind there, down by the beaked ships
his great avenger waited, a greater man by far—
395   that man was I, and I smashed your strength! And you—
the dogs and birds will maul you, shame your corpse
while Achaeans bury my dear friend in glory!"

Struggling for breath, Hector, his helmet flashing,

Epic Simile *What does this simile convey about Hector's attack?*

Vocabulary

barbaric (bär bar′ ik) *adj.* crude; wild in taste, style, or manner

363 **whetted:** sharpened.

364 **tempered:** hardened by reheating and cooling in oil; strengthened.

369 **barbaric:** This word choice is ironic because barbaric originally meant anyone not belonging to one's cultural group, which to a Greek would be a non-Greek.

370 **well-wrought:** fashioned with great effort and artistry. **blazoned:** in this use, adorned with ornate symbolic inscriptions and artwork.

372 **god of fire:** Hephaestus (hi fes′ təs), son of Zeus, god of fire and metalworking (blacksmithing). At Thetis's request, he had made armor for Achilles.

378–383 **scanning . . . off the shoulders:** Since the armor had once been his own, Achilles knew where to look for its one vulnerable spot.

said, "I beg you, beg you by your life, your parents—
400 don't let the dogs devour me by the Argive ships!
Wait, take the princely ransom of bronze and gold,
the gifts my father and noble mother will give you—
but give my body to friends to carry home again,
so Trojan men and Trojan women can do me honor
405 with fitting rites of fire° once I am dead."

405 **fitting rites of fire:** proper religious funeral services that included cremation of the body.

     Staring grimly, the proud runner Achilles answered,
"Beg no more, you fawning dog—begging me by my parents!
Would to god my rage, my fury would drive me now
to hack your flesh away and eat you raw—
410 such agonies you have caused me! Ransom?
No man alive could keep the dog-packs off you,
not if they haul in ten, twenty times that ransom
and pile it here before me and promise fortunes more—
no, not even if Dardan Priam should offer to weigh out
415 your bulk in gold! Not even then will your noble mother
lay you on your deathbed, mourn the son she bore . . .
The dogs and birds will rend you—blood and bone!"

     At the point of death, Hector, his helmet flashing,
said, "I know you well—I see my fate before me.
420 Never a chance that I could win you over . . .
Iron inside your chest, that heart of yours.
But now beware, or my curse will draw god's wrath
upon your head, that day when Paris and lord Apollo—
for all your fighting heart—destroy you at the
     Scaean Gates!"°

422–424 **beware . . . Scaean Gates:** Hector predicts the place and circumstances of Achilles' own death.

425   Death cut him short. The end closed in around him.
Flying free of his limbs
his soul went winging down to the House of Death,
wailing his fate, leaving his manhood far behind,
his young and supple strength. But brilliant Achilles
430 taunted Hector's body, dead as he was, "Die, die!
For my own death, I'll meet it freely—whenever Zeus
and the other deathless gods would like to bring it on!"

     With that he wrenched his bronze spear from the corpse,
laid it aside and ripped the bloody armor off the back.
435 And the other sons of Achaea, running up around him,

Analyze Cultural Context *According to Hector, what factors will bring about Achilles' death?*

crowded closer, all of them gazing wonder-struck
at the build and marvelous, lithe beauty of Hector.
And not a man came forward who did not stab
   his body,
glancing toward a comrade, laughing: "Ah, look
   here—
440   how much softer he is to handle now, this
   Hector,
than when he gutted our ships with roaring fire!"

               Standing over him, so they'd **gloat** and
                       stab his body.
But once he had stripped the corpse the proud
   runner Achilles
took his stand in the midst of all the Argive troops
445   and urged them on with a flight of winging orders:
"Friends—lords of the Argives, O my captains!
Now that the gods have let me kill this man
who caused us agonies, loss on crushing loss—
more than the rest of all their men combined—
450   come, let us ring their walls in armor, test them,
see what recourse the Trojans still may have in mind.
Will they abandon the city heights with this man fallen?
Or brace for a last, dying stand though Hector's gone?
But wait—what am I saying? Why this deep debate?
455   Down by the ships a body lies unwept, unburied—
Patroclus . . . I will never forget him,
not as long as I'm still among the living
and my springing knees will lift and drive me on.
Though the dead forget° their dead in the House of Death,
460   I will remember, even there, my dear companion.
                             Now,
come, you sons of Achaea, raise a song of triumph!
Down to the ships we march and bear this corpse on high—
we have won ourselves great glory. We have brought
magnificent Hector down, that man the Trojans
465   glorified in their city like a god!"
                       So he triumphed
and now he was bent on outrage, on shaming noble Hector.

Achilles dragging the body of Hector, c. 520–510 BC. attributed to The Anitope Group, Ancient Greece. Black-figure vase, height: 56 cm, diameter: 33 cm. Museum of Fine Arts, Boston.

459 the dead forget: a mental state oblivious to emotions, such as love or sorrow, was a characteristic of the dead in Greek mythology.

The Heroic Ideal *What compliment does Achilles pay Hector in lines 447–453?*

Piercing the tendons,° ankle to heel behind both feet,
he knotted straps of rawhide through them both,
lashed them to his chariot, left the head to drag

470 and mounting the car, hoisting the famous arms aboard,
he whipped his team to a run and breakneck on they flew,
holding nothing back. And a thick cloud of dust rose up
from the man they dragged, his dark hair swirling round
that head so handsome once, all tumbled low in the dust—

475 since Zeus had given him over to his enemies now
to be defiled in the land of his own fathers.

So his whole head was dragged down in the dust.
And now his mother began to tear her hair . . .
she flung her shining veil to the ground and raised

480 a high, shattering scream, looking down at her son.
Pitifully his loving father groaned and round the king
his people cried with grief and wailing seized the city—
for all the world as if all Troy were torched and smoldering
down from the looming brows of the citadel to her roots.

485 Priam's people could hardly hold the old man back,
frantic, mad to go rushing out the Dardan Gates.
He begged them all, groveling in the filth,
crying out to them, calling each man by name,
"Let go, my friends! Much as you care for me,

490 let me hurry out of the city, make my way,
all on my own, to Achaea's waiting ships!
I must implore that terrible, violent man . . .
Perhaps—who knows?—he may respect my age,
may pity an old man. He has a father too,

495 as old as I am—Peleus sired him once,
Peleus reared him to be the scourge of Troy
but most of all to me—he made my life a hell.
So many sons he slaughtered, just coming into bloom . . .
but grieving for all the rest, one breaks my heart the most

500 and stabbing grief for him will take me down to Death—
my Hector—would to god he had perished in my arms!
Then his mother who bore him—oh so doomed,
she and I could glut ourselves with grief."

So the voice of the king rang out in tears,
505 the citizens wailed in answer, and noble Hecuba
led the wives of Troy in a throbbing chant of sorrow:

467 **Piercing the tendons:** ironic,
because a wound in the tendon of
the heel, his only vulnerable spot,
will kill Achilles.

Analyze Cultural Context *What do these lines suggest about Zeus and the gods?*

The Siege of Troy: The Death of Hector, c. 1490. Biagio di Antonio. Oil on panel, 47 x 161 cm. Fitzwilliam Museum, University of Cambridge, UK.

<u>View the Art</u> Although this narrative painting represents the siege of Troy, the warriors wear Renaissance armor and the buildings reflect medieval and Renaissance architecture. What incident related to Hector's death is represented here? Why might di Antonio have chosen to portray this incident as he did?

"O my child—my desolation! How can I go on living?
What agonies must I suffer now, now *you* are dead and gone?
You were my pride throughout the city night and day—
510   a blessing to us all, the men and women of Troy:
throughout the city they saluted you like a god.
You, you were their greatest glory while you lived—
now death and fate have seized you, dragged you down!"

     Her voice rang out in tears, but the wife of Hector
515   had not heard a thing. No messenger brought the truth
of how her husband made his stand outside the gates.
She was weaving at her loom, deep in the high halls,
working flowered braiding into a dark red folding robe.
And she called her well-kempt women through the house
520   to set a large three-legged cauldron over the fire
so Hector could have his steaming hot bath
when he came home from battle—poor woman,
she never dreamed how far he was from bathing,
struck down at Achilles' hands by blazing-eyed Athena.
525   But she heard the groans and wails of grief from the
       rampart now
and her body shook, her shuttle° dropped to the ground,
she called out to her lovely waiting women, "Quickly—
two of you follow me—I must see what's happened.
That cry—that was Hector's honored mother I heard!
530   My heart's pounding, leaping up in my throat,

526 shuttle: a device used in weaving for passing thread through the loom.

Analyze Cultural Context *What does this line suggest about how the ancient Greeks viewed the relationship between gods and humans?*

the knees beneath me paralyzed—Oh I know it . . .
something terrible's coming down on Priam's children.
Pray god the news will never reach my ears!
Yes but I dread it so—what if great Achilles

535 has cut my Hector off from the city, daring Hector,
and driven him out across the plain, and all alone?—
He may have put an end to that fatal headstrong pride
that always seized my Hector—never hanging back
with the main force of men, always charging ahead,

540 giving ground to no man in his fury!"
                                        So she cried,
dashing out of the royal halls like a madwoman,
her heart racing hard, her women close behind her.
But once she reached the tower where soldiers massed
she stopped on the rampart, looked down and saw it all—

545 saw him dragged before the city, stallions galloping,
dragging Hector back to Achaea's beaked warships—
ruthless work. The world went black as night
before her eyes, she fainted, falling backward,
gasping away her life breath . . .

550 She flung to the winds her glittering headdress,
the cap and the coronet,° braided band and veil,
all the regalia° golden Aphrodite gave her once,
the day that Hector, helmet aflash in sunlight,
led her home to Troy from her father's house

555 with countless wedding gifts to win her heart.
But crowding round her now her husband's sisters
and brothers' wives supported her in their midst,
and she, terrified, stunned to the point of death,
struggling for breath now and coming back to life,

560 burst out in grief among the Trojan women: "O Hector—
I am destroyed! Both born to the same fate after all!
You, you at Troy in the halls of King Priam—
I at Thebes, under the timberline of Placos,°
Eetion's° house . . . He raised me as a child,

565 that man of doom, his daughter just as doomed—
would to god he'd never fathered me!
                                        Now you go down
to the House of Death, the dark depths of the earth,
and leave me here to waste away in grief, a widow
lost in the royal halls—and the boy only a baby,

570 the son we bore together, you and I so doomed.

---

551 coronet: a small crown.

552 regalia (ri gā′ lē ə): emblems or symbols indicating royalty.

563 Placos: mountain which dominates the landscape near Thebes.

564 Eetion: Andromache's father, king of Thebes, killed by Achilles during the sacking of that city.

The Heroic Ideal *Based on what you know about Hector, is Andromache's assessment of her husband accurate? Explain.*

Literary Element Epic Simile

An **epic simile** extends over several lines. For example, in lines 165–170, Homer develops a detailed comparison of Achilles to a "wild mountain hawk" and Hector to a "cringing dove":

> and Achilles went for him, fast, sure of his
>   speed
> as the wild mountain hawk, the quickest thing
>   on wings,
> launching smoothly, swooping down on a
>   cringing dove
> and the dove flits out from under, the hawk
>   screaming
> over the quarry, plunging over and over, his
>   fury
> driving him down to beak and tear his kill—

1. Find another example of an epic simile in this book of the epic. Identify the elements the simile compares.

2. How does your experience of reading an epic simile differ from that of reading a regular simile?

Review: Epic Hero

As you learned on page 193, **epic heroes** are larger-than-life figures who reflect the values of their cultures. In the *Iliad*, both Achilles and Hector function as epic heroes.

Partner Activity Working with a partner, review the events in this book of the epic. Then answer the following questions.

1. What values do Achilles and Hector reflect?

2. Do you admire Hector or Achilles more? Support your response with details from the text.

3. The Greeks and Trojans closely followed the exploits of their heroes. What figures in today's society attract similar attention from ordinary citizens?

Literature Online

Selection Resources For Selection Quizzes, eFlash-cards, and Reading-Writing Connection activities, go to glencoe.com and enter QuickPass code GLW6053u2.

Reading Strategy Analyze Cultural Context

SAT Skills Practice

Reread lines 598–599 ("glistening worms . . . corpse"). These lines suggest the Trojans

(A) believed the body could feel pain even after death

(B) did not draw a clear distinction between earthly life and the afterlife

(C) were indifferent to the decay of the body

(D) worshipped the earth and its natural cycles

(E) placed importance on the preparation and burial of bodies

Vocabulary Practice

Practice with Denotation and Connotation Denotation is the literal meaning of a word, while **connotation** is its implied meaning. For example, *aroma* has a positive connotation and *stench* has a negative connotation. Next to each vocabulary word below is a word with a similar denotation. Choose the word that has a more positive connotation.

1. **bereft**   without

2. **glistening**   shiny

3. **gloat**   rejoice

4. **barbaric**   unrefined

Academic Vocabulary

*Hector asked Achilles to respect his body; **nevertheless**, Achilles tied it to the chariot.*

Nevertheless is an academic word. More familiar words similar in meaning are *yet, still, but,* and *however.* To study this word further, complete the sentence below.

It rained on Saturday; **nevertheless**, my best friend and I were able to _____.

For more on academic vocabulary, see pages 36–37 and R83–R85.

Respond Through Writing

Expository Essay

Analyze Cause and Effect At the climax of the *Iliad*, Achilles and Hector meet in battle to determine the fate of Troy. Why does this event happen? Write an essay in which you analyze the cause-and-effect relationships that lead up to this decisive battle.

Understand the Task Cause and effect describes the relationship between an action and its consequence. The **effect**, or consequence, is a direct result of the **cause**, or action.

Prewrite To help organize your essay, list cause-and-effect relationships in a chart like the one below. Add as many rows as you need. Remember that just because one event precedes another does not mean the first event is the cause of the other. To help assess the gods' role in the battle, review the chart you made on page 210. Finally, write a thesis sentence to state your idea about cause-and-effect relationships.

Cause	Effect
Hector slays Patroclus.	Achilles vows revenge.

Draft Using the cause-and-effect relationships listed in your chart, determine how each one supports your thesis. The following frame may help you write your body paragraphs.

Apollo says, "There's a war to fight with the Trojans you stampeded, / look, they're packed inside their city walls, but you, / you've slipped away out here." In saying this, Apollo causes _____ by inciting _____.

Revise Exchange papers with a partner and evaluate each other's essays. Does the writer support a thesis? Are cause-and-effect relationships clearly explained? Provide comments for your partner and revise your essay according to his or her comments.

Edit and Proofread Proofread your paper, correcting any errors in grammar, spelling, and punctuation. Use the Grammar Tip in the side column to help you with participles.

Learning Objectives

In this assignment, you will focus on the following objectives:

Writing: Writing an expository essay.

Grammar: Understanding participles.

> **Grammar Tip**

Participles

A **participle** is a verb form that can function as an adjective. Identify the participle in the following sentence.

Resolved, Hector stands his ground.

Resolved, a verb form that describes Hector, is a participle. Present participles always end in *-ing (losing)*. Past participles often end in *-ed (wounded)*.

Participles may be used in phrases with prepositions and objects, as in the example below.

Priam watched Achilles hurtling over the plain.

Hurtling over the plain is a **participial phrase** that describes Achilles.

Homer Through the Ages

<table>
<tr><td>

Learning Objectives

For pages 232–233

In studying this text, you will focus on the following objectives:

Reading:

Understanding cultural and historical context.

Understanding the nature of translation.

</td></tr>
</table>

HOMER IS ONE OF THE MOST WIDELY TRANSLATED AUTHORS IN HISTORY. Today the *Iliad* appears in many different languages and literary forms. Almost every generation has seen a new translation of the *Iliad* and the *Odyssey* in English since the first complete translation of both epics was made by George Chapman in 1611 and 1616, respectively.

The Challenges of Translating

Why do translators feel the need to create these new versions, and what purpose do they serve? Before trying to answer these questions, it is necessary to consider some of the difficulties that arise when attempting to translate a piece of literature.

- A word might have the same meaning (denotation) in another language, but not the same associations and feelings (connotation).

- Idiomatic expressions—such as "he's pulling your leg"—are unique to their original language, and their meanings have little to do with the literal meaning of the words.

- Sentence structure and grammar vary from one language to another.

- Every translator will have a different idea of the author's meaning and intentions.

These challenges, the changes the English language has undergone over time, and the change in writing styles and taste of a given period give a sense of the many possible reasons translators might interpret the ancient works of Homer for readers of their time.

Translating Homer

The British poet Matthew Arnold noted that a good Homeric translation must try to capture the key elements of Homer's work: fast-paced storytelling, plainness and directness of expression and idea, and a highly noble style. Throughout the ages, translators have emphasized each of these qualities to differing degrees based on their own interests and the interests of their audiences.

Achilles at the Court of King Lycomedes with his Daughters, 1746. Pompeo Girolamo Batoni. Oil on canvas. Galleria degli Uffizi, Florence.

Iliad, Book I, lines 1–5

LITERAL TRANSLATION

Sing, O Goddess (Muse), (the) destroying anger
of Achilles, son of Peleus, which placed
    innumerable woes
to the Achaeans but (and) prematurely-sent many
    brave
souls of heroes to Hades and made them prey
to dogs and all birds of prey.

George Chapman's Translation, 1611

Achilles' baneful wrath resound, O Goddess, that
    imposed
Infinite sorrows on the Greeks, and many brave
    souls losed
From breasts heroic; sent them far to that invisible
    cave
That no light comforts; and their limbs to dogs and
    vultures gave.

Alexander Pope's Translation, 1720

Achilles' wrath, to Greece the direful spring
Of woes unnumber'd, heav'nly Goddess, sing!
That wrath which hurl'd to Pluto's gloomy reign
The souls of mighty chiefs untimely slain;
Whose limbs, unburied on the naked shore,
Devouring dogs and hungry vultures tore.

Richmond Lattimore's Translation, 1951

Sing goddess, the anger of Peleus'
    son Achilleus
and its devastation, which put pains
    thousandfold upon the Achaians
hurled in their multitudes to the
    house of Hades strong souls
of heroes, but gave their bodies to
    be the delicate feasting
of dogs, of all birds.

Hector and Andromache, 1924. Giorgio de Chirico. Oil on canvas, 89.5 x 60.3 cm. Private collection © Foundation Giorgio de Chirico/Licensed by VAGA, New York.

images. George Chapman and Alexander Pope chose to render Homer's style in rhyming couplets, the most elevated poetic form of their times. However, both these versions seem somewhat stilted to modern readers, who favor straightforward translations that read as if the works were originally written in English. Modern translators such as Richmond Lattimore and Robert Fagles have replaced the long similes used by Homer with quick, direct phrases.

A word-for-word translation gives the reader a sense of Homer's directness—his use of just a few words to establish that the poem is about human weakness and tragedy. But the awkwardness of the literal version fails to capture Homer's spirit and powerful

LOG ON **Literature** Online

Literature and Reading For more about the *Iliad* and the translators in this book, go to glencoe.com and enter QuickPass code GLW6053u2.

Respond and Think Critically

1. What do you consider the greatest challenge in translating Homer?

2. Robert Fagles translated the excerpts from the *Iliad* that you read earlier in this book. How would you compare his translation of the opening passage with the translations in this feature?

3. Choose a passage from Fagles's translation that you particularly admire. What examples of word choice and "quick, direct phrases" do you find particularly impressive, and why?

Historical Perspective
on the *Iliad*

Learning Objectives

For pages 234–240

In studying this text, you will focus on the following objectives:

Reading:
Analyzing and evaluating informational text.
Connecting to contemporary issues.

from
Echoes of the **Heroic Age**

Library Journal Best Books of the Year Winner   **Caroline Alexander**

Set a Purpose for Reading

Read to learn about possible connections between archaeological discoveries and the *Iliad*.

Build Background

Inspired by Homer's *Iliad,* Heinrich Schliemann in the late nineteenth century made one of the greatest finds in the history of archaeology: the sites of the ancient cities of Troy and Mycenae. In this excerpt from the magazine article "Echoes of the Heroic Age," Caroline Alexander discusses the relationship between the Trojan War and the excavations conducted by Heinrich Schliemann and Manfred Korfmann. Though Korfmann died in 2005, his team still continues his work at Troy.

Reading Strategy Evaluate Evidence

When you **evaluate evidence,** you judge the strength of the facts and details that support an argument. As you read, ask yourself, What are the claims, or main points, and the supporting evidence that the author provides? Use a two-column chart like the one below to list your findings.

Claims	Supporting Evidence

For Greeks of antiquity the *Iliad* related events from their own past; the Trojan War was taken as historical fact. Some believed they were descendants of Homer's heroes; Alexander the Great,[1] who slept with a copy of the *Iliad*, traced his maternal ancestry back to Achilles. But the reality is far more complex. The *Iliad* is not a "true story," nor does it offer a realistic picture of life in Greece's late Bronze Age—about 1600 to 1100 B.C.

Indeed, the *Iliad* was not composed in this period, known to historians as the Mycenaean Age,[2] but is the end result of an inspired oral poetic tradition spanning 500 years. Between the 13th century B.C., the height of the Mycenaean Age, and the age of Homer in the eighth century B.C., lie five centuries during which generations of unknown professional poets passed down

---

1. *Alexander the Great,* king of Macedonia from 336 to 323 B.C., defeated the Persian Empire and spread Greek culture to his conquered lands.
2. *Mycenaean Age* (mī sə nē´ ən) refers to a period during the late Bronze Age, from 1600 B.C. to 1100 B.C. Mycenae (mī sē´ nē) was a Greek city in the Peloponnese, the peninsula that forms the southern part of mainland Greece.

the epic-in-the-making. Each added something of his own genius, and the taste of the successive audiences who kept the *Iliad* in demand must have been of the same high standard as the skill of the bards themselves. The Greeks credited the final composition of this masterpiece to a poet they called *theios Homeros*—"divine Homer"—and we, as they, know nothing more about this person than his supposed name.

Most archaeologists and scholars study the late Bronze Age for its own sake, not because they seek to shed light on the *Iliad*. "I don't *care* about Homer!" an archaeologist in Greece said to me, exasperated by the popular view that she was searching for the Trojan War. Nonetheless, sophisticated modern studies of this period continue to yield unmistakably Homeric details, proving that the *Iliad*, though not a Bronze Age work, has preserved shards of Bronze Age history. Like the archaeologist, I was not in search of the Trojan War, but I was deeply interested in all those shards of history that give the *Iliad* its rich texture: The land around Troy itself in northwestern Turkey, the giant walls of Mycenae and its fabled gold, warships of the Bronze Age, weaponry and armaments, scraps of Mycenaean, the language of the Greek Bronze Age—these relics were my quest.

In a sense the *Iliad* is a tale of two cities: Troy, or "windy Ilion," the wealthy Asiatic city commanding the Dardanelles,[3] and "Mycenae of much gold," the city leading the united Greek invasion across the Aegean Sea to the gates of Troy. For centuries the wealth of these legendary cities was thought to exist only in the realm of imagination. But between 1870 and 1890 Heinrich Schliemann, an ambitious and ruthless businessman from Germany, put the "lost" cities on the map. Acting on the advice of a local amateur archaeologist (whom he did not bother to credit), Schliemann revealed the ruins of Troy, then found the gold of Mycenae.

The *Iliad's* every description of Mycenae speaks of its power. And from the base of the rocky acropolis on which Homer's "strong-founded citadel" stands, I looked up to discover that these descriptions still hold true. Even in decay the great fortress remains imperious, still commanding, as it did centuries ago, the mountain-ringed plain of Argos,[4] now a blur of purple-gold in the hazy heat. Making my way up the entrance ramp, I paused before the citadel's famous Lion Gate—posts and a lintel[5] of colossal stone overarched by two weathered heraldic lions. . . .

As an epic, the *Iliad* is mostly interested in the fate of kings and warriors, not of the common man. And while archaeologists have uncovered traces of the small timber and mud-brick dwellings of humble people, it is the relics of Mycenae's rich and powerful that are most in evidence. The massive walls enclosed a palatial administrative complex—houses, sanctuaries, storerooms, and royal courts with colorful frescoes and sculpted stone. Wandering through the vacant citadel, past walls that had collapsed into rubble, across a floor of beaten earth that had once been decorated with painted stucco and gypsum slabs, I felt a lingering air of regal might.

In the *Iliad* the king of Mycenae, Agamemnon, is also commander in chief of the Greek forces—not on account of any special qualifications but because he has

---

3. The *Dardanelles* (Hellespont) is a narrow strait that links the Black Sea with the Aegean Sea by way of the Sea of Marmara.

4. *Argos* is a city in the northeastern Peloponnese of Greece.
5. A *lintel* is a horizontal piece that spans an opening and is supported by two posts.

the direction of Manfred Korfmann of Germany's Tübingen University in partnership with the University of Cincinnati is reexcavating the entire site. The object of their scrutiny is not just Hisarlik, the hill on which the ruins of Troy stand, but also the coastal area and surrounding plain, where according to the *Iliad* the Greeks beached their curved ships and the war was waged. Troy's many levels—nine in all—range from 3000 B.C. to the Roman city of New Ilium in the early sixth century A.D.

According to one version of Greek tradition the Trojans were the descendants of the hero Teucer, who came from Crete, seeking a place to settle. The historical Trojans, however, may have been Luvians, an Anatolian[8] people who became vassals of the Hittites.[9] Animal bones show that the Trojans kept sheep, cattle, pigs, and horses, while carbonized seeds indicate that they cultivated barley in marshy valleys. The city had a thriving wool industry and traded throughout Central Asia, receiving horses from the steppes beyond the Black Sea, tin from Afghanistan. Whether or not Troy ever went to war with Mycenae, there certainly was trading contact between the two peoples. Mycenaean pottery at Troy dates as far back as 1500 B.C.

In the past, visitors to Troy have been struck by the smallness of the site, wondering how so insignificant a place could have entered legend. But directing me through high grass and cotton fields well beyond Schliemann's citadel, Korfmann pointed out a line of trenches that reveal one of his team's most exciting discoveries—the outer defenses of an entire lower town below the citadel. Here Korfmann's team located

---

8. *Anatolian* refers to the people of Anatolia, a peninsula that today is the Asian part of Turkey.
9. The *Hittites* were Indo-Europeans who lived in Anatolia around 2000 B.C. By 1340, they were a dominant power in the Middle East.

Fighting in the Trojan War, c. 525 BC. Relief, frieze, from north wall of Treasury of Sifnos, Delphi, Greece.

evidence of an encircling trench—some ten feet wide and eight feet deep—1,300 feet beyond the citadel walls. Increasing the known area of Troy VI by as much as 50 acres, the reconfigured city is almost ten times as large as Schliemann's citadel, containing a population of at least 6,000.

"Hittite documents refer to Taruisa," Korfmann told me. Taruisa has been identified by scholars with Troy. "*Tara* may be Luvian for 'wooden'—the city's name is perhaps a reference to the wooden houses of the lower town, which would have been conspicuous."

Yet the *Iliad* refers only to Troy's "well built walls" of stone such as Schliemann found on the citadel itself. These walls—and the damage done to them—have given archaeologists the most reliable key to the fate of the city.

Cracks and fire marks indicate that an earthquake destroyed the first Homeric candidate, Troy VI, around 1250 B.C. Soon afterward the same people who fled the earthquake returned to repair their city, creating a second settlement, Troy VIIa. The remains of small, cramped houses indicate that a larger population than before crowded inside the protective walls, while buried storage jars suggest to some scholars preparations for a siege. Flame-damaged walls indicate that about 70 years later a fierce fire destroyed this settlement. Was this the Troy, weakened by earthquake, that the invading Greeks finally sacked? Or had the Greeks attacked but not destroyed Troy VI in the wake of a natural disaster? Or was the fall of Troy entirely unrelated to the Homeric legend? . . .

The reconstruction below shows Mycenae's fortress in the late thirteenth century B.C., at the peak of its power.

Whether or not they played any role in Troy's destruction, the Mycenaeans did not long survive the city's fall. Why the apparently thriving Mycenaean civilization collapsed remains one of the most baffling questions of Bronze Age history. Pylos, Mycenae, Tiryns, Midea—nearly all the great palaces fell sometime around 1200 B.C. Some scholars have sought the cause in natural disasters, citing an earthquake such as destroyed Troy VI or even climatic change. Another theory has it that the Mycenaean economy, highly centralized and bureaucratic, became overextended and collapsed under its own weight. The downfall of Mycenaean palaces occurs at about the same time as the fall of numerous cities throughout the Aegean and eastern Mediterranean, and although there is no archaeological evidence of foreign invasion, a revolutionary change in fighting tactics may have given barbarian raiders a new advantage. Most scholars suggest there

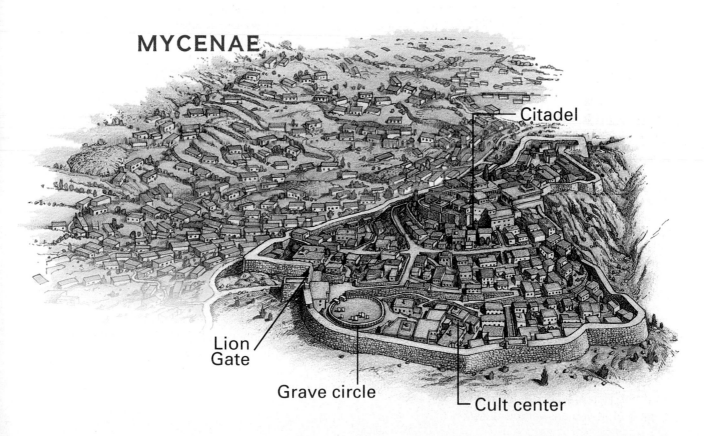

MYCENAE

Citadel

Lion Gate

Grave circle

Cult center

was a protracted decline, a slow trickling away of the population. . . .

The collapse of the Mycenaean world marked the beginning of several centuries traditionally known as the dark age of Greece, a period of shrinking populations, poverty, and cultural decline. Gone were the rich palaces with their colorful frescoes and imported luxuries. All the sophisticated arts of palace civilization were lost— monumental architecture, painting, metalwork, literacy. Yet it is this period of apparent cultural vacuum that transmitted two of the world's literary masterworks: the *Iliad* and the *Odyssey*. And while the *Iliad* bears evidence of its Mycenaean roots, it was the unknown poets of the dark age, centuries removed from the events they described, who fostered the great epic.

It is not difficult to imagine wayfarers from the fallen Mycenaean towns carrying their storytelling traditions with them during the 11th century B.C. As the generations passed, successive storytellers may have transformed a minor trade skirmish in Anatolia—or elsewhere—into an epic clash between Asiatic Troy and a unified force of Greek-speaking warriors, much as Britons[10] wistfully re-created the history of their clashes with invading Anglo-Saxons[11] into the legends of King Arthur.

The close of the eighth century B.C. revealed an entirely new human landscape. Everywhere populations had rebounded. Isolated settlements had given way to small city-states. Perhaps the characterization of the independent-minded hero Achilles and the *Iliad's* interest in different types of leadership reflect associated political change. Trade had revived and overseas colonization flourished. Above all, the new era revealed the epic poems attributed to Homer.

---

10. *Britons* refers to the Celtic people who inhabited Britain before the Anglo-Saxon invasions.
11. *Anglo-Saxons* refers to Germanic tribes who invaded England in the fifth century A.D. and controlled it until the Norman Conquest in A.D. 1066.

Respond and Think Critically

Respond and Interpret

1. Write a brief summary of the main ideas in this article before you answer the following questions. For help on writing a summary, see page 1147.

2. How would you compare the way ancient Greeks regarded the *Iliad* with the way modern scholars regard it?

3. (a)How does Alexander explain the origins of the *Iliad*? (b)Why does she call this epic poem "a tale of two cities"?

4. What artifacts discovered at Mycenae resemble items described by Homer in the *Iliad*?

5. (a)How many levels of Troy have been excavated? (b)What evidence suggests that Troy VIIa might be Homer's Troy? Refer to your chart from page 234 as you answer this question.

Analyze and Evaluate

6. What do you find most impressive about the discoveries of Schliemann and Korfmann? Explain.

7. (a)What claims does Alexander make about the historical Trojans? (b)How well does she support these claims?

8. Which of the theories about the collapse of the Mycenaean civilization seems most convincing? Explain.

Connect

9. How has your understanding of the *Iliad* changed as a result of reading this excerpt?

Before You Read

Lyric Poems

Meet **Sappho**
(c. 610–570 B.C.)

In the seventh century B.C., lyric poetry, a type of poetry with a highly individual voice, appeared in Greece. One of the earliest and greatest of the ancient Greek lyric poets was Sappho (sa′fō).

Greek Lyric Poet Sappho lived on Lesbos, a Greek island off the coast of what is now Turkey. Of noble birth, she had a daughter and at least two brothers whom she sometimes addressed in her poems. Some scholars believe that Sappho was in charge of a school that educated young noblewomen in the arts. Due to political disturbances on Lesbos, it seems likely she and her family went into exile in Sicily, where Greek colonists had founded the city of Syracuse. She later returned to Lesbos, where she died.

> "I do not expect my fingers
> to graze the sky"
>
> —Sappho, from Fragment 4

Greek lyric poets usually performed their work in private for friends and invited guests. They often sang or chanted their poetry, accompanying themselves on a harp-like instrument they called a *lyra*. In the dialect of Lesbos, Sappho composed both highly personal poems and more formal hymns and wedding songs. Her style was closer to everyday speech than to the more established literary style of her time. Though Lesbos produced several famous lyric poets, Sappho was early recognized as the greatest.

Legacy After her death, Sappho became famous throughout the Mediterranean world. She was honored with public statues. Greek and Roman authors imitated her poems, and Greek scholars collected her poetry in nine volumes. A poem attributed to the Greek philosopher Plato pays Sappho the ultimate tribute, classifying her among the goddesses of poetry: "Some say there are nine Muses: but they're wrong. Look at Sappho of Lesbos; she makes ten."

Unfortunately, much of Sappho's work was lost during the early Middle Ages. Only one complete poem and about 100 fragments were preserved as quotations in the works of other authors. Additional fragments have been discovered on archaeological digs in the twentieth century, including one fragment that appeared on a strip of papyrus removed from a mummified crocodile.

Sappho's poetry provides a rare glimpse of ancient Greece from a woman's perspective. Though only fragments of her work have survived, her intense, controlled verses have earned her a place as one of the world's greatest lyric poets.

Literature and Reading Preview

Connect to the Poems

What makes a person or thing look beautiful to you? Freewrite for a few minutes, explaining why you consider someone or something beautiful.

Build Background

Sappho's poems express intense personal feelings—love, anger, sorrow, and joy. She frequently used a verse form that came to be called the "sapphic stanza." It consists of four lines—three long and one shorter.

Set Purposes for Reading

Big Idea The Good Life

As you read, notice what Sappho's poetry reveals about the ancient Greeks' thoughts on the good life. Ask yourself, What matters personally to Sappho?

Literary Element Imagery

Imagery refers to the "word pictures" that authors create to evoke an emotional response. In creating effective images, authors use **sensory details**, or descriptions that appeal to one or more of the five senses: sight, hearing, touch, taste, and smell. As you read, ask yourself, How do the images in these poems contribute to the mood, or overall feeling?

Reading Strategy Paraphrase

When you **paraphrase**, you put something into your own words. Unlike a summary, a paraphrase is usually about the same length as the original passage. As you read, ask yourself, How does paraphrasing help you figure out the message of each poem?

....

Tip: Use a Paraphrase Chart Use a chart like the one below to record your paraphrase of each poem. Paraphrase each stanza of the longer poems.

Author's Words	My Paraphrase
"Most Beautiful of All the Stars"	Lovely evening star, at nightfall you send home the animals and children that have been away since dawn.

Learning Objectives

For pages 241–247

In studying this text, you will focus on the following objectives:

Literary Study: Analyzing imagery.

Reading: Paraphrasing.

Writing: Applying imagery.

Vocabulary

subtle (sut′əl) *adj.* hard to detect; p. 243 *The message of the poem was subtle and indirect.*

fasten (fas′ən) *v.* to attach firmly; p. 244 *He fastened the poster to the wall with masking tape.*

surpass (sər pas′) *v.* to exceed; p. 245 *We hope the results of the fund-raiser surpass those of previous years.*

....

Tip: Synonyms Synonyms are words that have nearly the same meaning. To determine whether two words are synonyms, see if one word can replace the other in a sentence. For example, in the sentence *The message of the poem was subtle and indirect*, the word *elusive* can replace *subtle*. Therefore, *elusive* and *subtle* are synonyms.

Lyric Poetry

Sappho
Translated by Jim Powell

Most Beautiful of All the Stars

Most beautiful of all the stars
O Hesperus,° bringing everything
the bright dawn scattered:
you bring the sheep, you bring the goat,
you bring the child back to her mother.

In My Eyes He Matches the Gods

In my eyes he matches the gods, that man who
sits there facing you—any man whatever—
listening from closeby to the sweetness of your
    voice as you talk, the

5   sweetness of your laughter: yes, that—I swear it—
sets the heart to shaking inside my breast, since
once I look at you for a moment, I can't
    speak any longer,

but my tongue breaks down, and then all at once a
10 **subtle** fire races inside my skin, my
eyes can't see a thing and a whirring whistle
    thrums at my hearing,

cold sweat covers me and a trembling takes
ahold of me all over: I'm greener than the
15 grass is and appear to myself to be little
    short of dying.

The Good Life *What matters to the speaker personally?*

Imagery *What sense(s) do these images primarily appeal to?*

Vocabulary

subtle (sut´ əl) *adj.* hard to detect

Sappho. Gustave Moreau. Watercolor, 18.4 x 12.4 cm. Victoria & Albert Museum, London.

View the Art In this watercolor, Gustave Moreau, a French symbolist painter, portrays Sappho in a melancholy moment. How does this image of Sappho match the one you get from her poems?

For My Mother Said

for my mother said

that when she was a girl if you
bound the locks of your hair in back,
gathered there in a circlet of plaited purple,°

5 that was truly a fine adornment,
but for blondes with hair yellower
than a torch it is better to **fasten** it

with fresh garlands of flowers in bloom,
and more recently there were headbands
10 decorated in Sardis,° elaborately
embroidered . . .°

4 circlet of plaited purple: circular ornament of woven or braided strands made from purple material. Purple was the most prized color of the ancient Mediterranean world.

10 Sardis: the capital of Lydia.
11 embroidered: decorated with ornamental needlework.

Some Say Thronging Cavalry

Some say thronging cavalry, some say foot soldiers,
others call a fleet the most beautiful of
sights the dark earth offers, but I say it's what-
      ever you love best.

5   And it's easy to make this understood by
everyone, for she who **surpassed** all human
kind in beauty, Helen,° abandoning her
      husband—that best of

men—went sailing off to the shores of Troy and
10 never spent a thought on her child or loving
parents: when the goddess seduced her wits and
      left her to wander,

she forgot them all, she could not remember
anything but longing, and lightly straying
15 aside, lost her way. But that reminds me
      now: Anactória,

she's not here, and I'd rather see her lovely
step, her sparkling glance and her face than gaze on
all the troops in Lydia° in their chariots and
20   glittering armor.

7 Helen: known as *Helen of Troy;* the wife of Menelaus, king of Sparta. Her abduction by Paris, a prince of Troy, triggered the Trojan War.

19 Lydia: wealthy kingdom in Asia Minor (present-day Turkey) in the sixth and seventh centuries B.C.

Paraphrase *Paraphrase the last stanza of this poem.*

Vocabulary

surpass (sər pas´) *v.* to exceed

Classical Greek Drama

THEATER MEANT FAR MORE THAN ENTERTAINMENT FOR THE PEOPLE of ancient Greece. It was part of their religion, a way of displaying loyalty to their city-state, and a method of honoring local heroes. It was also a major social event, a thrilling competition, and a place where important philosophical issues could be aired.

"The Athenian citizen took his drama seriously, not only because it was a part of a great religious festival, but because he loved talk and display and the tales the poets told."

—Vera Mowry Roberts, from *On Stage: A History of Theatre*

Greek drama is one of the oldest forms of drama we know. In ancient Greece, plays grew out of religion and myths. From the sixth century B.C., religious festivals featured a chorus, or group of actors, that danced and sang hymns to Dionysus (dī ə nē′ səs), the god of wine. In about 534 B.C., the lyric poet Thespis introduced the use of a single actor, separate from the chorus. (Actors today are still called thespians.) The chorus voiced the attitudes of the community while the actor delivered speeches, answered the chorus, and performed the story. In the early fifth century, the great dramatist Aeschylus (c. 524–456 B.C.) added a second actor to the stage; within a few years, his rival, Sophocles (496–406 B.C.), added a third. With these changes, drama—from the Greek word for *doing*, rather than *telling*—was born.

Reproductions of ancient Greek theater masks.

At the Theater

What would you have seen from the benches of an ancient Greek amphitheater? Up to 15,000 spectators might throng the Theater of Dionysus in Athens. Seated in the upper rows, a spectator was more than 55 yards from the stage below. The actors' gestures had to be exaggerated and dramatic, for no one in the back row could have interpreted slight movements.

Only men were allowed to perform. All the actors wore masks made of wool, linen, wood, or plaster. In the mid-fifth century B.C., the time of Sophocles, masks were fairly realistic representations of human faces. In later centuries, masks grew in size and became less realistic, featuring deep eye sockets and wide, gaping mouths, making actors appear larger against the background. Typically, tragic actors wore striking, richly decorated robes that set them apart from the audience. Chorus members wore more conventional costumes, which identified the roles they were playing: soldiers, priests, mourners, or even—in the case of comedies—frogs, birds, or wasps.

Ancient Greek theaters were open-air, so the lighting was natural. There were very few props. A hunter might carry a bow; an elderly man, a stick; a soldier, a sword and shield. These props served more as symbols to identify the character's role in the play than to imitate life. The violence—murder, suicide, and battles—almost always occurred offstage. Typically, a messenger would appear after the event and describe in gory detail what just happened.

The Golden Age

During the fifth century B.C., drama grew to be a vital part of life in Athens. The festival of Dionysus, the most important Greek religious festival, introduced a drama competition. The four greatest Greek dramatists—Aeschylus, Sophocles, Euripides (c. 480–406 B.C.), and Aristophanes (c. 448–c. 385 B.C.)—presented their plays at these festivals.

These dramatists—all from Athens—wrote plays in verse, based on themes familiar to their audiences. They retold myths, rewrote history, and ridiculed politicians. Aristophanes, the sole comic writer among the four Athenian masters, landed himself in legal trouble for boldly and uproariously satirizing society, politics, and even the gods. However, his three great contemporaries were all tragic poets, whose plays capture humankind's timeless struggle to find meaning and self-understanding.

Central to the tragedy is the fall of a great man (or woman, though her part would have been acted by a man). According to the Greek philosopher Aristotle, the tragic hero should be neither very good nor very bad. The hero's downfall is brought about by a flaw within his or her own character. In this way, the downfall of a hero would encourage audiences to examine their own lives, to define their beliefs, and to cleanse their emotions of pity and terror through compassion for the character.

LOG ON **Literature** Online

Literature and Reading For more about classical Greek drama, go to glencoe.com and enter QuickPass code GLW6053u2.

Restored seats in Theater of Dionysus. Athens.

Respond and Think Critically

1. In your opinion, what is the most significant difference between ancient Greek theater and modern American theater? Consider any American plays you have seen or read.

2. How did the purpose of Greek comedy differ from that of tragedy?

3. Why do you think Aristotle argued that the tragic hero should be a person neither especially good nor especially bad?

Eyes of Oedipus, 1945. Adolph Gottlieb. Oil on canvas. The Israel Museum, Jerusalem.

__View the Art__ Adolph Gottlieb is known for his pictograph style of painting in which shapes—often inspired by mythology—appear in a gridlike pattern. Based on the images in this painting, what do you think this play is about?

OEDIPUS THE KING

Sophocles
Translated by Robert Fagles

CHARACTERS

OEDIPUS: king of Thebes

A PRIEST: of Zeus

CREON: brother of Jocasta

A CHORUS: of Theban citizens and their LEADER

TIRESIAS: a blind prophet

JOCASTA: the queen, wife of Oedipus

A MESSENGER: from Corinth

A SHEPHERD

A MESSENGER: from inside the palace

ANTIGONE, ISMENE: daughters of Oedipus and Jocasta

GUARDS AND ATTENDANTS

PRIESTS OF THEBES

TIME AND SCENE: *The royal house of Thebes. Double doors dominate the façade; a stone altar stands at the center of the stage.*

Many years have passed since OEDIPUS *solved the riddle of the Sphinx and ascended the throne of Thebes, and now a plague has struck the city. A procession of* PRIESTS *enters; suppliants,° broken and despondent, they carry branches wound in wool° and lay them on the altar.*

The doors open. GUARDS *assemble.* OEDIPUS *comes forward, majestic but for a telltale limp, and slowly views the condition of his people.*

suppliants: people humbly asking a monarch to grant a request.
branches wound in wool: symbolic goodwill offerings to the gods.

OEDIPUS. Oh my children, the new blood of ancient Thebes,
why are you here? Huddling at my altar,
praying before me, your branches wound in wool.
Our city reeks with the smoke of burning incense,
5   rings with cries for the Healer° and wailing for the dead.
I thought it wrong, my children, to hear the truth
from others, messengers. Here I am myself—
you all know me, the world knows my fame:
I am Oedipus.

[*Helping a* PRIEST *to his feet.*]

                              Speak up, old man. Your years,
10   your **dignity**—you should speak for the others.
Why here and kneeling, what preys upon you° so?
Some sudden fear? some strong desire?
You can trust me; I am ready to help,
I'll do anything. I would be blind to misery
15   not to pity my people kneeling at my feet.

PRIEST. Oh Oedipus, king of the land, our greatest power!
You see us before you, men of all ages
clinging to your altars. Here are boys,
still too weak to fly from the nest,
20   and here the old, bowed down with the years,
the holy ones—a priest of Zeus° myself—and here
the picked, unmarried men, the young hope of Thebes.
And all the rest, your great family gathers now,
branches wreathed, massing in the squares,
25   kneeling before the two temples of queen Athena°
or the river-shrine where the embers glow and die
and Apollo sees the future in the ashes.°

                              Our city—
look around you, see with your own eyes—
our ship pitches wildly, cannot lift her head
30   from the depths, the red waves of death . . .
Thebes is dying. A blight° on the fresh crops
and the rich pastures, cattle sicken and die,
and the women die in labor, children stillborn,
and the plague, the fiery god of fever hurls down

5 **the Healer:** Apollo, god of sunlight, healing, prophecy, and archery.

11 **preys upon you:** troubles your mind.

21 **Zeus:** the chief Greek god.

25 **Athena:** also Pallas Athena, goddess of wisdom and the arts and sciences.
26–27 **river-shrine . . . in the ashes:** a nearby shrine where Apollo's priests read the future in the ashes left by burnt offerings.

31 **blight:** a disease that kills plants.

The Tragic Vision *One of the qualities of a tragic hero is nobility. How does Oedipus demonstrate this quality here?*

Vocabulary

dignity (dĭg′nə tē) *n.* worthiness; the quality of being worthy of honor.

35 on the city, his lightning slashing through us—
raging plague in all its **vengeance**, devastating
the house of Cadmus! And Black Death luxuriates°
in the raw, wailing miseries of Thebes.

Now we pray to you. You cannot equal the gods,
40 your children know that, bending at your altar.
But we do rate you first of men,
both in the common crises of our lives
and face-to-face encounters with the gods.
You freed us from the Sphinx; you came to Thebes
45 and cut us loose from the bloody tribute we had paid
that harsh, brutal singer. We taught you nothing,
no skill, no extra knowledge, still you triumphed.
A god was with you, so they say, and we believe it—
you lifted up our lives.
                                    So now again,
50 Oedipus, king, we bend to you, your power—
we implore you, all of us on our knees:
find us strength, rescue! Perhaps you've heard
the voice of a god or something from other men,
Oedipus . . . what do you know?
55 The man of experience—you see it every day—
his plans will work in a crisis, his first of all.

Act now—we beg you, best of men, raise up our city!
Act, defend yourself, your former glory!
Your country calls you savior now
60 for your zeal, your action years ago.
Never let us remember of your reign:
you helped us stand, only to fall once more.
Oh raise up our city, set us on our feet.
The omens were good that day you brought us joy—
65 be the same man today!
Rule our land, you know you have the power,
but rule a land of the living, not a wasteland.
Ship and towered city are nothing, stripped of men
alive within it, living all as one.

37 house of Cadmus: Thebes; Cadmus founded the city. **luxuriates:** indulges in pleasure; grows abundantly.

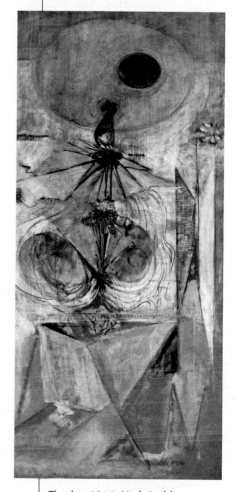

Tiresias, 1946. Mark Rothko. Oil on canvas, 79 3/4 x 40in. Collection of Christopher Rothko. ©ARS, NY.

Apply Background Knowledge *How did Oedipus save Thebes from the Sphinx?*

Vocabulary

vengeance (ven′jəns) n. revenge; the return of a harmful deed for a harmful deed

OEDIPUS.   My children,
70   I pity you. I see—how could
         I fail to see
      what longings bring you
         here? Well I know
      you are sick to death,
         all of you,
      but sick as you are,
         not one is sick as I.
      Your pain strikes
         each of you alone,
         each
75   in the confines of
         himself, no other.
         But my spirit
      grieves for the city, for
         myself and all of you.
      I wasn't asleep, dreaming.
         You haven't wakened me—
      I've wept through the nights, you
         must know that,
      groping, laboring over many paths of thought.
80   After a painful search I found one cure:
      I acted at once. I sent Creon,
      my wife's own brother, to Delphi—°
      Apollo the Prophet's oracle—° to learn
      what I might do or say to save our city.

85   Today's the day. When I count the days gone by
      it torments me . . . what is he doing?
      Strange, he's late, he's gone too long.
      But once he returns, then, then I'll be a traitor
      if I do not do all the god makes clear.

90   PRIEST. Timely words. The men over there
      are signaling—Creon's just arriving.

      OEDIPUS. [*Sighting* CREON, *then turning to the altar.*] Lord
         Apollo,
      let him come with a lucky word of rescue,
      shining like his eyes!

      PRIEST. Welcome news, I think—he's crowned, look,
95   and the laurel wreath is bright with berries.°

      OEDIPUS.   We'll soon see. He's close enough to hear—

Athenian red-figure kylix depicting Aegeus, King of Athens, consulting the Delphic Oracle. Staatliche Museen, Berlin.

82 **Delphi:** site of a shrine to Apollo; Delphi was the most famous oracle in ancient Greece.
83 **oracle:** a shrine at which questions might be answered about the hidden past or the future; the term *oracle* can also refer to the answer itself or to the priestess who gives the answer.

94–95 **crowned . . . with berries:** A crown of laurel was given as a prize for victory or excellence.

The Tragic Vision *What qualities does Oedipus exhibit in lines 77–79?*

[*Enter* CREON *from the side; his face is shaded with a wreath.*]

Creon, prince, my kinsman, what do you bring us?
What message from the god?

CREON.   Good news.
    I tell you even the hardest things to bear,
100   if they should turn out well, all would be well.

OEDIPUS. Of course, but what were the god's *words*?° There's
    no hope
    and nothing to fear in what you've said so far.

CREON. If you want my report in the presence of these . . .

[*Pointing to the* PRIESTS *while drawing* OEDIPUS *toward the palace.*]

    I'm ready now, or we might go inside.

OEDIPUS.   Speak out,
105   speak to us all. I grieve for these, my people,
    far more than I fear for my own life.

CREON.   Very well,
    I will tell you what I heard from the god.
    Apollo commands us —he was quite clear—
    "Drive the corruption from the land,
110   don't harbor° it any longer, past all cure,
    don't nurse it in your soil—root it out!"

OEDIPUS. How can we cleanse ourselves—what rites?°
    What's the source of the trouble?

CREON. Banish the man, or pay back blood with blood.
    Murder sets the plague-storm on the city.

115 OEDIPUS.   Whose murder?
    Whose fate does Apollo bring to light?

CREON.   Our leader,
    my lord, was once a man named Laius,°
    before you came and put us straight on course.

OEDIPUS.   I know—
    or so I've heard. I never saw the man myself.

120 CREON. Well, he was killed, and Apollo commands us
    now—
    he could not be more clear,
    "Pay the killers back—whoever is responsible."

OEDIPUS. Where on earth are they? Where to find it now,
    the trail of the ancient guilt so hard to trace?

101 the god's words: Apollo; it was believed that the god spoke through the voice of the priestess at the oracle.

110 harbor: to give shelter to, to conceal.

112 rites: religious ceremonies; symbolic acts often required to atone for a wrongdoing.

117 Laius: the king who immediately preceded Oedipus; first husband of Jocasta.

The Tragic Vision *How would you rate Oedipus as a leader so far?*

125   CREON. "Here in Thebes," he said.
     Whatever is sought for can be caught, you know,
     whatever is neglected slips away.

     OEDIPUS.   But where,
     in the palace, the fields or foreign soil,
     where did Laius meet his bloody death?

130   CREON. He went to consult an oracle, he said,
     and he set out and never came home again.

     OEDIPUS. No messenger, no fellow-traveler saw what
         happened?
     Someone to cross-examine?

     CREON.   No,
     they were all killed but one. He escaped,
135   terrified, he could tell us nothing clearly,
     nothing of what he saw—just one thing.

     OEDIPUS.   What's that?
     One thing could hold the key to it all,
     a small beginning give us grounds for hope.

     CREON. He said thieves attacked them—a whole band,
     not single-handed, cut King Laius down.

140   OEDIPUS.   A thief,
     so daring, so wild, he'd kill a king? Impossible,
     unless conspirators paid him off in Thebes.

     CREON. We suspected as much. But with Laius dead
     no leader appeared to help us in our troubles.

145   OEDIPUS. Trouble? Your *king* was murdered—royal blood!
     What stopped you from tracking down the killer
     then and there?

     CREON.   The singing, riddling Sphinx.
     She . . . persuaded us to let the mystery go
     and concentrate on what lay at our feet.

     OEDIPUS.   No,
150   I'll start again—I'll bring it all to light myself!
     Apollo is right, and so are you, Creon,
     to turn our attention back to the murdered man.
     Now you have *me* to fight for you, you'll see:
     I am the land's avenger by all rights°
155   and Apollo's champion° too.
     But not to assist some distant kinsman, no,

154 land's avenger by all rights:
As king, Oedipus has the authority
to punish crimes.

155 champion: one who defends
a worthy person or a just cause.

The Tragic Vision *What do these lines reveal about Oedipus?*

for my own sake I'll rid us of this corruption.
Whoever killed the king may decide to kill me too,
with the same violent hand—by avenging Laius
I defend myself.

[*To the* PRIESTS.]

160   Quickly, my children.
Up from the steps, take up your branches now.

[*To the* GUARDS.]

One of you summon the city here before us,
tell them I'll do everything. God help us,
we will see our triumph—or our fall.

[OEDIPUS *and* CREON *enter the palace, followed by the* GUARDS.]

165   PRIEST. Rise, my sons. The kindness we came for
Oedipus volunteers himself.
Apollo has sent his word, his oracle—
Come down, Apollo, save us, stop the plague.

[*The* PRIESTS *rise, remove their branches and exit to the side.*]

[*Enter a* CHORUS, *the citizens of Thebes, who have not heard the
news that* CREON *brings. They march around the altar, chanting.*]

CHORUS.   Zeus!
Great welcome voice of Zeus,° what do you bring?
170   What word from the gold vaults of Delphi
comes to brilliant Thebes? I'm racked with terror—
                                        terror shakes my heart
and I cry your wild cries, Apollo, Healer of Delos°
I worship you in dread . . . what now, what is your price?
175   some new sacrifice? some ancient rite from the past
come round again each spring?—
                        what will you bring to birth?°
Tell me, child of golden Hope
        warm voice that never dies!

180   You are the first I call, daughter of Zeus
deathless Athena—I call your sister Artemis,°
heart of the market place enthroned in glory,
                                guardian of our earth—
I call Apollo, Archer astride the thunderheads° of
        heaven—
185   O triple shield against death,° shine before me now!

169 voice of Zeus: Apollo, as the god of prophecy, spoke for his father, Zeus.

173 Delos: island birthplace of Apollo and a famous center of his worship.

174–177 worship you in dread . . . bring to birth: They fear what sacrifice the gods will demand from them to end the plague.

181 Artemis: goddess of the hunt and of the moon.

184 Archer: Apollo was sometimes referred to as "the distant deadly Archer," whose arrows caused disease or death. **astride the thunderheads:** riding atop storm clouds.
185 triple shield against death: Athena, Artemis, and Apollo.

Chorus *What group of people do you think the chorus represents?*

245   OEDIPUS. You pray to the gods? Let me grant your prayers.
       Come, listen to me—do what the plague demands:
       you'll find relief and lift your head from the depths.
       I will speak out now as a stranger to the story,
       a stranger to the crime. If I'd been present then,
250   there would have been no mystery, no long hunt
       without a clue in hand. So now, counted
       a native Theban years after the murder,
       to all of Thebes I make this proclamation:
       if any one of you knows who murdered Laius,
255   the son of Labdacus, I order him to reveal
       the whole truth to me. Nothing to fear,
       even if he must **denounce** himself,
       let him speak up
       and so escape the brunt of the charge—
260   he will suffer no unbearable punishment,
       nothing worse than exile, totally
       unharmed.

  [OEDIPUS *pauses, waiting for a reply.*]

                                 Next,
       if anyone knows the murderer is a stranger,
       a man from alien soil, come, speak up.
       I will give him a handsome reward, and lay
         up
265   gratitude in my heart for him besides.

  [*Silence again, no reply.*]

       But if you keep silent, if anyone
         panicking,
       trying to shield himself or friend or kin,
       rejects my offer, then hear what I will do.
       I order you, every citizen of the state
270   where I hold throne and power: banish
            this man—
       whoever he may be—never shelter him,
          never
       speak a word to him, never make him partner
       to your prayers, your victims burned to the gods.
       Never let the holy water touch his hands.
275   Drive him out, each of you, from every home.
       He is the plague, the heart of our corruption,

Oedipus and the Sphinx. Relief of Hellenistic sarcophagus. Ancient Art & Architecture Collection Ltd.

Vocabulary

denounce (di nouns´) *v.* to inform against; accuse publicly

as Apollo's oracle has revealed to me
just now. So I honor my obligations:
I fight for the god and for the murdered man.

280 Now my curse on the murderer. Whoever he is,
a lone man unknown in his crime
or one among many, let that man drag out
his life in agony, step by painful step—
I curse myself as well . . . if by any chance
285 he proves to be an intimate of our house,
here at my hearth, with my full knowledge,
may the curse I just called down on him strike me!

These are your orders: perform them to the last.
I command you, for my sake, for Apollo's, for this country
290 blasted root and branch by the angry heavens.
Even if god had never urged you on to act,
how could you leave the crime uncleansed so long?
A man so noble—your king, brought down in blood—
you should have searched. But I am the king now,
295 I hold the throne that he held then, possess his bed
and a wife who shares our seed . . . why, our seed
might be the same, children born of the same mother
might have created blood-bonds between us
if his hope of offspring hadn't met disaster—°
300 but fate swooped at his head and cut him short.
So I will fight for him as if he were my father,
stop at nothing, search the world
to lay my hands on the man who shed his blood,
the son of Labdacus descended of Polydorus,
305 Cadmus of old and Agenor,° founder of the line:
their power and mine are one.

                      Oh dear gods,
my curse on those who disobey these orders!
Let no crops grow out of the earth for them—
shrivel their women,° kill their sons,
310 burn them to nothing in this plague
that hits us now, or something even worse.
But you, loyal men of Thebes who approve my actions,
may our champion, Justice, may all the gods
be with us, fight beside us to the end!

296–299 our seed . . . disaster:
If Laius had fathered children before
his death, Oedipus would be
their stepfather.

305 Agenor: father of Cadmus.

309 shrivel their women: keep
them from bearing any more
children and carrying on the
family line.

The Tragic Vision *In what ways might this speech foretell the tragic hero's downfall?*

The Tragic Vision *What does this passage suggest about Oedipus's fate?*

TIRESIAS. I'd rather not cause pain for you or me.
So why this . . . useless interrogation?
You'll get nothing from me.

380 OEDIPUS.   Nothing! You,
you scum of the earth, you'd enrage a heart of stone!
You won't talk? Nothing moves you?
Out with it, once and for all!

TIRESIAS. You criticize my temper . . .° unaware
385   of the one *you* live with, you revile° me.

OEDIPUS. Who could restrain his anger hearing you?
What outrage—you spurn the city!

TIRESIAS. What will come will come.
Even if I shroud it all in silence.

390 OEDIPUS. What will come? You're bound to *tell* me that.

TIRESIAS. I'll say no more. Do as you like, build your anger
to whatever pitch you please, rage your worst—

OEDIPUS. Oh I'll let loose, I have such fury in me—
now I see it all. You helped hatch the plot,
395   you did the work, yes, short of killing him
with your own hands—and given eyes° I'd say
you did the killing single-handed!

TIRESIAS.   Is that so!
I charge you, then, submit to that decree
you just laid down: from this day onward
400   speak to no one, not these citizens, not myself.
You are the curse, the corruption of the land!

OEDIPUS. You, shameless—
aren't you appalled to start up such a story?
You think you can get away with this?

TIRESIAS.   I have already.
405   The truth with all its power lives inside me.

OEDIPUS. Who primed you° for this? Not your
prophet's trade.

TIRESIAS. You did, you forced me, twisted it out of me.

OEDIPUS. What? Say it again—I'll understand it better.

TIRESIAS. Didn't you understand, just now?

The Tragic Vision *Why does Oedipus suddenly turn against Tiresias?*

The Tragic Vision *Is fury a desirable quality in a leader, or is it a flaw? Explain.*

384 temper: Here, *temper* refers to character; the qualities that determine how a person behaves.
385 revile: abuse verbally.

396 and given eyes: (ironic) if I had knowledge of the past.

406 primed you: instructed you beforehand in what to say.

410   Or are you tempting me to talk?

OEDIPUS. No, I can't say I grasped your meaning.
     Out with it, again!

TIRESIAS. I say you are the murderer you hunt.

OEDIPUS. That obscenity, twice—by god, you'll pay.

415 TIRESIAS. Shall I say more, so you can really rage?

OEDIPUS. Much as you want. Your words are nothing—futile.

TIRESIAS. You cannot imagine . . . I tell you,
     you and your loved ones live together in infamy,
     you cannot see how far you've gone in guilt.

420 OEDIPUS. You think you can keep this up and never suffer?

TIRESIAS. Indeed, if the truth has any power.

OEDIPUS.   It does
     but not for you, old man. You've lost your power,
     stone-blind, stone-deaf—senses, eyes blind as stone!

TIRESIAS. I pity you, flinging at me the very insults
     each man here will fling at you so soon.

425 OEDIPUS.   Blind,
     lost in the night, endless night that nursed you!
     You can't hurt me or anyone else who sees the
     light—
     you can never touch me.

TIRESIAS.
         True, it is not your fate
     to fall at my hands. Apollo is quite enough,
430   and he will take some pains to work this
     out.

OEDIPUS. Creon! Is this conspiracy his
or yours?

TIRESIAS. Creon is not your downfall,
     no, you are your own.

OEDIPUS.
               O power—
     wealth and empire, skill
        outstripping skill
     in the heady° rivalries of life,
435   what envy lurks inside you!° Just

433–435 O power . . .
lurks inside you: competition for
power leads to jealousy.
434 heady: intoxicating; dizzying.

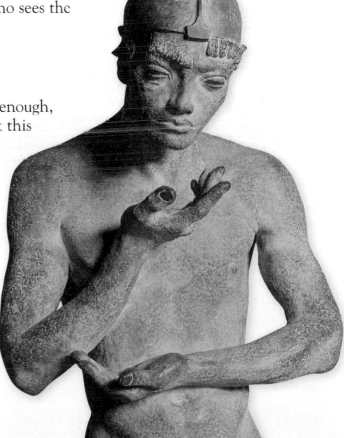

*Oedipus replying to the
Sphinx*, 1931. Glyn Philpot.
Bronze, height: 84 cm Tate
Gallery, London.

View the Art What do you
think the sculpture's hand
gestures and facial expression
suggest about Oedipus?

Apply Background Knowledge *Who are Oedipus's
loved ones?*

for this,
the crown the city gave me—I never sought it,
they laid it in my hands—for this alone, Creon,
the soul of trust, my loyal friend from the start
steals against me . . . so hungry to overthrow me
440   he sets this wizard on me, this scheming quack,
this fortune-teller peddling lies, eyes peeled
for his own profit—seer blind in his craft!

Come here, you pious fraud. Tell me,
when did you ever prove yourself a prophet?
445   When the Sphinx, that chanting Fury° kept her
     deathwatch here,
why silent then, not a word to set our people free?
There was a riddle, not for some passer-by to solve—
it cried out for a prophet. Where were you?
Did you rise to the crisis? Not a word,
450   you and your birds, your gods—nothing.
No, but I came by, Oedipus the ignorant,
I stopped the Sphinx! With no help from the birds,
the flight of my own intelligence hit the mark.

And this is the man you'd try to overthrow?
455   You think you'll stand by Creon when he's king?
You and the great mastermind—
you'll pay in tears, I promise you, for this,
this witch-hunt.° If you didn't look so senile
the lash° would teach you what your scheming means!

460   LEADER. I would suggest his words were spoken in anger,
Oedipus . . . yours too, and it isn't what we need.
The best solution to the oracle, the riddle°
posed by god—we should look for that.

TIRESIAS. You are the king no doubt, but in one respect,
465   at least, I am your equal: the right to reply.
I claim that privilege too.
I am not your slave. I serve Apollo.
I don't need Creon to speak for me in public.
                                 So,
you mock my blindness? Let me tell you this.

445 Fury: The Furies were three avenging spirits who punished crimes that were beyond the reach of human justice. This reference is used loosely by Oedipus; the Sphinx was not one of the Furies.

458 witch-hunt: false accusation; search for evidence that does not exist.
459 lash: whip.

462 solution to the . . . riddle: The precise meaning of an oracle was often vague or ambiguous (open to different interpretations).

The Tragic Vision *How would you describe Oedipus's opinion of himself? Could this be problematic? Explain.*

Chorus *What can you infer about the attitude of the chorus's leader?*

470   You with your precious eyes,
         you're blind to the corruption of your life,
         to the house° you live in, those you live with—
         who *are* your parents? Do you know? All unknowing
         you are the scourge of your own flesh and blood,
475   the dead below the earth and the living here above,
         and the double lash of your mother and your father's curse
         will whip you from this land one day, their footfall
         treading you down in terror,° darkness shrouding°
         your eyes that now can see the light!

                                   Soon, soon
480   you'll scream aloud—what haven won't reverberate?°
         What rock of Cithaeron° won't scream back in echo?
         That day you learn the truth about your marriage,
         the wedding-march that sang you into your halls,
         the lusty voyage home to the fatal harbor!°
485   And a load of other horrors you'd never dream
         will level you with yourself and all your children.

         There. Now smear us with insults—Creon, myself
         and every word I've said. No man will ever
         be rooted from the earth as brutally as you.

490   OEDIPUS. Enough! Such filth from him? Insufferable—°
         what, still alive? Get out—
         faster, back where you came from—vanish!

         TIRESIAS. I'd never have come if you hadn't called me here.

         OEDIPUS. If I thought you'd blurt out such absurdities,
495   you'd have died waiting before I'd had you summoned.

         TIRESIAS. Absurd, am I? To you, not to your parents:
         the ones who bore you found me sane enough.

         OEDIPUS. Parents—who? Wait . . . who is my father?

         TIRESIAS. This day will bring your birth and your
         destruction.

500   OEDIPUS. Riddles—all you can say are riddles, murk
         and darkness.

         TIRESIAS. Ah, but aren't you the best man alive at
         solving riddles?

The Tragic Vision *Why does Oedipus ask for Tiresias's help and then refuse it?*

Apply Background Knowledge *How does Tiresias turn Oedipus's reputation for solving riddles against him?*

---

472 **house:** in this use, a family including ancestors, descendants, and close relatives.

477–478 **footfall . . . in terror:** memory of what occurred will haunt you.
478 **shrouding:** covering; ironic, because a shroud is also used to cover the dead.
480 **you'll scream . . . reverberate:** you will find no escape from the horror.
481 **Cithaeron:** a remote mountain range.

484 **lusty voyage . . . harbor:** refers to the consummation of Oedipus's marriage to Jocasta.

490 **Insufferable:** unbearable; intolerable.

The Oracle. George Edward Robertson (b. 1864). Oil on canvas, 145.5 x 250.2 cm.
Private collection.

View the Art In this painting, Robertson depicts three people holding lyres—stringed
instruments associated with Apollo. Which figure in this painting do you think has come, like
Creon, to request a prophecy from the oracle? How can you tell?

OEDIPUS. Mock me for that, go on, and you'll reveal
    my greatness.

TIRESIAS. Your great good fortune, true, it was your ruin.

OEDIPUS. Not if I saved the city—what do I care?

TIRESIAS. Well then, I'll be going.

[*To his* ATTENDANT.]

505   Take me home, boy.

OEDIPUS. Yes, take him away. You're a nuisance here.
    Out of the way, the irritation's gone.

[*Turning his back on* TIRESIAS, *moving toward the palace.*]

TIRESIAS.   I will go,
    once I have said what I came here to say.
    I'll never shrink from the anger in your eyes—

510 you can't destroy me. Listen to me closely:
the man you've sought so long, proclaiming,
cursing up and down, the murderer of Laius—
he is here. A stranger,°
you may think, who lives among you,
515 he soon will be revealed a native Theban
but he will take no joy in the revelation.
Blind who now has eyes, beggar who now is rich,
he will grope his way toward a foreign soil,
a stick tapping before him step by step.

[OEDIPUS *enters the palace*.]

520 Revealed at last, brother and father both
to the children he embraces, to his mother
son and husband both—he sowed the loins
his father sowed,° he spilled his father's blood!

Go in and reflect on that, solve that.
525 And if you find I've lied
from this day onward call the prophet blind.

[TIRESIAS *and the* BOY *exit to the side*.]

CHORUS.   Who—
who is the man the voice of god denounces
resounding out of the rocky gorge of Delphi?
The horror too dark to tell,
530 whose ruthless bloody hands have done the work?
His time has come to fly
to outrace the stallions of the storm
his feet a streak of speed—
Cased in armor, Apollo son of the Father°
535 lunges on him, lightning-bolts afire!
And the grim unerring Furies
closing for the kill.
Look,
the word of god has just come blazing
flashing off Parnassus'° snowy heights!
540 That man who left no trace—
after him, hunt him down with all our strength!
Now under bristling timber
up through rocks and caves he stalks
like the wild mountain bull—

Apply Background Knowledge *Under what circumstances did Oedipus marry Jocasta?*

513 **stranger:** in its original sense, a stranger was a foreigner or a person in another's house as a guest or as an intruder.

522–523 **sowed the loins . . . sowed:** had children with the same woman with whom his father had children.

534 **the Father:** Zeus.

539 **Parnassus:** twin-peaked mountain near Delphi, sacred to Apollo and Dionysus.

Before You Read

Oedipus the King

Build Background

Greek dramas were based on myths and legends known and loved by Athenians. Favorite subjects included the Trojan War and such legendary figures as Oedipus, Agamemnon, and the Greek gods and goddesses. Because the audience already knew the ending of Oedipus's story, Sophocles could focus on developing character and creating dialogue rich in meaning and tinged with irony.

Literary Element Tragedy

A **tragedy** is a literary work in which the main character, or hero, is a person of great ability who experiences a downfall primarily because of a **tragic flaw:** a fault within his or her character. Excessive pride, or *hubris* (hyü′brəs), is the most common flaw. Ambition, jealousy, self-doubt, and anger are other weaknesses that can defeat the tragic hero. Even though he or she suffers defeat, and often death, the tragic hero ultimately gains some kind of insight into himself or herself. As you read, ask yourself, What tragic qualities does *Oedipus the King* reflect?

Reading Strategy Analyze Argument

Argument is a form of persuasion in which logic or reason is used to try to influence someone's ideas or actions. Logical reasoning may be either inductive or deductive. **Inductive** reasoning moves from the specific to the general; **deductive** reasoning moves from the general to the specific. As you read this section of *Oedipus the King*, ask yourself, What arguments do the characters construct and what reasons do they cite for acting and thinking as they do?

....

Tip: Examine Reasoning Use a chart like the one below to record the thesis statements and evidence the characters present.

Thesis	Evidence

Learning Objectives

For pages 274–290

In studying this text, you will focus on the following objectives:

Literary Study: Analyzing tragedy.

Reading: Analyzing argument.

Writing: Writing an essay.

Vocabulary

sullen (sul′ən) *adj.* showing resentment and ill humor by sulky withdrawal; p. 280 *My little brother was sullen because he was grounded.*

foreboding (fôr bō′ding) *n.* a feeling something bad or harmful will happen; p. 285 *Caroline had a foreboding the plane would crash.*

gauge (gāj) *v.* to estimate; judge; p. 286 *Actors try to gauge the audience's reactions to their lines.*

crucial (krōō′shəl) *adj.* essential; decisive; p. 287 *She made the crucial decision to become a writer.*

retract (ri trakt′) *v.* take back or deny; p. 287 *Harry realized it was too late to retract his cruel words.*

Tip: Synonyms Synonyms are words that have nearly the same meaning. For example, *glum* is a synonym of *sullen* because it is an adjective that also describes something that shows ill humor.

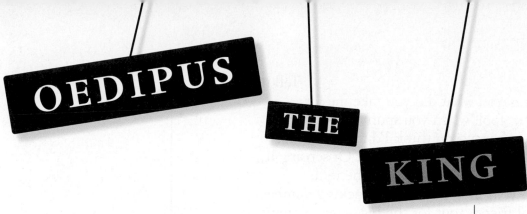

OEDIPUS THE KING

[*Enter* CREON *from the side*.]

CREON. My fellow-citizens, I hear King Oedipus
   levels terrible charges at me. I had to come.
575   I resent it deeply. If, in the present crisis,
   he thinks he suffers any abuse from me,
   anything I've done or said that offers him
   the slightest injury, why, I've no desire
   to linger out this life, my reputation a shambles.
580   The damage I'd face from such an accusation
   is nothing simple. No, there's nothing worse:
   branded a traitor in the city, a traitor
   to all of you and my good friends.

LEADER.   True,
   but a slur might have been forced out of him,
585   by anger perhaps, not any firm conviction.

CREON. The charge was made in public, wasn't it?
   I put the prophet up to spreading lies?

LEADER. Such things were said . . .
   I don't know with what intent, if any.

590 CREON. Was his glance steady, his mind right
   when the charge was brought against me?

LEADER. I really couldn't say. I never look
   to judge the ones in power.

[*The doors open.* OEDIPUS *enters*.]

                    Wait,
   here's Oedipus now.

OEDIPUS.   You—here? You have the gall
595   to show your face before the palace gates?
   You, plotting to kill me, kill the king—
   I see it all, the marauding° thief himself
   scheming to steal my crown and power!

597 **marauding**: roaming about in search of loot.

The Tragic Vision *Why has Oedipus reached this conclusion? What does his behavior suggest about his character?*

                                                      Tell me,
        in god's name, what did you take me for,
600   coward or fool, when you spun out your plot?
        Your treachery—you think I'd never detect it
        creeping against me in the dark? Or sensing it,
        not defend myself? Aren't you the fool,
        you and your high adventure. Lacking numbers,
605   powerful friends, out for the big game of empire—
        you need riches, armies to bring that quarry° down!

        CREON. Are you quite finished? It's your turn to listen
        for just as long as you've . . . instructed me.
        Hear me out, then judge me on the facts.

610   OEDIPUS. You've a wicked way with words, Creon,
        but I'll be slow to learn—from you.
        I find you a menace, a great burden to me.

        CREON. Just one thing, hear me out in this.

        OEDIPUS.   Just one thing,
        don't tell me you're not the enemy, the traitor.

615   CREON. Look, if you think crude, mindless stubbornness
        such a gift, you've lost your sense of balance.

        OEDIPUS. If you think you can abuse a kinsman,
        then escape the penalty, you're insane.

        CREON. Fair enough, I grant you. But this injury
620   you say I've done you, what is it?

        OEDIPUS. Did you induce me, yes or no,
        to send for that sanctimonious° prophet?

        CREON. I did. And I'd do the same again.

        OEDIPUS. All right then, tell me, how long is it now
        since Laius . . .

        CREON.   Laius—what did *he* do?

625   OEDIPUS.   Vanished,
        swept from sight, murdered in his tracks.

        CREON. The count of the years would run you far back . . .

        OEDIPUS. And that far back, was the prophet at his trade?

        CREON. Skilled as he is today, and just as honored.

        OEDIPUS. Did he ever refer to me then, at that time?

630   CREON.   No,
        never, at least, when I was in his presence.

606 **quarry:** something pursued or hunted; prey.

622 **sanctimonious:** exhibiting false virtue; hypocritical.

Tragedy *Why does Oedipus display such stubbornness here?*

OEDIPUS. But you did investigate the murder, didn't you?

CREON. We did our best, of course, discovered nothing.

OEDIPUS. But the great seer never accused me then—
 why not?

635 CREON. I don't know. And when I don't, *I* keep quiet.

OEDIPUS. You do know this, you'd tell it too—
 if you had a shred of decency.

CREON.   What?
 If I know, I won't hold back.

OEDIPUS.   Simply this:
 if the two of you had never put heads together,
640 we'd never have heard about *my* killing Laius.

CREON. If that's what he says . . . well, you know best.
 But now I have a right to learn from you
 as you just learned from me.

OEDIPUS.   Learn your fill,
 you never will convict me of the murder.

645 CREON. Tell me, you're married to my sister, aren't you?

OEDIPUS. A genuine discovery—there's no denying that.

CREON. And you rule the land with her, with equal power?

OEDIPUS. She receives from me whatever she desires.

CREON. And I am the third, all of us are equals?°

650 OEDIPUS. Yes, and it's there you show your stripes—
 you betray a kinsman.

CREON.   Not at all.
 Not if you see things calmly, rationally,
 as I do. Look at it this way first:
 who in his right mind would rather rule
655 and live in anxiety than sleep in peace?
 Particularly if he enjoys the same authority.
 Not I, I'm not the man to yearn for kingship,
 not with a king's power in my hands. Who would?
 No one with any sense of self-control.
660 Now, as it is, you offer me all I need,
 not a fear in the world. But if I wore the crown . . .
 there'd be many painful duties to perform,
 hardly to my taste.
       How could kingship
 please me more than influence, power
665 without a qualm? I'm not that deluded yet,

649 all of us are equals:
As the queen's brother, Creon is a member of the royal family with great influence and power.

to reach for anything but privilege outright,
profit free and clear.
Now all men sing my praises, all salute me,
now all who request your favors curry mine.°
670   I'm their best hope: success rests in me.
Why give up that, I ask you, and borrow trouble?
A man of sense, someone who sees things clearly
would never resort to treason.
No, I've no lust for conspiracy in me,
675   nor could I ever suffer one who does.

Do you want proof? Go to Delphi yourself,
examine the oracle and see if I've reported
the message word-for-word. This too:
if you detect that I and the clairvoyant°
680   have plotted anything in common, arrest me,
execute me. Not on the strength of one vote,
two in this case, mine as well as yours.
But don't convict me on sheer unverified surmise.°

How wrong it is to take the good for bad,
685   purely at random, or take the bad for good.
But reject a friend, a kinsman? I would as soon
tear out the life within us, priceless life itself.
You'll learn this well, without fail, in time.
Time alone can bring the just man to light;
690   the criminal you can spot in one short day.

LEADER.   Good advice,
my lord, for anyone who wants to avoid disaster.
Those who jump to conclusions may be wrong.

OEDIPUS. When my enemy moves against me quickly,
plots in secret, I move quickly too, I must,
695   I plot and pay him back. Relax my guard a moment,
waiting his next move—he wins his objective,
I lose mine.

CREON.   What do you want?
You want me banished?

OEDIPUS.   No, I want you dead.

---

669 curry mine: seek my approval, especially through flattery.

679 clairvoyant (klār voi´ənt): a seer, one who is able to apprehend what is not apparent to the five senses; psychic.

683 surmise: speculation; suspicion.

Analyze Argument *Is Creon's argument convincing? Explain.*

The Tragic Vision *Why might jumping to conclusions be considered a character flaw?*

CREON. Just to show how ugly a grudge can . . .

OEDIPUS.   So,
700   still stubborn? you don't think I'm serious?

CREON. I think you're insane.

OEDIPUS.   Quite sane—in my behalf.

CREON. Not just as much in mine?

OEDIPUS.   You—my mortal enemy?

CREON. What if you're wholly wrong?

OEDIPUS.   No matter—I must rule.

CREON. Not if you rule unjustly.

OEDIPUS.   Hear him,° Thebes, my city!

705   CREON. My city too, not yours alone!

LEADER. Please, my lords.

[Enter JOCASTA from the palace.]

                          Look, Jocasta's coming,
        and just in time too. With her help
        you must put this fighting of yours to rest.

JOCASTA. Have you no sense? Poor misguided men,
710   such shouting—why this public outburst?
        Aren't you ashamed, with the land so sick,
        to stir up private quarrels?

[To OEDIPUS.]

        Into the palace now. And Creon, you go home.
        Why make such a furor over nothing?

715   CREON. My sister, it's dreadful . . . Oedipus, your husband,
        he's bent on a choice of punishments for me,
        banishment from the fatherland or death.

OEDIPUS. Precisely. I caught him in the act, Jocasta,
        plotting, about to stab me in the back.

720   CREON. Never—curse me, let me die and be damned
        if I've done you any wrong you charge me with.

JOCASTA. Oh god, believe it, Oedipus,
        honor the solemn oath he swears to heaven.
        Do it for me, for the sake of all your people.

[The CHORUS begins to chant.]

725   CHORUS. Believe it, be sensible

704 Hear him: Oedipus suggests that Creon is advocating usurpation—the unlawful seizing of the throne from the rightful king.

Tragedy *What quality does Oedipus reveal in his response to Creon?*

JOCASTA. Tell me what's happened first.

CHORUS. Loose, ignorant talk started dark suspicions
755   and a sense of injustice cut deeply too.

JOCASTA. On both sides?

CHORUS.   Oh yes.

JOCASTA.   What did they say?

CHORUS. Enough, please, enough! The land's so racked
        already
    or so it seems to me . . .
    End the trouble here, just where they left it.

760   OEDIPUS. You see what comes of your good intentions now?
        And all because you tried to blunt my anger.

CHORUS.   My king,
    I've said it once, I'll say it time and again—
    I'd be insane, you know it,
    senseless, ever to turn my back on you.
765   You who set our beloved land—storm-tossed, shattered—
    straight on course. Now again, good helmsman,
    steer us through the storm!

[*The* CHORUS *draws away, leaving* OEDIPUS *and* JOCASTA *side by side.*]

JOCASTA.   For the love of god,
    Oedipus, tell me too, what is it?
    Why this rage? You're so unbending.

770   OEDIPUS. I will tell you. I respect you, Jocasta,
        much more than these . . .

[*Glancing at the* CHORUS.]

    Creon's to blame, Creon schemes against me.

JOCASTA. Tell me clearly, how did the quarrel start?

OEDIPUS. He says *I* murdered Laius—I am guilty.

775   JOCASTA. How does he know? Some secret knowledge
        or simple hearsay?

OEDIPUS.   Oh, he sent his prophet in
    to do his dirty work. You know Creon,
    Creon keeps his own lips clean.

JOCASTA.   A prophet?
    Well then, free yourself of every charge!

780   Listen to me and learn some peace of mind:
      no skill in the world,
      nothing human can penetrate the future.
      Here is proof, quick and to the point.

      An oracle came to Laius one fine day
785   (I won't say from Apollo himself
      but his underlings, his priests) and it said
      that doom would strike him down at the hands of a son,
      our son, to be born of our own flesh and blood. But Laius,
      so the report goes at least, was killed by strangers,
790   thieves, at a place where three roads meet . . . my son—
      he wasn't three days old and the boy's father°
      fastened his ankles, had a henchman° fling him away
      on a barren, trackless mountain.
                              There, you see?
      Apollo brought neither thing to pass. My baby
795   no more murdered his father than Laius suffered—
      his wildest fear—death at his own son's hands.
      That's how the seers and all their revelations
      mapped out the future. Brush them from your mind.
      Whatever the god needs and seeks
800   he'll bring to light himself, with ease.

      OEDIPUS.   Strange,
      hearing you just now . . . my mind wandered,
      my thoughts racing back and forth.

      JOCASTA. What do you mean? Why so anxious, startled?

      OEDIPUS. I thought I heard you say that Laius
805   was cut down at a place where three roads meet.

      JOCASTA. That was the story. It hasn't died out yet.

      OEDIPUS. Where did this thing happen? Be precise.

      JOCASTA. A place called Phocis,° where two branching roads,
      one from Daulia,° one from Delphi,
810   come together—a crossroads.

      OEDIPUS. When? How long ago?

      JOCASTA. The heralds no sooner reported Laius dead
      than you appeared and they hailed you king of Thebes.

791 the boy's father: Laius.
792 henchman: assistant.

808 Phocis: territory in central Greece.
809 Daulia: a city near Delphi.

Tragedy *What do you predict will happen when Jocasta shares this memory?*

Analyze Argument *What does Jocasta try to prove? Is she convincing? Explain.*

OEDIPUS. My god, my god—what have you planned
        to do to me?

JOCASTA. What, Oedipus? What haunts you so?

815 OEDIPUS.   Not yet.
        Laius—how did he look? Describe him.
        Had he reached his prime?

JOCASTA.   He was swarthy,°
        and the gray had just begun to streak his temples,
        and his build . . . wasn't far from yours.

OEDIPUS.   Oh no no,
820   I think I've just called down a dreadful curse
        upon myself—I simply didn't know!

JOCASTA. What are you saying? I shudder to look at you.

OEDIPUS. I have a terrible fear the blind seer can see.°
        I'll know in a moment. One thing more—

JOCASTA.   Anything,
825   afraid as I am—ask, I'll answer, all I can.

OEDIPUS. Did he go with a light or heavy escort,
        several men-at-arms, like a lord, a king?

JOCASTA. There were five in the party, a herald
        among them, and a single wagon carrying Laius.

OEDIPUS.   Ai—
830   now I can see it all, clear as day.
        Who told you all this at the time, Jocasta?

JOCASTA. A servant who reached home, the lone survivor.

OEDIPUS. So, could he still be in the palace—even now?

JOCASTA. No indeed. Soon as he returned from the scene
835   and saw you on the throne with Laius dead and gone,
        he knelt and clutched my hand, pleading with me
        to send him into the hinterlands,° to pasture,
        far as possible, out of sight of Thebes.
        I sent him away. Slave though he was,
840   he'd earned that favor—and much more.

OEDIPUS. Can we bring him back, quickly?

JOCASTA. Easily. Why do you want him so?

OEDIPUS.   I'm afraid,
        Jocasta, I have said too much already.
        That man—I've got to see him.

817 **swarthy:** having a dark or suntanned complexion.

823 **the blind seer can see:** can reveal hidden truths.

837 **hinterlands:** remote regions lying inland from the coast.

The Tragic Vision *Why does Oedipus now realize that the seer "sees"?*

JOCASTA.   Then he'll come.
845   But even I have a right, I'd like to think,
        to know what's torturing you, my lord.

        OEDIPUS.   And so you shall—I can hold nothing back from
                you,
            now I've reached this pitch of dark **foreboding**.
            Who means more to me than you? Tell me,
850   whom would I turn toward but you
        as I go through all this?

        My father was Polybus, king of Corinth.
        My mother, a Dorian,° Merope. And I was held
        the prince of the realm among the people there,
855   till something struck me out of nowhere,
        something strange . . . worth remarking perhaps,
        hardly worth the anxiety I gave it.
        Some man at a banquet who had drunk too much
        shouted out—he was far gone, mind you—
860   that I am not my father's son. Fighting words!
        I barely restrained myself that day
        but early the next I went to mother and father,
        questioned them closely, and they were enraged
        at the accusation and the fool who let it fly.
865   So as for my parents I was satisfied,
        but still this thing kept gnawing at me,
        the slander° spread—I had to make my move.
                                                And so,
            unknown to mother and father I set out for Delphi,
            and the god Apollo spurned me, sent me away
870   denied the facts I came for,
        but first he flashed before my eyes a future
        great with pain, terror, disaster—I can hear him cry,
        "You are fated to couple with° your mother,
            you will bring
        a breed of children into the light no man can
            bear to see—
875   you will kill your father, the one who gave you life!"
        I heard all that and ran. I abandoned Corinth,

---

853 Dorian: one of four cultural groups that occupied ancient Greece; the Dorians founded the city of Corinth.

867 slander: false speech meant to damage another's reputation.

873 couple with: marry.

Tragedy *How did Oedipus react to this prophecy before the play began? What was the result of his actions?*

Vocabulary

foreboding (fôr bō′ding) *n.* a feeling that something bad or harmful will happen

from that day on I **gauged** its landfall only
by the stars,° running, always running
toward some place where I would never see

880   the shame of all those oracles come true.
And as I fled I reached that very spot
where the great king, you say, met his death.
Now, Jocasta, I will tell you all.
Making my way toward this triple crossroad

885   I began to see a herald, then a brace° of colts
drawing a wagon, and mounted on the bench . . . a man,
just as you've described him, coming face-to-face,
and the one in the lead and the old man himself
were about to thrust me off the road—brute force—

890   and the one shouldering me aside, the driver,
I strike him in anger!—and the old man, watching me
coming up along his wheels—he brings down
his prod, two prongs straight at my head!
I paid him back with interest!

895   Short work, by god—with one blow of the staff
in this right hand I knock him out of his high seat,
roll him out of the wagon, sprawling headlong—
I killed them all—every mother's son!

Oh, but if there is any blood-tie

900   between Laius and this stranger . . .
what man alive more miserable than I?
More hated by the gods? *I* am the man
no alien, no citizen welcomes to his house,
law forbids it—not a word to me in public,

905   driven out of every hearth° and home.
And all these curses I—no one but I
brought down these piling° curses on myself!
And you, his wife, I've touched your body with these,
the hands that killed your husband cover you with blood.

910   Wasn't I born for torment? Look me in the eyes!
I am abomination°—heart and soul!
I must be exiled, and even in exile
never see my parents, never set foot
on native earth° again. Else I'm doomed

915   to couple with my mother and cut my father down . . .

877–878 gauged . . . the stars: never went near Corinth.

885 brace: matched pair.

905 hearth: fireplace; in ancient Greece, the most important part of the home.
907 piling: mounting.

911 abomination: something disgusting or loathsome; wickedness.

913–914 set foot . . . native earth: return to Corinth.

Polybus who reared me, gave me life.
                                    But why, why?
Wouldn't a man of judgment say—and wouldn't he
   be right—
some savage power has brought this down upon my head?

Oh no, not that, you pure and awesome° gods,
920   never let me see that day! Let me slip
from the world of men, vanish without a trace
before I see myself stained with such corruption,
stained to the heart.

LEADER. My lord, you fill our hearts with fear.
925   But at least until you question the witness,
do take hope.

OEDIPUS.   Exactly. He is my last hope—
I am waiting for the shepherd. He is **crucial**.

JOCASTA. And once he appears, what then? Why so urgent?

OEDIPUS. I'll tell you. If it turns out that his story
930   matches yours, I've escaped the worst.

JOCASTA. What did I say? What struck you so?

OEDIPUS.   You said *thieves*—
he told you a whole band of them murdered Laius.
So, if he still holds to the same number,
I cannot be the killer. One can't equal many.
935   But if he refers to one man, one alone,
clearly the scales come down on me:°
I am guilty.

JOCASTA.   Impossible. Trust me,
I told you precisely what he said,
and he can't **retract** it now;
940   the whole city heard it, not just I.
And even if he should vary his first report
by one man more or less, still, my lord,
he could never make the murder of Laius

919 **awesome**: in this use, deserving of fear and worship.

936 **scales**: an instrument of measurement made from two trays of equal weight on either side of a balanced center beam. **scales come down on me**: the weight of the evidence is against me.

The Tragic Vision *What does Oedipus mean by "some savage power"?*

Vocabulary

crucial (krōō′shəl) *adj.* essential; decisive
retract (ri trakt′) *v.* take back or deny

Oedipus kills Laertes on chariot, 3rd century AD. Marble relief from a Roman sarcophagus. Vatican Museums, Vatican State.

truly fit the prophecy. Apollo was explicit:
945 my son was doomed to kill my husband . . . my son,
poor defenseless thing, he never had a chance
to kill his father. They destroyed him first.

So much for prophecy. It's neither here nor there.
From this day on, I wouldn't look right or left.

950 OEDIPUS. True, true. Still, that shepherd,
someone fetch him—now!

JOCASTA. I'll send at once. But do let's go inside.
I'd never displease you, least of all in this.

[OEDIPUS *and* JOCASTA *enter the palace.*]

CHORUS. Destiny° guide me always
955 Destiny find me filled with reverence
pure in word and deed.
Great laws tower above us, reared on high
born for the brilliant vault of heaven—
Olympian° Sky their only father,
960 nothing mortal, no man gave them birth,
their memory deathless, never lost in sleep:
within them lives a mighty god, the god does not
grow old.°

954 Destiny: refers to a future that has been determined in advance and the outcome of which is inevitable.

957–962 Great laws . . . grow old: The gods have decreed certain unchanging laws that cannot be disobeyed.
959 Olympian: of or relating to Olympus, the highest mountain in Greece and home of the gods.

Analyze Argument *What is Jocasta's main point?*

The Tragic Vision *What do these lines suggest about the tragic vision of the play?*

Pride° breeds the tyrant
violent pride, gorging, crammed to bursting
965   with all that is overripe and rich with ruin—
clawing up to the heights, headlong pride
crashes down the abyss—sheer doom!
        No footing helps, all foothold lost and gone.°
But the healthy strife° that makes the city strong—
970   I pray that god will never end that wrestling:
god, my champion, I will never let you go.

But if any man comes striding, high and mighty
        in all he says and does,
no fear of justice, no reverence
975   for the temples of the gods—
        let a rough doom tear him down,
repay his pride, breakneck, ruinous pride!
If he cannot reap his profits fairly
        cannot restrain himself from outrage—
980   mad, laying hands on the holy things untouchable!

Can such a man, so desperate, still boast
he can save his life from the flashing bolts of god?
        If all such violence goes with honor now
        why join the sacred dance?°

985   Never again will I go reverent to Delphi,
        the inviolate° heart of Earth
or Apollo's ancient oracle at Abae
or Olympia° of the fires—
        unless these prophecies all come true
990   for all mankind to point toward in wonder.
King of kings, if you deserve your titles
        Zeus, remember, never forget!
You and your deathless, everlasting reign.

They are dying, the old oracles sent to Laius,
995   now our masters strike them off the rolls.°
        Nowhere Apollo's golden glory now—
        the gods, the gods go down.

⚜

963 **Pride:** here, the Greek concept of *hubris;* pride that goes beyond acceptable limits and brings on divine punishment.

966–968 **clawing up . . . lost and gone:** Hubris can make the mighty overreach and bring about their own doom.
969 **strife:** competition.

983–984 **If all such . . . why join the sacred dance:** If actions such as these go unpunished, why should anyone show reverence for the gods?
986 **inviolate:** pure.
987–988 **Abae or Olympia:** other famous shrines.

995 **rolls:** official records.

The Tragic Vision *How do the citizens of Thebes feel at this point in the play? Explain.*

OEDIPUS THE KING

[Enter JOCASTA *from the palace, carrying a suppliant's branch wound in wool.*]

JOCASTA. Lords of the realm, it occurred to me,
just now, to visit the temples of the gods,
1000   so I have my branch in hand and incense too.

Oedipus is beside himself. Racked with anguish,
no longer a man of sense, he won't admit
the latest prophecies are hollow as the old—
he's at the mercy of every passing voice
1005   if the voice tells of terror.
I urge him gently, nothing seems to help,
so I turn to you, Apollo, you are nearest.

[*Placing her branch on the altar, while an old herdsman enters from the side, not the one just summoned by the King but an unexpected* MESSENGER *from Corinth.*]

I come with prayers and offerings . . . I beg you,
cleanse us, set us free of defilement!
1010   Look at us, passengers in the grip of fear,
watching the pilot of the vessel go to pieces.

MESSENGER. [*Approaching* JOCASTA *and the* CHORUS.]
Strangers, please, I wonder if you could lead us
to the palace of the king . . . I think it's Oedipus.
Better, the man himself—you know where he is?

1015   LEADER. This is his palace, stranger. He's inside.
But here is his queen, his wife and mother
of his children.

MESSENGER.   Blessings on you, noble queen,
queen of Oedipus crowned with all your family—
blessings on you always!

1020   JOCASTA. And the same to you, stranger, you deserve it . . .
such a greeting. But what have you come for?
Have you brought us news?

MESSENGER.   Wonderful news—
for the house, my lady, for your husband too.

JOCASTA. Really, what? Who sent you?

MESSENGER.   Corinth.
1025 I'll give you the message in a moment.
      You'll be glad of it—how could you help it?—
      though it costs a little sorrow in the bargain.

JOCASTA. What can it be, with such a double edge?

MESSENGER. The people there, they want to make your
      Oedipus
1030 king of Corinth, so they're saying now.

JOCASTA. Why? Isn't old Polybus still in power?

MESSENGER. No more. Death has got him in the tomb.

JOCASTA. What are you saying? Polybus, dead?—dead?

MESSENGER.   If not,
      if I'm not telling the truth, strike me dead too.

1035 JOCASTA. [To a SERVANT.] Quickly, go to your master, tell
      him this!

      You prophecies of the gods, where are you now?
      This is the man that Oedipus feared for years,
      he fled him, not to kill him—and now he's dead,
      quite by chance, a normal, natural death,
1040 not murdered by his son.

OEDIPUS. [Emerging from the palace.] Dearest,
      what now? Why call me from the palace?

JOCASTA. [Bringing the MESSENGER closer.] Listen to him, see
      for yourself what all
      those awful prophecies of god have come to.

OEDIPUS. And who is he? What can he have for me?

1045 JOCASTA. He's from Corinth, he's come to tell you
      your father is no more—Polybus—he's dead!

OEDIPUS. [Wheeling on the MESSENGER.] What? Let me have
      it from your lips.

MESSENGER.   Well,
      if that's what you want first, then here it is:
      make no mistake, Polybus is dead and gone.

1050 OEDIPUS. How—murder? sickness?—what? what killed him?

Synthesize *Recall the oracle's prophecy. Why was Oedipus afraid of Polybus?*

MESSENGER.   A light tip of the scales can put old bones to
     rest.°

OEDIPUS.   Sickness then—poor man, it wore him down.

MESSENGER.   That,
     and the long count of years he'd measured out.

OEDIPUS.   So!
     Jocasta, why, why look to the Prophet's hearth,
1055 the fires of the future? Why scan the birds
     that scream above our heads? They winged me on
     to the murder of my father, did they? That was my doom?
     Well look, he's dead and buried, hidden under the earth,
     and here I am in Thebes, I never put hand to sword—
1060 unless some longing for me wasted him away,
     then in a sense you'd say I caused his death.
     But now, all those prophecies I feared—Polybus
     packs them off to sleep with him in hell!
     They're nothing, worthless.

JOCASTA.   There.
1065 Didn't I tell you from the start?

OEDIPUS.   So you did. I was lost in fear.

JOCASTA.   No more, sweep it from your mind forever.

OEDIPUS.   But my mother's bed, surely I must fear—

JOCASTA.   Fear?
     What should a man fear? It's all chance,
1070 chance rules our lives. Not a man on earth
     can see a day ahead, groping through the dark.
     Better to live at **random**, best we can.
     And as for this marriage with your mother—
     have no fear. Many a man before you,
1075 in his dreams, has shared his mother's bed.
     Take such things for shadows, nothing at all—
     Live, Oedipus,
     as if there's no tomorrow!

1051 **A light tip . . . to rest:** refers
to the frailty of old age, in which a
minor illness can be fatal.

The Tragic Vision *How does Jocasta's speech reflect the tragic vision of the
ancient Greeks?*

Vocabulary

random (ran´dəm) *n.* lack of careful choice or plan

OEDIPUS.
                                    Brave words,
    and you'd persuade me if mother
        weren't alive.
1080   But mother lives, so for all your
        reassurances
    I live in fear, I must.

JOCASTA.
                        But your father's death,
    that, at least, is a great blessing,
        joy to the eyes!

OEDIPUS. Great, I know . . . but I fear
    her—she's still alive.

MESSENGER. Wait, who is this woman,
    makes you so afraid?

1085   OEDIPUS. Merope, old man. The wife of
        Polybus.

MESSENGER. The queen? What's there to
    fear in her?

OEDIPUS. A dreadful prophecy, stranger,
    sent by the gods.

MESSENGER. Tell me, could you? Unless it's forbidden
    other ears to hear.

OEDIPUS.   Not at all.
1090   Apollo told me once—it is my fate—
    I must make love with my own mother,
    shed my father's blood with my own hands.
    So for years I've given Corinth a wide berth,
    and it's been my good fortune too. But still,
1095   to see one's parents and look into their eyes
    is the greatest joy I know.

MESSENGER.   You're afraid of that?
    That kept you out of Corinth?

OEDIPUS.   My father, old man—
    so I wouldn't kill my father.

MESSENGER.   So that's it.
    Well then, seeing I came with such good will, my king,
1100   why don't I rid you of that old worry now?

OEDIPUS. What a rich reward you'd have for that.

Oedipe et le Berger (Oedipus and the Shepherd). Honoré Daumier. 65.5 x 50 cm. Private collection.

View the Art This painting of Oedipus as an infant shows Honoré Daumier's talent for capturing movement and light. What feelings does the shepherd seem to have for the baby Oedipus? What details in the painting lead you to this conclusion?

Irony *What is ironic about Jocasta's reaction to Polybus's death?*

The time has come to reveal this once for all.

LEADER. I think he's the very shepherd you wanted to see,
a moment ago. But the queen, Jocasta,
she's the one to say.

1155 OEDIPUS.   Jocasta,
you remember the man we just sent for?
Is *that* the one he means?

JOCASTA.   That man . . .
why ask? Old shepherd, talk, empty nonsense,
don't give it another thought, don't even think—

1160 OEDIPUS. What—give up now, with a clue like this?
Fail to solve the mystery of my birth?
Not for all the world!

JOCASTA.   Stop—in the name of god,
if you love your own life, call off this search!
My suffering is enough.

OEDIPUS.   Courage!
1165 Even if my mother turns out to be a slave,
and I a slave, three generations back,
you would not seem common.

JOCASTA.   Oh no,
listen to me, I beg you, don't do this.

OEDIPUS. Listen to you? No more. I must know it all,
see the truth at last.

1170 JOCASTA.   No, please—
for your sake—I want the best for you!

OEDIPUS. Your best is more than I can bear.°

JOCASTA.   You're doomed—
may you never fathom who you are!

OEDIPUS. [*To a* SERVANT.] Hurry, fetch me the herdsman,
now!
1175 Leave her to glory in her royal birth.

JOCASTA. Aieeeeee—
                    man of agony—
that is the only name I have for you,
that, no other—ever, ever, ever!

1171 Your best . . . I can bear:
Not knowing the truth is unbearable.

Irony *How does Oedipus misread Jocasta's anxiety? What is ironic here?*

The Tragic Vision *Why do you suppose Oedipus has not yet solved the mystery of his identity?*

[Flinging through the palace doors. A long, tense silence follows.]

LEADER. Where's she gone, Oedipus?
1180   Rushing off, such wild grief . . .
I'm afraid that from this silence
something monstrous may come bursting forth.

OEDIPUS. Let it burst! Whatever will, whatever must!
I must know my birth, no matter how common
1185   it may be—must see my origins face-to-face.
She perhaps, she with her woman's pride
may well be mortified by my birth,
but I, I count myself the son of Chance,
the great goddess, giver of all good things—
1190   I'll never see myself disgraced. She is my mother!°
And the moons have marked me out, my blood-brothers,
one moon on the wane, the next moon great with
      power.°
That is my blood, my nature—I will never betray it,
never fail to search and learn my birth!

1195   CHORUS. Yes—if I am a true prophet
            if I can grasp the truth,
      by the boundless skies of Olympus,°
at the full moon of tomorrow, Mount Cithaeron
you will know how Oedipus glories in you—
1200   you, his birthplace, nurse, his mountain-mother!
And we will sing you, dancing out your praise—
you lift our monarch's heart!
      Apollo, Apollo, god of the wild cry
            may our dancing please you!
                        Oedipus—
1205   son, dear child, who bore you?
Who of the nymphs° who seem to live forever
mated with Pan,° the mountain-striding Father?
Who was your mother? who, some bride of Apollo
the god who loves the pastures spreading toward the sun?
1210   Or was it Hermes,° king of the lightning ridges?
Or Dionysus, lord of frenzy, lord of the barren peaks—
did he seize you in his hands, dearest of all his lucky
      finds?—
      found by the nymphs, their warm eyes dancing, gift
to the lord who loves them dancing out his joy!°

1188–1190 I count myself . . . She is my mother: Oedipus believes that he has always had good fortune and therefore has nothing to fear.
1191–1192 the moons . . . great with power: What has seemed to be misfortune has always led to triumph.

1197 by . . . Olympus: by all that is holy.

1205–1214 who bore you . . . dancing out his joy: In mythology, mysterious children often turn out to be the offspring of gods. The Chorus imagines this might be the case with Oedipus.
1206 nymphs: minor female deities who lived in forests, on hills, or in rivers.
1207 Pan: god of fields, forests, and herdsmen, who often was involved romantically with woodland nymphs.
1210 Hermes: god of science, travelers, and vagabonds; pictured with winged helmet and sandals, he was the messenger of the gods.

Irony *How is Oedipus's claim an example of dramatic irony?*

Oedipus and the Shepherd. Olivier Theatre.

[OEDIPUS *strains to see a figure coming from the distance. Attended by* PALACE GUARDS, *an old* SHEPHERD *enters slowly, reluctant to approach the king.*]

1215   OEDIPUS. I never met the man,
my friends . . . still,
    if I had to guess, I'd say
    that's the shepherd,
    the very one we've looked
    for all along.
    Brothers in old age, two
    of a kind,
    he and our guest here.
    At any rate
1220   the ones who bring him in
    are my own men,
    I recognize them.

[*Turning to the* LEADER.]

                 But you
    know more than I,
    you should, you've seen the man before.

  LEADER. I know him, definitely. One of Laius' men,
    a trusty shepherd, if there ever was one.

1225   OEDIPUS. You, I ask you first, stranger,
    you from Corinth—is this the one you mean?

  MESSENGER. You're looking at him. He's your man.

  OEDIPUS. [*To the* SHEPHERD.] You, old man, come over here—
    look at me. Answer all my questions.
    Did you ever serve King Laius?

1230   SHEPHERD.   So I did . . .
    a slave, not bought on the block though,
    born and reared in the palace.

  OEDIPUS. Your duties, your kind of work?

  SHEPHERD. Herding the flocks, the better part of my life.

1235   OEDIPUS. Where, mostly? Where did you do your grazing?

SHEPHERD.   Well,
  Cithaeron sometimes, or the foothills round about.

OEDIPUS. This man—you know him? ever see him there?

SHEPHERD. [*Confused, glancing from the* MESSENGER *to the King.*]
  Doing what?—what man do you mean?

OEDIPUS. [*Pointing to the* MESSENGER.] This one here—ever
  have dealings with him?

1240 SHEPHERD. Not so I could say, but give me a chance,
  my memory's bad . . .

MESSENGER. No wonder he doesn't know me, master.
  But let me refresh his memory for him.
  I'm sure he recalls old times we had

1245 on the slopes of Mount Cithaeron;
  he and I, grazing our flocks, he with two
  and I with one—we both struck up together,
  three whole seasons, six months at a stretch
  from spring to the rising of Arcturus° in the fall,

1250 then with winter coming on I'd drive my herds
  to my own pens, and back he'd go with his
  to Laius' folds.°

  [*To the* SHEPHERD.]

                        Now that's how it was,
  wasn't it—yes or no?

SHEPHERD.   Yes, I suppose . . .
  it's all so long ago.

MESSENGER.   Come, tell me,
1255 you gave me a child back then, a boy, remember?
  A little fellow to rear, my very own.

SHEPHERD. What? Why rake up that again?

MESSENGER. Look, here he is, my fine old friend—
  the same man who was just a baby then.

1260 SHEPHERD. Damn you, shut your mouth—quiet!

OEDIPUS. Don't lash out at him, old man—
  you need lashing° more than he does.

SHEPHERD.   Why,
  master, majesty—what have I done wrong?

OEDIPUS. You won't answer his question about the boy.

1265 SHEPHERD. He's talking nonsense, wasting his breath.

1249 **Arcturus:** a star in the northern sky; its rising, or reappearance, in mid-September signaled the end of summer.
1252 **folds:** enclosure or pen for livestock.

1261–1262 **lash out . . . lashing:** a play on words; **lash out** means "verbally abuse" while **lashing** refers to a whipping.

Irony *Why is the shepherd's response to the messenger so vehement?*

OEDIPUS. So, you won't talk willingly—
    then you'll talk with pain.

[*The* GUARDS *seize the* SHEPHERD.]

SHEPHERD. No, dear god, don't torture an old man!

OEDIPUS. Twist his arms back, quickly!

SHEPHERD.   God help us, why?—
1270   what more do you need to know?

OEDIPUS. Did you give him that child? He's asking.

SHEPHERD. I did . . . I wish to god I'd died that day.

OEDIPUS. You've got your wish if you don't tell the truth.

SHEPHERD. The more I tell, the worse the death I'll die.

1275 OEDIPUS. Our friend here wants to stretch things out,°
        does he?

[*Motioning to his men for torture.*]

SHEPHERD. No, no, I gave it to him—I just said so.

OEDIPUS. Where did you get it? Your house? Someone else's?

SHEPHERD. It wasn't mine, no, I got it from . . . someone.

OEDIPUS. Which one of them?

[*Looking at the citizens.*]

                                      Whose house?

SHEPHERD.   No—
1280   god's sake, master, no more questions!

OEDIPUS. You're a dead man if I have to ask again.

SHEPHERD. Then—the child came from the house . . .
        of Laius.

OEDIPUS.   A slave? or born of his own blood?

SHEPHERD.   Oh no,
        I'm right at the edge, the horrible truth—I've got to say it!

1285 OEDIPUS. And I'm at the edge of hearing horrors, yes, but I
        must hear!

SHEPHERD. All right! His son, they said it was—his son!
        But the one inside, your wife,
        she'd tell it best.

1275 stretch things out: a play on words; in one sense, it means "delay," and in another, it refers to torture—stretching limbs to unnatural limits, as on a rack.

Synthesize *Is Oedipus's treatment of the shepherd out of character? Explain.*

The Tragic Vision *Why does Oedipus insist on hearing the truth, no matter how horrible it might be?*

OEDIPUS. My wife—
1290   *she* gave it to you?

SHEPHERD. Yes, yes, my king.

OEDIPUS. Why, what for?

SHEPHERD. To kill it.

OEDIPUS. Her own child,
1295   how could she?

SHEPHERD. She was afraid—
        frightening prophecies.

OEDIPUS. What?

SHEPHERD.   They said—
        he'd kill his parents.

1300 OEDIPUS. But you gave him to this old man—why?

SHEPHERD. I pitied the little baby, master,
        hoped he'd take him off to his own country,
        far away, but he saved him for this, this fate.
        If you are the man he says you are, believe me,
        you were born for pain.

1305 OEDIPUS.   O god—
        all come true, all burst to light!
        O light—now let me look my last on you!°
        I stand revealed at last—
        cursed in my birth, cursed in marriage,
1310   cursed in the lives I cut down with these hands!

[*Rushing through the doors with a great cry. The Corinthian*
MESSENGER, *the* SHEPHERD *and* ATTENDANTS *exit slowly to the side.*]

CHORUS. O the generations of men
        the dying generations—adding the total
        of all your lives I find they come to nothing . . .
                does there exist, is there a man on earth
1315   who seizes more joy than just a dream, a vision?
        And the vision no sooner dawns than dies
        blazing into **oblivion**.

1307 **O light . . . on you:** let me
die now; it also foreshadows his
own torment.

Irony *What is ironic about the shepherd's simple act of kindness long ago?*

Synthesize *How has the prophecy been fulfilled?*

Vocabulary

oblivion (ə bliv′ē ən) *n.* state of having been forgotten

You are my great example, you, your life,
your destiny, Oedipus, man of misery—
I count no man blest.°

1320   You outranged all men!
     Bending your bow to the breaking-point
you captured priceless glory, O dear god,
and the Sphinx came crashing down,
                         the virgin, claws hooked
1325 like a bird of omen singing, shrieking death—
like a fortress reared in the face of death
you rose and saved our land.

     From that day on we called you king
we crowned you with honors, Oedipus, towering over all—
1330 mighty king of the seven gates of Thebes.
But now to hear your story—is there a man more
     agonized?
More wed to pain and frenzy? Not a man on earth,
the joy of your life ground down to nothing
O Oedipus, name for the ages—
1335   one and the same wide harbor served you
                         son and father both
son and father came to rest in the same bridal chamber.
How, how could the furrows your father plowed
bear you, your agony, harrowing° on
in silence O so long?

1340   But now for all your power
Time, all-seeing Time has dragged you to the light,
judged your marriage monstrous from the start—
the son and the father tangling, both one—
O child of Laius, would to god
1345   I'd never seen you, never never!
     Now I weep like a man who wails the dead
and the dirge comes pouring forth with all my heart!
I tell you the truth, you gave me life
my breath leapt up in you
1350 and now you bring down night upon my eyes.°

[Enter a MESSENGER from the palace.]

MESSENGER. Men of Thebes, always first in honor,

1311–1320 O the generations . . .
I count no man blest: The human
struggle is pointless, and happiness
is just a fleeting illusion; the fate of
Oedipus is a perfect example.

1338 **harrowing:** a play on words;
in one sense, it means "cultivating
soil," and in another, it means
"vexing or tormenting."

1348–1350 **you gave me . . .
upon my eyes:** You saved Thebes,
and now you have caused its ruin.

The Tragic Vision *How does the chorus feel about Oedipus's downfall?*

Oedipus abandoned on Mount Cithaeron by the shepherd. 3rd century AD. Ancient Rome. Marble relief from a sarcophagus. Catican Museums, Vatican State.

View the Art This relief was used to decorate a sarcophagus, a type of coffin that was popular with upper-class members of Greco-Roman society. What is the mood of this relief, and how does it parallel the mood at this point in the play?

          what horrors you will hear, what you will see,
          what a heavy weight of sorrow you will shoulder . . .
          if you are true to your birth, if you still have
1355   some feeling for the royal house of Thebes.
          I tell you neither the waters of the Danube
          nor the Nile can wash this palace clean.
          Such things it hides, it soon will bring to light—
          terrible things, and none done blindly now,
1360   all done with a will. The pains
          we **inflict** upon ourselves hurt most of all.

    LEADER. God knows we have pains enough already.
        What can you add to them?

    MESSENGER. The queen is dead.

    LEADER.   Poor lady—how?

1365 MESSENGER. By her own hand. But you are spared the worst,
        you never had to watch . . . I saw it all,
        and with all the memory that's in me
        you will learn what that poor woman suffered.

        Once she'd broken in through the gates,
1370   dashing past us, frantic, whipped to fury,

Vocabulary

inflict (in flikt′) *v.* to give or cause

ripping her hair out with both hands—
straight to her rooms she rushed, flinging herself
across the bridal-bed, doors slamming behind her—
once inside, she wailed for Laius, dead so long,
1375 remembering how she bore his child long ago,
the life that rose up to destroy him, leaving
its mother to mother living creatures
with the very son she'd borne.
Oh how she wept, mourning the marriage-bed
1380 where she let loose that double brood—monsters—
husband by her husband, children by her child.

                                        And then—
but how she died is more than I can say. Suddenly
Oedipus burst in, screaming, he stunned us so
we couldn't watch her agony to the end,
1385 our eyes were fixed on him. Circling
like a maddened beast, stalking, here, there,
crying out to us—
                        Give him a sword! His wife,
no wife, his mother, where can he find the mother earth
that cropped two crops at once, himself and all his
    children?
1390 He was raging—one of the dark powers pointing the way,
none of us mortals crowding around him, no,
with a great shattering cry—someone, something leading
    him on—
he hurled at the twin doors and bending the bolts back
out of their sockets, crashed through the chamber.
1395 And there we saw the woman hanging by the neck,
cradled high in a woven noose, spinning,
swinging back and forth. And when he saw her,
giving a low, wrenching sob that broke our hearts,
slipping the halter° from her throat, he eased her down,   1399 **halter:** rope or strap.
1400 in a slow embrace he laid her down, poor thing . . .
then, what came next, what horror we beheld!

He rips off her brooches, the long gold pins
holding her robes—and lifting them high,
looking straight up into the points,
1405 he digs them down the sockets of his eyes, crying, "You,
you'll see no more the pain I suffered, all the pain
    I caused!

Too long you looked on the ones you never should
    have seen,°
blind to the ones you longed to see, to know!° Blind
from this hour on! Blind in the darkness—blind!"

1410   His voice like a dirge, rising, over and over
raising the pins, raking them down his eyes.
And at each stroke blood spurts from the roots,
splashing his beard, a swirl of it, nerves and clots—
black hail of blood pulsing, gushing down.

1415   These are the griefs that burst upon them both,
coupling man and woman. The joy they had so lately,
the fortune of their old ancestral house
was deep joy indeed. Now, in this one day,
wailing, madness and doom, death, disgrace,
1420   all the griefs in the world that you can name,
all are theirs forever.

       LEADER.   Oh poor man, the misery—
has he any rest from pain now?

[A voice within, in torment.]

       MESSENGER.   He's shouting,
"Loose the bolts, someone, show me to all of Thebes!
My father's murderer, my mother's——"
1425   No, I can't repeat it, it's unholy.
Now he'll tear himself from his native earth,°
not linger, curse the house with his own curse.
But he needs strength, and a guide to lead him on.
This is sickness more than he can bear.

[The palace doors open.]

                                  Look,
1430   he'll show you himself. The great doors are opening—
you are about to see a sight, a horror
even his mortal enemy would pity.

[Enter OEDIPUS, blinded, led by a boy. He stands at the palace steps,
as if surveying his people once again.]

       CHORUS.   O the terror—
the suffering, for all the world to see,
the worst terror that ever met my eyes.
1435   What madness swept over you? What god,

1407 the ones you never should have seen: Laius as his victim and Jocasta as his wife.
1408 the ones you longed . . . to know: Laius and Jocasta as his parents.

1426 tear . . . his native earth: leave Thebes.

Synthesize *Who called Oedipus blind earlier in the play? What might Oedipus gain though he has lost his physical sight?*

what dark power leapt beyond all bounds,
beyond belief, to crush your wretched life?—
godforsaken, cursed by the gods!
I pity you but I can't bear to look.
1440   I've much to ask, so much to learn,
so much fascinates my eyes,
but you . . . I shudder at the sight.

OEDIPUS.   Oh, Ohh—
the agony! I am agony—
where am I going? where on earth?
1445   where does all this agony hurl me?
where's my voice?—
    winging, swept away on a dark tide—
My destiny, my dark power, what a leap you made!

CHORUS. To the depths of terror, too dark to hear, to see.

1450 OEDIPUS. Dark, horror of darkness
my darkness, drowning, swirling around me
crashing wave on wave—unspeakable, irresistible
    headwind, fatal harbor! Oh again,
the misery, all at once, over and over
1455 the stabbing daggers, stab of memory
raking me insane.

CHORUS.   No wonder you suffer
twice over, the pain of your wounds,
the lasting grief of pain.

OEDIPUS.   Dear friend, still here?
Standing by me, still with a care for me,
1460   the blind man? Such compassion,
    loyal to the last. Oh it's you,
I know you're here, dark as it is
I'd know you anywhere, your voice—
it's yours, clearly yours.

CHORUS.   Dreadful, what you've done . . .
1465 how could you bear it, gouging out your eyes?
What superhuman power drove you on?

OEDIPUS. Apollo, friends, Apollo—
he ordained my agonies—these, my pains on pains!
    But the hand that struck my eyes was mine,
1470   mine alone—no one else—

The Tragic Vision *What images does Sophocles use in these lines to convey Oedipus's overwhelming suffering?*

I did it all myself!
What good were eyes to me?
Nothing I could see could bring me joy.

CHORUS. No, no, exactly as you say.

OEDIPUS.   What can I ever see?
1475   What love, what call of the heart
can touch my ears with joy? Nothing, friends.
Take me away, far, far from Thebes,
quickly, cast me away, my friends—
this great murderous ruin, this man cursed to heaven,
1480   the man the deathless gods hate most of all!

CHORUS. Pitiful, you suffer so, you understand so much . . .
I wish you'd never known.

OEDIPUS.   Die, die—
whoever he was that day in the wilds
who cut my ankles free of the ruthless pins,
1485   he pulled me clear of death, he saved my life
for this, this kindness—
Curse him, kill him!
If I'd died then, I'd never have dragged myself,
my loved ones through such hell.

CHORUS. Oh if only . . . would to god.

1490 OEDIPUS.   I'd never have come to this,
my father's murderer—never been branded
mother's husband, all men see me now! Now,
loathed by the gods, son of the mother I defiled
coupling in my father's bed, spawning lives in the loins
1495 that spawned my wretched life. What grief can crown this
grief?
It's mine alone, my destiny—I am Oedipus!

CHORUS. How can I say you've chosen for the best?
Better to die than be alive and blind.

OEDIPUS. What I did was best—don't lecture me,
1500   no more advice. I, with *my* eyes,
how could I look my father in the eyes
when I go down to death? Or mother, so abused . . .
I have done such things to the two of them,
crimes too huge for hanging.
Worse yet,

Synthesize *Whom does Oedipus curse?*

1505   the sight of my children, born as they were born,
    how could I long to look into their eyes?
    No, not with these eyes of mine, never.
    Not this city either, her high towers,
    the sacred glittering images of her gods—
1510   I am misery! I, her best son, reared
    as no other son of Thebes was ever reared,
    I've stripped myself, I gave the command myself.°
    All men must cast away the great blasphemer,°
    the curse now brought to light by the gods,
1515   the son of Laius—I, my father's son!

    Now I've exposed my guilt, **horrendous** guilt,
    could I train a level glance on you,° my countrymen?
    Impossible! No, if I could just block off my ears,
    the springs° of hearing, I would stop at nothing—
1520   I'd wall up my loathsome body like a prison,
    blind to the sound of life, not just the sight.
    Oblivion—what a blessing . . .
    for the mind to dwell a world away from pain.

    O Cithaeron, why did you give me shelter?
1525   Why didn't you take me, crush my life out on the spot?
    I'd never have revealed my birth to all mankind.

    O Polybus, Corinth, the old house of my fathers,
    so I believed—what a handsome prince you raised—
    under the skin, what sickness to the core.
1530   Look at me! Born of outrage, outrage to the core.

    O triple roads—it all comes back, the secret,
    dark ravine, and the oaks closing in
    where the three roads join . . .
    You drank my father's blood, my own blood
1535   spilled by my own hands—you still remember me?
    What things you saw me do? Then I came here
    and did them all once more!
                Marriages! O marriage,
    you gave me birth, and once you brought me into

1512 I've stripped . . . command myself: Oedipus issued the proclamation that decreed the murderer's punishment.

1513 blasphemer: one who has shown contempt for something sacred.

1517 train a level glance on you: look you in the eye.

1519 springs: here, source.

Synthesize *How has Oedipus kept the promise he made to his people at the beginning of the play?*

Vocabulary

horrendous (hô ren′dəs) *adj.* horrible; frightful

the world
you brought my sperm rising back, springing to light
1540   fathers, brothers, sons—one murderous breed—
brides, wives, mothers. The blackest things
a man can do, I have done them all!

                                    No more—
it's wrong to name what's wrong to do. Quickly,
for the love of god, hide me somewhere,
1545   kill me, hurl me into the sea
where you can never look on me again.

[Beckoning to the CHORUS as they shrink away.]

                                    Closer,
it's all right. Touch the man of sorrow.
Do. Don't be afraid. My troubles are mine
and I am the only man alive who can sustain° them.

1549 sustain: here, suffer; Oedipus is suggesting that his troubles are not contagious and cannot be transmitted to others by touch.

[Enter CREON from the palace, attended by palace GUARDS.]

1550   LEADER. Put your requests to Creon. Here he is,
just when we need him. He'll have a plan, he'll act.
Now that he's the sole defense of the country
in your place.

OEDIPUS.   Oh no, what can I say to him?
How can I ever hope to win his trust?
1555   I wronged him so, just now, in every way.
You must see that—I was so wrong, so wrong.

CREON. I haven't come to mock you, Oedipus,
or to criticize your former failings.

[Turning to the GUARDS.]

                                    You there,
have you lost all respect for human feeling?
1560   At least revere the Sun, the holy fire
that keeps us all alive. Never expose a thing
of guilt and holy dread so great it appalls
the earth, the rain from heaven, the light of day!
Get him into the halls—quickly as you can.
1565   Piety° demands no less. Kindred alone
should see a kinsman's shame. This is obscene.

OEDIPUS. Please, in god's name . . . you wipe my fears away,
coming so generously° to me, the worst of men.
Do one thing more, for your sake, not mine.

1565 Piety: loyalty to natural or fundamental obligations, often used with respect to religious devotion.

1568 coming so generously: Creon's kindness goes beyond what Oedipus has any right to expect.

Synthesize Why does the kingship now pass to Creon?

1570 CREON. What do you want? Why so insistent?

OEDIPUS. Drive me out of the land at once, far from sight,
where I can never hear a human voice.

CREON. I'd have done that already, I promise you.
First I wanted the god to clarify my duties.

1575 OEDIPUS. The god? His command was clear, every word:
death for the father-killer, the curse—
he said destroy me!

CREON. So he did. Still, in such a crisis
it's better to ask precisely what to do.

1580 OEDIPUS. You'd ask the oracle about a man like me?°

CREON. By all means. And this time, I assume,
even you will obey the god's decrees.

OEDIPUS.   I will,
I will. And you, I command you—I beg you . . .
the woman inside, bury her as you see fit.

1585 It's the only decent thing,
to give your own the last rites. As for me,
never condemn the city of my fathers
to house my body, not while I'm alive, no,
let me live on the mountains, on Cithaeron,

1590 my favorite haunt, I have made it famous.
Mother and father marked out that rock
to be my everlasting tomb—buried alive.
Let me die there, where they tried to kill me.

Oh but this I know: no sickness can destroy me,

1595 nothing can. I would never have been saved
from death—I have been saved
for something great and terrible, something strange.
Well let my destiny come and take me on its way!

About my children, Creon, the boys at least,

1600 don't burden yourself. They're men;°
wherever they go, they'll find the means to live.
But my two daughters, my poor helpless girls,
clustering at our table, never without me
hovering near them . . . whatever I touched,

1605 they always had their share. Take care of them,
I beg you. Wait, better—permit me, would you?

1580 ask the oracle . . . me: refers to the practice of consulting oracles only for matters of utmost importance. Oedipus now thinks he is unworthy; ironic, because the oracle has already played a large role in Oedipus's life.

1600 They're men: refers to the boys' gender and the opportunities open to males in ancient Greek society; it is not a reference to their age.

The Tragic Vision *How has Oedipus's attitude toward his fate changed?*

Just to touch them with my hands and take
our fill of tears. Please . . . my king.
Grant it, with all your noble heart.
1610 If I could hold them, just once, I'd think
I had them with me, like the early days
when I could see their eyes.

[ANTIGONE *and* ISMENE, *two small children, are led in from the palace*
by a nurse.]

                                        What's that?
O god! Do I really hear you sobbing?—
my two children. Creon, you've pitied me?
1615 Sent me my darling girls, my own flesh and blood!
Am I right?

CREON.   Yes, it's my doing.
I know the joy they gave you all these years,
the joy you must feel now.

OEDIPUS.   Bless you, Creon!
May god watch over you for this kindness,
better than he ever guarded me.
1620   Children, where are you?
Here, come quickly—

[*Groping for* ANTIGONE *and* ISMENE, *who approach their father*
cautiously, then embrace him.]

                        Come to these hands of mine,
your brother's hands, your own father's hands°
that served his once bright eyes so well—
that made them blind. Seeing nothing, children,
1625 knowing nothing, I became your father,
I fathered you in the soil that gave me life.

How I weep for you—I cannot see you now . . .
just thinking of all your days to come, the bitterness,
the life that rough mankind will thrust upon you.
1630 Where are the public gatherings you can join,
the banquets of the clans? Home you'll come,
in tears, cut off from the sight of it all,
the brilliant rites unfinished.
And when you reach perfection, ripe for marriage,
1635 who will he be, my dear ones? Risking all
to shoulder the curse that weighs down my parents,
yes and you too—that wounds us all together.

1622 your brother's . . . father's
hands: because Oedipus married
his mother and had children with
her, these children are both sisters
and daughters to him.

Synthesize *How might Sophocles' audience, who would have known the future*
misfortune of Oedipus's daughters, have responded to these lines?

What more misery could you want?
Your father killed his father, sowed his mother,
1640   one, one and the selfsame womb sprang you—
he cropped the very roots of his existence.°

Such disgrace, and you must bear it all!
Who will marry you then? Not a man on earth.
Your doom is clear: you'll wither away to nothing,
single, without a child.

[*Turning to* CREON.]

1645   Oh Creon,
you are the only father they have now . . .
we who brought them into the world
are gone, both gone at a stroke—
Don't let them go begging, abandoned,
1650   women without men. Your own flesh and blood!
Never bring them down to the level of my pains.
Pity them. Look at them, so young, so **vulnerable**,
shorn of everything—you're their only hope.
Promise me, noble Creon, touch my hand.

[*Reaching toward* CREON, *who draws back.*]

1655   You, little ones, if you were old enough
to understand, there is much I'd tell you.
Now, as it is, I'd have you say a prayer.
Pray for life, my children,
live where you are free to grow and season.°
1660   Pray god you find a better life than mine,
the father who begot you.

CREON.   Enough.
You've wept enough. Into the palace now.

OEDIPUS.   I must, but I find it very hard.

CREON.   Time is the great healer, you will see.

1665   OEDIPUS.   I am going—you know on what condition?

CREON.   Tell me. I'm listening.

OEDIPUS.   Drive me out of Thebes, in exile.

CREON.   Not I. Only the gods can give you that.

1641 cropped . . . existence: fathered children by his own mother.

1659 season: mature; age properly.

Synthesize *What does this plea suggest about the position of women in ancient Greek society?*

Vocabulary

vulnerable (vul′nər ə bəl) *adj.* weak; unable to defend oneself

OEDIPUS. Surely the gods
hate me so much—

CREON. You'll get your
wish at once.

1670 OEDIPUS.
You consent?

CREON. I try to say what
I mean; it's my habit.

OEDIPUS. Then take me
away. It's time.

CREON. Come along, let
go of the children.

OEDIPUS.
No—
don't take them away
from me, not now!
No no no!

[*Clutching his daughters as the* GUARDS *wrench them loose and take
them through the palace doors.*]

1675 CREON. Still the king, the master of all things?
No more: here your power ends.
None of your power follows you through life.

[*Exit* OEDIPUS *and* CREON *to the palace. The* CHORUS *comes forward
to address the audience directly.*]

CHORUS. People of Thebes, my countrymen, look on
Oedipus.
He solved the famous riddle with his brilliance,
1680 he rose to power, a man beyond all power.
Who could behold his greatness without envy?
Now what a black sea of terror has overwhelmed him.
Now as we keep our watch and wait the final day,°
count no man happy till he dies, free of pain at last.°

[*Exit in procession.*]

Head of Oedipus, 2nd-3rd
century AD. Relief on a
Roman mausoleum.

Rheinisches Landesmuseum,
Trier, Germany.

1683 watch: period of time
during which a person is employed
to protect someone or something.
keep . . . final day: try to live
our lives in keeping with honor
and duty.
1684 count no man . . . at last:
Do not call any man happy until
he dies, because up until that
point his fate is unknown and no
one can predict what the future
holds in store.

The Tragic Vision *Why do you think Sophocles includes this final detail about Oedipus?*

The Tragic Vision *In what way do the chorus's final lines summarize the tragic vision?*

After You Read

Respond and Think Critically

Respond and Interpret

1. What was your reaction to the end of the play?

2. (a)What does the messenger tell Oedipus about his birth? (b)At this point, what is the worst outcome Oedipus foresees?

3. (a)Why does Jocasta try to prevent Oedipus from questioning the shepherd? (b)Why do you think Jocasta kills herself?

4. How does Oedipus explain his decision to blind himself?

Analyze and Evaluate

5. Do you think Oedipus should have figured out the truth about his past sooner? Explain.

6. In your opinion, should Oedipus be banished from Thebes? Explain.

7. What do you predict will happen to Thebes after Oedipus's fall from power?

8. In a dramatic work, the **climax** is the point of greatest interest or emotional intensity. What is the climax of *Oedipus the King*?

Connect

9. **Big Idea** **The Tragic Vision** In your opinion, is Oedipus responsible for his downfall, or is he a victim of fate? Explain.

10. **Connect to Today** How might the experiences of a modern audience at a performance of *Oedipus the King* differ from those of Sophocles' original audience?

Daily Life & Culture

The Delphic Oracle

The ancient Greeks believed the gods revealed the future in mysterious ways. The most important shrine of the gods was the oracle at Delphi, sacred to Apollo. An oracle was a priest or priestess who reported the responses of a god to human petitioners. (The word *oracle* also referred to the response itself and to the shrine of the god.) Delphi, now a famous archaeological site, is located on the lower plateau of Mount Parnassus in central Greece. Apollo was thought to convey his messages to a priestess, known as the Pythia, while she experienced an ecstatic trance. An official interpreter wrote down her frenzied prophecies, which were cryptic and open to conflicting interpretations.

Consulting the god Apollo at Delphi, vase fragment, 4th century BC. Classical Greek. Museo Nazionale Taranto, Italy.

Group Activity Discuss the following questions in a small group.

1. To what extent are the actions and reactions of the characters in this play dependent on oracular prophesies?

2. What are some examples of prophecy in today's society?

Literary Element | Irony

ACT Skills Practice

Why is it ironic that Oedipus forces the shepherd to speak?

A. Jocasta tries to prevent Oedipus from doing it.

B. The shepherd is unwilling to tell what he knows.

C. The shepherd's revelations will destroy Oedipus.

D. The chorus warns Oedipus not to do it.

Review: Tragedy

As you learned on page 274, a **tragedy** is a play in which the main character is brought to ruin or suffers a great sorrow. The **tragic hero** is typically a person of dignified or heroic stature whose downfall is at least partly caused by a flaw or an error in judgment.

Partner Activity Meet with another classmate to discuss how you would rate each statement below. Use this rating system:

strongly disagree	disagree	agree	strongly agree
★	★★	★★★	★★★★

Support your ratings with evidence from the play.

1. Oedipus should have remained in Corinth.

2. Oedipus should never have murdered anyone.

3. Oedipus's tragic flaw is excessive pride, or *hubris.*

LOG ON ▶ **Literature** Online

Selection Resources For Selection Quizzes, eFlash-cards, and Reading-Writing Connection activities, go to glencoe.com and enter QuickPass code GLW6053u2.

Reading Strategy | Synthesize

Synthesizing details, sidenote information, biographical and cultural information, and your own prior knowledge can help you interpret a drama. Review the chart you made on page 291 and answer the following questions.

1. When were the seeds of Oedipus's downfall originally sown?

2. Violent events in classical Greek drama almost always occurred offstage. How would the effect of Oedipus's blinding have been different for the audience if it had been shown on stage?

Vocabulary Practice

Practice with Word Origins Create a word map, like the one below, for each boldfaced vocabulary word. Use a dictionary for help.

random	oblivion	inflict
horrendous	vulnerable	

EXAMPLE:

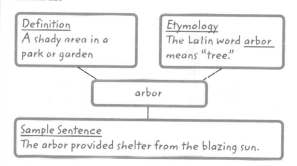

> **Definition**
> A shady area in a park or garden
>
> **Etymology**
> The Latin word *arbor* means "tree."
>
> **arbor**
>
> **Sample Sentence**
> The arbor provided shelter from the blazing sun.

Academic Vocabulary

*Based on a **hypothesis** he forms, Oedipus accuses Creon of conspiracy.*

Hypothesis is an academic word. Familiar words that are similar in meaning include *theory* and *assumption.* To further explore the meaning of this word, answer the following question: If you were a detective trying to solve a crime, how might you develop a **hypothesis**?

For more on academic vocabulary, see pages 36–37 and R83–R85.

Respond Through Writing

Expository Essay

Learning Objectives

In this assignment, you will focus on the following objectives:

Writing: Writing an expository essay.

Grammar: Understanding ellipsis points.

Analyze Irony Sophocles' mastery of dramatic irony is evident in *Oedipus the King*, a timeless tragedy. In an essay, analyze Sophocles' use of dramatic irony and describe its overall effect. Support your ideas with examples from the text.

Understand the Task Dramatic irony occurs when the reader or audience knows something important a character does not know.

Prewrite Before you begin to write, fill out a chart like the one below. Add as many rows as you need.

Example	Ironic Meaning	Effect on Reader
"Oedipus . . . what do you know?" (line 54)	The chorus asks Oedipus for knowledge, but he doesn't even know who he is.	The reader senses the people of Thebes are in terrible danger.

Draft Formulate a clear thesis, supported by valid and relevant evidence. Develop an engaging introduction, a body, and a conclusion. Use smooth transitions to build coherence. Your body paragraphs should provide examples of dramatic irony and describe their effect on the reader. You may find it helpful to use sentence frames as you write. For example, you might state your thesis as follows.

In Oedipus the King, *Sophocles' use of dramatic irony creates an overall effect of _____.*

Revise Exchange papers with a classmate and evaluate each other's essays. Does the writer clearly state and support a thesis? Are there accurate and detailed references to the text? Provide comments for your partner and revise your essay according to his or her comments.

Edit and Proofread Proofread your paper, correcting any errors in grammar, spelling, and punctuation. Use the Grammar Tip in the side column to help you with using ellipsis points in quoted material.

> **Grammar Tip**
>
> ### Ellipsis Points
>
> Ellipsis points, or a series of three spaced periods, indicate the omission of material from a quotation. For example, notice the ellipses in the following quotation from lines 150–159 of the play:
>
> *"I'll bring it all to light myself! . . . by avenging Laius / I defend myself."*
>
> The ellipses sharpen the focus of the quotation, highlighting the irony.
>
> Use three ellipsis points if the omitted material occurs at the beginning of a sentence. If the omitted material is in the middle or at the end of a sentence, use any necessary punctuation plus the ellipsis points.

Vocabulary Workshop

Jargon

Literature Connection In the following quotation from *The Poetics*, Aristotle uses Oedipus as an example of the ideal type of tragic hero, whose downfall is the result of what he calls *hamartia*.

> *"There remains, then, the intermediate kind of personage, a man not eminently virtuous and just, whose misfortune, however, is brought upon him not by wickedness or worthlessness but through some* hamartia.*"*

What does the term *hamartia* mean? Context clues can provide some help. In the above sentence, *hamartia* is contrasted with "wickedness" and "worthlessness"; therefore the word does not refer to immorality. If you check in a dictionary, you will see *hamartia* is often translated as "tragic flaw" or "tragic mistake."

Such technical terms specific to a particular trade or field are called **jargon**. Because Aristotle's study of tragedy has been very influential, *hamartia* has become an important term in dramatic criticism. When you first encounter such technical terms in a passage, you will often be provided with an appositive definition. For example, *"Greek theater had its origin in the* dithyramb, *a hymn sung in honor of the god Dionysus."*

Law and medicine are two fields that use jargon.

Legal Jargon	Medical Jargon
sidebar—conference between opposing lawyers and the judge during a trial	**meds**—medications or drugs
nolo—short for nolo contendere, plea by which a defendant admits guilt	**crash cart**—wheeled hospital cart with basic equipment necessary to save someone's life in an emergency

Practice Identify the jargon pertaining to drama in each of the following sentences. Then write what you think each of these technical terms might mean. Check your guesses in a dictionary.

1. Oedipus, the protagonist of Sophocles' play, is king of Thebes.
2. Like many tragic heroes, the proud, reckless Oedipus suffers from hubris.
3. Behind the acting area was the skene, which served as the permanent setting for all plays.

Learning Objectives

In studying this workshop, you will focus on the following objective:

Vocabulary: Understanding jargon.

Jargon

Jargon is the specialized or technical language of a trade.

Test-Taking Tip

When you encounter unfamiliar jargon in a text, first check to see if an appositive definition is provided. Then look for clues in the subject of the text and the context of the sentence.

LOG ON ▶ **Literature** Online

Vocabulary For more vocabulary practice, go to glencoe.com and enter QuickPass code GLW6053u2.

Before You Read

Pericles' Funeral Oration

Meet **Thucydides**
(c. 460–c. 404 B.C.)

One of the greatest historians of the Western world was also one of the first—Thucydides (thoo̅ sid′ə dēz′). Little is known about his life; even the dates of his birth and death must be inferred from references in his writing. He was likely born in or near Athens to a wealthy, upper-class family. In 424 B.C., Thucydides was elected one of the ten *strategoi*, or high-ranking military leaders, of the year. He was put in command of the Athenian fleet based in the northern Aegean Sea. His responsibility was to defend the city of Amphipolis. When the Spartans captured the city, Thucydides was sent into exile. He returned to Athens after the war ended and is believed to have died shortly thereafter.

ended with the defeat of Athens in 404 B.C. and the eclipse of Athenian civilization.

Thucydides, who began this work just before 431 B.C., told his readers he believed the war would be "more worthy of relation than any that had preceded it." In his attempt to present an accurate account, he interviewed participants and eyewitnesses from both sides, sifted through statements others had made, and presented his results in concise, chronological order. He often reported the exact words of significant political speeches, including Pericles' funeral oration. Thucydides is celebrated as the first historian to apply truly rigorous standards of accuracy to his work.

Thucydides never completed the *History*: his account stops abruptly more than six years before the war ended. This abruptness has led to speculation that he may have died suddenly—and perhaps violently—a victim of social upheaval after the war.

> "I shall be content if [the History of the Peloponnesian War] is judged useful by those inquirers who desire an exact knowledge of the past as an aid to the interpretation of the future . . ."
>
> —Thucydides from Book I,
> *History of the Peloponnesian War*

His Life's Work Thucydides' *History of the Peloponnesian War*, his life's work, narrates the conflict between Athens and Sparta in the fifth century B.C. At that time Greece was a collection of city-states, each with its own government and sphere of influence. The struggle

LOG ON **Literature** Online

Author Search For more about Thucydides, go to glencoe.com and enter QuickPass code GLW6053u2.

Literature and Reading Preview

Connect to the Speech

Why do some speeches continue to inspire people through the ages? Write a journal entry in which you describe the qualities of a memorable speech you have heard or read.

Build Background

The most powerful city-state in Greece in the fifth century B.C. was Athens. The enduring achievements of Athens owe much to the leadership of Pericles, who was elected more than fifteen times to the office of general. Shortly after the outbreak of the war with Sparta in 431 B.C., Pericles delivered this eulogy to honor those slain in battle.

Set Purposes for Reading

Big Idea The Heroic Ideal

As you read, notice how Pericles' eulogy reflects the heroic ideal of the ancient Greeks. Ask yourself, What qualities does Pericles consider heroic?

Literary Element Argument

Argument is a type of persuasive writing or speaking in which reason is used to influence ideas or actions. Pericles includes several arguments in his eulogy to the Athenian war dead. As you read, ask yourself, What is his purpose for including them?

Reading Strategy Analyze Rhetorical Devices

Rhetoric is the art of using language to present facts and ideas to persuade an audience. **Rhetorical devices** are techniques speakers and authors use to evoke an emotional response in the audience. Rhetorical devices include the use of repetition, connotative words, parallelism, and emotional appeals.

Tip: Take Notes In a chart like the one below, identify examples of rhetorical devices as you read the eulogy.

Example	Rhetorical Devices	Purpose
the words "honor," "courage," and "valiant/valiantly"	Connotative words and repetition	To reinforce the idea of Athenian nobility and the justness of its cause

Learning Objectives

For pages 320–332

In studying this text, you will focus on the following objectives:

Literary Study: Analyzing argument.

Reading: Analyzing rhetorical devices.

Listening and Speaking: Delivering a speech.

Vocabulary

incredulous (in krej′ə ləs) *adj.* doubting; skeptical; p. 323 *The incredulous crowd doubted the speaker's foolish claims.*

versatility (vur′sə til′ə tē) *n.* ability to do many things well; p. 326 *The athlete showed versatility by excelling in several sports.*

tangible (tan′jə bəl) *adj.* real; actual; definite; p. 326 *The guard saw tangible evidence of damage.*

consummation (kon′sə mā′shən) *n.* end; completion; p. 327 *The author's consummation of his life's work was a trilogy of novels.*

commiserate (kə miz′ə rāt′) *v.* sympathize with; pity; p. 329 *I can commiserate with you during this difficult time.*

Our constitution is called a democracy because power is in the hands **not of a minority but of the whole people.**

However, the fact is that this institution was set up and approved by our forefathers, and it is my duty to follow the tradition and do my best to meet the wishes and the expectations of every one of you.

'I shall begin by speaking about our ancestors, since it is only right and proper on such an occasion to pay them the honor of recalling what they did. In this land of ours there have always been the same people living from generation to generation up till now, and they, by their courage and their virtues, have handed it on to us, a free country. They certainly deserve our praise. Even more so do our fathers deserve it. For to the inheritance they had received they added all the empire we have now, and it was not without blood and toil that they handed it down to us of the present generation. And then we ourselves, assembled here today, who are mostly in the prime of life, have, in most directions, added to the power of our empire and have organized our State in such a way that it is perfectly well able to look after itself both in peace and in war.

'I have no wish to make a long speech on subjects familiar to you all: so I shall say nothing about the warlike deeds by which we acquired our power or the battles in which we or our fathers gallantly[4] resisted our enemies, Greek or foreign. What I want to do is, in the first place, to discuss the spirit in which we faced our trials and also our constitution and the way of life which has made us great. After that I shall speak in praise of the dead, believing that this kind of speech is not inappropriate to the present occasion, and that this whole assembly, of citizens and foreigners, may listen to it with advantage.

'Let me say that our system of government does not copy the institutions of our neighbors. It is more the case of our being a model to others, than of our imitating anyone else. Our constitution is called a democracy because power is in the hands not of a minority but of the whole people. When it is a question of settling private disputes, everyone is equal before the law; when it is a question of putting one person before another in positions of public responsibility, what counts is not membership of a particular class, but the actual ability which the man possesses. No one, so long as he has it in him to be of service to the state, is kept in political obscurity because of poverty. And, just as our political life is free and open, so is our day-to-day life in our relations with each other. We do not get into a state with our next-door neighbor if he enjoys himself in his own way, nor do we give him the kind of black looks which, though they do no real harm, still do hurt people's feelings. We are free

---

4. *Gallantly* means "nobly or bravely."

Argument *Why is Pericles reluctant to deliver the funeral oration?*

Analyze Rhetorical Devices *How does Pericles appeal to his audience in this passage?*

Argument *What reasons support the claim that the Athenian government is a model to others?*

and tolerant in our private lives; but in public affairs we keep to the law. This is because it commands our deep respect.

'We give our obedience to those whom we put in positions of authority, and we obey the laws themselves, especially those which are for the protection of the oppressed, and those unwritten laws which it is an acknowledged shame to break.

'And here is another point. When our work is over, we are in a position to enjoy all kinds of recreation for our spirits. There are various kinds of contests and sacrifices regularly throughout the year; in our own homes we find a beauty and a good taste which delight us every day and which drive away our cares. Then the greatness of our city brings it about that all the good things from all over the world flow in to us, so that to us it seems just as natural to enjoy foreign goods as our own local products.

'Then there is a great difference between us and our opponents, in our attitude towards military security. Here are some examples: Our city is open to the world, and we have no periodical deportations in order to prevent people observing or finding out secrets which might be of military advantage to the enemy. This is because we rely, not on secret weapons, but on our own real courage and loyalty. There is a difference, too, in our educational systems. The Spartans, from their earliest boyhood, are submitted to the most laborious training in courage; we pass our lives without all these restrictions, and yet are just as ready to face the same dangers as they are. Here is a proof of this: When the Spartans invade our land, they do not come by themselves, but bring all their allies with them; whereas we, when we launch an attack abroad, do the job by ourselves, and, though fighting on foreign soil, do not often fail to defeat opponents who are fighting for their own

hearths and homes. As a matter of fact none of our enemies has ever yet been confronted with our total strength, because we have to divide our attention between our navy and the many missions on which our troops are sent on land. Yet, if our enemies engage a detachment of our forces and defeat it, they give themselves credit for having thrown back our entire army; or, if they lose, they claim that they were beaten by us in full strength. There are certain advantages, I think, in our way of meeting danger voluntarily, with an easy mind, instead of with a laborious training, with natural rather than with state-induced courage. We do not have to spend our time practicing to meet sufferings which are still in the future; and when they are actually upon us we show ourselves just as brave as these others who are always in strict training. This is one point in which, I think, our city deserves to be admired. There are also others:

'Our love of what is beautiful does not lead to extravagance; our love of the things of the mind does not make us soft. We regard wealth as something to be properly used, rather than as something to boast about. As for poverty, no one need be ashamed to admit it: the real shame is in not taking practical measures to escape from it. Here each individual is interested not only in his own affairs but in the affairs of the state as well: even those who are mostly occupied with their own business are extremely well-informed on general politics—this is a peculiarity of ours: we do not say that a man who takes no interest in politics is a man who minds his own business; we say that he has no business here at all. We Athenians, in our own persons, take our decisions on policy or submit them to proper

---

Argument *Reread this paragraph. Why does Pericles consider Athens better militarily than other city-states?*

discussions: for we do not think that there is an incompatibility between words and deeds; the worst thing is to rush into action before the consequences have been properly debated. And this is another point where we differ from other people. We are capable at the same time of taking risks and of estimating them beforehand. Others are brave out of ignorance; and, when they stop to think, they begin to fear. But the man who can most truly be accounted brave is he who best knows the meaning of what is sweet in life and of what is terrible, and then goes out undeterred to meet what is to come.

'Again, in questions of general good feeling there is a great contrast between us and most other people. We make friends by doing good to others, not by receiving good from them. This makes our friendship all the more reliable, since we want to keep alive the gratitude of those who are in our debt by showing continued goodwill to them: whereas the feelings of one who owes us something lack the same enthusiasm, since he knows that, when he repays our kindness, it will be more like paying back a debt than giving something spontaneously. We are unique in this. When we do kindnesses to others, we do not do them out of any calculations of profit or loss: we do them without afterthought, relying on our free liberality. Taking everything together then, I declare that our city is an education to Greece, and I declare that in my opinion each single one of our citizens, in all the manifold⁵ aspects of life, is able to show himself the rightful lord and owner of his own person, and do this, moreover, with exceptional grace and exceptional **versatility**. And to show that this is no empty boasting for the present occasion, but real **tangible** fact, you have only to consider the power which our city possesses and which has been won by those very qualities which I have mentioned. Athens, alone of the states we know, comes to her testing time in a greatness that surpasses what was imagined of her. In her case, and in her case alone, no invading enemy is ashamed at being defeated, and no subject can complain of being governed by people unfit for their responsibilities. Mighty indeed are the marks and monuments of our empire which we have left. Future ages will wonder at us, as the present age wonders at us now. We do not need the praises of a Homer, or of anyone else whose words may delight us for the moment, but whose estimation of facts will fall short of what is really true. For our adventurous spirit has forced an entry into every sea and into every land; and everywhere we have left behind us everlasting memorials of good done to our friends or suffering inflicted on our enemies.

'This, then, is the kind of city for which these men, who could not bear the thought of losing her, nobly fought and nobly died. It is only natural that every one of us who survive them should be willing to undergo hardships in her service. And it was for this reason that I have spoken at such length about our city, because I wanted to make it clear that for us there is more at stake than

---

5. *Manifold* means "of many kinds or parts; many and various."

The Heroic Ideal *What does Pericles consider true heroism?*

Argument *According to Pericles, why is Athens "an education to Greece"?*

Argument *Why should Athenians be willing to sacrifice for Athens?*

Vocabulary

versatility (vur´ sə til´ ə tē) *n.* ability to do many things well

tangible (tan´ jə bəl) *adj.* real; actual; definite

Combat scene, 5th century BC. Marble relief. British Museum, London.

View the Art Why do you think the soldiers in this relief are taking the man on the horse away? How does their action reflect Pericles' view on Athenians?

there is for others who lack our advantages; also I wanted my words of praise for the dead to be set in the bright light of evidence. And now the most important of these words has been spoken. I have sung the praises of our city; but it was the courage and gallantry of these men, and of people like them, which made her splendid. Nor would you find it true in the case of many of the Greeks, as it is true of them, that no words can do more than justice to their deeds.

Analyze Rhetorical Devices *What idea, introduced at the beginning of the speech, does Pericles echo here? What purpose might this repetition serve?*

'To me it seems that the **consummation** which has overtaken these men shows us the meaning of manliness in its first revelation and in its final proof. Some of them, no doubt, had their faults; but what we ought to remember first is their gallant conduct against the enemy in defence of their native land. They have blotted out evil with good, and done more service to the commonwealth than they ever did harm in their private lives. No one of these men weakened because he wanted to go on enjoying his wealth: no one put off the awful day in the

Vocabulary

consummation (kon´sə mā´shən) *n.* end; completion

When one is alive, one is always liable to the jealousy of one's competitors, but when one is out of the way, the honor one receives is
sincere and unchallenged.

present here. Instead I shall try to comfort them. They are well aware that they have grown up in a world where there are many changes and chances. But this is good fortune—for men to end their lives with honor, as these have done, and for you honorably to lament them: their life was set to a measure where death and happiness went hand in hand. I know that it is difficult to convince you of this. When you see other people happy you will often be reminded of what used to make you happy too. One does not feel sad at not having some good thing which is outside one's experience: real grief is felt at the loss of something which one is used to. All the same, those of you who are of the right age must bear up and take comfort in the thought of having more children. In your own homes these new children will prevent you from brooding over those who are no more, and they will be a help to the city, too, both in filling the empty places, and in assuring her security. For it is impossible for a man to put forward fair and honest views about our affairs if he has not, like everyone else, children whose lives may be at stake. As for those of you who are now too old to have children, I would ask you to count as gain the greater part of your life, in which you have been happy, and remember that what remains is not long, and let your hearts be lifted up at the thought of the fair fame of the dead. One's sense of honor is the only thing that does not grow old, and the last pleasure, when one is worn out with age, is not, as the poet said, making money, but having the respect of one's fellow men.

'As for those of you here who are sons or brothers of the dead, I can see a hard struggle in front of you. Everyone always speaks well of the dead, and, even if you rise to the greatest heights of heroism, it will be a hard thing for you to get the reputation of having come near, let alone equalled, their standard. When one is alive, one is always liable[6] to the jealousy of one's competitors, but when one is out of the way, the honor one receives is sincere and unchallenged.

'Perhaps I should say a word or two on the duties of women to those among you who are now widowed. I can say all I have to say in a short word of advice. Your great glory is not to be inferior to what God has made you, and the greatest glory of a woman is to be least talked about by men, whether they are praising you or criticizing you. I have now, as the law demanded, said what I had to say. For the time being our offerings to the dead have been made, and for the future their children will be supported at the public expense by the city, until they come of age. This is the crown and prize which she offers, both to the dead and to their children, for the ordeals which they have faced. Where the rewards of valor are the greatest, there you will find also the best and bravest spirits among the people. And now, when you have mourned for your dear ones, you must depart.' ∾

---

6. *Liable* means "subject to the possibility; susceptible."

Argument *Is Pericles' argument here convincing? Explain.*

After You Read

Respond and Think Critically

Respond and Interpret

1. What passages in this speech impressed you most, and why?

2. (a)Why does Pericles disapprove of the custom of giving a solemn public speech to honor the Athenian war dead? (b)According to Pericles, why do these dead possess the grandest of all sepulchres?

3. (a)How do the Athenians and Spartans differ in their military training? (b)Why do you think Pericles emphasizes these differences?

4. (a)What is the Athenian attitude toward wealth and poverty? (b)Toward participation in public life?

Analyze and Evaluate

5. Ancient Greek culture often promoted the ideal of the "golden mean," referring to moderation and balance in all aspects of life. As described by Pericles, how might the Athenian lifestyle be regarded as an example of this ideal? Cite several examples from the speech.

6. What do Pericles' comments on the women and children in the audience suggest about family life in ancient Athens?

7. Why does Pericles devote so much space in his speech to describing the virtues of Athenians and their city? Explain.

Connect

8. **Big Idea** **The Heroic Ideal** How does Pericles' description of courage and honor illustrate the ancient Greek concept of the heroic ideal?

9. **Connect to Today** How would you compare Pericles' description of Athenian democracy with American democratic government today? Explain.

Literary Element Argument

SAT Skills Practice

According to Pericles, which of the following elements make Athenian society and culture superior?

(A) Athenian government, lifestyle, education, lack of militarism, and philosophy

(B) Athenian government, lifestyle, education, and lack of militarism

(C) Athenian government, lifestyle, education, and architecture

(D) Athenian lifestyle, education, and lack of militarism

(E) Athenian lifestyle, education, and athletics

Review: Tone

As you learned on page 25, **tone** is a reflection of an author's attitude toward his or her subject. Tone may reflect a variety of attitudes, such as sympathy, objectivity, seriousness, bitterness, or humor. Several elements—including diction, imagery, and figures of speech—help convey tone.

Partner Activity Meet with a partner to determine Pericles' tone toward Athens in his funeral oration. Use a web like the one below to identify the elements that help convey the tone.

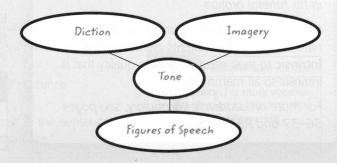

from the *Apology*

Meet **Plato**

(C. 427–347 B.C.)

Born into a distinguished family in Athens, Plato (plā´tō) was groomed for a career in politics. He put aside that life, however, to follow Socrates (470–399 B.C.), a philosopher who claimed that a divine voice led him to challenge the statements of people who pretended to be wise. For Socrates, true wisdom meant recognizing that one was ignorant. His probing questions and nontraditional approach eventually got him in trouble with the authorities.

In 399 B.C., during a period of political turmoil in Athens, some leaders accused Socrates of undermining Athenian patriotism. At the age of 70, he was charged with ignoring the gods and corrupting the youth of Athens and was sentenced to death by poison. His ideals and wisdom continue to live on largely because of the writings of Plato.

Socratic Dialogues Most of Plato's surviving writings are dialogues, in which he uses the techniques of drama to express philosophical ideas. Socrates is the central figure in these dialogues, and he uses a question-and-answer format, which later became known as the Socratic method, to uncover the truth. The early dialogues, such as the *Apology*, portray the historical Socrates, although Plato likely refined the ideas that Socrates expresses. In the later dialogues, Plato often appears to use Socrates as a mouthpiece for his own ideas. The most influential of the Socratic dialogues was the *Republic*, which examines the nature of justice.

Philosopher for the Ages Deeply distraught over Socrates' execution, Plato knew his fellow Athenians had acted out of ignorance. He concluded that what they needed was an

> "*God orders me to fulfill the philosopher's mission of searching into myself and other men.*"
>
> —Socrates, in Plato's *Apology*

education in philosophy. To achieve that goal, Plato established the Academy, a large, park-like school. With its open spaces and shaded walkways, the Academy offered an idyllic setting where students and teachers could exchange and discuss ideas.

Like his mentor Socrates, Plato was committed to using reason in a relentless search to discover the truth. Many of the basic concepts of Western philosophy can be traced to him. A brilliant literary stylist and a profound thinker, he has inspired authors and philosophers for more than 2,000 years. As the nineteenth–century American thinker Ralph Waldo Emerson observed, "Plato is philosophy, and philosophy Plato."

 Literature Online

Author Search For more about Plato, go to glencoe.com and enter QuickPass code GLW6053u2.

Literature and Reading Preview

Connect to the Speech

Who is the wisest person you have known? With a partner, discuss what it means to be wise.

Build Background

The *Apology* (a formal explanation for actions or beliefs) is a collection of speeches that Socrates made in his defense. After he was found guilty, the jury asked him to propose an alternative punishment. Socrates replied that Athens should reward him with a pension for his services as a gadfly, or pest. The following excerpt is from the speech Socrates gave to the jury after it sentenced him to death.

Set Purposes for Reading

Big Idea The Good Life

In this speech, Socrates shares his views about the Athenian people, government, and life and death. As you read, ask yourself, What values does Socrates consider worth living—and dying—for?

Literary Element Formal Speech

In a **formal speech**, the speaker tries to influence the audience's behavior, beliefs, and attitudes. The main purpose of a formal speech is to persuade, although it can also inform and entertain. As you read, ask yourself, What views does Socrates express, and how does he support them?

Reading Strategy Analyze Persuasion

When you **analyze persuasion**, you identify and examine the techniques that speakers or authors use to sway the audience. These techniques may include defending an idea, refuting the opposition, promoting a new idea, or inspiring listeners to take action. As you read, ask yourself, What persuasive techniques does Socrates use?

··

Tip: Chart Persuasive Techniques As you read the excerpt from the *Apology*, use a chart to list examples of defending an idea, refuting the opposition, promoting a new idea, and inspiring listeners to take action.

Defending	Refuting	Promoting	Inspiring

Vocabulary

detractor (di trak′ tər) *n.* one who speaks ill of someone or something; p. 336 *Many detractors criticized the mayor's proposed tax increases.*

acquittal (ə kwit′ əl) *n.* a setting free from a criminal charge by verdict, sentence, or other legal process; p. 336 *No one expects an acquittal in the trial of the alleged murderer.*

censure (sen′ shər) *v.* to find fault with and criticize; p. 338 *The manager censured the athletes for breaking curfew.*

intimation (in′ tə mā′ shən) *n.* an indirect suggestion; p. 338 *There were intimations that the team would soon move to a new city.*

from the

APOLOGY

from the Dialogues

PLATO ❧ Translated by Benjamin Jowett

Not much time will be gained, O Athenians, in return for the evil name which you will get from the **detractors** of the city, who will say that you killed Socrates, a wise man; for they will call me wise, even although I am not wise, when they want to reproach you. If you had waited a little while, your desire would have been fulfilled in the course of nature. For I am far advanced in years, as you may perceive, and not far from death. I am speaking now not to all of you, but only to those who have condemned me to death. And I have another thing to say to them: You think that I was convicted because I had no words of the sort which would have procured my **acquittal**—I mean, if I had thought fit to leave nothing undone or

unsaid. Not so; the deficiency which led to my conviction was not of words—certainly not. But I had not the boldness or impudence or inclination to address you as you would have liked me to do, weeping and wailing and lamenting, and saying and doing many things which you have been accustomed to hear from others, and which, as I maintain, are unworthy of me. I thought at the time that I ought not to do anything common or mean when in danger: nor do I now repent of the style of my defense; I would rather die having spoken after my manner, than speak in your manner and live. For neither in war nor yet at law ought I or any man to use every way of escaping death. Often in battle there can be no doubt that if a man will throw away

Vocabulary

detractor (di trak′ tər) *n.* one who speaks ill of someone or something

acquittal (ə kwit′ əl) *n.* a setting free from a criminal charge by verdict, sentence, or other legal process

Analyze Persuasion *Which persuasive technique does Socrates use here?*

Formal Speech *Formal speeches contain topic sentences and details to support them. How does Socrates support this statement in the next few lines?*

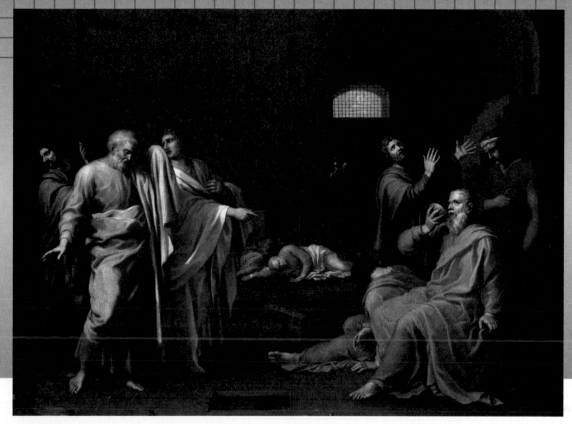

The Death of Socrates, 1650. Charles Alphonse Dufresnoy. Oil on canvas, 122 x 155 cm. Galleria Palatina Palazzo Pitti, Florence.

<u>View the Art</u> In this painting, Socrates' disciples express their grief as he carries out his death sentence by drinking hemlock. How do the attitudes of the subjects influence the mood of the painting?

his arms, and fall on his knees before his pursuers, he may escape death; and in other dangers there are other ways of escaping death, if a man is willing to say and do anything. The difficulty, my friends, is not to avoid death, but to avoid unrighteousness; for that runs faster than death. I am old and move slowly, and the slower runner has overtaken me, and my accusers are keen and quick, and the faster runner, who is unrighteousness, has overtaken them. And now I depart hence[1] condemned by you to suffer the penalty of death,—they too go their ways condemned by the truth to suffer the penalty of villainy and wrong; and I must abide by my award—let them abide by theirs. I suppose that these things may be regarded as fated,—and I think that they are well.

And now, O men who have condemned me, I would fain[2] prophesy to you; for I am about to die, and in the hour of death men are gifted with prophetic power. And I prophesy to you who are my murderers, that immediately after my departure punishment far heavier than you have inflicted on me will surely await you. Me you have killed because you wanted to escape the accuser, and not to give an account of your lives. But that will not be as you suppose:

---

1. Here, *hence* means "from this world or life."

The Good Life *What can you infer about Socrates' values in life?*

2. *Fain* means "willingly" or "with pleasure."

far otherwise. For I say that there will be more accusers of you than there are now; accusers whom hitherto I have restrained: and as they are younger they will be more inconsiderate with you, and you will be more offended at them. If you think that by killing men you can prevent someone from **censuring** your evil lives, you are mistaken; that is not a way of escape which is either possible or honorable; the easiest and the noblest way is not to be disabling others, but to be improving yourselves. This is the prophecy which I utter before my departure to the judges who have condemned me.

Friends, who would have acquitted me, I would like also to talk with you about the thing which has come to pass, while the magistrates are busy, and before I go to the place at which I must die. Stay then a little, for we may as well talk with one another while there is time. You are my friends, and I should like to show you the meaning of this event which has happened to me. O my judges—for you I may truly call judges—I should like to tell you of a wonderful circumstance. Hitherto the divine faculty[3] of which the internal oracle[4] is the source has constantly been in the habit of opposing me even about trifles, if I was going to make a slip or error in any matter; and now as you see there has come upon me that which may be thought, and is generally believed to be, the last and worst evil. But the oracle made no sign of opposition, either when I was leaving my house in the morning, or when I was on my way to the court, or while I was speaking, at anything which I was going to say; and yet I have often been stopped in the middle of a speech, but now in nothing I either said or did touching the matter in hand has the oracle opposed me. What do I take to be the explanation of this silence? I will tell you. It is an **intimation** that what has happened to me is a good, and that those of us who think that death is an evil are in error. For the customary sign would surely have opposed me had I been going to evil and not to good.

Let us reflect in another way, and we shall see that there is great reason to hope that death is a good; for one of two things—either death is a state of nothingness and utter unconsciousness, or, as men say, there is a change and migration of the soul from this world to another. Now if you suppose that there is no consciousness, but a sleep like the sleep of him who is undisturbed even by dreams, death will be an unspeakable gain. For if a person were to select the night in which his sleep was undisturbed even by dreams, and were to compare with this the other days and nights of his life, and then were to tell us how many days and nights he had passed in the course of his life better and more pleasantly than this one, I think that any man, I will not say a private man, but even the great king will not find many such days or nights, when compared with the others. Now if death be of such a nature, I say that

---

3. *Faculty* means "an inherent or natural ability."
4. Socrates uses *internal oracle* as a metaphor for the human conscience.

Vocabulary

: **censure** (sen′ shər) *v.* to find fault with and criticize

Vocabulary

: **intimation** (in′ tə mā′ shən) *n.* an indirect suggestion

to die is gain; for eternity is then only a single night. But if death is the journey to another place, and there, as men say, all the dead abide, what good, O my friends and judges can be greater than this? If indeed when the pilgrim arrives in the world below, he is delivered from the professors of justice in this world, and finds the true judges who are said to give judgment there, Minos and Rhadamanthus and Aeacus[5] and Triptolemus,[6] and other sons of God who were righteous in their own life, that pilgrimage will be worth making. What would not a man give if he might converse with Orpheus[7] and Musaeus and Hesiod and Homer?[8] Nay, if this be true, let me die again and again. I myself, too, shall have a wonderful interest in there meeting and conversing with Palamedes, and Ajax the son of Telamon, and any other ancient hero who has suffered death through an unjust judgment; and there will be no small pleasure, as I think, in comparing my own sufferings with theirs. Above all, I shall then be able to continue my search into true and false knowledge; as in this world, so also in the next; and I shall find out who is wise, and who pretends to be wise, and is not. What would not a man give, O judges, to be able to examine the leader of the great Trojan expedition; or Odysseus[9] or Sisyphus,[10] or numberless others, men and women too! What infinite delight would there be in conversing with them and asking them questions! In another world they do not put a man to death for asking questions: assuredly not. For besides being happier than we are, they will be immortal, if what is said is true.

Wherefore, O judges, be of good cheer about death, and know of a certainty, that no evil can happen to a good man, either in life or after death. He and his are not neglected by the gods; nor has my own approaching end happened by mere chance. But I see clearly that the time had arrived when it was better for me to die and be released from trouble; wherefore the oracle gave no sign. For which reason, also, I am not angry with my condemners, or with my accusers; they have done me no harm, although they did not mean to do me any good; and for this I may gently blame them.

Still I have a favor to ask of them. When my sons are grown up, I would ask you, O my friends, to punish them; and I would have you trouble them, as I have troubled you, if they seem to care about riches, or anything, more than about virtue; or if they pretend to be something when they are really nothing,—then reprove them, as I have reproved you, for not caring about that for which they ought to care, and thinking that they are something when they are really nothing. And if you do this, both I and my sons will have received justice at your hands.

The hour of departure has arrived, and we go our ways—I to die, and you to live. Which is better God only knows. ☙

---

5. *Minos, Rhadamanthus,* and *Aeacus* were rulers known for their wisdom and fairness. After their deaths, they became judges in Hades, the underworld.
6. *Triptolemus* taught agriculture and was known for his compassion.
7. In Greek mythology, *Orpheus* was a musician so gifted that his melodies could charm animals, trees, and rocks.
8. *Musaeus, Hesiod,* and *Homer* were renowned Greek poets.
9. *Palamedes, Ajax,* and *Odysseus* were Greek warriors famed for their heroic exploits during the Trojan War.
10. *Sisyphus* was a crafty king who tried to trick death. For his deceitfulness, he was condemned in the underworld to roll a huge stone uphill forever. Each time it reached the crest, the stone rolled back down, forcing Sisyphus to begin again.

The Good Life *What does this passage indicate about Socrates' vision of the good life?*

For pages 342–345

In studying this text, you will focus on the following objectives:

Reading:
Distinguishing fact from opinion.
Using text features.
Analyzing informational text.

Set a Purpose for Reading

Read to learn how the teachings of Socrates are being applied in today's world.

Preview the Article

1. Read the **deck,** the large type after the title. What sorts of issues do you predict these groups discuss?

2. What do you already know about Socrates and the Socratic method?

Reading Strategy

Distinguish Fact from Opinion

A **fact** is a statement that can be proven with evidence. An **opinion** is a personal judgment that cannot be proven true or false. As you read this article, ask yourself, What is the relationship between stated facts and the opinions of individuals? Use a chart like the one below to record your findings.

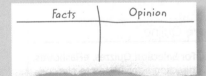

Facts	Opinion

TIME

All the Right QUESTIONS

Discussion groups based on the teachings of Socrates are reviving the art of conversation.

By ANITA HAMILTON

THERE'S A BUZZ IN THE AIR AT THE EL DIABLO COFFEE CO. in Seattle, Washington, and it's not just coming from the aroma of the shop's Cuban-style espresso drinks. On a recent Wednesday evening, as most patrons sat quietly reading books or tapping away on their laptop computers, about 15 people gathered in a circle discussing philosophy. "When is violence necessary?" asked one. "What is a well-lived life?" asked another, as the group enjoyed a well-caffeinated, intellectual debate.

Known as a Socrates Café, the group at El Diablo is just one of 150 or so that meet in coffee shops, bookstores, libraries, churches and community centers across the country. Founded by Christopher Phillips, a former journalist and teacher, the cafés are designed to get people talking about philosophical issues. Using a kind of Socratic method, the cafés encourage people to develop their views by asking questions, being open to challenges, and considering alternative answers. Adhering to Socrates' belief that the unexamined life is not worth living, the cafés focus on exchanging ideas, not using them to compete with or belittle other participants. "Instead of just yelling back and forth, we take a few steps back and examine people's underlying values. People can ask why to their heart's content," says Phillips.

While a modern-day discussion group based on the teachings of a thinker from the 5th century B.C. may seem outdated, Socrates Cafés have found a surprisingly large and diverse following.

In Seattle, participants meet and talk in a local coffeehouse.

Ann States

Meetings have been held everywhere from a Navajo Nation reservation in Ganado, Arizona, to an airplane terminal in Providence, Rhode Island. Ongoing groups have formed in prisons, senior centers, and homeless shelters. International groups have even popped up in Afghanistan, Finland, and Spain. What's the attraction? "People who get off on ideas come to this," says Fred Korn, a retired philosophy professor, who attends the Wednesday night meetings at El Diablo. "Outside of college, there's not a lot of opportunity to get together with people who want to talk about ideas," he says.

For Phillips, the dialogue groups are about much more than good conversation. "It's grassroots

> *"The whole idea is not that we have to find a final answer; it's that we keep thinking."*
>
> —Christopher Phillips
> Founder, Socrates Café

democracy," he says. "It's only in a group setting that people can hash out their ideas about how we should act not just as an individual but as a society." To avoid divisive dead-end arguments, the cafés frequently turn current events into broader philosophical questions. For example, rather than asking whether the U.S. and its allies should have invaded Iraq, a group asked, "What is a just war?"

Phillips first came up with the idea for such sessions while studying political philosophy at the College of William and Mary in Williamsburg, Virginia. Several days a week after class, he and other students would meet with a favorite professor at a local restaurant in order to discuss philosophical issues. Often other people would overhear their heated discussions and join in. "I thought, 'Wouldn't it be wonderful just to have these great conversations all the time?'" he says.

After quitting work as a writer, Phillips held his first Socrates Café at a Borders bookstore in Wayne, New Jersey, in the summer of 1996. Within a month, he met a woman named Cecilia, who was the only person to show up at one meeting. "We held a dialogue on the question What is love? and fell in love," he says. Married in 1998, the couple put their belongings in storage and travel year-round helping form new groups around the country.

The mood, tone and topic of discussion for each café vary greatly, depending on the participants. Typically, the topic is decided by group vote, and anyone can suggest an idea. At El Diablo, the mostly middle-aged crowd (ages 25 to 66) settled on a tough one: Do countries with greater power have a greater responsibility to act fairly? "Is any act that a nation makes in its own self-interest ever moral?" asked Matt Waller, a technical writer. "I say no." "Well, what's the nature of self-interest?" responds housepainter Steve Crawford. "Nations don't exist in a vacuum, certainly not in today's world." After two hours of discussion, no conclusion was reached, but that's not the point. "It's exercise of the mind," says Margaret Friedman, a writer and real estate agent who took part in the exchange.

At a Chicago, Illinois, homeless shelter for women called Deborah's Place, the discussion turns deeply

Photo Caption TK

Portrait statuette of Socrates, c. 200 AD. British Museum, London.

personal with the question What's the role of courage in love? A woman replies, "The courage to walk away." Another says, "To walk away and not become a stalker. When I was 21 and in love with someone who was 19, that was the hardest thing I ever had to do." Launched three years ago with the question Why do bad things happen to good people?, the café at the shelter has been going strong ever since. "Just listening and participating made me grow a lot and care about myself when before I didn't," says Jackie Grayer, a Deborah's Place resident who regularly attends meetings.

While Phillips believes the cafés can benefit anyone, one of his favorite groups is children. One morning he met with seven kids ranging in age from 6 to 16 at Children's Hospital in Oakland, California. Wearing multicolored hospital gowns and fuzzy slippers, the children were bashful about answering direct questions at first. But Phillips was determined to begin a conversation. After making jokes about his own "uncool" haircut and asking a couple of easy questions like "What's four plus three?" and "Do you like to draw?", he finally got his audience warmed up and eased them on to the heavier topic of truth, lies, and secrets. "When is it not better to tell the truth?" Phillips asked his now rapt audience. "When is it good to lie?" Mariela, who has severe asthma, replied, "When you're trying to help somebody escape from something like slavery."

Philosophy is important for kids of all ages, Phillips says later, because "it gives them this great chance to sculpt their moral code, to figure out clearly who they are and who they want to be . . . The whole idea is not that we have to find a final answer; it's that we keep thinking about these things." One question at a time.

—**With reporting by Laura A. Locke/Oakland, Eli Sanders/ Seattle and Leslie Whitaker/ Chicago**

Respond and Think Critically

Respond and Interpret

1. Write a brief summary of this article's main ideas before you answer the following questions. For help on writing a summary, see page 1147.

2. (a)How do the Socrates Café groups approach philosophical discussion? (b)How do the groups approach current political issues?

3. (a)Where are some of the places Socrates Café groups have formed? (b)How are the groups different from one another? How are they similar?

Analyze and Evaluate

4. (a)Describe how two different people mentioned in the article support the philosophical opinions they put forth. Do they use facts? Explain. (b)Do you agree with their opinions? Explain.

5. (a)Do you think there are criteria you can use to determine whether one opinion is more valid than another? Explain. (b)Do you think it is possible for people to reach consensus on the types of questions mentioned in this article? Explain.

Connect

6. After reading the *Apology* and this article, do you think Socrates' philosophical methods are as relevant today as they were in ancient Greece? Explain.

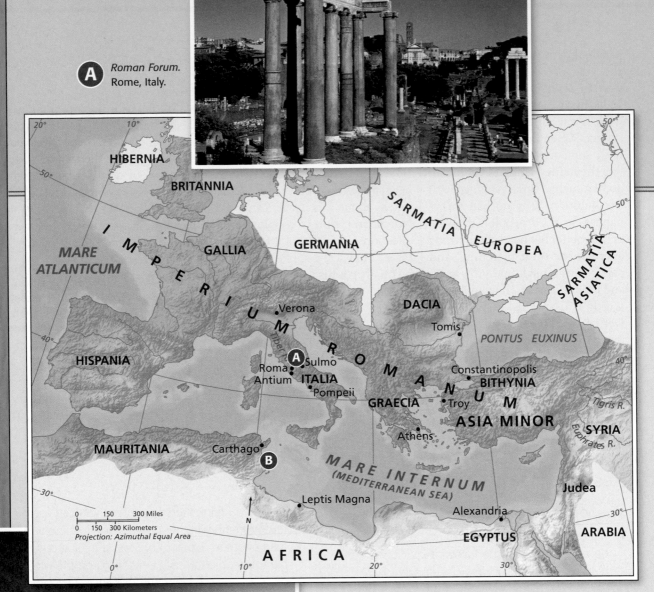

A *Roman Forum.*
Rome, Italy.

B *El Jem*, Roman amphitheatre

LOG
ON ▶ **Literature** Online

Literature and Reading For more about the history
and literature of this period, go to glencoe.com and
enter QuickPass code GLW6053u2.

PART TWO

ANCIENT ROME

800 B.C.–A.D. 500

Being There

Although only a small farming town in the beginning, Rome had great natural advantages. The seven hills on which it was built offered protection from its more powerful neighbors. Its location

The Knucklebone Player, late 2nd century AD. Roman school. Marble, height: 70 cm. Antikensammlung, Staatliche Museen zu Berlin, Germany.

fifteen miles up the Tiber River offered easy access to the sea, and its position at the crossing of several trade routes brought foreign goods and ideas. As Rome expanded, Romans improved the lands they gained. They paved roads, constructed great aqueducts to carry water, built cities, encouraged trade, and applied the rule of law. Rome developed from a city state into one of the largest empires in history.

Looking Ahead

In literature, as in other areas, the Romans learned from the Greeks. They adapted poetic forms the Greeks had established, such as the epic, ode, and lyric. Roman authors, however, also developed poetic forms of their own, such as satire, which mocks the follies of the time.

Keep the following questions in mind as you read:

▣ How did Greek philosophy help shape Roman thought?

▣ What were the basic features of Roman religion?

▣ What were living conditions like in imperial Rome?

TIMELINE 800 B.C.–A.D. 500

ROMAN LITERATURE

800 B.C.

Virgil and the Muses from Sousse

300 B.C.

c. 254
Comic playwright Plautus is born

70
Epic poet Virgil is born

◀ **51**
Julius Caesar publishes his *Gallic Wars*

38
Lyric poet Horace meets Maecenas, his patron

▲ **23**
Horace publishes the first three books of his *Odes*

19
Virgil dies, leaving the *Aeneid* unfinished

ROMAN EVENTS

800 B.C.

753
Legendary date of Rome's founding

616
Etruscans rule Rome

509
Rome becomes a republic

450
The Twelve Tables, the basis of Roman law, is codified

312
Appian Way, first Roman road, is built

300 B.C.

264 ▶
First Punic War begins

216
Hannibal defeats Romans at Cannae

146
Rome destroys Carthage

73
Spartacus leads a slave revolt

44
Julius Caesar is assassinated

27
Octavian is named emperor

WORLD EVENTS

800 B.C.

612
Babylonians conquer the Assyrian Empire

539
Cyrus the Great conquers the Babylonian Empire

▲ **sixth century**
Lao-tzu, founder of Taoism, dies

c. 500
Nok culture emerges in western Africa

300 B.C.

141
Han emperor Wu Ti comes to the throne in China

Head from Nok, Nigerian culture

A.D. 1

8
Augustus banishes Ovid

14
Augustus Caesar dies; Golden Age of Latin literature ends

79
Naturalist Pliny the Elder dies during eruption of Mt. Vesuvius

A.D. 300

c. 120
Historian Tacitus dies

A.D. 1

c. 30
Jesus is crucified in Jerusalem

64
Fire destroys much of Rome

79
Eruption of Mt. Vesuvius destroys Pompeii ▼

122
Construction of Hadrian's Wall begins

180
Marcus Aurelius dies; *Pax Romana* ends

A.D. 300

313
Emperor Constantine legalizes Christianity

330
Constantine makes Constantinople the imperial capital

380
Theodosius makes Christianity Rome's state religion

▲

410
Visigoths sack Rome

476
Western Roman Empire ends

A.D. 300

320
Chandra Gupta founds Gupta dynasty in India

c. 400 ▲
Hopewell culture begins decline in the Ohio River Valley

Reading Check

Analyze Graphic Information About how many years elapsed between Rome's founding and the end of the Roman Empire?

For pages 346–357

In studying this text, you will focus on the following objectives:

Literary Study: Analyzing literary periods.

Reading: Evaluating historical influences.
Connecting to the literature.

ANCIENT
ROME
800 B.C.—A.D. 500

Historical, Social, and Cultural Forces

The Great Cameo of France, 1st century AD. Roman. Agate. Bibliotheque Nationale, Paris.

The Land of Italy

Italy is a long, narrow peninsula that juts into the Mediterranean Sea. Divided by a mountain range running down its length, Italy still has large fertile plains ideal for farming. One of these is the plain of Latium, on which the city of Rome is located. The Latin-speaking peoples who inhabited this region had migrated into the peninsula sometime between about 1500 and 1000 B.C. After about 800 B.C., other peoples, including the Etruscans and the Greeks, began settling in Italy. The Etruscans ruled the early Romans from about 616 to 509 B.C.

The Roman Republic

In 509 B.C. the Romans overthrew the last Etruscan king and established a republic. For the next 200 years, the city strove to control the rest of Italy. Later, in the Punic Wars, the Romans fought against the city of Carthage in Northern Africa for control of the Mediterranean. In 146 B.C., the Romans set fire to Carthage and sold its people into slavery.

As Rome expanded its conquests, civil war erupted because its political leaders vied for power.

The greatest of these leaders was Julius Caesar, a brilliant soldier who used his military success as a springboard to seize control of Rome. In 44 B.C., Caesar was assassinated. Octavian, his nephew and adopted son, later defeated the forces of Mark Antony and Cleopatra at the Battle of Actium in 31 B.C. Four years later, the Roman Senate awarded Octavian the title of *Augustus* ("revered one") and named him *imperator* (the source of the English word *emperor*), or commander in chief.

Augustus ushered in an era of peace and prosperity, known as the *Pax Romana*, "Roman peace." During this period, which lasted almost two centuries, literature, art, and architecture flourished.

> *"I came. I saw. I conquered."*
>
> —Julius Caesar, describing one of his victories

The Roman Empire

At its greatest extent, early in the second century, the Roman Empire extended from northern Britain to what is now Iraq and included a population estimated at more than 50 million. The Romans were open to the cultures of the peoples they conquered. In particular, they admired the intellectual achievements of the Greeks and spread Greek culture throughout their lands.

After the death of the successful ruler Marcus Aurelius in A.D. 180, a series of inept or cruel leaders used military strength to seize the imperial throne. However, beginning in A.D. 284, the emperors Diocletian and then Constantine helped restore order and stability to the empire. Rome remained the capital of the Western Roman Empire; Byzantium, renamed Constantinople (modern Istanbul), became the capital of the Eastern Roman Empire. The Western Roman Empire suffered increasing pressure as Germanic barbarian hordes invaded its frontiers. Finally, in A.D. 476, with the deposition of the Roman emperor, the Western Roman Empire came to an end.

Italian warrior, reconstruction. 4th century BC. Private collection.

Big Idea 1
Seize the Day

Human skeleton, 1st century AD. Roman. Mosaic pavement. Musée Archéologique, Naples.

What principles should guide human life? Should people primarily observe social traditions, seek insight in religion, or cultivate the use of reason? Is it better to throw caution to the wind in an attempt to live fully in the present moment? The ancient Romans addressed these questions and others like them.

Epicureanism

Two important influences on Roman thought were Epicureanism and Stoicism, schools of philosophy that developed in Greece around 300 B.C. Epicureanism (e pi kyū′rē ə ni zəm) took its name from its founder, Epicurus, who taught that the purpose of life is personal happiness, or the pursuit of pleasure. To achieve pleasure and freedom from anxiety, one must live prudently and virtuously. The greatest expression in Latin literature of Epicurus's ideas was the philosophical poem *De rerum natura* ("On the Nature of Things") by the Roman poet Lucretius.

> *"Even as we speak, envious time has passed:*
> *Seize the day, putting as little trust as possible in tomorrow!"*
>
> —Horace, from *Odes,* Book I, 11

The Golden Mean and *Carpe Diem*

Epicureanism also influenced the Roman poet Horace (see pages 363–366). In his poems, he urged readers to live virtuously by following the "golden mean"—that is, by steering a middle course and thereby avoiding extremes of behavior such as rashness and cowardice. Horace coined the phrase *carpe diem,* or seize the day, to capture the sweetness and brevity of human life—and the importance of living in the here and now. As Horace observed in a letter to a friend, "Amid hopes and cares, amid fears and passions, believe that every day that has dawned is your last."

Stoicism

Stoicism (stō ə si′zəm), a school of Greek philosophy opposed to Epicureanism, also influenced Roman thought. The name derives from the Greek word *stoa* (or "porch"), a reference to the site in the marketplace of Athens where Zeno, the founder of this school, taught his followers. Stoicism emphasized the importance of doing one's duty, living according to nature, and mastering emotions. It preached indifference to everything but virtue. This philosophy, which reinforced traditional Roman values such as self-control, family loyalty, and love of country, influenced many Roman writers, including the emperor Marcus Aurelius.

Reading Check

Compare and Contrast What are the similarities and differences between Epicureanism and Stoicism?

Roman Myth

The earliest Roman religious practices involved rituals in the home presided over by the paterfamilias, the father of the family. These rituals centered on the worship of the guardian spirits, including family ancestors and minor divinities known as the household gods.

State Religion

Augustus restored traditional festivals to revive the state religion, which focused on the public worship of gods and goddesses, including Jupiter, Juno, Venus, and Mars. In addition, beginning with Augustus, the Roman Senate sometimes declared emperors to be divine, thus linking religion and patriotism.

To honor Augustus and proclaim the destiny of Rome, Virgil (see pages 376–398) composed his epic poem, the *Aeneid*. It traced the ancestry of the Romans to Aeneas, a Trojan prince who sailed to Italy after Troy fell to the Greeks. His descendants were Romulus and Remus, twins who, according to legend, founded Rome in 753 B.C.

Kore or Hera enthroned sprinkling the peplos and nuptial diadem. 5th century BC. Terracotta. Museo Archeologico, Taranto, Italy.

Like the Greeks, the Romans believed in many gods. They assumed the peoples whom they conquered worshipped the same gods, only under different names. For example, the Romans took the Greek Zeus as their own Jupiter.

The Romans believed their success in establishing an empire was a manifestation of divine favor. As the Roman statesman Cicero asserted in the first century B.C., "We have overcome all the nations of the world, because we have realized that the world is directed and governed by the gods." At the same time, the Romans generally tolerated other religions.

> *"Rome shall extend her empire to earth's end, her ambition to the sky...."*
>
> —Virgil, from the *Aeneid*, Book VI

Christianity

An exception to this policy of religious tolerance was Christianity. Ironically, early Christians often were accused of atheism, since they denied the existence of the pagan gods. Eventually, however, Christians gained respect for their work in feeding the poor and tending the sick. And the virtues they taught—piety, hard work, courage—were those the Romans had always admired. By the time the emperor Constantine legalized Christianity, it had already become widespread. In A.D. 380, Theodosius declared Christianity the official religion of the Roman Empire.

Reading Check

Make Generalizations How did the Romans respond to the religions of other peoples?

Neaera Reading a Letter from Catullus, 1894 Henry J. Hudson. Oil on canvas 155.5 x 104.5 cm. Bradford City Art Gallery & Museum, England.

View the Art In this painting, Henry Hudson, a nineteenth-century painter of portraits and figures, may have wanted to suggest an imaginary love affair between Catullus and the nymph Neaera, who appears in the *Odyssey*. What are some of the details the artist uses to indicate his subject is from ancient Rome?

Poems of Catullus

Translated by Carl Sesar

My woman says there's nobody she'd rather marry
than me, not even Jupiter[1] himself if he asked her.
She says, but what a woman says to a hungry lover
you might as well scribble in wind and swift water.

My mind's sunk so low, Lesbia, because of you,
wrecked itself on your account so bad already,
I couldn't like you if you were the best of women,
or stop loving you, no matter what you do.

I hate her and I love her. Don't ask me why.
It's the way I feel, that's all, and it hurts.

---

1. *Jupiter*, also called Jove, is the chief Roman god. He is the god
   of light, the sky, and the weather. In Greek mythology, he is known
   as Zeus.

Speaker *What idea does the speaker convey with the word
scribble in this image?*

Make Generalizations *What generalization might you make
about the speaker's personality based on this statement?*

Literature and Reading Preview

Connect to the Poem

What is the best piece of practical advice you have ever received? Freewrite for a few minutes about these "words of wisdom" and explain why you consider them important.

Build Background

The ode "Better to Live, Licinius" is probably addressed to the brother-in-law of Maecenas, Horace's patron. Aulus Terentius Varro Murena (formerly known as Licinius Murena) rose to the consulship, Rome's highest official position, in 23 B.C. The emperor Augustus soon had him removed from office because of his outspoken political views. Murena was executed the following year for allegedly conspiring against Augustus.

Set Purposes for Reading

Big Idea Seize the Day

In Horace's time, Romans led a cultured lifestyle reflected in the theme "seize the day." As you read, ask yourself, What connections do you see between this poem and that theme?

Literary Element Ode

An **ode** is a lyric poem, or a song, with an elevated style and exalted or enthusiastic tone. Before Horace, most odes were written to glorify public figures or to commemorate important events. Horace developed a more meditative and personal type of ode. As you read, ask yourself, What characteristics of an ode does this poem reflect?

Reading Strategy Interpret Imagery

Imagery refers to the word pictures that authors create to evoke emotional responses. In creating imagery, authors use sensory details that appeal to sight, hearing, touch, taste, or smell. When you **interpret** imagery, you analyze these word pictures and determine the emotional responses they evoke in the reader. As you read, ask yourself, What do the images in this poem mean?

Tip: Take Notes As you read the poem, use a chart like the one below to make associations between images.

Image (line)	Appeals to Sense of . . . (line)	Emotional Response

Learning Objectives

For pages 363–366

In studying this text, you will focus on the following objectives:

Literary Study: Analyzing ode.

Reading: Interpreting imagery.

Writing: Writing a letter.

Vocabulary

moderation (mod′ə rā′shən) *n.* avoiding or limiting excesses or extremes; self-control; p. 365 *His limited income forced him to practice moderation when he went shopping.*

stern (sturn) *adj.* harsh or severe in manner; firm or unyielding; p. 365 *His stern look revealed his disapproval of our conduct.*

swell (swel) *v.* to increase in size or volume; expand; p. 365 *Pumping air into the tire caused it to swell.*

Tip: Word Usage When you encounter a new word, it might help you to ask a question about that word. For example, What jobs might require a **stern** attitude?

Better to Live, Licinius

Horace
Translated by Joseph P. Clancy

Better to live, Licinius, not always
rushing into deep water, and not, when fear
of storms makes you shiver, pushing too close to
    the dangerous coast.

5 A man who prizes golden **moderation**
stays safely clear of the filth of a run-down
building, stays prudently out of a palace
    others will envy.

The giant pine is more often troubled by the
10 wind, and the tallest towers collapse with a
heavier fall, and bolts of lightning strike the
    tops of the mountains.

Hopeful in the bad times, fearful in the good times,
that is the man who has readied his heart for
15 the turn of the dice. Jupiter brings back foul
    winters; he also

takes them away. No, if things are bad now, they
will not remain that way: sometimes Apollo
wakes the silent Muse with his lyre° and is not
20   always an archer.

When troubles come, show that you have a stout heart
and a **stern** face: but see that you have the good sense
to take in sail° when it **swells** in a wind that's
    a little too kind.

A Boat, 2nd century AD. Roman relief from a stone sarcophagus. Museo della Civilta Romana, Rome.

18–19 Apollo: god of sunlight, prophecy, archery, music, and poetry, was also guardian of the **Muses,** who presided over the arts. As god of music he is often shown playing a **lyre,** a harp-like instrument.

23 to take in sail: to roll up the sail on a boat to reduce speed.

Seize the Day *Why does Horace admire this type of person?*

Ode *Why might these references to Apollo and the Muse be fitting in this poem?*

Vocabulary

moderation (mod′ə rā′shən) *n.* avoiding or limiting excesses or extremes; self-control

stern (sturn) *adj.* harsh or severe in manner; firm or unyielding

swell (swel) *v.* to increase in size or volume; expand

THE STORY OF *Pyramus* AND *Thisbe*

from the Metamorphoses

Ovid

Translated by Rolfe Humphries

"Next door to each other, in the brick-walled city
Built by Semiramis, lived a boy and girl,
Pyramus, a most handsome fellow, Thisbe,
Loveliest of all those Eastern° girls. Their nearness
5   Made them acquainted, and love grew, in time,
So that they would have married, but their parents
Forbade it. But their parents could not keep them
From being in love: their nods and gestures showed it—
You know how fire **suppressed** burns all the fiercer.
10 There was a chink° in the wall between the houses,
A flaw the careless builder had never noticed,
Nor anyone else, for many years, **detected**,
But the lovers found it—love is a finder, always—
Used it to talk through, and the loving whispers
15 Went back and forth in safety. They would stand
One on each side, listening for each other,
Happy if each could hear the other's breathing,
And then they would scold the wall: 'You envious barrier,
Why get in our way? Would it be too much to ask you
20 To open wide for an embrace, or even
Permit us room to kiss in? Still, we are grateful,
We owe you something, we admit; at least

4 **Eastern:** The Roman Empire extended from the Atlantic Ocean on the west to the eastern rim of the Mediterranean Sea. To ancient Romans, people who lived in southwest Asia were *Eastern*.

10 **chink:** a small slit or opening in a wall.

Narrative Poetry *What elements of a short story does Ovid introduce at the beginning of the poem?*

Narrative Poetry *What does the dialogue in these lines tell you about the characters?*

Vocabulary

suppress (sə pres′) *v.* keep in or hold back
detect (di tekt′) *v.* discover or determine something

You let us talk together.' But their talking
Was **futile**, rather; and when evening came
25　They would say Good-night! and give the good-night kisses
That never reached the other.
　　　　　　　　　　　　　"The next morning
Came, and the fires of night burnt out, and sunshine
Dried the night frost, and Pyramus and Thisbe
Met at the usual place, and first, in whispers,
30　Complained, and came—high time!—to a decision.
That night, when all was quiet, they would fool
Their guardians, or try to, come outdoors,
Run away from home, and even leave the city.
And, not to miss each other, as they wandered
35　In the wide fields, where should they meet? At Ninus'
Tomb,° they supposed, was best; there was a tree there,
A mulberry-tree,° loaded with snow-white berries,
Near a cool spring. The plan was good, the daylight
Was very slow in going, but at last
40　The sun went down into the waves,° as always,
And the night rose, as always, from those waters.

And Thisbe opened her door, so **sly**, so cunning,
There was no creaking of the hinge, and no one
Saw her go through the darkness, and she came,
45　Veiled, to the tomb of Ninus, sat there waiting
Under the shadow of the mulberry-tree.
Love made her bold. But suddenly, here came something!—
A lioness, her jaws a crimson froth
With the blood of cows, fresh-slain, came there for water,
50　And far off through the moonlight Thisbe saw her
And ran, all scared, to hide herself in a cave,
And dropped her veil as she ran. The lioness,
Having quenched her thirst, came back to the woods,
　　and saw
The girl's light veil, and mangled it and mouthed it
55　With bloody jaws. Pyramus, coming there
Too late, saw tracks in the dust, turned pale, and paler
Seeing the bloody veil. 'One night,' he cried,
'Will kill two lovers, and one of them, most surely,

36 Ninus' Tomb: Ninus was an Assyrian king and the husband of Semiramis (sə mir′ ə mis). He founded the Assyrian capital, Nineveh. After his death, Semiramis erected a temple on the outskirts of Babylon—Ninus' tomb.
37 mulberry trees: Asian trees cultivated as ornamental trees and for their sweet, edible fruits.
40 The sun went down into the waves: refers to the horizon on which the sun appears to set. Babylon was located between the Tigris and Euphrates Rivers.

Seize the Day *Do the lovers live for the moment, or not? Explain.*

Vocabulary

futile (fu′ til) *adj.* useless; worthless; ineffectual
sly (slī) *adj.* clever; wily; secretive

Deserved a longer life. It is all my fault,
60 I am the murderer, poor girl; I told you
To come here in the night, to all this terror,
And was not here before you, to protect you.
Come, tear my flesh, devour my guilty body,
Come, lions, all of you, whose lairs lie hidden
65 Under this rock! I am acting like a coward,
Praying for death.' He lifts the veil and takes it
Into the shadow of their tree; he kisses
The veil he knows so well, his tears run down
Into its folds: 'Drink my blood too!' he cries,
70 And draws his sword, and plunges it into his body,
And, dying, draws it out, warm from the wound.
As he lay there on the ground, the spouting blood
Leaped high, just as a pipe sends water spurting
Through a small hissing opening, when broken
75 With a flaw in the lead,° and all the air is sprinkled.
The fruit of the tree, from that red spray, turned crimson,
And the roots, soaked with the blood, dyed all the berries
The same dark hue.
                    "Thisbe came out of hiding,
Still frightened, but a little fearful, also,
80 To disappoint her lover. She kept looking
Not only with her eyes, but all her heart,
Eager to tell him of those terrible dangers,
About her own escape. She recognized
The place, the shape of the tree, but there was something
85 Strange or peculiar in the berries' color.
Could this be right? And then she saw a quiver
Of limbs on bloody ground, and started backward,
Paler than boxwood,° shivering, as water
Stirs when a little breeze ruffles the surface.
90 It was not long before she knew her lover,
And tore her hair, and beat her innocent bosom
With her little fists, embraced the well-loved body,
Filling the wounds with tears, and kissed the lips
Cold in his dying. 'O my Pyramus,'
95 She wept, 'What evil fortune takes you from me?
Pyramus, answer me! Your dearest Thisbe
Is calling you. Pyramus, listen! Lift your head!'

75 a flaw in the lead: compares the way water issues from a broken pipe to how blood spurts from a wound.

88 boxwood: a shrub used for hedges and borders.

Narrative Poetry *What does Pyramus's speech reveal about his character? What else does the speech add to the story?*

Identify Sequence *What might have been prevented had Thisbe returned sooner to the tomb?*

Night and Sleep, 1878. Evelyn de Morgan. Oil on canvas. De Morgan Foundation, London.

View the Art Evelyn de Morgan (1855–1919) was one of the few female English Pre-Raphaelite painters. These painters strove to attain a naturalistic style of art. What is the mood of this painting? What part of the story does it reflect?

He heard the name of Thisbe, and he lifted
His eyes, with the weight of death heavy upon them,
100   And saw her face, and closed his eyes.

                           "And Thisbe
Saw her own veil, and saw the ivory scabbard°
With no sword in it, and understood. 'Poor boy,'
She said, 'So, it was your own hand,
Your love, that took your life away. I too
105   Have a brave hand for this one thing, I too
Have love enough, and this will give me strength
For the last wound. I will follow you in death,
Be called the cause and comrade of your dying.
Death was the only one could keep you from me,
110   Death shall not keep you from me. Wretched parents
Of Pyramus and Thisbe, listen to us,

101 **scabbard:** a sheath for a sword or dagger.

Narrative Poetry *What does Thisbe's speech reveal about her?*

Seize the Day *Why does Thisbe decide to take her life?*

Pyramus and Thisbe, 1472 Lucas Cranach
the Elder. Oil on canvas. Neue Residenz,
Bamberg, Germany.

Listen to both our prayers, do not begrudge us,
Whom death has joined, lying at last together
In the same tomb. And you, O tree, now shading
115 The body of one, and very soon to shadow
The bodies of two, keep in remembrance always
The sign of our death, the dark and mournful color.'
She spoke, and fitting the sword-point at her breast,
Fell forward on the blade, still warm and reeking
120 With her lover's blood. Her prayers touched the gods,
And touched her parents, for the mulberry fruit
Still reddens at its ripeness, and the ashes
Rest in a common urn."°

123 urn: a vessel, typically an
ornamental vase on a pedestal. Urns
are often used for preserving the
ashes of the dead after cremation.

After You Read

Respond and Think Critically

Respond and Interpret

1. Were you surprised by the outcome of this poem? Explain.

2. (a)Why must Pyramus and Thisbe talk through a chink in a wall? (b)What does the narrator suggest with the remark, "You know how fire suppressed burns all the fiercer"?

3. (a)Why does Thisbe run off after she arrives at the tomb of Ninus? (b)Why does Pyramus blame himself for Thisbe's "death"?

4. (a)Identify an assumption in "The Story of Pyramus and Thisbe" that has tragic consequences. (b)What leads the character to make the incorrect assumption?

Analyze and Evaluate

5. In your opinion, what factors led to the deaths of Pyramus and Thisbe?

6. **Myths** often explain some aspect of nature. In what way does the end of the poem function as a myth?

Connect

7. **Big Idea** **Seize the Day** What does Ovid's poem suggest about love? (b)How does the poem reflect the theme of living for the moment? Support your answer with details from the poem.

8. **Connect to Today** If you were updating the story of Pyramus and Thisbe, what elements would you change?

Literary Element **Narrative Poetry**

A **narrative poem** has a plot that centers on a conflict.

1. What is the main conflict in "The Story of Pyramus and Thisbe"?

2. A **lyric poem** is a brief, songlike poem expressing personal thoughts and feelings. How would you compare the experience of reading a lyric poem with that of reading a narrative poem?

Reading Strategy **Identify Sequence**

Review the sequence chain you filled in on page 369. Then answer the following questions.

1. Which events, if their sequence were different, would change the outcome of the plot?

2. How might this poem be different if it were told in reverse, rather than chronological, order?

LOG ON ▶ **Literature** Online

Selection Resources For Selection Quizzes, eFlashcards, and Reading-Writing Connection activities, go to glencoe.com and enter QuickPass code GLW6053u2.

Vocabulary Practice

Practice with Denotation and Connotation
Although the words *cheap* and *inexpensive* have similar denotations, the word *cheap* has negative connotations but *inexpensive* generally does not. In each pair of words below, choose the one with negative connotations.

1. suppress   curb
2. detect   expose
3. futile   impractical
4. sly   clever

Writing

Write a Summary Write a brief summary of "The Story of Pyramus and Thisbe." Before writing, look back at your sequence chain on page 369 to review the important events. In your summary, use signal words such as *then, next, later,* and *finally* to show the order of events.

from the *Aeneid*

Meet **Virgil**
(70–19 B.C.)

V irgil, ancient Rome's greatest poet, grew up on a farm in northern Italy, near what is now the town of Mantua. Shy and gentle, he preferred the peace of the countryside to the bustle of the city and celebrated rural life in many of his poems. Virgil attended school in Cremona and Milan and later went to Rome to study mathematics, medicine, and rhetoric (the art of persuasion).

Rome's Honored Poet The assassination of Julius Caesar in 44 B.C. triggered civil war in Rome. To escape the turmoil, Virgil moved to Naples, where he lived in a house Maecenas, his wealthy patron, had given him. Thanks to Maecenas, Virgil was able to devote himself to philosophy and literary pursuits.

Virgil's connection with Maecenas proved fortunate in another way. His patron was a close adviser to Octavian, who later became the emperor Augustus. Probably prompted by Maecenas, Octavian took an interest in the young poet. After Octavian had defeated his rivals and seized control of the Roman Empire, he urged Virgil to compose a patriotic poem to honor Rome. To glorify the city and its new ruler, Virgil wrote the *Aeneid*, a twelve-book epic in Latin.

The National Epic Modeling the *Aeneid* on the Homeric epics the *Iliad* and the *Odyssey*, Virgil drew upon the ancient legend of Troy. Virgil's hero is Aeneas, a Trojan prince who escapes from Troy and visits Carthage in North Africa, where he falls in love with Queen Dido. He then travels to Italy, where he conquers the Latins and establishes a new nation. Aeneas's descendants are destined to found

Rome and create a worldwide empire. Although the *Aeneid* celebrates Rome's long tradition of military conquest, Virgil does not overlook the tragic side of warfare.

Virgil began writing the Aeneid at age 40. In 19 B.C. he set out on a voyage to Greece with the intention of revising the poem he spent eleven years composing, but he became gravely ill. On his deathbed he requested his unrevised manuscript be burned. Fortunately, Emperor Augustus ordered the poem be published. The *Aeneid* secured Virgil's literary reputation and has profoundly influenced Western culture through the ages.

> "At the heart of things there are tears."
>
> —Virgil, the *Aeneid*

LOG ON ▶ **Literature** Online

Author Search For more about Virgil, go to glencoe.com and enter QuickPass code GLW6053u2.

Literature and Reading Preview

Connect to the Epic

What does it mean to be a hero? Write a journal entry about someone you consider heroic and why.

Build Background

Aeneas is the son of Venus, the goddess of love and beauty, and Anchises, a mortal. At a feast in his honor, Aeneas reluctantly agrees to tell Queen Dido the story of Troy's destruction, the event that prompted his search for a new homeland.

Set Purposes for Reading

Big Idea Roman Myth

Virgil created a mythical past for Italy linked to Aeneas, whom he portrays as the ideal Roman hero. As you read, ask yourself, What qualities of a hero does Aeneas embody?

Literary Element Imagery

Imagery refers to the "word pictures" authors create to evoke an emotional response. In creating effective images, authors use sensory details, or descriptions that appeal to one or more of the five senses: sight, hearing, touch, taste, and smell. As you read, ask yourself, What images does Virgil create to help you visualize Aeneas's experiences?

Reading Strategy Make and Verify Predictions

When you **make predictions**, you make educated guesses about what will happen later in a literary work. You then **verify predictions** by looking for textual evidence that confirms their accuracy. As you read, ask yourself, What predictions can I make about the outcomes of events in this epic?

Tip: Take Notes Use a chart like the one below to make and verify predictions as you read.

Prediction	Evidence for Prediction	Verification

Learning Objectives

For pages 376–398

In studying this text, you will focus on the following objectives:

Literary Study: Analyzing imagery

Reading: Making and verifying predictions

Vocabulary

dupe (do͞op) v. to deceive or delude; p. 381 *He duped her into giving away all her money.*

impel (im pel´) v. to urge forward as if through moral pressure; p. 384 *She was impelled to tell her parents the truth.*

defile (di fīl´) v. to make unclean; p. 386 *The vandals defiled the holy shrine, scrawling hateful messages on the walls.*

suppliant (sə´plē´ənt) n. one who asks humbly and earnestly; p. 386 *The suppliant pleaded with the court to hear his testimony.*

Tip: Context Clues When you come across an unfamiliar term, pay close attention to the surrounding words. For example, in the sentence *The vandals defiled the holy shrine, scrawling hateful messages on the walls, defiled* must mean "to make unclean" because "vandals" wrote "hateful messages."

from **Book Two:**

THE FINAL HOURS OF TROY FROM THE AENEID

VIRGIL   TRANSLATED BY ROBERT FAGLES

Procession of the Trojan Horse into Troy, 1727. Giovanni Battista Tiepolo. Oil on canvas. National Gallery, London.

IN THE TENTH YEAR OF THE TROJAN WAR, *the Greeks built a large wooden horse, which they claimed was an offering to ensure their safe passage home. After hiding warriors inside the horse's belly, the Greek forces pretended to sail away. Some Trojans wanted to bring the horse into their city, but others urged caution. The debate was interrupted by a captured Greek named Sinon (sī′nən), whose lies convinced the Trojans to drag the horse inside. Under cover of darkness, Sinon set free the hidden Greeks, who then dropped out of the horse and opened Troy's gates to their fellow warriors. Aeneas was asleep at the time, dreaming that the dead Trojan hero Hector told him to take his household gods and abandon the city. (The Romans believed household gods, or Penates (pə nā′tēz), protected the pantry, and their images were worshipped in every household.) Aeneas awoke to the sound of battle.*

"But now.
chaos—the city begins to reel with cries of grief,
louder, stronger, even though father's palace
stood well back, screened off by trees, but still
the clash of arms rings clearer, horror on the attack.
5 I shake off sleep and scrambling up to the pitched roof
I stand there, ears alert, and I hear a roar like fire
assaulting a wheatfield, whipped by a Southwind's fury,
or mountain torrent in full spate,° flattening crops,
leveling all the happy, thriving labor of oxen,
10 dragging whole trees headlong down in its wake—
and a shepherd perched on a sheer rock outcrop
hears the roar, lost in amazement, struck dumb.
No doubting the good faith of the Greeks now,
their treachery plain as day.
                        "Already, there,
15 the grand house of Deiphobus° stormed by fire,
crashing in ruins—
                        "Already his neighbor Ucalegon°
up in flames—
                        "The Sigean straits° shimmering back the blaze,
the shouting of fighters soars, the clashing blare of trumpets.
Out of my wits, I seize my arms—what reason for arms?
20 Just my spirit burning to muster troops for battle,
rush with comrades up to the city's heights,
fury and rage driving me breakneck on
as it races through my mind
what a noble thing it is to die in arms!
                        "But now, look,
25 just slipped out from under the Greek barrage of spears,
Panthus, Othrys' son, a priest of Apollo's° shrine
on the citadel—hands full of the holy things,
the images of our conquered gods—he's dragging along
his little grandson, making a wild dash for our doors.
30 'Panthus, where's our stronghold? our last stand?'—
words still on my lips as he groans in answer:
'The last *day* has come for the Trojan people,
no escaping this moment. Troy's no more.
Ilium,° gone—our awesome Trojan glory.
35 Brutal Jupiter° hands it all over to Greece,

---

8 spate: here, a flood.

15 Deiphobus (dē′ ə phō′ bəs): a son of Priam.

16 Ucalegon (ū kal′ ə gən): a Trojan elder.

17 Sigean straits: waterways near Troy.

26 Panthus: Trojan elder. **Apollo:** god of sunlight, healing, prophecy, archery, music, and poetry. He favored the Trojans.

34 Ilium (il′ ē əm): Troy.

35 Jupiter: chief god and the god of the sky and weather; he favored Troy but knew it could not be saved.

Imagery *What senses does Virgil appeal to in this description?*

Greeks are lording over our city up in flames.
The horse stands towering high in the heart of Troy,
disgorging its armed men, with Sinon in his glory,
gloating over us—Sinon fans the fires.
40   The immense double gates are flung wide open,
Greeks in their thousands mass there, all who ever
sailed from proud Mycenae.° Others have choked
the cramped streets, weapons brandished now
in a battle line of naked, glinting steel
45   tense for the kill. Only the first guards
at the gates put up some show of resistance,
fighting blindly on.'

                                                        "Now

like a wolfpack out for blood on a foggy night,
driven blindly on by relentless, rabid hunger,
50   leaving cubs behind, waiting, jaws parched—
so through spears, through enemy ranks we plow
to certain death, striking into the city's heart,
the shielding wings of the darkness beating round us.
Who has words to capture that night's disaster,
55   tell that slaughter? What tears could match
our torments now? An ancient city is falling,
a power that ruled for ages, now in ruins.
Everywhere lie the motionless bodies of the dead,
strewn in her streets, her homes and the gods' shrines
60   we held in awe. And not only Trojans pay the price in
    blood—
at times the courage races back in their conquered hearts
and they cut their enemies down in all their triumph.
Everywhere, wrenching grief, everywhere, terror
and a thousand shapes of death…

MISTAKEN FOR GREEKS, *Aeneas and his companions are able to destroy a Greek faction. Then, encouraged by their victory, they try a new strategy. They disguise themselves in Greek armor and continue fighting.*

                                               "But, oh
65   how wrong to rely on gods dead set against you!
Watch: the virgin daughter of Priam, Cassandra,°

66 **Priam** (prī′ əm): King of Troy and father of Hector and many others.
Cassandra (kə săn′ drə): prophetess whose predictions, though always true, were never believed.

Imagery *Virgil uses a simile to create an image of the Trojans. What does he compare them with?*

Cassandra, 1898. Evelyn De Morgan. Oil on canvas, 97.7 x 48.2 cm. The De Morgan Centre, London.

torn from the sacred depths of Minerva's° shrine,
dragged by the hair, raising her burning eyes
to the heavens, just her eyes, so helpless,
70   shackles kept her from raising her gentle hands.
Coroebus° could not bear the sight of it—mad with rage
he flung himself at the Greek lines and met his death.
Closing ranks we charge after him, into the thick of battle
and face our first disaster. Down from the temple roof
75   come showers of lances hurled by our own comrades there,
duped by the look of our Greek arms, our Greek crests
that launched this grisly slaughter. And worse still,
the Greeks roaring with anger—we had saved Cassandra—
attack us from all sides! Ajax,° fiercest of all and
80   Atreus' two sons and the whole Dolopian° army,
wild as a rampaging whirlwind, gusts clashing,

67 Minerva (mi nur′və): goddess of wisdom and the arts and sciences.

71 Coroebus (kər ō′ ə bəs): Trojan ally who loves Cassandra.

79 Ajax: Ajax the Lesser, a great warrior in the Greek army.
80 Atreus' two sons: Agamemnon and Menelaus. **Dolopian:** referring to a kingdom ruled by Achilles' father.

Vocabulary

dupe (do͞op) *v.* to deceive or delude

the West- and the South- and Eastwind riding high
on the rushing horses of the Dawn, and the woods howl
and Nereus, thrashing his savage trident,° churns up
85   the sea exploding in foam from its rocky depths.
And those Greeks we had put to rout,° our ruse
in the murky night stampeding them headlong on
throughout the city—back they come, the first
to see that our shields and spears are naked lies,
90   to mark the words on our lips that jar with theirs.

    "And there, I tell you, a pitched battle flares!
You'd think no other battles could match its fury,
nowhere else in the city were people dying so.
Invincible Mars° rears up to meet us face-to-face
95   with waves of Greeks assaulting the roofs, we see them
choking the gateway, under a tortoise-shell of shields,
and the scaling ladders cling to the steep ramparts—
just at the gates the raiders scramble up the rungs,
shields on their left arms thrust out for defense,
100   their right hands clutching the gables.°
Over against them, Trojans ripping the tiles
and turrets° from all their roofs—the end is near,
they can see it now, at the brink of death, desperate
for weapons, some defense, and these, these missiles they
    send
105   reeling down on the Greeks' heads—the gilded beams,
the inlaid glory of all our ancient fathers.
Comrades below, posted in close-packed ranks,
block the entries, swordpoints drawn and poised.
My courage renewed, I rush to relieve the palace,
110   brace the defenders, bring the defeated strength.

    "There was a secret door, a hidden passage
linking the wings of Priam's house—remote,
far to the rear. Long as our realm still stood,
Andromache,° poor woman, would often go this way,
115   unattended, to Hector's° parents, taking the boy
Astyanax° by the hand to see grandfather Priam.
I slipped through the door, up to the jutting roof
where the doomed Trojans were hurling futile spears.
There was a tower soaring high at the peak toward the sky,
120   our favorite vantage point for surveying all of Troy

84 Nereus: (nēr′ē əs): sea god;
the old man of the sea. **trident:**
three-pronged spear carried by the
sea god.
86 put to rout: to defeat or to
force to retreat.

94 Mars: god of war.

100 gables: triangular architectural
sections.

102 turrets: small tower-shaped
projections on a building.

114 Andromache (an drom′ə
kē): Hector's wife.
115 Hector: Troy's greatest hero,
killed by Achilles.
116 Astyanax (as tī′ə naks): the
young son of Hector and
Andromache.

Imagery *What image is used in this description? What do you visualize as you
read this passage?*

and the Greek fleet and camp. We attacked that tower
with iron crowbars, just where the upper-story planks
showed loosening joints—we rocked it, wrenched it free
of its deep moorings and all at once we heaved it toppling
125 down with a crash, trailing its wake of ruin to grind
the massed Greeks assaulting left and right. But on
came Greek reserves, no letup, the hail of rocks,
the missiles of every kind would never cease.

     "There at the very edge of the front gates
130 springs Pyrrhus, son of Achilles, prancing in arms,
aflash in his shimmering brazen° sheath like a snake
buried the whole winter long under frozen turf,
swollen to bursting, fed full on poisonous weeds
and now it springs into light, sloughing° its old skin
135 to glisten sleek in its newfound youth, its back slithering,
coiling, its proud chest rearing high to the sun,
its triple tongue flickering through its fangs.
Backing him now comes Periphas, giant fighter,
Automedon too, Achilles' henchman, charioteer
140 who bore the great man's armor—backing Pyrrhus,
the young fighters from Scyros° raid the palace,
hurling firebrands at the roofs. Out in the lead,
Pyrrhus seizes a double-axe and batters the rocky sill
and ripping the bronze posts out of their sockets,
145 hacking the rugged oaken planks of the doors,
makes a breach, a gaping maw,° and there, exposed,
the heart of the house, the sweep of the colonnades,°
the palace depths of the old kings and Priam lie exposed
and they see the armed sentries bracing at the portals.

150   "But all in the house is turmoil, misery, groans,
the echoing chambers ring with cries of women,
wails of mourning hit the golden stars.
Mothers scatter in panic down the palace halls
and embrace the pillars, cling to them, kiss them hard.
155 But on he comes, Pyrrhus with all his father's force,
no bolts, not even the guards can hold him back—
under the ram's repeated blows the doors cave in,
the doorposts, prised° from their sockets, crash flat.

Imagery *What does this image suggest about Pyrrhus?*

Make and Verify Predictions *What do you predict Pyrrhus will do after break-ing into the palace?*

131 **brazen:** made of brass.

134 **sloughing:** shedding an outer layer of dead skin.

141 **Scyros** (skīʹrəs): island in the Aegean Sea off Greece; birthplace of Pyrrhus.

146 **maw:** an opening.
147 **colonnades:** a series of columns placed at intervals.

158 **prised:** forced loose.

Force makes a breach and the Greeks come storming
   through,
160 butcher the sentries, flood the entire place with men-at-
   arms.
No river so wild, so frothing in spate, bursting its banks
to overpower the dikes, anything in its way, its cresting
tides stampeding in fury down on the fields to sweep
the flocks and stalls across the open plain.
165 I saw him myself, Pyrrhus crazed with carnage
and Atreus' two sons just at the threshold—
                                   "I saw
Hecuba° with her hundred daughters and daughters-in-law,
saw Priam fouling with blood the altar fires
he himself had blessed.
                    "Those fifty bridal-chambers
170 filled with the hope of children's children still to come,
the pillars proud with trophies, gilded with Eastern gold,
they all come tumbling down—
and the Greeks hold what the raging fire spares.

   "Perhaps you wonder how Priam met his end.
175 When he saw his city stormed and seized, his gates
wrenched apart, the enemy camped in his palace depths,
the old man dons his armor long unused, he clamps it
round his shoulders shaking with age and, all for nothing,
straps his useless sword to his hip, then makes
180 for the thick of battle, out to meet his death.
At the heart of the house an ample altar stood,
naked under the skies,
an ancient laurel° bending over the shrine,
embracing our household gods within its shade.
185 Here, flocking the altar, Hecuba and her daughters
huddled, blown headlong down like doves by a black storm—
clutching, all for nothing, the figures of their gods.
Seeing Priam decked in the arms he'd worn as a young man,
'Are you insane?' she cries, 'poor husband, what **impels** you
190 to strap that sword on now? Where are you rushing?
Too late for such defense, such help. Not even
my own Hector, if *he* came to the rescue now . . .
Come to me, Priam. This altar will shield us all
or else you'll die with us.'

167 Hecuba (hek′yə bə):
Priam's wife.

183 laurel: evergreen shrub or
tree.

Vocabulary

impel (im pel′) *v.* to urge forward as if through moral pressure

Aeneas and his Father Fleeing Troy, c. 1635. Simon Vouet. Oil on canvas, 140.3 x 110 cm. San Diego Museum of Art, CA.

View the Art This painting shows Aeneas's wife (clutching the household gods) and son watching as Aeneas lifts Anchises onto his shoulders. What does the painting suggest about the relationship between Aeneas and his father?

"With those words,
195 drawing him toward her there, she made a place
for the old man beside the holy shrine.
                  "Suddenly,
look, a son of Priam, Polites,° just escaped
from slaughter at Pyrrhus' hands, comes racing in
through spears, through enemy fighters, fleeing down
200 the long arcades and deserted hallways—badly wounded,
Pyrrhus hot on his heels, a weapon poised for the kill,
about to seize him, about to run him through and pressing
home as Polites reaches his parents and collapses,
vomiting out his lifeblood before their eyes.
205 At that, Priam, trapped in the grip of death,
not holding back, not checking his words, his rage:

197 **Polites** (pə lī′ tēz): young Trojan warrior.

Make and Verify Predictions *Pyrrhus murders Polites before Priam's very eyes. What do you predict Priam will do now?*

'You!' he cries, 'you and your vicious crimes!
If any power on high recoils at such an outrage,
let the gods repay you for all your reckless work,
210   grant you the thanks, the rich reward you've earned.
You've made me see my son's death with my own eyes,
defiled a father's sight with a son's lifeblood.
You say you're Achilles' son? You lie! Achilles
never treated his enemy Priam so. No, he honored
215   a **suppliant's** rights, he blushed to betray my trust,
he restored my Hector's bloodless corpse for burial,
sent me safely home to the land I rule!'
                                        "With that
and with all his might the old man flings his spear—
but too impotent now to pierce, it merely grazes
220   Pyrrhus' brazen shield that blocks its way
and clings there, dangling limp from the boss,
all for nothing. Pyrrhus shouts back: 'Well then,
down you go, a messenger to my father, Peleus'° son!
Tell him about my vicious work, how Neoptolemus°
225   degrades his father's name—don't you forget.
Now—die!'
"That said, he drags the old man
straight to the altar, quaking, slithering on through
slicks of his son's blood, and twisting Priam's hair
in his left hand, his right hand sweeping forth his sword—
230   a flash of steel—he buries it hilt-deep in the king's flank.
      "Such was the fate of Priam, his death, his lot on earth,
with Troy blazing before his eyes, her ramparts down,
the monarch who once had ruled in all his glory
the many lands of Asia, Asia's many tribes.
235   A powerful trunk is lying on the shore.
The head wrenched from the shoulders.
A corpse without a name.
                            "Then, for the first time
the full horror came home to me at last. I froze.
The thought of my own dear father filled my mind
240   when I saw the old king gasping out his life

---

223 **Peleus** (pē′lē əs): father of Achilles.
224 **Neoptolemus:** (nē op tôl′ə məs′): another name for Pyrrhus.

Imagery *What images help you visualize Priam's death?*

Vocabulary

defile (di fīl′) *v.* to make unclean
suppliant (sə′plē′ənt) *n.* one who asks humbly and earnestly

with that raw wound—both men were the same age—
and the thought of my Creusa,° alone, abandoned,
our house plundered, our little Iulus'° fate.
I look back—what forces still stood by me?

245 None. Totally spent in war, they'd all deserted,
down from the roofs they'd flung themselves to earth
or hurled their broken bodies in the flames.

["So,

at just that moment I was the one man left
and then I saw her, clinging to Vesta's° threshold,
250 hiding in silence, tucked away—Helen of Argos.
Glare of the fires lit my view as I looked down,
scanning the city left and right, and there she was . . .
terrified of the Trojans' hate, now Troy was overpowered,
terrified of the Greeks' revenge, her deserted husband's
    rage—
255 that universal Fury, a curse to Troy and her native land
and here she lurked, skulking, a thing of loathing
cowering at the altar: Helen. Out it flared,
the fire inside my soul, my rage ablaze to avenge
our fallen country—pay Helen back, crime for crime.

260   " 'So, this woman,' it struck me now, 'safe and sound
she'll look once more on Sparta, her native Greece?
She'll ride like a queen in triumph with her trophies?
Feast her eyes on her husband, parents, children too?
Her retinue fawning round her, Phrygian° ladies, slaves?
265 That—with Priam put to the sword? And Troy up in flames?
And time and again our Dardan° shores have sweated blood?
Not for all the world. No fame, no memory to be won
for punishing a woman: such victory reaps no praise
but to stamp this abomination out as she deserves,
270 to punish her now, they'll sing my praise for that.
What joy, to glut° my heart with the fires of vengeance,
bring some peace to the ashes of my people!'

    "Whirling words—I was swept away by fury now]
when all of a sudden there my loving mother stood

---

242 **Creusa** (krē ū′ sə): wife of Aeneas.
243 **Iulus** (ū′ ləs): son of Aeneas and Creusa, also called Ascanius.

249 **Vesta:** goddess of the hearth and household activities.

264 **retinue:** retainers who accompany a high-ranking individual. **Phrygian** (frij′ ē ən): people from a region near Troy.
266 **Dardan:** Trojan.

271 **glut:** to fill beyond capacity, or satiate.

Roman Myth *What qualities of the ideal Roman hero does Aeneas possess?*

Make and Verify Predictions *Do you think Aeneas will kill Helen? Explain.*

275 before my eyes, but I had never seen her so clearly,
her pure radiance shining down upon me through the night,
the goddess in all her glory, just as the gods behold
her build, her awesome beauty. Grasping my hand
she held me back, adding this from her rose-red lips:
280 'My son, what grief could incite such blazing anger?
Why such fury? And the love you bore me once,
where has it all gone? Why don't you look first
where you left your father, Anchises, spent with age?
Do your wife, Creusa, and son Ascanius still survive?
285 The Greek battalions are swarming round them all,
and if my love had never rushed to the rescue,
flames would have swept them off by now or
enemy sword-blades would have drained their blood.
Think: it's not that beauty, Helen, you should hate,
290 not even Paris,° the man that you should blame, no,
it's the gods, the ruthless gods who are tearing down
the wealth of Troy, her toppling crown of towers.
Look around. I'll sweep it all away, the mist
so murky, dark, and swirling around you now,
295 it clouds your vision, dulls your mortal sight.
You are my son. Never fear my orders.
Never refuse to bow to my commands.
                                        " 'There,
yes, where you see the massive ramparts shattered,
blocks wrenched from blocks, the billowing smoke and
      ash—
300 it's Neptune° himself, prising loose with his giant trident
the foundation-stones of Troy, he's making the walls quake,
ripping up the entire city by her roots.
                              " 'There's Juno,°
cruelest in fury, first to commandeer the Scaean Gates,°
sword at her hip and mustering comrades, shock troops
305 streaming out of the ships.
                              " 'Already up on the heights—
turn around and look—there's Pallas° holding the fortress,
flaming out of the clouds, her savage Gorgon° glaring.
Even Father himself, he's filling the Greek hearts
with courage, stamina—Jove in person spurring the gods
310 to fight the Trojan armies!

290 **Paris:** the prince of Troy
whose kidnapping of Helen
triggered the Trojan War.

300 **Neptune:** the god of the sea.

302 **Juno:** chief goddess and
protector of marriage; wife of
Jupiter, she favored the Greeks.
303 **Scaean Gates** (skē′ ən): set
of gates in the walls surrounding
Troy.

306 **Pallas:** Athena, the Greek
goddess of war and wisdom.
307 **Gorgon:** refers to Medusa, a
monster whose appearance turned
beholders to stone. Here, her head
is attached to Pallas's shield.

Imagery *What image does Venus use to describe the destruction of Troy?*

"　'Run for your life, my son.
Put an end to your labors. I will never leave you,
I will set you safe at your father's door.'

　"Parting words. She vanished into the dense night.
And now they all come looming up before me,
315　terrible shapes, the deadly foes of Troy,
the gods gigantic in power.
　　　　　　　　　　"Then at last
I saw it all, all Ilium settling into her embers,
Neptune's Troy, toppling over now from her roots
like a proud, veteran ash on its mountain summit,
320　chopped by stroke after stroke of the iron axe as
woodsmen fight to bring it down, and over and
over it threatens to fall, its boughs shudder,
its leafy crown quakes and back and forth it sways
till overwhelmed by its wounds, with a long last groan
325　it goes—torn up from its heights it crashes down
in ruins from its ridge . . .
Venus leading, down from the roof I climb
and win my way through fires and massing foes.
The spears recede, the flames roll back before me.

330　　"At last, gaining the door of father's ancient house,
my first concern was to find the man, my first wish
to spirit him off, into the high mountain range,
but father, seeing Ilium razed from the earth,
refused to drag his life out now and suffer exile.
335　'You,' he argued, 'you in your prime, untouched by age,
your blood still coursing strong, you hearts of oak,
you are the ones to hurry your escape. Myself,
if the gods on high had wished me to live on,
they would have saved my palace for me here.
340　Enough—more than enough—that I have seen
one sack of my city, once survived its capture.
Here I lie, here laid out for death. Come say
your parting salutes and leave my body so.
I will find my own death, sword in hand:
345　my enemies keen for spoils will be so kind.
Death without burial? A small price to pay.
For years now, I've lingered out my life,
despised by the gods, a dead weight to men,

Imagery *What word picture does Virgil create here?*

ever since the Father of Gods and King of Mortals
350   stormed at me with his bolt and scorched me with its fire.'

    "So he said, planted there. Nothing could shake him now.
But we dissolved in tears, my wife, Creusa, Ascanius,
the whole household, begging my father not to pull
our lives down with him, adding his own weight
355   to the fate that dragged us down.
He still refuses, holds to his resolve,
clings to the spot. And again I rush to arms,
desperate to die myself. Where could I turn?
What were our chances now, at this point?
360   'What!' I cried. 'Did you, my own father,
dream that I could run away and desert you here?
How could such an outrage slip from a father's lips?
If it please the gods that nothing of our great city
shall survive—if you are bent on adding your own death
365   to the deaths of Troy and of all your loved ones too,
the doors of the deaths you crave are spread wide open.
Pyrrhus will soon be here, bathed in Priam's blood,
Pyrrhus who butchers sons in their fathers' faces,
slaughters fathers at the altar. Was it for this,
370   my loving mother, you swept me clear of the weapons,
free of the flames? Just to see the enemy camped
in the very heart of our house, to see my son, Ascanius,
see my father, my wife, Creusa, with them, sacrificed,
massacred in each other's blood?
                                        'Arms, my comrades,
375   bring me arms! The last light calls the defeated.
Send me back to the Greeks, let me go back
to fight new battles. Not all of us here
will die today without revenge.'
                                        "Now buckling on
my sword again and working my left arm through
380   the shieldstrap, grasping it tightly, just as I
was rushing out, right at the doors my wife, Creusa,
look, flung herself at my feet and hugged my knees

Make and Verify Predictions *Do you predict Anchises will leave with Aeneas or remain in his palace? Explain.*

Roman Myth *What does this passage suggest about the Roman attitude toward the role of the warrior and the importance of courage?*

and raised our little Iulus up to his father.
'If you are going off to die,' she begged,
385   'then take us with you too,
to face the worst together. But if your battles
teach you to hope in arms, the arms you buckle on,
your first duty should be to guard our house.
Desert us, leave us now—to whom? Whom?
390   Little Iulus, your father and your wife,
so I once was called.'
                                "So Creusa cries,
her wails of anguish echoing through the house
when out of the blue an omen strikes—a marvel!
Now as we held our son between our hands
395   and both our grieving faces, a tongue of fire,
watch, flares up from the crown of Iulus' head,
a subtle flame licking his downy hair, feeding
around the boy's brow, . . .

IN ADDITION TO THE MAGIC FLAME *that illuminates Iulus's hair, a shooting star streaks across the sky and lands in the forests near Mount Ida. These supernatural signs deeply move Anchises.*

Won over at last, my father rises to his full height
400   and prays to the gods and reveres that holy star:
'No more delay, not now! You gods of my fathers,
now I follow wherever you lead me, I am with you.
Safeguard our house, safeguard my grandson Iulus!
This sign is yours: Troy rests in your power.
405   I give way, my son. No more refusals.
I will go with you, your comrade.'
                                "So he yielded
but now the roar of flames grows louder all through Troy
and the seething floods of fire are rolling closer.
'So come, dear father, climb up onto my shoulders!
410   I will carry you on my back. This labor of love
will never wear me down. Whatever falls to us now,

Imagery *What senses do these details appeal to?*

we both will share one peril, one path to safety.
Little Iulus, walk beside me, and you, my wife,
follow me at a distance, in my footsteps.
415 Servants, listen closely . . .
Just past the city walls a grave-mound lies
where an old shrine of forsaken Ceres° stands
with an ancient cypress growing close beside it—
our fathers' reverence kept it green for years.
420 Coming by many routes, it's there we meet,
our rendezvous. And you, my father, carry
our hearth-gods now, our fathers' sacred vessels.
I, just back from the war and fresh from slaughter,
I must not handle the holy things—it's wrong—
425 not till I cleanse myself in running springs.'

                                        "With that,
over my broad shoulders and round my neck I spread
a tawny lion's skin for a cloak, and bowing down,
I lift my burden up. Little Iulus, clutching
my right hand, keeps pace with tripping steps.
430 My wife trails on behind. And so we make our way
along the pitch-dark paths, and I who had never flinched
at the hurtling spears or swarming Greek assaults—
now every stir of wind, every whisper of sound
alarms me, anxious both for the child beside me
435 and burden on my back. And then, nearing the gates,
thinking we've all got safely through, I suddenly
seem to catch the steady tramp of marching feet
and father, peering out through the darkness, cries:
'Run for it now, my boy, you must. They're closing in,
440 I can see their glinting shields, their flashing bronze!'

    "Then in my panic something strange, some enemy power
robbed me of my senses. Lost, I was leaving behind
familiar paths, at a run down blind dead ends
when—
            "Oh dear god, my wife, Creusa—
445 torn from me by a brutal fate! What then,
did she stop in her tracks or lose her way?
Or exhausted, sink down to rest? Who knows?
I never set my eyes on her again.

Roman Myth *What does this passage suggest about the Roman attitude toward the gods?*

417 forsaken Ceres: the goddess of grain, whose daughter Proserpina was stolen by Pluto and taken to the underworld.

Aeneas Carrying His Father Anchises from the Blazing City of Troy. Daniel Van Heil. Oil on copper, 18.2 x 25.4 cm. Private collection.

View the Art This painting was done on a copper plate, a medium that allows painters to create rich, glowing colors. What impression do the color and lighting create in this painting?

    I never looked back, she never crossed my mind—
450 Creusa, lost—not till we reached that barrow
    sacred to ancient Ceres where, with all our people
    rallied at last, she alone was missing. Lost
    to her friends, her son, her husband—gone forever.
    Raving, I blamed them all, the gods, the human race—
455 what crueler blow did I feel the night that Troy went down?
    Ascanius, father Anchises, and all the gods of Troy,
    entrusting them to my friends, I hide them well away
    in a valley's shelter, don my burnished gear
    and back I go to Troy . . .

Roman Myth *What can you infer about the ideal Roman hero from this passage?*

460 my mind steeled to relive the whole disaster,
retrace my route through the whole city now
and put my life in danger one more time.

                              "First then,
back to the looming walls, the shadowy rear gates
by which I'd left the city, back I go in my tracks,
465 retracing, straining to find my footsteps in the dark,
with terror at every turn, the very silence makes me cringe.
Then back to my house I go—if only, only she's gone
     there—
but the Greeks have flooded in, seized the entire place.
All over now. Devouring fire whipped by the winds
470 goes churning into the rooftops, flames surging
over them, scorching blasts raging up the sky.
On I go and again I see the palace of Priam
set on the heights, but there in colonnades
deserted now, in the sanctuary of Juno, there
475 stand the elite watchmen, Phoenix,° ruthless Ulysses°
guarding all their loot. All the treasures of Troy
hauled from the burning shrines—the sacramental tables,
bowls of solid gold and the holy robes they'd seized
from every quarter—Greeks, piling high the plunder.
480 Children and trembling mothers rounded up
in a long, endless line.

                    "Why, I even dared fling
my voice through the dark, my shouts filled the streets
as time and again, overcome with grief I called out
'Creusa!' Nothing, no reply, and again 'Creusa!'
485 But then as I madly rushed from house to house,
no end in sight, abruptly, right before my eyes
I saw her stricken ghost, my own Creusa's shade.
But larger than life, the life I'd known so well.
I froze. My hackles° bristled, voice choked in my throat,
490 and my wife spoke out to ease me of my anguish:
'My dear husband, why so eager to give yourself
to such mad flights of grief? It's not without
the will of the gods these things have come to pass.
But the gods forbid you to take Creusa with you,
495 bound from Troy together. The king of lofty Olympus°
won't allow it. A long exile is your fate . . .
the vast plains of the sea are yours to plow

---

475 **Phoenix** (fē′niks): a Greek leader who had been Achilles' tutor.
475 **Ulysses** (ū′lis′ēz): Odysseus, the king of Ithaca; Greek leader known for his strategems.

489 **hackles:** hairs on the back of the neck.

495 **Olympus:** Mount Olympus, the highest mountain in Greece and the home of the gods.

Make and Verify Predictions *What do you predict Creusa's ghost will say to her husband?*

until you reach Hesperian land, where Lydian Tiber°
flows with its smooth march through rich and loamy fields,
500   a land of hardy people. There great joy and a kingdom
are yours to claim, and a queen to make your wife.
Dispel your tears for Creusa whom you loved.
I will never behold the high and mighty pride
of their palaces, the Myrmidons,° the Dolopians,
505   or go as a slave to some Greek matron, no, not I,
daughter of Dardanus° that I am, the wife of Venus' son.
The Great Mother of Gods detains me on these shores.
And now farewell. Hold dear the son we share,
we love together.'
          "These were her parting words
510   and for all my tears—I longed to say so much—
dissolving into the empty air she left me now.
Three times I tried to fling my arms around her neck,
three times I embraced—nothing . . . her phantom
sifting through my fingers,
515   light as wind, quick as a dream in flight.
                            "Gone—
and at last the night was over. Back I went to my people
and I was amazed to see what throngs of new companions
had poured in to swell our numbers, mothers, men,
our forces gathered for exile, grieving masses.
520   They had come together from every quarter,
belongings, spirits ready for me to lead them
over the sea to whatever lands I'd choose.
And now the morning star was mounting above
the high crests of Ida,° leading on the day.
525   The Greeks had taken the city, blocked off every gate.
No hope of rescue now. So I gave way at last and
lifting my father, headed toward the mountains."

Imagery *What do the similes in this passage suggest about Aeneas's actions?*

Roman Myth *How does the ideal Roman hero respond to adversity?*

498 Hesperian: (he sper′ē ən):
of the land to the west where the
sun sets, known as the "land of the
evening"; Italy, the peninsula on
which Rome is located. **Tiber**
(tī′ bər): the river that flows
through Rome, Italy: at that time,
controlled by Etruscans, who may
have come from Lydia (lī′ dē ə), in
Asia Minor.
504 Myrmidons: the followers of
Achilles.
506 Dardanus: thought to be the
founder of Troy.

524 Ida: mountain near Troy.

Respond Through Writing

Expository Essay

Analyze Imagery Virgil's poetry is known for its powerful visual imagery, or word pictures. In an essay of 1,500 words, analyze the imagery used to describe the fall of Troy in Book Two of the *Aeneid*. Build your essay around a thesis that states the overall effect the imagery creates.

Understand the Task The **thesis** states your paper's main idea or what you're trying to prove or support.

Prewrite Virgil often uses figurative language to create images. Use a chart like the one below to note passages containing figurative comparisons. Once you have identified several of these passages, look for patterns in the imagery.

Passage	Comparison	Type of Imagery
"I hear a roar like fire … and a shepherd perched on a sheer rock outcrop." (lines 6–11)	The sound of fighting is compared with a grassfire and a flood	Violent forces in nature

Draft Formulate a clear thesis and provide valid and relevant evidence to support it. Develop an introduction, a body, and a conclusion. Use transitional words and phrases to achieve coherence. You may find it helpful to use sentence frames as an organizational tool while drafting your essay. For example, the thesis statement might follow this format:

In Book Two of the Aeneid, *Virgil uses visual imagery to create an overall pattern of* _____.

Revise In your revision, identify and address complexities within the *Aeneid*. For example, you may need to account for any images that do not fit neatly into the pattern identified in your thesis. Use the rubric on page 1292 to check other elements of your essay.

Edit and Proofread Proofread your paper, correcting any errors in spelling, grammar, and punctuation. Use the Grammar Tip in the side column to help you with the comparative and superlative degrees of adjectives and adverbs.

> **Grammar Tip**

Comparative and Superlative Degrees of Adjectives and Adverbs

Adjectives such as *strong* and adverbs such as *forcefully* are in the **positive** form. These forms change to reflect the number of things compared.

The **comparative** form of an adjective (*stronger*) or an adverb (*more forcefully*) shows two things being compared:

The Greek army moves more forcefully than a flooded river.

The **superlative** form of an adjective (*strongest*) or an adverb (*most forcefully*) shows three or more things being compared:

Ajax is the strongest of all the Greeks.

Vocabulary Workshop

Greek and Latin Word Origins

Learning Objectives

In this workshop, you will focus on the following objective:

Vocabulary: Understanding word origins.

Literature Connection The *Aeneid* includes references to many Roman deities, which highlight the fact that ancient Rome did not have a monotheistic belief system. *Monotheistic*, meaning "having one God," comes from the Greek root *mono (mon)*, meaning "one, single, or alone." Many words related to fields such as political science and medicine have Greek and Latin origins. Becoming familiar with a few common roots can help you determine the meanings of unfamiliar words.

Word	Definition	Origin	Discipline
agoraphobia	fear of open spaces	Greek, *phobia*, "fear; aversion"	Medicine
flexor	muscle that bends a limb	Latin, *flect (flex)*, "bend"	Medicine
fracture	break or crack	Latin, *fract (frag)*, "break"	Medicine
hypothermia	below normal body temperature	Greek, *hypo*, "under"	Medicine
macrocosm	larger world; universe	Greek, *macro*, "large"	Political science
microsurgery	surgery performed with microscopes and tiny instruments	Latin, *micro*, "small"	Medicine
regicide	act of killing a king	Latin, *cide*, "killing"	Political science

Etymology

Etymology is the history of a word. A word **root** is the original basis for a word.

Test-Taking Tip

When you encounter an unfamiliar term on a test, try to identify the root. It may help you determine the meaning of the word.

Practice Using a dictionary and the chart above, find the origin and meaning of the root and the definition of each of the following words.

1. hypoglycemia   **4.** polytheism

2. claustrophobia   **5.** creed

3. genocide

Vocabulary For more vocabulary practice, go to glencoe.com and enter QuickPass code GLW6053u2.

Comparing Literature

Across Time and Place

Compare Literature About Disasters

Disasters evoke our deepest fears and expose our hidden frailties. The three authors compared here—Tacitus, Takashi Nagai, and Wisława Szymborska—vividly describe disasters that occurred in different times and places.

Learning Objectives

For pages 400–415

In studying these texts, you will focus on the following objectives:

Literary Study:
Comparing themes. Analyzing author's purpose.

Reading:
Comparing cultural contexts. Recognizing bias.

Writing: Writing a mission statement.

COMPARE THE `Big Idea` **The Imperial City**

These three literary works focus on a city in the throes of a disaster. Tacitus reveals the conditions in ancient Rome that led to a fire spreading out of control, Nagai describes the chaos in Nagasaki immediately after an atomic explosion, and Szymborska explores the thoughts of a famous biblical character as the city of Sodom is destroyed. As you read, ask yourself, What details do the authors reveal about these three cities?

COMPARE Style

Each of these authors uses different styles and literary techniques to re-create a calamity and reflect on its meaning. As you read, ask yourself, What literary techniques contribute to the style of each work?

COMPARE Cultures

Tacitus in ancient Rome, Nagai in Japan near the end of World War II, and Szymborska in modern Poland—these authors represent different cultures. As you read, ask yourself, What cultural values and beliefs do these authors reflect in their work?

The Destruction of Sodom and Gomorrah. Attributed to Joachim Patinir. Oil on panel. Ashmolean Museum, University of Oxford, UK.

 Literature Online

Author Search For more about Tacitus, Takashi Nagai, and Wislawa Szymborska, go to glencoe.com and enter QuickPass code GLW6053u2.

Before You Read

The Burning of Rome

Meet **Tacitus**

(C. A.D. 56–C. 120)

Although he was a successful politician and lawyer, Tacitus (tas′i təs), is best known as the historian of the early Roman Empire. He lived during a turbulent time in Rome, when the democratic rule of the republic was replaced by the absolute rule of the Roman emperor. Having experienced emperors who abused their power, Tacitus found himself confronting their evil deeds more than singing their praises in his histories.

Born into a wealthy family, Tacitus rose to political prominence during Emperor Domitian's reign (A.D. 81–96). He saw many fellow senators destroyed by this tyrannical emperor, which no doubt influenced his view of imperialism. Despite his pessimism, however, Tacitus rose to the position of governor of Asia, Rome's most important province.

Role of the Historian Tacitus's first major work was the *Histories*. Of the original fourteen volumes, only four complete books remain. This work, which covers the period from A.D. 69 to the assassination of Emperor Domitian in A.D. 96, is one of the most detailed histories in Greek and Roman literature.

His second major work is the sixteen-volume *Annals*, which covers the years A.D. 14–68, from the death of Augustus to the death of Nero. In this historical and literary masterpiece, Tacitus portrays the fire that ravaged Rome in A.D. 64 as vividly as an eyewitness, although in fact he relied on sources such as public records and earlier historical accounts. He recorded virtuous and evil actions, rumors and first-hand accounts,

> "It seems to me a historian's foremost duty to ensure that merit is recorded, and to confront evil deeds and words with the fear of posterity's denunciations."
>
> —Tacitus, from the *Annals*

believing his words would punish the bad, reward the good, and instruct future generations.

Today, Tacitus's works continue to be valued for their vivid pictures of imperial Rome. His friend Pliny the Younger accurately predicted, "Your histories will be immortal."

LOG ON **Literature** Online

Author Search For more about Tacitus, go to glencoe. com and enter QuickPass code GLW6053u2.

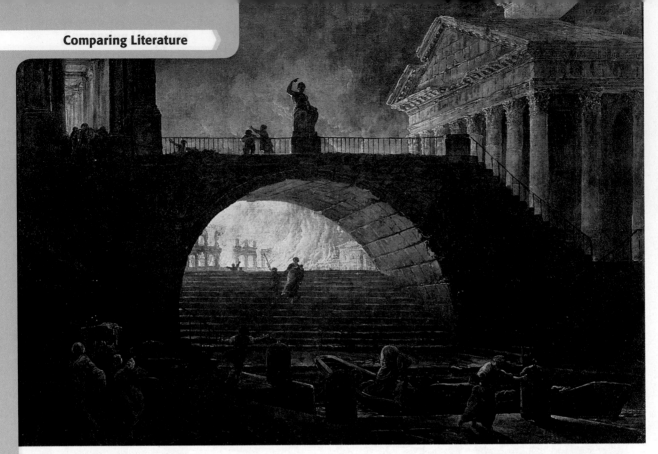

The Burning of Rome. Robert Hubert. Oil on canvas, 76 x 93 cm. Musée des Beaux-Arts André Malraux, Le Havre, France.

involved. Finally, with no idea where or what to flee, they crowded on to the country roads, or lay in the fields. Some who had lost everything—even their food for the day—could have escaped, but preferred to die. So did others, who had failed to rescue their loved ones. Nobody dared fight the flames. Attempts to do so were prevented by menacing gangs. Torches, too, were openly thrown in, by men crying that they acted under orders. Perhaps they had received orders. Or they may just have wanted to plunder unhampered.

Nero was at Antium.[2] He only returned to the city when the fire was approaching the mansion he had built to link the Gardens of Maecenas to the Palatine. The flames could not be prevented from overwhelming the whole of the Palatine, including his palace. Nevertheless, for the relief of the homeless, fugitive masses he threw open the Field of Mars,[3] including Agrippa's public buildings, and even his own Gardens. Nero also constructed emergency accommodation for the destitute multitude. Food was brought from Ostia and neighboring towns, and the price of corn was cut. Yet these measures, for all their popular character, earned no gratitude. For a rumor had spread that, while the city was burning, Nero had gone to his private stage and, comparing modern calamities with ancient, had sung of the destruction of Troy.[4]

---

2. *Antium* (now Anzio) is an ancient coastal city about 30 miles south of Rome. It was Nero's birthplace.

Recognize Bias *What does Tacitus suspect is the cause of the fire? Explain.*

---

3. The *Field of Mars* was a grassy area used for athletic and military events honoring Mars, the Roman god of war.
4. *Troy* was an ancient city of Asia Minor. Its destruction by the Greeks is told in the *Aeneid,* an epic poem by Virgil.

By the sixth day enormous **demolitions** had confronted the raging flames with bare ground and open sky, and the fire was finally stamped out. But before panic had subsided, or hope revived, flames broke out again in the more open regions of the city. Here there were fewer casualties; but the destruction of temples and pleasure arcades was even worse. This new conflagration caused additional ill feeling because it started on Tigellinus's[5] estate. For people believed that Nero was ambitious to found a new city to be called after himself.

Of Rome's fourteen districts only four remained intact. Three were leveled to the ground. The other seven were reduced to a few scorched and mangled ruins. To count the mansions, blocks, and temples destroyed would be difficult. They included shrines of remote antiquity, the precious spoils of countless victories, Greek artistic masterpieces, and authentic records of old Roman genius. All the splendor of the rebuilt city did not prevent the older generation from remembering these irreplaceable objects. It was noted that the fire had started on July 19th, the day on which the Senonian Gauls[6] had captured and burned the city.

But Nero profited by his country's ruin to build a new palace. Its wonders were not so much customary and commonplace luxuries like gold and jewels, but lawns and lakes and faked rusticity—woods here,

open spaces and views there. With their cunning, impudent artificialities, Nero's architects and contractors outbid Nature.

They also fooled away an emperor's riches. For they promised to dig a navigable canal from Lake Avernus to the Tiber estuary,[7] over the stony shore and mountain barriers. The only water to feed the canal was in the Pontine marshes. Elsewhere, all was **precipitous** or waterless. Moreover, even if a passage could have been forced, the labor would have been unendurable and unjustified. But Nero was eager to perform the incredible; so he attempted to excavate the hills adjoining Lake Avernus. Traces of his frustrated hopes are visible today.

In parts of Rome unfilled by Nero's palace, construction was not—as after the burning by the Gauls—without plan or demarcation. Street fronts were of regulated dimensions and alignment, streets were broad, and houses spacious. Their height was restricted, and their frontages protected by colonnades. Nero undertook to erect these at his own expense, and also to clear debris from building sites before transferring them to their owners. He announced bonuses, in

Visual Vocabulary
A *colonnade* is a series of columns set at regular intervals that usually supports a roof.

---

5. *Tigellinus* was a close adviser and friend of Nero.
6. The *Gauls* were Celtic-speaking peoples who lived in modern-day northern Italy, France, and Germany. The *Senonian Gauls* captured and burned Rome in 390 B.C.

Author's Purpose *What do these details reveal about Tacitus's purpose for writing?*

Vocabulary

demolition (dem′ə lish′ən) *n.* an act of tearing down or breaking to pieces; destruction

---

7. The *Tiber estuary* is the section of the Tiber River—which flows through Rome—that meets the sea.

Recognize Bias *What does this passage suggest about Tacitus's opinion of Nero?*

Vocabulary

precipitous (pri sip′ə təs) *adj.* having very steep sides

Build Background

Near the end of World War II, the United States dropped atomic bombs over the cities of Hiroshima and Nagasaki in Japan. In the following excerpt, Dr. Takashi Nagai—a physician who specialized in radiology—describes his experience helping victims of the Nagasaki attack. Nagai was born in 1908 and worked at the Nagasaki Medical College, located only 700 meters from the area directly beneath the explosion. Several months after the explosion, Nagai was diagnosed with leukemia—the result of his exposure to radiation from the bombing—and died in 1951.

From *The Bells of* NAGASAKI

Takashi Nagai

Translated by William Johnston

On August 9, 1945, at two minutes past eleven in the morning, a plutonium atomic bomb exploded at an altitude of some five hundred meters over Matsuyama in the center of the Urakami district of Nagasaki.[1] Tremendous energy was released. And this energy, a tempestuous blast of air traveling at a rate of two thousand meters per second, smashed, pulverized, and blew apart anything in its path. The void created at the center of the explosion sucked up everything on the ground, carrying it high into the sky, and hurled it back violently against the earth. The heat of 9000° Fahrenheit burned the surrounding area. Fragments of incandescent metal rained down in balls of fire immediately setting everything alight.

It is estimated that thirty thousand people lost their lives and that more than one hundred thousand received light or serious wounds, while countless others were afflicted with atomic diseases caused by radiation. In some cases the symptoms of these diseases appeared immediately; in others they appeared much later.

The cloud of smoke in the sky, caused by the bomb and the debris that had been sucked up, hid the rays of the sun, bringing a total darkness like an eclipse. After about three minutes, however, as this immense cloud of smoke and dirt grew bigger, it scattered and became less dense. And once again light and heat filtered down to the earth.

As I have already said, I myself was buried beneath a heap of debris. But finally I managed to extricate myself by my own efforts and make my way to the photography room where I found Professor Fuse with Nurse Hashimoto, the chief nurse, and the others. They all ran to me. "Oh, good! Good!" they kept shouting as they threw their arms around me joyfully.

I looked at their faces one by one. How precious life is, I reflected. How good that you are alive!

---

1. *Matsuyama* is a port city on Shikoku Island, east of Kyushu, Nagasaki's island. The *Urakami district* of Nagasaki was an industrial zone named after the Urakami River, on which Nagasaki is situated.

"But people are missing," I said. "What about Yamashita? What about Inoue? What about Umezu? Let's look for the others and help them. Come back here in five minutes." And with that we left the room and scattered in all directions.

Professor Fuse and Shiro went to the developing room. Pulling away pieces of rubble and looking underneath, they kept shouting: "Hey! Hey!" and strained their ears. But there was no answer. "Moriguchi, are you alive?" roared Shiro. But all was silent.

Choro brought back Umezu seriously wounded. He had found him amidst the instruments in the radiotherapy room. Covered with blood, Umezu threw himself down in the corridor. "I've lost my eyes," he whimpered.

"Don't talk nonsense! Your eyes are all right," said Choro, examining the wound. Above his eyes was a deep gash and there were cuts all over his body.

"It's all right, it's all right," said the chief nurse encouragingly as she applied iodine, put some gauze on the wound, and skill-fully bandaged it.

I took Umezu's pulse and gave some instructions about how we should treat the wounded.

"Doctor, help me!"
"Give me medicine!"
"Look at this wound!"
"Doctor, I'm cold. Give me clothes!"

A strange group of naked human beings crowded around us, all shouting. These were the people who somehow survived when everybody and everything was swept into the air and hurled in all directions by the explosion.

Since the bomb had fallen just when the outpatients were coming in great numbers for consultation, this part of the corridor and the waiting room were littered with an enormous number of fallen people. Their clothes had been torn off; their skin was cut and peeling away. Covered with dirt and smoke, they were gray like phantoms, and it was difficult to believe they were human or that they belonged to this world.

> *"I looked at their faces one by one. How precious life is, I reflected."*

Some, in whom a spark of life remained, extricated themselves from the vast and motionless heap of dead flesh and crawled up to me. Clinging to my feet, they cried: "Doctor, help me! Doctor, help me!" Someone held up a wrist from which blood was pouring profusely. "Mommy! Mommy!" screamed a little girl as she ran this way and that. And mothers, writhing in agony, kept calling the names of their children. "Where's the exit?" roared a big man as he ran around. "Stretcher! Stretcher!" shouted agitated students. And the whole place fell into deeper and deeper turmoil and confusion.

We began emergency treatment. But we quickly ran out of bandages and had to tear shirts, using the strips to bind the wounds.

No sooner had we treated ten or twenty victims than from behind came more and more shouting, "Help me! Help me!" On and on they came and it seemed there was no limit to their number. Since I had to keep one hand pressed tightly against my own wounded forehead, I found it difficult to work. Whenever I removed this hand in order to attend to a patient's wound, the blood would spurt out like red ink from a water pistol, splattering the wall and the

Remains of the Nagasaki Medical College, August 1945. Japan.

shoulder of the chief nurse. An artery in my temple had been cut. But since it was a small artery, I thought my body would hold out for about three hours. Sometimes I felt my own pulse and then went on treating the patients. . . .

I did some serious thinking. The place had become a bloody field of battle. We were the ambulance corps. Our real work was just beginning; we must stand with determination. Doubtless the enemy would continue to drop these bombs. Within a week he would invade our shores and fighting would break out. This was no time for wavering. If we fell into confusion, we would be able to do nothing. We must assemble the core staff members and get organized. We must make sure we had sufficient supplies of medicine and food. We must prepare a camp. After that, we had to establish an efficient system of communi-cations and choose a suitable place in the country for a hospital. Sooner or later Nagasaki would be bombarded from the sea. We must get the patients quickly away and reassemble in a nearby valley.

I looked out the window. I could see nothing but a forest of fire. The whole neighborhood had become one great mass of flames. The fire had even spread to one corner of the building in which we were, and now we could hear the crackling of the approaching flames. . . .

Already twenty minutes had elapsed since the explosion, and Urakami had become a flaming landscape. From the center of the hospital, flames were spreading through the whole campus. The only place free from fire was the hill on the east side of the hospital. Pumps, hoses, water tanks, energetic people—anything or anyone capable of quenching those flames had vanished in a moment. Only one possibility remained: to allow the flames to spread and spread.

Even the survivors were penetrated by powerful radioactive rays. Their clothes were torn and many of them were completely naked. From downtown they ran, climbing the mountain with tottering steps in an effort to escape the flames. Two children passed by dragging their father. A young woman ran clutching a headless child. An aged couple, hand in hand, slowly climbed the mountain. As she ran, a girl's clothes burst into flames and she fell writhing in a ball of fire. On top of a roof that was enveloped in flames, I saw a man dancing and singing wildly: he was out of his mind. Some people kept looking back, looking back as they ran; others did not even turn their heads. A girl was scolding her little sister who lagged behind, but the little one begged her to wait. And from behind the flames pressed on.

About one in ten people had had the good fortune to survive. The others lay charred and dead beneath the wreckage of their burned houses.

As the fire roared on, the direction of the wind changed and from far and near it carried the sound of voices incessantly crying for help. I stood aghast, with folded arms, contemplating the spectacle. Never in my life had I felt so deeply my own impotence. Was there no way of helping these suffering people who were rushing to death before my very eyes? . . .

Was it not for today that we practiced with those stretchers and gave all those lectures on relief work? And now we were confronted with total failure. Like a mosquito whose legs have been plucked off, like a crab whose claws have been torn

away, we faced a multitude of wounded people, helpless and empty-handed. It was really primitive medicine that we were now reduced to. Our knowledge, our love, our hands—we had only these with which to save the people. Crestfallen and depressed, I climbed the steps and, standing in the entrance, surveyed the whole situation once more.

Discouraged though I was, I knew that around me stood doctors and nurses and students—about twenty people in all—who would work till they dropped. The groups of two who had gone from room to room to pick up the wounded now returned and put them in the coal shed beside the entrance. This was the only place that was safe from falling sparks.

I stood helplessly in the middle of them, doing nothing. The fire was becoming more and more violent. Black smoke swirled round and round in the sky; and the thick cloud, reflecting the color of the fire, glowed with an ominous red light. It was an utterly disheartening scene. . . .

Dr. Nagai and the other survivors carry the wounded to safety outdoors, but are unable to save the school and its resources.

The university had become one big ball of fire. It was indeed the end. The president, Professor Tsuno, had suffered serious wounds. No one had seen the director of the hospital, Professor Naito, and it was presumed that he had met the same fate as the hospital itself. According to the students' reports, only Professors Koyano and Cho were safe. Almost all the others had vanished, though someone reported that Professors Kitamura and Hasegawa had been rescued by hospital workers and had been seen covered with blood climbing the hill at the back. Eighty per cent of the

Mother and Son Living in Nagasaki Ruins, September 14, 1945. Nagasaki, Japan.

students and nurses had died. Among those who survived, many were seriously wounded. Combining my group, consisting mainly of people from the surgery department, and another group from the dermatology and pediatrics departments working at the rear entrance area, the total number of survivors was about fifty.

Since we despaired of any survivors from the rooms of fundamental medicine, we had to admit that in terms of personnel and equipment the university was utterly destroyed. We who were standing on the hill looking at the last traces of that burning university, we were the heroic soldiers of the era of Showa.[2]

From one of the hospital rooms, Dr. Okura brought out a big white sheet. Taking a handful of the blood that was dripping from my chin, I traced a huge circular sun on the sheet, which now became a Japanese flag. Attaching this "Rising Sun" to a bamboo pole, we lifted it up and watched it flutter loudly as the hot wind blew all around.

With sleeves rolled up and a white band around his head, young Nagai grasped the pole with both hands and raised the flag high in the air. And then he moved slowly forward carrying the bloody Rising Sun up that hill covered with black smoke. And we all followed in solemn and silent procession. It was five o'clock in the afternoon.

Thus our Nagasaki School of Medicine lost the battle and was reduced to ashes. ✍

---

2. In Japanese history, the *Showa* period (meaning "Bright Peace") lasted for the duration of the reign of emperor Hirohito (1926–1989). The early Showa period lasted from 1926 until the end of World War II in 1945.

> **Discussion Starter**
>
> In a small group, discuss what world leaders might learn from reading Dr. Nagai's account of the Nagasaki bombing. How did reading this memoir increase your knowledge of the devastation caused by a nuclear explosion?

Build Background

According to Genesis 19 in the Bible, Sodom and Gomorrah were the twin cities of sin. God's angels found only one virtuous man living in Sodom—Lot. The angels told him to flee with his family and not look back at Sodom, a city doomed to fiery destruction. Disregarding the angels' warning, Lot's wife looked back at the burning city and was transformed into a pillar of salt. In the following poem, Wisława Szymborska (vis läʹvä shim bôrʹskä) imagines this biblical character examining her motives for looking back.

Lot's Wife

Lot's Wife Looks Back (Burning), 1991. Albert Herbert. Oil on board. Private collection.

Wisława Szymborska
Translated by Adam Czerniawski

> I looked back supposedly curious.
> But besides curiosity I might have had other reasons.
> I looked back regretting the silver dish.
> Through carelessness—tying a sandal strap.
> 5 In order not to keep staring at the righteous nape[1]
> of my husband, Lot.
> Because of sudden conviction that had I died
> he wouldn't have stopped.
> Being humble yet disobedient.

---

1. The *nape* is the back of the neck.

Biographical Narrative

> ▶ **Writing Process**

You may think of new ideas at any stage of a writing process. Feel free to return to earlier stages as you write.

Prewrite

Draft

Revise

Focus Lesson:
Action Verbs

Edit and Proofread

Focus Lesson: Verb Tense

Present

 **Literature** Online

Writing and Research For prewriting, drafting, and revising tools, go to glencoe.com and enter QuickPass code GLW6053u2.

Literature Connection In "The Burning of Rome," Tacitus reveals the infamous character of the Roman emperor Nero.

> *"For a rumor had spread that, while the city was burning, Nero had gone to his private stage and, comparing modern calamities with ancient, had sung of the destruction of Troy."*

Similar to a fictional narrative, Tacitus's story contains a specific setting, point of view, plot, and characters. Yet the narrative is nonfiction because the people and events are historical. As in any narrative, imagery, vivid details, and realistic dialogue bring the characters of a biographical narrative to life. To write a successful biographical narrative, you will need to learn the goals of narrative writing and the strategies to achieve those goals.

Rubric

Goals	Strategies
To narrate a significant incident in a person's life	☑ Explore the meaning of a particular incident
To use specific details to describe the person and the experience	☑ Describe appearances, movements, sensory images, personal feelings, shifts in perspective, and settings in concrete detail
	☑ Use dialogue to bring a character to life
To narrate the events and actions in a logical order	☑ Use narrative details to narrate the events in chronological order
	☑ Pace the action to match changes in time, space, or mood
To connect with an audience	☑ Use a thoughtful, but natural, style
	☑ Capture the audience's interest and imagination

Write a biographical narrative of at least 1,000 words about a true story or series of events involving a friend, family member, historical figure, or another real person to reveal his or her unique character.

Audience: your school or community

Purpose: to reveal the unique personality of a familiar person or public figure

Analyze a Professional Model

In the excerpt below, Mary Renault recounts Alexander the Great's conquest of the Sogdian Rock, a fortress in central Asia. Renault's use of precise narrative and descriptive details reveals the unique character of Alexander. The comments in the margin point out features you might want to include in your own biographical narrative.

Real-World Connection

You may be required to use nonfiction narrative skills to tell facts about your life when you apply to college or for a job. The main points you present about your experiences and your character, along with the supporting details, may be used to judge your merits as a future student or an employee.

from *The Nature of Alexander* by Mary Renault

Everything of importance fell on [Alexander]. He could not delegate to an establishment he was in process of constructing as he went.

He was founding more cities, deeply concerned with them both as viable communities, and as his own memorials. Kandahar still echoes his name. On choice of site hung the settlers' welfare, even their lives. . . .

The country was full of precipitous cliffs and summits, fortified from remote antiquity in the perennial cycles of blood feud and tribal war. From time to time some especially sensational and ingenious siege gets detailed description. It was impossible for Alexander to hear that a strongpoint was impregnable without regarding it as a personal challenge. This showed a perceptive grasp of war psychology in Sogdiana, where courage, strength and success were essentials of status and of survival.

The most notorious of such pinnacles was the Sogdian Rock; high, sheer, and riddled at the top with caves well stocked with

Introduction
Capture your reader's interest in the subject's character and experiences.

Setting
Use details of setting to help the reader visualize your subject's world.

Personal Feelings
Make your subject come alive by revealing his or her feelings.

Conclusion

Discuss how the episode you have presented reveals your subject's character.

food and water. Its chieftain, Oxyartes, was away raising the countryside, leaving his family and garrison in the charge of his son. The single path to the top was entirely commanded from above. The area was under snow.

Alexander offered a parley [conference]. Two envoys climbed down, laughed in his face, and told him not to waste his time unless his men had wings. That settled the matter. He called for volunteers who were expert climbers, and got 300. At night, helped by the snow which would have etched out all the ledges, they were to ascend the steepest, unguarded face, a "very severe." The first man up would get 12 talents, a sum on which to be comfortable for life; the next 11; and so through the first twelve. Iron tent pegs for pitons, mallets, and ropes got them up, in spite of snow-numbed fingers, with a loss of one in ten. In Sogdiana, to have conceded failure might have cost lives by the thousand.

Stunned at dawn by the sight of an unknown force above him, the chief's son surrendered, and everyone was spared. A feast was offered, at which the ladies of the family performed a dance for the conqueror. Among them was the chief's daughter, Roxane. Alexander fell in love with her at first sight. Quixotically renouncing the right of capture which neither friend nor foe would have questioned, he asked for her hand in marriage.

Political expediency has been suggested, but does not convince. No doubt had she been disastrously unsuitable—married for instance—he would have mastered his feelings; but everything points to an authentic *coup de foudre* [love at first sight]. . . . It would seem that falling in love with a woman was a new and exhilarating experience, and, ever the explorer, he was eager to pursue it without delay.

Reading-Writing Connection Think about the writing techniques you just encountered and try them out in the biographical narrative you write.

Prewrite

Choose a Subject As you consider a person you might write about, ask yourself which particular traits stand out and make that person unique. Then think of an incident that helped you see or understand your subject in a new way.

Reveal Character Like a fictional narrative, your biographical narrative should involve specific characters, have a specific setting, and be told from a particular point of view. Try to reveal the personality of your character through his or her actions and interactions with others, rather than simply explaining what that person is like. Use conversation, or dialogue, to make your characters more lifelike. In addition, dialogue lets readers form their own opinions about a character as they "listen in" to the conversation.

Use a Cluster Diagram Use a cluster diagram like the one below to help you plan your narrative. Start by putting your subject's name in the center, and then list general events in his or her life. Move outward to more specific aspects of these events.

Use Vivid Description

Avoid general descriptions or vague characterizations, such as "Claudia is loud and brash." Instead, *demonstrate* your character's nature through specific observations and precise language.

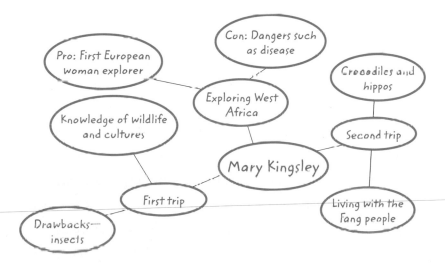

Round Out Your Character You are familiar with the character you are writing about, but your audience may need additional background information to feel the full impact of your narrative. Select details that will help capture your audience's interest and imagination.

Share Your Ideas Meet with a partner to help develop your writing voice. Take turns telling each other the most vivid details about your character and the incident you will write about. As you write, aim for a natural, highly descriptive voice to narrate your experience.

Avoid Plagiarism

As you work on your narrative, you might conduct research about a historical figure. Remember it is wrong to copy directly from another source and present another person's work as your own. Make sure you credit a quotation properly if you wish to incorporate one in your essay.

For more on avoiding plagiarism, see pages R33–R34.

Word Choice

The following academic vocabulary word is used in the student model.

encounter (en koun′tər) *n.* an unexpected or casual meeting; *One of her most memorable encounters on this trip was with a crocodile.*

Using academic vocabulary may help strengthen your writing. Try to use one or two academic vocabulary words in your essay. See the complete list on pages R83–R85.

Revise

Peer Review After you complete your draft, read it aloud for a partner. Use the checklist below to evaluate and strengthen each other's biographical narrative.

Checklist
☑ Do you present main points about your subject's life?
☑ Does your essay have a clear beginning, middle, and end?
☑ Do you narrate events in chronological order and/or tell main ideas in a logical order?
☑ Do you use descriptive details and other precise language?
☑ Do you supply any necessary background information readers need?
☑ Do you write in a conversational tone that allows your voice to come through?

Focus Lesson

Action Verbs

Action verbs tell what someone or something does. When the subject of the sentence performs the action, the action verb is in the active voice. Keep your writing in the active voice as often as possible. Avoid the passive voice, which consists of a form of *to be* plus the past participle.

Draft:

Then she continued her journey into the interior. The strange sights and sounds of the vast tropical forest, and the lives of its animals and human inhabitants, were very interesting to Kingsley. Walking or using a dugout canoe, she moved northward until she reached present-day Nigeria.

Revision:

Then she journeyed[1] into the interior. The strange sights and sounds of the vast tropical forest, and the lives of its animals and people, enchanted[2] Kingsley. Striding[3] along or paddling[3] a dugout canoe, she explored[3] northward until she reached present-day Nigeria.

1 Replace wordy verb constructions with precise verbs.
2 Use active voice whenever possible.
3 Avoid vague writing by using precise action verbs.

Edit and Proofread

Get It Right When you have completed the final draft of your narrative, proofread it for errors in grammar, usage, mechanics, and spelling. Refer to the Language Handbook, pages R40–R59, as a guide.

> **Focus Lesson**

Verb Tense

As you edit your biographical narrative, make sure that your verb tenses are formed correctly and that any shifts in tense are accurate.

Original: There is an incorrect shift in tense.

Kingsley nursed Boer prisoners until she catches a fever and dies, on June 3, 1900.

Improved: Make sure the tenses of verbs in the same sentence match each other.

Kingsley nursed Boer prisoners until she caught a fever and died, on June 3, 1900.

Original: The tense of the sentence does not show that events occurred at different times.

She read about West Africa in her father's library, and she decided to visit this mysterious region.

Improved: Shift from the past tense to the past perfect tense to show that her reading took place before her decision to go to Africa.

She had read about West Africa in her father's library, and she decided to visit this mysterious region.

Present/Publish

Make a Good Impression After you finish editing and proofreading, look over your essay one last time. Make sure the paper is typed and double-spaced with readable fonts and appropriate margins. Give it an interesting title and check with your teacher about any additional presentation guidelines.

Peer Review Tips

A classmate may ask you to read his or her narrative. Take notes as you read so you can give constructive feedback. Use the following questions to get started.

- Do you get a clear sense of the subject?
- Is the tone engaging?
- Are there vivid details?

Word-Processing Tip

If you are typing your narrative on a computer, make sure you use appropriate margin sizes. Half an inch for all margins is usually adequate. Margins too wide or too narrow can be distracting for readers.

Writer's Portfolio

Place a clean copy of your biographical narrative in your portfolio to review later.

LOG ON ▶ **Literature** Online

Writing and Research For editing and publishing tools, go to glencoe.com and enter QuickPass code GLW6053u2.

Do Your Research

Before creating a photo- or art-essay, research art and photo exhibits. What is it about these exhibits that speaks to the audience and stands out above everyday images? You should incorporate these elements into your presentation.

Speaking, Listening, and Viewing Workshop

Photo-Essay

Literature Connection

> *"You will find him depicted as one of the four kings on the standard French pack of playing cards; you will find the map of his empire on every Greek school map, and every taverna wall; he's on Sicilian carnival carts, Ethiopian bridal cloths, Byzantine church murals, and on paintings from Moghul India."*

Alexander the Great has been the subject of an extraordinary variety of artwork, as shown in the quotation above by Michael Wood from *In the Footsteps of Alexander the Great*. Examine the image below. What does it reveal about the artist's view of Alexander?

You can collect and combine art or photographs to present the significance of a historical figure in a photo-essay.

> **Assignment**   **Present a Photo- or Art-Essay**
>
> Plan and deliver a photo- or art-essay on a historical figure.

The Dying Alexander the Great, 356-323 BC. Marble. Ancient Art and Architecture Collection Ltd.

Plan Your Presentation

Just like written essays, your photo- or art-essay needs to have a main idea. Choose a historical person you would like to represent and decide what you want to express about that individual. For example, if you decide to present legends about Alexander the Great, you might collect medieval images showing him flying through air or exploring underwater. Your presentation should be compelling and interesting to gain and keep your audience's attention. Follow these guidelines when presenting an art- or photo-essay.

- **Research the topic well.** You should be prepared to answer any questions the audience may have about your historical figure and each image you present.

- **Allow enough time to prepare.** Think about how many pieces you would like to have in your essay, as well as what kinds of images would best suit your purpose.

- **Decide how you will showcase your work.** Will you use an easel, poster board, a slide projector, or a computer presentation?

Create Meaning in Visual Media

It is often said a picture is worth a thousand words. Your pictures need to be able to "speak" to the audience, or convey emotion and feeling.

Presentation Tips

Use the following checklist to evaluate your presentation.

- Did you remember not to block the visuals?

- Did you face the audience and not the visuals?

- Did you vary the tone of your visuals, incorporating both humor and serious images when appropriate?

Techniques for Presenting a Photo- or Art-Essay

Verbal Techniques	Nonverbal Techniques
☑ **Volume** Speak loudly and clearly so your audience can understand any background information you provide.	☑ **Eye Contact** Make frequent eye contact with the audience. However, you should also look at the photographs or art to draw attention to important details.
☑ **Pace** Allow the audience enough time to view and react to each image before moving on to the next one.	☑ **Gestures** Point out key details in your art, but be careful not to block your essay when presenting.
☑ **Tone** The tone of your speech should match the tone of your photo- or art-essay. If your essay is of a serious nature, you should speak in a dignified, serious tone. More light-hearted essays can be presented with a more informal tone.	☑ **Display** Use an easel or poster board to display your images. The art and photographs should be presented in such a way that your entire audience can view them.

LOG ON ▶ **Literature** Online

Speaking, Listening, and Viewing For project ideas, templates, and presentation tips, go to glencoe.com and enter QuickPass code GLW6053u2.

Assessment

English–Language Arts

Reading: Nonfiction

Carefully read the following passage. Use context clues to help you define any words with which you are unfamiliar. Pay close attention to credibility, cultural context, the author's purpose, and his use of literary devices. Then, on a separate sheet of paper, answer the questions on pages 429–433.

from *Julius Caesar* by Suetonius

Now Caesar's approaching murder was foretold to him by unmistakable signs. . . . Shortly before his death, as he was told, the herds of horses which he had dedicated to the river Rubicon when he crossed it, and had let loose without a keeper, stubbornly refused to graze and wept copiously. Again,
5   when he was offering sacrifice, the soothsayer Spurinna warned him to beware of danger, which would come not later than the Ides of March. On the day before the Ides of that month, a little bird called the king-bird flew into the Hall of Pompey with a sprig of laurel, pursued by others of various kinds from the grove hard by, which tore it to pieces in the hall. In fact the
10   very night before his murder he dreamt now that he was flying above the clouds, and now that he was clasping the hand of Jupiter; and his wife Calpurnia thought that the pediment of their house fell, and that her husband was stabbed in her arms; and on a sudden the door of the room flew open of its own accord.
15   Both for these reasons and because of poor health he hesitated for a long time whether to stay at home and put off what he had planned to do in the Senate; but at last, urged by Decimus Brutus not to disappoint the full meeting, which had for some time been waiting for him, he went forth almost at the end of the fifth hour; and when a note revealing the plot was handed
20   him by someone on the way, he put it with others which he held in his left hand, intending to read them presently. Then, after many victims had been slain, and he could not get favorable omens, he entered the Senate in defiance of portents, laughing at Spurinna and calling him a false prophet, because the Ides of March were come without bringing him harm. Spurinna
25   replied that they had of a truth come, but they had not gone.
As he took his seat, the conspirators gathered about him as if to pay their respects, and straightway Tillius Cimber, who had assumed the lead, came nearer as though to ask something; and when Caesar with a gesture put him off to another time, Cimber caught his toga by both shoulders; then as

30 Caesar cried, "Why, this is violence!" one of the Cascas stabbed him from one
side just below the throat. Caesar caught Casca's arm and ran it through with
his stylus, but as he tried to leap to his feet, he was stopped by another
wound. When he saw that he was beset on every side by drawn daggers, he
muffled his head in his robe, and at the same time drew down its lap to his
35 feet with his left hand, in order to die more decently, with the lower part of
his body also covered. And in this way he was stabbed with three and twenty
wounds, uttering not a word, but merely a groan at the first stroke, though
some have written that when Marcus Brutus rushed at him, he said in Greek,
"You too, my child?" All the conspirators made off, and he lay there lifeless for
40 some time, until finally three common slaves put him on a litter and carried
him home, with one arm hanging down. And of so many wounds none
turned out to be mortal, in the opinion of the physician Antistius, except the
second one in the breast.

1. In the opening paragraph, what warning does
   Caesar receive of his approaching death?
   A. One of the conspirators informs Caesar.
   B. Strange events suggest something bad will
   happen.
   C. Caesar's friends warn him in person.
   D. Caesar receives a letter from a friend.

2. Suetonius introduces the horses in lines 2–4
   to show that:
   F. Caesar loves animals.
   G. Caesar is generous.
   H. the animals sense Caesar's impending
   death.
   J. Caesar believes deeply in the Roman
   gods.

3. As it is used in line 5, the word *soothsayer*
   most nearly means:
   A. doctor.
   B. fortune-teller.
   C. bodyguard.
   D. murderer.

4. The accounts of Caesar and Calpurnia in
   lines 9–14 suggest that:
   F. Calpurnia is going to be an accomplice in
   Caesar's murder.
   G. Spurinna's warnings have a positive effect
   on Caesar.
   H. Caesar and his wife have premonitions of
   his death.
   J. Caesar knows how he is going to die.

5. The discussion of the days leading up to
   Caesar's assassination in paragraph 1 suggests
   that the Romans:

   I. were apathetic toward their animals.
   II. were always thinking about death.
   III. believed in omens and fortune-telling.

   A. II only
   B. III only
   C. I and III only
   D. II and III only

6. Caesar eventually decides to meet with the Senate because:
   F. Decimus Brutus convinces him the Senate has been waiting long enough.
   G. he fails to read the letter that warns of the plot.
   H. he is in poor health and prefers to be with others.
   J. he no longer believes in omens of any sort.

7. As it is used in line 23, the word *portents* most nearly means:
   A. enemies.
   B. victims.
   C. prophets.
   D. forewarnings.

8. Caesar scoffs at Spurinna and calls him a false prophet because:

   I. the Ides of March have arrived without incident.
   II. Caesar wants to give an impression of confidence.
   III. none of Spurinna's prophecies ever came true.

   F. I only
   G. III only
   H. I and II only
   J. I, II, and III

9. As it is used in line 32, the word *stylus* most nearly means:
   A. a sharp-pointed pen
   B. a sandal
   C. a long robe
   D. a heavy club

10. At what point does Caesar try to dismiss one of the senators?
    F. after he cries "Why, this is violence!"
    G. before the conspirators gathered about him
    H. after the first attack
    J. before Tillius Cimber grabs his toga

11. Why does Caesar draw his toga to his feet?
    A. to protect his legs from wounds
    B. to keep from being cold
    C. to die with dignity
    D. to avoid falling

12. When does Caesar let out a groan?
    F. as the first wound is inflicted
    G. after the twenty-third wound was inflicted
    H. after Marcus Brutus rushed at him
    J. after he muffled his head in his robe

13. After reading Suetonius's account, what generalization can you make about Caesar?
    A. He knows all of the conspirators intimately.
    B. He is proud and stoic.
    C. He has great respect for the physician Antistius.
    D. He often disagrees with his wife Calpurnia.

14. What is the author's primary purpose in this passage?
    F. to entertain
    G. to inform
    H. to persuade
    J. to express feelings

15. According to the physician Antistius, what is the cause of Caesar's death?
    A. his inability to fight back
    B. only some of the 23 blows
    C. Caesar's failure to heed bad omens
    D. the second wound in Caesar's breast

Vocabulary Skills: Sentence Completion

For each item in the Vocabulary Skills section, choose the word or words that best complete the sentence. Write your answers on a separate sheet of paper.

1. Seeking _____, the Persians once again invaded Greece ten years after the culmination of the battle at Marathon.
   A. vengeance
   B. munificence
   C. moderation
   D. demolition

2. For a Greek soldier, leaving weapons and armor in the hands of the enemy was considered _____ behavior, likely to be _____ by fellow Greeks.
   F. ignominious…denounced
   G. incredulous…dignity
   H. stern…intimation
   J. tangible…versatility

3. The Greek poet Sappho hoped her writings would be remembered rather than fall into _____.
   A. foreboding
   B. droves
   C. detractor
   D. oblivion

4. Athens _____ all other Greek city-states in the brilliance of its civilization.
   F. appeased
   G. inflicted
   H. surpassed
   J. retracted

5. Theater was a _____ and _____ element of the culture of ancient Athenians, who used it to explore everything from religious experiences to social questions.
   A. horrendous…ignominious
   B. sullen…incredulous
   C. crucial…tangible
   D. random…vulnerable

6. In their struggle with Carthage, the Romans _____ help from other peoples of Italy.
   F. swelled
   G. enlisted
   H. surpassed
   J. censured

7. The assassins surrounded Julius Caesar and _____ 23 wounds, leaving him dead and his supporters and family _____.
   A. appeased…suppliant
   B. fastened…sinister
   C. enlisted…horrendous
   D. inflicted…bereft

8. Breaking out on July 18, A.D. 64, the Great Fire of Rome had _____ results, bringing the city to the brink of disaster.
   F. vulnerable
   G. subtle
   H. dire
   J. futile

9. Epicureanism _____ people to avoid pain and to seek wisdom in seclusion, withdrawing from public life.
   A. impelled
   B. defiled
   C. detected
   D. suppressed

10. Roman gladiatorial combats were fights to the death, never _____ as too violent by their bloodthirsty audiences.
    F. duped
    G. denounced
    H. detected
    J. gloated

Grammar and Writing Skills: Sentence Improvement

Read carefully through the following passage from the first draft of a student's essay. For Questions 1–8, choose the best alternative for each word or phrase that is underlined and numbered. If you think the original version is best, choose "NO CHANGE." Then answer Questions 9 and 10. Write your answers on a separate sheet of paper.

[1]

The defeat and destruction of Rome <u>was</u> the lifelong goal of the Carthaginian general Hannibal. <u>Brave</u>
1
<u>brilliant, cunning, resourceful and relentless</u>, he was the most dangerous enemy the Romans ever
2
faced. When Hannibal was a child, his father made him swear before the gods that he would never
stop fighting Rome. That promise Hannibal kept <u>under</u> all his victories and his final defeat.
3

[2]

<u>When he grew up, Hannibal first seizes</u> one of Rome's allied cities in Spain, an act of war. His next
4
move was even <u>bolder; to attack Italy itself.</u> Leading 40,000 soldiers and about forty elephants,
5
Hannibal marched out of Spain. He <u>crossed southern Gaul and reached</u> the foot of the Alps in the
6
fall of 218 B.C. <u>Before, he reached northern Italy, cold, ice, hunger, sickness, and attacks</u> by mountain
7
peoples killed half of Hannibal's army and most of his elephants.

[3]

[1] Although the Carthaginians were usually outnumbered, Hannibal led his troops to a series of victories against Roman armies. [2] Determined to stop him, Rome's leaders sent out the most powerful force they had ever assembled, an army estimated to have been as large as 100,000 men. [3] Luring his enemies into a trap, Hannibal surrounded and destroyed nearly the entire Roman army. [4] In early August 216 B.C., the Romans met <u>Hannibal's troops near the town of Cannae in southeastern</u>
8
<u>Italy.</u> [5] Roman armies were organized into units known as legions, centuries, and cohorts.

1. **A.** NO CHANGE
   B. were
   C. had been
   D. are

2. **F.** NO CHANGE
   G. Brave, brilliant, cunning, resourceful, and relentless
   H. Brave and brilliant, cunning, resourceful, and relentless
   J. Brave, brilliant, cunning, resourceful, relentless

3. **A.** NO CHANGE
   B. over
   C. into
   D. through

4. **F.** NO CHANGE
   G. When he grows up, Hannibal will first seize
   H. When he grew up, Hannibal first seized
   J. Growing up, Hannibal first seized

5. **A.** NO CHANGE
   B. bolder, to attack Italy itself.
   C. bolder—to attack Italy itself.
   D. bolder to attack Italy itself.

6. **F.** NO CHANGE
   G. crossed southern Gaul, and reached
   H. crosses southern Gaul, and reaches
   J. had crossed southern Gaul and reaches

7. **A.** NO CHANGE
   B. Before he reached northern Italy, cold, ice, hunger, sickness, and attacks
   C. Before, he reached northern Italy cold, ice, hunger, sickness, and attacks
   D. Before he reached northern Italy, cold ice, hunger sickness, and attacks

8. **F.** NO CHANGE
   G. Hannibal's troops near the town of Cannae, in southeastern Italy
   H. Hannibal troops near the town of Cannae in southeastern Italy
   J. Hannibals troops near the town of Cannae in Southeastern Italy

9. Which of the following sequences of sentences will make Paragraph 3 most logical?
   A. 1, 2, 4, 5, 3
   B. 2, 1, 3, 4, 5
   C. 3, 4, 1, 2, 3
   D. 1, 2, 5, 4, 3

Question 10 refers to the preceding passage as a whole.

10. The writer has been asked to write an essay that includes an introduction, a body, and a conclusion about what motivated Hannibal. Would this essay fulfill that assignment?
    F. Yes; the writer explains Hannibal's motivations and includes an introduction, a body, and a conclusion.
    G. No; the writer does not discuss Hannibal's motivations.
    H. No; the writer does not include an introduction.
    J. No; the writer discusses what motivated Hannibal but does not include a conclusion.

Essay: Writing Situation

Which of the individuals you encountered in this unit seems the most heroic?

Directions for Writing

Remember that the Greek heroic ideal stressed all-around excellence, including physical power, intellectual ability (often viewed as cunning), and moral strength (such as bravery and endurance). Select one of the figures from this unit, either a real person (such as Socrates) or an imaginary character (such as Oedipus), and analyze how this individual reflects or departs from the Greek heroic ideal.

Remember to:

- Write about the assigned topic.
- Make your writing thoughtful and interesting.
- Make sure each sentence you write contributes to your composition as a whole.
- Make sure your ideas are clear and easy for the reader to follow.
- Write about your ideas in depth so the reader is able to develop a good understanding of what you are saying.

- Proofread your writing to correct errors in spelling, capitalization, punctuation, grammar, and sentence structure.

 Literature Online

Assessment For additional test practice, go to glencoe.com and enter QuickPass code GLW6053u2.

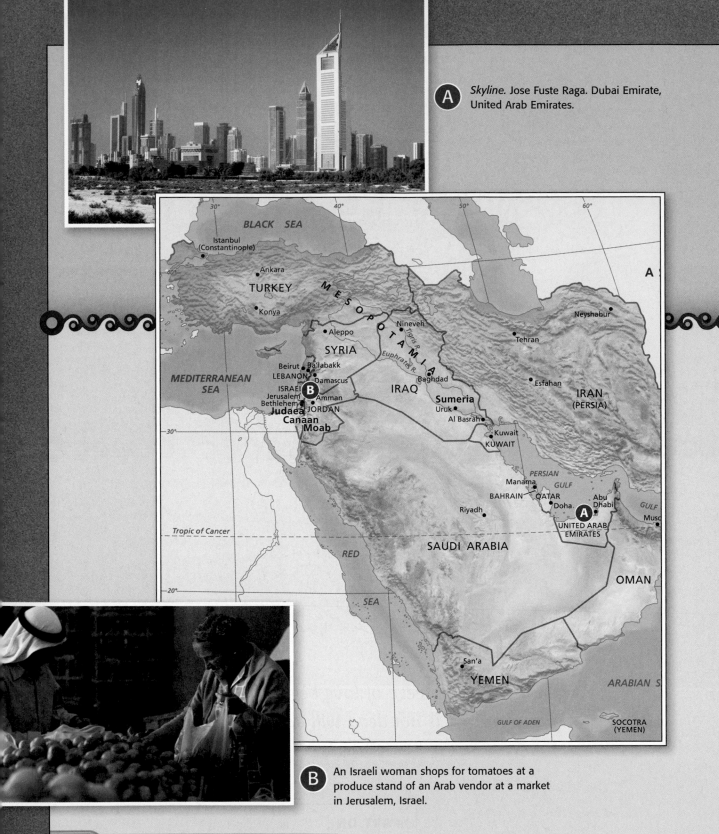

A *Skyline.* Jose Fuste Raga. Dubai Emirate, United Arab Emirates.

B An Israeli woman shops for tomatoes at a produce stand of an Arab vendor at a market in Jerusalem, Israel.

LOG ON ▶ **Literature** Online

Literature and Reading For more about the history and literature of this period, go to glencoe.com and enter QuickPass code GLW6053u3.

Southwest Asia

3500 B.C.—Present

Being There

The western edge of southwest Asia borders the Mediterranean Sea. To the north and the east, the land rises into rugged, snowcapped mountain ranges. Vast deserts occupy much of the southern part of the region. In the center lies the valley of the Tigris and the Euphrates rivers, known in the ancient world as Mesopotamia. The people of southwest Asia have a long and rich cultural history.

Looking Ahead

Some of the world's earliest civilizations arose in Mesopotamia more than 5,000 years ago. Later, three major religions—Judaism, Christianity, and Islam—originated in the region. Religion remains an important and often divisive force in contemporary southwest Asia. The region is primarily Muslim, with the exception of the Jewish state of Israel and some small Christian communities.

Keep the following questions in mind as you read:

- How did the sacred scriptures of Judaism, Christianity, and Islam develop?

- How did Persian poetry develop, and what are some of its main themes?

- How have recent political and cultural events affected the contemporary literature of southwest Asia?

Southwest Asia

Learning Objectives

For pages 436–447

In studying this text, you will focus on the following objectives:

Literary Study: Analyzing literary periods.

Reading: Evaluating historical influences.
Connecting to the literature.

3500 B.C.–Present

Historical, Social, and Cultural Forces

Ancient Mesopotamia

Ancient Mesopotamian farmers benefited greatly from the fresh water provided by the Tigris and the Euphrates rivers. This water allowed them to grow a surplus of food, which fed a growing population—including the rulers, the priests, and the scribes who eventually created and organized the world's first city-states, around 3000 B.C. The technical and intellectual achievements of the ancient Mesopotamians included the plow, the wheel, the sailboat, the 60-minute hour, and the world's first writing system.

As the city-states of ancient Mesopotamia grew, they came into conflict with one another. Around 2334 B.C., a ruler named Sargon conquered Mesopotamia and created the world's first empire. Over the next 3,000 years, a long series of empires—Babylonian, Assyrian, Persian, Macedonian, Parthian, and Sassanid—rose and fell in this region.

Judaism and Christianity

The Jewish people emerged as a distinct cultural group between 1200 B.C. and 1000 B.C. They established the ancient kingdom of Israel on the Mediterranean coast and practiced the faith known today as Judaism. At the time, Judaism was unique among the religions of southwest Asia because of its tenet that there is only one God. Because of this, the ancient Jews had to struggle to preserve both their religion and their political independence from powerful neighbors such as the Babylonians and the Assyrians. By the first century A.D., Israel had become part of the Roman Empire. Under Roman rule, a Jewish prophet named Jesus, who stressed the importance of tolerance, love, and charity, was crucified as a revolutionary. His followers, who believed Jesus to be the son of God, became known as Christians (from *Christos,* "anointed one," a Greek title for Jesus).

Laylat al-Qadr Celebrated. Kazuyoshi Nomachi. Mecca, Saudi Arabia.

Islam

Islam became the predominant religion throughout southwest Asia after the Islamic empire expanded in the seventh century A.D. Muhammad, the founder of Islam (*Islam* is Arabic for "submission"), was born about A.D. 570 in the city of Mecca on the Arabian Peninsula. Muslims believe that Muhammad was a prophet through whom Allah (God) revealed himself as he had done earlier through Jewish prophets such as Moses and Jesus. Muhammad taught that Islam was a more fundamental unifying force than nationality or kinship. Muslim power in southwest Asia remained strong until the 1700s, when it began a long decline that would continue into modern times.

> *"There is no god but God; Muhammad is the messenger of God."*
>
> —Islamic profession of faith

Islamic Civilization

The early Arab empire was prosperous and was supported by an extensive trade network. It was home to flourishing cities, including Cairo and Baghdad. The Abassids, a line of Muslim rulers, built Baghdad to be their capital city. Under their rule, Arab civilization reached a cultural high point. They were great patrons of the arts and made Baghdad one of the most splendid cities in the world. Muslim scholars preserved ancient works while making new contributions to history, literature, philosophy, and science. In the mid-thirteenth century, Mongol invaders overran the Abbasid Empire, capturing and destroying Baghdad in 1258. As a result, the new center of Islamic civilization became Cairo, Egypt. Later, the Ottoman and Persian empires dominated southwest Asia.

Modern Islam

After World War I, the Arabic provinces of the Ottoman Empire came under British and French control. By the late 1940s, all these areas had regained their independence. In the former Ottoman province of Palestine, Jewish settlers established the State of Israel in 1948. Since then, there has been nearly continual tension between Israel and its Arab neighbors, punctuated by several wars. Southwest Asia has also been troubled by conflicts between various Muslim states, such as the Iran-Iraq War of the 1980s.

Abbasid Plaque, 12th century. Iraq or Iran. Ivory. Louvre, Paris.

Islamic Art

An early collection of Muhammad's sayings warned against any attempt to imitate God by creating pictures of living beings. As a result, from early times, no depictions of humans or animals appear in Islamic art, and no representation of the prophet Muhammad ever adorns a mosque, or an Islamic house of worship. Instead, most Islamic art consists of Arabic letters, shapes derived from plants and flowers, and abstract figures. These motifs are repeated in geometric patterns called *arabesques* that cover the surfaces of objects and buildings. Arts and crafts, such as pottery, metalwork, and carpet weaving, are much appreciated and given high status. Calligraphy, the creation of beautiful handwriting, became a high art in Islamic civilization.

The miniature, a pictorial tradition developed in Persia, was an exception to the avoidance of portraying people and animals in Islamic art. Persian miniature painting was usually done to illustrate works of literature. Persian artists used rich, jewel-like colors to paint elaborate pictures showing scenes from epic poems, romances, fables, and other works.

> *"I came in like a cloud, and I left like a wind."*
>
> —Rumi

Bowl, 13th century. Persian School. Stone-paste with lustre over glaze. Ashmolean Museum, University of Oxford, UK.

Whirling Dervish Performing. Hans Georg Roth. Istanbul, Turkey. ▶

Religious Dance

In Islam, dance is not considered appropriate religious expression. The one exception is the tradition of dancing practiced by Sufi dervishes. (*Sufis* got their name from the Arabic word *suf*, or "wool," which refers to the woolen cloaks worn by early dervishes as a sign of their poverty—*dervish* is Persian for "beggar.") Sufism is a religious movement that seeks to attain a direct experience of God through contemplation and other practices. One of these practices is a whirling dance whose goal is to put dervishes into a trance in which they can experience a mystical union with God. For seven centuries, this tradition has been kept alive by the order of Mevlevi (or Mawlawi) dervishes, founded by the great Sufi poet Rumi (see pages 511–515) in the thirteenth century.

Religious Architecture

Many of the most beautiful buildings in southwest Asia were built for religious use. Cities such as Aleppo in Syria and Esfahān in Iran contain magnificent mosques and shrines. There are also beautiful Christian churches (notably in Istanbul, Turkey), which often feature Byzantine artwork, such as frescoes and mosaics. The region also contains great surviving temples of the ancient world, such as Baalbek in Lebanon.

Hagia Sophia. Murat Taner. Istanbul, Turkey.

PREVIEW **Big Ideas** of Southwest Asia

1 The Secret of Life	**2** The Search for Wisdom	**3** The Violence of Change
Southwest Asia was the birthplace of three great world religions, Judaism, Christianity, and Islam. The sacred texts of these faiths often explore and reveal different ideas about the secrets of life. **See page 444**	Medieval Persia gave rise to an extraordinarily rich collection of literature, including the skeptical poetry of Omar Khayyám and the mystical writings of Jalal al-Din Rumi. In their works, these poets explore wisdom and how it is achieved. **See page 445**	In the twentieth century, southwest Asia became a focus of great political, social, and economic change, which has led to violent conflicts among Muslims, Israelis, and Westerners that continue to this day. **See page 446**

The Secret of Life

Page from a Hebrew Bible with birds, 1299. Instituto da Biblioteca Nacional, Lisbon, Portugal.

What is the most essential function of writing? For many cultures, it has been the recording of religious tenets and traditions. Sacred texts form a basic element of the literature of southwest Asia, dating back to some of the earliest written records in the world. From the beginning, these religious writings spoke to fundamental human concerns, such as how the world was created and what happens to the soul after death.

The First Literature

The first writing to appear in Mesopotamia—and possibly in the world—probably took the form of pictographs (pictures representing ideas or words). As part of an ancient record-keeping system, merchants marked wedge-shaped symbols representing different goods onto wet clay tablets. By 3000 B.C., Mesopotamian scribes were using a writing system based on these symbols. Modern scholars refer to this script as *cuneiform* ("wedge-shaped"). Archaeologists have discovered thousands of cuneiform tablets. Among them is the world's oldest literary masterpiece, the epic of *Gilgamesh* (see pages 448–466), which relates the quest of a legendary Mesopotamian king for the secret of eternal life.

> "He went on a long journey, was weary, worn out with labor, and returning engraved on a stone the whole story."
>
> —from *Gilgamesh*

People of the Book

Judaism, Christianity, and Islam share a belief in one God and a basis in sacred texts believed to be revealed by God. One of these texts, the Islamic Qur'an (kô rän´), describes Jews, Christians, and Muslims as "people of the book." The traditions of the Jewish people are preserved in their sacred text, the Tanakh, or Hebrew Bible (see pages 470–485). The Jews believed that God gave a code of laws, the Ten Commandments, to Moses. By obeying these laws, an individual can establish a personal relationship with God.

Jesus, the Jewish founder of Christianity, taught that to achieve salvation, people needed not only to obey God's laws, but also to be transformed by love for one another. Accounts of the life and the teachings of Jesus, along with other religious texts, circulated among early Christian communities and were later gathered together as the New Testament (see pages 486–490), the second part of the Christian Bible. (Parts of the Hebrew Bible form the first part, known to Christians as the Old Testament.) Muslims believe that those who desire to achieve salvation and life after death must subject themselves to the will of Allah as revealed in the Qur'an (see pages 491–495), Islam's sacred text.

Reading Check

Make Generalizations Why are Jews, Christians, and Muslims known as "people of the book"?

Big Idea 2
The Search for Wisdom

What is wisdom? Is it simply shrewdness and common sense? Is it based on a mature understanding of human limits and the fleeting nature of happiness? Or is it a profound insight into the underlying reality of things? Medieval Persian literature explores wisdom in all its forms.

Farhad carrying Shirin and her horse. Miniature from *Khusrau u Shirin.* Victoria & Albert Museum, London.

Islamic Persia

Muslim armies conquered Persia within twenty years of Muhammad's death in 632. Because Islam requires that believers read the Qur'an in Arabic, many Arabic words entered the Persian language after the Muslim conquest. The Persians preserved their own language, however, unlike many conquered peoples who adopted Arabic. By the middle of the tenth century, the Muslim empire had grown weak. Native princes regained control of Persia, and nationalist feeling reawakened. One result of this shift in power was a revival of Persian literature.

> "The Moving Finger writes; and, having writ,
> Moves on: nor all your Piety nor Wit
> Shall lure it back to cancel half a Line,
> Nor all your Tears wash out a Word of it."
> —from the *Rubáiyát*

Persian Literature

Persians regarded poetry as the highest form of literature. Therefore, it is not surprising that a poet was largely responsible for the revival of Persian literature. This poet, Firdusi, was born about 935. He combined traditional Persian myth, legend, and history in an epic poem, the *Shah Nameh* (Persian for "Book of Kings"). In short, rhyming couplets, Firdusi told the story of Persia from the time of its mythical kings, through the conquests of Alexander the Great, and up to the Arab conquest. The *Shah Nameh* became the Persian national epic and the inspiration for many masterpieces of Persian miniature painting.

Some of the works of Islamic literature that are most familiar to Western readers were produced in Persia during the Middle Ages. Among them is the famous collection known as the *Rubáiyát* (Persian for "quatrains") by Persian poet, scientist, and mathematician Omar Khayyám (see pages 505–510). Another well-known medieval Persian poet is thirteenth-century Sufi mystic Rumi (see pages 511–515), author of *The Masnavi*, a large collection of Sufi sermons and fables in verse. Many of the stories in the vast collection of tales known as *The Thousand and One Nights* (see pages 496–504) are also Persian in origin.

Reading Check

Analyze Cause-and-Effect Relationships How did the weakening of Muslim control in Persia lead to a revival of Persian literature?

Big Idea 3
The Violence of Change

Periods of rapid political and cultural change are difficult for those who experience them, whether the changes are ultimately positive or not. When such periods are accompanied by violence and the outcome remains uncertain, they can be almost unendurable.

A Region of Conflict

The Industrial Revolution, which began in the 1700s, made European nations very powerful. Using their economic and military strength, they gained power over the Muslim peoples of southwest Asia. In the decades following World War II, Muslim nations regained their independence, and some states became enriched by oil revenues. Persistent political problems trouble the region, however, and many Muslims resent what they see as the West's hostility toward traditional Islamic values. These political and cultural conflicts have often erupted into violence.

The creation of the Jewish state of Israel in 1948 and disputes over land rights have also led to many conflicts. Since Israel's formation, Israelis have fought several wars with neighboring Muslim countries. Palestinian Arabs displaced by the Israelis have staged violent protest movements known as *intifadas* (Arabic for "uprisings") against Israel. Additionally, religious and cultural movements and ethnic disputes have led to conflicts such as the Iran-Iraq War, which lasted from 1980 to 1988. Finally, Muslim nations and groups have fought with some Western countries, as evidenced by the two American-led wars against Iraq.

> "Put it on record.
>   I am an Arab.
> I am a name without a title . . ."
>
> —Mahmoud Darwish, from "Identity Card"

The Flag Bearer, 1955. Avigdor Arikha. Oil on canvas. Israel Museum, Jerusalem.

A Literature of Conflict

The modern literature of southwest Asia is permeated with themes that derive from the region's conflicts. This is especially true of the poetry written by Hebrew poets Yehuda Amichai (see pages 524–527) and Dahlia Ravikovitch (see pages 520–523). Both of these poets received international acclaim for their explorations of the physical and emotional repercussions of war. A prominent voice of Palestinian resistance to Israel, Mahmoud Darwish spent many years living in exile before returning to the Palestinian territory of the West Bank in 1996. In her acclaimed graphic novel *Persepolis*, Iranian illustrator and author Marjane Satrapi (see pages 532–541) has explored her own recollections of the Iranian Revolution and the ways in which it changed Iran and impacted her friends and family.

Reading Check

Analyze Cause-and-Effect Relationships What is one cause of the recent conflicts in southwest Asia?

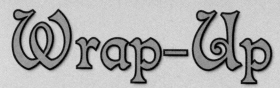

Wrap-Up

Legacy of the Region

Some of the most influential cultural and religious ideas in the world originated in southwest Asia. The ancient Mesopotamians developed what was probably the world's first system of writing and used it to produce a rich literary tradition, including the world's oldest literary masterpiece, *Gilgamesh*. Judaism, Christianity, and Islam all arose in southwest Asia. Their beliefs, values, traditions, and sacred scriptures have had an extraordinary impact on world history.

Islam became the driving force and the cultural basis for an empire that—at its greatest extent around A.D. 750—stretched from Spain to the borders of China. Islamic civilization both preserved and transformed the cultures of the peoples within the Muslim empire. One of the greatest of these cultures was Persia's, which gave rise to poets Omar Khayyám and Rumi and was the source of many of the tales in *The Thousand and One Nights*.

Since World War II, southwest Asia has been the scene of violent protests, acts of terrorism, and wars. Bitter conflicts continue to plague the region.

They have been transported swiftly, from *The Arabian Nights,* 1939. Roger Broders. Colour engraving. Private collection.

Cultural and Literary Links

- The Hebrew Bible and the Christian New Testament have profoundly influenced Western civilization.

- After *The Thousand and One Nights* was translated into European languages, characters such as Sindbad the Sailor, Ali Baba, and Aladdin took their place among the most popular of all fairy-tale figures.

- The *Rubáiyát* became popular outside Persia after Edward FitzGerald translated it in the nineteenth century.

LOG ON ▶ **Literature** Online

Unit Resources For additional skills practice, go to glencoe.com and enter QuickPass code GLW6053u3.

Activities

Use what you have learned about the region to do one of these activities.

1. **Follow Up** Go back to Looking Ahead on page 437 and answer the questions.

2. **Contrast Literary Periods** In the United States, the Civil War era gave rise to classic works, including *The Red Badge of Courage* and *Incidents in the Life of a Slave Girl*. Compare and contrast the causes of the Civil War with the sources of conflict authors in southwest Asia have explored.

3. **Build Visual Literacy** Create a visual display showing how different illustrators have

depicted tales from *The Thousand and One Nights*.

4. **Take Notes** Use this study organizer to keep track of the literary elements you learn in this part.

FOLDABLES Study Organizer   **BOUND BOOK**

Before You Read

from *Gilgamesh*

The epic of *Gilgamesh* is the greatest surviving literary work of ancient Mesopotamia (a region centered in what is now Iraq). Mesopotamia was home to a series of important ancient cultures, including the Sumerians', the Babylonians', and the Assyrians'. Each of these cultures played a role in the development and preservation of the *Gilgamesh* epic.

History and Myth *Gilgamesh* is a series of separate tales that describe the exploits of the epic hero Gilgamesh. Although the epic projects him into the realm of myth, Gilgamesh was an actual person who ruled the ancient Sumerian city-state of Uruk around 2700 B.C. Historians believe that Sumerian storytellers began to recount tales of Gilgamesh's adventures and accomplishments soon after his death. However, these stories may not have been written down for nearly 1,000 years. Sometime between 2000 and 1600 B.C., the tales were recorded in Akkadian, the language of the Babylonian Empire, which had conquered the Sumerian city-states.

A Lost Epic By the seventh century B.C., the Assyrians dominated the Mesopotamian region. Assyrian emperor Ashurbanipal had the tales recorded on clay tablets and stored in his library at the palace at Nineveh. Assyria was destroyed soon after his rule, and the tablets were lost for nearly 2,500 years. They were unearthed in the mid-1800s by archaeologist Hormuzd Rassam. This discovery brought international recognition to one of the oldest and most important epics in the world. Since the nineteenth century, many other tablets and fragments of *Gilgamesh* have been discovered.

> *"Humans are born, they live, then they die,*
> *this is the order that the gods have decreed."*
> —from *Gilgamesh*

The Story of the Epic Exposed to the dangers of flood, drought, and warfare, the Mesopotamians seem to have believed that earthly life was fleeting and fraught with peril. In the epic, Gilgamesh is strong and handsome, but he is also a tyrant. After his subjects beg the gods to end his oppression, the gods create a powerful man named Enkidu to conquer Gilgamesh. Although they battle at first, the two men become friends and eventually succeed in killing a monster named Humbaba on a dangerous mission to a sacred forest. They then incur the wrath of the gods, who send a dream to Enkidu as he lies sick in bed. The dream shows that misery and sorrow are the fate of healthy men. Gilgamesh watches over his friend for twelve days, but Enkidu dies. The excerpt you are about to read begins as Gilgamesh is grieving for his friend.

Literature and Reading Preview

Connect to the Epic

With a partner, discuss what qualities you look for in a friend. How might these qualities contribute to a lasting friendship?

Build Background

The influence of oral tradition on *Gilgamesh* is evident in many features of the epic's style, such as repetition. For example, Utnapishtim is often called "the Distant One." Oral storytellers use repetition to remember details about characters and places.

Set Purposes for Reading

Big Idea | The Secret of Life

As you read *Gilgamesh*, ask yourself, What does this epic convey about the meaning of life?

Literary Element | Epic Hero

An **epic hero** is a courageous person (usually a man) of high social status who embodies the ideals of his people. His story is told in an **epic,** a long narrative poem that recounts his adventures, which often entail a quest and supernatural beings. As you read the epic, ask yourself, How does Gilgamesh fit the definition of an epic hero?

Reading Strategy | Visualize

When you **visualize**, you picture characters, scenes, and actions in your mind. You use the sensory details described by the author to imagine how various items in the text, such as flowers or food, might smell, look, or taste.

Tip: Make a Sketch Using a chart like this one, make sketches of various characters and other details from the epic.

Text	Sketch
"Two scorpion people were posted at the entrance . . ."	

Learning Objectives

For pages 448–466

In studying this text, you will focus on the following objectives:

Literary Study: Analyzing epic hero.

Reading: Visualizing.

Vocabulary

ravaged (rav′ijd) *adj.* devastated; ruined; p. 454 *The continued warfare left the city in a ravaged state.*

treacherous (trech′ər əs) *adj.* hazardous; dangerous; p. 458 *We barely survived the treacherous drive through the blizzard.*

prevail (pri vāl′) *v.* to gain ascendancy through strength or superiority; to triumph; p. 459 *The runner knew she would prevail if she focused on the finish line.*

antidote (an′ti dōt′) *n.* something that relieves, prevents, or counteracts; p. 462 *Alex found yoga to be an antidote to stress.*

Tip: Word Origins Word origins are the history and development of words. Also called **etymologies,** they are often included in dictionary entries. For example, the entry for *prevail* states*:* [ME, fr. L *praevalēre,* fr. *prae*- pre + *valēre* to be strong]. This means that *prevail* came from a Middle English (ME) word that derived from Latin (L).

Their auras shimmered over the mountains.
When Gilgamesh saw them, he was pierced with dread,
25   but he steadied himself and headed toward them.

The scorpion man called out to his wife,
"This one who approaches—he must be a god."

The scorpion woman called back to him,
"He is two-thirds divine and one-third human."

30   The scorpion man said, "What is your name?
How have you dared to come here? Why
have you traveled so far, over seas and mountains
difficult to cross, through wastelands and deserts
no mortal has ever entered? Tell me
35   the goal of your journey. I want to know."
"Gilgamesh is my name," he answered,
"I am the king of great-walled Uruk
and have come here to find my ancestor

Ashurbanipal on a Horse, Hunting Lion, c. 668-627 BC. Sumeria. Relief from the North Palace at Nineveh.

View the Art This relief is from Ashurbanipal's throne-room suite at the Palace of Nineveh. The reliefs discovered there are some of the finest existing Assyrian sculpture. How might the man on the horse remind you of Gilgamesh?

Utnapishtim, who joined the assembly
40   of the gods, and was granted eternal life.
He is my last hope. I want to ask him
how he managed to overcome death."

The scorpion man said, "No one is able
to cross the Twin Peaks, nor has anyone ever
45   entered the tunnel into which the sun
plunges when it sets and moves through the earth.
Inside the tunnel there is total darkness:
deep is the darkness, with no light at all."

The scorpion woman said, "This brave man,
50   driven by despair, his body frost-chilled,
exhausted, and burnt by the desert sun—
show him the way to Utnapishtim."

The scorpion man said, "Ever downward
through the deep darkness the tunnel leads.
55   All will be pitch black before and behind you,
all will be pitch black to either side.
You must run through the tunnel faster than the wind.
You have just twelve hours. If you don't emerge
from the tunnel before the sun sets and enters,
60   you will find no refuge from its deadly fire.
Penetrate into the mountains' depths,
may the Twin Peaks lead you safely to your goal,
may they safely take you to the edge of the world.
The gate to the tunnel lies here before you.
65   Go now in peace, and return in peace." . . .

Before him the garden of the gods appeared,
with gem-trees of all colors, dazzling to see.
There were trees that grew rubies, trees with lapis
lazuli° flowers, trees that dangled
70   gigantic coral clusters like dates.
Everywhere, sparkling on all the branches,
were enormous jewels: emeralds, sapphires,
hematite, diamonds, carnelians,° pearls.
Gilgamesh looked up and marveled at it all.

69 lapis lazuli: (lap´is laz´ə lē) a deep blue semiprecious stone.

73 hematite: (hem´ə tīt´) a reddish-brown to black mineral. **carnelians:** (kär nēl´yəns) red or reddish-orange semiprecious stones often set in jewelry.

Visualize *What mood do the sensory details create in this passage?*

Visualize *What details in this stanza help you visualize the scene? To what sense do these images appeal?*

75　At the edge of the ocean, the tavern keeper
　　Shiduri was sitting. Her face was veiled,
　　her golden pot-stand and brewing vat
　　stood at her side. As Gilgamesh came
　　toward her, worn out, his heart full of anguish,
80　she thought, "This desperate man must be
　　a murderer. Why else is he heading
　　straight toward me?" She rushed into her tavern,
　　locked the door, then climbed to the roof.
　　Gilgamesh heard the noise, he looked up
85　and saw her standing there, staring at him.
　　"Why did you lock yourself in?" he shouted.
　　"I want to enter now. If you don't let me,
　　I will smash your locks and break down your door."

　　Shiduri answered, "You seemed so wild
90　that I locked my door and climbed to the roof.
　　Tell me your name now. Where you are going?"

　　"Gilgamesh is my name," he said.
　　"I am the king of great-walled Uruk.
　　I am the man who killed Humbaba
95　in the Cedar Forest, I am the man
　　who triumphed over the Bull of Heaven."°

　　Shiduri said, "Why are your cheeks so hollow
　　and your features so **ravaged**? Why is your face
　　frost-chilled, and burnt by the desert sun?
100　Why is there so much grief in your heart?
　　Why are you worn out and ready to collapse,
　　like someone who has been on a long, hard journey?"

　　Gilgamesh said, "Shouldn't my cheeks
　　be hollow, shouldn't my face be ravaged,
105　frost-chilled, and burnt by the desert sun?
　　Shouldn't my heart be filled with grief?
　　Shouldn't I be worn out and ready to collapse?
　　My friend, my brother, whom I loved so dearly,
　　who accompanied me through every danger—

96 Bull of Heaven: this bull was unleashed on Uruk by Ishtar's father, the sky god Anu, after Gilgamesh refused to become Ishtar's lover. The bull killed hundreds of people, but Enkidu and Gilgamesh eventually killed it.

Epic Hero *What qualities of an epic hero does Gilgamesh possess?*

Vocabulary

ravaged (rav′ijd) *adj.* devastated; ruined

Gilgamesh, having learnt the whereabouts of the Plant of Life which confers immortality, sets out to find it, 1924. Artist unknown.

110   Enkidu, my brother, whom I loved so dearly,
     who accompanied me through every danger—
     the fate of mankind has overwhelmed him.
     For six days I would not let him be buried,
     thinking, 'If my grief is violent enough,
115   perhaps he will come back to life again.'
     For six days and seven nights I mourned him,
     until a maggot fell out of his nose.
     Then I was frightened, I was terrified by death,
     and I set out to roam the wilderness.
120   I cannot bear what happened to my friend—
     I cannot bear what happened to Enkidu—
     so I roam the wilderness in my grief.
     How can my mind have any rest?

     My beloved friend has turned into clay—
125   my beloved Enkidu has turned into clay.
     And won't I too lie down in the dirt
     like him, and never arise again?"

The Secret of Life *What does this passage reveal about the ancient Mesopotamian attitude toward death?*

Why are you worn out and ready to collapse,
200 like someone who has been on a long, hard journey?" . . .

Gilgamesh said,
"I must find Utnapishtim,"
whom men call 'The Distant One.' I must ask him
how he managed to overcome death.
I have wandered the world, climbed the most **treacherous**
205 mountains, crossed deserts, sailed the vast ocean,
and sweet sleep has rarely softened my face.

I have worn myself out through ceaseless striving,
I have filled my muscles with pain and anguish.
I have killed bear, lion, hyena, leopard,
210 tiger, deer, antelope, ibex,° I have eaten
their meat and have wrapped their rough skins around me.
And what in the end have I achieved?
When I reached Shiduri the tavern keeper,
I was filthy, exhausted, heartsick. Now let
215 the gate of sorrow be closed behind me,
and let it be sealed shut with tar and pitch." . . .

Utnapishtim said,
"Yes: the gods took Enkidu's life.
But man's life *is* short, at any moment
it can be snapped, like a reed in a canebrake.°
220 The handsome young man, the lovely young woman—
in their prime, death comes and drags them away.
Though no one has seen death's face or heard
death's voice, suddenly, savagely, death
destroys us, all of us, old or young.
225 And yet we build houses, make contracts, brothers
divide their inheritance, conflicts occur—
as though this human life lasted forever.
The river rises, flows over its banks
and carries us all away, like mayflies

210 **ibex:** (ī′bex) wild mountain goat with curving horns that is native to Europe, Asia, and northern Africa.

219 **canebrake:** thicket of cane.

Epic Hero *How does the description in lines 204–208 characterize Gilgamesh as an epic hero?*

The Secret of Life *What does this stanza reveal about the Mesopotamian view of death?*

Vocabulary

treacherous (trech′ər əs) *adj.* hazardous; dangerous

230 floating downstream: they stare at the sun,
then all at once there is nothing.

"The sleeper and the dead, how alike they are!
Yet the sleeper wakes up and opens his eyes,
while no one returns from death. And who
235 can know when the last of his days will come?
When the gods assemble, they decide your fate,
they establish both life and death for you,
but the time of death they do not reveal."

Gilgamesh said to Utnapishtim,
240 "I imagined that you would look like a god.
But you look like me, you are not any different.
I intended to fight you, yet now that I stand
before you, now that I see who you are,
I can't fight, something is holding me back.
245 Tell me, how is it that you, a mortal,
overcame death and joined the assembly
of the gods and were granted eternal life?"
Utnapishtim said, "I will tell you
a mystery, a secret of the gods. . . ."

*Utnapishtim describes a time when the gods decided to
send a flood. Ea, the god of wisdom, told him to build a ship
out of his house to save his life and take examples of every
living creature aboard the ship. The god Enlil boarded the ship
and touched the forehead of both Utnapishtim and his wife
and made them immortal. Enlil sent them to the mouth of the
rivers to live.*

The Return

250 "Now then, Gilgamesh, who will assemble
the gods for *your* sake? Who will convince them
to grant you the eternal life that you seek?
How would they know that you deserve it?
First pass this test: Just stay awake
255 for seven days. **Prevail** against sleep,
and perhaps you will prevail against death."

Vocabulary

prevail (pri vāl´) *v.* to gain ascendancy through strength or superiority;
to triumph

So Gilgamesh sat down against a wall
to begin the test. The moment he sat down,
sleep swirled over him, like a fog.

260 Utnapishtim said to his wife,
"Look at this fellow! He wanted to live
forever, but the very moment he sat down,
sleep swirled over him, like a fog."

His wife said, "Touch him on the shoulder, wake him,
265 let him depart and go back safely
to his own land, by the gate he came through."

Utnapishtim said, "All men are liars.
When he wakes up, watch how he tries to deceive us.
So bake a loaf for each day he sleeps,
270 put them in a row beside him, and make
a mark on the wall for every loaf."

She baked the loaves and put them beside him,
she made a mark for each day he slept.
The first loaf was rock-hard, the second loaf
275 was dried out like leather, the third had shrunk,
the fourth had a whitish covering, the fifth
was spotted with mold, the sixth was stale,
the seventh loaf was still on the coals
when he reached out and touched him. Gilgamesh
280 woke with a start and said, "I was almost
falling asleep when I felt your touch."

Utnapishtim said, "Look down, friend,
count these loaves that my wife baked and put here
while you sat sleeping. This first one, rock-hard,
285 was baked seven days ago, this leathery one
was baked six days ago, and so on for all
the rest of the days you sat here sleeping.
Look. They are marked on the wall behind you."

Gilgamesh cried out, "What shall I do,
290 where shall I go now? Death has caught me,
it lurks in my bedroom, and everywhere I look,
everywhere I turn, there is only death."

Epic Hero *How does this action contrast with Gilgamesh's earlier heroic feats?*

Nile Mosaic (detail). Late 2nd century BC. Museo Archeologico Prenestino, Palestrina, Italy.

Utnapishtim said to the boatman,
"This is the last time, Urshanabi,
295 that you are allowed to cross the vast ocean
and reach these shores. As for this man,
he is filthy and tired, his hair is matted,
animal skins have obscured his beauty.
Bring him to the tub and wash out his hair,
300 take off his animal skin and let
the waves of the ocean carry it away,
moisten his body with sweet-smelling oil,
bind his hair in a bright new headband,
dress him in fine robes fit for a king.
305 Until he comes to the end of his journey
let his robes be spotless, as though they were new."
He brought him to the tub, he washed out his hair,
he took off his animal skin and let
the waves of the ocean carry it away,
310 he moistened his body with sweet-smelling oil,
he bound his hair in a bright new headband,
he dressed him in fine robes fit for a king.

Visualize *To what senses does this image appeal?*

Then Gilgamesh and Urshanabi
boarded, pushed off, and the little boat
315 began to move away from the shore.

But the wife of Utnapishtim said, "Wait,
this man came a very long way, he endured
many hardships to get here. Won't you
give him something for his journey home?"

320 When he heard this, Gilgamesh turned the boat
around, and he brought it back to the shore.
Utnapishtim said, "Gilgamesh,
you came a very long way, you endured
many hardships to get here. Now
325 I will give you something for your journey home,
a mystery, a secret of the gods.
There is a small spiny bush that grows
in the waters of the Great Deep, it has sharp spikes
that will prick your fingers like a rose's thorns.

330 If you find this plant and bring it to the surface,
you will have found the secret of youth."

Gilgamesh dug a pit on the shore
that led down into the Great Deep. He tied
two heavy stones to his feet, they pulled him
335 downward into the water's depths.
He found the plant, he grasped it, it tore
his fingers, they bled, he cut off the stones,
his body shot up to the surface, and the waves
cast him back, gasping, onto the shore.

340 Gilgamesh said to Urshanabi,
"Come here, look at this marvelous plant,
the **antidote** to the fear of death.
With it we return to the youth we once had.
I will take it to Uruk, I will test its power
345 by seeing what happens when an old man eats it.
If that succeeds, I will eat some myself
and become a carefree young man again."

Humbaba, demon, genie and guardian of the cedar forests of the Lebanon range, 20th-16th century BC. Terracotta. Louvre, Paris.

The Secret of Life *What is the goal of Gilgamesh's quest?*

Vocabulary

antidote (an′ti dōt′) n. something that relieves, prevents, or counteracts

At four hundred miles they stopped to eat,
at a thousand miles they pitched their camp.
350   Gilgamesh saw a pond of cool water.
He left the plant on the ground and bathed.
A snake smelled its fragrance, stealthily
it crawled up and carried the plant away.
As it disappeared, it cast off its skin.

355   When Gilgamesh saw what the snake had done,
he sat down and wept. He said to the boatman,
"What shall I do now? All my hardships
have been for nothing. O Urshanabi,
was it for this that my hands have labored,
360   was it for this that I gave my heart's blood?
I have gained no benefit for myself
but have lost the marvelous plant to a reptile.
I plucked it from the depths, and how could I ever
manage to find that place again?
365   And our little boat—we left it on the shore."

At four hundred miles they stopped to eat,
at a thousand miles they pitched their camp.
When at last they arrived, Gilgamesh
said to Urshanabi, "This is
370   the wall of Uruk, which no city on earth can equal.
See how its ramparts gleam like copper in the sun.
Climb the stone staircase, more ancient than the mind can
    imagine
approach the Eanna Temple, sacred to Ishtar,
a temple that no king has equaled in size or beauty,
375   walk on the wall of Uruk, follow its course
around the city, inspect its mighty foundations,
examine its brickwork, how masterfully it is built,
observe the land it encloses: the palm trees, the gardens,
the orchards, the glorious palaces and temples, the shops
380   and marketplaces, the houses, the public squares."

The Secret of Life *What is the lesson of Gilgamesh's journey?*

Visualize *What does the description of Uruk in lines 369–372 imply about Gilgamesh and his city?*

Respond Through Writing

Expository Essay

Learning Objectives

In this workshop, you will focus on the following objectives:

Writing: Writing an expository essay.

Grammar: Understanding sentence types.

Analyze Epic Hero In an expository essay of at least 1,500 words, analyze the heroic qualities Gilgamesh displays and compare and contrast these qualities with those of the costumed crime fighters and other heroes of modern popular culture. In your conclusion, evaluate whether Gilgamesh is a hero by today's standards.

Understand the Task When you **compare** and **contrast** two things, you identify similarities and differences between them.

Prewrite To begin organizing your thoughts, create a Venn diagram like the one below to note Gilgamesh's heroic qualities, the qualities of pop culture heroes, and the qualities they share.

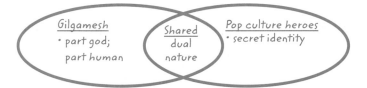

Gilgamesh
• part god;
part human

Shared
dual
nature

Pop culture heroes
• secret identity

Draft As you begin writing, evaluate the quality of your sources and make sure you convey information from these sources accurately and coherently. Review the story and your research notes to gather evidence to support your thesis.

Revise As you revise, be sure to use transitional words and phrases to clearly signal comparisons (*likewise*) and contrasts (*but, however*). Also, check to ensure that you have used literary terms, such as epic hero, accurately and that you have addressed any potential misunderstandings your readers may have. Use the rubric on page 1292 to check other elements of your review.

Edit and Proofread Proofread your paper, correcting any errors in spelling, grammar, and punctuation. Use the word count feature on your computer to determine whether your paper is at least 1,500 words. Review the Grammar Tip in the side column for information on sentence types.

> ## Grammar Tip
>
> ### Sentence Types
> English has four types of sentences, classified according to the kinds of messages they express.
>
> A **declarative sentence** makes a statement.
>
> *Gilgamesh was a legendary king of Uruk.*
>
> An **imperative sentence** gives a command or makes a request.
>
> *Please feast and rejoice.*
>
> An **interrogative sentence** asks a question.
>
> *Where are you going?*
>
> An **exclamatory sentence** expresses strong feeling or emotion.
>
> *"Despair is in my heart!"*
>
> As you write, try to use a variety of these sentence types.

Grammar Workshop

Pronoun-Antecedent Agreement

Learning Objectives

In this workshop, you will focus on the following objective:

Grammar: Understanding correct pronoun-antecedent agreement.

Literature Connection In the sentence "Humans are born, they live, then they die" from *Gilgamesh,* the pronoun *they* refers to *humans.* This pronoun is plural because its antecedent is plural. **Incorrect pronoun shifts** occur when a writer uses a pronoun of one person or number and then illogically shifts to a pronoun in another person or number. Another type of agreement problem occurs when a pronoun has no clearly stated antecedent.

PROBLEM 1 A pronoun does not agree with its antecedent in person.

Shiduri asks <u>Gilgamesh</u> why <u>you</u> look so ravaged.

SOLUTION Replace the incorrect pronoun with a pronoun that agrees with its subject in person.

Shiduri asks <u>Gilgamesh</u> why <u>he</u> looks so ravaged.

PROBLEM 2 A pronoun does not agree with its antecedent in number.

<u>Gilgamesh</u> faces many obstacles in <u>their</u> quest for immortality

SOLUTION Replace the incorrect pronoun with a pronoun that agrees with its subject in number.

<u>Gilgamesh</u> faces many obstacles in <u>his</u> quest for immortality.

PROBLEM 3 A pronoun has no clearly stated antecedent.

Gilgamesh mourns for Enkidu, <u>which</u> leads to his decision to seek Utnapishtim.

SOLUTION Replace the incorrect pronoun with an appropriate noun.

Gilgamesh mourns for Enkidu, and his <u>grief</u> leads to his decision to seek Utnapishtim.

Pronouns and Antecedents

A **pronoun** is a word that takes the place of a noun, a group of words acting as a noun, or another pronoun. The word or group of words a pronoun refers to is called its **antecedent.**

Tip

Use gender-neutral language, such as *his* or *her* and *he* or *she,* when the gender of an antecedent is unknown. For example, *A doctor faces many challenges in his or her lifetime.* You can also make the pronoun and antecedent plural: *Doctors face many challenges in their lifetimes.*

Language Handbook

For more on pronouns, see the Language Handbook, p. R40.

Proofread For each sentence below, write the correct form of the pronoun or the correct rephrasing of the sentence on a separate sheet of paper.

1. Gilgamesh was a legendary king of the Sumerians who was famous for (his, their) strength and courage.
2. Ancient scribes wrote the stories of Gilgamesh on clay tablets, and (your, these records) survived.
3. Gilgamesh meets Shiduri, who says (him, he) should try to enjoy life.

LOG ON ▶ **Literature** Online

Grammar For more grammar practice, go to glencoe.com and enter QuickPass code GLW6053u3.

Learning Objectives

For pages 468–469

In studying this text, you will focus on the following objectives:

Literary Study: Analyzing literary genres.

Reading:

Evaluating historical influences.

Connecting to the literature.

Sacred Texts

S ACRED TEXTS ARE WRITINGS THAT ARE CLOSELY LINKED WITH A specific religion or religious tradition. These texts, which include poetry, epics, parables, songs, and sermons, are often revered as holy.

Many sacred texts, such as the Bible, are regarded as divine revelations, directly communicated from God to humans. Other sacred texts are the written records of an oral teaching or a sermon given by a religious leader. Sacred texts have also originated from oral tradition; these texts developed over time until they were written down. For many religions, the oral dimension of sacred texts remains important and is still incorporated into religious rituals through reciting, chanting, and singing.

Sacred texts compiled centuries ago continue to play a vital role in Judaism, Christianity, Islam, Hinduism, and Buddhism, the five major religions of the modern world. However, such scriptures are not characteristic of all religions. For example, ancient Greeks and Romans had hundreds of myths based on their gods, but these stories tended to be told orally, rather than written down.

The Tanakh

The Tanakh, or Hebrew Bible, consists of three books: the Torah, the Nevi'im, and the Ketuvim. These books are seen as a repository of the laws, rituals, and history of Israel. The Torah consists of the first five books of the Bible and is the book of Hebrew law. The Nevi'im is a collection of visions and sermons of Jewish prophets, including Samuel, Joshua, and Ezekiel. The Ketuvim is a collection of psalms, proverbs, and history.

Moses and the Plague of Locusts. German woodcut from the Gutenberg Bible. Victoria & Albert Museum, London.

> *"In the beginning God created the heaven and the earth. And the earth was without form, and void; and darkness was upon the face of the deep."*
>
> —from the book of Genesis, in the Bible

The Christian Bible

The Bible (from Greek *biblia,* "books") is said to be the most widely read book in the world. Christianity is rooted in Judaism, so the Christian Bible contains the Tanakh, called the Old Testament by Christians, as well as additional books called the New Testament. The New Testament (see page 486) includes books on the life, death, and teachings of Christianity's central figure, Jesus Christ. The four primary books of the New Testament are called the Gospels.

The Qur'an

The Qur'an (kô rän´) (see pages 491–495) is the holy book of Islam. Muslims believe that the contents of the Qur'an are the actual words of God (in Arabic, *Allah*) as they were revealed to the prophet Muhammad from A.D. 610 to A.D. 632. The word *Qur'an* (also spelled *Koran*) is Arabic for "recitation" or "oral reading." The written text of the Qur'an was standardized within 30 years of Muhammad's death. Today, the Qur'an helps guide the lives of more than 1.3 billion Muslims around the globe.

Koran, Surah al-Rum, verses 24 and 25, 11th century. Persian. Kufic writing. Victoria and Albert Museum, London.

> *"Praise be to God, Lord of the Universe,*
> *The Compassionate, the Merciful,*
> *Sovereign of the Day of Judgement!"*
>
> —from "The Exordium," in the Qur'an

The Vedas

Unlike Judaism, Christianity, and Islam, Hinduism, the traditional religion of India, acknowledges a number of gods and goddesses. The oldest sacred texts of Hinduism are called the Vedas (from Sanskrit, meaning "knowledge"). They are believed by Hindus to be the eternal truth as it was revealed to ancient seers. The Vedas contain four collections of hymns and verses composed by various authors from about 1500 B.C. to 1000 B.C. The oldest and most revered of the four collections is the Rig-Veda (see pages 558–562), which contains more than 1,000 hymns. Another important sacred Hindu text is the Bhagavad Gita, a philosophical dialogue that appears within the epic poem the *Mahabharata*.

Buddhist Texts

Buddhism has hundreds of sacred texts, some of which were initially passed on orally, rather than written down. The texts are primarily written in Pali, a dialect considered the Buddha's own language. The sacred texts of Buddhism include the *Dhammapada*, a popular work on Buddhist doctrine; the *Suttanipata*, a collection of 55 poems; and the *Theragatha* and the *Therigatha*, hymns written by senior monks and nuns.

Literature Online

Literature and Reading For more about sacred texts, go to glencoe.com and enter QuickPass code GLW6053u3.

Respond and Think Critically

1. How do sacred texts vary from stories passed down through oral tradition?

2. What are some similarities among the sacred texts of these five major religions?

3. Based on your knowledge of sacred texts and world cultures, what might be the benefits of reading the sacred texts of different world religions?

Genesis 6–9:

The Flood

from the King James *version of the* Bible

Noah releasing the white dove (detail). 13th century. Mosaic. San Marco, Venice.

Chapter 6

And it came to pass, when men began to multiply on the face of the earth, and daughters were born unto them, that the sons of God saw the daughters of men that they were fair; and they took them wives of all which they chose. And the Lord said, "My Spirit shall not always strive with man, for that he also is flesh: yet his days shall be an hundred and twenty years." There were giants in the earth in those days; and also after that, when the sons of God came in unto the daughters of men, and they bare children to them, the same became mighty men which were of old, men of renown.

And God saw that the wickedness of man was great in the earth, and that every imagination of the thoughts of his heart was only evil continually. And it repented the Lord that he had made man on the earth, and it grieved him at his heart. And the Lord said, "I will destroy man whom I have created from the face of the earth; both man, and beast, and the creeping thing, and the fowls of the air; for it repenteth me that I have made them." But Noah found grace in the eyes of the Lord.

These are the generations of Noah: Noah was a just man and perfect in his generations, and Noah walked with God. And Noah begat three sons, Shem, Ham, and Japheth.

The earth also was **corrupt** before God, and the earth was filled with violence. And God looked upon the earth, and, behold, it was corrupt; for all flesh had corrupted his way upon the earth. And God said unto Noah, "The end of all flesh is come before me; for the earth is filled with violence through them; and, behold, I will destroy them with the earth. Make thee an ark of gopher wood; rooms shalt thou make in the ark, and shalt pitch it within and without

Vocabulary

corrupt (kə rupt´) *adj.* morally unsound; evil

with pitch.[1] And this is the fashion which thou shalt make it of: The length of the ark shall be three hundred cubits,[2] the breadth[3] of it fifty cubits, and the height of it thirty cubits. A window shalt thou make to the ark, and in a cubit shalt thou finish it above; and the door of the ark shalt thou set in the side thereof; with lower, second, and third stories shalt thou make it.

"And, behold, I, even I, do bring a flood of waters upon the earth, to destroy all flesh, wherein is the breath of life, from under heaven; and every thing that is in the earth shall die. But with thee will I establish my **covenant;** and thou shalt come into the ark, thou, and thy sons, and thy wife, and thy sons' wives with thee. And of every living thing of all flesh, two of every sort shalt thou bring into the ark, to keep them alive with thee; they shall be male and female. Of fowls after their kind, and of cattle after their kind, of every creeping thing of the earth after his kind, two of every sort shall come unto thee, to keep them alive. And take thou unto thee of all food that is eaten, and thou shalt gather it to thee; and it shall be for food for thee, and for them." Thus did Noah according to all that God commanded him, so did he.

Chapter 7

And the Lord said unto Noah, "Come thou and all thy house into the ark; for thee have I seen righteous before me in this generation. Of every clean beast[4] thou shalt take to thee by sevens, the male and his female: and of beasts that are not clean by two, the male and his female. Of fowls also of the air by sevens, the male and the female; to keep seed alive upon the face of all the earth. For yet seven days, and I will cause it to rain upon the earth forty days and forty nights; and every living substance that I have made will I destroy from off the face of the earth." And Noah did according unto all that the Lord commanded him.

And Noah was six hundred years old when the flood of waters was upon the earth. And Noah went in, and his sons, and his wife, and his sons' wives with him, into the ark, because of the waters of the flood. Of clean beasts, and of beasts that are not clean, and of fowls, and of every thing that creepeth upon the earth. There went in two and two unto Noah into the ark, the male and the female, as God had commanded Noah. And it came to pass after seven days, that the waters of the flood were upon the earth.

In the six hundredth year of Noah's life, in the second month, the seventeenth day of the month, the same day were all the fountains of the great deep broken up, and the windows of heaven were opened.

And the rain was upon the earth forty days and forty nights. In the selfsame day entered Noah, and Shem, and Ham, and Japheth, the sons of Noah, and Noah's wife, and the three wives of his sons with

---

1. *Pitch* is a black, tarlike substance that was used as a waterproofing compound.
2. A *cubit* equals about eighteen inches.
3. *Breadth* is another word for *width*.

4. According to Jewish religious law, *clean beasts* are beasts that are fit to eat and are acceptable to be used for sacrifices—this excludes pigs, reptiles, amphibians, rodents, carnivorous animals, most insects, and all shellfish.

Theme *How does this sentence underscore the theme of the story?*

Question *What is confusing about God's instructions here, given what he told Noah earlier?*

Vocabulary

covenant (kuv´ə nənt) *n.* an agreement, a pact

Question *How does this information conflict with information at the beginning of the story? How might you explain the apparent contradiction?*

them, into the ark; they, and every beast after his kind, and all the cattle after their kind, and every creeping thing that creepeth upon the earth after his kind, and every fowl after his kind, every bird of every sort. And they went in unto Noah into the ark, two and two of all flesh, wherein is the breath of life. And they that went in, went in male and female of all flesh, as God had commanded him: and the Lord shut him in.

And the flood was forty days upon the earth; and the waters increased, and bare up the ark, and it was lift up above the earth. And the waters prevailed, and were increased greatly upon the earth; and the ark went upon the face of the waters. And the waters prevailed exceedingly upon the earth; and all the high hills, that were under the whole heaven, were covered. Fifteen cubits upward did the waters prevail; and the mountains were covered. And all flesh died that moved upon the earth, both of fowl, and of cattle, and of beast, and of every creeping thing that creepeth upon the earth, and every man: all in whose nostrils was the breath of life, of all that was in the dry land, died. And every living substance was destroyed which was upon the face of the ground, both man, and cattle, and the creeping things, and the fowl of heaven; and they were destroyed from the earth: and Noah only remained alive, and they that were with him in the ark. And the waters prevailed upon the earth an hundred and fifty days.

Chapter 8

And God remembered Noah, and every living thing, and all the cattle that was with him in the ark: and God made a wind to pass over the earth, and the waters assuaged;

the fountains also of the deep and the windows of heaven were stopped, and the rain from heaven was restrained; and the waters returned from off the earth continually: and after the end of the hundred and fifty days the waters were abated. And the ark rested in the seventh month, on the seventeenth day of the month, upon the mountains of Ararat. And the waters decreased continually until the tenth month: in the tenth month, on the first day of the month, were the tops of the mountains seen.

And it came to pass at the end of forty days, that Noah opened the window of the ark which he had made: and he sent forth a raven, which went forth to and fro, until the waters were dried up from off the earth. Also he sent forth a dove from him, to see if the waters were **abated** from off the face of the ground. But the dove found no rest for the sole of her foot, and she returned unto him into the ark; for the waters were on the face of the whole earth: then he put forth his hand, and took her, and pulled her in unto him into the ark. And he stayed yet another seven days; and again he sent forth the dove out of the ark; and the dove came in to him in the evening; and, lo, in her mouth was an olive leaf plucked off: so Noah knew that the waters were abated from off the earth. And he stayed yet other seven days; and sent forth the dove; which returned not again unto him any more.

And it came to pass in the six hundredth and first year, in the first month, the first day of the month, the waters were dried up from off the earth: and Noah removed the covering of the ark, and looked, and, behold, the face of the ground was dry. And in the second month, on the seven and twentieth day of the month, was the earth dried.

The Secret of Life *What reassuring lesson would readers of the Bible learn from this passage?*

And God spake unto Noah, saying, "Go forth of the ark, thou, and thy wife, and thy sons, and thy sons' wives with thee. Bring forth with thee every living thing that is with thee, of all flesh, both of fowl, and of cattle, and of every creeping thing that creepeth upon the earth; that they may breed abundantly in the earth, and be fruitful, and multiply upon the earth." And Noah went forth, and his sons, and his wife, and his sons' wives with him: every beast, every creeping thing, and every fowl, and whatsoever creepeth upon the earth, after their kinds, went forth out of the ark.

And Noah builded an altar unto the Lord; and took of every clean beast, and of every clean fowl, and offered burnt offerings on the altar. And the Lord smelled a sweet savor;[5] and the Lord said in his heart, I will not again curse the ground any more for man's sake; for the imagination of man's heart is evil from his youth: neither will I again smite[6] any more every thing living, as I have done. While the earth remaineth, seedtime and harvest, and cold and heat, and summer and winter, and day and night shall not cease.

Chapter 9

And God blessed Noah and his sons, and said unto them, "Be fruitful, and multiply, and replenish the earth. And the fear of you and the dread of you shall be upon every beast of the earth, and upon every fowl of the air, upon all that moveth upon the earth, and upon all the fishes of the sea; into your hand are they delivered. Every moving thing that liveth shall be meat for you; even as the green herb have I given you all things. But flesh with the life thereof, which is the blood thereof, shall ye not eat. And surely your blood of your lives will I require; at the hand of every beast will I require it, and at the hand of man; at the hand of every man's brother will I require the life of man. Whoso sheddeth man's blood, by man shall his blood be shed: for in the image of God made he man. And you, be ye fruitful, and multiply; bring forth abundantly in the earth, and multiply therein.

And God spake unto Noah, and to his sons with him, saying, "And I, behold, I establish my covenant with you, and with your seed after you; and with every living creature that is with you, of the fowl, of the cattle, and of every beast of the earth with you; from all that go out of the ark, to every beast of the earth. And I will establish my covenant with you; neither shall all flesh be cut off any more by the waters of a flood; neither shall there any more be a flood to destroy the earth."

And God said, "This is the token of the covenant which I make between me and you and every living creature that is with you, for perpetual generations: I do set my bow in the cloud, and it shall be for a token of a covenant between me and the earth. And it shall come to pass, when I bring a cloud over the earth, that the bow shall be seen in the cloud: and I will remember my covenant, which is between me and you and every living creature of all flesh; and the waters shall no more become a flood to destroy all flesh. And the bow shall be in the cloud; and I will look upon it, that I may remember the everlasting covenant between God and every living creature of all flesh that is upon the earth. ❧

---

5. A *savor* is a smell or an odor.
6. *Smite* means "strike down" or "attack."

Question *What does the size of Noah's sacrifice indicate?*

The Book of Ruth

from the King James version of the Bible

Chapter 1

Now it came to pass in the days when the judges ruled, that there was a famine in the land. And a certain man of Bethlehem-Judah went to **sojourn** in the country of Moab, he, and his wife, and his two sons. And the name of the man was Elimelech, and the name of his wife Naomi,[1] and the name of his two sons Mahlon and Chilion, Ephrathites[2] of Bethlehem-Judah. And they came into the country of Moab, and continued there.

And Elimelech Naomi's husband died; and she was left, and her two sons. And they took them wives of the women of Moab; the name of the one was Orpah, and the name of the other Ruth: and they dwelled there about ten years. And Mahlon and Chilion died also both of them; and the woman was left of her two sons and her husband.

Then she arose with her daughters-in-law, that she might return from the country of Moab: for she had heard in the country of Moab how that the Lord had visited his people in giving them bread. Wherefore she went forth out of the place where she was, and her two daughters-in-law with her; and they went on the way to return unto the land of Judah.

And Naomi said unto her two daughters-in-law, "Go, return each to her mother's house: the Lord deal kindly with you, as ye have dealt with the dead, and with me. The Lord grant you that ye may find rest, each of you in the house of her husband." Then she kissed them; and they lifted up their voice, and wept. And they said unto her, "Surely we will return with thee unto thy people."

And Naomi said, "Turn again, my daughters: why will ye go with me? Are there yet any more sons in my womb, that they may be your husbands? Turn again, my daughters, go your way; for I am too old to have a husband. If I should say, I have hope, if I should have a husband also tonight, and should also bear sons; would ye tarry[3] for them till they were grown?

---

1. In Hebrew, *Naomi* means "beautiful," "pleasant," or "delightful."
2. *Ephrathites* are citizens of Bethlehem.

---

3. *Tarry* means "wait" or "remain."

The Secret of Life *What hope does Naomi express for her daughters-in-law by instructing them to turn back?*

Parallelism *Identify an example of both parallelism and repetition in these lines.*

Vocabulary

sojourn (sō′jurn) *v.* to stay or reside temporarily

Would ye stay for them from having husbands? Nay, my daughters; for it grieveth me much for your sakes that the hand of the Lord is gone out against me."

And they lifted up their voice, and wept again: and Orpah kissed her mother-in-law; but Ruth clave[4] unto her. And she said, "Behold, thy sister-in-law is gone back unto her people, and unto her gods: return thou after thy sister-in-law." And Ruth said, "Entreat me not to leave thee, or to return from following after thee: for whither thou goest, I will go; and where thou lodgest, I will lodge: thy people shall be my people, and thy God my God: where thou diest, will I die, and there will I be buried: the Lord do so to me, and more also, if ought but death part thee and me." When she saw that she was steadfastly minded to go with her, then she left speaking unto her. So they two went until they came to Bethlehem.

And it came to pass, when they were come to Bethlehem, that all the city was moved about them, and they said, "Is this Naomi?" And she said unto them, "Call me not Naomi, call me Mara:[5] for the Almighty hath dealt very bitterly with me. I went out full, and the Lord hath brought me home again empty: why then call ye me Naomi, seeing the Lord hath testified against me, and the Almighty hath afflicted me?"

So Naomi returned, and Ruth the Moabitess, her daughter-in-law, with her, which returned out of the country of Moab: and they came to Bethlehem in the beginning of barley harvest.

Chapter 2

And Naomi had a kinsman of her husband's, a mighty man of wealth, of the family of Elimelech; and his name was Boaz.[6]

And Ruth the Moabitess said unto Naomi, "Let me now go to the field, and **glean** ears of corn after him in whose sight I shall find grace." And she said unto her, "Go, my daughter." And she went, and came, and gleaned in the field after the reapers: and her hap[7] was to light on a part of the field belonging unto Boaz, who was of the kindred of Elimelech.

And, behold, Boaz came from Bethlehem, and said unto the reapers, "The Lord be with you." And they answered him, "The Lord bless thee." Then said Boaz unto his servant that was set over the reapers, "Whose damsel is this?" And the servant that was set over the reapers answered and said, "It is the Moabitish damsel that came back with Naomi out of the country of Moab: And she said, 'I pray you, let me glean and gather after the reapers among the sheaves': so she came, and hath continued even from the morning until now, that she tarried a little in the house."

Then said Boaz unto Ruth, "Hearest thou not, my daughter? Go not to glean in another field, neither go from hence, but abide here fast by my maidens: Let thine eyes be on the field that they do reap, and go thou after them: have I not charged the young men that they shall not touch thee? And when thou art athirst, go unto

---

4. *Clave* is an archaic form of the verb *cleaved,* meaning "adhered or clung to."
5. *Mara* means "bitter."

6. In Hebrew, the name *Boaz* is associated with the word for strength. *Boaz* is also the name of a pillar in a great temple built by Solomon, the son and successor of King David.
7. *Hap* means "luck" or "lot."

Vocabulary

glean (glēn) *v.* to gather what's left by reapers; to gather slowly, bit by bit; to discover or find out slowly

the vessels, and drink of that which the young men have drawn."

Then she fell on her face, and bowed herself to the ground, and said unto him, "Why have I found grace in thine eyes, that thou shouldest take knowledge of me, seeing I am a stranger?"

And Boaz answered and said unto her, "It hath fully been shewed me, all that thou hast done unto thy mother-in-law since the death of thine husband and how thou hast left thy father and thy mother, and the land of thy nativity, and art come unto a people which thou knewest not heretofore. The Lord recompense[8] thy work, and a full reward be given thee of the Lord God of Israel, under whose wings thou art come to trust."

Then she said, "Let me find favor in thy sight, my lord; for that thou hast comforted me, and for that thou hast spoken friendly unto thine handmaid, though I be not like unto one of thine handmaidens."

And Boaz said unto her, "At mealtime come thou hither, and eat of the bread, and dip thy morsel in the vinegar." And she sat beside the reapers: and he reached her parched corn, and she did eat, and was sufficed, and left.

And when she was risen up to glean, Boaz commanded his young men, saying, "Let her glean even among the sheaves, and reproach her not: And let fall also some of the handfuls of purpose for her, and leave them, that she may glean them, and rebuke her not."

So she gleaned in the field until even, and beat out that she had gleaned: and it was about an ephah[9] of barley. And she took it up, and went into the city: and her mother-in-law saw what she had gleaned: and she brought forth, and gave to her that she had reserved after she was sufficed. And her mother-in-law said unto her, "Where hast thou gleaned today? And where wroughtest thou? Blessed be he that did take knowledge of thee." And she shewed her mother-in-law with whom she had wrought, and said, "The man's name with whom I wrought today is Boaz."

And Naomi said unto her daughter-in-law, "Blessed be he of the Lord, who hath not left off his kindness to the living and to the dead." And Naomi said unto her, "The man is near of kin unto us, one of our next kinsmen." And Ruth the Moabitess said, "He said unto me also, 'Thou shalt keep fast by my young men, until they have ended all my harvest.'" And Naomi said unto Ruth her daughter-in-law, "It is good, my daughter, that thou go out with his maidens, that they meet thee not in any other field." So she kept fast by the maidens of Boaz to glean unto the end of barley harvest and of wheat harvest; and dwelt with her mother-in-law.

Chapter 3

Then Naomi her mother-in-law said unto her, "My daughter, shall I not seek rest for thee, that it may be well with thee? And now is not Boaz of our kindred, with whose maidens thou wast? Behold, he **winnoweth** barley tonight in the threshing floor. Wash thyself therefore, and anoint thee, and put

---

8. *Recompense* (rek′əm pens′) means "repay."

The Secret of Life *Explain the meaning of this reference as it applies to Ruth's faith.*

Respond to Characters *What character traits does Boaz reveal in these instructions to his workers? How do you think readers are meant to respond to Boaz?*

---

9. An *ephah* is a Hebrew unit of measure that equals a little more than a bushel.

Vocabulary

winnow (win′ō) *v.* to remove by exposing to air currents; to free from lighter particles; to sift; to separate

thy raiment[10] upon thee, and get thee down to the floor: but make not thyself known unto the man, until he shall have done eating and drinking. And it shall be, when he lieth down, that thou shalt mark the place where he shall lie, and thou shalt go in, and uncover his feet, and lay thee down; and he will tell thee what thou shalt do." And she said unto her, "All that thou sayest unto me I will do."

And she went down unto the floor, and did according to all that her mother-in-law bade her. And when Boaz had eaten and drunk, and his heart was merry, he went to lie down at the end of the heap of corn: and she came softly, and uncovered his feet, and laid her down. And it came to pass at midnight, that the man was afraid, and turned himself: and, behold, a woman lay at his feet.

And he said, "Who art thou?" And she answered, "I am Ruth thine handmaid: spread therefore thy skirt over thine handmaid; for thou art a near kinsman."

And he said, "Blessed be thou of the Lord, my daughter: for thou hast shewed more kindness in the latter end than at the beginning, inasmuch as thou followedst not young men, whether poor or rich. And now, my daughter, fear not; I will do to thee all that thou requirest: for all the city of my people doth know that thou art a virtuous woman. And now it is true that I am thy near kinsman: howbeit there is a kinsman nearer than I. Tarry this night, and it shall be in the morning, that if he will perform unto thee the part of a kinsman, well; let him do the kinsman's part: but if he will not do the part of a kinsman to thee, then will I do the part of a kinsman to thee, as the Lord liveth: lie down until the morning."

Ruth parting from Naomi, 1803. William Blake. Wash, pencil, coloured chalk. Southampton City Art Gallery, Hampshire, UK.

<u>View the Art</u> Poet William Blake was one of England's greatest religious artists. This watercolor depicts Naomi, Ruth, and Orpah. How would you describe the contrast between Ruth and Orpah?

And she lay at his feet until the morning: and she rose up before one could know another. And he said, "Let it not be known that a woman came into the floor." Also he said, "Bring the vail that thou hast upon thee, and hold it." And when she held it, he measured six measures of barley, and laid it on her: and she went into the city.

And when she came to her mother-in-law, she said, "Who art thou, my daughter?" And she told her all that the man had done to her. And she said, "These six measures of barley gave he me; for he said to me, 'Go not empty unto thy mother-in-law.'" Then said she, "Sit still, my daughter, until thou know how the matter will fall: for the man will not be in rest, until he have finished the thing this day."

---

10. *Raiment* (rā′mənt) is another word for clothing.

The Secret of Life *What might be one secret to a good life, according to this passage?*

Literary Element | Parallelism

SAT Skills Practice

1. Ruth's response to Naomi, "thy people shall be my people, and thy God my God," is best described as an example of parallel

    (A) words

    (B) metaphors

    (C) clauses

    (D) similes

    (E) sentences

2. Naomi's blessing of her daughters-in-law, "the Lord deal kindly with you, as ye have dealt with the dead, and with me," is best described as an example of parallel

    (A) tenses

    (B) sentences

    (C) clauses

    (D) images

    (E) words

Review: Theme

As you learned on page 471, the **theme** of a literary work is its main insight or central message about life. As a sacred text, the story of Ruth is meant to teach a lesson or present a central idea about Judaism.

Partner Activity With a partner, discuss the theme of the book of Ruth. Then answer the following questions.

1. What do you think is the central idea or lesson to be learned in the book of Ruth?

2. What evidence from the story can you cite to support your opinion?

Reading Strategy | Respond to Characters

When you **respond** to characters, you note your initial reactions to them, as well as details that linger in your mind. Refer to the chart you made on page 477 and then answer these questions.

1. (a) What qualities does Naomi demonstrate? What qualities does Boaz demonstrate?
   (b) What words or actions reveal these qualities?

2. Was your response to Ruth favorable or unfavorable? Explain.

Vocabulary Practice

Practice with Denotation and Connotation
The **denotation** of a word is its literal definition. A word's **connotations**, or implied meanings, are often related to the intensity of a word's meaning. With a partner, identify connotations by completing a graphic organizer for each boldfaced vocabulary word.

sojourn   glean   winnow   redeem

EXAMPLE:

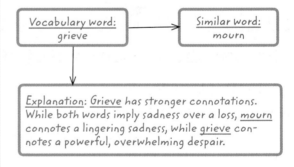

Academic Vocabulary

*Naomi and Ruth become poor when they are widowed; Boaz marries Ruth and **restores** the living conditions of the two women.*

Restore is an academic word. In more casual conversation, you may hear someone say that a judge **restored** order in a court. Using context clues in the sentence above, try to figure out the meaning of this word.

For more on academic vocabulary, see pages 36–37 and R83–R85.

Respond Through Writing

Persuasive Essay

Argue a Position When Ruth moved to Judah with Naomi, she became an immigrant who needed help to survive in her new community. Imagine you are Ruth, and in a persuasive essay, convince your fellow Judeans to provide the resources you need as a newcomer. Present arguments and evidence in favor of your position.

Understand the Task An **argument** is a logical statement supported by evidence that is used to defend a position in persuasive writing.

Prewrite Before you draft your paper, research possible resources you might benefit from as an immigrant. Record and organize your research in a chart like the one below. Then use your research to create logical arguments.

Ruth's Needs	Resources
Instruction in local customs	

Draft Formulate a clear thesis, with credible and relevant evidence to support it. Refer to your experiences (as Ruth) in your essay. Make sure your arguments are structured logically and that they anticipate opposing arguments or biases your readers may have. Sometimes it is helpful to use sentence frames as you write. For example, your introduction will include your thesis, which might be stated as follows:

Like me, immigrants in your community want to fit in, but may need _____ to help them do so.

Revise As you revise, make sure you have used persuasive techniques, such as appeals to ethics or emotions, to convince your readers.

Edit and Proofread Proofread your paper, correcting any errors in spelling, grammar, and punctuation. Review the Grammar Tip in the side column for information on infinitives and infinitive phrases.

The Parable of the Prodigal Son

from the **King James** *version of the* **Bible**

And he[1] said, "A certain man had two sons: and the younger of them said to his father, 'Father, give me the portion of goods that falleth to me.' And he divided unto them his living. And not many days after the younger son gathered all together, and took his journey into a far country, and there wasted his substance with riotous living. And when he had spent all, there arose a mighty famine in that land; and he began to be in want. And he went and joined himself to a citizen of that country; and he sent him into his fields to feed swine.[2] And he would fain[3] have filled his belly with the husks that the swine did eat: and no man gave unto him.

"And when he came to himself, he said, 'How many hired servants of my father's have bread enough and to spare, and I perish with hunger! I will arise and go to my father, and will say unto him, "Father, I have sinned against heaven, and before thee, and am no more worthy to be called thy son: make me as one of thy hired servants." '

"And he arose, and came to his father. But when he was yet a great way off, his father saw him, and had compassion, and ran, and fell on his neck, and kissed him. And the son said unto him, 'Father, I have sinned against heaven, and in thy sight, and am no more worthy to be called thy son.' But the father said to his servants, 'Bring forth the best robe, and put it on him; and put a ring on his hand, and shoes on his feet: and bring hither the fatted calf, and kill it; and let us eat, and be merry: for this my son was dead, and is alive again; he was lost, and is found.' And they began to be merry.

"Now his elder son was in the field: and as he came and drew nigh to the house, he heard music and dancing. And he called one of the servants, and asked what these things meant. And he said unto him, 'Thy brother is come; and thy father hath killed the fatted calf, because he hath received

---

1. Here, *he* refers to Jesus Christ.
2. *Swine* (or pigs) are considered unclean animals in Jewish belief.
3. *Fain* means "willingly" or "gladly."

Parable *Based on this opening sentence, what might be the topic of this parable? Why might this be an effective topic to use to teach a lesson?*

Make Inferences About Theme *What might the father's reaction to his son's return reveal about the theme?*

The return of the Prodigal Son, 1773. Pompeo Batoni. Oil on canvas, 173 x 122 cm. Kunsthistorisches Museum, Vienna, Austria.

View the Art Batoni was renowned in eighteenth-century Rome for his ornate depictions of mythological and historical subjects. How does his portrayal of the prodigal son and his father compare with how you imagine these men looked and dressed?

him safe and sound.' And he was angry, and would not go in: therefore came his father out, and intreated[4] him. And he answering said to his father, 'Lo, these many years do I serve thee, neither transgressed I at any time thy commandment: and yet thou never gavest me a kid,[5] that I might make merry with my friends: but as soon as this thy son was come, which hath devoured thy living with harlots, thou hast killed for him the fatted calf.' And he said unto him, 'Son, thou art ever with me, and all that I have is thine. It was meet that we should make merry, and be glad: for this thy brother was dead, and is alive again; and was lost, and is found.' " ∾

---

4. *Intreated* is a variant spelling of *entreated,* which means "begged" or "pleaded."
5. A *kid* is a young goat.

The Secret of Life *What might be the metaphorical and religious meaning of the father's statement to his older son?*

After You Read

Respond and Think Critically

Respond and Interpret

1. Did the ending of the parable surprise you? Why or why not?

2. (a)What request does the younger son make to his father? (b)What does the father's response to this request reveal about the father?

3. (a)What is the younger son forced to do when he runs out of money? (b)What is particularly humiliating about his situation?

4. (a)How does the father respond to his older son's comments? (b)What point do you think the father is making?

Analyze and Evaluate

5. Do you think the older son's reaction to the welcoming festivities is justified? Why or why not?

6. *Prodigal* has several meanings, including "wasteful" and "overly generous." Considering these definitions, how might *prodigal* describe both the father and the younger son?

Connect

7. **Big Idea** **The Secret of Life** What lessons about family and other close relationships does this parable teach?

8. **Connect to Today** Why might this parable continue to influence readers today?

Literary Element Parable

Review the **parable**, paying attention to its structural elements. Then answer the questions below.

1. What elements of this story help identify it as a parable?

2. (a)What lesson does the father teach the older son? (b)How might you interpret this lesson symbolically?

Reading Strategy Make Inferences About Theme

When you **make inferences about theme**, you identify an insight about life that is implied through the events in a text. Refer to the chart you made on page 487 and answer the following questions.

1. (a)Describe the conflicts that unfold in the parable. (b)How are the conflicts resolved?

2. What insights about life are implied in the story?

LOG ON ▶ **Literature** Online

Selection Resources For Selection Quizzes, eFlashcards, and Reading-Writing Connection activities, go to glencoe.com and enter QuickPass code GLW6053u3.

Academic Vocabulary

*The **framework** of "The Parable of the Prodigal Son" is one of repentance and forgiveness.*

In the sentence above, *framework* means "the basic structure of ideas." For example, the *framework* of a new law is based on constitutional rights. To further explore the meaning of this word, answer this question: What is the **framework** of the United States government?

For more on academic vocabulary, see pages 36–37 and R83–R85.

⚡ Writing

Write a Parable Write a short **parable** that teaches a lesson about modern life. Develop a plot in which the characters and the conflict can be interpreted on both literal and symbolic levels. After you draft your parable, exchange papers with a peer and review each other's work, offering comments for revision.

Before You Read

from the *Qur'an*

The Qur'an (kô rän´) is the holy book of Islam, believed by Muslims to be the sacred word of Allah, or God. According to Muslim belief, Allah revealed the Qur'an to Muhammad ("the Glorified One"), the prophet who founded Islam. Muhammad was born in A.D. 570 to a merchant family in Mecca (also spelled Makkah), a thriving city on one of the major caravan trade routes across Arabia. He was orphaned by the age of six and was raised by family members, eventually becoming a manager on a caravan trade route, a husband, and a father.

The Word of God Muhammad's sense of justice and devotion to prayer were renowned. He sometimes retreated into the desert and the hills to pray. According to Muslim tradition, during one such retreat around A.D. 610, Allah sent the angel Gabriel to Muhammad and told him to recite what Gabriel said. The Qur'an, whose title means "recitation" in Arabic, came out of these revelations over 23 years. Muhammad's followers eventually wrote them down.

A New Religion Gabriel's messages called on Muhammad to forsake the gods of his people and start a new religion marked by devotion to a single deity, pious conduct, and submission to the will of Allah. Muhammad came to believe that Allah had already revealed himself in part through Moses and Jesus—and thus through the traditions of Judaism and Christianity. He believed, however, that the final revelations of Allah were now being given to him. While Muhammad was able to convert some followers, he also met with much opposition. For the rest of his life, both in Mecca and in the city of Yathrib (now called Medina), Muhammad worked to spread the word of Allah. In the century after Muhammad's death in A.D. 632, Islam spread rapidly, and the Islamic Empire expanded until it stretched from Spain to the borders of India.

> "To God belong the East and the West;
> whithersoever you turn, there is the
> Face of God;
> God is All-embracing,
> All-knowing. . . ."
>
> —from the Qur'an

A Difficult Masterpiece Within 30 years after Muhammad's death, the Qur'an was compiled into a standard written text. The book consists of 114 chapters (called *suras*), which vary in length from hundreds of verses to only one or two lines. Except for the brief opening sura—"The Exordium" (or introduction)—these chapters are arranged approximately according to length, beginning with the longer ones. Notoriously difficult to translate, the Qur'an established the classical form of the Arabic language and is regarded as a literary masterpiece.

Literature and Reading Preview

Connect to the Sacred Text

Why might a person choose to live compassionately? In your journal, reflect on this question.

Build Background

Set forth in the Qur'an, the fundamental doctrines of Muslim religious belief are known as "the five pillars of Islam": acknowledging Allah as the only God, praying five times a day, fasting from dawn to dusk during the holy month of Ramadan, giving alms to the poor, and making a pilgrimage to Mecca at least once in a lifetime, if the believer has the means.

Set Purposes for Reading

Big Idea The Secret of Life

Sacred texts often reveal how one can attain fulfillment and enlightenment. As you read this sacred text, ask yourself, What Islamic ideas on how to live well does it reveal?

Literary Element Antithesis

Antithesis is the balanced contrast of two phrases or ideas, as illustrated in lines 7–8 of "The Exordium":

> The path of those whom You have favored,
> Not of those who have incurred Your wrath…

In this passage, "those whom you have favored" is the opposite of "those who have incurred your wrath." As you read "Daylight," ask yourself, What is an example of antithesis, and how does it contribute to the verse?

Reading Strategy Interpret Imagery

Imagery refers to descriptive language that appeals to one or more of the five senses: sight, hearing, touch, taste, and smell. When you **interpret imagery,** you examine how it contributes to the underlying ideas in the text. As you read, ask yourself, What are some examples of images, and what do they mean?

Tip: Take Notes Use a chart like the one below to help you interpret images.

Image	Sensory Response	Meaning
"the straight path"	a well-marked trail leading to your destination	Following Allah's word will lead one toward a righteous lifestyle.

Learning Objectives

For pages 491–495

In studying this text, you will focus on the following objectives:

Literary Study: Analyzing antithesis.

Reading: Interpreting imagery.

Writing: Writing a memo.

Vocabulary

incur (in kur′) *v.* to bring upon oneself; p. 494 *She incurred large library fines by failing to return her books on time.*

abhor (ab hōr′) *v.* to detest; p. 494 *His bad attitude led many people to abhor the basketball player.*

chide (chīd) *v.* to scold; p. 494 *The babysitter had to chide the girls for making so much noise.*

Tip: Context Clues You can often figure out the meaning of words by looking at their **context,** the words and sentences that surround them. For example, in the sample sentence above for *chide,* the phrase "making so much noise" suggests that *chide* means "scold."

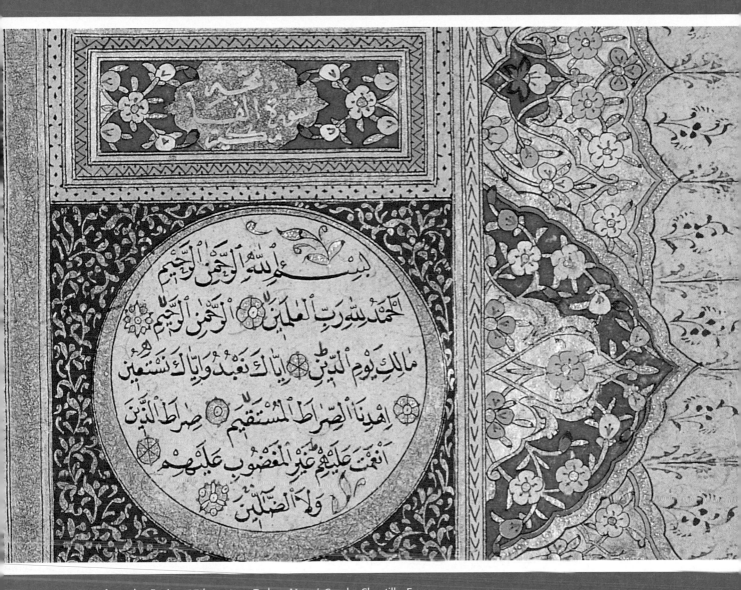

Page from the Qur'an, 17th century, Turkey. Musée Condé, Chantilly, France.

from the Qur'an

Translated by N. J. Dawood

The Exordium

*In the Name of God
the Compassionate the Merciful*

Praise be to God, Lord of the Universe,
The Compassionate, the Merciful,
Sovereign of the Day of Judgement!
You alone we worship, and to You alone
we turn for help.
Guide us to the straight path,
The path of those whom You have favored,
Not of those who have **incurred** Your wrath,
Nor of those who have gone astray.

Daylight

*In the Name of God,
the Compassionate, the Merciful*

By the light of day, and by the dark of night, your Lord
has not forsaken you, nor does He **abhor** you.
The life to come holds a richer prize for you than this
present life. You shall be gratified with what your Lord will
give you.
Did He not find you an orphan and give you shelter?
Did He not find you in error and guide you?
Did He not find you poor and enrich you?
Therefore do not wrong the orphan, nor **chide** away the
beggar. But proclaim the goodness of your Lord.

The Secret of Life *What does this description of God suggest about the Islamic view of life?*

Antithesis *What antithesis is presented here? What quality of God's does this antithesis emphasize?*

Vocabulary

incur (in kur´) *v.* to bring upon oneself
abhor (ab hôr´) *v.* to detest
chide (chīd) *v.* to scold

After You Read

Respond and Think Critically

Respond and Interpret

1. What insights into Islam have you gained by reading these suras?

2. (a)In lines 6–9 of "The Exordium," who has not followed the "straight path"? (b)What does the straight path represent?

3. (a)What two images are in the first line of "Daylight"? (b)Why might these images begin the sura, and what is their significance?

4. (a)What promise is given to the faithful in lines 3–5 of "Daylight"? (b)Who seems to be the intended audience for this sura?

Analyze and Evaluate

5. What kind of **tone**, or attitude toward the subject matter, does "The Exordium" set for the Qur'an as a whole? Use evidence from the text to support your response.

6. How would you state the **theme**, or main message, of "Daylight"?

Connect

7. **Big Idea** **The Secret of Life** How is a Muslim life best lived according to these two suras?

8. **Connect to Today** "Daylight" maintains that people should respect one another, especially those who are less fortunate. How does modern society demonstrate this value?

Literary Element Antithesis

Authors often emphasize important ideas through the use of **antithesis,** or the balanced contrast of two phrases or ideas.

1. What important idea in "The Exordium" is emphasized through the use of antithesis?

2. In what lines of "Daylight" is antithesis used?

Reading Strategy Interpret Imagery

The pattern of **imagery** in a literary work can help convey the meaning of that work. Refer to your chart from page 492 and then answer the following questions.

1. What is the dominant image in "The Exordium"?

2. Why does "Daylight" provide contrasting images such as *orphan* and *shelter* and *poor* and *rich*?

LOG ON ▶ **Literature** Online

Selection Resources For Selection Quizzes, eFlash-cards, and Reading-Writing Connection activities, go to glencoe.com and enter QuickPass code GLW6053u3.

Vocabulary Practice

Practice with Context Clues Read the following sentences and identify the context clues that help you determine the meaning of each boldfaced vocabulary word.

1. David **incurred** large debt because of his poor money management skills and expensive tastes.

2. Always the opposite of her sister, Jenna loved the headlining band, while Gina **abhorred** it.

3. His coach would **chide** him every time he made a mistake, so Eric lost his confidence.

Writing

Write a Memo How well do your classmates get along with one another? Think about this question and write a memo to your class with ideas on how to improve interpersonal relationships. Try to mirror the ideas conveyed in "Daylight" and use **antithesis** to emphasize key ideas.

The Second Voyage of
Sindbad the Sailor

from The Thousand and One Nights

Translated by N. J. Dawood

The Travellers Rescue by the Rukh (detail) from the *Ajaib al-Makhukat*, 14th century. Freer Gallery of Art, Washington, DC.

For some time after my return to Baghdad I continued to lead a joyful and carefree life, but it was not long before I felt an irresistible longing to travel again about the world and to visit distant cities and islands in quest of profit and adventure. So I bought a great store of merchandise and, after making preparations for departure, sailed down the Tigris to Basrah.[1] There I embarked, together with a band of merchants, in a fine new vessel, well-equipped and manned by a sturdy crew, which set sail the same day.

Aided by a favorable wind, we voyaged for many days and nights from port to port and from island to island, selling and bartering our goods, and haggling with merchants and officials wherever we cast anchor. At length Destiny carried our ship to the shores of an uninhabited island, rich in fruit and flowers, and jubilant with the singing of birds and the murmur of crystal streams.

Here passengers and crew went ashore, and we all set off to enjoy the delights of the island. I strolled through the green meadows, leaving my companions far behind, and sat down in a shady **thicket** to eat a simple meal by a spring of water. Lulled by the soft and fragrant breeze which blew around me, I lay upon the grass and presently fell asleep.

I cannot tell how long I slept, but when I awoke I saw none of my fellow-travelers, and soon realized that the ship had sailed away without anyone noticing my absence.

---

1. In Sindbad's time, Baghdad was a thriving city whose merchants traded in many kingdoms. To set out on a trading expedition, sailors traveled down the Tigris River from Baghdad to *Basrah,* a port near where the Tigris and the Euphrates rivers meet.

Point of View *What details in this sentence indicate that the story will be told from the first-person point of view?*

Identify Problem and Solution *What factors lead to Sindbad's problem?*

Vocabulary

thicket (thik′it) *n.* a dense growth of shrubs, underbrush, or small trees

I ran in frantic haste towards the sea, and on reaching the shore saw the vessel, a white speck upon the vast blue ocean, dissolving into the far horizon.

Broken with terror and despair, I threw myself upon the sand, wailing: "Now your end has come, Sindbad! The jar that drops a second time is sure to break!" I cursed the day I bade farewell to the joys of a contented life and bitterly repented my folly in venturing again upon the hazards and hardships of the sea, after having so narrowly escaped death in my first voyage.

At length, resigning myself to my doom, I rose and, after wandering about aimlessly for some time, climbed into a tall tree. From its top I gazed long in all directions, but could see nothing save the sky, the trees, the birds, the sands, and the boundless ocean. As I scanned the interior of the island more closely, however, I gradually became aware of some white object looming in the distance. At once I climbed down the tree and made my way towards it. Drawing nearer, I found to my astonishment that it was a white dome of extraordinary dimensions. I walked all round it, but could find no door or entrance of any kind; and so smooth and slippery was its surface that any attempt to climb it would have been **fruitless**. I walked round it again, and, making a mark in the sand near its base, found that its circumference measured more than fifty paces.

Whilst I was thus engaged the sun was suddenly hidden from my view as by a great cloud and the world grew dark around me. I lifted up my eyes towards the sky, and was **confounded** to see a gigantic bird with enormous wings which, as it flew through the air, screened the sun and hid it from the island.

The sight of this prodigy[2] instantly called to my mind a story I had heard in my youth from pilgrims and adventurers—how in a far island dwelt a bird of monstrous size called the roc, which fed its young on elephants; and at once I realized that the white dome was no other than a roc's egg. In a twinkling the bird alighted upon the egg, covering it completely with its wings and stretching out its legs behind it on the ground. And in this posture it went to sleep. (Glory to Him who never sleeps!)

Rising swiftly, I unwound my turban from my head, then doubled it and twisted it into a rope with which I securely bound myself by the waist to one of the great talons of the monster. "Perchance this bird," I thought, "will carry me away to a civilized land; wherever I am set down, it will surely be better than a solitary island."

Visual Vocabulary
A *turban* is a headdress made of a long cloth wound about the head.

I lay awake all night, fearing to close my eyes lest the bird should fly away with me while I slept. At daybreak the roc rose from the egg, and, spreading its wings, took to the air with a terrible cry. I clung fast to its talon as it winged its flight through the void and soared higher and higher until it almost touched the heavens. After some

---

The Search for Wisdom *What does Sindbad's action here reveal about his ability to search out new information?*

fruitless (frōōt′lis) *adj.* unproductive; useless; sure to end in failure

---

2. Here, *prodigy* means "an event or a thing so rare or extraordinary as to inspire wonder."

confound (kən found′) *v.* to confuse or bewilder

Draco (detail) (constellation of the Northern Hemisphere) from the *Ajaib al-Makhukat* , 14th century. Freer Gallery of Art, Washington, DC.

time it began to drop, and sailing swiftly downwards came to earth on the brow of a steep hill.

Trembling with fear, I hastened to untie my turban before the roc became aware of my presence. Scarcely had I released myself when the monster darted off towards a great black object lying near and, clutching it in its fearful claws, took wing again. As it rose in the air I was astonished to see that this was a serpent of immeasurable length; and with its prey the bird vanished from sight.

Looking around, I found myself on a precipitous hillside overlooking an exceedingly deep and vast valley. On all sides towered craggy mountains whose beetling[3] summits no man could ever scale. I was stricken with fear and repented my rashness. "Would I had remained in that island!" I thought to myself. "There at least I lacked neither fruit nor water, while these barren steeps offer nothing to eat or drink. No sooner do I escape from one peril than I find myself in another more grievous. There is no strength or help save in Allah!"

When I had made my way down the hill I marvelled to see the ground thickly cov-ered with the rarest diamonds, so that the entire valley blazed with a glorious light. Here and there among the glittering stones, however, coiled deadly snakes and vipers, dread keepers of the fabulous treasure. Thicker and longer than giant palm-trees, they could have swallowed whole elephants at one gulp. They were crawling back into their sunless dens, for by day they hid themselves from their enemies the rocs and the eagles and moved about only at night.

Overwhelmed with horror, and oblivious of hunger and fatigue, I roamed the valley all day searching with infinite caution for a shelter where I might pass the night. At dusk I came upon a narrow-mouthed cave, into which I crawled, blocking its entrance from within by a great stone. I thought to myself: "Here I shall be safe tonight. When tomorrow comes, let Destiny do its worst."

Scarcely had I advanced a few steps, when I saw at the far end of the cave an enormous serpent coiled in a great knot round its eggs. My hair stood on end and I was transfixed with terror. Seeing no way of escape, however, I put my trust in Allah and kept vigil all night. At daybreak I rolled back the stone and staggered out of the cave, reeling like a drunken man.

---

3. *Beetling* means "overhanging" or "projecting."

Identify Problem and Solution *Why is Sindbad's new problem worse than his original one?*

The Search for Wisdom *Do you think Sindbad's decision here is wise? Explain.*

As I thus stumbled along I noticed a great joint of flesh come tumbling down into the valley from rock to rock. Upon closer inspection I found this to be a whole sheep, skinned and drawn. I was deeply perplexed at the mystery, for there was not a soul in sight; but at that very moment there flashed across my mind the memory of a story I had once heard from travelers who had visited the Diamond Mountains— how men obtained the diamonds from this treacherous and inaccessible valley by a strange device. Before sunrise they would throw whole carcasses of sheep from the top of the mountains, so that the gems on which they fell penetrated the soft flesh and became embedded in it. At midday rocs and mighty vultures would swoop down upon the mutton and carry it away in their talons to their nests in the mountain heights. With a great clamor the merchants would then rush at the birds and force them to drop the meat and fly away, after which it would only remain to look through the carcasses and pick out the diamonds.

As I recalled this story a plan of escape formed in my mind. I selected a great quantity of priceless stones and hid them all about me, filling my pockets with them and pressing them into the folds of my belt and garments. Then I unrolled my turban, stuffed it with more diamonds, twisted it into a rope as I had done before, and, lying down below the carcass, bound it firmly to my chest. I had not remained long in that position when I suddenly felt myself lifted from the ground by the talons of a huge vulture which had tightly closed upon the meat. The bird climbed higher and higher and finally alighted upon the top of a mountain. As soon as it began to tear at the flesh there arose from behind the neighboring rocks a great **tumult**, at which the bird took fright and flew away. At once I freed myself and sprang to my feet, with face and clothes all bloody.

I saw a man come running to the spot and stop in alarm as he saw me. Without uttering a word he cautiously bent over the carcass to examine it, eyeing me suspiciously all the while; but finding no diamonds, he wrung his hands and lifted up his arms, crying: "O heavy loss! Allah, in whom alone dwell all power and majesty, defend us from the wiles of the Evil One!"

Before I could explain my presence the man, shaking with fear, turned to me and asked: "Who are you, and how came you here?"

"Do not be alarmed, sir," I replied, "I am no evil spirit, but an honest man, a merchant by profession. My story is an extraordinary one, and the adventure which has brought me to these mountains surpasses in wonder all the marvels that men have seen or heard of. But first pray accept some of these diamonds, which I myself gathered in the fearful valley below."

I took some splendid jewels from my pocket and offered them to him, saying: "These will bring you all the riches you can desire."

The owner of the bait was overjoyed at the unexpected gift; he warmly thanked me and called down blessings upon me. Whilst we were thus talking, several other merchants came up from the mountain-side. They crowded round us, listening in amazement to my story, and congratulated me, saying: "By Allah, your escape was a miracle; for no man has ever set foot in that valley and returned alive. Allah alone be praised for your salvation."

Identify Problem and Solution *What role might the diamonds play in solving Sindbad's problems?*

Capricornus (detail) from the *Ajaib al-Makhukat of al-Kawzwini,* 14th century. Freer Gallery of Art, Washington DC.

The merchants then led me to their tent. They gave me food and drink and there I slept soundly for many hours. Early next day we set out from our tent and, after journeying over a vast range of mountains, came at length to the seashore. After a short voyage we arrived in a pleasant, densely wooded island, covered with trees so huge that beneath one of them a hundred men could shelter from the sun. It is from these trees that the aromatic substance known as camphor[4] is extracted. The trunks are hollowed out, and the sap oozes drop by drop into vessels which are placed beneath, soon curdling into a crystal gum.

In that island I saw a gigantic beast called the karkadan, or rhinoceros, which grazes in the fields like a cow or buffalo. Taller than a camel, it has a single horn in the middle of its forehead, and upon this horn Nature has carved the likeness of a man. The karkadan attacks the elephant and, impaling it upon its horn, carries it aloft from place to place until its victim dies. Before long, however, the elephant's fat melts in the heat of the sun and, dripping down into the karkadan's eyes, puts out its sight, so that the beast blunders

helplessly along and finally drops dead. Then the roc swoops down upon both animals and carries them off to its nest in the high mountains. I also saw many strange breeds of buffalo in that island.

I sold a part of my diamonds for a large sum and exchanged more for a vast quantity of merchandise. Then we set sail and, trading from port to port and from island to island, at length arrived safely in Basrah. After a few days' sojourn there I set out upstream to Baghdad, the City of Peace.

Loaded with precious goods and the finest of my diamonds, I hastened to my old street and, entering my own house, rejoiced to see my friends and kinsfolk. I gave them gold and presents, and distributed alms[5] among the poor of the city.

I soon forgot the perils and hardships of my travels and took again to sumptuous living. I ate well, dressed well, and kept open house for innumerable gallants and boon[6] companions.

From far and near men came to hear me speak of my adventures and to learn the news of foreign lands from me. All were astounded at the dangers I had escaped and wished me joy of my return. Such was my second voyage.

Tomorrow, my friends, if Allah wills, I shall relate to you the extraordinary tale of my third voyage.

The famous mariner ended. The guests marvelled at his story.

When the evening feast was over, Sindbad the Sailor gave Sindbad the Porter a hundred pieces of gold, which he took with thanks and many blessings, and departed, lost in wonderment at all he had heard. ∾

---

4. *Camphor* is used in lotions and medicines.

5. *Alms* are money, food, or other items given to aid the poor.
6. *Boon* describes people who are sociable and make good company.

The Search for Wisdom *Based on this sentence, how did people during this time learn about the world?*

After You Read

Respond and Think Critically

Respond and Interpret

1. Which parts of the story did you find most entertaining? Why?

2. (a)Briefly describe the roc and its egg. (b)How do Sindbad's descriptions help create suspense?

3. (a)How does Sindbad escape from the roc's island? (b)What does his plan of escape suggest about his character?

4. (a)How do merchants obtain diamonds from the Diamond Mountains? (b)How does their method help Sindbad escape?

5. (a)What does Sindbad do with his riches when he returns home? (b)What do his actions reveal about him?

Analyze and Evaluate

6. **Irony** occurs when something is the opposite of what is expected. What is ironic about Sindbad's situation after the roc deposits him in the Diamond Mountains?

7. (a)**Hyperbole** is exaggeration or overstatement for effect. What are some examples of hyperbole in the story? (b)What effects does this literary device have on the tale?

Connect

8. **Big Idea** **The Search for Wisdom** What does this story reveal about the ways in which people gain information and the sources to which they turn for knowledge and inspiration?

9. **Connect to Today** What elements of Sindbad's story are common in contemporary adventure books and stories?

Literary Element **Point of View**

"The Second Voyage of Sindbad the Sailor" is told from the **first-person** point of view. Other points of view include the **third-person omniscient,** in which an outside narrator is all knowing, and the **third-person limited,** in which the events are described as only one character perceives them.

1. What effect does the first-person point of view have on "The Second Voyage of Sindbad the Sailor"?

2. How would the story be different if it had been told from the third-person point of view?

Review: Imagery

As you learned on page 242, **imagery** is language that creates "word pictures" in the reader's mind and evokes emotional responses. Imagery appeals to one or more of the five senses and can enhance the reader's enjoyment of a literary work.

Partner Activity With a partner, find examples of imagery in the story. Work together to create a chart like the one below. For each of the five senses listed, find corresponding imagery in the text that appeals to that sense.

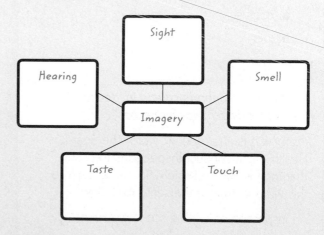

Reading Strategy — Identify Problem and Solution

ACT Skills Practice

Sindbad makes a mark in the sand at the base of the roc's egg to:

A. claim the egg later as his property.

B. leave some memento of his stay on the island.

C. determine the egg's circumference.

D. be able to identify the egg later.

Vocabulary Practice

Practice with Analogies Choose the correct word to complete each analogy.

1. beach : sand :: thicket :
   a. shrubs   **c.** lumber
   b. nests   **d.** fruit

2. enormous : massive :: fruitless :
   a. meaningful   **c.** chaotic
   b. pointless   **d.** priceless

3. peace : calm :: tumult :
   a. mob   **c.** din
   b. party   **d.** crime

4. thrill : entertain :: confound :
   a. confuse   **c.** discover
   b. join   **d.** destroy

Academic Vocabulary

*In this story, Sindbad's careful **inspection** of his surroundings helps him escape.*

Inspection is an academic word. The Board of Health might conduct **inspections** to ensure that food is handled safely. To further explore this word, complete the sentence below.

An inspection of a crime scene would include _____, _____, and _____.

For more on academic vocabulary, see pages 36–37 and R83–R85.

Connect to *Art*

 Write a Report

Assignment Persian miniatures are vivid paintings that were used to illustrate Persian manuscript books in the Middle Ages. Research this art form and write a brief report on the style and the subjects of the miniatures. In your report, compare the pictorial style of the miniatures with the narrative style of *The Thousand and One Nights*.

Investigate Develop a research plan, such as deciding what search terms—for example, "Iranian painting"—may be helpful. Generate ideas from multiple sources, such as art history books and the Internet. Keep a record of the bibliographical information about your sources and use a chart like the one below to record your notes.

Painting	Subject	Style
Illustration from Persian epic the Shah-nama ("Book of Kings")	Combat between warrior heroes Sohrab and Rustum	Bright colors, flat (little perspective), every area filled with ornamental detail

Create Illustrate your report with specific examples of the Persian miniatures about which you are writing. Photocopy or scan the images you want to use or download examples you find on the Internet.

Report Compile the information you have gathered and write your report, making sure to incorporate relevant historical and cultural background. Include a works cited list, or bibliography, using your teacher's preferred form for citations.

Before You... d

from the *Rubái...*

Meet **Omar Khayyám**
(1048–1131)

Ironically, Omar Khayyám, the best-known Persian poet in the Western world, was famous in his own lifetime as an astronomer and a mathematician. The word *khayyám* means "tent maker," but Khayyám—whose name may have been derived from his father's occupation—was a brilliant scholar versed in philosophy, medicine, and astronomy.

A Man of Many Talents The details of Khayyám's life are vague, but modern scholars believe he was born in the Persian city of Nishapur (now Neyshabur in Iran), which was the intellectual capital of Islam at the time. While in his twenties, Khayyám wrote a scholarly work on algebra that caught the attention of Sultan Malik-shah, who asked him to join a learned group that was reforming the Islamic calendar. Their work resulted in the Jalali calendar, which remains the most accurate calendar in the world.

Despite his impressive accomplishments in mathematics and astronomy, Khayyám's fame in the West rests largely on a collection of four-line poems he wrote using a popular medieval Persian poetic form called the *ruba´i* (*ruba´i* means "quatrain"; the plural form is *rubáiyát*). Typically, the first two lines of a *ruba´i* introduce a problem or a situation, the third creates tension or surprise, and the fourth offers resolution, sometimes with an unexpected slant or twist.

A Rediscovered Poet Khayyám's poetry, which never developed a significant audience during his lifetime, remained largely unknown to readers outside of Persia for hundreds of years. In the mid-1800s, however, copies of Khayyám's verses were discovered in the Bodleian Library at Oxford University in England. Struck by the

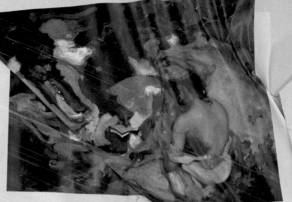

Omar Khayyám, Persian Astrono... ...oet (detail). S... rank Brangwyn. Oil on canvas. Private coll... ion.

> "Ah, make the most of what we yet
> may spend,
> Before we too into the Dust
> descend . . ."
>
> —from *The Rubáiyát of Omar Khayyám*

beauty and emotional depth of the poems, British poet Edward FitzGerald (1809–1893) translated them into English and published them as *The Rubáiyát of Omar Khayyám* in 1859. Although it was little noticed at first, the *Rubáiyát* gradually found an enthusiastic readership. FitzGerald's translation increased in popularity, and he later published several revised and expanded editions.

In the late nineteenth and early twentieth centuries, publishers all over the world created illustrated editions of the *Rubáiyát*. These editions helped make Khayyám a world-renowned poet more than 700 years after his death.

Literature and Reading Preview

Connect to the Poems

Why might people believe that certain pleasures ~~~~y be denied or enjoyed only moderately? Write a~~~~ about your thoughts on this question.

Build Background

FitzGerald wanted modern readers to ~~~~ this, he often incor- ~~emotionally to the *Rubáiyát*. To ac~~~~ed from the original porated contemporary images th~~~s so that they appear to Persian. He also arranged the ~~ugh it is unlikely that be an account of a single d~~~ment. Khayyám intended this ar~~~

Set Purposes f~~ Reading

Big Idea The ~~search for Wisdom

As you read, ask yourself, Does it seem wise to always seek refuge in pleasure and to live for the moment?

Literary Element Rhyme Scheme

Rhyme scheme is the pattern that end rhymes form in a stanza or a poem. Rhyme scheme is designated by the assign- ment of a different letter of the alphabet for each rhyme. As you read the verses from the *Rubáiyát*, ask yourself, What is the rhyme scheme of each *ruba'í*?

Reading Strategy Clarify Meaning

To **clarify meaning** as you read, it often helps to reread difficult passages or to read more slowly if you are confused. When reading poetry, you should follow the syntax, or arrange- ment, of the lines to track complete thoughts. As you read, ask yourself, Do I understand the meaning of this line or quatrain?

Tip: Track Word Order Pay particular attention to lines that do not follow normal word-order patterns. Use a chart like this to track inverted, or reverse, word order in Khayyám's verses.

Khayyám's Word Order	Normal Word Order
"Myself when young did eagerly frequent"	"When I was young I eagerly frequented"

Learning Objectives

For pages 505–510

In studying this text, you will focus on the following objectives:

Literary Study: Analyzing rhyme scheme.

Reading: Clarifying meaning.

Writing: Reporting on literary criticism.

Vocabulary

waive (wāv) v. to reject, decline, or give up; p. 507 *The suspect wanted to defend himself, so he chose to waive his right to be silent.*

conspire (kən spīr´) v. to join in agreement; to plot; p. 508 *The younger siblings decided to conspire against their self-absorbed older brother.*

Tip: Word Usage When you encounter a new word, it might help you to ask yourself a question about it. For example, when might you *conspire* with a friend?

Literature and Reading Preview

Connect to the Poems

Why might people believe that certain pleasures in life should be denied or enjoyed only moderately? Write a journal entry about your thoughts on this question.

Build Background

FitzGerald wanted modern readers to be able to respond emotionally to the *Rubáiyát*. To accomplish this, he often incorporated contemporary images that differed from the original Persian. He also arranged the quatrains so that they appear to be an account of a single day, although it is unlikely that Khayyám intended this arrangement.

Set Purposes for Reading

Big Idea The Search for Wisdom

As you read, ask yourself, Does it seem wise to always seek refuge in pleasure and to live for the moment?

Literary Element Rhyme Scheme

Rhyme scheme is the pattern that end rhymes form in a stanza or a poem. Rhyme scheme is designated by the assignment of a different letter of the alphabet for each rhyme. As you read the verses from the *Rubáiyát*, ask yourself, What is the rhyme scheme of each *ruba'i*?

Reading Strategy Clarify Meaning

To **clarify meaning** as you read, it often helps to reread difficult passages or to read more slowly if you are confused. When reading poetry, you should follow the syntax, or arrangement, of the lines to track complete thoughts. As you read, ask yourself, Do I understand the meaning of this line or quatrain?

....

Tip: Track Word Order Pay particular attention to lines that do not follow normal word-order patterns. Use a chart like this to track inverted, or reverse, word order in Khayyám's verses.

Khayyám's Word Order	Normal Word Order
"Myself when young did eagerly frequent"	"When I was young I eagerly frequented"

Learning Objectives

For pages 505–510

In studying this text, you will focus on the following objectives:

Literary Study: Analyzing rhyme scheme.

Reading: Clarifying meaning.

Writing: Reporting on literary criticism.

Vocabulary

waive (wāv) v. to reject, decline, or give up; p. 507 *The suspect wanted to defend himself, so he chose to waive his right to be silent.*

conspire (kən spīr′) v. to join in agreement; to plot; p. 508 *The younger siblings decided to conspire against their self-absorbed older brother.*

....

Tip: Word Usage When you encounter a new word, it might help you to ask yourself a question about it. For example, when might you *conspire* with a friend?

from the Rubáiyát

Omar Khayyám
Translated by Edward FitzGerald

Shah Abbas I and a Courtier (detail). Persian school. Fresco. Chehel Sotun Isfahan, Iran.

I

Awake! for Morning in the Bowl of Night°
Has flung the Stone° that puts the Stars to Flight:
    And Lo! the Hunter of the East has caught
The Sultán's Turret° in a Noose of Light.

VII

Come, fill the Cup, and in the Fire of Spring
The Winter Garment of Repentance fling:
    The Bird of Time has but a little way
To fly—and Lo! the Bird is on the Wing.

XII

"How sweet is mortal Sovranty!"°—think some:
Others—"How blest the Paradise to come!"
    Ah, take the Cash in hand and **waive** the Rest;
Oh, the brave Music of a *distant* Drum!

XIII

Look to the Rose that blows about us—"Lo,
Laughing," she says, "into the World I blow:
    At once the silken Tassel of my Purse
Tear, and its Treasure on the Garden throw."

XVII

They say the Lion and the Lizard keep
The Courts where Jamshy'd° gloried and drank deep;
    And Bahrám,° that great Hunter—the Wild Ass
Stamps o'er his Head, and he lies fast asleep.

I, 1 **Bowl of Night:** the night sky.
I, 2 **Stone:** the rising sun.

I, 4 **Turret:** a small, often ornamental, tower projecting from a larger structure.

XII, 1 **Sovranty:** freedom from external control (spelled *sovereignty* in Standard English).

XVII, 2 **Jamshy'd:** In Persian mythology, he was a king of celestial beings condemned to live as a mortal being.
XVII, 3 **Bahrám:** legendary king who was killed while hunting an ass.

Rhyme Scheme *Which three lines in this verse rhyme?*

Clarify Meaning *How might you rearrange this line to follow a more standard sentence structure?*

Vocabulary

waive (wāv) *v.* to reject, decline, or give up

OMAR KHAYYÁM **507**

XXVII

Myself when young did eagerly frequent
Doctor and Saint, and heard great Argument
   About it and about: but evermore
Came out by the same Door as in I went.

XXVIII

With them the Seed of Wisdom did I sow,
And with my own hand labor'd it to grow:
   And this was all the Harvest that I reap'd—
"I came like Water, and like Wind I go."

LXVIII

We are no other than a moving row
Of Magic Shadow-shapes that come and go
   Round with the Sun-illumined Lantern held
In Midnight by the Master of the Show.

LXIX

But helpless Pieces of the Game He plays
Upon this Checker-board of Nights and Days;
   Hither and thither moves, and checks, and slays,
And one by one back in the Closet lays.

LXXI

And much as Wine has play'd the Infidel,
And robb'd me of my Robe of Honor—well,
   I often wonder what the Vintners° buy
One half so precious as the Goods they sell.

XCIX

Ah, Love! could you and I with Him **conspire**
To grasp this sorry Scheme of Things entire,
   Would not we shatter it to bits—and then
Re-mold it nearer to the Heart's Desire!

A Dancing Girl with a Tambourine. Qajar school.
Oil on canvas. Private collection.

LXXI, 3. Vintners: sellers of wine and liquor.

The Search for Wisdom *What does this verse suggest about the role of well-educated people in the search for wisdom?*

Rhyme Scheme *How does the rhyme scheme in this verse differ from the usual ruba'i pattern?*

After You Read

Respond and Think Critically

Respond and Interpret

1. What images linger in your mind after reading these verses?

2. (a)What time of day is **personified**, or given human characteristics, in ruba'i I? (b)What part of the human life cycle might this time of day represent?

3. (a)In ruba'i VII, what does the speaker urge readers to do? (b)What reason does the speaker give?

4. (a)What is the **theme**, or overall message, of ruba'i XVII? (b)What image develops this theme?

Analyze and Evaluate

5. (a)Does the speaker agree with the beliefs of others whom he quotes in ruba'i XII? (b)What does his response to these beliefs suggest about him?

6. (a)What image does Khayyám create in ruba'i LXVIII? (b)What does this image suggest about the speaker's view of human life?

Connect

7. **Big Idea** **The Search for Wisdom** Critics have said that the knowledge that death is inevitable drives the love of life displayed in the *Rubáiyát*. In your opinion, is this view accurate? Explain.

8. **Connect to the Author** Omar Khayyám was a brilliant scholar educated in a variety of subjects. How might his broad education have contributed to the verses of the *Rubáiyát* excerpted here?

Literary Element Rhyme Scheme

Poems are often structured around a particular **rhyme scheme,** or a regular pattern of rhyme. Rhyme schemes are analyzed by assigning a different letter of the alphabet to each rhyme, beginning with the letter *a*, as in the following example from the *Rubáiyát*:

Awake! for Morning in the Bowl of <u>Night</u> *a*

Has flung the Stone that puts the Stars to <u>Flight</u>: *a*

And Lo! the Hunter of the East has <u>caught</u> *b*

The Sultán's Turret in a Noose of <u>Light</u>. *a*

1. What rhyme scheme appears most frequently in the *Rubáiyát*?

2. Do you think the verses would be more or less effective if all the lines rhymed with one another? Explain.

Review: Speaker

As you learned on page 359, a poem's **speaker** is the person or being who is speaking, similar to a narrator in a work of prose. The speaker is sometimes the poet but can also be a fictional person or even an object. The speaker communicates a particular **tone,** or attitude, in the poem by using specific word choice, or **diction.**

1. Choose a verse from the *Rubáiyát* and explain how the **diction** contributes to the speaker's tone.

2. Review the chart you made on page 506 to restate inverted word order in normal English. How do your restatements affect the tone of the lines?

3. What are three or four adjectives you might use to describe the speaker of the *Rubáiyát*?

Reading Strategy Clarify Meaning

SAT Skills Practice

The speaker introduces Jamshy'd and Bahrám in ruba'i XVII to

(A)   celebrate their power and glory

(B)   emphasize the passing of fame

(C)   evoke the greatness of the past

(D)   create a desert landscape

(E)   evoke a mood of despair

Vocabulary Practice

Practice with Usage Respond to the statements below to gain a better understanding of the meaning of each boldfaced vocabulary word from the verses.

1. Why might a country refuse to **waive** the right to free speech?

2. How might citizens **conspire** to overthrow a tyrant?

Academic Vocabulary

The speaker of the Rubáiyát *believes that people should live without* **inhibitions** *and should enjoy life fully.*

Inhibition is an academic word. In more casual conversation, you might say that a person who is afraid to dance in front of people has an **inhibition.** To further explore the meaning of this word, complete the sentence below.

My inhibitions prevented me from _____.

For more on academic vocabulary, see pages 36–37 and R83–R85.

LOG ON ▶ **Literature** Online

Selection Resources For Selection Quizzes, eFlashcards, and Reading-Writing Connection activities, go to glencoe.com and enter QuickPass code GLW6053u3.

Research and Report

⚡ Literary Criticism

Assignment Evaluate a passage of literary criticism that comments on the outlook on life expressed in Khayyám's poetry. Write a short response in which you explain whether you agree or disagree with the critic, using evidence from the *Rubáiyát.* Present your response to the class in a report.

Prepare Use the Internet and the library to research credible literary criticism that has been written on Khayyám's poetry. Choose an appropriate passage to evaluate and then formulate a thesis you can support with valid, relevant evidence from the text. Use a chart like the one below to match different points made by the critic with your opinions and the evidence you will use to support them.

Critic's Statement	My Opinion	Evidence
"In spite of the labels which some commentators have tried to pin on him, Omar was not a mystic." (Louis Untermeyer)	I agree	Khayyám notes that people should not take refuge in paradise but instead should "…take the Cash in hand and waive the Rest."

Report Make sure your report includes logical arguments that will inform and persuade your listeners. When you present the report, make eye contact, speak loudly and clearly, and maintain good posture. Use appropriate tones of voice to clarify logical appeals and to enhance emotional ones.

Evaluate In a short paragraph, evaluate your delivery of the report. Consider the quality of your research and your use of verbal and nonverbal techniques.

Before You Read

The Counsels of the Bird

Meet **Rumi**
(1207–1273)

According to Islamic tradition, when the famous Persian poet Farid ud-Din Attar was very old, he met Jalal al-Din Rumi (rü′mē), who was then only a child, and proclaimed that Rumi would become a great leader. Although this story may be a myth, Rumi did become an exceptionally influential Islamic poet and mystic. His poetry has inspired Muslims and non-Muslims alike from the thirteenth century to the present.

Early Life Rumi was born in 1207 in the city of Balkh (now a part of northern Afghanistan). He and his family fled westward when the Mongol armies of Genghis Khan invaded the area. The family eventually settled in the city of Konya (in present-day Turkey), where the king had invited Rumi's father to teach at a madrassa, or religious school. When his father died in 1231, Rumi filled his position at the madrassa, and gained acclaim as a teacher of Sufism, an Islamic mystical movement.

Spiritual Friendship In 1244, Rumi's life changed permanently when he met a wandering mystic named Shams al-Din Tabrizi. Shams's religious teachings and spirituality inspired Rumi, and the men became inseparable. This friendship caused jealousy in the Sufi community, especially when Rumi began to neglect his Sufi disciples and his family. In 1248, Shams vanished mysteriously—modern historians agree he was murdered, likely by men jealous over his relationship with Rumi. Distraught by his friend's disappearance, Rumi began to write thousands of verses of poetry that expressed feelings of love and loss. He signed these poems in Shams's name—a Sufi gesture that signified the spiritual bond between the two men.

> "Beyond this world and life we know there is Someone watching over us. To know Him is not in our power. But once in a glimpse I saw that we are His shadow and our shadow is the world."
>
> —Rumi

The Masnavi Rumi's most famous work is *The Masnavi* ("couplets" in Arabic), a huge collection of Sufi sermons and fables in verse. *The Masnavi* is regarded by some as Islam's most important spiritual literature after the Qur'an. It asserts that God is present in everything—all people, places, and objects—yet also describes the difficulty many people have experiencing a personal relationship with God. Poet and translator Jonathan Star observed of Rumi, "…his every word came from a place of love and inspiration, a place where the soul and its Creator are one."

Literature Online

Author Search For more about Rumi, go to glencoe.com and enter QuickPass code GLW6053u3.

Literature and Reading Preview

Connect to the Poem

Have you ever ignored a piece of advice? Freewrite for a few minutes about this advice and why you ignored it.

Build Background

Sufis sought to find truth and knowledge through a personal experience with God. They embraced poverty and wore *sufs*, or patched cloaks of rough wool, as a sign of their unworldliness. Rumi founded the Mevlevi order of Sufis, whose ritual prayer (called *dhikr*) involves spinning dances set to music. This garnered them the nickname "whirling dervishes" (*dervish* is Persian for "beggar").

Set Purposes for Reading

Big Idea The Search for Wisdom

As you read, ask yourself, How does the bird in the poem use wisdom to gain his freedom?

Literary Element Maxim

A **maxim** is a short saying that contains a general truth, a fundamental principle, or a rule of conduct about morality, personal behavior, or human experience. Such statements existed throughout history—for example, in the works of the philosopher Confucius, the biblical book of Proverbs, and the oral traditions of Africa. As you read, ask yourself, What maxims does the bird offer the man?

Reading Strategy Make Generalizations About Characters

When you **make generalizations about characters,** you draw conclusions about them based on details in the text. As you read, ask yourself, What generalizations can I make about the bird and the man based on their words and actions?

....

Tip: Track Words and Actions In a chart like the one below, track the words and actions of the bird and the man.

Character	Words and Actions	Generalization
Man	Captured bird by wiles and snares	Man is cunning enough to trap bird

Vocabulary

deem (dēm) *v.* to regard in a certain way; p. 514 *She did not deem him worthy of her attention.*

assertion (ə sur′shən) *n.* a forceful or confident statement of fact or belief; p. 514 *The alumni believed the coach's assertion that the team would win the championship.*

prosperity (pros per′ə tē) *n.* the state of being successful; p. 514 *Her prosperity was due to her dedicated work ethic and high-paying job.*

....

Tip: Antonyms Antonyms are words with opposite meanings. For example, *poverty,* or the lack of money and material possessions, is an antonym of *prosperity.* Antonyms are always the same part of speech.

A Bird. Persian Miniature.

The Counsels of the *Bird*
from The Masnavi

Rumi
Translated by E. H. Winfield

A man captured a bird by wiles and snares;
The bird said to him, "O noble sir,
In your time you have eaten many oxen and sheep,
And likewise sacrificed many camels;
5   You have never become satisfied with their meat,
So you will not be satisfied with my flesh.
Let me go, that I may give you three counsels,
Whence you will see whether I am wise or foolish.
The first of my counsels shall be given on your wrist,
10 The second on your well-plastered roof,
And the third I will give you from the top of a tree.

Make Generalizations About Characters *Think about the locations the bird mentions. What generalization can you make about the bird from what he proposes here?*

On hearing all three you will **deem** yourself happy.
As regards the counsel on your wrist, 'tis this,—
'Believe not foolish **assertions** of any one!' "

15 When he had spoken this counsel on his wrist, he flew
Up to the top of the roof, entirely free.
Then he said, "Do not grieve for what is past;
When a thing is done, vex not yourself about it."
He continued, "Hidden inside this body of mine

20 Is a precious pearl, ten drachms° in weight.
That jewel of right belonged to you,
Wealth for yourself and **prosperity** for your children.
You have lost it, as it was not fated you should get it,
That pearl whose like can nowhere be found."

25 Thereupon the man, like a woman in her travail,°
Gave vent to lamentations and weeping.
The bird said to him, "Did I not counsel you, saying,
'Beware of grieving over what is past and gone?'
When 'tis past and gone, why sorrow for it?

30 Either you understood not my counsel or are deaf.
The second counsel I gave you was this, namely,
'Be not misguided enough to believe foolish assertions.'
O fool, altogether I do not weigh three drachms,
How can a pearl of ten drachms be within me?"

35 The man recovered himself and said, "Well then,
Tell me now your third good counsel!"
The bird replied, "You have made a fine use of the others,
That I should waste my third counsel upon you!
To give counsel to a sleepy ignoramus

40 Is to sow seeds upon salt land.
Torn garments of folly and ignorance cannot be patched.
O counselors, waste not the seed of counsel on them!"

20 **drachm:** about half an ounce.

25 **a woman in her travail:** a woman in labor.

The Search for Wisdom *What do you think the man has learned from the counsels of the bird?*

Maxim *What general truth does this maxim reveal?*

Vocabulary

deem (dēm) *v.* to regard in a certain way
assertion (ə sur′shən) *n.* a forceful or confident statement of fact or belief
prosperity (pros per′ə tē) *n.* the state of being successful

After You Read

Respond and Think Critically

Respond and Interpret

1. Did the ending of the poem surprise you? Explain why or why not.

2. (a)What advice does the bird give when he is on the man's wrist? (b)Why might the bird have given this advice first?

3. How does the man react to the loss of the pearl?

Analyze and Evaluate

4. **Irony** is a contrast between expectations and reality. What irony do you see in the conclusion of the poem?

5. What is the **theme,** or message, of the poem?

Connect

6. **Big Idea** **The Search for Wisdom** Translators Jonathan Star and Shahram Shiva observe that with Rumi's verse, "one must always be aware of the meaning behind the meaning, and the veils behind the veils." How do meanings hide behind meanings in "The Counsels of the Bird"?

7. **Connect to the Author** Rumi was well known as a teacher, particularly of Islamic mysticism. How might his career as a teacher have influenced the way he wrote this poem?

Literary Element Maxim

Maxims are most effective when they state truths with wit, fresh imagery, and penetrating insight.

1. Reread the maxim in lines 17–18. What general truth does it teach?

2. Restate the third counsel of the bird (lines 39–41) in your own words. What, if anything, is lost by rewording it? Explain.

Reading Strategy Make Generalizations About Characters

When you **make generalizations about characters,** you will better understand them.

1. (a)What generalizations can you make about the bird's character? (b)What or whom might the bird represent?

2. (a)What generalizations can you make about the man's character? (b)What or whom might he represent?

LOG ON ▶ **Literature** Online

Selection Resources For Selection Quizzes, eFlashcards, and Reading-Writing Connection activities, go to glencoe.com and enter QuickPass code GLW6053u3.

Vocabulary Practice

Practice with Antonyms With a partner, brainstorm three antonyms for each boldfaced vocabulary word below. Then discuss your choices with your classmates. Be prepared to explain why you chose your antonyms.

deem   **assertion**   **prosperity**

EXAMPLE: evade
Antonyms: participate; join; contribute
Sample explanation: A person who *evades* avoids taking part in something, while a person who *contributes* does take part.

Writing

Write a Maxim What truths have you learned through experience? Write a list of five or more maxims that express these truths, using the maxims in "The Counsels of the Bird" as models. Try to use metaphors to make your maxims memorable. Make sure the details in your maxims relate to broad truths by creating a graphic organizer similar to the one you filled out on page 512.

Before You Read

Elegy for a Woman of No Importance

Meet **Nāzik al-Malā'ikah**
(1922–2007)

Nāzik al-Malā'ikah (nä′zēk äl′mäl i′khä), a poet and a literary critic, was one of the most notable women authors in the Middle East. Al-Malā'ikah began to challenge the traditional structure of Arabic poetry with the publication of her first volume of free-verse poetry, *The Lover of Night*, in 1947.

Al-Malā'ikah was born in Baghdad, the capital of Iraq, in 1923 and was the first of her parents' seven children. Her mother was a poet who wrote under the pseudonym Um Nizar, and her father was a grammar teacher, a poet, and the editor of a twenty-volume encyclopedia. Her parents inspired al-Malā'ikah's love of literature and language at an early age; she wrote her first classical Arabic poem at the age of ten, under her father's guidance. Al-Malā'ikah graduated from a college in Baghdad and went on to study at Princeton University and the University of Wisconsin in the United States. Al-Malā'ikah's earliest published poems, which were printed while she was in college, revealed her inclination toward modernist poetics.

Cultural Influences Al-Malā'ikah was strongly influenced by her society and often responded to current events. One of her best-known poems, "Cholera," centers on the effects of a cholera epidemic that struck Egypt in 1947. Al-Malā'ikah later said of the poem, "I woke up and lay in bed listening to the broadcaster on the radio, who said that the number of the dead in Egypt had reached 1,000. I was overwhelmed by a profound sadness and deep distress. I jumped out of bed, took out a pen and paper . . . and began to compose 'Cholera'. . ."

> "Why do we fear words?
> Some words are secret bells,
>   the echoes
> of their tone announce the start
>   of a magic
> And abundant time"
>
> —Nāzik al-Malā 'ikah,
> from "Love Song for Words"

"Cholera" was one of al-Malā'ikah's first free-verse poems. Although she defended the free-verse movement, she believed that poems should retain some form of meter and often a rhyme scheme. She remained a prominent figure in Arabic modernism throughout the 1950s, but by the late 1960s, her poetry became less experimental. She spent 40 years teaching in Iraqi schools and universities but left Iraq in 1970 after Saddam Hussein came to power and spent the rest of her life in exile in Kuwait and Egypt. Al-Malā'ikah published several volumes of poetry, including *Splinters and Ashes*, *Bottom of the Wave*, and *The Sea Changes its Colors*.

 LOG ON ▶ **Literature** Online

Author Search For more about Nāzik al-Malā'ikah, go to glencoe.com and enter QuickPass code GLW6053u3.

Literature and Reading Preview

Connect to the Poem

Imagine you are considered to be a person of no importance. What would your emotions be? How would the goals of your life change? Respond to these questions in a journal entry.

Build Background

The following poem is an **elegy,** a poem mourning a death or another great loss. The elegy, which is named after an ancient Greek metrical form, is one of the most enduring forms of poetry. Although elegies originally dealt with famous people, al-Malā'ikah mourns the loss of a woman no one will miss.

Set Purposes for Reading

Big Idea The Violence of Change

As you read, ask yourself, What kind of society do the images in the poem portray?

Literary Element Personification

Personification is the attribution of human qualities or thoughts to an animal, an object, or an idea. Poets often use personification to bring energy to a poem, to help readers visualize and relate to the events, or to establish the mood and tone of the work. As you read, ask yourself, How does personification reinforce the indifferent reaction to the woman's death?

Reading Strategy Analyze Tone

When you **analyze** the **tone** of a poem, you look for the literary elements that help you understand the author's or speaker's attitude toward the subject. These elements include word choice, imagery, and figures of speech. As you read, ask yourself, What do the literary elements contribute to the tone?

....

Tip: Note Literary Elements Use a chart like the one below to identify literary elements and describe their effects.

Passage	Literary Element	Effect
"No face turned pale, no lips trembled"	Imagery	Suggests loneliness

Learning Objectives

For pages 516–519

In studying this text, you will focus on the following objectives:

Literary Study: Analyzing personification.

Reading: Analyzing tone.

Writing: Writing an elegy.

Vocabulary

vague (vāg) *adj.* unclear; without form; indistinct; p. 518 *The driving instructor gave vague, confusing instructions on how to parallel park.*

murmur (mur'mər) *v.* to say something in an indistinct voice; to say something quietly and cautiously; p. 518 *The crowd began to murmur when the guest speaker did not appear on stage.*

shrill (shrill) *adj.* high-pitched; p. 518 *The shrill ringing of the fire alarm startled everyone.*

....

Tip: **Synonyms** Synonyms are words with similar meanings. For example, the words *shrill* and *piercing* are synonyms. Replacing a word with a synonym can make the meaning more precise, but not all synonyms can be used to replace one another.

Elegy for a Woman of **No Importance**

Nāzik al-Malā'ikah

Translated by Chris Knipp and Mohammad Sadiq

Solitude, 1991. Al-Adhamy, Firyal.
Watercolour on paper. Private collection.

When she died no face turned pale, no lips trembled
doors heard no retelling of her death
no curtains opened to air the room of grief
no eyes followed the coffin to the end of the road—
5   only, hovering in the memory, a **vague** form
        passing in the lane

The scrap of news stumbled in the alleyways
its whisper, finding no shelter,
lodged obscurely in an unseen corner.
The moon **murmured** sadly.

10 Night, unconcerned, gave way to morning
light came with the milk cart and the call to fasting°
with the hungry mewing of a cat of rags and bones
the **shrill** cries of vendors in the bitter streets
the squabbling of small boys throwing stones
15 dirty water spilling along the gutters
smells on the wind
which played about the rooftops
playing in deep forgetfulness
playing alone

11 call to fasting: begins each day during Ramadan, the month during which Muslims fast from sunrise to sunset.

Personification *What is the author personifying in these lines? What effect does this create?*

After You Read

Respond and Think Critically

Respond and Interpret

1. How did you feel about the woman's death after reading the poem?

2. (a)According to lines 1–5, how does the woman's neighborhood react to her death? (b)What do these lines suggest about the woman's status in the neighborhood?

3. (a)Based on lines 11–15, what do you think the setting of the poem might be? (b)How does the setting contribute to the meaning of the poem?

Analyze and Evaluate

4. (a)What images of loneliness does al-Malā'ikah use in the poem? (b)Why might this imagery be an effective way to convey the mood of the poem?

5. Why might the poet have chosen not to name the woman or to give details of her life?

6. What is the speaker truly mourning? Explain.

7. In your opinion, would the author agree that the woman was "of no importance"? Explain.

Connect

8. **Big Idea** **The Violence of Change** What type of society does this poem reflect?

9. **Connect to the Author** Al-Malā'ikah was well known for her free-verse poetry that does not follow a regular rhythm or rhyme scheme. How does this style influence the effect of the poem?

Literary Element **Personification**

Poets often use **personification** to highlight an idea or create a striking description.

1. Identify at least four examples of personification in this poem.

2. How do these examples reinforce the ideas of solitude and indifference?

Reading Strategy **Analyze Tone**

Tone is a reflection of the author's or speaker's attitude toward the subject—for example, sympathy, amusement, or superiority.

1. What is the tone of the poem?

2. What literary elements create this tone?

LOG ON ▶ **Literature** Online

Selection Resources For Selection Quizzes, eFlash-cards, and Reading-Writing Connection activities, go to glencoe.com and enter QuickPass code GLW6053u3.

Vocabulary Practice

Practice with Synonyms A synonym is a word that has the same or nearly the same meaning as another word. With a partner, match each boldfaced vocabulary word below with its synonym. Use a thesaurus or a dictionary to check your answers. You will not use all the answer choices.

1. vague	a. sing	d. mumble
2. murmur	b. mock	e. muted
3. shrill	c. uncertain	f. blaring

Writing

Write an Elegy Write an elegy about a loss you have suffered. Include images that express your feelings and set an appropriate mood. Use personification to help readers better visualize your imagery. To get ideas for other literary elements to use, look at the chart you filled out on page 517.

The Sound of Birds at Noon

Dahlia Ravikovitch
Translated by Chana Bloch and Ariel Bloch

This chirping
is not in the least **malicious.**
They sing without giving us a thought
and they are as many
5   as the seed of Abraham.[1]
They have a life of their own,
they fly without thinking.
Some are **rare,** some common,
but every wing is grace.
10   Their hearts aren't heavy
even when they peck at a worm.
Perhaps they're light-headed.
The heavens were given to them
to rule over day and night
15   and when they touch a branch,
the branch too is theirs.
This chirping is entirely free of malice.
Over the years
it even seems to have
20   a note of **compassion.**

---

1. The *seed of Abraham* refers to Genesis 22:17, in which God promises that Abraham's descendants will be "as numerous as the stars in the sky and the grains of sand on the seashore."

Enjambment *How does this line break affect your understanding of the poem's time frame?*

Vocabulary

malicious (mə lish′əs) *adj.* marked by a desire to cause pain, injury, or distress to another

rare (rār) *adj.* distinctive or seldom seen

compassion (kəm pash′ən) *n.* sympathetic awareness of another's distress

After You Read

Respond and Think Critically

Respond and Interpret

1. What images in the poem do you find most striking or memorable? Explain.

2. (a)In lines 1–2, how does the speaker characterize the song of the birds? (b)Why might this characterization surprise readers?

3. (a)What two things are compared in lines 4–5? (b)What impression does this simile create?

Analyze and Evaluate

4. (a)In lines 6–11, which of the birds' qualities impress the speaker? (b)Why might the speaker admire these particular qualities?

5. (a)How does line 17 echo lines 1–2? (b)In your opinion, what effect does this echo create?

Connect

6. **Big Idea** **The Violence of Change** Based on the last lines of the poem, do you think the speaker would advocate a change brought about by violence? Explain.

7. **Connect to the Author** Ravikovitch once joked that ". . . a slice of bread with butter and honey on an oilcloth-covered breakfast table solves any problem better than an elusive poem." What does this quotation suggest about her reasons for writing antiwar poetry?

Literary Element Enjambment

Enjambment allows the poet to break lines at points where people would normally pause in conversation and also to emphasize ideas and images.

1. In what lines of "The Sound of Birds at Noon" does Ravikovitch use enjambment?

2. How do the line breaks give the poem a conversational quality?

Reading Strategy Recognize Author's Purpose

To recognize an author's purpose, look for clues to help you infer if the author wrote to persuade, inform, explain, describe, or entertain.

1. How might lines 10–11 reveal Ravikovitch's purpose?

2. Why do you think Ravikovitch ended the poem with the words "a note of compassion"?

Vocabulary Practice

Practice with Context Clues Identify the context clues in the following sentences that help you determine the meaning of each boldfaced vocabulary word.

1. Alex's babysitter quit because she was tired of his **malicious** comments and cruel tricks.

2. As natural resources grow scarce, there may come a day when oil is considered a **rare** treasure.

3. The nurse's **compassion,** or awareness of another's distress, led her to treat the patient gently.

Writing

Write a Poem Write a descriptive poem that compares a particular animal behavior with a specific human interaction. As you write, use sensory details to describe the distinctive characteristics of your subject. Use **enjambment** to create a rhythm that mimics everyday speech. Create a graphic organizer like the one on page 521 to help you link the details in your poem to a larger statement about society.

THE DIAMETER OF THE BOMB

Yehuda Amichai

Translated by Chana Bloch
and Stephen Mitchell

Eulogy, 1996. Nissan Engel. Mixed media.
Private collection.

The diameter of the bomb was thirty centimeters
and the diameter of its effective **range** about seven meters,
with four dead and eleven wounded.
And around these, in a larger circle
5   of pain and time, two hospitals are scattered
and one graveyard. But the young woman
who was buried in the city she came from,
at a distance of more than a hundred kilometers,
enlarges the circle **considerably**,
10   and the **solitary** man mourning her death
at the distant shores of a country far across the sea
includes the entire world in the circle.
And I won't even mention the crying of orphans
that reaches up to the throne of God and
15   beyond, making
a circle with no end and no God.

Analyze Cause-and-Effect Relationships *How does this image reflect the changes caused by the terrorists?*

Diction *Why might Amichai have repeated the word* no *in this line? What is its effect?*

After You Read

Respond and Think Critically

Respond and Interpret

1. (a)Based on the title, what did you expect the poem to be about? (b)Did the poem meet your expectations? Explain.

2. (a)What specific facts about the bombing does the poem's speaker present in lines 1–3? (b)How do these details contrast with the details in lines 4–16?

3. (a)What is included as the circle grows in lines 4–12? (b)What is the effect of the **imagery** in these lines?

4. (a)Who and what are included in the circle by the end of the poem? (b)How do lines 13–16 provide the emotional climax, or a high point, to the poem?

Analyze and Evaluate

5. The image of an ever-widening circle unifies the poem. In your opinion, is this image appropriate for the subject matter? Explain.

6. (a)How does the speaker feel about the people's suffering? (b)Based on the speaker's attitude, what is the theme of the poem?

Connect

7. **Big Idea** **The Violence of Change** (a)What might cause a person or a group to use violence? (b)What advice might you give to someone who says violence brings change?

8. **Connect to Today** Recall another act of terrorism that you know about. How does the theme of this poem apply to that incident?

Literary Element Diction

Authors often vary their **diction**. For example, a scientist would use more technical diction with scientists than with the general public.

1. (a)What is the tone of lines 1–3? (b)Which words and phrases contribute to this tone?

2. (a)What is the tone of lines 4–16? (b)How does the diction help build this tone?

Reading Strategy Analyze Cause-and-Effect Relationships

Remember that a single cause may have several effects, and one effect may have multiple causes.

1. List three effects caused by the bomb.

2. (a)How do the effects of the bomb expand throughout the world? (b)In your opinion, which effect is most devastating?

LOG ON ▶ **Literature** Online

Selection Resources For Selection Quizzes, eFlashcards, and Reading-Writing Connection activities, go to glencoe.com and enter QuickPass code GLW6053u3.

Vocabulary Practice

Practice with Analogies For each of these analogies, determine the relationship between the first pair of words. Apply that relationship to the second pair to complete the analogy.

1. expansion : enlargement :: range :

    a. danger **b.** depth   **c.** path   **d.** limit

2. completely : partially :: considerably :

    a. largely **b.** scarcely **c.** easily **d.** slowly

3. religious : minister :: solitary :

    a. hermit **b.** musician **c.** farmer **d.** soldier

Writing

Write an Essay Write an expository essay about the effects of terrorism in one part of the world. Consider the graphic organizer you filled out on page 525 as you examine the cause-and-effect relationships associated with terrorist acts. As you write, pay close attention to your diction.

BUTTERFLIES

Fawziyya Abu Khalid

The Waiting Horseman, 1990. Suad Al-Attar. Oil on canvas. Private collection.

When you abandoned me,
I didn't need an elegy°
because you had planted
a flight of butterflies in my heart
whose path I follow
like a bedouin who knows
how to perfectly trace the footsteps
   of his truant mare.°

2 elegy: a song or a poem that expresses sadness and grief, usually for a person who has died.

8 truant mare: a female horse that has strayed.

Connect to Personal Experience *In your opinion, does this reference to a Bedouin make the poem inaccessible to readers unfamiliar with Saudi culture? Explain.*

After You Read

Respond and Think Critically

Respond and Interpret

1. Would you recommend this poem to other readers? Why or why not?

2. (a)According to the first line of the poem, what has happened to the speaker? (b)What do you think the speaker means by "I didn't need an elegy"?

3. (a)What has been planted in the speaker's heart? (b)What feelings might this metaphor express?

Analyze and Evaluate

4. (a)Can you tell whether the speaker in "Butterflies" is a man or a woman? Explain. (b)Do you need to know the speaker's gender to understand the poem? Why or why not?

5. How would you describe the tone of the poem? Support your answer with details from the text.

6. How does the poet's **diction,** or word choice, affect your perception of the speaker's feelings?

Connect

7. **Big Idea** **The Violence of Change** (a)What change has taken place in the speaker's life? (b)In what way does the speaker's reaction to this change indicate that dramatic upheavals can have positive effects?

8. **Connect to the Author** Abu Khalid left Saudi Arabia to study in the United States but eventually returned home. What ideas about departure and return are evident in "Butterflies"?

Literary Element Simile

Poets use **similes,** a type of **figurative language,** to create vivid images and suggest meaning.

1. What is the **simile,** or comparison, in lines 4–8?

2. What does this simile suggest about the speaker's relationship with the person addressed?

Reading Strategy Connect to Personal Experience

Connecting events, emotions, and characters to your own life can help you explore a literary work more deeply. Refer to the Venn diagram you made on page 529 and then answer these questions.

1. Do you and the speaker have anything in common? Explain.

2. Rewrite the last three lines of the poem, using a simile that relates to your own life.

LOG ON ▶ **Literature** Online

Selection Resources For Selection Quizzes, eFlashcards, and Reading-Writing Connection activities, go to glencoe.com and enter QuickPass code GLW6053u3.

Academic Vocabulary

In "Butterflies," the speaker addresses a person who has **abandoned** her.

Abandon is an academic word. Synonyms include desert, forsake, and leave. To study this word further, fill out a graphic organizer like the one below.

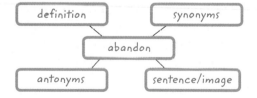

For more on academic vocabulary, see pages 36–37 and R83–R85.

Writing

Write an Essay Reflect on an event that was particularly emotional for you, such as the end of a friendship. Write an essay describing this event, how you felt, and what you learned. Use a **simile** in your essay to add interest and enliven the style.

 # THE LETTER

I'D NEVER READ AS MUCH AS I DID DURING THAT PERIOD.

MY FAVORITE AUTHOR WAS ALI ASHRAF DARVISHIAN, A KIND OF LOCAL CHARLES DICKENS. I WENT TO HIS CLANDESTINE BOOK-SIGNING WITH MY MOTHER.

FER ME FRIEND KOUROSH.

WHY DOES HE SPEAK LIKE THAT?

IT'S JUST HIS KURDISH ACCENT.

HE TOLD SAD BUT TRUE STORIES: REZA BECAME A PORTER AT THE AGE OF TEN.

LEILA WOVE CARPETS AT AGE FIVE.

HASSAN, THREE YEARS OLD, CLEANED CAR WINDOWS.

GET DOWN FROM THERE, STUPID!

I FINALLY UNDERSTOOD WHY I FELT ASHAMED TO SIT IN MY FATHER'S CADILLAC.

THE REASON FOR MY SHAME AND FOR THE REVOLUTION IS THE SAME: THE DIFFERENCE BETWEEN SOCIAL CLASSES.

BUT NOW THAT I THINK OF IT... WE HAVE A MAID AT HOME!!!

HER

THIS IS MEHRI.

SHE WAS EIGHT YEARS OLD WHEN SHE HAD TO LEAVE HER PARENTS' HOME TO COME TO WORK FOR US. JUST LIKE REZA, LEILA AND HASSAN.

WE HAVE TOO MANY CHILDREN, 14 OR 15 INCLUDING HER.

SHE WILL EAT WELL AT YOUR HOUSE.

WE WILL TAKE CARE OF HER.

SHE WAS JUST TEN YEARS OLD WHEN I WAS BORN...SHE TOOK CARE OF ME.

SHE PLAYED WITH ME.

AND SHE ALWAYS FINISHED MY FOOD.

SHE ALSO TOLD ME STORIES ABOUT JACKALS THAT SCARED ME.

AND IT CAME CLOSER! AND IT CAME CLOSER!

IN OTHER WORDS, WE GOT ALONG WELL.

MEHRI HAD A REAL SISTER, ONE YEAR YOUNGER, WHO WORKED AT MY UNCLE'S HOUSE.

AFTER A FEW VISITS, SHE FELL IN LOVE WITH HIM TOO.

HER JEALOUSY WAS MORE THAN SHE COULD BEAR AND SHE TOLD MEHRI'S STORY TO MY UNCLE, WHO TOLD IT TO MY GRANDMA, WHO TOLD IT TO MY MOM. THAT IS HOW THE STORY REACHED MY FATHER...

...WHO DECIDED TO CLARIFY THE SITUATION.

WHEN I FINALLY UNDERSTOOD THE REASONS FOR THE REVOLUTION I MADE MY DECISION.

TOMORROW WE ARE GOING TO DEMONSTRATE.

WE ARE NOT ALLOWED!

DON'T WORRY! WE ARE GOING ANYWAY!

SO THE NEXT DAY...

TAKE CARE!

MEHRI, DON'T FORGET TO COOK HER SOME CHICKEN.

YES, MADAM.

SEE YOU LATER!

FOR ONCE SHE DIDN'T INSIST ON COMING WITH US.

THERE IS THE DEMONSTRATION...

WE SHOUTED FROM MORNING TILL NIGHT.

After You Read

Respond and Think Critically

Respond and Interpret

1. What was your immediate response to Satrapi's graphic style? Explain.

2. What realization does Satrapi have about her shame and the revolution?

3. What aspect of oppression in Iran is represented by Mehri's job and her age when she took it?

4. (a)How does Satrapi react when the neighbor rejects Mehri? (b)What does her reaction reveal about her feelings for Mehri? Explain.

Analyze and Evaluate

5. (a)How does Satrapi graphically convey the emotions and violence of the demonstrations? (b)Do you think these images are effective? Explain.

6. (a)Why do you think Satrapi makes the imprint of slaps remain on her face and on Mehri's face on page 540? (b)What statement do you think Satrapi is making about violence?

Connect

7. **Big Idea** **The Violence of Change** Based on "The Letter," how would you describe the time of the Iranian Revolution?

8. **Connect to the Author** Satrapi states that she prefers drawing in black and white because "there is no bluff" in it. What do you think her statement means?

Literary Element Symbol

Some **symbols** have well-known meanings. Other symbols may be created by an author based on what he or she values and is trying to convey.

Partner Activity With a partner, discuss what the letter in this excerpt symbolizes. Consider the role social class plays in the excerpt.

Reading Strategy Identify Genre

Satrapi, like many other graphic novelists, uses her medium to meld humor with social commentary.

1. How do the elements of the graphic novel help advance the plot throughout the "The Letter"?

2. Do you think this graphic novel would be more or less effective if it were told as a conventional narrative without illustrations? Explain.

Vocabulary Practice

Practice with Synonyms With a partner, brainstorm three synonyms for each boldfaced vocabulary word below. Be prepared to explain your choices.

clandestine   devoted   demonstrate

EXAMPLE: inquire
Synonyms: ask, question, query

Sample explanation: When you inquire about a product, you ask about it.

Writing

Write a Graphic Story *Persepolis* shows how key events in Satrapi's life changed her perspective on the world. Using her work as a model, create a short graphic novel, using images, panels, speech balloons, and symbols to tell a story from your life. Look at the graphic organizer you filled out on page 533 as you consider how to apply this genre's elements.

Regarding RANIA

Blazing a trail for Arab women, Jordan's stylish queen has redefined her role to become an agent of political change. But in the face of traditionalist opposition, she can push women's issues only so far.

By SCOTT MACLEOD

Learning Objectives

For pages 542–545

In studying this text, you will focus on the following objectives:

Reading: Connecting to contemporary issues.

Using text features.

Analyzing informational text.

Set a Purpose for Reading

Read to learn about how one Arab woman is fighting for the rights of women in her society.

Preview the Article

1. Read the deck—the brief text beneath the article's title—and view the photographs on pages 543 and 544. What impression of Rania do these features give you?

2. Skim the entire article, reading the first sentence of each paragraph. What conflicts might the article address?

Reading Strategy Connect to Contemporary Issues

When you **connect to contemporary issues,** you relate what you read to what you already know about current events and ideas. As you read, ask yourself:

• How does this information fit with what I already know about the Middle East?

• What new information does this article teach me about current events, ideas, and conflicts?

STEPPING OUT OF HER GUNMETAL-GRAY SUV AND striding into the compound of Kamalia School for Girls in Amman, Jordan, Rania al Abdullah doesn't fit the prim, cautious image of an Arab queen. For one thing, she's wearing a tight-fitting metallic gold top, matching pants, and two-inch heels, and her glossy brown hair brushes across her shoulders as she walks. For another, rather than standing around exchanging pleasantries, she's walking briskly to her appointment like the busy head of a corporation heading to a board meeting. Nor could she seem more unlike the audience that awaits her inside the school: 28 teenage girls in drab blue uniforms, half of them with their hair fully covered with scarves in the tradition of conservative Muslims.

The Jordanian queen's exposed hair and modern style are social and political statements, of course, advertising her belief that the veil worn by many Muslim women as a part of their religious beliefs should be a matter of personal choice. Rania usually chooses not to. But she isn't at the school to lecture anybody about fashion or faith. She's marking the start of Human Rights Day at one of many events being held in schools across the kingdom of Jordan. The nationwide observance—never before held in an Arab world famous for its violations of basic freedoms—was Rania's idea, just one of many modernizing notions and programs she works for.

After greeting the students, Rania reads aloud a passage about the rights of women, drawn from the United Nations' Universal Declaration of Human Rights. "Freedom means no discrimination on the basis of race, language, religion, politics, or origin, with no differences between men and women," she says in a teacherly way. "Everyone is equal." To the queen's delight, one of the girls responds by quoting Islam's prophet Muhammad on women's equality. Others throw up their hands in a competition to join in. Long after Rania has left, the girls still have stars in their eyes. "She talks to us about freedom, that nobody can take it away from us," beams Rula Nasser. The 10th grader pauses for a moment, then adds: "She's amazing!"

No Western queen or first lady would get such a glowing review just for reading from a legal document. But in the Arab world, where most rulers' wives follow the conservative line in dress and behavior, Rania is a rarity: a powerful woman who uses that power to push a forward-looking, modern agenda. While other Arab wives typically limit their public profile to supporting uncontroversial charities, Rania uses her influence on controversial issues that have brought her praise from modernists, criticism from traditionalists—and attention from well beyond the borders of tiny Jordan. "She's a mover and shaker," says one of the Arab press's leading commentators, Abdul Rahman al Rashid, columnist for the London, England–based *Asharq al Awsat*. "She's not a woman who

INSPIRATION Posing with starstruck students at Amman's Kamalia School for Girls on Human Rights Day

Khalil Mazraawi—AFP/Getty

wants media attention, but one who wants to deliver a program. It is not easy to change things, but she is making noise and delivering what she promises."

The secret to Rania's transformative approach to the monarchy may be her background. She was not raised to be a queen. Her parents are Palestinian—her father was a children's doctor—and she earned a living as part of Amman's middle class, working as a marketing executive for Apple Computer before meeting and marrying then Prince Abdullah in 1993. After becoming queen in 1999 she turned into an international fashion symbol (Italian designer Giorgio Armani said she "has the body of a model, and she holds herself like the queen she is—what more could you want?"). But recently she has evolved into someone even more impressive and hard to define. After a recent earthquake reduced the Iranian town of Bam to rubble, she supervised the loading of

relief supplies onto a Jordanian transport plane and then rode on it to Iran to comfort the victims. She's on the governing board of the World Economic Forum (WEF), the only Arab helping to guide that group of global political and business leaders.

Rania and her husband, King Abdullah II, teamed up with the WEF and U.S. tech company Cisco Systems to launch the Jordan Education Initiative, which teaches people in the Middle East how to learn with the Internet. Her favorite part of the project is Jordan's 10 Cisco Networking Academies. There, high-tech skills are taught to 600 students—almost two-thirds of them women. And thanks to Rania's urging, Arab satellite channels now broadcast public-service ads aimed at boosting women's participation in public life.

Rania's most controversial work is done behind the scenes in Amman, where she quietly urges the king and leading Jordanian

QUEEN RANIA attends the Red Cross gala evening during her visit to London in June.

politicians to establish social and political reforms, many of them aimed at improving the circumstances of women. In 2003, her promptings helped lead to an increase in the number of women holding leadership positions in Jordanian politics. The following year six seats were reserved for women in the newly elected 110-seat Chamber of Deputies. The king had also appointed seven women to the 55-seat Senate and included three women in his government's 21-member cabinet. "She comes and pushes the case," says Abdullah. "She'll say, 'I'm just reminding you, if we are going to give women more of a role, for them to feel a stronger part of society, how about trying to push the envelope?'"

There's plenty of pushing left to be done. In a series of interviews with TIME, Rania described a Middle East where many women's lives remain disadvantaged by inequality. "One of the main obstacles preventing the Arab world from advancing is the exclusion of women," she says. "Sometimes people ask, 'Do you have an agenda?' Yes, I do have a gender agenda. The more you include women, the more people will get used to the fact that yes they are capable, yes they are part of the scene."

But the same traditions that suppress Arab women also place limits on what Rania can achieve. Jordan's conservative politicians have struck many of her modernizing programs down. Also in 2003,

parliament rejected proposals she supported to equalize divorce rights and increase the marrying age of girls from 15 to 18. Rania has also tried and failed to persuade politicians to end a regulation that prevents Jordanian mothers from handing down citizenship to their children. Without citizenship, which can be passed down only by fathers in Jordan, children cannot get state-sponsored education and medical care.

Officials close to the queen say that the setbacks in parliament have taught her not to expect overnight success. "My disappointments," Rania says, "have come mainly from my own impatience. [Reform] requires changes from within society. If society still believes that a woman's place is in the home, you are not going to get change." Even so, she is firmly convinced that "now is the time to confront these issues."

She has already witnessed plenty of change. Rania al Yasin was born in Kuwait in August 1970. Her family remained in Kuwait until Iraq invaded the tiny oil-rich nation in 1990. The Yasins left and never went back. Rania earned a business degree from the American University in Cairo, Egypt, before joining her parents in Amman in 1991. She worked in marketing, first for Citibank, then for Apple. She met Abdullah, oldest son of Jordan's then King Hussein, at a dinner party in 1992, and they married the following year.

She was not expected to become queen. On his deathbed, King Hussein decided to pass over his brother Hassan, who had been next in line for the throne, and instead make Abdullah his heir.

That decision caught Rania—and all of Jordan—by surprise. "A whole new life and responsibility was suddenly placed on my shoulders," she recalls. "You start feeling insecure. You feel you have to prove yourself."

The traditional role of the Arab wife would have required the new queen to limit herself to the raising of their three children. Instead, the king asked her to develop programs on human rights, women's rights, children's rights, education, and health. As a result, Rania set up a separate office, which has a staff of 20, including researchers, speechwriters, schedulers, and media advisers. Many of the people who work in the office are modern young Jordanian women like herself. Although she rarely states her political positions in public, Abdullah says he frequently asks for Rania's advice. "I come home at night, and I have a problem with education or health, and I need somebody to [discuss them with]," he says.

If her discussions with Abdullah have become political, Rania's early public image was centered on her looks and her wardrobe. There were comparisons to former U.S. First Lady Jacqueline Kennedy and Great Britain's Princess Diana, and she became a favorite of celebrity interviewers, gossip columnists, and fashion magazines on both sides of the Atlantic. The media attention led to some criticism in Amman, where Rania's fondness for designer dresses and expensive European vacations is considered inappropriate for the queen of a poor country. The gossips call her "the handbag queen," and even serious commentators in Jordan complain about the costly lifestyle of the royal family. She calls the criticism "part of the turf," but adds: "If the gossip gets out of hand, I may have to look at myself and ask, Am I doing something wrong?"

She has done a lot that is right. Shortly after Abdullah's coronation, she agreed to become a spokeswoman for the global finance movement, which seeks to give power to Third World women by providing them with loans to start small businesses. She has since traveled the globe promoting the Washington, D.C.-based Foundation of International Community Assistance, holding lunches with women in Washington and Hollywood and delivering aid to women in battle zones like Kosovo.

These days, Rania is entirely at home in a room filled with powerful world leaders. When she was invited to address the Economic Forum in Saudi Arabia—where discrimination against women is so pervasive that they are barred from most occupations—she boldly accepted. When the day came, Jordan's queen presented a blunt message. Instead of a speech on business, Rania wanted to talk about something "a little more relevant": the need to include Arab women in all aspects of life. "We must face up to hard truths," she said from the podium. "It will not help to wring our hands, point fingers, or clench our fists. First, we must *all* participate." For women across the Arab world, it was a call to action from one of their own.

**—Updated 2007,
From TIME Atlantic**

Respond and Think Critically

Respond and Interpret

1. Write a brief summary of the main ideas in this article before you answer the following questions. For help on writing a summary, see page 1147.

2. (a)What are some of Rania's political accomplishments? (b)What obstacles has she faced in trying to institute reforms?

3. (a)How are Rania's politics and public persona untraditional? (b)What criticisms has she faced in Jordan?

Analyze and Evaluate

4. How might Rania's background have influenced her political opinions?

5. (a)Why do you think Rania has gained international attention? (b)Why might she be viewed differently in the West than in the Middle East?

Connect

6. How does the description of gender conflict in this article relate to the other literature you have read in Unit 3, Part 1?

Timeline 2500 B.C.—Present

SOUTH CENTRAL ASIAN LITERATURE

3000 B.C.

c. 1500
Earliest Vedas appear

1000 B.C.

c. 750–550
Upanishads are compiled

c. 563 ▶
Siddhārtha Gautama
(the Buddha) is born
in India

500
Classical Sanskrit begins
to develop

c. 300
Ramayana is composed

SOUTH CENTRAL ASIAN EVENTS

3000 B.C.

c. 2600
First Indus Valley cities
are established

c. 1700
Indus Valley cities are
abandoned

c. 1500
Indo-European tribes
occupy northern India

1000 B.C.

326
Alexander the Great
invades India

◀ **c. 265–238**
Emperor Aśoka promotes
Buddhism

WORLD EVENTS

3000 B.C.

c. 3000
Cuneiform writing
is developed

c. 2589–2566
Pharaoh Khufu builds
Great Pyramid at Giza

1450s–c. 1425
Pharaoh Thutmose III
expands Egyptian Empire

1000 B.C.

c. 509
Roman Republic
is founded

221
Ch'in Shih Huang Ti
becomes first Chinese
emperor
▼

LOG ON ▶ **Literature** Online

Literature and Reading To explore the Interactive
Timeline, go to glencoe.com and enter QuickPass code
GLW6053u3

100 Years of Indian Cinema
Celebrated on Postage Stamps

A.D. 1   **A.D. 1000**   **A.D. 2000**

c. 400
Present text of
Mahabharata takes form

1440
Mystical poet Kabir is born

c. 1529
Bābur writes his memoirs

1913
Rabindranath Tagore wins
the Nobel Prize in
Literature

1935
R. K. Narayan publishes
the first of his Malgudi
fiction

2005
Poet and novelist Amrita
Pritam dies

A.D. 1   **A.D. 2000**

c. 380–415
Candra Gupta II rules
northern India

712
Muslims invade India

Mughal Flask
(metalwork)

1498 ▲
Portuguese explorer Vasco
da Gama reaches India

1526
Bābur establishes Mogul
Empire

1653
Shāh Jāhan completes
the Taj Mahal

1885
Indian National Congress
is formed

1947
British India is partitioned
into India and Pakistan

1948 ▶
Mohandas Gandhi is
assassinated

1984
Union Carbide disaster
takes place in Bhopul,
India

2004
Tsunami devastates Indian
Ocean coastal areas

A.D. 1   **A.D. 1000**   **A.D. 2000**

313
Constantine I legalizes
Christianity in Rome

552
Buddhism is introduced
to Japan

c. 610
Muhammad, founder of
Islam, begins preaching

1517
Martin Luther posts
95 theses in Germany

▼

1762
Catherine the Great
becomes ruler of Russia

1945
World War II ends

Reading Check

Analyze Graphic Information About how long
after Babur formed the Mogul Empire did he write
his memoirs?

South Central Asia

3500 B.C.—Present

Historical, Social, and Cultural Forces

The Indus Civilization

Between 3000 B.C. and 1500 B.C., the valleys of the Indus River system in present-day Pakistan supported a flourishing civilization that stretched from the Himalaya mountain range to the coast of the Arabian Sea. Archaeologists have found the remains of more than 1,000 settlements in this region. The well-planned cities of the Indus civilization indicate a highly organized society. Eventually, however, natural disasters, a shift in the course of the Indus River, and climate change weakened the Indus civilization, whose cities seem to have been largely abandoned by 1700 B.C.

The Indo-Europeans

What remained of the Indus Valley civilization was destroyed in about 1500 B.C. by migrating peoples (now referred to as the Indo-Europeans or Aryans) who had crossed the Hindu Kush mountain range from their homelands on the plains of central Asia. The Indo-Europeans were herders with a strong warrior tradition. They gradually abandoned herding for farming as they extended their control over most of India. Their early literature, which includes hymns and heroic legends, reveals that between 1500 B.C and 400 B.C., India was plagued by continual warfare. Various tribal leaders, known as *rajas* ("kings" in Sanskrit), carved out small states and fought one another, attacking fortresses and seizing women, cattle, and treasure.

Seal depicting a mythological animal and pictographic symbols, 3000-1500 BC. Stone. Mohenjo-Daro, Indus Valley, Pakistan.

Invaders and Empire-Builders

Alexander the Great crossed the Indus River in 326 B.C. after he had heard of the riches of India. He defeated some native rulers in fierce battles, but his soldiers grew weary of fighting and refused to advance farther into the region, forcing him to withdraw. Alexander's conquests set the stage for India's first empire-builders, the Mauryan dynasty. At its height under Aśoka, who ruled from 265 B.C. to 238 B.C., the Mauryan Empire included most of India. After Aśoka's death, the Mauryan Empire declined and was succeeded for centuries by warring kingdoms.

In A.D. 321, a prince named Candragupta created a new state in the central Ganges Valley. His successors, the Guptas, expanded their rule into an empire. Under a series of efficient rulers—especially Candra Gupta II, who reigned from 380 to 415—the Gupta Empire marked a golden age of Indian civilization. The great Sanskrit poet Kalīdāsa lived during the Gupta dynasty. The famous murals of the Ajanta Caves in western India also date from the Gupta period.

> *"The mighty army of Delhi was laid in the dust in the course of half a day."*
>
> —Bābur describing his victory over the Indians in his *Autobiography*

The last great conqueror to establish an Indian empire was Bābur, who defeated the sultan of Delhi at the battle of Panipat in 1526. Bābur was a descendant of the Mongol conqueror Genghis Khan, and the line of rulers he established is known as the Mogul (Persian, for "Mughul") dynasty. The greatest Mogul emperor was Bābur's grandson Akbar, who ruled from 1556 to 1605. A great soldier, Akbar was also a wise and humane ruler who established a policy of religious toleration that helped reconcile the many sects in his empire.

Maharana Raj Singh I of Mewar, c.1670. Indian School. Gouache with gold on paper. Ashmolean Museum, University of Oxford, UK.

British Rule and Modern India

By the early 1700s, the power of the Mogul rulers was waning. The arrival of the British hastened the decline of the Mogul Empire. British authority in India was exercised by the East India Company, a private company empowered by the British crown to act on its behalf for more than two centuries. By the mid-nineteenth century, the company controlled much of India, hiring Indian soldiers, known as sepoys, to protect its interests. A rebellion by the sepoys prompted Britain to tighten its control by establishing direct rule of India.

The British created a modern infrastructure in south central Asia, building railroads, a court system, hospitals, and schools, but they also exploited the region economically and treated the people they ruled as social and cultural inferiors. In 1885, a small group of Indians formed the Indian National Congress, which demanded that Indians share in the governing process. After World War I, political leader Mohandas Gandhi began using nonviolent methods of civil disobedience to protest British rule. By the 1940s, the Muslim League had begun to believe in the need for the creation of a separate Muslim state. In 1947, British India was divided into two independent nations: India (officially secular with a Hindu majority) and Pakistan (officially Muslim).

Religion dominates all aspects of life in south central Asia. Hindus make up about 80 percent of the population, while Muslims account for about 10 percent. India is the birthplace of Jainism, which stresses spirituality through discipline, and Sikhism, which began as a Hindu movement. Although India is also the birthplace of Siddhārtha Gautama, the founder of Buddhism, Sri Lanka and Bhutan are the only Buddhist countries in south central Asia today.

Hinduism

Hindus worship many gods, whom they believe to be the various forms of Brahman, a single, universal, and divine spirit. The most important forms of Brahman are the three gods that form the "Hindu trinity": Brahma, the creator; Vishnu, the preserver; and Shiva, the destroyer. Hindus believe the soul goes through a series of rebirths, each based on a person's actions in the previous life. The force that is generated by these actions and that determines how that person will be reborn is called *karma*. Karma, in turn, is ruled by *dharma*, the divine law that requires all people to fulfill the duties of their station in life. Eventually, a person who lives well and fulfills his or her dharma can break out of this cycle, and the person's *atman*, or soul, will unite with the universal spirit.

Radha and Krishna embrace in a grove of flowering trees, c.1780. Watercolor on paper. Victoria & Albert Museum, London.

Classical Literature

The earliest literature of south central Asia— the Vedas, the *Mahabharata*, and the *Ramayana*— was first composed and transmitted through oral tradition and later written down in Sanskrit, the classical language of India. The Vedas, which contain four collections of hymns, are the most important sacred texts in Hinduism. The *Mahabharata* is an epic that tells the story of a set of cousins who battle over a kingdom in northern India. In one section of this vast narrative, the Hindu god Krishna delivers a sermon on moral duty. This sermon, known as the Bhagavad Gita, or "Song of God," is the most famous poem in Indian literature. The second great Sanskrit epic, the *Ramayana*, tells the story of the god-king Rama, whose dharma is to defeat the demon Ravana.

> *"The Eternal in man cannot kill: the Eternal in man cannot die."*
>
> —from the Bhagavad Gita

An increased emphasis on spirituality within Hinduism in the thirteenth to seventeenth centuries inspired many fine poets such as Tulsīdās, who translated the *Ramayana* into Hindi (a language descended from Sanskrit); the blind poet Surdas; and the Rajput princess and mystical poet Mirabai. Another mystical poet was Kabir, a Muslim who sought to combine the spiritual elements of Islam and Hinduism and urged people to overcome the prejudices of the caste system.

Reading Check

Make Generalizations What is the spiritual goal of Hinduism?

Big Idea 2
A Place in Society

Women carry vessels containing water in the village of Kundaliya.

For generations, Indian society has been defined by the caste system, which classifies people based on the social group into which they are born. Until recently, people's jobs, homes, and spouses were determined by this inherited status. For Indian women, religious beliefs have also led to strictly defined roles and rules of conduct.

The Caste System

The invasion of India by the Indo-Europeans resulted in a system of class divisions that separated the conquerors from the conquered. Over time, these divisions developed into the traditional Hindu caste system. The castes were divided by occupation: priests (Brahmans), rulers and soldiers (Kshatriyas), merchants and farmers (Vaishyas), and peasants and laborers (Sudras). At the bottom were the "untouchables," who were made to do tasks other Indians would not accept, such as handling dead bodies. The degrading aspects of the caste system were ruled illegal when newly independent India adopted its constitution in 1950, although the castes themselves still exist. More social mobility exists now than ever before, fueled in part by economic growth and by people who have obtained higher education.

Village Life

While the caste system is not as pervasive as it once was, it still continues in many places, particularly rural areas. Despite the growth of urban districts, many people in south central Asia live in villages and farm or herd animals. Families of the same caste tend to live near one another, with the lowest castes at the fringes of the villages. In the past, families often created alliances with families of other castes and traded specialized services, such as carpentry, barbering, or officiating at religious rites. These hereditary alliances could be traced back over many generations.

> "A woman must never be independent."
>
> —The Laws of Manu

Family Life

Traditionally, three or four generations of one family lived in a single home. These households typically included a man and wife, their sons and their sons' wives, unmarried daughters, and the children of their sons. In some urban centers today, the nuclear family is the more standard arrangement.

Religious beliefs have defined the lives and roles of Indian women throughout history. The Laws of Manu, which are followed by many traditional Hindus, state that a woman is always subject to her father, husband, or son. Some Indian women have also followed *purdah*, a belief that began in Islam but was adopted by many Hindus. Purdah requires women to live mostly in seclusion and to wear veils in the presence of nonfamily members. In recent times, however, Indian women have become increasingly active in many professions, including medicine and business.

Reading Check

Analyze Cause-and-Effect Relationships How have modern political and social conditions affected the caste system?

Big Idea 3
A Complex Heritage

What would it be like to live in a country with 22 official state and national languages? That is only one aspect of modern India's cultural complexity.

South Central Asia Today

Like other regions around the world, south central Asia has undergone a number of positive changes over the past few decades. India, for example, has achieved extraordinary technological development and the noticeable growth of a middle class. However, there are also serious problems, including overpopulation, poverty, and ethnic and religious conflict. Unlike its neighbor India, Pakistan was a completely new nation when it attained independence in 1947. Its early years were marked by internal conflicts, particularly the hostility between East and West Pakistan. In 1971,

East Pakistan declared its independence and, after a bloody civil war, became the new nation of Bangladesh. Both Pakistan (as West Pakistan is now known) and Bangladesh, however, have had difficulty establishing stable governments.

The Languages of a Subcontinent

More than twenty major languages are spoken in south central Asia, along with hundreds of other languages and dialects. Sanskrit was the dominant language until about A.D. 1000 and is the language of Hindu sacred literature. The official national language of India (Hindi) and that of Pakistan (Urdu) are both descended from Sanskrit. English, introduced by the British, is also widely spoken in south central Asia, particularly between people of different language backgrounds.

Modern South Asian Literature

Poetry was the major form of literature in south central Asia until the British introduced modern European literary forms such as the novel and the short story. Rabindranath Tagore, who won the Nobel Prize in 1913, and Prem Chand, who wrote novels and short stories about rural life, were among the first Indian authors to explore these new forms. Hindi and Urdu are the most widely read languages of south central Asia, but each of the region's other languages—some spoken by millions of people—have their own literatures. English is not identified with a specific ethnic group, but offers writers a worldwide audience. Several major authors, such as R. K. Narayan, wrote in English. Tagore wrote his work in Bengali (the language of Bangladesh), but often translated his works into English himself.

Rickshaws jostling for work. Thierry Prat. Calcutta, India.

Reading Check

Analyze Cause-and-Effect Relationships
Why does English continue to be used in south central Asia?

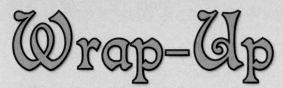

Wrap-Up

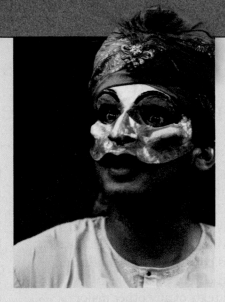

Actor Jacob Rajan in *Krishnan's Diary*. Robbie Jack. Edinburgh, Scotland.

Legacy of the Region

India's ancient civilization had a great effect on other cultures. Since monks originally carried it to China, Korea, Southeast Asia, and Japan, Buddhism has remained active in all four areas. More than 375 million people worldwide practice some form of it today, making Buddhism the world's fourth-largest religion.

Indian nationalist Mohandas Gandhi's nonviolent resistance to political oppression has had a powerful influence on civil rights and on human rights leaders around the world, including Martin Luther King Jr., Nelson Mandela of South Africa, and Aung San Suu Kyi of Myanmar.

Cultural and Literary Links

● The fables of the *Panchatantra* were among the sources used by seventeenth-century French author Jean de La Fontaine (see page 602).

● The *Mahabharata* was the basis for a nine-hour theatrical version (and a five-hour film) created by British director Peter Brook.

● The conventions of classical Sanskrit drama, with its emphasis on music and dancing, have greatly influenced the modern Indian Bollywood movies that are becoming popular with Western audiences.

Literature Online

Unit Resources For additional skills practice, go to glencoe.com and enter QuickPass code GLW6053u3.

Activities

Use what you have learned about the region to do one of these activities.

1. Follow Up Go back to Looking Ahead on page 547 and answer the questions.

2. Contrast Literary Periods During the seventeenth- and eighteenth-century European movement known as the Enlightenment, authors and scholars explored how reason could be used to achieve knowledge and contentment. Research an author from this period and write an essay comparing and contrasting his or her arguments with what you have learned about the search for enlightenment in south central Asia.

3. Speaking/Listening Tragedy was not permitted in classical Indian drama, in which the imitation of

defeat and death was not seen as providing a catharsis for the audience as in Western tragedy. Working with other students, research classical Indian theater and discuss how it is like and unlike Western theater.

4. Take Notes You might try using this organizer to explore your responses to the literary works in this part.

FOLDABLES
Study Organizer

BOUND BOOK

from the Rig-Veda

Translated by Wendy Doniger O'Flaherty

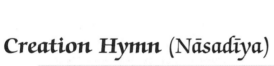

Creation Hymn (Nāsadīya)

1   There was neither non-existence nor existence then;
    there was neither the realm of space nor the sky
    which is beyond. What stirred? Where? In whose
    protection? Was there water, bottomlessly deep?

2   There was neither death nor immortality then. There
    was no **distinguishing** sign of night nor of day. That
    one breathed, windless, by its own **impulse**. Other
    than that there was nothing beyond.

3   Darkness was hidden by darkness in the beginning;
    with no distinguishing sign, all this was water. The
    life force that was covered with emptiness, that one
    arose through the power of heat.

Paradox *Explain the paradox in this line.*

Vocabulary

distinguishing (dis ting′ gwish ing) *adj.* marking as different; characterizing
impulse (im′ puls) *n.* a sudden desire or feeling that makes one want to act

Indra, 7th-8th century. Wall
painting. National Museum of
India, New Delhi.

View the Art Indra, god of
thunder and war, was the
supreme ruler of the Vedic
gods. He was the defender of
gods and humans against the
forces of evil. What qualities
might you associate with
Indra, based on this painting?

4 Desire came upon that one in the beginning; that was the first seed of mind. Poets seeking in their heart with wisdom found the bond of existence in non-existence.

5 Their cord was extended across. Was there below? Was there above? There were seed-placers; there were powers. There was impulse beneath; there was giving-forth above.

6 Who really knows? Who will here **proclaim** it? Whence was it produced? Whence is this creation? The gods came afterwards, with the creation of this universe. Who then knows whence it has arisen?

7 Whence this creation has arisen—perhaps it formed itself, or perhaps it did not—the one who looks down on it, in the highest heaven, only he knows—or perhaps he does not know.

Analyze Connotation *Which words and phrases in this passage are associated with fertility and growth? How do these words help clarify the speaker's view of creation?*

Vocabulary

proclaim (prə klām′) *v.* to announce publicly; to make known; to declare

Vishnu sleeping between the two periods of cosmic evolution, 17th century. Rajasthan, India. Painting on paper, 30 x 24 cm. National Gallery, Prague.

After You Read

Respond and Think Critically

Respond and Interpret

1. Did the story of creation offered in this hymn surprise you? Explain.

2. (a)In stanza 3, how does the speaker describe conditions before creation? (b)What do these conditions reveal about the Hindu understanding of creation?

3. (a)How does the speaker describe the relationship of the gods to creation? (b)What does this imply about the gods and their involvement in creation?

4. (a)What conclusions does the speaker draw about creation? (b)What does this tell you about the Hindu attitude toward dogma (absolute belief) in religion?

Analyze and Evaluate

5. (a)What is the "cord" mentioned in stanza 5? (b)What does this image suggest about Hindu views of oral tradition?

6. (a)What can you infer about Hinduism from the questions asked in stanza 6? (b)What might be the purpose of this stanza?

Connect

7. **Big Idea** **The Search for Enlightenment** What is the value of a creation hymn that questions the origin of the universe?

8. **Connect to Today** Critical thinking is a crucial skill used in countless professions in contemporary society. What lessons does this hymn offer about the value of critical thinking?

Literary Element Paradox

A **paradox** states an apparent contradiction that actually reflects reality. For example, the statement "You must be cruel to be kind" sounds contradictory, but sometimes unkind words may benefit someone.

Partner Activity With a partner, identify examples of paradox in "Creation Hymn" and explain them.

Reading Strategy Analyze Connotation

By examining the **connotations**, or implied meanings, of key words in a literary work, you can better explore its main ideas. Review the chart you made on page 559 and then answer these questions.

1. What are the connotations of the word *poet*?

2. Why might "poets" be mentioned in "Creation Hymn?"

Vocabulary Practice

Practice with Analogies Choose the word that best completes each analogy.

1. similar : akin :: distinguishing :
   - **a.** separating
   - **b.** expensive
   - **c.** noble
   - **d.** merging

2. conviction : reservation :: impulse :
   - **a.** energetic
   - **b.** sudden
   - **c.** surprising
   - **d.** premeditation

3. enact : law :: proclaim :
   - **a.** whisper
   - **b.** announcement
   - **c.** shout
   - **d.** dialogue

Writing

Write a List Think about the big questions that people ponder, and then list three or more that you would like answered. Include a paradox in one question; for example, you might frame a question as: How can _____ be both _____ and _____?

LOG ON **Literature** Online

Selection Resources For Selection Quizzes, eFlashcards, and Reading-Writing Connection activities, go to glencoe.com and enter QuickPass code GLW6053u3.

Before You Read
Hundred Questions from the Mahabharata

The *Mahabharata* (mə hä′bär′ə tə), one of India's most revered epics, is approximately seven times the length of the *Iliad* and the *Odyssey* combined, making it one of the longest literary works in the world. It is of great religious, philosophical, and historical importance to Indian culture. The epic describes a feud between two rival groups of cousins, the Pandavas and the Kauravas, who are descendants of King Bharat (*Mahabharata* is a Sanskrit word meaning "great epic of the Bharata dynasty").

In the epic, the five Pandava (pän dä′vä) brothers lose their kingdom in northern India and all their wealth to the Kauravas (kôr ä′vəs), who cheat them by using loaded dice in a game of chance. The Pandavas are exiled for twelve years, after which time they battle the Kauravas to regain their kingdom. In the end, the Pandavas win, but the destruction is so great that their victory is hollow.

Tales Within a Tale The feud between the cousins is the main story within the epic, but many episodes and digressions, including myths, legends, stories, and religious ideas, are interwoven with the tale. The most famous of the digressions is the Bhagavad Gita (bä′gə väd′ gē′tə), the most important Hindu religious text, which emphasizes aspects of Hindu philosophy. The central focus of the *Mahabharata* is the Hindu concept of *dharma* (där′mə), which is a sacred code of conduct and duty. Hindus believe that people preserve the natural order of the universe by fulfilling their responsibilities according to their station in life.

> "*What is found here, may be found elsewhere. What is not found here, will not be found elsewhere.*"
>
> —the *Mahabharata*

The Creation of the *Mahabharata* Hindu tradition maintains that a wise man named Vyasa dictated the Sanskrit verses of the *Mahabharata* to Ganesha, the god of wisdom, who wrote them down. Compiled in its present form about A.D. 400, the *Mahabharata* contains about 100,000 verses and is divided into books called *parvas*. "Hundred Questions" is an episode from the third book, *Aranya-parva* ("Forest"), in which the Pandava brothers have nearly completed their twelve-year exile in a forest.

For many generations, the epic was preserved through oral tradition, although it is unlikely that any one storyteller ever told the entire epic in one sitting. The following version is from the prose retelling of the epic by the modern Indian author R. K. Narayan.

CHARACTERS IN THE EPIC

Pandava Brothers

YUDHISTIRA (yōō dē′stē rə) eldest brother and hero of the epic

BHIMA (bē′mə) second brother and strongest character in the epic

ARJUNA (är′jōō nə) third brother and greatest warrior of the epic

NAKULA (nä′k ōō lə) one of the twins born to Madri

SAHADEVA (sä hä dā′və) second twin born to Madri

Others

BRAHMA one of the major gods of Hinduism

DURYODHANA (dōōr yō′də nə) eldest of the 100 Kaurava brothers, cousins and rivals of the Pandavas

KUNTHI mother of Yudhistira, Bhima, and Arjuna

MADRI mother of Nakula and Sahadeva

YAMA god of justice, father of Yudhistira

The Pandavas were in a hopeful mood when they came back to their original starting point, Dwaitavana, after their prolonged pilgrimage. Dwaitavana was rich in fruits and roots, and the Pandavas lived on sparse diets, performing **austerities** and practicing rigid vows.

They managed to live, on the whole, a tranquil life—until one day a brahmin arrived in a state of great agitation. He had lost a churning staff and two faggots[1] of a special kind, with which he produced the fire needed for his religious activities. All his hours were normally spent in the performance of rites. But that day, he wailed, "A deer of extraordinary size, with its antlers spreading out like the branches of a

tree, dashed in unexpectedly, lowered its head, and stuck the staff and the faggots in its horns, turned round, and vanished before I could understand what was happening. I want your help to recover those articles of prayer, for without them I will not be able to perform my daily rites. You can see its hoof marks on the ground and follow them."

As a kshatriya, Yudhistira felt it his duty to help the brahmin, so with his brothers, he set out to chase the deer. They followed its hoof marks and eventually spotted it, after a long chase. But when they shot their arrows, the deer sprang away, tempted them to follow it here and there, and suddenly vanished without a trace. They were by

---

1. A *faggot* is a bundle of sticks.

Vocabulary

austerity (ôs ter′ə tē) *n.* a morally strict act

Apply Background Knowledge *Based on the background information you have read, why do think Yudhistira helps the brahmin?*

this time drawn far into the forest and, feeling fatigued and thirsty, they sat under a tree to rest.

Yudhistira told his youngest brother, Nakula, "Climb this tree and look for any sign of water nearby."

Presently, Nakula cried from the top of the tree, "I see some green patches and also hear the cries of cranes . . . must be a water source." He came down and proceeded towards a crystal-clear pond, sapphire-like, reflecting the sky. He fell down on his knees and splashed the water on his face. As he did this, a loud voice, which seemed to come from a crane standing in the water, cried, "Stop! This pond is mine. Don't touch it until you answer my questions. After answering, drink or take away as much water as you like." Nakula's thirst was so searing that he could not wait. He bent down and, cupping his palms, raised the water to his lips. He immediately collapsed, and lay, to all purposes, dead.

After a while, Yudhistira sent his brother, Sahadeva, to see what was delaying Nakula's return. He too rushed forward eagerly at the sight of the blue pond, heard the warning, tasted the water, and fell dead.

Arjuna followed. On hearing the voice, he lifted his bow, shot an arrow in the direction of the voice, and approached the water's edge. The voice said, "Don't be foolhardy. Answer me first before you touch the water."

Arjuna, surveying with shock and sadness the bodies of his younger brothers, replied, "When you are silenced with my arrows, you will cease to question. . . ." Driven to desperation with thirst and enraged at the spectacle of his dead brothers, he sent a rain of arrows in all directions. As the voice continued to warn, "Don't touch," he stooped and took the water to his lips and fell dead.

Next came Bhima. He saw his brothers lying dead, and swung his mace and cried back when he heard the voice, "O evil power, whoever you may be, I will put an end to you presently, but let me first get rid of this deadly thirst. . . ." Turning a deaf ear to the warning, he took the water in the cup of his palm and with the first sip fell dead, the mace rolling away at his side.

Yudhistira himself presently arrived, passing through the forest where no human being had set foot before except his brothers. He was struck by the beauty of the surroundings—enormous woods, resonant with the cry of birds, the occasional grunt of a bear, or the light tread of a deer on dry leaves—and then he came upon the magnificent lake, looking as if made by heavenly hands. There on its bank he saw his brothers.

He wept and lamented aloud. Both the **poignancy** and the mystery of it tormented him. He saw Arjuna's bow and Bhima's mace lying on the ground, and reflected, "Where is your promise to split Duryodhana's thigh?[2] What was the meaning of the gods' statement at Arjuna's birth that no one could vanquish him?" How was he to explain this calamity to Kunthi?

---

2. Bhima promised to *split Duryodhana's thigh* after the Pandavas had lost everything to their cousins in the game of dice.

Vocabulary

poignancy (poin′yən sē) *n.* the quality of painfully affecting one's feelings

Pancha Pandava, the five hero brothers of the Mahabharata. India. Painted stone relief. Surya Temple, Somnath, Mumbai.

View the Art This relief was created for Surya Temple—in Hinduism, Surya is both the sun and the sun god. He is also believed to be the father of Manu, the forefather of the human race. Why might the artist of this relief have chosen to represent the Pandavas almost identically?

A little later he said to himself, "This is no ordinary death. I see no marks of injury on any of them. What is behind it all?" Could it be that Duryodhana had pursued them, and had his agents at work? He observed the dead faces; they bore no discoloration or sign of decay. He realized that his brothers could not have been killed by mortals, and concluded that there must be some higher power responsible. Resolving not to act hastily, he considered all the possibilities, and stepped into the lake to perform the rites for the dead.

The voice now said, "Don't act rashly; answer my questions first and then drink and take away as much water as you like. If you disregard me, you will be the fifth corpse here. I am responsible for the deaths of all these brothers of yours; this lake is mine and whoever ignores my voice will die. Take care!"

Yudhistira said humbly, "What god are you to have vanquished these invincible brothers of mine, gifted and endowed with **inordinate** strength and courage? Your feat is great and I bow to you in homage, but please explain who you are and why you have slain these innocent slakers of thirst? I do not understand your purpose, my mind is agitated and curious. Please tell me who you are."

At this request he saw an immense figure materializing beside the lake, towering over the surroundings. "I am a yaksha.³ These brothers of yours, though warned, tried to force their way in and have paid for it with their lives. If you wish to live, don't drink this water before you answer my questions."

Yudhistira answered humbly, "O yaksha, I will not covet what is yours. I will not touch this water without your sanction, in spite of my thirst. I will answer your questions as well as I can."

The yaksha asked, "What makes the sun rise? . . . What causes him to set?"

Apply Background Knowledge *Why does Yudhistira suspect Duryodhana and his agents?*

Epic Hero *How are Yudhistira's actions consistent with those of an epic hero?*

---

3. A *yaksha* is a spirit that guards the world's wealth. The feminine spelling is *yakshi.*

Vocabulary

inordinate (in ôrʹ də nit) *adj.* excessive

Yudhistira answered, "The Creator Brahma makes the sun rise, and his dharma causes the sun to set. . . ."

Yudhistira had to stand a gruelling test. He had no time even to consider what to say, as the questions came in a continuous stream. Yudhistira was afraid to delay an answer or plead ignorance. Some of the questions sounded **fatuous**, some of them profound, some obscure but packed with layers of significance. Yudhistira was constantly afraid that he might upset the yaksha and provoke him to commit further damage, although one part of his mind reflected, "What worse fate can befall us?"

Without giving him time to think, the questions came, sometimes four at a time in one breath. Their range was unlimited, and they jumped from one topic to another.

"What is important for those who sow? What is important for those who seek prosperity?" Before Yudhistira could complete his sentence with "Rain," he also had to be answering the next question with "Offspring. . . ."

The yaksha went on to ask, "What is weightier than the earth?"

"Mother."

"Higher than the heavens?"

"Father."

"Faster than the wind?"

"Mind."

"What sleeps with eyes open?"

"Fish."

"What remains immobile after being born?"

"Egg."

"Who is the friend of the exile?"

"The companion on the way."

"Who is the friend of one about to die?"

"The charity done in one's lifetime."

"Who is that friend you could count as God given?"

"A wife."

"What is one's highest duty?"

"To refrain from injury."

To another series of questions on renunciation, Yudhistira gave the answers: "Pride, if renounced, makes one agreeable; anger, if renounced, brings no regret; desire, if renounced, will make one rich; **avarice**, if renounced, brings one happiness. True tranquility is of the heart. . . . Mercy may be defined as wishing happiness to all creatures. . . . Ignorance is not knowing one's duties. . . . Wickedness consists in speaking ill of others."

"Who is a true brahmin? By birth or study or conduct?"

"Not by birth, but by knowledge of the scriptures and right conduct. A brahmin born to the caste, even if he has mastered the Vedas,[4] must be viewed as of the lowest caste if his heart is impure."

There were a hundred or more questions in all. Yudhistira felt faint from thirst, grief, and suspense, and could only whisper his replies. Finally, the yaksha asked, "Answer four more questions, and you may find your brothers—at least one of them—revived. . . . Who is really happy?"

"One who has scanty means but is free from debt; he is truly a happy man."

"What is the greatest wonder?"

"Day after day and hour after hour, people die and corpses are carried along, yet the onlookers never realize that they are also to die one day, but think they will live forever. This is the greatest wonder of the world."

---

4. The *Vedas*—sacred Hindu writings—are believed to contain eternal truths that were divinely revealed.

Vocabulary

fatuous (fach′ o͞o əs) *adj.* silly; foolish

Vocabulary

avarice (av′ ər is) *n.* greed

Babur racing with two companions during the flight from Samarqan (detail), ca. 1590-1592. The Pierpont Morgan Library, New York.

"What is the Path?"

"The Path is what the great ones have trod. When one looks for it, one will not find it by study of scriptures or arguments, which are contradictory and conflicting."

At the end of these answers, the yaksha said, "From among these brothers of yours, you may choose one to revive."

Yudhistira said, "If I have only a single choice, let my young brother, Nakula, rise."

The yaksha said, "He is after all your stepbrother. I'd have thought you'd want Arjuna or Bhima, who must be dear to you."

"Yes, they are," replied Yudhistira. "But I have had two mothers. If only two in our family are to survive, let both the mothers have one of their sons alive. Let Nakula also live, in fairness to the memory of my other mother Madri."

The yaksha said, "You have indeed pleased me with your humility and the judiciousness of your answers. Now let all your brothers rise up and join you."

The yaksha thereafter revived all his brothers and also conferred on Yudhistira the following boon:[5] "Wherever you may go henceforth, with your brothers and wife, you will have the blessing of being unrecognized." The yaksha was none other than Yama, the God of Justice, and father of Yudhistira, who had come to test Yudhistira's strength of mind and also to bless him with the power to remain incognito—[6] a special boon in view of the conditions laid down for the last year of exile. ❧

---

5. A *boon* is a blessing.
6. If someone is *incognito,* he or she can escape notice.

The Search for Enlightenment *Based on Yudhistira's answer here, what does he seem to believe about enlightenment?*

Epic Hero *Which of Yudhistira's qualities enabled him to save himself and his brothers?*

After You Read

Respond and Think Critically

Respond and Interpret

1. Which of the yaksha's questions surprised you most? Why?

2. (a)What happens to the first four Pandava brothers at the pond? (b)How would you characterize their actions?

3. (a)What happens to Yudhistira at the pond? (b)What do his actions reveal about him?

4. (a)What kinds of questions does the yaksha ask Yudhistira? (b)What seems to be the yaksha's intent in asking these questions?

Analyze and Evaluate

5. (a)Why is the yaksha pleased with Yudhistira? (b)How does the yaksha's offer to reward Yudhistira constitute a final test of Yudhistira's character?

6. (a)Why does Yudhistira save his stepbrother Nakula? (b)What does this decision reveal about Yudhistira's character?

7. What do you think is the most important question the yaksha poses to Yudhistira? Explain.

Connect

8. **Big Idea** The Search for Enlightenment How does this excerpt from the *Mahabharata* reflect Hindu religious beliefs?

9. **Connect to Today** What kinds of tests of character does modern life pose? Describe a situation from your own experience that tested your character.

Visual Literacy

Graphic Organizer

To better understand "Hundred Questions," use a graphic organizer to arrange your notes based on the three paths to salvation, according to Hindu belief.

- The path of duty requires the proper performance of religious and ethical duties.
- The path of knowledge involves the study of philosophical texts and the practice of contemplation.
- The path of devotion involves mystical self-surrender to deities.

You can organize your notes on specific events and dialogue according to which path they exemplify. Complete a chart like this one.

The Path of Duty	The Path of Knowledge	The Path of Devotion
Yudhistira's duty as a kshatriya is to help the brahmin chase the deer.		

Group Activity Discuss the following questions with classmates. Refer to your chart and cite evidence from the excerpt.

1. Do your classmates agree with the way you classified events and dialogue? If not, discuss why your classifications differ and see whether you can reach a consensus.

2. Working together, think of other actions the Pandavas might take to fulfill each path.

ACT Skills Practice

1. What is the main insight suggested by the paragraph on page 568 that begins "A little later he said to himself . . ."?

   A. Yudhistira is spared by the gods because he is considered to be divine.

   B. Yudhistira lacks compassion for his family members.

   C. Yudhistira is the most perceptive and thoughtful of all of the brothers.

   D. Yudhistira is obsessed with performing the funeral rites quickly.

2. In the paragraph on page 569 that begins "Not by birth, but by knowledge of the scriptures . . ." Yudhistira demonstrates that he:

   F. is more dedicated to study than to action.

   G. has a reasoned understanding of religious principles.

   H. is unsure of himself.

   J. is strong only in his physical stature.

Review: Theme

As you learned on page 471, the **theme** of a literary work is its central idea about life. Some works have a **stated theme,** which the author expresses directly, but most works have an **implied theme,** which the author reveals gradually through events, dialogue, or description.

Partner Activity With a partner, discuss what might be the theme of "Hundred Questions." Consider how the events in the story demonstrate the theme.

LOG ON ▶ **Literature** Online

Selection Resources For Selection Quizzes, eFlash-cards, and Reading-Writing Connection activities, go to glencoe.com and enter QuickPass code GLW6053u3.

The meaning of a literary work becomes more apparent when you **apply background knowledge** to your reading. For example, applying the background knowledge you have learned about Hinduism can help you better understand the meanings of "Hundred Questions."

Partner Activity Review the three background facts given in the Reading Strategy chart on page 564. With a partner, discuss how each fact gives you insight into the story.

Vocabulary Practice

Practice with Antonyms With a partner, match each boldfaced vocabulary word below with its antonym. Use a thesaurus or a dictionary to check your answers. You will not use all the answer choices.

1. austerity   **a.** solemn

2. poignancy   **b.** sensible

3. inordinate   **c.** moderate

4. fatuous   **d.** indifference

5. avarice   **e.** self-indulgence

                    f. generosity

                    g. dryness

Academic Vocabulary

In the Mahabharata, *the Pandava brothers have no* **alternative** *but to help the brahmin chase the deer, since he is from a higher caste.*

Alternative is an academic word. In more casual conversation, someone might say certain types of music are an **alternative** to what is frequently played on the radio. To further explore the meaning of this word, answer the question below.

What are two examples of **alternative** energy sources?

For more on academic vocabulary, see pages 36–37 and R83–R85.

Respond Through Writing

Research Report

Investigate the Epic Investigate how the ideas of the *Mahabharata* are interpreted in modern India by researching how the epic is depicted in a variety of forms, such as movies, plays, and art. Write a research report of 1,500 words or more on this topic.

Understand the Task When you **investigate,** you research background information and uncover insights from multiple sources.

Prewrite As you begin researching multiple sources and compiling notes, consider moving from handwritten notes to an electronic spreadsheet. This way, you can use various software features to sort information and make it easier to find when you begin drafting. Create a classification chart like the one below to organize your research notes.

Music	Theater	Film	Art
The epic describes types of folk music that are common in Indian society today. Dancing such as bhangra is an outgrowth of this music.			

Draft As you write, support your thesis with evidence from "Hundred Questions" and from credible primary and secondary sources. Be sure to convey information accurately and coherently. Anticipate potential misunderstandings by providing cultural context for terms that might be unfamiliar to your reader, such as *dharma*.

Revise To complement your report, try including photos of art or dance related to the epic. After you finish your draft, exchange papers with a partner and evaluate each other's work, checking for clarity, organization, and supporting evidence.

Edit and Proofread Proofread your paper, correcting any errors in spelling, grammar, and punctuation. Use the Grammar Tip in the side column to help you correct any problems with italics.

Grammar Tip

Italics

Writers often use italics (characters set in type that slants to the right) to highlight or emphasize certain words or thoughts in a text. Using italics is appropriate in a number of situations.

foreign words: *dharma*

special emphasis: Rather than physical strength, it is the *moral* strength of Yudhistira that inspires Hindus.

titles of books, plays, artworks, longer musical compositions, and longer poems: *Mahabharata*

The *Mahabharata* as Shadow Play

I**N A VILLAGE HOME ON THE INDONESIAN ISLAND OF JAVA AT MIDNIGHT,** a few dozen people sit in front of a long screen lit from behind, watching vibrant shadow images of the Pandava brothers as they fight a bloody battle against their cousins, the Kauravas.

These Indonesian villagers know the stories of the *Mahabharata* well, although most of them do not know Sanskrit and have never read the epic. Instead, they have learned the *Mahabharata* from watching *wayang kulit*—Indonesian shadow puppet plays. The name of this performing art derives from the Javanese words for "shadow" (*wayang*) and "skin" (*kulit*), which refers to the water buffalo leather from which the puppets are crafted. *Wayang kulit* is considered to be the most prestigious performing art in Indonesia.

Staging a Shadow Play

Staging a shadow puppet performance of the *Mahabharata* is no simple task. A performance may last for eight or nine hours, beginning around nine in the evening and continuing until dawn. The performance often takes place in the home of a wealthy sponsor in a rural village, where shadow plays are often commissioned for weddings and other special occasions. In urban areas, the plays are frequently performed at local auditoriums.

Wayang shadow puppets, 2002. Bali Province, Indonesia.

> "*The* wayang *plays retain a ceremonial, mystical aspect which suggests that originally they may have been a religious ritual performed by the head of the family to invoke the aid and advice of ancestral spirits.*"
>
> —Bil Baird, *The Art of the Puppet*

The key figure of the *wayang kulit* is the *dalang*, a skilled artist who functions as the storyteller, the puppeteer, a singer, the sound effects technician, and the director. For the entire performance, the dalang sits cross-legged on the floor and works the leather puppets, which have been intricately carved and painted to indicate particular characters and their personalities. These puppets are animated by sticks—one for the body and one for each arm.

The puppets are kept in a large wooden chest that doubles as a sound effects box. The dalang holds one hammer between the toes of his right foot and another in his left hand and strikes the wood or a small bronze plate on the chest to set a rhythm or to punctuate dramatic moments. The dalang is accompanied by singers and, often, by an Indonesian gamelan orchestra that includes drums, gongs, and a variety of other percussion instruments.

Bringing a Story to Life

In addition to manipulating the puppets and creating sound effects, the dalang narrates the story and sings lines of classical poetry or songs. The dalang speaks all the parts and interprets the characters by giving them distinctive voices and ways of moving. For example, Arjuna, the greatest warrior in the epic, might move fluidly across the stage, while his wife Draupadi takes small, dainty steps. During battle scenes, Arjuna shoots a bow, while his brother Bhima, the strongest character in the epic, strikes opponents with a big club. The dalang also imitates the chatter of monkeys, the grunts of pigs, and the neighing of horses.

Although parts of every shadow play are standardized, much of the dalang's work involves improvisation. Working without a script, the dalang creates dialogue, weaves subplots into the main story, and injects jokes and slapstick into the story. If there is an orchestra, it plays music throughout the performance. The dalang chooses from a repertoire of more than 100 musical selections that fit certain types of scenes, characters, or other elements of drama.

Wayang kulit is second in popularity only to televised soccer matches among forms of entertainment in Indonesia. Contemporary Indonesisans often refer to characters from the *Mahabharata*; an Indonesian might say another person is "like Bhima"—that is, honest, brave, and strong. Through the magic of *wayang kulit*, the story, the characters, and the moral messages of the *Mahabharata* have become ingrained in the culture of Indonesia.

Javanese Shadow Puppet Maker. Yogyakarta, Java, Indonesia.

Literature Online

Literature and Reading For more about the *Mahabharata* as shadow play and the translators in this book, go to glencoe.com and enter QuickPass code GLW6053u3.

Respond and Think Critically

1. How would watching a shadow puppet performance of the *Mahabharata* differ from reading the epic?

2. What do you think is the most challenging aspect of the dalang's performance?

3. Why do you think *wayang kulit* continues to be popular in Indonesia?

Cultural Perspective
on the *Mahabharata*

Learning Objectives

For pages 576–581

Reading:
Analyzing cultural context.
Making connections across literature.
Analyzing informational text.

from Homer in India

William Dalrymple

Thomas Cook Travel Book Award Winner

Set a Purpose for Reading

Read to learn about the function of storytellers and the oral epic tradition in modern India.

Build Background

Scottish author and historian William Dalrymple is known for skillfully combining travel memoir with historical investigation. From 1989 to 1995, Dalrymple lived in Delhi, a city in northern India. While there, he wrote his critically acclaimed book *City of Djinns: A Year in Delhi*. Ten years later, he returned and became interested in the culture of the *bhopas*, traditional storytellers in the Indian state of Rajasthan who retell the *Mahabharata* and other ancient epics from memory. In the following excerpt from an article in the *New Yorker* magazine, Dalrymple describes this unique oral tradition.

Reading Strategy Analyze Cultural Context

When you **analyze cultural context,** you look closely at how a particular culture shaped the form, style, and themes of a literary tradition or text. In this article, Dalrymple examines a unique oral tradition to reveal insights about the history, beliefs, and daily life of the people who value it. As you read, keep track of how this excerpt reveals various aspects of Rajasthani culture.

W hile I was staying at Rohet,[1] I heard about what seemed to be the most remarkable survival of all: the existence of several orally transmitted epic poems. Unlike the ancient epics of Europe—the *Iliad*, the *Odyssey*, *Beowulf*, and the *Nibelungenlied* (the basis of Wagner's "Ring Cycle"[2])—which were now the province only of academics and literature classes, the epics of Rajasthan were still very much alive. They were preserved by a caste of wandering *bhopas*— shamans and bards—who travelled from village to village, staging performances.

"The *bhopa* is a normal villager until the god Pabuji comes to him," one of the aunts explained. "Then he has great power. People bring him the possessed, and Pabuji cures them."

"How?" I asked.

---

1. *Rohet* refers to Rohet Garh, an early seventeenth-century fortress. While in Rajasthan, Dalrymple stays with the family who lives at Rohet Garh, including two elderly aunts.
2. Richard *Wagner* (1813–1883) was a German composer. One of his most famous works is *The Ring of the Nibelung,* or the *Ring Cycle.*

"Sometimes the *bhopa* just says a mantra over them. He tries to make the spirit speak—to reveal who he is. But," she added ominously, "sometimes he has to beat the possessed person with his rods, or cut him and draw blood."

One afternoon, during a long walk through the desert, I met a *bhopa*. He was very old and dressed in a tatty white kurtadhoti.[3] He had a cataract in his left eye, and he parted his great fan of beard outward at the center of his chin. This man worked as a village exorcist,[4] but I had heard that there were still many other *bhopas*, out in the wild places of the desert, whose job it was to recite the great epics, some of them many thousands of stanzas long. . . .

While the *Mahabharata* is today the most famous of the Indian epics, it was originally only one of a large number. During the Mogul period, for example, one of the most popular was the Muslim epic *Dastan-i Amir Hamza*, or the *Story of Hamza*. The brave and chivalrous Hamza, the paternal uncle of the Prophet, journeys from Iraq to Sri Lanka, via Mecca, Tangiers, and Byzantium, on the way falling in love with various beautiful Persian and Greek princesses, and all the while avoiding the traps laid for him by his terrible foe, the dastardly magician Zumurrud Shah.

Over the centuries, the factual underpinning of the story was covered in layers of fantastic subplots and a cast of dragons, giants, and sorcerers—in one of its most popular forms, the tale encompassed three hundred and sixty stories. Today, however, while children in Persia, Pakistan, and parts of India may be acquainted with some episodes, the *Story of Hamza* as a whole no longer really exists as an oral epic. There are fears that the *Mahabharata* and other Hindu epics could share that fate in the twenty-first century, surviving in written or recorded forms only.

Given all this, it seemed extraordinary to find in modern Rajasthan performers who were still the guardians of an entire self-contained oral culture. Apart from anything else, I longed to know how the *bhopas*, who were always simple villagers— ploughmen, cowherds, and so on—and often illiterate, could remember such colossal quantities of verse. Recently, having moved back to Delhi after an absence of ten years, I decided to go in search of the *bhopas* who had preserved this ancient tradition. It would, I felt, be a little like meeting Homer in the flesh.

There were several full-fledged Rajasthani epic poems that the *bhopas* performed, but two were especially popular. One told the tale of the deeds, feuds, life, death, and avenging of Pabuji, a semi-divine warrior and incarnate[5] god who died protecting a goddess's cattle against demonic rustlers. The other—four times its size, much more ambitious, and with similarities to both the *Iliad* and "Once Upon a Time in the West"—was the tale of a humble cattle herder named Sawai Bhoj, of the Bagravat clan; he eloped with an incarnate goddess, who had taken the form of a beautiful young wife of an elderly Rajput raja, and so sparked a monumental caste war. This ultimately led to the bloody death of Sawai Bhoj and twenty-two of his twenty-three brothers— deaths that were avenged, Sicilian style, by Sawai Bhoj's son, Dev Narayan, the legend's hero. Both epics—like the *Dastan-i Amir Hamza* and the *Mahabharata*—seemed to be

---

3. A *kurtadhoti* is a traditional outfit worn by Hindu men. It consists of a knee-length, loose shirt and a long, draped loincloth that looks like baggy pants.
4. An *exorcist* is a person who frees others from possession by evil spirits.

5. Something *incarnate* has a bodily form.

Bhopa Family Dancing, New Delhi, India.

Before long, Laxmi Chundawat arrived with her guests, and she gave the signal for Mohan to begin. He picked up his fiddle—an instrument called a *ravanhattha*—as his wife held up the lamp to illuminate the *phad*. Mohan played an instrumental overture, then, accompanied by his son on the *dholak* (a drum), he began to sing in a voice full of solemnity and sadness. Every so often, as Patasi held up the lamp, he would stop, point with his bow to an illustration on the *phad*, and then recite a line of explanatory verse, all the while plucking at the string with his thumb.

At the end of each *sloka*, Patasi would step forward, fully veiled, and sing the next stanza, before handing the song back to her husband. As the story unfolded, and the husband and wife passed the *slokas* back and forth, the tempo increased, and Mohan began to whirl and dance, jiggling his hips and stamping his feet so as to ring the bells, and shouting out, "Aa-ha! Hai! Wa-hai!"

During the performance, I asked another guest, who understood Mewari, one of the five major dialects of Rajasthan, if he could check Mohan Bhopa's rendition against a transcription by John D. Smith, of Cambridge University, of a version performed in a different part of Rajasthan in the nineteen-seventies. Give or take a couple of turns of phrase, the two versions were identical, he said. And there was nothing homespun about Mohan Bhopa's language, he added. It was delivered in a fine and courtly diction. . . .

After Mohan had sung for a couple of hours, there was a break while the Rani's guests headed off for dinner. I asked Mohan whom he normally performed for—the local landowners, perhaps? No, he said, it was usually cowherds and his fellow-villagers. Their motives, as he described them, were less to hear the poetry than to use him as a sort of supernatural veterinary service.

such as those at Dunhuang, you'll see images of itinerant monks and storytellers with the scrolls they used then. The *phads* are the last survival of that tradition. The *bhopas* like to say that the *phad* of Dev Narayan is so full of bravery that when you tell the tale the grass gets burned around it." . . .

At first, I didn't notice the *bhopa* and his family, squatting in the shadows. Mohan Bhopa was a tall, dark-skinned man of about sixty, with a bristling gray handlebar mustache. He wore a long red robe and a tightly tied red turban. He was barefoot and there were bells attached to his ankles. Beside Mohan was his wife, Patasi, her face shrouded in a red peaked veil. As Mohan supervised, she swept the ground around the *phad* and sprinkled it with water. Then she prepared the wick of an oil lamp and both of them raised their palms in reverence to the deity of the scroll.

"People call me in whenever their animals fall sick," he said. "Camels, sheep, buffalo, cows—any of these. Pabuji is very powerful at curing sickness in beasts. He is also good at curing any child who is possessed by a djinn."[6]

"So does Pabuji enter you while you perform?"

"How can I do it unless the spirit comes?" Mohan said. "You are educated. I am not, but I never forget the words, thanks to Pabuji. As long as I invoke him at the beginning, all will be well. Wherever we perform, the demons run away. No ghosts, no spirits can withstand the power of this story." . . .

This, it seemed to me, was the key, and the answer to the question of how it was that the Rajasthani epics were still living in a way that the *Iliad* and the other epics of the West were not. The poems remained religious rituals, and the *bhopas* were still receptacles for the messages of the gods, able to penetrate the wall—in India always a fairly porous wall—between the divine and the mundane.

Moreover, the gods in question were not impossibly distant and metaphysical beings but deified locals with whom the herders could relate and who could understand their needs. The Gujars[7] certainly took care to propitiate[8] the great "national" gods, like Shiva and Vishnu, whom they understood as controlling the continuation of the wider cosmos. For everyday needs, however, they prayed to the less remote, less awesome figures of their local herder gods and heroes who—along with the almost numberless pantheon of sprites and god-lings, tree spirits and water nymphs that are worshipped and propitiated in every Indian village—know the things that the great gods cannot: the till and soil of the local fields and the sweet water of the wells, the needs and thirsts of the cattle and the goats; and they are believed to guard and regulate the ebb and flow of daily life. ❧

---

6. A *djinn* is a spirit with supernatural power over humans.

7. The *Gujars* are a Rajasthani herding caste.
8. *Propitiate* means "appease" or "pacify."

Respond and Think Critically

Respond and Interpret

1. Write a brief summary of the main ideas in this article before you answer the following questions. For help on writing a summary, see page 1147.

2. (a)Summarize the duties of the *bhopas*. (b)Would you characterize the *bhopas'* function as practical, spiritual, or both? Explain.

3. (a)Who does Mohan Bhopa say is his primary audience? (b)How would you describe the social status of the *bhopas?*

Analyze and Evaluate

4. (a)A **bias** is an assumption that stems from one's cultural values or prejudices. Which of his own biases does Dalrymple reveal as he speaks to Mohan Bhopa? (b)How do Dalrymple's findings prove his biases to be false? Explain.

5. According to Dalrymple, how does the close relationship between the divine and the mundane help explain the survival of the Rajasthani epic tradition?

6. According to Dalrymple, why do European epics lack popular appeal?

Connect

7. Does having read Dalrymple's article enhance your understanding of the "Hundred Questions"? Explain.

Rama's army in battle with monkeys, 1713. British Library, London.

Rama and Ravana in Battle
from the Ramayana

Translated by R. K. Narayan

Every moment, news came to Ravana of fresh disasters in his camp. One by one, most of his commanders were lost. No one who went forth with battle cries was heard of again. Cries and shouts and the wailings of the widows of warriors came over the chants and songs of triumph that his courtiers arranged to keep up at a loud pitch in his assembly hall. Ravana became restless and abruptly left the hall and went up on a tower, from which he could obtain a full view of the city. He surveyed the scene below but could not stand it. One who had spent a lifetime in destruction, now found the gory spectacle intolerable. Groans and wailings reached his ears with deadly clarity; and he noticed how the monkey hordes[1] reveled in their bloody handiwork. This was too much for him. He felt a terrific rage rising within him, mixed with some admiration for Rama's valor. He told himself, "The time has come for me to act by myself again."

---

1. *Hordes* are large groups or crowds.

Monitor Comprehension *Do the monkey hordes support Rama or Ravana? How do you know?*

He hurried down the steps of the tower, returned to his chamber, and prepared himself for the battle. He had a ritual bath and performed special prayers to gain the benediction[2] of Shiva;[3] donned his battle dress, matchless armor, armlets, and crowns. He had on a protective armor for every inch of his body. He girt his sword-belt and attached to his body his accoutrements[4] for protection and decoration.

When he emerged from his chamber, his heroic appearance was breathtaking. He summoned his chariot, which could be drawn by horses or move on its own if the horses were hurt or killed. People stood aside when he came out of the palace and entered his chariot. "This is my resolve," he said to himself:

"Either that woman Sita, or my wife Mandodari, will soon have cause to cry and roll in the dust in grief. Surely, before this day is done, one of them will be a widow."

The gods in heaven noticed Ravana's determined move and felt that Rama would need all the support they could muster. They requested Indra[5] to send down his special chariot for Rama's use. When the chariot appeared at his camp, Rama was deeply impressed with the **magnitude** and brilliance of the vehicle. "How has this come to be here?" he asked.

"Sir," the charioteer answered, "my name is Matali. I have the honor of being the charioteer of Indra. Brahma, the four-faced god and the creator of the Universe, and Shiva, whose power has emboldened Ravana now to challenge you, have commanded me to bring it here for your use. It can fly swifter than air over all obstacles, over any mountain, sea, or sky, and will help you to emerge victorious in this battle."

Rama reflected aloud, "It may be that the rakshasas[6] have created this illusion for me. It may be a trap. I don't know how to view it." Whereupon Matali spoke convincingly to dispel the doubt in Rama's mind. Rama, still hesitant, though partially convinced, looked at Hanuman[7] and Lakshmana and asked, "What do you think of it?" Both answered, "We feel no doubt that this chariot is Indra's; it is not an illusory creation."

Rama fastened his sword, slung two quivers full of rare arrows over his shoulders, and climbed into the chariot.

The beat of war drums, the challenging cries of soldiers, the trumpets, and the rolling chariots speeding along to confront each other, created a deafening mixture of noise. While Ravana had instructed his charioteer to speed ahead, Rama very gently ordered his chariot-driver, "Ravana is in a rage; let him perform all the antics he desires and exhaust himself. Until then be calm; we don't have to hurry forward. Move slowly and calmly, and you must strictly follow my instructions; I will tell you when to drive faster."

Ravana's assistant and one of his staunchest supporters, Mahodara—the giant among giants in his physical appearance—begged Ravana, "Let me not be a

2. A *benediction* is a blessing.
3. *Shiva* is the Hindu god of destruction and reproduction.
4. *Accoutrements* (ə kōō´trə mənts) are equipment and accessories.
5. *Indra* is one of the chief Hindu gods, associated with rain and thunderbolts.

The Search for Enlightenment *Why is Shiva an appropriate god for Ravana to pray to at this time?*

Conflict *What indicates that the conflict between Rama and Ravana is nearing its climax?*

Vocabulary

magnitude (mag´nə tōōd´) *n.* great size or importance

6. *Rakshasas* are demons capable of changing their forms at will.
7. *Hanuman* is the leader of the army of monkeys fighting on Rama's side.

mere spectator when you confront Rama. Let me have the honor of grappling with him. Permit me to attack Rama."

"Rama is my sole concern," Ravana replied. "If you wish to engage yourself in a fight, you may fight his brother Lakshmana."

Noticing Mahodara's purpose, Rama steered his chariot across his path in order to prevent Mahodara from reaching Lakshmana. Whereupon Mahodara ordered his chariot-driver, "Now dash straight ahead, directly into Rama's chariot."

The charioteer, more practical-minded, advised him, "I would not go near Rama. Let us keep away." But Mahodara, obstinate and intoxicated with war fever, made straight for Rama. He wanted to have the honor of a direct encounter with Rama himself in spite of Ravana's advice; and for this honor he paid a heavy price, as it was a moment's work for Rama to destroy him, and leave him lifeless and shapeless on the field. Noticing this, Ravana's anger mounted further. He commanded his driver, "You will not slacken[8] now. Go." Many ominous signs were seen now—his bow-strings suddenly snapped; the mountains shook; thunders rumbled in the skies; tears flowed from the horses' eyes; elephants with decorated foreheads moved along dejectedly. Ravana, noticing them, hesitated only for a second, saying, "I don't care. This mere mortal Rama is of no account, and these omens do not concern me at all." Meanwhile, Rama paused for a moment to consider his next step; and suddenly turned towards the armies supporting Ravana, which stretched away to the horizon, and destroyed them.

He felt that this might be one way of saving Ravana. With his armies gone, it was possible that Ravana might have a change of heart. But it had only the effect of spurring Ravana on; he plunged forward and kept coming nearer Rama and his own doom.

Rama's army cleared and made way for Ravana's chariot, unable to stand the force of his approach. Ravana blew his conch[9] and its shrill challenge reverberated through space. Following it another conch, called "Panchajanya," which belonged to Mahavishnu[10] (Rama's original form before his present incarnation), sounded of its own accord in answer to the challenge, agitating the universe with its vibrations. And then Matali picked up another conch, which was Indra's, and blew it. This was the signal indicating the commencement of the actual battle. Presently Ravana sent a shower of arrows on Rama; and Rama's followers, unable to bear the sight of his body being studded with arrows, averted their heads. Then the chariot horses of Ravana and Rama glared at each other in hostility, and the flags topping the chariots—Ravana's ensign of the Veena[11] and Rama's with the whole universe on it—clashed, and one heard the stringing and twanging of bow-strings on both sides, overpowering in volume all other sound. Then followed a shower of arrows from Rama's own bow. Ravana stood gazing at the chariot sent by Indra and swore, "These gods, instead of supporting me, have gone to the support of this petty human being. I will teach them a lesson. He is not fit to be killed with my

---

8. To *slacken* means "to let up or grow weaker."

9. A *conch* is a seashell used as a horn.
10. *Mahavishnu* is another name for Vishnu.
11. A *veena* (also spelled *vina*) is a stringed musical instrument.

Monitor Comprehension *Summarize how Mahodara meets his end.*

Conflict *What internal conflict does Rama seem to be having?*

arrows but I shall seize him and his chariot together and fling them into high heaven and dash them to destruction." Despite his oath, he still strung his bow and sent a shower of arrows at Rama, raining in thousands, but they were all invariably shattered and neutralized by the arrows from Rama's bow, which met arrow for arrow. Ultimately Ravana, instead of using one bow, used ten with his twenty arms, multiplying his attack tenfold; but Rama stood unhurt.

Ravana suddenly realized that he should change his tactics and ordered his charioteer to fly the chariot up in the skies. From there he attacked and destroyed a great many of the monkey army supporting Rama. Rama ordered Matali, "Go up in the air. Our young soldiers are being attacked from the sky. Follow Ravana, and don't slacken."

There followed an aerial pursuit at dizzying speed across the dome of the sky and rim of the earth. Ravana's arrows came down like rain; he was bent upon destroying everything in the world. But Rama's arrows diverted, broke, or neutralized Ravana's. Terror-stricken, the gods watched this pursuit. Presently Ravana's arrows struck Rama's horses and pierced the heart of Matali himself. The charioteer fell. Rama paused for a while in grief, undecided as to his next step. Then he recovered and resumed his offensive. At that moment the divine eagle Garuda was seen perched on Rama's flagpost, and the gods who were watching felt that this could be an auspicious[12] sign.

After circling the globe several times, the duelling chariots returned, and the fight continued over Lanka. It was impossible to be very clear about the location of the battleground as the fight occurred here, there, and everywhere. Rama's arrows pierced Ravana's armor and made him

Rama on Hanuman fighting Ravana, c. 1820. Tamil Nadu. Album painting on paper. British Museum, London.

wince. Ravana was so insensible to pain and impervious to attack that for him to wince was a good sign, and the gods hoped that this was a turn for the better. But at this moment, Ravana suddenly changed his tactics. Instead of merely shooting his arrows, which were powerful in themselves, he also invoked several supernatural forces to create strange effects: He was an adept in the use of various asthras[13] which could be made dynamic with special incantations.[14] At this point, the fight became one of attack with supernatural powers, and parrying of such an attack with other supernatural powers.

13. *Asthras* are special weapons with supernatural powers.
14. *Incantations* are chants and magic spells.

Monitor Comprehension *How has the physical conflict escalated at this point?*

12. *Auspicious* (ôs pish´ əs) means "favorable; predictive of success."

Ravana realized that the mere aiming of shafts with ten or twenty of his arms would be of no avail because the mortal whom he had so contemptuously thought of destroying with a slight effort was proving formidable, and his arrows were beginning to pierce and cause pain. Among the asthras sent by Ravana was one called "Danda," a special gift from Shiva, capable of pursuing and pulverizing its target. When it came flaming along, the gods were struck with fear. But Rama's arrow neutralized it.

Now Ravana said to himself, "These are all petty weapons. I should really get down to proper business." And he invoked the one called "Maya"—a weapon which created illusions and confused the enemy.

With proper incantations and worship, he sent off this weapon and it created an illusion of reviving all the armies and its leaders—Kumbakarna and Indrajit[15] and the others—and bringing them back to the battlefield. Presently Rama found all those who, he thought, were no more, coming on with battle cries and surrounding him. Every man in the enemy's army was again up in arms. They seemed to fall on Rama with victorious cries. This was very confusing and Rama asked Matali, whom he had by now revived, "What is happening now? How are all these coming back? They were dead." Matali explained, "In your original identity you are the creator of illusions in this universe. Please know that Ravana has created phantoms to confuse you. If you make up your mind, you can dispel them immediately." Matali's explanation was a great help. Rama at once invoked a weapon called "Gnana"—which means "wisdom" or "perception." This was a very rare weapon, and he sent it forth. And all the terrifying armies who seemed to have come on in such a great mass suddenly evaporated into thin air.

Ravana then shot an asthra called "Thama," whose nature was to create total darkness in all the worlds. The arrows came with heads exposing frightening eyes and fangs, and fiery tongues. End to end the earth was enveloped in total darkness and the whole of creation was paralyzed. This asthra also created a deluge of rain on one side, a rain of stones on the other, a hailstorm showering down **intermittently**, and a tornado sweeping the earth. Ravana was sure that this would arrest Rama's enterprise. But Rama was able to meet it with what was named "Shivasthra." He understood the nature of the phenomenon and the cause of it and chose the appropriate asthra for counteracting it.

Ravana now shot off what he considered his deadliest weapon—a trident endowed with extraordinary destructive power, once gifted to Ravana by the gods. When it started on its journey there was real panic all round. It came on flaming toward

Visual Vocabulary
A *trident* is a three-pronged spear.

Rama, its speed or course unaffected by the arrows he flung at it.

When Rama noticed his arrows falling down ineffectively while the trident sailed towards him, for a moment he lost heart. When it came quite near, he uttered a certain mantra[16] from the depth of his being and while he was breathing out that

---

15. *Kumbakarna* and *Indrajit* are the brother and son of Ravana, respectively.

16. A *mantra* is a chant or a prayer.

Vocabulary

intermittently (in´tər mit´ənt lē) *adv.* on and off again; coming at intervals

incantation, an esoteric[17] syllable in perfect timing, the trident collapsed. Ravana, who had been so certain of vanquishing Rama with his trident, was astonished to see it fall down within an inch of him, and for a minute wondered if his adversary might not after all be a divine being although he looked like a mortal. Ravana thought to himself, "This is, perhaps, the highest God. Who could he be? Not Shiva, for Shiva is my supporter; he could not be Brahma, who is four faced; could not be Vishnu, because of my immunity from the weapons of the whole trinity.[18] Perhaps this man is the **primordial** being, the cause behind the whole universe. But whoever he may be, I will not stop my fight until I defeat and crush him or at least take him prisoner."

With this resolve, Ravana next sent a weapon which issued forth monstrous serpents vomiting fire and venom, with enormous fangs and red eyes. They came darting in from all directions.

Rama now selected an asthra called "Garuda" (which meant "eagle"). Very soon thousands of eagles were aloft, and they picked off the serpents with their claws and beaks and destroyed them. Seeing this also fail, Ravana's anger was roused to a mad pitch and he blindly emptied a quiverful of arrows in Rama's direction. Rama's arrows met them half way and turned them round so that they went back and their sharp points embedded themselves in Ravana's own chest.

Ravana was weakening in spirit. He realized that he was at the end of his resources. All his learning and equipment in weaponry were of no avail and he had practically come to the end of his special gifts of destruction. While he was going down thus, Rama's own spirit was soaring up. The combatants were now near enough to grapple with each other and Rama realized that this was the best moment to cut off Ravana's heads. He sent a crescent-shaped arrow which sliced off one of Ravana's heads and flung it far into the sea, and this process continued; but every time a head was cut off, Ravana had the benediction of having another one grown in its place. Rama's crescent-shaped weapon was continuously busy as Ravana's heads kept cropping up. Rama lopped off his arms but they grew again and every lopped-off arm hit Matali and the chariot and tried to cause destruction by itself, and the tongue in a new head wagged, uttered challenges, and cursed Rama. On the cast-off heads of Ravana devils and minor demons, who had all along been in terror of Ravana and had obeyed and pleased him, executed a dance of death and feasted on the flesh.

Ravana was now desperate. Rama's arrows embedded themselves in a hundred places on his body and weakened him. Presently he collapsed in a faint on the floor of his chariot. Noticing his state, his charioteer pulled back and drew the chariot aside. Matali whispered to Rama, "This is the time to finish off that demon. He is in a faint. Go on. Go on."

But Rama put away his bow and said, "It is not fair warfare to attack a man who is in a faint. I will wait. Let him recover," and waited.

---

17. *Esoteric* (es′ ə ter′ ik) means "secret; understood by only a few."
18. *Trinity* here refers to the three gods Shiva, Brahma, and Vishnu.

The Search for Enlightenment *What does Ravana begin to suspect at this point? Why does he begin to suspect it?*

Monitor Comprehension *Summarize the kinds of weapons the two adversaries have used against each other so far.*

Vocabulary

primordial (prī môr′ dē əl) *adj.* original; existing from the beginning

When Ravana revived, he was angry with his charioteer for withdrawing, and took out his sword, crying, "You have disgraced me. Those who look on will think I have retreated." But his charioteer explained how Rama suspended the fight and forebore[19] to attack when he was in a faint. Somehow, Ravana appreciated his explanation and patted his back and resumed his attacks. Having exhausted his special weapons, in desperation Ravana began to throw on Rama all sorts of things such as staves, cast-iron balls, heavy rocks, and oddments he could lay hands on. None of them touched Rama, but glanced off and fell ineffectually. Rama went on shooting his arrows. There seemed to be no end of this struggle in sight.

Now Rama had to pause to consider what final measure he should take to bring this campaign to an end. After much thought, he decided to use "Brahmasthra," a weapon specially designed by the Creator Brahma on a former occasion, when he had to provide one for Shiva to destroy Tripura, the old monster who assumed the forms of flying mountains and settled down on habitations and cities, seeking to destroy the world. The Brahmasthra was a special gift to be used only when all other means had failed. Now Rama, with prayers and worship, invoked its fullest power and sent it in Ravana's direction, aiming at his heart rather than his head; Ravana being vulnerable at heart. While he had prayed for indestructibility of his several heads and arms, he had forgotten to strengthen his heart, where the Brahmasthra entered and ended his career.

Rama watched him fall headlong from his chariot face down onto the earth, and that was the end of the great campaign. Now one noticed Ravana's face aglow with a new quality. Rama's arrows had burnt off the layers of dross,[20] the anger, conceit, cruelty, lust, and egotism which had encrusted his real self, and now his personality came through in its pristine form—of one who was devout and capable of tremendous attainments. His constant meditation on Rama, although as an adversary, now seemed to bear fruit, as his face shone with serenity and peace. Rama noticed it from his chariot above and commanded Matali, "Set me down on the ground." When the chariot descended and came to rest on its wheels, Rama got down and commanded Matali, "I am grateful for your services to me. You may now take the chariot back to Indra."

Surrounded by his brother Lakshmana and Hanuman and all his other war chiefs, Rama approached Ravana's body, and stood gazing on it. He noted his crowns and jewelery scattered piecemeal on the ground. The decorations and the extraordinary workmanship of the armor on his chest were blood-covered. Rama sighed as if to say, "What might he not have achieved but for the evil stirring within him!"

At this moment, as they readjusted Ravana's blood-stained body, Rama noticed to his great shock a scar on Ravana's back and said with a smile, "Perhaps this is not an episode of glory for me as I seem to have killed an enemy who was turning his back and retreating. Perhaps I was wrong in

19. To *forbear* means "to refrain from; to hold oneself back." *Forebore* (or *forbore*) is the past tense of the word.

20. *Dross* means "waste matter; surface scum."

The Search for Enlightenment *What indicates that Ravana has at last achieved enlightenment?*

Conflict *Why does Rama seem unsure about the glory of having won the conflict as he did?*

Vocabulary

pristine (pris′tēn) *adj.* pure; unspoiled

Lakshmana Consulting the Heads of the Monkey Armies, 19th century. Indian school. Gouache on paper. Private collection.

View the Art How do the monkey hordes in this painting compare with how you visualize them?

shooting the Brahmasthra into him." He looked so concerned at this supposed lapse on his part that Vibishana, Ravana's brother, came forward to explain. "What you have achieved is unique. I say so although it meant the death of my brother."

"But I have attacked a man who had turned his back," Rama said. "See that scar."

Vibishana explained, "It is an old scar. In ancient days, when he paraded his strength around the globe, once he tried to attack the divine elephants that guard the four directions. When he tried to catch them, he was gored in the back by one of the tuskers and that is the scar you see now; it is not a fresh one though fresh blood is flowing on it."

Rama accepted the explanation. "Honor him and cherish his memory so that his spirit may go to heaven, where he has his place. And now I will leave you to attend to his funeral arrangements, befitting his grandeur." ∾

The Search for Enlightenment *According to Hinduism, why does Ravana deserve a place in heaven?*

Comparing Literature

Across Time and Place

Learning Objectives

For pages 594–606

In studying these texts, you will focus on the following objectives:

Literary Study:
Comparing themes.
Analyzing moral.

Reading:
Comparing cultural contexts.
Previewing.

Writing: Writing a fable.

Compare Literature About Lessons

Fables—which are common to almost all cultures—teach lessons about human behavior. The following fables were written hundreds of years apart from one another in India, Greece, France, and the United States, yet each one contains a lesson on common sense.

COMPARE THE Big Idea **The Search for Enlightenment**

These fables feature characters, both human and nonhuman, who believe they have attained wisdom. The fates of these characters prompt readers to question their own behavior and enlightenment. As you read, ask yourself, What can I learn from the fates of these characters?

COMPARE Fables

The stories in the *Panchatantra* and Aesop's fables began as oral tales. La Fontaine (lə fon tān′) and Thurber wrote fables for a highly sophisticated audience. As you read, ask yourself, What is the style of each fable?

COMPARE Cultures

A fable reflects the culture in which it was created. The four cultures represented in the following fables have different values, social customs, and intellectual ideas, yet the lesson in each fable is universal. As you read, ask yourself, What cultural values and beliefs does each fable reflect?

A peri (fantastic creature) holding an effigy of the sun rides a composite Lion. Indian miniature on paper. The Pierpont Morgan Library, NY.

LOG ON ▶ **Literature** Online

Author Search For more about Aesop, Jean de la Fontaine, and James Thurber, go to glencoe.com and enter QuickPass code GLW6053u3.

Before You Read

The Lion-Makers from the *Panchatantra*

India

The *Panchatantra* (pun′ chə tän′trə) is a collection of ancient Indian fables or stories that contain lessons about living wisely. The Sanskrit words *pancha tantra* mean "five chapters," which describes the way the collection is arranged. Each of the five chapters in the collection contains a variety of brief fables told within a single frame story.

> *"In what can wisdom not prevail?*
> *In what can resolution fail?*
> *What cannot flattery subdue?*
> *What cannot enterprise put through?"*
>
> —*Panchatantra*

Warriors fighting a lion-griffin, 5th century AD. Stone relief. Museum, Sarnath, Uttar Pradesh, India.

Moral Tales *The Lion-Makers* is set within the frame story of a king who asks a learned Brahman, or Hindu priest, to teach his three foolish sons about interpersonal relationships and the art of ruling. The Brahman, named Vishnusharman (vish′noo shär′mən), teaches the boys with stories that are instructive and entertaining. Most of them are animal fables or fables involving both humans and animals.

An Ancient Collection The stories of the *Panchatantra* were probably first collected and written down around 200 B.C. Many of the stories in the collection were originally passed down through oral tradition for much longer. As the stories were collected, they were classified into five chapters, each with a different theme: losing friends, winning friends, handling international relations, losing profits and possessions, and the consequences of hasty actions.

The *Panchatantra* Outside India Over time, the fables of the *Panchatantra* spread through Asia and Europe, inspiring storytellers in many lands. They were translated into Persian as early as the sixth century and into Arabic, Greek, Hebrew, Latin, German, and Italian during the Middle Ages. In 1570, the *Panchatantra* became the first Indian work to be translated into English. Related stories of some of the tales can be found in many other works of world literature, including *The Thousand and One Nights* (see page 496), Aesop's fables (see page 600), Geoffrey Chaucer's *The Canterbury Tales*, and Giovanni Boccaccio's *Decameron* (see page 926).

Literature and Reading Preview

Connect to the Fable

Do you think common sense is as valuable as formal education? Discuss this question with a partner.

Build Background

The verse proverbs of the *Panchatantra* can be easily memorized, and the collection was intended as a *niti-shastra* (ni′ tē shä strə), or a "textbook on the wise conduct of life." The word *niti* means "worldly wisdom," and to achieve this state, a person needs to be determined, physically secure, free from want, intelligent, and in possession of good friends. A person with *niti* uses cleverness and wit, rather than force.

Set Purposes for Reading

Big Idea The Search for Enlightenment

As you read, ask yourself, How can people gain enlightenment through observing the world around them?

Literary Element Moral

A **moral** is a practical lesson about right or wrong conduct taught in a fable or a parable. In some fables, the author states the moral explicitly; in others, the reader must infer the moral from what happens in the story. Sometimes, the moral is written as an **epigram,** a short, pointed verse or saying. As you read, ask yourself, How do the events in this fable lead to the moral?

Reading Strategy Preview

You can **preview** a work of literature by noting the title and the subtitle and by looking ahead to any subheads, illustrations, and conclusions. Previewing can help you recognize the topic of a work, its organization, and sometimes its theme. Before you begin "The Lion-Makers," ask yourself, How can I preview this story to better understand it when I begin reading?

Tip: Predict An **epigraph** is a quotation at the beginning of a literary work that often provides a hint of what is to come. Use the checklist below to preview the fable and make predictions.

- ☑ Preview this fable. What might the story be about, based on the title and the illustrations?

- ☑ According to the epigraph, what will this fable be about?

Vocabulary

scholarship (skol′ ər ship′) *n.* academic achievement or knowledge; p. 597 *Claude was known for his scholarship—he was well read in many subjects.*

attainment (ə tān′ mənt) *n.* accomplishment; p. 597 *Ms. Lowndes, who started a business, was proud of this attainment.*

nullity (nul′ ə tē) *n.* a mere nothing; something insignificant; p. 598 *Many religions hold that no living thing is a nullity and that all life is sacred.*

Tip: Word Parts You can often determine the meanings of unfamiliar words by examining their parts. For example, a *scholar* is a person who studies. The suffix *-ship* refers to a status level. Therefore, *scholarship* can mean the status of a person who is well studied, or "academic achievement."

from the
Panchatantra

Translated by Arthur W. Ryder

Lion at Rest, ca. 1585. India school. Ink, colors, silver, and gold on paper, Overall: 20.3 x 15.2 cm. The Metropolitan Museum of Art, NY.

Indeed, there is wisdom in the saying:

> **Scholarship** *is less than sense;*
> *Therefore seek intelligence:*
> *Senseless scholars in their pride*
> *Made a lion; then they died.*

"How was that?" asked the wheel-bearer. And the gold-finder told the story of

---

Vocabulary

scholarship (skol′ər ship′) *n.* academic achievement or knowledge

The Lion-Makers

In a certain town were four Brahmans who lived in friendship. Three of them had reached the far shore of all scholarship, but lacked sense. The other found scholarship distasteful; he had nothing but sense.

One day they met for consultation. "What is the use of **attainments**," said they, "if one does not travel, win the favor of kings, and acquire money? Whatever we do, let us all travel."

Vocabulary

attainment (ə tān′mənt) *n.* accomplishment

But when they had gone a little way, the eldest of them said: "One of us, the fourth, is a dullard,[1] having nothing but sense. Now nobody gains the favorable attention of kings by simple sense without scholarship. Therefore we will not share our earnings with him. Let him turn back and go home."

Then the second said: "My intelligent friend, you lack scholarship. Please go home." But the third said: "No, no. This is no way to behave. For we have played together since we were little boys. Come along, my noble friend. You shall have a share of the money we earn."

With this agreement they continued their journey, and in a forest they found the bones of a dead lion. Thereupon one of them said: "A good opportunity to test the ripeness of our scholarship. Here lies some kind of creature, dead. Let us bring it to life by means of the scholarship we have honestly won."

Then the first said: "I know how to assemble the skeleton." The second said: "I can supply skin, flesh, and blood." The third said: "I can give it life."

So the first assembled the skeleton, the second provided skin, flesh, and blood. But while the third was intent on giving the breath of life, the man of sense advised against it, remarking: "This is a lion. If you bring him to life, he will kill every one of us."

"You simpleton!" said the other, "it is not I who will reduce scholarship to a **nullity**." "In that case," came the reply,

Prince Salim surprised by lion while hunting, c.1595–1600, Mughal. Christie's Images.

View the Art Prince Salim, the future Jahangir, or "World-Conqueror," ruled the Mogul Empire from 1605 until his death in 1627. This painting shows a lion leaping at Prince Salim, who defends himself with a staff. How does the mood of this painting compare with the mood of the fable?

"wait a moment, while I climb this convenient tree."

When this had been done, the lion was brought to life, rose up, and killed all three. But the man of sense, after the lion had gone elsewhere, climbed down and went home.
"And that is why I say:
      Scholarship is less than sense, . . .
and the rest of it." ❧

---

1. A *dullard* is someone with no imagination or intelligence.

The Search for Enlightenment *What opinion about enlightenment does this statement express?*

Vocabulary

nullity (nul′ə tē) *n.* a mere nothing; something insignificant

---

Moral *How can you tell that this is the moral of the fable?*

After You Read

Respond and Think Critically

Respond and Interpret

1. What was your reaction to this fable? Explain.

2. (a)What do the Brahmans seek on their travels? (b)Why do the first two Brahmans want to exclude the fourth Brahman from their travels?

3. (a)What do the Brahmans discover in the forest, and what do the first three decide to do? (b)Why does the fourth Brahman disagree with their plan?

Analyze and Evaluate

4. (a)Do you think the first three Brahmans are most disadvantaged by their education, their lack of common sense, or their pride? Explain. (b)Do you think the fourth Brahman is saved by his *lack* of education? Explain.

5. In your opinion, does this fable mean that people should *not* try to educate themselves? Explain.

Connect

6. **Big Idea** **The Search for Enlightenment** Who is truly enlightened in this story? What does this say about how enlightenment is achieved?

7. **Connect to Today** Do you think the moral of "The Lion-Makers" is relevant to contemporary society? Explain.

Literary Element **Moral**

A **moral** is the equivalent of a theme, or main idea.

1. Where is the moral of "The Lion-Makers" explicitly stated?

2. State the moral in your own words.

Reading Strategy **Preview**

When you preview a text, you form a mental picture of what the work is about and how it is organized. Review the chart you made on page 596.

Partner Activity Skim the "The Lion-Makers" and look for elements that stand out, such as the title, the epigraph, the subhead, and the illustrations. List these elements and discuss what they might lead a reader to expect from the fable.

LOG ON ▶ **Literature** Online

Selection Resources For Selection Quizzes, eFlashcards, and Reading-Writing Connection activities, go to glencoe.com and enter QuickPass code GLW6053u3.

Vocabulary Practice

Practice with Word Parts For each boldfaced vocabulary word, identify the word with a shared word part in the right column. Write each word and underline the part both words share. Then explain how the words are related.

1. scholarship   purity

2. attainment   school

3. nullity   accomplishment

EXAMPLE: re<u>ce</u>de   pro<u>ce</u>ed

Recede means "to go back"; *proceed* means "to go forward."

Writing

Write a Fable Using "The Lion-Makers" as a model, write a fable that presents a moral. In your fable, use elements of the *Panchatantra* (such as nonhuman characters), describe a specific setting, and include figurative language.

Build Background

Aesop (ē′sop) was supposedly a Greek slave in the sixth century B.C. who was famous for telling witty and powerful fables. These fables expressed values that were widely held among ancient Greeks, many of which are still held by people today. Aesop's tales continue to delight and instruct people of all ages and many common phrases can be traced to them, including "sour grapes," "a wolf in sheep's clothing," and "killing the goose that laid the golden egg."

The Dog and the Wolf

Aesop
Retold by Joseph Jacobs

A gaunt Wolf was almost dead with hunger when he happened to meet a Housedog who was passing by. "Ah, Cousin," said the Dog, "I knew how it would be; your irregular life will soon be the ruin of you. Why do you not work steadily as I do, and get your food regularly given to you?"

"I would have no objection," said the Wolf, "if I could only get a place."

"I will easily arrange that for you," said the Dog; "come with me to my master and you shall share my work."

So the Wolf and the Dog went towards the town together. On the way there the Wolf noticed that the hair on a certain part of the Dog's neck was very much worn away, so he asked him how that had come about.

Aesop Hund und Wolf (Dog and Wolf), 15th century. Illuminated manuscript.

"Oh, it is nothing," said the Dog. "That is only the place where the collar is put on at night to keep me chained up; it chafes a bit, but one soon gets used to it."

"Is that all?" said the Wolf. "Then good-bye to you, Master Dog."

"Better starve free than be a fat slave." ∾

💬 Discussion Starter

"The Dog and the Wolf" is a **beast fable,** one that features animals that behave like humans. Why might Aesop have used animals to teach lessons about human behavior? How are animals used in contemporary culture to represent human behavior? Discuss these questions with a group.

Build Background

In seventeenth-century France, fables were considered a minor literary form, unworthy of sophisticated readers. Jean de la Fontaine (zhän də lä fon tän') challenged this notion in the three collections of fables he published over a 26-year period. He enhanced the dramatic impact of these brief tales through subtle characterization and rich imagery. Within a single fable, he could shift from tragic to comic styles. La Fontaine often suggested rather than stated the morals of his fables, allowing readers to draw their own conclusions.

The Oak and the Reed

Jean de la Fontaine

Translated by James Michie

One day the oak said to the reed:
"You have good cause indeed
To accuse Nature of being unkind.
To you a wren¹ must seem
5 An intolerable burden, and the least puff of wind
That chances to wrinkle the face of the stream
Forces your head low; whereas I,
Huge as a Caucasian peak,² defy
Not only the sun's glare, but the worst the weather can do.
10 What seems a breeze to me is a gale for you.
Had you been born in the lee³ of my leaf-sheltered ground,
You would have suffered less, I should have kept you warm;
But you reeds are usually found
On the moist borders of the kingdom of the storm.
15 It strikes me that to you Nature has been unfair."
"Your pity," the plant replied, "springs from a kind heart.
But please don't be anxious on my part.
Your fear of the winds ought to be greater than mine.
I bend, but I never break. You, till now, have been able to bear
20 Their fearful buffets⁴ without flexing your spine.
But let us wait and see." Even as he spoke,

---

1. A *wren* is a very small European bird.
2. *Caucasian peak* refers to the Caucasus mountains, which lie between Russia, Turkey, and Iran, and contain the highest mountains in Europe.
3. The *lee* is the side (as of a tree) that is sheltered from the wind.
4. *Buffets* (buf′əts) means "blows."

The Great Piece of Turf, 1503. Albrecht Dürer. Watercolor. Albertina Graphic Collection, Vienna.

View the Art Albrecht Dürer, painter and printmaker, was a central figure of the German Renaissance. His careful observation of nature in this watercolor is characteristic of Renaissance art. How does he portray the beauty of ordinary things? Which character in "The Oak and the Reed" does this watercolor suggest? Explain.

From the horizon's nethermost gloom
The worst storm the north had ever bred in its womb
      Furiously awoke.
25 The tree stood firm, the reed began to bend.
The wind redoubled[5] its efforts to blow—
      So much so
      That in the end
It uprooted the one that had touched the sky with its head,
30 But whose feet reached to the region of the dead.

---

5. *Redoubled* means "intensified."

💬 Discussion Starter

A Chinese proverb states, "A wise man adapts himself to circumstances, as water shapes itself to the vessel that contains it." How might this proverb relate to the theme of "The Oak and the Reed"? How might it relate to the themes of "The Lion-Makers" and "The Dog and the Wolf"? Discuss these questions in a group.

Build Background

Twentieth-century American author and illustrator James Thurber commented that "Every writer is fascinated by the fable form; it's short, concise and can say a great deal about life." However, Thurber's fables do not include clear-cut prescriptions for moral behavior. Instead, they often parody well-known sayings—for example, "There is no safety in numbers, or in anything else" and "You can fool too many of the people too much of the time."

The Elephant

Who Challenged the World

James Thurber

An elephant who lived in Africa woke up one morning with the conviction that he could defeat all the other animals in the world in single combat, one at a time. He wondered that he hadn't thought of it before. After breakfast he called first on the lion. "You are only the King of Beasts," bellowed the elephant, "whereas I am the Ace!" and he demonstrated his prowess by knocking the lion out in fifteen minutes, no holds barred. Then in quick succession he took on the wild boar, the water buffalo, the rhinoceros, the hippopotamus, the giraffe, the zebra, the eagle, and the vulture, and he conquered them all. After that the elephant spent most of his time in bed eating peanuts, while the other animals, who were now his slaves, built for him the largest house any animal in the world had ever had. It was five stories high, solidly made of the hardest woods to be found in Africa. When it was finished, the Ace of Beasts moved in and announced that he could pin back the ears of any animal in the world. He challenged all comers to meet him in the basement of the big house, where he had set up a prize ring ten times the regulation size.

Several days went by and then the elephant got an anonymous letter accepting his challenge. "Be in your basement tomorrow afternoon at three o'clock," the message read. So at three o'clock the next day the elephant went down to the basement to meet his mysterious opponent, but there was no one there, or at least no one he could see. "Come out from behind whatever you're behind!" roared the elephant. "I'm not behind anything," said a tiny voice. The elephant tore around the basement, upsetting barrels and boxes, banging his head against the furnace pipes, rocking the house on its foundations, but he could not find his opponent. At the end of an hour the elephant roared that the whole business was a trick and a deceit—probably ventriloquism—and that

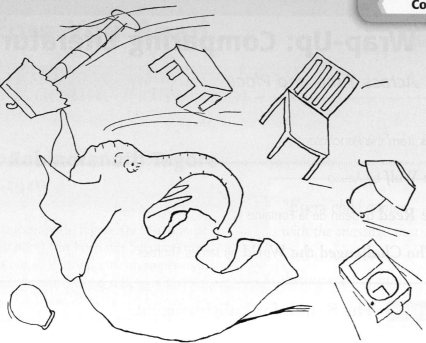

The Elephant Who Challenged the World. James Thurber. Illustration.

he would never come down to the basement again. "Oh, yes you will," said the tiny voice. "You will be down here at three o'clock tomorrow and you'll end up on your back." The elephant's laughter shook the house. "We'll see about that," he said.

The next afternoon the elephant, who slept on the fifth floor of the house, woke up at two-thirty o'clock and looked at his wristwatch. "Nobody I can't see will ever get me down to the basement again," he growled, and went back to sleep. At exactly three o'clock the house began to tremble and quiver as if an earthquake had it in its paws. Pillars and beams bent and broke like reeds, for they were all drilled full of tiny holes. The fifth floor gave way completely and crashed down upon the fourth, which fell upon the third, which fell upon the second, which carried away the first as if it had been the floor of a berry basket. The elephant was precipitated into the basement, where he fell heavily upon the concrete floor and lay there on

his back, completely unconscious. A tiny voice began to count him out. At the count of ten the elephant came to, but he could not get up. "What animal are you?" he demanded of the mysterious voice in a quavering tone which had lost its menace. "I am the termite," answered the voice.

The other animals, straining and struggling for a week, finally got the elephant lifted out of the basement and put him in jail. He spent the rest of his life there, broken in spirit and back.

Moral: The battle is sometimes to the small, for the bigger they are the harder they fall. ❧

Quickwrite

How does Thurber's use of humor compare with the use of humor in the other fables you have read? What might be the advantages and the disadvantages of using humor in a fable? Write a paragraph or two addressing these questions. Use evidence from the fables to support your response.

My five years' old daughter Mini cannot live without chattering. I really believe that in all her life she has not wasted a minute in silence. Her mother is often vexed at this, and would stop her prattle, but I would not. To see Mini quiet is unnatural, and I cannot bear it long. And so my own talk with her is always lively.

One morning, for instance, when I was in the midst of the seventeenth chapter of my new novel, my little Mini stole into the room, and putting her hand into mine, said: "Father! Ramdayal the door-keeper calls a crow a krow! He doesn't know anything, does he?"

Before I could explain to her the differences of language in this world, she was embarked on the full tide of another subject. "What do you think, Father? Bhola says there is an elephant in the clouds, blowing water out of his trunk, and that is why it rains!"

And then, darting off anew, while I sat still making ready some reply to this last saying, "Father! what relation is Mother to you?"

"My dear little sister in the law!" I murmured involuntarily to myself, but with a grave face contrived to answer: "Go and play with Bhola, Mini! I am busy!"

The window of my room overlooks the road. The child had seated herself at my feet near my table, and was playing softly, drumming on her knees. I was hard at work on my seventeenth chapter, where Protrap Singh, the hero, had just caught Kanchanlata, the heroine, in his arms, and was about to escape with her by the third story window of the castle, when all of a sudden Mini left her play, and ran to the window, crying, "A Kabuliwallah! a Kabuliwallah!"

Sure enough in the street below was a Kabuliwallah, passing slowly along. He wore the loose soiled clothing of his people, with a tall turban; there was a bag on his back, and he carried boxes of grapes in his hand.

I cannot tell what were my daughter's feelings at the sight of this man, but she began to call him loudly. "Ah!" I thought, "he will come in, and my seventeenth chapter will never be finished!" At which exact moment the Kabuliwallah turned, and looked up at the child. When she saw this, overcome by terror, she fled to her mother's protection, and disappeared. She had a blind belief that inside the bag, which the big man carried, there were perhaps two or three other children like herself. The peddler meanwhile entered my doorway, and greeted me with a smiling face.

So precarious was the position of my hero and my heroine, that my first impulse was to stop and buy something, since the man had been called. I made some small purchases, and a conversation began about Abdurrahman, the Russians, the English, and the Frontier Policy.

As he was about to leave, he asked: "And where is the little girl, sir?"

And I, thinking that Mini must get rid of her false fear, had her brought out.

She stood by my chair, and looked at the Kabuliwallah and his bag. He offered her nuts and raisins, but she would not be tempted, and only clung the closer to me, with all her doubts increased.

This was their first meeting.

One morning, however, not many days later, as I was leaving the house, I was startled to find Mini, seated on a bench near

Visual Vocabulary

A *sari* is a garment worn by women of southern Asia. It is made from several yards of lightweight cloth draped so that one end forms a skirt and the other a shoulder or head covering.

the door, laughing and talking, with the great Kabuliwallah at her feet. In all her life, it appeared, my small daughter had never found so patient a listener, save her father. And already the corner of her little *sari* was stuffed with almonds and raisins, the gift of her visitor. "Why did you give her those?" I said, and taking out an eight-anna bit,[1] I handed it to him. The man accepted the money without **demur**, and slipped it into his pocket.

Alas, on my return an hour later, I found the unfortunate coin had made twice its own worth of trouble! For the Kabuliwallah had given it to Mini, and her mother catching sight of the bright round object, had pounced on the child with: "Where did you get that eight-anna bit?"

"The Kabuliwallah gave it to me," said Mini cheerfully.

"The Kabuliwallah gave it you!" cried her mother much shocked. "Oh, Mini! how could you take it from him?"

I, entering at the moment, saved her from impending disaster, and proceeded to make my own inquiries.

It was not the first or second time, I found, that the two had met. The Kabuliwallah had overcome the child's first terror by a judicious bribery of nuts and almonds, and the two were now great friends.

They had many quaint jokes, which afforded them much amusement. Seated in front of him, looking down on his gigantic frame in all her tiny dignity, Mini would ripple her face with laughter, and begin: "O Kabuliwallah, Kabuliwallah, what have you got in your bag?"

And he would reply, in the nasal accents of the mountaineer: "An elephant!" Not much cause for merriment, perhaps; but how they both enjoyed the witticism! And for me, this child's talk with a grown-up man had always in it something strangely fascinating.

Then the Kabuliwallah, not to be behindhand, would take his turn: "Well, little one, and when are you going to the father-in-law's house?"[2]

Now most small Bengali maidens have heard long ago about the father-in-law's house; but we, being a little new-fangled, had kept these things from our child, and Mini at this question must have been a trifle bewildered. But she would not show it, and with ready tact replied: "Are *you* going there?"

Amongst men of the Kabuliwallah's class, however, it is well known that the words *father-in-law's house* have a double meaning. It is a euphemism for *jail*, the place where we are well cared for, at no expense to ourselves. In this sense would the sturdy peddler take my daughter's question. "Ah," he would say, shaking his fist at an invisible policeman, "I will thrash my father-in-law!" Hearing this, and picturing the poor discomfited relative, Mini would

---

1. An *eight-anna bit* is a small coin.

Vocabulary

demur (di mur´) *n.* a hesitation or an objection

---

2. Traditionally, when women in India marry, they go to live with their husband's family, or to their *father-in-law's house.*

Analyze Cultural Context *Why do you think the narrator and his wife chose not to tell Mini about the father-in-law's house?*

there was a sense of ablution[7] in the air, and the sun-rays looked like pure gold. So bright were they that they gave a beautiful radiance even to the **sordid** brick walls of our Calcutta lanes. Since early dawn today the wedding-pipes had been sounding, and at each beat my own heart throbbed. The wail of the tune, Bhairavi, seemed to intensify my pain at the approaching separation. My Mini was to be married tonight.

From early morning noise and bustle had pervaded the house. In the courtyard the canopy had to be slung on its bamboo poles; the chandeliers with their tinkling sound must be hung in each room and verandah. There was no end of hurry and excitement. I was sitting in my study, looking through the accounts, when someone entered, saluting respectfully, and stood before me. It was Rahmun the Kabuliwallah. At first I did not recognize him. He had no bag, nor the long hair, nor the same vigor that he used to have. But he smiled, and I knew him again.

"When did you come, Rahmun?" I asked him.

"Last evening," he said, "I was released from jail."

The words struck harsh upon my ears. I had never before talked with one who had wounded his fellow, and my heart shrank within itself, when I realized this, for I felt that the day would have been better-omened had he not turned up.

"There are ceremonies going on," I said, "and I am busy. Could you perhaps come another day?"

At once he turned to go; but as he reached the door he hesitated, and said: "May I not see the little one, sir, for a moment?" It was his belief that Mini was

still the same. He had pictured her running to him as she used, calling "O Kabuliwallah! Kabuliwallah!" He had imagined too that they would laugh and talk together, just as of old. In fact, in memory of former days he had brought, carefully wrapped up in paper, a few almonds and raisins and grapes, obtained somehow from a countryman, for his own little fund was dispersed.

I said again: "There is a ceremony in the house, and you will not be able to see anyone today."

The man's face fell. He looked wistfully at me for a moment, said "Good morning," and went out.

I felt a little sorry, and would have called him back, but I found he was returning of his own accord. He came close up to me holding out his offerings and said: "I brought these few things, sir, for the little one. Will you give them to her?"

I took them and was going to pay him, but he caught my hand and said: "You are very kind, sir! Keep me in your recollection. Do not offer me money!—You have a little girl, I too have one like her in my own home. I think of her, and bring fruits to your child, not to make a profit for myself."

Saying this, he put his hand inside his big loose robe, and brought out a small and dirty piece of paper. With great care he unfolded this, and smoothed it out with both hands on my table. It bore the impression of a little hand. Not a photograph. Not a drawing. The impression of an ink-smeared hand laid flat on the paper. This touch of his own little daughter had been always on his heart, as he had come year after year to Calcutta, to sell his wares in the streets.

Tears came to my eyes. I forgot that he was a poor Kabuli fruit-seller, while I was—

---

7. *Ablution* (əblōō′shən) means "cleansing."

Vocabulary

sordid (sôr′did) *adj.* dirty; squalid; wretched

Characterization *What does this revelation add to your understanding of the Kabuliwallah's character?*

but no, what was I more than he? He also was a father.

That impression of the hand of his little Pārbati[8] in her distant mountain home reminded me of my own little Mini.

I sent for Mini immediately from the inner apartment. Many difficulties were raised, but I would not listen. Clad in the red silk of her wedding-day, with the sandal paste on her forehead, and adorned as a young bride, Mini came, and stood bashfully before me.

The Kabuliwallah looked a little staggered at the apparition. He could not revive their old friendship. At last he smiled and said: "Little one, are you going to your father-in-law's house?"

But Mini now understood the meaning of the word "father-in-law," and she could not reply to him as of old. She flushed up at the question, and stood before him with her bride-like face turned down.

I remembered the day when the Kabuliwallah and my Mini had first met, and I felt sad. When she had gone, Rahmun heaved a deep sigh, and sat down on the floor. The idea had suddenly come to him that his daughter too must have grown in this long time, and that he would have to make friends with her anew. Assuredly he would not find her, as he used to know her. And besides, what might not have happened to her in these eight years?

The marriage-pipes sounded, and the mild autumn sun streamed round us. But Rahmun sat in the little Calcutta lane, and saw before him the barren mountains of Afghanistan.

I took out a bank-note, and gave it to him, saying: "Go back to your own daughter, Rahmun, in your own country, and may the happiness of your meeting bring good fortune to my child!"

Having made this present, I had to curtail some of the festivities. I could not have the electric lights I had intended, nor the military band, and the ladies of the house were despondent at it. But to me the wedding feast was all the brighter for the thought that in a distant land a long-lost father met again with his only child. ∾

First Marriage, 1988. Shanti Panchal. Watercolor on paper. Bradford Art Galleries and Museums, West Yorkshire, UK.

View the Art Shanti Panchal is well known for his multihued, watercolor images of Indian life. How do the two figures in the foreground, or front, of the painting reflect Mini and the narrator and their reactions to the Kabulliwallah at the end of the story?

8. *Pārbati* (par bä′tē) is another name for the goddess Durga in a reincarnated form; *her distant mountain home* refers to Mount Kailas.

Analyze Cultural Context *What does this description reveal about Indian marriage customs? What might be the significance of Mini's appearance for the Kabuliwallah?*

Characterization *How has Mini changed since she was a small girl? To what do you attribute this change?*

Respond Through Writing

Reflective Essay

Compare Events When Mini is a young girl, the Kabuliwallah and she share jokes about going to the father-in-law's house. On her wedding day, the Kabuliwallah tries to revive their old joke, but Mini no longer finds it funny. Compare two events in your life that reflect how an idea or a value you once had changed over time. As you write, use narration, exposition, and description to explore this shift.

Understand the Task When you **reflect,** you look back at a specific experience to better understand its larger meaning.

Prewrite To choose two events that reflect how your perceptions changed, review old journal entries, flip through photo albums, or talk to friends. Create a Venn diagram like the one below to see how you can use an event from "The Kabuliwallah" as a springboard to craft your own reflection.

Mini getting ready to leave home after her marriage

- looking forward to independence
- saying good-bye to old friends
- fear of meeting new people

leaving home for summer camp

Draft As you write your reflection, pay attention to your word choice, sentence structure, and tone. Your writing should connect the events and the ideas you discuss to broader generalizations about life; for example, you might draw on the idea that people often learn valuable lessons through a coming-of-age experience. Your writing should reflect the significance and the emotions of your experience.

Revise Be sure that you have drawn clear comparisons between the two events and your old and new perceptions. Trade papers with a partner and ask him or her if the connections you made between your ideas and a broader generalization about life are apparent in your writing.

Edit and Proofread Proofread your paper, correcting any errors in grammar, spelling, and punctuation. Use the Grammar Tip in the side column to help you use dashes.

Learning Objectives

In this assignment, you will focus on the following objectives:

Writing: Writing a reflective essay.

Grammar: Understanding dashes.

Grammar Tip

Em Dashes and En Dashes

Em dashes (—) can indicate an abrupt break or change in thought.

They got along like old friends—at least when they first met.

Em dashes can also be used to set off a parenthetical statement.

The Fourth of July party lasted for three hours—only one of which included fireworks—in the state park.

Remember that an em dash is different from an en dash (–), which indicates a range of numbers, including dates, times, pages, and so on. In this usage the dash means "through" or "to." For example:

The Vietnam War (1954–75)

Before You Read

India

Like the Sun

Meet **R. K. Narayan**

(1906–2001)

R. K. Narayan was born in the southern Indian city of Madras (now called Chennai) to a family of the Brahman caste, the highest-ranking social class in India. Although he loathed the English schools he was forced to attend, he learned to love the English language, and it eventually became his language of choice when writing. Narayan believed that English is "a very adaptable language . . . [that] can take on the tint of any country." He taught for a short time but eventually decided to become a writer, relying on newspaper and magazine writing to earn a living while he wrote his novels. He set many of his works in a fictional village called Malgudi, which was based upon Mysore, the village where he grew up.

> "For human beings the greatest source of strength lies in each other's presence."
>
> —R. K. Narayan

A Favor from an Admirer At first, Narayan had a difficult time getting his writing published because there was little support at the time for Indian authors who wrote in English. He had little luck with publishers in India, and English publishers initially rebuffed him. Narayan gave the manuscript of his first novel to a friend who was studying at Oxford University in England, and his friend passed the manuscript along to acclaimed British novelist Graham Greene. Greene so admired Narayan's prose that he personally recommended it to publisher Hamish Hamilton, who published the novel, renamed *Swami and Friends*, in 1935. The book became a critical success. One review in the British press lauded the novel as "an entirely delightful story" that depicts life in an Indian school and provides a vivid glimpse into Indian life and culture.

Tragedy and Transcendence In 1939, Narayan's wife, Rajam, died of typhoid. Narayan sank into a period of profound depression and believed he would never write again. By caring for the couple's daughter, Narayan eventually recovered. His acclaimed, mostly autobiographical novel *The English Teacher*, published in 1945, describes this turning point in his life. Narayan went on to become one of the most respected fiction authors in India. His legacy includes an impressive group of novels and short story collections, essays, memoirs, and prose retellings of two Indian epics, the *Mahabharata* (see pages 563–573) and the *Ramayana* (see pages 582–593). His work for publications such as the *New Yorker* magazine and his unique brand of storytelling earned him an international audience.

LOG ON **Literature** Online

Author Search For more about R. K. Narayan, go to glencoe.com and enter QuickPass code GLW6053u3.

R. K. NARAYAN **619**

The bell rang and the boys burst out of the class.

Sekhar paused for a moment outside the headmaster's room to button up his coat; that was another subject the headmaster always sermonized about.

He stepped in with a very polite "Good evening, sir."

The headmaster looked up at him in a very friendly manner and asked, "Are you free this evening?"

Sekhar replied, "Just some outing which I have promised the children at home—"

"Well, you can take them out another day. Come home with me now."

"Oh . . . yes, sir, certainly . . ." And then he added timidly, "Anything special, sir?"

"Yes," replied the headmaster, smiling to himself . . . "You didn't know my weakness for music?"

"Oh, yes, sir . . ."

"I've been learning and practicing secretly, and now I want you to hear me this evening. I've engaged a drummer and a violinist to accompany me—this is the first time I'm doing it full-dress and I want your opinion. I know it will be valuable."

Sekhar's taste in music was well known. He was one of the most dreaded music critics in the town. But he never anticipated his musical inclinations would lead him to this trial. . . . "Rather a surprise for you, isn't it?" asked the headmaster. "I've spent a fortune on it behind closed doors. . . ." They started for the headmaster's house. "God hasn't given me a child, but at least let him not deny me the consolation of music," the headmaster said, pathetically, as they walked. He incessantly chattered about music: how he began one day out of sheer boredom; how his teacher at first laughed at him, and then gave him hope; how his ambition in life was to forget himself in music.

At home the headmaster proved very ingratiating. He sat Sekhar on a red silk carpet, set before him several dishes of delicacies, and fussed over him as if he were a son-in-law of the house. He even said, "Well, you must listen with a free mind. Don't worry about these test papers." He added half humorously, "I will give you a week's time."

"Make it ten days, sir," Sekhar pleaded.

"All right, granted," the headmaster said generously. Sekhar felt really relieved now—he would attack them at the rate of ten a day and get rid of the nuisance.

The headmaster lighted incense sticks. "Just to create the right atmosphere," he explained. A drummer and a violinist, already seated on a Rangoon mat, were waiting for him. The headmaster sat down between them like a professional at a concert, cleared his throat, and began an alapana,[2] and paused to ask, "Isn't it good Kalyani?"[3] Sekhar pretended not to have heard the question. The headmaster went on to sing a full song composed by Thyagaraja[4] and followed it with two more. All the time the headmaster was singing, Sekhar went on commenting within himself, He croaks like a dozen frogs. He is bellowing like a buffalo. Now he sounds like loose window shutters in a storm.

The incense sticks burnt low. Sekhar's head throbbed with the medley of sounds that had assailed his eardrums for a couple of hours now. He felt half

---

2. An *alapana* is a musical improvisation.
3. *Kalyani* means "music."
4. *Thyagaraja* (thyä´gä rä zhä) was an Indian composer (1767–1847) known for his devotional songs.

stupefied. The headmaster had gone nearly hoarse, when he paused to ask, "Shall I go on?" Sekhar replied, "Please don't, sir, I think this will do. . . ." The headmaster looked stunned. His face was beaded with perspiration. Sekhar felt the greatest pity for him. But he felt he could not help it. No judge delivering a sentence felt more pained and helpless. Sekhar noticed that the headmaster's wife peeped in from the kitchen, with eager curiosity. The drummer and the violinist put away their burdens with an air of relief. The headmaster removed his spectacles, mopped his brow, and asked, "Now, come out with your opinion."

"Can't I give it tomorrow, sir?" Sekhar asked tentatively.

"No. I want it immediately—your frank opinion. Was it good?"

"No, sir . . ." Sekhar replied.

"Oh! . . . Is there any use continuing my lessons?"

"Absolutely none, sir . . ." Sekhar said with his voice trembling. He felt very unhappy that he could not speak more soothingly. Truth, he reflected, required as much strength to give as to receive.

All the way home he felt worried. He felt that his official life was not going to be smooth sailing hereafter. There were questions of **increment** and confirmation and so on, all depending upon the headmaster's goodwill. All kinds of worries seemed to be in store for him. . . . Did not Harischandra[5] lose his throne, wife, child, because he would speak nothing less than the absolute Truth whatever happened?

At home his wife served him with a sullen face. He knew she was still angry with

Flute Player. Lincoln Seligman. Oil on canvas. Private collection.

him for his remark of the morning. Two casualties for today, Sekhar said to himself. If I practice it for a week, I don't think I shall have a single friend left.

He received a call from the headmaster in his classroom next day. He went up apprehensively.

"Your suggestion was useful. I have paid off the music master. No one would tell me the truth about my music all these days. Why such antics at my age! Thank you. By the way, what about those test papers?"

"You gave me ten days, sir, for correcting them."

"Oh, I've reconsidered it. I must positively have them here tomorrow. . . ." A hundred papers in a day! That meant all night's sitting up! "Give me a couple of days, sir . . ."

"No. I must have them tomorrow morning. And remember, every paper must be thoroughly **scrutinized**."

"Yes, sir," Sekhar said, feeling that sitting up all night with a hundred test papers was a small price to pay for the luxury of practicing Truth. ∾

---

5. *Harischandra* (ha´rē shän´drä) was a king who sacrificed his kingdom for the *Sat Panth*, or the Path of Truth.

Vocabulary

stupefied (stoo´pə fīd) *adj.* stupid, groggy, or insensible
increment (ing´krə mənt) *n.* something gained or added in a series, usually at regular intervals

A Complex Heritage *Do you think Sekhar's personal philosophy differs from the social norms in his culture? Explain.*

Vocabulary

scrutinize (skroōt´ən īz´) *v.* to examine with close attention to detail

Literature and Reading Preview

Connect to the Story

How are the traditions of different ethnic groups reflected in American society? Do you think preserving these cultural heritages is important? Discuss these questions with a partner.

Build Background

Under British colonial rule, many Indians—particularly those who were members of the higher Indian castes—were sent to Western-style schools. The British hoped to create a class of Indians who could help interpret British policies for the rest of the population. Many Western-educated Indians became government administrators, political leaders, and professionals.

Setting Purposes for Reading

Big Idea A Complex Heritage

As you read, ask yourself, How does this story illustrate the cultural identity crises faced by many Indians under British colonial rule?

Literary Element Autobiography

An **autobiography** is the story of a person's life written by that person. Autobiographies can give insights into the author's view or himself or herself and the society in which he or she lived. As you read, ask yourself, What insights does this story convey about the author and her society?

Reading Strategy Connect to Contemporary Issues

When you **connect,** you link what you read to events in your own life or in the world around you. As you read, ask yourself, What elements of this story relate to contemporary issues?

Tip: Track Connections Use a chart like the one below to keep track of the ways Rau's story connects to contemporary issues.

Story Event	Contemporary Issue	Shared Significance
A girl in Santha's class tries to fit in by wearing a cotton dress.	Schools in England recently banned Muslim girls from wearing full-faced veils to school.	People are sometimes forced to reject their traditions to accommodate the cultural values of others.

Learning Objectives

For pages 625–634

In studying this text, you will focus on the following objectives:

Literary Study: Analyzing autobiography.

Reading: Connecting to contemporary issues.

Listening and Speaking: Delivering a speech.

Vocabulary

provincial (prə vin′shəl) *adj.* belonging or peculiar to a particular province; local; lacking sophistication or polish; p. 628 *The student came from a provincial town and had difficulty coping with the challenges of urban living.*

insular (in′sə lər) *adj.* isolated; narrow-minded; p. 628 *His wealthy, insular upbringing made him indifferent to the problems faced by homeless people.*

incomprehensible (in′kom pri hen′sə bəl) *adj.* unintelligible; indiscernible; not understood; p. 629 *Her sloppy handwriting made the letter incomprehensible.*

sedately (si dāt′lē) *adv.* in a dignified or serious manner; calmly; solemnly; p. 631 *The president walked sedately to the podium.*

tepid (tep′id) *adj.* lukewarm; halfhearted; p. 631 *The soft drink tasted tepid because it had been left on the counter for an hour.*

Head Mistress, 2005. Lincoln Seligman. Acrylic. Private collection.

By Any Other Name

Santha Rama Rau

At the Anglo-Indian day school in Zorinabad to which my sister and I were sent when she was eight and I was five and a half, they changed our names. On the first day of school, a hot, windless morning of a north Indian September, we stood in the headmistress's study and she said, "Now you're the new girls. What are your names?"

My sister answered for us. "I am Premila, and she"—nodding in my direction—"is Santha."

The headmistress had been in India, I suppose, fifteen years or so, but she still smiled her helpless inability to cope with Indian names. Her rimless half-glasses glittered, and the precarious bun on the top of her head trembled as she shook her

---

A Complex Heritage *What difficulties might students face at an "Anglo-Indian" school?*

head. "Oh, my dears, those are much too hard for me. Suppose we give you pretty English names. Wouldn't that be more jolly? Let's see, now—Pamela for you, I think." She shrugged in a baffled way at my sister. "That's as close as I can get. And for *you*" she said to me, "how about Cynthia? Isn't that nice?"

My sister was always less easily intimidated than I was, and while she kept a stubborn silence, I said, "Thank you," in a very tiny voice.

We had been sent to that school because my father, among his responsibilities as an officer of the civil service, had a tour of duty to perform in the villages around that steamy little **provincial** town, where he had his headquarters at that time. He used to make his shorter inspection tours on horseback, and a week before, in the stale heat of a typically postmonsoon day,[1] we had waved good-bye to him and a little procession—an assistant, a secretary, two bearers,[2] and the man to look after the bedding rolls and luggage. They rode away through our large garden, still bright green from the rains, and we turned back into the twilight of the house and the sound of fans whispering in every room.

Up to then, my mother had refused to send Premila to school in the British-run establishments of that time, because, she

used to say, "you can bury a dog's tail for seven years and it still comes out curly, and you can take a Britisher away from his home for a lifetime and he still remains **insular**." The examinations and degrees from entirely Indian schools were not, in those days, considered valid. In my case, the question had never come up, and probably never would have come up if Mother's extraordinary good health had not broken down. For the first time in my life, she was not able to continue the lessons she had been giving us every morning. So our Hindi books were put away, the stories of the Lord Krishna[3] as a little boy were left in midair, and we were sent to the Anglo-Indian school.

That first day at school is still, when I think of it, a remarkable one. At that age, if one's name is changed, one develops a curious form of dual personality. I remember having a certain detached and disbelieving concern in the actions of "Cynthia," but certainly no responsibility. Accordingly, I followed the thin, erect back of the headmistress down the veranda to my classroom feeling, at most, a passing interest in what was going to happen to me in this strange, new atmosphere of School.

The building was Indian in design, with wide verandas opening onto a central courtyard, but Indian verandas are usually whitewashed, with stone floors. These, in the tradition of British schools, were

---

1. A *postmonsoon day* is a day that occurs just after a monsoon, or heavy rainfall.
2. *Bearers* are porters who carry the equipment and supplies for a journey.

Autobiography *What does the description of her voice indicate about Santha's emotional state at this point?*

Vocabulary

provincial (prə vin′shəl) *adj.* belonging or peculiar to a particular province; local; lacking sophistication or polish

---

3. *Lord Krishna* is an incarnation of the Hindu god Vishnu.

Connect to Contemporary Issues *What cultural biases are revealed here? Do biases like this exist in modern American society? Explain.*

Autobiography *Why do you think Santha feels only a passing interest in what will happen to her at school?*

Vocabulary

insular (in′sə lər) *adj.* isolated; narrow-minded

painted dark brown and had matting on the floors. It gave a feeling of extra intensity to the heat.

I suppose there were about a dozen Indian children in the school—which contained perhaps forty children in all—and four of them were in my class. They were all sitting at the back of the room, and I went to join them. I sat next to a small, solemn girl who didn't smile at me. She had long, glossy-black braids and wore a cotton dress, but she still kept on her Indian jewelry—a gold chain around her neck, thin gold bracelets, and tiny ruby studs in her ears. Like most Indian children, she had a rim of black kohl around her eyes. The cotton dress should have looked strange, but all I could think of was that I should ask my mother if I couldn't wear a dress to school, too, instead of my Indian clothes.

Visual Vocabulary
Kohl is a cosmetic that women in southwest and south central Asia use to darken the edges of their eyelids.

I can't remember too much about the proceedings in class that day, except for the beginning. The teacher pointed to me and asked me to stand up. "Now, dear, tell the class your name."

I said nothing.

"Come along," she said, frowning slightly. "What's your name, dear?"

"I don't know," I said, finally.

The English children in the front of the class—there were about eight or ten of them—giggled and twisted around in their chairs to look at me. I sat down quickly and opened my eyes very wide, hoping in that way to dry them off. The little girl with the braids put out her hand and very lightly touched my arm. She still didn't smile.

Most of that morning I was rather bored.

I looked briefly at the children's drawings pinned to the wall, and then concentrated on a lizard clinging to the ledge of the high, barred window behind the teacher's head. Occasionally it would shoot out its long yellow tongue for a fly, and then it would rest, with its eyes closed and its belly palpitating, as though it were swallowing several times quickly. The lessons were mostly concerned with reading and writing and simple numbers—things that my mother had already taught me—and I paid very little attention. The teacher wrote on the easel blackboard words like "bat" and "cat," which seemed babyish to me; only "apple" was new and **incomprehensible**.

When it was time for the lunch recess, I followed the girl with braids out onto the veranda. There the children from the other classes were assembled. I saw Premila at once and ran over to her, as she had charge of our lunchbox. The children were all opening packages and sitting down to eat sandwiches. Premila and I were the only ones who had Indian food—thin wheat chapatties,[4] some vegetable curry, and a bottle of buttermilk. Premila thrust half of it into my hand and whispered fiercely that I should go and sit with my class, because that was what the others seemed to be doing.

The enormous black eyes of the little Indian girl from my class looked at my food longingly, so I offered her some. But she only shook her head and plowed her way solemnly through her sandwiches.

---

4. *Chapatties* (chä pät′ēz) are pancake-shaped, unleavened breads common to northern India.

A Complex Heritage *Why do you think the Indian girl declines Santha's offer?*

Vocabulary

incomprehensible (in′kom pri hen′sə bəl) *adj.* unintelligible; indiscernible; not understood

Slide, Mysore, 2001. Andrew Macara. Oil on canvas. Private collection.

View the Art Macara considers himself to be a self-taught artist. How does the mood of this painting compare with the mood of the excerpt?

I was very sleepy after lunch, because at home we always took a siesta. It was usually a pleasant time of day, with the bedroom darkened against the harsh afternoon sun, the drifting off into sleep with the sound of Mother's voice reading a story in one's mind, and, finally, the shrill, fussy voice of the ayah[5] waking one for tea.

At school, we rested for a short time on low, folding cots on the veranda, and then we were expected to play games. During the hot part of the afternoon we played indoors, and after the shadows had begun to lengthen and the slight breeze of the evening had come up we moved outside to the wide courtyard.

I had never really grasped the system of competitive games. At home, whenever we played tag or guessing games, I was always allowed to "win"—"because," Mother used to tell Premila, "she is the youngest, and we have to allow for that." I had often heard her say it, and it seemed quite reasonable to me, but the result was that I had no clear idea of what "winning" meant.

When we played twos-and-threes that afternoon at school, in accordance with my training, I let one of the small English boys catch me, but was naturally rather puzzled when the other children did not return the courtesy. I ran about for what seemed like hours without ever catching anyone, until it was time for school to close. Much later I learned that my attitude was called "not being a good sport," and I stopped allowing myself to be caught, but it was not for years that I really learned the spirit of the thing.

---

5. An *ayah* is a governess or a nanny.

When I saw our car come up to the school gate, I broke away from my classmates and rushed toward it yelling, "Ayah! Ayah!" It seemed like an eternity since I had seen her that morning—a wizened, affectionate figure in her white cotton sari, giving me dozens of urgent and useless instructions on how to be a good girl at school. Premila followed more **sedately**, and she told me on the way home never to do that again in front of the other children.

When we got home we went straight to Mother's high, white room to have tea with her, and I immediately climbed onto the bed and bounced gently up and down on the springs. Mother asked how we had liked our first day in school. I was so pleased to be home and to have left that peculiar Cynthia behind that I had nothing whatever to say about school, except to ask what "apple" meant. But Premila told Mother about the classes, and added that in her class they had weekly tests to see if they had learned their lessons well.

I asked, "What's a test?"

Premila said, "You're too small to have them. You won't have them in your class for donkey's years." She had learned the expression that day and was using it for the first time. We all laughed enormously at her wit. She also told Mother, in an aside, that we should take sandwiches to school the next day. Not, she said, that *she* minded. But they would be simpler for me to handle.

That whole lovely evening I didn't think about school at all. I sprinted barefoot across the lawns with my favorite playmate, the cook's son, to the stream at the end of the garden. We quarreled in our usual way, waded in the **tepid** water under the lime trees, and waited for the night to bring out the smell of the jasmine. I listened with fascination to his stories of ghosts and demons, until I was too frightened to cross the garden alone in the semidarkness. The ayah found me, shouted at the cook's son, scolded me, hurried me in to supper—it was an entirely usual, wonderful evening.

It was a week later, the day of Premila's first test, that our lives changed rather abruptly. I was sitting at the back of my class, in my usual inattentive way, only half listening to the teacher. I had started a rather guarded friendship with the girl with the braids, whose name turned out to be Nalini (Nancy, in school). The three other Indian children were already fast friends. Even at that age it was apparent to all of us that friendship with the English or Anglo-Indian children was out of the question. Occasionally, during the class, my new friend and I would draw pictures and show them to each other secretly.

The door opened sharply and Premila marched in. At first, the teacher smiled at her in a kindly and encouraging way and said, "Now, you're little Cynthia's sister?"

Premila didn't even look at her. She stood with her feet planted firmly apart and

---

A Complex Heritage *Does Premila really believe it would be simpler to take sandwiches to school, or does she have another reason for requesting them? Explain.*

sedately (si dāt′lē) *adv.* in a dignified or serious manner; calmly; solemnly

Connect to Contemporary Issues *Why might this division be readily apparent to the Indian children? How does this passage relate to issues students face in school today?*

tepid (tep′id) *adj.* lukewarm; halfhearted

her shoulders rigid, and addressed herself directly to me. "Get up," she said. "We're going home."

I didn't know what had happened, but I was aware that it was a crisis of some sort. I rose obediently and started to walk toward my sister.

"Bring your pencils and your notebook," she said.

I went back for them, and together we left the room. The teacher started to say something just as Premila closed the door, but we didn't wait to hear what it was.

In complete silence we left the school grounds and started to walk home. Then I asked Premila what the matter was. All she would say was "We're going home for good."

It was a very tiring walk for a child of five and a half, and I dragged along behind Premila with my pencils growing sticky in my hand. I can still remember looking at the dusty hedges, and the tangles of thorns in the ditches by the side of the road, smelling the faint fragrance from the eucalyptus trees and wondering whether we would ever reach home. Occasionally a horse-drawn tonga[6] passed us, and the women, in their pink or green silks, stared at Premila and me trudging along on the side of the road. A few coolies[7] and a line of women carrying baskets of vegetables on their heads smiled at us. But it was nearing the hottest time of day, and the road was almost deserted. I walked more and more slowly, and shouted to Premila, from time to time, "Wait for me!" with increasing peevishness. She spoke to me only once, and

that was to tell me to carry my notebook on my head, because of the sun.

When we got to our house the ayah was just taking a tray of lunch into Mother's room. She immediately started a long, worried questioning about what are you children doing back here at this hour of the day.

Mother looked very startled and very concerned, and asked Premila what had happened.

Premila said, "We had our test today, and she made me and the other Indians sit at the back of the room, with a desk between each one."

Mother said, "Why was that, darling?"

"She said it was because Indians cheat," Premila added. "So I don't think we should go back to that school."

Mother looked very distant, and was silent a long time. At last she said, "Of course not, darling." She sounded displeased.

We all shared the curry she was having for lunch, and afterward I was sent off to the beautifully familiar bedroom for my siesta. I could hear Mother and Premila talking through the open door.

Mother said, "Do you suppose she understood all that?"

Premila said, "I shouldn't think so. She's a baby."

Mother said, "Well, I hope it won't bother her."

Of course, they were both wrong. I understood it perfectly, and I remember it all very clearly. But I put it happily away, because it had all happened to a girl called Cynthia, and I never was really particularly interested in her. ❧

---

6. A *tonga* is a horse-drawn, two-wheeled vehicle for two to four people.

7. *Coolies* are unskilled laborers or porters who work for low wages. The term is considered derogatory today.

Autobiography *Why does Santha refer to herself in the third person here?*

After You Read

Respond and Think Critically

Respond and Interpret

1. Do you think Premila's decision to pull herself and her sister out of school is appropriate? Explain.

2. (a)How are the Indian students treated at the school? (b)What does this treatment reveal about the teachers' attitude toward them?

3. (a)Until the day of the test, how does Premila behave at school? (b)Why might she behave this way?

4. (a)On the day of the test, why does Premila leave school and take Santha with her? (b)What does this action reveal about Premila's character?

5. (a)What does Santha understand at the end of the story? (b)What reason does Santha give for claiming that she put the incident "happily away"?

Analyze and Evaluate

6. An **allusion** is a reference to something from history or from another work of literature, music, or art. The title of this story alludes to lines from William Shakespeare's play *Romeo and Juliet*: "What's in a name? that which we call a rose / By any other name would smell as sweet." (a) What do these lines mean? (b)How does this meaning apply to Rau's story?

7. (a)Why does the girls' mother worry that Santha understood Premila's reason for leaving school? (b)What does this reveal about the way Santha and Premila were raised?

Connect

8. **Big Idea** **A Complex Heritage** Can you think of any other ethnic groups whose cultural traditions were deeply affected by colonial powers? Explain.

9. **Connect to the Author** What insights does Rau's autobiography give into her personality and values? Support your answer with evidence from the text.

Literary Element Autobiography

SAT Skills Practice

The primary purpose of the first four paragraphs of the text is to

(A) inform the reader about the benefits of colonial education in India

(B) entertain the reader with an anecdote about childhood

(C) persuade the reader to empathize with Santha and Premila

(D) describe the thoughts of the headmistress

(E) show the playfulness of the children

Review: Imagery

As you learned on page 377, **imagery** is the "word pictures" authors create to evoke particular emotional responses. To create effective imagery, authors use **sensory details**—descriptions that appeal to one or more of the five senses (sight, hearing, touch, taste, and smell).

Partner Activity With a partner, review the text and answer the following questions.

1. Find words and phrases that describe the physical appearance of the headmistress. What do these descriptions suggest about Rau's view of her?

2. Find words and phrases that describe the climate and the weather conditions. How do these descriptions contribute to the tone and the mood of the story?

3. What images does Rau use to describe her life at home? What tone and mood do these images convey?

Before You Read

The Wagon

Meet **Khalida Asghar**
(born 1938)

Technology creates the potential for both unprecedented achievement and unfathomable disaster. Khalida Asghar (kä lē′dä ash′gär) explores the consequences of modern technology in her highly original and imaginative fiction.

A Newly Formed Country Asghar was born in Lahore in a region of India that later became a Pakistani province. However, at the time of Asghar's birth, Pakistan was not a separate country. Pakistan was created when the partition of 1947 divided the Indian subcontinent along religious lines—Pakistan for the Muslim population and India for the Hindu one. At first, Pakistan was divided into East Pakistan and West Pakistan, which were separated by 1,000 miles of Indian territory. In 1971, after a nine-month civil war, East Pakistan became the independent nation of Bangladesh.

> "'The Wagon' . . . is an abstractly psychological story that has a powerfully hallucinatory effect on the reader even in translation."
>
> —Vinay Dharwadker

An Interrupted Career During the early 1960s, Asghar began to compose short stories in Urdu, the national language of Pakistan. "The Wagon," a short story she wrote early in her career, is considered a modern classic of Urdu

Gabba woollen mat (detail of woman making gabba). Pakistani school.

literature. In this story, Asghar uses a surrealistic approach and an eerie tone to address the problems that can stem from technological advances and human ambivalence. Asghar got married in 1965 and proceeded to publish very few stories for more than a decade. She resumed her career in 1981 with a book of short fiction. Since then, she has published two more short story collections and a short novel, *Kaghazi Ghat*. Some translations of her stories have appeared in anthologies such as *Hoops of Fire: Fifty Years of Fiction by Pakistani Women*; *The Tale of the Old Fisherman*; *Modern Literatures of the Non-Western World: Where the Waters Are Born*; and *Global Voices: Contemporary Literature from the Non-Western World*. In her more recent fiction, she often examines the place of women in Pakistani society, which men have traditionally dominated. Asghar began her career writing under her maiden name but has since written under the name Khalida Husain.

LOG ON ▶ **Literature** Online

Author Search For more about Khalida Asghar, go to glencoe.com and enter QuickPass code GLW6053u3.

Literature and Reading Preview

Connect to the Story

How would it feel to live in a place that was no longer healthy or pleasant because of an environmental hazard? Write a journal entry imagining how you might feel and what you might do in this situation.

Build Background

When Asghar wrote "The Wagon" in the early 1960s, fear of a nuclear holocaust was at an all-time high. Additionally, the effects of industry and manmade chemicals on the environment were starting to be better understood. "The Wagon" eerily foreshadows some of the environmental and nuclear disasters that were to come. One of the most tragic of these disasters occurred in Bhopal, India, in December 1984, when an insecticide plant leaked, killing 3,000 people almost immediately and between 15,000 and 20,000 people over time.

Set Purposes for Reading

Big Idea A Complex Heritage

As you read, ask yourself, What details in the story reveal how technology has changed the modern world?

Literary Element Narrator

The **narrator** is the person who tells a story. The narrator may be a character in the story or may be outside the story. The narrator may speak in the first person (using the pronoun *I*) or in the third person. As you read the story, ask yourself, What clues does the narrator reveal about his state of mind?

Reading Strategy Identify Ambiguities

When you **identify ambiguities**, you look for details in a literary work that cannot be explained in a single, clear way. Monitoring such ambiguities can help you discover hidden meanings in a text. As you read "The Wagon," ask yourself, Why might the ambiguities in this story be significant?

Tip: Track Details Use a chart to record your best explanations for the ambiguities in the story. In your chart, set up the details as questions and your explanations as answers.

Question	Answer #1	Answer #2
Why do the men's faces look "curiously alike"?	They are related.	They have similar concerns and habits.

Learning Objectives

For pages 636–650

In studying this text, you will focus on the following objectives:

Literary Study: Analyzing narrator.

Reading: Identifying ambiguities.

Vocabulary

impervious (im pur′vē əs) *adj.* not easily affected or disturbed; p. 639 *The comedian seemed impervious to the bad reviews.*

inexorable (i nek′sər ə bəl) *adj.* relentless; unyielding; p. 639 *The inexorable effects of aging had begun to slow Thomas down.*

pungent (pun′jənt) *adj.* having a sharp or stinging quality, especially affecting the sense of taste or smell; p. 643 *The pungent odor left by the skunk stung our nostrils.*

surge (surj) *n.* a strong, sudden increase or flow; p. 648 *She was getting tired, but a surge of energy enabled her to finish her long swim.*

Tip: Context Clues When you read an unfamiliar word, pay close attention to the context, or setting, in which it appears. For example, in the sentence *The pungent odor left by the skunk stung our nostrils,* you can determine that *pungent* means "having a sharp quality" because the odor "stung our nostrils."

laughed and said, "Must be peasants, on their way to the city to have a good time."

An air of strangeness surrounded these men. Zakiya, of course, could not have known it: one really had to look at them to feel the weird aura.[1]

The next day I waited impatiently for the evening. I walked to the bridge, expecting them to show up. And they did, just as the daylight ebbed away. They leaned over the bridge and watched the sun go down, indifferent to the sound of traffic. Their absorption in the scene made it impossible to talk to them. I waited until the sun had gone down completely and the men had started to return. This would be the time to ask them what it was they expected to find in the vanishing sun and the marshes of the receding river.

When the sun had sunk all the way, the men gave one another a sad, mute look, lowered their heads and started off. But, instead of returning to the village, they took the road to the city. Their shoes were covered with dust and their feet moved on rhythmically together.

I gathered my faltering courage and asked them, "Brothers! what village do you come from?"

The man with the snub nose turned around and stared at me for a while. Then the three exchanged glances, but none of them bothered to answer my question.

"What do you see over there . . . on the bridge?" I asked. The mystery about the three men was beginning to weigh heavily upon me now. I felt as though molten lead had seeped into my legs—indeed into my whole body, and that it was only a matter of time before I'd crumble to the ground reeling from a spell of dizziness.

Again they did not answer. I shouted at them in a choking voice, "Why are you always staring at the sunset?"

No answer.

We reached the heavily congested city road. The evening sounds grew closer. It was late October, and the air felt pleasantly cool. The sweet scent of jasmine wafted in, borne by the breeze.

As we passed the octroi post,[2] the old man with snow-white hair suddenly spoke, "Didn't you see? Has nobody in the city seen . . . ?"

"Seen what?"

"When the sun sets, when it goes down all the way . . . ?" asked the hoary[3] old man, rearranging his mantle over his shoulders.

Visual Vocabulary
A *mantle* is a loose, sleeveless piece of clothing.

"When the sun goes down all the way?" I repeated. "What about it? That happens every day!"

I said that very quickly, afraid that the slightest pause might force them back into their impenetrable silence.

"We knew that, we knew it would be that way. That's why we came. That other village, there, too . . ." He pointed toward the east and lowered his head.

"From there we come . . ." said the snub-nosed man.

"From where?" I asked, growing impatient. "Please tell me clearly."

The third man peered back at me over his shoulder. The scar on his forehead suddenly seemed deeper than before. He said,

---

1. An *aura* is a distinctive character or atmosphere surrounding a person or thing.

Identify Ambiguities *What is the ambiguity here? Why can't the narrator make Zakiya understand the men's strangeness?*

2. An *octroi* is a local customs tax, payable on goods moved within a country; it is collected at an *octroi post*.

3. *Hoary* means "gray or white with age."

Red Townscape, 1961. Francis Newton Souza. Oil on canvas. Private collection.

"We didn't notice, nor, I believe, did you. Perhaps nobody did. Because, as you say, the sun rises and sets every day. Why bother to look? And we didn't, when day after day, there, over there," he pointed in the direction of the east, "the sky became blood-red and so bright it blazed like fire even at nightfall. We just failed to notice . . ." He stopped abruptly, as if choking over his words. "And now this redness," he resumed after a pause, "it keeps spreading from place to place. I'd never seen such a phenomenon before. Nor my elders. Nor, I believe, did they hear their elders mention anything quite like that ever happening."

Meanwhile the darkness had deepened. All I could see of my companions were their white flowing robes; their faces became visible only when they came directly under the pale, dim light of the lampposts. I turned around to look at the stretch of sky over the distant Ravi. I was stunned: it was glowing red despite the darkness.

"You are right," I said, to hide my puzzlement, "we really did fail to notice that." Then I asked, "Where are you going?"

"To the city, of course. What would be the point of arriving there *afterwards?*"

A sudden impulse made me want to stay with them, or to take them home with me. But abruptly, they headed off on another road, and I remembered I was expected home soon. Munna would be waiting on the front porch for his daily sweets and Zakiya must be feeling irritated by my delay.

The next day I stopped at the bridge to watch the sunset. I was hoping to see those three men. The sun went down completely, but they didn't appear. I waited impatiently

A Complex Heritage *What does this statement indicate about the culture of the three men? What does it indicate about the nature of the phenomenon?*

for them to show up. Soon, however, I was entranced by the sunset's last magical glow.

The entire sky seemed covered with a sheet soaked in blood, and it scared me that I was standing all alone underneath it. I felt an uncanny presence directly behind me. I spun around. There was nobody. All the same, I felt sure there was someone—standing behind my back, within me, or perhaps, somewhere near.

Vehicles, of all shapes and sizes, rumbled along in the light of the street lamps. Way back in the east, a stretch of evening sky still blazed like a winding sheet of fire, radiating heat and light far into the closing darkness. I was alarmed and scurried home. Hastily I told Zakiya all I'd seen. But she laughed off the whole thing. I took her up to the balcony and showed her the red and its infernal bright glow against the dark night sky. That sobered her up a little. She thought for a while, then remarked, "We're going to have a storm any minute—I'm sure."

The next day in the office, as I worked, bent over my files, I heard Mujibullah ask Hafiz Ahmad, "Say, did you see how the sky glows at sunset these days? Even after it gets dark? Amazing, isn't it?"

All at once I felt I was standing alone and defenseless under that bloodsheet of a sky. I was frightened. Small drops of sweat formed on my forehead. As the evening edged closer, a strange restlessness took hold of me. The receding Ravi, the bridge, the night sky and the sun frightened me; I wanted to walk clear out of them. And yet, I also felt irresistibly drawn toward them.

I wanted to tell my colleagues about the three peasants who in spite of their distinctly individual faces somehow looked alike; about how they had come to the city accompanying this strange redness, had drawn my attention to it, and then dropped out of sight; and about how I'd searched in vain for them everywhere. But I couldn't.

Mujibullah and Hafiz Ahmad, my office-mates, had each borrowed about twenty rupees from me some time ago, which they conveniently forgot to return, and, into the bargain, had stopped talking to me ever since.

On my way home when I entered the bridge, a strange fear made me walk briskly, look away from the sun, and try to concentrate instead on the street before me. But the blood-red evening kept coming right along. I could feel its presence everywhere. A flock of evening birds flew overhead in a "V" formation. Like the birds, I too was returning home. Home—yes, but no longer my haven against the outside world; for the flame-colored evening came pouring in from its windows, doors, even through its walls of solid masonry.

I now wandered late in the streets, looking for the three peasants. I wanted to ask them where that red came from. What was to follow? Why did they leave the last settlement? What shape was it in? But I couldn't find them anywhere. Nobody seemed to care.

A few days later I saw some men pointing up to the unusual red color of the evening. Before long, the whole city was talking about it. I hadn't told a soul except Zakiya. How they had found out about it was a puzzle to me. Those three peasants must be in the city—I concluded. They have got to be.

The red of evening had now become the talk of the town.

Chaudhri Sahib, who owns a small bookshop in Mozang Plaza, was an old acquaintance of mine. People got together at his shop for a friendly chat every evening. Often, so did I. But for some time now,

Narrator *What does this passage reveal about the narrator's willingness to talk to others? How might it contribute to a better understanding of his relationship with the three men?*

Coming from Rajasthan, 1984. Balraj Khanna. Acrylic on canvas. Arts Council Collection, Hayward Gallery, London.

about where I wanted to be. I began to feel heavy and listless.

All the same, I did go back to the bookshop once again that evening. Most of the regulars had already gathered. Chaudhri Sahib asked, "What do you think about it, fellows? Is it all due to the atomic explosions as they say? The rumor also has it that pretty soon the earth's cold regions will turn hot and the hot ones cold and the cycle of seasons will also be upset."

I wanted to tell them about my encounter with the three villagers but felt too shy to talk before so many people. Just then a **pungent** smell, the likes of which I'd never smelled before, wafted in from God knows where. My heart sank and a strange, sweet sort of pain stabbed my body. I felt nauseous, unable to decide whether it was a stench, a pungent aroma, or even a wave of bittersweet pain. I threw the newspaper down and got up to leave.

"What's the matter?" asked Chaudhri Sahib.

"I must go. God knows what sort of smell that is."

"Smell? What smell?" Chaudhri Sahib sniffed the air.

I didn't care to reply and walked away.

That offensive smell, the terrifying wave of pain, followed me all the way home. It

since my first encounter with those mantle-wrapped oracular[4] figures, I had been too preoccupied with my own thoughts to go there. No matter where I went, home or outside, I felt restless. At home, an inexorable urge drove me outdoors; outdoors, an equally strong urge sent me scrambling back home, where I felt comparatively safer. I became very confused

---

4. *Oracular* means "prophetic."

Narrator *What conclusions can you draw about the physical and mental state of the narrator? What may be causing his behavior?*

Identify Ambiguities *How might you account for the discrepancy in reactions to the stench the narrator notices?*

Vocabulary

pungent (pun′jənt) *adj.* having a sharp or stinging quality, especially affecting the sense of taste or smell

me. It was an oversized wagon pulled by a pair of scrawny white oxen with leather blinders over their eyes and thick ropes strung through their steaming nostrils. A wooden cage sat atop the base of the wagon, its interior hidden behind black curtains—or were they just swaying walls of darkness?

Two men, sitting outside the cage enclosure in the front of the wagon, drove the two emaciated, blindfolded animals. I couldn't make out their faces, partly because of the darkness, but partly also because they were buried in folds of cloth thrown loosely around them. Their heads drooped forward and they seemed to have dozed off, overcome by fatigue and sleep.

Behind them the interior of the curtained wagon swelled with darkness and from the heart of that darkness shot out the nauseating stench which cut sharper than a sword . . . Before I knew it, the wagon had creaked past me, flooding my senses with its cargo of stink. My head swirled. I jumped off the main road onto the dirt sidewalk . . . and vomited.

I had no idea whether the people in the city had also seen the eerie wagon. If they had, what must have they endured? I had the hardest time getting home after what I had seen. Once inside the house, I ran to my bed and threw myself on it. Zakiya kept asking me what had happened, but a blind terror sealed my lips.

A few days later a small news item appeared in the local papers. It railed against the local Municipal Office for allowing garbage carts to pass through busy streets in the evening. Not only did muck-wagons pollute the air, they also hurt the fine olfactory sense of the citizenry.

Identify Ambiguities *How do these ambiguous details about the wagon contribute to the suspense of the story?*

I took a whole week off from work. During those seven days, though hardly fit to go out and observe firsthand the plight of the city, I was nonetheless kept posted of developments by local newspapers. Groups of concerned citizens demanded that the municipal authorities keep the city clear of the muck-wagons or, if that was impossible, assign them routes along less busy streets.

On the seventh day I ventured out. A change was already visible. Wrecked by insomnia and exhaustion, people strained themselves to appear carefree and cheerful, but managed only to look painfully silly. Suddenly I recalled that in the morning I had myself looked no different in the mirror.

About this time, the number of entertainment programs and movies shot up as never before. People swarmed to box offices—often hours before a show— where they formed long lines and patiently waited to be let in, and then filed out from the entertainment still looking pale and ridiculous.

In the office, no matter how hard I tried, I couldn't concentrate on work. Intermittently, the image of the muck-wagon lumbering down the streets flashed across my mind. Was it really one of those municipal dump-carts? No. It couldn't be. Municipal dump-carts never looked like that eerie wagon, with its sleepy drivers, a pair of blindfolded bony oxen, black curtains and the outrageously nauseating smell. What on earth could give off such an odd smell—at once fragrant and foul!

An insane desire suddenly overwhelmed me: to rush up to the wagon, lift up those swaying curtains, and peek inside. I must discover the source of the stench!

The Couple, 1984. Hind Nasser (Jordan). Oil on canvas, 90 x 100 cm. Collection of the Mango Family.

View the Art How do the colors in this painting affect your response to it? How does color affect the characters in the story?

Coming to the bridge my feet involuntarily slowed down. There was still some time before sunset and the waves of the pain-filled odor came faster and stronger. I leaned over the bridge, an unknown fear slowly rising in my throat. The bottomless swamp, its arms ominously outstretched, seemed to be dragging me down toward it. I was afraid I might jump into the swamp, sink with the sun and become buried forever in that sprawling sheet of blood.

I became aware of something approaching me—or was I myself drawing closer to something? . . . Something awaited by all men—those before and those after us. My whole body felt as though it was turning into a piece of granite, with no escape from the bridge, the miasma,[6] the sun, for now they all seemed inseparable from my being. Helplessly, I looked around myself and almost dropped dead.

The three men were coming towards me from the direction of the countryside. As before, they were wrapped in their flowing white robes and walked with their amazingly identical gait. I kept staring at them with glassy eyes until they walked right up to me and stopped. The hoary old man was

Narrator *How has the narrator changed since the beginning of the story?*

6. A *miasma* is a heavy vaporous emanation or atmosphere.

Literary Element | Narrator

Whether the narrator speaks in the first person or the third person, you need to ask yourself, Can I trust what this narrator tells me? A **reliable narrator** is one who can be trusted. An **unreliable narrator** is one whose point of view the reader distrusts—perhaps because the narrator reveals clues that he or she is unstable, dishonest, naïve, or otherwise questionable.

1. At one point in the story, the narrator seems haunted by the memory of the "muck-wagon" and begins to question his own perceptions. Do you agree with the narrator that what he saw could not have been an ordinary municipal dump-cart? Support your answer with evidence from the story.

2. Do you think the narrator is reliable or unreliable? Explain.

Review: Plot

As you learned on page 84, **plot** is the sequence of events in a work of fiction. The plot begins with **exposition,** which introduces the story's characters, setting, and conflict, then leads to **rising action** (which develops the conflict), a **climax,** and ends with **falling action** and **resolution.**

Partner Activity With a partner, discuss the various plot elements of this story. Then fill in a plot diagram like the one below with a description of each plot element in this story. Discuss how you feel about the ending. Is there a true resolution?

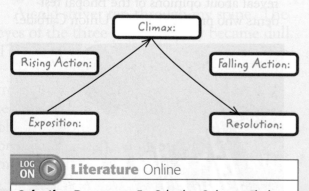

Climax:

Rising Action:

Falling Action:

Exposition:

Resolution:

LOG ON ▶ **Literature** Online

Selection Resources For Selection Quizzes, eFlash-cards, and Reading-Writing Connection activities, go to glencoe.com and enter QuickPass code GLW6053u3.

Reading Strategy | Identify Ambiguities

SAT Skills Practice

On page 639, the passage "Their outfits suggested that they were well-to-do villagers, and their dust-coated shoes that they had trudged for miles just to watch the sun as it set over the marshes of the receding Ravi" creates ambiguity by:

(A) identifying the Ravi but not the time of day.

(B) noting that the men walked far but giving an odd reason for their journey.

(C) creating a contrast between the men's clothing and their shoes.

(D) using nonspecific adjectives.

(E) placing the villagers in unfamiliar territory.

Vocabulary Practice

Practice with Context Clues Look back at pages 638–648 to find context clues for the vocabulary words below. Record your findings in a graphic organizer like the one here.

impervious   inexorable   pungent   surge

EXAMPLE:

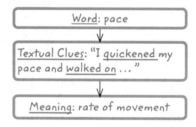

Word: pace

Textual Clues: "I quickened my pace and walked on ... "

Meaning: rate of movement

Academic Vocabulary

*"The Wagon" suggests the serious effects that **technology** can have on the environment.*

Technology is an academic word. In more casual conversation, a person might say that consumers look forward to advances in computer **technology.** To further explore the meaning of the word, answer this question: What is a career that involves developing new **technologies**?

For more on academic vocabulary, see pages 36–37 and R83–R85.

Respond Through Writing

Editorial

Learning Objectives

In this assignment, you will focus on the following objectives:

Writing: Writing an editorial.

Grammar: Using colons.

Offer a Solution Imagine you live in the city depicted in "The Wagon" and are fed up with the ambiguous stench. Write an editorial that offers a solution to the community's indifference to this pollution. Make an appeal to reason in your editorial that is supported by concrete details from the story and by your own inferences about this mysterious problem.

Understand the Task An **editorial** is an article that expresses the personal ideas and opinions of the writer. In an editorial, you **appeal to reason,** or use facts and evidence to convince your readers of a rational conclusion.

Prewrite Develop your editorial around a main point; for example, you could issue a call to action such as a protest or a letter-writing campaign. Write down your ideas as you brainstorm, and note the pros and cons of each idea. For inspiration, read editorials from a variety of newspapers and magazines. You will want to create an engaging opening, which journalists call the "lead."

Draft As you write, maintain a coherent link between problems in the village and the solutions you propose. Be sure your arguments are arranged logically and are supported with convincing evidence. It may be helpful to review details from the story to speculate on the cause of the problem and what can be done to solve it. Organize your notes in a graphic organizer like the one below.

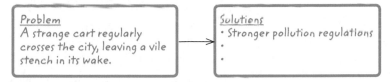

Revise As you revise, pretend you are someone who disagrees with your viewpoint. Consider the flaws that person might see in your argument and address these concerns in your revision. Also, make sure to use direct quotations from the story and provide corresponding attributions.

Edit and Proofread Proofread your paper, correcting any errors in grammar, spelling, and punctuation. Use the Grammar Tip in the side column to help you use colons.

> **Grammar Tip**
>
> **Colons**
> Colons can help introduce a list.
>
> *The sanitation department needs resources: laptop computers, infrared sensors, and more workers.*
>
> Colons can also be used to introduce material that illustrates, explains, or restates the preceding material.
>
> *The cause of the riot was apparent: people were fed up with the unsanitary conditions.*
>
> Finally, a colon can be used to introduce long or formal quotations and is often preceded by such words as *this, these, the following,* or *as follows.*

Writing Workshop

Reflective Essay

Learning Objectives

For pages 652–659

In this workshop, you will focus on the following objectives:

Writing: Writing a reflective essay using the writing process.

Understanding how to use sensory details.

Grammar: Understanding how to correct unclear pronoun references.

Writing Process

At any stage of a writing process, you may think of new ideas. Feel free to return to earlier stages as you write.

Prewrite

Draft

Revise

Focus Lesson: Sensory Details

Edit and Proofread

Focus Lesson: Unclear Pronoun References

Present

Writing and Research For prewriting, drafting, and revising tools, go to glencoe.com and enter QuickPass code GLW6053u3.

Literature Connection

*"They have a life of their own,
they fly without thinking.
Some are rare, some common,
but every wing is grace."*

In these lines from Dahlia Ravikovitch's poem "The Sound of Birds at Noon," the speaker's observations of birds lead her to reflect on human behavior. Authors use many forms of writing—poems, autobiographies, memoirs, and short essays—to reflect, or provide interpretations and explanations of the significance of an experience or an observation. A good reflective essay can make your audience feel the impact of even a small or an ordinary incident in your life. To write a successful reflective essay, you will need to meet the goals and learn the strategies listed below.

Rubric

Goals	Strategies
To present a meaningful experience from your life	☑ Reflect on a memorable experience or observation from your past.
To present a clear setting and sequence of events	☑ Give background details on the setting and your role in the incident. ☑ Narrate the events in a logical order.
To make the experience seem real to the reader	☑ Describe appearances, movements, sensory images, and personal feelings in concrete detail. ☑ Use action verbs and precise nouns.
To connect with an audience	☑ Use the first-person point of view. ☑ Use a tone appropriate to the experience or the observation you describe.

Assignment: Reflect on an Observation

Write a reflective essay of at least 1,000 words about an observation you have made or an experience you have had. As you move through the stages of writing, keep your audience and purpose in mind.

Audience: classmates and peers

Purpose: to explore the meaning and the effect of a personal observation or experience

Real-World Connection

You may be required to retell a personal experience when you apply to college or for a job. Your ability to present your experience and reflect upon its significance may be used to judge your merits as a student or an employee.

Analyze a Professional Model

The Taj Mahal is a white marble mausoleum, or tomb, in northern India. Built by a seventeenth-century emperor, it is one of the most magnificent structures in the world. In the following excerpt, author Salman Rushdie reflects on his experience of seeing the monument for the first time. Using vivid descriptions, he shows how the observation led him to an unexpected insight about the power of reality over imitation. As you read, note the comments in the margin; they point out features you might want to include in your own reflective essay.

from *"The Taj Mahal"* by Salman Rushdie

When you arrive at the outer walls of the gardens in which the Taj is set, it's as if every hustler and hawker in Agra is waiting for you to make the familiarity-breeds-contempt problem worse, peddling imitation Mahals of every size and price. This leads to a certain amount of shoulder-shrugging disenchantment. Recently, a British friend who was about to make his first trip to India told me that he had decided to leave the Taj off his itinerary because of its over-exposure. If I urged him not to, it was because of my own vivid memory of pushing my way for the first time through the jostling crowd, not only of imitation-vendors but also of prescribed readings, past all the myriad hawkers of meaning and interpretation, and into the presence of the *thing-in-itself*, which utterly overwhelmed me and made all my notions about its devaluation feel totally and completely redundant.

Narrative Elements

Include elements of narrative, such as setting, in your reflection.

Tone

Match your tone to your subject. An ironic tone can draw your reader in and reveal the more humorous aspects of your experience.

First-Person Point of View

Write your reflection from the first-person point of view.

Background Information

Explain what occurred or how you felt before the incident to help the reader more fully understand the significance of your experience.

Descriptive Details

Try to *show* your reader what happened, rather than simply telling.

Conclusion

Use your current perspective to reflect on the meaning of the observation or the experience.

I had been skeptical about the visit. One of the legends of the Taj is that the hands of the master masons who built it were cut off by the emperor, so that they could never build anything lovelier. Another is that the mausoleum was constructed in secrecy behind high walls, and a man who tried to sneak a preview was blinded for his interest in architecture. My personal imagined Taj was somewhat tarnished by these cruel tales.

The building itself left my skepticism in shreds, however. Announcing itself as itself, insisting with absolute force on its sovereign authority, it simply obliterated the million million counterfeits of it and glowingly filled, once and forever, the place in the mind previously occupied by its simulacra [superficial representations].

And this, finally, is why the Taj Mahal must be seen: to remind us that the world is real, that the sound is truer than the echo, the original more forceful than its image in a mirror. The beauty of beautiful things is still able, in these image-saturated times, to transcend imitations. And the Taj Mahal is, beyond the power of words to say it, a lovely thing, perhaps the loveliest of things.

Reading-Writing Connection Think about the writing techniques you just encountered and try them out in the reflective essay you write.

Prewrite

Choose a Topic As you brainstorm topics, break down your life into different periods and think about which experiences you remember most vividly from each period. Ask yourself which experiences had the most meaning or significance, and choose the one that is most interesting to you and that you feel comfortable sharing.

Describe Vividly Your goal in writing a reflective essay is to make the experience or the observation seem real for your reader. Make a list of details that you remember from the experience you chose. Then look over your list and replace general or vague descriptions with language that *shows* the details to the reader: vivid and specific nouns and verbs, sensory details, and comparisons.

Make an Outline Your next step is to organize your ideas for the beginning, the middle, and the end of your essay. You may find it helpful to narrate your experience in chronological order, or you may wish to skip back and forth between your past experience and your present reflections, as Rushdie does. Use a graphic organizer like the one below to arrange your essay.

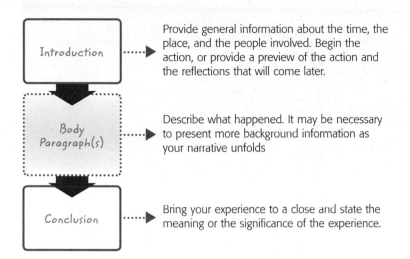

Introduction → Provide general information about the time, the place, and the people involved. Begin the action, or provide a preview of the action and the reflections that will come later.

Body Paragraph(s) → Describe what happened. It may be necessary to present more background information as your narrative unfolds

Conclusion → Bring your experience to a close and state the meaning or the significance of the experience.

Share Ideas Meet with a partner to discuss your topic. To help develop your writing voice, listen to your speaking voice as you describe the significance of the experience you chose. Write down words and phrases that capture your voice.

Draft

Structure Your Essay As you write, remember that your essay should have a clear beginning, middle, and end. Depending on your topic, you may need only three paragraphs, one for each part of the essay. Some topics may call for several middle paragraphs that include both narration and reflection. For topics that require lengthier narration, use transitional words such as *first, next*, and *then* to connect parts of the narration.

Analyze a Workshop Model

On the next page, you will read a final draft of a reflective essay. Read the essay and answer the questions in the margin. Use the answers to these questions to guide you as you write.

Focus on Significance

Remember that the goal of a reflective essay is not to simply recount an exciting or unusual event, but to reflect on the larger significance or meaning of an incident. To decide whether an event would make a good topic for your essay, ask yourself, How has the event changed my ideas or outlook?

Avoid Plagiarism

As you work on your essay, you might remember the words of another writer who perfectly captured an idea you want to convey. Copying these words, however, is wrong unless you give credit to the source.

Monarch Madness

Last year during February vacation, my family and I went to visit my grandmother, who lives in Toluca, a city just west of Mexico City. This was my first time in Mexico. Having lived in Los Angeles all my life, I was fascinated by Mexico's landscape and its natural beauty. The most memorable part of the visit was a trip we took to a nearby place called Angangueo. There we saw the greatest show on Earth: the migration of the monarch butterflies.

Before we went, Grandma gave us a little bit of background. She told us Angangueo is the home of a monarch butterfly sanctuary. Every winter, butterflies make the long journey to Angangueo from North America. Some travel as far as 1,800 miles. Perhaps even more amazing, every year the butterflies come back to the very same place. Most of these butterflies live two years, which means they make this trip twice.

Our trip to the sanctuary began with a ride in a flatbed truck up a rural mountainside. Several trucks and buses were also making the trip up the bumpy, narrow road. We sat in the truck with several other Mexican families. Everyone seemed happy and expectant. Still, none of us were prepared for the great thrill that awaited us.

Once we got within a quarter-mile of the sanctuary, we became part of a whole army of people hiking the final distance to the sanctuary at the top of the mountain. The last part of the climb took us through a congested area of stands where busy merchants were selling butterfly souvenirs, frying fragrant meats, and making spicy tamales and empanadas. We saw a vendor selling ice-cold green and pink drinks. They were too tantalizing to resist, because we had all become thirsty from our long journey in the hot sun.

At first, we spotted a few small groups of monarchs flying in the air overhead, clustering on the grass, or sitting together in a bush. Never having seen as many as five or ten monarchs together, we thought this was a big deal. But by the time we had climbed just ten feet higher into the sanctuary, we began to see a vast sea of orange. Butterflies covered entire trees, weighing down their branches. They filled the sky—a blizzard of butterflies. They landed on tourists' arms and heads, including my own, and were crushed under our feet, despite everyone's best efforts to avoid stepping on them.

My binoculars brought into focus whole tree trunks and boughs that were covered on every square inch with monarchs. Individual butterflies would have come into close view, except for the fact that the monarchs were all on top of one another, the way bees swarm in a hive or termites form a dense mass of insect bodies in a nest. As I looked through my binoculars, I repeatedly found myself exclaiming out loud—and often to no one! My family was scattered on all parts of the trail, oohing and aahing.

If I had to guess how many monarchs I saw in just that one day, I would say millions. I would guess, though I do not know this, that some trees held ten thousand or more. And I would say that seeing those monarchs was just as thrilling and memorable as seeing a million sparkling diamonds. I was more awed by the butterflies that day than by earthquakes and thunderstorms that I have experienced. From the trip to Angangueo, I gained an appreciation for more delicate natural spectacles.

Exposition / Description

Narrative Elements

What elements of narration, or storytelling, do you find in this paragraph?

Sensory Details

What senses does the writer appeal to in this paragraph?

Descriptive Details

Which nouns, verbs, and phrases in this paragraph help you imagine the scene?

Tone

How would you describe the writer's tone? What does it tell you about the experience?

Conclusion

How do you know that this experience was significant to the writer?

Revise

Peer Review After you complete your draft, have a peer reviewer read it. Have him or her identify which parts are most memorable and interesting, and which parts seem vague or unclear. Ask your partner to make suggestions about where to add background information, sensory details, or reflection. Remember to refer to the traits of strong writing and consider how they apply to your essay. Use the checklist below to evaluate your writing.

Checklist

- ☑ Do you reflect, or look back, on a meaningful experience?
- ☑ Do you use the first-person point of view throughout your essay?
- ☑ Do you narrate events in a logical order ?
- ☑ Do you have an introduction that sets up the topic and a conclusion that summarizes your reflections?
- ☑ Do you use sensory details, precise nouns, and action verbs?
- ☑ Do you make the significance of your experience clear?
- ☑ Is your tone appropriate for your topic?

> ## Focus Lesson

Sensory Details

Sensory details are words or phrases that appeal to one of the five senses. Well-chosen sensory details help your readers feel they are experiencing the scenes you describe. Notice how the sensory details added to the passage below contribute to the narrative and to the overall impression the writer is trying to create.

Draft:

The last part of the climb took us through a congested area of stands where merchants were selling souvenirs and food.

Revision:

The last part of the climb took us through a congested area of stands where busy merchants were selling butterfly souvenirs, <u>frying fragrant meats,</u>[1] and making <u>spicy tamales and empanadas.</u>[2] We saw a vendor selling <u>ice-cold green and pink drinks.</u>[3]

1: Appeals to Smell   **2: Appeals to Taste**   **3: Appeals to Touch and Sight**

Traits of Strong Writing

Follow these traits of strong writing to express your ideas effectively.

Ideas

Organization

Voice

Word Choice

Sentence Fluency

Conventions

Presentation

For more information on using the Traits of Strong Writing, see pages R28–R30.

Word Choice

The following academic vocabulary word is used in the student model.

individual (in′də vij′ŏŏ əl) *adj.* single; distinct; *The writer had trouble focusing on individual butterflies because so many were clustered together.*

Using academic vocabulary may help strengthen your writing. Try to use one or two academic vocabulary words in your essay. See the complete list on pages R83–R85.

Writing and Research For editing and publishing tools, go to glencoe.com and enter QuickPass code GLW6053u3.

Edit and Proofread

Get It Right When you have completed the final draft of your reflective essay, proofread it for errors in grammar, usage, mechanics, and spelling. Refer to the Language Handbook, pages R40–R59, as a guide.

> **Focus Lesson**

Unclear Pronoun References

A pronoun must always refer to a noun or a pronoun that appears earlier in the piece of writing. Make sure each of your pronouns refers to the closest noun or pronoun before it. Below are examples of how to correct unclear pronoun references.

Original: The sentence contains an unclear pronoun reference.

The author intends the pronoun *They* to refer to *ice-cold green and pink drinks,* but as it is used, it refers to the antecedent *spicy tamales and empanadas.*

The last part of the climb took us through a congested area of stands where busy merchants were selling butterfly souvenirs, frying fragrant meats, selling ice-cold green and pink drinks, and making spicy tamales and empanadas. They were too tantalizing to resist, because we had all become thirsty from our long journey in the hot sun.

Improved: Replace the pronoun with the exact noun to which it refers.

. . . selling ice-cold green and pink drinks, and making spicy tamales and empanadas. The drinks were too tantalizing to resist, . . .

Present/Publish

Final Check After you have finished editing and proofreading, make sure your essay is double-spaced with an appropriate font and margins. Give it an interesting title and check to see if your teacher has any additional presentation guidelines.

Peer Review Tip

A classmate may ask you to read his or her essay. Take notes as you read so you can give constructive feedback. Use the following questions to get started.

- Do you get a clear sense of the subject and its significance?

- Are there vivid details?

Word-Processing Tip

If you are typing your story on a computer, make sure you use an appropriate font and size. Choose a font that is easy to read and not too ornate or distracting. Many word-processing programs default to a 12-point size, which is usually adequate.

Writer's Portfolio

Place a clean copy of your reflective essay in your portfolio to review later.

Speaking, Listening, and Viewing Workshop

Reflective Presentation

Literature Connection Salman Rushdie uses an impassioned tone in his essay on the Taj Mahal, writing that the building itself "simply obliterated the million million counterfeits of it." Imagine how reading these words aloud could add to their emotional charge. An oral presentation can make your written reflections come alive for your audience. Visual aids—for example, a large, glossy photograph—are another way to show your audience what you experienced. In this workshop, you will learn how to use an oral presentation and visuals to express the significance of the events in your reflective essay.

> **Assignment**   **Deliver a Reflective Essay** Adapt your reflective essay into an oral presentation that uses appropriate voice, gestures, and visual aids.

Plan Your Presentation

Think of your presentation not as simply a spoken version of your essay, but as a chance to share your most important ideas with a live audience.

- Start by reading your essay aloud, keeping your audience in mind. Which parts of your essay sound best read aloud? Which seem to reflect your speaking style? Which images or incidents are most captivating?

- Next, go through your essay and highlight the parts you think will lend themselves best to oral delivery. Focus on the most important highlights instead of trying to present each idea.

- Adapt your essay into a script. Use the script as a study guide for remembering ideas and particularly effective phrases.

- Make note cards that include a few words and phrases that will remind you of your main points.

Focus on Main Points

Your audience cannot go back and reread parts of your presentation, as they can with an essay, so you will want to reinforce your most important ideas throughout the presentation. Look through your script and cut any details that are not related to your main points. Come back to your main ideas at the end of your presentation and restate them for your audience.

Speaking Frames

As you prepare your reflection, think about using some of the following frames to get started.

- I'd always felt that _____, until I _____.

- Like _____ [character/author], I have had the experience of _____.

Literature Online

Speaking, Listening, Viewing For project ideas, templates, and presentation tips, go to glencoe.com and enter QuickPass code GLW6053u3

Create Your Visuals

Visual aids can be a powerful way to reach your audience. Look through your script and identify images that will help your audience connect to your experience. You can use photographs or even video clips to show your audience places or things that might otherwise be difficult to visualize. Use a graphic organizer like the one below to plan your visual aids. Be sure to discuss your visuals in your presentation, and write prompts on your note cards that cue you to display each image at the correct time.

drawing of a mountain trail → picture of a monarch butterfly taking flight → photo of me surrounded by butterflies

Rehearse

After you have rehearsed on your own, present your reflection to a friend or a family member. If your teacher has given your presentation a time limit, ask the friend or the family member to time you—you may need to cut parts of your presentation to stay within the limit. Ask your friend or your family member to provide suggestions about how you could improve each of the techniques listed in the chart below.

Techniques for Presenting a Reflection

Verbal Techniques	Nonverbal Techniques
☑ **Tone** Match your tone to your subject, whether it is light or serious.	☑ **Eye Contact** Make frequent eye contact with your audience.
☑ **Pace** Speak slowly enough so the audience can react to your ideas.	☑ **Posture** Avoid leaning or slouching.
☑ **Volume** Speak loudly and clearly so your audience can understand you.	☑ **Gestures** Make natural gestures, but do not move so much that it becomes distracting.
☑ **Emphasis** Vary your emphasis, stressing important words and ideas.	☑ **Visual Aids** Present your visuals prominently, and be sure not to block them while you speak.

Presentation Tips

Use the following checklist to evaluate your presentation.

- Did you vary your tone and use natural gestures?
- Did you make eye contact with the audience?
- Did you remember not to block the visuals?
- Did you face the audience and not the visuals?

Independent Reading

Literature of the Region

THE TRADITIONAL LITERATURES OF SOUTHWEST AND SOUTH CENTRAL ASIA HAVE HAD A profound and far-reaching effect on the world from ancient times to the present. The stories of the Bible, the tales of *The Thousand and One Nights*, the fables of the *Panchatantra*, and other traditional narratives from this region have spread throughout the world, providing wisdom, inspiration, and entertainment.

Shahnameh

Ferdowsi

The national epic of Iran, the *Shahnameh*, or "Book of Kings" (1010), is a vast narrative that presents Iranian history from the creation of the world until Muslim Arab armies conquered Persia in the seventh century A.D. Writing several centuries after the Muslim conquest, the poet Ferdowsi (also spelled Firdowsi) collected and transmitted in verse form the myths and legends of his country. Though historical in nature, the epic contains many episodes and beings from the realm of fantasy including curses, supernatural creatures, and enormous birds.

Siddhartha

Hermann Hesse

German author Hermann Hesse was a prolific novelist who focused on the idea that humans could find their true selves only by unfettering themselves from the confines of society. Hesse's interest in Eastern philosophy heavily influenced his most critically acclaimed work of fiction, *Siddhartha* (1922). The novella tells the story of a young Indian mystic who gives up everything he knows and sets off on a quest to find the true meaning of life. In one sense, this is a detective story in which Siddhartha searches for clues to unravel the mystery of self.

Nectar in a Sieve

Kamala Markandaya

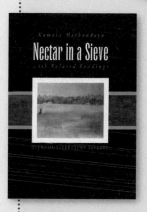

With strength and dignity, an Indian peasant woman, Rukmani, survives many hardships in life, including monsoons, drought, and famine, as India embarks upon modernization in the second half of the twentieth century.

A House for Mr. Biswas

V. S. Naipaul

Set in Trinidad in the mid-twentieth century, *A House for Mr. Biswas* draws from the author's childhood experiences as a Hindu Indian living in what was then a British colony.

Shabanu: Daughter of the Wind

Suzanne Fisher Staples

A Newbery Honor Book, Staples's first novel describes a young woman's experience growing up in the traditional nomadic culture of Pakistani desert dwellers.

CRITICS' CORNER

" . . . [T]he Nights *not only celebrates the power of stories, but offers a vision of the very act of story-telling itself as nothing less than an art form which offers both its practitioners and its listeners an opportunity to order, comprehend, define, and delimit (at least temporarily) an otherwise chaotic and incomprehensible world of experience. It is by telling stories and by hearing stories told, the* Nights *seems to say, that we come to know our world, each other, and— ultimately—our own selves.*"

—Robert L. Mack, from the Introduction to *Arabian Nights' Entertainments*

The Thousand and One Nights

Perhaps the most famous collection of tales in all world literature, *The Thousand and One Nights* (c. 700s–1500s) has no author. It is often referred to as *The Arabian Nights*, but many of its tales come from Persia and India. The frame narrative tells of Scheherazade, a brave and clever woman who outwits a brutal sultan by telling him stories night after night to prevent him from killing her.

Create a Visual Display

Read one of the books listed on these pages and create a visual display about the book for your classmates. Find or create images that represent the characters, plot, and setting. Present your display to the class.

Assessment

English–Language Arts

Reading: Fiction and Poetry

Carefully read the following two passages. Use context clues to help you define any words with which you are unfamiliar. Pay close attention to the **author's purpose, themes,** and use of **literary devices** in each text. Then, on a separate sheet of paper, answer the questions on page 666.

from *"The Raj Seal"* by Rabindranath Tagore

The elder brother of the new family was its guiding light. Everyone at home and in the neighborhood revered his opinions on all matters. He was a BA[1] and had a capable mind, but a fat salary and a position of authority did not appeal to him, neither did the whole business of contacts and patronage;
5 the British kept their distance from him, and he, likewise, preferred to keep them at arm's length. Thus, though his presence dazzled his domestic circle, he exerted little influence further afield.

Earlier, he had spent three years away in England. The courtesy of English people there had so captivated him that he had forgotten the humiliating
10 condition of his country and had returned home suited and booted in the English style.

His family had been a bit embarrassed at first, but soon they began to say that no one wore sahib's clothes as well as their elder brother. In due course, the glory of English dress penetrated to their very hearts.

15 The brother's own idea when he came back was: "I shall set the first example of how to be on equal terms with the British." By always bowing and scraping when we meet them, he maintained, we simply make ourselves inferior and at the same time do the sahibs an injustice.

He had brought back many cordial testimonials from important figures
20 in England, and so in Bengal he managed to attain some slight position in the councils of the British. Accompanied by his wife, he partook of English tea, dinner, sports and humor. His success made his blood tingle and go to his head.

It was around this time, on the occasion of the opening of a new railway
25 line, that some respectable native gentlemen, a favored few, were invited by the company to travel along the new track with the lieutenant-governor. The elder brother of the family was among them.

On the way back a railway sergeant insulted the party by compelling them to leave their special carriage. The brother, dressed in his usual English attire,

---

1. A *BA* is a person who has a bachelor of arts degree.

30 was about to get out when the official politely said, "Why are you getting up?
You may stay."

The privilege puffed him up a little, to begin with. But as the carriage rolled
on and the arid ashen-colored fields of Bengal rolled by, the dying glow of
the sun setting on the western horizon seemed like a shameful stain across

35 the whole country; the mind of the lonely passenger, observing it unwinkingly,
felt abashed. The thought of his Motherland cleft his whole heart and made
his eyes sting with tears.

An old story came to his mind. An ass was pulling a temple car along the
sacred way, and the passers-by, prostrating themselves in the dust before it

40 were offering their *pranams*.[2] "They are all worshipping me," the foolish
ass thought.

"There's only one small difference between that ass and me," the elder
brother told himself. "I have at last realized that it is not my person the British
sahibs respect, but the jacket weighing on my shoulders."

45 As soon as he reached home, he called everyone together, lit a fire and
cast into it all his English clothes, one by one, as sacrificial offerings.

---

2. *Pranams* are respectful gestures of greeting.

"Clockwork Doll" by Dahlia Ravikovitch
Translated by Chana Bloch and Ariel Bloch

That night, I was a clockwork doll
and I whirled around, this way and that,
and I fell on my face and shattered to bits
and they tried to fix me with all their skill.

5 Then I was a proper doll once again
and I did what they told me, poised and polite.
But I was a doll of a different sort,
an injured twig that dangles from a stem.

And then I went to dance at the ball,
10 but they left me alone with the dogs and cats
though my steps were measured and rhythmical.

And I had blue eyes and golden hair
and a dress all the colors of garden flowers,
and a trimming of cherries on my straw hat.

Items 1–6 apply to the passage from "The Raj Seal."

1. The statement in lines 8–11 ("The courtesy... style") suggests that the elder brother returns from England wearing English clothing because
   (A) he wants to show his power over his family
   (B) he has forgotten the customs of his country
   (C) he abhors the fashion of his own country
   (D) he has a strong desire to mock the English
   (E) he has long wanted to return to his homeland

2. In line 18, "sahibs" most nearly means
   (A) servants
   (B) family members
   (C) friends
   (D) masters
   (E) distant cousins

3. The primary purpose of the author's use of highly descriptive language in lines 32–37 is to
   (A) offer details about the landscape of Bengal
   (B) explain why the English love India
   (C) link the brother's passionate emotional reactions to his love for his homeland
   (D) show that the brother is a very sensitive young man
   (E) highlight the brother's loneliness

4. In line 36, "abashed" most nearly means
   (A) proud
   (B) ashamed
   (C) annoyed
   (D) startled
   (E) ignored

5. What does the brother do once he realizes the English value his clothes, not his character?
   (A) He throws away his English clothes.
   (B) He burns his English clothes one piece at a time.
   (C) He says his *pranams*.
   (D) He spends more time with his family.
   (E) He thinks of all the time he has wasted.

6. Which statement best expresses the moral of the story of the ass and the temple car (lines 38–41)?
   (A) It is important to respect animals.
   (B) Beauty leads to popularity.
   (C) One should not mistake the admiration of possessions for true respect.
   (D) People and animals are very similar.
   (E) One should never feel embarrassed.

Items 7–10 apply to "Clockwork Doll."

7. Which statement best describes how others treat the speaker?
   (A) They give her freedom.
   (B) They buy her gifts.
   (C) They try to control her behavior.
   (D) They physically injure her.
   (E) They treat her fairly.

8. What is the tone in lines 1–3?
   (A) hopeful
   (B) lively
   (C) angry
   (D) peaceful
   (E) straightforward

9. The "injured twig" in line 8 refers to
   (A) the speaker as a proper doll
   (B) the speaker as a clockwork doll
   (C) the speaker's feelings
   (D) the speaker as a doll of a different sort
   (E) a girl with blue eyes

10. Which of the following themes do the excerpt from "The Raj Seal" and the poem "Clockwork Doll" share?
    (A) People should not treat other humans like animals.
    (B) Conforming to expectations will not necessarily bring respect.
    (C) Physical appearance is never important.
    (D) Isolation is an unavoidable experience.
    (E) Solving problems requires a group effort.

Vocabulary Skills: Sentence Completion

For each item in the Vocabulary Skills section, choose the word or words that best complete the sentence. Write your answers on a separate sheet of paper.

1. Mohandas Gandhi's nonviolent resistance movement posed a _____ threat to British rule in India.
   (A) devoted
   (B) formidable
   (C) fatuous
   (D) stupefied
   (E) clandestine

2. Colonial schools offered Indian students the chance to pursue Western-style education; however, prejudiced teachers often _____ their students inferior.
   (A) demonstrated
   (B) deemed
   (C) waived
   (D) incurred
   (E) confounded

3. Many have _____ the caste system, focusing on the "untouchables" and their inability to break free of their _____ position.
   (A) incurred…arid
   (B) demonstrated…rare
   (C) ravaged…range
   (D) scrutinized…fettered
   (E) prevailed…treacherous

4. A(n) _____ characteristic of ancient Sumerian cities was their thick walls, which made them _____ to intruders.
   (A) inexorable…inordinate
   (B) primordial…pungent
   (C) fruitless…pristine
   (D) pristine…stupefied
   (E) distinguishing…impervious

5. According to Jewish tradition, the Israelites made a _____ with God, promising, in exchange for divine blessing, not to _____ their religious duties.
   (A) covenant…shirk
   (B) prosperity…prevail
   (C) demur…conspire
   (D) nullity…waive
   (E) austerity…sojourn

6. The years since Israel _____ itself an independent nation have been marked by unrest and _____ between Israelis and Arabs.
   (A) proclaimed…tumult
   (B) abhorred…thicket
   (C) chided…compassion
   (D) demonstrated…poignancy
   (E) redeemed…magnitude

7. The ancient Mesopotamians gained economic _____ by irrigating the _____ lands of southwest Asia.
   (A) impulse…rare
   (B) prosperity…arid
   (C) increment…inordinate
   (D) demur…shrill
   (E) range…primordial

8. Impatient for religious freedom, activists _____ for the formation of a Muslim state.
   (A) demonstrated
   (B) proclaimed
   (C) shirked
   (D) deemed
   (E) murmured

Grammar and Writing Skills: Paragraph Improvement

Read the following sentences carefully. Pay close attention to **pronouns**, **sentence types**, **punctuation**, and **introductory phrase**s. Then, on a separate sheet of paper, choose the letter of the section that shows a grammatical mistake or choose E if there is no error.

1. Biotechnology <u>is</u> an emerging industry in India, **A** <u>whose</u> economic <u>growth rate</u> continues <u>to</u> **A**   **B**   **C** <u>increase</u> each year. <u>No error</u> **D**   **E**

2. Jean Piaget <u>was</u> a <u>Swiss</u> philosopher and **A**   **B** developmental psychologist <u>know</u> primarily for **C** his <u>work with children</u>. <u>No error</u> **D**   **E**

3. The avocado, <u>that</u> originated in Mexico and **A** Guatemala, became a <u>profit-turning</u> crop for **B** California farmers in the <u>1970s</u> when **C** Americans began a <u>love affair</u> with guacamole **D** that continues today. <u>No error</u> **E**

4. <u>Without</u> talented structural engineers, **A** <u>postmodern</u> architects such as Frank Gehry **B** would not <u>be able to</u> create <u>his</u> revolutionary **C**   **D** buildings. <u>No error</u> **E**

5. <u>As</u> materials for tents, <u>sleeping bags and</u> **A**   **B** <u>backpacks</u> become more <u>lightweight</u>, pack **C** weights for hikers and backpackers continue <u>to</u> **D** drop. <u>No error</u> **E**

6. Giuseppe Garibaldi, a revolutionary leader who <u>help</u> unify Italy in the 1860s, <u>has been</u> vilified **A**   **B** by some <u>historians</u> and celebrated <u>by</u> others. **C**   **D** <u>No error</u> **E**

7. Internet banks <u>are</u> able to offer investors higher **A** interest rates <u>then</u> traditional banks because **B** they <u>employ</u> fewer workers and do not have to **C** pay rent for <u>branch locations</u>. <u>No error</u> **D**   **E**

8. *Moai*, the giant stone statues <u>on</u> Easter Island in **A** the <u>South Pacific</u>, <u>are</u> carved from <u>volcanic</u> ash **B**   **C**   **D** sometime after A.D. 1000. <u>No error</u> **E**

9. From <u>1967 to 1976</u>, when the dunk was <u>banned</u> **A**   **B** in college basketball, centers such as Lew Alcindor and Bill Walton had to develop <u>shots</u> <u>like the sky hook</u> to make use of <u>his</u> height. **C**   **D** <u>No error</u> **E**

10. The <u>antelope</u> jackrabbit, an inhabitant of the **A** Sonoran and Chihuahuan deserts, <u>uses</u> its large **B** ears to radiate heat from <u>its</u> body, a process <u>that</u> **C**   **D** regulates its body temperature. <u>No error</u> **E**

Essay

Think carefully about the following excerpt and the writing assignment below.

"Tears came to my eyes. I forgot that he was a poor Kabuli fruit-seller, while I was—but no, what was I more than he? He also was a father."

—Rabindranath Tagore, from "The Kabuliwallah"

Assignment: Write an essay in which you analyze the relationship between the narrator of "The Kabuliwallah" and the Kabuliwallah. In your essay, consider how social classes and economic divisions affect the characters. Present your ideas in a logical order and use evidence from the story to support your views. As you write, keep in mind that your essay will be checked for **ideas, organization, voice, word choice, sentence fluency, conventions,** and **presentation.**

Remember to:

- Write about the assigned topic.

- Make your writing thoughtful and interesting.

- Make sure each sentence you write contributes to your composition as a whole.

- Make sure your ideas are clear and easy for the reader to follow.

- Write about your ideas in depth so the reader is able to develop a good understanding of what you are saying.

- Proofread your writing to correct errors in spelling, capitalization, punctuation, grammar, and sentence structure.

LOG ON ▶ **Literature** Online

Assessment For additional test practice, go to glencoe.com and enter QuickPass code GLW6053u3.

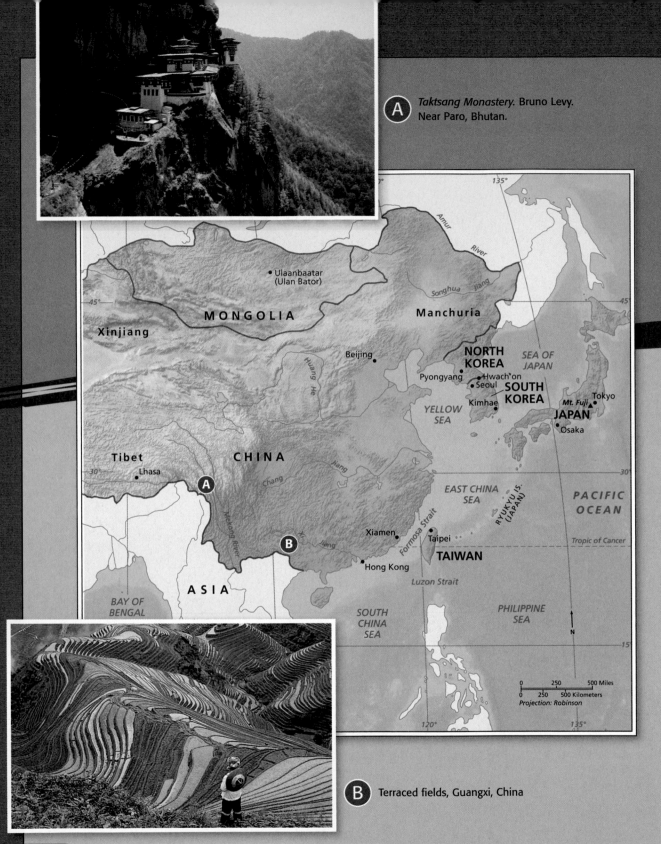

A Taktsang Monastery. Bruno Levy. Near Paro, Bhutan.

B Terraced fields, Guangxi, China

LOG ON ▶ Literature Online

Literature and Reading For more about the history and literature of this period, go to glencoe.com and enter QuickPass code GLW6053u4.

PART ONE

East Asia

2000 B.C.–Present

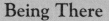

Terracotta Army, Qin Dynasty, 210 BC; horses and carriage

Being There

East Asia stretches from the windswept plains of Mongolia and the lofty plateau of Tibet, through the rich agricultural lands of eastern China, across the Yellow Sea to the mountainous peninsula of Korea, and finally to the island country of Japan. The diverse countries in the region have been bound together for centuries by culture and history. China's most fertile land is found in the eastern third of the country, where the majority of the people live. Today, South Korea is one of Asia's most technologically developed countries. Though densely populated, Japan is the most prosperous nation in Asia.

Looking Ahead

China, one of the world's oldest civilizations, has greatly influenced the culture and history of East Asia. Much of this influence stems from the philosophies of Confucianism and Taoism. From very early times, Korea and Japan followed Chinese models in government, the arts, and other areas, including familial and social structures.

Keep the following questions in mind as you read:

- How did the worldviews of Confucianism and Taoism differ?
- How did the institution of the family shape East Asian cultures?
- How have East Asian cultures responded to change?

Timeline

2000 B.C.–Present

EAST ASIAN LITERATURE

2000 B.C.

c. 1400 ▶
Earliest known Chinese written records are developed

1000 B.C.

c. 1000
Chinese begin poems in the *Book of Songs*

c. 759
Japanese compile massive poetry anthology the *Man'yo-shu* ("Collection of Ten Thousand Leaves")

6th century
Lao-tzu, founder of Taoism, lives

551
Confucius is born in China

213
Chinese emperor Qin Shihuangdi orders the destruction of most books

c. 105
Chinese invent paper

EAST ASIAN EVENTS

2000 B.C.

1900
First Chinese cities are founded

c. 1766 ▶
Shang, first historical Chinese dynasty, comes to power

1600
Chinese discover how to make bronze

Shang Dynasty Elephant-Shaped Zun. Bronze. Hunan Provincial Museum, Changsha City, China.

1000 B.C.

220 ▶
Chinese emperor Qin Shihuangdi orders the building of the Great Wall

206
Han dynasty is founded in China

WORLD EVENTS

2000 B.C.

1792–1750
Hammurabi establishes code of law in Babylon

c. 1500 ▶
Olmec civilization begins in Mexico

1000 B.C.

432
Parthenon is completed in Greece

LOG ON ▶ **Literature** Online

Literature and Reading To explore the Interactive Timeline, go to glencoe.com and enter QuickPass code GLW6053u4.

A.D. 1

701
Chinese poet Li Po is born

712
Chinese poet Tu Fu is born

868
Earliest printed book is made in China

990s
Sei Shōnagon writes *The Pillow Book* in China

A.D. 1000

1644
Japanese poet Matsuo Bashō is born

1949
Chinese poet Bei Dao is born

1968
Yasunari Kawabata becomes first Japanese author to win the Nobel Prize in Literature

2000
Gao Xingjian becomes first Chinese author to win the Nobel Prize in Literature ▶

A.D. 1

c. 65
Buddhism is introduced to China from India

552
Buddhism is introduced to Japan

794
Japan's capital is moved to Heian (later Kyoto)

▲
1260–1294
Mongol empire reaches its peak under Kublai Khan

1592–1598
Koreans fight off Japanese invasions

1854
Commodore Perry opens Japan to the West

1905
Japan defeats Russia in Russo-Japanese War

1945
Korea is divided into North and South Korea

1949
Communists take control in China

1997
Hong Kong reverts to mainland China rule

A.D. 1

476
Western Roman Empire falls

c. early ninth century
First Maori arrive in New Zealand ▼

A.D. 1000

1099
Crusaders capture Jerusalem

1521
Spanish conquer Aztec Empire

1869
Suez Canal is completed in Egypt

1901
First Nobel Prizes are awarded

1948
State of Israel is formed

▲
1994
Nelson Mandela becomes president of South Africa

Reading Check

Analyze Graphic Information How many years after the Nobel Prizes were established was the first prize in literature awarded to a Japanese author? to a Chinese author?

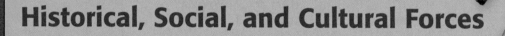

East Asia

2000 B.C.–Present

Historical, Social, and Cultural Forces

Early China

China's geographical isolation and lack of outside contact allowed it to develop one culture across many regions and preserve a strong sense of national identity. From the beginning of its recorded history until the early 1900s, China was governed by dynasties, or lines of rulers from the same family. The Shang, China's first dynasty, came to power around 1766 B.C.

Perhaps the most important cultural contribution of early China was the creation and development of the Chinese written language. By Shang times, the Chinese had developed a simple script that is the ancestor of the highly complex written language of today.

Warring States

The Shang rulers were succeeded around 1045 B.C. by the Zhou dynasty, which lasted for almost 800 years. During its final centuries, Zhou China fragmented into a number of small states that challenged the Zhou ruler. This decline led to a long and bloody conflict known as the "Period of Warring States," which began in 475 B.C. This disorder ended when the ruler of the state of Qin (chin) conquered his rivals in 221 B.C. and became

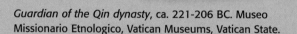

Guardian of the Qin dynasty, ca. 221-206 BC. Museo Missionario Etnologico, Vatican Museums, Vatican State.

Qin Shihuangdi (chin′shir′hwäng′dē′), China's first emperor. A tireless, ruthless ruler, Qin Shihuangdi exercised both great vision and great brutality in his effort to strengthen and unify China. He instituted a uniform writing system and code of laws, but he also ordered the destruction of most books and executed scholars who opposed his policies.

> "The King of Qin has the heart of a tiger or a wolf. Once he really has his way, he will hold the whole world captive."
>
> —Sima Qian,
> from *The Records of the Grand Historian*

The Golden Age of China

The period from the T'ang dynasty (A.D. 618–907) through the Ming dynasty (1368–1644) was a golden age of Chinese literature and art. The invention of printing during the T'ang dynasty helped to make literature more readily available and popular. The T'ang dynasty is viewed as the great age of poetry in China. The poets Li Po (see pages 694–699) and Tu Fu (see pages 703–706) were both prolific during this period.

Japan

As with China, geography significantly influenced the development of Japan. Isolated on their island chain, the ancient Japanese were close enough to the mainland to conduct a kind of cultural exchange with China, but far enough away to retain their political and cultural independence. From China, the Japanese absorbed Buddhism, the Chinese writing system, and T'ang poetry. These influences combined with Japan's native religious system of Shinto ("the way of the gods"), which focuses on harmony with nature and reverence for deities and spiritual elements of nature.

By about A.D. 400, the leader of the Yamato clan established the first unified Japanese state. Over the succeeding centuries, emperors became largely ceremonial figureheads, and the heads of various ruling clans exercised the real political power. In 794 the imperial capital was moved to the city of Heian, which was later called Kyoto. The aristocrats of the Heian court created a culture that still reflected Chinese influence but was increasingly Japanese in character. This period was Japan's golden age of literature.

Beginning in 1156, a series of civil wars broke out between two great clans that lasted for more than 30 years. When it was over, the emperor bestowed on the head of the victorious clan the title of *shogun*, or "general," which became hereditary. Japan remained a feudal society governed by a series of shogunates until the mid-1860s.

Under this feudal system, powerful lords governed large territories. Military retainers called samurai, who lived according to a strict code of honor and behavior called the Bushido ("The Way of the Warrior"), supported the lords. Besides the development of military skills, the Bushido emphasized such virtues as loyalty, courage, honor, frugality, and self-discipline.

Modern East Asia

In the twentieth century, China, Korea, and Japan underwent massive social, political, and technological changes. During the first half of the century, China endured revolution, civil war, and occupation by the Japanese during World War II. In 1949 the People's Republic of China was established, ruled by communist leader Mao Tse-tung (mau′ dzə′ doong′). Mao's government achieved some important social reforms; Chinese women, for example, gained new freedoms. Attempts in the 1950s to improve farming, however, led to famine, and the Cultural Revolution—Mao's effort to renew a revolutionary spirit throughout the country in the 1960s and 1970s—resulted in widespread abuses and stifled creativity. Since Mao's death in 1976, modified capitalist techniques have been used to encourage growth in industry and agriculture.

Shojiro with a sword, 1924. Natori Shunsen. Colour woodblock print. Private collection.

Jade carving of Immortal with Crane holding Ling Zhi Fungus, 18th century. Oriental Museum, Durham University, UK.

The Chinese often draw from a variety of traditions in responding to life. As an old Chinese proverb says, "The wise become Confucian in good times, Buddhist in bad times, and Taoist in old age."

Confucianism

Born in 551 B.C., Confucius (see pages 684–688) was deeply troubled by the violence and moral decay of his time. He presented a series of ideas, known as Confucianism, to restore social order. This philosophy became the backbone of Chinese culture. According to Confucianism, the key to life was to behave in harmony with the *Tao* (dou) or "Way," the principle of order in the universe. Five basic relationships, each with its own code of ethics, encapsulate this order: parent and child, husband and wife, old and young, friend and friend, ruler and subject.

According to Confucianism, rulers had a duty to be virtuous and subjects had a duty to be loyal. The Chinese believed their rulers governed according to the "Mandate of Heaven." If rulers were fair and effective, they received a divine mandate, or authority to rule. If rulers did not govern properly—as indicated by poor crops or losses in battle—they lost the mandate to someone else who then started a new dynasty.

Taoism

In Chinese tradition, Lao-tzu (see pages 689–693), or the "Old Master," was a contemporary of Confucius. Scholars cannot confirm if Lao-tzu actually existed, but the ideas associated with him became known as Taoism (dou′iz′əm) and gained popularity in the fifth and fourth centuries B.C. A belief in the *Tao Te Ching* links Taoism and Confucianism, yet each philosophy defines it in sharply contrasting ways. Taoism encourages people to ignore the dictates of society, live spontaneously, and not interfere with nature. To the Taoist, wisdom is represented by the principle of *wu wei* (wōō′wā′), meaning "nonaction" or "letting things take their natural course."

> *"The world is sacred.*
> *It can't be improved.*
> *If you tamper with it, you'll ruin it.*
> *If you treat it like an object, you'll*
>   *lose it."*
>
> —Lao-tzu, from the *Tao Te Ching*

Buddhism

When Buddhism was introduced to China from India during the first century A.D., it mixed with the indigenous philosophies of Confucianism and Taoism. Buddhism later spread to Korea and Japan. The fundamental principle of Buddhist *dharma*, or doctrine, is that a person should live a pure and upright life without becoming attached to worldly desires.

Reading Check

Compare and Contrast How do Confucianism and Taoism differ in their approach to the *Tao*?

Big Idea 2
Family and Tradition

The first group most of us experience is the family, and our ideas about what society will expect are based on values learned at home. The family was the most important social unit in ancient China and became the foundation for traditional Chinese values. In Japan, tradition also manifested itself in the royal court.

Filial Piety

As in most agricultural societies, the ancient Chinese viewed the family as the basic economic and social unit. However, the family took on an almost sacred quality as a symbol of the entire social order. Confucianism, China's most influential philosophical tradition, was one of the major factors that contributed to the central position of the family. At the heart of Confucianism was the idea of "filial piety," the duty of family members to subordinate their needs and desires to those of the male head of the family. Male supremacy was a key element in the social system of ancient China.

> *"The duty of children to their parents is the foundation from which all virtues spring."*
>
> —Confucius, from *The Analects*

The World of the Courtier

Beginning in the early seventh century A.D., the rulers of Japan sent cultural missions to China to further adopt Chinese styles and customs. A century after the imperial court was established at Heian in 794, the Japanese decided to end these missions. In the period that followed, an elite group of about 3,000 Japanese aristocrats, calling themselves "dwellers among the clouds," created Heian culture. Although these aristocrats still deeply admired Chinese culture, Japanese elements began to predominate in Heian court life, whose focus was a quest for beauty.

The Heian court's cultivation of the beautiful pervaded all activities, from elegantly wrapping a gift to carefully choosing the colors of the garments courtiers wore. People devoted hours each day to writing letters in pristine script, as beautiful calligraphy was believed to display the writer's character. During this period the women who wrote diaries, journals, essays, letters, and fiction produced much of Japan's earliest prose literature. These include Sei Shōnagon's journal, *The Pillow Book* (see pages 716–728), and the world's first novel, *The Tale of Genji* by Murasaki Shikibu—a masterpiece of Japanese literature.

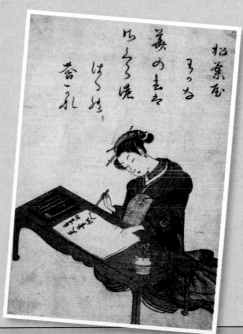

A courtesan writing, 1770. Suzuki Harunobu. British Library, London.

Reading Check

Analyze Cause-and-Effect Relationships How did the end of the Japanese cultural missions to China affect the development of Heian culture?

Big Idea 3
Moments of Reflection

Depictions of nature in Western cultures tend to portray timelessness, power, danger, and mystery. In contrast, Chinese and Japanese literature emphasize the delicacy and fleetingness of natural beauty.

> *On a withered branch*
> *a crow has settled—*
> *autumn nightfall*
>
> —Bashō,
> translated by Harold G. Henderson

Snowfall over Ukimodo Shrine at Katata, from *Eight Views of Omi,* 1918. Ito Shinsui. Colour woodblock print. British Library, London, UK.

Nature and Feeling

This famous haiku by Bashō vividly conveys the passing of the seasons. Its mood is reflective and melancholy, suggesting the fleeting nature of life. The natural imagery and universal theme of this haiku relate to a cultural touchstone. As Professor Yuriko Saito observes of Japan, "This frequent association between transience of nature and transience of human life stems from the conviction that nature and man are essentially the same, rooted in the same principle of existence."

From the Heian period to the present, Japanese poets have used two very brief poetic forms, the tanka (see pages 712–715) and the haiku (see pages 738–742) to capture glimpses of nature that express how swiftly all things pass. These reflections have cultural underpinnings in Shintoism and Buddhism, including Zen Buddhism, which convey the interrelation of nature and human life. Ki no Tsurayuki, a Japanese author of the Heian period, noted that this type of poetic reflection strikes people "when they [are] startled into thoughts on the brevity of their lives by seeing the dew on the grass or the foam on the water."

Traditional Chinese poetry similarly employs natural imagery to express human frailty. In a lyric by the great T'ang poet Tu Fu, for example, he compares himself to a tiny shore-bird dwarfed by the vastness of its surroundings: "Flitting, flitting, what am I like / But a sand-snipe in the wide, wide world!"

Time and Memory

The emphasis in traditional Chinese and Japanese poetry on the transitory nature of human life coexists with the frequent use of dreams, personal memories, and meditations on the distant past. For instance, in Tu Fu's "Jade Flower Palace" (see pages 703–706), the speaker reflects on the ruins of an ancient palace. These writings often set the span of a human life against the backdrop of the natural world, including the relative longevity of such things as mountains and the slow, relentless effects of erosion. In other instances, this literature focuses on the brief lifespan of flora and fauna in relation to humans. Both approaches create poignant views on the passage of time and elegant reflections on the beauty and brevity of life.

Reading Check

Make Generalizations How would you characterize the depiction of nature in traditional Chinese and Japanese literature?

Wrap-Up

Legacy of the Periods

Confucian ideals remain essential to the Chinese, despite communist attacks on "old ideas" during the Cultural Revolution of the late 1960s. Like Confucianism, Taoism continues to influence the Chinese worldview. The Chinese often draw from both traditions in responding to life.

The literature of the Heian court, particularly *The Tale of Genji*, has helped define Japanese culture. Episodes from *The Tale of Genji* are as familiar to the Japanese as scenes from Shakespeare's plays are to Westerners.

The view that both nature and human life are fleeting is essential to the cultures of East Asia.

Scene from the Tale of Genji, 16th century. Japanese school. Ink colour and gold leaf on paper. Brooklyn Museum of Art, NY.

Cultural and Literary Links

The writings of Confucius and his disciple Mencius were favorite reading of the nineteenth-century American authors known as the Transcendentalists, particularly Ralph Waldo Emerson and Henry David Thoreau.

Irish poet W. B. Yeats modeled two of his later plays on Japanese Noh drama, to which the American poet Ezra Pound introduced him.

Early twentieth-century British and American poets known as the Imagists wrote brief, concrete lyrics inspired by Japanese haiku.

LOG ON ▶ **Literature** Online

Unit Resources For additional skills practice, go to glencoe.com and enter QuickPass code GLW6053u4.

Activities

Use what you have learned about the period to do one of these activities.

1. **Follow Up** Go back to the Looking Ahead on page 673 and answer the questions.

2. **Contrast Literary Periods** Research American Transcendentalism and compare its views about virtue and wisdom with those presented in this introduction.

3. **Build Visual Literacy** Research ancient and modern illustrations for *The Tale of Genji*. Create a visual display exhibiting the different styles artists have used in interpreting the characters and episodes.

4. **Take Notes** You might try using this study organizer to keep track of the Big Ideas in this part.

 FOLDABLES Study Organizer **THREE-TAB BOOK**

Big Idea 1 Big Idea 2 Big Idea 3

Before You Read

from the *Analects*

Meet **Confucius**

(551 B.C.–479 B.C.)

No individual has had a greater influence on Chinese culture and thought than the philosopher and teacher Confucius (kən fū′shəs). Until the early twentieth century, his collection of teachings, the *Analects*, was required reading for Chinese government officials. For more than 2,000 years, the Chinese Empire felt the influence of his emphasis on duty and responsibility.

> *"I am not one who was born in the possession of knowledge; I am one who is fond of antiquity, and earnest in seeking it there."*
>
> —Confucius

The Master Confucius was born in eastern China in 551 B.C. during a period of great upheaval. War had broken out, and the social order had broken down. Though his birth name was K'ung Qiu, he later became known by the title "Master K'ung" (K'ung-fu-tzu), which was Westernized as "Confucius." Although Confucius was born into poverty, he was well-educated. Consumed with a desire for knowledge, he eagerly learned everything he could, and by age fifteen he considered himself a scholar.

In his early thirties, Confucius began teaching his philosophies, and he went on to devote his entire life to education and scholarship. He believed preserving traditions and practicing moderation and benevolence was the only way to save Chinese society. He is regarded as the first person in China to believe that education should be available to all people, not just the wealthy or noble classes.

Spreading the Word During his forties and fifties, Confucius traveled throughout China in an attempt to gain an important government position through which he could integrate his philosophies and spur social change. Though he was appointed magistrate and served in a few minor positions, he could not convince any rulers to accept his philosophies of reform. When he was 67, Confucius returned home to teach his philosophies to his followers, who numbered well into the thousands.

Confucius died at the age of 73, leaving no records of his sayings and beliefs. His followers collected his teachings and published them posthumously, and they continued to spread his philosophies throughout the world.

 Literature Online

Author Search For more about Confucius, go to glencoe.com and enter QuickPass code GLW6053u4.

Literature and Reading Preview

Connect to the Sacred Text

In this excerpt, Confucius states, "Never do to others what you would not like them to do to you." What does this saying mean to you? Discuss this question with a partner.

Build Background

At the core of Confucianism are the concepts of *jen* and *li. Jen*, meaning "love," "goodness," "humanness" or "benevolence," is Confucianism's most important virtue. *Li* means "ritual," "etiquette," or simply "good manners." In Confucian philosophy, relationships function smoothly when correct etiquette, or *li*, is observed.

Set Purposes for Reading

Big Idea Virtue and Wisdom

As you read, ask yourself, What emphasis does Confucius place on duty, morality, and respect?

Literary Element Maxim

A **maxim** is a short saying that contains a general truth or gives practical advice about how to behave and live morally. As you read, look for the maxims Confucius includes and ask yourself, What general truths or advice is he expressing?

Reading Strategy Make Generalizations

A **generalization** is a general statement or rule. When you make a generalization, you gather details from a text and then form a broad statement that can apply to life in general, or to several situations. As you read, ask yourself, How do Confucius's statements apply to life in general?

Tip: Convert Information Use a graphic organizer like the one below to record key details that reveal what is important to Confucius. Then convert those details into a generalization about how Confucius believes people should behave.

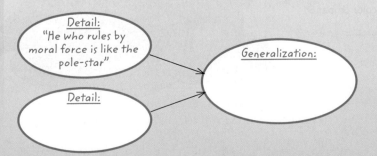

Detail: "He who rules by moral force is like the pole-star"

Detail:

Generalization:

Vocabulary

homage (hom′ij) *n.* the honor or respect that is shown to another person; p. 687 *The priests paid homage to the Pope when they visited the Vatican.*

docile (dos′əl) *adj.* easily taught; obedient; p. 687 *The docile students listened attentively to the tour guide as he explained one of Picasso's paintings.*

dictates (dik′tāts) *n.* principles that must be followed; p. 687 *The dictates of society state that we should not steal.*

extent (ıks tent′) *n.* amount or distance; p. 687 *The judge punished the thief to the greatest extent of the law.*

Tip: Synonyms Synonyms are words that have the same, or similar, meaning. They can often serve as context clues. For example, in the sentence *The docile students listened attentively to the guide, docile* must mean "easily taught" if the students listened attentively.

After You Read

Respond and Think Critically

Respond and Interpret

1. Which of Confucius's maxims did you find most memorable or intriguing? Explain.

2. (a)What simile does Confucius use in the first saying? (b)How do you interpret this simile?

3. What do you think Confucius means when he compares some sons' treatment of their parents to their treatment of dogs and horses?

4. (a)In the fifth saying, what kind of person does Confucius say will find happiness? (b)How does he view ill-gotten wealth? (c)Do you agree or disagree with his views? Explain.

Analyze and Evaluate

5. (a)How does Confucius say people should behave every day? (b)How is this saying central to his philosophy?

6. (a)Why do you think Confucius teaches that a simple life will lead to happiness? (b)What is he implying about people and their values?

Connect

7. **Big Idea** **Virtue and Wisdom** What proverbs or sayings have you heard that express sentiments similar to those of Confucius?

8. **Connect to Today** Do you think Confucius's ideas about people and society are still relevant today? Why or why not?

Literary Element Maxim

Many of the ideas contained in the *Analects* are conveyed as **maxims**. Throughout the centuries, philosophers and writers have often used maxims to offer instruction on morality and behavior.

1. What maxim is included in the second saying?

2. Why might Confucius say this maxim represents his teachings better than his other sayings?

Reading Strategy Make Generalizations

Refer to the web diagram you made on page 685 as you answer the following questions.

1. What generalization can you make about Confucius's views on society?

2. (a)What generalization can you make about the way people behaved at the time? (b)Does this differ from how people behave today? Explain.

LOG ON ▶ **Literature** Online

Selection Resources For Selection Quizzes, eFlashcards, and Reading-Writing Connection activities, go to glencoe. com and enter QuickPass code GLW6053u4.

Vocabulary Practice

Practice with Synonyms With a partner, match each boldfaced vocabulary word below with its synonym. Use a thesaurus or dictionary to check your answers.

1. homage   a. rules

2. docile   b. reverence

3. dictates   c. degree

4. extent   d. passive

🚀 **Writing**

Write Guidelines To establish a productive and fair environment, many groups create guidelines, or a code of conduct, that explain how people should behave and treat one another. Using Confucius's sayings as a model, write guidelines for a group of classmates, co-workers, or teammates. Feel free to diverge from Confucius's views when you disagree with them and present a few of your points as **maxims**.

Before You Read

from the *Tao Te Ching*

Meet **Lao-tzu**
(sixth century B.C.)

> "*Manifest plainness,*
> *Embrace simplicity,*
> *Reduce selfishness,*
> *Have few desires.*"
>
> —Lao-tzu,
> from Verse 19 of the *Tao Te Ching*

The life of Lao-tzu (lou´dzu´), the legendary author of the *Tao Te Ching* (dou´tā´ching´), is shrouded in mystery. Some scholars question whether he lived at all, and if he did, whether he was the author of the *Tao Te Ching*. To many followers of Taoism (dou´i´zəm), which is a way of approaching life based on the *Tao Te Ching*, Lao-tzu was a mythical figure who could adopt different personalities and who lived more than 200 years. Modern followers of Taoism embrace the philosophy credited to Lao-tzu: living a peaceful life of nonaction in harmony with nature.

A Legendary Meeting According to a biography written around 100 B.C. by the ancient Chinese historian Ssu-ma Ch'ien, Lao-tzu lived around 600 B.C. and served as a *shih* (a scholar of astrology and divination) to the kingdom of Chou (jō). In the biography, Ssu-ma Ch'ien says that while Lao-tzu was at the royal court, he met with Confucius (see pages 684–688) and criticized him for his pride and ambition. Ssu-ma Ch'ien goes on to say the chastened younger philosopher was so impressed by Lao-tzu he later spoke to his followers admiringly of him. While modern scholars doubt such a meeting took place, the story speaks to the relationship between Confucianism and Taoism in China.

Recording the Tao Another celebrated story in Ssu-ma Ch'ien's biography describes a trip Lao-tzu embarked on late in life. According to the biography, Lao-tzu left the royal court and rode off to the west, eventually coming to a gate in the wall at the edge of the kingdom. There the keeper of the gate asked him to write down his knowledge. Lao-tzu complied, recording his ideas in the 81-verse *Tao Te Ching* ("classic of the way of power"). Scholars, however, believe the *Tao Te Ching* was compiled by followers of Taoism in the fourth and third centuries B.C. Regardless of the authorship of the *Tao Te Ching*, its profound influence on Chinese culture and the cultures of many other Asian nations is undisputed.

Taoism spread as both a religion and a philosophy. Some religious Taoists sought to gain longevity, wealth, and even immortality through various mystical practices. However, it is as a philosophy, a way of approaching and understanding the world, that Taoism has had its greatest influence.

Literature and Reading Preview

Connect to the Sacred Text

Is violence ever necessary? If so, under what circumstances? Freewrite for a few minutes about this question.

Build Background

Taoism arose in response to the same conditions—war, chaos, and corruption—that produced Confucianism. But while Confucius hoped to reform society by promoting a strict code of social behavior, Lao-tzu recommended living in harmony with the natural world. At the heart of his philosophy is the principle of *wu wei* (wōō′wā′), meaning "nonaction" or "letting things take their natural course." Rather than inaction, *wu wei* stresses living free from worldly desires and in accordance with the underlying harmony of nature.

Set Purposes for Reading

Big Idea Virtue and Wisdom

As you read, ask yourself, What ideas in the *Tao Te Ching* illustrate the Taoist belief in nonaction and letting things take their natural course?

Literary Element Parallelism

Parallelism is the use of a series of words, phrases, or lines that have similar grammatical structure. Authors employ this technique in a literary work to emphasize an idea or emotion, to convey a sense of unity or balance, or to create a musical effect. As you read, look for examples of parallelism and ask yourself, What purposes might these uses of parallelism serve?

Reading Strategy Question

When you **question**, you ask yourself regularly whether you are comprehending what you read. It is similar to a running dialogue you conduct with yourself that helps you understand a text and connect it to your own experiences. As you read, ask yourself, Do I understand each section of the text?

....

Tip: Take Notes Use a chart like the one shown to record the questions that occur to you and your answers to them.

Questions	Answers
Why are weapons tools of fear?	People use them to defend themselves when they are afraid of being attacked.

Learning Objectives

For pages 689–693

In studying this text, you will focus on the following objectives:

Literary Study: Analyzing parallelism.

Reading: Questioning.

Writing: Writing a blog.

Vocabulary

detest (di test′) *v.* dislike intensely; hate; p. 691 *Used to doing as he pleased at home, the boy detested his aunt's rules.*

endure (en door′) *v.* continue to exist; last; p. 692 *If you take good care of yourself, you have a better chance of enduring for a long time.*

tamper (tam′pər) *v.* meddle improperly; p. 692 *To trick their mother into letting them stay up late, the children tampered with the settings on the clock.*

....

Tip: Analogies To complete an analogy, decide on the relationship represented by the first pair of words. Then apply that relationship to the second pair of words. For example, in the analogy *endure : continue :: terminate : end*, both sets of words are synonyms.

from the

TAO TE CHING

Lao-tzu
Translated by Stephen Mitchell

31

Weapons are the tools of violence;
all decent men **detest** them.

Weapons are the tools of fear;
a decent man will avoid them
5   except in the direst[1] necessity
and, if compelled, will use them
only with the utmost restraint.
Peace is his highest value.
If the peace has been shattered,
10   how can he be content?
His enemies are not demons,
but human beings like himself.
He doesn't wish them personal harm.
Nor does he rejoice in victory.
15   How could he rejoice in victory
and delight in the slaughter of men?

He enters a battle gravely,
with sorrow and with great compassion,
as if he were attending a funeral.

---

1. *Direst* (dīr′est) refers to an extreme condition of urgency
or desperation.

Virtue and Wisdom *How do these lines illustrate Taoist beliefs?*

Vocabulary

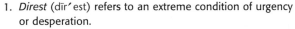

detest (di test′) *v.* dislike intensely; hate

Bronze Horseman with Spears. Eastern
Han Dynasty, 2nd century A.D. Height: 53 cm.
National Museum, Beijing, China.

Before You Read

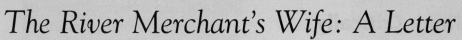

The River Merchant's Wife: A Letter

Meet **Li Po**
(701–762)

> "[Li Po is] an immortal banished from heaven."
>
> —Ho Chih-chang, contemporary of Li Po

L i Po's (lē′ pō′) vast talent, personal charisma, and eccentric lifestyle made his life the stuff of legend. One story, likely true, says the poet died when he fell out of a boat and drowned while trying to grasp the moon's reflection in the water, an appropriately poetic story for such a colorful character.

A Vagabond Life Li Po grew up in the south-western province of Szechwan (sech′wän′). A well-educated young man from a good family, he chose not to take the test for imperial service most young men in his position took. Having shown an early talent for writing poetry, he probably could have had a career as a court poet, but he had other plans.

When Li Po was about 24 years old, he set out on his own. He lived as a hermit for a time, spending several years practicing Taoism in the mountains. Then he began a series of journeys that took him all over China. A colorful and intriguing personality, he made many friends during his travels. Among his friends were government officials, other hermits, and fellow poets, including Tu Fu (see page 703).

Skilled Swordsman, Banished Poet As he traveled, Li Po served as a wandering knight and honed his skill as a swordsman. During this time, his fame as a poet grew, and even the emperor came to admire him. When he was in his early forties, Li Po joined a group of distinguished court poets in Ch'ang-an, the T'ang dynasty capital. He kept this position for two years, until his wild behavior prompted his hosts to dismiss him.

In his mid-fifties, Li Po served as an unofficial poet laureate with the military expedition of Prince Lin, the emperor's sixteenth son. After the prince came under suspicion for wanting to set up an independent kingdom, Li Po abandoned him, and the prince was later executed. Because of his association with the prince, Li Po was arrested and imprisoned for a short time, and by the summer of 758, he was banished from the province. However, the sentence was revoked as he was on his way into exile, and he returned to eastern China.

Li Po's work was praised both during and after his lifetime for its lyrical style, rich imagery, and expression of emotion. His work endures for its moving reflections on nature, friendship, soli-tude, and the passage of time.

Literature Online

Author Search For more about Li Po, go to glencoe.com and enter QuickPass code GLW6053u4.

Literature and Reading Preview

Connect to the Poem

How would you feel if someone you loved had been gone for five months? Write a journal entry exploring this question.

Build Background

Many believe China's greatest poetry was written during the T'ang dynasty (A.D. 618–907), when Li Po lived. Two common types of T'ang verse are the "occasion poem" and the "character poem." Poets wrote occasion poems when extending an invitation or after seeing a friend. Character poems, such as "The River-Merchant's Wife: A Letter," describe character types of the period.

Set Purposes for Reading

Big Idea Family and Tradition

As you read the poem, ask yourself, How are ancient Chinese traditions, such as arranged marriages and loyalty, portrayed?

Literary Element Tone

The **tone** of a literary work is the author's or speaker's attitude toward his or her audience or subject. A work's tone can usually be described with a single adjective, such as sympathetic or critical, formal or informal, silly or serious, angry or calm. An author uses word choice, punctuation, sentence structure, and figures of speech to convey tone. As you read the poem, ask yourself, What clues indicate the speaker's attitude toward the subject matter?

Reading Strategy Visualize

Imagine a friend is describing her vacation—the bright sunshine of a clear fall afternoon, the foothills ablaze with crimson-leafed maple trees. You can picture the scene even though you've never been there because you're **visualizing** what your friend saw, or forming a mental picture of what she's describing. To visualize when you read, pay attention to concrete nouns, sensory details, adjectives, and active verbs. As you read the poem, ask yourself, What would this scene look like?

....

Tip: Focus on Details Create a chart like this one to keep track of the details that help you visualize the characters and the setting.

Stanza	Character Details	Setting Details
1	Hair cut straight across forehead	Near front gate, pulling flowers

Learning Objectives

For pages 694–699

In studying this text, you will focus on the following objectives:

Literary Study: Analyzing tone.

Reading: Visualizing.

Listening and Speaking: Presenting an oral interpretation.

Sakasai Ferry, plate 67 from the series *One Hundred Famous Views of Edo,* 1857. Ando or Utagawa Hiroshige. Woodblock print. Brooklyn Museum of Art, NY.

After You Read

Respond and Think Critically

Respond and Interpret

1. What images or lines from this poem did you find particularly memorable? Explain.

2. (a)According to lines 7–10, how did the speaker feel after she first married? (b)According to lines 11–14, how did her feelings change over time?

3. (a)How long has the speaker's husband been gone? (b)Was he eager to leave? Cite passages from the poem to support your response.

4. (a)What do the moss, falling leaves, and butterflies signify to the speaker? (b)Why might the butterflies hurt her?

Analyze and Evaluate

5. (a)In lines 26–29, what does the speaker say she will do? (b)What do these lines reveal about her feelings toward her husband?

6. (a)How would you describe the overall **mood**, or feeling, of this poem? (b)Which images in the poem help convey that mood?

Connect

7. **Big Idea** **Family and Tradition** What does this poem reveal about ancient Chinese traditions regarding love and marriage?

8. **Connect to Today** (a)How are the social customs and habits described in this poem different from or similar to those in the United States today? (b)What advantages and disadvantages do you see in each system?

Literary Element Tone

SAT Skills Practice

1. The word choice in lines 1–6 gives the first stanza a tone of

   (A) regretfulness

   (B) playfulness

   (C) nostalgia

   (D) sorrowfulness

   (E) jubilation

2. The sentence structure in line 25 ("They hurt me. I grow older.") reflects the speaker's

   (A) detachment

   (B) bitterness

   (C) annoyance

   (D) hopefulness

   (E) disappointment

Review: Setting

As you learned on page 108, **setting** is the time and place in which the events of a poem or story take place. The setting includes the physical surroundings as well as the ideas, customs, values, and beliefs of the people who live there.

Partner Activity Meet with a classmate and discuss the setting of this poem. With your partner, complete a chart like the one below. Fill it in with details from the poem and what those details suggest about the setting.

Detail	Setting
Bamboo stilts	Bamboo suggests China; stilts as a child's toy suggest the past
Narrator is married at age fourteen to a man she calls "My Lord."	

Reading Strategy   Visualize

Reread lines 19–25, and **visualize** the young woman who has fallen in love with her husband and misses him in his absence. How does she appear to you? How is she dressed? How is her hair arranged? Does she look sad, tired, or upset? As you visualize the scene, you can add details the author has not included.

1. Make a list of concrete nouns, sensory details, adjectives, and other words that help you visualize these lines.

2. Make a storyboard, or a series of sketches, that illustrates what you visualize when you read these lines.

Academic Vocabulary

*Li Po **displays** the passage of time in his poem through such imagery as moss growing by the gate and leaves falling.*

Display is a commonly used academic word. In more familiar usage, a store seeking an employee might **display** a "Help Wanted" sign in its window. To further explore the meaning of this word, answer the following question: In what sort of situation have you been called upon to **display** leadership skills?

For more on academic vocabulary, see pages 36–37 and R83–R85.

Silk embroidery panel with flowers and ducks found in Dunhuang caves, China, 9th-10th century. British Museum, London.

Listening and Speaking

Oral Interpretation

Assignment Poets write for both the ear and the eye. With this in mind, read "The River-Merchant's Wife: A Letter" aloud and explain your interpretation of it.

Prepare Reread the poem to make sure you grasp its meaning. Take notes and keep in mind the details you recorded in your chart on page 695 to help your audience visualize the poem.

Perform Type your own copy of the poem, re-creating it exactly. Use this copy as your script; highlight key words you want to emphasize, mark where you should pause, and note the tone you want to use.

EXAMPLE:

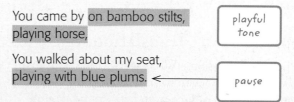

You came by on bamboo stilts, playing horse,   *playful tone*

You walked about my seat, playing with blue plums. ←   *pause*

Follow your script as you recite, and try to reflect the tone of the poem in your vocal and physical presentation. When you finish reading, explain your interpretation of the poem and how you tried to express it through your reading.

Evaluate Write a paragraph assessing the effectiveness of your oral interpretation and describe if and how you better understand the poem's meaning and style after this experience. Look at the rubric on page 167 to help rate your presentation.

LOG ON ▶ **Literature** Online

Selection Resources For Selection Quizzes, eFlashcards, and Reading-Writing Connection activities, go to glencoe.com and enter QuickPass code GLW6053u4.

Creating a Work of Beauty

"THE RIVER MERCHANT'S WIFE: A LETTER" IS EZRA POUND'S translation—the most beloved translation—of Li Po's poem "The Song of Ch'ang-Kan." Yet many scholars would call it a new work, not a translation, because Pound did not render Li Po's lines word-for-word. He also made a number of changes in the grammar, structure, and meaning of the original. Others consider Pound's version to be a translation of superior quality, believing it best captures the spirit and formal beauty of Li Po's original Chinese. A translator's decision whether to mirror the original text or depart from it is one aspect of the art of translation.

Approaches to Translation

The poet and translator W. S. Merwin has written that when he first began to translate poetry as a student, he sought advice from Ezra Pound. Pound urged Merwin to "get as close to the original as possible" and to focus on "the seed," not "the leaves," of the work. Sometimes getting close to the original source means not interpreting it literally, but rather encapsulating its spirit, or seed. One can see this paradox at work in Pound's translation of Li Po's poem.

Li Po	藍	藍	河	旁	草
Chinese	Sei	Sei	Ka	Han	So
Fenollosa	blue	blue	river	bank side	grass
Pound	Blue, blue is the grass about the river				

Knowing virtually no Chinese, Pound based his translation on notes acquired from the American scholar Ernest Fenollosa (1853–1908). In various notebooks, Fenollosa had written lines from Chinese poems, the equivalent English words, and explanatory notes. Pound transformed these jottings into lines of exquisite beauty.

As the example below suggests, though Pound did not render the Chinese poem word-for-word, he managed to convey its essential meaning. Pound's mastery of poetry guided his work, enabling him, for instance, to capture the modest and naive voice of a young Chinese woman in "The River Merchant's Wife: A Letter." It also helped him—despite his ignorance of Chinese—to convey the clear, concise style and fresh imagery of Li Po's poem.

Sound and Sense

A good translator must not only understand other cultures, but have a feel for the music of language. One translation may be more accurate than others, but if it lacks the music of the original, it may not be the best. Wai-lim Yip's version of Li Po's poem, for example, is closer to the original than Pound's, but it lacks the musical phrasing of Pound's translation. Pound often ignored the literal meaning of a Chinese character—for instance, writing "blue plums" where other translators wrote "green plums"—to achieve a softer, more melodious effect. By making such choices, he created a work of elegance and beauty. Three translations of the beginning of Li Po's poem follow.

Witter Bynner

My hair had hardly covered my forehead.
I was picking flowers, playing by my door,
When you, my lover, on a bamboo horse,
Came trotting in circles and throwing green plums.
We lived near together on a lane in Ch'ang-kan,
Both of us young and happy-hearted.

Wai-lim Yip

My hair barely covered my forehead.
I played in front of the gate, plucking flowers,
You came riding on a bamboo-horse
And around the bed we played with green plums.
We were then living in Ch'ang-kan.
Two small people, no hate nor suspicion.

Florence Ayscough and Amy Lowell

When the hair of your Unworthy One first began
    to cover her forehead.
She picked flowers and played in front of the door.
Then you, my Lover, came riding a bamboo horse.
We ran round and round the bed, and tossed about
    the sweetmeats of green plums.
We both lived in the village of Ch'ang Kan.
We were both very young, and knew neither
    jealousy nor suspicion.

Untitled (A Chinese girl seated looking out of the window), 18th century. attr. to Lam Qua. Oil on canvas. Private collection.

LOG ON **Literature** Online

Literature and Reading For more about translations of Li Po's poem and the translators in this book, go to glencoe.com and enter QuickPass code GLW6053u4.

Respond and Think Critically

1. Why might focusing too much on "the leaves" of a poem—the accuracy of individual words—create a less effective translation?

2. Compare Pound's translation of the opening lines of Li Po's poem on page 697 with the versions above. In your opinion, which translation is most like Pound's? Explain.

3. How is Pound's translation unique?

4. What poetic devices does Pound use to lend a musical quality to his translation?

After You Read

Respond and Think Critically

Respond and Interpret

1. After reading lines 1–19, how did you respond to the question at the end of the poem?

2. What does the condition of the palace tell you about the people who lived there?

3. How would you characterize the prince's lifestyle, based on lines 11–16?

Analyze and Evaluate

4. In your opinion, how well does the poem evoke a sense of compassion?

5. Tu Fu wrote many poems criticizing imperial opulence and power. Do you think this is one of them? Cite examples from the poem to support your answer.

Connect

6. **Big Idea** **Moments of Reflection** What do you think the speaker means by the words "The future / Slips imperceptibly away"?

7. **Connect to Today** What connections can you make between the prince and his ruined palace and a contemporary situation or person?

Literary Element **Imagery**

Tu Fu uses **imagery** to help readers visualize and experience a palace in a state of ruin. The imagery also helps fuel the **mood**, or overall feeling, of the poem.

1. (a)Which images in the poem appeal to your sense of hearing? (b)How do these images contribute to the poem's mood?

2. (a)How do you interpret the image of "green ghost fires" in line 6? (b)How might it relate to the rest of the poem?

Reading Strategy **Make Inferences About Theme**

When you **infer** you make a calculated guess about what an author wants the reader to take away from the details in a literary work.

1. What can you infer about the poem's theme from the description of the ruined palace?

2. (a)Do you think the speaker eventually completed the poem mentioned in line 17? Explain. (b)What can you infer about the poem's theme from this detail?

Academic Vocabulary

*In this poem, Tu Fu reflects on the **termination** of a palace's era of glory.*

Termination is an academic word. In a business context, dismissing an employee is often referred to as **termination**. To further explore the meaning of this word, answer the following question: What do you look forward to at the **termination** of the school year?

For more on academic vocabulary, see pages 36–37 and R83–R85.

Writing

Write a Story How do you imagine the prince described in the poem? Based on Tu Fu's details, write a story about his life. Use imagery to show what the palace might have been like when it was new. Present specific details that lead the reader to a broader statement about life and time. Refer to the chart you made on page 704 for help.

LOG ON ▶ **Literature** Online

Selection Resources For Selection Quizzes, eFlashcards, and Reading-Writing Connection activities, go to glencoe. com and enter QuickPass code GLW6053u4.

Build Background

Percy Bysshe Shelley (1792–1822) is one of the greatest English Romantic poets. The Romantics valued imagination above all else and often wrote about past eras. "Ozymandias" alludes to King Ramses II, who ruled Egypt during the thirteenth century B.C. and was dubbed "the Great." He built his own funerary temple, the Ramesseum, on the west bank of the Nile. Today, all that remains of the temple are fragments of a 57-foot statue of Ramses II and carvings showing war scenes.

Ozymandias

Percy Bysshe Shelley

I met a traveler from an antique land
Who said: Two vast and trunkless legs of stone
Stand in the desert . . . Near them, on the sand,
Half sunk, a shattered visage[1] lies, whose frown,
5 And wrinkled lip, and sneer of cold command,
Tell that its sculptor well those passions read
Which yet survive, stamped on these lifeless things,
The hand[2] that mocked[3] them, and the heart[4]
    that fed:
And on the pedestal these words appear:
10 "My name is Ozymandias, king of kings:
Look on my works, ye Mighty, and despair!"
Nothing beside remains. Round the decay
Of that colossal wreck, boundless and bare
The lone and level sands stretch far away.

The head of a massive granite statue of the seated Ramses II sits on the ground at the Ramesseum, the pharoah's mortuary temple on the west bank of the Nile River at Thebes.

---

1. A *visage* is a face.
2. Here, *hand* refers to the hand of the sculptor.
3. *Mocked* means "imitated" or "derided."
4. *Heart* refers to the heart of Ozymandias.

💬 Discussion Starter

The England of Shelley's time was a rapidly industrializing, blossoming empire that reached its peak near the end of the nineteenth century. How might living in this era have influenced Shelley in writing "Ozymandias"? What do you think the poem is saying about heroes? Discuss these questions with a small group.

of winter, where sleepy sailors scrub the decks, pail in hand and one eye on the black-and-white television in the distance; of the old booksellers who lurch from one financial crisis to the next and then wait shivering all day for a customer to appear; of the barbers who complain that men don't shave as much after an economic crisis; of the children who play ball between the cars on cobblestoned streets; of the covered women who stand at remote bus stops clutching plastic shopping bags and speak to no one as they wait for the bus that never arrives; of the empty boathouses of the old Bosphorus villas; of the teahouses packed to the rafters with unemployed men; . . . of the city walls, ruins since the end of the Byzantine Empire; of the markets that empty in the evenings; of the dervish lodges, the *tekkes*, that have crumbled; of the seagulls perched on rusty barges caked with moss and mussels, unflinching under the pelting rain; of the tiny ribbons of smoke rising from the single chimney of a hundred-year-old mansion on the coldest day of the year; . . . of a cobble-stone staircase with so much asphalt poured over it that its steps have disappeared; of marble ruins that were for centuries glorious street fountains but now stand dry, their faucets stolen; of the apartment buildings in the side streets where during my childhood middle-class families—of doctors, lawyers, teachers, and their wives and children—would sit in their apartments listening to the radio in the evenings, and where today the same apartments are packed with knitting and button machines and young girls working all night long for the lowest wages in the city to meet urgent orders; of the view of the Golden Horn, looking toward Eyüp from the Galata Bridge; of the *simit* vendors on the pier who gaze at the view as they wait for customers; of everything being broken, worn out, past its prime; of the storks flying south from the Balkans and northern and western Europe as autumn nears, gazing down over the entire city as they waft over the Bosphorus and the islands of the Sea of Marmara; . . . I speak of them all.

It is by seeing *hüzün*, by paying our respects to its manifestations in the city's streets and views and people, that we at last come to sense it everywhere. On cold winter mornings, when the sun suddenly falls on the Bosphorus and that faint vapor begins to rise from the surface, the *hüzün* is so dense you can almost touch it, almost see it spread like a film over its people and its landscapes. . . .

Hüzün teaches endurance in times of poverty and deprivation; it also encourages us to read life and the history of the city in reverse. It allows the people of Istanbul to think of defeat and poverty not as a historical end point but as an honorable beginning, fixed long before they were born. So the honor we derive from it can be rather misleading. But it does suggest that Istanbul does not bear its *hüzün* as an incurable illness that has spread throughout the city, as an immutable poverty to be endured like grief, or even as an awkward and perplexing failure to be viewed and judged in black and white; it bears its *hüzün* with honor. ❧

✍ Quickwrite

Pamuk refers to Istanbul's past as he describes its current poverty and overcrowding. How does he connect Istanbul's history to its modern state? What aspects of the excerpt reflect an industrialized society? Write a paragraph responding to these questions.

Wrap-Up: Comparing Literature

Across Time and Place

- *Jade Flower Palace* by Tu Fu

- *Ozymandias* by Percy Bysshe Shelley

- from *Istanbul: Memories and the City* by Orhan Pamuk

COMPARE THE [Big Idea] Moments of Reflection

Group Activity All three authors use specific images to reflect on the meaning of life and the power of time. In a small group, discuss the following questions. Cite evidence from the texts to support your points.

1. What images stand out in each of these works? Which do you think are most effective, and why?

2. Compare and contrast the speakers in each of these works. Which do you think most effectively reflect on the past and present? Why?

3. What do you find similar about the content of Shelley's and Tu Fu's poems? How is Pamuk's reflection different?

COMPARE Style

Writing How do the styles of these three literary works differ? Write a brief essay discussing how the style of each text contributes to its effect. Consider elements such as word choice, sentence structure, imagery, and tone.

COMPARE Historical Context

Speaking and Listening Historical context plays a key role in each of these works. Tu Fu and Shelley both comment on vanished leaders or civilizations, while Pamuk describes the mood of people living in contemporary Istanbul in the shadow of a glorious former empire. Review the author biography information on page 703 and the Build Background notes on page 707 and 708. Research the cultures of each author. Prepare an oral report for the class about the historical context of each work.

A guide stands beside one of the two Colossi of Memnon. The Colossi stand over 60 feet high. Luxor, Egypt.

Selection Resources For Selection Quizzes, eFlashcards, and Reading-Writing Connection activities, go to glencoe.com and enter QuickPass code GLW6053u4.

Tanka

Translated by Geoffrey Bownas
and Anthony Thwaite

When I Went to Visit
Ki no Tsurayuki

When I went to visit
The girl I love so much,
That winter night
The river blew so cold
That the plovers were crying.

Forsaking the Mists
Lady Ise

Forsaking the mists
That rise in the spring,
Wild geese fly off.
They have learned to live
In a land without flowers.

Mount Fuji Reflected in Lake Misaica. From the series '36 Views of Mount Fuji'. Woodblock print. Leeds Museums and Art Galleries, UK.

Was It That I Went to Sleep
Ono no Komachi

Was it that I went to sleep
Thinking of him,
That he came in my dreams?
Had I known it a dream
I should not have wakened.

Mood *What mood does this image suggest to you?*

Trailing on the Wind
Saigyō

Trailing on the wind,
The smoke from Mount Fuji
Melts into the sky.
So too my thoughts—
Unknown their resting place.

Moments of Reflection *How does this image suggest the fleeting nature of life?*

After You Read

Respond and Think Critically

Respond and Interpret

1. What images or lines in these poems did you find most appealing? Explain.

2. (a)Who is the speaker visiting in Tsurayuki's poem? (b)What do the last two lines suggest about the outcome of his visit?

3. (a)In "Forsaking the Mists," where does the speaker say the geese have learned to live? (b)What do you think the speaker means by this?

4. (a)In Komachi's poem, what does the speaker wish she had not done? (b)Why do you think she feels this way?

5. (a)In Saigyō's poem, to what does the speaker compare his thoughts? (b)What might this imply about the speaker's state of mind?

Analyze and Evaluate

6. (a)What emotions are evoked in the last two lines of "Forsaking the Mists"? (b)What do you think this poem might be suggesting about people?

7. What, in your opinion, are the benefits and limitations of the tanka form?

Connect

8. **Big Idea** **Moments of Reflection** What attitude do these poems convey about change and the passage of time?

9. **Connect to the Author** How might "Trailing on the Wind" reflect Saigyō's experiences as a wandering monk?

Literary Element **Mood**

An author's choice of images and words helps to create mood.

1. How do the images in Tsurayuki's poem contribute to the mood?

2. What mood does Saigyō's tanka evoke?

Reading Strategy **Interpret Imagery**

Imagery refers to language that appeals to one or more of the senses. Review the imagery equations you made on page 713.

1. List three examples of imagery in these tanka, and explain to which sense each one appeals.

2. How do these images help you determine the symbolic meanings of the poems?

Academic Vocabulary

*In "Forsaking the Mists," spring **coincides** with hope and adventure as the geese fly away.*

Coincide is an academic word. In more casual conversation, someone might say two friends whose birthdays **coincide** should celebrate together. Using context clues, try to figure out the meaning of *coincide* in the sentence above about the tanka.

For more on academic vocabulary, see pages 36–37 and R83–R85.

Writing

Write a Tanka Recall a time when you were struck by a thought, sensation, or emotion you didn't want to forget. Write a tanka that captures that moment. Use word choice and imagery that contribute to the **mood** you want to establish. Review the tanka form before you begin.

from

The Pillow Book

Sei Shōnagon
Translated by Ivan Morris

Hateful Things

One is in a hurry to leave, but one's visitor keeps chattering away. If it is someone of no importance, one can get rid of him by saying, "You must tell me all about it next time"; but, should it be the sort of visitor whose presence commands one's best behavior, the situation is hateful indeed.

One finds that a hair has got caught in the stone on which one is rubbing one's inkstick, or again that gravel is lodged in the inkstick, making a nasty, grating sound.

Someone has suddenly fallen ill and one summons the exorcist.[1] Since he is not at home, one has to send messengers to look for him. After one has had a long fretful wait, the exorcist finally arrives, and with a sigh of relief one asks him to start his incantations.[2] But perhaps he has been exorcizing too many evil spirits recently; for hardly has he installed himself and begun praying when his voice becomes drowsy. Oh, how hateful!

A man who has nothing in particular to recommend him discusses all sorts of subjects at random as though he knew everything.

An elderly person warms the palms of his hands over a brazier[3] and stretches out the wrinkles. No young man would dream of behaving in such a fashion; old people can really be quite shameless. I have seen some dreary old creatures actually resting their feet on the brazier and rubbing them against the edge while they speak. These are the kind of people who in visiting someone's house first use their fans to wipe away the dust from the mat and, when they finally sit on it, cannot stay still but are forever spreading out the front of their hunting costume or even tucking it up under their knees. One might suppose that such behavior was restricted to people of humble station; but I

---

1. An *exorcist* is someone who expels evil spirits.
2. *Incantations* are verbal charms spoken or sung as part of a ritual of magic.

Diary *Why do you think Shōnagon writes down these annoyances even though she knows her diary will not make the situations change?*

---

3. A *brazier* (brā′zhər) is a pan that holds burning coals.

Girl with a Mirror, c. 1790 Kitagawa Utamaro. Colour woodblock print. British Library, London.

have observed it in quite well-bred people, including a Senior Secretary of the Fifth Rank in the Ministry of Ceremonial and a former Governor of Suruga.

I hate the sight of men in their cups[4] who shout, poke their fingers in their mouths, stroke their beards, and pass on the wine to their neighbors with great cries of "Have some more! Drink up!" They tremble, shake their heads, twist their faces, and **gesticulate** like children who are singing, "We're off to see the Governor." I have seen really well-bred people behave like this and I find it most distasteful.

To envy others and to complain about one's own lot; to speak badly about people;

---

4. The phrase *in their cups* means they have had too much to drink.

Draw Conclusions About Author's Culture *What conclusion can you draw about the organization of the court from this secretary's official title?*

dog have imagined that this would be his fate? We all felt sorry for him. "When Her Majesty was having her meals," recalled one of the ladies-in-waiting, "Okinamaro always used to be in attendance and sit opposite us. How I miss him!"

It was about noon, a few days after Okinamaro's banishment, that we heard a dog howling fearfully. How could any dog possibly cry so long? All the other dogs rushed out in excitement to see what was happening. Meanwhile a woman who served as a cleaner in the Palace latrines ran up to us. "It's terrible," she said. "Two of the Chamberlains are flogging a dog. They'll surely kill him. He's being punished for having come back after he was banished. It's Tadataka and Sanefusa who are beating him." Obviously the victim was Okinamaro. I was absolutely wretched and sent a servant to ask the men to stop; but just then the howling ceased. "He's dead," one of the servants informed me. "They've thrown his body outside the gate."

That evening, while we were sitting in the Palace bemoaning Okinamaro's fate, a wretched-looking dog walked in; he was trembling all over, and his body was fearfully swollen.

"Oh dear," said one of the ladies-in-waiting. "Can this be Okinamaro? We haven't seen any other dog like him recently, have we?"

We called to him by name, but the dog did not respond. Some of us insisted that it was Okinamaro, others that it was not. "Please send for Lady Ukon," said the Empress, hearing our discussion. "She will certainly be able to tell." We immediately went to Ukon's room and told her she was wanted on an urgent matter.

"Is this Okinamaro?" the Empress asked her, pointing to the dog.

"Well," said Ukon, "it certainly looks like him, but I cannot believe that this loathsome creature is really our Okinamaro. When I called Okinamaro, he always used to come to me, wagging his tail. But this dog does not react at all. No, it cannot be the same one. And besides, wasn't Okinamaro beaten to death and his body thrown away? How could any dog be alive after being flogged by two strong men?" Hearing this, Her Majesty was very unhappy.

When it got dark, we gave the dog something to eat; but he refused it, and we finally decided that this could not be Okinamaro.

On the following morning I went to attend the Empress while her hair was being dressed and she was performing her ablutions.[6] I was holding up the mirror for her when the dog we had seen on the previous evening slunk into the room and crouched next to one of the pillars. "Poor Okinamaro!" I said. "He had such a dreadful beating yesterday. How sad to think he is dead! I wonder what body he has been born into this time. Oh, how he must have suffered!"

At that moment the dog lying by the pillar started to shake and tremble, and shed a flood of tears. It was astounding. So this really was Okinamaro! On the previous night it was to avoid betraying himself that he had refused to answer to his name. We were immensely moved and pleased. "Well, well, Okinamaro!" I said, putting down the mirror. The dog stretched himself flat on the floor and yelped loudly, so that the Empress beamed with delight. All the ladies gathered round, and Her Majesty summoned Lady Ukon. When the Empress

---

6. The phrase *performing her ablutions* means that she was bathing.

Draw Conclusions About Author's Culture *Why do the members of the court come to this conclusion about Okinamaro's identity?*

explained what had happened, everyone talked and laughed with great excitement.

The news reached His Majesty, and he too came to the Empress's room. "It's amazing," he said with a smile. "To think that even a dog has such deep feelings!" When the Emperor's ladies-in-waiting heard the story, they too came along in a great crowd. "Okinamaro!" we called, and this time the dog rose and limped about the room with his swollen face. "He must have a meal prepared for him," I said. "Yes," said the Empress, laughing happily, "now that Okinamaro has finally told us who he is."

The Chamberlain, Tadataka, was informed, and he hurried along from the Table Room. "Is it really true?" he asked. "Please let me see for myself." I sent a maid to him with the following reply: "Alas, I am afraid that this is not the same dog after all." "Well," answered Tadataka, "whatever you say, I shall sooner or later have occasion to see the animal. You won't be able to hide him from me indefinitely."

Before long, Okinamaro was granted an Imperial pardon and returned to his former happy state. Yet even now, when I remember how he whimpered and trembled in response to our sympathy, it strikes me as a strange and moving scene; when people talk to me about it, I start crying myself.

To have spoken about someone not knowing that he could overhear. This is embarrassing even if it be a servant or some other completely insignificant person.

To hear one's servants making merry. This is equally annoying if one is on a journey and staying in cramped quarters or at home and hears the servants in a neighboring room.

Parents, convinced that their ugly child is adorable, pet him and repeat the things he has said, imitating his voice.

An ignoramus who in the presence of some learned person puts on a knowing air and converses about men of old.

A man recites his own poems (not especially good ones) and tells one about the praise they have received—most embarrassing.

Lying awake at night, one says something to one's companion, who simply goes on sleeping.

Visual Vocabulary
A *zither* is a stringed instrument that is placed horizontally and is plucked with the fingers.

In the presence of a skilled musician, someone plays a zither just for his own pleasure and without tuning it.

A son-in-law who has long since stopped visiting his wife runs into his father-in-law in a public place.

Embarrassing Things

While entertaining a visitor, one hears some servants chatting without any restraint in one of the back rooms. It is embarrassing to know that one's visitor can overhear. But how to stop them?

A man whom one loves gets drunk and keeps repeating himself.

Pleasing Things

Finding a large number of tales that one has not read before. Or acquiring the second volume of a tale whose first volume one has enjoyed. But often it is a disappointment.

Family and Tradition *What sort of court or society traditions would lead Shōnagon to make such a statement?*

Someone has torn up a letter and thrown it away. Picking up the pieces, one finds that many of them can be fitted together.

One has had an upsetting dream and wonders what it can mean. In great anxiety one consults a dream-interpreter, who informs one that it has no special significance.

A person of quality is holding forth about something in the past or about a recent event that is being widely discussed. Several people are gathered round him, but it is oneself that he keeps looking at as he talks.

A person who is very dear to one has fallen ill. One is miserably worried about him even if he lives in the capital and far more so if he is in some remote part of the country. What a pleasure to be told that he has recovered!

I am most pleased when I hear someone I love being praised or being mentioned approvingly by an important person.

A poem that someone has composed for a special occasion or written to another person in reply is widely praised and copied by people in their notebooks. Though this is something that has never yet happened to me, I can imagine how pleasing it must be.

A person with whom one is not especially intimate refers to an old poem or story that is unfamiliar. Then one hears it being mentioned by someone else and one has the pleasure of recognizing it. Still later, when one comes across it in a book, one thinks, "Ah, this is it!" and feels delighted with the person who first brought it up.

I feel very pleased when I have acquired some Michinoku paper, or some white, decorated paper, or even plain paper if it is nice and white.

A person in whose company one feels awkward asks one to supply the opening or closing line of a poem. If one happens to recall it, one is very pleased. Yet often on such occasions one completely forgets something that one would normally know.

I look for an object that I need at once, and I find it. Or again, there is a book that I must see immediately; I turn everything upside down, and there it is. What a joy!

When one is competing in an object match (it does not matter what kind), how can one help being pleased at winning?

I greatly enjoy taking in someone who is pleased with himself and who has a self-confident look, especially if he is a man. It is amusing to observe him as he alertly waits for my next repartee;[7] but it is also interesting if he tries to put me off my guard by adopting an air of calm indifference as if there were not a thought in his head.

I realize that it is very sinful of me, but I cannot help being pleased when someone I dislike has a bad experience.

It is a great pleasure when the ornamental comb that one has ordered turns out to be pretty.

I am more pleased when something nice happens to a person I love than when it happens to myself.

Entering the Empress's room and finding that ladies-in-waiting are crowded round her in a tight group, I go next to a pillar which is some distance from where she is sitting. What a delight it is when Her Majesty summons me to her side so that all the others have to make way! ❧

---

7. *Repartee* is an interchange of witty remarks.

Diary *If she feels it is sinful, why do you think Shōnagon makes such an admission?*

Family and Tradition *Is court tradition working in Shōnagon's favor, or against her? Explain.*

Woman surrounded by Calligraphy. Utagawa Kunisada (Japan, 1786-1864). Color woodblock print. Private collection.

View the Art During the eighteenth century in Japan, many courtesans who were celebrated for their artistic compositions were depicted in woodblock prints. How is the woman in the painting like the narrator?

Respond Through Writing

Autobiographical Narrative

Learning Objectives

In this assignment, you will focus on the following objectives:

Writing: Writing an autobiographical narrative.

Grammar: Understanding gerunds.

Apply Description Write an autobiographical narrative, using *The Pillow Book* as a model. Apply Shōnagon's style to your narrative by presenting vivid descriptions and observations relating to the culture you live in and your attitude toward your environment.

Understand the Task When you **apply**, you use an author's form or style as a model for your own writing.

Prewrite Generate lists to organize your thoughts before writing your narrative. Consult the diagram you made on page 717 and use a chart like the one below to record your impressions; you can use the categories listed or create your own. List specific objects or situations that provoke strong responses in you, as Shōnagon does.

Hateful Things	Embarrassing Things	Pleasing Things	Scary Things
loud chewing	tripping on the sidewalk	popping bubble wrap	shark movies

Then refine and filter your initial thoughts into a coherent whole, eliminating items that do not provoke a strong emotional response or do not lend themselves to description.

Draft Use your chart to create a sequential outline for your narrative. Remember that in this narrative, you are both describing events and commenting on their cultural significance. Pace the action to show changes in time and mood.

Revise Review your writing to ensure your scenes and incidents take place in specific, vivid settings. Also be sure you have portrayed your characters and elaborated your descriptions with concrete and sensory details. Trade papers with a partner and ask him or her to describe a scene based on your draft. If your partner's description falls short of your experience, revise your narrative to make it more vivid and specific.

Edit and Proofread Proofread your paper, correcting any errors in spelling, grammar, and punctuation. Review the Grammar Tip in the side column to help you use gerunds.

Grammar Tip

Gerunds

In the sentence *Rehearsing exhausts me, exhausts* is the verb. While *rehearsing* appears to be a verb, it is actually a gerund, or a verb form ending in *-ing* functioning as a noun. In the sentence *Crossing the school parking lot can be difficult, crossing* is the gerund and *crossing the school parking lot* is the complete gerund phrase, which functions as the subject.

You might use gerunds in your autobiographical narrative to name things you describe, such as swimming, eating, gossiping, and so on.

Grammar Workshop

Commas with Interjections and Parenthetical Expressions

Learning Objective

In this workshop, you will focus on the following objective:

Grammar: Understanding how to use commas with interjections and parenthetical expressions.

Literature Connection In this passage from *The Pillow Book*, Sei Shōnagon uses the interjection "Ah" to express delight.

> "Still later, when one comes across it in a book, one thinks, 'Ah, this is it!' and feels delighted with the person who first brought it up."

Interjections are words that express emotion or exclamation, such as *ah, oh, ouch,* and *oh well*. Most interjections occur at the beginning of a sentence. Because these expressions have no grammatical connection to other words in the sentence, they should be set off with a comma.

Similarly, authors can set off **parenthetical expressions**—side thoughts—with commas. Here is an example from *The Pillow Book*: "And besides, wasn't Okinamaro beaten to death and his body thrown away?" "And besides" is a parenthetical expression. Parenthetical expressions include phrases such as *in fact, on the contrary,* and *by the way*.

PROBLEM 1 A comma is missing with an interjection.

Oh what happened to poor Lady Uma?

SOLUTION Oh, what happened to poor Lady Uma?

PROBLEM 2 Commas are missing with a parenthetical expression at the beginning of a sentence.

In fact Sei Shōnagon had strong opinions.

SOLUTION In fact, Sei Shōnagon had strong opinions.

PROBLEM 3 Commas are missing with a parenthetical expression in the middle of a sentence.

Lady Murasaki on the other hand felt Sei Shōnagon acted improperly.

SOLUTION Lady Murasaki, on the other hand, felt Sei Shōnagon acted improperly.

Revise Rewrite the following sentences, adding commas where needed.

1. After all the ladies-in-waiting could be highly competitive.
2. The palace cat on the other hand lived a life of leisure.
3. Ah I see that Sei Shōnagon came from a literary family.

Interjections and Parenthetical Expressions

Interjections express emotion or exclamation. **Parenthetical expressions** are side thoughts that add information. Both need commas to separate them from the rest of a sentence.

Tip

Overuse of interjections and parenthetical expressions can make your writing appear overly casual and informal, so use them sparingly when writing for a test or an assignment.

Language Handbook

For more on **commas**, see the Language Handbook, p. R40.

LOG ON ▶ **Literature** Online

Grammar For more grammar practice, go to glencoe.com and enter QuickPass code GLW6053u4.

Before You Read

Zen Parables

In Buddhist legend, Bodhidharma, the monk credited with founding Zen Buddhism, stared at a wall for nine years to achieve enlightenment. Besides promoting the virtue of patience, this legend illustrates one of the core principles of Zen—that one must look beyond the logic of everyday life to attain enlightenment. Zen, a Japanese school of Buddhism, asserts each individual has the potential to reach an enlightened state characterized by tranquility, fearlessness, and spontaneity.

The Rise of Zen Bodhidharma (bō di där´mə) is said to have traveled from India to China during the sixth century. In China, his ideas mixed with Taoist philosophy to create the *Ch'an* school of Buddhism. Ch'an was introduced to Japan in 1191 and developed into what is now called Zen.

Unlike religions that emphasize worship or the study of scripture, Zen focuses on guidance toward *satori* (sä tō´rē), or enlightenment—total self-realization and liberation from ignorance and worldly desires. Zen Buddhists believe that people who achieve satori have reached a higher state of awareness.

Parables and Koans Zen masters do not teach their students by telling them facts and testing them on their knowledge. Instead, they use parables, or short stories that illustrate Zen principles. Some Zen masters use riddle-like questions called *koans* (kō´änz´) to stimulate their search for enlightenment. Famous koans include "What did your face look like before you were born?" and "What is the sound of one hand clapping?" Because such questions have no logical answers, contemplating them forces students to move beyond reason.

"Zen has entered internally into every phase of the cultural life of the people."

—Daisetz T. Suzuki, from
Zen and Japanese Culture

The Impact of Zen The Zen values of discipline and fearlessness influenced the samurai culture that developed in the twelfth century. Samurai adopted the Zen art of swordsmanship, which emphasizes unity of the mind, body, and spirit. To this day, the Zen ideal of simplicity permeates Japanese arts as diverse as architecture, dance, and gardening.

Literature and Reading Preview

Connect to the Parables

Do you believe you should always follow certain rules, or does correct behavior vary from situation to situation? Freewrite for a few minutes in response to this question.

Build Background

Buddhists believe people who achieve satori have tapped into a deeper part of their intuition that signifies a profound "waking up" of the individual's consciousness. However, the most direct way to attain enlightenment is through a form of sitting meditation called *zazen* (*za*: "sitting," *zen*: "absorption"). In practicing zazen, the sitter remains alert, but refrains from clinging to any thought, keeping the mind perfectly clear.

Set Purposes for Reading

Big Idea Virtue and Wisdom

As you read, ask yourself, How do these parables define virtue and wisdom? What principles do they share with Taoism?

Literary Element Parable

A **parable** is a brief story that illustrates a moral or lesson. Parables often contain a **paradox**, an apparent contradiction of logic that actually reveals an underlying truth. As you read the parables, ask yourself, How is paradox used to prompt the reader to question conventional thinking?

Reading Strategy Apply Background Knowledge

When you **apply background knowledge**, you use what you've learned about a subject or time period to gain a deeper understanding of a text. Your background knowledge includes information about the cultural forces that underpin a piece of literature. As you read, ask yourself, How can I use what I know about Zen Buddhism to interpret these parables?

Tip: Track Details In a chart like the one below, keep track of how you use background knowledge to interpret details in the parables.

Background Knowledge	Detail	Interpretation
Zen Buddhists believe in nonattachment.	Banzo tells Matajuro never to speak of fencing or touch a sword.	Matajuro can master swordsmanship only by freeing his mind.

Vocabulary

intersection (in′tər·sek shən) *n.* a place where roads cross one another; p. 732 *When the light turned green, I drove through the busy intersection.*

anticipate (an·tis′ə·pāt′) *v.* expect; consider in advance; p. 734 *If there is an accident on the highway, drivers should anticipate delays.*

seldom (sel′dəm) *adv.* rarely; p. 734 *Michael seldom went to the movies, preferring to stay at home and read.*

Tip: Word Usage When you encounter a new word, it might be useful to answer a specific question about the word. For example, What kind of road does not have **intersections**?

Matajuro Yagyu was the son of a famous swordsman. His father, believing that his son's work was too mediocre to **anticipate** mastership, disowned him.

So Matajuro went to Mount Futara and there found the famous swordsman Banzo. But Banzo confirmed the father's judgment. "You wish to learn swordsmanship under my guidance?" asked Banzo. "You cannot fulfill the requirements."

"But if I work hard, how many years will it take me to become a master?" persisted the youth.

"The rest of your life," replied Banzo.

"I cannot wait that long," explained Matajuro. "I am willing to pass through any hardship if only you will teach me. If I become your devoted servant, how long might it be?"

"Oh, maybe ten years," Banzo relented.

"My father is getting old, and soon I must take care of him," continued Matajuro. "If I work far more intensively, how long would it take me?"

"Oh, maybe thirty years," said Banzo.

"Why is that?" asked Matajuro. "First you say ten and now thirty years. I will undergo any hardship to master this art in the shortest time!"

"Well," said Banzo, "in that case you will have to remain with me for seventy years. A man in such a hurry as you are to get results **seldom** learns quickly."

"Very well," declared the youth, understanding at last that he was being rebuked for impatience, "I agree."

Matajuro was told never to speak of fencing and never to touch a sword. He cooked for his master, washed the dishes, made his bed, cleaned the yard, cared for the garden, all without a word of swordsmanship.

Three years passed. Still Matajuro labored on. Thinking of his future, he was sad. He had not even begun to learn the art to which he had devoted his life.

But one day Banzo crept up behind him and gave him a terrific blow with a wooden sword.

The following day, when Matajuro was cooking rice, Banzo again sprang upon him unexpectedly.

After that, day and night, Matajuro had to defend himself from unexpected thrusts. Not a moment passed in any day that he did not have to think of the taste of Banzo's sword.

He learned so rapidly he brought smiles to the face of his master. Matajuro became the greatest swordsman in the land. ❧

Apply Background Knowledge *How are Banzo's responses typical of a Zen master?*

Parable *How does the parable illustrate the Zen principle of patience?*

Vocabulary

anticipate (an tis′ ə pāt′) *v.* expect; consider in advance

seldom (sel′ dəm) *adv.* rarely

After You Read

Respond and Think Critically

Respond and Interpret

1. What was your reaction to the ending of "Muddy Road"?

2. (a)In "Muddy Road," what does Tanzan do to upset Ekido? (b)Why does it upset him?

3. In "The Taste of Banzo's Sword," how does Banzo respond to Matajuro's promises to work hard?

4. (a)What does Banzo have Matajuro do for the first three years of his training? (b)Why might Banzo require this?

Analyze and Evaluate

5. (a)What does Tanzan mean by his question at the end of "Muddy Road"? (b)What general lesson might this question convey?

6. (a)In "The Taste of Banzo's Sword," what qualities must Matajuro develop to become the greatest swordsman in the land? (b)Why do you think Banzo's teaching methods are successful?

Connect

7. **Big Idea** Virtue and Wisdom (a)What message about virtue does "Muddy Road" convey? (b)What message about attaining wisdom does "The Taste of Banzo's Sword" convey?

8. **Connect to Today** In your opinion, do the lessons of these parables apply to today's world? Explain.

Literary Element Parable

Zen parables often use **paradoxes,** or apparent contradictions, to teach lessons.

1. (a)How does Tanzan's question at the end of "Muddy Road" contradict logic? (b)In what deeper sense are his words true?

2. Identify a paradox in "The Taste of Banzo's Sword."

Reading Strategy Apply Background Knowledge

Your **background knowledge** can help you interpret characters' actions in a literary work.

1. What principle of Zen Buddhism might Tanzan demonstrate by carrying the girl across the road? Explain.

2. Relate the legend about Bodhidharma on page 730 to "The Taste of Banzo's Sword."

LOG ON ▶ **Literature** Online

Selection Resources For Selection Quizzes, eFlashcards, and Reading-Writing Connection activities, go to glencoe.com and enter QuickPass code GLW6053u4.

Vocabulary Practice

Practice with Word Usage Respond to these statements to help you explore the meanings of the vocabulary words from the parables.

1. Make a list of things besides roads that can form an **intersection**.

2. Describe a situation in which you had to **anticipate** an occurrence or event.

3. Give an example of something that **seldom** occurs.

Writing

Write a Parable Write a parable of your own that expresses a Zen principle. Look back at the chart you filled out on page 731 to review the background information you'll need to keep in mind as you write. Then think of a modern situation to which a Zen principle might apply.

Japanese Drama: Noh and Kabuki

STILL PERFORMED TODAY, NOH AND KABUKI PLAYS PROVIDE A GLIMPSE into traditional Japanese culture. Noh, the elaborate classical theater of Japan, evolved more than 600 years ago from ancient religious rituals. Both Noh (also spelled No) and Kabuki, which developed later, involve rich, all-day spectacles of music, dance, and mime that show the influence of the Japanese court tradition.

Noh mask of jealous woman. Hanya.

And I spent my heart on the glimpse of a moon that slipped through the boughs of an autumn tree.

—Seami Motokiyo, from *The Damask Drum*

Noh Plays

Noh, the traditional theater of Japanese nobility, developed its permanent form in the fourteenth century. The form grew out of Zen Buddhist religious festivals and retains a strong spiritual element, using powerful gestures and meditative silences to tell stories. A typical Noh play has only three or four roles, all performed by men on a small, bare stage. The actors, in contrast, wear elaborate costumes and masks. A Noh play usually tells the tale of a restless ghost. The main character is a spirit, or *shite* (shē′tā), often in human form, who is tortured by memories from a troubled life. A secondary character, called a *waki* (wä′kē), asks questions of the *shite*. Throughout the play, a chorus echoes the words of the main characters, who dance and gesture to the music of a flute player and drummers. Most action in a Noh play is symbolic. For example, a character may take only a few steps to indicate he is on a long journey. Noh drama has influenced such authors as the Irish poet and dramatist W. B. Yeats, who wrote a number of plays in this form, including *Four Plays for Dancers* (1921).

Seami Motokiyo

The most famous of the Noh actor-playwrights, Seami Motokiyo (1363–1443), wrote about 90 of the approximately 230 Noh plays typically performed today. According to Seami, among the most important aspects of Noh drama are the moments of "no action," in which actors captivate their audiences by conveying a sense of spiritual or mental strength. Describing such moments, Seami wrote, "In the art of the Noh . . . the different types of miming are artificial things. What holds the parts together is the mind." In one of Seami's best-known plays, *The Damask Drum*, a beautiful princess tells an aged gardener if he beats a drum in a garden so hard it can be heard in her palace, she will visit him. When the old man realizes the futility of the task, he drowns himself. With its tragic outcome, stylized gestures, and mystical time shifts, this play is typical of the Noh aesthetic.

Kabuki Theater

Kabuki, a theater created for the common people, arose around 1600, eventually replacing Noh as Japan's most popular dramatic form. A group of female performers originated the style. However, the government viewed Kabuki as excessively provocative and banned women from performing in 1629. Today, Kabuki, like Noh, exists as an all-male art form. Unlike Noh plays, Kabuki plays are extravagant and unrestrained. They usually have a historical or domestic focus and feature lower-class heroes who resist oppression by the nobility. For example, the famous *Chushingura* (1748) tells the story of a band of samurai who revenge the death of their lord. Like Noh, Kabuki makes use of dance, music, and stylized gestures. However, Kabuki performers wear no masks and constantly interact with the audience. A Kabuki stage has passageways projecting into the audience on the left and right, which means the actors can encircle the audience. Kabuki programs continue from morning to night, accompanied by a continuous coming and going of the audience. Sometimes performers stop and address the crowd directly. Occasionally members of the audience break into the performance to praise a favorite scene or to call out the name of a favorite performer.

Contemporary Renditions

Twentieth-century playwright Mishima Yukio (1925–1970), reacting to what he saw as a deadening in modern Japanese culture, wrote his own version of *The Damask Drum*, in which he used the central image from the Seami play in a modern setting. Today's international performances of Noh and Kabuki range from classical renderings of Seami to Kabuki versions of Shakespeare plays. Recent productions of *Kabuki Othello* (1986) and *Kabuki Lady Macbeth* (2005) illustrate the appeal of these forms in the West.

Japanese Kabuki actor Kankuro Nakamura (foreground) performs with his sons Kantaro and Hichinosuke.

Literature Online

Literature and Reading For more about Noh and Kabuki, go to glencoe.com and enter QuickPass code GLW6053u4.

Respond and Think Critically

1. How are Noh and Kabuki dramas similar? How do they differ?

2. Why might Seami have believed "no action" was one of the most powerful elements of Noh?

3. Review the information on Greek drama on pages 248–249. How does Noh drama compare with Greek tragedy?

4. What do the conventions and subjects of Noh and Kabuki dramas reflect about Japanese culture?

Haiku

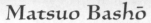

Young Woman in a Summer Shower, 1765. Suzuki Haranobu (Japanese, 1724-1770). Woodblock print, 28.6 x 22 cm. Clarence Buckingham Collection, The Art Institute of Chicago, IL.

Matsuo Bashō
Translated by Harold G. Henderson

Poverty's child—
    he starts to grind the rice,
       and gazes at the moon.

The sun's way:
    hollyhocks turn toward it
       through all the rain of May.

Yosa Buson
Translated by Geoffrey Bownas
and Anthony Thwaite

Spring rain:
Telling a tale as they go,
Straw cape, umbrella.

Spring rain:
Soaking on the roof
A child's rag ball.

Kobayashi Issa
Translated by Geoffrey Bownas and
Anthony Thwaite

The world of dew is
A world of dew . . . and yet,
And yet . . .

Melting snow:
And on the village
Fall the children.

Form *Review the background information on page 739. How is this opening line typical of the haiku form?*

Analyze Imagery *What action does this image convey?*

After You Read

Respond and Think Critically

Respond and Interpret

1. What do you think of the haiku form? Do you find it puzzling or enjoyable? Explain.

2. (a)What images in Buson's poems follow the words "Spring rain"? (b)What moods or emotions do these images suggest?

3. (a)What can you infer about the life of the boy in the first poem by Bashō? (b)What might cause him to gaze at the moon?

4. (a)Where do the hollyhocks turn in the second poem by Bashō? (b)What do you think is the significance of their action?

Analyze and Evaluate

5. **Connotations** are the associations a word brings to mind beyond its dictionary definition. Describe all the connotations that words in one of the haiku have for you.

6. (a)What *kigo,* or season word, is present in the second poem by Buson? (b)In light of your associations with this season, did you find the poem surprising? Explain.

7. (a)Do you find the last line of the second poem by Issa surprising? Explain. (b)What does this line reveal about the speaker's attitude toward the subject matter?

Connect

8. **Big Idea** **Moments of Reflection** What universal themes about nature do these haiku reflect?

9. **Connect to the Author** Do you think Issa's poems reflect the sorrows he experienced in his life? Explain.

Literary Element Form

Poets use **form,** such as the haiku's arrangement of lines, to enhance the emotional and thematic effects of their poems.

1. (a)Where do the **caesuras,** or pauses, occur in the two haiku by Bashō? (b)What are the effects of the caesuras?

2. What is the effect of the break between the second and third lines of the second haiku by Issa?

3. What do you think might be gained or lost by rewriting these haiku as longer, free-verse poems?

Review: Diction

As you learned on page 525, **diction** is an author's word choice. In a short poem such as a haiku, the poet must select each word very carefully, considering its meanings and connotations. Translators of haiku also must select words carefully to preserve the spirit of the original. Two translators of the same poem may interpret it very differently.

Partner Activity Meet with a partner to read and compare these two different translations of a haiku by Bashō. Then discuss the following questions.

Poverty's child—
he starts to grind the rice,
and gazes at the moon.
—Harold G. Henderson translation

The young farm-child
interrupts rice husking to
gaze up at the moon
—Sam Hamill translation

1. (a)How would you describe the diction in each of these translations? (b)What effects does the diction in each create? Support your response with examples from the translations.

2. Which translation do you prefer? Explain.

Their careers span the great flowering of the haiku form. Bashō lived in the latter half of the seventeenth century, Buson in the middle of the eighteenth, Issa at the end of the eighteenth and the beginning of the nineteenth. Much of what has been done with this small form, they did. . . .

The *hokku,* as it was called in Bashō's time, emerged, almost accidentally, from the practice of linked verse. It was, from the beginning, very attentive to time and place. It tended to begin with a theme from classical poetry—the poetry of the Heian court—that was associated with a season of the year. It then added an image that seemed to penetrate to the essence of the classical theme. The spirit of haiku required that the language be kept plain. "The function of haikai," Bashō once said, "is to rectify common speech." It also demanded accurate and original images, drawn mostly from common life. "The old verse can be about willows," Bashō also said, "Haikai requires crows picking snails in a rice paddy." He insisted on poetry as a serious calling. One of the fascinations of his life is that it amounted to years of immensely subtle thinking about how to give resonance and depth to the image, which he worked out in practice in his own work and with his friends and students. "A poet," he said, "needs to discipline himself every day."

The insistence on time and place was crucial for writers of haiku. The seasonal reference was called a *kigo* and a haiku was thought to be incomplete without it. In Bashō's poem quoted above, for example, the phrase *aki fukaki,* "deep autumn" or "autumn deepens" is traditional and had accumulated resonances and associations from earlier poetry as well as from the Japanese way of thinking about time and change. So does the reference to snow—

yuki, which can also mean "snowfall"— in Buson's poems. It is always connected to a sense of exposure to the elements, for which there is also a traditional phrase, *fuyuzare,* which means "winter bareness." The practice was sufficiently codified and there was even a rule that the seasonal reference should always appear either in the first or third unit of the three phrase poem. Buson's poem—it is typical of him— violates that rule and an attentive reader might be led to ask what the connection is between the unexpected snow in the second line and the tethered horse or the rather mysterious snow in both stirrups. In the same way, the spiders in Issa's poem were a traditional mid-summer theme.

These references were conventional and widely available. They were the first way readers of the poems had of locating themselves in the haiku. Its traditional themes— deep autumn, a sudden summer shower, the images of rice seedlings and plum blossoms, of spring and summer migrants like the mountain cuckoo and the bush warbler, of the cormorant-fishermen in summer, and the apprentices on holiday in the spring—gave a powerful sense of a human place in the ritual and cyclical movement of the world.

If the first level of a haiku is its location in nature, its second is almost always some implicit Buddhist reflection on nature. One of the striking differences between Christian and Buddhist thought is that in the Christian sense of things, nature is fallen,[1] and in the Buddhist sense it isn't. Another is that, because there is no creator-being in Buddhist cosmology, there

---

1. The Christian doctrine of the Fall says ever since the time humans first sinned and were banished from an earthly paradise, the natural world has been harsh, imperfect, and distant from God.

Evening Snow on the Asuka Mountain, from *Eight Views of Environs of Edo,* c.1838. Ando or Utagawa Hiroshige. Woodblock colour print. Brooklyn Museum of Art, New York.

is no higher plane of meaning to which nature refers. At the core of Buddhist metaphysics are three ideas about natural things: that they are transient; that they are contingent; and that they suffer. Though the melancholy of autumn is as traditional an experience in European poetry as it is Japanese, it is not fundamentally assimilated into the European system of thought. English poets had a word for these feelings, they called them "moods." When Wordsworth or Keats[2] writes about being "in pensive or in wayward mood," you know that they're doing one of the jobs of the artist, trying to assimilate psychological states for which

the official culture didn't have a language. Bashō's Japan did. The old Japanese phrase that sums up the transience of things, "swirling petals, falling leaves," was a religious thought.

Bashō's "Deep autumn" is a poem about the transience of things, and Bashō has connected it to a particular expression of spiritual loneliness. Buson's "Tethered horse" would, for Japanese readers, connect it through the image of a snowstorm to our mortal bareness, and the horse's tether would lead a reader to think quite naturally that suffering is a condition of creatures. Issa's busy spiders make their webs in a

2. William Wordsworth (1770–1850) and John Keats (1795–1821) were English Romantic poets.

ROBERT HASS **745**

Flowers and insects. Painting, hanging scroll. The Trustees of the Chester Beatty Library, Dublin.

world peculiarly contingent on the whims of housekeepers with their own notions of useful activity, and they happened to be spared by the moods of summer, which in turn make the argument for a kind of compassion. All three poems represent quite traditional Japanese ways of thinking about being.

But what has fascinated all readers about them is that they are also something more, or other, than that. They have a quality of actuality, of the moment seized on and rendered purely, and because of this they seem to elude being either traditional images of nature or ideas about it. The formal reason for this mysteriousness is that they don't usually generalize their images. When the *hokku* became detached from linked verse, it also cast off the room the *tanka* provided for drawing a moral (though not all *tanka* do moralize, of course) and what was left was the irreducible mysteriousness of the images themselves. . . .

So much has been written by western commentators about the connection between haiku and Zen that I'm not inclined to say much about it here. A short version would be to say that Zen provided people training in how to stand aside and leave the meaning-making activity of the ego to its own devices. Not resisting it, but seeing it as another phenomenal thing, like bush warblers and snow fall, though more intimate to us. Trying to find this quality in every haiku, however, romanticizes them and the culture they came from. It tends to make one rush to their final mysteriousness and silence. I know that for years I didn't see how deeply personal these poems were or, to say it another way, how much they have the flavor—Bashō might have said "the scent"—of a particular human life, because I had been told and wanted to believe that haiku were never subjective.... Better to sink down through the levels of these poems—their attention to the year, their ideas about it, the particular human consciousness the poems reflect, Bashō's profound loneliness and sense of suffering, Buson's evenness of temper, his love for the materials of art and for the color and shape of things, Issa's pathos and comedy and anger. One returns to their mysteriousness anyway. ॐ

Respond and Think Critically

Respond and Interpret

1. Write a brief summary of the main ideas in this excerpt before you answer the following questions. For help in writing a summary, see page 1147.

2. (a)What is a *kigo*? (b)Why is it helpful to know about Japanese literary tradition in order to fully understand the meaning of a *kigo*?

3. (a)According to Hass, what are the three main Buddhist ideas about nature? (b)What does Hass mean when he says "there is no higher plane of meaning to which nature refers" in Buddhist thought?

4. (a)What is the relationship between the haiku form and the tanka form? (b)How does Hass use this relationship to explain the effects of haiku?

Analyze and Evaluate

5. Hass writes that looking for the Zen influence "in every haiku . . . romanticizes them and the culture they came from." What does this suggest about Hass's attitude toward using generalizations to understand literature?

6. (a)Which does Hass seem to think is a more important influence on these poets' work—their individual personalities, or their cultural traditions? Explain. (b)Which of these elements do you think is more important to take into account when interpreting literature? Explain.

Connect

7. Did Hass's individual characterizations of Bashō, Buson, and Issa change your understanding of the haiku on page 740? Explain.

ANSWER

Bei Dao

Translated by Donald Finkel with Chen Xueliang

The scoundrel carries his baseness around like an ID card.
The honest man bears his honor like an epitaph.
Look—the gilded° sky is swimming
with **undulant** reflections of the dead.

5   They say the ice age ended years ago.
Why are there icicles everywhere?
The Cape of Good Hope° has already been found.
Why should all those sails contend on the Dead Sea?

I came into this world with nothing
10   but paper, rope, and shadow.
Now I come to be judged,
and I've nothing to say but this:

Listen. *I don't believe!*
OK. You've **trampled**
15   a thousand enemies underfoot. Call me
a thousand and one.

I don't believe the sky is blue.
I don't believe what the thunder says.
I don't believe dreams aren't real,
20   that beyond death there is no **reprisal**.

3 gilded: deceptively attractive. A meaning no longer in use is "smeared with blood."

7 Cape of Good Hope: a rocky outcrop at the southernmost point in Africa.

Figurative Language *Why do you think the speaker compares his own time to the ice age?*

Virtue and Wisdom *If this poem serves as the speaker's "answer," what do you think the question was?*

Vocabulary

undulant (un′ jə lənt) *adj.* having a wavy form or motion

trample (tram′ pəl) *v.* to walk upon and damage by crushing or bruising; to stomp

reprisal (ri prī′ zəl) *n.* the act of using force in retaliation for damage or loss suffered

Tien An Men Square Peaceful Protesters Carry the Statue of Democracy. Jacques Langevin. Beijing, China.

If the sea should break through the sea-wall,
let its brackish° water fill my heart.
If the land should rise from the sea again,
we'll choose again to live in the heights.

25   The earth revolves. A **glittering** constellation
pricks the vast defenseless sky.
Can you see it there? that ancient ideogram—°
   the eye of the future, gazing back.

22 **brackish:** salty.

26 **ideogram:** a character or a symbol representing an idea. It is one type of pictograph.

This nearly blind grandmother, simply from having heard the jay's voice, spoke as if she had seen everything. Yoshiko was filled with wonder.

When, clearing away the breakfast things, Yoshiko went into the kitchen, the jay was singing from the roof of the neighbor's house.

In the back garden, there was a chestnut tree and two or three persimmon trees. When she looked at the trees, she saw that a light rain was falling. It was the sort of rain that you could not tell was falling unless you saw it against the dense foliage.

The jay, shifting its perch to the chestnut tree, then flying low and skimming the ground, returned again to its branch, singing all the while.

The mother bird could not fly away. Was it because her chick was somewhere around there?

Worrying about it, Yoshiko went to her room. She had to get herself ready before the morning was over.

In the afternoon, her father and mother were coming with the mother of Yoshiko's fiancé.

Sitting at her mirror, Yoshiko glanced at the white stars under her fingernails. It was said that, when stars came out under your nails, it was a sign that you would receive something, but Yoshiko remembered having read in the newspaper that it meant a deficiency of vitamin C or something. The job of putting on her makeup went fairly pleasantly. Her eyebrows and lips all became unbearably winsome.[3] Her kimono,[4] too, went on easily.

She'd thought of waiting for her mother to come and help with her clothes, but it was better to dress by herself, she decided.

Her father lived away from them. This was her second mother.

When her father had divorced her first mother, Yoshiko had been four and her younger brother two. The reasons given for the divorce were that her mother went around dressed in flashy clothes and spent money wildly, but Yoshiko sensed dimly that it was more than that, that the real cause lay deeper down.

Her brother, as a child, had come across a photograph of their mother and shown it to their father. The father hadn't said anything but, with a face of terrible anger, had suddenly torn the photograph to bits.

When Yoshiko was thirteen, she had welcomed the new mother to the house. Later, Yoshiko had come to think that her father had endured his loneliness for ten years for her sake. The second mother was a good person. A peaceful home life continued.

When the younger brother, entering upper school, began living away from home in a dormitory, his attitude toward his stepmother changed noticeably.

"Elder sister, I've met our mother. She's married and lives in Azabu. She's really beautiful. She was happy to see me."

Hearing this suddenly, Yoshiko could not say a word. Her face paled, and she began to tremble.

From the next room, her stepmother came in and sat down.

"It's a good thing, a good thing. It's not bad to meet your own mother. It's only natural. I've known for some time that this day would come. I don't think anything particular of it."

---

3. *Winsome* means "charming."
4. A *kimono* is a long robe with wide sleeves and a broad sash, traditionally worn in Japan.

Family and Tradition *How do Yoshiko's thoughts here defy traditional folkloric knowledge?*

Conflict *What does this action suggest about the relationship between the mother and the father?*

But the strength seemed to have gone out of her stepmother's body. To Yoshiko, her emaciated stepmother seemed pathetically frail and small.

Her brother abruptly got up and left. Yoshiko felt like smacking him.

"Yoshiko, don't say anything to him. Speaking to him will only make that boy go bad." Her stepmother spoke in a low voice.

Tears came to Yoshiko's eyes.

Her father summoned her brother back home from the dormitory. Although Yoshiko had thought that would settle the matter, her father had then gone off to live elsewhere with her stepmother.

It had frightened Yoshiko. It was as if she had been crushed by the power of masculine indignation and resentment. Did their father dislike even them because of their tie to their first mother? It seemed to her that her brother, who'd gotten to his feet so abruptly, had inherited the frightening male **intransigence** of his father.

And yet it also seemed to Yoshiko that she could now understand her father's sadness and pain during those ten years between his divorce and remarriage.

And so, when her father, who had moved away from her, came back bringing a marriage proposal, Yoshiko had been surprised.

"I've caused you a great deal of trouble. I told the young man's mother that you're a girl with these circumstances and that, rather than treating you like a bride,[5] she

Japanese Grey robe decorated with flowers and birds. Leeds Museums and Art Galleries, UK..

should try to bring back the happy days of your childhood."

When her father said this kind of thing to her, Yoshiko wept.

If Yoshiko married, there would be no woman's hand to take care of her brother and grandmother. It had been decided that the two households would become one. With that, Yoshiko had made up her mind. She had dreaded marriage on her father's account, but, when it came down to the actual talks, it was not that dreadful after all.

When her preparations were completed, Yoshiko went to her grandmother's room.

"Grandmother, can you see the red in this kimono?"

---

5. *". . . rather than treating you like a bride"* refers to the fact that brides in arranged marriages were traditionally treated harshly by the husband's mother.

Family and Tradition *How is Yoshiko's father fulfilling his traditional family role, even though he lives apart from his children?*

Literary Element Conflict

Conflict is the struggle that lies at the center of a story's plot. In a story that has a standard plot structure, the central conflict reaches a climax and is resolved at the end. "The Jay," however, does not follow this typical plot development. Instead, the story portrays a slice of family life and leaves several conflicts unresolved.

1. (a)What conflicts exist between Yoshiko and the men in this story? (b)Are any of these conflicts resolved? Explain.

2. (a)How would you characterize the relationships between Yoshiko and the women in the story? (b)How do these relationships compare with those Yoshiko has with the men in her family?

3. (a)How do the characters in this story deal with their feelings? Give specific examples. (b)How does this affect the resolution or lack of resolution of the conflicts?

Review: Mood

As you learned on page 713, **mood** is the emotional quality of a literary work. An author's choice of language, subject matter, setting, and tone, as well as certain sound devices, contributes to a work's mood. Kawabata's stories are respected for their focused and subtle mood, which often recalls the tightness of Japanese poetic forms such as the **tanka** (see pages 712–715) and **haiku** (see pages 738–742).

Partner Activity Meet with a classmate and discuss the following questions.

1. How would you describe the mood of "The Jay"?

2. What details in the story contribute to this mood?

LOG ON ▶ **Literature** Online

Selection Resources For Selection Quizzes, eFlash-cards, and Reading-Writing Connection activities, go to glencoe.com and enter QuickPass code GLW6053u4.

Reading Strategy Review

ACT Skills Practice

What is Yoshiko waiting for when the story occurs?

A. Her father and stepmother's arrival

B. Her reunion with her mother

C. Her meeting with her fiancé

D. The return of her brother

Vocabulary Practice

Practice with Word Origins Create a word map like the one below for each boldfaced vocabulary word. Use a dictionary for help.

furtively   intransigence
assiduously   plaintively

EXAMPLE:

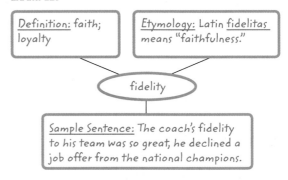

Academic Vocabulary

*Yoshiko deserves some **credit** for considering her family's welfare in deciding to marry.*

Credit has many meanings. Synonyms include *commendation, recognition,* and *acclaim.* Using context clues, try to figure out the meaning of *credit* in each of the following sentences and explain the difference between the meanings.

1. Though I helped my sister with her science fair project, she didn't give me **credit** for it.

2. Because I overpaid my library fines, I have an outstanding **credit** of five dollars.

For more on academic vocabulary, see pages 36–37 and R83–R85.

Respond Through Writing

Expository Essay

Learning Objectives

In this assignment, you will focus on the following objectives:

Writing: Writing an expository essay.

Grammar: Understanding coordinating conjunctions.

Evaluate Style At the end of "The Jay" the reader doesn't know precisely why Yoshiko wants her father and stepmother to see the birds. Kawabata often ends his stories like this, without a clear resolution. In an expository essay, evaluate how effectively his style contributes to the ambiguous ending of this story.

Understand the Task When you **evaluate** a story, you make a reasoned judgment or form an opinion about it. Something that is **ambiguous** has more than one possible meaning.

Prewrite To help organize your essay, select categories you want to use to assess elements of Kawabata's style, such as word choice, imagery, or mood. Rank his performance in each category using the numbered scale below—one being the least effective and five being the most effective—and take notes about your judgments. Use these notes to shape your thesis.

Draft In your essay, offer examples of Kawabata's style. You might use sentence frames like these to help you:

Some examples of _____ in the story are _____, _____, and _____.

Images such as _____ and _____ contribute to Kawabata's style by _____.

Evaluate how well Kawabata's style contributes to the ambiguous ending of the story. Did it add to or detract from your experience? Did it make the ending more or less ambiguous than it might otherwise have been? Use a timeline like the one on page 754 to sequence your essay properly.

Revise Trade papers with a classmate and critique one another's essays. Check that the details your partner cites support his or her evaluation. If an aspect of the essay isn't working, offer alternative suggestions.

Edit and Proofread Proofread your paper, correcting any errors in spelling, grammar, and punctuation. Review the Grammar Tip in the side column for information about using coordinating conjunctions.

Grammar Tip

Coordinating Conjunctions

Use coordinating conjunctions such as *and, but, or, so, nor, yet*, and *for* to combine two sentences that contain equally important ideas. This can make your sentences more varied and fluid.

Original: *The ending left me confused. The image of the birds presents an interesting comparison.*

Combined: *The ending left me confused, but the image of the birds presents an interesting comparison.*

Beside a Chrysanthemum

Sŏ Chŏngju

Translated by David R. McCann

Bridal panel, 19th century. Korean school. Red satin. Victoria and Albert Museum, London.

To bring one chrysanthemum
to flower, the cuckoo has cried
since spring.

To bring one chrysanthemum to bloom,
5　　thunder has rolled
through black clouds.

Flower, like my sister returning
from distant, youthful byways°
of throat-tight longing
10　　to stand by the mirror:

for your yellow petals to open,
last night such a frost fell,
and I did not sleep.

8 **Byways:** small, infrequently traveled roads.

Simile *How does this comparison expand the meaning of the poem?*

After You Read

Respond and Think Critically

Respond and Interpret

1. What images did you find most striking? Explain.

2. (a)What three things had to happen for the chrysanthemum to bloom? (b)What might these things have in common?

3. (a)What can you infer about the time of year from line 12? (b)What might be the significance of the chrysanthemum's blooming at this time?

4. (a)Why might the speaker not have slept the night before? (b)What does this suggest about the connection between the human and natural worlds?

Analyze and Evaluate

5. (a)Why might the chrysanthemum remind the speaker of his or her sister? (b)What emotional effects do lines 8–9 create?

6. What is the connection between the chrysanthemum and the other natural phenomena the speaker describes?

Connect

7. **Big Idea** **Moments of Reflection** How does the poet use nature to convey a message about the connection between beauty and pain?

8. **Connect to the Author** What do you think Sŏ Chŏngju would have thought about the haiku you studied earlier (pages 738–741)?

Literary Element **Simile**

Similes help readers make connections between things that at first may seem dissimilar.

1. (a)What two things are compared in the third stanza? (b)What do you think are the "distant, youthful byways / of throat-tight longing"?

2. Why might the speaker connect the chrysanthemum to these "distant, youthful byways"?

Reading Strategy **Analyze Speaker**

Refer to the chart you made on page 763.

1. What can you infer about the speaker's relationship with nature?

2. Addressing an inanimate object or an idea is called **apostrophe**. What does the use of apostrophe in the last two stanzas suggest about the speaker's attitude toward the chrysanthemum?

Academic Vocabulary

Sŏ reverses chronology by starting with the blooming chrysanthemum and then describing the natural phenomena that preceded it.

Reverse is a word often used in academic contexts. In more casual usage, you might say someone put a car in **reverse** to back out of a parking space. To further explore the meaning of this word, answer this question: What is an example of a court case in which a legal act or ruling has been **reversed**?

For more on academic vocabulary, see pages 36–37 and R83–R85.

Writing

Write a Letter Have the speaker and his sister had a falling out, or do they get along well? Write a letter from the speaker to his sister. Include details that suggest the speaker's personality and a simile to connect the details to larger issues.

ASSEMBLY LINE

Shu Ting

Translated by Carolyn Kizer

Smoke rises from chimneys at the Chongqing Iron and Steel Factory. Photograph. Chongqing Municipality, China.

In time's assembly line
Night presses against night.
We come off the factory night-shift
In line as we march towards home.
5   Over our heads in a row
The assembly line of stars
Stretches across the sky.
Beside us, little trees
Stand numb in assembly lines.

10   The stars must be exhausted
After thousands of years
Of journeys which never change.
The little trees are all sick,

Choked on smog and **monotony**,
15   Stripped of their color and shape.
It's not hard to feel for them;
We share the same **tempo** and rhythm.

Yes, I'm numb to my own existence
As if, like the trees and stars
20   —perhaps just out of habit
—perhaps just out of sorrow,
I'm unable to show concern
For my own manufactured fate.

Metaphor *What is "time's assembly line"?*

Analyze Diction *What do the speaker's words suggest about her life?*

Vocabulary

monotony (mə not′ ən ē) *n.* tiresome sameness
tempo (tem′ pō) *n.* pattern or rate of movement

After You Read

Respond and Think Critically

Respond and Interpret

1. How did you feel after reading this poem?

2. (a)Which images from nature are described in terms of an assembly line? (b)Why does the speaker see nature in these terms?

3. (a)What sensations does the speaker ascribe to the stars and trees? (b)What does the speaker mean by "we share the same tempo and rhythm"?

4. (a)What has made the speaker numb to his or her own existence? (b)How do you interpret the phrase "my own manufactured fate"?

Analyze and Evaluate

5. How does the speaker extend the idea of an assembly line beyond factory walls?

6. (a)Shu Ting uses the phrase "assembly line" twice in the first stanza. How does this repetition reinforce the meaning of the poem? (b)Where else in the poem does Shu Ting use repetition effectively? Explain.

7. (a)Why do you think Shu Ting uses the pronoun *we*, rather than *I*, in the first two stanzas? (b)What is the effect of the pronoun *I* in the final stanza?

Connect

8. **Big Idea** **Virtue and Wisdom** In this poem, how does the speaker's work affect her?

9. **Connect to Today** Do you think the feelings expressed in "Assembly Line" apply only to people in China, or are they universal? Explain.

Literary Element Metaphor

In contrast to a simile, a **metaphor** implies a comparison instead of stating it directly.

1. What does the metaphor "assembly line of stars" in line 6 suggest about the stars?

2. How does Shu Ting develop the assembly-line metaphor in the second stanza?

Reading Strategy Analyze Diction

Review the chart you made on page 767 and then answer the following questions.

1. (a)What words does the speaker use to describe the trees in lines 13–15? (b)What do these words suggest about the speaker's own experience?

2. Would you describe Shu Ting's diction in "Assembly Line" as complex or simple? Explain.

Vocabulary Practice

Practice with Usage Respond to these statements to help you explore the meanings of the vocabulary words from the poem.

1. Describe something that is an example of **monotony**.

2. What type of **tempo** do you prefer in music? Name a song you like that demonstrates this tempo.

Writing

Write an Essay "Assembly Line" suggests the relationship between work and life—a topic explored by many authors. For instance, Henry Wadsworth Longfellow wrote, "Taste the joy / That springs from labor," while Alfred, Lord Tennyson stated, "Ah, why should life / all labor be?" With which quote do you agree more? Write a brief essay that explores your response. Include a **metaphor** in your essay.

TIME

A New Day DAWNS

An industrial city that was among the most polluted in Japan has become an environmental role model.

By BRYAN WALSH

S HE BEGAN HIS DAILY COMMUTE, YOICHI Kaminaga could look down the mountainside on which he lived and see the layer of smoky red, black, and brown air that hid the city of Kitakyushu below. It was the 1960s, and smoke soared from hundreds of factories in this western Japanese city that produced raw materials for the country's manufacturing boom. But if the impact of rapid industrial growth on the environment was already visible in Kitakyushu, that didn't mean it was understood. "I had to go down through the smoke when I was coming to work, and it smelled awful," says Kaminaga, who worked at a brick factory. "But we didn't feel it was dangerous. It meant for us that we were producing a lot for the country. Now I realize that we were destroying the environment."

By the 1960s, Kitakyushu, one of the nation's main industrial centers, was possibly Japan's most polluted city, at a time when the country was an environmental nightmare. But Kitakyushu was also one of the first major Japanese cities to clean itself up, when local housewives debated, protested, and shamed officials and companies into controlling the pollution. Step out of Kitakyushu's new international airport today and you'll see blue sky and clean water next to factories that puff smoke as gently as a professor's pipe.

Across Japan, urban pollution has been controlled to a remarkable degree. Kitakyushu stands out among the country's success stories. The city's effort to reduce pollution is an example of Japan's path to becoming environmentally aware and an antipollution experience for other Asian cities to follow. "We want to help those cities before they suffer as much as we did," says Koichi Sueyoshi, Kitakyushu's long-time mayor. "I believe [other cities] can clean up because we were able to do it, and we can be the role model."

Kitakyushu wasn't always a model to follow. A documentary produced by one of the city's women's groups in 1965 shows the city's factories, charcoal-polluted skies, filthy apartment buildings, and children who looked like chimney cleaners. When the film was made, some 100 tons of dust fell per sq km some months in Kitakyushu's most polluted districts. The narrator of the documentary declares: "Industrial development should not take place at the cost of the people."

It was a simple but revolutionary statement that would inspire the changes to come. In the 1950s and '60s, the housewives of Kitakyushu—organized into numerous women's associations across the city—were the first to recognize the damage uncontrolled development brought to their families. "They could never get their laundry white from all the soot," says Yoshiko Misumi, the president of an organization that has studied the women's movement in Kitakyushu. "Their children would get sick. That's what pushed them."

Because most of the women were married to factory workers or executives, they were in the awkward position of protesting the very businesses that put food on their tables. So rather than dem-

At the Kitakyushu industrial center, industry and housing vie for space. Heavy pollution plagues the people who live nearby.

onstrating in the streets, they began to carefully gather evidence. Working with supportive university professors, the women spent months calculating the pollution with homemade experiments. They measured how much soot dust accumulated on drying bedsheets and recorded how often children were absent from school with illnesses caused by breathing polluted air. They even tossed a live goldfish into a bowl of water taken from Kitakyushu's industrial Dokai Bay, otherwise known as the "Sea of Death." (The fish died instantly.)

Led by resourceful women like Akiko Mori, a teacher recognized decades later by the United Nations for her work to improve the environment, the Kitakyushu's

GREEN FUTURE Kitakyushu's once-polluted Dokai Bay area as it appears today.

women's associations took their research data to city officials and industry executives and demanded action. One factory manager dismissed the movement, saying, "Citizens should endure a certain degree of pollution." But the women knew better, and by the mid-'60s public opinion, in Kitakyushu and elsewhere, began to swing their way. "They said it was in everyone's interest to do something, because the pollution was affecting everyone," says Beverly Yamamoto, a professor at Osaka University who has studied the movement. "They backed that up with hard data."

If industry was slow to respond at first, city politicians were quicker. They knew the women's groups were planning to turn pollution into an issue during upcoming elections. Shortly after the national government passed Japan's first real pollution laws in 1967, Kitakyushu began establishing even tougher regulations. Factories there installed over 1,000 air cleaners between 1967 and 1978, and in the early 1970s they switched to fuels that created less smog.

In 1972 the city began to clean the bottom of Dokai Bay, which had been seriously contaminated with mercury. Equally important, the local government strictly enforced regulations to control pollution. One policy required companies to reduce the amount of smog-causing sulfur dioxide produced by their factories by 20–40% on days when weather conditions made smog formation likely.

The citizens of Kitakyushu also began to use less coal. As a result, dust levels fell nearly 75% from 1970–75. Kitakyushu's pioneering housewives had made the difference. "If there had been no women's movement, our work to reduce pollution would have been significantly delayed," says Reiji Hitsumoto, an environmental official with the city government.

In 1990, Kitakyushu became the first Japanese city to win the United Nations Environmental Program's (UNEP) Global 500 Award. The award recognizes the environmental achievements of individuals and organizations around the world. Kitakyushu's concerned citizens had learned that if they express their views, they could save even the most polluted city.

Kitakyushu is sharing that lesson with developing cities struggling with the effects of industrialization on the environment. Since 1980 Kitakyushu, with the help of the Japan International Cooperation Agency, has sent environmental consultants to developing countries. The consultants help local governments plan and practice anti-pollution measures based on the Kitakyushu model. Thousands of environmental officers from abroad have also visited Kitakyushu to be trained in pollution control methods. They learn everything from how to dispose of garbage and other waste to insuring cleaner industrial production.

The results can be seen in Dalian, a city in northeastern China that was once a carbon copy of the polluted Kitakyushu of the 1960s. Over the past 15 years, Kitakyushu has trained factory managers from Dalian, refitted plants there with cleaner industrial technology and conducted a survey that helped the local government to develop a model environmental zone. The cooperation has paid off. Under Kitakyushu's guidance Dalian joined the UNEP's honor roll in 2001. Officials in Dalian hope their success will be a model for other Chinese cities to follow.

The transformation of Kitakyushu and Dalian is powerful proof that even cities that once measured their success solely by how well industries performed can discover the importance of environmental-friendly economic growth. "Combining environmental efforts with economic benefits has become a vital international issue," says Hiro Mizoguchi, the director of Kitakyushu's Office for International Environmental Cooperation. "I definitely think it can be accomplished, and our effort is part of that."

For Kitakyushu, this commitment to a cleaner future is now an important part of its character. The city that once accepted pollution as an ordinary part of urban life now even boasts its own environment museum, where former factory workers like Kaminaga teach schoolchildren about the importance of a clean environment. "People here feel about the environment the way they used to about production," he says. "I'm proud of my city."

— **With reporting by Yuki Oda/ Kitakyushu Updated 2007.**

Respond and Think Critically

Respond and Interpret

1. Write a brief summary of the main ideas in this article before you answer the following questions. For help in writing a summary, see page 1147.

2. (a)Who led the environmental movement in Kitakyushu? (b)How did they influence public opinion?

3. (a)What problems did pollution create for the citizens of Kitakyushu? (b)Why might it have taken so long for anti-pollution efforts to take hold?

4. (a)How did the city's industries and government reduce pollution? (b)What does this suggest about the potential for efforts to control pollution in other places?

Analyze and Evaluate

5. (a)How did the activists in Kitakyushu organize themselves? (b)What does their example suggest about grassroots organizations?

6. (a)How does Kitakyushu serve as a role model to Dalian, China, and the world? (b)Is it important to have a global discussion about environmental pollution? Why or why not?

Connect

7. What similarities do you see between the pollution in Kitakyushu and the pollution described in Shu Ting's poem "Assembly Line"?

Timeline 500 B.C.–Present

SOUTHEAST ASIAN AND PACIFIC LITERATURE

500 B.C.

after 111
Chinese writing system is introduced into Vietnam

A.D. 1

c. 870
Javanese version of the *Ramayana* is composed

A.D. 1000

◄ **1113**
Earliest surviving text in the Burmese language is carved in stone

c. 1250
Earliest surviving Thai literature is written

1380
Nguyen Trai is born in Vietnam

SOUTHEAST ASIAN AND PACIFIC EVENTS

500 B.C.

c. 500
Dong Son culture is established in northern Vietnam

c. 250
First Buddhist missionaries arrive in Southeast Asia

111
China conquers what is now northern Vietnam

A.D. 1

c. 100
Funan, the first great Southeast Asian kingdom, is established in Cambodia

c. 400
Easter Island is settled
▼

c. 800
First Maori arrive in New Zealand

802
Khmer state is founded in Cambodia

939
Vietnam regains independence from China

A.D. 1000

c. 1150
Construction of Angkor Wat is completed in Cambodia

1238
First Thai kingdom is founded

WORLD EVENTS

500 B.C.

490
Greeks defeat Persians at the Battle of Marathon

c. 483
Siddhārtha Gautama, founder of Buddhism, dies

A.D. 1

c. 1
Bantu people begin to migrate east and south from Central Africa

711
Islamic armies invade Spain

800
Charlemagne is crowned Holy Roman Emperor

c. 900
Rise of Toltec civilization in Mexico

▲

c. 985
First Viking settlements are established in Greenland

1275–1292
Marco Polo visits China

1492
Christopher Columbus reaches America

 Literature Online

Literature and Reading To explore the Interactive Timeline, go to glencoe.com and enter QuickPass code GLW6053u4.

A.D. 1500

1651
Roman alphabet for writing the Vietnamese language is introduced

1765
Nguyen Du, author of Vietnamese epic *The Tale of Kieu*, is born

1922
Katherine Mansfield's *The Garden Party* is published

1973
Patrick White becomes the first Australian to win the Nobel Prize in Literature

1991
Pro-democracy activist Aung San Suu Kyi of Myanmar wins the Nobel Peace Prize

NATIONAL LEAGUE FOR DEMOCRACY

◀ 1642
Dutch explorer Tasman is first European to sight New Zealand

1779 ▶
Explorer Captain James Cook dies after fruitless search for the Northwest Passage

Captain Cook's Tiki, 18th Century

1858–1893
France takes control of Indochina

1979
Vietnamese army overthrows Khmer Rouge government in Cambodia

1602
Dutch East India Company is formed

1788
British establish prison colony in New South Wales, Australia

A.D. 1500

1789
French Revolution begins

1869
Suez Canal is completed

1912
Last Chinese emperor abdicates

1957
Soviet Union launches *Sputnik I* satellite

Reading Check

Analyze Graphic Information About how many years after the death of Siddhārtha Gautama did Buddhist missionaries begin arriving in Southeast Asia?

Learning Objectives

For pages 774–785

In studying this text, you will focus on the following objectives:

Literary Study: Analyzing literary periods.

Reading: Evaluating historical influences.
Connecting to the literature.

Southeast Asia and the Pacific

500 B.C.–Present

Historical, Social, and Cultural Forces

A Complex Region

Southeast Asia is a complex region reflecting a rich mixture of peoples, cultures, and religions. The earliest settlers arrived from the north and west thousands of years ago, traveling down through Indochina and eventually spreading as far east as Polynesia. Mountain ranges and river valleys divide the nations of Southeast Asia. These geographical barriers may explain why the region was never unified under a single government. Instead, distinctive cultures with different languages and religions developed.

A Mixture of Faiths

The religions of Southeast Asia and the Pacific islands often combine many layers of cultural influences. The oldest beliefs are animistic, requiring the performance of ceremonies and rituals to communicate with gods, spirits, and ancestors. Later, Indian missionaries and merchants carried both Buddhist and Hindu traditions to Indonesia. In Myanmar, Thailand, Laos, and Cambodia, most people practice a variety of Buddhism that is in many ways close to the Buddha's original teachings. In Vietnam, the influence of Confucian thought has been strong.

In the thirteenth century, Arab traders played a large part in converting Malaysia and most of Indonesia to Islam. Today, only the people of Bali retain a form of

Hinduism, but Indian traditions are still very evident throughout Indonesian music, dance, theater, and textile arts. (See "The *Mahabharata* as Shadow Play," pages 574–575.) Christianity, introduced by European missionaries, is widespread in the Philippines and the Pacific islands.

Buddha Park, 1958. Bunleua Sulilat. Vientiane, Laos.

Ancient Kingdoms

Before A.D. 1500, a number of states developed in Southeast Asia, adapting political models from India and China. The Vietnamese were one of the first peoples in Southeast Asia to develop their own state. After the Chinese conquered Vietnam in 111 B.C., they tried for centuries to make it part of China. The Vietnamese clung to their own identity, however, and in A.D. 939 they finally overthrew Chinese rule.

> *"How dare you bandits trespass on our soil?*
> *You shall meet your undoing at our hands."*
>
> —Traditional Vietnamese poem

In the ninth century A.D., the kingdom of Angkor arose in what is now Cambodia. This kingdom was formed when a powerful ruler named Jayavarman united the Khmer (kə mer′) people and established his capital at Angkor Thom. Although surrounded by enemies, Angkor, or the Khmer Empire, remained the most powerful state in Southeast Asia for several centuries.

The Spice Trade

Some Southeast Asian states, such as the Sultanate of Melaka (located in present-day Malaysia and Indonesia), supported themselves chiefly through trade. During the Middle Ages, the demand for spices enriched these trading states. Merchant fleets from India, the Arabian Peninsula, and, later, Europe sailed to the Indonesian islands. There they bought cloves, pepper, nutmeg, cinnamon, and precious woods, such as teak and sandalwood, which wealthy Chinese and Europeans desired.

Western Imperialism

For centuries, the European presence in Southeast Asia was confined to a few trading and missionary outposts. This situation changed dramatically in the mid-nineteenth century, however, when the

Arrival of the French in the Bay of Haiphong, 1884. Vietnamese school. Private collection.

"new imperialism" resulted in the European colonization of much of Southeast Asia. From 1858 to 1893, France gained control of Vietnam, Cambodia, and Laos, creating French Indochina. After World War II, Vietnamese nationalists under communist leader Ho Chi Minh fought against the French. In 1954, France withdrew from Vietnam, and the country was divided into communist North Vietnam and noncommunist South Vietnam, which soon waged civil war. The United States intervened in support of South Vietnam, but eventually withdrew its troops. By 1975, the communists ruled all of Vietnam.

Postcolonial Southeast Asia

Many colonies in Southeast Asia achieved independence after World War II. In 1946, the United States granted independence to the Philippines. Two years later, Burma (now Myanmar), a British colony, became independent. In 1949, the Netherlands recognized the independence of Indonesia. Malaya, another British colony, became independent in 1957 (and became part of Malaysia in 1963). Many of these nations, however, have been plagued by ethnic and religious conflicts, political corruption, and repressive governments. For example, the military government in Myanmar has repressed free speech. Moreover, it continues to keep under house arrest Aung San Suu Kyi, an activist for democracy and the winner of the 1991 Nobel Peace Prize.

The Struggle to Survive

How might the history of some Southeast Asian nations, marked by repeated struggles for independence, have helped shape their national characters?

Vietnamese Nationalism

In 111 B.C., China's powerful Han emperor Wu-Ti conquered what is now northern Vietnam. Attempts to impose Chinese culture on the Vietnamese, however, soon met with determined resistance. In A.D. 39, two noblewomen, Trung Trac and her sister Trung Nhi, organized a revolt against local Chinese rulers. At first successful, the sisters eventually were defeated by a Han army, after which China tightened its control over Vietnam. Still, the Trung sisters were regarded as national heroes and are still celebrated today. Even after regaining independence in A.D. 939, Vietnam endured periodic Chinese invasions. These centuries of struggle against a foreign power helped shape the Vietnamese national character. It is marked by a fierce streak of independence and a staunch refusal to yield to foreign rule.

> "To slay the people's foe and wreak revenge,
> Two sisters lifted arms for their just cause . . .
> While streams and hills endure, their shrine shall stand:
> A monument to peerless womanhood."
>
> —Traditional Vietnamese poem

Children Caught up in the Fall of Saigon, April 29, 1975. Jacques Pavlovsky. South Vietnam.

The Khmer Rouge

In 1975, the Khmer Rouge, a radical communist faction, used guerrilla warfare to seize control of Cambodia. It installed its military leader, Pol Pot, as prime minister and enacted a series of measures designed to bring about a classless society. Under the Khmer Rouge, more than one million Cambodians died from execution, torture, disease, or starvation. In 1979, Vietnamese forces ousted the Khmer Rouge from power. Pin Yathay describes the sufferings inflicted by the Khmer Rouge in Cambodia in *Stay Alive, My Son* (see pages 819–827). After Pol Pot's death in 1998, the last remnants of the Khmer Rouge disbanded.

Literature of Southeast Asia

A consistent theme in contemporary Southeast Asian literature is the struggle of the author to express a personal identity amid social and political change. Important modern authors include novelist Pramoedya Ananta Toer of Indonesia and democracy activist Aung San Suu Kyi of Myanmar, winner of the Nobel Peace Prize.

Reading Check

Analyze Cultural Context What Vietnamese cultural values does the heroic status of the Trung sisters reflect?

Big Idea 2
Place and Identity

The idea of remoteness, of "getting away from it all," may call to mind an array of images, such as a country landscape with a still pond reflecting the stars, or a mysterious island with huge waves battering its shores. The literatures of Southeast Asia and the Pacific often express remoteness, exploring connections between place and identity.

Fields and Gardens

Chinese literature distinguished different types of remoteness. Some poets wrote about "fields and gardens," describing a gentle, familiar rural world. Others portrayed the wilder, more distant landscapes of "mountains and water." The poets of the "fields and gardens" tradition often celebrated the joys of retiring to a place close to nature and far from the city. This tradition influenced Vietnamese authors such as Nguyen Trai, whose "Bamboo Hut" (see pages 786–789) describes a simple rural refuge.

> "My life
> to begin where the nightmare ended
> and crosses stand like islands:
> Upolu, Savii, Apolima, and
>   Manono
> are scented with morning."
>
> —Albert Wendt

Island Worlds

The Pacific Ocean covers a third of the Earth's surface. Scattered across its millions of square miles are groups of tiny islands—tens of thousands of them, including the islands of Melanesia, Micronesia, and Polynesia, a region known as

Threadfin Butterfly Fish Swimming. Stuart Westmorlan. Fakarava Atoll, French Polynesia.

Oceania. In spite of the distances separating these islands, their languages, social structures, and beliefs are remarkably consistent. Oceania was settled by Asian voyagers who came in open canoes. Navigating by the stars and other natural features, they populated almost all the scattered islands of the vast ocean. Until about 500 years ago, Oceania was isolated from most of the outside world. As a result, its cultures developed their own identities and perspectives. Its literature often evokes a distinct type of remoteness, conveying an attitude toward nature that combines reverence and fear. Kauraka Kauraka of the Cook Islands (see pages 829–833) expresses this attitude in describing "the waves that destroy us / the waves that create new lands." Oceanic literature also draws upon rich oral traditions in which different animals symbolize places. Authors such as Albert Wendt (see pages 829–833) celebrate the uniqueness of Pacific island culture.

Reading Check

Compare and Contrast How does the Chinese "fields and gardens" approach to nature differ from that of the literature of the Pacific islands?

Before You Read

The Bamboo Hut

Meet Nguyen Trai

(1380–1442)

N guyen Trai (noo yin′trī) led a life full enough for several people. He excelled as a soldier, politician, historian, geographer, scholar, and poet.

Nguyen's childhood was marked by the loss of his mother when he was five years old. He then lived with his maternal grandfather, who died a short time later. Despite his difficult life, Nguyen earned his master's degree at the age of twenty. He was serving as the deputy head provincial administrator of Ha Dong province when Vietnam was invaded by China in 1407. In 1418, he joined the Vietnamese resistance under the general Le Loi.

> "Better conquer hearts than citadels."
>
> —Nguyen Trai

Soldier, Statesman, and Poet Nguyen's skill as a military strategist helped his people achieve a decisive victory that restored Vietnamese independence. According to legend, he used honey to write the message "Le Loi for the people, Nguyen Trai for Le Loi" on the leaves of trees. When ants ate the parts of the leaves covered in honey, they carved out the message. The enemy, however, assumed supernatural forces had inscribed it.

Following his heroics in helping Vietnam achieve independence, Nguyen Trai was appointed to a high government position. He wrote a famous poetic account of the war, titled

Phoenix Ewer, 14th-15th century. Vietnamese school. Stoneware with underglaze cobalt blue decoration, H. 11 1/2 in. The Metropolitan Museum of Art, NY.

the *Proclamation of Victory over the Chinese.* The Chinese invaders had destroyed books and works of art in an attempt to wipe out Vietnamese culture. After the occupation, the entire culture had to be rebuilt. At the forefront of this effort, Nguyen Trai wrote poetry in *chu nom* (choo′nôm′), a written form of the Vietnamese language based on Chinese characters. By using *chu nom,* he hoped to create a national literature in simple, direct language everyone in his country could understand.

Fall from Power After fighting to free Vietnam from foreign domination and then to rebuild its culture, Nguyen Trai retired to a simple life in the country. Still, he served as an adviser to the king, and some members of the court were jealous of his influence. Accused of planning to kill the king, Nguyen Trai was executed along with his entire family. Today he is honored as a hero in Vietnam.

LOG ON **Literature** Online

Author Search For more about Nguyen Trai, go to glencoe.com and enter QuickPass code GLW6053u4.

Literature and Reading Preview

Connect to the Poem

Where do you go when you want to get away from the world? Write a journal entry describing an ideal place to be alone with your thoughts.

Build Background

Bamboo—a tall, treelike plant that is actually a grass—has long been praised in the literature and art of East and Southeast Asia. Bamboo grows in hollow, jointed stalks. The sturdy and fast-growing bamboo stems provide an ideal material for building. They are used to make houses and rafts, scaffoldings for construction sites, and a variety of smaller items ranging from furniture to walking sticks.

Set Purposes for Reading

Big Idea Place and Identity

The Chinese poetic ideal of living a simple rural life away from the world's bustle deeply influenced traditional Vietnamese poetry. As you read, ask yourself, How does this poem reflect that influence?

Literary Element Imagery

Imagery is the word pictures that help evoke an emotional response. In creating images, authors use sensory details or descriptions that appeal to one or more of the five senses. As you read, ask yourself, What do the images in the poem reveal about the speaker's life?

Reading Strategy Analyze Structure

When you **analyze structure**, you identify the pattern of oranization an author uses to present his or her ideas. "The Bamboo Hut" is made up of four two-line sentences. As you read, ask yourself, Why did the poet choose this structure?

Tip: Take Notes In a chart like the one below, write down an analysis of each sentence in this poem.

Sentence	Structure	Main Idea	Supporting Details
1	Two-part sentence divided by dash; first part gives physical details		

Bamboo, Momoyama Period, ca.1568-1615. Japanese school. Ink on paper. Private collection.

The Bamboo Hut

Plum Blossoms, 1972. Guan Tianying (Bonnie Kwan Huo). Watercolor, 37.5 x 15 cm. Private collection.

Nguyen Trai

Translated by Nguyen Ngoc Bich
with Burton Raffel and W. S. Merwin

A bamboo hut and a plum tree bower—[1]
That's where I spend my days, far from the world's talk.
For meals, only some pickled cabbage,
But I've never cared for the life of damask[2] and silk.
There's a pool of water for watching the moon,
And land to plough into flower beds.
Sometimes I feel inspired on snowy nights—
That's when I write my best poems, and sing.

---

1. A *bower* (bou′ər) is a shelter (as in a garden) made with tree boughs.
2. *Damask* (dam′əsk) is a rich, patterned fabric.

Analyze Structure *What line in the poem does this line echo?*

After You Read

Respond and Think Critically

Respond and Interpret

1. Can you identify with the speaker's feelings in this poem? Explain.

2. (a)Where does the speaker spend his days? (b)What does the speaker like about this place?

3. What can you infer about the speaker's view of work from the last four lines?

Analyze and Evaluate

4. Do you think the poet is the speaker in this poem? Why or why not?

5. The **theme** of a literary work is its main idea. What do you think is the theme of this poem?

Connect

6. **Big Idea** **Place and Identity** How would you describe the relationship between the speaker and nature in this poem?

7. **Connect to Today** (a)What might be the modern-day equivalents of a bamboo hut? of a life of damask and silk? (b)Do you think most Americans would choose "a bamboo hut and a plum tree bower" over a life of luxury? Explain.

Literary Element **Imagery**

Authors use **imagery** to convey how things look, taste, feel, sound, and smell. Nguyen's imagery helps the reader picture the speaker's surroundings.

1. Based on the imagery in the poem, what kind of life does the speaker live?

2. What images help you picture the speaker's environment and lifestyle? Explain.

Reading Strategy **Analyze Structure**

The **structure** of "The Bamboo Hut" is four sentences, each of which is two lines long. Review the chart you made on page 787. Then answer the following questions.

1. How would you state the main idea of the second sentence?

2. (a)What structural similarities can you find in the first and fourth sentences? (b)What does the contrast between the words "talk" and "sing" suggest?

Academic Vocabulary

Trai's poem suggests that a simple lifestyle that fosters creativity is **sufficient** *for happiness.*

Sufficient is an academic word. In more familiar usage, you might say that a piece of fruit is often a **sufficient** snack. To study this word, fill out a graphic organizer like the one below.

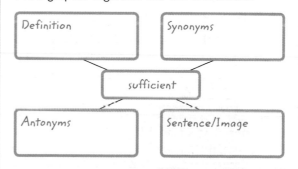

For more on academic vocabulary, see pages 36–37 and R83–R87.

Writing

Write a Poem Write a poem about an ideal spot "far from the world's talk." Include imagery and figures of speech to describe the kind of life you would lead in your ideal spot. Share your poem with your classmates.

Before You Read

The Doll's House

Meet **Katherine Mansfield**

(1888–1923)

K atherine Mansfield lived only 34 years, but in her short life she became one of the greatest short story authors and an innovator in the form. Although she lived in Europe as an adult, she often returned to her childhood home in New Zealand in her fiction.

Born Kathleen Mansfield Beauchamp (bē′chəm), she grew up in Karori, a rural New Zealand village not far from the nation's capital, Wellington. The daughter of a wealthy banker, she nevertheless attended local New Zealand schools, rubbing elbows with children from families far less privileged than her own.

> "I want to write about my own country till I simply exhaust my store."
>
> —Katherine Mansfield

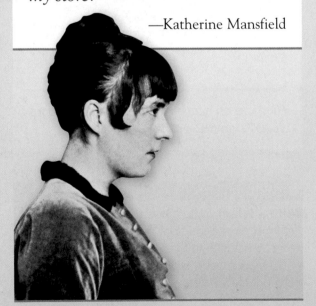

Setbacks and Success Independent from childhood, she moved to London at nineteen to start a writing career. Her life there got off to a rough start. She married hastily and left her husband after only a few days, then became increasingly disillusioned. In 1911 her life improved—Mansfield published her first book and met her future second husband, John Middleton Murry, editor of two magazines that published her stories.

The death of her soldier brother in 1915 affected Mansfield deeply. Dedicating herself to preserving her memories of him and their shared childhood, she wrote a series of short stories that beautifully portray her family life in New Zealand. Regarded today as masterpieces of the short story form, they were published in 1920 in the collection *Bliss and Other Stories*.

Illness and Critical Acclaim Mansfield contracted tuberculosis in her late twenties. Despite her illness, she continued to write, producing some of her best works while desperately seeking a cure for her illness. During this period she published the critically acclaimed collection *The Garden Party*. She completed her last story only months before her death in France.

Mansfield revolutionized the concept of the short story, moving it away from the strictures of plot and external action. She was able to capture the meaning of a relationship, illuminating the inner truth of a character's life. Her stories have been called delicate and profound. "I choose not only the length of every sentence, but even the sound of every sentence," she wrote. "I choose the rise and fall of every paragraph."

LOG ON ▶ **Literature** Online

Author Search For more about Katherine Mansfield, go to glencoe.com and enter QuickPass code GLW6053u4.

Literature and Reading Preview

Connect to the Story

How much does a person's social class affect his or her status in your school or community? Write a journal entry in response to this question.

Build Background

During the late 1800s, class differences in New Zealand were far more pronounced than they are today. Because there were few schools in rural areas, wealthy New Zealanders sent their children to the same schools the poor attended. However, the wealthy still made harsh judgments based on social status.

Set Purposes for Reading

Big Idea Cultures in Conflict

As you read, ask yourself, What conflicts does the class system in the story create?

Literary Element Symbol

A **symbol** is a person, a place, or a thing that stands for itself and something beyond itself, often an abstract quality or idea. For example, a red heart is a common symbol for love; a dove is a common symbol for peace. As you read, ask yourself, What symbols support this story's message, or theme?

Reading Strategy Analyze Sensory Details

In creating effective images, authors use **sensory details,** or descriptions that appeal to one or more of the five senses: sight, hearing, touch, taste, and smell. As you read, ask yourself, How do the sensory details influence the tone and meaning?

Tip: Make a Chart In a chart like the one below, keep track of the sensory appeal of the details in "The Doll's House."

Detail	Sense	Effect
"A dark, oily spinach green, picked out with bright yellow"	Sight; also perhaps taste and touch	Helps the reader visualize and emotionally respond to the doll's house.

Learning Objectives

For pages 790–800

In studying this text, you will focus on the following objectives:

Literary Study: Identifying symbol.

Reading: Analyzing sensory details.

Vocabulary

congealed (kən jēld´) *adj.* thickened; changed from a liquid to a solid state; p. 793 *As the temperature dropped, it was difficult to stir the congealed paint.*

marvelous (märv´ə ləs) *adj.* extraordinary; causing wonder; p. 793 *Her marvelous performance exceeded my expectations.*

flag (flag) *v.* to decline in interest or attraction; p. 796 *After a few hours at the carnival, the children's excitement began to flag.*

titter (ti´tər) *v.* to laugh nervously; p. 796 *The guests tittered at their host's little joke.*

imploring (im plôr´ing) *adj.* begging or beseeching; p. 798 *With an imploring look, the prisoner pleaded for mercy.*

Tip: Context Clues When you come upon an unfamiliar term, examine the surrounding words to determine its possible meaning. For example, in the sentence *With an imploring look, the prisoner pleaded for mercy, imploring* must mean "entreating" because the prisoner is pleading for mercy.

Suffragette's House. Tirzah Ravilious (1908-1951). Private collection.

The Doll's House

Katherine Mansfield

When dear old Mrs. Hay went back to town after staying with the Burnells she sent the children a doll's house. It was so big that the carter and Pat carried it into the courtyard, and there it stayed, propped up on two wooden boxes beside the feed room door. No harm could come to it: it was summer. And perhaps the smell of paint would have gone off by the time it had to be taken in. For, really, the smell of paint coming from that doll's house ("Sweet of old Mrs. Hay, of course; most sweet and generous!")—but the smell of paint was quite enough to make anyone seriously ill, in Aunt Beryl's opinion. Even before the sacking was taken off. And when it was . . .

There stood the Doll's house, a dark, oily, spinach green, picked out with bright yellow. Its two solid little chimneys, glued on to the roof, were painted red and white, and the door, gleaming with yellow varnish, was like a little slab of toffee. Four windows, real windows, were divided into panes by a broad streak of green. There was actually a tiny porch, too, painted yellow, with big lumps of **congealed** paint hanging along the edge.

But perfect, perfect little house! Who could possibly mind the smell. It was part of the joy, part of the newness.

"Open it quickly, someone!"

The hook at the side was stuck fast. Pat pried it open with his penknife, and the whole house front swung back, and—there you were, gazing at one and the same moment into the drawing room and dining room, the kitchen and two bedrooms. That is the way for a house to open! Why don't all houses open like that? How much more exciting than peering through the slit of a door into a mean little hall with a hatstand and two umbrellas! That is—isn't it?—what you long to know about a house when you put your hand on the knocker. Perhaps it is the way God opens houses at the dead of night when He is taking a quiet turn with an angel . . .

"O-oh!" The Burnell children sounded as though they were in despair. It was too **marvelous**; it was too much for them. They had never seen anything like it in their lives. All the rooms were papered. There were pictures on the walls, painted on the paper, with gold frames complete. Red carpet covered all the floors except the kitchen; red plush chairs in the drawing room, green in the dining room; tables, beds with real bedclothes, a cradle, a stove, a dresser with tiny plates and one big jug. But what Kezia liked more than anything, what she liked frightfully, was the lamp. It stood in the middle of the dining room table, an exquisite little amber lamp with a white globe. It was even filled all ready for lighting, though, of course, you couldn't light it. But there was something inside that looked like oil and moved when you shook it.

The father and mother dolls, who sprawled very stiff as though they had fainted in the drawing room, and their two little children asleep upstairs, were really too big for the doll's house. They didn't look as though they belonged. But the lamp

---

Analyze Sensory Details *To what senses does this passage appeal?*

Vocabulary

congealed (kən jēld´) *adj.* thickened; changed from a liquid to a solid state

---

Symbol *Why does the little lamp attract Kezia's attention?*

Vocabulary

marvelous (märv´ə ləs) *adj.* extraordinary; causing wonder

was perfect. It seemed to smile at Kezia, to say, "I live here." The lamp was real.

The Burnell children could hardly walk to school fast enough the next morning. They burned to tell everybody, to describe, to—well—to boast about their doll's house before the school-bell rang.

"I'm to tell," said Isabel, "because I'm the eldest. And you two can join in after. But I'm to tell first."

There was nothing to answer. Isabel was bossy, but she was always right, and Lottie and Kezia knew too well the powers that went with being eldest. They brushed through the thick buttercups at the road edge and said nothing.

"And I'm to choose who's to come and see it first. Mother said I might."

For it had been arranged that while the doll's house stood in the courtyard they might ask the girls at school, two at a time, to come and look. Not to stay to tea, of course, or to come traipsing[1] through the house. But just to stand quietly in the courtyard while Isabel pointed out the beauties, and Lottie and Kezia looked pleased . . .

Visual Vocabulary
Palings are the stakes or pickets that form a fence.

But hurry as they might, by the time they had reached the tarred palings of the boys' playground the bell had begun to jangle. They only just had time to whip off their hats and fall into line before the roll was called. Never mind. Isabel tried to make up for it by looking very important and mysterious and by whispering behind her hand to the girls near her, "Got something to tell you at playtime."

Playtime came and Isabel was surrounded. The girls of her class nearly fought to put their arms round her, to walk away with her, to beam flatteringly, to be her special friend. She held quite a court under the huge pine trees at the side of the playground. Nudging, giggling together, the little girls pressed up close. And the only two who stayed outside the ring were the two who were always outside, the little Kelveys. They knew better than to come anywhere near the Burnells.

For the fact was, the school the Burnell children went to was not at all the kind of place their parents would have chosen if there had been any choice. But there was none. It was the only school for miles. And the consequence was all the children of the neighborhood, the Judge's little girls, the doctor's daughters, the storekeeper's children, the milkman's, were forced to mix together. Not to speak of there being an equal number of rude, rough little boys as well. But the line had to be drawn somewhere. It was drawn at the Kelveys. Many of the children, including the Burnells, were not allowed even to speak to them. They walked past the Kelveys with their heads in the air, and as they set the fashion in all matters of behavior, the Kelveys were shunned by everybody. Even the teacher had a special voice for them, and a special smile for the other children when Lil Kelvey came up to her desk with a bunch of dreadfully common-looking flowers.

They were the daughters of a spry, hard-working little washerwoman, who went

---

1. *Traipsing* means "walking around idly or aimlessly."

Cultures in Conflict *What conflict does this general attitude toward the Kelvey girls suggest?*

about from house to house by the day. This was awful enough. But where was Mr. Kelvey? Nobody knew for certain. But everybody said he was in prison. So they were the daughters of a washerwoman and a jailbird. Very nice company for other people's children! And they looked it. Why Mrs. Kelvey made them so conspicuous was hard to understand. The truth was they were dressed in "bits" given to her by the people for whom she worked. Lil, for instance, who was a stout, plain child, with big freckles, came to school in a dress made from a green art-serge tablecloth of the Burnells', with red plush sleeves from the Logans' curtains. Her hat, perched on top of her high forehead, was a grown-up woman's hat, once the property of Miss Lecky, the postmistress. It was turned up at the back and trimmed with a large scarlet quill. What a little guy[2] she looked! It was impossible not to laugh. And her little sister, our Else, wore a long white dress, rather like a nightgown, and a pair of little boy's boots. But whatever our Else wore she would have looked strange. She was a tiny wishbone of a child, with cropped hair and enormous solemn eyes—a little white owl. Nobody had ever seen her smile; she scarcely ever spoke. She went through life holding on to Lil, with a piece of Lil's skirt screwed up in her hand. Where Lil went, our Else followed. In the playground, on the road going to and from school, there was Lil marching in front and our Else holding on behind. Only when she wanted anything, or when she was out of breath, our Else gave Lil a tug, a twitch, and Lil stopped and turned round. The Kelveys never failed to understand each other.

Now they hovered at the edge; you couldn't stop them listening. When the little girls turned round and sneered, Lil, as usual, gave her silly, shamefaced smile, but our Else only looked.

And Isabel's voice, so very proud, went on telling. The carpet made a great sensation, but so did the beds with real bedclothes, and the stove with an oven door.

When she finished Kezia broke in. "You've forgotten the lamp, Isabel."

"Oh, yes," said Isabel, "and there's a teeny little lamp, all made of yellow glass, with a white globe that stands on the dining room table. You couldn't tell it from a real one."

"The lamp's best of all," cried Kezia. She thought Isabel wasn't making half enough of the little lamp. But nobody paid any attention. Isabel was choosing the two who were to come back with them that afternoon and see it. She chose Emmie Cole and Lena Logan. But when the others knew they were all to have a chance, they couldn't be nice enough to Isabel. One by one they put their arms round Isabel's waist and walked her off. They had something to whisper to her, a secret. "Isabel's my friend."

Only the little Kelveys moved away forgotten; there was nothing more for them to hear.

Days passed, and as more children saw the doll's house, the fame of it spread. It became the one subject, the rage. The one question was, "Have you seen Burnells' doll's house? Oh, ain't it lovely!" "Haven't you seen it? Oh, I say!"

---

2. In British slang, a *guy* is an ugly, shabbily dressed person.

Analyze Sensory Details *What effect does this description of Lil create?*

Symbol *What does the doll's house represent to the Burnells' classmates?*

KATHERINE MANSFIELD **795**

Even the dinner hour was given up to talking about it. The little girls sat under the pines eating their thick mutton sandwiches and big slabs of johnny cake[3] spread with butter. While always, as near as they could get, sat the Kelveys, our Else holding on to Lil, listening too, while they chewed their jam sandwiches out of a newspaper soaked with large red blobs.

"Mother," said Kezia, "can't I ask the Kelveys just once?"

"Certainly not, Kezia."

"But why not?"

"Run away, Kezia; you know quite well why not."

At last everybody had seen it except them. On that day the subject rather **flagged**. It was the dinner hour. The children stood together under the pine trees, and suddenly, as they looked at the Kelveys eating out of their paper, always by themselves, always listening, they wanted to be horrid to them. Emmie Cole started the whisper.

"Lil Kelvey's going to be a servant when she grows up."

"O-oh, how awful!" said Isabel Burnell, and she made eyes at Emmie.

Emmie swallowed in a very meaning way and nodded to Isabel as she'd seen her mother do on those occasions.

"It's true—it's true—it's true," she said.

Then Lena Logan's little eyes snapped. "Shall I ask her?" she whispered.

"Bet you don't," said Jessie May.

"Pooh, I'm not frightened," said Lena.

Suddenly she gave a little squeal and danced in front of the other girls. "Watch! Watch me! Watch me now!" said Lena. And sliding, gliding, dragging one foot, giggling behind her hand, Lena went over to the Kelveys.

Lil looked up from her dinner. She wrapped the rest quickly away. Our Else stopped chewing. What was coming now?

"Is it true you're going to be a servant when you grow up, Lil Kelvey?" shrilled Lena.

Dead silence. But instead of answering, Lil only gave her silly, shamefaced smile. She didn't seem to mind the question at all. What a sell[4] for Lena! The girls began to **titter**.

Lena couldn't stand that. She put her hands on her hips; she shot forward. "Yah, yer father's in prison!" she hissed, spitefully.

This was such a marvelous thing to have said that the little girls rushed away in a body, deeply, deeply excited, wild with joy. Someone found a long rope, and they began skipping. And never did they skip so high, run in and out so fast, or do such daring things as on that morning.

In the afternoon Pat called for the Burnell children with the buggy and they drove home. There were visitors. Isabel and Lottie, who liked visitors, went upstairs to change their pinafores. But Kezia thieved out at the back. Nobody was about; she began to swing on the big white gates of the courtyard. Presently, looking along the road, she saw two little dots. They grew bigger, they were coming towards her. Now she could see that one was in front and one

---

3. A *johnny cake* is a flat, crisp cake made of cornmeal.

Analyze Sensory Details *What does the contrast in the little girls' lunches suggest about their class differences?*

Vocabulary

flag (flag) *v.* to decline in interest or attraction

---

4. In British slang, a *sell* is a great disappointment.

Vocabulary

titter (ti′tər) *v.* to laugh nervously

The Road to the school on Edam. **Max Liebermann.** Oil on canvas. Pushkin Museum, Moscow.

<u>View the Art</u> Liebermann was an important German Impressionist. He often focused on light and color in his paintings. How does the mood of this painting compare with the mood of the story?

close behind. Now she could see that they were the Kelveys. Kezia stopped swinging. She slipped off the gate as if she was going to run away. Then she hesitated. The Kelveys came nearer, and beside them walked their shadows, very long, stretching right across the road with their heads in the buttercups. Kezia clambered back on the gate; she had made up her mind; she swung out.

"Hullo," she said to the passing Kelveys.

They were so astounded that they stopped. Lil gave her silly smile. Our Else stared.

"You can come and see our doll's house if you want to," said Kezia, and she dragged one toe on the ground. But at that Lil turned red and shook her head quickly.

"Why not?" asked Kezia.

Lil gasped, then she said, "Your ma told our ma you wasn't to speak to us."

Cultures in Conflict *What does Lil understand about social tensions in the community?*

"Oh, well," said Kezia. She didn't know what to reply. "It doesn't matter. You can come and see our doll's house all the same. Come on. Nobody's looking."

But Lil shook her head still harder.

"Don't you want to?" asked Kezia.

Suddenly there was a twitch, a tug at Lil's skirt. She turned round. Our Else was looking at her with big, **imploring** eyes; she was frowning; she wanted to go. For a moment Lil looked at our Else very doubtfully. But then our Else twitched her skirt again. She started forward. Kezia led the way. Like two little stray cats they followed across the courtyard to where the doll's house stood.

"There it is," said Kezia.

There was a pause. Lil breathed loudly, almost snorted; our Else was still as stone.

"I'll open it for you," said Kezia kindly. She undid the hook and they looked inside.

"There's the drawing room and the dining room, and that's the—"

"Kezia!"

Oh, what a start they gave!

"Kezia!"

It was Aunt Beryl's voice. They turned round. At the back door stood Aunt Beryl, staring as if she couldn't believe what she saw.

"How dare you ask the little Kelveys into the courtyard?" said her cold, furious voice. "You know as well as I do, you're not allowed to talk to them. Run away, children, run away at once. And don't come back again," said Aunt Beryl. And she stepped into the yard and shooed them out as if they were chickens.

"Off you go immediately!" she called, cold and proud.

They did not need telling twice. Burning with shame, shrinking together, Lil huddling along like her mother, our Else dazed, somehow they crossed the big courtyard and squeezed through the white gate.

"Wicked, disobedient little girl!" said Aunt Beryl bitterly to Kezia, and she slammed the doll's house to.

The afternoon had been awful. A letter had come from Willie Brent, a terrifying, threatening letter, saying if she did not meet him that evening in Pulman's Bush, he'd come to the front door and ask the reason why! But now that she had frightened those little rats of Kelveys and given Kezia a good scolding, her heart felt lighter. That ghastly pressure was gone. She went back to the house humming.

When the Kelveys were well out of sight of Burnells', they sat down to rest on a big red drainpipe by the side of the road. Lil's cheeks were still burning; she took off the hat with the quill and held it on her knee. Dreamily they looked over the hay paddocks, past the creek, to the group of wattles[5] where Logan's cows stood waiting to be milked. What were their thoughts?

Presently our Else nudged up close to her sister. But now she had forgotten the cross lady. She put out a finger and stroked her sister's quill; she smiled her rare smile.

"I seen the little lamp," she said, softly.

Then both were silent once more. ❧

---

5. *Wattles* are branches or poles woven together to make walls.

Cultures in Conflict *How does Aunt Beryl serve as a spokesperson for the entire community?*

Vocabulary

imploring (im plôr´ ing) *adj.* begging or beseeching

Analyze Sensory Details *What do these details suggest about the setting of the final scene?*

After You Read

Respond and Think Critically

Respond and Interpret

1. What was your reaction to the way the Kelvey girls are treated?

2. (a)Describe the Burnells' doll's house. Why does it remain outside? (b)What do the Burnell children think of their new doll's house?

3. (a)Under what conditions are the girls' school friends allowed to see the doll's house? (b)Why do the Burnells set such strict conditions?

4. (a)What rule must the Burnell girls obey regarding the Kelvey sisters? Why? (b)What effect do adult prejudices have on the Burnell girls and some of the other girls at school?

Analyze and Evaluate

5. (a)How is Kezia different from her family? Support your answer with details from the story.

(b)What do you think Kezia will be like when she grows up? Why?

6. What is significant about Else's statement at the end of the story?

7. The **theme**, or main idea, of a story can often be expressed as a general statement. How would you express the theme of this story?

Connect

8. **Big Idea** **Cultures in Conflict** What does the story suggest about the way economic or class differences can affect people?

9. **Connect to Today** The children in this story yield to peer pressure in their admiration of Isabel and their rejection of the Kelvey sisters. What qualities must a young person have to resist peer pressure in today's world?

Daily Life & Culture

Society in Miniature

Like their clothes, children's toys may reflect the socioeconomic class of their owners, as suggested in Mansfield's story. In the 1800s, children of wealth enjoyed dolls with finely detailed heads and hands of bisque (unglazed china), porcelain, or molded wax. Doll's houses were also indicative of status. Well-to-do children might play with elaborate doll's houses beautifully furnished. As with children's dolls, many of these houses were meant for show rather than play. Poor children, needless to say, seldom, if ever, had the luxury of playing with doll's houses.

Group Activity Discuss the following questions.

1. Does the doll's house in this story seem intended as a toy or as a display piece? Explain.

2. The doll's house in this story is described on p. 793 as a "perfect little house." In your opinion, is it perfect? Explain.

Before You Read

Rainforest and *River Bend*

Meet **Judith Wright**
(1915–2000)

"The true function of an art and a culture," Australian poet Judith Wright once wrote, "is to interpret us to ourselves, and to relate us to the country and society in which we live." She carried out this sentiment in her poetry, her commitment to the environment, and her involvement in politics.

Love for the Land Wright was born into a family that had lived in Australia since the nineteenth century. Her connection to the natural world was formed during her childhood on a ranch in the mountains of New South Wales. For Wright, it was not family but the land itself that would become the greatest influence on her life.

The Poet Emerges As a young child, Wright was educated at home, but when she began her studies at the New England Girls' School, one of her teachers recognized and encouraged her talent for writing. During her last year at school, she broke her pelvis in a riding accident. When doctors told her she would be unable to have children, Wright remembered one of her favorite childhood books, *My Brilliant Career*, which describes a young woman who decides not to get married so she can maintain her independence. Wright knew she could have a fulfilling life as an author. In the mid-1940s Wright began to compose poetry and was published in several literary journals, including *Meanjin Papers*. Tired of the old "literature of nostalgia," she believed the time had come to make Australia a spiritual and literary home for its people.

Artist and Activist Wright's beautifully crafted, lyrical poems present a world in which humans and nature are bonded together, but she was also aware of the connection between art

"As a poet you have to imitate somebody, but as I had a beautiful landscape outside that I loved so much and was in so much . . . it was my main object from the start."

—Judith Wright

and politics. She was an outspoken opponent of uranium mining and nuclear power. She devoted much of her time to advocating for the rights of Aboriginal people of Australia and for the protection of natural resources. Some of Wright's critics claimed her politics began to overshadow the artistic merits of her poetry, but she insisted the two were not separate. She was one of the first to deliver a scholarly paper analyzing the work of Aboriginal writers. Her final public act came just before her death when she led a march across the Sydney Harbor Bridge during bitterly cold winter weather. She and the other marchers were demonstrating for reconciliation for Australia's Aboriginal population.

 Literature Online

Author Search For more about Judith Wright, go to glencoe.com and enter QuickPass code GLW6053u4.

Literature and Reading Preview

Connect to the Poems

To what aspects of the natural world do you think people are most strongly connected? Discuss this question with a small group. Consider the power and strength of nature, as well as its subtle characteristics.

Build Background

The Aborigines of Australia lived off the land without adversely affecting it. But since the arrival of Europeans, much of the land has been cleared for lumbering or farming. In Wright's native state of New South Wales, the forest that was once prevalent now covers only 10 percent of the land.

Set Purposes for Reading

Big Idea Place and Identity

As you read the poems, ask yourself, How do the poems show that humans, animals, and plants are interconnected?

Literary Element Meter and Rhythm

Meter is a regular pattern of stressed (marked ′) and unstressed (marked ˘) syllables that give a line of poetry a **rhythm**, or pattern of beats. The basic metrical unit is called the **foot**, which usually consists of one stressed syllable and one or more unstressed syllables. As you read the poems, ask yourself, How do meter and rhythm create a musical effect?

Reading Strategy Clarify Meaning

When you **clarify meaning**, you examine difficult sections of text to clear up what is confusing. As you read, ask yourself, Do I understand the ideas in each part of the text? If your answer is "no," ask yourself questions about the text, reread more slowly, and look up unfamiliar words in a dictionary.

Tip: Take Notes Use a chart like the one below to record your interpretations of excerpts from Wright's poems.

Excerpt	Questions	My Interpretation
"We cannot understand that call <u>unless we move into his dream</u>, where all is one and one is all and <u>frog and python are the same.</u>"	What does it mean to "move into" the frog's dream? How can a frog and a python be the same?	We need to enter a mindset in which we can see the unity of all creatures.

Vocabulary

mutter (mut′ər) *v.* to speak in a low voice or indistinctly with lips partially closed; p. 804 *Andrea saw the grade written on her test and began to mutter behind her hand.*

forage (fôr′ij) *v.* to hunt or search for food; p. 804 *The raccoons like to forage for scraps near the garbage cans.*

perpetual (pər pech′oo əl) *adj.* everlasting; eternal; p. 804 *The forest of giant redwoods seems to exist in perpetual silence.*

Tip: Word Usage When you encounter a new word, it might help you to answer a specific question about the word. For example, When might you **mutter** a comment as opposed to saying it clearly?

Before You Read

Municipal Gum

Meet **Oodgeroo of the tribe Noonuccal**
(1920–1993)

Oodgeroo of the tribe Noonuccal (ōōd′jer ōō nōō′noo kəl) adopted her tribal name in 1988 to protest bicentennial celebrations of the European settlement in Australia. She characterized the 200 years of settlement as years of destruction and carnage, writing, "From the Aboriginal point of view, what is there to celebrate?"

> "Change is the law. The new must oust the old."
>
> —Oodgeroo of the tribe Noonuccal

Early Life Noonuccal was born Kathleen (Kath) Ruska, a member of the Noonuccal tribe of Stradbroke Island, Queensland, in northeastern Australia. When she was thirteen, financial pressures forced her to leave school and take a job as a servant. She wrote that, for an Aborigine at that time, "there wasn't the slightest possibility of getting 'a better job' [even] if you stayed on at school." During World War II, she worked for the Australian Women's Army Service. She was promoted to corporal, but had to resign from the service because of chronic middle ear infections. In 1942, she married Bruce Walker, with whom she had a son in 1946.

Aboriginal Voice After the war, Noonuccal began to gain wide recognition for her poetry and for her celebration of her heritage. With her first book, *We Are Going* (1964), she became the first Aboriginal poet ever published. It became one of the best-selling poetry collections in Australian history. She wrote of the collection, "I felt poetry would be the breakthrough for the Aboriginal people because they were storytellers and song-makers, and I thought poetry would appeal to them more than anything else. It was more of a book of their voices that I was trying to bring out, and I think I succeeded in doing this."

Tireless Activist In addition to writing, Noonuccal worked as a political and environmental activist throughout her life. In the 1960s, she served as the Queensland State Secretary of the Federal Council for the Advancement of Aborigines and Torres Strait Islanders, a group created to combat racism and ensure citizenship and voting rights for indigenous people. In 1970, she returned to her homeland of Minjerriba on Stradbroke Island and purchased property that became an open air classroom for Aboriginal culture and society. That same year, she was appointed a Member of the Order of the British Empire for her work advancing Aboriginal rights. However, she returned the honor in 1987 to protest Australia's bicentennial celebration. She is famous for poetry that expresses anger over European-Australian racism and conveys nostalgia for the lost Aboriginal ways of life.

LOG ON ▶ **Literature** Online

Author Search For more about Oodgeroo of the tribe Noonuccal, go to glencoe.com and enter QuickPass code GLW6053u4.

Literature and Reading Preview

Connect to the Poem

How can something change when it is taken out of its natural habitat? Write a journal entry about this question.

Build Background

When Europeans arrived in Australia in the late eighteenth century, they encountered one of the world's oldest cultures, dating back at least 42,000 years. The Aborigines (ab′ə rij′ə nēs) are hunter-gatherers who perform rituals to honor the earth and who live in close connection with Australia's animal and plant species. These include the native gum tree, or eucalyptus, which remains a symbol of the country and its people.

Set Purposes for Reading

Big Idea Cultures in Conflict

As you read, ask yourself, How have colonization and urbanization affected the Australian landscape?

Literary Element End Rhyme

Rhyme is the repetition of sound in words that appear close to one another. **End rhyme** occurs at the ends of lines. As you read, ask yourself, What are the patterns of end rhymes in the poem? Read the poem out loud and consider how the end rhyme contributes to the poem's emotional impact.

Reading Strategy Connect to Personal Experience

When you **connect to personal experience**, you make connections between details in a literary work and your life to help you understand the work. As you read, ask yourself, How do the ideas in "Municipal Gum" relate to my experiences?

Tip: Make a Web Use a web like the one below to record your thoughts as you read.

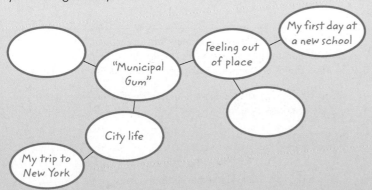

Learning Objectives

For pages 806–809

In studying this text, you will focus on the following objectives:

Literary Study: Analyzing end rhyme.

Reading: Connecting to personal experience.

Writing: Writing an internal monologue.

Vocabulary

listless (list′lis) *adj.* showing disinterest; spiritless; p. 808 *Stuck indoors on a rainy day, Laura grew listless.*

dolorous (dō′lər əs) *adj.* marked by sadness or grief; p. 808 *The dolorous love song had the audience in tears.*

Tip: Denotation and Connotation
A word's denotation is its literal meaning, while its connotations are its implied meanings. For example, the word *listless* literally means "disinterested," but it has a stronger connotation than the word *disinterested.*

Municipal Gum

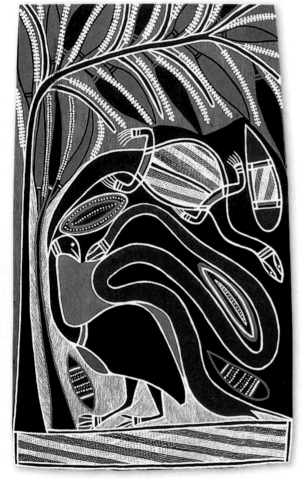

The Tree of Life and His Totems. David Malangi (b. 1934). Bark painting Aham Land, Northern Territory, Australia.

Oodgeroo of the tribe Noonuccal
(Kath Walker)

Gumtree in the city street,
Hard bitumen¹ around your feet,
Rather you should be
In the cool world of leafy forest halls
5   And wild bird calls.
Here you seem to me
Like that poor cart-horse
Castrated,² broken, a thing wronged,
Strapped and buckled, its hell prolonged,
10   Whose hung head and **listless** mien³ express
Its hopelessness.
Municipal gum, it is **dolorous**
To see you thus
Set in your black grass of bitumen—
15   O fellow citizen,
What have they done to us?

---

1. *Bitumen* (bĭ tōō´mən) can mean "tar" or "asphalt."
2. *Castrated* means "impotent" or "lacking in vitality."
3. *Mien* (mēn) is a person's manner or appearance.

End Rhyme *How does the use of end rhyme enhance your sense of the speaker's emotions?*

Vocabulary

listless (list´lis) *adj.* showing disinterest; spiritless
dolorous (dō´lər əs) *adj.* marked by sadness or grief

After You Read

Respond and Think Critically

Respond and Interpret

1. What images from this poem did you find the most memorable? Explain.

2. (a)How does the speaker contrast the life of a city gum tree and that of a gum tree in the forest? (b)What does this suggest about the Noonuccal tribe's beliefs?

3. (a)What might the gum tree and cart-horse represent? (b)How would you state the **theme**, or message, of this poem?

Analyze and Evaluate

4. (a)What **metaphor** does the author use in line 14? (b)How does this metaphor reinforce the poem's theme?

5. What can you infer about the speaker's relationship with, and attitude toward, the natural world? Explain.

6. (a)What do the last two lines of the poem suggest? (b)How effective do you find these two lines? Explain.

Connect

7. **Big Idea** **Cultures in Conflict** How does this poem illustrate the conflict between Aboriginal values and European values?

8. **Connect to the Author** Noonuccal changed her name to reflect her culture. What kinds of things do people do today to celebrate their heritage and define themselves?

Literary Element **End Rhyme**

Poets use **end rhyme** to create rhythm, to stress particular ideas, or to amuse their audiences.

1. What idea does the poet express through the end rhymes in lines 8–9?

2. How does the end rhyme add to the overall effect of the poem?

Reading Strategy **Connect to Personal Experience**

Connecting to personal experience allows you to better understand pieces of literature.

1. (a)Describe a situation in which you felt out of place. (b)What aspects of the situation were most uncomfortable?

2. To what extent were the emotions you experienced similar to those in the poem?

LOG ON ▶ **Literature** Online

Selection Resources For Selection Quizzes, eFlashcards, and Reading-Writing Connection activities, go to glencoe.com and enter QuickPass code GLW6053u4.

Vocabulary Practice

Practice with Denotation and Connotation
Each of the boldfaced vocabulary words below is listed with a word that has a similar denotation. Choose the word that has the stronger connotation.

1. listless   bored

2. dolorous   miserable

Writing

Write an Internal Monologue Write an internal monologue from the point of view of the tree in "Municipal Gum." If the tree had a voice, what do you think it would say about being displaced? As you plan, think about your experiences observing the overlap of urban and rural features, such as strip malls along country roads. Consult your web on page 807 for ideas and use sensory details to capture how the tree experiences its environment.

Clouds on the Sea

Ruth Dallas

Lowry Bay, New Zealand, 1954. Roland Wakelin. Oil on board. Private collection.

I walk among men with tall bones,
With shoes of leather, and pink faces;
I meet no man holding a begging
   bowl;
All have their dwelling places.

5 In my country
Every child is taught to read and
   write,
Every child has shoes and a warm
   coat,
Every child must eat his dinner,
No one must grow any thinner;
10 It is considered remarkable and not
   nice
To meet bed-bugs or lice.
Oh we live like the rich
With music at the touch of a switch,

Light in the middle of the night,
15 Water in the house as if from a spring.
Hot, if you wish, or cold, anything
For the comfort of the flesh,
In my country. Fragment
Of new skin at the edge of the world's
   ulcer.

20 For the question
That troubled you as you watched the
   reapers
And a poor woman following,
Gleaning the ears on the ground,
*Why should I have grain and this
   woman none?*
25 No satisfactory answer has been
   found.

Summarize *How would you summarize the main idea of this stanza?*

Cultures in Conflict *What do these lines tell you about class divisions in New Zealand?*

After You Read

Respond and Think Critically

Respond and Interpret

1. Which lines in the poem were most surprising to you? Explain.

2. (a)Describe the appearance of the men in lines 1–2. (b)Based on this description, what can you infer about their identity?

3. (a)According to the second stanza, what is life like in New Zealand? (b)How does this description contrast with that of the woman in the third stanza?

4. (a)What question troubles the "you" in the final stanza? (b)Who do you think the "you" is?

Analyze and Evaluate

5. How would you contrast the **mood** of the second stanza with that of the final stanza?

6. (a)How do you interpret the **metaphor** in lines 18–19? (b)What effect does this metaphor create?

Connect

7. **Big Idea** **Cultures in Conflict** How does the situation described in this poem reflect a culture clash in New Zealand?

8. **Connect to Today** Is the situation described by Dallas relevant only to New Zealand, or does it apply to contemporary American society? Explain.

Literary Element Speaker

A poet can express his or her ideas and opinions through a **speaker.** You can find clues about a speaker's identity and attitudes when you pay attention to elements such as tone and diction.

1. How would you describe the speaker's **tone** (the attitude he or she takes toward the subject)?

2. Do you think Dallas shares the speaker's views? Explain.

Reading Strategy Summarize

Refer to the chart you made on page 811 and then answer the following questions.

1. Summarize what the adults and children of New Zealand have, according to the poem.

2. How would you summarize the **theme** expressed in the final stanza?

Academic Vocabulary

*The speaker in "Clouds on the Sea" makes a clear **differentiation** between the rich and the poor, but she struggles to find an underlying reason for the gap between these two groups.*

Differentiation is an academic word. Identical twins may look alike, but the **differentiation** in their personalities marks them as individuals. The word *differentiation* is also used in biology. Use context clues to figure out the meaning of *differentiation* in the following sentence.

During **differentiation**, the cells of an embryo develop into separate and specific tissues.

For more on academic vocabulary, see pages 36–37 and R83–R85.

Writing

Write an Essay Using "Clouds on the Sea" as a springboard, research policies that address social and economic inequality in New Zealand. Present your findings in a brief expository essay. In one of your body paragraphs, compare New Zealand's policies with similar ones in the United States.

Thoughts of Hanoi

Nguyen Thi Vinh

Translated by Nguyen Ngoc Bich with Burton Raffel and W. S. Merwin

The night is deep and chill
as in early autumn. Pitchblack,
it thickens after each lightning flash.
I dream of Hanoi:
5   Co-ngu° Road
ten years of separation
the way back sliced by a frontier of hatred.
I want to bury the past
to burn the future
10 still I **yearn**
still I fear
those endless nights
waiting for dawn.

Brother,
15 how is Hang Dao° now?
How is Ngoc Son° temple?
Do the trains still run
each day from Hanoi
to the neighboring towns?
20 To Bac-ninh, Cam-giang, Yen-bai,°
the small villages, islands
of brown thatch in a **lush** green sea?
The girls
      bright eyes
25   **ruddy** cheeks
      four-piece dresses
         raven-bill scarves
      sowing harvesting
         spinning weaving
30 all year round,
the boys
      ploughing
         transplanting
      in the fields

5 Co-ngu: (kôʹəng)

15 **Hang Dao:** (hän dou)
16 **Ngoc Son:** (nyokʹsun)

20 **Bac-ninh:** (bäkʹnēn);
Cam-giang: (kämʹyē än); **Yen-bai:** (yinʹbī)

> **Vocabulary**
>
> **yearn** (yurn) *v.* to desire or long
> **lush** (lush) *adj.* luxuriant; thick with vegetation
> **ruddy** (rudʹē) *adj.* having a rosy or reddish complexion

---

Activate Prior Knowledge *In light of what you know about Vietnam's history, how do you interpret these lines?*

35   in their shops
     running across
         the meadow at evening
     to fly kites
         and sing alternating songs.

40   Stainless blue sky,
        jubilant voices of children
     stumbling through the alphabet,
        village graybeards strolling to the temple,
     grandmothers basking in twilight sun,
45   chewing betel° leaves
     while the children run—

     Brother,
     how is all that now?
     Or is it **obsolete**?
50   Are you like me,
     reliving the past,
     imagining the future?
     Do you count me as a friend
     or am I the enemy in your eyes?
55   Brother, I am afraid
     that one day I'll be with the
         March-North Army°
     meeting you on your way to the South.
     I might be the one to shoot you then
     or you me
60   but please
     not with hatred.

     For don't you remember how it was,
     you and I in school together,
     plotting our lives together?
65   Those roots go deep!

     Brother, we are men,
     conscious of more
     than material needs.
     How can this happen to us
70   my friend
     my foe?

45 **betel** (bē′təl) **leaves:** a mild stimulant from a type of pepper tree; the habit of chewing them, although diminishing, is still widespread in southeast Asia.

56 **March-North Army:** the South Vietnamese army at the time of the Vietnam War.

Ham Rong Bridge, 1970. Vu Giang Huong. Woodcut on rice paper, 12 x 16 7/8 in. Collection of the Artist.

Flashback *Why are the speaker's memories of Hanoi so idyllic?*

The Struggle to Survive *How are the speaker's values in conflict with the demands of the war?*

Vocabulary

jubilant (jōō′bə lənt) *adj.* joyful; rejoicing
obsolete (ob′sə lēt′) *adj.* outdated; no longer in use

After You Read

Respond and Think Critically

Respond and Interpret

1. How would you answer the final question if you were the speaker's friend?

2. (a)What questions about Hanoi does the speaker ask the person addressed as "Brother"? (b)What scenes from his past does the speaker recall?

3. (a)In lines 50–64, what does the speaker wonder about Brother? (b)What emotion frightens the speaker?

Analyze and Evaluate

4. (a)Nguyen begins "Thoughts of Hanoi" with an image of a dark, lightning-filled sky. What do you think this image might represent?

(b)Why might the poem begin with such an image?

5. How would you describe the **style**—the expressive qualities, including word choice and sentence arrangement—of this poem?

6. What is the effect of the poet's use of a series of unanswered questions?

Connect

7. **Big Idea** The Struggle to Survive
How does this poem illustrate how civil war affects individuals?

8. **Connect to Today** What recent conflicts in the world have caused divisions among people?

Literary Element Flashback

Authors often use **flashbacks** to provide background information, to create tension, or to create a contrast with the present situation being described.

1. Why might Nguyen have wanted to paint a picture of Hanoi before the war?

2. How does the tone of the flashback differ from the tone of the rest of the poem?

Reading Strategy Activate Prior Knowledge

Consult the chart you made on page 815 and then answer the following questions.

1. (a)What situations have you heard of in which former friends became enemies? (b)How could such a change of feelings be prevented?

2. Discuss what you know about the Vietnam War. How might this knowledge help you understand and connect to the poem?

LOG ON ▶ **Literature** Online

Selection Resources For Selection Quizzes, eFlashcards, and Reading-Writing Connection activities, go to glencoe.com and enter QuickPass code GLW6053u4.

Vocabulary Practice

Practice with Synonyms With a partner, match each boldfaced vocabulary word below with its synonym. Use a thesaurus or dictionary to check your answers.

1. yearn   a. archaic
2. lush   b. flushed
3. ruddy   c. crave
4. jubilant   d. euphoric
5. obsolete   e. flourishing

Writing

Write a Letter Write a letter to the speaker in "Thoughts of Hanoi" in which you answer the question posed at the end of the poem as if you are the "Brother." Activate your prior knowledge about the Vietnam War and personal experiences of separation from loved ones to stimulate your thinking. In your letter, use **flashbacks** to show how you (as the "Brother") felt about the speaker in the past and how you remember life before the war.

Before You Read

Feeding the Fire of Enmity
from *Stay Alive, My Son*

Cambodia

Meet **Pin Yathay**
(born 1953)

When he was in his early twenties, Pin Yathay (pin yä′tī) worked as an engineer in Cambodia's Ministry of Public Works. In April 1975, communist guerrillas known as the Khmer Rouge (kə mer′rōōzh) took control of Phnom Penh (pə näm′pen′), the capital of Cambodia. At first, Thay (the short version of his name) welcomed them because he hoped they would restore order to his nation. Thay's hopes for an improved Cambodia, however, soon turned into a nightmare.

False Promises Claiming a U.S. bombing of Phnom Penh was imminent, the Khmer Rouge ordered three million people, including those in hospitals, out of the country's cities, promising them they could soon return to their homes. Instead, they were transported to rural labor camps, where they were forced to do hard labor for at least twelve hours a day, digging canals and building irrigation systems. Rations were limited to about a half a pound of rice a day for eight people. Malnourished and exhausted, many died.

Others were taken to detention centers, where many were killed if they knew a second language, were educated, or even wore glasses. The Khmer Rouge sought to eradicate the intellectuals and rebuild Cambodia as a classless peasant society where all resources would be shared equally. In pursuit of this goal, the Khmer Rouge changed schools and places of worship into labor and re-education camps. Singing, dancing, and praying were outlawed. Being immodest or stealing was punishable by death. Banks, money, and private property were abolished. All religions were outlawed. Estimates

"Through our suffering, I want . . . my readers to see how fine-sounding ideals of justice and equality can be perverted by fanatics to create brutal oppression. . ."

—Pin Yathay

vary, but it is believed that between one and three million people died, or about one third of the population of Cambodia. Yathay himself lost seventeen members of his family. The atrocities continued until Vietnam invaded Cambodia in 1979, ending the Khmer Rouge dictatorship.

A Father's Directive Among the family members Yathay lost during the Khmer Rouge's reign of terror was his father. Lying on his deathbed, Yathay's father said to him, "Stay alive, my son." These words, which Yathay later spoke to his own son, became the title of his memoir.

 Literature Online

Author Search For more about Pin Yathay, go to glencoe.com and enter QuickPass code GLW6053u4.

Literature and Reading Preview

Connect to the Memoir

Have you ever felt you were treated unjustly by someone in a position of authority? Discuss this question with a partner.

Build Background

From 1970 to 1975, Cambodia was ruled by an army general named Lon Nol, who had seized power from the previous ruler, Prince Sihanouk, in a *coup* (kü')—a sudden, violent overthrow of the government. In 1975, the Khmer Rouge overthrew Lon Nol's regime with the support of the North Vietnamese and the exiled Prince Sihanouk. In 1976, a Khmer Rouge leader named Pol Pot became prime minister of Cambodia. Under his leadership, the country's entire population was forced to live and work as peasants in rural camps. Those who disobeyed orders or behaved in a "counterrevolutionary" way were killed.

Set Purposes for Reading

Big Idea The Struggle to Survive

As you read, ask yourself, How does the narrator cope with the constant threat of death?

Literary Element Protagonist and Antagonist

The **protagonist** is the central character in a literary work, the one around whom the action revolves. The **antagonist** is the person or force that works against the protagonist. As you read, ask yourself, What details influence my feelings about the protagonist and antagonist?

Reading Strategy Question

Skilled readers **ask questions** to deepen their understanding of a text. When a detail of setting, a bit of dialogue, or even a vocabulary word puzzles you, ask questions about what it means. As you read, ask yourself questions such as "Why is this idea important?"

....

Tip: Make a KWL Chart Use a KWL chart to record your questions and answers.

What I Know	What I Want to Know	What I Learned
Rice is an important food staple in Southeast Asia.	How did people survive when their food rations were insufficient?	They were forced to obtain rice illegally.

Vocabulary

frantically (fran'tik lē) *adv.* in a manner marked by fast and nervous activity; p. 823 *Helen frantically tried to pick up all the marbles before someone slipped on them and fell.*

prelude (prel'ūd) *n.* an event preceding and preparing for a more important matter; p. 823 *The appetizers were a prelude to the feast.*

accomplice (ə kom'plice) *n.* a participant in a crime or wrongdoing; p. 824 *The robber's accomplice stayed in the car and kept the motor running.*

plausible (plô'zə bəl) *adj.* appearing worthy of belief; p. 824 *Late for class for the third time that week, Mike did not have a plausible excuse.*

taint (tānt) *v.* to contaminate morally; to corrupt; p. 825 *"Your actions taint our society," said the judge.*

....

Tip: Word Parts Knowledge of word parts can help you understand unfamiliar words. Knowing that the prefix *pre-* in *prelude* means "before" can help you understand the entire word.

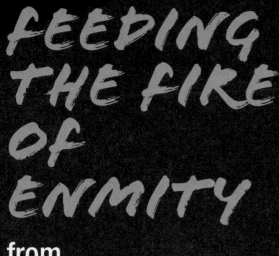

FEEDING THE FIRE OF ENMITY

from
Stay Alive, My Son

Pin Yathay

Boys in the Field, 1991. Monirith Chhea. Oil on canvas, 58x 48 in. Collection of the artist.

For the first couple of months in Leach[1]—November and December 1976—we survived as we had in Veal Vong,[2] by supplementing our rations buying rice on the black market,[3] with the occasional addition of sugar, fruit and fish. Though our hoard of spare clothing and jewelry inherited from my family was running low, I still had dollars, and these were valued in Leach. A hundred dollars bought fifteen cans of rice (a hundred-dollar bill being once again the basic unit of currency).

My job was clearing trees, along with a hundred other men. Our first assignment involved a scheme that was typical of the way the Khmer Rouge did things. We were marched off to a rice field in which grew a scattering of fruit trees and bushes. It looked like a perfectly serviceable rice field

to me, perhaps better than most because it supported the fruit trees as well, mostly rather fine mangoes and tamarinds.

Our leader, Comrade Run, explained our task with obvious pride. Apparently, at harvest time the place was infested with sparrows that gorged themselves on the rice. The sparrows nested in the fruit trees. Eager to display true revolutionary initiative, to apply the sacred spirit of self-sufficiency that Angkar[4] demanded, Comrade Run planned an assault on the sparrows. How? By destroying their nests. And how again? By cutting down the fruit trees. While people were dying of hunger a mile away, we were out chopping down fruit trees. The damage wrought by the

4. According to the author, *Angkar* (ang'kär), represents "the faceless all-pervading authority" of the new government.

Protagonist and Antagonist *Who is the antagonist? What clues in this passage indicate this?*

1. *Leach* (le'ich)
2. *Veal Vong* (vil vong)
3. The *black market* is illegal trade in goods and foods.

sparrows was nothing compared to the damage we did to Leach's fruit harvest.

After that notable objective was achieved, we were turned loose on the forest to make new clearings. We were divided into ten groups. I belonged to a group of twelve who were considered the best workers and thus designated Group No. 1. In the morning, we walked in columns to the work site. At noon, there was an hour's break for lunch, then we returned to work until six p.m. At night, when the moon shone, we worked up until ten or eleven p.m. We would return to the village every tenth day to rest, but also to attend a political meeting.

There was, however, another unofficial side to our lives. Out in our forest camp, I and two others hung our hammocks a little apart from the rest, in the hope of having some peace, away from constant supervision. Sometimes, when our comrades and our group leader were fast asleep, we would sneak away two at a time to go back to the village. The third always stayed in his hammock to tell any snooping Khmer Rouge that the other two had gone into the forest to relieve themselves. On these trips, I would pass through a number of Leach's other subsidiary camps, each one a collection of eight foot by ten foot bamboo huts, thatched with palm leaves and raised on stilts. It was on these occasions I was able to continue making exchanges. I would make a deal on the way in with a broker— as in Veal Vong, the brokers were well-known to the New People[5]—go home to see Any,[6] collect clothing, jewelry, or dollars, and pick up the extra cans of rice on my way back. Any was the focus of this activity. Seeing her and talking with her was my only pleasure, my only strength.

We were life itself to each other, each other's only hope.

We were forbidden to have extra food, but we managed. Though not allowed to cook rice, we could boil water, so when we saw our group leader, Run, coming, we would snatch up a water can, and put it on the fire, whipping away any rice that was cooking and hiding it in the bushes. Thus, whenever it was my turn to go back to the village, I could take cooked rice to Any, returning to the forest camp before dawn, so that on waking up no one noticed my absence.

One rest day, I decided to stay in my hut rather than go to the political meeting. It was foolhardy, but all I had to do was remain out of sight until I heard the gong, which rang to call the children to eat—an hour or so before the adults' meal—and also signified the end of the meeting. Then it would take the men about an hour to get back to camp. It would be easy for me to drift back in time for the communal meal.

When I left, I took with me in my scarf one can's worth of newly bought raw rice which I intended to cook that evening. At the campsite, however, I found to my surprise that everyone had eaten. Apparently, the meeting had been shorter than usual and my workmates had returned and eaten early. For a moment I was taken aback, thinking I was about to go hungry, until I saw that they had kept some rice aside for me. I was touched—in those harsh conditions, it was more than I would have expected. Eager for food, I unthinkingly put my scarf containing the rice into the nearest hammock and sat down to eat about twenty yards away.

Question *Why do you think the workers were not allowed to cook rice?*

Question *Why is Yathay so moved by his comrades' generosity?*

---

5. The *New People* refers to former urban dwellers like Pin Yathay.
6. *Any* is the author's wife.

Just then, the owner of the hammock, a friend of mine called Chorn, came back, went to lie down, and sat right on the bundle of rice. He jumped up in surprise, and prodded the scarf. His jaw dropped. "Rice!" he said, in an appalled voice. Possessing extra rice was a major offense, and here was a whole bundle of it in his hammock. In panic, he held the scarf up and shouted, "But it's not mine! This rice doesn't belong to me! Who left rice in my hammock?"

You would have thought he was holding a bomb. I flapped my hand and mouthed **frantically** at him to attract his attention. Too late—the camp chief, the boss of the whole operation, was already on his way across to us. Seeing him, Chorn protested even more loudly: "It's not my rice! It's not my rice!" He kept repeating the words over and over, as if they were some sort of incantation.

"Whose is it then?" the chief asked. "And whose scarf is it? You're sure they're not yours?"

"No! I found them under me when I lay in my hammock."

The chief turned to the rest of us. "Whose rice is this?" he asked, his gaze wandering from one to another.

Everyone knew the scarf was mine. Sooner or later the truth would come out.

I stood up. "Comrade, the rice is mine."

Then Run, my immediate supervisor, the group leader, whose responsibility it was to deal with the situation, stepped forward. It would, in normal circumstances, have been the **prelude** to my death. Fortunately, however, Run and I were not complete strangers. Two weeks before I had seen Run sitting in front of his house, looking utterly crushed. When I asked him what the matter was, he said, "It's my wife, Thay. She's very sick. She's in such pain she sometimes screams for relief."

"Have you no medicine for her?" I asked.

"I've tried our medicines, but they're not effective," he said. He was obviously a very worried man, for he had tried everything available to a Khmer Rouge. At once, I saw there was a chance here to get some extra rations, for I knew someone who could obtain some tetracyclin, an antibiotic.[7] There were doctors among the New People who still did what they could for us. They brought their medicines into the black market, as others provided food, clothing, jewelry, or watches. One tablet of tetracyclin was worth a can of rice. I would ask two cans—one for me, one for my supplier. But I had to proceed cautiously.

"Comrade, have you tried foreign medicine?" It was a harmless way to suggest the idea. If he disapproved of foreign medicine, I wouldn't be trapped. But he leaped at it.

"Comrade, do you happen to have any? Do you know where to get any?"

"Not me," I said innocently, placing my hand on my heart. "I don't want to be mixed up in anything illegal. I have never seen any foreign medicines, but I've heard about them in the camp."

He couldn't care less about my guilt or innocence. He just wanted his wife to be free of the pain. "Try to do something for me, Thay! My wife cries all the time. I don't know what to do. I'm desperate."

I said I would do my best.

The next day, having done precisely nothing, I told him that, despite the risks involved, I had contacted a man who had two tablets of tetracyclin. Not, of course, that I could guarantee a complete cure . . .

7. An *antibiotic* is a medicine derived from a microorganism that inhibits or kills another microorganism.

Question *Why is Yathay so cautious with Run after it is clear Run is willing to disobey the law?*

"How can I get them?"

"The man wants two cans' worth of rice for one tablet. I can arrange that for you."

"Come back tomorrow. I'll find the rice. Don't let me down."

So we became **accomplices**. I found him the tablets, and he gave me the rice. The two of us shared a secret. If one of us betrayed his promise, in the eyes of the authorities we would both be guilty.

Now here was Run, bombarding me with questions as he had to in the presence of the camp leader and a whole crowd of others. "The rice is yours? Where did it come from? Why did you leave the rice in your comrade's hammock? Do you want to eat more than others? You're a counterrevolutionary, is that it?"

I was on a knife-edge. Run had the power of life and death over me, and nobody would have reproached him for having me killed. He had reason enough—theft and black-marketeering were capital offenses.[8] Moreover, I knew he had another reason to show himself as an intransigent[9] leader—by having me killed, he could get rid of a witness to his own crime. "Who sold you the rice?" he shouted. "You must denounce the person who sold it to you!"

I certainly didn't want to do that. The only thing I could do was make up something **plausible** and then somehow turn the conversation to my advantage. "A soldier," I said. "I exchanged a pair of trousers for it with a soldier who was passing on his bicycle." No, I had no idea of his name. I had never seen him before. "Anyway, comrade, the rice was not for me."

Run was taken aback. "I don't understand. Why did you bring the rice here then?"

"I was going to trade it to find medicine for my *wife*," I said, looking him in the eye.

There was the briefest of pauses.

"She's getting worse," I went on. "Angkar's medicines have not cured her. I have to find some tablets. You know how it is."

I could see that he did.

"But why did you bring the rice to the worksite?"

"I told you: I thought perhaps one of us had medicine."

"Who then?"

"Oh! I didn't have anybody special in mind, comrade. I—"

At this point, the camp leader interrupted. "This is a serious crime, comrades! Comrade Run, it is up to you to decide how to punish Comrade Thay."

Run tied my elbows behind my back, and led me away. From their terrified expressions, it was obvious my friends thought I was going to my death.

Run pushed me towards his hammock, away from the others, and told me to squat down in front of him. He sat back and began to lecture me. I would have expected nothing less, and lowered my head, playing my role as the ritual phrases of condemnation poured over me. "Thay, you are a counterrevolutionary . . . you participated in exchanges . . . you don't know how to get rid of individualist leanings . . . you

---

8. *Capital offenses* are crimes punishable by death.
9. *Intransigent* means "unwilling to compromise or come to an agreement."

Vocabulary

accomplice (ə kom′plice) *n.* a participant in a crime or wrongdoing

plausible (plô′zə bəl) *adj.* appearing worthy of belief

The Struggle to Survive *Why does Yathay make up the story about planning to trade the rice for medicine? How does he think it will help save his life?*

Protagonist and Antagonist *What details in this passage indicate Yathay is the protagonist?*

taint our group . . . you've been in reeducation for more than a year and a half, yet you have remained a counterrevolutionary . . ." and on and on for an hour or more.

It occurred to me as he talked that he seemed to be so taken up with the need to show himself as strong that he was in danger of forgetting the favor I'd done him. If he went on like that, he would leave himself no other course but to have me cudgeled to death in the forest or sent off to a reeducation camp. I thought I'd better take action.

As he drew breath, I said in a low voice, "Comrade, remember your sick wife. Remember my efforts to help you. If you hurt me, I will denounce you." I looked up at him, so there could be no doubt about my seriousness. "If I die, you die."

His eyes widened, and the color drained from his face, and I knew I had a chance.

In a second or two, he resumed the look of an austere and inflexible leader, his face impassive.[10] For another quarter of an hour, he continued his harangue,[11] his voice growing louder and louder. It became clear to me that he was putting on a show for everyone to hear, especially the camp leader. I began to relax, wondering how he could retract his accusations without loss of face.

"Thay, you are a counterrevolutionary, but fortunately for you, you are a good worker." Then he began to praise me, still talking in a loud voice—"I have noticed you are the first to wake in the mornings and that you are the best worker," and on and on he went about how I gave every-

Seven Women in the Field, 1990. Monirith Chhea. Oil on canvas, 58 x 64 in. Collection of the artist.

View the Art Like Pin Yathay, Monirith Chhea is haunted by his memories of Cambodia during the Khmer Rouge regime. How does the artist use different shapes to create a mood in this painting? How is this mood present in the memoir?

thing I had to my work. It was such an astonishing performance that I could hardly believe our undeclared conspiracy would not be discovered. Never had the most assiduous[12] Khmer Rouge, the most perfect revolutionary, been garlanded with such praise. An hour before I was criminal scum; now Comrade Run found it hard to do justice to my merits. And he concluded: "As a result, this time—and only this time—I will ask the chief to give you a warning so that you can cleanse yourself. It will be a serious warning, Thay. The next time, you will become fertilizer on our rice fields."

After that, it only remained for the camp leader to give me a brief, formal warning—"Don't do it again! Next time, you'll be fertilizer"—and I was saved. ✍

---

10. An *impassive* face is calm and shows no emotion.
11. A *harangue* is a long, blustering, noisy, or scolding speech.

Question *Why is Yathay worried that Run feels a need to prove his strength?*

Vocabulary

taint (tānt) *v.* to contaminate morally; to corrupt

---

12. *Assiduous* means "busy, diligent, or persevering."

Vocabulary Workshop

Denotation and Connotation

Literature Connection In this passage from *Stay Alive, My Son* by Pin Yathay, a leader refers to the Cambodian workers as "comrades."

> *"At this point, the camp leader interrupted. 'This is a serious crime, comrades! Comrade Run, it is up to you to decide how to punish Comrade Thay.'"*

The **denotation**, or dictionary definition, of *comrade* is "friend, companion, or associate," but in this context it has a charged, political **connotation**, or association. The Khmer Rouge used the word to describe citizens of their communist society and to convey a sense of equality. The word took on different connotations, however, when it was used to help justify the Khmer Rouge's brutal policies. Pin Yathay uses the word to contrast the ideal definition with reality. Because words with strong connotations can be used to distort reality, it is important to recognize how they can be used. Bias, hyperbole, and propaganda all make use of connotations.

Language that expresses a one-sided point of view demonstrates **bias**. Try substituting *stood up to* for *betrayed* in the following sentence. Notice how *stood up to* produces a positive bias, while *betrayed* produces a negative one.

> *The soldier betrayed his superiors by refusing to fight.*

Hyperbole is exaggerated language used to make a point.

> *A shift in political power would mean the death of all our freedoms.*

Language used to influence public opinion is called **propaganda**.

> *In our glorious city, citizens live as harmoniously as brothers and sisters.*

Loaded Words

Loaded words express strong connotations and emotions. Some reveal **bias**, or a one-sided point of view, while others use **hyperbole**, or exaggeration, to make a point. **Propaganda** is persuasive language that may distort the truth.

Test-Taking Tip

When you read a text, ask yourself, "What is the author's purpose?" Once you have determined the author's purpose, look for words or phrases that are used to make you think or feel a certain way.

Practice For each passage, underline words that have strong connotations and determine the persuasive techniques.

1. "Our first assignment involved a scheme that was typical of the way the Khmer Rouge did things. We were marched off to a rice field…"
2. "'Thay, you are a counterrevolutionary . . . you participated in exchanges . . . you don't know how to get rid of individualist leanings . . . you taint our group . . .'"
3. "'I will ask the chief to give you a warning so that you can cleanse yourself. It will be a serious warning, Thay. The next time, you will become fertilizer on our rice fields.'"

Vocabulary For more vocabulary practice, go to glencoe.com and enter QuickPass code GLW6053u4.

Before You Read

Moana and *Island*

Meet **Kauraka Kauraka** and **Albert Wendt**

The Pacific islands have a strong tradition of oral literature. So strong, in fact, their written literature didn't truly begin to blossom until the 1960s. During the 1970s, such authors as Albert Wendt began to react against the European image of their culture: "Up to now, most literature about us [the Pacific islanders] has been written by outsiders—much of it superficial and distorted and over romantic and racist. We now want to examine ourselves and our way of life ourselves."

Albert Wendt (born 1939) The person most responsible for the emergence of Pacific island written literature is Wendt, a novelist and poet from the republic of Western Samoa. Wendt blends Polynesian oral traditions with European literary heritage to portray islanders and their way of life. According to Wendt, at the heart of indigenous writing are "the techniques of oral storytelling . . . and indigenous philosophies and visions." Much of his writing responds to colonialism and the injustices the Pacific islanders have continued to face long after their indepen-

dence. His work addresses the feelings of exile—due to both geography and culture—they have experienced because of other people's ideas and myths about their way of life.

Wendt and other Pacific island authors believe they should write about islanders and for islanders, and thus value the importance of integrating the oral tradition of their culture into their work. These myths, legends, songs, chants, and tales of magic allow them to express their way of life. While this literature is written in English, which allows the authors to speak to a wide audience, its language reflects the influence of Pacific culture and spoken literature.

Kauraka Kauraka (1951–1997) Born in Rarotonga, the main island of the Cook Islands, Kauraka Kauraka was one of the best known Pacific island authors. The Cooks, consisting of fifteen volcanic islands, form a self-governing state in the South Pacific. Previously controlled by New Zealand, the Cook Islands—like much of the Pacific—are home to a culture shaped by the intersection of local tradition and colonial rule. Through his verse and his work as an anthropologist with the Ministry of Cultural Development, Kauraka studied and brought attention to the people of the Cook Islands and their rich oral traditions. He published stories, nonfiction, and six poetry collections in both English and the Cook Islands Maori language. His writings are renderings of myths and legends about the land, the sea, and the gods, as well as original works. Kauraka's poems often convey a profound sense of loss while simultaneously expressing great pride in his homeland.

> "I belong to Oceania . . . and it nourishes my spirit, helps to define me, and feeds my imagination."
>
> —Albert Wendt

LOG ON ▶ **Literature** Online

Author Search For more about Albert Wendt and Kauraka Kauraka, go to glencoe.com and enter QuickPass code GLW6053u4.

Literature and Reading Preview

Connect to the Poems

What do you think of when you hear the words *island* and *ocean*? Freewrite for a few minutes about the images that appear in your mind when you think about these words.

Build Background

The Pacific island nations occupy some 34,000 square miles of land spread over millions of square miles of ocean. Their inhabitants came from Asia by way of Indonesia thousands of years ago. The more than 10,000 islands include two general types. Volcanos usually produced mountainous, forested islands. Islands that grew from coral reefs are usually smaller and lower, with sparse vegetation and limited fresh water.

Set Purposes for Reading

Big Idea Place and Identity

As you read, ask yourself, How are the poetry and the authors influenced by the landscape?

Literary Element Form

A poem's **form**—or structure—contributes to its theme and reflects its subject. Pacific island poets and many other modern authors use loosely structured poetic forms, or free verse. They vary line length, stanzas, rhythm, rhyme, repetition, and word placement to emphasize their ideas and emotions and convey meaning. As you read, ask yourself, How does the form of these poems contribute to their themes and subjects?

Reading Strategy Recognize Author's Purpose

An **author's purpose** is his or her reason for writing. Authors typically write to persuade, to inform, to explain, to entertain, or to describe. The purpose is often revealed in the title, form, word choice, tone, and content. As you read, ask yourself, What clues reveal the author's purpose?

Tip: Cluster Details Use a cluster diagram like the one below to help you determine the poets' purposes.

Learning Objectives

For pages 829–833

In studying these texts, you will focus on the following objectives:

Literary Study: Analyzing form.

Reading: Recognizing author's purpose.

Writing: Creating a brochure.

Vocabulary

graceful (grās′fəl) *adj.* showing effortless beauty or movement; p. 831 *The dancer's movements were graceful and fluid.*

frail (frāl) *adj.* easily broken or damaged; fragile; p. 832 *The hikers carefully inched across the frail bridge, hoping it would not snap under their weight.*

Tip: Analogies When you read an analogy question, you should read it as a sentence that shows the relationship between two words. For example, in the analogy *dancer : graceful :: scholar : _____*, the sentence showing the relationship is "A dancer is graceful." To complete the analogy, you would read "A scholar is [smart]."

Moana

Kauraka Kauraka

Name of the Great Ocean
the dark blue sea
the mysterious
Moana-Nui-o-Kiva
5 Moana-Vai-a-Vare[1]
mysterious ocean
Moana our daughter
graceful rider through space
from Havaiki[2]
10 today you have earned
the keys to enter
the four rooms
of the mysterious
ocean of life
15 many will call upon
your name for guidance
for interpretation
of these mysteries
Moana our sister
20 you were born and raised
in the mysterious ocean
we look to you for understanding
of the fish we eat
the waves that destroy us
25 the waves that create new lands
for us
Moana our daughter
Moana our sister
Moana our mother

Seashells on the Seashore. Brian Kere (Solomon Islands, b. 1960). Mixed media, 90 x 64 cm. The International Museum of 20th Century Arts, Laguna Beach, CA.

---

1. Lines 4–5 refer to the Pacific Ocean.
2. *Havaiki* (hä vä ē′kē) is the legendary homeland of the Maori. Cook Islanders are considered a branch of the Maori people.

Place and Identity *What can you infer about the ocean from each comparison?*

Vocabulary

graceful (grās′fəl) *adj.* showing effortless beauty or movement

ISLAND

Albert Wendt

This island was a **frail** tremor snared
in stingray seas dark with threat of storm.
The tremor was strong enough
to give us birth.

Lava pouring into ocean, Volcanoes Nat'l Park, Big Island, Hawaii. Art Wolfe. Photograph.

After You Read

Respond and Think Critically

Respond and Interpret

1. What feelings did you experience while reading these poems? Explain.

2. (a)Who or what is Moana? (b)Why do you think the speaker of "Moana" repeatedly refers to Moana as "mysterious"?

3. (a)The **speaker** of a poem is the voice that talks to the reader. What do the speaker of "Moana" and the people expect from Moana? (b)How would you describe the relationship between the people and Moana?

4. What does the speaker in "Island" say the island once was?

Analyze and Evaluate

5. What does Wendt's description of the ocean as "stingray seas" suggest about the region?

6. (a)What examples of **alliteration** can you find in "Island"? (b)How does alliteration contribute to the poem's overall effect?

7. (a)How are "Moana" and "Island" similar as creation stories? (b)How do they differ?

Connect

8. **Big Idea** **Place and Identity** What does the Moana myth tell of the culture that created it?

9. **Connect to Today** How do people in your community feel about local geography? Explain.

Literary Element Form

The **form** of a poem is the way it is arranged on a page, such as the placement of words and phrases, the length of lines, and the shape of stanzas.

1. Explain the form of "Moana." How does the form relate to the meaning of the poem?

2. How does the form of "Moana" reflect the culture and ideas of the Pacific islands? Explain.

Reading Strategy Recognize Author's Purpose

Use the diagram you made on page 830 to help you answer the following questions.

1. Consider Kauraka's word choice in "Moana." How do the words convey his purpose?

2. How does the length of "Island" relate to the author's purpose?

Vocabulary Practice

Practice with Analogies Identify the pair of words that best expresses the relationship in the original pair.

1. graceful : fluid ::
a. stars : night   **c.** adult : baby
b. adventure : explore   **d.** peaceful : tranquil

2. frail : sturdy ::
a. delightful : unpleasant   **c.** lamb : sheep
b. excitement : joy   **d.** cook : stove

Writing

Create a Brochure Using the library and the Internet, research the role the ocean plays in the daily life of Pacific islanders. As you research, note essential facts and interesting information about the ocean. Then create a brochure summarizing your findings. You might format your brochure with a three-column layout, include photographs, and present some of your information in bulleted lists.

Writing Process

At any stage of a writing process, you may think of new ideas. Feel free to return to earlier stages as you write.

Prewrite

Draft

Revise

Focus Lesson: Evidence

Edit and Proofread

Focus Lesson: Parallelism

Present

LOG ON ▶ **Literature** Online

Writing and Research For prewriting, drafting, and other revising tools, go to glencoe.com and enter QuickPass code GLW6053u4.

⚡ Writing Workshop

Persuasive Speech

Literature Connection In the following passage from the *Analects,* Confucius makes a point about the state of family relationships by using a memorable comparison and a powerful rhetorical question.

> "'Filial sons' nowadays are people who see to it that their parents get enough to eat. But even dogs and horses are cared for to that extent. If there is no feeling of respect, wherein lies the difference?"

In a persuasive speech, you use such rhetorical devices, along with well-reasoned arguments, to convince an audience to take your side on a particular issue. To write an effective persuasive speech, you will need to study the goals and strategies listed below.

Rubric

Goals	Strategies
To present a clearly stated opinion on an issue	☑ Give background information on the issue. ☑ State your opinion at the beginning of the speech.
To explain and support your opinion	☑ Give reasons for your opinion in a logical order. ☑ Use facts and examples to support your reasons.
To convince and engage your audience	☑ Use logical, emotional, and ethical appeals. ☑ Use rhetorical devices. Persuade your audience to act.
To anticipate and address counterarguments	☑ Describe other points of view. ☑ Respond to these points of view with reasoned arguments.

Write a persuasive speech of at least 1,000 words about an issue in your community that you feel strongly about. As you move through the stages of writing, keep your audience and purpose in mind.

Audience: your school or community

Purpose: to use logical arguments and detailed evidence to persuade an audience to act

Analyze a Professional Model

In the following persuasive speech, given in 1969, former congress-woman Shirley Chisholm urges the House of Representatives to spend government money on social programs in the United States rather than on the Vietnam War. Pay close attention to the comments in the margin. They point out features you might want to include in your own persuasive speech.

from *"The Business of America Is War"*
by Shirley Chisholm

Mr. Speaker, on the same day President Nixon announced he had decided the United States will not be safe unless we start to build a defense system against missiles, the Head Start program[1] in the District of Columbia was cut back for the lack of money.

As a teacher, and as a woman, I do not think I will ever understand what kind of values can be involved in spending nine billion dollars—and more, I am sure—on elaborate, unnecessary and impractical weapons when several thousand disadvantaged children in the nation's capital get nothing.

When the new administration took office, I was one of the many Americans who hoped it would mean that our country would benefit from the fresh perspectives, the new ideas, the different priorities of a leader who had no part in the mistakes of the past. Mr. Nixon has said things like this:

---

1. *Head Start* is a program, run by the U.S. Department of Health and Human Services, that provides services to children from low-income families.

Real-World Connection

At various points in your life, you will need to use persuasive skills to ensure that your voice is heard in your community. To influence a local project, policy, or problem, you must be able to articulate and defend your opinions clearly.

Ethical Appeal

Appeal to your audience's sense of right and wrong.

Draft

Develop Your Tone Following your outline, draft your speech from start to finish. Use a formal and respectful tone.

Analyze a Workshop Model

Here is a final draft of a persuasive speech. Read the speech and answer the questions in the margin. Use the answers to these questions to guide you as you write.

Writing Frames

As you read the workshop model, think about the writer's use of the following persuasive writing frames.

What these objectors fail to realize is ____.

Studies have shown that ____.

Try using these kinds of frames to offer counterarguments to those who may disagree with your ideas.

Thesis Statement

How does the writer's thesis statement appeal to those who are not yet convinced?

Counterarguments

How does the writer strengthen his or her position by addressing this counterargument?

Sleepy Students: Waking Up to the Solution

Walk into almost any Franklin High classroom in the first few hours of the day, and you'll see students struggling to keep their eyes open. A survey taken last year showed that Franklin High students sleep an average of 6.5 hours per night—2.5 hours less than the recommended amount for teenagers. In light of research showing that people need a good night's sleep to think and learn properly, these findings are disturbing. However, many members of this community have decried a proposed measure to address these issues. The measure, which would change Franklin High's starting time from 7:00 A.M. to 8:00 A.M., would give students an extra hour of sleep and could significantly improve their lives.

Opponents of the later starting time have blamed students' sleep habits, rather than Franklin High's current schedule, for the fact that students are so sleepy. Several community members have argued that we should focus on teaching students to go to bed earlier. While it is true that students need to be taught good sleep habits, studies have shown that teenagers actually remain alert later at night than adults. In addition, they continue producing melatonin, the chemical responsible for sleepiness, far longer into the morning than adults. These findings explain why Franklin High's current schedule doesn't work. Pushing back the starting time is the only way to truly address the problem.

Pushing back Franklin's starting time would also sharpen students' minds and promote learning. Educational researcher Kyla Wahlstrom conducted a four-year study of two Minneapolis school districts, both of which pushed back their starting times by about an hour. Students reported they were going to bed at the same time as they had before the change and so were getting an extra hour of sleep each night. The extra hour made a difference: teachers at the schools reported that "students were more alert and ready for learning." These findings are consistent with research showing we need sleep to retrieve long-term memories, to learn new material, and to perform complex mental tasks. They make it clear that a later starting time could have a significant academic benefit for Franklin High.

Several of the most vocal objectors to the proposed schedule change have been coaches, who argue that the later starting time would interfere with after-school sports. What these objectors fail to realize is that the new schedule could actually strengthen sports. Every season, Franklin High coaches complain about team members being tired during practices. Just as an extra hour of sleep has been shown to improve students' attendance and alertness in class, it is bound to improve their performance in sports as well.

Perhaps the most important reason to accept the proposed schedule change is that it would help keep students safe. Studies have shown that sleep deprivation puts teenagers at a higher risk for depression and other behavior issues. However, students report less depression when their schools introduce later starting times. As U.S. Rep. Zoe Lofgren of California states, later starting times "could do more to improve education and reduce teen accidents and crime than many more expensive initiatives." If pushing back Franklin High's starting time can make students happier and healthier, it is our duty to accept the costs.

Let's put aside our fear of change and embrace this simple measure that could benefit students, teachers, coaches, and parents alike.

Persuasion

Logical Appeal

How does the writer appeal to the audience's reason here?

Supporting Evidence

How does the writer use facts to support his or her position?

Rhetorical Devices

How do the writer's rhetorical questions help support his or her point?

Conclusion

How does the writer tailor the conclusion to his or her audience?

Speaking, Listening, and Viewing Workshop

Persuasive Presentation

Literature Connection Confucius delivered all his teachings orally. Only after his death did his followers attempt to capture his clever rhetorical devices and powerful delivery in writing. In this workshop, you will do the opposite: you will translate your persuasive writing into engaging spoken language. To do this, you will need to streamline your writing into concise statements and use techniques such as tone and gestures to enhance your arguments.

Assignment	**Deliver a Persuasive Speech** Adapt a persuasive essay into a speech and present it to an audience, using nonverbal techniques such as eye contact, body language, voice, and gestures for emphasis.

Speaking Frames

As you prepare your speech, think about using some of the following frames to get started.

- My own view is that _____, because _____.
- For example, _____ shows that _____.
- For these reasons, _____ should be _____.

Hook Your Audience

Your arguments are more likely to convince audience members if your topic interests them. Rather than launching directly into your thesis statement, look for a particular anecdote or fact in your written speech that will grab your audience's attention. Use this "hook" to open your speech.

Plan Your Presentation

In writing your persuasive speech, you clarified your thinking and created logical, ordered arguments. Now your goal is to develop an engaging speaking style to present your viewpoint. Follow these steps to prepare your persuasive speech for oral delivery.

- Read your speech aloud several times. Take note of sections where you stumble and think about how you might revise them using simpler, more straightforward language.

- Use a highlighter to note the thesis and the main arguments of your speech. Use a different color highlighter to highlight the key pieces of evidence that support your arguments. Cross out details that are not persuasive enough or that would be unnecessary for a speech.

- Write your main arguments and pieces of evidence on note cards. Refer to the note cards as you rehearse. Your goal is to become familiar enough with your material that you will be arguing from your own expertise, rather than reading from your note cards, in your final presentation.

Create Visual Aids

Visual aids add interest to your persuasive speech and can serve as evidence. The types of visual aids you use will depend on the types of appeals you make. A graph or a chart might best enhance a logical argument based on scientific data, while a powerful photograph might best strengthen an emotional appeal. Limit yourself to one or two visual aids that directly support your main arguments. Use a chart like the one below to brainstorm ideas.

Argument	Visual Aid	Purpose of Visual Aid
Starting school an hour later would have academic benefits	Graph showing improved attendance at other schools	To show that attendance could also improve at our school

Rehearse

Take turns rehearsing speeches with a partner. Use the following techniques to assess one another's speeches.

- Identify the thesis and the main arguments. If you are unable to identify these, work with your partner to find clearer ways of stating his or her main points.

- Ask questions and offer additional counterarguments. Your partner's presentation will be stronger if he or she has prepared responses to many possible objections.

- Evaluate the effectiveness of your partner's speech. How convincing were the arguments? Which rhetorical devices were most powerful?

Finally, keep in mind the following verbal and nonverbal delivery techniques while rehearsing.

Techniques for Delivering a Persuasive Speech

Verbal Techniques	Nonverbal Techniques
☑ **Tone** Vary your tone to draw attention to important points.	☑ **Eye Contact** Look directly at your audience.
☑ **Enunciation** Speak clearly.	☑ **Posture** Avoid leaning or slouching.
☑ **Emphasis** Stress important ideas.	☑ **Gestures** Use gestures to emphasize your points.
☑ **Pace** Speak slowly.	☑ **Visual Aids** Do not block your visual aids.

Presentation Tips

Use the following checklist to evaluate your presentation.

- Did you vary the tone of your presentation, adding emphasis where needed?
- Did you make eye contact with the audience?
- Did you remember not to block the visuals?
- Did you face the audience and not the visuals?

LOG ON ▶ **Literature** Online

Speaking, Listening, and Viewing For project ideas, templates, and presentation tips, go to glencoe.com and enter QuickPass code GLW6053u4.

Media Impact: **Propaganda Poster**

Activity

Listening and Speaking

Meet in a small group to discuss the following questions:

1. What is the basic message of this propaganda poster?

2. How would you describe the colors the artist used in this poster?

3. Review the list of logical fallacies on page 845. Which fallacy do you think best applies to the message in this poster? Explain your choice.

4. How does the image reflect the caption of the poster?

Build Background Propaganda posters are usually very simple. They are intended to convey one clear idea. In this poster from the 1960s, Chairman Mao Tse-tung, one of the key leaders of the communist revolution in China, is celebrated as the center of Chinese life. Mao adapted Soviet Union-style communism to his own purposes in China.

Design Element

Mao is the focal point here. Notice how brightly the sun is shining on his yellow shirt.

Symbol

Mao, the great teacher, is surrounded by young people, who symbolize China's future. They are eagerly listening to his every word. Notice how most of them are looking at the seated Mao.

Design Element

The backdrop is an open space near water. Notice the warm colors of the ground and the brightness of the beautiful blue sky that surrounds Mao and his students.

紧 跟 毛 主 席　在 大 风 大 浪 中 锻 炼 成 长

Closely following Chairman Mao, let us train and develop in strong winds and strong waves.

Text Feature

The caption uses metaphors—"strong winds and strong waves"—to suggest Mao's powerful influence on shaping young minds.

Literature Online

Media Literacy For project ideas, templates, and media analysis guides, go to glencoe.com and enter QuickPass code GLW6053u4.

Media Impact: **News Transcript**

Build Background In the past two decades, China not only has become one of the most powerful economic forces in the world, but also has developed one of the largest militaries in the world. In this radio news report, broadcast the week before China celebrated the 80th anniversary of the founding of the People's Liberation Army by men like Mao Tse-tung, a National Public Radio reporter visited Beijing's Military Museum to see an exhibit of China's newest weaponry and military technology.

TRANSCRIPT

REPORTER ANTHONY KUHN: The exhibit features *Top Gun*-style videos showing China's latest military hardware in action. Out in the parking lot are tanks, fighter jets, and a vehicle that looks an awful lot like a Hum-Vee. The videos of new submarines and missiles highlight the Chinese military's shifting emphasis from fighting defensive wars on its own turf to projecting power beyond its borders.

[Short quote of Chinese soldier explaining a new technology in Chinese]

KUHN: One young soldier shows off China's advances in military satellite technology. With a few touches on a large screen, the view zooms in from miles above down to a Chinese city with clearly marked buildings and streets. So how accurate is the map, I ask, and when did the military start using these things?

[Short quote of soldier answering Kuhn's question in Chinese]

KUHN: "It's not convenient for me to say," he replies. It's not clear from the exhibit just how much of China's army, known as the PLA, actually has such advanced weaponry and information technology. Experts say that while some elite units have it, much of China's military lags behind the U.S. by a generation or more.

Activity

Listening and Speaking

Take notes as you watch a local TV newscast about a political event. Then respond to the following questions:

1. What visual images did you find striking? Why?

2. Did anyone shown on the newscast use propaganda? If so, give examples.

3. Was the news report objective? Why or why not?

Cultural Perspective

The reporter uses a reference to an American military movie to describe the style of the videos.

Sound Reasoning

The reporter makes a reasonable statement about the purpose of the exhibit based on the facts he has learned.

Objective Reporting

The soldier's answer to the reporter's question reveals the tight control the Chinese government maintains over its citizens.

Sources

The reporter cites experts in Chinese military history to add validity to his report.

Assessment

English–Language Arts

Reading: Fiction

Carefully read the following passage. Use context clues to help you define any words with which you are unfamiliar. Pay close attention to **themes, cultural context, author's purpose,** and the use of **literary devices**. Then, on a separate sheet of paper, answer the questions on pages 851–852.

"Peach-Blossom Spring" by T'ao Ch'ien

Translated by David Hinton

During the T'ai-yüan years [376–397 A.D.] of the Chin Dynasty, there was a man in Wu-ling who caught fish for a living. One day he went up a stream, and soon didn't know how far he'd gone. Suddenly, he came upon a peach orchard in full bloom. For hundreds of feet, there was nothing but peach
5　trees crowding in over the banks. And in the confusion of fallen petals, there were lovely, scented flowers. The fisherman was amazed. Wanting to see how far the orchard went, he continued on.

　　The trees ended at the foot of a mountain, where a spring fed the stream from a small cave. It seemed as if there might be a light inside, so the fisher-
10　man left his boat and stepped in. At first, the cave was so narrow he could barely squeeze through. But he kept going and, after a few dozen feet, it opened out into broad daylight. There, on a plain stretching away, austere houses were graced with fine fields and lovely ponds. Dikes and paths crossed here and there among mulberries and bamboo. Roosters and dogs
15　called back and forth. Coming and going in the midst of all this, there were men and women tending the fields. Their clothes were just like those worn by the people outside. And whether they were old with white hair or children in pigtails, they were all happy and of themselves content.

　　When they saw the fisherman, they were terribly surprised and asked
20　where he had come from. Once he had answered all their questions, they insisted on taking him back home. And soon, they had set out wine and killed chickens for dinner. When the others in the village heard about this man, they all came to ask about him. They told him how, long ago, to escape those years of turmoil during the Ch'in Dynasty [221–207 B.C.], the village
25　ancestors gathered their wives and children, and with their neighbors came to this distant place. And never leaving, they'd kept themselves cut-off from the people outside ever since. So now they wondered what dynasty it was. They'd never heard of the Han [203 B.C.–A.D. 220], let alone Wei [A.D. 386–535] or Chin. As the fisherman carefully told them everything he knew,

30 they all sighed in sad amazement. Soon, each of the village families had invited him to their house, where they also served wine and food.

After staying for some days, the fisherman prepared to leave these people. As he was going, they said *There's no need to tell the people outside.* He returned to his boat and started back, careful to remember each pace along
35 the way.

When he got back home, he went to tell the prefect what had happened, and the prefect sent some men to retrace the route with him. They tried to follow the landmarks he remembered, but they were soon lost and finally gave up the search.

40 Liu Tzu-chi, who lived in Nan-yang, was a recluse of great honor and esteem. When he heard about this place, he joyfully prepared to go there. But before he could, he got sick and passed away. Since then, no one's asked the Way.

1. What is the author's primary purpose in describing the peach orchard in lines 3–7?
   A. to show the danger of being drawn in by beauty
   B. to comment on the joys of cultivating plants
   C. to set a mood of confusion and distress
   D. to create an atmosphere of mystery and beauty

2. Why does the fisherman enter the small cave?
   F. He thinks he sees a light inside.
   G. He is enticed by the lovely, scented flowers.
   H. He is amazed.
   J. He wants to see the extent of the orchard.

3. Where does the fisherman find the village?
   A. in the middle of a peach orchard
   B. at the top of a mountain
   C. inside a large cave at the beginning of a stream
   D. past the peach orchard, through a small cave at the beginning of the stream

4. From the second paragraph, what can be inferred about the author's view of nature?
   F. The author sees nature as a constant threat to humans.
   G. The author thinks humans should live in harmony with nature.
   H. The author believes that humans inevitably destroy nature.
   J. The author finds humans more interesting than nature.

5. As it is used in line 18, the word *content* most nearly means:
   A. subject matter.
   B. satisfied.
   C. substance.
   D. ignorant.

6. At what point do the villagers set out wine and kill chickens?
   F. after they insist on taking the fisherman back home
   G. after the fisherman leaves
   H. before the fisherman answers all of their questions
   J. before they see the fisherman

7. How do the people in the village react when the fisherman arrives?
   A. They are frightened and confused.
   B. They treat him irreverently and ridicule him.
   C. They are intrigued and ask him many questions.
   D. They immediately begin telling him the story of their escape from the outside world.

8. The residents of the village cut themselves off from the outside world because:

   I. they wanted to explore uncharted lands.
   II. they were banished by the leaders of the Ch'in Dynasty.
   III. they wanted to escape turmoil.

   F. I only
   G. II only
   H. III only
   J. II and III

9. According to the passage, the phrase "sad amazement" (line 30) implies that:
   A. the villagers are surprised and disappointed at their lack of knowledge about the outside world.
   B. the villagers wholeheartedly regret having left the outside world.
   C. the villagers are frustrated with their own ignorance about the outside world.
   D. the villagers are melancholy by nature.

10. What is the most likely explanation for the villagers' warning that "there's no need to tell the people outside" (line 33)?
    F. They think outsiders already know about their society.
    G. They are afraid they will be punished for fleeing if they are discovered.
    H. They are ashamed of their simple way of life.
    J. They fear that contact with the outside world would destroy their way of life.

11. As it is used in line 36, the word *prefect* most nearly means:
    A. monk
    B. high official
    C. fisherman
    D. servant

12. At what point did the ancestors of the villagers escape to the secret place?
    F. During the T'ai-yüan years of the Chin Dynasty
    G. After the Han Dynasty
    H. After the Wei Dynasty
    J. During the Ch'in Dynasty

13. What is the main insight suggested by the statement in lines 37–39 ("They tried... search")?
    A. The people from outside are uninterested in the past.
    B. The men are unable to trace the route because the village does not exist.
    C. The place the men are searching for remains a mystery.
    D. The fisherman dreams up the village and its inhabitants and tells the prefect in order to gain respect.

14. Which of the following best states the theme of this story?
    F. Cutting oneself off from society leads to sadness and ignorance.
    G. True adventurers do not need plans or directions to guide them.
    H. Society has lost its connection to the peaceful, harmonious lifestyle of the past.
    J. We are actually not so different from those we view as outsiders.

Vocabulary Skills: Sentence Completion

For each item in the Vocabulary Skills section, choose the word or words that best complete the sentence. Write your answers on a separate sheet of paper.

1. Although Confucius's _____ for moral behavior are strict, they are not yet _____, for many people still follow them today.
   - **A.** extents…undulant
   - **B.** accomplices…glittering
   - **C.** reprisals…perpetual
   - **D.** dictates…obsolete

2. Zen masters teach their students to _____ long periods of meditation.
   - **F.** endure
   - **G.** flag
   - **H.** banish
   - **J.** chastise

3. Although he had served as a statesman and a soldier, Nguyen Trai was accused of being a(n) _____ in a murder plot against the king.
   - **A.** accomplice
   - **B.** intransigence
   - **C.** prelude
   - **D.** tempo

4. Samurai _____ follow a training regimen, refrain from pursuing their own pleasures, and show allegiance only to their lords.
   - **F.** assiduously
   - **G.** frantically
   - **H.** plaintively
   - **J.** furtively

5. Because of a severe shortage of food, citizens under the rule of the Khmer Rouge often had to _____ to stay alive.
   - **A.** detest
   - **B.** tamper
   - **C.** forage
   - **D.** trample

6. Bei Dao _____ for freedom, so he resigned from the Red Guards and joined the pro-democracy movement.
   - **F.** banished
   - **G.** foraged
   - **H.** tainted
   - **J.** yearned

7. Because of China's _____ economic growth in recent years, experts _____ that the country's economy will soon surpass that of Germany.
   - **A.** trivial…flag
   - **B.** vigorous…anticipate
   - **C.** glittering…gesticulate
   - **D.** congealed…yearn

8. The Maori, the indigenous people of New Zealand, paid _____ to their gods by decorating their bodies and faces with tattoos.
   - **F.** prelude
   - **G.** homage
   - **H.** extent
   - **J.** tempo

9. A trek through one of New Zealand's national parks is not for the _____, but strong hikers will enjoy exploring the majestic volcanoes and _____ rain forests.
   - **A.** docile…imploring
   - **B.** frail…lush
   - **C.** marvelous…ruddy
   - **D.** inquisitive…congealed

10. Outback Australia, a brutal expanse of desert, is _____ visited by city dwellers.
    - **F.** frantically
    - **G.** plaintively
    - **H.** seldom
    - **J.** assiduously

Grammar and Writing Skills: Paragraph Improvement

Read carefully through the following passage from the first draft of a student's essay. Choose the best answer to each question or the best alternative for each word or phrase that is underlined and numbered. If you think the original version is best, choose "NO CHANGE." Write your answers on a separate sheet of paper.

Though teenagers make up only 6.4 percent of all drivers in the United States, they account <u>by</u> 14
1
percent of all drivers in fatal accidents (Allstate 1). <u>Traffic deaths of these mean wasting</u> potential and
2
devastation to families. Preventing these deaths should be a top priority in our state. However, lawmakers have proposed a misguided solution to this many-layered problem: raising the driving age from 16 to 18. This law would not reduce <u>the</u>
3
<u>number of fatal crashes, and it would only</u> create a new set of obstacles for teenagers trying to achieve independence.

Of course, lawmakers are right to draw our attention to the high teen accident rate. "Teen drivers ages 16 to 19 are four times more likely than older drivers to crash" (Insurance Institute for Highway Safety 2005). However, it does not make sense to attribute this higher incidence of crashes to immaturity. <u>Two thirds of teens killed in car crashes</u>
4

<u>in 2003 were males (Allstate 2)</u>. People become good drivers not because they are mature but
5
because they <u>extensively</u> have practiced.
6

<u>So</u> raising the driving age would only cause there to be more inexperienced drivers, who would be just as likely to crash as their younger counterparts. Instead of taking away a 16-year-old's chance to drive, authorities would be better off requiring he or she to spend extra hours behind the wheel with an instructor's supervision before obtaining a license.**7**

8
[1] Students with working parents often <u>needed</u> to provide their own after-school transportation. [2] Raising the driving age would also place unfair constraints on teenagers' activities. [3] Without the ability to drive, they would be forced to give up their activities. [4] Many high school students live in areas without reliable public transportation, but
9
<u>enjoy participating in after-school clubs, working part time, or to play sports.</u>

---

1. **A.** NO CHANGE
    B. for
    C. into
    D. to

2. **F.** NO CHANGE
    G. These deaths in traffic means wasted
    H. These traffic deaths mean wasted
    J. Traffic deaths of these sorts mean wasting

3. **A.** NO CHANGE
   B. the number of fatal crashes, would only
   C. the number of fatal crashes; it would only
   D. the number of fatal crashes; and it would only

4. **F.** NO CHANGE
   G. Two-thirds of car crashes in 2003 involved male teens (Allstate 2).
   H. Male teens accounted for about two thirds of teen car crash victims in 2003.
   J. OMIT the underlined portion

5. **A.** NO CHANGE
   B. (Place after *because*)
   C. (Place after *practiced*)
   D. (Place after *have*)

6. **F.** NO CHANGE
   G. (Begin new paragraph) To summarize,
   H. (Begin new paragraph) In addition,
   J. (Do NOT begin new paragraph) So

7. Suppose the writer changed the verb *taking* in the preceding sentence to *snatching*. This change would make the sentence more:
   A. biased
   B. straightforward
   C. positive
   D. ambiguous

8. **F.** NO CHANGE
   G. will be needed
   H. needing
   J. need

9. **A.** NO CHANGE
   B. enjoy participating in after-school clubs, work part time, or to play sports
   C. enjoy participating in after-school clubs, working part time, or sports
   D. enjoy participating in after-school clubs, working part time, or playing sports

10. Which is the logical sequence of sentences in Paragraph 4?
    F. 4, 3, 2, 1
    G. 2, 1, 4, 3
    H. 3, 4, 1, 2
    J. 1, 2, 4, 3

Essay

In the *Tao Te Ching*, Lao-Tzu writes, "Do you want to improve the world? / I don't think it can be done / . . . If you tamper with it, you'll ruin it." Write a brief persuasive essay in which you argue for or against Lao-Tzu's claim. Be sure to include real-life examples to support your position. As you write, keep in mind that your essay will be evaluated for **ideas, organization, voice, word choice, sentence fluency, conventions, and presentation.**

Checklist for Your Writing

This checklist will help you do your best work. Make sure you do the following:

- ☑ Read the essay prompt carefully.
- ☑ Organize your writing with an introduction, a body, and a conclusion.
- ☑ Use specific evidence and logical reasoning to support your ideas.
- ☑ Use precise language that is appropriate for your audience and purpose.
- ☑ Edit for sentence fluency and conventions.

LOG ON ▶ **Literature** Online

Assessment For additional test practice, go to glencoe.com and enter QuickPass code GLW6053u4.

Le Trait d'Union, 1942. René Magritte. Oil on Canvas, 60 x 150 cm. Private collection. © ARS, NY.

View the Art Magritte is known for his Surrealist paintings. What might the birds in this painting represent?

EUROPE

A.D. 400–PRESENT

Nel mezzo del camin di nostra vita, mi ritrovai
per una selva oscura, che la diritta via era smarrita.

*Midway in our life's journey, I went astray from
the straight road and woke to find myself alone in
a dark wood.*

—Dante, from the *Inferno*

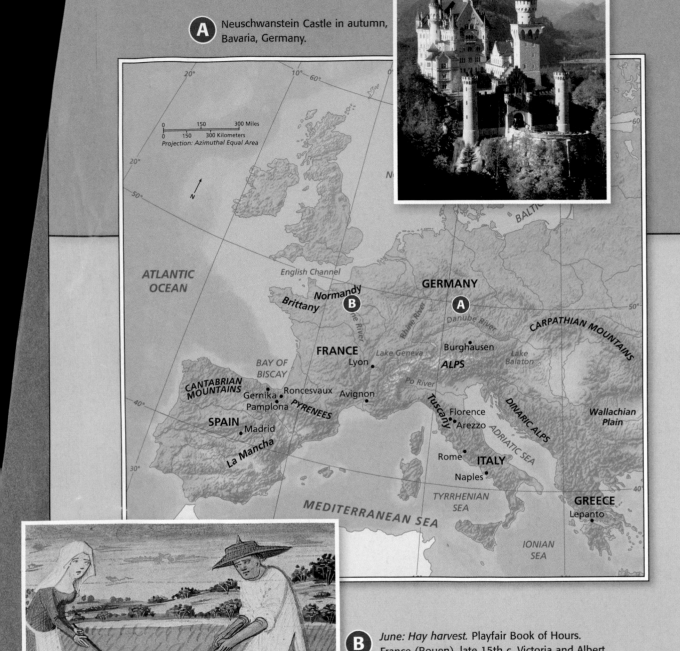

A Neuschwanstein Castle in autumn, Bavaria, Germany.

B *June: Hay harvest.* Playfair Book of Hours. France (Rouen), late 15th c. Victoria and Albert Museum, London.

LOG ON ▶ **Literature** Online

Literature and Reading For more about the history and literature of this period, go to glencoe.com and enter QuickPass code GLW6053u5.

EARLY EUROPE

A.D. 400–1650

Seal of Landgrave Johann, 14th century AD. Wax. Germanisches Nationalmuseum, Nuremberg, Germany.

Being There

On a world map, Europe is little more than a peninsula on the northwest corner of Asia. A band of fertile plains stretches through the center, from the Atlantic Ocean to Russia. The region to the north is rugged and chilly. The central plains and the north were the home of Celtic and Germanic peoples. The region to the south, which has a mild climate, runs along the coast of the Mediterranean Sea and provided the setting for the classical Greek and Roman civilizations.

Looking Ahead

When the Western Roman Empire collapsed in the 400s, few people in Europe identified themselves as Europeans. Their languages, religious beliefs, and ways of life defined them from their neighbors. By the year 1000, however, a European civilization had begun to emerge from the traditions of the Germanic and Celtic peoples, the legacy of Roman civilization, and Christianity.

Keep the following questions in mind as you read:

○ What did Germanic and Celtic traditions contribute to the development of medieval romance?

○ How did Christianity shape medieval civilization?

○ How did the Renaissance change the direction of European civilization?

TIMELINE A.D. 400–1650

400   900

c. 405
Vulgate (Latin) translation
of the Bible is completed

c. 750
Beowulf is composed

780s–790s
Charlemagne encourages
revival of learning

1222–1223
Snorri Sturluson writes the
Prose Edda in Iceland

▲

c. 1314
Dante completes the
Divine Comedy in Italy

c. 1353
Boccaccio completes
the *Decameron* in Italy

EARLY EUROPEAN EVENTS

400   900

496
Clovis, king of the Franks,
converts to Christianity

732
Christians stop Arab
expansion northward
into France

c. 790
Viking raids begin in
Western Europe

1054
East-West Schism divides
Roman and Byzantine
Christians

1066 ▶
French-speaking Normans
conquer England

1215
King John signs the Magna
Carta in England

1241
Mongols invade
central Europe

WORLD EVENTS

400   900

▲
300–900
Maya civilization
flourishes in Central
America

c. 1000
Vikings reach
North America

1095
Christians launch the First
Crusade against Muslims

c. 1150
Temple of Angkor Wat
completed in Cambodia

LOG ON ▶ **Literature** Online

Literature and Reading To explore the Interactive
Timeline, go to glencoe.com and enter QuickPass code
GLW6053u5.

Viking bridle
mount

1400

c. 1445
Gutenberg develops the first printing press in Europe

1485
Sir Thomas Malory's *Le Morte d'Arthur* is published

1513
Machiavelli writes *The Prince* in Italy

1516
Sir Thomas More's *Utopia* is published

1605
Part 1 of Cervantes's *Don Quixote* is published in Spain

1623
First Folio of Shakespeare is published in England

1668–1694
French poet Jean de La Fontaine publishes the *Fables*

1400

c. 1478
Moscow gains freedom from Mongol control

1517
Martin Luther ignites the Protestant Reformation

1526
Ottoman Turks conquer Hungary

1543 ▲
Copernicus publishes his theory of the sun-centered universe

1588
English navy defeats the Spanish Armada

c. 1600
Italian musicians create the first operas

1626
St. Peter's Basilica completed in Rome

1400

1411–1413
Chinese ships begin traveling to Arabia and Africa

1492
Christopher Columbus makes his first voyage to America

c. 1500
Songhay Empire reaches its peak in Africa

1526
Mogul dynasty under Babur begins in India
▼

c. 1600 ▲
Japanese dramatists create the Kabuki form of theater

c. 1650
Taj Mahal is completed in India

Reading Check

Analyze Graphic Information Which of the following authors' works first appeared before the invention of printing, and which first appeared after? (a)Shakespeare; (b)Dante; (c)Cervantes; (d)Boccaccio; (e)Machiavelli

Learning Objectives

For pages 858–869

In studying this text, you will focus on the following objectives:

Literary Study: Analyzing literary periods.

Reading:
Evaluating historical influences.
Connecting to the literature.

EARLY EUROPE

A.D. 400–1650

Historical, Social, and Cultural Forces

The Early Middle Ages

Germanic peoples had begun to move into the lands of the Western Roman Empire by the third century. In A.D. 476, a date often seen as the fall of the Western Empire, the Germanic ruler Odaacer deposed the Roman emperor. (The

Eastern, or Byzantine Empire, based in Constantinople, would survive until 1453.) Over the next few centuries, a series of Germanic states rose and fell in Western Europe, but only the kingdom of the Franks endured. The most powerful Frankish ruler was Charlemagne, who greatly expanded his territory and created the Carolingian Empire. At its height in the early 800s, his empire covered much of western and central Europe. Charlemagne's political strength was matched by his desire to promote learning throughout his kingdom. His efforts led to a revival of education and culture called the Carolingian Renaissance.

The High Middle Ages

By the eleventh and twelfth centuries, a medieval civilization had developed that combined the traditions of the Germanic and Celtic peoples, the heritage of Roman civilization, and the institutions of the Christian Church. The church shaped every aspect of people's lives, providing predictable rituals that gave medieval life its structure. The church also established monasteries where men dedicated themselves to lives of work, prayer, and study. Monasteries became centers

Glorification of the Virgin (detail) North Rose Window, Chartres Cathedral, France.

of learning in which schools were established and books were copied by hand. Another fundamental medieval institution was feudalism. This system of social organization was useful in a time of frequent warfare. Nobles maintained private armies of knights by granting them land in exchange for military service.

The Decline of Medieval Civilization

Beginning in the fourteenth century, a series of events shattered medieval civilization. In 1347, an outbreak of bubonic plague, called "the Black Death," spread throughout Europe, killing perhaps a third of the population before it ended. Between 1337 and 1453 England and France fought the Hundred Years' War, devastating parts of France and draining both countries economically. Finally, the Great Schism, a struggle over the leadership of the church that began in 1378, divided Europe and weakened the church's authority.

The Rise of the Renaissance

As medieval civilization declined, however, a new cultural revolution known as the Renaissance began to reshape Europe. The Renaissance emerged in Italian city-states in the mid-1300s and spread throughout Europe in the decades to come. A major factor that contributed to the rise of this movement, and to the philosophy known as humanism, was a renewed interest in the classical civilizations of ancient Greece and Rome. Humanists believed humanity held a central place in the divine order and asserted that there were no limits to what individuals could accomplish.

> *"Men can do all things if they will."*
>
> —Leon Battista Alberti

The Spread of the Renaissance

One of the most important factors in the spread of Renaissance ideas was the development of printing. In the mid-1400s, Europeans learned how to print with movable metal type. Johannes Gutenberg played a crucial role in this process. The Gutenberg Bible, printed around 1455, was the first European book produced from movable type. By 1500, there were more than 1,000 printers in Europe, and almost 40,000 titles had been published. The printing of books encouraged scholarly research and increased the public's desire for knowledge, impacting European society and literacy.

Portrait of a Lady as the Magdalen, c. 1490 - c. 1540. Master of the Female Half Lengths. Flemish tempera on panel. Sotheby's, London.

Architecture

Most of the great achievements of medieval and Renaissance architecture were religious buildings. Romanesque architecture, dominant from about 1000 to about 1150, emphasized rounded forms and arches. Large buildings in this style needed massive walls to support their weight. Builders in the Gothic style, which succeeded Romanesque, developed pointed arches and exterior bracing that allowed them to erect much higher, thinner walls that often featured magnificent stained glass windows. The Gothic style of architecture created an overall impression of extraordinary lightness. Medieval cathedral builders adorned both Romanesque and Gothic buildings with carvings, usually illustrating biblical stories. They also sought inspiration from ancient Roman and Greek models. Churches and other buildings in the Renaissance style frequently included Doric or Corinthian columns (see page 185) and other classical elements in their decoration.

Music

During the Middle Ages and the Renaissance, European music became increasingly varied, complex, and secular. Originally developed around 600, Gregorian chant was the dominant form of

"It is fitting that the body, simultaneously with the soul, repeatedly sings praises to God through the voice."

—Hildegard of Bingen

medieval music. Chants were religious music, often sung by monks. Performers sang in unison or with simple harmonies and used few instruments. Composers remained anonymous, and tunes evolved from one performance to the next. One exception to the anonymity of medieval composers was the German nun Hildegard of Bingen, who wrote about 80 musical works. By the 1200s, minstrels traveling from one noble's court to another sang about love, war, and other worldly themes. A century later, musicians played instruments, such as the lute, independently, rather than solely to accompany a singer. By the 1500s, individual composers, such as Italian Giovanni Palestrina, were becoming popular.

Duomo Cathedral, Florence, Italy

Boy playing
the lute.
Michelangelo
Merisi da
Caravaggio.
Hermitage,
St. Petersburg,
Russia.

Renaissance Painting

Prior to the Renaissance, painting was a minor art
in Europe, often used to illustrate books. Medieval
artists usually created biblical and other religious
images that were colorful but flat. Renaissance
painters explored new subject matter and artistic
techniques. For example, they revived the classical tradition of portraiture, painting vivid, revealing images of their subjects' faces—and sometimes
of their own. Renaissance artists also revolutionized painting by rediscovering the techniques of
perspective. Using these techniques, Renaissance
painters arranged forms and colors to create the
appearance of depth on a flat surface.

Annunciation. Hans Vredeman de Vries 1598.
Oak, 221 x 140 cm. Kunsthistorisches Museum,
Vienna, Austria.

PREVIEW **Big Ideas** of Early Europe

1 From Myth to Romance	**2** The Vision of Faith	**3** The Renaissance and Humanism
After the collapse of the Western Roman Empire, a new civilization took shape in Western Europe that combined elements of Christianity, Roman heritage, and Germanic and Celtic heroic traditions. Literature of this period often celebrates the courageous adventures and chivalric virtues of knights. **See pages 866**	After the fall of Rome, the Christian Church became the greatest power in Europe. The church controlled every aspect of medieval life and culture. Medieval literature expressed the beliefs and values of Christianity, and sought to harmonize scientific reason with religious faith. **See page 867**	With the decline of medieval civilization in the mid-1300s, a new cultural spirit known as the Renaissance reshaped European civilization. Developing in Italy and spreading throughout Europe, Renaissance literature expressed a cultural outlook called humanism, which celebrated human freedom and the joys of this world. **See page 868**

From Myth to Romance

The knight in armor is the most familiar symbol of the Middle Ages. Some of the basic features of the culture of knighthood expressed in medieval epics and romances came from the traditions of the Celtic and Germanic peoples of Europe.

Celtic and Germanic Peoples

Before its collapse, the Western Roman Empire was home to a variety of peoples who spoke Celtic and Germanic languages. The Celts originally inhabited wide areas of western and central Europe. Conquered first by the Romans and later by Germanic groups, they survived only in regions at the edge of Europe, including Ireland, Scotland, Wales, and Brittany. Germanic peoples, particularly the Franks, eventually occupied much of the former territory of the Western Roman Empire.

> *"Franks are good men; like vassals brave they'll stand. . ."*
>
> —from the *Song of Roland*

Lords and Vassals

Among the most enduring contributions of the Germanic peoples to the emerging civilization of the Middle Ages was the idea of honor. The bond of loyalty between a warrior and his lord, even in times of struggle, represented a commitment to an ideal vision of nobility, pride, and courage. Early Norse myths such as *Ragnarok* (see pages 870–875), for example, celebrated the devotion to heroism in spite of a guaranteed loss. In Germanic society, warriors swore an oath of loyalty to their leaders, who rewarded them with gold, weapons, horses, and other prized gifts. This idea of loyalty between a warrior and his lord survived in the medieval institution of feudalism. To become a

Two knights fighting, c1415. Their armour includes scale, mail and plate, which in the case of the man on the right, has proved inadequate. Shelfmark ID: Cotton Nero E ii part 1. Folio No: 1. British Library, London.

vassal, a knight performed an act of homage to his lord. In feudal society, loyalty to one's lord was the chief virtue. This relationship can be seen in the greatest medieval epic, the *Song of Roland* (see pages 877–885).

The Rise of Romance

One of the principal Celtic contributions to later medieval culture was the legend of King Arthur. Although he may have been a Celtic chieftain in Britain who briefly withstood invading Germanic peoples in the early 500s, the legend of Arthur grew over the centuries until he was portrayed as a great leader. The tales of King Arthur and his knights of the Round Table were one of the principal cycles of medieval romance, a literary form that developed in France during the 1100s. In prose or verse, the medieval romance related stories of knights in combat and in love. These stories exhibited the ideals of chivalry, the knightly code that required courage, loyalty, and honor. Medieval romances also presented the values of courtly love, which celebrated romantic passion and the unswerving devotion of a knight to his lady.

Reading Check

Analyze Cause-and-Effect Relationships How did Germanic values contribute to the development of feudalism?

Big Idea 2
The Vision of Faith

Adoration of the Magi, detail from one of four tabernacle reliquaries. Fra Angelico. Museo di S. Marco, Florence.

The tall spires of Gothic cathedrals that soared above many towns in the Middle Ages are apt symbols of the domination of medieval life by the Christian Church.

The Power of the Church

By the end of the 300s, Christianity had become the supreme religion of the Roman Empire. As the Western Roman Empire fell apart in 476, the church played an increasingly important role in the growth of European civilization. As feudalism developed, church officials were often feudal lords who held worldly as well as spiritual power. One of the most extraordinary expressions of Christianity's power in the world was the Crusades. In 1095, Pope Urban II launched the first of a long series of Christian military expeditions to regain the Holy Land of Palestine from the Muslims. Though this goal ultimately failed, the extensive efforts of Christian crusaders demonstrate the strength of the church's leadership in medieval Europe.

Christian Belief

In the Middle Ages, the sacraments of the church were a crucial part of ordinary people's lives from birth to death. The sacraments were seen as the principal means for receiving God's grace and therefore necessary for salvation. Only the clergy could administer the sacraments, so every Christian depended on the clergy to achieve salvation. Other religious practices were widespread, including the veneration of Christian saints. Relics, or bones of saints or objects connected with them, were used to heal people or produce other miracles. Pilgrimages to sacred Christian shrines were also widespread.

> *"But now was turning my desire and will,*
> *Even as a wheel that equally is moved,*
> *The Love which moves the sun and the other stars."*
> —Dante, from the *Paradiso*

Christian Thought

Through its control of education and the copying of books, the church shaped the development of intellectual life in the Middle Ages. Theology was the most highly regarded area of study at medieval universities. One of the most influential intellectual traditions in the Middle Ages was scholasticism, which sought to reconcile faith and reason—to show that what was accepted on faith was in harmony with what could be learned through reason and experience. In his religious epic the *Divine Comedy* (see pages 898–914), the Italian poet Dante expressed this medieval attempt to reconcile the world of faith with the world of experience.

Reading Check

Make Generalizations How did the Christian Church dominate European life in the Middle Ages?

Before You Read

Ragnarok: The Twilight of the Gods

Meet **Snorri Sturluson**

(1179–1241)

Chess piece king and queen, 12th century BC. Walrus ivory. Isle of Lewis, Outer Hebrides.

The apocalyptic story of "Ragnarok: The Twilight of the Gods" includes a series of vicious winters, an era of moral chaos, and an epic battle between giants and gods. The myth is part of an anonymous collection of heroic poems called the *Poetic Edda* originally compiled in writing around the tenth century. The *Poetic Edda* reflects the pagan values of its Nordic audience and was a main source for Snorri Sturluson's *Prose Edda*. In this work written three centuries later for Christian readers, Sturluson aims to teach his fellow writers about the older style and expression of early Icelandic *skalds* (court poets) and to bring contemporary relevance to ancient myths. It is fitting, therefore, that this excerpt from Sturluson's Christian retelling of the pagan Ragnarok myth describes a turning point in history. In the battle, as in medieval Iceland, one world ends as another begins.

Political Intrigue Snorri Sturluson was born in western Iceland to a politically active family. He grew up in Oddi in the home of Iceland's most powerful chieftain. Sturluson married an heiress in 1199, moved to Reykjaholt in 1206, and later became president of the Icelandic high court. During this period, he forged a political relationship with King Haakan IV of Norway to further his own political ambitions in Iceland. This maneuver proved to be Sturluson's undoing, as the Norwegian king became suspicious of Sturluson's motives and had him assassinated.

The *Eddas* Though his personal and political life was turbulent, Sturluson had a celebrated literary career as a poet and historian. In addition to the *Prose Edda*, he is credited with writing the *Heimskringla*, a massive work chronicling the history of the kings of Norway from ancient times to the late twelfth century. He also authored *Egil's Saga*, a biography of the tenth-century poet Egill Skallagrimsson, an ancestor of Sturluson's. The *Prose Edda*, however, represents Sturluson's most significant literary contribution. Written at a time long after Christianity had superseded pagan beliefs in Western Europe, it includes a prologue in which the author advises his readers on how to approach the myths:

> "Remember, these tales . . . must be revered as ancient tradition, but are neither to be believed nor to be tampered with."
>
> —Snorri Sturluson

Scholars theorize that Sturluson may have included this advice to protect himself from criticism by the clergy—who were determined to eliminate any influence of pagan beliefs on Icelandic society—while at the same time promoting a respect and love for the myths.

LOG ON ▶ **Literature** Online

Author Search For more about Snorri Sturluson, go to glencoe.com and enter QuickPass code GLW6053u5.

Literature and Reading Preview

Connect to the Myth

What other stories have you read about the end of the world? Discuss these stories with a partner. Consider how they are similar to and different from "Ragnarok: The Twilight of the Gods."

Build Background

The universe of Norse mythology was composed of three realms. Asgard, the home of the gods (the Aesir), was at the top; Midgard, the home of men, was in the middle; and Niflheim, the home of the dead, was at the bottom. The gods and human heroes of Norse myths fought in vain against the forces of evil (giants and monstrous creatures), anticipating the rise of a new world that would follow the destruction of the old world.

Set Purposes for Reading

Big Idea From Myth to Romance

As you read "Ragnarok," ask yourself, What details reveal characteristics of mythology?

Literary Element Description

Description is a detailed portrayal of a person, a place, an object, or an event. Good descriptive writing includes imagery that appeals to the senses. As you read, ask yourself, Which descriptions are especially vivid and powerful?

Reading Strategy Summarize

When you **summarize**, you state the main ideas and events of a text in your own words and in a logical sequence. Summarizing helps you determine whether you've understood what the text is about. As you read, ask yourself, What happened in each paragraph and section?

Tip: Take Notes As you read, answer these questions to help you summarize.

- ☑ Who are the characters?
- ☑ What are they doing?
- ☑ When and where do they do it?
- ☑ How and why do they do it?

Vocabulary

misery (miz′ər ē) *n.* unhappy state of mind; great distress; wretchedness; p. 873 *Everyone who endured the hurricane experienced misery and suffering.*

sever (sev′ər) *v.* cut or break apart; separate; divide; p. 873 *The worker severed the cord that bound the stack of wheat, freeing up the sheaves.*

writhe (rīth) *v.* twist the body violently; contort; p. 874 *The wounded man writhed in pain, twisting and turning uncontrollably on the ground.*

asunder (ə sun′dər) *adv.* into parts; into different pieces; p. 874 *Displeased with what she had written, the author tore the manuscript asunder and threw away the pieces.*

Tip: Word Usage When you encounter a new word, you can gain a better understanding of it by asking yourself a question. For example, What might cause someone to feel *misery*?

Ragnarok:
The Twilight of the Gods

from The Prose Edda

Snorri Sturluson
Translated by Jean I. Young

Valhalla and the Midgard Serpent (detail), 1680. Icelandic
School. Arni Magnusson Institute, Reykjavik, Iceland.

NORSE GLOSSARY

FENRIR A monstrous wolf bound in chains by the gods until Ragnarok; offspring of Loki

MIDGARD SERPENT A sea serpent encircling Midgard in the waters surrounding it and so large he bites his own tail; offspring of Loki

NAGLFAR Ship that transports the giants to the final conflict

HRYM (also called Thrym) leader of the frost giants

MUSPELL A southern region of fire

SONS OF MUSPELL Fire giants who live in Muspell

SURT Giant who guards Muspell; leader of the sons of Muspell

BIFROST A rainbow bridge connecting Midgard to Asgard

VIGRID A vast plain on which the final conflict takes place

LOKI Considered a god, but born of two giants; father of Fenrir and the Midgard Serpent; evil mischief maker bound by the gods until Ragnarok

HEL (also called Niflheim) The underworld or land of the dead presided over by an evil goddess of the same name who is an offspring of Loki

HEIMDALL Watchman of the gods who guarded the entry to Asgard

ODIN (also called Wodan, Woden, and Wotan) Leader of the gods; protector of heroes in his hall Valhalla; god of poetry

MIMIR God of wisdom whose head and speech were preserved after he was killed by rival gods

MIMIR'S WELL Well or spring of wisdom located at the roots of Yggdrasil and guarded by Mimir's head

AESIR Collective name for the group of gods who live in Asgard

EINHERJAR Dead warriors who reside in Valhalla within Asgard

YGGDRASIL The World Tree; a giant ash tree that supports the universe

THOR God of thunder, second only to Odin in rank; son of Odin and guardian of the gods

FREY God of fertility; ruler of the sun and rain

SKIRNIR Frey's messenger or servant

GARM A monstrous hound bound in chains

GNIPAHELLIR A cave at the entrance to Hel

TYR God of war, considered the bravest of the gods; son of Odin

VIDAR Son of Odin; a survivor of the final conflict

"First will come the winter called Fimbulvetr. Snow will drive from all quarters, there will be hard frosts and biting winds; the sun will be no use. There will be three such winters on end with no summer between. Before that, however, three other winters will pass accompanied by great wars throughout the whole world. Brothers will kill each other for the sake of gain, and no one will spare father or son in manslaughter. As it says in the *Sibyl's Vision*:

> Brothers will fight
> and kill each other,
> men will know **misery,**
> an axe-age, a sword-age,
> shields will be cloven,
> a wind-age, a wolf-age,
> before the world's ruin.

"Then will occur what will seem a great piece of news, the wolf will swallow the sun and that will seem a great disaster to men. Then another wolf will seize the moon and that one too will do great harm. The stars will disappear from heaven. Then this will come to pass, the whole surface of the earth and the mountains will tremble so [violently] that trees will be uprooted from the ground, mountains will crash down, and all fetters and bonds will be snapped and **severed.** The wolf Fenrir will get loose then. The sea will lash against the land

Summarize *What events will take place during the first set of winters before the end of the world?*

Vocabulary

misery (miz′ər ē) *n.* unhappy state of mind; great distress; wretchedness
sever (sev′ər) *v.* cut or break apart; separate; divide

because the Miðgarð Serpent is **writhing** in giant fury trying to come ashore. At that time, too, the ship known as Naglfar will become free. It is made of dead men's nails, so it is worth warning you that, if anyone dies with his nails uncut, he will greatly increase the material for that ship which both gods and men devoutly hope will take a long time building. In this tidal wave, however, Naglfar will be launched. The name of the giant steering Naglfar is Hrym. The wolf Fenrir will advance with wide open mouth, his upper jaw against the sky, his lower on the earth (he would gape more widely still if there were room) and his eyes and nostrils will blaze with fire. The Miðgarð Serpent will blow so much poison that the whole sky and sea will be spattered with it; he is most terrible and will be on the other side of the wolf.

"In this din the sky will be rent **asunder** and the sons of Muspell ride forth from it. Surt will ride first and with him fire blazing both before and behind. He has a very good sword and it shines more brightly than the sun. When they ride over Bifröst, however—as has been said before—that bridge will break. The sons of Muspell will push forward to the plain called Vígríð and the wolf Fenrir and the Miðgarð Serpent will go there too. Loki and Hrym with all the frost giants will also be there by then, and all the family of Hel will accompany Loki. The sons of Muspell, however, will form a host in themselves and that a very bright one. The plain Vígríð is a hundred and twenty leagues in every direction.

"When these things are happening, Heimdall will stand up and blow a great blast on the horn Gjöll and awaken all the gods and they will hold an assembly.

Then Óðin will ride to Mímir's spring and ask Mímir's advice for himself and his company. The ash Yggdrasil will tremble and nothing in heaven or earth will be free from fear. The Æsir and all the Einherjar will arm themselves and press forward on to the plain. Óðin will ride first in a helmet of gold and a beautiful coat of mail and with his spear Gungnir, and he will make for the wolf Fenrir. Thór will advance at his side but will be unable to help him, because he will have his hands full fighting the Miðgarð Serpent. Frey will fight against Surt and it will be a hard conflict before Frey falls; the loss of the good sword that he gave to Skírnir will bring about his death. Then the hound Garm, which was bound in front of Gnipahellir, will also get free; he is the worst sort of monster. He will battle with Týr and each will kill the other. Thór will slay the Miðgarð Serpent but stagger back only nine paces before he falls down dead, on account of the poison blown on him by the serpent. The wolf will swallow Óðin and that will be his death. Immediately afterwards, however, Víðar will stride forward and place one foot on the lower jaw of the wolf. On this foot he will be wearing the shoe which has been in the making since the beginning of time; it consists of the strips of leather men pare off at the toes and heels of their shoes, and for this reason people who want to help the Æsir must throw away these strips. Víðar will take the wolf's upper jaw in one hand and tear his throat asunder and that will be the wolf's death. Loki will battle with Heimdall and each will kill the other. Thereupon Surt will fling fire over the earth and burn up the whole world. ❧

Description *Describe Fenrir and the Midgard Serpent.*

Vocabulary

writhe (rīth) *v.* twist the body violently; contort
asunder (ə sun′dər) *adv.* into parts; into different pieces

From Myth to Romance *Who is Odin, and why will he ask Mimir for advice?*

Summarize *Beginning with this sentence and continuing to the myth's end, briefly summarize the outcomes of the individual battles.*

After You Read

Respond and Think Critically

Respond and Interpret

1. What part of this myth made the strongest impression on you? Explain.

2. (a)Identify the beings that roam the land during the upheaval on Earth. (b)Do they represent forces of good or evil? Explain. (Use information from the glossary on page 873 to support your answer.)

3. (a)On what battlefield does the final conflict take place? (b)Where is this battlefield located? How do you know?

Analyze and Evaluate

4. (a)What is the battle's final outcome? (b)Based on what you've learned about Norse mythology, why was this outcome inevitable?

5. Based on what you know about other mythologies (Greek and Roman, for example), why is it significant that gods die in this myth?

6. What might evil's triumph over good in this myth indicate about the ancient Norse outlook on life?

Connect

7. **Big Idea** **From Myth to Romance** How are the characters, events, and ideas in this myth similar to and different from myths of other cultures with which you are familiar?

8. **Connect to Today** This myth uses Icelandic winters and local creatures such as wolves to represent destructive forces. What images of destruction might exist in a modern end of the world story?

Literary Element Description

Description involves a detailed portrayal of a person, a place, an object, or an event.

1. What is particularly menacing about Fenrir and the Midgard Serpent?

2. (a)Which individual battle do you think is described most graphically? (b)Do you think the description is effective? Why or why not?

Reading Strategy Summarize

A **summary** is a boiled-down, distilled, and refined statement of the key details in a text.

1. Identify the characters and places in this myth.

2. In your own words, briefly summarize the plot of this myth. Use your notes from page 871.

LOG ON ▶ **Literature** Online

Selection Resources For Selection Quizzes, eFlashcards, and Reading-Writing Connection activities, go to glencoe.com and enter QuickPass code GLW6053u5.

Vocabulary Practice

Practice with Word Usage Respond to these statements to help you explore the meanings of the vocabulary words from the myth.

1. Identify an event that has caused **misery**.

2. Explain how you might **sever** something.

3. Name something that makes you **writhe**.

4. Explain how you might put two things **asunder**.

Writing

Write a Description Write your own description about an event that would mark a dramatic turning point in history. Set your description in the future, but make it resemble an event that could really happen. Be sure to use details to paint a picture of the event and appeal to all the senses as Sturluson does.

Vocabulary Workshop

Words from Norse Myth

Literature Connection Though Odin, leader of the Norse gods, met his end in the final conflict of Ragnarok, we still pay tribute to him on our calendar. The English word *Wednesday* comes from the Old English word *Wodnesdaeg*, which means "Woden's day" (Odin's day). In addition, our words *Tuesday, Thursday,* and *Friday* are named for the Norse deities Tyr, Thor, and Freya/Frigg.

Tracing the etymology, or origin, of a word can help you understand how words from other cultures enter our language. Modern English has its roots in Old English, the language of the Anglo-Saxons who lived in England during the early Middle Ages. The development of Old English was influenced in part by the Scandinavian Vikings who invaded and settled the British Isles. Thus, it is not surprising that many English words can be traced directly or through Old English to Norse origins. For example, the word "berserk" comes from the Norse word meaning "bear shirt." Below is a chart of English words and their definitions, along with their etymologies showing the Norse words from which they were derived.

Word Origins

Word origins, or etymologies, are the history and development of words. **Word roots** are the part of the word from which the core meaning is derived.

Test-Taking Tip

When you do not know the meaning of a word, consider its root and origin. Thinking about how a word was derived can help you understand its meaning.

English Word	Etymology
skill *n.* ability gained by practice; expertise	from Middle English *skil,* meaning "cause, reason"; from Old Norse *skil,* "knowledge, distinction"
husband *n.* a married man	from Old English *husbonda,* meaning "master of the house"; from Old Norse *husbondi,* meaning "householder, peasant who owns land"
ski *n.* one of a pair of long, flat, thin pieces of wood, plastic, or metal used for gliding over snow	from Norwegian *ski* (same meaning); from Old Norse *skith,* meaning "stick of wood"

Practice Match the English words below with their meanings from their Norse origins. Use a dictionary to check your answers.

1. sky   a. whip
2. gape   b. butcher's meat
3. stagger   c. open the mouth wide
4. fling   d. cloud
5. slaughter   e. push

LOG ON ▶ **Literature** Online

Vocabulary For more vocabulary practice, go to glencoe.com and enter QuickPass code GLW6053u5.

Before You Read

from the *Song of Roland*

The *Song of Roland*, often called the national epic of France, is the earliest known example of the genre of medieval French poetry called *chansons de geste*, or "songs of deeds." The poem, whose authorship is unknown, was composed around the year 1100, but is based on a historical event from centuries earlier that grew into a legend passed down from one generation to the next.

The Empire Charlemagne (shär′ lə mān′), or Charles the Great, was king of the Franks (an early Germanic tribe) from 768 to 814. After years of campaigning against various warring kings and city-states, he managed to establish a unified state in Western Europe, an area roughly equivalent to the ancient Roman Empire. In 800, Pope Leo III crowned Charlemagne as the first emperor in the West since the fall of Rome. He was a civilized king instrumental in spreading Christianity, art, and learning throughout Western Europe. His domain later became known as the Holy Roman Empire, and in one form or another, it lived on until 1806.

The Story Behind the Epic In Charlemagne's time, Arab Muslims ruled Spain. Agreeing to intercede between two of their warring factions, Charlemagne led a siege on the Spanish city of Saragossa in 778. But his Spanish campaign was a disaster, and he was forced to retreat. With his army, he crossed the Pyrenees Mountains that divide France and Spain. There, in the narrow pass at Roncevaux (rawns voh′), his rear guard was attacked and destroyed by local mountaineers known as Basques. One of the soldiers killed in this battle was a commander named Roland.

The Legend Grows Approximately 300 years later, in the eleventh century, Roland was celebrated in an epic poem. During this time, Europe was in the throes of the Crusades, the series of holy wars fought by Christians hoping to reclaim the city of Jerusalem from the Muslims and restore it as a center of Christianity. Feelings against Muslims ran high throughout Europe. In the legend of Roland, the attackers were no longer Christian Basques, but Muslims—the pagan "Saracens" referred to in the poem. Their force had grown from a small local band of mountaineers to a fierce army 400,000 strong. The conflict itself had swollen into an epic battle between Christianity and Islam, reflecting the large-scale battles fought during the Crusades. Roland, who had played only a minor role in the actual Spanish expedition, was now Charlemagne's nephew, his most valiant chieftain—and a legendary epic hero.

> "'The end! The end of the world is upon us!' . . . it is the worldwide grief for the death of Roland."
>
> —from the *Song of Roland*

Olifant, 1st 1/2 11th century. Musee Paul Dupuy, Toulouse, France.

Literature and Reading Preview

Connect to the Epic

Which of these two qualities do you think is more valuable in a leader: the ability to set an example through individual excellence, or the ability to make sure the whole team functions smoothly as a unit? Discuss this question with a partner.

Build Background

Ganelon, Roland's stepfather, became furious because Roland had recommended him for the dangerous job of Charlemagne's ambassador to the Saracen king Marsilion. Turning traitor, Ganelon encouraged Marsilion to attack the rear guard of Charlemagne's army, and also persuaded Charlemagne to place Roland in command of that rear guard. As this excerpt opens, Roland, his loyal friend Oliver, and a small detachment of troops are trapped in a mountain pass at Roncevaux, under surprise attack by the Saracen army.

Set Purposes for Reading

Big Idea From Epic to Romance

As you read, ask yourself, What medieval values does Roland represent?

Literary Element Epic

An **epic** is a long narrative poem that describes the adventures of a larger-than-life hero. Medieval epics include characteristics such as formal speeches, supernatural elements, battle descriptions, and repetition of key words. As you read, ask yourself, What epic conventions are apparent in this work?

Reading Strategy Evaluate Characters

When you **evaluate characters,** you judge their qualities and compare them with those of other characters in a literary work. As you read, ask yourself, What details can help me assess each character?

Tip: Sort Details In a chart like the one below, list details about Roland. Then decide which qualities those details suggest.

Details	Qualities
Roland earlier refused to blow the horn.	pride; foolhardiness
Roland tries to break his sword so that pagans cannot use it.	

Learning Objectives

For pages 877–885

In studying this text, you will focus on the following objectives:

Literary Study: Analyzing epic.

Reading: Evaluating characters.

Writing: Writing a character sketch.

Vocabulary

refuge (ref′ūj) *n.* shelter or protection from danger; p. 879 *As the floodwaters rose, townspeople sought refuge by fleeing to higher ground.*

torment (tôr′ment) *n.* great pain or suffering; p. 879 *Psychologists say people who inflict torment on animals are emotionally troubled.*

exult (ig zult′) *v.* to rejoice greatly; p. 881 *Our team exulted after defeating a strong opponent.*

strut (strut) *v.* to walk in a proud manner; p. 882 *The player who scored the touchdown strutted in the end zone.*

feign (fān) *v.* to make a false show of; pretend; p. 882 *Did you feign being sick so you could skip school and avoid that math test?*

Tip: Word Origins Etymologies trace a word's development from its language of origin to its current meaning and usage. For example, *feign* ultimately derives from the Latin *fingere,* meaning "to form, shape, or alter."

from the
Song of Roland

Translated by
Frederick Goldin

Charlemagne battling the Neapolitans. French Illumination from the History of Emperors. Bibliotheque de l'Arsenal, Paris.

❧110❧

The battle is fearful and full of grief.
Oliver and Roland strike like good men,
the Archbishop°, more than a thousand blows,
and the Twelve Peers° do not hang back, they strike!
5   the French fight side by side, all as one man.
The pagans die by hundreds, by thousands:
whoever does not flee finds no **refuge** from death,
like it or not, there he ends all his days.
And there the men of France lose their greatest arms;
10   they will not see their fathers, their kin again,
or Charlemagne, who looks for them in the passes.
Tremendous **torment** now comes forth in France,
a mighty whirlwind, tempests of wind and thunder,
rains and hailstones, great and immeasurable,
15   bolts of lightning hurtling and hurtling down:
it is, in truth, a trembling of the earth.
From Saint Michael-in-Peril to the Saints,
from Besançon to the port of Wissant,°
there is no house whose veil of walls does not crumble.

3 Archbishop: Turpin, archbishop of Reims and chaplain for Charlemagne's forces.

4 Twelve Peers: Charlemagne's top military leaders.

17–18 Saint Michael . . . Wissant: By naming cities in various parts of France, the song suggests the battle's far-reaching impact.

Epic *What details in this stanza suggest that this battle is one of epic proportions?*

Vocabulary

refuge (ref′ūj) *n.* shelter or protection from danger
torment (tôr′ment) *n.* great pain or suffering

20 A great darkness at noon falls on the land,
there is no light but when the heavens crack.
No man sees this who is not terrified,
and many say: "The Last Day! Judgment Day!
The end! The end of the world is upon us!"
25 They do not know, they do not speak the truth:
it is the worldwide grief for the death of Roland.°

❧ 130 ❧

And Roland says: "We are in a rough battle.
I'll sound the olifant,° Charles will hear it."
Said Oliver: "No good vassal would do it.
30 When I urged it, friend, you did not think it right.
If Charles were here, we'd come out with no losses.
Those men down there—no blame can fall on them."
Oliver said: "Now by this beard of mine,
If I can see my noble sister, Aude,°
35 once more, you will never lie in her arms!"

❧ 131 ❧

And Roland said: "Why are you angry at me?"
Oliver answers: "Companion, it is your doing.
I will tell you what makes a vassal good:
    it is judgment, it is never madness;
40 restraint is worth more than the raw nerve of a fool.
Frenchmen are dead because of your wildness.
And what service will Charles ever have from us?
If you had trusted me, my lord would be here,
we would have fought this battle through to the end,
45 Marsilion would be dead, or our prisoner.
Roland, your prowess—had we never seen it!°
    And now, dear friend, we've seen the last of it.
No more aid from us now for Charlemagne,
a man without equal till Judgment Day,
50 you will die here, and your death will shame France.
We kept faith, you and I, we were companions;
    and everything we were will end today.
We part before evening, and it will be hard."

26 death of Roland: Roland has not died at this point, but the narrative suggests that the natural world is already mourning his coming death.

28 olifant (also spelled *oliphant*): a horn made of an elephant's tusk.

34 Aude: Oliver's sister, is engaged to marry Roland.

41–46 Frenchmen . . . seen it: When Roland's troops were ambushed, Oliver had begged Roland to sound his horn and call for help immediately, but out of pride Roland had refused.

Epic *How does the narrator emphasize Roland's importance?*

Evaluate Characters *What judgment can you make about Roland's character based on Oliver's claims?*

✦132✦

Turpin the Archbishop hears their bitter words,
55 digs hard into his horse with golden spurs
and rides to them; begins to set them right:
"You, Lord Roland, and you, Lord Oliver,
I beg you in God's name do not quarrel.
To sound the horn could not help us now, true,
60 but still it is far better that you do it:
let the King come, he can avenge us then—
these men of Spain must not go home **exulting!**
Our French will come, they'll get down on
    their feet,
and find us here—we'll be dead, cut to pieces.
65 They will lift us into coffins on the backs of mules,
and weep for us, in rage and pain and grief,
and bury us in the courts of churches;
and we will not be eaten by wolves or pigs or dogs."
Roland replies, "Lord, you have spoken well."

✦134✦

70 And now the mighty effort of Roland the Count:
he sounds his olifant; his pain is great,
and from his mouth the bright blood comes
    leaping out,
and the temple bursts in his forehead.
That horn, in Roland's hands, has a mighty voice:
75 King Charles hears it drawing through the passes.
Naimon° heard it, the Franks listen to it.
And the King said: "I hear Count Roland's horn;
he'd never sound it unless he had a battle."
Says Ganelon: "Now no more talk of battles!
80 You are old now, your hair is white as snow,
the things you say make you sound like a child.
You know Roland and that wild pride of his—
what a wonder God has suffered it so long!
Remember? he took Noples without your command:

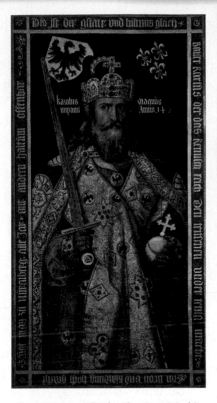

Charlemagne (Charles the Great) in his coronation robes, 16th century. after Albrecht Dürer. Oil on Canvas, 213 x 113 cm. Kunsthistorisches Museum, Vienna.

View the Art Charlemagne brought order and Christian culture to the western part of the former Roman Empire. How has the artist tried to give a sense of the emperor's personality?

76 Naimon: one of Charlemagne's dukes.

Epic *Why might Roland's blowing of the horn be considered heroic?*

Vocabulary

exult (ig zult´) *v.* to rejoice greatly

85   the Saracens rode out, to break the siege;
      they fought with him, the great vassal Roland.
      Afterwards he used the streams to wash the blood
      from the meadows: so that nothing would show.
      He blasts his horn all day to catch a rabbit,
90   he's **strutting** now before his peers and bragging—
      who under heaven would dare meet him on the field?
      So now: ride on! Why do you keep on stopping?
      The Land of Fathers° lies far ahead of us."

93 Land of Fathers: Ganelon is referring to France.

❧168❧

Now Roland feels that death is very near.
95   His brain comes spilling out through his two ears;
      prays to God for his peers: let them be called;
      and for himself, to the angel Gabriel;°
      took the oliphant: there must be no reproach!
      took Durendal his sword in his other hand,
100   and farther than a crossbow's farthest shot
      he walks toward Spain, into a fallow° land,
      and climbs a hill: there beneath two fine trees
      stand four great blocks of stone, all are of marble;
      and he fell back, to earth, on the green grass,
105   has fainted there, for death is very near.

97 Gabriel: The archangel Gabriel served as God's messenger.

101 fallow: plowed but not sown with seed.

❧169❧

      High are the hills, and high, high are the trees;
      there stand four blocks of stone, gleaming of marble.
      Count Roland falls fainting on the green grass,
      and is watched, all this time, by a Saracen:
110   who has **feigned** death and lies now with the others,
      has smeared blood on his face and on his body;
      and quickly now gets to his feet and runs—
      a handsome man, strong, brave, and so crazed with pride
      that he does something mad and dies for it:
115   laid hands on Roland, and on the arms of Roland,

Epic *Read the rest of this stanza. How does Roland continue to prove himself a true epic hero?*

Vocabulary

strut (strut) *v.* to walk in a proud manner
feign (fān) *v.* to make a false show of; pretend

and cried: "Conquered! Charles's nephew conquered!
I'll carry this sword home to Arabia!"
As he draws it, the Count begins to come round.

❧170❧

Now Roland feels: *someone taking his sword!*
120 opened his eyes, and had one word for him:
"I don't know you, you aren't one of ours";
grasps that olifant that he will never lose,
strikes on the helm° beset with gems in gold,

123 **helm:** helmet.

shatters the steel, and the head, and the bones,
125 sent his two eyes flying out of his head,
dumped him over stretched out at his feet dead;
and said: "You nobody! how could you dare
lay hands on me—rightly or wrongly: how?
Who'll hear of this and not call you a fool?
130 Ah! the bell-mouth of the olifant is smashed,
the crystal and the gold fallen away."

❧173❧

Roland the Count strikes down on a dark rock,
and the rock breaks, breaks more than I can tell,
and the blade grates, but Durendal will not break,
135 the sword leaped up, rebounded toward the sky.
The Count, when he sees that sword will not be broken,
softly, in his own presence, speaks the lament:
"Ah Durendal, beautiful, and most sacred,
the holy relics in this golden pommel!
140 Saint Peter's tooth and blood of Saint Basile,
a lock of hair of my lord Saint Denis,
and a fragment of blessed Mary's robe:
your power must not fall to the pagans,
you must be served by Christian warriors.
145 May no coward ever come to hold you!
It was with you I conquered those great lands

Evaluate Characters *What does Roland's interaction with the Saracen in this stanza indicate about his character?*

From Epic to Romance *What does Roland fear will happen to Durendal? What might his attitude toward his sword reveal about medieval values?*

Before You Read

Bisclavret: The Lay of the Werewolf

Meet **Marie de France**

(late twelfth century)

Marie de France, the earliest known French woman poet, is considered one of the finest poets of her century. Although little is known about her life, historians believe she was aristocratic and knew several languages, including French, English, and Latin. She likely spent many years in England, and may have been the half-sister of Henry II, who ruled from 1154 to 1189.

A Preserver of Culture Although it was customary at the time for authors to remain anonymous, Marie's name appears on three works of twelfth-century French literature. These works are the *Lais,* from which this poem is taken; the *Fables,* a collection of fables translated from English into Old French; and *St. Patrick's Purgatory,* the life of a saint translated from Latin into French. Without Marie's work, these tales would not have survived.

A Keen Observer Marie is best known for her twelve *lais,* short narrative poems written in rhyming couplets and intended to be sung. In these "lays," whose subjects range from love to adventure, Marie presents details of twelfth-century western European court life, including descriptions of the speech and behavior of noble men and women.

A Noble Purpose Marie's purpose in writing these lays was to preserve the oral literature sung by the minstrels who came from Brittany. She explains that she "called to mind those lays I had heard so often . . . I would not that they should perish, forgotten, by the roadside. In my turn, therefore, I have made of them a song, rhymed as well as I am able, and often has their shaping kept me sleepless in my bed."

> "He to whom God has granted wisdom and eloquence in speech ought not to hide these gifts in silence, but gladly to make use of them."
>
> —Marie de France

Ahead of Her Time Everyday women in medieval Europe were generally regarded as inferior to men, but the "courtly love" tradition idealized the concept of femininity. The lover, smitten by the beauty and virtue of his lady, worshipped her from afar. Marie de France wrote within this tradition, but she gave it a new twist by portraying female characters who possess their own personalities. For her, a relationship between a man and a woman should be based on genuine affection. In an age when most marriages were based on economics or politics, this attitude set her apart from the norm.

LOG ON ▶ **Literature** Online

Author Search For more about Marie de France, go to glencoe.com and enter QuickPass code GLW6053u5.

Literature and Reading Preview

Connect to the Poem

Have you ever known or read about a person who had a hidden side to his or her personality? Write a journal entry that describes how you might react if you discovered a hidden personality trait in someone you were close to.

Build Background

In "Bisclavret," a wife's discovery that her husband is a werewolf causes serious problems in their marriage. In folklore, a werewolf is a human being who turns into a wolf at times and devours animals or people. Legends about werewolves were common in European folklore. Medieval intellectuals dismissed werewolves as creatures of the imagination, but common people believed such creatures were real.

Set Purposes for Reading

Big Idea From Myth to Romance

As you read "Bisclavret," ask yourself, How do medieval superstitions, customs, and traditions form the background of the tale?

Literary Element Suspense

Suspense is the tension or excitement a reader feels about what will happen next in a story. Authors often create a feeling of suspense by putting the central character in a threatening or dangerous situation and raising questions in the reader's mind about what will happen next. As you read the poem, ask yourself, What specific details help create suspense?

Reading Strategy Monitor Comprehension

When you **monitor comprehension,** you pause during reading to determine if you fully understand what is happening in a text. As you pause, you might make predictions, ask questions, paraphrase, and summarize. If you find you cannot complete any of these tasks satisfactorily, go back and reread the parts that are giving you trouble. As you read, ask yourself, What can I do to improve my understanding of the text?

....

Tip: Take Notes Use a chart like the one below to ask yourself questions about the plot and answer those questions with evidence from the text.

Question	Answer
Why is the wife upset?	Her husband is gone for three days a week, and she doesn't know where he goes.

Learning Objectives

For pages 886–897

In studying this text, you will focus on the following objectives:

Literary Study: Analyzing suspense.

Reading: Monitoring comprehension.

Listening and Speaking: Performing a skit.

Vocabulary

savage (sav′ij) *adj.* wild; untamed, and often fierce; p. 888 *After the savage attack by the dog, Alicia had to undergo several surgeries.*

rational (rash′ən əl) *adj.* able to reason; p. 892 *Despite the chaotic surroundings, Denise remained rational.*

grudge (gruj) *n.* a feeling of hatred or resentment; p. 894 *Simon had a grudge against Kathy for years because of her cruelty toward him when they were children.*

....

Tip: Context Clues When you read an unfamiliar word, pay close attention to the context, or setting, in which it appears. One type of context clue is an explanation, such as "This beast is rational—he has a mind" (page 892). This sentence indicates that the beast is able to reason.

[when he became a werewolf].

70 "Wife," he replied, "I go stark naked."
"Tell me, then, for God's sake, where your clothes are."
"That I won't tell you;
for if I were to lose them,
and then be discovered,
75 I'd stay a werewolf forever.
I'd be helpless
until I got them back.
That's why I don't want their hiding place to be known."
"My lord," the lady answered,
80 "I love you more than all the world;
you mustn't hide anything from me
or fear me in any way:
that doesn't seem like love to me.
What wrong have I done? For what sin of mine
85 do you mistrust me about anything?
Do the right thing and tell me!"
She harassed and bedeviled him so,°
that he had no choice but to tell her.
"Lady," he said, "near the woods,
90 beside the road that I use to get there,
there's an old chapel
that has often done me good service;
under a bush there is a big stone,
hollowed out inside;
95 I hide my clothes right there
until I'm ready to come home."
The lady heard this wonder
and turned scarlet from fear;
she was terrified of the whole adventure.
100 Over and over she considered
how she might get rid of him;
she never wanted to sleep with him again.
There was a knight of that region
who had loved her for a long time,
105 who begged for her love,
and dedicated himself to serving her.
She'd never loved him at all,
nor pledged her love to him,
but now she sent a messenger for him,
110 and told him her intention.
"My dear," she said, "cheer up!

87 **harassed and bedeviled:**
exhausted by persistent questioning.

> *What wrong have I done? For what sin of mine do you mistrust me about anything?*

Monitor Comprehension *What do you think of the wife at this point? Has your opinion changed since she was first introduced? Explain.*

I shall now grant you without delay
what you have suffered for;
you'll meet with no more refusals—
115 I offer you my love and my body;
make me your mistress!"
He thanked her graciously
and accepted her promise,
and she bound him to her by an oath.
120 Then she told him
how her husband went away and what happened to him;
she also taught him the precise path
her husband took into the forest,
and then she sent the knight to get her husband's clothes.
125 So Bisclavret was betrayed,
ruined by his own wife.
Since people knew he was often away from home
they all thought
this time he'd gone away forever.
130 They searched for him and made inquiries
but could never find him,
so they had to let matters stand.
The wife later married the other knight,
who had loved her for so long.
135 A whole year passed
until one day the king went hunting;
he headed right for the forest
where Bisclavret was.
When the hounds were unleashed,
140 they ran across Bisclavret;
the hunters and the dogs
chased him all day,
until they were just about to take him
and tear him apart,
145 at which point he saw the king
and ran to him, pleading for mercy.
He took hold of the king's stirrup,
kissed his leg and his foot.
The king saw this and was terrified;
150 he called his companions.
"My lords," he said, "come quickly!
Look at this marvel—
this beast is humbling itself to me.
It has the mind of a man, and it's begging me for mercy!

*Wolf-Beast from December:
Book of Hours,* 15th century.
Workshop of the Bedford
Master, French illuminated
manuscript. The Huntington
Library, San Marino, CA.

Suspense *How does this passage create a feeling of suspense?*

Before You Read

from *the Inferno* from the *Divine Comedy*

Meet **Dante Alighieri**
(1265–1321)

I n *La Vita Nuova* (The New Life), a collection of poems joined by autobiographical prose commentaries, the young Dante Alighieri describes the one true love of his life. Historians believe this love was Beatrice Portinari, the daughter of a wealthy Florentine banker. Dante first encountered her at a party when he was only nine and she a year younger. He recalls being overwhelmed by her beauty and gentle manner. He met her again nine years later, but she did not share his romantic feelings, and his inferior social position precluded any realistic possibility of marriage. She became instead a source of literary inspiration, embodying his ideal of spiritual perfection. In *Il Paradiso* (Paradise), the last section of Dante's epic the *Divine Comedy*, it is Beatrice who guides the poet in the final stage of his journey to salvation and Heaven.

Personal History Born in Florence, a European center of wealth and culture, Dante received an excellent education in classic literature and religious studies. When he was about eighteen, he married Gemma Donati, fulfilling a marriage contract his father had arranged when Dante was twelve. As a young man, Dante was active in Florence's political life, serving in the military and holding public office. When a rival political faction assumed power in 1301, Dante was banished. He never returned to the city, and it is not known whether he ever saw his wife and family again. For the remaining twenty years of his life, Dante lived in various other parts of Italy, accepting the hospitality of friends and patrons. He died at the home of a friend in Ravenna after contracting malaria.

"*Consider your origin; you were not born to live like brutes, but to follow virtue and knowledge.*"

—Dante Alighieri

Literary History Dante wrote the *Divine Comedy* during his exile. He composed the poem in modern Italian instead of Latin, which most major contemporary authors used. In doing so, he made the poem accessible to many Italians and established Italian as a literary language. In the *Divine Comedy*, Dante strove to persuade readers to live better lives through faith by showing them the consequences of evil and the rewards of salvation. He titled the epic *La Commedia*, not because it was humorous but rather because it had a happy ending. After his death, Dante's literary reputation steadily grew, and he became known throughout Italy as the *divino poeta* (divine poet). Today, the *Divine Comedy* is considered one of the masterpieces of Western literature.

LOG ON ▶ **Literature** Online

Author Search For more about Dante Alighieri, go to glencoe.com and enter QuickPass code GLW6053u5.

Literature and Reading Preview

Connect to the Poem

In your opinion, how should people be punished for wrongdoing? Freewrite for a few minutes about this question.

Build Background

The *Divine Comedy* is divided into three parts—*Inferno* (Hell), *Purgatorio* (Purgatory), and *Paradiso* (Paradise). Dante used a verse form called *terza rima*—three-line stanzas in which the first and third lines rhyme and the second line rhymes with the first line of the next stanza. The episodes you are about to read are from the *Inferno*. Dante's vision of Hell includes nine levels, each level for different kinds of sinners. The First Circle is Limbo, for unbaptized spirits. The next four circles punish those who committed the lesser sins of lust, gluttony, avarice, and wrathfulness. With the Sixth Circle, the extreme torments begin for heretics, murderers, seducers, thieves, hypocrites, liars, and finally (frozen in the ice of the Ninth Circle) betrayers.

Set Purposes for Reading

Big Idea The Vision of Faith

As you read, ask yourself, Which details represent the beliefs and values of Christianity in medieval Italy?

Literary Element Allegory

In an **allegory,** actions, objects, and people represent moral qualities, universal struggles, or abstract ideas such as love or virtue. A popular allegorical motif is the journey or quest. As you read, ask yourself, What is Dante's allegorical purpose?

Reading Strategy Analyze Sound Devices

Poets use **sound devices** such as **rhythm** (meter), **rhyme, alliteration** (repetition of consonant sounds at the beginnings of words), **consonance** (repetition of consonant sounds, typically at the end of non-rhyming words), and **assonance** (repetition of the same or similar vowel sounds in stressed syllables) to create mood or reinforce meaning. As you read, ask yourself, What do these devices contribute to the poem?

Tip: Group Details In a chart like the one below, list examples of sound devices and describe their effects.

Example of Sound Device	Effect on Mood or Meaning
Line 4—alliteration: "grinning, grotesque"	The "gr" sound reinforces the fearsome sight of Minos.

Vocabulary

verdict (vur′dikt) *n.* decision; judgment; p. 901 *My teacher's verdict was proof she doubted my excuse.*

anguish (ang′gwish) *n.* severe physical or mental pain; suffering; p. 902 *Though she affected a stiff upper lip, our aunt could not hide the anguish of her loss.*

reel (rēl) *v.* stand or move unsteadily; sway from a blow or shock; p. 905 *The stunned boxer reeled from the force of his opponent's punches.*

nimble (nim′bəl) *adj.* surefooted; light and quick; p. 909 *The hikers crossed the shallow creek with nimble steps, treading lightly on the exposed rocks.*

Tip: Synonyms Words that have the same or nearly the same meaning are synonyms. For example, the words *verdict* and *judgment* are synonyms. Synonyms are always the same part of speech.

it is his fate to enter every door.
    This has been willed where what is willed must be,
    and is not yours to question. Say no more."

25 Now the choir of **anguish**, like a wound,
    strikes through the tortured air. Now I have come
    to Hell's full lamentation,° sound beyond sound.

I came to a place stripped bare of every light
    and roaring on the naked dark like seas
30   wracked by a war of winds. Their hellish flight

of storm and counterstorm through time foregone,°
    sweeps the souls of the damned before its charge.
    Whirling and battering it drives them on,

and when they pass the ruined gap of Hell
35   through which we had come, their shrieks begin anew.
    There they blaspheme° the power of God eternal.

And this, I learned, was the never ending flight
    of those who sinned in the flesh, the carnal° and lusty
    who betrayed reason to their appetite.

40 As the wings of wintering starlings bear them on
    in their great wheeling° flights, just so the blast
    wherries° these evil souls through time foregone.

Here, there, up, down, they whirl and, whirling, strain
    with never a hope of hope to comfort them,
45   not of release, but even of less pain.

As cranes go over sounding their harsh cry,
    leaving the long streak of their flight in air,
    so come these spirits, wailing as they fly.

And watching their shadows lashed by wind, I cried:
50   "Master, what souls are these the very air
    lashes with its black whips from side to side?"

27 **lamentation:** wailing out of grief and pain.

31 **time foregone:** time past.

36 **blaspheme** (blas fēm´): to insult or show a lack of reverence for God.

38 **carnal:** interested only in physical pleasure.

41 **wheeling:** to fly around in circles.

42 **wherries:** transports quickly, as in a light, low rowboat.

Analyze Sound Devices *What example of alliteration here suggests the sound of roaring mentioned in line 29? How is this effect achieved?*

Vocabulary

anguish (ang´gwish) *n.* severe physical or mental pain; suffering

"The first of these whose history you would know,"
    he answered me, "was Empress of many tongues.
    Mad sensuality corrupted her so

55 that to hide the guilt of her debauchery°
    she licensed all depravity alike,
    and lust and law were one in her decree.

    She is Semiramis° of whom the tale is told
    how she married Ninus and succeeded him
60   to the throne of that wide land the Sultans° hold.

    The other is Dido;° faithless to the ashes
    of Sichaeus, she killed herself for love.
    The next whom the eternal tempest lashes

    is sense-drugged Cleopatra. See Helen° there,
65   from whom such ill arose. And great Achilles,°
    who fought at last with love in the house of prayer.

    And Paris. And Tristan."° As they whirled above
    he pointed out more than a thousand shades
    of those torn from the mortal life by love.

70 I stood there while my Teacher one by one
    named the great knights and ladies of dim time;
    and I was swept by pity and confusion.

    At last I spoke: "Poet, I should be glad
    to speak a word with those two swept together°
75   so lightly on the wind and still so sad."

    And he to me: "Watch them. When next they pass,
    call to them in the name of love that drives
    and damns them here. In that name they will pause."

    Thus, as soon as the wind in its wild course
80   brought them around, I called: "O wearied souls!
    if none forbid it, pause and speak to us."

    As mating doves that love calls to their nest
    glide through the air with motionless raised wings,
    borne by the sweet desire that fills each breast—

55 debauchery: excessive indulgence in sensual pleasures; behavior lacking virtue or morality

58 Semiramis (sə mir′ə mis): According to legend, Semiramis built Babylon. Her sin was her love affair with her own son.

60 Sultans: Muslim rulers of the area that was Babylon in Dante's day.

61 Dido: The queen of Carthage, unfaithful to the memory of her dead husband Sichaeus, fell in love with Aeneas; when he abandoned her, she killed herself.

64 Helen: the queen of Sparta. Helen left her husband Menelaus for Paris (line 67), the prince of Troy.

65 Achilles: In the Trojan War, the Greek hero Achilles fell so deeply in love with Polyxena, a Trojan, that he planned to switch sides. On his way to marry Polyxena, he was killed by Paris.

67 Tristan: In a famous love story of the Middle Ages, Tristan loved and died with Isolde, the wife of his uncle, King Mark.

74 those two swept together: The narrator sees Paolo and Francesca suffering together and wants to speak to them. In 1275 Francesca entered into a political marriage with Giovanni Malatesta. She fell in love with Giovanni's younger brother, Paolo, who was himself married. Their affair continued for several years, until Giovanni discovered them together and killed them.

The Vision of Faith *Why do you think Dante includes historical and literary characters from antiquity in his description of Hell?*

I looked up, thinking to see Lucifer°
    as I had left him, and I saw instead
90   his legs projecting high into the air.

Now let all those whose dull minds are still vexed
    by failure to understand what point it was
    I had passed through, judge if I was perplexed.

"Get up. Up on your feet," my Master said.
95   "The sun already mounts to middle tierce,°
    and a long road and hard climbing lie ahead."

It was no hall of state we had found there,
    but a natural animal pit hollowed from rock
    with a broken floor and a close and sunless air.

100 "Before I tear myself from the Abyss,"°
    I said when I had risen, "O my Master,
    explain to me my error in all this:

where is the ice? and Lucifer—how has he
    been turned from top to bottom: and how can the sun
105   have gone from night to day so suddenly?"

And he to me: "You imagine you are still
    on the other side of the center where I grasped
    the shaggy flank of the Great Worm of Evil

which bores through the world—you were while I climbed
        down,
110   but when I turned myself about, you passed
    the point to which all gravities are drawn.

You are under the other hemisphere where you stand;
    the sky above us is the half opposed
    to that which canopies the great dry land.

115 Under the midpoint of that other sky
    the Man° who was born sinless and who lived
    beyond all blemish, came to suffer and die.

Allegory *What does "the sky above us" represent?*

88 Lucifer: light-bearer. The name is a reminder that Satan once had a place of honor among the angels of Heaven.

95 middle tierce: The Roman Catholic Church divided the day into canonical hours. Tierce (or terce) named the period from 6:00 A.M. to 9:00 A.M., so middle tierce would be about 7:30 A.M. As they have crossed Satan, the travelers have moved ahead half a day (it was twilight in line 68; see also line 120).

100 Abyss (ə bis′): a very deep gulf or pit. The Bible uses the term more specifically to refer to the hellish depths of the earth.

116 Man: Jesus. Virgil is also explaining that they now are on the other side of the world from Jerusalem, the city in which Jesus was crucified.

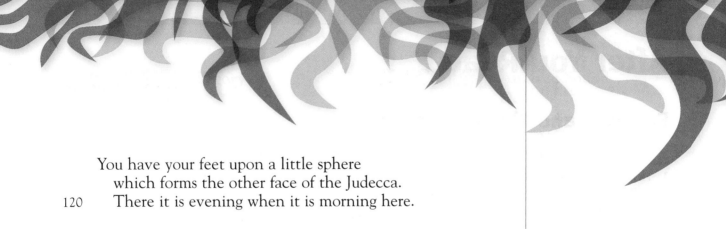

You have your feet upon a little sphere
    which forms the other face of the Judecca.
120   There it is evening when it is morning here.

And this gross Fiend and Image of all Evil
    who made a stairway for us with his hide
    is pinched and prisoned in the ice-pack still.

On this side he plunged down from heaven's height,
125   and the land that spread here once hid in the sea
    and fled North to our hemisphere for fright;

and it may be that moved by that same fear,
    the one peak° that still rises on this side
    fled upward leaving this great cavern here."

130 Down there, beginning at the further bound
    of Beelzebub's° dim tomb, there is a space
    not known by sight, but only by the sound

of a little stream° descending through the hollow
    it has eroded from the massive stone
135   in its endlessly entwining lazy flow."

My Guide and I crossed over and began
    to mount that little known and lightless road
    to ascend into the shining world again.

He first, I second, without thought of rest
140   we climbed the dark until we reached the point
    where a round opening brought in sight the blest

and beauteous shining of the Heavenly cars.°
And we walked out once more beneath the Stars.

128 one peak: the Mount of Purgatory. In Roman Catholic belief, souls spend a time of suffering in Purgatory and thus are cleansed to enter Heaven.

131 Beelzebub: another name of Satan—literally, lord of the flies.

133 little stream: This may refer to the river Lethe (lē′thē), the stream from which souls drank to forget the sorrows of their earthly lives. If so, Virgil may be suggesting that the stream carries memories of sin away from purified souls and into Hell.

142 cars: chariots; figuratively, Dante is referring to the planets and stars.

Analyze Sound Devices *Identify the sound device in this line and explain its effect.*

Let us recall two examples. First, the best-known episode of the *Inferno*, the story of Paolo and Francesca in the fifth canto. I would not presume to summarize what Dante has said—it would be irreverent for me to say in other words what Dante has said for always in his Italian—but I'd like simply to recall the circumstances.

Dante and Virgil arrive at the second circle. There they see the whirlwind of souls and smell the stench of sin, the stench of punishment. There is Minos,[4] twining his tail around himself to indicate to which circle the condemned must descend. It is physically disagreeable, deliberately ugly, because it is understood that in Hell nothing can be beautiful.

In that circle where the lustful are punished there are great, illustrious names. I say "great names" because Dante, when he began the canto, had not yet reached the perfection of his art, the point where the characters became something more than their names. But halfway through the canto, Dante makes his great discovery: the possibility of a dialogue between the souls of the dead and Dante himself, who will respond and judge in his fashion. No, he will not judge them. He knows that he is not the Judge, that the Judge is the Other, the third speaker, the Divinity.

Well then: there are Helen, Achilles, Paris, Tristan, and other luminaries.[5] But Dante sees two whom he does not know, less illustrious, and who belong to the contemporary world: Paolo and Francesca. He knows that they have both died as adulterers. He calls to them and they come, "*quali colombe dal disio chiamate.*"[6] Here we have two sinners, and Dante compares them to two doves called by desire, because sensuality must also be the essence of the scene. They draw near, and Francesca, who is the only one to speak— Paolo cannot—thanks him for calling them and speaks these pathetic words: "*Se fosse amico il Re dell'universo/ noi pregheremmo lui per la tua pace,*" if we were friends of the King of the universe—she cannot say God, because that name is forbidden in Hell and Purgatory—we would pray for your peace, since you have taken pity on our misfortune.

Francesca tells her story, and she tells it twice. The first time she tells it in a reserved fashion, but she insists that she is still in love with Paolo. Repentance is forbidden in Hell. She knows she has sinned and must continue to be faithful to her sin, which gives her a heroic grandeur. It would be terrible if she repented, if she denied what happened. Francesca knows the punishment is just; she accepts it, and continues to love Paolo.

Dante is curious about one thing. "*Amor condusse noi ad una morte*": Paolo and Francesca were executed together. Dante is not interested in adultery, nor in the way they were discovered and brought to justice. What interests him is something more intimate, and that is how they knew they were in love, how they fell in love, how they reached the time of the sweet sighs. He asks them. . . .

This is what Dante wants to know; he wants them to tell him how it happened. She tells how, to entertain themselves one day, they were reading about Lancelot and

---

4. Minos is a mythological Greek king. Dante presents him as a monster who points each sinner toward the proper circle of Hell.
5. A *luminary* is an admired or inspirational person.

6. *Quali colombe dal disio chiamate* means "As doves, called onward by desire."

how he complained of love. They were alone and suspected nothing. They did not suspect they were in love. And they were reading a story from the *Matière de-Bretagne*, one of those books conceived by the British in France after the Saxon invasion—one of those books that fed the madness of Alonso Quijano[7] and revealed their guilty love to Paolo and Francesca. Well: Francesca states that at times they blushed. Then, "*quando leggemmo il disiato riso*,"[8] when we read how the longed-for smile was kissed by such a lover, this one, who will never be separated from me, kissed my mouth, *tutto tremante*.[9]

There is something that Dante does not say, but which one feels at a distance from the episode and perhaps gives it its virtue. Dante relates the fate of the two lovers with an infinite pity, and we sense that he envies their fate. Paolo and Francesca are in Hell and he will be saved, but they have loved and he never won the love of the woman he loved, Beatrice. There is a certain injustice to this, and Dante must feel it as something terrible, now that he is separated from her. In contrast, these two sinners are together. They cannot speak to each other, they turn in the black whirlwind without hope, yet they are together. When she speaks, she says "we," speaking for the two of them, another form of being together. They are together for eternity; they share Hell—and that, for Dante, must have been a kind of Paradise.

We know that he is quite moved. He then collapses as though he were dead. ∾

---

7. In Miguel de Cervantes's *Don Quixote,* the character Alonso Quijano avidly reads chivalric romances, becoming so engaged in them he confuses reality and fantasy and starts to regard himself as a great knight.
8. *Quando leggemmo il disiato riso* means "When we read about the longed-for mouth."
9. *Tutto tremante* means "all trembling."

Respond and Think Critically

Respond and Interpret

1. Write a brief summary of the main ideas in this essay before you answer the following questions. For help on writing a summary, see page 1147.

2. (a)What emotions does Borges say Dante shows toward the lovers? (b)Why does Borges believe Dante feels this way?

Analyze and Evaluate

3. (a)According to Borges, how are Paolo and Francesca heroic or noble? (b)How does this relate to what Borges says is unique about Dante's writing?

4. (a)Why is Paolo and Francesca's Hell "a kind of Paradise" to Dante? (b)How does this relate to his vision of Paradise, discussed in the background information on page 898?

5. (a)How did reading this essay deepen or change your understanding of the *Inferno*? (b)Do you think it is fair to assume biographical information about Dante can contribute to a reader's understanding of his writings? Explain.

Connect

6. How does Dante's love for Beatrice compare with the love between Paolo and Francesca?

Literature and Reading Preview

Connect to the Poem

How does time affect our feelings for someone we love? Freewrite for a few minutes about this question.

Build Background

Many of the sonnets in Petrarch's collected poems, the *Canzoniere,* are about Petrarch's love for a mysterious woman named Laura. The *Canzoniere* is organized to show the conflicted emotions Petrarch experienced while Laura lived and the grief he felt following her death.

Set Purposes for Reading

Big Idea **The Renaissance and Humanism**

As you read, ask yourself, Which descriptions of Laura represent a blending of the sacred and the secular?

Literary Element **The Petrarchan Sonnet**

The **Petrarchan,** or **Italian, sonnet** is divided into a group of eight lines, called the octave, and a group of six lines, called the sestet, with a turn between the two parts. The **octave** describes a problem or a situation and has the rhyme scheme *abba, abba.* The **turn** is the shift from the problem to the resolution. The problem or situation is resolved in the **sestet,** which can have varying rhyme schemes, such as *cde cde, cde dce,* or *cdc dcd.*

Reading Strategy Interpret Imagery

When you **interpret imagery,** you use your knowledge of the world to find meaning in images beyond the literal level. As you read, ask yourself, What are the literal and symbolic meanings of the poem's images?

....

Tip: Use a Web As you read, use a web to record images from the poem and note your interpretations.

speaker has great reverence for Laura

golden hair

Vocabulary

pity (pit′ē) *n.* sympathy for another's suffering; p. 921 *I felt pity for the stray dog whimpering outside my door.*

dreary (drēr′ē) *adj.* dull or sorrowful; p. 921 *After the third rainy day of our camping trip, we were all in a dreary mood.*

....

Tip: Synonyms Synonyms are words with the same or similar meanings. For example, *tangle, twist,* and *snarl* express differently the idea of combining in a messy way. Authors often choose from among several synonyms, each with its own shade of meaning, to express their ideas accurately.

Young woman at Her Toilet, 1515 (detail). Giovanni Bellini. Oil on panel.
Kunsthistorisches Museum, Vienna.

Laura
from Canzoníere

Petrarch
Translated by Morris Bishop

She used to let her golden hair fly free
   For the wind to toy and tangle and molest;
   Her eyes were brighter than the radiant west.
   (Seldom they shine so now.) I used to see
5 **Pity** look out of those deep eyes on me.
   ("It was false pity," you would now protest.)
   I had love's tinder° heaped within my breast;
   What wonder that the flame burned furiously?
She did not walk in any mortal way,
10   But with angelic progress;° when she spoke,
   Unearthly voices sang in unison.
She seemed divine among the **dreary** folk
   Of earth. You say she is not so today?
   Well, though the bow's unbent,° the wound bleeds on.

Canzoníere (kan zō nē′ ər):
the Italian word for songs.

7 tinder: material used to start
a fire.

10 progress: here, a forward
movement.

14 unbent: An archer bends
a bow into a curve before firing
an arrow.

Interpret Imagery *To what does the speaker compare
Laura's eyes? What might this image symbolize?*

Vocabulary

pity (pit′ē) *n.* sympathy for another's suffering
dreary (drēr′ē) *adj.* dull or sorrowful

After You Read

Respond and Think Critically

Respond and Interpret

1. What image of Laura did you find most memorable? Explain.

2. (a)According to lines 1–4, how has Laura's appearance changed? (b)What caused this change?

3. (a)The last line contains an **allusion** to Cupid, the god of love who shoots lovers with arrows. Which words in line 14 make the allusion? (b)Explain the metaphor in that line.

Analyze and Evaluate

4. (a)What is being personified in lines 1–2? (b)How effective are these lines in describing Laura's personality? Explain.

5. (a)What is the function of the comments enclosed within parentheses in lines 4 and 6? (b)Do they achieve this goal? Explain.

6. (a)What does this poem say about love, aging, and death? (b)Do you agree or disagree with the speaker's sentiments? Explain.

Connect

7. **Big Idea** The Renaissance and Humanism (a)Is Laura depicted as human, divine, or both? Explain. (b)How does this poem exemplify the concerns of Renaissance humanism?

8. **Connect to Today** How does this poem's theme have meaning for today's readers?

Literary Element The Petrarchan Sonnet

In the **Italian sonnet**, or **Petrarchan sonnet**, the octave usually presents a single **theme**, or message, and the sestet expands or develops it.

1. (a)What is the rhyme scheme of the octave? (b)How does it change in the last six lines?

2. What is the main idea expressed in the octave? in the sestet?

Reading Strategy Interpret Imagery

Look at the web you made on page 920 and then answer the following questions.

1. (a)What picture does line 3 create? (b)What does this image suggest about Laura?

2. (a)Identify the metaphor in lines 7–8. (b)What does it tell you about the speaker's love?

LOG ON ▶ **Literature** Online

Selection Resources For Selection Quizzes, eFlashcards, and Reading-Writing Connection activities, go to glencoe.com and enter QuickPass code GLW6053u5.

Vocabulary Practice

Practice with Synonyms With a partner, match each boldfaced vocabulary word below with its synonym. Use a thesaurus or dictionary to check your answers. You will not use all the answer choices.

1. pity   a. sympathy   d. dismal

2. dreary   b. snarl   e. sorrow

                  c. unravel

Writing

Write a Sonnet Petrarch wrote this sonnet to describe how he and Laura had changed. Think of a person you know who has changed since you have known him or her, or a situation that is different now than when it began. Write a sonnet about this person or situation, using the rhyme scheme and structure of the Petrarchan sonnet. Include figurative language, such as metaphors and similes.

Build Background

The French poet Louise Labé (c. 1524–1566) wrote within the Petrarchan tradition, but she provided her own perspective. In the typical Petrarchan love sonnet, the male speaker yearns for an idealized, aloof, and inaccessible lady. The lady's beauty is praised in extravagant terms, but she is portrayed as a prized object rather than as a thinking and feeling subject. Using a female speaker with a male beloved, Louise Labé challenged these conventions. In the dedication to her single volume of poetry, she made the revolutionary move of urging women to set aside their domestic activities, fine clothes, and jewelry, in order to study literature and culture.

Sonnet 8

Louise Labé
Translated by Willis Barnstone

The Pained Heart or *Sigh No More, Ladies*, 1868. Arthur Hughes (England 1832-1915). Oil on canvas, 94 x 110 cm. The Maas Gallery, London.

I live, I die, I burn myself and drown.
I am extremely hot in suffering cold:
my life is soft and hardness
    uncontrolled.
When I am happy, then I ache
    and frown.
5   Suddenly I am laughing while I cry
and in my pleasure I endure
    deep grief:
my joy remains and slips out
    like a thief.
Suddenly I am blooming and turn dry.
So Love inconstantly leads me
    in vain
10 and when I think my sorrow has
    no end
unthinkingly I find I have no pain.
But when it seems that joy is in
    my reign
and an ecstatic hour is mine to spend,
He comes and I, in ancient
    grief, descend.

Quickwrite

How does Labé describe the experience of being in love? How do you think her experience is affected by the fact she is a woman? Based on your knowledge of the Petrarchan sonnet and the portrayal of women in Renaissance literature and art, how might this poem be evidence that Labé was a feminist in the context of her time?

Build Background

Born in New York City in 1950 and raised in the Dominican Republic, the award-winning author Julia Alvarez is known for writing poems and novels that probe the qualities of identity. In *Homecoming* (1984), which contains the sonnet you are about to read, Alvarez explores her identity as a woman and her fascination with traditional verse forms. One of her goals is to write sonnets that portray women as independent voices rather than "love objects." As Alvarez writes, "My idea of traditional forms is that as women much of our heritage is trapped in them. But the cage can turn into a house if you house-keep it the right way." To this end, Alvarez varies the traditional conventions of the sonnet, experimenting with loose rhythms and slant rhyme.

Secretly
I am building in the heart

Julia Alvarez

Portrait of Joan Salvat-Papasseit, 1918. Rafael Perez Barradas. Collection of Gustau Camps, Barcelona.

Secretly I am building in the heart
a delicate structure like one of those
cardhouses or Popsicle palaces
kids build, patiently piecing each part
5 together, fingers pinching a small tube
of glue, eyes straining to perceive what
new thing I am making that takes so
    much time
    to finish if there's finish in these
    things.
  And making it out of nothing but what
10 are ruins from an earlier effort
  and tempted constantly to believe that
  a readymade is better, and yet I've
  labored with my heart to outlast the
    heart
  with this thing I'm creating out of love.

Discussion Starter

Although this sonnet refers to traditional subjects such as "love" and the "heart," the object of the speaker's love is very different from the usual beloved. What is the speaker "building"? What does she mean when she says she has "labored with my heart to outlast the heart"? Discuss these questions with a group.

Wrap-Up: Comparing Literature

Across Time and Place

- *Laura* from *Canzoniere* by Petrarch

- *Sonnet 8* by Louise Labé

- *Secretly I am building in the heart* by Julia Alvarez

Lovers with Daisies (Les Amoreux aux Marguerites), 1949-1950. Marc Chagall. Private collection.© ARS, NY.

COMPARE THE `Big Idea` The Renaissance and Humanism

Visual Display During the Renaissance, details and experiences of everyday life moved to the forefront of art and literature. How do Renaissance depictions of such worldly subjects as work, love, and marriage compare with contemporary illustrations? Using Internet and print sources, create a collage of images from the cultures of Petrarch (Renaissance Italy), Labé (Renaissance France), and Alvarez (present-day United States) that celebrate love in the context of everyday life. Present your display to the class and discuss the similarities and differences between the images and the cultural values they suggest. Make sure you give proper credit to your sources.

COMPARE Sonnets

Writing Write a brief essay comparing the three poets' use of the sonnet form. Consider elements such as meter, rhyme, and the turn between the octave and the sestet. In addition, consider the authors' style, tone, and diction. Be sure to address how Alvarez both adheres to and breaks from the traditional sonnet form, and discuss passages in the poem that might explain her reasons for these artistic decisions.

COMPARE Responses to Love

Group Activity With a small group, answer the following questions. Cite evidence from the poems to defend your points.

1. What motivates each speaker to write?

2. In your opinion, how would each speaker define "love"?

3. How can you apply the background information (see pages 920, 923, and 924) to help you understand the speakers' views of love?

Literature Online

Author Search For information about Francesco Petrarch, Louise Labé, and Julia Alvarez, go to glencoe.com and enter QuickPass code GLW6053u5.

The lady paused a little at this, and began to think what she should do. She knew that Federigo had loved her for a long time, and yet had never had one glance from her, and she said to herself:

"How can I send or go and ask for this falcon, which is, from what I hear, the best that ever flew, and moreover his support in life? How can I be so thoughtless as to take this away from a gentleman who has no other pleasure left in life?"

Although she knew she was certain to have the bird for the asking, she remained in embarrassed thought, not knowing what to say, and did not answer her son. But at length love for her child got the upper hand and she determined that to please him in whatever way it might be, she would not send, but go herself for it and bring it back to him. So she replied:

"Be comforted, my child, and try to get better somehow. I promise you that tomorrow morning I will go for it, and bring it to you."

The child was so delighted that he became a little better that same day. And on the morrow the lady took another woman to accompany her, and as if walking for exercise went to Federigo's cottage, and asked for him. Since it was not the weather for it, he had not been hawking for some days, and was in his garden employed in certain work there. When he heard that Monna Giovanna was asking for him at the door, he was greatly astonished, and ran there happily. When she saw him coming, she got up to greet him with womanly charm, and when Federigo had courteously saluted her, she said:

"How do you do, Federigo? I have come here to make amends for the damage you have suffered through me by loving me more than was needed. And in token of this, I intend to dine today familiarly with you and my companion here."

"Madonna," replied Federigo humbly, "I do not remember ever to have suffered any damage through you, but received so much good that if I was ever worth anything it was owing to your worth and the love I bore it. Your generous visit to me is so precious to me that I could spend again all that I have spent; but you have come to a poor host."

So saying, he modestly took her into his house, and from there to his garden. Since there was nobody else to remain in her company, he said:

"Madonna, since there is nobody else, this good woman, the wife of this workman, will keep you company, while I go to set the table."

Now, although his poverty was extreme, he had never before realized what necessity he had fallen into by his foolish extravagance in spending his wealth. But he repented of it that morning when he could find nothing with which to do honor to the lady, for love of whom he had entertained vast numbers of men in the past. In his anguish he cursed himself and his fortune and ran up and down like a man out his senses, unable to find money or anything to pawn.[7] The hour was late and his desire to honor the lady extreme, yet he would not apply to anyone else, even to his own workman; when suddenly his eye fell upon his falcon, perched on a bar in the sitting room. Having no one to whom he could

Visual Vocabulary
Madonna is an Italian term of respect once used to address a lady. The term is also used as a name for the Virgin Mary.

---

7. To *pawn* something is to deposit it with someone as security for a loan.

appeal, he took the bird, and finding it plump, decided it would be food worthy such a lady. So, without further thought, he wrung its neck, made his little maid servant quickly pluck and prepare it, and put it on a spit to roast. He spread the table with the whitest napery,[8] of which he had some left, and returned to the lady in the garden with a cheerful face, saying that the meal he had been able to prepare for her was ready.

The lady and her companion arose and went to table, and there together with Federigo, who served it with the greatest devotion, they ate the good falcon, not knowing what it was. They left the table and spent some time in cheerful conversation, and the lady, thinking the time had now come to say what she had come for, spoke fairly[9] to Federigo as follows:

"Federigo, when you remember your former life and my chastity, which no doubt you considered harshness and cruelty, I have no doubt that you will be surprised at my **presumption** when you hear what I have come here for chiefly. But if you had children, through whom you could know the power of parental love, I am certain that you would to some extent excuse me.

"But, as you have no child, I have one, and I cannot escape the common laws of mothers. Compelled by their power, I have come to ask you—against my will, and against all good manners and duty—for a gift, which I know is something especially dear to you, and reasonably so, because I know your straitened[10] fortune has left you no other pleasure, no other recreation, no other consolation. This gift is your falcon, which has so fascinated my child that if I do not take it to him, I am afraid his present illness will grow so much worse that I may lose him. Therefore I beg you, not by the love you bear me (which holds you to nothing), but by your own nobleness, which has shown itself so much greater in all courteous usage than is wont in other men, that you will be pleased to give it to me, so that through this gift I may be able to say that I have saved my child's life, and thus be ever under an obligation to you."

When Federigo heard the lady's request and knew that he could not serve her, because he had given her the bird to eat, he began to weep in her presence, for he could not speak a word. The lady at first thought that his grief came from having to part with his good falcon, rather than from anything else, and she was almost on the point of retraction. But she remained firm and waited for Federigo's reply after his lamentation. And he said:

"Madonna, ever since it has pleased God that I should set my love upon you, I have felt that Fortune has been **contrary** to me in many things, and have grieved for it. But they are all light in comparison with what she has done to me now, and I shall never be at peace with her again when I reflect that you came to my poor house, which you never deigned to visit when it was rich, and asked me for a little gift, and Fortune has so acted that I cannot give it to you. Why this cannot be, I will briefly tell you.

---

8. *Napery* is another word for table linens–tablecloths, napkins, and so on.
9. Here, *fairly* describes a pleasant, charming way of speaking.

Analyze Plot *How does this part of the rising action develop the conflict and build suspense?*

presumption (pri zump′shən) *n.* attitude or conduct that oversteps the bounds of propriety or courtesy

---

10. *Straitened,* here, alludes to Federigo's fortune being almost used up.

Analyze Plot *What is this part of the plot called? Why?*

contrary (kon′trer ē) *adj.* unfavorable

Reading Strategy Analyze Plot

ACT Skills Practice

Why does Monna decide to marry Federigo at the end of the story?

A. Federigo threw lavish banquets and spent all his money trying to woo her.

B. She pities Federigo because he has loved her for so long and not received so much as a glance from her.

C. She is grateful to Federigo because he saved her son's life.

D. Federigo showed tremendous generosity in killing his prized falcon to honor her.

Vocabulary Practice

Practice with Word Usage Respond to these questions and statements to help you explore the meanings of the vocabulary words from the story.

1. Describe someone who is universally **revered**.

2. What type of people live a **chaste** life?

3. What does it mean to live **penuriously**?

4. What is a **presumption** you might make about a stranger?

5. How might someone behave if he or she is being **contrary**?

Academic Vocabulary

*The story of Federigo's falcon expresses a **core** humanistic value—the belief in the power of goodwill to overcome obstacles.*

Core is an academic word with a variety of uses. For example, someone might say most people believe honesty and integrity are **core** values. Using context clues, figure out the meaning of the word *core* in the sample sentence above. Check your guess in a dictionary.

For more on academic vocabulary, see pages 36–37 and R83–R85.

Listening and Speaking

Oral Report

Assignment Early in this story, the queen says Fortune does not distribute rewards evenly. At one point, Federigo adds, "I have felt that Fortune has been contrary to me in many things, and have grieved for it." Present an oral report in which you compare medieval and Renaissance ideas about fate and human potential, and describe how these ideas are evident in the story.

Prepare Identify electronic and print resources you can use to research this topic. Before you begin your research, generate some questions. Here are some examples:

- How did ideas about fate affect people's daily lives during the Middle Ages?

- Why did the humanists create new theories about fate and human potential?

- Who was the goddess Fortuna, and what was the "Wheel of Fortune"?

The Wheel of Fortune. Chretien Legouais. Ovid Moralise. 14th century BC. Bibliotheque Municipale, Rouen, France.

As you research, take notes that address your questions. Rehearse your speech several times and check for coherence. Does your report flow well? If not, try switching the order in which you present ideas. Practice using body language and hand gestures to emphasize your main points.

Report Present your report to the class. Focus on communicating effectively through ideas, voice, and body language. Consider using visual aids like the one above.

Evaluate Write a paragraph in which you assess your oral report's effectiveness.

Before You Read

from *Don Quixote*

Meet **Miguel de Cervantes**
(1547–1616)

Soldier, slave, civil servant, satirist—Miguel de Cervantes (mē gel′dā sər vän′tāz) was all these things—and the most celebrated author in Spanish literature. He was born in Alcalá, near Madrid, the fourth of seven children. His family was of minor nobility, but poor, and the family moved frequently as the father traveled looking for work. However, young Cervantes became an enthusiastic reader and published his first poems at age 21.

Soldier, Slave In 1570 Cervantes enlisted as a soldier with Spanish military forces stationed in Italy. Fighting valiantly against the Turks in the battle of Lepanto, he was wounded in the chest and permanently lost the use of his left hand. Returning by sea to Spain with letters of commendation to the king, he was captured by Barbary pirates and sold into slavery. He tried to escape several times.

Civil Servant, Novelist Eventually his high ransom was paid, and Cervantes returned to Spain. He married and found a job as purchasing agent for the navy. During this period he had a number of plays produced, but none brought him the fame and fortune he desired. At this time, he was also at work on a book-length fictional prose narrative in what was then a new literary form, the novel. Part I of *Don Quixote* was published in 1605 and was an immediate success. Since he had sold the publishing rights, however, Cervantes made no more financial profit. By the time Part II was published in 1615, the first part had seen many subsequent editions. Together the two parts of the work became the world's most frequently published novel, and Cervantes was one of the world's most esteemed authors.

> "*It can be said that all prose fiction is a variation on the theme of* Don Quixote."
>
> —Lionel Trilling

His Great Work The Spanish philosopher Miguel de Unamuno has remarked that Cervantes's novel embodies the spirit and genius of the Spanish people. *Don Quixote* is also one of the world's great parodies. The work is structured as a series of adventures that bring its hero into contact with a wide variety of human types and situations. This structure allowed Cervantes to mock old-fashioned notions of chivalry and to explore the unstable boundaries between reality and imagination, between sanity and insanity. Is Quixote mad, as the narrator claims? Or is he a simple, pure soul who attempts to make the world a better place by following his own vision of reality? Readers have been debating that question for centuries.

LOG ON **Literature** Online

Author Search For more about Miguel de Cervantes, go to glencoe.com and enter QuickPass code GLW6053u5.

colored coarse cloth. He had a housekeeper past forty, a niece not yet twenty, and a man-of-all-work who did everything from saddling the horse to pruning the trees. Our gentleman was approximately fifty years old; his complexion was weathered, his flesh scrawny, his face gaunt, and he was a very early riser and a great lover of the hunt. Some claim that his family name was Quixada, or Quexada, for there is a certain amount of disagreement among the authors who write of this matter, although reliable conjecture seems to indicate that his name was Quexana. But this does not matter very much to our story; in its telling there is absolutely no deviation from the truth.

And so, let it be said that this aforementioned gentleman spent his times of leisure—which meant most of the year—reading books of chivalry with so much devotion and enthusiasm that he forgot almost completely about the hunt and even about the administration of his estate; and in his rash curiosity and folly he went so far as to sell acres of arable land in order to buy books of chivalry to read, and he brought as many of them as he could into his house; and he thought none was as fine as those composed by the worthy Feliciano de Silva,[3] because the clarity of his prose and complexity of his language seemed to him more valuable than pearls, in particular when he read the declarations and missives of love, where he would often find written: *The reason for the unreason to which my reason turns so weakens my reason that with reason I complain of thy beauty.* And also when he

read: . . . *the heavens on high divinely heighten thy divinity with the stars and make thee deserving of the deserts thy greatness deserves.*

With these words and phrases the poor gentleman lost his mind, and he spent sleepless nights trying to understand them and extract their meaning, which Aristotle[4] himself, if he came back to life for only that purpose, would not have been able to **decipher** or understand. Our gentleman was not very happy with the wounds that Don Belianís gave and received, because he imagined that no matter how great the physicians and surgeons who cured him, he would still have his face and entire body covered with scars and marks. But, even so, he praised the author for having concluded his book with the promise of unending adventure, and he often felt the desire to take up his pen and give it the conclusion promised there; and no doubt he would have done so, and even published it, if other greater and more persistent thoughts had not prevented him from doing so. He often had discussions with the village priest—who was a learned man, a graduate of Sigüenza—regarding who had been the greater knight, Palmerín of England or Amadís of Gaul; but Master Nicolás, the village barber, said that none was the equal of the Knight of Phoebus, and if any could be compared to him, it was Don Galaor, the brother of Amadís of Gaul, because he was moderate in everything: a knight who was not affected, not as weepy as his brother, and incomparable in questions of courage.

In short, our gentleman became so

---

3. *Feliciano de Silva* was the author of several novels of chivalry. The names of the authors and heroes that follow in this paragraph are all typical of the romantic literature of the period.

Make Inferences About Theme *What kind of tone does the narrator use here?*

---

4. The Greek philosopher *Aristotle* (384–322 B.C.) was considered to possess one of the greatest minds of the ancient world.

decipher (di sī′fər) *v.* to translate; figure out

caught up in reading that he spent his nights reading from dusk till dawn and his days reading from sunrise to sunset, and so with too little sleep and too much reading his brains dried up, causing him to lose his mind. His fantasy filled with everything he had read in his books, enchantments as well as combats, battles, challenges, wounds, courtings, loves, torments, and other impossible foolishness, and he became so convinced in his imagination of the truth of all the countless grandiloquent[5] and false inventions he read that for him no history in the world was truer. He would say that El Cid Ruy Díaz had been a very good knight but could not compare to Amadís, the Knight of the Blazing Sword, who with a single backstroke cut two ferocious and colossal giants in half. He was fonder of Bernardo del Carpio because at Roncesvalles he had killed the enchanted Roland by availing himself of the tactic of Hercules when he crushed Antaeus, the son of Earth, in his arms.[6] He spoke highly of the giant Morgante because, although he belonged to the race of giants, all of them haughty and lacking in courtesy, he alone was amiable and well-behaved. But, more than any of the others, he admired Reinaldos de Montalbán, above all when he saw him emerge from his castle and rob anyone he met, and when he crossed the sea and stole the idol of Mohammed made all of gold, as recounted in his history. He would have traded his housekeeper, and even his niece, for the chance to strike a blow at the traitor Guenelon.

The truth is that when his mind was completely gone, he had the strangest thought any lunatic in the world ever had, which was that it seemed reasonable and necessary to him, both for the sake of his honor and as a service to the nation, to become a knight errant[7] and travel the world with his armor and his horse to seek adventures and engage in everything he had read that knights errant engaged in, righting all manner of wrongs and, by seizing the opportunity and placing himself in danger and ending those wrongs, winning eternal **renown** and everlasting fame. The poor man imagined himself already wearing the crown, won by the valor of his arm, of the empire of Trebizond at the very least; and so it was that with these exceedingly agreeable thoughts, and carried away by the extraordinary pleasure he took in them, he hastened to put into effect what he so fervently desired. And the first thing he did was to attempt to clean some armor that had belonged to his great-grandfathers and, stained with rust and covered with mildew, had spent many long years stored and forgotten in a corner. He did the best he could to clean and repair it, but he saw that it had a great defect, which was that instead of a full sallet[8] helmet with an attached neckguard, there was only a simple headpiece; but he compensated for this with his industry, and out of pasteboard he fashioned a kind of half-helmet that, when attached

---

5. *Grandiloquent* language is high-flown and overwrought.
6. *tactic of Hercules . . . in his arms.* The Roman hero Hercules defeated the giant Anteus, who derived his strength from his contact with the earth, by holding him up in the air.

7. A *knight errant* traveled about in search of adventure.
8. A *sallet* was a type of light helmet with or without a visor and a piece over the neck.

The Renaissance and Humanism *How does Don Quixote plan to contribute to humankind?*

Vocabulary

renown (ri noun′) n. a state of being widely acclaimed

that Sancho could supply himself with whatever he thought he would need. He ordered him in particular to bring along saddlebags, and Sancho said he certainly would bring them and also planned to take along a donkey he thought very highly of because he wasn't one for walking any great distance. As for the donkey, Don Quixote had to stop and think about that for a while, wondering if he recalled any knight errant who had with him a squire riding on a donkey, and none came to mind, yet in spite of this he resolved to take Sancho along, intending to obtain a more honorable mount for him at the earliest opportunity by appropriating the horse of the first **discourteous** knight he happened to meet. He furnished himself with shirts and all the other things he could, following the advice the innkeeper had given him; and when this had been accomplished and completed, without Panza taking leave of his children and wife, or Don Quixote of his housekeeper and niece, they rode out of the village one night, and no one saw them, and they traveled so far that by dawn they were certain they would not be found even if anyone came looking for them.

Sancho Panza rode on his donkey like a patriarch,[12] with his saddlebags, and his wineskin, and a great desire to see himself governor of the ínsula his master had promised him. Don Quixote happened to follow the same direction and route he had followed on his first sally, which was through the countryside of Montiel, and he rode there with less difficulty than he had the last time, because at that hour of the morning the sun's rays fell obliquely and did not tire them.

CHAPTER VIII
Regarding the good fortune of the valorous Don Quixote in the fearful and never imagined adventure of the windmills, along with other events worthy of joyful remembrance

As they were talking, they saw thirty or forty of the windmills found in that countryside, and as soon as Don Quixote caught sight of them, he said to his squire:

"Good fortune is guiding our affairs better than we could have desired, for there you see, friend Sancho Panza, thirty or more enormous giants with whom I intend to do battle and whose lives I intend to take, and with the spoils we shall begin to grow rich, for this is righteous warfare, and it is a great service to God to remove so evil a breed from the face of the earth."

"What giants?" said Sancho Panza.

"Those you see over there," replied his master, "with the long arms; sometimes they are almost two leagues[13] long."

"Look, your grace," Sancho responded, "those things that appear over there aren't giants but windmills, and what looks like their arms are the sails that are turned by the wind and make the grindstone move."

"It seems clear to me," replied Don Quixote, "that thou art not well-versed in the matter of adventures: these are giants; and if thou art afraid, move aside and start to pray whilst I enter with them in fierce and unequal combat."

And having said this, he spurred his horse, Rocinante, paying no attention to

---

12. A *patriarch* is the oldest and most respected member of a family.

Vocabulary

discourteous (dis kur′tē əs) *adj.* impolite

---

13. A *league* is a measure of distance of about three miles.

Parody *How does Sancho Panza's advice parody the traditional relationship between a knight and his squire?*

Don Quixote and the Windmill. Francisco J. Torromé (Spainish fl.1890-1908) Bonhams, London.

the shouts of his squire, Sancho, who warned him that, beyond any doubt, those things he was about to attack were windmills and not giants. But he was so convinced they were giants that he did not hear the shouts of his squire, Sancho, and could not see, though he was very close, what they really were; instead, he charged and called out:

"Flee not, cowards and base creatures, for it is a single knight who attacks you."

Just then a gust of wind began to blow, and the great sails began to move, and, seeing this, Don Quixote said:

"Even if you move more arms than the giant Briareus, you will answer to me."

And saying this, and commending himself with all his heart to his lady Dulcinea, asking that she come to his aid at this critical moment, and well-protected by his shield, with his lance in its socket, he charged at Rocinante's full gallop and attacked the first mill he came to; and as he thrust his lance into the sail, the wind moved it with so much force that it broke the lance into pieces and picked up the horse and the knight, who then dropped to the ground and were very badly battered. Sancho Panza hurried to help as fast as his donkey could carry him, and when he reached them he discovered that Don Quixote could not move because he had taken so hard a fall with Rocinante.

"God save me!" said Sancho. "Didn't I tell your grace to watch what you were doing, that these were nothing but windmills, and only somebody whose head was full of them wouldn't know that?"

"Be quiet, Sancho my friend," replied Don Quixote. "Matters of war, more than any others, are subject to continual change; moreover, I think, and therefore it is true, that the same Frestón the Wise who stole my room and my books has turned these giants into windmills in order to deprive

Make Inferences About Theme *How does this statement contribute to your understanding of the story's theme?*

Literary Element Parody

A **parody** is a humorous imitation of a literary work that aims to point out the work's shortcomings. A parody may imitate the plot, characters, or style of another work. Parody often goes hand in hand with **satire,** or writing that comments humorously on human flaws, ideas, social customs, or institutions in order to change them.

1. How can you tell Cervantes is parodying the style of Feliciano de Silva?

2. What is the target of Cervantes's satire when the narrator describes Don Quixote's lofty goals?

Review: Plot

As you learned on page 84, **plot** refers to the sequence of events in a story. Because this literary work is an excerpt of a long novel, you do not have access to the entire plot. You do, however, have a substantial amount of the **exposition,** which introduces the story's characters, setting, and situation, as well as a portion of what is called the **rising action.**

Partner Activity Work with a classmate to summarize these elements in the exposition of *Don Quixote.* You can create a chart like this one to help organize your thoughts.

Characters:
_____

Setting:
_____

Situation:
_____

Rising Action:
_____

LOG ON ▶ **Literature** Online

Selection Resources For Selection Quizzes, eFlash-cards, and Reading-Writing Connection activities, go to glencoe.com and enter QuickPass code GLW6053u5.

Reading Strategy Make Inferences About Theme

SAT Skills Practice

Based on his parody of chivalric romances, what can you infer about Cervantes's theme?

(A) Chivalric romances idealize a past that may never have existed.

(B) Chivalry is worth preserving.

(C) Chivalric romances are a realistic portrayal of life.

(D) Chivalry needs to be updated if it is to survive in the future.

(E) Chivalry is an important means to equal rights for women.

Vocabulary Practice

Practice with Word Parts For each bold-faced vocabulary word in the left column, identify the related word with a shared word part in the right column. Write each word and underline the part they have in common. Use a printed or online dictionary to look up the meaning of the related word. Then explain how it is related to the vocabulary word.

1. abstinence   renew

2. decipher   abstain

3. renown   decode

4. discourteous   discredit

5. enmity   enemy

Academic Vocabulary

In Don Quixote, *Cervantes introduces a fake* **quotation** *from a writer of chivalric romances to parody the absurd literary style of these works.*

Quotation is an academic term. To further explore the meaning of this word, answer the following question: How might you use a **quotation** in a biographical sketch? in an editorial?

For more on academic vocabulary, see pages 36–37 and R83–R85.

Respond Through Writing

Reflective Essay

Explore Theme What theme do you think Cervantes is expressing through the character of Don Quixote? Explore this question in a 1,500-word reflective essay, in which you reference *Don Quixote* and your own experience.

Understand the Task In a **reflective essay,** you examine details from your experience and reading to present a thought about life.

Prewrite Before you draft your essay, create a concept map like the one below to organize your ideas about Don Quixote. Then identify experiences of your own that seem to link with those of Don Quixote and add them to your concept map. You might derive these experiences from a variety of sources, including brainstorming, journals, and discussions. As you plan, use the graphic organizer you filled out on page 936.

• Don Quixote—courageous but foolish
• Me—trying to be an actor

Don Quixote—hero or lunatic?

Draft Formulate a clear thesis statement, relating Cervantes's theme to your own experiences. In your body paragraphs, make reference to Don Quixote and your own experience. Your conclusion should restate your thesis and provide closure by using Cervantes's theme and your own experience as the basis for a reflection on life.

Revise Use the following checklist in revising your essay.

- Does my thesis clearly state how Cervantes expresses his theme and how it relates to my own experience?
- Do I use details from *Don Quixote* and my own experience?
- Does my conclusion link Cervantes's theme and my own experience?

Edit and Proofread Proofread your paper, correcting any errors in spelling, grammar, and punctuation. Use your computer's word count feature to check that your essay is about 1,500 words. Review the Grammar Tip in the side column for information on using hyphens.

Learning Objectives

In this assignment, you will focus on the following objectives:

Writing: Writing a reflective essay.

Grammar: Understanding how to use hyphens.

> ### Grammar Tip

> #### Hyphens

> One common use of hyphens is to separate compound words, such as *good-bye.*

> Hyphens are also used to join two modifying words into a single compound modifier, such as *lean-faced.* Remember that expressions consisting of an adverb ending in *–ly* and an adjective—such as *extravagantly worded*—are not hyphenated.

TIMELINE 1650–PRESENT

EUROPEAN LITERATURE

1650

1666
French playwright Molière's *The Misanthrope* is first performed

1750

1759 ▶
French author Voltaire publishes *Candide*

1827
Heinrich Heine publishes *The Book of Songs* in Germany

1832
German author Goethe publishes *Faust, Part II*

1850

1862
French author Victor Hugo publishes *Les Misérables*

1865–1869
Russian author Leo Tolstoy publishes *War and Peace*

1879
Henrik Ibsen's *A Doll's House* is first performed

EUROPEAN EVENTS

1650

1661
Louis XIV begins a massive renovation of the Palace of Versailles in France

c. 1668
Anton van Leeuwenhoek develops simple microscope

1707
England and Scotland unite as Great Britain

1750

1762
Catherine the Great becomes ruler of Russia

1804
Napoleon Bonaparte becomes emperor of France

1821
Greeks begin war for independence

1845
Potato blight starts a five-year famine in Ireland
▼

1850

1861
Russian Czar Alexander II frees the serfs

1918
World War I ends

1919–1920
European countries establish the League of Nations

WORLD EVENTS

1650

c. 1650
Taj Mahal completed in India

c. 1697
Ashanti Empire formed in Africa

1752 ▲
Ben Franklin invents the lightning rod

1775
American Revolution begins

1808
Spanish colonies in the Americas begin winning independence

1825
Java War begins between Indonesians and Dutch colonialists

1850

1853
First railroad line in India is completed

1903
The Wright brothers fly the first airplane

1910
The Mexican Revolution begins

LOG ON ▶ **Literature** Online

Literature and Reading To explore the Interactive Timeline, go to glencoe.com and enter QuickPass code GLW6053u5.

1950

1900–1903
French author Colette publishes her *Claudine* novels

1904
Anton Chekhov's *The Cherry Orchard* is first performed

1907 ▶
Anna Akhmatova begins writing poetry in Russia

1973
The first parts of Aleksandr Solzhenitsyn's *The Gulag Archipelago* are published

▲

2006
Turkish author Orhan Pamuk wins the Nobel Prize in Literature

1945
World War II ends

THE VICTORY OF THE UNITED NATIONS IS ASSURED

1955
Eastern European countries sign the Warsaw Pact

1957
Soviet Union launches *Sputnik I*, the first artificial satellite

▲

1989
Germany opens the Berlin Wall

1991
Soviet Union dissolves into separate republics

1993
The European Union is formed

1999
Eleven European countries adopt a single currency

2005
Terrorist bombings in London claim more than 50 lives

1950

1918–1919
Worldwide influenza epidemic kills 20 million people

1957
African colonies win independence

1956
Cuban Revolution begins

1969
Apollo XI lands on the moon

1978
Israel and Egypt sign a peace treaty

1994 ▶
Nelson Mandela is elected president of South Africa

2003
War in Iraq begins

Reading Check

Analyze Graphic Information How many years separate the first plane flight and the first landing on the moon?

Learning Objectives

For pages 948–959

In studying this text, you will focus on the following objectives:

Literary Study: Analyzing literary periods.

Reading: Evaluating historical influences.
Connecting to the literature.

MODERN EUROPE

1650–PRESENT

Historical, Social, and Cultural Forces

The Enlightenment

The Enlightenment dominated philosophy and literature in the late 1600s and 1700s. Faith in human reason and skepticism toward traditional religion characterized this broad movement. Also referred to as Rationalism and "The Age of Reason," the Enlightenment stimulated an outburst of scientific and intellectual inquiry that included Denis Diderot's monumental *Encyclopédie* and Sir Isaac Newton's investigation into the laws of motion. The Enlightenment also shook the political establishment in challenging the "divine right" of kings. These ideas laid the foundation for a modern worldview based on secularism and the rights of the individual. The arguments of such Enlightenment figures as John Locke and Jean-Jacques Rousseau helped shape the ideals behind the American Revolution, the Declaration of Independence, and the French Revolution.

The Industrial Revolution

In the 1700s and 1800s, Europeans began to radically change the way they made goods. Instead of making them by hand and with simple tools, they increasingly used power-driven machines. This change, called the Industrial Revolution, affected

people's lives in many ways. The mass production of such goods as shoes, clothes, and furniture gave people more products they could afford. This new technology came at a human cost, however, as factory workers, including children, endured brutal conditions and long workdays. In the late 1700s, authors associated with the literary movement known as Romanticism began to respond to this change by turning toward nature and the imagination. In the mid-1800s, Realist authors brought attention to the problems of the working class.

A Forge, 1893. Fernand Corman. Oil on canvas. Musee d'Orsay, Paris.

Nationalism

In the 1800s, political borders rarely matched cultural borders. Europe, like most of the world, consisted of tiny kingdoms and sprawling multi-ethnic empires. For example, German-speaking people lived throughout 300 states, while the vast Austrian Empire included Hungarians, Poles, Czechs, Serbs, and other ethnic groups. Europeans felt more loyal to their region or their ruler than to their nationality or ethnic background. However, the idea of nationalism, which comprises a sense of devotion to a nation and a feeling everyone who shares a language and a culture should be in a single separate state, was spreading. Politicians began to exploit ethnic rivalries. People began to embrace, and to even kill and die for, their national identity. These developments propelled Napoleon Bonaparte's drive to conquer Europe in the name of France. During the Napoleonic Wars between 1792 and 1815, France staged a series of invasions, including a failed attempt to conquer Russia. Despite Napoleon's defeat, the trend of nationalism spread throughout Europe. Germany, Italy, and Russia each developed strong dictatorships fueled by nationalist sentiment.

French troops stand guard along the trenches. Undated photograph, ca. 1914-1919.

"What is the throne?—a bit of wood gilded and covered with velvet. I am the state—I alone am the representative of the people."

—Napoleon

The Two World Wars

A complex system of alliances led to the outbreak of World War I (1914–1918). This war pitted the Allies (Britain, France, Russia, Italy, Japan, and the United States) against the Central Powers (Germany, Austria-Hungary, and the Turkish Ottoman Empire). During World War I, armies unleashed new technologies—such as machine guns, tanks, and poisonous gas—that contributed to the deaths of more than 20 million people.

The peace that followed the "Great War" was short-lived, as poor economic conditions in Germany caused by World War I contributed to Adolf Hitler's rise to power. His *blitzkrieg* ("lightning war") invasions of Poland, Belgium, The Netherlands, and France propelled Europe into World War II. Fought between 1939 and 1945, this conflict further devastated Europe. The Axis Powers—Italy, Germany, and Japan—overwhelmed much of the world before the Allies—led by Britain, Russia, and the United States—eventually thwarted them. In World War II, gas chambers, conventional bombs, and atomic weapons killed more than 50 million people. World War II included the Holocaust, one of the darkest periods in European history, as Hitler's Nazi party used racist ideology to justify the systematic killing of six million Jews.

Since World War II, Europe has worked to heal its wounds and prevent future conflicts through political diplomacy. This spirit has created a range of groups, including the United Nations (UN), the European Economic Community (EEC), and the European Union (EU), which was established in 1993 and absorbed the EEC. Today, European countries are moving toward standardizing currencies and other government functions across the continent while maintaining their distinct ethnic traditions.

Modern Films

Motion pictures developed in the late 1800s, following the work of British photographer Eadweard Muybridge, who rigged a row of separate cameras to take a series of photographs of a running horse. Muybridge attached strings to the shutters of the cameras, and as the horse ran by it broke the strings, triggering the shutters in succession. The result was the first motion picture. Inventors in other countries soon developed more portable devices to make films. The Lumière brothers—famous for their early motion picture cameras and projectors—showed their first motion picture in Paris in 1895. Since the 1950s, movie directors such as Italy's Federico Fellini and France's François Truffaut have created films that demonstrate the enduring appeal of great art.

Modern Music

Inspired by the nationalism spreading through Europe, many composers in the 1800s and 1900s incorporated folk styles into their music to celebrate the histories of their countries. Often, they challenged listeners with new harmonies, scales, and rhythms. In 1913, Russian composer Igor Stravinsky's score for the ballet *The Rite of Spring* proved too much for some audiences. The driving rhythms and jarring harmonies outraged many

listeners, who responded with boos and catcalls, pushing, shoving, and even fistfights. One critic called the score "the most irritating friction and squeaking that can be imagined." Yet European composers continued to push avant-garde boundaries. The French composer Pierre Boulez incorporated serialism (repeating patterns) into his music, while the Austrian composer Arnold Schoenberg invented twelve-tone music and created atonal works that purposely lacked harmony.

Modern Painting

During the first half of the 1800s, European painters continued to develop the styles and methods they inherited from earlier generations. The

Improvisation Painting, 1914. Wassily Kandinsky.

Galloping Horse, plate 628 from *Animal Locomotion,* 1887. Eadweard Muybridge.

> *"To listen is an effort, and just to hear is no merit. A duck hears also."*
>
> —Igor Stravinsky

middle of the century, however, saw the rise of the Impressionists. These artists, including Claude Monet and Pierre Auguste Renoir, rejected the importance of traditional subject matter and artistic practices. Instead, they brought their painting outdoors and aimed to manipulate color, texture, and tone in new ways. In the early 1900s artists made even more revolutionary efforts. Pablo Picasso, for example, rejected the traditional emphasis on portraying an object's surface. Instead of showing an object from a single perspective, he showed it from several angles in the same painting. One critic described Marcel Duchamp's 1912 painting *Nude Descending a Staircase* as "an explosion in a shingle factory." While such painters as Picasso and Duchamp shocked viewers by what they showed, other painters shocked people by what they left out of their work. Vassily Kandinsky and Piet Mondrian created nonrepresentational, abstract paintings—works that combined colors, lines, and forms without portraying any particular real-world object.

Nude Descending a Staircase, No.2, 1912. Marcel Duchamp. Oil on canvas. Philadelphia Museum of Art, Pennsylvania.

PREVIEW **Big Ideas** of Modern Europe

1 From the Enlightenment to Romanticism

The Enlightenment marked an outburst of intellectual freedom and scientific inquiry in the late 1600s. By the late 1700s, a new cultural movement known as Romanticism emphasized nature, passion, and the imagination.

See page 956

2 Realism and Modernism

By the mid-1800s, Realism, a reaction to Romanticism, changed the shape of literature. Realist authors sought to re-create the texture of everyday life and address the problems of ordinary people. In the late 1800s and early 1900s, Modernist authors broke tradition with experimental techniques and an interest in the unpredictable side of human nature.

See page 957

3 Postwar Europe

World War II resulted in millions of deaths and left much of Europe in ruins. The horrors of the Holocaust and the threat of nuclear war seemed to challenge all traditional values. Postwar European authors responded in a variety of ways to these events, from expressions of hope to celebrations of human absurdity.

See page 958

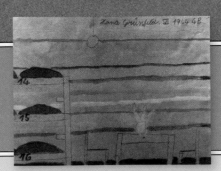

Drawings by Jewish children while at Terezin ghetto: both later died at Auschwitz concentration camp.

Big Idea 3
Postwar Europe

War often spurs dramatic changes in literature. The collective exhaustion that Europeans felt following World War II led many to lose faith in traditional ideas.

> "Everything had to be reassessed because everything had changed. With one stroke, mankind's achievements seemed to have been erased."
> —Elie Wiesel

Holocaust Literature

Elie Wiesel's response to the atrocities of the Nazi death camp Auschwitz echoes the concerns of many post–World War II authors. The Holocaust represented the Nazis' "final solution to the Jewish question" (as phrased by the Nazis) and led to the killing of six million Jews. Postwar authors detailed the horrors of the Holocaust to give voice to the voiceless victims of the period and to ensure the world would never forget the tragedy. Elie Wiesel (see pages 1063–1071) has documented the horrors of the Holocaust through both nonfiction and fiction. Engraved in the U.S. Holocaust Memorial Museum are his words: "For the dead and the living, we must bear witness."

The Diary of Anne Frank (originally published in 1947) is another masterpiece of Holocaust literature. Frank was a young Jewish girl who recorded her experiences while hiding from Nazi forces in The Netherlands. Frank eventually died in a concentration camp only weeks before Allied forces liberated the camp. The graphic novelist Art Spiegelman, born in Poland to Jewish parents who survived Auschwitz, created *Maus* (published from 1980 to 1985), a pivotal work in the rise of the graphic novel and a poignant telling of the Holocaust.

Gulags, Existentialism, and the Absurd

Following World War II, tense political conditions persisted in many parts of Europe. The Cold War that emerged between nuclear superpowers Russia and the United States caused many people to live in daily fear of nuclear attack. In Russia, Joseph Stalin's Communist Party created the Gulag political prisons and restricted the freedom of authors such as Aleksandr Solzhenitsyn (see pages 1072–1075), whom they viewed as a threat to authority.

Existentialism, a philosophy that investigates the meaning of existence, reflected the anxiety of this period. Many Existentialists concluded life was essentially meaningless and absurd. A related movement in drama called "Theater of the Absurd" flourished in the 1950s and 60s. It presented confused and anxious characters wandering through a meaningless world. The French author Albert Camus (see pages 1056–1062) emerged as the spokesman for these complex responses to the world. However, rather than describing a world of bottomless despair, Camus argued that once people realize the underlying meaninglessness of the world they can begin to make choices that give meaning to their lives.

Reading Check

Interpret How does Holocaust literature honor those who died in Nazi concentration camps?

WRAP-UP

Legacy of the Period

The literary movement of Romanticism contributed to European and American culture a belief in the spiritual power of nature, the importance of the imagination, and the dignity of the artist. Realism extended Romantic ideals and inspired such social changes as better working conditions. Modernists wanted people to see life in a new way—they strove to break away from traditional forms and often explored the power of the subconscious. The Modernist desire to experiment remains alive in literature today.

Cultural and Literary Links

 Many famous American authors, including Ernest Hemingway and Gertrude Stein, moved to Paris at the beginning of the twentieth century. These authors drew from modern European art and literature. For example, Stein applied the innovations of Cubist painting to her groundbreaking poems.

Portrait of Gertrude Stein, 1906. Pablo Picasso. Oil on canvas. Metropolitan Museum of Art, NY.

 Anton Chekhov wrote more than 600 short stories in his lifetime. When interviewed in 1987, ten well-known authors, including Eudora Welty, Nadine Gordimer, and Raymond Carver, cited him as a key influence.

LOG ON ▶ **Literature** Online

Unit Resources For additional skills practice, go to glencoe.com and enter QuickPass code GLW6053u5.

Activities

 Use what you have learned about the period to do one of these activities.

1. Follow Up Go back to the Looking Ahead on page 949 and answer the questions.

2. Contrast Cultures The literature of modern Europe takes many forms, including short stories, novels, and poetry. Write several paragraphs in which you select one of these forms and contrast it with the same form in another culture you have studied in this book. Consider such literary elements as theme, form, and diction.

3. Speaking/Listening With classmates, organize a panel discussion with representatives from the Enlightenment, the Romantic, Realism, and Modernism periods, and postwar Europe. Choose a moderator to lead the discussion and have each representative explain his or her views on subjects such as war, the nature of good and evil, or reality.

4. Take Notes Use this graphic organizer to record your responses to the literary works in this part.

FOLDABLES
Study Organizer   **BOUND BOOK**

Before You Read

from *Candide*

France

Meet **Voltaire**
(1694–1778)

> "Let us work without arguing... it's the only way to make life endurable."
>
> —Voltaire

Voltaire (vol tār´) spent his life fighting the injustices of the legal system, the cruelties of war, the intolerance of religions, and the callousness of society toward its poor. To this day, he remains one of France's most influential thinkers.

Jailed for Satire Known by his pen name Voltaire, he was born François-Marie Arouet to middle-class parents. In college Voltaire became interested in literature, theater, and fashionable Parisian society, and he soon became popular among Paris intellectuals with the publication of several short satirical poems. After King Louis XIV died in 1715, his five-year-old great-grandson acceded to the throne as Louis XV, with the Duc d'Orléans serving as regent, or acting ruler. Voltaire was accused of satirizing the regent and was imprisoned in the Bastille. While there he wrote a tragic drama, *Oedipe*, which was staged in Paris upon his release and became a great success.

Jail and Exile Voltaire continued to criticize the behavior of the nobility, which earned him a second jail term and exile to England. He thrived within the more permissive environment of England, a country whose intellectuals proved to be more tolerant of free thought than his countrymen. Voltaire admired the works of the scientist Sir Isaac Newton and the social philosopher John Locke and enjoyed the company of satirical authors Jonathan Swift and Alexander Pope. When he returned to Paris, Voltaire wrote *Lettres philosophiques*, which embodies eighteenth-century rationalism. He argued that the purpose of life is not to achieve heaven through penitence, but rather to bring happiness to all people through advancements in the arts and sciences. Because he praised England so enthusiastically, his French contemporaries were again displeased. His *Essay on the Morals and the Spirit of the Nations* was banned and Voltaire was sent into a second exile.

Famed as a "Saint of Reason" Although he stayed away from Paris for most of his remaining years, Voltaire's outspoken criticism of social injustices brought him trouble wherever he lived. After extensive travels throughout Europe, Voltaire retired to an estate near Geneva, Switzerland, and another in Tourney, France, just over the border; by crossing the border he could escape either country's authorities. He continued to write about multiple subjects in various genres, earning both praise and criticism from important literary and political figures. His satirical novel *Candide*, published in 1759, became his most famous work. At age 83, just before his death, Voltaire returned to Paris in triumph for the production of his last play. Years after his death and after the French Revolution of 1789—a revolution influenced in part by Voltaire's ideas for social reform—his body was interred in the Panthéon in Paris, a site of honor reserved for France's most famous figures.

 LOG ON **Literature** Online

Author Search For more about Voltaire, go to glencoe.com and enter QuickPass code GLW6053u5.

Literature and Reading Preview

Connect to the Novel

Have you ever felt yourself the victim of injustice? How did you react? Discuss these questions with a small group.

Build Background

Candide is Voltaire's response to the ideas of German philosopher Gottfried Wilhelm Leibniz (līb′nits), who was the model for Dr. Pangloss, the tutor of Candide (kon dēd′) and Cunegonde (koo′nə gond). The students initially accept Dr. Pangloss's pronouncement that "all is for the best . . . in this best of all possible worlds," and consequently endure every imaginable humiliation. Candide and Cunegonde grow more realistic as Votaire ridicules Dr. Pangloss's optimistic philosophy.

Set Purposes for Reading

Big Idea From the Enlightenment to Romanticism

As you read the excerpt from *Candide,* ask yourself, How does Voltaire's novel both represent and satirize eighteenth-century Enlightenment ideas and intellectual inquiry?

Literary Element Satire

Writing that comments on human flaws, ideas, social customs, or institutions is called **satire**. Often humorous, sometimes biting, satire often promotes reform. As you read, ask yourself, Whom or what does Voltaire satirize in this work?

Reading Strategy Apply Background Knowledge

Sometimes **background knowledge** helps a reader understand the historical context or the implied message of a work. For example, knowing that Dr. Pangloss is based on a real person can enhance your enjoyment. As you read, ask yourself, What was happening in the world when this novel was written?

Tip: Record Influences Review the part introduction on pages 948–959 to get a sense of the context of the novel. Record your notes for easy reference as you read.

Background	Candide
Constant warring in Europe	Candide conscripted for Bulgarian army

Learning Objectives

For pages 960–968

In studying this text, you will focus on the following objectives:

Literary Study: Analyzing satire.

Reading: Applying background knowledge.

Vocabulary

candor (kan′dər) *n.* honesty or frankness; openness; p. 963 *With the candor of a child, my little sister told me how strange my outfit looked.*

pensive (pen′siv) *adj.* thoughtful; p. 964 *I think Leon's pensive look is from worrying about exams.*

vivacity (vi vas′ə tē′) *n.* liveliness; animation; p. 964 *There's a charming vivacity in the voice of the play's main actor.*

consternation (kon′stər nā′shən) *n.* great fear or shock; upset; p. 964 *The smoke coming through the window caused much consternation among the shoppers.*

clemency (klem′ən sē) *n.* mercy; leniency, especially toward an enemy; p. 966 *The judge was determined to show little clemency toward the convicted robbers.*

Tip: Word Origins Word origins, or etymologies, may give clues to a word's meaning. The word *vivacity*, for example, comes from a Latin word that refers to life. Knowing this etymology can help you determine the word's meaning.

of all possible Baronesses. " 'Tis demonstrated," said he, "that things cannot be otherwise; for, since everything is made for an end, everything is necessarily for the best end. Observe that noses were made to wear spectacles; and so we have spectacles. Legs were visibly instituted to be breeched, and we have breeches.[6] Stones were formed to be quarried and to build castles; and My Lord has a very noble castle; the greatest Baron in the province should have the best house; and as pigs were made to be eaten, we eat pork all the year round; consequently, those who have asserted that all is well talk nonsense; they ought to have said that all is for the best." Candide listened attentively and believed innocently; for he thought Mademoiselle Cunegonde extremely beautiful, although he was never bold enough to tell her so. He decided that after the happiness of being born Baron of Thunder-ten-tronckh, the second degree of happiness was to be Mademoiselle Cunegonde; the third, to see her every day; and the fourth to listen to Doctor Pangloss, the greatest philosopher of the province and therefore of the whole world. One day when Cunegonde was walking near the castle, in a little wood which was called The Park, she observed Doctor Pangloss in the bushes, giving a lesson in experimental physics to her mother's waiting-maid, a very pretty and docile[7] brunette. Mademoiselle Cunegonde had a great inclination for science and watched breathlessly the reiterated[8] experiments she witnessed; she observed clearly the Doctor's sufficient reason, the effects and the causes, and returned home very much excited, **pensive**, filled with the desire of learning, reflecting that she might be the sufficient reason of young Candide and that he might be hers. On her way back to the castle she met Candide and blushed; Candide also blushed. She bade[9] him good morning in a hesitating voice; Candide replied without knowing what he was saying. Next day, when they left the table after dinner, Cunegonde and Candide found themselves behind a screen; Cunegonde dropped her handkerchief, Candide picked it up; she innocently held his hand; the young man innocently kissed the young lady's hand with remarkable **vivacity**, tenderness and grace; their lips met, their eyes sparkled, their knees trembled, their hands wandered. Baron Thunder-ten-tronckh passed near the screen, and, observing this cause and effect, expelled Candide from the castle by kicking him in the backside frequently and hard. Cunegonde swooned;[10] when she recovered her senses, the Baroness slapped her in the face; and all was in **consternation** in the noblest and most agreeable of all possible castles.

---

9. *Bade* is the past tense of *bid*, in the sense of "to give, express, or declare."
10. *Swooned* means "fainted."

Apply Background Knowledge *Why does the Baron expel Candide from his castle?*

Vocabulary

pensive (pen′siv) *adj.* thoughtful
vivacity (vi vas′ə te′) *n.* liveliness; animation
consternation (kon′stər nā′shən) *n.* great fear or shock; upset

---

6. *Breeches* are pants or trousers.
7. *Docile* means "easy to manage or teach."
8. *Reiterated* means "repeated."

Satire *What kind of logical argument does Voltaire satirize here?*

CHAPTER II

What Happened to Candide Among the Bulgarians[11]

Candide, expelled from the earthly paradise, wandered for a long time without knowing where he was going, turning up his eyes to Heaven, gazing back frequently at the noblest of castles which held the most beautiful of young Baronesses; he lay down to sleep supperless between two furrows in the open fields; it snowed heavily in large flakes. The next morning the shivering Candide, penniless, dying of cold and exhaustion, dragged himself toward the neighboring town, which was called Waldberghoff-trarbk-dikdorff. He halted sadly at the door of an inn. Two men dressed in blue noticed him. "Comrade," said one, "there's a well-built young man of the right height." They went up to Candide and very civilly invited him to dinner. "Gentlemen," said Candide with charming modesty, "you do me a great honor, but I have no money to pay my share." "Ah, sir," said one of the men in blue, "persons of your figure and merit never pay anything; are you not five feet five tall?" "Yes, gentlemen," said he, bowing, "that is my height." "Ah, sir, come to table; we will not only pay your expenses, we will never allow a man like you to be short of money; men were only made to help each other." "You are in the right," said Candide, "that is what Doctor Pangloss was always telling me, and I see that everything is for the best." They begged him to accept a few crowns,[12] he took them and wished to give them an I O U; they refused to take it and all sat down to table. "Do you not love tenderly . . . ." "Oh, yes," said he. "I love Mademoiselle Cunegonde tenderly." "No," said one of the gentlemen. "We were asking if you do not tenderly love the King of the Bulgarians." "Not a bit," said he, "for I have never seen him." "What! He is the most charming of Kings, and you must drink his health." "Oh, gladly, gentlemen." And he drank. "That is sufficient," he was told. "You are now the support, the aid, the defender, the hero of the Bulgarians; your fortune is made and your glory assured." They immediately put irons on his legs and took him to a regiment.[13] He was made to turn to the right and left, to raise the ramrod[14] and return the ramrod, to take aim, to fire, to double up, and he was given thirty strokes with a stick; the next day he drilled not quite so badly, and received only twenty strokes; the day after, he only had ten and was looked on as a prodigy[15] by his comrades. Candide was completely mystified and could not make out how he was a hero. One fine spring day he thought he would take a walk, going straight ahead, in the belief that to use his legs as he pleased was a

---

12. *Crowns* are coins of various worth in different countries.
13. Candide is being forced into military service, in a Bulgarian *regiment,* or army unit.
14. A *ramrod* is a rod used to force (ram) gunpowder and ammunition into the barrel of a musket or firearm.
15. A *prodigy* is a person of unusual talent or genius.

> **Satire** *What kind of military recruiting practices do the two men in blue demonstrate in this passage?*

---

11. *The Bulgarians* here refers to Frederick the Great's Prussian army.

Prelude. Oil on canvas. Boilly, Louis Leopold (1761-1845). Pushkin Museum, Moscow.

---

privilege of the human species as well as of animals. He had not gone two leagues[16] when four other heroes, each six feet tall, fell upon him, bound him and dragged him back to a cell. He was asked by his judges whether he would rather be thrashed thirty-six times by the whole regiment or receive a dozen lead bullets at once in his brain. Although he protested that men's wills are free and that he wanted neither one nor the other, he had to make a choice; by virtue of that gift of God which is called *liberty*, he

---

16. A *league* is a measure of distance roughly equivalent in some countries to three miles.

From the Enlightenment to Romanticism *How does Candide demonstrate his belief in Dr. Pangloss's version of Enlightenment philosophy?*

---

determined to run the gauntlet[17] thirty-six times and actually did so twice. There were two thousand men in the regiment. That made four thousand strokes which laid bare the muscles and nerves from his neck to his backside. As they were about to proceed to a third turn, Candide, utterly exhausted, begged as a favor that they would be so kind as to smash his head; he obtained this favor; they bound his eyes and he was made to kneel down. At that moment the King of the Bulgarians came by and inquired the victim's crime; and as this King was possessed of a vast genius, he perceived from what he learned about Candide that he was a young metaphysician[18] very ignorant in worldly matters, and therefore pardoned him with a **clemency** which will be praised in all newspapers and all ages. An honest surgeon healed Candide in three weeks with the ointments recommended by Dioscorides.[19] He had already regained a little skin and could walk when the King of the Bulgarians went to war with the King of the Abares.[20] ◐

---

17. In being forced to *run the gauntlet*, Candide must run between two rows of men who will beat him as he passes.
18. A *metaphysician* is a person who studies metaphysics, or the nature of reality.
19. *Dioscorides* (dī'əs kor ē dəs) was a Greek physician and pharmacologist of the first century A.D.
20. *Abares* here refers to the French.

From the Enlightenment to Romanticism *Why would this doctor treat Candide with ancient Greek remedies?*

Vocabulary

clemency (klem'ən sē) *n.* mercy; leniency, especially toward an enemy

After You Read

Respond and Think Critically

Respond and Interpret

1. What surprised you most about this excerpt? Why?

2. (a)What is Candide's status at Baron Thunder-ten-tronckh's castle? (b)Summarize the circumstances that cause Candide to be expelled from the castle.

3. (a)How does Dr. Pangloss prove that "everything is made for an end"? (b)What conclusion does he draw from these examples?

4. (a)Why do the two men in blue comment on Candide's height? (b)Why do they want to meet him?

5. (a)Why can't Candide walk away from the Bulgarian regiment? (b)What are his options, and what is his choice?

Analyze and Evaluate

6. (a)How does the setting of this excerpt affect the plot? (b)Could the story take place in another time or place? Explain.

7. (a)Are Voltaire's characters three-dimensional and believable? Explain. (b)Why do you think Voltaire might have drawn his characters with the amount of detail he did?

Connect

8. **Big Idea** **From the Enlightenment to Romanticism** How does Dr. Pangloss demonstrate that he is a product of the Enlightenment? Explain.

9. **Connect to the Author** Voltaire, like Candide, suffered for his beliefs. How do you think the author's personal experiences might have affected his attitude toward his main character?

Primary Source Quotation

The Real Pangloss

Candide's tutor, Dr. Pangloss, is a satirical portrait of Gottfried Wilhelm Leibniz (1646–1716), a German philosopher, mathematician, metaphysician, historian, political adviser, and logician. One of his major areas of investigation involved the question of good and evil: Why does God allow horrible events such as murders, wars, and natural disasters? He concluded that:

"God has chosen the best of all possible worlds."

Humans who object that this cannot be the best of worlds because of the suffering in it are merely shortsighted, he argues; there is no way for us to know what may be the greatest good for all creation, and what seems to us to be evil may in fact be necessary on the cosmic scale. In *Candide*, Voltaire satirizes Leibniz's philosophy as simplistic, and to prove his point, he brutalizes his characters, kills them off, and brings them back to life, as if to say, "*Now* what do you think of your 'best of all possible worlds'?"

Gottfried Wilhelm von Leibniz.

Group Activity Discuss the following questions with your classmates.

1. How might you prove this is the best of all possible worlds?

2. How might you prove this is *not* the best of all possible worlds?

SAT Skills Practice

The primary satirical purpose of Chapter II is to

(A) illustrate the brutality of the Bulgarians

(B) show the punishment for desertion

(C) show that Candide adheres to what he has learned and what he knows to be true

(D) introduce the King of the Bulgarians

(E) question the concept of heroism

Review: Narrator

As you learned on page 637, a **narrator** is the person who tells a story. The narrator may be a character in the story or remain outside the story. The narrator's **point of view** may have a great effect on the story and the impressions it creates.

Narrative Points of View	
First Person	Narrator a character in story; uses *I* and *me*
Third-Person Omniscient	Narrator all-knowing; tells thoughts and feelings
Third-Person Limited	Narrator describes events as only one character perceives them

Partner Activity Work with a classmate to answer the following questions.

1. From what point of view is *Candide* told?

2. Describe the narrator's voice in terms of diction, tone, and concern for the characters and events.

3. In your opinion, what effect does Voltaire's use of the narrator have on his satirical effect?

LOG ON ▶ **Literature** Online

Selection Resources For Selection Quizzes, eFlash-cards, and Reading-Writing Connection activities, go to glencoe.com and enter QuickPass code GLW6053u5.

Reading Strategy Apply Background Knowledge

Use your background knowledge to answer these questions. Consult the chart you made on page 961.

1. Why does Candide readily accept the hospitality of the "two men dressed in blue"?

2. How does "liberty" figure in Candide's having to run the gauntlet?

Vocabulary Practice

Practice with Word Origins Studying the etymology, or origin and history, of a word can help you better understand and explore its meaning. Create a word map like the one below for each boldfaced vocabulary word from the novel. Use a dictionary for help.

candor   pensive   vivacity
consternation   clemency

EXAMPLE:

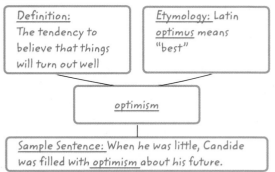

Academic Vocabulary

In Candide, *Voltaire uses the misadventures of his innocent hero to* **demonstrate** *the defects of European society.*

Demonstrate is an academic term meaning "to clearly show the nature of something by using examples." To further explore the meaning of this word, answer this question: What examples would you use to **demonstrate** flaws in society today?

For more on academic vocabulary, see pages 36–37 and R83–R85.

Respond Through Writing

Expository Essay

Learning Objective

In this assignment, you will focus on the following objectives:

Writing: Writing an expository essay.

Grammar: Understanding active and passive voice.

Analyze Cause and Effect In *Candide*, Voltaire uses cause-and-effect relationships as one of his satirical strategies. For example, the Baroness is widely respected because she weighs 350 pounds. In a 1,500-word expository essay, explain how Voltaire uses cause and effect in Chapters 1 and 2 of *Candide* and analyze how this contributes to the overall tone of his fiction.

Understand the Task The **tone** of a literary work is the attitude an author takes toward the audience, a subject, or a character.

Prewrite Use a graphic organizer like the one below to get started. Then plan a sequence for presenting these details within your essay.

Cause: The Baron's castle has a door and windows	Effect: He is one of the most powerful lords in Westphalia

Relation to Tone: Here Voltaire pokes fun at Westphalia by saying that simply having a castle with a door and windows makes the Baron one of Westphalia's most powerful lords. This exemplifies Voltaire's satiric tone.

Draft Structure your body paragraphs so that each presents a separate example of Voltaire's use of cause and effect. Include supporting evidence from the text to back up your ideas and explain how this evidence is meaningful.

Revise Review your draft to make sure you look beyond the literal meaning of the events in *Candide* in considering how causes and effects reflect a particular tone. Review the text as well as the background material on pages 960–961 to see if you left out any essential ideas. Before handing in your work, consider including a visual element within your essay. For example, you might create a map of Candide's travels annotated with various causes and effects and their meanings.

Edit and Proofread Proofread your paper, correcting any errors in spelling, grammar, and punctuation. Use the word count feature on a computer to determine that your paper is at least 1,500 words. Review the Grammar Tip in the side column for information on active and passive voice.

> **Grammar Tip**

Active and Passive Voice

An action verb is in the **active voice** when the subject of the verb performs the action. It is in the **passive voice** when its action is performed on the subject.

Voltaire attacked the social evils of his time. [active]

The social evils of his time were attacked by Voltaire. [passive]

The active voice usually creates a stronger impression than the passive. Passive voice can be effective when you do not want to call attention to who performed the action.

The Faust Legend

YOU HAVE PROBABLY HEARD THE EXPRESSIONS "SELL YOUR SOUL" OR "make a deal with the devil." These sayings originate with the Faust (foust) legend, a medieval tale in which a man trades his soul for knowledge. The legend of Faust (also called Faustus or Doctor Faustus) has been retold for more than four centuries.

"*Fate has given this man a spirit*
Which is always pressing onwards, beyond control,
And whose mad striving overleaps
All joys of the earth between pole and pole.
Him shall I drag through the wilds of life
And through the flats of meaninglessness,
I shall make him flounder and gape and stick
And to tease his insatiableness
Hang meat and drink in the air before his watering lips;
In vain he will pray to slake his inner thirst,
And even had he not sold himself to the devil
He would be equally accursed."

—Mephistopheles, from *Faust* by Johann Wolfgang von Goethe

Faust and Mephistopheles, 1826-1827. (Ferdinand Victor) Eugene Delacroix. Wallace Collection, London, UK.

Rise of Faust

A real person in Germany, about whom little is known inspired the Faust legend. Several public documents and letters from the early sixteenth century mention a boastful wandering magician named George Faust, and accounts from several decades later tell of a Johannes Faust—probably the same man—who called the devil his "brother-in-law." By the mid-sixteenth century, people had begun to tell fantastical stories of a magician who had been given magical powers by the devil. In 1587, the earliest printed collection of these tales appeared. Known as the *Faustbuch*, or "Faust Book," it portrays Faust as a bold and selfish man who desires superhuman powers and knowledge. With the aid of a devil named Mephistopheles (mef´ ə stof´ ə lēz´) (also known as Mephisto), Faust performs astounding feats of magic until he plunges to hell. Using dark humor, the *Faustbuch* stresses Christian values and warns of the consequences of a sinful life.

The first major literary adaptation of the legend was *The Tragical History of Doctor Faustus*, written in 1589 by the English dramatist Christopher Marlowe. The play portrays Faust as a "Renaissance man," obsessed with worldly knowledge and experience. The play retains the humor, sorcery, and final punishment found in the original tales. However, Marlowe's Doctor Faustus is an admirable man corrupted by power, rather than the power-hungry Faust depicted in the original.

Goethe's *Faust*

Johann Wolfgang von Goethe (gur′tə) embraced the heroic aspects of the Faust legend in his poetic drama *Faust* (1808–1832), which is considered the legend's greatest retelling. Growing up in Frankfurt am Main, Germany, in the mid-eighteenth century, Goethe became fascinated by the Faust legend after seeing it performed as a puppet play. An early version of Goethe's *Faust* reflects the ideas of the *Sturm und Drang*, or "Storm and Stress," movement. This movement spurred German Romanticism, which embraced the values of individualism and imagination. Goethe cast his Faust as a Romantic hero: idealistic, emotional, and hungry for knowledge.

Goethe's *Faust* transformed the traditionally bleak ending of the legend. A merciful God praises Faust's quest for knowledge and saves him from the fires of hell. The work also portrays the devil Mephistopheles in a new light—he is ironic, witty, and cynical. Part epic and part drama, Goethe's *Faust* includes an impressive range of verse forms, and critics view it as an ironic comment on the goals and limits of the Western intellectual tradition.

Modern Adaptations

The most highly regarded twentieth-century retelling of the Faust legend is the 1947 novel *Doctor Faustus* by the German author Thomas Mann. Narrating the life of a composer who makes a pact with the devil, the novel also serves as an allegory for the intellectual decline of Germany in the period before World War II.

In modern times, the Faust legend has been the basis for comic books, orchestral compositions, and films, including a famous 1926 version by the German director F. W. Murnau.

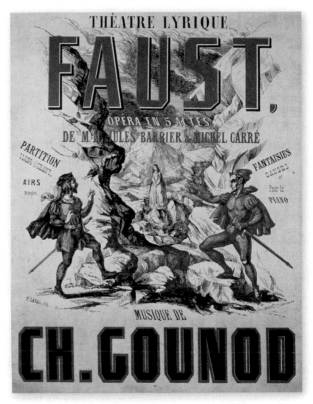

Opera Poster advertising *Faust*, 1875. T. Laval. Lithograph from engraving.

Literature Online

Literature and Reading For more about the Faust legend, go to glencoe.com and enter QuickPass code GLW6053u5.

Respond and Think Critically

1. How did the Faust legend reinforce religious beliefs in the Middle Ages?

2. How did Romanticism influence Goethe's version of the legend?

3. What makes Goethe's version unique?

4. Why do you think the Faust legend continues to captivate people?

The Lorelei

Heinrich Heine
Translated by Aaron Kramer

> I cannot explain the sadness
> That's fallen on my breast.
> An old, old fable haunts me,
> And will not let me rest.
>
> 5   The air grows cool in the twilight,
> And softly the Rhine flows on;
> The peak of a mountain sparkles
> Beneath the setting sun.
>
> More lovely than a vision,
> 10   A girl sits high up there;
> Her golden jewelry glistens,
> She combs her golden hair.
>
> With a comb of gold she combs it,
> And sings an evensong;[1]
> 15   The wonderful melody reaches
> A boat, as it sails along.
>
> The boatman hears, with an anguish
> More wild than was ever known;
> He's blind to the rocks around him;
> 20   His eyes are for her alone.
>
> —At last the waves devoured
> The boat, and the boatman's cry;
> And this she did with her singing,
> The golden Lorelei.

---

1. *Evensong* is a prayerful song sung late in the afternoon or in the evening.

Rhyme *What examples of true and slant rhyme can you find in this stanza?*

Analyze Sound Devices *Identify the assonance in lines 11–13. How does it add to the poem?*

The Siren, 1879. Charles Landelle (French 1821-1908). Oil on canvas. Russell-Cotes Art Gallery and Museum, Bournemouth, UK.

After You Read

Respond and Think Critically

Respond and Interpret

1. Which images from this poem linger in your mind? Share your response with the class.

2. (a)What is the "old, old fable" that has been troubling the speaker? (b)Why do you think he is troubled by this?

3. (a)What does the girl in the legend do? (b)Do you think she is a real person? Explain.

Analyze and Evaluate

4. (a)In creating the image of the girl, which features does the poet emphasize? (b)Why do you think he uses this imagery?

5. (a)How is the ending of the poem ironic, or unexpected? (b)How does this irony connect to the poem's theme?

Connect

6. **Big Idea** **From the Enlightenment to Romanticism** (a)What do you think the girl's singing symbolizes? (b)In what way does this reflect the ideals of the Romantic period?

7. **Connect to Today** Does "The Lorelei" remind you of any contemporary poems or songs you know? Explain.

Literary Element Rhyme

When words sound similar but do not rhyme exactly (like *alone* and *belong*), they are called **half-rhymes** or **slant rhymes**. A poem's rhyme scheme can be expressed by letters indicating the pattern of rhymes that occur at the ends of lines (for example, *aabb* or *abab*).

1. What is the rhyme scheme of "The Lorelei"?

2. Identify two examples of half-rhyme in this translation of the poem.

Reading Strategy Analyze Sound Devices

An unstressed syllable at the end of a line is called a feminine ending, while a stressed syllable at the end of a line is known as a masculine ending.

1. Read the poem aloud to yourself. Which lines have feminine endings?

2. Identify an example of consonance in line 7 and of assonance in lines 18–20.

Academic Vocabulary

"More lovely than a vision, / A girl sits high up there"

—Heinrich Heine, "The Lorelei"

Vision is an academic word. In more casual conversation, you might say you have 20/20 vision if you have perfect eyesight. To explore this word further, write and answer a question about "The Lorelei" using the word *vision*.

For more on academic vocabulary, see pages 36–37 and R83–R85.

Writing

Write a Poem Heine uses sound devices to make "The Lorelei" pleasing to the ear. Using Heine's style as a model, write a poem about an experience you've had with something beautiful. Refer to the chart you made on page 973 about sound devices in "The Lorelei" for devices to use in your own poem.

RUSSIA 1812

Napoleon's Retreat From Moscow. Adolf Northen (German, 1828–1876) Private collection.

from THE EXPIATION

Victor Hugo
Translated by Robert Lowell

The snow fell, and its power was multiplied.
For the first time the Eagle° bowed its head—
dark days! Slowly the Emperor returned—
behind him Moscow! Its onion domes° still burned.
5   The snow rained down in blizzards—rained and froze.
Past each white waste a further white waste rose.
None recognized the captains or the flags.
Yesterday the Grand Army, today its dregs!
No one could tell the vanguard from the flanks.°
10 The snow! The hurt men struggled from the ranks,
hid in the bellies of dead horse, in stacks
of shattered caissons. By the bivouacs,°
one saw the picket° dying at his post,

2 Eagle: Napoleon, who took the eagle as his standard. Napoleon required his troops to swear by this standard that they would conquer or die.

4 onion domes: domes of Eastern Orthodox churches.

9 vanguard: the front division of an army. **flanks:** an army's sides.

12 caissons (kā´ sənz): chests that hold ammunition or carts for ammunition. **bivouacs:** temporary encampments.

13 picket: here, a sentry.

Visualize *What is the predominant color in this description? What emotions does this scene evoke?*

still standing in his saddle, white with frost,
15   the stone lips frozen to the bugle's mouth!
Bullets and grapeshot° mingled with the snow,
that hailed . . . The Guard, surprised at shivering, march
in a dream now; ice rimes° the gray mustache.
The snow falls, always snow! The driving mire
20   submerges; men, trapped in that white empire,
have no more bread and march on barefoot—gaps!
They were no longer living men and troops,
but a dream drifting in a fog, a mystery,
mourners parading under the black sky.
25   The **solitude**, vast, terrible to the eye,
was like a mute avenger everywhere,
as snowfall, floating through the quiet air,
buried the huge army in a huge shroud.°
Could anyone leave this kingdom? A crowd—
30   each man, **obsessed** with dying, was alone.
Men slept—and died! The beaten mob sludged on,
ditching the guns to burn their carriages.
Two foes. The North, the Czar. The North was worse.
In hollows where the snow was piling up,
35   one saw whole regiments fallen asleep.
Attila's dawn, Cannaes of Hannibal!°
The army marching to its funeral!
Litters,° wounded, the dead, deserters—swarm,
crushing the bridges down to cross a stream.
40   They went to sleep ten thousand, woke up four.°
Ney,° bringing up the former army's rear,
hacked his horse loose from three disputing Cossacks . . .
All night, the *qui vive?*° The alert! Attacks;
retreats! White ghosts would wrench away our guns,
45   or we would see dim, terrible squadrons,
circles of steel, whirlpools of savages,
rush sabering through the camp like dervishes.°
And in this way, whole armies died at night.

The Emperor was there, standing—he saw.
50   This oak already trembling from the axe,
watched his glories drop from him branch by branch:

16 grapeshot: small metal balls fired from cannons.

18 rime: to cover with ice.

28 shroud: a sheet in which a corpse is wrapped before burial.

36 Attila: ruler of the Huns (c. 406–453). Called "the Scourge of God," he plagued both the Roman and Byzantine empires. **Hannibal:** the Carthaginian general (247–183 B.C.) also fought against Rome. Hugo suggests that the winter (the North) gave Napoleon as much trouble as Attila and Hannibal gave ancient Rome.

38 Litters: stretchers.

40 ten thousand, woke up four: Napoleon's losses during this trek might have been as many as 500,000 soldiers (in an army of 600,000 to 700,000).

41 Ney (Nā): Napoleon's second in command during this campaign.

43 *qui vive* (kē vēv): "long live who?" is the challenge of a sentry in French (similar to "who goes there?").

47 dervishes: a sect of Islam that is known for the whirling dances performed (sometimes with sabers, or swords) in religious ceremonies.

Antagonist *How does Hugo describe the snow? How has it become the men's antagonist?*

Visualize *What has happened to these men? How do you visualize them?*

Vocabulary

solitude (sol′ə tōōd′) *n.* state of being alone; isolation

obsessed (əb sesd′) *adj.* having an excessive concern

Reading Strategy Visualize

"Russia 1812" is a narrative poem, or a poem that tells a story. Hugo uses descriptive language to help the reader **visualize** the setting, the characters, and the action.

1. (a)What do the descriptions help you "see" and understand about the men and the war? (b)What do the details suggest about the war?

2. (a)What is the theme of the poem? (b)How do the details help you understand the theme?

Vocabulary Practice

Practice with Synonyms A **synonym** is a word that has the same or nearly the same meaning as another word. With a partner, match each boldfaced vocabulary word below with its synonym. Use a thesaurus or dictionary to check your answers. You will not use all the answer choices.

1. solitude
2. obsessed

a. dismal
b. isolation
c. preoccupied
d. comradeship

Academic Vocabulary

*Hugo presents key **aspects** of Napoleon's character, including his stubborn pride, even in the face of defeat.*

Aspects is an academic word with a variety of uses. One of the many **aspects** of writing a good story is character development. Write and answer a question about "Russia 1812" using this word.

For more on academic vocabulary, see pages 36–37 and R83–R85.

Listening and Speaking

Oral Interpretation

Assignment Present an oral interpretation of "Russia 1812" to convey Hugo's attitude toward Napoleon and the war.

Prepare As you review Hugo's narrative poem, use the following checklist to develop your interpretation of the poem:

- What is the historical background of "Russia 1812"?
- Who is the speaker?
- What type of imagery predominates?
- What metaphors are used?

Familiarize yourself with the sound devices and rhythm in the poem. Practice your oral interpretation a few times, experimenting with different tones, volumes, speeds, and other vocal devices. Use facial expressioons and gestures to reflect the meaning of your words. Try to increase your fluency, or ease with which you read, each time you read the poem. You may wish to record your practice readings.

You may want to introduce visual effects into your oral interpretation (such as art depicting the retreat from Moscow). If you do, be sure these effects do not overshadow your presentation. Refer to the graphic organizer you filled out on page 977 as you consider how you want your listener to visualize your interpretation.

Perform Present your interpretation in front of the class, varying the tone of your voice to keep your audience's attention.

Evaluate Write a paragraph in which you assess the effectiveness of your oral interpretation. Use the rubric on page 167 to help in this self-evaluation.

LOG ON **Literature** Online

Selection Resources For Selection Quizzes, eFlashcards, and Reading-Writing Connection activities, go to glencoe. com and enter QuickPass code GLW6053u5.

Before You Read

How Much Land Does a Man Need?

Meet **Leo Tolstoy**
(1828–1910)

When he was an old man, Leo Tolstoy sometimes made visitors uncomfortable; it often seemed as if he could read their minds. His profound psychological insight is also apparent in his fiction. One of Russia's greatest novelists, Tolstoy was a master at portraying people's thoughts and feelings.

Life on the Estate Tolstoy came from an aristocratic family. His parents died before he was ten, and he lost his grandmother and a beloved aunt within the next few years. Even so, he always remembered a "blissful" early life under the care of another aunt and a favorite cousin. He inherited the family's 2,000-acre estate when he was nineteen, and he wrote his first two books while serving as an officer in the Russian army.

At age 34, Tolstoy married the eighteen-year-old daughter of family friends, settling down on his estate. Within fifteen years, he wrote his two masterpieces, the novels *War and Peace* and *Anna Karenina*. Shortly after finishing *Anna Karenina*, a spiritual crisis led him to renounce these novels. For a while, he wrote only nonfiction works about religion and morality. Eventually he returned to fiction, producing moral tales written in a simplified style. By the end of his life, Tolstoy was revered throughout the world as an artist and a philosopher.

Sudden Prophet Inspired by the religious faith of Russian peasants, Tolstoy underwent a spiritual awakening in his early fifties. He eventually rejected the doctrines of the Russian Orthodox Church and was excommunicated. In a series of essays, Tolstoy set forth a new system of beliefs based on the New Testament Gospels. He stressed the importance of pacifism, simple living, and self-improvement through physical work. He eventually gave up all claim to his land holdings, believing it was wrong to own property. His son Ilya described the effect of Tolstoy's spiritual crisis: "From the fun-loving, lively head of our family he was transformed before our eyes into a stern, accusatory prophet." Tolstoy's ideas of civil disobedience influenced the young Mahatma Gandhi, who used them to lead the people of India to independence from Great Britain.

Unhappiness at home led Tolstoy to flee on October 28, 1910, and he died of pneumonia a few days later. The quest of his life was captured in his last words: "To seek, always to seek . . ." .

> "An artist is an artist because he sees things not as he wishes to see them but as they really are."
>
> —Leo Tolstoy

Literature and Reading Preview

Connect to the Story

How can you tell the difference between what you want and what you need? Discuss this question with a small group. Consider why people often want much more than they need.

Build Background

Until 1861, when Czar Alexander II emancipated the peasants, millions worked on Russian farms under a system called serfdom. Serfs lived in virtual slavery and were tied to the land; if a landowner sold a section of property, the serfs working that area were also sold. Serfs had few legal rights—they could not leave, change jobs, or marry without the landowner's permission—and they were often beaten or sent to serve in the army. After the abolition of serfdom, they were supposed to receive land, but landowners and local authorities often gave them the smallest or least productive plots.

Set Purposes for Reading

Big Idea Realism and Modernism

As you read, ask yourself, How does Tolstoy describe the everyday lives and problems of his ordinary characters?

Literary Element Structure

Structure is the order or pattern an author uses to present ideas. The most common structure for a narrative is chronological order, in which events are told in the order they happen. Other kinds of writing, such as persuasive or expository writing, might use a cause-and-effect or problem-solution structure. As you read the story, ask yourself, How does Tolstoy's structure contribute to the story's message?

Reading Strategy Make Inferences About Theme

When you **make inferences about theme,** you look for clues that suggest the author's message about life. Those clues can be found in the events, dialogue, and descriptions that make up the story. As you read, ask yourself, What details point to clues about the author's message?

Tip: Note Details As you read, note details that contribute to the theme in a chart like the one below.

Detail	Theme

Vocabulary

disparage (dis par′ij) *v.* speak badly of; p. 985 *Eve disparaged my contribution to the potluck dinner.*

discord (dis′kôrd) *n.* angry or quarrelsome disagreement; lack of harmony; p. 986 *Discord between the two sisters disrupted the happiness of the family reunion.*

trespass (tres′pəs) *v.* illegally enter property; p. 987 *The guard's yell stopped them from trespassing.*

arable (ar′ə bəl) *adj.* fit for growing crops; p. 989 *Hoping to raise corn, hay, and lettuce, the Potter family bought twenty acres of arable land.*

disperse (dis purs′) *v.* scatter or spread in many directions; p. 993 *After the party, the guests dispersed to their own homes.*

Tip: Context Clues When you read an unfamiliar word, pay close attention to the context, or setting, in which it appears. One type of context clue is a contrast, such as "The younger sister . . . disparaged the life of a tradesman, and stood up for that of a peasant."

How Much Land Does a Man Need?

Leo Tolstoy

Translated by Louise and Aylmer Maude

Ploughing the Field, 1871. Mikhail Konstantinovich Klodt von Juergensburg. Oil on canvas. State Russian Museum, Moscow.

An elder sister came to visit her younger sister in the country. The elder was married to a tradesman in town, the younger to a peasant in the village. As the sisters sat over their tea talking, the elder began to boast of the advantages of town life: saying how comfortably they lived there, how well they dressed, what fine clothes her children wore, what good things they ate and drank, and how she went to the theater, promenades, and entertainments.

The younger sister was piqued, and in turn **disparaged** the life of a tradesman, and stood up for that of a peasant.

"I would not change my way of life for yours," said she. "We may live roughly, but at least we are free from anxiety. You live in better style than we do, but though you often earn more than you need, you are very likely to lose all you have. You know the proverb, 'Loss and gain are brothers twain.' It often happens that people who are wealthy one day are begging their bread the next. Our way is safer. Though a peasant's life is not a fat one, it is a long one. We shall never grow rich, but we shall always have enough to eat."

The elder sister said sneeringly:

"Enough? Yes, if you like to share with the pigs and the calves! What do you know of elegance or manners! However much your goodman may slave, you will die as you are living—on a dung heap—and your children the same."

"Well, what of that?" replied the younger. "Of course our work is rough and coarse. But, on the other hand, it is sure, and we need not bow to any one. But you, in your towns, are surrounded by temptations; today all may be right, but tomorrow the Evil One[1] may tempt your husband with cards, wine, or women, and all will go to ruin. Don't such things happen often enough?"

Pakhom, the master of the house, was lying on the top of the stove and he listened to the women's chatter.

"It is perfectly true," thought he. "Busy as we are from childhood tilling mother earth, we peasants have no time to let any nonsense settle in our heads. Our only trouble is that we haven't land enough. If I had plenty of land, I shouldn't fear the Devil himself!"

The women finished their tea, chatted a while about dress, and then cleared away the tea-things and lay down to sleep.

But the Devil had been sitting behind the stove, and had heard all that was said. He was pleased that the peasant's wife had led her husband into boasting, and that he had said that if he had plenty of land he would not fear the Devil himself.

"All right," thought the Devil. "We will have a tussle. I'll give you land enough; and by means of that land I will get you into my power."

II

Close to the village there lived a lady, a small landowner who had an estate of about three hundred acres. She had always lived on good terms with the peasants until she engaged as her steward an old soldier, who took to burdening the people with fines. However careful Pakhom tried to be, it happened again and again that now a horse of his got among the lady's oats, now a cow strayed into her garden, now his calves found their way into her meadows—and he always had to pay a fine.

Pakhom paid up, but grumbled, and going home in a temper, was rough with his family. All through that summer, Pakhom had much trouble because of this steward, and he was even glad when winter came and the cattle had to be stabled. Though he grudged the fodder when they could no longer graze on the pasture-land, at least he was free from anxiety about them.

In the winter the news got about that the lady was going to sell her land and that the keeper of the inn on the high road was bargaining for it. When the peasants heard this they were very much alarmed.

"Well," thought they, "if the innkeeper gets the land, he will worry us with fines worse than the lady's steward. We all depend on that estate."

So the peasants went on behalf of their commune,[2] and asked the lady not to sell the land to the innkeeper, offering her a better price for it themselves. The lady agreed to let them have it. Then the peasants tried to arrange for the commune to buy the whole estate, so that it might be held by them all in common. They met twice to discuss it, but could not settle the matter; the Evil One sowed **discord** among them and they could not agree. So they decided to buy the land individually, each according to his means; and the lady agreed to this plan as she had to the other.

---

2. In some rural areas, farmers organize into *communes* for mutual support. Members of the commune also may own or use property or equipment in common.

---

1. The *Evil One* is the Devil.

Structure *Why does Tolstoy begin a new section of the story here? How does this division help develop the plot?*

Presently Pakhom heard that a neighbor of his was buying fifty acres, and that the lady had consented to accept one half in cash and to wait a year for the other half. Pakhom felt envious.

"Look at that," thought he, "the land is all being sold, and I shall get none of it." So he spoke to his wife.

"Other people are buying," said he, "and we must also buy twenty acres or so. Life is becoming impossible. That steward is simply crushing us with his fines."

So they put their heads together and considered how they could manage to buy it. They had one hundred rubles laid by.

They sold a colt and one half of their bees, hired out one of their sons as a laborer and took his wages in advance; borrowed the rest from a brother-in-law, and so scraped together half the purchase money.

Having done this, Pakhom chose out a farm of forty acres, some of it wooded, and went to the lady to bargain for it. They came to an agreement, and he shook hands with her upon it and paid her a deposit in advance. Then they went to town and signed the deeds; he paying half the price down, and undertaking to pay the remainder within two years.

So now Pakhom had land of his own. He borrowed seed, and sowed it on the land he had bought. The harvest was a good one, and within a year he had managed to pay off his debts both to the lady and to his brother-in-law. So he became a landowner, ploughing and sowing his own land, making hay on his own land, cutting his own trees, and feeding his cattle on his own pasture. When he went out to plough his fields, or to look at his growing corn, or at his grass-meadows, his heart would fill with joy. The grass that grew and the flowers that bloomed there seemed to him unlike any that grew elsewhere. Formerly, when he had passed by that land, it had appeared the same as any other land, but now it seemed quite different.

III

So Pakhom was well-contented, and everything would have been right if the neighboring peasants would only not have **trespassed** on his corn-fields and meadows. He appealed to them most civilly, but they still went on: now the communal herdsmen would let the village cows stray into his meadows, then horses from the night pasture would get among his corn. Pakhom turned them out again and again, and forgave their owners, and for a long time he forbore[3] to prosecute any one. But at last he lost patience and complained to the district court. He knew it was the peasants' want of land, and no evil intent on their part, that caused the trouble, but he thought:

"I cannot go on overlooking it or they will destroy all I have. They must be taught a lesson."

So he had them up, gave them one lesson, and then another, and two or three of the peasants were fined. After a time Pakhom's neighbors began to bear him a grudge for this, and would now and then let their cattle on to his land on purpose. One peasant even got into Pakhom's wood at night and cut down five young lime trees

---

3. *Forbore* means "refrained from or held back."

Vocabulary

trespass (tres′pəs) *v.* illegally enter property

for their bark. Pakhom passing through the wood one day noticed something white. He came nearer and saw the stripped trunks lying on the ground, and close by stood the stumps where the trees had been. Pakhom was furious.

"If he had only cut one here and there it would have been bad enough," thought Pakhom, "but the rascal has actually cut down a whole clump. If I could only find out who did this, I would pay him out."[4]

He racked his brains as to who it could be. Finally he decided: "It must be Simon—no one else could have done it." So he went to Simon's homestead to have a look round, but he found nothing, and only had an angry scene. However, he now felt more certain than ever that Simon had done it, and he lodged a complaint. Simon was summoned. The case was tried, and retried, and at the end of it all Simon was acquitted, there being no evidence against him. Pakhom felt still more aggrieved, and let his anger loose upon the elder and the judges.

"You let thieves grease your palms," said he. "If you were honest folk yourselves you would not let a thief go free."

So Pakhom quarrelled with the judges and with his neighbors. Threats to burn his building began to be uttered. So though Pakhom had more land, his place in the commune was much worse than before.

About this time a rumor got about that many people were moving to new parts.

"There's no need for me to leave my land," thought Pakhom. "But some of the others might leave our village and then there would be more room for us. I would take over their land myself and make my estate a bit bigger. I could then live more

The Wheat Harvest, 1914. Sinaida Yewgenyevna Serebryakova. Oil sketch. Private collection.

View the Art Serebryakova spent much of her youth at her family's country estate, Neskuchnoye. It was there that she first became captivated by the life of peasants. What do you think these peasants' lives are like? How might they be similar to the lives of the peasants in the story?

at ease. As it is, I am still too cramped to be comfortable."

One day Pakhom was sitting at home when a peasant, passing through the village, happened to call in. He was allowed to stay the night, and supper was given him. Pakhom had a talk with this peasant and asked him where he came from. The stranger answered that he came from beyond the Volga,[5] where he had been working. One word led to another, and the man went on to say that many people were settling in those parts. He told how some people from his village had settled there. They had joined the commune, and had had twenty-five acres per man granted them. The land was so good, he said, that the rye

---

4. To *pay him out* means that Pakhom wants to hurt the person for the wrong he has done.

Make Inferences About Theme *What does this passage suggest about how Pakhom's possessions are affecting his life?*

5. The *Volga* is a river in western Russia.

sown on it grew as high as a horse, and so thick that five cuts of a sickle made a sheaf. One peasant, he said, had brought nothing with him but his bare hands, and now he had six horses and two cows of his own.

Pakhom's heart kindled with desire. He thought:

"Why should I suffer in this narrow hole, if one can live so well elsewhere? I will sell my land and my homestead here, and with the money I will start afresh over there and get everything new. In this crowded place one is always having trouble. But I must first go and find out all about it myself."

Towards summer he got ready and started. He went down the Volga on a steamer to Samara,[6] then walked another three hundred miles on foot, and at last reached the place. It was just as the stranger had said. The peasants had plenty of land: every man had twenty-five acres of communal land given him for his use, and any one who had money could buy, besides, at two shillings an acre as much good freehold[7] land as he wanted.

Having found out all he wished to know, Pakhom returned home as autumn came on, and began selling off his belongings. He sold his land at a profit, sold his homestead and all his cattle, and withdrew from membership of the commune. He only waited till the spring, and then started with his family for the new settlement.

IV

As soon as Pakhom and his family reached their new abode, he applied for admission into the commune of a large village. He stood treat to the elders[8] and obtained the necessary documents. Five shares of communal land were given him for his own and his sons' use: that is to say—125 acres (not all together, but in different fields) besides the use of the communal pasture. Pakhom put up the buildings he needed, and bought cattle. Of the communal land alone he had three times as much as at his former home, and the land was good cornland. He was ten times better off than he had been. He had plenty of **arable** land and pasturage, and could keep as many head of cattle as he liked.

At first, in the bustle of building and settling down, Pakhom was pleased with it all, but when he got used to it he began to think that even here he had not enough land. The first year, he sowed wheat on his share of the communal land and had a good crop. He wanted to go on sowing wheat, but had not enough communal land for the purpose, and what he had already used was not available; for in those parts wheat is only sown on virgin soil or on fallow land.[9] It is sown for one or two years, and then the land lies fallow till it is again overgrown with prairie grass. There were many who wanted such land and there was not enough for all; so that people quarrelled about it. Those who were better off wanted it for growing wheat, and those who were poor wanted it to let to dealers, so that they might raise money to pay their taxes. Pakhom wanted to sow more wheat, so he rented land from a

---

6. *Samara* is a city on the Volga.
7. Pakhom could purchase and then sell *freehold* land to anyone he liked.

Realism and Modernism *How does this passage reflect economic changes during this period in Russia?*

8. When Pakhom *stood treat to the elders,* he treated the elder members of the council to food and drink.
9. *Virgin soil* is land that has never been farmed; *fallow land* is land that is being rested after producing a harvest.

Structure *What pattern of behavior is Pakhom beginning to exhibit? What problems might this cause later?*

dealer for a year. He sowed much wheat and had a fine crop, but the land was too far from the village—the wheat had to be carted more than ten miles. After a time Pakhom noticed that some peasant-dealers were living on separate farms and were growing wealthy; and he thought:

"If I were to buy some freehold land and have a homestead on it, it would be a different thing altogether. Then it would all be nice and compact."

The question of buying freehold land recurred to him again and again.

He went on in the same way for three years, renting land and sowing wheat. The seasons turned out well and the crops were good, so that he began to lay money by. He might have gone on living contentedly, but he grew tired of having to rent other people's land every year, and having to scramble for it. Wherever there was good land to be had, the peasants would rush for it and it was taken up at once, so that unless you were sharp about it you got none. It happened in the third year that he and a dealer together rented a piece of pasture land from some peasants; and they had already ploughed it up, when there was some dispute and the peasants went to law about it, and things fell out so that the labor was all lost.

"If it were my own land," thought Pakhom, "I should be independent, and there would not be all this unpleasantness."

So Pakhom began looking out for land which he could buy; and he came across a peasant who had bought thirteen hundred acres, but having got into difficulties was willing to sell again cheap. Pakhom bargained and haggled with him, and at last they settled the price at 1,500 rubles, part in cash and part to be paid later. They had all but clinched the matter when a passing dealer happened to stop at Pakhom's one day to get a feed for his horses. He drank tea with Pakhom and they had a talk. The dealer said that he was just returning from the land of the Bashkirs,[10] far away, where he had bought thirteen thousand acres of land, all for 1,000 rubles. Pakhom questioned him further, and the tradesman said:

"All one need do is to make friends with the chiefs. I gave away about one hundred rubles worth of silk robes and carpets, besides a case of tea, and I gave wine to those who would drink it; and I got the land for less than a penny an acre." And he showed Pakhom the title-deeds, saying:

"The land lies near a river, and the whole prairie is virgin soil."

Pakhom plied him with questions, and the tradesman said:

"There is more land there than you could cover if you walked a year, and it all belongs to the Bashkirs. They are as simple as sheep, and land can be got almost for nothing."

"There now," thought Pakhom, "with my one thousand rubles, why should I get only thirteen hundred acres, and saddle myself with a debt besides? If I take it out there, I can get more than ten times as much for the money."

Pakhom inquired how to get to the place, and as soon as the tradesman had left him, he prepared to go there himself. He left his wife to look after the homestead, and started on his journey taking his man[11]

---

10. The *Bashkirs* (bäsh´kērs) are a nomadic people of western Russia.
11. Pakhom's *man* is his male servant.

Make Inferences About Theme *What causes Pakhom's discontent?*

Make Inferences About Theme *The title of this story is a question. How might Pakhom answer it at this point?*

with him. They stopped at a town on their way and bought a case of tea, some wine, and other presents, as the tradesman had advised. On and on they went until they had gone more than three hundred miles, and on the seventh day they came to a place where the Bashkirs had pitched their tents. It was all just as the tradesman had said. The people lived on the steppes,[12] by a river, in felt-covered tents. They neither tilled the ground, nor ate bread. Their cattle and horses grazed in herds on the steppe. The colts were tethered behind the tents, and the mares were driven to them twice a day. The mares were milked, and from the milk kumiss[13] was made. It was the women who prepared kumiss, and they also made cheese. As far as the men were concerned, drinking kumiss and tea, eating mutton, and playing on their pipes, was all they cared about. They were all stout and merry, and all the summer long they never thought of doing any work. They were quite ignorant, and knew no Russian, but were good-natured enough.

As soon as they saw Pakhom, they came out of their tents and gathered round their visitor. An interpreter was found, and Pakhom told them he had come about some land. The Bashkirs seemed very glad; they took Pakhom and led him into one of the best tents, where they made him sit on some down cushions placed on a carpet, while they sat round him. They gave him some tea and kumiss, and had a sheep killed, and gave him mutton to eat. Pakhom took presents out of his cart and distributed them among the Bashkirs, and divided the tea amongst them. The Bashkirs were delighted. They talked a great deal among themselves, and then told the interpreter to translate.

"They wish to tell you," said the interpreter, "that they like you, and that it is our custom to do all we can to please a guest and to repay him for his gifts. You have given us presents, now tell us which of the things we possess please you best, that we may present them to you."

"What pleases me best here," answered Pakhom, "is your land. Our land is crowded and the soil is exhausted; but you have plenty of land and it is good land. I never saw the like of it."

The interpreter translated. The Bashkirs talked among themselves for a while. Pakhom could not understand what they were saying, but saw that they were much amused and that they shouted and laughed. Then they were silent and looked at Pakhom while the interpreter said:

"They wish me to tell you that in return for your presents they will gladly give you as much land as you want. You have only to point it out with your hand and it is yours."

The Bashkirs talked again for a while and began to dispute. Pakhom asked what they were disputing about, and the interpreter told him that some of them thought they ought to ask their chief about the land and not act in his absence, while others thought there was no need to wait for his return.

VI

While the Bashkirs were disputing, a man in a large fox-fur cap appeared on the scene. They all became silent and rose to

---

12. *Steppes* are vast land areas and are usually level and treeless.
13. *Kumiss* (koo´mis) is a beverage made from fermented horse milk.

Structure *Here and elsewhere in section V, Tolstoy describes a way of life very different from Pakhom's. How does Tolstoy use the compare-contrast structure to develop the story?*

Make Inferences About Theme *Describe the Bashkirs' attitude toward land ownership.*

Landscape. I.S. Ostroukhov (Russiaian, 1858-1929). Oil on Canvas, 17 1/2 x 23 in. Private collection.

their feet. The interpreter said, "This is our chief himself."

Pakhom immediately fetched the best dressing-gown and five pounds of tea, and offered these to the chief. The chief accepted them, and seated himself in the place of honor. The Bashkirs at once began telling him something. The chief listened for a while, then made a sign with his head for them to be silent, and addressing himself to Pakhom, said in Russian:

"Well, let it be so. Choose whatever piece of land you like; we have plenty of it."

"How can I take as much as I like?" thought Pakhom. "I must get a deed to make it secure, or else they may say, 'It is yours,' and afterwards may take it away again."

"Thank you for your kind words," he said aloud. "You have much land, and I only want a little. But I should like to be sure which bit is mine. Could it not be measured and made over[14] to me? Life and death are in God's hands. You good people give it to me, but your children might wish to take it away again."

"You are quite right," said the chief. "We will make it over to you."

"I heard that a dealer had been here," continued Pakhom, "and that you gave him a little land, too, and signed title-deeds to that effect. I should like to have it done in the same way."

The chief understood.

---

14. Here, *made over* means "legally changed from one owner to another."

"Yes," replied he, "that can be done quite easily. We have a scribe,[15] and we will go to town with you and have the deed properly sealed."

"And what will be the price?" asked Pakhom.

"Our price is always the same: one thousand rubles a day."

Pakhom did not understand.

"A day? What measure is that? How many acres would that be?"

"We do not know how to reckon it out," said the chief. "We sell it by the day. As much as you can go round on your feet in a day is yours, and the price is one thousand rubles a day."

Pakhom was surprised.

"But in a day you can get round a large tract of land," he said.

The chief laughed.

"It will all be yours!" said he. "But there is one condition: If you don't return on the same day to the spot whence you started, your money is lost."

"But how am I to mark the way that I have gone?"

"Why, we shall go to any spot you like, and stay there. You must start from that spot and make your round, taking a spade with you. Wherever you think necessary, make a mark. At every turning, dig a hole and pile up the turf; then afterwards we will go round with a plough from hole to hole. You may make as large a circuit as you please, but before the sun sets you must return to the place you started from. All the land you cover will be yours."

Pakhom was delighted. It was decided to start early next morning. They talked a while, and after drinking some more kumiss and eating some more mutton, they had tea again, and then the night came on. They gave Pakhom a feather bed to sleep on, and the Bashkirs **dispersed** for the night, promising to assemble the next morning at daybreak and ride out before sunrise to the appointed spot.

VII

Pakhom lay on the feather bed, but could not sleep. He kept thinking about the land.

"What a large tract I will mark off!" thought he. "I can easily do thirty-five miles in a day. The days are long now, and within a circuit of thirty-five miles what a lot of land there will be! I will sell the poorer land, or let it to peasants, but I'll pick out the best and farm it. I will buy two ox teams, and hire two more laborers. About a hundred and fifty acres shall be ploughland, and I will pasture cattle on the rest."

Pakhom lay awake all night, and dozed off only just before dawn. Hardly were his eyes closed when he had a dream. He thought he was lying in that same tent and heard somebody chuckling outside. He wondered who it could be, and rose and went out, and he saw the Bashkir chief sitting in front of the tent holding his sides and rolling about with laughter. Going nearer to the chief, Pakhom asked: "What are you laughing at?" But he saw that it was no longer the chief, but the dealer who had recently stopped at his house and had told him about the land. Just as Pakhom was going to ask, "Have you been here long?" he saw that it was not the dealer, but the peasant who had come up from the Volga, long ago, to Pakhom's old home. Then he saw that it was not the peasant

---

15. Here, a *scribe* is an official secretary or recorder of legal documents.

Make Inferences About Theme *What bargain does the chief strike with Pakhom? How do you think Pakhom will respond?*

Vocabulary

disperse (dis purs´) v. scatter or spread in many directions

either, but the Devil himself with hoofs and horns, sitting there and chuckling, and before him lay a man barefoot, prostrate on the ground, with only trousers and a shirt on. And Pakhom dreamt that he looked more attentively to see what sort of a man it was that was lying there, and he saw that the man was dead, and that it was himself! He awoke horror-struck.

"What things one does dream," thought he.

Looking round he saw through the open door that the dawn was breaking.

"It's time to wake them up," thought he. "We ought to be starting."

He got up, roused his man (who was sleeping in his cart), bade him harness; and went to call the Bashkirs.

"It's time to go to the steppe to measure the land," he said.

The Bashkirs rose and assembled, and the chief came too. Then they began drinking kumiss again, and offered Pakhom some tea, but he would not wait.

"If we are to go, let us go. It is high time," said he.

VIII

The Bashkirs got ready and they all started: some mounted on horses, and some in carts. Pakhom drove in his own small cart with his servant and took a spade with him. When they reached the steppe, the morning red was beginning to kindle. They ascended a hillock (called by the Bashkirs a *shikhan*) and dismounting from their carts and their horses, gathered in one spot. The chief came up to Pakhom and stretching out his arm towards the plain;

"See," said he, "all this, as far as your eye can reach, is ours. You may have any part of it you like."

Pakhom's eyes glistened: it was all virgin soil, as flat as the palm of your hand, as black as the seed of a poppy, and in the hollows different kinds of grasses grew breast high.

The chief took off his fox-fur cap, placed it on the ground and said:

"This will be the mark. Start from here, and return here again. All the land you go round shall be yours."

Pakhom took out his money and put it on the cap. Then he took off his outer coat, remaining in his sleeveless undercoat. He unfastened his girdle[16] and tied it tight below his stomach, put a little bag of bread into the breast of his coat, and tying a flask of water to his girdle, he drew up the tops of his boots, took the spade from his man, and stood ready to start. He considered for some moments which way he had better go—it was tempting everywhere.

"No matter," he concluded, "I will go towards the rising sun."

He turned his face to the east, stretched himself, and waited for the sun to appear above the rim.

"I must lose no time," he thought, "and it is easier walking while it is still cool."

The sun's rays had hardly flashed above the horizon, before Pakhom, carrying the spade over his shoulder, went down into the steppe.

Pakhom started walking neither slowly nor quickly. After having gone a thousand yards he stopped, dug a hole, and placed pieces of turf one on another to make it more visible. Then he went on; and now that he had walked off his stiffness he quickened his pace. After a while he dug another hole.

Structure *The author reveals an essential element of the story through a dream sequence. What is revealed? How is it important?*

---

16. Here, a *girdle* is a length of cloth used as a belt or back support.

Pakhom looked back. The hillock could be distinctly seen in the sunlight, with the people on it, and the glittering tyres of the cartwheels. At a rough guess Pakhom concluded that he had walked three miles. It was growing warmer; he took off his undercoat, flung it across his shoulder, and went on again. It had grown quite warm now; he looked at the sun, it was time to think of breakfast.

"The first shift is done, but there are four in a day, and it is too soon yet to turn. But I will just take off my boots," said he to himself.

He sat down, took off his boots, stuck them into his girdle, and went on. It was easy walking now.

"I will go on for another three miles," thought he, "and then turn to the left. This spot is so fine, that it would be a pity to lose it. The further one goes, the better the land seems."

He went straight on for a while, and when he looked round, the hillock was scarcely visible and the people on it looked like black ants, and he could just see something glistening there in the sun.

"Ah," thought Pakhom, "I have gone far enough in this direction, it is time to turn. Besides I am in a regular sweat, and very thirsty."

He stopped, dug a large hole, and heaped up pieces of turf. Next he untied his flask, had a drink, and then turned sharply to the left. He went on and on; the grass was high, and it was very hot.

Pakhom began to grow tired: he looked at the sun and saw that it was noon.

"Well," he thought, "I must have a rest."

He sat down, and ate some bread and drank some water; but he did not lie down, thinking that if he did he might fall asleep. After sitting a little while, he went on again. At first he walked easily: the food had strengthened him; but it had become terribly hot and he felt sleepy, still he went on, thinking: "An hour to suffer, a lifetime to live."

He went a long way in this direction also, and was about to turn to the left again, when he perceived a damp hollow: "It would be a pity to leave that out," he thought. "Flax would do well there." So he went on past the hollow, and dug a hole on the other side of it before he turned the corner. Pakhom looked towards the hillock. The heat made the air hazy: it seemed to be quivering, and through the haze the people on the hillock could scarcely be seen.

"Ah!" thought Pakhom, "I have made the sides too long; I must make this one shorter." And he went along the third side, stepping faster. He looked at the sun: it was nearly halfway to the horizon, and he had not yet done two miles of the third side of the square. He was still ten miles from the goal.

"No," he thought, "though it will make my land lopsided, I must hurry back in a straight line now. I might go too far, and as it is I have a great deal of land."

So Pakhom hurriedly dug a hole, and turned straight towards the hillock.

IX

Pakhom went straight towards the hillock, but he now walked with difficulty. He was done up with the heat, his bare feet were cut and bruised, and his legs began to fail. He longed to rest, but it was impossible if he meant to get back before sunset. The sun waits for no man, and it was sinking lower and lower.

"Oh dear," he thought, "if only I have not blundered trying for too much! What if I am too late?"

Make Inferences About Theme *Why does Pakhom keep changing his plans?*

Literary Element | Structure

ACT Skills Practice

When does Pakhom know he will die and never use the land he worked so hard to gain?

A. when the dealer tells him about the Bashkirs

B. when the chief tells him he can have the land he can walk around in a day

C. when he is running toward the hillock and remembers his dream

D. when the Bashkirs wave at him to hurry back

Review: Irony

As you learned on page 291, **irony** is a contrast between appearance and reality or between expectation and outcome. **Situational irony** occurs when something happens that is different from what the characters, readers, or audience expect. **Dramatic irony** occurs when the reader or audience knows something a character does not.

Partner Activity Meet with a classmate and discuss the use of irony in this story. Working together, complete a chart like the one below. Fill it in with examples of irony. Then tell what type of irony each one is and explain how you know.

Example	Type	Explanation
The Devil overhears Pakhom's boast.	Dramatic	The reader knows about it, but Pakhom does not.
Pakhom dies just as he reaches his goal.		

LOG ON ▶ **Literature** Online

Selection Resources For Selection Quizzes, eFlash-cards, and Reading-Writing Connection activities, go to **glencoe.com** and enter QuickPass code GLW6053u5.

Reading Strategy | Make Inferences About Theme

This story is an **allegory**, a story in which the characters, settings, and events represent ideas or qualities beyond themselves. The theme of this story is the answer to the question posed in the title. Review the chart you made on page 984.

1. What do the Bashkirs represent? What does Pakhom represent?

2. What values do you think Tolstoy is trying to teach?

Vocabulary Practice

Practice with Context Clues Look back at pages 985–996 to find context clues for the boldfaced vocabulary words below. Record your findings in a chart like the one here.

disparage	discord	trespass
arable	disperse	

EXAMPLE:

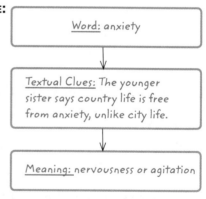

Word: anxiety

↓

Textual Clues: The younger sister says country life is free from anxiety, unlike city life.

↓

Meaning: nervousness or agitation

Academic Vocabulary

*In this short story, Tolstoy makes an **assessment** about the destructive power of greed.*

Assessment is an academic term. A synonym for *assessment* is *evaluation*. To further explore the meaning of this word, answer the following question: What might a teacher look for when doing an assessment of a student's writing?

For more on academic vocabulary, see pages 36–37 and R83–R85.

Respond Through Writing

Persuasive Essay

Argue a Position "How Much Land Does a Man Need?" has the effect of a parable, a story that teaches a moral lesson. The lesson of Pakhom's fate seems to be about the danger of greed. However, some readers might see him as ambitious and independent. Write a 1,500-word persuasive essay that supports or challenges Tolstoy's lesson.

Understand the Task A **persuasive essay** expresses a writer's opinion and tries to make readers agree and perhaps even take action.

Prewrite Before you draft your essay, use a chart like the one below to organize arguments for and against the lesson of Tolstoy's story. Then, decide which position seems stronger.

Arguments for Tolstoy's Lesson	Arguments Against Tolstoy's Lesson
Ambitious individuals often create envy and resentment that damages community life.	Without ambitious individuals, the economic life of a community stagnates.

Draft To persuade your audience that your position is valid, provide reasons in your body paragraphs and support them with evidence. In your conclusion, summarize your position and end with a call to action.

Revise In your revision, you may want to strengthen your arguments with appeals to ethics or emotions. For example, you might ask readers to think about how the pioneer spirit affected American history:

What would have happened to the future of the United States if Americans had just stopped at the Mississippi River, unwilling to face the challenges of the prairies, mountains, and deserts?

Use the rubric on page 834 of the Writing Workshop on persuasive speeches to check other elements of your review.

Edit and Proofread Proofread your paper, correcting any errors in spelling, grammar, and punctuation. Use the word count feature on your computer to check that your essay is 1,500 words. Review the Grammar Tip in the side column for information on sentence structure.

Main and Subordinate Clauses

A **main clause** contains a subject and predicate and can stand alone as a complete sentence. A **subordinate clause** contains a subject and predicate but does not express a complete thought.

Tip

You can identify a subordinate clause by looking for a subordinating conjunction or a relative pronoun followed by a subject and a predicate.

Subordinating Conjunctions	Relative Pronouns
after	that
as	whatever
because	which
before	whichever
since	who
unless	whom
until	whoever
when	whose

Language Handbook

For more on **main and subordinate clauses,** see Language Handbook, pp. R40–R59.

Literature Online

Grammar For more Grammar practice, go to glencoe.com and enter QuickPass code GLW6053u5.

Grammar Workshop

Main and Subordinate Clauses

Literature Connection The following sentence by Leo Tolstoy uses both a main and a subordinate clause: "While the Bashkirs were disputing, a man in a large fox-fur cap appeared on the scene."

A **main clause** contains a subject and a predicate, expresses a complete thought, and can stand alone as a sentence. A **subordinate clause** contains a subject and a predicate, but does not express a complete thought and cannot stand alone as a sentence. In the sentence above, *a man in a large fox-fur cap appeared on the scene* is the main clause. *While the Bashkirs were disputing* is the subordinate clause. Three types of subordinate clauses are described below.

Adverb Clauses An adverb clause modifies a verb, adjective, or another adverb from the main clause. Adverb clauses are usually signaled by **subordinating conjunctions,** such as *because, until,* and *when.*

> <u>Because he wanted all of the land,</u> Pakhom walked as far as he could.

[The underlined adverb clause modifies the verb *walked*.]

Adjective Clauses An adjective clause modifies a noun or pronoun from the main clause of the sentence. Adjective clauses are usually signaled by relative pronouns, such as *who, what,* or *that.*

> The eldest sister, <u>who lived in the city,</u> bragged about her life.

[The underlined adjective clause modifies the noun *sister.*]

Noun Clauses A noun clause is a special kind of subordinate clause that functions as a noun *within* a main clause. Noun clauses are usually signaled by relative pronouns.

> <u>What Pakhom did</u> was foolish.

[The underlined noun clause is the subject of the verb *was.*]

Proofread Identify the main and subordinate clauses in each of the following sentences. Then identify whether the subordinate clause is an adverb clause, an adjective clause, or a noun clause.

1. Pakhom, who lived in the village, was proud of his way of life.
2. When he saw the sun beginning to sink, Pakhom started to walk faster.
3. Greedy people often lose what they have.

Before You Read

The Bet

Meet **Anton Chekhov**
(1860–1904)

> "*The artist is not meant to be a judge of his characters and what they say; his only job is to be an impartial witness.*"
>
> —Anton Chekhov

As a doctor, the Russian author Anton Chekhov (chek′ ôf) saw many sides of the human experience in his brief life. His stories and plays reveal not only what life was like during his lifetime, but what it means to be human in any era.

A Childhood Without Childhood "The father of the modern short story," Anton Pavlovich Chekhov was born in a seaport town in southern Russia. Chekhov recalls his father as a stern figure who tyrannized young Anton and his two older brothers. Chekhov's mother, on the other hand, was a wonderful storyteller who passed along to him her gift for words. The family struggled financially for years, and Chekhov's father fled to Moscow in 1875 to escape his debts. Chekhov stayed behind with his mother and younger siblings to finish his schooling. Before long, his mother lost the house to an unscrupulous local bureaucrat and

joined her husband in Moscow. Chekhov eked out a living by tutoring younger pupils at his school. Life was difficult; as he wrote later, "There was no childhood in my childhood." His luck improved, however, when he won a scholarship to study medicine at Moscow University.

Writing from Necessity While he was still a student, Chekhov published a series of short fictional sketches in humor magazines. He wrote less out of love for the craft than to ease the financial hardship of his family. However, it was in these short pieces that some of his lifelong subjects began to emerge. His stories often feature the petty tyranny of government bureaucrats and other authority figures, the suffering of the poor, and the ironies inherent in human relationships. Chekhov became wildly popular as a humorist. Though continuing his medical practice, Chekhov gradually became more comfortable with his literary work. Medicine eventually took a back seat to writing.

A Man of the Theater In 1887 Chekhov began working on a play that he later titled *Ivanov*. It was produced to great acclaim later the same year. Chekhov responded to this latest success with characteristic modesty—he left town. Over the next seventeen years, however, he penned the four masterworks that would make him famous: *The Seagull* (1896), *Uncle Vanya* (1897), *Three Sisters* (1901), and *The Cherry Orchard* (1904). Chekhov also fell in love with an actress, Olga Knipper. They were married in 1901, even though Chekhov had tuberculosis. His illness worsened over the next three years and finally took his life, silencing one of Russia's literary giants.

Literature Online

Author Search For more about Anton Chekhov, go to glencoe.com and enter QuickPass code GLW6053u5.

Literature and Reading Preview

Connect to the Story

Have you ever spent a long period of time alone? How is isolation good and bad for a person? Write a journal entry that describes your thoughts during your period of isolation.

Build Background

Chekhov achieved great fame and popularity in Russia, but by the 1880s many critics began to rebuke him for his failure to espouse a political point of view. Although he was the grandson of serfs, Chekhov never became a political writer. He preferred to explore the details of human experience. As his writing matured, his themes encompassed more humanitarian issues, such as starvation or marital and child abandonment.

Set Purposes for Reading

Big Idea Realism and Modernism

As you read "The Bet," ask yourself, How do Chekhov's ordinary characters reveal the complexities of human behavior?

Literary Element Character

A **character** is a person portrayed in a literary work. A **main character** is central to the story and is typically fully developed. A **minor character** displays few personality traits. As you read "The Bet," ask yourself, Why does the author never give names to the two main characters?

Reading Strategy Analyze Cause-and-Effect Relationships

A **cause-and-effect relationship** always deals with the question "Why?" Sometimes a cause-and-effect relationship can have a single cause and a single effect. Other times, an effect causes other effects in a **causal chain**. Identifying these relationships can help you better understand what you read. As you read, ask yourself, Why did each event happen?

....

Tip: Use a Graphic Organizer Use a graphic organizer like the one below to track the chain of causes and effects as you read.

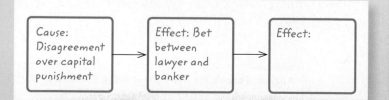

Learning Objectives

For pages 1001–1011

In studying this text, you will focus on the following objectives:

Literary Study: Analyzing character.

Reading: Analyzing cause-and-effect relationships.

Vocabulary

humane (hū mān′) *adj.* marked by compassion, sympathy, or consideration for humans or animals; p. 1003 *Annie is very humane; she treats all animals kindly.*

compulsory (kəm pul′sər ē) *adj.* mandatory; enforced; p. 1004 *To graduate to the next level, students took a compulsory test.*

indiscriminately (in′dis krim′ə nit lē) *adv.* randomly; haphazardly; p. 1006 *In trying to get the driver's attention, the police officer waved her arms indiscriminately.*

emaciated (i mā′shē āt id) *adj.* thin and feeble; p. 1007 *The elderly man was so emaciated he looked like a skeleton.*

ethereal (i thēr′ē əl) *adj.* otherworldly; p. 1008 *Her pale face looked ethereal in the moonlight.*

....

Tip: Connotation and Denotation The **connotation** of a word is its suggested or implied meaning. The **denotation** is its literal definition. For example, *thin* means *emaciated,* but *emaciated* has a stronger connotation than *thin.*

The Bet

Anton Chekhov
Translated by Constance Garnett

The Artist's Dinner Party, 1903. Viggo Johansen. Oil on canvas. National Museum, Stockholm, Sweden.

I

It was a dark autumn night. The old banker was walking up and down his study and remembering how, fifteen years before, he had given a party one autumn evening.

There had been many clever men there, and there had been interesting conversations. Among other things they had talked of capital punishment. The majority of the guests, among whom were many journalists and intellectual men, disapproved of the death penalty.

They considered that form of punishment out of date, immoral, and unsuitable for Christian States. In the opinion of some of them the death penalty ought to be replaced everywhere by imprisonment for life.

"I don't agree with you," said their host the banker. "I have not tried either the death penalty or imprisonment for life, but if one may judge à *priori*,[1] the death penalty is more moral and more **humane** than imprisonment for life. Capital punishment kills a man at once, but lifelong imprisonment kills him slowly. Which executioner is the more humane, he who kills you in a few minutes or he who drags the life out of you in the course of many years?"

"Both are equally immoral," observed one of the guests, "for they both have the same object—to take away life. The State is not God. It has not the right to take away what it cannot restore when it wants to."

---

1. *À priori* (ā′ prī ôr′ī) is a Latin term referring to reasoning based on ideas assumed to be true.

Among the guests was a young lawyer, a young man of five-and-twenty. When he was asked his opinion, he said:

"The death sentence and the life sentence are equally immoral, but if I had to choose between the death penalty and imprisonment for life, I would certainly choose the second. To live anyhow is better than not at all."

A lively discussion arose. The banker, who was younger and more nervous in those days,[2] was suddenly carried away by excitement; he struck the table with his fist and shouted at the young man:

"It's not true! I'll bet you two millions you wouldn't stay in solitary confinement for five years."

"If you mean that in earnest," said the young man, "I'll take a bet, but I would stay not five but fifteen years."

"Fifteen? Done!" cried the banker. "Gentlemen, I stake two millions!"

"Agreed! You stake your millions and I stake my freedom!" said the young man.

And this wild, senseless bet was carried out! The banker, spoiled and frivolous, with millions beyond his reckoning, was delighted at the bet. At supper he made fun of the young man, and said:

"Think better of it, young man, while there is still time. To me two millions are a trifle, but you are losing three or four of the best years of your life. I say three or four, because you won't stay longer. Don't forget either, you unhappy man, that voluntary confinement is a great deal harder to bear than **compulsory**. The thought that you have the right to step out in liberty at any moment will poison your whole existence in prison. I am sorry for you."

And now the banker, walking to and fro, remembered all this, and asked himself: "What was the object of that bet? What is the good of that man's losing fifteen years of his life and my throwing away two millions? Can it prove that the death penalty is better or worse than imprisonment for life? No, no. It was all nonsensical and meaningless. On my part it was the caprice of a pampered man, and on his part simple greed for money. . . ."

Then he remembered what followed that evening. It was decided that the young man should spend the years of his captivity under the strictest supervision in one of the lodges in the banker's garden. It was agreed that for fifteen years he should not be free to cross the threshold of the lodge, to see human beings, to hear the human voice, or to receive letters and newspapers. He was allowed to have a musical instrument and books, and was allowed to write letters, to drink wine, and to smoke. By the terms of the agreement, the only relations he could have with the outer world were by a little window made purposely for that object. He might have anything he wanted—books, music, wine, and so on—in any quantity he desired by writing an order, but could only receive them through the window. The agreement provided for every detail and every trifle that would make his imprisonment strictly solitary, and bound the young

---

2. Even as he grew old, however, the banker continued to take risks with his money.

Analyze Cause-and-Effect Relationships *If the effect of the exchange between the lawyer and the banker is the bet itself, what is the cause?*

Character *Based on his opinion and the way he speaks, what assumptions can you make about the banker?*

Analyze Cause-and-Effect Relationships *What single cause does the banker assume will bring about the lawyer's losing the bet?*

Vocabulary

compulsory (kəm pul′sər ē) *adj.* mandatory; enforced

Evening in the Ukraine, 1878. Arkhip Ivanovich Kuindzhi. Oil on canvas, 81 x 163 cm.
State Russian Museum, St. Petersburg.

View the Art Arkhip Kuindzhi, a nineteenth-century landscape painter, was fascinated by the almost concrete effects of light. How might the setting of this painting be similar to the setting of the story?

man to stay there *exactly* fifteen years, beginning from twelve o'clock of November 14, 1870, and ending at twelve o'clock of November 14, 1885. The slightest attempt on his part to break the conditions, if only two minutes before the end, released the banker from the obligation to pay him two millions.

For the first year of his confinement, as far as one could judge from his brief notes, the prisoner suffered severely from loneliness and depression. The sounds of the piano could be heard continually day and night from his lodge. He refused wine and tobacco. Wine, he wrote, excites the desires, and desires are the worst foes of the prisoner; and besides, nothing could be more dreary than drinking good wine and seeing no one. And tobacco spoilt the air of his room. In the first year the books he

sent for were principally of a light character; novels with a complicated love plot, sensational and fantastic stories, and so on.

In the second year the piano was silent in the lodge, and the prisoner asked only for the classics. In the fifth year music was audible again, and the prisoner asked for wine. Those who watched him through the window said that all that year he spent doing nothing but eating and drinking and lying on his bed, frequently yawning and angrily talking to himself. He did not read books. Sometimes at night he would sit down to write; he would spend hours writing, and in the morning tear up all that he had written. More than once he could be heard crying.

In the second half of the sixth year the prisoner began zealously studying languages, philosophy, and history. He threw himself eagerly into these studies—so much so that the banker had enough to do to get him the books he ordered. In the course of four years some six hundred volumes were procured at his request. It was during this period that the banker received the following letter from his prisoner:

"My dear Jailer, I write you these lines in six languages. Show them to people who know the languages. Let them read them. If they find not one mistake I implore you to fire a shot in the garden. That shot will show me that my efforts have not been thrown away. The geniuses of all ages and of all lands speak different languages, but the same flame burns in them all. Oh, if you only knew what unearthly happiness my soul feels now from being able to understand them!" The prisoner's desire was fulfilled. The banker ordered two shots to be fired in the garden.

Then after the tenth year, the prisoner sat immovably at the table and read nothing but the Gospel. It seemed strange to the banker that a man who in four years had mastered six hundred learned volumes should waste nearly a year over one thin book easy of comprehension. Theology and histories of religion followed the Gospels.

In the last two years of his confinement the prisoner read an immense quantity of books quite **indiscriminately**. At one time he was busy with the natural sciences, then he would ask for Byron or Shakespeare. There were notes in which he demanded at the same time books on chemistry, and a manual of medicine, and a novel, and some treatise on philosophy or theology. His

reading suggested a man swimming in the sea among the wreckage of his ship, and trying to save his life by greedily clutching first at one spar and then at another.

------ ◆ **II** ◆ ------

The old banker remembered all this, and thought:

"Tomorrow at twelve o'clock he will regain his freedom. By our agreement I ought to pay him two millions. If I do pay him, it is all over with me: I shall be utterly ruined."

Fifteen years before, his millions had been beyond his reckoning; now he was afraid to ask himself which were greater, his debts or his assets. Desperate gambling on the Stock Exchange, wild speculation, and the excitability which he could not get over even in advancing years, had by degrees led to the decline of his fortune, and the proud, fearless, self-confident millionaire had become a banker of middling rank, trembling at every rise and fall in his investments. "Cursed bet!" muttered the old man, clutching his head in despair. "Why didn't the man die? He is only forty now. He will take my last penny from me, he will marry, will enjoy life, will gamble on the Exchange; while I shall look at him with envy like a beggar, and hear from him every day the same sentence: 'I am indebted to you for the happiness of my life, let me help you!' No, it is too much! The one means of being saved from bankruptcy and disgrace is the death of that man!"

It struck three o'clock, the banker listened; everyone was asleep in the house, and nothing could be heard outside but the

---

Character *What does the lawyer's mastery of languages reveal about his character?*

Vocabulary

indiscriminately (in´dis krim´ə nit lē) *adv.* randomly; haphazardly

Realism and Modernism *How does Chekhov's description of the banker's behavior and motivations reflect the overall sensibilities of Realism?*

rustling of the chilled trees. Trying to make no noise, he took from a fireproof safe the key of the door which had not been opened for fifteen years, put on his overcoat, and went out of the house.

It was dark and cold in the garden. Rain was falling. A damp cutting wind was racing about the garden, howling and giving the trees no rest. The banker strained his eyes, but could see neither the earth nor the white statues, nor the lodge, nor the trees. Going to the spot where the lodge stood, he twice called the watchman. No answer followed. Evidently the watchman had sought shelter from the weather, and was now asleep somewhere either in the kitchen or in the greenhouse.

"If I had the pluck to carry out my intention," thought the old man, "suspicion would fall first upon the watchman."

He felt in the darkness for the steps and the door, and went into the entry of the lodge. Then he groped his way into a little passage and lighted a match. There was not a soul there. There was a bedstead with no bedding on it, and in the corner there was a dark cast-iron stove. The seals on the door leading to the prisoner's rooms were intact.

When the match went out the old man, trembling with emotion, peeped through the little window. A candle was burning dimly in the prisoner's room. He was sitting at the table. Nothing could be seen but his back, the hair on his head, and his hands. Open books were lying on the table, on the two easy chairs, and on the carpet near the table.

Five minutes passed and the prisoner did not once stir. Fifteen years' imprisonment had taught him to sit still. The banker tapped at the window with his finger, and the prisoner made no movement whatever in response. Then the banker cautiously broke the seals off the door and put the key in the keyhole. The rusty lock gave a grating sound and the door creaked. The banker expected to hear at once footsteps and a cry of astonishment, but three minutes passed and it was as quiet as ever in the room. He made up his mind to go in.

At the table a man unlike ordinary people was sitting motionless. He was a skeleton with the skin drawn tight over his bones, with long curls like a woman's, and a shaggy beard. His face was yellow with an earthy tint in it, his cheeks were hollow, his back long and narrow, and the hand on which his shaggy head was propped was so thin and delicate that it was dreadful to look at it. His hair was already streaked with silver, and seeing his **emaciated**, aged-looking face, no one would have believed that he was only forty. He was asleep. . . . In front of his bowed head there lay on the table a sheet of paper on which there was something written in fine handwriting.

"Poor creature!" thought the banker, "he is asleep and most likely dreaming of the millions. And I have only to take this half-dead man, throw him on the bed, stifle him a little with the pillow, and the most conscientious expert would find no sign of a violent death. But let us first read what he has written here. . . ."

The banker took the page from the table and read as follows:

"Tomorrow at twelve o'clock I regain my freedom and the right to associate with other men, but before I leave this room and see the sunshine, I think it necessary to say a few words to you. With a clear conscience I tell you, as before God, who beholds me, that I despise freedom and life and health, and all that in your books is called the good things of the world.

Vocabulary

emaciated (i mā′shē āt id) *adj.* thin and feeble

Literary Element | Character

A **flat character** has only one or two dominant traits. **Round characters** are more fully developed; like real people, there are many sides to their personalities. Characters who change significantly as the plot unfolds are called **dynamic characters.** **Static characters** remain essentially the same, even though their outward circumstances might change. For example, a character who experiences great hardship but remains cheerful throughout a story is a static character.

1. Is the banker a flat or round character? Explain.

2. Is the lawyer a static or dynamic character? Explain.

3. Who are the story's minor characters?

Review: Mood

As you learned on page 713, **mood** is the overall feeling of a literary work. An author's choice of language, subject matter, setting, and tone contribute to the mood. In Chekhov's stories and plays, it often seems that not much is happening. But he creates a strong sense of mood as he explores the inner worlds of his characters and the way they think and live.

Partner Activity With a partner, read the following quotation from the story. Discuss the mood it evokes.

> *"What was the object of that bet? What is the good of a man's losing fifteen years of his life and my throwing away two millions? Can it prove that the death penalty is better or worse than imprisonment for life? No, no. It was all nonsensical and meaningless."*

LOG ON ▶ **Literature** Online

Selection Resources For Selection Quizzes, eFlashcards, and Reading-Writing Connection activities, go to glencoe.com and enter QuickPass code GLW6053u5.

Reading Strategy | Analyze Cause-and-Effect Relationships

SAT Skills Practice

Why did the banker plan to kill the man in the cell?

(A) The banker had to prove that long imprisonment does kill a man.

(B) The banker took out a life insurance policy on the man and needed the money.

(C) The banker was wary of the man's wisdom, gained from years of reading and solitude.

(D) The banker was afraid the man would kill him.

(E) The banker's fortunes had failed in the last fifteen years, and paying his bet would bankrupt him.

Vocabulary Practice

Practice with Denotation and Connotation
Denotation is the dictionary meaning of a word. **Connotation** is its implied meaning. Complete a graphic organizer like this one for each boldfaced vocabulary word.

humane   compulsory   emaciated
ethereal   indiscriminately

EXAMPLE:

> Vocabulary word: zealous → Similar word: eager
>
> Explanation: Zealous has the stronger connotation. A zealous person is very enthusiastic about one thing, and an eager person might not be as enthusiastic.

Academic Vocabulary

The young man in "The Bet" agrees to be **isolated** *from the world for fifteen years.*

Isolated is an academic word with a variety of uses. For example, in chemistry an **isolated** substance is something that has been separated from a mixture. To further explore this word, answer the following question: Have you ever felt **isolated** from other people? Explain.

For more on academic vocabulary, see pages 36–37 and R83–R85.

Respond Through Writing

Summary

Learning Objectives

In this assignment, you will focus on the following objectives:

Writing: Writing a summary.

Grammar: Using absolute phrases.

Report Story Events To fully grasp "The Bet," you need to be able to summarize the events of the story. A **summary** is a short retelling of events in chronological order. Write a summary of "The Bet," telling the main events of the story in proper sequence. Your summary should be about 100 words and should not include your personal feelings, just the facts. Be sure to report the cause-and-effect relationships in the story.

Understand the Task In a **plot summary,** you report the main story events and explain the main conflicts and their resolutions.

Prewrite To help you get organized before you write, refer to the chart you made on page 1002. Then make a cause-and-effect chain to review the key events of the story.

Draft Use your chain to create a time-based structure in your summary. Keep in mind that a summary includes only important details. For instance, you could say that the banker lacks money to pay the bet, but not that he lost money on the Stock Exchange. Here is a summary of Katherine Mansfield's "The Doll's House" (see pages 790–801).

The Burnell sisters receive an exquisite dollhouse, which must be kept in the courtyard. The youngest sister, Kezia, especially loves a tiny lamp in the house. The only girls from school who are not invited to see the dollhouse are the Kelveys, who are shunned because of their low social class. One day when Kezia is alone in the courtyard, the Kelveys come walking down the road. Kezia invites them to look at the dollhouse. While they are looking, Kezia's aunt yells at the children and the Kelveys leave. The younger Kelvey sister, Else, says she saw the lamp Kezia loves.

Revise When you finish your draft, get feedback from someone who has read the story and someone who has not. The person who has read the story should check for inaccuracies in your summary. The person who has not read the story should understand the basic story from your summary. Revise your summary to reflect your readers' comments.

Edit and Proofread Proofread your paper, correcting any errors in spelling, grammar, and punctuation. Review the Grammar Tip in the side column for ideas on using absolute phrases.

> **Grammar Tip**

Absolute Phrases

An absolute phrase modifies an entire sentence, rather than a specific word. These phrases have no grammatical relation to the rest of the sentence, and they consist of nouns or pronouns along with participles and related modifiers. In the following example, the absolute phrase is underlined:

His money depleting, the banker worries how he can pay if he loses the bet.

The lawyer turned to books, his mind reeling in solitude.

In some absolute phrases, the participle *being* is understood rather than stated: *The jail sentence* [being] *over,* the lawyer could have claimed his money.

The Symbolist Poets

I N THE LATE NINETEENTH CENTURY, A GROUP OF FRENCH POETS CREATED daring, emotional poems rich with symbols, or details with both literal and figurative meanings. Known as the Symbolists, these authors revolutionized poetry with their experimental rejection of strict forms and classical subjects.

Baudelaire and Mallarmé

The writings of Charles Baudelaire (bō də lär′) mark a turning point from the Romanticism that dominated poetry in the early 1800s and the emergence of Symbolism later in the century. Like the Romantics, Baudelaire (1821–1867) wrote emotionally charged poetry. However, he disliked Romanticism's direct statement of emotions and its focus on nature. Inspired by the American author Edgar Allan Poe's use of symbols, Baudelaire created rich images to suggest, rather than directly state, the harshness of urban life. Although critics today consider Baudelaire one of the finest nineteenth-century poets, his work appalled many

of his contemporaries. When his collection *The Flowers of Evil* was published in 1857, six of the poems were banned, and Baudelaire was accused of obscenity and blasphemy.

One of the few poets of the day to embrace Baudelaire's sordid urban landscapes was Stéphane Mallarmé (mal′ är mā), who emerged as a leader of the Symbolists. In such works as *Divagations* (1897), Mallarmé (1842–1898) bends language into lines of poetry without clear meaning. Through the use of fantastic images and musical sound patterns, Mallarmé believed poets could give their readers glimpses of deep emotional and mental realities that could not be described directly. He said "To *name* an object is to take away three-fourths of the pleasure given by a poem. The pleasure consists in guessing little by little: to *suggest* it, that is the ideal."

Rimbaud and Verlaine

An arrogant and volatile genius from a young age, Arthur Rimbaud (rom bō′) (1854–1891) saw himself as a poetic "seer," or prophet. Along with his friend Paul Verlaine (vär len), he wanted to break free of the conventional ways poets described the world. Rimbaud created brilliant free verse and prose poems in his teenage years that matched his brash vision. However, Rimbaud left poetry behind before the age of twenty, and in 1875 he began a series of adventures as a merchant and gunrunner in Africa. The following poem exemplifies Rimbaud's use of symbolism.

Seated portrait of symbolist poet Stephane Mallarme. Nadar. Photograph.

My Bohemia

A Fantasy

Arthur Rimbaud
Translated by Wyatt Mason

And so off I went, fists thrust in the torn pockets
Of a coat held together by no more than its name.
O Muse, how I served you beneath the blue;
And oh what dreams of dazzling love I dreamed!

My only pair of pants had a huge hole.
—Like some dreaming Tom Thumb, I sowed
Rhyme with each step. My inn was the Big Dipper.
—My stars rustled in the sky.

Roadside on warm September nights
I listened as drops of dew fell
On my forehead like fortifying wine;

And there, surrounded by streaming shadows,
* I rhymed*
Aloud, and as if they were lyres, plucked the laces
Of my wounded shoes, one foot beneath my heart.

Like Rimbaud, Paul Verlaine (1844–1896) began
his career by imitating contemporary forms. Soon,
however, he began exploring the musical properties
of language. This impulse led to the 1874 collection
Songs Without Words. Rimbaud's stormy friendship
with Verlaine ended violently in 1873, when, in
a fit of rage, Verlaine shot and wounded Rimbaud.
Verlaine served two years in prison for the act. In
1886, under the mistaken belief his friend had died,
Verlaine published Rimbaud's collection *Illumi
nations*, which was written during their travels
together. This image-rich collection of prose poems
made Rimbaud famous.

The Symbolist Legacy

Spurred by the innovations of Mallarmé, Rimbaud,
and Verlaine, Symbolism gained momentum in the
1880s, when many Symbolist journals and magazines
began to appear. Although the movement declined
around the turn of the century, it laid the foundations
for modern British and American poetry. Imagism—
an American poetic movement of the early twentieth
century led by Ezra Pound—applied Symbolist
principles to the presentation of images. The work of
William Butler Yeats, T. S. Eliot, and Virginia Woolf
was also influenced by the Symbolist poets.

The Poor Fisherman, 1881. Pierre Puvis de Chavannes. Oil on
canvas. Musee d'Orsay, Paris.

Literature Online

Literature and Reading For more about the
Symbolist poets, go to glencoe.com and enter QuickPass
code GLW6053u5.

Respond and Think Critically

1. How does Baudelaire's poetry differ from that
   of the Romantics?

2. (a)What poetic techniques did the Symbolists
   embrace? (b)What poetic conventions did
   they reject?

3. (a)What role does the imagination play in the life
   of the speaker of "My Bohemia"? (b)What does
   this tell you about the concerns of the Symbolists?

4. Do the images in "My Bohemia" appeal more to
   emotion or to logic? Explain.

In the Circus, 1932. Lill Tschudi. Linocut. Private collection.

FIRST SORROW

Franz Kafka
Translated by Willa and Edwin Muir

A trapeze artist—this art, practiced high in the vaulted domes of the great variety theaters, is admittedly one of the most difficult humanity can achieve—had so arranged his life that, as long as he kept working in the same building, he never came down from his trapeze by night or day, at first only from a desire to perfect his skill, but later because custom was too strong for him. All his needs, very **modest** needs at that, were supplied by relays of attendants who watched from below and sent up and hauled down again in specially constructed containers whatever he required. This way of living caused no particular inconvenience to the theatrical people, except that, when other turns were on the stage, his being still up aloft, which could not be dissembled, proved somewhat distracting, as also the fact that, although at such times he mostly kept very still, he drew a stray glance here and there from the public. Yet the management overlooked this, because he was an extraordinary and unique artist. And of course they recognized that this mode of life was no mere prank, and that only in this way could he really keep himself in constant practice and his art at the pitch of its perfection.

Besides, it was quite healthful up there, and when in the warmer seasons of the year the side windows all around the dome of the theater were thrown open and sun and fresh air came pouring irresistibly into the dusky vault, it was even beautiful. True, his social life was somewhat limited, only sometimes a fellow acrobat swarmed up the ladder to him, and then they both sat on the trapeze, leaning left and right against the supporting ropes, and chatted, or builders' workmen repairing the roof exchanged a few words with him through an open window, or the fireman, inspecting the emergency lighting in the top gallery, called over to him something that sounded respectful but could hardly be made out. Otherwise nothing disturbed his **seclusion**; occasionally, perhaps, some theater hand straying through the empty theater of an afternoon gazed thoughtfully up into the great height of the roof, almost beyond eyeshot, where the trapeze artist, unaware that he was being observed, practiced his art or rested.

The trapeze artist could have gone on living peacefully like that, had it not been for the inevitable journeys from place to place, which he found extremely trying. Of course his manager saw to it that his sufferings were not **prolonged** one moment more than necessary; for town travel, racing automobiles were used, which whirled him, by night if possible or in the earliest hours of the morning, through the empty streets at breakneck speed, too slow all the same for the trapeze artist's impatience; for railways journeys, a whole compartment was reserved, in which the trapeze artist, as a possible though wretched alternative to his usual way of living, could pass the time up on the luggage rack; in the next town on their circuit, long before he arrived, the trapeze was already slung up in the theater and all the doors leading to the stage were flung wide open, all corridors kept free—yet the manager never knew a happy moment until the trapeze artist set his foot

---

Respond to Characters *What type of person is the trapeze artist?*

Tone *What is ironic about the narrator's observation? What is the narrator's attitude?*

Vocabulary

modest (mod′ist) *adj.* unassuming; plain; simple

Vocabulary

seclusion (si kloo′zhən) *n.* solitude; privacy; isolation
prolong (prə lông′) *v.* lengthen in time or space; draw out

on the rope ladder and in a twinkling, at long last, hung aloft on his trapeze.

Despite so many journeys having been successfully arranged by the manager, each new one embarrassed him again, for the journeys, apart from everything else, got on the nerves of the artist a great deal.

Once when they were again traveling together, the trapeze artist lying on the luggage rack dreaming, the manager leaning back in the opposite window seat reading a book, the trapeze artist addressed his companion in a low voice. The manager was immediately all attention. The trapeze artist, biting his lips, said that he must always in future have two trapezes for his performace instead of only one, two trapezes opposite each other. The manager at once agreed. But the trapeze artist, as if to show that the manager's consent counted for as little as his refusal said that never again would he perform on only one trapeze, in no circumstances whatever. The very idea that it might happen at all seemed to make him shudder. The manager, watchfully feeling his way, once more emphasized his entire agreement, two trapezes were better than one, besides it would be an advantage to have a second bar, more variety could be introduced into the performance. At that the trapeze artist suddenly burst into tears. Deeply **distressed**, the

manager sprang to his feet and asked what was the matter, then getting no answer climbed up on the seat and caressed him, cheek to cheek, so that his own face was bedabbled by the trapeze artist's tears. Yet it took much questioning and soothing endearment until the trapeze artist sobbed: "Only the one bar in my hands—how can I go on living!" That made it somewhat easier for the manager to comfort him; he promised to wire from the very next station for a second trapeze to be installed in the first town on their circuit; reproached himself for having let the artist work so long on only one trapeze; and thanked and praised him warmly for having at last brought the mistake to his notice. And so he succeeded in reassuring the trapeze artist, little by little, and was able to go back to his corner. But he himself was far from reassured, with deep uneasiness he kept glancing secretly at the trapeze artist over the top of his book. Once such ideas began to torment him, would they ever quite leave him alone? Would they not rather increase in urgency? Would they not threaten his very existence? And indeed the manager believed he could see, during the apparently peaceful sleep which had succeeded the fit of tears, the first **furrows** of care engraving themselves upon the trapeze artist's smooth, childlike forehead. ∾

Respond to Characters *Why do journeys bother the trapeze artist? Does his irritation seem reasonable? Explain.*

Vocabulary

distressed (dis tres′d) *adj.* anxious; anguished; upset

Realism and Modernism *Why does the manager want to comfort the trapeze artist? Support your answer with evidence from the story.*

Vocabulary

furrows (fur′ōs) *n.* grooves or tracks cut in the earth by a plow; wrinkles

After You Read

Respond and Think Critically

Respond and Interpret

1. Do you sympathize or identify more with the trapeze artist or his manager? Explain.

2. (a)Why does the trapeze artist stay on his trapeze night and day? (b)Does this make him happy? Support your answer with evidence from the story.

3. (a)What request does the trapeze artist make of his manager during one journey? (b)Why does he make this request?

4. (a)Why is the manager worried at the end of the story? (b)What prompts him to have this thought?

Analyze and Evaluate

5. At the end of the story, is the manager concerned only for the trapeze artist, or might he also be concerned for himself? Explain.

6. (a)What is the significance of the story's title? (b)What moment in the story does it describe?

7. Why do you think Kafka chose to refer to his characters by what they do ("the artist" and "the manager") rather than by actual names?

Connect

8. **Big Idea** Modernism and Realism
(a)How is the trapeze artist's way of life and his request to the manager a metaphor for the uncertainties of modern life? (b)Explain the significance of the story's last four sentences.

9. **Connect to the Author** Kafka continually focused on the estrangement of the individual from society in his works. How is this topic reflected in "First Sorrow"?

Literary Element Tone

Authors deliberately write with a certain tone to convey particular impressions, moods, or ideas. Sometimes a work can have more than one tone.

1. (a)What is the narrator's attitude toward the trapeze artist's situation? (b)What words or phrases help convey the narrator's tone?

2. Tone often influences a work's **mood,** or overall feeling. What mood is created by the change in tone in the story's last paragraph?

Review: Theme

As you learned on page 927, **theme** is the message about life in a literary work. In some works, such as fables and folk tales, the theme is directly stated, usually in the form of a moral at the end. In most works, however, the theme is implied. The reader is responsible for analyzing what happens in order to identify the message the author wishes to convey.

Partner Activity Meet with another classmate to discuss the theme of "First Sorrow."

1. (a)What might the trapeze artist's enjoyment of his craft and his dislike of traveling symbolize? (b)What might the artist's request and the manager's concern represent?

2. What is the theme of "First Sorrow"?

Programme for the Cirque Rancy, 19th century. Tamagno. Colour lithograph. Musee de la Ville de Paris, Musee Carnavalet, Paris.

Reading Strategy — Respond to Characters

ACT Skills Practice

How does the trapeze artist change by the end of the story?

A. He does not want to stay on his trapeze all the time.

B. He will only perform on one trapeze.

C. He refuses to travel anymore.

D. He has begun to worry about things.

Vocabulary Practice

Practice with Word Usage Respond to these statements to help you explore the meanings of the vocabulary words from the story.

1. Describe the behavior of a **modest** person.

2. Explain what you would do if you wanted **seclusion.**

3. Name an experience you've had that you wished you could **prolong.**

4. Identify something that has recently caused you to be **distressed.**

5. Explain what a **furrow** looks like.

Academic Vocabulary

*At the end of the story, the **aggregate** of the trapeze artist's thoughts and actions reveal a man struggling to cope with himself.*

Aggregate is an academic word. More familiar words that are similar in meaning are *total*, *whole*, and *collection*. To further explore the meaning of *aggregate*, answer the following question: What is the **aggregate** of your experience in school this year?

For more on academic vocabulary, see pages 36–37 and R83–R85.

Write with Style

Apply Tone

Assignment The term *Kafkaesque* refers to a nightmarishly complex, bizarre, or illogical situation. Invent a Kafkaesque situation and create a character, such as the trapeze artist in "First Sorrow," who exists in this situation and has an internal life hidden from most people. Write a story about this character, applying the tone Kafka used in "First Sorrow."

Get Ideas You might scan newspaper articles or observe people in public to choose the subject of your story. Choose someone to be your main character who piques your interest so you can invent a life for him or her. Create a chart like the one you filled out on page 1015 to help you respond to your character.

Give It Structure Many modern short stories, including Kafka's "First Sorrow," include an **epiphany,** or sudden revelation, as the climax of the story. Consider building your narrative around an epiphany that relates to the theme of the story. You can diagram your ideas about the epiphany, as in the example below.

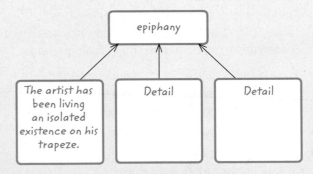

Look at Language Evaluate the tone of your story and check the tone against that of "First Sorrow."

LOG ON ▶ **Literature** Online

Selection Resources For Selection Quizzes, eFlashcards, and Reading-Writing Connection activities, go to glencoe.com and enter QuickPass code GLW6053u5.

Before You Read

Lot's Wife

Meet **Anna Akhmatova**
(1888–1966)

Portrait of Anna Akhmatova, 1914. Natan Isaevic Altman. The State Russian Museum.

Anna Akhmatova (uk mä′tə və) has been called the greatest woman poet to hail from the former Soviet Union. Highly regarded for her intimate yet sophisticated poems about life, love, and politics, Akhmatova suffered greatly under communism. She said, "Fate did not leave anything out for me. Everything anyone could possibly experience fell to my lot."

*"I'm not of those who left their country
For wolves to tear it limb from limb."*

—Anna Akhmatova

A New Voice Akhmatova began writing poetry at age eleven. She published her first poem in 1907 in a literary magazine founded by the poet Nikolai Gumilyov. In 1910, after repeated proposals, Akhmatova married Gumilyov, who soon emerged as the leader of the Acmeists. This small group of early twentieth-century Russians believed that poets were not mystics but rather patient craftspeople building their art word by word. Rejecting the principles of French Symbolism and its metaphorical language, the Acmeists focused on human emotions and aesthetic beauty. Akhmatova was an active member of the group and soon garnered fame with the 1912 publication of her collection of poems, *Vecher.* For many, her simplistic approach to exploring the intimacy of love, jealousy, parting, and death captured the tragic spirit of the time. However, other critics defined her poetic voice as a combination of "a harlot and a nun."

Surrounded by Totalitarianism In 1914, with the start of World War I, the world—and Akhmatova's poetic voice—began to change. Surrounded by totalitarianism and tragedy, her themes became less personal and feminine and increasingly prophetic. In her poem "Molitva," the speaker pleads with God for peace: "This I

pray at your liturgy / After so many tormented days, / So that the stormcloud over darkened Russia / Might become a cloud of glorious rays."

In 1921, the Communists executed Gumilyov and later imprisoned her son. Although she remained loyal to her country through these trials (even taking a firm stance against emigration), she became politically suspect because her works focused on love and God, subjects that were taboo to Communists. Her works were censored, and she published nothing in the Soviet Union from 1923 until 1940. When she wrote about Stalin's reign of terror in a cycle of poems called *Requiem,* she and a few trusted friends memorized passages because writing them down would have been too dangerous. *Requiem* was finally published in Russia in 1989. Following Stalin's death in 1953, Akhmatova slowly began to publish her poems, translations, and essays, and the years preceding her death brought a renewed interest in her work.

LOG ON **Literature** Online

Author Search For more about Anna Akhmatova, go to glencoe.com and enter QuickPass code GLW6053u5.

Literature and Reading Preview

Connect to the Poem

How would you react if you were forced to leave your home? List several objects, people, or places you might miss most.

Build Background

According to the biblical story, God sent angels to Sodom after hearing of the town's wickedness. They found only one virtuous man living there—Lot. The angels told him to flee with his family, warning them to avert their eyes from Sodom. However, Lot's wife looked back at the burning city and was turned into a pillar of salt. Akhmatova wrote the poem "Lot's Wife" sometime between 1922 and 1924. During this period, she sometimes used biblical and literary allusions to suggest themes that could not be discussed openly. Although she suffered greatly under communism, she had strong feelings for her homeland. On the following page, "Lot's Wife" appears both in English and in the original Russian.

Set Purposes for Reading

Big Idea Realism and Modernism

As you read, ask yourself, What does this poem suggest about the Soviet people and the choices they had to make?

Literary Element Rhyme Scheme

The **rhyme scheme** is the pattern that end rhymes form in a stanza or poem. You can mark the rhyme scheme by assigning a different letter to each new rhyme. For example, the first four lines of "Lot's Wife" have an *abab* rhyme scheme. As you read, ask yourself, What is the rhyme scheme of each stanza of this poem?

Reading Strategy Connect to Personal Experience

When you **connect to personal experience**, you link what you read to events in your own life or to your personal beliefs or feelings. Connecting literature to your own experiences and knowledge can help you understand the meaning and purpose of a work. As you read, ask yourself, How would I feel if I were forced to leave my home and never return?

....

Tip: Categorize Details In a chart like the one below, list details from the poem and connect them to your own experiences.

Detail	My Experience
Lot is ordered to leave his home.	

Learning Objectives

For pages 1021–1024

In studying this text, you will focus on the following objectives:

Literary Study: Analyzing rhyme scheme.

Reading: Connecting to personal experience.

Writing: Writing a character sketch.

Lot Fleeing from Sodom, 1810. Benjamin West. Oil on panel. The Detroit Institute of Arts, MI.

LOT'S *Wife*

Anna Akhmatova
Translated by Richard Wilbur

The just man followed then his angel guide
Where he strode on the black highway, hulking
    and bright;
But a wild grief in his wife's bosom cried,
Look back, it is not too late for a last sight

5 *Of the red towers of your native Sodom, the square
Where once you sang, the gardens you shall mourn,
And the tall house with empty windows where
You loved your husband and your babes were born.*

She turned, and looking on the bitter view
10 Her eyes were welded shut by mortal pain;
Into transparent salt her body grew,
And her quick feet were rooted in the plain.

Who would waste tears upon her? Is she not
The least of our losses, this unhappy wife?
15 Yet in my heart she will not be forgot
Who, for a single glance, gave up her life.

~

И праведник шел за посланником Бога,
Огромный и светлый, по черной горе.
Но громко жене говорила тревога:
Не поздно, ты можешь еще посмотреть

5 На красные башни родного Содома,
На площадь, где пела, на двор, где пряла,
На окна пустые высокого дома,
Где милому мужу детей родила.

Взглянула—и, скованы смертною болю,
10 Глаза ее больше смотреть не могли;
И сделалось тело прозрачною солью,
И быстрые ноги к земле приросли.

Кто женщину эту оплакивать будет?
Не меньшей ли мнится она из утрат?
15 Лишь сердце мое никогда не забудет
Отдавшую жизнь за единственный взгляд.

Lot and His Daughters Leaving Sodom, 17th century. Louis de Caullery (Flemish, 1580-1621). Oil on canvas. Rafael Valls Gallery, London.

Realism and Modernism *What idea does this stanza express? How is it different from the first three stanzas?*

Literature and Reading Preview

Connect to the Story

How do you deal with grief or loss? Write a journal entry in response to this question.

Build Background

Turning against its German and Austro-Hungarian allies, Italy joined World War I on the side of Britain, France, and Russia. Italy's wartime efforts proved unsuccessful. During its three-year involvement in World War I, an estimated 650,000 Italians died, and nearly one million were wounded. Italy eventually surrendered to German forces and withdrew its troops from the war. Pirandello was personally aware of the anguish the war caused many families—his own son was a prisoner of war.

Set Purposes for Reading

Big Idea Realism and Modernism

As you read, ask yourself, How does Pirandello focus on the problems of ordinary people in this story?

Literary Element Dialogue

Dialogue is conversation between characters. In "War," Pirandello uses dialogue to illustrate various attitudes of parents toward their children. Each passenger speaks philosophically about his or her personal tragedy. As you read, ask yourself, How does Pirandello use dialogue to show how the characters cope with their losses?

Reading Strategy Recognize Author's Purpose

Authors typically write for one or more reasons: to persuade, to inform, to explain, to entertain, and to describe. As you read, ask yourself, What was Pirandello's purpose for writing "War"?

Tip: Chart Details In a chart like the one below, list details about the characters in the story. Then use your notes to draw a conclusion about Pirandello's position on the war.

Woman's Husband	Man with Two Sons	Fat Man	Woman in Mourning
He claims the world is nasty and tells the passengers about their son.	Explains that a father loves his children equally and therefore his suffering is double.		

Learning Objectives

For pages 1025–1031

In studying this text, you will focus on the following objectives:

Literary Study: Analyzing dialogue.

Reading: Recognizing author's purpose.

Writing: Applying dialogue.

Vocabulary

console (kən′sōl′) *v.* to alleviate a person's grief, sense of loss, or trouble; to comfort; p. 1028 *Nothing could console her after her husband died.*

disillusion (dis′i lōō′zhən) *n.* the state of being freed from misleading images or naïve trust; p. 1029 *His friend's betrayal filled him with sadness and disillusion.*

distorted (dis tôr′tid) *adj.* twisted out of normal or original shape or condition; p. 1029 *His distorted face and swollen eyes were signs of grief.*

Tip: Word Parts Use your knowledge of word parts to figure out the meanings of new words. Two vocabulary words—*disillusion* and *distorted*—for example, have the prefix *dis-*, meaning "two" or "apart." When you look at a word, check to see if there is a root word and any affixes—prefixes or suffixes.

WAR

Luigi Pirandello
Translated by Samuel Putnam

The Railway Carriage-Blackout. Kenneth Rowntree (1915-1997). Watercolour on paper. Fry Art Gallery, Saffron Walden, Essex, UK.

The passengers who had left Rome by the night express had had to stop until dawn at the small station of Fabriano in order to continue their journey by the small old-fashioned "local" joining the main line with Sulmona.

At dawn, in a stuffy and smoky second-class carriage in which five people had already spent the night, a bulky woman in deep mourning, was hoisted in—almost like a shapeless bundle. Behind her—puffing and moaning, followed her husband—a tiny man, thin and weakly, his face death-white, his eyes small and bright and looking shy and uneasy.

Having at last taken a seat he politely thanked the passengers who had helped his wife and who had made room for her; then he turned round to the woman trying to pull down the collar of her coat and politely inquired:

"Are you all right, dear?"

The wife, instead of answering, pulled up her collar again to her eyes, so as to hide her face.

"Nasty world," muttered the husband with a sad smile.

And he felt it his duty to explain to his traveling companions that the poor woman was to be pitied for the war was taking away from her her only son, a boy of twenty to whom both had devoted their entire life, even breaking up their home at Sulmona to follow him to Rome where he had to go as a student, then allowing him to volunteer for war with an assurance, however, that at least for six months he would not be sent to the front, and now, all of a sudden, receiving a wire saying that he was due to leave in three days' time and asking them to go and see him off.

The woman under the big coat was twisting and wriggling, at times growling like a wild animal, feeling certain that all those explanations would not have aroused even a shadow of sympathy from those people who—most likely—were in the same plight as herself. One of them, who had been listening with particular attention, said:

"You should thank God that your son is only leaving now for the front. Mine has been sent there the first day of the war. He has already come back twice wounded and been sent back again to the front."

Realism and Modernism *Why does Pirandello describe the setting this way? What does it tell you about the characters?*

"What about me? I have two sons and three nephews at the front," said another passenger.

"Maybe, but in our case it is our *only* son," ventured the husband.

"What difference can it make? You may spoil your only son with excessive attentions, but you cannot love him more than you would all your other children if you had any. Paternal love is not like bread that can be broken into pieces and split amongst the children in equal shares. A father gives *all* his love to each one of his children without discrimination, whether it be one or ten, and if I am suffering now for my two sons, I am not suffering half for each of them but double. . . ."

"True . . . true . . ." sighed the embarrassed husband, "but suppose (of course we all hope it will never be your case) a father has two sons at the front and he loses one of them, there is still one left to **console** him . . . while . . ."

"Yes," answered the other, getting cross, "a son left to console him but also a son left for whom he must survive, while in the case of the father of an only son if the son dies the father can die too and put an end to his distress. Which of the two positions is the worse? Don't you see how my case would be worse than yours?"

"Nonsense," interrupted another traveler, a fat, red-faced man with bloodshot eyes of the palest gray.

He was panting. From his bulging eyes seemed to spurt inner violence of an uncontrolled vitality which his weakened body could hardly contain.

"Nonsense," he repeated, trying to cover his mouth with his hand so as to hide the two missing front teeth. "Nonsense. Do we give life to our children for our own benefit?"

The other travelers stared at him in distress. The one who had had his son at the front since the first day of the war sighed: "You are right. Our children do not belong to us, they belong to the Country. . . ."

"Bosh," retorted the fat traveler. "Do we think of the Country when we give life to our children? Our sons are born because . . . well, because they must be born and when they come to life they take our own life with them. This is the truth. We belong to them but they never belong to us. And when they reach twenty they are exactly what we were at their age. We too had a father and mother, but there were so many other things as well . . . girls, cigarettes, illusions, new ties . . . and the Country, of course, whose call we would have answered—when we were twenty—even if father and mother had said no. Now, at our age, the love of our Country is still great, of course, but stronger than it is the love for our children. Is there any one of us here who wouldn't gladly take his son's place at the front if he could?"

There was a silence all round, everybody nodding as to approve.

"Why then," continued the fat man, "shouldn't we consider the feelings of our children when they are twenty? Isn't it natural that at their age they should consider the love for their Country (I am speaking of decent boys, of course) even greater than the love for us? Isn't it natural that it should be so, as after all they must look upon us as upon old boys who cannot move any more and must stay at home? If Country exists, if Country is a natural necessity like bread, of which each of us must eat in order not to die of hunger, somebody must go to defend it. And our sons go, when they are twenty, and they

---

Dialogue *What do you learn about the characters through this conversation?*

Vocabulary

console (kən′sōl′) *v.* to alleviate a person's grief, sense of loss, or trouble; to comfort

Dialogue *What is the main idea of the fat man's arguments?*

don't want tears, because if they die, they die inflamed and happy (I am speaking, of course, of decent boys). Now, if one dies young and happy, without having the ugly sides of life, the boredom of it, the pettiness, the bitterness of **disillusion** . . . what more can we ask for him? Everyone should stop crying: everyone should laugh, as I do . . . or at least thank God—as I do—because my son, before dying, sent me a message saying that he was dying satisfied at having ended his life in the best way he could have wished. That is why, as you see, I do not even wear mourning. . . ."

He shook his light fawn[1] coat as to show it; his livid lip over his missing teeth was trembling, his eyes were watery and motionless and soon after he ended with a shrill laugh which might well have been a sob.

"Quite so . . . quite so . . ." agreed the others.

The woman who, bundled in a corner under her coat, had been sitting and listening had—for the last three months—tried to find in the words of her husband and her friends something to console her in her deep sorrow, something that might show her how a mother should resign herself to send her son not even to death but to a probable danger of life. Yet not a word had she found amongst the many which had been said . . . and her grief had been greater in seeing that nobody—as she thought—could share her feelings.

But now the words of the traveler amazed and almost stunned her. She suddenly realized that it wasn't the others who were wrong and could not understand her but herself who could not rise up to the same height of those fathers and mothers willing to resign themselves, without crying, not only to the departure of their sons but even to their death.

She lifted her head, she bent over from her corner trying to listen with great attention to the details which the fat man was giving to his companions about the way his son had fallen as a hero, for his King and his Country, happy and without regrets. It seemed to her that she had stumbled into a world she had never dreamed of, a world so far unknown to her and she was so pleased to hear everyone joining in congratulating that brave father who could so stoically[2] speak of his child's death.

Then suddenly, just as if she had heard nothing of what had been said and almost as if waking up from a dream, she turned to the old man, asking him:

"Then . . . is your son really dead?"

Everybody stared at her. The old man, too, turned to look at her, fixing his great, bulging, horribly watery light gray eyes, deep in her face. For some little time he tried to answer, but words failed him. He looked and looked at her, almost as if only then—at that silly, incongruous question—he had suddenly realized at last that his son was really dead . . . gone forever . . . forever. His face contracted, became horribly **distorted**, then he snatched in haste a handkerchief from his pocket and, to the amazement of everyone, broke into harrowing,[3] heart-rending, uncontrollable sobs. ◌

2. *Stoically* means "indifferently to emotional pain."
3. *Harrowing* means "extremely distressing; agonizing."

Recognize Author's Purpose *What does this description suggest about people's attitude toward the war?*

1. This coat would be pale grayish-brown in color.

Vocabulary

disillusion (dis'i loo'zhən) *n.* the state of being freed from misleading images or naïve trust

Vocabulary

distorted (dis tôr'tid) *adj.* twisted out of normal or original shape or condition

After You Read

Respond and Think Critically

Respond and Interpret

1. Were you surprised by the fat man's reaction at the end of the story? Explain.

2. (a)Why are the husband and wife traveling to Sulmona? (b)Why does the wife wriggle under her coat as the husband explains their situation?

3. (a)How does the fat man feel about the debate between the husband and the other passengers? (b)Why hasn't the fat man mourned the death of his son?

4. (a)What effect does the fat man's speech have on the woman? (b)Why do you think she reacts as she does to the fat man's speech?

Analyze and Evaluate

5. An **epiphany** is a sudden, unexpected moment of insight. Who do you think has the epiphany in this story, the woman or the fat man? Explain.

6. **Tone** is the attitude a narrator takes toward a subject or character. Do you think the narrator's tone remains consistent in this story? Explain.

7. According to one critic, Pirandello created characters who "adopt multiple identities, or 'masks,' in an effort to reconcile social demands with personal needs." Do you think this statement describes the characters in "War"? Explain.

Connect

8. **Big Idea** **Realism and Modernism** (a)Which details of the setting contribute to the story's realism? (b)What is realistic about the portrayal of the characters?

9. **Connect to the Author** Pirandello's wife suffered from mental illness for years, and many of his literary works deal with the relationship between madness and sanity. Do you think he saw the fat man as sane or insane? Explain.

Literary Element Dialogue

The conversations between characters, or **dialogue,** can contribute to characterization, create mood, advance the plot, and develop theme. Dialogue should be convincing; what a character says must be appropriate to his or her personality, background, and intelligence. In "War," Pirandello uses dialogue to present a realistic exchange of ordinary people's ideas and opinions about war and its costs. Consult your chart about author's purpose on page 1026 and consider how the dialogue reveals Pirandello's purpose.

1. (a)What does their dialogue reveal about the personalities of the two men who have sons at the front? (b)Is their dialogue natural? Explain.

2. How does the dialogue in "War" serve as an exchange of ideas?

Review: Characterization

As you learned on page 608, the methods an author uses to reveal the personality of a character is called **characterization.** Authors may describe a character and make explicit statements about him or her. They may also reveal a character through his or her words, thoughts, and actions and through what other characters think and say about the character.

Partner Activity Work with a partner to analyze Pirandello's characterization of the fat man and the woman.

1. (a)What does Pirandello's description of the fat man reveal about the character? (b)What do the fat man's actions reveal about his feelings?

2. (a)How does Pirandello describe the woman? (b)What do her actions reveal about her feelings and opinions? (c)How does Pirandello signal her change in mood?

Recognize Author's Purpose

SAT Skills Practice

Pirandello uses the fat man's apparent resignation to his son's death to show that

(A) He never loved his son.

(B) Many people do not understand the effects of the war.

(C) He believes his country will win the war.

(D) People do not support the war.

(E) He is trying to keep his son's death a secret.

Vocabulary Practice

Practice with Word Parts For each bold-faced vocabulary word in the left column, identify the related word with a shared word part in the right column. Write each word and underline the part they have in common. Use a printed or online dictionary to look up the meaning of the related word. Then explain how it is related to the vocabulary word.

1. **console**   consolidate
2. **disillusion**   distract
3. **distorted**   illusory

Academic Vocabulary

The husband and wife in "War" are **persistent** *in following their son.*

Persistent is an academic word. Similar words include *stubborn, determined,* and *resolute.* Complete a four-square organizer like the one below for *persistent.*

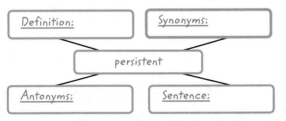

For more on academic vocabulary, see pages 36–37 and R83–R85.

Write with Style

Apply Dialogue

Assignment Dialogue drives the narration and characterization in "War." We find out most details about characters and their circumstances through their words. Apply Pirandello's use of dialogue in a 1,000-word story about a group of strangers.

Get Ideas Choose a controversial topic. Then create a group of characters and list details about them. You can use real people for inspiration.

Give It Structure Determine your purpose for writing the story. How do you want to affect your readers? Present the dialogue in a sequence that allows your ideas to flow in a dramatic way. Also explain the setting and context of your story.

EXAMPLE:

> Gabriel and Greta stopped when they reached the bus stop. "Did we miss it?"
>
> "I don't think so," said Gabriel.
>
> While they caught their breath, they noticed an older man sitting on the bench. This was Mr. Brown.
>
> "Excuse me, are you waiting for Bus 52?" asked Greta. Gabriel wondered why she would ask a stranger.
>
> "I am," said Mr. Brown. "It's late."
>
> The three waited for some time. Gabriel wrung his hands. "We have to go. We should have gone before. Let's get a taxi."
>
> "I don't know," said Greta. "We're already here, and we probably have some time." Gabriel looked at her. "Let's just wait a little longer."
>
> "What if it never comes? Ever think of that? Are we just going to wait here?"
>
> "It all comes, if you wait long enough," said Mr. Brown.
>
> And so they stood in the afternoon sun.

Look at Language Read your story aloud. Does the dialogue sound real? Check your attribution tags and the punctuation. Remember to begin a new paragraph and use a new set of quotation marks every time the speaker changes.

LOG ON ▶ **Literature** Online

Selection Resources For Selection Quizzes, eFlashcards, and Reading-Writing Connection activities, go to glencoe.com and enter QuickPass code GLW6053u5.

Before You Read

Two Memories of Sido

Meet **Colette**
(1873–1954)

Sidonie-Gabrielle Colette (kô let′), known simply as Colette, grew up in a small village in the Burgundy region of France. Her much-loved mother taught her to appreciate the sights, sounds, tastes, textures, and colors of the French countryside. Her skill at sensual description is one of the distinguishing aspects of her writing.

First Marriage At age twenty, Colette married the author and critic Henri Gauthier-Villars (gō′ tē ā ve yär), better known as "Willy." Fifteen years older, he soon recognized her literary talent and encouraged—some say forced—her to write salacious stories based on her childhood. These novels center on the fortunes of a young heroine named Claudine and were so popular that they inspired many commercial products, such as Claudine clothing, soap, perfume, and haircuts (matching Colette's). There was even a musical based on the character. In spite of this success, Colette did not benefit financially from her work. Her husband published the stories under his own name and kept the royalties.

Moving On After leaving Willy, Colette found herself on shaky financial ground. She performed in music halls and continued to write fiction and journalism. A second marriage also ended in divorce, but her third husband, Maurice Goudeket, proved to be a faithful and loving companion. Her happiness turned to despair, however, when Goudeket was arrested and imprisoned by the Nazis during World War II. Colette also endured crippling arthritis, which eventually confined her to her Paris apartment.

Finding Her Voice Colette is widely admired for her precise style, her evocative descriptions of nature, and her insight into relations between men and women. She also wrote several memoirs about her life, using diverse experiences—from hairdressing to performing as a mime—as sources for her work. In many of these autobiographical writings, her mother took on a larger-than-life role. Although her writing and life were controversial, Colette received high honors from the French literary establishment. At her death in 1954, she was given a state funeral, an unprecedented honor at the time for a female French author. Her literary reputation continues to grow, supported by her more than 50 novels and novellas along with an even greater number of short stories.

"*The day necessity put a pen in my hand, and in return for my written pages I was given a little money, I realized that every day thereafter I would slowly, tractably, patiently have to write ...*"

—Colette

 Literature Online

Author Search For more about Colette, go to glencoe.com and enter QuickPass code GLW6053u5.

Literature and Reading Preview

Connect to the Story

What do you think you will be like when you are elderly? Discuss this question with a partner.

Build Background

Colette's memoirs offer an endearing portrait of her mother, Sidonie, who showed a deep respect for everything that "germinates, blossoms, or flies." Sido (sē dō′), as Colette called her, was not a typical country wife. Her unconventional views about religion and morality had a great influence on Colette. Sido taught Colette how to read before the age of three and supported her writing throughout her life.

Set Purposes for Reading

Big Idea Realism and Modernism

As you read, ask yourself, How does the narrator weave the texture of everyday life and the problems of ordinary people into the text?

Literary Element Autobiography

An **autobiography** is a person's account of his or her own life. Told from the first-person point of view, autobiographies can offer revealing insights into a person's view of himself or herself. Colette's autobiography also incorporates elements of a **biography,** or an account of a person's life written by someone else. As you read, ask yourself, How does Colette reveal information about her own values as she portrays her mother?

Reading Strategy Analyze Characterization

When you **analyze characterization,** you consider the ways an author reveals a character's personality. An author can build characterization through a character's actions, words, and habits or through imagery and other literary elements. As you read, ask yourself, How does Colette reveal her mother's character?

Tip: Use a Graphic Organizer Use a chart to keep track of how the author reveals her mother's character.

Method	Example	What It Reveals
Dialogue	"Too quickly? What do you call too quickly? I was going down quickly. Have I time to go downstairs majestically like the Sun King?"	She's always busy.

Learning Objectives

For pages 1032–1039

In studying this text, you will focus on the following objectives:

Literary Study: Analyzing autobiography.

Reading: Analyzing characterization.

Vocabulary

elasticity (i las′tis′ə tē) *n.* the quality of being easily adaptable or adjustable, so as to fit changes or new circumstances; p. 1035 *Sharon, with her usual elasticity, was able to fit the new activities into her already packed schedule.*

undaunted (un dôn′tid) *adj.* courageously firm or resolute, especially in the face of danger or difficulty; not discouraged; p. 1036 *Carlos was undaunted by the rough terrain, so he continued running.*

respites (res′pits) *n.* periods of temporary relief, rest, or delay; p. 1036 *The hikers required frequent respites on their four-day hike.*

Tip: Antonyms Antonyms are words that have opposite or nearly opposite meanings. For example, the words *defiance* and *submission* are antonyms.

Two Memories of Sido

from EARTHLY pARAdISE

Colette
Translated by Una Vincenzo Troubridge and Enid McCleod

THE TiME CAME . . .

The time came when all her strength left her. She was amazed beyond measure and would not believe it. Whenever I arrived from Paris to see her, as soon as we were alone in the afternoon in her little house, she had always some sin to confess to me. On one occasion she turned up the hem of her dress, rolled her stocking down over her shin, and displayed a purple bruise, the skin nearly broken.

"Just look at that!"

"What on earth have you done to yourself this time, Mother?"

She opened wide eyes, full of innocence and embarrassment.

"You wouldn't believe it, but I fell downstairs!"

"How do you mean—'fell'?"

"Just what I said. I fell, for no reason. I was going downstairs and I fell. I can't understand it."

"Were you going down too quickly?"

"Too quickly? What do you call too quickly? I was going down quickly. Have I time to go downstairs majestically like the Sun King?[1] And if that were all . . . But look at this!"

On her pretty arm, still so young above the faded hand, was a scald forming a large blister.

"Oh goodness! Whatever's that!"

"My footwarmer."

"The old copper footwarmer? The one that holds five quarts?"

"That's the one. Can I trust anything, when that footwarmer has known me for forty years? I can't imagine what possessed it, it was boiling fast, I went to take it off the fire, and crack, something gave in my wrist. I was lucky to get nothing worse than the blister. But what a thing to happen! After that I let the cupboard alone. . . ."

She broke off, blushing furiously.

"What cupboard?" I demanded severely.

My mother fenced, tossing her head as though I were trying to put her on a lead.

---

1. Louis XIV (1638–1715), King of France, was known as the *Sun King.*

Autobiography *Who is described in the first paragraph? What period in the person's life is described?*

Analyze Characterization *How does Colette's use of imagery help you understand her mother?*

At the Cafe, 1949. Tsuguharu Foujita. Oil oncanvas, 76 x 64 cm. Musee National d'Art Moderne, Paris. Licensed by ARS, NY.

"Oh, nothing! No cupboard at all!"

"Mother! I shall get cross!"

"Since I've said, 'I let the cupboard alone,' can't you do the same for my sake? The cupboard hasn't moved from its place, has it? So, shut up about it!"

The cupboard was a massive object of old walnut, almost as broad as it was high, with no carving save the circular hole made by a Prussian bullet that had entered by the right-hand door and passed out through the back panel.

"Do you want it moved from the landing, Mother?"

An expression like that of a young she-cat, false and glittery, appeared on her wrinkled face.

"I? No, it seems to me all right there—let it stay where it is!"

All the same, my doctor brother and I agreed that we must be on the watch. He saw my mother every day, since she had followed him and lived in the same village, and he looked after her with a passionate devotion which he hid. She fought against all her ills with amazing **elasticity**, forgot them, baffled them, inflicted on them signal if temporary defeats, recovered, during entire days, her vanished strength; and the sound of her battles, whenever I spent a few days with her, could be heard all over the house till I was irresistibly reminded of a terrier tackling a rat.

At five o'clock in the morning I would be awakened by the clank of a full bucket being set down in the kitchen sink immediately opposite my room.

"What are you doing with that bucket, Mother? Couldn't you wait until Josephine arrives?"

And out I hurried. But the fire was already blazing, fed with dry wood. The milk was boiling on the blue-tiled charcoal stove. Nearby, a bar of chocolate was melting in a little water for my breakfast, and, seated squarely in her cane[2] armchair, my mother was grinding the fragrant coffee which she roasted herself. The morning hours were always kind to her. She wore their rosy colors in her cheeks. Flushed with a brief return to health, she would gaze at the rising sun, while the church bell rang for early Mass, and rejoice at having tasted, while we still slept, so many forbidden fruits.

The forbidden fruits were the overheavy bucket drawn up from the well, the firewood split with a billhook on an oaken block, the spade, the mattock, and above all the double steps propped against the gable

---

2. *Cane* furniture is made by weaving the hollow woody stems of reeds.

Analyze Characterization *How does Sido react to her various ailments? How does her daughter react? What do their reactions reveal about each of them?*

Vocabulary

elasticity (i las´tis´ə tē) *n.* the quality of being easily adaptable or adjustable, so as to fit changes or new circumstances

A Woman Sitting at Her Writing Desk. Anna Ancher. Oil on canvas, 48.5 x 39.5 cm. Private collection.

__View the Art__ Ancher was known for her paintings of domestic interiors. How might this woman remind you of Colette or Sido?

window of the woodhouse. There were the climbing vine whose shoots she trained up to the gable windows of the attic, the flowery spikes of the too-tall lilacs, the dizzy cat that had to be rescued from the ridge of the roof. All the accomplices of her old existence as a plump and sturdy little woman, all the minor rustic[3] divinities who once obeyed her and made her so proud of doing without servants, now assumed the appearance and position of adversaries. But they reckoned without that love of combat which my mother was to keep till the end of her life. At seventy-one, dawn still found her **undaunted**, if not always undamaged. Burnt by the fire, cut with the pruning knife, soaked by melting snow or spilled

---

3. The narrator describes the plants and the cat as being almost godlike in importance in this country (*rustic*) setting.

water, she had always managed to enjoy her best moments of independence before the earliest risers had opened their shutters. She was able to tell us of the cats' awakening, of what was going on in the nests, of news gleaned,[4] together with the morning's milk and the warm loaf, from the milkmaid and the baker's girl, the record in fact of the birth of a new day.

It was not until one morning when I found the kitchen unwarmed, and the blue enamel saucepan hanging on the wall, that I felt my mother's end to be near. Her illness knew many **respites**, during which the fire flared up again on the hearth, and the smell of fresh bread and melting chocolate stole under the door together with the cat's impatient paw. These respites were periods of unexpected alarms. My mother and the big walnut cupboard

Visual Vocabulary
A *gable* is a triangular corner in a roof.

were discovered together in a heap at the foot of the stairs, she having determined to transport it in secret from the upper landing to the ground floor. Whereupon my elder brother insisted that my mother should keep still and that an old servant should sleep in the little house. But how could an old servant prevail against a vital energy so youthful and mischievous that it contrived to tempt and lead astray a body already half

---

4. *Gleaned* means "gathered."

Analyze Characterization *What are Sido's greatest strengths—and how do they sometimes backfire?*

Vocabulary

undaunted (un dôn′tid) *adj.* courageously firm or resolute, especially in the face of danger or difficulty; not discouraged

respites (res′pits) *n.* periods of temporary relief, rest, or delay

body already half fettered[5] by death? My brother, returning before sunrise from attending a distant patient, one day caught my mother red-handed in the most wanton[6] of crimes. Dressed in her nightgown, but wearing heavy gardening sabots,[7] her little gray septuagenarian's plait of hair[8] turning up like a scorpion's tail on the nape of her neck, one foot firmly planted on the crosspiece of the beech trestle, her back bent in the attitude of the expert jobber,[9] my mother, rejuvenated by an indescribable expression of guilty enjoyment, in defiance of all her promises and of the freezing morning dew, was sawing logs in her own yard.

"Sir, you ask me..."

"Sir,

"You ask me to come and spend a week with you, which means I would be near my daughter, whom I adore. You who live with her know how rarely I see her, how much her presence delights me, and I'm touched that you should ask me to come and see her. All the same I'm not going to accept your kind invitation, for the time being at any rate. The reason is that my pink cactus is probably going to flower. It's a very rare plant I've been given, and I'm told that in our climate it flowers only once every four years. Now, I am already a very old woman, and if I went away when my pink cactus is about to flower, I am certain I shouldn't see it flower again.

"So I beg you, sir, to accept my sincere thanks and my regrets, together with my kind regards."

This note, signed "Sidonie Colette, née[10] Landoy," was written by my mother to one of my husbands, the second. A year later she died, at the age of seventy-seven.

Whenever I feel myself inferior to everything about me, threatened by my own mediocrity, frightened by the discovery that a muscle is losing its strength, a desire its power, or a pain the keen edge of its bite, I can still hold up my head and say to myself: "I am the daughter of the woman who wrote that letter—that letter and so many more that I have kept. This one tells me in ten lines that at the age of seventy-six she was planning journeys and undertaking them, but that waiting for the possible bursting into bloom of a tropical flower held everything up and silenced even her heart, made for love. I am the daughter of a woman who, in a mean, close-fisted, confined little place, opened her village home to stray cats, tramps, and pregnant servant girls. I am the daughter of a woman who many a time, when she was in despair at not having enough money for others, ran through the wind-whipped snow to cry from door to door, at the houses of the rich, that a child had just been born in a poverty-stricken home to parents whose feeble, empty hands had no swaddling clothes[11] for it. Let me not forget that I am the daughter of a woman who bent her head, trembling, between the blades of a cactus, her wrinkled face full of ecstasy over the promise of a flower, a woman who herself never ceased to flower, untiringly, during three quarters of a century." ❧

---

5. *Fettered* means "chained" or "shackled."
6. Anything done in a *wanton* way displays mischief—and, sometimes, cruelty.
7. *Sabots* (sa bōz′) is French for wooden shoes.
8. A *septuagenarian* (sep′tōō ə jə nār′ē ən) is a person in his or her seventies; a *plait of hair* is a braid.
9. The mother would bend in the position of an expert woodcutter, one foot braced on the horizontal piece of a bench made of beech wood.

Realism and Modernism *How does this passage reflect the early twentieth-century issue of independence and women's rights?*

---

10. *Née* (nā) is French for "born" and is used to identify a married woman's maiden name.
11. *Swaddling clothes* are narrow strips of cloth wrapped around an infant to restrict its movement.

Autobiography *What lesson does Colette learn from her mother's life?*

After You Read

Respond and Think Critically

Respond and Interpret

1. What adjectives come to mind when you think of Sido?

2. (a)According to Sido, why did she fall? (b)What is another interpretation of the reason for her fall?

3. (a)When her daughter asks whether she wants the cupboard moved from the landing, what is Sido's response? (b)How do her words contradict her wishes?

4. (a)What collective term does Colette use to describe the bucket, firewood, and other objects used in Sido's labor? (b)What does Colette mean by this?

5. (a)When does Colette feel her mother is close to dying? (b)Why does she feel this way?

Analyze and Evaluate

6. Do you think Colette idealizes Sido? Explain.

7. (a)Do you think Colette and her brother should have taken stronger measures to protect Sido from injury? Explain. (b)What does their decision to let Sido make her own decisions reveal about the family's relationship?

Connect

8. **Big Idea** **Realism and Modernism** Colette repeats the phrase "I am the daughter of a woman who . . ." How does her pride in her mother reflect the spirit of the times?

9. **Connect to the Author** In writing this autobiography, Colette makes a significant change to the facts of the cactus incident. In the real letter, her mother mentions the blooming flower, but agrees to visit her daughter. (a)Why do you think Colette chose to make this change? (b)What does this reveal about an author's freedom to alter history?

Primary Source Quotation

Delight in the Ordinary

Colette said her journals and memoirs were closer to random groupings of observations and reflections than a strict chronological retelling.

"I do not possess the knack of writing a proper journal. The art of selection, of noting things of mark, retaining the unusual while discarding the commonplace, has never been mine, since most of the time I am stimulated and quickened by the ordinary."

Colette, 1896. Jacques Fernand Humbert. Oil on canvas. Private collection.

Group Activity

Think about the quotation by Colette in relation to "Two Memories of Sido." Then answer these questions with a group.

1. What details in "Two Memories of Sido" might be considered "commonplace"?

2. Do you think these details make the work more or less appealing? Explain.

Literary Element Autobiography

ACT Skills Practice

1. How does the author feel about Sido?

  A. Sido should give up making breakfast.

  B. Sido is too old to live alone.

  C. Sido does not let her illness and old age hinder her ambitions.

  D. Sido can do everything she used to do, if she tries hard enough.

2. Colette is proud of her mother because she:

  F. lives life to the fullest.

  G. is utterly dependent on her.

  H. is deeply religious.

  J. obeys all her instructions.

Review: Repetition

As you learned on page 79, **repetition** is the recurrence of sounds, words, phrases, lines, or stanzas in a speech or literary work.

Partner Activity With a partner, complete a diagram like the one below. Fill it in with examples that complete the repeated phrase "I am the daughter of a woman who . . ." Then, discuss the effect of this repetition on the reader. How does it reveal the author's feelings about her mother?

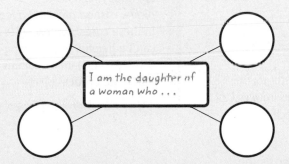

I am the daughter of a woman who . . .

LOG ON ▶ **Literature** Online

Selection Resources For Selection Quizzes, eFlashcards, and Reading-Writing Connection activities, go to glencoe.com and enter QuickPass code GLW6053u5.

Reading Strategy Analyze Characterization

An author can use **direct characterization** by simply telling the reader what the character is like. More often, however, authors use **indirect characterization** by describing a character's behavior or physical appearance, telling what the character says and thinks, revealing what other characters say and think about the character, and showing a character's effect on other people.

1. (a)Why does Sido describe her mother's expression as "guilty enjoyment" when she is discovered sawing logs? (b)How effective is this image as a way of characterizing Sido? Explain.

2. List three additional examples of indirect characterization. Explain how each example reveals something about Sido and about Colette's attitude toward her.

Vocabulary Practice

Practice with Antonyms With a partner, brainstorm three antonyms for each boldfaced vocabulary word below. Then discuss your choices with your classmates. Be prepared to explain why you chose your words.

elasticity   undaunted   respites

EXAMPLE: majestic

Antonyms: humble, modest, unimposing
Explanation: A majestic person would make a show of descending the stairs, but a humble person would not.

Academic Vocabulary

*Colette suggests there are spiritual **dimensions** to Sido's personality, as Sido's accomplices are "rustic divinities" and her face is "full of ecstasy."*

Dimensions is an academic word. In more casual conversation, someone might say they had to measure the **dimensions** of a room to see if new furniture would fit. To further explore this word, answer the following question: What are the **dimensions** of your personality?

For more on academic vocabulary, see pages 36–37 and R83–R85.

Respond Through Writing

Biographical Narrative

Apply Characterization Colette describes her mother, Sido, as her role model because she does not allow old age and illness to dampen her vitality. Write a 500-word profile of someone whose example you would like to follow. You might choose someone you know personally, someone famous, a fictional character, or a historical figure. Your profile should include both direct and indirect characterization.

Understand the Task A **profile** is an abridged biography, or a short descriptive article about someone.

Prewrite Research to learn about your subject. If you know the person, you might interview him or her. If you do not know your subject, you might use the Internet to conduct research. Organize your information in a storyboard like the one below. In the top panels draw pictures related to key ideas you want to include in your profile. In the bottom panels include a caption that explains the relevance of the image.

Draw an early memory of your subject	Draw an example of your subject in action.	Draw an example of your subject among others.
Note how this memory has affected you.	Note how this action relates to the reason your subject is a good role model.	Note how your subject has affected the lives of others.

Draft As you write, refer to the chart you made about methods of characterization on page 1033. Use figurative language and imagery to describe your subject's character and behavior. Include specific details about places and events.

Revise Check your draft against the storyboard you created. Is the sequence of events correct? Do you shift tone when appropriate, and are transitions clear? Do you effectively convey information to the reader?

Edit and Proofread Proofread your paper, correcting any errors in spelling, grammar, and punctuation. Use the word count feature on your computer to check that your profile is 500 words. Review the Grammar Tip in the side column for information on using idioms.

Grammar Tip

Idioms

An **idiom** is a word or phrase that has a different figurative meaning from its literal meaning. The phrase *out of the question* is so familiar to most English speakers that they know immediately it means "not to be considered" or "impossible." (However, someone who is not fluent in English might interpret the phrase literally.)

Some idioms cannot be interpreted so easily: *stuck up, happy as a clam, in a pickle, cost an arm and a leg.* In these cases, context clues can be helpful. In your narrative, try using familiar idioms that match your subject.

Before You Read

The Guitar

Meet **Federico García Lorca**
(1898–1936)

Federico García Lorca's life was cut short by tragedy. Yet during his brief but brilliant career, he became one of Spain's preeminent modern authors.

Musical Roots The first of four children, García Lorca was born into a wealthy family in Andalusia, a rural region in southern Spain. Although his family moved to the city of Granada when García Lorca turned ten, his heart remained in the Andalusian countryside. García Lorca was not a successful student—he took nine years to obtain his bachelor's degree at the University of Granada—but he thrived as a musician. He particularly excelled at composing and playing the piano. While still in his teens, he began to experiment with poetry and drama. He soon developed a style all his own, juxtaposing genres with a strong sense of musicality.

> *"I have a huge storehouse of childhood recollections in which I can hear the people speaking. This is poetic memory, and I trust it implicitly."*
>
> —Federico García Lorca

Life in Madrid In 1919, García Lorca relocated to Madrid and moved into the Residencia de Estudiantes. There he met a group who would one day include the best-known artists of their generation, such as surrealist painter Salvador Dalí and filmmaker Louis Buñuel. It was at this time García Lorca established himself as a member of Madrid's literary elite, specifically the "Generation of 1927." García Lorca became notorious for purposely holding up publication of his books. He preferred to perform his own plays and poetry, and his florid style of presentation won him many admirers.

Success and a Tragic End In 1928, García Lorca published *Gypsy Ballads*, a collection of poems inspired by traditional Spanish songs. It was his first unqualified literary success, but fame did not suit García Lorca's personality. He was a private person, and the spotlight robbed him of his solitude during an especially difficult period in his personal life. His relationship with Dalí disintegrated and he experienced a spiritual crisis and depression. A visit to the United States and Cuba in 1929 improved his spirits; he returned to Spain with renewed energy in 1930, took over as head of the theater company La Barraca, and wrote a play (*Once Five Years Pass*, 1931). Other plays soon followed, including the tragedies *Blood Wedding* and *The House of Bernarda Alba*.

In 1936, the Spanish Civil War broke out. Within the first few months of the war, García Lorca, a liberal intellectual with a controversial personal life, was labeled a radical. He was arrested and, without benefit of a trial, shot to death by Nationalist soldiers. His death stunned the world, especially since his poetry had never been obviously political. Fifty years later, Spain erected a monument at the site of the assassination to commemorate García Lorca's accomplishments.

LOG ON ▶ **Literature** Online

Author Search For more about Federico García Lorca, go to glencoe.com and enter QuickPass code GLW6053u5.

Literature and Reading Preview

Connect to the Poem

What kind of music evokes strong emotions for you? Write a journal entry that describes how the beat of the music, the sound of the instruments, or the rhythm of the lyrics affect your mood.

Build Background

García Lorca wrote a book of poetry entitled *Poem of the Deep Song*. In it, he sought to capture the emotional power of the native Andalusian flamenco music of his boyhood. While some flamenco music is festive, García Lorca preferred the more somber aspects of the form *cante jondo* (kän te hōn′dō) ("deep song"). The guitar, an instrument associated with Spain and Spanish culture for centuries, plays a central role in this music. Most of the poems in García Lorca's collection are written in short, irregular lines that echo the forceful energy of flamenco.

Set Purposes for Reading

Big Idea Realism and Modernism

As you read, ask yourself, How does the poet use the memory of a musical style to evoke the complexity of human passion?

Literary Element Sound Devices

Sound devices are poetic techniques that appeal to the ear. Authors use sound devices to create a sense of rhythm, to emphasize particular sounds, or to add to the musical quality of their writing. As you read "The Guitar" aloud, ask yourself, What rhythm and musicality do I hear?

Reading Strategy Analyze Style

When you **analyze** an author's **style,** you examine the combination of unique expressive qualities such as word choice and the use of figurative language and imagery. Style can reveal an author's attitude and purpose. As you read, ask yourself, What elements of the poem contribute to García Lorca's style?

Tip: Compare Words As you read, consider the concrete words and phrases García Lorca uses in place of less specific ones. Create a chart like the one below.

Ineffective	Effective
General: weapons	*Specific:* five swords
Abstract: injured	*Concrete:* gravely wounded

Learning Objectives

For pages 1041–1044

In studying this text, you will focus on the following objectives:

Literary Study: Analyzing sound devices.

Reading: Analyzing style.

Writing: Writing a song.

Guitar and Flowers, 1912. Juan Gris. Oil on canvas, 44 1/8 x 27 5/8 in. Bequest of Anna Erickson Levene, in memory of her husband Dr. Phoebus Aaron Theodor Levene. The Museum of Modern Art, NY.

The Guitar

Federico García Lorca
Translated by Robert Bly

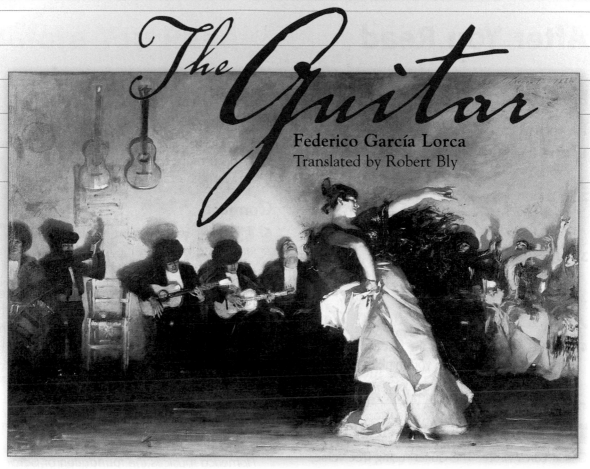

El Jaleo, 1882 John Singer Sargent. Isabella Stewart Gardner Museum, Boston.

The crying of the guitar
starts.
The goblets[1]
of the dawn break.
5   The crying of the guitar
starts.
No use to stop it.
It is impossible
to stop it.
10   It cries repeating itself
as the water cries,
as the wind cries
over the snow.

It is impossible
15   to stop it.
It is crying for things
far off.
The warm sand of the South
that asks for white camellias.[2]
20   For the arrow with nothing to hit,
the evening with no dawn coming,
and the first bird of all dead
on the branch.
Guitar!
25   Heart wounded, gravely,
by five swords.

---

1. A *goblet* is a drinking glass with a stem.

Sound Devices *What effect does this repetition create? How does it affect the mood of the poem?*

2. The *camellia* (kə mēl′yə) is an evergreen shrub or tree with sweet-smelling flowers.

Realism and Modernism *These lines cry out in pain and yet they reflect the poet's joy in the music. How does this reflect the contradictory themes of the Modernist movement?*

FEDERICO GARCÍA LORCA   **1043**

Literature and Reading Preview

Connect to the Poem

Have you ever witnessed a natural phenomenon—a sunset, a deer in the woods—that made you consider your place in the world? Freewrite for a few minutes about how a moment in nature gave you a new perspective on your own life.

Build Background

Czesław Miłosz wrote many descriptions of landscapes. As a boy, he wanted to become a naturalist, and this interest carried over into his poetry. As he once claimed: "The forests, the valleys and the rivers which I saw in my childhood possess for me a strong evocative force." Unlike many poets, however, Miłosz refused to idealize nature in his work. He said American authors tend to emphasize the beauty of nature, whereas he felt, "nature is extremely cruel, or at least indifferent."

Set Purposes for Reading

Big Idea Postwar Europe

Miłosz's poem "Encounter" takes the form of a memory of a lost event in a lost location. As you read the poem, ask yourself, How does the passage of time affect the speaker's relationship with the "encounter" in the poem?

Literary Element Title

The **title** is the name of a literary work. A title can help explain a setting, provide insight into the theme, or describe the action that will take place in the work. As you read, ask yourself, What kind of feeling does the word "encounter" connote to me?

Reading Strategy Interpret Imagery

Imagery is the "word pictures" authors create to evoke an emotional response in readers. To create effective imagery, authors use **sensory details,** or descriptions that appeal to one or more of the five senses. As you read, ask yourself, What details are clues that guide me to the work's meaning?

....

Tip: Note Details Use a chart like the one below to note details that appeal to your sense of sight (visual) and to your sense of hearing (aural).

Visual	Aural
frozen fields, dawn, red wing, darkness...	

Winter Sunday in Dalecarlia, 1899. Gustaf Ankarcrona (Swedish, 1869-1933). Oil on canvas, 64 x 109 cm. Private collection.

Encounter

Czesław Miłosz
Translated by the author and Lillian Vallee

We were riding through frozen fields in a wagon at dawn.
A red wing rose in the darkness.

And suddenly a hare ran across the road.
One of us pointed to it with his hand.

That was long ago. Today neither of them is alive,
Not the hare, nor the man who made the gesture.

O my love, where are they, where are they going.
The flash of a hand, streak of movement, rustle of pebbles.
I ask not out of sorrow, but in wonder.

Jechaliśmy przed świtem po zamarzłych polach,
Czerwone skrzydło wstawało, jeszcze noc.

I zając przebiegł nagle tuż przed nami,
A jeden z nas pokazał go ręką.

To było dawno. Dzisiaj już nie żyją
Ni zając, ani ten co go wskazywał.

Miłości moja, gdzież są, dokąd idą
Błysk ręki, linia biegu, szelest grud—
Nie z żalu pytam, ale z zamyślenia.

Interpret Imagery *To which sense do these images appeal? Which words convey the images?*

Postwar Europe *How does the tone of this poem reflect the cultural outlook of post–World War II Europe?*

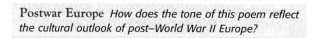

Literature and Reading Preview

Connect to the Poem

In what ways are you connected to people around the world? Discuss this question with a small group.

Build Background

In 1938 the Turkish government accused Hikmet of using his poetry to promote disloyalty and sentenced him to prison. While serving his sentence, he produced a large body of work, including "The World, My Friends, My Enemies, You, and the Earth." He enclosed poems in letters to friends and relatives who then circulated them in manuscript form. Although an international protest campaign helped win Hikmet's release, his poetry was not published in Turkey until after his death.

Set Purposes for Reading

Big Idea Modernism and Realism

Like many Modernist authors, Hikmet wrote poems that were at once personal and public. As you read, ask yourself, How does the speaker illustrate this idea of public and private in the poem?

Literary Element Free Verse

Free verse is a form of poetry that has no fixed pattern of meter, rhyme, line length, or stanza arrangement. Although poets who write free verse ignore traditional rules, they use techniques such as repetition and alliteration to create musical patterns. As you read, ask yourself, How do the line breaks and punctuation help you understand the poem's meaning?

Reading Strategy Monitor Comprehension

When you **monitor comprehension,** you check in with yourself as you read to see if you fully grasp the ideas in a literary work. To do this, you will find it helpful to divide the work into sections and pause to ask questions after reading each one. If necessary, reread the section. As you read, ask yourself, What is the main idea and emotion in each section?

....

Tip: Chart Questions In a chart like the one below, list your questions and answers as you read Hikmet's poem.

Question: Who is the speaker in the poem?	Question:	Question:
Answer: The poet himself	Answer:	Answer:

Vocabulary

dimension (di men′shən) *n.* a measure of physical form or proportion; p. 1051 *Given the dimensions of the boat, it was clear it would seat only three people.*

mere (mēr) *adj.* being nothing more or less than; p. 1052 *Though it was a mere three miles to town, it was farther than we were willing to walk.*

nautical (nô′ti kəl) *adj.* of or relating to sailors or ships; p. 1052 *The restaurant features a nautical theme—from its all-seafood menu to the servers' sailor caps.*

....

Tip: Word Usage When you encounter a new word, ask yourself a question about it to help you understand what it means. For example, you might ask, What are the dimensions of my bedroom?

The World, My Friends, My Enemies, You, and the Earth

Nazim Hikmet

Translated by Randy Blasing and Mutlu Konuk

Parana, Brazil I, 1995.
Deirdre Kelly. Screenprint
and collage, 75 x 72 cm.
Hardware Gallery, London.

I'm wonderfully happy I came into the world,
I love its earth, its light, its struggle, and its bread.
Even though I know its **dimensions** from pole to pole to the
centimeter,

Learning Objectives

For pages 1054–1055

In studying this text, you will focus on the following objectives:

Reading: Analyzing cultural and historical context. Understanding the nature of language.

The Dream of a Common Language

MOST OF THE EUROPEAN UNION HAS BEEN ABLE TO ADOPT A SINGLE currency, but it still has 23 official languages, a record-keeper's nightmare. At the United Nations, every word spoken at an official meeting must be translated and printed in six langages, at an estimated cost of hundreds of millions of dollars a year. Why can't Europe—and the rest of the world—agree on a single language for all communication?

For centuries, many people have promoted the idea of adopting one language for use in international communication. Simple, easy-to-learn languages have been invented for that purpose, with Esperanto, a phonetic language derived from Romance language roots, being the best known. But nations cannot agree on a single international language, either an existing one or a new one. Why do Europeans—and the rest of the world—resist a proposal that could save time, effort, money, and misunderstanding?

Welcome

Albanian	*Misardhje*
Basque	*Ongi-etorri*
Bulgarian	Доốрѐ дошьл
Danish	*Velkommen*
Dutch	*Welkom*
Esperanto	*Bonveno*
French	*Bienvenue*
German	*Willkommen*
Hungarian	*Isten hozott*
Irish Gaelic	*Fáilte*
Italian	*Benvenuto*
Norweigian	*Velkommen*
Polish	*Witajcie*
Portuguese	*Bem-vindo*
Russian	Доốрó пожáловать
Serbian	*Dobro si dosao*
Slovenian	*Dobrodôsel*
Spanish	*Bienvenido*
Swedish	*Välkommen*

The Politics of Language

Europe is a small continent—not much larger than the United States—but its people are divided into many nations and speak about 60 different languages. The political and cultural differences among Europeans have played a part in igniting the two world wars of the twentieth century. Not surprisingly, Europe has been the center of the Esperanto movement, whose proponents believe that international understanding and tolerance would be furthered if everyone spoke the same language.

Although Esperanto has been the most successful language invented for international use, it has failed to catch on. In the twentieth century, as nationalism grew in Europe, many governments viewed the Esperanto movement as a threat to their national identity and goals. Esperanto faced competition from national languages as well as other invented languages.

Since World War II, English has become the international language of commerce, science, and technology because English-speakers have dominated those fields. Even so, the world's nations have not adopted English as the single official language for international forums. Many governments equate adopting a language with allowing one culture to dominate others. According to this view, language equals control.

European currency: one Euro coin

LEARN ESPERANTO & MEET WORKERS FROM FORTY COUNTRIES AT THE S.A.T. CONGRESS 3-7 AUG. 1930 CONWAY HALL LONDON

SECRETARY JOEL SULSKY 19 LEYTON RD HARPENDEN

Learn Esperanto and Meet Workers from Forty Countries, 1930. Poster.

The issue of cultural domination would seem to strengthen the case for adopting a neutral, invented language; however, many people object to invented languages on principle. They claim that invented languages lack the richness, vitality, and expressiveness that existing languages have accumulated over time. They resist giving up a "natural" language for an "artificial" one.

Language and National Pride

Each of the world's languages has evolved over a long period of time, and each reflects the history and the culture of its speakers. Each language contains many words and expressions that have gained associations and feelings (connotations) specific to a given culture. Such aspects of a language cannot be easily translated or imported into an invented language.

Many English words, for example, have connotations that either are lacking or are different in other languages. Take the word *red*, for instance. In English, the word is associated with blood, passion, and anger, as in the expression "seeing red." In Russian, on the other hand, the word connotes beauty, and the name *Red Square* suggests beautiful architecture. In Russian, a "red girl" is a beautiful girl. In Chinese, the word *red* is associated with joy and celebration.

English, like other languages, contains thousands of culture-specific idioms that are difficult, if not impossible, to translate. An **idiom** is an expression that has a meaning other than its literal one, such as "barking up the wrong tree." An idiom such as this would be meaningless if translated literally into another language.

Each language has so many culture-specific elements that help to define its speakers to the world and to themselves. Take away a people's language, and you take away part of their being. A Welsh proverb expresses this idea: "A nation without a language is a nation without a heart."

LOG ON ▶ **Literature** Online

Literature and Reading For more about common language and the translators in this book, go to glencoe.com and enter the QuickPass code GLW6053u5.

Respond and Think Critically

1. (a) How many official languages are spoken in Europe? (b) How does this affect political relations between nations?

2. (a) What is Esperanto? (b) Why are some Europeans reluctant to speak it?

3. What idioms do you use that might be difficult to translate into another language?

4. Which do you think is a better solution to the international language problem—using an existing language or an invented one? Explain.

The
MYTH of
SISYPHUS

Albert Camus
Translated by Justin O'Brien

Sisyphos, 1547-1548. Titian (Tiziano Vecellio). Canvas, 237 x 216 cm. Museo del Prado, Madrid.

The gods had condemned Sisyphus to ceaselessly rolling a rock to the top of a mountain, whence the stone would fall back of its own weight. They had thought with some reason that there is no more dreadful punishment than futile and hopeless labor.

If one believes Homer, Sisyphus was the wisest and most **prudent** of mortals. According to another tradition, however, he was disposed to practice the profession of highwayman. I see no contradiction in this. Opinions differ as to the reasons why he became the futile laborer of the underworld. To begin with, he is accused of a certain levity[1] in regard to the gods. He stole their secrets. Aegina, the daughter of Aesopus, was carried off by Jupiter. The father was shocked by that disappearance and complained to Sisyphus. He, who knew of the abduction, offered to tell about it on condition that Aesopus would give water to the citadel of Corinth.[2] To the celestial thunderbolts he preferred the benediction[3] of water. He was punished for this in the underworld. Homer tells us also that Sisyphus had put Death in chains. Pluto could not endure the sight of his deserted, silent empire. He dispatched the god of war, who liberated Death from the hands of her conqueror.

It is said also that Sisyphus, being near to death, rashly wanted to test his wife's love. He ordered her to cast his unburied body into the middle of the public square. Sisyphus woke up in the underworld. And there, annoyed by an obedience so contrary to human love, he obtained from Pluto permission to return to earth in order to chastise his wife. But when he had seen again the face of this world, enjoyed water and sun, warm stones and the sea, he no longer wanted to go back to the infernal darkness.

---

1. *Levity*, a lack of seriousness, borders on mocking disrespect.

Vocabulary

prudent (pro͞od′ənt) *adj.* sensible; sound in judgment

2. According to Greek mythology, Sisyphus was the king of the city of *Corinth*; a *citadel* is a city's most important fort.
3. Here, *benediction* is something that causes goodness or well-being.

Recalls, signs of anger, warnings were of no avail. Many years more he lived facing the curve of the gulf, the sparkling sea, and the smiles of earth. A decree of the gods was necessary. Mercury came and seized the impudent man by the collar and, snatching him from his joys, led him forcibly back to the underworld, where his rock was ready for him.

You have already grasped that Sisyphus is the absurd hero. He *is*, as much through his passions as through his torture. His **scorn** of the gods, his hatred of death, and his passion for life won him that unspeakable penalty in which the whole being is exerted toward accomplishing nothing. This is the price that must be paid for the passions of this earth. Nothing is told us about Sisyphus in the underworld. Myths are made for the imagination to breathe life into them. As for this myth, one sees merely the whole effort of a body straining to raise the huge stone, to roll it and push it up a slope a hundred times over; one sees the face screwed up, the cheek tight against the stone, the shoulder bracing the clay-covered mass, the foot wedging it, the fresh start with arms outstretched, the wholly human security of two earth-clotted hands. At the very end of his long effort measured by skyless space and time without depth, the purpose is achieved. Then Sisyphus watches the stone rush down in a few moments toward that lower world whence he will have to push it up again toward the summit. He goes back down to the plain.

It is during that return, that pause, that Sisyphus interests me. A face that toils so close to stones is already stone itself! I see that man going back down with a heavy yet measured step toward the torment of which he will never know the end. That hour like a breathing space which returns as surely as his suffering, that is the hour of consciousness. At each of those moments when he leaves the heights and gradually sinks toward the lairs of the gods, he is superior to his fate. He is stronger than his rock.

If this myth is tragic, that is because its hero is conscious. Where would his torture be, indeed, if at every step the hope of succeeding upheld him? The workman of today works every day in his life at the same tasks, and this fate is no less absurd. But it is tragic only at the rare moments when it becomes conscious. Sisyphus, proletarian[4] of the gods, powerless and rebellious, knows the whole extent of his wretched condition: it is what he thinks of during his descent. The lucidity that was to constitute his torture at the same time crowns his victory. There is no fate that cannot be surmounted by scorn.

If the descent is thus sometimes performed in sorrow, it can also take place in joy. This word is not too much. Again I fancy Sisyphus returning toward his rock, and the sorrow was in the beginning. When the images of earth cling too tightly to memory, when the call of happiness becomes too insistent, it happens that melancholy rises in man's heart: this is the rock's victory, this is the rock itself. The boundless grief is too heavy to bear. These are our nights of Gethsemane.[5] But crushing truths perish

---

4. A *proletarian* is an industrial wage-earner.
5. According to the Bible, *Gethsemane* (geth sem′ə nā) is the olive grove where Jesus Christ contemplated his possible death on the eve of his arrest.

Determine Main Idea and Supporting Details *How does this detail support the main idea?*

Postwar Europe *How does Camus connect Greek myths to the conditions in postwar Europe?*

Reading Strategy · Determine Main Idea and Supporting Details

SAT Skills Practice

What is the meaning of the last line, "One must imagine Sisyphus happy"?

(A) Sisyphus hopes he will finish his task soon.

(B) Sisyphus is happy because he chastised his wife.

(C) Sisyphus will be rewarded for his devotion.

(D) Sisyphus is actually master of his own fate.

(E) Sisyphus will never realize his own absurdity, and so lives in blissful ignorance.

Vocabulary Practice

Practice with Word Origins Studying the origin and history of a word can help you better understand its meaning. Using a dictionary, create a word map for each vocabulary word.

prudent scorn myriad fidelity negate

EXAMPLE:

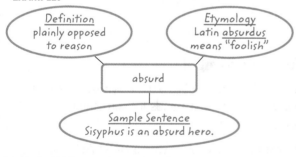

Academic Vocabulary

*In this essay, Camus presents a **justification** for the plight of Sisyphus: that pushing the rock gives meaning to Sisyphus's life.*

Justification is an academic word that often occurs in writing related to current events. For example, an editorial might say an unprovoked attack creates a **justification** for going to war. To further explore the meaning of this word, complete the following statement.

_____ is my justification for _____.

For more on academic vocabulary, see pages 36–37 and R83–R85.

Write with Style

 Apply Symbolism

Assignment Review the way Camus uses symbolism and allusion to argue that even an absurd life has meaning. With this strategy in mind, write an essay to persuade your readers to change their perspective on an issue of your choosing.

Get Ideas Page through your journal or brainstorm to find a topic about which you think many people should alter their perspective. Consider what you think is wrong with most people's view, and make a list of things that could change their minds. When you begin to compile ideas, sort them into a main idea and supporting details chart. Use the chart you filled out on page 1057 as a model. After organizing your ideas, create a plan for your essay that addresses purpose, audience, and the time frame you have to complete the essay.

Give It Structure Refer to your prewriting notes as you draft your essay. Use an organizer like the one below to structure your essay.

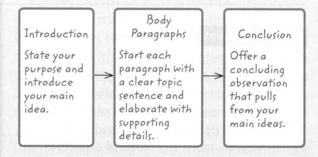

Look at Language While modeling your own writing on Camus' style, remember to maintain your own voice. Try developing your unique style by using sentence variety and combining short sentences into longer, more complex ones (see pages 90–91).

LOG ON ▶ **Literature** Online

Selection Resources For Selection Quizzes, eFlashcards, and Reading-Writing Connection activities, go to glencoe.com and enter QuickPass code GLW6053u5.

Before You Read

from Night

Meet **Elie Wiesel**
(born 1928)

Elie Wiesel (el′ ē vē zel′) lived in Sighet, Romania, until 1944, when Nazi soldiers rounded up the town's Jews for extermination. Until that day, the residents of Sighet had been relatively insulated from the outside world, living lives of prayer and contemplation, and had no idea of the horrors to come.

Peace Before the Holocaust Wiesel recalls his early childhood as happy. Synagogues, day schools, and Jewish newspapers flourished in the community of Sighet. Wiesel started *kheder* (religious elementary school) when he was three years old. He studied secular subjects, played the violin, and eventually found a local scholar with whom he could study Kabbalah, a mystical interpretation of Hebrew scriptures. He recalls that in Sighet, he and the other inhabitants "spoke Yiddish among ourselves, responded to others in Romanian or Hungarian or Ruthenian, and we prayed in Hebrew."

> *"We must always take sides. Neutrality helps the oppressor, never the victim."*
>
> —Elie Wiesel

Auschwitz When he was fifteen, Wiesel, his parents, and his three sisters were deported to Auschwitz, a concentration camp in Poland. His mother and younger sister were gassed to death immediately. He and his father were sent to the slave-labor division of Auschwitz, and eight months later were part of a death march to Buchenwald. His father died just a few months before liberation in April 1945. The American military evacuated Wiesel, along with other child survivors, and brought them to France. He was sent to a home for Jewish child survivors and was later reunited with his two older sisters.

Giving Voice to Memory After liberation, Wiesel vowed to keep silent about the horrors he had witnessed. He continued his education at the Sorbonne in France. While studying in Paris, he began work as a journalist, writing stories for the Yiddish newspaper *Zion in Kamf* and the Israeli newspaper *Yedi'ot Akharonot*. Journalism put him in contact with a critical figure, French writer François Mauriac. In 1954, at Mauriac's behest, Wiesel broke his silence and finally gave voice to his memories. Wiesel wrote and published his Yiddish memoir, *Un Di Velt Hot Geshvign* ("And the World Kept Silent"), in 1956. Under Mauriac's guidance, Wiesel revised the text and translated it into French under the title *La Nuit* in 1958; in 1960 this seminal work was translated into English as *Night*.

Wiesel moved to the United States in 1956 and was naturalized as a citizen in 1963. As a result of his prolific writing and lecturing, Wiesel has become one of the most visible and renowned Holocaust survivors, eventually winning the Nobel Peace Prize in 1986.

LOG ON ▶ **Literature** Online

Author Search For more about Elie Wiesel, go to glencoe.com and enter QuickPass code GLW6053u5.

until we can go into the showers . . . You'll come and get me."

I could have screamed in anger. To have lived and endured so much; was I going to let my father die now? Now that we would be able to take a good hot shower and lie down?

"Father!" I howled. "Father! Get up! Right now! You will kill yourself . . ."

And I grabbed his arm. He continued to moan:

"Don't yell, my son . . . Have pity on your old father . . . Let me rest here . . . a little . . . I beg of you, I'm so tired . . . no more strength . . ."

He had become childlike: weak, frightened, vulnerable.

"Father," I said, "you cannot stay here."

I pointed to the corpses around him; they too had wanted to rest here.

"I see, my son. I do see them. Let them sleep. They haven't closed an eye for so long . . . They're exhausted . . . exhausted . . ."

His voice was tender.

I howled into the wind:

"They're dead! They will never wake up! Never! Do you understand?"

This discussion continued for some time. I knew that I was no longer arguing with him but with Death itself, with Death that he had already chosen.

The sirens began to wail. Alert. The lights went out in the entire camp. The guards chased us toward the blocks. In a flash, there was no one left outside. We were only too glad not to have to stay outside any longer, in the freezing wind. We let ourselves sink into the floor. The cauldrons at the entrance found no takers. There were several tiers of bunks. To sleep was all that mattered.

When I woke up, it was daylight. That is when I remembered that I had a father. During the alert, I had followed the mob, not taking care of him. I knew he was running out of strength, close to death, and yet I had abandoned him.

I went to look for him.

Yet at the same time a thought crept into my mind: If only I didn't find him! If only I were relieved of this responsibility, I could use all my strength to fight for my own survival, to take care only of myself . . . Instantly, I felt ashamed, ashamed of myself forever.

I walked for hours without finding him. Then I came to a block where they were distributing black "coffee." People stood in line, quarreled.

A **plaintive** voice came from behind me: "Eliezer, my son . . . bring me . . . a little coffee . . ."

I ran toward him.

"Father! I've been looking for you for so long . . . Where were you? Did you sleep? How are you feeling?"

He seemed to be burning with fever. I fought my way to the coffee cauldron like a wild beast. And I succeeded in bringing back a cup. I took one gulp. The rest was for him.

I shall never forget the gratitude that shone in his eyes when he swallowed this beverage. The gratitude of a wounded animal. With these few mouthfuls of hot water, I had probably given him more satisfaction than during my entire childhood . . .

He was lying on the boards, ashen, his lips pale and dry, shivering. I couldn't stay

Evaluate Characters *What does this passage reveal about Wiesel's character and his inner conflict? How does he react to his feelings?*

Postwar Europe *How does Wiesel's statement indicate his purpose in writing about his experiences in the Holocaust?*

Vocabulary

plaintive (plān′ tiv) *adj.* expressive of suffering or distress

with him any longer. We had been ordered to go outside to allow for cleaning of the blocks. Only the sick could remain inside.

We stayed outside for five hours. We were given soup. When they allowed us to return to the blocks, I rushed toward my father:

"Did you eat?"

"No."

"Why?"

"They didn't give us anything . . . They said that we were sick, that we would die soon, and that it would be a waste of food . . . I can't go on . . ."

I gave him what was left of my soup. But my heart was heavy. I was aware that I was doing it grudgingly.

Just like Rabbi Eliahu's[3] son, I had not passed the test.

Every day, my father was getting weaker. His eyes were watery, his face the color of dead leaves. On the third day after we arrived in Buchenwald, everybody had to go to the showers. Even the sick, who were instructed to go last.

When we returned from the showers, we had to wait outside a long time. The cleaning of the blocks had not been completed.

From afar, I saw my father and ran to meet him. He went by me like a shadow, passing me without stopping, without a glance. I called to him, he did not turn around. I ran after him:

"Father, where are you running?"

He looked at me for a moment and his gaze was distant, otherworldly, the face of a stranger. It lasted only a moment and then he ran away.

Father and Child, 1946. Ben Shahn. Tempera on cardboard, 39 7/8 x 30 in. Gift of James Thrall Soby. The Museum of Modern Art, NY.© VAGA, NY.

Suffering from dysentery, my father was prostrate on his cot, with another five sick inmates nearby. I sat next to him, watching him; I no longer dared to believe that he could still **elude** Death. I did all I could to give him hope.

All of a sudden, he sat up and placed his feverish lips against my ear:

"Eliezer . . . I must tell you where I buried the gold and silver . . . In the cellar . . . You know . . ."

And he began talking, faster and faster, afraid of running out of time before he could tell me everything. I tried to tell him that it was not over yet, that we would be going home together, but he no longer wanted to listen to me. He *could* no longer listen to me. He was worn out. Saliva mixed with blood was trickling from his lips. He had closed his eyes. He was gasping more than breathing.

---

3. Earlier, Eliezer had witnessed *Rabbi Eliahou's* son purposefully leaving his father behind to die. Eliezer had prayed for the strength never to betray his own father in this way.

Evaluate Characters *What does this action reveal about Wiesel's character?*

For a ration of bread I was able to exchange cots to be next to my father. When the doctor arrived in the afternoon, I went to tell him that my father was very ill.

"Bring him here!"

I explained that he could not stand up, but the doctor would not listen. And so, with great difficulty, I brought my father to him. He stared at him, then asked curtly:

"What do you want?"

"My father is sick," I answered in his place . . . "Dysentery . . ."

"That's not my business. I'm a surgeon. Go on. Make room for the others!"

My protests were in vain.

"I can't go on, my son . . . Take me back to my bunk."

I took him back and helped him lie down. He was shivering.

"Try to get some sleep, Father. Try to fall asleep . . ."

His breathing was labored. His eyes were closed. But I was convinced that he was seeing everything. That he was seeing the truth in all things.

Another doctor came to the block. My father refused to get up. He knew that it would be of no use.

In fact, that doctor had come only to finish off the patients. I listened to him shouting at them that they were lazy good-for-nothings who only wanted to stay in bed . . . I considered jumping him, strangling him. But I had neither the courage nor the strength. I was **riveted** to my father's agony. My hands were aching, I was clenching them so hard. To strangle the doctor and the others! To set the whole world on fire! My father's murderers! But even the cry stuck in my throat.

On my return from the bread distribution, I found my father crying like a child:

"My son, they are beating me!"

"Who?" I thought he was delirious.

"Him, the Frenchman . . . and the Pole . . . They beat me . . ."

One more stab to the heart, one more reason to hate. One less reason to live.

"Eliezer . . . Eliezer . . . tell them not to beat me . . . I haven't done anything . . . Why are they beating me?"

I began to insult his neighbors. They mocked me. I promised them bread, soup. They laughed. Then they got angry; they could not stand my father any longer, they said, because he no longer was able to drag himself outside to relieve himself.

The following day, he complained that they had taken his ration of bread.

"While you were asleep?"

"No. I wasn't asleep. They threw themselves on me. They snatched it from me, my bread . . . And they beat me . . . Again . . . I can't go on, my son . . . Give me some water . . ."

I knew that he must not drink. But he pleaded with me so long that I gave in. Water was the worst poison for him, but what else could I do for him? With or without water, it would be over soon anyway . . .

"You, at least, have pity on me . . ."

Have pity on him! I, his only son . . .

A week went by like that.

"Is this your father?" asked the *Blockälteste*.

"Yes."

Memoir *What do the doctor's words reveal about the Nazis' treatment of the prisoners?*

Vocabulary

rivet (riv´ it) *v.* fixed firmly; completely engrossed

Evaluate Characters *What does this passage reveal about the prisoners who were abusing Eliezer's father?*

"He is very sick."

"The doctor won't do anything for him."

He looked me straight in the eye:

"The doctor *cannot* do anything more for him. And neither can you."

He placed his big, hairy hand on my shoulder and added:

"Listen to me, kid. Don't forget that you are in a concentration camp. In this place, it is every man for himself, and you cannot think of others. Not even your father. In this place, there is no such thing as father, brother, friend. Each of us lives and dies alone. Let me give you good advice: stop giving your ration of bread and soup to your old father. You cannot help him anymore. And you are hurting yourself. In fact, you should be getting *his* rations . . ."

I listened to him without interrupting. He was right, I thought deep down, not daring to admit it to myself. Too late to save your old father . . . You could have two rations of bread, two rations of soup . . .

It was only a fraction of a second, but it left me feeling guilty. I ran to get some soup and brought it to my father. But he did not want it. All he wanted was water.

"Don't drink water, eat the soup . . ."

"I'm burning up . . . Why are you so mean to me, my son? . . . Water . . ."

I brought him water. Then I left the block for roll call. But I quickly turned back. I lay down on the upper bunk. The sick were allowed to stay in the block. So I would be sick. I didn't want to leave my father.

All around me, there was silence now, broken only by moaning. In front of the block, the SS were giving orders. An officer passed between the bunks. My father was pleading:

"My son, water . . . I'm burning up . . . My insides . . ."

"Silence over there!" barked the officer.

"Eliezer," continued my father, "water . . ."

The officer came closer and shouted to him to be silent. But my father did not hear. He continued to call me. The officer wielded his club and dealt him a violent blow to the head.

I didn't move. I was afraid, my body was afraid of another blow, this time to *my* head.

My father groaned once more, I heard: "Eliezer . . ."

I could see that he was still breathing—in gasps. I didn't move.

When I came down from my bunk after roll call, I could see his lips trembling; he was murmuring something. I remained more than an hour leaning over him, looking at him, etching his bloody, broken face into my mind.

Then I had to go to sleep. I climbed into my bunk, above my father, who was still alive. The date was January 28, 1945.

I woke up at dawn on January 29. On my father's cot there lay another sick person. They must have taken him away before daybreak and taken him to the crematorium. Perhaps he was still breathing . . .

No prayers were said over his tomb. No candle lit in his memory. His last word had been my name. He had called out to me and I had not answered.

I did not weep, and it pained me that I could not weep. But I was out of tears. And deep inside me, if I could have searched the recesses of my feeble conscience, I might have found something like: Free at last! . . .⌒

Evaluate Characters *What does this passage reveal about the head of the block?*

Memoir *Think about the way Wiesel chooses to reveal his father's death. How does this indirect description affect you?*

After You Read

Respond and Think Critically

Respond and Interpret

1. What detail or incident in this excerpt did you find most disturbing? Explain.

2. (a)How does Wiesel's father react when he hears about the hot showers? (b)Why does Wiesel insist that his father follow him to the showers?

3. (a)How do the other inmates treat the father after he comes down with dysentery? (b)Why do the other inmates behave this way?

4. (a)What advice does the head of the block offer Wiesel? (b)Why does Wiesel feel guilty after hearing this advice?

5. (a)How does Wiesel's father die? (b)Why does Wiesel say that his father's last word was a call he did not answer?

Analyze and Evaluate

6. (a)**Foreshadowing** occurs when an author provides hints about what will happen later in a text. What details foreshadow the death of Wiesel's father? (b)How well does the foreshadowing prepare you for what happens?

7. Do you think Wiesel's guilty feelings about his father are justified? Why or why not?

Connect

8. **Big Idea** **Postwar Europe** How did the events Wiesel describes lead him and other authors to question basic values that most people take for granted?

9. **Connect to Today** Do you think the message of Wiesel's memoir is still relevant today? Explain.

Literary Element Memoir

Traditionally, autobiography has been distinguished from **memoir**, but the two types of writing are closely related. A memoir is a type of autobiographical writing that usually focuses on the author's involvement in historically or culturally significant events, either as an eyewitness or a participant. Consult the chart you made on page 1064 then answer the following questions.

1. How might this memoir differ if it were written by someone other than Wiesel?

2. Based on this excerpt from *Night*, what was Wiesel's purpose in writing the book?

3. Some people deny the Holocaust ever occurred. How might you use Wiesel's writing to respond to that view?

LOG ON ▶ **Literature** Online

Selection Resources For Selection Quizzes, eFlashcards, and Reading-Writing Connection activities, go to glencoe. com and enter QuickPass code GLW6053u5.

Review: Conflict

As you learned on page 754, **conflict** is the central struggle between two opposing forces in a literary work. It can be **external**, when a character struggles against an outside force. It can also be **internal**, when the struggle takes place within the mind of a character torn between opposing feelings, desires, or goals.

Partner Activity Meet with a classmate and discuss the external and internal conflicts Wiesel experiences. Working with your partner, complete a chart like the one below.

When?	Conflict	External or Internal
Day of arrival at Buchenwald		
Morning after arrival at Buchenwald		

Reading Strategy — Evaluate Characters

SAT Skills Practice

What does Eliezer's reaction to the advice from the head of the block reveal about him?

(A) He is selfish and stingy.

(B) He is trusting and cooperative.

(C) He is easily shocked.

(D) He listens to his elders.

(E) He is compassionate and selfless.

Vocabulary Practice

Practice with Synonyms A synonym is a word that has the same or nearly the same meaning as another word. With a partner, match each boldfaced vocabulary word below with its synonym. Use a thesaurus or dictionary to check your answers. You will not use all the answer choices.

1. plaintive
2. elude
3. rivet

a. fasten
b. mournful
c. fitfully
d. hinge
e. escape

Academic Vocabulary

Wiesel's humanitarian work promotes an **ideology** *of justice and equality.*

Ideology is an academic word with which you may be familiar from social studies classes. In the sentence above, *ideology* means "a set of principles and thoughts that guide an individual or a group." To further explore the meaning of this word, answer the following question: Do you hold any **ideologies?** If so, what are they?

For more on academic vocabulary, see pages 36–37 and R83–R85.

Research and Report

Internet Connection

Assignment Use the Internet to research Wiesel's impact on the world through his humanitarian efforts related to the Holocaust. Deliver an oral report on your findings.

Get Ideas Create questions to guide your research. Through your research questions, generate key words that will lead to specific results and give you reliable information to include in your report.

Research Question	Key Word
What was life like at Buchenwald prison camp, where Eliezer and his father were sent?	"Buchenwald camp"
How has Elie Wiesel promoted education about the Holocaust?	"Elie Wiesel" AND "Holocaust education"

Use Boolean search techniques, which offer different ways to combine words. Searching for "Holocaust memorials" tells the computer to find every book or articles with exactly those words. By removing the quotation marks, you will get documents where the words "Holocaust" and "memorials" appear, but not necessarily together. Use AND to link search items and NOT to exclude others. For example, searching Wiesel AND "Nobel Prize" will produce documents in which both "Wiesel" and "Nobel Prize" appear. Searching Wiesel AND "Nobel Prize" NOT Holocaust will produce documents in which "Wiesel" and "Nobel Prize" appear, and "Holocaust" does not.

Research Evaluate the reliability of your sources and take careful notes. Then organize them in relation to your key words. Place Wiesel, his writings, and his humanitarian work in context, such as the creation of Holocaust memorials. Also address criticism of Wiesel and his work.

Report Use effective eye contact, tone, and body language to express yourself. Offer your own analysis of what you found in your Internet sources.

Before You Read

Freedom to Breathe

Meet **Aleksandr Solzhenitsyn**
(born 1918)

W hen Aleksandr Solzhenitsyn was awarded the Nobel Prize, he did not accept the award in person, fearing he would not be allowed to return home. However, he prepared an acceptance speech in which he stated that world literature can help nations discover "the true history of another" and spare it "from repeating the same cruel mistakes."

Childhood and Education Solzhenitsyn was born in Kislovodsk, Russia, one year after the outbreak of the Russian Revolution. His father died before Solzhenitsyn was born. Solzhenitsyn grew up in Rostov, where his mother earned a modest living as a stenographer. Though he was interested in literature, family and financial circumstances led him to pursue studies in mathematics and physics at the University of Rostov. During World War II, he served in the military, rising to the rank of captain of artillery.

Imprisonment and Exile Late in the war, Solzhenitsyn was arrested for writing letters in which he criticized Soviet leader Joseph Stalin. After eight years in prison, he was exiled to southern Kazakhstan for three years, where he worked as a teacher and began to write.

After emerging from exile in 1956, Solzhenitsyn continued teaching and writing. In 1961, when the new Soviet leader Nikita Khrushchev launched an attack on Stalinism and established a more open policy toward artistic expression, Solzhenitsyn took a chance. He arranged to have his novel *One Day in the Life of Ivan Denisovich* published in *Novy Mir* (*New World*), a prestigious literary and political journal. When it appeared in 1962, it quickly became a success, but also generated much controversy. The inner

> "*Lies can prevail against much in this world, but never against art.*"
>
> Aleksandr Solzhenitsyn

executive committee of the Communist Party openly criticized and harassed Solzhenitsyn and strongly objected to his grim depictions of Soviet oppression. After Khrushchev's fall from power, the attacks intensified. In 1965, the secret police seized Solzhenitsyn's papers, and later, Soviet authorities tried to ban his work from being published in foreign countries.

Solzhenitsyn was expelled from Russia in 1974, shortly after parts of *The Gulag Archipelago*, his historical account of the horrors of the Stalin-era Soviet labor camps, were published in Paris. After living briefly in Switzerland, he settled in Vermont. In 1989, influenced by Mikhail Gorbachev's policy of *glasnost* (openness), *Novy Mir* published government-approved excerpts from *The Gulag Archipelago*. In 1990, Soviet authorities reinstated Solzhenitsyn's citizenship. Four years later Solzhenitsyn returned to his homeland, having outlasted the Soviet regime.

 Literature Online

Author Search For more about Aleksandr Solzhenitsyn, go to glencoe.com and enter QuickPass code GLW6053u5.

Literature and Reading Preview

Connect to the Poem

What images do you associate with the word *freedom*? List several descriptive words or phrases that come to mind.

Build Background

Solzhenitsyn spent the last days of his imprisonment in a Gulag labor camp in a bitterly cold area of northern Kazakhstan. In *The Gulag Archipelago*, he describes his release and journey into exile. Although officially he was a free man, his activities were still restricted. The night of his release, having not yet obtained lodging, he stayed at MGB headquarters (department of safeguard), and the guards allowed him to spend the night outside. The poem "Freedom to Breathe," which he wrote later, appears in his book *Stories and Prose Poems*, first published in English in 1971.

Set Purposes for Reading

Big Idea Postwar Europe

As you read, ask yourself, How does Solzhenitsyn respond to political conditions in the post–World War II Soviet Union?

Literary Element Prose Poetry

A **prose poem** is a short prose composition that uses rhythm, imagery, figurative language, and other poetic devices to express an idea or emotion. Unlike metrical and free verse, prose poetry does not have line breaks; instead, the sentences appear in standard paragraph form. As you read "Freedom to Breathe," ask yourself, Which poetic devices does Solzhenitsyn use to express his feelings about freedom?

Reading Strategy Visualize

Poets use sensory language (words that appeal to sight, sound, taste, smell, and touch) to help readers picture an idea or feeling they want to convey. In "Freedom to Breathe," Solzhenitsyn creates a variety of pictures which, taken together, help the reader visualize his ideas about freedom. As you read, ask yourself, What images help me visualize Solzhenitsyn's experience?

....

Tip: Track Sensory Language As you read the poem, use a chart to jot down words or groups of words that appeal to the senses. By each example, describe the picture the words create.

Example of Sensory Language	Picture It Creates
apple tree in blossom, grass glistens with moisture, sweet fragrance pervades the air	pleasant, satisfying images of nature

L'Envol, 1968-1971. Marc Chagall (Russian, 1887–1985). Oil on canvas ,125 x 90 cm. Private collection. ©ARS

FREEDOM TO *breathe*

Aleksandr Solzhenitsyn

Translated by Michael Glenny

A shower fell in the night and now dark clouds drift across the sky, occasionally sprinkling a fine film of rain.

I stand under an apple tree in blossom and I breathe. Not only the apple tree but the grass round it glistens with moisture; words cannot describe the sweet fragrance that pervades the air. I inhale as deeply as I can, and the aroma invades my whole being; I breathe with my eyes open, I breathe with my eyes closed—I cannot say which gives me the greater pleasure.

This, I believe, is the single most precious freedom that prison takes away from us: the freedom to breathe freely, as I now can. No food on earth, no wine, not even a woman's kiss is sweeter to me than this air steeped in the fragrance of flowers, of moisture and freshness.

No matter that this is only a tiny garden, hemmed in by five-story houses like cages in a zoo. I cease to hear the motorcycles backfiring, radios whining, the burble of loud-speakers. As long as there is fresh air to breathe under an apple tree after a shower, we may survive a little longer.

Apple Trees in Bloom, 1904. Kazimir Severinovich Malevich (Russian, 1878-1935). Oil on canvas, 55 x 70 cm. State Russian Museum, St. Petersburg.

Visualize *Describe the scene. To what senses do the images appeal?*

Prose Poetry *What examples of figurative language can you find in this paragraph? Describe each example.*

After You Read

Respond and Think Critically

Respond and Interpret

1. The speaker describes a setting that gives him great pleasure. What memories of pleasurable moments from your own experience did his description evoke?

2. (a)How would you describe the setting at the beginning of "Freedom to Breathe"? (b)Why might Solzhenitsyn have included the setting's details in the last paragraph?

3. (a)What does the sweet fragrance of the flowers and the grass inspire the speaker to do? (b)What might Solzhenitsyn be suggesting about a person's connection to nature?

4. (a)According to the speaker, what is the most precious freedom prison takes away? (b)What, in your opinion, does this statement mean?

Analyze and Evaluate

5. What can you infer has happened to the speaker in the past?

6. **Tone** is a speaker's attitude toward the subject. What is the tone of "Freedom to Breathe"?

7. In the last sentence of the poem, what does the speaker imply about freedom?

Connect

8. **Big Idea** **Postwar Europe** What might the speaker's reverence for freedom imply about prison conditions in the Russian Gulag?

9. **Connect to the Author** (a)What biographical connection can you make between the speaker in the poem and Solzhenitsyn? (b)How would you interpret the last sentence of the poem?

Literary Element Prose Poetry

A **prose poem** allows a poet to express poetical ideas without following the usual rules of poetic form.

1. (a)Identify one example of parallel structure in the poem. (b)What purpose does it serve?

2. (a)Read the last paragraph aloud at a moderate speed. What rhythm is created? (b)What purpose might this rhythm serve?

Reading Strategy Visualize

When you **visualize**, you picture an author's ideas or descriptions in your mind.

1. (a)Identify examples of imagery that appeal to sight. (b)To which ones does the speaker seem to respond favorably? To which unfavorably?

2. (a)What images in the last paragraph appeal to hearing? (b)What might they represent?

Academic Vocabulary

*Solzhenitsyn writes about the **bond** between nature and people.*

*Bond is an academic word. In more casual conversation, you might talk about the **bond** among friends or family members. Using context clues, figure out the meaning of bond in the sentence above. Check your guess in a dictionary.*

For more on academic vocabulary, see pages 36–37 and R83–R85.

Writing

Write a Prose Poem Think of a time when doing something simple, like breathing, gave you great pleasure. Write a prose poem about that experience, using "Freedom to Breathe" as a model. Use sensory language and poetic devices to convey your feelings. Refer to the chart you made on page 1073 to help create original details for your poem.

Set a Purpose for Reading

Read to learn about six people who have revolutionized politics, the arts, science, and technology. Consider how their lives relate to the drastic changes that have occurred in postwar Europe.

Preview the Article

1. Scan the headings of the paragraphs. What do you already know about the people discussed in this article?

2. Skim the photos and their captions. What is similar and what is different about the people in the images?

Reading Strategy **Evaluate Historical Influences**

As you read, assess how the people profiled in this article created turning points in history, and trace how their actions affected others. Use a chart like the one below.

Person	Turning Point	Influence
King Juan Carlos	Spoke Catalan	Spread democratic ideals

TIME

60 Years of Risk Takers

OVER THE PAST 60 YEARS, MANY EXTRAORDINARY people have emerged from the turmoil, creativity, and chaos of a period that witnessed the aftermath of world war, the collapse of communism, the failure of old certainties, and the rise of new fears.

Some fought battles against repression and prejudice. Others tapped into the energies of the era to produce new technologies and innovative art forms. Still others introduced us to exciting new worlds and environments. Many of these agents of change took risks—with ideas, with conventions, sometimes with life itself. All of them changed our world for the better.

Aleksandr Solzhenitsyn

His powerful account of life in the Soviet Union's Gulag gave a voice to victims of oppression.

By YURI ZARAKHOVICH

His is a story about the power of the written word. In 1945, Aleksandr Solzhenitsyn was sentenced to eight years in the labor camps for criticizing the Soviet Union's dictator Joseph Stalin in letters to a friend. Seventeen years later, he turned his experience into *One Day in the Life of Ivan Denisovich*, the first literary work to describe the brutalities of prison under Stalin.

The book propelled Solzhen-itsyn to fame, but after the praise came persecution. Solzhenitsyn's books were banned and the writer was watched by the KGB, the Soviet intelligence agency. Yet he still kept writing, secretly sending novels abroad where they could be published. The first part of his epic three-volume work, *The Gulag Archipelago,* was published in Paris in 1973. It enraged the Soviet government and Solzhenitsyn was exiled abroad, which for a Russian writer, he said, amounted to a spiritual death.

That death was to last for 20 years. Now back home after the collapse of the communist government in 1991, Solzhenitsyn is still unwilling to stay quiet. He turned down new Russia's highest state award to protest "the all-out plundering of the country" he felt had been condoned by the regime that followed the Soviets.

But he doesn't believe in blaming bad government for all ills. On Feb. 12, 1974, the same day the KGB broke into his apartment to arrest him, *Live Not by Lies* was published. It was a roadmap on how to fight oppression: "It is not they who are to blame for everything—we are to blame ourselves, we alone . . . And the simplest key to liberation is this: personal nonparticipation in lies." It's a philosophy that is today just as relevant in his homeland—and in the wider world—as it was in Russia's totalitarian past.

Jacques-Yves Cousteau

Pioneering filmmaker and environmentalist, he showed the world the wonders of the deep.

By CATHERINE MAYER

Sailors tell tales of a magical world beneath the sea. Until Jacques-Yves Cousteau developed the aqualung SCUBA diving equipment, that world was off-limits to all but submariners and professional divers in clunky suits and helmets, sucking on air delivered by hosepipe. But with his self-contained breathing equipment and body-hugging wet suit, Cousteau became a "manfish" and was soon sending reports from this gloriously strange environment.

His many films, books, and long-running TV series—including *The Undersea World of Jacques Cousteau*—entranced people across the world. His 1956 film *Le Monde du Silence* (The Silent

Jacques Cousteau, French undersea explorer and oceanographer, shown in 1971 photo.

Bettmann/Corbis

World) won an Academy Award and was the first documentary to win the Palme d'Or award at the Cannes Film Festival. The documentary is hardly an advertisement for environmental best practices—the captain and his crew from the good ship *Calypso* are shown taking rides on turtles and casually killing sharks. Nevertheless, when Cousteau died, aged 87, in 1997, he was widely regarded as one of the fathers of environmentalism for his work as an oceanographer and vocal opposition to France's nuclear test program.

His was a life seemingly destined for greatness. Long before rising to public attention, Cousteau had already received France's top award, the Légion d'Honneur (the

Legion of Honor), for aiding the anti-Nazi French Resistance during World War II. His enduring legacy was to make the world aware of the beauty and fragility of the sea. "I spent my life amazed by nature and dazzled by the experiences of life," he said. And his achievements continue to amaze and dazzle.

King Juan Carlos

Groomed to take over from a dictator, he used his power to transform Spain into a democracy.

By JAMES GRAFF

European royalty has struggled to stay relevant in the modern age.

One monarch who succeeded is King Juan Carlos of Spain, whose sure sense of personal and national destiny helped his country turn itself into a democracy.

That happy result was hardly predestinated. Juan Carlos was born in exile in 1938. His father gave up control of his son's education to General Francisco Franco, the dictator who succeeded the royals after years of civil war, hoping this would encourage Franco to restore the crown. Juan Carlos was named Franco's eventual successor in 1969, but democrats had no great expectations of him. They realized their mistake once he took the throne upon Franco's death in 1975. Within four months he created a sensation by speaking Catalan, a language Franco had repressed. He then worked hard to have a centrist Prime Minister selected and began to introduce democratic reforms at a rapid pace. Spain's democratic constitution was ratified in 1978.

There was another test to come. After a series of terrorist bombings by Basques, an ethnic group that wants to secede from Spain, a conservative faction in the military tried to take control of the government in 1981. Many of them believed they were acting on the King's behalf. But Juan Carlos ordered military units back to their barracks, and without his support, the attempt collapsed. Four days later, 3 million people marched in cities throughout Spain in support of democracy. Their slogan, almost universally, was "*¡Viva el Rey!*" (Long live the King). That sentiment has persisted, more quietly, ever since.

Nobel peace prize winner Mother Teresa of Calcutta embraces nine month old Christina Ott

Mother Teresa

The Saint of Calcutta spread her love to the unwanted, the homeless, and the abandoned.

By DOMINIQUE LAPIERRE

My first sight of her was in her hospice of the Pure Heart in Calcutta, India decades ago. She was on her knees feeding, with a spoon and a plate of rice, a man who looked more like a corpse than a human being. Suddenly, she sensed my presence behind her. She turned around and abruptly handed me her plate: "Go on feeding this man," she said, "and love him." Those words—and actions—reflect Mother Teresa's message. To love those who have never been loved. To love the unwanted, the homeless, the abandoned, as if each one were Jesus Christ himself. For nearly 40 years, the Saint of Calcutta spread her message throughout India and the rest of the world.

And yet, from her arrival in Calcutta in 1929 as a young Albanian nun of the Loreto missionary order, her life had begun in a very different way. For years, she taught history and geography in Loreto schools in Calcutta and elsewhere. But on Sept. 10, 1946, she experienced a calling while on a train taking her to a retreat in Darjeeling at the foot of the Himalayas. The inner voice told her to give up the comfort of her surroundings, and to go share the life of the inhabitants of the nearest slum. She wrote to the Vatican for permission, and went to the bazaar to buy a cheap piece of white cotton cloth bordered with blue. This humble sari was to become the uniform of the exceptional group she then set up to serve the poorest of the poor, wherever they were: the homeless, the hungry, lepers, unwanted babies, AIDS victims. In 1979, she was awarded the Nobel Peace Prize.

Today, Mother Teresa's Missionaries of Charity carry on her ideal of compassion to all suffering human beings—with the same message I heard from her lips the very first day I met her in Calcutta: "Love them."

John Lydon

As the frontman of the ultimate British punk band the Sex Pistols, he inspired a new generation—and terrified an old one.

By HUGH PORTER

Londoners watching a local early-evening TV talk show dropped their forks. It was 1976 and they had expected the usual, easily digestible broadcast. Instead, they were served up musical revolution with their beans on toast. "They are punk rockers. The new craze, they tell me," announced the host Bill Grundy of his guests, the Sex Pistols. Grundy couldn't hide his

John Lydon, a.k.a. Johnny Rotten, is shown in a head shoulders photo

Lynn Goldsmith/CORBIS

contempt, pushing the band to respond outrageously. Viewers were witnessing a clash of generations, but the Pistols challenged not only their conservative elders but mainstream rock and its enduring hippie influences.

As the Pistols' lead singer, John Lydon—a.k.a. Johnny Rotten—wore the very heart of punk on his torn sleeve. He meant it then. He still does. Britain in the mid-1970s was strike-ridden and divided, and happy songs about love and sunshine seemed hopelessly out of tune with the times. The country needed punk, and it couldn't have happened without Lydon. He had the attitude and the look, and he was also articulate. His lyrics, delivered with a snarl, were social commentaries, often witty, often nasty. It made him as threatening to some as he was inspiring to others.

Always the outsider, Lydon was born to Irish parents in a north London slum, surviving the illness spinal meningitis as a 7-year-old and then enduring a strict Catholic schooling. In August 1975, now a scrawny youth with green locks, he was spotted on London's King's Road and asked to audition for a pop band. Lydon became Rotten, the TV clash guaranteed fame, and terrified town councils forbid the Pistols from performing. By the summer of 1977, they had taken on Britain's head of state. Their alternative anthem, God Save the Queen—with its reference to "her fascist regime" and "no future" refrain—was released as the country celebrated the 25th anniversary of Queen Elizabeth II's reign. "We had declared war on the entire country—without meaning to," said Lydon.

> **"His lyrics, delivered with a snarl, were social commentaries, often witty, often nasty."**
>
> —Hugh Porter

Six months later it was all over: the Pistols had split up and punk was beginning to be adopted by the mainstream. "It became acceptable and absorbed back into the system," said Lydon. He instantly rejected his insider status by forming a new band, Public Image Ltd, whose post-punk experimentation with new sounds and genres was massively influential and produced eight albums over 14 years. These days Lydon, perhaps inspired by his early encounter with Grundy, is a frequent TV presence, his gift for controversy undimmed by the passing years.

Linus Torvalds

By giving away his software, the Finnish programmer earned a place in history.

By PETER GUMBEL

Linus Torvalds was just 21 when he changed the world. Working out of his family's apartment in Finland's capital, Helsinki, in 1991, he wrote the beginnings of a new computer operating system called Linux. He then posted the system for free on the Internet—and invited anyone interested to help improve it. Today Linux powers everything from supercomputers to mobile phones around the world, and Torvalds has achieved fame as the godfather of the open-source movement. Followers believe software code should be shared and developed in a collaborative, or group, effort rather than being kept locked up by a single owner.

Some of Torvalds' supporters portray him as a sort of anti-Bill Gates, but the significance of Linux is much bigger than merely a criticism of Microsoft. Sharing core technologies could lead to a huge reduction in some business costs, freeing up money for more innovative investments elsewhere.

Torvalds continues to keep a close eye on Linux's development and has made some money from two companies that use the system in their products. But his success isn't just measured in dollars. There's an asteroid named after him, as well as an annual software festival. Torvalds' parents were student radicals in the 1960s and his father, a communist, even spent a year studying in Moscow. But it's their son who has turned out to be the real revolutionary.

—from TIME Atlantic

Linus Torvalds Holding Laptop Computer

Jim Sugar/Corbis

Respond and Think Critically

Respond and Interpret

1. Write a brief summary of the main ideas in each profile before you answer the following questions. For help on writing a summary, see page 1147.

2. (a)What punishment did Aleksandr Solzhenitsyn face in the Soviet Union? (b)Do you think people must face such obstacles to initiate change? Why or why not?

3. (a)Compare and contrast Mother Teresa's early life with her later life in India. (b)Mother Teresa believed she had to "give up the comfort of her surroundings." Do you think this is necessary in order to give to those less fortunate than yourself? Why or why not?

4. (a)What was unique about the way in which Torvalds developed Linux? (b)What quality does this reveal about Torvalds's character?

Analyze and Evaluate

5. (a)What was contradictory about Jacques-Yves Cousteau's work? (b)Is it possible to still be highly regarded for your achievements despite your faults? Explain.

6. (a)How is John Lydon's story different from the other profiles in this article? (b)Does it surprise you that his achievements were included in the article? Explain.

Connect

7. After World War II in Europe, many people lost faith in traditional ideals. Which of these risk takers may have been affected by this kind of change?

Writing Workshop

Biographical Investigation

Learning Objectives

For pages 1082–1091

In this workshop, you will focus on the following objectives:

Writing: Writing a biographical investigation using the writing process. Understanding how to develop coherent paragraphs.

Grammar: Understanding how to use commas correctly.

▶ **Writing Process**

At any stage of a writing process, you may think of new ideas. Feel free to return to earlier stages as you write.

Prewrite

Draft

Revise

Focus Lesson: Coherent Paragraphs

Edit and Proofread

Focus Lesson: Commas

Present

LOG ON ▶ **Literature** Online

Writing and Research For prewriting, drafting, and revising tools, go to glencoe.com and enter QuickPass code GLW6053u5.

Literature Connection Dante casts himself as the main character of the *Divine Comedy*, indirectly linking many details in the poem to emotions and experiences from his life.

> "Then turning to those spirits once again,
> I said: 'Francesca, what you suffer here
> melts me to tears of pity and of pain . . .'"

Researching Dante's life can give you a context for understanding his portrayal of Hell. Learning about authors' lives can reveal insights into their writing, because authors often use their real-life experiences as sources for their work. One function of a **research report** is to investigate how an author's historical period, beliefs, and personal experiences affected his or her work. To write this kind of report, use the strategies below.

Rubric

Goals	Strategies
To present a clear thesis	☑ Narrow and clarify the focus of your essay.
	☑ Revise your thesis statement as needed.
To support your thesis with historical evidence	☑ Make connections between the author's life and the literary text.
To organize your research logically	☑ Structure your essay with a clear introduction, body, and conclusion.
	☑ Organize your evidence into paragraphs with clear topic sentences.
To use evidence effectively and correctly	☑ Take notes on a variety of sources.
	☑ Quote, paraphrase, and summarize information and credit sources.
To present your own ideas on the topic	☑ Comment on experts' ideas.
	☑ Present your own insights.

Assignment: Connect an Author's Life and Work

Write a research paper of at least 1,000 words in which you investigate the relationship between an author's life and his or her work. As you move through the stages of writing, keep your audience and purpose in mind.

Audience: peers, classmates, and teacher

Purpose: research an author's life and make connections with his or her work

Prewrite

Narrow Your Topic Review the literary works in this unit and think about which authors' lives intrigue you. Depending on the author you choose and the amount of research available, you may want to narrow your focus to a particular theme or element of a single work or a specific aspect of the author's life. To help narrow your focus, make a list of questions and choose one or two of them. For example, if you choose to write about the connection between Dante's life and his poetry, you might ask questions like these:

▶ Was Beatrice modeled on a woman in Dante's life?

▶ How did Dante know so much about different aspects of human experience?

▶ Is Dante himself the main character in the *Divine Comedy*?

Gather Information Identify a variety of sources, including books, reputable Internet sites, and encyclopedias (see page R32 for more on reliable sources). A **primary source** is an original document from the time period you are researching. Autobiographies or letters written by your author or by people who knew the author are particularly useful primary sources. A **secondary source** is a document, such as an encyclopedia entry, by a person who had no personal involvement in the events you are writing about.

As you research, think about your paper's **thesis,** or central idea. Look for patterns and contradictions in your sources, and think about what conclusions you can draw about your topic.

Take Notes As you investigate your topic, take notes on four different kinds of note cards. Color-code or label them so you know exactly what type of information—bibliography, summary, paraphrase, or quotation— appears on each note card. Be sure to record page numbers to indicate where you found the information. This will help you manage the information you gather. (For more on how to use note cards effectively, see page R32–R33.)

Real-World Connection

Many activities in life require the ability to gather research, take notes, and synthesize information. Whether you are investigating a career or choosing a college, your ability to evaluate information will help you make informed decisions.

Avoid Plagiarism

As you research, you might come across a phrase or sentence that says exactly what you want to say. If this happens, be sure to show your readers the source of your ideas. Plagiarizing, or presenting someone else's words or ideas as your own, is dishonest. It is important to distinguish between a paraphrase, a quote, or a summary when you take notes. Include quotation marks to indicate direct quotes. If you summarize or paraphrase, you must give the author due credit.

Cite Your Sources

As you write your draft, indicate each source with parenthetical citations. Typically, parenthetical citations include the author's last name and the page number **(Stade 411)**. If you mention the author's name in a sentence, you only need to cite the page number. For sources with no author listed, give a shortened version of the title in parentheses. (For more about citations and creating a works-cited list, see pages R34–R37.)

▶ **Bibliography note cards** Write the complete publishing information for each source on a separate card.

▶ **Summary note cards** Write the author's last name and the source's title, and then write down the source's main ideas.

▶ **Paraphrase note cards** Write the author's last name and the source's title, and then retell information from the source in your own words.

▶ **Quotation note cards** Write the author's last name and the source's title, and then copy the passage exactly.

Create an Outline Use your note cards to create an outline for your paper. Your outline is a plan for the body of your paper, which should expand upon and provide support for a main idea. Organize note cards with similar topics into groups, and arrange the groups in a logical order. Use each group as a main topic in your outline. Once you have created a general outline, insert specific evidence from your note cards to support each main topic. Cite the sources as in the example below.

Outline Form

I. Main topic

  A. Subtopic

    1. Evidence

  B. Subtopic

  C. Subtopic

II. Main topic

  A. Subtopic

  B. Subtopic

III. Main topic

  A. Subtopic

  B. Subtopic

I. Dante's pain over lost love

  A. Falls in love with Beatrice, whose premature death causes Dante enormous grief

    1. "Dante called her Beatrice, the bringer of blessings, the one who brought bliss to all who looked upon her" (Stade 411).

  B. After Beatrice's death, embarks on a period of intense study and learning

  C. Love of Beatrice transforms into love of philosophy, which influences the *Divine Comedy*

II. Dante's political disappointments

  A. Enters public life during period of political strife between Black and White Guelfs

  B. Develops deep hatred for policies of Pope Boniface VIII

III. Dante's exile from Florence

  A. Experiences loneliness and difficulty

  B. Benefits from exile

Develop a Thesis Statement Once you have organized your research into an outline, write your thesis statement—the central idea you will prove in your paper. Your thesis statement should be a one- or two-sentence synthesis of the main topics in your outline.

Draft

Create Structure As you draft, use your outline to guide your writing. Write at least one paragraph for each main topic in your outline. Include a topic sentence and supporting details in each paragraph. Your conclusion should restate your thesis in a different way, recount your main points, or provide a final thought-provoking idea.

Analyze a Workshop Model

Here is a final draft of a biographical investigation. Read the essay and answer the questions in the margin. Use your answers to these questions to guide you as you write.

Suffering and Creativity: The Life of Dante Alighieri

The hardships and triumphs of authors' lives often become the foundations for their fiction. Dante Alighieri experienced great tragedy and change during his life, including a deeply felt heartache over a lost love, political betrayals, and exile from his home in Florence, Italy. Narrating in the first person and casting himself as the protagonist, Dante translated his experiences into the *Divine Comedy*, one of the greatest works in Western literature.

When he was just nine years old, Dante fell in love with the daughter of the noble Florentine Folco Portinari. George Stade explains that Dante called this girl Beatrice, meaning "the bringer of blessings, the one who brought bliss to all who looked upon her" (411). Beatrice was perhaps the most powerful force in Dante's life and art, but his love for her was never returned—Beatrice married another man. Although Dante eventually married as well, he continued to idealize Beatrice throughout his life. Her premature death caused him enormous grief.

Writing Frames

As you read the workshop model, think about the following persuasive frames.

- The writer's argument that ____ is supported by ____ ____, and ____.

- The writer argues ____, and I agree, because ____.

Try using frames like these as you write your paper.

Thesis Statement

What makes this thesis statement effective?

Citations

Why does the writer include only the page number in this parenthetical citation?

The loss of Beatrice influenced Dante's religious and philosophical development, eventually leading him to the vision of Heaven he presents in his last work, the *Divine Comedy*. Searching for comfort after the death of Beatrice, Dante turned away from the love poetry he had written in his youth and embarked on a period of intense study and learning. He read the work of the Greek political philosopher Cicero and the medieval philosopher Boethius. Dante admits in the *Convivio*, a philosophical work published sometime between 1304 and 1307, that this reading was very difficult for him at first. Still, he kept at it. Also in the *Convivio*, he writes:

> And as it may happen that a man looking for silver accidentally hits on gold . . . so I, seeking consolation, found not only a remedy for my sorrow but the language of authors and sciences and books; reflecting on which I judged that philosophy—the lady of these authors and sciences and books—was a very great thing. And I imagined it as a noble lady, whom I could not represent to myself in any attitude but one of compassion; with the result that my sense of truth was so drawn to her that I could not take my eyes off her. (qtd. in Foster 45)

This quotation describes how Dante's early romantic love of Beatrice transformed into a love of philosophy, which would become the driving force behind his later poetry. Reynolds remarks that, in his maturity, Dante portrayed Beatrice not as "the scornful young woman" of the early poems, but as a figure who led him to higher philosophical truths (112). Dante's intellectual development, she explains, "led him to create a new Beatrice [in the *Divine Comedy*], beatified and invested with the divine qualities he had already associated with her but which formerly he had not understood" (112).

Well before Dante wrote the *Divine Comedy*, however, he became involved in the political life of Florence. Florence was a thriving economic, artistic, and political center in Dante's time, and the poet felt a deep love for his city, despite the feuding and conspiracies that characterized public life. In 1295, he sought

---

Block Quotations

Why might the writer have chosen to include a quotation of this length?

Explanations

Why is this sentence an effective way to transition from the block quotation to the next sentence?

Secondary Sources

How does this secondary source help reinforce the writer's point?

Main Ideas

Which sentence in this paragraph states the main idea?

public office as a member of the physician's guild. However, his timing was disastrous. The Guelfs, the ruling party in Florence, had recently divided into two warring factions: the Blacks, who supported papal rule, and the Whites, who felt that religious and political rule should remain separate. Dante, a White Guelf, felt deep distress over this state of affairs—a distress he expresses memorably in Canto 26 of the *Inferno*, where he writes that Florence's political unrest is so well-known that the city's name is spread "throughout Hell" (Alighieri 220). On May 1, 1300, the turmoil reached a boiling point, and violence broke out between the Black and White Guelfs. As a result, many of Dante's fellow White Guelfs were exiled. Dante makes these devastating events the backdrop for the *Divine Comedy*, setting his epic during Easter Week of 1300 (Reynolds 36).

The pain and bitterness Dante felt at this time come through most obviously in his hate-filled portrayal of Pope Boniface VIII in the *Divine Comedy*. Elected in 1294, Boniface helped the Black Guelfs stage a 1301 coup of Florence; he was also accused by Dante and others of simony, or selling religious titles for profit (Reynolds 41). As Ricardo J. Quinones points out, Dante hated Boniface because his actions defied one of Dante's primary beliefs: that politics and religion must be kept separate to preserve the purity of the church (Quinones 80). In the *Inferno*, Dante goes out of his way to criticize Boniface's behavior, having one soul mention that the pope is expected in Hell. He even has St. Peter rail against Boniface in the *Paradiso* (Reynolds 384–385). Dante was a devout Christian and hated Boniface for corrupting the title of pope. However, there was another, more personal cause for his feelings. He seems to have seen Boniface as directly responsible for his next major misfortune: his devastating exile from Florence.

Exposition

Paraphrase

Why is a direct quotation not necessary here?

The graceful Cathedral of Santa Maria del Fiore, and its baptistery and campanile, form the heart of Florence, Italy.

Dante's exile, a pivotal event in his life, provided much of the spiritual and creative inspiration for the *Divine Comedy*. Following Boniface's Black Guelf takeover, Dante was banished on charges of political corruption. If he returned to Florence, he would risk being captured and burned alive. At first, Dante was able to find comfort in a community of fellow exiles, but after quarrelling with them over failed attempts at regaining power, he was left on his own (Reynolds 49). He then began a lonely and difficult period of travel in northern Italy, "fulfilling diplomatic assignments, when he could find them, on behalf of lords who received him grudgingly and those who really opened their doors to him" (*Dante: His Life* 19–20). Of this period, Dante himself remarked, "Truly I have been a ship without a sail and without a rudder, driven to many ports and river mouths and shores by the dry wind of miserable poverty . . ." (qtd. in *Dante: His Life* 5). The "dark wood" Dante finds himself in at the beginning of the *Inferno* may represent the sense of despair and uncertainty he felt in exile—he did not know, at the time of writing, whether he would ever be allowed to return to Florence.

Though Dante's exile was painful, it led to several positive developments in his life. First, the solitude afforded him the opportunity to resume his writing. By most accounts, he began writing the *Comedy* to sustain and comfort himself in the first years of his exile. Then, from 1312 on, he found patronage in the courts of several noblemen (Hollander 6), a turn of events that provided him with a new level of stability and security. When he wrote the joyful final canto of the *Paradiso* just before his death in 1321, he was probably living under some of the happiest conditions of his life (Hollander 6).

Like Dante's life, the *Divine Comedy* describes a difficult journey that has more than its share of disappointments, hardships, and revelations. In fact, Dante's difficult experiences were his primary motivation for pursuing philosophy and writing. If Dante had not experienced the pain of lost love, the bitterness of political betrayal, and the longing for home, he may never have achieved such poetic

---

Primary Sources

Why might the writer have chosen to use a direct quotation here rather than paraphrasing?

Synthesize

What original ideas does the writer offer?

Paragraph Structure

How does the writer use details to support the main idea of this paragraph?

greatness. His *Divine Comedy* demonstrates that personal difficulties can often be translated into works of supreme beauty.

Works Cited

Alighieri, Dante. <u>Inferno</u>. Trans. John Ciardi. New Brunswick: Rutgers UP, 1954.

"Dante." <u>Encyclopedia Britannica</u>. 2007. Encyclopedia Britannica Online. 23 Jan. 2007 <http://www.britannica.com/eb/article-22147>.

"Florence." <u>Encyclopedia Britannica</u>. 2007. Encyclopedia Britannica Online. 19 Jan. 2007 <http://www.britannica.com/eb/article-22454>.

Foster, Kenelm. "The Mind in Love: Dante's Philosophy." <u>Dante: A Collection of Critical Essays</u>. Ed. John Freccero. Englewood Cliffs: Prentice-Hall, 1965. 43–60.

"Guelf and Ghibelline." <u>Encyclopedia Britannica</u>. 2007. Encyclopedia Britannica Online. 23 Jan. 2007 <http://www.britannica.com/eb/article-9038359>.

Hollander, Robert. <u>Dante: A Life in Works</u>. New Haven: Yale UP, 2001.

Quinones, Ricardo J. <u>Dante Alighieri</u>. Updated ed. Twayne's World Authors Series. New York: Simon & Schuster Macmillan, 1998.

Reynolds, Barbara. <u>Dante: The Poet, the Political Thinker, the Man</u>. Emeryville: Shoemaker & Hoard, 2006.

Salvadori, Giuseppina T., and Bernice L. Lewis, trans. <u>Dante: His Life, His Times, His Works</u>. New York: American Heritage, 1968.

Stade, George, ed. "Dante Alighieri." <u>European Writers: Selected Authors</u>. Vol. 1. New York: Scribner, 1992. 411–415.

Exposition

Conclusion

What makes this conclusion effective?

Variety of Sources

How might this encyclopedia entry have been helpful to the writer?

Reliable Sources

What indicates that this source is reliable?

Revise

Peer Review Have a peer review your draft to identify its strengths and weaknesses. Use the checklist below to evaluate your own writing.

Checklist

☑ Do you begin with a well-defined thesis statement?

☑ Do you connect information about the author's life to his or her writing?

☑ Do you include direct quotations and cite sources accurately?

☑ Do you provide your own insights on the topic?

> **Focus Lesson**

Coherent Paragraphs

As you revise, delete unimportant details, rearrange the order of ideas, or improve transitions to make a paragraph flow better.

Draft:

By most accounts, Dante began writing the *Comedy* to sustain and comfort himself in the first years of his exile. <u>Though his exile was painful, it led to several positive developments in his life. The solitude afforded him the opportunity to resume his writing.</u> From 1312 on, he found patronage in the courts of several noblemen (Hollander 6), a turn of events that provided him with a new level of stability and security. . . . <u>Dante's death, at the age of 56, was caused by malarial fever (Hollander 4).</u>

Revision:

<u>Though Dante's exile was painful, it led to several positive developments in his life.</u> First,[1] <u>the solitude afforded him the opportunity to resume his writing.</u>[2] By most accounts, he began writing the *Comedy* to sustain and comfort himself in the first years of his exile. Then,[1] from 1312 on, he found patronage in the courts of several noblemen (Hollander 6), a turn of events that provided him with a new level of stability and security. . . . ~~Dante's death, at the age of 56, was caused by malarial fever (Hollander 4).~~[3]

1: Link ideas with transitional phrases	2: Improve the flow of ideas	3: Delete unrelated details

Edit and Proofread

Get It Right When you have completed the final draft of your research report, proofread it for errors in grammar, usage, mechanics, and spelling. Refer to the Language Handbook, pages R40–R59, as a guide.

> **Focus Lesson**

Commas

Commas are often used to separate transitional words and phrases. Use commas after introductory expressions (at the beginning of a sentence) and on either side of interrupters (in the middle of a sentence).

Original: *Like Dante's life* is an introductory transitional phrase.

Like Dante's life the Divine Comedy describes a difficult journey that has more than its share of disappointments, hardships, and revelations.

Improved: Add a comma after the introductory transitional phrase.

Like Dante's life, the Divine Comedy describes a difficult journey that has more than its share of disappointments, hardships, and revelations.

Original: The transitional word *however* is an interrupter.

Well before Dante wrote the Divine Comedy however, he became involved in the political life of Florence.

Solution: Add another comma before the interrupter.

Well before Dante wrote the Divine Comedy, however, he became involved in the political life of Florence.

Present/Publish

Final Check Before turning in your paper, check that it is at least 1,000 words. Make sure all your in-text citations are in the proper format and include an alphabetical works cited list with full bibliographic information for each of your sources (see pages R35–R37). You may wish to bind your research report in a folder with a cover sheet that gives the title of the paper and your name. Check with your teacher for additional presentation guidelines, such as page numbering and margins.

Peer Review Tips

If you review a classmate's essay, look for their thesis, main points, and supporting details.

- Circle his or her thesis statement in pencil.
- Use sticky notes to point out the topic sentence in each paragraph.
- Underline the supporting details for each main point.

Word-Processing Tip

If you are typing your essay on a computer, use a professional font style. Make sure it is properly sized and easy to read. Many creative fonts are appropriate for large posters, but can be difficult to read in smaller sizes.

Writer's Portfolio

Place a clean copy of your research report in your portfolio to review later.

Develop Your Presentation

Avoid Plagiarism

Correctly credit each image, video clip, and sound, along with all your print sources, in your Works Cited list. (See pages R34–37 for standardized citation styles.)

Follow these steps to build your presentation.

- **_Focus on your purpose._** Your main purpose is to inform. All the sounds and images should clearly and accurately present main ideas that explain your thesis and give strong support to back it up.

- **_Make your thesis clear._** Because your thesis is the most important idea you will present, consider displaying your thesis at the beginning of your presentation and restating it at the end.

- **_Remember the audience and occasion._** Think about other ways to help your audience understand and follow your presentation. If you are using unfamiliar or technical terms, think about explaining them. Consider using diagrams, maps, graphs, or charts.

- **_Write your narration._** Remember that, in most cases, your images and sounds will not speak for themselves. Create a narration that clearly conveys your main ideas and helps your audience make links between the different parts of your presentation.

- **_Edit for conciseness._** Add interest and information where needed. Delete unnecessary or distracting ideas, images, and sounds.

Organize Your Presentation

Next, create a storyboard. Draw one frame of the storyboard for each slide, card, or transparency you will use. Begin with a title and author frame, and end with a Works Cited frame that includes all your research sources, as well all your visual and sound sources. In the remainder of the storyboard frames, list in order the ideas for the images, sounds, and text you will use.

- title
- Gustav Doré illustration
<u>Medieval religious music</u>

- thesis
<u>bring music down</u>
- image of Dante

- image of Beatrice
- dramatic reading— quote from Stade tell main idea and details
<u>Medieval religious music</u>

- page from an illuminated manuscript
- dramatic reading— quote from *Convivio* tell main idea and details

---

- picture of Boniface or Guelfs
<u>clashing sounds/minor chords</u>
tell main idea/details

- title page of *Divine Comedy* narrate main idea and details
<u>glorious/celebratory religious music c. 1300</u>

- dramatic reading of quotation from *Dante: His Life*
- map showing exile tell main idea and details

- thesis
- Works Cited
<u>music from opening frame</u>

Here are two examples of slides based on ideas mapped out in the model storyboard.

"Suffering and Creativity" The Life of Dante Alighieri

by Silvia Diaz

ITALY

Florence ●

Dante's exile from Florence, Italy
Inspiration for scenes in the *Divine Comdey*

Rehearse and Deliver Your Presentation

A successful multimedia presentation depends, in large part, on timing. Rehearse several times in order to be sure that all your images, sound, and narration work smoothly together. Once you have the timing down, give your presentation to one or two classmates or family members. Find out whether they can state your thesis and the main ideas that support it. Use their feedback to help you make adjustments to your pace, to your volume, or to specific slides.

As you rehearse and deliver your presentation, keep the presentation techniques below in mind. When you are an audience member, keep the listening and viewing techniques in mind.

Techniques for Delivering a Multimedia Presentation

Presentation Techniques	Listening and Viewing Techniques
☑ **Pace** Because your audience is not familiar with your research or your images, allow more time to convey information.	☑ **Posture** Show your enthusiasm in the presentation by sitting upright in your seat and keeping your head up. Try not to doodle, tap, or fidget.
☑ **Volume** Your audience must be able to hear you at all times. Be sure your music and sound effects do not drown out or overpower your words.	☑ **Movement and Facial Expression** Maintain a look on your face that says, "I'm interested." As appropriate, use subtle movements such as a nod to show you are engaged.

Evaluation Checklist

☑ Does the presentation flow smoothly and keep you interested from beginning to end?

☑ Is the thesis clear? Are the main ideas that support it clear?

☑ Do the images and sounds work well to convey or complement the thesis and main ideas?

☑ Does the presentation reflect careful editing and rehearsing?

Assessment

English–Language Arts

Reading: Fiction

Carefully read the following passage. Use context clues to help you define any words with which you are unfamiliar. Pay close attention to **themes, cultural context, author's purpose,** and the use of **literary devices**. Then, on a separate sheet of paper, answer the questions on page 1100.

from *Crime and Punishment* by Fyodor Dostoevsky

Towards the end of a sultry afternoon early in July a young man came out of his little room in Stolyarny Lane and turned slowly and somewhat irresolutely in the direction of Kamenny Bridge.

5   He had been lucky enough to escape an encounter with his landlady on the stairs. His little room, more like a cupboard than a place to live in, was tucked away under the roof of the high five-storied building. The landlady, who let him the room and provided him with dinners and service,
10 occupied a flat on the floor below, and every time he went out he was forced to pass the door of her kitchen, which nearly always stood wide open. He went past each time with an uneasy, almost frightened, feeling that made him frown with shame. He was heavily in debt to his landlady
15 and shrank from meeting her.

It was not that he was a cowed or naturally timorous person, far from it; but he had been for some time in an almost morbid state of irritability and tension. He had cut himself off from everybody and withdrawn so completely
20 into himself that he now shrank from every kind of contact. He was crushingly poor, but he no longer felt the oppression of his poverty. For some time he had ceased to concern himself with everyday affairs. He was not really afraid of any landlady, whatever plots he might think she
25 was hatching against him, but to have to stop on the stairs and listen to all her chatter about trivialities in which he refused to take any interest, all her complaints, threats, and insistent demands for payment, and then to have to extricate himself, lying and making excuses—no, better to
30 creep downstairs as softly as a cat and slip out unnoticed.

This time, however, he reached the street feeling astonished at the intensity of his fear of his landlady.

'To think that I can contemplate such a terrible act and yet be afraid of such trifles,' he thought, and he smiled
35 strangely. 'Hm…yes…a man holds the fate of the world in his two hands, and yet, simply because he is afraid, he just lets things drift—that is a truism…I wonder what men are most afraid of…Any new departure, and especially a *new word*—that is what they fear most of all…But I am talking
40 too much. That's why I don't act, because I am always talking. Or perhaps I talk so much just because I can't act. I have got into a habit of babbling to myself during this last month, while I have been lying in a corner for days on end, thinking…fantastic nonsense. And why have I come out
45 now? Can I really be capable of *that*? Am I really serious? No, of course I'm not serious. So I am just amusing myself with fancies, children's games? Yes, perhaps I am only playing a game.'

The heat in the streets was stifling. The stuffiness,
50 the jostling crowds, the bricks and mortar, scaffolding and dust everywhere, and that peculiar summer stench so familiar to everyone who cannot get away from St. Petersburg into the country, all combined to aggravate the disturbance of the young man's nerves. The intolerable
55 reek from the public houses, so numerous in that part of the city, and the sight of the drunken men encountered at every turn, even though this was not a holiday, completed the mournfully repellant picture. An expression of the deepest loathing passed across the young man's delicate features.
60 (He was, by the way, a strikingly handsome young man, with fine dark eyes, brown hair, and a slender well-knit figure, taller than the average.) Soon, however, he relapsed again into profound thought, or rather into a sort of abstraction, and continued on his way in complete and
65 willful unconsciousness of his surroundings. Once or twice he muttered something to himself in a manner that, as he had just confessed, had grown habitual with him. He himself realized that at times his thoughts were confused and that he was very weak; he had eaten practically nothing
70 for two days.

1. What does the young man's behavior toward his landlady suggest?
   (A) That he is a cruel and intolerant man
   (B) That he has recently lost a great deal of money
   (C) That he is antisocial by nature
   (D) That there has been an unsettling change in his mental state
   (E) That he is painfully shy

2. In line 16, "timorous" most nearly means
   (A) outgoing
   (B) fearful
   (C) dishonest
   (D) emotional
   (E) depraved

3. The statement in lines 31–32 serves primarily to
   (A) show that the young man has been steadily going crazy
   (B) suggest that the intensity of his fear of his landlady is a positive force in his life
   (C) justify the young man's actions
   (D) portray the young man in a negative light
   (E) show that this particular instance was especially frightening for the young man

4. The young man's comment in lines 33–34 ("To think…trifles") has a tone of
   (A) playful surprise
   (B) total detachment
   (C) strict formality
   (D) ironic self-pity
   (E) utter despair

5. According to the young man, what do men fear most?
   (A) A new word
   (B) Truisms
   (C) People who babble to themselves
   (D) Fantastic nonsense
   (E) Death

6. The primary purpose of the fifth paragraph is to
   (A) show the abysmal conditions in which the young man lived
   (B) offer details that will encourage the reader to sympathize with the young man
   (C) show the young man's interior monologue, which is an example of his feverish mind at work
   (D) prove that the young man has completely lost his mind
   (E) suggest that the landlady's strict demeanor has driven the young man mad

7. What is the main idea in lines 49–54 ("The heat…nerves")?
   (A) The streets of St. Petersburg are stiflingly hot.
   (B) Many inhabitants of St. Petersburg do not have enough money to leave during the summer.
   (C) The summer stench and dust are unbearable.
   (D) The bricks, mortar, and scaffolding show there is construction in St. Petersburg.
   (E) The heat, stuffiness, crowds, bricks and mortar, scaffolding and dust, and stench combine to further irritate the young man's nerves.

8. The author's use of a parenthetical statement in lines 60–62 ("He was…average") serves primarily to
   (A) show that the protagonist is very popular
   (B) contrast the protagonist's attractive appearance with his confused mental state
   (C) suggest that the protagonist is on the path to recovery
   (D) emphasize the protagonist's flair for drama
   (E) de-emphasize the protagonist's reveries

Vocabulary Skills: Sentence Completion

For each item in the Vocabulary Skills section, choose the word or words that best complete the sentence. Write your answers on a separate sheet of paper.

1. Crying out in _____, the souls of the lustful drift through a whirlwind in Dante's *Inferno*.
   (A) grudge
   (B) torment
   (C) respites
   (D) scorn
   (E) solitude

2. When he began to see Laura as a _____ earthly distraction, Petrarch stopped presenting her as a _____, goddess-like figure in his poetry.
   (A) contrary...discourteous
   (B) nautical...obsessed
   (C) savage...rational
   (D) mere...revered
   (E) myriad...plaintive

3. Knights swore never to be _____, but to show politeness and _____ to their lords.
   (A) rational...elasticity
   (B) discourteous...fidelity
   (C) chaste...solitude
   (D) prudent...vivacity
   (E) distorted...consternation

4. Because they were only given the least _____, most undesirable plots of land, Russian peasants had to live quite _____ for many years.
   (A) arable...penuriously
   (B) nimble...indiscriminately
   (C) prudent...clemency
   (D) contrary...distressed
   (E) compulsory...asunder

5. Europe is home to _____ cultural groups, and there has often been strife and _____ between them.
   (A) nimble...disillusion
   (B) humane...presumption
   (C) myriad...discord
   (D) modest...elasticity
   (E) compulsory...renown

6. Dante was _____ with Beatrice for many years, as evidenced by the repeated references to her in his work.
   (A) obsessed
   (B) plaintive
   (C) undaunted
   (D) compulsory
   (E) discourteous

7. After he was deported from Russia for _____ the communist government, Aleksandr Solzhenitsyn sought _____ in the United States.
   (A) reeling...abstinence
   (B) consoling...seclusion
   (C) negating...furrows
   (D) disparaging...refuge
   (E) deciphering...renown

8. Marie de France has received great _____ and praise for her well-crafted poems.
   (A) anguish
   (B) renown
   (C) seclusion
   (D) verdict
   (E) discord

Grammar and Writing Skills:
Sentence Improvement

Read the following sentences carefully. Pay close attention to the writer's **sentence structure, transitions,** and use of **punctuation**. Then, on a separate sheet of paper, write the letter of the answer that correctly fixes each underlined portion.

1. Rosie the Riveter, an image that appeared on posters during World War II, <u>quickly became a cultural icon</u>.
   (A) quickly became a cultural icon
   (B) became quickly a cultural icon
   (C) quickly become a cultural icon
   (D) have become quickly a cultural icon
   (E) quickly becoming a cultural icon

2. Many different portable audio devices <u>has been used to play music</u> over the years, including cassette players, CD players, and MP3 players.
   (A) has been used to play music
   (B) been used to play music
   (C) have been used to play music
   (D) should be used to play music
   (E) is used to play music

3. <u>The Golden Gate Bridge the second longest suspension bridge in the United States,</u> connects San Francisco to Marin County.
   (A) The Golden Gate Bridge the second longest suspension bridge in the United States,
   (B) The Golden Gate Bridge the second, longest suspension bridge in the United States,
   (C) The Golden Gate Bridge the second longest suspension bridge, in the United States,
   (D) The Golden, Gate Bridge the second longest suspension bridge, in the United States,
   (E) The Golden Gate Bridge, the second longest suspension bridge in the United States,

4. Wolfgang Amadeus Mozart wrote over 600 compositions <u>before dying at the age of 35.</u>
   (A) before dying at the age of 35.
   (B) before the age of 35 when he had been dying.
   (C) dying before the age of 35.
   (D) at the age of 35 dying.
   (E) at the age of 35 when he had died.

5. Many different types of hot breakfast cereals, such as oatmeal, grits, and porridge, <u>is eaten around the world.</u>
   (A) is eaten around the world.
   (B) should be eaten around the world.
   (C) has eaten around the world.
   (D) are eaten around the world.
   (E) have eaten around the world.

6. The Lhasa apso is <u>a small furry dog originally bred in Tibet and now very popular</u> in the United States.
   (A) a small furry dog originally bred in Tibet and now very popular
   (B) a small, furry dog, originally bred in Tibet and now very popular
   (C) a small, furry dog originally bred in Tibet and now very popular
   (D) a small furry dog, originally bred in Tibet and now very popular
   (E) a small furry dog originally bred in Tibet, and now very popular

7. Although salmon is not a traditional Japanese food, many American sushi chefs serve the fish in their maki rolls and <u>as sashimi; a slice of raw fish</u> accompanied by condiments.
   (A) as sashimi; a slice of raw fish
   (B) as sashimi, a slice of raw fish
   (C) as sashimi a slice of raw fish
   (D) like sashimi, a slice of raw fish
   (E) like sashimi; a slice of raw fish

8. Because fixed gear bicycles do not have a free wheel, riders do not have the luxury of <u>coasting; instead, they must pedal all the time.</u>
   (A) coasting; instead, they must pedal all the time.
   (B) coasting—instead they must pedal all the time.
   (C) coasting, instead they must be pedaling all the time.
   (D) coasting, instead; they must pedal all the time.
   (E) coasting; instead they must pedal all the time.

9. Swedish filmmaker Ingmar Bergman, perhaps best known for his stark portrayal of medieval Europe in "The Seventh Seal," <u>has died in 2007 at the age of 89.</u>
   (A) has died in 2007 at the age 89.
   (B) in 2007 has died at the age of 89.
   (C) dying at 89 in 2007.
   (D) died in 2007 at the age of 89.
   (E) at the age of 89, in 2007, had died.

10. The sticky note was created by accident when Dr. Spencer Silver made a <u>weak adhesive whose glue did not leave a residue.</u>
    (A) a weak adhesive whose glue did not leave a residue.
    (B) a weak adhesive which did not leave a glue.
    (C) a weak adhesive that did not leave a residue.
    (D) a weak adhesive that leave no residue.
    (E) a weak adhesive which leaves no residue.

Essay

Think carefully about the following excerpt and the writing assignment below.

"Too late to save your old father . . . You could have two rations of bread, two rations of soup . . .
   It was only a fraction of a second, but it left me feeling guilty. I ran to get some soup and brought it to my father."

—Elie Wiesel, from *Night*

Write an essay in which you analyze Elie Wiesel's internal conflict in *Night*. What factors cause his conflict? What values does the conflict illustrate? How is the conflict resolved, or is it left unresolved? Be sure to include specific examples from the text in your essay. As you write, keep in mind that your essay will be evaluated for **ideas, organization, voice, word choice, sentence fluency, conventions,** and **presentation.**

A Quechua woman with llamas. Cuzco, Peru.

B The remains of an Inca settlement stand at Machu Picchu, Peru, ca. 1440.

LOG ON ▶ **Literature** Online

Literature and Reading For more about the history and literature of this period, go to glencoe.com and enter QuickPass code GLW6053u6.

THE EARLY AMERICAS

3000 B.C.– A.D. 1900

Mask, representing the God Quetzalcoatl or Tonatiuh, c.1500. Aztec school. Turquoise and shell on wood. British Museum, London.

Being There

The two connecting continents of North and South America stretch nearly 10,000 miles from north to south. The first settlers arrived in the Americas perhaps 30,000 years ago. With the domestication of crops such as corn and potatoes, the cultures of the original settlers, who were hunters and gatherers, gradually developed into advanced civilizations, culminating in the Aztec and Inca empires. The Spanish conquistadors overthrew these empires in the early 1500s.

Looking Ahead

In the centuries following the Spanish conquest, Native American and European elements blended in the cultures of the Americas. Native American oral and written records were preserved in the Spanish language. European soldiers and settlers wrote accounts of their experiences in the New World. Colonial writers adapted European literary forms such as the epic and the sonnet.

Keep the following questions in mind as you read:

- What role did storytelling have in Native American tradition?
- Why did Native Americans and European settlers come into conflict?
- How did European literature develop in the Americas?

Learning Objectives

For pages 1106–1117

In studying this text, you will focus on the following objectives:

Literary Study: Analyzing literary periods.

Reading: Evaluating historical influences.
Connecting to the literature.

THE EARLY AMERICAS

3000 B.C.–1900

Historical, Social, and Cultural Forces

Hunters and Farmers

The oldest and most widespread lifestyle found among Native Americans was that of nomadic hunters. In North America, groups moved with the seasons, following bison and caribou or traveling to lake areas to trap migrating ducks and geese. In winter, people lived on dried food. Along the northwest coast, where fish were abundant, people were able to establish permanent settlements, leading to the artistic achievements of groups including the Haida and Tlingit.

The domestication of vegetables such as corn, squash, and beans led to the rise of farming-based societies. With the growth of farming, more groups established permanent towns and villages—although hunting remained an important food resource for most groups. Permanent homes and a more secure food supply allowed peoples such as the Natchez to develop complex societies and artistic forms. From about 900 to 1200, the Mississippians erected huge mounds at a site known as Cahokia in what is now Illinois.

City Builders

The Maya, Aztec, and Inca are the best known of the urban-oriented civilizations of early America. Other groups included the Olmec, the Toltec, and the Zapotec. At sites such as Chichén Itzá and Palenque, in present-day Mexico, and Tikal in present-day Guatemala, the ancient Maya erected plazas, temples, and huge pyramids—symbolic sacred mountains—where thousands gathered for religious ceremonies and festivals. The Aztec capital Tenochtitlán (tä nōch tē′tiahn), which may have included about 400,000 inhabitants at its height in 1519, rivaled other great cities of that period in size

Mayan Stone Relief of Xoc Performing a Blood-Letting Ritual. ca. 8th century.

and magnificence. From their capital city of Cuzco, located in the Andes in what is now Peru, the Incas ruled an empire that extended more than 2,500 miles along the Pacific coast of South America.

Religion and Sacrifice

Religion dominated these advanced civilizations. Mayan kings were spiritual, as well as political, leaders. They performed rituals and ceremonies to appease the gods. Like the ancient Greeks, the Maya believed that the movements of the sun, moon, and planets were journeys undertaken by the gods. Because the gods controlled nature, charting the movements of the heavenly bodies was crucial. To do so, Mayan priests learned to excel at mathematics and astronomy. Images on temples, sacred objects, and pottery provide clues about ancient Mayan beliefs and practices.

Religion motivated the Aztecs to wage war and offer sacrifice. Borrowing beliefs from the Maya and the Toltecs, the Aztecs held that human sacrifice was necessary to propitiate the gods and prevent natural disasters. Like the Aztecs, Inca priests sometimes offered human victims to their gods.

> *"I found very many islands peopled with inhabitants beyond number."*
>
> —Christopher Columbus,
> in a 1493 letter

Exploration, Conquest, and Colonization

After Christopher Columbus's fleet reached the islands of the Caribbean in 1492, European nations turned their attention to the Western Hemisphere. Eager for fame and gold, Spanish soldier-explorers known as *conquistadors* overthrew the empires of the Aztec and the Inca within a few decades. By the 1600s, Spain's empire in the New World included much of North and South America. Under Spanish rule, Native American peoples declined rapidly because of disease and mistreatment. To replace a

Battle With Natives in the Early French and Portuguese Colonization of Brazil, 1562. Theodor de Bry. Service Historique de la Marine, Chateau de Vincennes, France.

dwindling labor force, the Spanish introduced enslaved Africans to their colonies.

Over time, the merging of Native American, European, and African peoples in Spain's American colonies gave rise to a new culture. The center of this new culture was Mexico City, the capital of New Spain, which had been erected on the ruins of the Aztecs' Tenochtitlán. At its peak in the 1700s, this colonial capital contained many elegant homes and public buildings as well as splendid churches and convents.

Latin American Revolutions

In the early 1800s, region after region in Latin America rebelled against Spanish colonial rule. Military leaders such as Venezuela's Simón Bolívar and Argentina's José de San Martín led liberation movements, and by 1825 most of the modern-day nations of Latin America had won their independence from Portugal and Spain. An exception was Cuba, which—despite a series of uprisings in the late 1800s—did not become an independent republic until 1902. One of the Cuban rebel leaders was the poet José Martí (see pages 1169–1172), who in 1895 was killed fighting for independence from Spain.

Pottery and Ceramics

The tradition of pottery-making in the Americas is more than 5,000 years old; the earliest known examples, from Ecuador, date from about 3200 B.C. Most pottery was made by the coil method and shaped into bowls, vases, and spouted jars. The Moche (mō´cheh) culture, which flourished on the north coast of Peru from the first to the eighth centuries, excelled at making vessels in the shape of animals and human heads. These portrait jars, some of them depictions of Moche rulers, were executed with exceptional skill.

Architecture

Ceremonial pyramids topped by temples were constructed throughout Central and South America. Some of the most elaborate were built by the Maya, who rank among history's greatest builders. The Maya had little technology—they built their cities using only stone and bone tools—but great ingenuity. Many Mayan temples were built on top of artificial mounds. Each building consisted of a massive base, a series of terraces or stairs, and a single-storied temple on top. In later years, sometimes a palace occupied the place of the temple. The entire building was covered with white stucco and brilliantly decorated. Often the interior was painted with frescoes.

The Aztecs of Mexico built their capital, Tenochtitlán, on artificial islands connected by causeways to the shore. In 1521, when the Spaniards under Hernán Cortés first glimpsed this city with its plazas and pyramids, soldiers such as Bernal Díaz del Castillo were stunned by its size and beauty. In the Andes Mountains, the Inca built entire cities from huge blocks of granite, fitting the stones together so skillfully that a knife blade could not fit between them. Even in ruins, the temples and palaces of the Aztec and the Inca remain among the wonders of the world.

A Mochica vase depicting a warrior stands in a museum in Peru.

The figure of a Chac-Mool, ready to receive the hearts of victims of human sacrifice, gazes at Kukulcan Pyramid. Height of the Pyramid 30 m. Chichén Itzá, Yucatán, Mexico.

Music and Dance

Early American music and dance share many characteristics, despite distinctive regional variations. Dances were commonly associated with planting and harvesting ceremonies, hunting trips, war, and religious ceremonies. Other common dance characteristics included:

 a two-part rhythm, alternating between a strong and a weak beat

- dancers assuming a slightly bent-over posture, with raised knees
- flat-footed movements

Percussion instruments included a variety of drums and rattles made of deer hoofs or turtle shells. Wind instruments included conch-shell trumpets, used in religious ceremonies, and many types of flutes, the best known of which are the panpipes used in the Andes. Native American peoples were quick to adopt the stringed instruments introduced by Europeans, developing their own traditions of guitar, violin, and harp playing.

Ballet Folklorico de Mexico Performance in Mexico City. ▶

bu
magnars excavating a cemetery on
belonge found hundreds of funeral
the regions of the dead wrapped in
year-old texame clear that these
desert-like conture, which thrived in
cloths were cloak.D. 400. The 2,000-
tions of animals an because of the
This visual imagery w.gion. Many of the
ing among people who with representa-
hd imaginary.
communicat-
n language.

PREVIEW Big Ideas of The Early Americas

1 Gods and Mortals

The early Americas were home to hundreds of native civilizations, from the tribal groups of North America to the Maya, Aztec, and Inca civilizations of Central and South America. The oral and written literature of these peoples explores the origin of humanity and tells of the interrelations between people, animals, and gods.

See page 1114

2 Cultures in Conflict

The voyages of Christopher Columbus in the 1490s inaugurated an era of European exploration and conquest that reshaped the Americas. Written accounts of the initial encounters between natives and explorers reflect the striking contrasts between their values and ways of living.

See page 1115

3 Transplanting Traditions

A complex mixture of indigenous and European elements shaped Latin American culture. Authors transplanted such European traditions as the sonnet and Romanticism into literature that expressed new perspectives on gender, identity, and displacement, including the effects of exile.

See page 1116

out the world share
story patterns, known
The myexample, a creator god
charA series of worlds
as àent one is a plot pattern
is a charactetypes also appear in the
existing beearly Americas.
archetype
mytholo

> the story of the beginning,
> "there was not one bird,
> ne fish,
> not ne mountain."
>
> —from the Popol Vuh

Creators and Nature Gods

The Maya creation myth was preserved in the Popol Vuh (see pages 1120–1129), or "Council Book," a collection of Maya myths recorded soon after the Spanish Conquest. The Maya believed that the creator god had tried several times to make creatures capable of worshipping the gods. After destroying creatures made from mud and wood, the creator god finally formed humans out of corn. According to the ancient Aztecs, several previous worlds, or "suns," had perished because of flood, fire, wind, or supernatural beasts. The Aztecs believed the present world would be destroyed by earthquake.

The mythologies of the Maya, Aztecs, and Incas included a large number of gods and goddesses, many of which embodied forces of nature. For example, the Maya god Huracan was both the creator and the god of storms. (His name is the basis for the word *hurricane*.) The Aztec god Quetzalcoatl was associated with winds, rain, and the planet Venus. The central Inca god was Inti, the divine sun, who was believed to be the ancestor of the Inca rulers.

Quetzalcoatl with black beard rising from the jaws of earth. Museo Nacional de Antropologia e Historia, Mexico City, D.F., Mexico.

Oral Traditions

Although the Maya and the Aztecs had well-developed systems of writing, most Native American peoples did not. To preserve their myths, histories, and legends, they had to transmit them orally from one generation to the next, telling and retelling them at tribal ceremonies. In Native American oral traditions, the trickster is a character archetype that appears in many tales. Frequently depicted as an animal with speech and other human traits, this figure is not only troublesome but also clever and creative. Two prominent Native American tricksters are Coyote and Raven.

Reading Check

Make Generalizations What might tricksters such as Coyote and Raven reveal about the Native American attitude toward nature?

Big Idea 2
Cultures in Conflict

The European exploration, conquest, and settlement of the Americas had both positive and negative consequences for the cultures of the native peoples. For one thing, it led to the founding of new nations. Moreover, the reintroduction of the horse—exterminated by early American hunters—revolutionized transportation. The production of furs and other raw materials expanded, as people sought items to trade for European manufactured goods. European colonization, however, was also the prologue to the destruction of many Native American societies. Spain had two goals for its overseas empire—to acquire wealth and to spread Christianity. These goals proved disastrous for native peoples.

Cruelty and Disease

Under the *encomienda* system, a brutal type of forced labor established by Spanish rulers in their American colonies, landowners had the right to use Native Americans as enslaved workers. Many of those enslaved later died from mistreatment or overwork. Deadly diseases introduced from Europe also took a terrible toll. Exposed to smallpox and measles for the first time, millions of Native Americans died during the first 50 years of Spanish rule. The Spanish priest Bartolomé de Las Casas, who had firsthand knowledge of Spain's brutal colonial policies, protested the abuses of Native Americans in his *Brief Report on the Destruction of the Indies*.

> "Long before they heard the word Spaniard, *the Indians had properly organized states, wisely ordered by excellent laws, religion, and custom.*"
>
> —Bartolomé de Las Casas, from *The Destruction of the Indies*

Destruction of Records

The Spanish also destroyed much of the culture of the Maya and the Aztecs, including written records contained in painted books known as *codices*. Written largely in pictographic scripts, these books were the property of priests, nobles, and rulers. They contained information on mythic and secular histories, genealogies, and tax and tribute accounts. They also provided information on when to plant and harvest, and when and how to conduct rituals. During the Spanish Conquest, religious authorities ordered the destruction of hundreds of codices, condemning them as pagan relics. The few codices that survived provide a vital record of Aztec and Maya civilizations.

American Indians Carrying Goods for the Conquerors. From Diego Duran's History of the American Indians, 1579. Manuscript, fol. 204v. Biblioteca Nacional, Madrid.

Reading Check

Analyze Cause-and-Effect Relationships How did the Spanish goal of Christianizing Native Americans contribute to the destruction of their written records?

Cracking The Maya Code

CRACKING THE CODE OF MAYA HIEROGLYPHIC WRITING IS AMONG THE great achievements of the late twentieth century. But why, given the nearly 200-year history of Maya archaeology, did the code take so long to crack? The answer lies in the difficulty of deciphering an ancient script and in mistaken assumptions made about its nature.

The Mystery of the Maya

Among the peoples of pre-Columbian America, only the Maya developed a complete script or system of writing. To the Maya, writing was a sacred gift from the great creator god Itzamná. Knowledge of this gift belonged exclusively to members of the Maya elite and the priesthood, many of whom were scribes. Educated in both painting and writing, these artist-authors drew hieroglyphs on pottery, walls, and sculptures and in painted books called codices (the plural of *codex*). They also carved these writings into stone buildings and on stelae (stē′le)—commemorative stone slabs or pillars. Near the glyphs, they often created artistic scenes that serve as illustrations of the text.

By the time the Spaniards conquered Maya territory in the early 1500s, Maya civilization was in decline and the population was dispersed. However, the deserted Maya centers remained full of hieroglyphs.

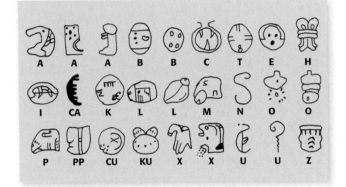

The Spanish Bishop Diego de Landa used these to create an "alphabet" of Maya writing, in which he paired one or more hieroglyphs with a letter or consonant-vowel combination. He published his findings in a book called *Account of the Affairs of Yucatán*. This book disappeared until 1862, but even when it was rediscovered, scholars paid little attention to it.

Mayan hieroglyphic text panel, Palenque Mayan ruins, Chiapas, Mexico. Classic Period, 750 AD.

Cracking the Code

Why was Landa's "alphabet" ignored for so long? The field of Maya studies was dominated by a few scholars who insisted Maya writing was primarily "picture writing." That is, they viewed each hieroglyph as a picture representing a particular word or idea. They didn't believe the glyphs had any relation to the Mayan language. But in 1952, a Russian scholar named Yuri Knorosov, who had never even seen a Maya ruin, showed that Maya writing reflects spoken language. Using Landa's "alphabet" and modern Maya dictionaries, Knorosov showed that the Maya script consists of both symbols that express ideas and symbols that express sounds.

Besides using the alphabetic system shown on the opposite page, the Maya combined symbols in a number of ways. These characters illustrate five different ways to write the Maya word for "jaguar."

The ancient scribes organized the glyphs into blocks placed in horizontal and vertical rows. In each block, they wrote one or more glyphs. As the example on the left shows, a block might include a logogram (a glyph that represents a whole word, in this case *jaguar*) combined with phonetic signs (signs representing the sounds of syllables), or just phonetic signs.

Since Knorosov's discovery, scholars have unlocked the meaning of many more glyphs. In so doing, they have disproved the belief that the glyphs primarily record astronomical and mythological events. Many actually describe the history of the Maya kings—their birth, accession to the throne, marriages, children, military conquests, participation in bloodletting rites and human sacrifice, and deaths. This new information shattered the long-cherished view of the ancient Maya as a peaceful, star-gazing people. They were, we now know, constantly at war and capable of great cruelty toward their enemies. Yet they also developed a very rich and sophisticated culture.

Deciphering Other Ancient Scripts

Maya hieroglyphic writing is not the only script that long eluded scholars. Egyptian hieroglyphic writing—a complex script with many similarities to Maya writing—also proved difficult to crack (see pages 34–35). As ancient Egyptian culture died out, and with it knowledge of Egyptian writing (the last example of ancient Egyptian writing is from A.D. 394), people began entertaining the mistaken notion that it was picture writing. This belief persisted until 1822, when a young Frenchman named Jean François Champollion proved the glyphs are largely phonetic, or based on the sounds of the spoken language. In so doing, he paved the way for the breaking of other early scripts, which scholars now realize all have phonetic components.

Respond and Think Critically

1. What steps might you take in trying to figure out an inscription in an unknown language?

2. (a) What is your impression of the glyphs used to spell the word *jaguar*? (b) What, in your opinion, are the strengths and weaknesses of each type of glyph?

3. Compare Maya hieroglyphic writing with the Egyptian writing on pages 34–35. Which script do you think would be most difficult to decipher? Why?

Before You Read

from the *Popol Vuh*

The Maya created one of the most advanced civilizations of pre-Columbian America. At the height of their power, they occupied more than 40 cities in southern Mexico, Guatemala, and northern Belize. Their civilization flourished from about A.D. 250 to about 900, the classic period of Mayan culture. Working with stone tools, they built pyramids, temples, and palaces, which they ornamented with carvings and hieroglyphic writing. In addition, the Maya were skilled in astronomy and mathematics.

> *"Here we shall inscribe . . . the Ancient Word . . . how things were put in shadow and brought to light . . ."*
>
> —from the Popol Vuh

Mayan Civilization The earliest Mayan settlements, established about 1500 B.C., were small farming communities that grew mainly corn, beans, and squash. By the time of the classic period, however, these communities had been transformed into a network of magnificent cities that featured ceremonial buildings, public plazas, and sports facilities. At its peak, Mayan civilization may have numbered two million people.

The remains of temples and other artifacts provide evidence of an artistic culture unequaled by any other Native American people. Mayan art is strikingly narrative, rich in color and detail. Hieroglyphic texts reveal astonishing intellectual achievements. The Maya developed a complex calendar based on astronomical calculations that enabled them to chart the positions of heavenly bodies and to predict solar eclipses. The calendar includes both an eighteen-month solar year (with each month containing twenty days) and a 260-day sacred year.

Religion was important to ancient Mayan culture. The Maya worshipped a variety of deities, including nature gods and goddesses. Each day of the sacred calendar was associated with a god or goddess. The Maya fasted, prayed, and offered ritual sacrifices—both animal and human—to seek divine favor.

Relic from a Lost Civilization Tragically, the Maya abandoned their magnificent cities by the year 900 and retired to the countryside. Why they did so remains a mystery. By the middle of the 1500s, Spanish forces had completely conquered the Maya.

Fortunately, the Popol Vuh (pō pəl vu´), a sacred text of the ancient Maya, survived the Spanish Conquest and the burning of Mayan books. Some Christian-trained Maya wrote down the Popol Vuh in the Roman alphabet. Around 1700 a friar named Francisco Ximénez copied this version and translated it into Spanish. Modern editions of the Popol Vuh are based on his copy.

Map of the Maya Area. Nigel Hughes. Watercolour on paper. Private collection.

Literature and Reading Preview

Connect to the Sacred Text

What stories have you heard about the creation of human beings? Discuss this question with a small group.

Build Background

The Popol Vuh, or "Council Book," is an important source of information about ancient Mayan culture and history. It was written in Quiché (kē chāʹ), a language a Mayan group in Guatemala spoke. The Quiché people believed that the Popol Vuh enabled their leaders to see into the future. The book contains stories about mythological heroes and an account of creation. It also relates the history of the Quiché people up to the Spanish Conquest, around 1550.

Set Purposes for Reading

Big Idea Gods and Mortals

The literature of the peoples of the early Americas explored the origin of humanity and the relationship between humans and the gods. As you read, ask yourself, What does this creation myth reveal about the Maya?

Literary Element Myth

A **myth** is a traditional story that explains some aspect of human society or the natural world. Creation myths explain the origin of the world and its inhabitants. As you read, ask yourself, What mythic elements appear in this excerpt from the Popol Vuh?

Reading Strategy Clarify Meaning

When you **clarify meaning**, you apply a variety of comprehension strategies to help you understand difficult passages of a text. These strategies include rereading confusing sections, reading slowly and carefully, drawing on personal background, questioning, predicting, summarizing, paraphrasing, and constructing graphic organizers. As you read, ask yourself, Which strategies help clarify the meaning of this creation myth?

Tip: Apply Comprehension Strategies Use a chart like the one below to clarify the meaning of difficult passages.

Difficult Passage	Simplified Meaning
The face of the earth is not clear.	The Earth does not yet exist.

Vocabulary

conception (kən sepʹshən) *n.* thought; idea; design; plan; p. 1123 *The old plan for the stadium is better known than the new conception.*

edible (edʹə bəl) *adj.* fit to eat; p. 1126 *Even though the mushrooms looked safe to eat, they were not edible.*

Tip: Context Clues When you come across an unfamiliar word, pay close attention to the surrounding words and try to determine a possible meaning. For example, in the sentence *Even though the mushrooms looked safe to eat, they were not edible,* edible must mean "safe to eat," the phrase that describes the mushrooms' appearance.

The Creation of Man, page from *Popol Vuh.* Diego Rivera. Watercolor on paper. Museo Casa Diego Rivera (INBA), Guanajuato, Mexico.

from the

Translated by Dennis Tedlock

his is the beginning of the Ancient Word, here in this place called Quiché. Here we shall inscribe, we shall implant the Ancient Word, the potential and source for everything done in the citadel[1] of Quiché, in the nation of Quiché people. . . .

This is the account, here it is:

Now it still ripples, now it still murmurs, ripples, it still sighs, still hums, and it is empty under the sky.

Here follow the first words, the first eloquence:

There is not yet one person, one animal, bird, fish, crab, tree, rock, hollow, canyon, meadow, forest. Only the sky alone is there; the face of the earth is not clear. Only the sea alone is pooled under all the sky; there is nothing whatever gathered together. It is at rest; not a single thing stirs. It is held back, kept at rest under the sky.

Whatever there is that might be is simply not there: only the pooled water, only the calm sea, only it alone is pooled.

Whatever might be is simply not there: only murmurs, ripples, in the dark, in the night. Only the Maker, Modeler alone, Sovereign Plumed Serpent, the Bearers, Begetters are in the water, a glittering light. They are there, they are enclosed in quetzal feathers, in blue-green.

Thus the name, "Plumed Serpent."

Feathered Serpent. Postclassical. Stone. Museo Nacional de Antropologia e Historia, Mexico City, D.F.

They are great knowers, great thinkers in their very being.

And of course there is the sky, and there is also the Heart of Sky. This is the name of the god, as it is spoken.

And then came his word, he came here to the Sovereign Plumed Serpent, here in the blackness, in the early dawn. He spoke with the Sovereign Plumed Serpent, and they talked, then they thought, then they worried. They agreed with each other, they joined their words, their thoughts. . . .

"Let it be this way, think about it: this water should be removed, emptied out for the formation of the earth's own plate and platform, then should come the sowing, the dawning of the sky-earth. But there will be no high days and no bright praise for our work, our design, until the rise of the human work, the human design," they said.

And then the earth arose because of them, it was simply their word that brought it forth. For the forming of the earth they said "Earth." It arose suddenly, just like a cloud, like a mist, now forming, unfolding. Then the mountains were separated from the water, all at once the great mountains came forth. By their genius alone, by their cutting edge alone they carried out the **conception** of the mountain-plain, whose face grew instant groves of cypress and pine.

---

1. A *citadel* is a fortress that commands a city or a stronghold.

Myth *Who are these characters? What form do they take?*

Vocabulary

conception (kən sep´shən) *n.* thought; idea; design; plan

And the Plumed Serpent was pleased with this:

"It was good that you came, Heart of Sky, Hurricane, and Newborn Thunderbolt, Sudden Thunderbolt. Our work, our design will turn out well," they said.

And the earth was formed first, the mountain-plain. The channels of water were separated; their branches wound their ways among the mountains. The waters were divided when the great mountains appeared.

Such was the formation of the earth when it was brought forth by the Heart of Sky, Heart of Earth, as they are called, since they were the first to think of it. The sky was set apart, and the earth was set apart in the midst of the waters.

Such was their plan when they thought, when they worried about the completion of their work. . . .

And then they gave out homes to the deer and birds:

"You, the deer: sleep along the rivers, in the canyons. Be here in the meadows, in the thickets, in the forests, multiply yourselves. You will stand and walk on all fours," they were told. So then they estab-

Man standing on a turtle, The Creator of the World. Mayan. Earthenware. Private collection.

Clarify Meaning *How would you paraphrase this sentence?*

lished the nests of the birds, small and great:

"You, precious birds: your nests, your houses are in the trees, in the bushes. Multiply there, scatter there, in the branches of trees, the branches of bushes," the deer and birds were told.

When this deed had been done, all of them had received a place to sleep and a place to stay. So it is that the nests of the animals are on the earth, given by the Bearer, Begetter. Now the arrangement of the deer and birds was complete.

And then the deer and birds were told by the Maker, Modeler, Bearer, Begetter:

"Talk, speak out. Don't moan, don't cry out. Please talk, each to each, within each kind, within each group," they were told— the deer, birds, puma, jaguar, serpent.

"Name now our names, praise us. We are your mother, we are your father. Speak now:

'Hurricane,
Newborn Thunderbolt, Sudden Thunderbolt,
Heart of Sky, Heart of Earth,
Maker, Modeler,
Bearer, Begetter,'

speak, pray to us, keep our days,"[2] they were told. But it didn't turn out that they spoke like people: they just squawked, they just chattered, they just howled. It wasn't apparent what language they spoke; each one gave a different cry. When the Maker, Modeler heard this:

"It hasn't turned out well, they haven't spoken," they said among themselves. "It hasn't turned out that our names have been named. Since we are their mason and

2. *Keep our days* refers to the Mayan sacred calendar. Each day was associated with one of the gods. The Maya consulted the calendar to guide their worship.

Gods and Mortals *Why are the gods displeased?*

sculptor, this will not do," the Bearers and Begetters said among themselves. So they told them:

"You will simply have to be transformed. Since it hasn't turned out well and you haven't spoken, we have changed our word:

"What you feed on, what you eat, the places where you sleep, the places where you stay, whatever is yours will remain in the canyons, the forests. Although it turned out that our days were not kept, nor did you pray to us, there may yet be strength in the keeper of days, the giver of praise whom we have yet to make. Just accept your service, just let your flesh be eaten.

"So be it, this must be your service," they were told when they were instructed—the animals, small and great, on the face of the earth.

And then they wanted to test their timing again, they wanted to experiment again, and they wanted to prepare for the keeping of days again. They had not heard their speech among the animals; it did not come to fruition and it was not complete.

And so their flesh was brought low: they served, they were eaten, they were killed—the animals on the face of the earth.

After informing the animals what their function on earth will be, the gods attempt to create humans. Working with earth and mud, they sculpt a body, but it keeps separating, loosening, and dissolving. Discouraged, the gods decide to carve humans out of wood. The woodcarvings look and talk like humans but are empty-headed and have no hearts. They neither remember nor praise the gods. Discouraged again, the gods destroy the woodcarvings—crushing and pulverizing them—and set out to discover the right ingredients for making humans.

And here is the beginning of the conception of humans, and of the search for the ingredi-ents of the human body. So they spoke, the Bearer, Begetter, the Makers, Modelers named Sovereign Plumed Serpent:

"The dawn has approached, preparations have been made, and morning has come for the provider, nurturer, born in the light, begotten in the light. Morning has come for humankind, for the people of the face of the earth," they said. It all came together as they went on thinking in the darkness, in the night, as they searched and they sifted, they thought and they wondered.

And here their thoughts came out in clear light. They sought and discovered what was needed for human flesh. It was only a short while before the sun, moon, and stars were to appear above the Makers and Modelers. Split Place, Bitter Water Place[3] is the name: the yellow corn, white corn came from there.

And these are the names of the animals who brought the food: fox, coyote, parrot, crow. There were four animals who brought the news of the ears of yellow corn and white corn. They were coming from over there at Split Place, they showed the way to the split.

And this was when they found the staple[4] foods.

And these were the ingredients for the flesh of the human work, the human design, and the water was for the blood. It became human blood, and corn was also used by the Bearer, Begetter.

And so they were happy over the provisions of the good mountain, filled with sweet things, thick with yellow corn, white corn, and thick with pataxte and cacao,

---

3. *Split Place, Bitter Water Place* refers to a high mountain in Guatemala near the Mexican border. Those who live near it today believe corn originated there.
4. *Staple* means "primary."

Gods and Mortals *According to Mayan belief, what symbolizes human flesh? What symbolizes blood?*

Young Maize God, c. 775 Honduras. Height 89.7 cm. British Museum, London.

View the Art Since corn, or maize, was the Maya's most important food, it is not surprising that the maize god was of great importance in Mayan culture. How does the artist suggest that this sculpture depicts a god?

countless zapotes, anonas, jocotes, nances, matasanos,[5] sweets—the rich foods filling up the citadel named Split Place, Bitter Water Place. All the **edible** fruits were there: small staples, great staples, small plants, great plants. The way was shown by the animals.

And then the yellow corn and white corn were ground, and Xmucane did the grinding nine times. Food was used, along with the water she rinsed her hands with,[6]

---

5. *Pataxte and cacao, . . . nances, matasanos:* Pataxte and cacao are seeds used to make cocoa and chocolate. Zapotes, anonas, jocotes, nances, and matasanos are all tropical fruits.
6. *Xmucane . . . rinsed her hands with:* Xmucane is one of the two seers the gods consult earlier in the story. Women ground corn to make corn cakes. They would rinse off the particles of corn meal that stuck to their hands during the grinding.

Vocabulary

edible (ed′ə bəl) *adj.* fit to eat

---

for the creation of grease; it became human fat when it was worked by the Bearer, Begetter, Sovereign Plumed Serpent, as they are called.

After that, they put it into words:

> the making, the modeling of our first mother-
> father,
> with yellow corn, white corn alone for the flesh,
> food alone for the human legs and arms,
> for our first fathers, the four human works.

It was staples alone that made up their flesh.

These are the names of the first people who were made and modeled.

This is the first person: Jaguar Quitze.
And now the second: Jaguar Night.
And now the third: Not Right Now.
And the fourth: Dark Jaguar.

And these are the names of our first mother-fathers. They were simply made and modeled, it is said; they had no mother and no father. We have named the men by themselves. No woman gave birth to them, nor were they begotten by the builder, sculptor, Bearer, Begetter. By sacrifice alone, by genius alone they were made, they were modeled by the Maker, Modeler, Bearer, Begetter, Sovereign Plumed Serpent. And when they came to fruition, they came out human:

They talked and they made words.
They looked and they listened.
They walked, they worked.

They were good people, handsome, with looks of the male kind. Thoughts came into existence and they gazed; their vision came all at once. Perfectly they saw, perfectly they knew everything under the sky, whenever they looked. The moment they turned around and looked around in the

---

Clarify Meaning *What does this sentence mean? What clues help clarify the meaning?*

sky, on the earth, everything was seen without any obstruction. They didn't have to walk around before they could see what was under the sky; they just stayed where they were.

As they looked, their knowledge became intense. Their sight passed through trees, through rocks, through lakes, through seas, through mountains, through plains. Jaguar Quitze, Jaguar Night, Not Right Now, and Dark Jaguar were truly gifted people.

And then they were asked by the builder and mason:

"What do you know about your being? Don't you look, don't you listen? Isn't your speech good, and your walk? So you must look, to see out under the sky. Don't you see the mountain-plain clearly? So try it," they were told.

And then they saw everything under the sky perfectly. After that, they thanked the Maker, Modeler:

"Truly now,
double thanks, triple thanks
that we've been formed, we've been given
our mouths, our faces,
we speak, we listen,
we wonder, we move,
our knowledge is good, we've understood
what is far and near,
and we've seen what is great and small
under the sky, on the earth.
Thanks to you we've been formed,
we've come to be made and modeled,
our grandmother, our grandfather,"

they said when they gave thanks for having been made and modeled. They understood everything perfectly, they sighted the four sides, the four corners in the sky, on the earth, and this didn't sound good to the builder and sculptor:

"What our works and designs have said is no good:

'We have understood everything, great and small,' they say." And so the Bearer, Begetter took back their knowledge:

"What should we do with them now? Their vision should at least reach nearby, they should see at least a small part of the face of the earth, but what they're saying isn't good. Aren't they merely 'works' and 'designs' in their very names? Yet they'll become as great as gods, unless they procreate, proliferate at the sowing, the dawning, unless they increase."

"Let it be this way: now we'll take them apart just a little, that's what we need. What we've found out isn't good. Their deeds would become equal to ours, just because their knowledge reaches so far. They see everything," so said

the Heart of Sky, Hurricane,
Newborn Thunderbolt, Sudden Thunderbolt,
Sovereign Plumed Serpent,
Bearer, Begetter,
Xpiyacoc, Xmucane,
Maker, Modeler,

as they are called. And when they changed the nature of their works, their designs, it was enough that the eyes be marred by the Heart of Sky. They were blinded as the face of a mirror is breathed upon. Their vision flickered. Now it was only from close up that they could see what was there with any clarity.

And such was the loss of the means of understanding, along with the means of knowing everything, by the four humans. The root was implanted.

And such was the making, modeling of our first grandfather, our father, by the Heart of Sky, Heart of Earth. ∾

Myth *What limitation does this turn of events help explain?*

Gods and Mortals *What do the gods do to impair the understanding of the first people?*

Modifiers

A **misplaced modifier** is a word or a phrase that makes a sentence unclear because the modifier is in the wrong place. A **dangling modifier** doesn't modify anything in a sentence.

Tip

To avoid misplaced and dangling modifiers, think about the meaning of the sentence. Draw an arrow from the modifier to the word or phrase it modifies.

Language Handbook

For more about **modifers,** see Language Handbook, p. R40.

 **Literature** Online

Grammar For more grammar practice, go to glencoe.com and enter QuickPass code GLW6053u6.

Grammar Workshop

Misplaced and Dangling Modifiers

Literature Connection A **misplaced modifier** is a word or phrase appearing in the wrong place in a sentence. Read the sentence below from the Popol Vuh.

> *"The dawn has approached, preparations have been made, and morning has come for the provider, nurturer, born in the light, begotten in the light."*

If the modifier *born in the light, begotten in the light* were moved to the beginning of the sentence, it would read: *Born in the light, begotten in the light, the dawn has approached . . .* The phrase would then incorrectly modify the word *dawn*, instead of *nurturer*. A sentence may also have a **dangling modifier**, which seems logically to modify no word at all. For example in the sentence *Bare and silent, there was no life,* "bare and silent" is dangling.

PROBLEM 1 A misplaced modifier

Separated from the water, the Makers formed mountains.

SOLUTION Place the modifier as close as possible to the word it modifies.

The Makers formed mountains separated from the water.

PROBLEM 2 A dangling modifier

Blinded, their understanding was now limited.

SOLUTION Supply a word that the dangling modifier can sensibly modify.

Blinded, the humans now had limited understanding.

Revise Rewrite the following sentences on a separate piece of paper to correct misplaced or dangling modifiers. If a sentence needs no revision, write *correct.*

1. Enclosed in quetzal feathers, The Serpent, the Bearers, and Begetters are in the water.
2. Emptied out of the earth, now there was no water to be found.
3. Into two divisions, the waters parted the mountains.
4. Devoured, gone were the animals.

Before You Read

Coyote Finishes His Work

Meet **Barry Lopez**
(born 1945)

Author and photographer Barry Lopez finds many of the subjects for his writing in nature and the environment. He has written about the desert in *Desert Notes: Reflections in the Eye of a Raven* (1976) and the Arctic vastness in *Arctic Dreams* (1986). In 1978 he published the best-selling *Of Wolves and Men.* Two works of fiction, *River Notes: The Dance of Herons* (1979) and *Winter Count* (1981), have also been well received. In addition to his nature writing, Lopez is acclaimed for his retellings of Native American tales.

Influence of Nature Lopez grew up primarily in rural southern California. Living near the desert, he developed a keen interest in nature. Lopez recalls that "encounters with coyotes, jackrabbits, and even rattlesnakes were not unusual." In college, Lopez began to merge his interest in nature with his passion for literature.

Reteller of Folktales While attending the University of Oregon, Lopez met Professor Barre Toelken. Toelken introduced him to the study of natural history and geography as well as to a number of creative people including "senior Native American men, itinerant Asian poets, black jazz musicians, and translators." Native American culture particularly impressed Lopez because of the close relationship it fostered between humanity and nature.

"Coyote Finishes His Work" is from Lopez's collection *Giving Birth to Thunder, Sleeping with His Daughter: Coyote Builds North America* (1977). According to Lopez, "Coyote is a creature of *oral* literature and mutable." In other words, because the original coyote folktales were

> "If I were asked what I want to accomplish as a writer, I would say it's to contribute to a literature of hope."
>
> —Barry Lopez

not written down, they were subject to alteration as one generation passed them down orally to the next. Stories about coyote were told "all over North America—in Cheyenne tipis, Mandan earth lodges, Inupiak igloos, Navajo hogans and Sia pueblos—with much laughter and guffawing and with exclamations of surprise and awe." In his Native American folktale retellings, Lopez strives to preserve the stories' connections to tribal identity, their entertainment values, and their reinforcement of moral beliefs.

LOG ON ▶ **Literature** Online

Author Search For more about Barry Lopez, go to glencoe.com and enter QuickPass code GLW605306.

Literature and Reading Preview

Connect to the Folktale

What qualities do you associate with coyotes? Discuss this question with a group.

Build Background

Whether creator, teacher, hero, or trickster, Coyote appears in a number of stories throughout the folklore traditions of the North American Plains Indians. In these stories, Coyote displays a variety of traits (foolishness, cleverness, playfulness, wisdom, strength, resourcefulness), all of which he uses—sometimes accidentally—to set the world right.

Set Purposes for Reading

Big Idea Gods and Mortals

Native American literature tells of the interrelations between people, animals, and gods. As you read, ask yourself, What do these interrelations suggest about Native American values?

Literary Element Motif

A **motif** is an element that recurs throughout a work or several works and is related to its theme. In most folklore traditions, the **trickster figure** (see pages 38–51) is a motif. Tricksters represent that part of human nature that wants to break rules and stir up trouble. As you read, ask yourself, How does the motif of the trickster help shape this folktale?

Reading Strategy Draw Conclusions About Culture

When you **draw conclusions about culture,** you make broad statements about the culture the work reflects, using clues found in the dialogue, the narrator's commentary, and the details of the plot. As you read, ask yourself, What can I conclude about the cultural background of this folktale?

....

Tip: Take Notes In a graphic organizer like the one below, write down details and a broad statement about the culture.

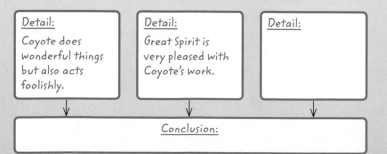

Detail:	Detail:	Detail:
Coyote does wonderful things but also acts foolishly.	Great Spirit is very pleased with Coyote's work.	

Conclusion:

Learning Objectives

For pages 1131–1135

In studying this text, you will focus on the following objectives:

Literary Study: Analyzing motif.

Reading: Drawing conclusions about culture.

Writing: Writing a graphic story.

Vocabulary

inhabit (in hab′it) *v.* to reside or live in; p. 1133 *A rare species of finches inhabits the island.*

revive (ri vīv′) *v.* to recover; to come back to life; p. 1134 *After several days in a coma, Jacob revived and began to speak.*

....

Tip: Word Parts Knowing a word's derivation often provides a clue to its meaning. For example, knowing the word *revive* is composed of the Latin prefix *re-,* which means "again," and the verb *vivere,* which means "to live," may help you remember that *revive* means "to recover" or "to live again."

COYOTE FINISHES HIS WORK

Retold by Barry Lopez

Brush Poppers, 1984. Jaune Quick-to-See Smith Flathead/Shoshone/Cree Tribes. Pastel on paper, 30 x 22 in. Marilyn Butler Gallery, Sante Fe, NM.

From the very beginning, Coyote was traveling around all over the earth. He did many wonderful things when he went along. He killed the monsters and the evil spirits that preyed on the people. He made the Indians, and put them out in tribes all over the world because Old Man Above wanted the earth to be **inhabited** all over, not just in one or two places.

He gave all the people different names and taught them different languages. This is why Indians live all over the country now and speak in different ways.

He taught the people how to eat and how to hunt the buffalo and catch eagles. He taught them what roots to eat and how to make a good lodge and what to wear. He taught them how to dance.

Gods and Mortals *What do these details suggest about the interrelations between people and animals?*

Sometimes he made mistakes, and even though he was wise and powerful, he did many foolish things. But that was his way.

Coyote liked to play tricks. He thought about himself all the time, and told everyone he was a great warrior, but he was not. Sometimes he would go too far with some trick and get someone killed. Other times, he would have a trick played on himself by someone else. He got killed this way so many times that Fox and the birds got tired of bringing him back to life. Another way he got in trouble was trying to do what someone else did. This is how he came to be called Imitator.

Coyote was ugly too. The girls did not like him. But he was smart. He could change himself around and trick the women. Coyote got the girls when he wanted.

One time, Coyote had done everything he could think of and was traveling from one place to another place, looking for other things that needed to be done. Old Man saw him going along and said to himself, "Coyote has now done almost everything he is capable of doing. His work is almost done. It is time to bring him back to the place where he started."

So Great Spirit[1] came down and traveled in the shape of an old man. He met Coyote. Coyote said, "I am Coyote. Who are you?"

Old Man said, "I am Chief of the earth. It was I who sent you to set the world right."

"No," Coyote said, "you never sent me. I don't know you. If you are the Chief, take that lake over there and move it to the side of that mountain."

"No. If you are Coyote, let me see you do it."

Coyote did it.

"Now, move it back."

Coyote tried, but he could not do it. He thought this was strange. He tried again, but he could not do it.

Chief moved the lake back.

Coyote said, "Now I know you are the Chief."

Old Man said, "Your work is finished, Coyote. You have traveled far and done much good. Now you will go to where I have prepared a home for you."

Then Coyote disappeared. Now no one knows where he is anymore.

Old Man got ready to leave, too. He said to the Indians, "I will send messages to the earth by the spirits of the people who reach me but whose time to die has not yet come. They will carry messages to you from time to time. When their spirits come back into their bodies, they will **revive** and tell you their experiences.

"Coyote and myself, we will not be seen again until Earth-woman[2] is very old. Then we shall return to earth, for it will require a change by that time. Coyote will come along first, and when you see him you will know I am coming. When I come along, all the spirits of the dead will be with me. There will be no more Other Side Camp.[3] All the people will live together. Earth-mother will go back to her first shape and live as a mother among her children. Then things will be made right."

Now they are waiting for Coyote. ∾

---

1. *Great Spirit* is the creator; in this case, it is Old Man Above.

Motif *What can you infer about the trickster figure?*

Draw Conclusions About Culture *What can you conclude about the Native American view of the supernatural?*

2. *Earth-woman* is Earth personified as a woman and, figuratively, the mother of all people.
3. *Other Side Camp* is a place where the spirits of the dead reside.

Vocabulary

revive (ri vīv′) *v.* to recover; to come back to life

After You Read

Respond and Think Critically

Respond and Interpret

1. Which details or incidents in this folktale did you find most interesting? Explain.

2. (a)How was Coyote foolish? (b)On whom did he depend for rescue when his foolishness went too far?

3. (a)How does Old Man prove to Coyote that he is the Chief of the earth? (b)Why does Old Man decide to send Coyote away from the world?

Analyze and Evaluate

4. (a)What does the incident of the mountain and the lake suggest about Coyote's power? (b)To what extent does Old Man guide Coyote's actions throughout the tale?

5. Tales such as "Coyote Finishes His Work" were originally passed down orally rather than in written form. How does the author's style suggest the oral nature of this tale?

Connect

6. **Big Idea** **Gods and Mortals** Based on this folktale, what values do you think are important to Native Americans?

7. **Connect to Today** (a)What trickster figures can you identify in modern literature or in popular culture? (b)Do these figures serve a useful function in society? Explain.

Literary Element Motif

In Native American folklore, the **trickster motif** is most commonly found in the character of Coyote. Although Coyote never shows concern for others, his actions often end up benefiting them.

1. What elements of the trickster motif does Coyote embody in this story?

2. Overall, do you think Coyote is a force for good or for evil? Explain.

Reading Strategy Draw Conclusions About Culture

Look back at the chart you made on page 1132, and then answer the following questions.

1. What conclusions can you draw about the spiritual belief system presented in this myth?

2. Which details support your conclusions?

Vocabulary Practice

Practice with Word Parts For each vocabulary word in the left column, identify the related word with a shared part in the right column. Write each word and underline the part they have in common. Use a printed or online dictionary to look up the meaning of the related word. Then explain how it is related to the vocabulary word.

1. inhabit   revitalize

2. revive   habitation

EXAMPLE: discon<u>sol</u>ate, <u>sol</u>ace

Solace means "comfort." A disconsolate person is one who cannot be comforted.

Writing

Write a Graphic Story How do you imagine people might receive Coyote when he returns to usher in the Earth's final transformation? Create a graphic story of three or four panels that tells the story of Coyote's return as you imagine it. If possible, use dialogue in your story.

FROM THE VOYAGE OF CHRISTOPHER COLUMBUS

CHRISTOPHER COLUMBUS

TRANSLATED BY JOHN CUMMINS

THURSDAY, 11 OCTOBER. Course wsw.[1] A heavy sea, the roughest in the whole voyage so far. We saw petrels,[2] and a green reed close to the ship, and then a big green fish of a kind which does not **stray** far from the shoals.[3] On the Pinta they saw a cane and a stick, and they picked up another little piece of wood which seemed to have been worked with an iron tool; also a piece of cane and another plant which grows on land, and a little board. On the Niña too they saw signs of land, and a thorn branch laden with red fruits, apparently newly cut. We were all filled with joy and relief at these signs. Sailed twenty-eight and a half leagues before sunset. After sunset I resumed our original course westward, sailing at about nine knots. By two o'clock in the morning we had sailed about sixty-eight miles, or twenty-two and a half leagues.

When everyone aboard was together for the *Salve Regina*,[4] which all seamen say or sing in their fashion, I talked to the men about the grace which God had shown us by bringing us in safety, with fair winds and

---

1. *WSW* is the abbreviation for West-South-West, one point on a mariner's compass.
2. *Petrels* (pe′trəlz) are seabirds that can fly far from land.
3. *Shoals* (shōlz) are sandbanks or sandbars that make the water shallow.

Vocabulary

stray (strā) *v.* to wander away; to go off course

---

4. *Salve Regina* (Latin for "Hail Holy Queen") is a prayer addressed to Mary, the mother of Jesus.

Recognize Bias *How do Columbus's religious views influence his interpretation of events?*

Santa Maria, 1939. André Bauchant. Oil on canvas, 73 x 100 cm. Private collection.

no obstacles, and by comforting us with signs which were more plentiful every day. I urged them to keep a good watch and reminded them that in the first article of the sailing instructions issued to each ship in the Canaries[5] I gave orders not to sail at night after we had reached a point seven hundred leagues from there; I was sailing on because of everyone's great desire to sight land. I warned them to keep a good lookout in the bows and told them that I would give a silk doublet[6] to the man who first sighted land, as well as the prize of 10,000 *maravedis*[7] promised by Your Majesties.

I was on the poop deck[8] at ten o'clock in the evening when I saw a light. It was so indistinct that I could not be sure it was land, but I called Pedro Gutiérrez, the Butler of the King's Table, and told him to look at what I thought was a light. He looked, and saw it. I also told Rodrigo Sánchez de Segovia, Your Majesties' observer on board, but he saw nothing because he was standing in the wrong place. After I had told them, the light appeared once or twice more, like a wax candle rising and falling. Only a few people thought it was a sign of land, but I was sure we were close to a landfall.

---

5. The *Canaries* are the Canary Islands. Owned by Spain, the Canaries are located in the Atlantic Ocean about 70 miles west of North Africa.
6. A *doublet* ia a man's close-fitting jacket.

7. A *maravedi* (mä rä vā′ dē) was a Spanish gold coin.
8. A *poop deck* is a short deck above the main deck at the stern of a boat or ship.

Then the Pinta, being faster and in the lead, sighted land and made the signal as I had ordered. The first man to sight land was called Rodrigo de Triana. The land appeared two hours after midnight, about two leagues away. We furled all sail except the *treo*, the mainsail with no bonnets, and jogged off and on until Friday morning, when we came to an island. We saw naked people, and I went ashore in a boat with armed men, taking Martín Alonso Pinzón and his brother Vicente Yáñez, captain of the Niña. I took the royal standard, and the captains each took a banner with the Green Cross which each of my ships carries as a device, with the letters F and Y, surmounted by a crown, at each end of the cross.

Visual Vocabulary
A *device* is a symbolic design, or emblem, often accompanied by a motto. Heralds— official messengers— carried a device to identify the noble family they represented.

When we stepped ashore we saw fine green trees, streams everywhere and different kinds of fruit. I called to the two captains to jump ashore with the rest, who included Rodrigo de Escobedo, secretary of the fleet, and Rodrigo Sánchez de Segovia, asking them to bear **solemn** witness that in the presence of them all I was taking possession of this island for their Lord and Lady the King and Queen, and I made the necessary declarations which are set down at greater length in the written testimonies.

Soon many of the islanders gathered round us. I could see that they were people who would be more easily converted to our

Journal *How might this information be useful later in Columbus's official report at court?*

Vocabulary

solemn (sol′əm) *adj.* serious; gravely important

Holy Faith by love than by **coercion,** and wishing them to look on us with friendship I gave some of them red bonnets and glass beads which they hung round their necks, and many other things of small value, at which they were so delighted and so eager to please us that we could not believe it. Later they swam out to the boats to bring us parrots and balls of cotton thread and darts, and many other things, exchanging them for such objects as glass beads and hawk bells. They took anything, and gave willingly whatever they had.

However, they appeared to me to be a very poor people in all respects. They go about as naked as the day they were born, even the women, though I saw only one, who was quite young. All the men I saw were quite young, none older than thirty, all well built, finely bodied and handsome in the face. Their hair is coarse, almost like a horse's tail, and short; they wear it short, cut over the brow, except a few strands of hair hanging down uncut at the back.

Some paint themselves with black, some with the color of the Canary Islanders, neither black nor white, others with white, others with red, others with whatever they can find. Some have only their face painted, others their whole body, others just their eyes or nose. They carry no weapons, and are ignorant of them; when I showed them some swords they took them by the blade and cut themselves. They have no iron; their darts are just sticks without an iron head, though some of them have a fish tooth or something else at the tip.

Cultures in Conflict *Does Columbus show respect for the islanders here? Explain.*

Recognize Bias *What criterion does Columbus use to judge the wealth of the islanders?*

Vocabulary

coercion (kō ur′shən) *n.* force; repression

They are all the same size, of good stature, dignified and well formed. I saw some with scars on their bodies, and made signs to ask about them, and they indicated to me that people from other islands nearby came to capture them and they defended themselves. I thought, and still think, that people from the mainland come here to take them prisoner. They must be good servants, and intelligent, for I can see that they quickly repeat everything said to them. I believe they would readily become Christians; it appeared to me that they have no religion. With God's will, I will take six of them with me for Your Majesties when I leave this place, so that they may learn Spanish.

I saw no animals on the island, only parrots.

SATURDAY, 13 OCTOBER. In the early morning many of the islanders came to the beach, all young, as I have said, tall and handsome, their hair not curly, but flowing and thick, like horsehair. They are all broader in the forehead and head than any people I have ever seen, with fine, large eyes. None of them is black; they are rather the same color as the folk on the Canary Islands, which is what one might expect, this island being on the same latitude as Hierro in the Canaries, which lies due E. Their legs are very straight, and they are all the same height, not stout in the belly but well shaped. They came out to the ship in *almadías* made from a tree trunk, like a long boat, all of a piece, wonderfully shaped in the way of this land, some big enough to carry forty or fifty men, others smaller, with only one man. They row them with paddles like a baker's shovel, very swiftly, and if the boat overturns they all jump into the sea to turn it over again and bale it out with gourds. They brought us balls of cotton thread and parrots and darts and other little things which it would be **tedious** to list, and exchanged everything for whatever we offered them.

I kept my eyes open and tried to find out if there was any gold, and I saw that some of them had a little piece hanging from a hole in their nose. I gathered from their signs that if one goes south, or around the south side of the island, there is a king with great jars full of it, enormous amounts. I tried to persuade them to go there, but I saw that the idea was not to their liking.

I decided to wait until tomorrow and then to set off to the southwest, for many of them seemed to be saying that there is land to the s and sw and NW, and that the people from the NW often come to attack them, and continue to the sw in search of gold

Vocabulary

tedious (tē′dē əs) *adj.* tiresome because of length or dullness; boring

and precious stones. This island is large and very flat, with green trees and plenty of water; there is a large lake in the middle, no mountains, and everything is green and a delight to the eye. The people are very gentle; they are so eager for our things that if we refuse to give them something without getting something in exchange they seize what they can and jump into the water with it. But they will give whatever they have for anything one gives them; they even bargained for pieces of broken plate and broken glasses. I saw them take three Portuguese *ceotís*, the equivalent of one Castilian *blanca*,[9] for sixteen balls of cotton which must have contained more than an *arroba*[10] of thread. I had forbidden anyone to take this, except that I had given orders to take it all for Your Majesties if it was in sufficient quantity. It grows on this island, though in the little time available I could not swear to this, and the gold they wear hanging from their noses is also from the island, but so as not to waste time I wish to set off to see if I can reach the island of Cipango.

It is now after nightfall and they have all gone ashore in their *almadías*.

SUNDAY, 14 OCTOBER. I gave orders at daybreak for the small boat of the Santa María and the boats of the two caravels to be got ready, and went along the coast to the northeast to examine the eastward part of the island, and the villages, of which I saw two or three. The people kept coming down to the beach, calling to us and giving thanks to God. Some brought us water, some food; others, seeing that I did not wish to go ashore, swam out to us, and we understood them to be asking if we had come from Heaven. One old man climbed into the boat, and the others, men and women, kept shouting, "Come and see the men who have come from Heaven; bring them food and drink."

Many men and women came, each bringing something and giving thanks to God, throwing themselves on the ground and raising their hands in the air. They called to us to go ashore, but I was afraid of a great reef which encircles the whole island, though between it and the shore there is a deep harbor big enough to hold every ship in Christendom, with a very narrow entrance channel. There are certainly shoals within this reef, but the sea inside it is as calm as a millpond.

I bestirred myself to explore all this this morning so as to be able to give Your Majesties a description of it all, and also of a possible site for a fort. I saw a piece of land which is virtually an island; there are six houses on it, and it could be converted into an island with a couple of days' work, although I do not see the necessity. These people have little knowledge of fighting, as Your Majesties will see from the seven I have had captured to take away with us so as to teach them our language and return them, unless Your Majesties' orders are that they all be taken to Spain or held captive on the island itself, for with fifty men one could keep the whole population in subjection and make them do whatever one wanted.

Near the islet I have described there are groves of the most beautiful trees I ever saw; so green, with their leaves like those in Castile in April and May. There is also plenty of water. I explored the whole harbor, and then returned to the ship and set

---

9. *Ceotis* (thā ō tēs′) and *blanca* (blän′ kä) are coins. *Castilian,* often used as a synonym for "Spanish," refers to Castile, a large region of central Spain.

10. An *arroba* (ä rō′ bä) is a unit of measurement equal to about 25 pounds.

Recognize Bias *Does Columbus consider the islanders intelligent? Explain.*

Cultures in Conflict *How do the islanders regard the Spanish sailors?*

sail. I saw so many islands that I could not decide which to go to first. The men I had captured told me by signs that there are so many that they cannot be counted; they gave me the names of over a hundred. I therefore looked for the largest, and decided to sail for it, which is what I am doing now. It must be about five leagues from this island of San Salvador.[11] Some of the others are nearer, some further away. They are all very flat and fertile, with no mountains, and they are all populated and make war on one another, though these people are very simple, and very finely made.

MONDAY, 15 OCTOBER. Last night I lay to[12] for fear of approaching land to anchor before morning, not knowing if the coast was free from shoals, and intending to increase sail at dawn. The distance was more than five leagues, nearer seven, and the tide set us back, so that it would be around noon when I reached the island. I found that the arm of the island nearest San Salvador runs N–S, and is five leagues long, and the other, along which I sailed, runs E–W for over ten leagues.

From this island I sighted another larger one to the west, so I increased sail to press on all day until nightfall, for otherwise I could not have reached the western cape. I named this island Santa María de la Concepción. I anchored off the western cape just before sunset to find out if there was any gold there. The prisoners I took on San Salvador kept telling me that the people of this island wore great gold bracelets and legbands, but I thought it was all invention to enable them to escape. However, my intention being not to pass by any island without taking possession of it, although taking possession of one might be taken to serve for them all, I anchored and remained there until today, Tuesday.

At daybreak I armed the boats and went ashore. There were numerous people, naked and similar to those on San Salvador. They let us go about on the island and gave us whatever I asked for. The wind was strengthening from the southeast, so I decided not to linger, but set off to return to the ship. A large *almadía* was alongside the Niña, and one of the men from San Salvador who was aboard the caravel jumped into the sea and went off in it (another had jumped overboard the previous night). Our boat set off after the *almadía*, which paddled away so fast that no boat ever built could have outpaced it, even with a considerable start. Anyway, it reached the shore and they abandoned it. Some of my men landed in pursuit, and the islanders all fled like chickens. The *almadía* was taken back on board the Niña.

By now another small *almadía* was approaching the Niña from a different headland with one man in it who had come to barter a ball of cotton. He did not want to come aboard, so some of the sailors jumped into the sea and captured him. I saw all this from the deck of the sterncastle,[13] so I sent for him; I gave him a red bonnet and put a few little green glass beads on his arm and hung two bells from his ears. I had him put back in his *almadía*, which had also been taken aboard the ship's boat, and sent him back ashore. I then made sail to go to the other large island which I could see to the westward, and I ordered the other *almadía* which the Niña was towing astern[14] to be set adrift.

---

11. *San Salvador* (sän säl′və dôr) is one of the islands of the Bahamas in the Caribbean Sea. It is believed to be the place where Columbus first landed, on October 12, 1492.
12. *Lay to* means "kept the ship in place at sea with the front facing toward the wind."

Recognize Bias *Why does Columbus think his captives are lying about the gold?*

13. The *sterncastle* is part of the upper deck toward the stern, or rear of a ship.
14. Here, *astern* means "behind."

SAT Skills Practice

1. Columbus's intended audience for his journal entries was

   (A) the Italian clergy

   (B) King Ferdinand and Queen Isabella of Spain

   (C) his brother Bartholomew in Lisbon

   (D) the upper classes of Europe

   (E) his wife and son

2. Columbus's main purpose for writing these journal entries was to

   (A) document events for the historical record

   (B) finally prove himself a success

   (C) convince the church to send missionaries to convert the natives

   (D) assure his patrons that their investment was worthwhile

   (E) establish himself as an author

Review: Setting

As you learned on page 108, **setting** is the time and place in which the events of a literary work occur.

Partner Activity Discuss the following questions with a classmate.

1. List some of the details Columbus provides to describe the landscape.

2. How do the great distance of the Bahamas from Spain and the islands' relative isolation influence the events described in the journal?

3. What is the cultural context of Columbus's point of view and his actions?

LOG ON ▶ **Literature** Online

Selection Resources For Selection Quizzes, eFlashcards, and Reading-Writing Connection activities, go to glencoe.com and enter QuickPass code GLW6053u6.

Reading Strategy Recognize Bias

Review the chart you filled in on page 1137. Then answer the following items.

1. Cite some descriptions of the islanders that seem objective and neutral.

2. In one sentence, summarize Columbus's bias as reflected in these journal entries.

Vocabulary Practice

Practice with Word Usage Respond to these statements to help explore the meanings of the vocabulary words from the text.

1. Explain what might happen if you **strayed** off course while hiking in the woods.

2. Describe a **solemn** event.

3. Relate a situation in which you observed someone using **coercion** to get his or her way.

4. Give three examples of tasks you find **tedious**.

5. Name things that might cause a driver to **veer** while driving down a street.

Academic Vocabulary

New information about Columbus's treatment of Native Americans has forced many readers to make **adjustments** to their perspectives on his voyages.

Adjustment is a word that has many meanings. Using context clues, figure out the meaning of adjustment in each sentence below. Then explain the difference between the two meanings.

1. After the insurance company made an **adjustment**, the doctor sent a bill to the patient for the remaining cost of her services.

2. Some economists predicted a market **adjustment** even before the dot-com bubble burst.

For more on academic vocabulary, see pages 36–37 and R83–R85.

Respond Through Writing

Summary

Report Main Ideas and Events When you write a summary of a nonfiction work, you restate the main ideas or events. In about 100 words, summarize the first entry from Columbus's journal.

Understand the Task When you **restate,** you retell written or spoken text in your own words without stating opinions.

Prewrite Note answers to the questions *who? what? when? where? why?* and *how?* in a chart. The chart below was created to summarize the excerpt from *Stay Alive, My Son* on pages 821–825.

Who	Pin Yathay
What	the memoir <u>Stay Alive, My Son</u>
When	1987
Where	a Cambodian work camp
Why	to show the brutality of the Khmer Rouge by relating his own experiences
How	

Draft Draw upon the answers to the six questions as you draft your summary. Below is a summary of the excerpt from *Stay Alive, My Son.*

In this excerpt from Stay Alive, My Son, *Pin Yathay describes his experiences in a Cambodian work camp to show the brutality and ineffectiveness of the Khmer Rouge. Yathay recounts a time when he was ordered to cut down fruit trees that could have provided food for the hungry workers. He then describes how he was caught with an illegally obtained can of rice and turned over to his group's leader, Run. Facing punishment by death, Yathay reminded Run that he had helped him obtain antibiotics illegally two weeks earlier. Run then spared Yathay because he feared for his own life.*

Revise Have a partner read your summary and ask him or her to circle the answers to the six questions listed above. If your partner cannot find the answers to all the questions, revise your summary accordingly.

Edit and Proofread Proofread your paper, correcting any errors in grammar, spelling, and punctuation. Use the Grammar Tip in the side column for help with using commas with appositives.

Learning Objectives

In this assignment, you will focus on the following objectives:

Writing: Writing a summary.

Grammar: Understanding commas with appositives.

Grammar Tip

Commas with Appositives

An appositive is a noun or a pronoun that is placed next to another noun or pronoun to identify it or give additional information about it. In the sentence *The group leader, Run, asks Yathay for help,* the name *Run* is an appositive. It is set off by commas because it gives information that is not essential to the meaning of the sentence. Usually an appositive follows the noun or pronoun it identifies or explains.

Before You Read

from *The Broken Spears: The Aztec Account of the Conquest of Mexico*

For hundreds of years, historians based their understanding of the Spanish Conquest of the Aztec Empire almost exclusively on accounts provided by the Spanish explorer Hernán Cortés and his soldier Bernal Díaz del Castillo. Then in 1962, *The Broken Spears: The Aztec Account of the Conquest of Mexico* told the story of the conquest from the Aztecs' perspective.

The Spanish Conquest By the early 1500s, just before the Spanish invasion, the Aztec Empire rivaled the empires of the other great Meso-American cultures that had preceded it. From Tenochtitlán (tae nōch′tēt län′), the Aztec capital city, Motecuhzoma II (ruled an advanced agricultural and trading society of nearly six million people.

Then in 1519, Cortés and his forces landed on the east coast of Mexico and made their way to the Aztec capital. These invaders demolished Tenochtitlán, leveling temples and burning many

> *"Broken spears lie in the roads;*
> *we have torn our hair in grief.*
> *The houses are roofless now, and*
>   *their walls*
> *are red with blood."*
>
> from *The Broken Spears*

of the Aztec codices (hieroglyphic texts). The conquerors considered it their Christian duty to destroy all artifacts of the Aztecs' pagan religion. Some Spanish missionaries, however, managed to salvage a few codices. They then taught an alphabetic version of Nahuatl (nä wä′təl), the Aztec language, to the conquest's survivors. Working together, the Spanish missionaries and their Aztec pupils recorded accounts of the Spanish invasion as well as native songs, poems, and narratives.

The Broken Spears *The Broken Spears,* compiled by Miguel Leon-Portilla, contains excerpts from several of the more than 40 Aztec manuscripts that survived the conquest. The first thirteen chapters present chronological accounts, beginning with the arrival of the Spanish and ending with the destruction of Tenochtitlán. Chapter Fourteen is a brief summary of the conquest taken from a single source that provides information not found anywhere else. The last chapter contains "songs of sorrow," elegies written by post-conquest survivors lamenting the fall of their city.

The excerpts from *The Broken Spears* that follow are divided into two parts. Part I describes the Aztecs' reaction to the arrival of the Spanish; Part II describes the battles leading to the fall of Tenochtitlán.

Aztec Empire located on an Island in the Lake of Texcoco. Franz Hogenbergh and Georg Braun. Colored engraving. Biblioteca Marciana, Venice.

Literature and Reading Preview

Connect to the History

What accounts about exploration and conquest have you read? Discuss this question with a small group.

Build Background

The Aztecs were the last of a series of nomadic groups to migrate to the fertile Valley of Mexico. They founded Tenochtitlán in 1325 on an island in Lake Texcoco (**tes kō′kō**), the site of present-day Mexico City. Gradually, the Aztecs expanded and consolidated their power through alliances with or conquests of other groups, including the forced annexation of Tlatelolco (**tlä tə lōl′kō**), a nearby commercial center that became part of the capital.

Set Purposes for Reading

Big Idea Cultures in Conflict

Written accounts of the initial encounters between native peoples and explorers reflect the striking contrasts between their values and ways of living. As you read, ask yourself, What are the contrasts between the Spanish explorers and the Aztecs?

Literary Element Setting

The **setting** is the time and place in which the events of a literary work occur. Setting includes not only the physical surroundings, but also the ideas, customs, values, and beliefs of a particular time and place. As you read, ask yourself, How does the setting influence the conflict between the Spaniards and the Aztecs?

Reading Strategy Analyze Cultural Context

When you **analyze cultural context,** you determine how the values and beliefs of the people living in a particular time and place affect the work. As you read, ask yourself, How do the Aztecs' values and beliefs influence their response to events?

....

Tip: Track Events In a chart like the one below, list events, the Aztecs' response, and the reason for their response.

Event	Aztecs' Response	Reason for Response
The Aztecs sight a ship offshore.	They assume the ship is a mountain.	They have seen mountains before but not a ship.

Learning Objectives

For pages 1148–1160

In studying this text, you will focus on the following objectives:

Literary Study: Analyzing setting.

Reading: Analyzing cultural context.

Listening and Speaking: Conducting an interview.

Vocabulary

haste (hast) *n.* quickness of action or movement; hurry; p. 1151 *Arriving late at the airport, we proceeded to the gate with great haste.*

humility (hū mil′ə tē) *n.* modesty; meekness; p. 1152 *With deep humility, the performer bowed to acknowledge the applause.*

straggler (strag′lər) *n.* one who lags behind or strays from a group; p. 1156 *The stragglers trailed the other runners by several blocks.*

epidemic (ep′ə dem′ik) *n.* rapid spread of disease affecting many people; p. 1157 *A flu epidemic made many students miss school.*

sustenance (sus′tə nəns) *n.* food; nourishment; means of support; p. 1157 *Lost, the camper desperately sought water and sustenance.*

Shield, c.1500. Aztec. Feathers, sheet-gold, agave paper, leather, and reed. Museum fur Volkerkunde, Vienna.

from
The Broken Spears

Edited by Miguel Leon-Portilla
Translated by Lysander Kemp

When the Spanish explorer Hernán Cortés and his troops arrived in Mexico, they first landed at Tabasco on the southeastern coast, where they made contact with local Indians. They then sailed up the coast, landing at what is now Veracruz. From there, they marched west into the interior of Mexico toward Tenochtitlán. Along the way, Cortés enlisted the aid of Indian groups who had been conquered by the Aztecs and resented their control, most notably the Tlaxcala nation. The conquest of the Aztec Empire took three years and was complicated by internal strife on both sides. The excerpts in Part I describe the Aztecs' reaction to the arrival of strangers in their land.

I.

A Macehual Arrives from the Gulf Coast

A few days later a *macehual* [common man] came to the city from Mictlancuauhtla. No one had sent him, none of the officials; he came of his own accord. He went directly to the palace of Motecuhzoma and said to him: "Our lord and king, forgive my boldness. I am from Mictlancuauhtla. When I went to the shores of the great sea,[1] there was a mountain range or small mountain floating in the midst of the water, and moving here and there without touching the shore. My lord, we have never seen the like of this, although we guard the coast and are always on watch."

Motecuhzoma thanked him and said: "You may rest now."

Motecuhzoma said to his *petlacalcatl*:[2] "Take him to the prison, and guard him well." Then he called for a *teuctlamacazqui* [priest] and appointed him his grand emissary. He said to him: "Go to Cuetlaxtlan, and tell the official in charge of the village that it is true, strange things have appeared on the great sea. Tell him to investigate these things himself, so as to learn what they may signify. Tell him to do this as quickly as he can, and take the ambassador Cuitlalpitoc with you."

When they arrived in Cuetlaxtlan, the envoys spoke with the official in charge there, a man named Pinotl. He listened to them with great attention and then said: "My lords, rest here with me, and send your attendants out to the shore." The attendants went out and came back in great **haste** to report that it was true: they had seen two towers or small mountains floating on the waves of the sea. The grand emissary said to Pinotl: "I wish to see these things in person, in order to learn what they are, for I must testify to our lord as an eyewitness. I will be satisfied with this and will report to him exactly what I see." Therefore he went out to the shore with Cuitlalpitoc, and they saw what was floating there, beyond the edge of the water. They also saw that seven or eight of the strangers had left it in a small boat and were fishing with hooks and lines.

The grand emissary and Cuitlalpitoc climbed up into a broad-limbed tree. From there they saw how the strangers were catching fish and how, when they were done, they returned to the ship in their small boat. The grand emissary said: "Come, Cuitlalpitoc." They climbed down from the tree and went back to the village, where they took hasty leave of Pinotl. They returned as swiftly as possible to the great city of Tenochtitlan, to report to Motecuhzoma what they had observed.

---

1. *The great sea* is the Gulf of Mexico in the Atlantic Ocean.
2. A *petlacalcatl* was the king's head steward or servant.

Setting *What detail in the setting frightens the commoner?*

haste (hāst) *n.* quickness of action or movement; hurry

two captives were then sacrificed before his eyes: their breasts were torn open, and the messengers were sprinkled with their blood.[8] This was done because the messengers had completed a difficult mission: they had seen the gods, their eyes had looked on their faces. They had even conversed with the gods!

The Messengers' Report

When the sacrifice was finished, the messengers reported to the king. They told him how they had made the journey, and what they had seen, and what food the strangers ate. Motecuhzoma was astonished and terrified by their report, and the description of the strangers' food astonished him above all else.

He was also terrified to learn how the cannon roared, how its noise resounded, how it caused one to faint and grow deaf. The messengers told him: "A thing like a ball of stone comes out of its entrails: it comes out shooting sparks and raining fire. The smoke that comes out with it has a pestilent odor, like that of rotten mud. This odor penetrates even to the brain and causes the greatest discomfort. If the cannon is aimed against a mountain, the mountain splits and cracks open. If it is aimed against a tree, it shatters the tree into splinters. This is a most unnatural sight, as if the tree had exploded from within."

The messengers also said: "Their trappings and arms are all made of iron. They dress in iron and wear iron casques[9] on their heads. Their swords are iron; their bows are iron; their shields are iron; their spears are iron. Their deer[10] carry them on their backs wherever they wish to go. These deer, our lord, are as tall as the roof of a house.

"The strangers' bodies are completely covered, so that only their faces can be seen. Their skin is white, as if it were made of lime. They have yellow hair, though some of them have black. Their beards are long and yellow, and their moustaches are also yellow. Their hair is curly, with very fine strands.

"As for their food, it is like human food. It is large and white, and not heavy. It is something like straw, but with the taste of a cornstalk, of the pith of a cornstalk. It is a little sweet, as if it were flavored with honey; it tastes of honey, it is sweet-tasting food.

"Their dogs are enormous, with flat ears and long, dangling tongues. The color of their eyes is a burning yellow; their eyes flash fire and shoot off sparks. Their bellies are hollow, their flanks long and narrow. They are tireless and very powerful. They bound here and there, panting, with their tongues hanging out. And they are spotted like an ocelot."

Visual Vocabulary
An *ocelot* is a medium-sized wildcat.

When Motecuhzoma heard this report, he was filled with terror. It was as if his heart had fainted, as if it had shriveled. It was as if he were conquered by despair.

---

8. *The two captives . . . with their blood:* The captives were slaves captured in war for the purpose of being used for ritual sacrifices. Human sacrifices were an important element of the Aztecs' religion. They believed that the gods needed the blood from sacrifices to make them strong.

Analyze Cultural Context *Why does the king think it necessary to offer human sacrifices?*

Setting *What unfamiliar sights, sounds, and smells do the messengers report in this paragraph?*

9. A *casque* is a helmet.
10. *Deer* refers to the troops' horses. The messenger mistakes them for deer because he has never seen a horse.

Cultures in Conflict *Why do you think Motecuhzoma is filled with terror after hearing the messengers' report?*

Aztec Bird God. Gold. Private collection.

The excerpts in Part II describe Cortés's initial arrival in Tenochtitlán and subsequent events. It is told by survivors of the Tlaltelolco district of the city and, as such, reflects the local pride and bias that influenced their descriptions of the conflict.

II.

The Arrival of Cortés

Year 1-Canestalk. The Spaniards came to the palace at Tlayacac. When the Captain[11] arrived at the palace, Motecuhzoma sent the Cuetlaxteca to greet him and to bring him two suns as gifts. One of these suns was made of the yellow metal, the other of the white.[12] The Cuetlaxteca also brought him a mirror to be hung on his person, a gold collar, a great gold pitcher, fans and ornaments of quetzal[13] feathers and a shield inlaid with mother-of-pearl.

The envoys made sacrifices in front of the Captain. At this, he grew very angry. When they offered him blood in an "eagle dish," he shouted at the man who offered it and struck him with his sword. The envoys departed at once.

All the gifts which the Cuetlaxteca brought to the Captain were sent by Motecuhzoma. That is why the Cuetlaxteca went to meet the Captain at Tlayacac: he was only performing his duties as a royal envoy.

Then the Captain marched to Tenochtitlan. He arrived here during the month called Bird, under the sign of the day 8-Wind. When he entered the city, we

---

11. *Captain* refers to Cortés.
12. *Yellow metal, the other of the white* means "gold and silver."
13. A *quetzal* (ket säl´) is a Central American bird, brilliantly colored, with long, flowing tail feathers.

Cultures in Conflict *Why might the sacrifices offend Cortés?*

gave him chickens, eggs, corn, tortillas and drink. We also gave him firewood, and fodder for his "deer." Some of these gifts were sent by the lord of Tenochtitlan, the rest by the lord of Tlatelolco.

Later the Captain marched back to the coast, leaving Don Pedro de Alvarado—The Sun—in command.

The Massacre in the Main Temple

During this time, the people asked Motecuhzoma how they should celebrate their god's fiesta. He said: "Dress him in all his finery, in all his sacred ornaments."

During this same time, The Sun commanded that Motecuhzoma and Itzcohuatzin, the military chief of Tlatelolco, be made prisoners. The Spaniards hanged a chief from Acolhuacan named Nezahualquentzin. They also murdered the king of Nauhtla, Cohualpopocatzin, by wounding him with arrows and then burning him alive.

For this reason, our warriors were on guard at the Eagle Gate. The sentries from Tenochtitlan stood at one side of the gate, and the sentries from Tlatelolco at the other. But messengers came to tell them to dress the figure of Huitzilopochtli.[14] They left their posts and went to dress him in his sacred finery: his ornaments and his paper clothing.

When this had been done, the celebrants began to sing their songs. That is how they celebrated the first day of the fiesta. On the second day they began to sing again, but without warning they were all put to death. The dancers and singers were completely unarmed. They brought only their embroidered cloaks, their turquoises,

their lip plugs, their necklaces, their clusters of heron feathers, their trinkets made of deer hooves. Those who played the drums, the old men, had brought their gourds of snuff and their timbrels.[15]

The Spaniards attacked the musicians first, slashing at their hands and faces until they had killed all of them. The singers—and even the spectators—were also killed. This slaughter in the Sacred Patio went on for three hours. Then the Spaniards burst into the rooms of the temple to kill the others: those who were carrying water, or bringing fodder for the horses, or grinding meal, or sweeping, or standing watch over this work.

The king Motecuhzoma, who was accompanied by Itzcohuatzin and by those who had brought food for the Spaniards, protested: "Our lords, that is enough! What are you doing? These people are not carrying shields or *macanas*.[16] Our lords, they are completely unarmed!"

The Sun treacherously murdered our people on the twentieth day after the Captain left for the coast. We allowed the Captain to return to the city in peace. But on the following day we attacked him with all our might, and that was the beginning of the war.

The Night of Sorrows

The Spaniards attempted to slip out of the city at night, but we attacked furiously at the Canal of the Toltecs, and many of them died. This took place during the fiesta of Tecuilhuitl. The survivors gathered first at Mazatzintamalco and waited for the **stragglers** to come up.

---

14. *Huitzilopochtli* was the Aztec god of war, and the special protector of the people of Tenochtitlán.

Cultures in Conflict *How might the Spaniards justify their slaughter of those at the festival?*

15. A *timbrel* is a small drum.
16. *Macanas* are clubs or cudgels.

Vocabulary

straggler (strag′lər) *n.* one who lags behind or strays from a group

Year 2-Flint. This was the year in which Motecuhzoma died.[17] Itzcohuatzin of Tlatelolco died at the same time.

The Spaniards took refuge in Acueco, but they were driven out by our warriors. They fled to Teuhcalhueyacan and from there to Zoltepec. Then they marched through Citlaltepec and camped in Temazcalapan, where the people gave them hens, eggs and corn. They rested for a short while and marched on to Tlaxcala.

Soon after, an **epidemic** broke out in Tenochtitlan. Almost the whole population suffered from racking coughs and painful, burning sores.

The Siege of Tenochtitlan

Now the Spaniards began to wage war against us. They attacked us by land for ten days, and then their ships appeared. Twenty days later, they gathered all their ships together near Nonohualco, off the place called Mazatzintamalco. The allies from Tlaxcala and Huexotzinco set up camp on either side of the road.

Our warriors from Tlatelolco immediately leaped into their canoes and set out for Mazatzintamalco and the Nonohualco road. But no one set out from Tenochtitlan to assist us: only the Tlatelolcas were ready when the Spaniards arrived in their ships. On the following day, the ships sailed to Xoloco.

The fighting at Xoloco and Huitzillan lasted for two days. While the battle was under way, the warriors from Tenochtitlan began to mutiny. They said: "Where are our chiefs? They have fired scarcely a single arrow! Do they think they have fought like men?" Then they seized four of their own leaders and put them to death. The victims were two captains, Cuauhnochtli and Cuapan, and the priests of Amantlan and Tlalocan. This was the second time that the people of Tenochtitlan killed their own leaders.

The Flight to Tlatelolco

The Spaniards set up two cannons in the middle of the road and aimed them at the city. When they fired them, one of the shots struck the Eagle Gate. The people of the city were so terrified that they began to flee to Tlatelolco. They brought their idol Huitzilopochtli with them, setting it up in the House of the Young Men. Their king Cuauhtemoc[18] also abandoned Tenochtitlan. Their chiefs said: "Mexicanos! Tlatelolcas! All is not lost! We can still defend our houses. We can prevent them from capturing our storehouses and the produce of our lands. We can save the **sustenance** of life, our stores of corn. We can also save our weapons and insignia, our clusters of rich feathers, our gold earrings and precious stones. Do not be discouraged; do not lose heart. We are Mexicanos! We are Tlatelolcas!"

The Fighting Is Renewed

The Spaniards made ready to attack us, and the war broke out again. They assembled

---

17. *Motecuhzoma died:* The circumstances of Motecuhzoma's death are not known. Historians theorize that he may have died of injuries sustained during the Aztec rebellion.

Analyze Cultural Context *What might this statement suggest about the relationship between the Tlatelolcas and the other residents of Tenochtitlán?*

Vocabulary

epidemic (ep′ə dem′ik) *n.* rapid spread of disease affecting many people

---

18. *Cuauhtemoc* became king of the Aztecs after the death of Motecuhzoma.

Vocabulary

sustenance (sus′tə nəns) *n.* food; nourishment; means of support

their forces in Cuepopan and Cozcacuahco. A vast number of our warriors were killed by their metal darts. Their ships sailed to Texopan, and the battle there lasted three days. When they had forced us to retreat, they entered the Sacred Patio, where there was a four-day battle. Then they reached Yacacolco.

The Tlatelolcas set up three racks of heads in three different places. The first rack was in the Sacred Patio of Tlilancalco [Black House], where we strung up the heads of our lords the Spaniards. The second was in Acacolco, where we strung up Spanish heads and the heads of two of their horses. The third was in Zacatla, in front of the temple of the earth-goddess Cihuacoatl, where we strung up the heads of Tlaxcaltecas.

The women of Tlatelolco joined in the fighting. They struck at the enemy and shot arrows at them; they tucked up their skirts and dressed in the regalia of war.

The Spaniards forced us to retreat. Then they occupied the market place. The Tlatelolcas—the Jaguar Knights, the Eagle Knights, the great warriors—were defeated, and this was the end of the battle. It had lasted five days, and two thousand Tlatelolcas were killed in action. During the battle, the Spaniards set up a canopy for the Captain in the market place. They also mounted a catapult on the temple platform.

Epic Description of the Besieged City

And all these misfortunes befell us.
We saw them and wondered at them;
we suffered this unhappy fate.

     Broken spears lie in the roads;
     we have torn our hair in our grief.

The houses are roofless now, and their walls are red with blood.

Worms are swarming in the streets and plazas, and the walls are splattered with gore.
The water has turned red, as if it were dyed, and when we drink it,
it has the taste of brine.

We have pounded our hands in despair against the adobe walls,
for our inheritance, our city, is lost and dead.
The shields of our warriors were its defense, but they could not save it.

We have chewed dry twigs and salt grasses;
we have filled our mouths with dust and bits
   of adobe;
we have eaten lizards, rats and worms. . . .

The City Falls

Cuauhtemoc said to the fortune tellers: "Please come forward. What do you see in your books?"

One of the priests replied: "My prince, hear the truth that we tell you. In only four days we shall have completed the period of eighty days. It may be the will of Huitzilopochtli that nothing further shall happen to us. Let us wait until these four days have passed."

But then the fighting broke out again. The captain of Huitznahuac—the same Huasteco who had brought in Xochitl—renewed the struggle. The enemy forced us to retreat to Amaxac. When they also attacked us there, the general flight began. The lake was full of people, and the roads leading to the mainland were all crowded.

Thus the people of Tenochtitlan and Tlatelolco gave up the struggle and abandoned the city. We all gathered in Amaxac. We had no shields and no *macanas*, we had nothing to eat and no shelter. And it rained all night. ✍

Analyze Cultural Context *What does this reveal about the Aztecs' attitude toward women?*

Cultures in Conflict *Why do you think the Aztecs gave up the fight?*

After You Read

Respond and Think Critically

Respond and Interpret

1. What details about the Aztecs or the conquest impressed you most? Why?

2. (a)When the messengers confirm the sighting of strangers, what objects does Motecuhzoma order to be made? (b)What might he want to do with them?

3. (a)Why do you think the narrator refers to Don Pedro de Alvarado as "The Sun"? (b)How do you think the narrator regards The Sun after he murders Aztecs?

4. (a)What do the citizens of Tenochtitlán do when Cortés returns to the city? (b)Why does the narrator say this moment "was the beginning of the war"?

Analyze and Evaluate

5. (a)Why do you think Cortés was able to receive assistance from Indian groups within the Aztec Empire? (b)What does this suggest about the power of the Aztecs?

6. How does the tone of the poem on page 1158 differ from the tone of the prose sections of the narrative? Support your response with evidence from the text.

Connect

7. **Big Idea** **Cultures in Conflict** (a)Why do you think Cortés and his troops were able to defeat the Aztecs? (b)Under what circumstances might the Aztecs have been victorious?

8. **Connect to Today** Why is it important for modern readers to understand the Aztecs' perspective on the Spanish Conquest?

Literary Element Setting

ACT Skills Practice

1. "The great sea" is significant in the narrative because it is:

   I. the route by which the Spaniards arrived.

   II. the location of the first Spaniard sightings.

   III. the route Quetzalcoatl used to leave Mexico.

   A. II only

   B. I and II only

   C. I and III only

   D. I, II, and III

2. The details of setting in the poem at the end of the narrative suggest a feeling of:

   F. exhilaration.

   G. mystery.

   H. devastation.

   J. prosperity.

Review: Point of View

As you learned on page 497, **point of view** is the relationship of the narrator to the literary work. Though the narrators of this historical account occasionally use first-person pronouns, the excerpts are told mainly from the **third-person** point of view. At times, the narrator is omniscient or all-knowing, as when describing Motecuhzoma's reaction to the messengers' report.

Partner Activity Working with a partner, discuss the following questions.

1. What cultural limitations affected the Aztec narrators' descriptions of the Spaniards?

2. The account in Part II is told by different Tlatelolco narrators. What details reveal a point of view specific to them?

Reading Strategy Analyze Cultural Context

Analyzing the cultural context of a text helps you identify the values and beliefs that influenced the work. Look back at the chart you made on page 1149, and then answer the following questions.

1. How did the cultural beliefs and practices of the Aztecs influence their treatment of the Spaniards? Cite examples from the text.

2. How did the Aztecs' view of the world work to their disadvantage in their dealings with the Spaniards?

Vocabulary Practice

Practice with Analogies Choose the word that best completes each analogy. Use a dictionary if you need help.

1. haste : speed :: hurry :
   a. politeness **b.** swiftness **c.** sensibleness

2. humility : pomposity :: envy :
   a. scorn **b.** timidity **c.** admiration

3. straggler : stray :: achiever :
   a. succeed **b.** withdraw **c.** criticize

4. epidemic : outbreak :: offense :
   a. defense **b.** insult **c.** delight

5. sustenance : starvation :: wealth :
   a. excess **b.** poverty **c.** luxury

Academic Vocabulary

The legend of the return of Quetzalcoatl influenced the Aztecs' **interpretation** *of the Spaniards' arrival.*

Interpretation is an academic word. In the justice system, lawyers and judges use their **interpretations** of laws to determine which actions are crimes. To further explore the meaning of this word, describe a time when your **interpretation** of an event or a literary character was inaccurate, and explain why.

For more on academic vocabulary, see pages 36–37 and R83–R85.

Listening and Speaking

 Interview

Assignment *The Broken Spears* is a compilation of several firsthand accounts of the conquest of Mexico. These primary sources changed the perspectives of many readers who had been familiar only with secondhand accounts. Conduct interviews with your peers and others in your community to determine what they know about the Spanish Conquest of the Aztec Empire. Then write a report based on the interviews.

Prepare Write a list of relevant questions phrased in mature, sensitive, and respectful language. Questions should reflect your understanding of the topic. Leave space under each for answers.

Interview Take notes on your subjects' responses to your questions. Follow these tips:

- Allow your subject to respond completely; don't interrupt.

- Make frequent eye contact.

- Adjust your tone of voice or body language in response to your subject.

- If necessary, ask further questions to clarify information.

- Review your subject's statements as a final check.

- Thank your subject for his or her cooperation.

Report Organize your interview notes to compile information for a short report. In your report, include your own reflections on the validity and reliability of each of your subjects' statements. Point out any contradicting information from interview subjects.

Evaluate Write a paragraph reflecting on your performance as an interviewer and outlining ideas for how to extract more in-depth answers if you were to re-interview your subjects.

 Literature Online

Selection Resources For Selection Quizzes, eFlash-cards, and Reading-Writing Connection activities, go to glencoe.com and enter QuickPass code GLW6053u6.

Vocabulary Workshop

Denotation and Connotation

Literature Connection In the excerpts from *The Broken Spears*, the narrator recounts Motecuhzoma's reaction to the news of the arrival of the Spanish conquistadors: "He was filled with terror. It was as if his heart had fainted, as if it had shriveled. It was as if he were conquered by despair." The narrator could have used words other than *terror*. For instance, he could have spoken of *trepidation* or *anxiety*—after all, those words have a meaning similar to *terror*. But they also have subtle differences. Words can have similar **denotations** (dictionary definitions) but different **connotations** (suggested ideas, images, or feelings).

A semantic chart like the one below can help you look more closely at the similarities, differences, and shades of meaning of the words *terror*, *trepidation*, and *anxiety*. Follow these instructions to complete the chart.

- Write the words you will analyze in the first column.

- Check a dictionary to find the definition for each word. Write the definitions in the second column.

- In the third column, record ideas, images, or feelings you associate with each word. For example, you may associate *terror* with acts of violence carried out by subversive groups. Such associations are a word's connotations.

Word	Denotation	Connotation
terror		
trepidation		
anxiety		

Learning Objectives

In this workshop, you will focus on the following objective:

Vocabulary: Understanding denotation and connotation.

Denotation and Connotation

The **denotation** of a word is its literal meaning; the **connotation** of a word is its implied meaning.

Test-Taking Tip

If you are asked a word's denotation on a test, think about how you would define the word to someone else. To identify the word's connotations, think about the images and ideas the word brings to mind.

Practice Use what you have learned about denotation and connotation to complete the activities below.

1. Complete this semantic chart on a separate sheet of paper. With your classmates, discuss the denotations and connotations of the three words. Why do you think the narrator chose to describe Motecuhzoma's reaction as *terror* and not as *trepidation* or *anxiety*?

2. Find three or four similar words used to describe a character's reaction in another literary work in Unit 6, Part 1. Create a semantic chart for these words. Share your completed charts with your classmates.

LOG ON ▶ **Literature** Online

Vocabulary For more vocabulary practice, go to glencoe.com and enter QuickPass code GLW6053u6.

Literature of the Conquest Era

MUCH OF THE INFORMATION WE HAVE ABOUT THE SPANISH Conquest of the Americas was written by the conquerors themselves. However, a few accounts are told from a Native American point of view.

Aztec Records

For hundreds of years following the Spanish Conquest of the Aztecs, the only version of this tragic history was that of the victors. The Aztecs left two types of documentary records, however. The first are the pictographic books known as *codices*. The Aztec codices created before the Spanish Conquest are entirely pictorial and largely devoted to religious ritual. Later codices were created under Spanish supervision; some of these were copies of pre-Conquest records that are now lost. These post-Conquest codices sometimes include Spanish commentary as well as pictographs and contain important information on Aztec history and culture. The second type of Aztec records are books written in Nahuatl, the language of the Aztecs, but using the Latin alphabet the Spanish had taught the Native Americans. In these books, the Aztecs preserved poems, songs, histories, and other traditions they had memorized in their own schools prior to the Spanish Conquest.

Hernán Cortés and Bernal Díaz del Castillo

In 1519, long before his forces had completed their conquest of the Aztec Empire, Hernán Cortés began sending reports to Spain in the form of lengthy letters to the Spanish ruler, Charles V. Cortés was an excellent writer, and his letters present a vivid, detailed, and carefully constructed version of the events of his expedition, designed to heighten his own achievements and silence his political enemies. The five letters of Cortés are among the most

Aztec feather artisan, mid 16th century. Bernardino de Sahagun. Illustration. Biblioteca Medicea-Laurenziana, Florence.

important primary sources about the Spanish Conquest of what is now Mexico.

Another important source is the account written by one of Cortés's men, Bernal Díaz del Castillo. He began writing *The True History of the Conquest of New Spain* in the early 1550s, but it was only after reading another account of the conquest, with which he disagreed, that he became motivated to complete his own. Díaz believed his personal involvement as a member of the expedition made him better qualified to describe it.

Bartolomé de Las Casas

In the years following the Spanish Conquest, many people began to protest against the brutality of the *encomienda* system through which Spanish colonists exacted forced labor from Native Americans. One prominent advocate for native peoples was Bartolomé de Las Casas, Bishop of Chiapas, an "Apostle of the Indies." As a young man on the Caribbean island of Hispaniola, Las Casas was horrified by Spanish mistreatment of Native Americans. He later wrote several books describing their destruction. His books were read throughout Europe, creating pressure on the Spanish government to change their policies.

Hernando Cortez. Museo Ciudad Mexico.

> *"Surely God will wreak his fury and anger against Spain some day for the unjust wars waged against the Indians."*
>
> —Bartolomé de Las Casas

Garcilaso de La Vega

Between 1532 and the early 1570s, the Spanish conquered the Inca Empire, destroying much of Inca civilization in the process. The source for much of what is known about the early history of the Incas is Garcilaso de la Vega's *Royal Commentaries of the Incas*, published between 1608 and 1617. Born in Peru in 1539, de la Vega, later known as "El Inca," was the son of an Inca princess and a Spanish conquistador. He grew up hearing his mother's relatives and friends retelling the ancient myths and legends of the Incas, which became the basis for his account. *The Royal Commentaries* is divided into two parts: the first deals with Inca history and civilization, the second with the Spanish conquest of Peru.

Alonso de Ercilla y Zúniga

Born in Spain in 1533, Alonso de Ercilla y Zúniga arrived in South America in 1555 and served with the Spanish in their long struggle against the Araucanian (or Mapuche) people of southern Chile and Argentina. The Native Americans were led by a brave, skillful warrior named Lautaro, who successfully resisted the Spanish until he was defeated and killed. He is one of the main characters in *La Araucana*, an epic poem in which Ercilla describes the Spanish campaigns in which he fought. Although Ercilla believed the Native Americans were wrong to resist Spanish authority once they had accepted it, his epic presents a sympathetic account of their struggle.

Literature and Reading For more about the literature of the Conquest Era, go to glencoe.com and enter QuickPass code GLW6053u6.

Respond and Think Critically

1. If you could ask one of these writers a question, who would it be and what would you ask?

2. How did the Aztec codices created before the Spanish Conquest differ from those produced after it?

3. (a)What seems to be the most characteristic form of Spanish literature of the Conquest Era? (b)Why do you think this was so?

Before You Read

Sonnet 145

Meet **Sor Juana Inés de la Cruz** (1651–1695)

Sor Juana Inés de la Cruz (sôr hwä′nä ē nās′ dā lä kruz′) was the first major author of European descent born in Latin America. She always maintained that women were intellectually equal to men—a controversial view at the time.

Child Prodigy Born in a village outside Mexico City, Sor Juana began reading at age three. Using her grandfather's extensive library, she taught herself Latin, literature, science, theology, and foreign languages. She was so eager to learn that when she was eight she asked her parents to let her disguise herself as a boy so she could attend the University of Mexico. Unfortunately, women had little opportunity to pursue education in colonial Mexico.

Conflict with Church Authorities When she was about seventeen, she decided to become a nun so that she could concentrate on her studies. For about two decades in the convent, Sor Juana wrote religious, philosophical, and love poems as well as plays. She also read widely and performed scientific experiments. Then her life took a sudden turn.

In 1690, the Bishop of Puebla invited Sor Juana to write an essay explaining her theological criticisms. Sor Juana obliged but insisted her essay should not be made public. The bishop, however, published the work, which many people found offensive. In response, Sor Juana wrote a passionate treatise defending a woman's right to pursue knowledge and learning. This treatise set some prominent church figures against her. Although she defended both her opinions and her right to express them with vigor, criticism continued. Angered by the

> "Have [women] not a rational soul as men do? Well, then, why cannot a woman profit by the privilege of enlightenment as they do?"
>
> —Sor Juana Inés de la Cruz

authorities' unyielding opposition, Sor Juana decided to stop writing altogether. She sold her books and research materials—more than 4,000 volumes, considered the largest library in Mexico—and gave the money to the poor. Then she devoted herself to caring for the sick. She died while nursing the victims of an epidemic.

 Literature Online

Author Search For more about Sor Juana Inés de la Cruz, go to glencoe.com and enter QuickPass code GLW6053u6.

Literature and Reading Preview

Connect to the Poem

Have you ever felt surprised or uncomfortable about your own image in a photograph? Write a journal entry explaining why you think your image made you feel that way.

Build Background

Sor Juana wrote a number of poems about portraits. In Sonnet 145, she addresses a painting of herself. Her modesty is reflected in the poem's full title: "She attempts to minimize the praise occasioned by a portrait of herself inscribed by truth, which she calls passion."

Set Purposes for Reading

Big Idea **Transplanting Traditions**

Colonial Latin American authors adapted traditional European forms such as the sonnet to express their perspectives. As you read, ask yourself, What perspectives does the speaker express in this sonnet?

Literary Element **Metaphor**

A **metaphor** is a figure of speech that compares two seemingly unlike things. Unlike a **simile,** a metaphor implies the comparison rather than stating it directly, so there is no use of a connective word such as *like* or *as.* As you read, ask yourself, What metaphors can I identify in this sonnet?

Reading Strategy **Paraphrase**

When you **paraphrase,** you put something you have read or heard into your own words. Paraphrasing is a useful strategy for breaking down difficult text and making it easier to understand. As you read, ask yourself, What passages can I clarify by paraphrasing them?

Tip: Take Notes In a chart like the one below, note difficult passages and your paraphrases of them.

Passages	My Paraphrases
"colorful deceit, / that so immodestly displays art's favors."	This portrait reflects not the truth but the artist's trickery.

Learning Objectives

For pages 1164–1168

In studying this text, you will focus on the following objectives:

Literary Study: Analyzing metaphor.

Reading: Paraphrasing.

Writing: Applying metaphor.

Vocabulary

fallacious (fə lā′shəs) *adj.* erroneous; p. 1166 *The research paper received a failing grade because it had several fallacious references.*

mitigate (mit′ə gāt′) *v.* to lessen; p. 1166 *The darkening clouds increased, rather than mitigated, our fear that a tornado was coming.*

artifice (är′tə fis) *n.* ingenious deception; p. 1166 *The celebrity used dark glasses, a wide-brimmed hat, and other artifices to escape detection.*

ploy (ploi) *n.* a trick or tactic; p. 1166 *He used a ploy to get me to invest in that wild scheme.*

Tip: Synonyms Synonyms are words that have nearly the same meaning. To determine whether two words are synonyms, see if one word can replace the other in a sentence. For example, in the sentence *The research paper received a failing grade because it had several fallacious references,* the word *misleading* can replace *fallacious.* Therefore, *misleading* and *fallacious* are synonyms.

When you **paraphrase,** you restate ideas in your own words. Look back at the chart you made on page 1165, and then answer the following questions.

1. Think about the connotations of the words *colorful* (line 1), *deceit* (line 1), and *cunning* (line 4). Write at least three words you might use to paraphrase each of these words.

2. How would you paraphrase the first six lines of the poem?

Vocabulary Practice

Practice with Synonyms A synonym is a word that has the same or nearly the same meaning as another word. With a partner, match each boldfaced vocabulary word below with its synonym. Use a thesaurus or dictionary to check your answers. You will not use all the answer choices.

1. fallacious
2. mitigate
3. artifice
4. ploy

a. trickery
b. learned
c. misleading
d. soften
e. stratagem
f. strengthen

Academic Vocabulary

Critical **comments** *about Sor Juana often focus on her feminist ideals.*

Comment is an academic word. The word is also used in more casual settings—for example, an online message-board posting is called a **comment.** To further explore the meaning of this word, describe a time when a peer's **comment** pleased you, and explain why.

For more on academic vocabulary, see pages 36–37 and R83–R85.

Write with Style

 Apply Metaphor

Assignment In Sonnet 145, Sor Juana uses metaphors, such as a flower and a corpse, to express the emptiness she sees in a portrait of herself. Write a poem in which you use a variety of metaphors to express the different ways the people in your life seem to regard you.

Get Ideas Create a web like the one below in which you identify the people in your life. Try to imagine how each one sees you. Then create a metaphor to express that person's view.

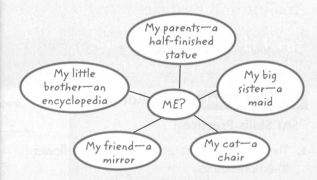

Give It Structure Once you have created metaphors expressing how the people in your life see you, begin assembling these metaphors into a poem.

Look at Language In revising your draft, strengthen your metaphors by creating precision and interest through supporting details. Use language in natural, fresh, and vivid ways.

EXAMPLE:

To my parents, I'm a half-done statue they've struggled to mold for years.

Just can't get the features right; something's still wrong with the ears.

 Literature Online

Selection Resources For Selection Quizzes, eFlash-cards, and Reading-Writing Connection activities, go to glencoe.com and enter QuickPass code GLW6053u6.

Before You Read

Two Countries

Meet **José Martí**
(1853–1895)

Born in Havana, Cuba, José Martí (hō zā′ mär tē′) devoted his life to Cuba's struggle for independence from Spain. When he was sixteen, he became a political prisoner, and the colonial government in Cuba sentenced him to hard labor at the quarries in Havana for his political activities. After he was released, he spent almost all of his adult life in exile, living in various countries in Europe and Latin America. In 1881 he moved to New York City, where he wrote poetry and worked as a journalist. He continued to write articles for Latin American journals, chronicling events such as the building of the Brooklyn Bridge. Through these writings he sought to help Latin Americans develop their understanding of the United States. While in New York, he also helped form the Cuban Revolution Party.

Revolutionary Hero Though uprooted from his homeland, Martí always remained true to the cause of Cuban independence. In 1891, he published "Nuestra America," a provocative essay that called for an alliance of the middle class, working class, and peasantry against Spanish landholders in Cuba and American-based businesses that profited there. A passionate speaker, he rallied support for Cuban emancipation, organized political groups in the United States and Central America, and fostered Cuban patriotism and pride. In April 1895, he took part in the Cuban Revolutionary Party's military invasion of Cuba. He died a month later on the battlefield—seven years before his dream of Cuban independence became a reality.

> "What matters in poetry is to feel, regardless of whether it resembles what others have felt; and what is felt anew, is new."
>
> —José Martí

Suffering Artist Martí believed that art grows out of suffering. He wrote that pain "matures poetry . . . Man needs to suffer. When he lacks real pain, he creates it. Pain purifies and prepares." Critics have praised his imagery, which he said came to him through visions. His innovative prose style greatly influenced Latin American authors in the twentieth century.

LOG ON ▶ **Literature** Online

Author Search For more about José Martí, go to glencoe.com and enter QuickPass code GLW6053u6.

Literature and Reading Preview

Connect to the Poem

How might you react if tragedy befell your homeland? Discuss this question with a partner.

Build Background

After Columbus's arrival in 1492, Cuba became a Spanish colony. By the mid-nineteenth century, however, many Cubans resented the Spanish colonial government. A bitter struggle for independence broke out in 1868 and lasted ten years. A second conflict erupted in 1895. Then in 1898, the United States declared war on Spain, and at the war's end Spain withdrew from Cuba. The last U.S. troops left the island in 1902, when the Republic of Cuba was declared.

Set Purposes for Reading

Big Idea Transplanting Traditions

Latin American authors transplanted European traditions to express new perspectives. As you read, ask yourself, How would you describe the author's vision of his homeland?

Literary Element Juxtaposition

Juxtaposition refers to the placing of two or more distinct elements of a literary work—for example, words, phrases, images, lines, or passages—next to or close to one another. For example, in line 1 of "Two Countries," Martí uses this technique to emphasize his plight of living in exile: "I have two countries: Cuba and the night." As you read, ask yourself, What other examples of juxtaposition can I identify?

Reading Strategy Analyze Figures of Speech

When you **analyze figures of speech,** you look critically at types of figurative language such as metaphor, personification, or simile. By analyzing figures of speech, you can better explore the theme and tone of a poem. As you read, ask yourself, what figures of speech does Martí use to support his theme?

Tip: Chart Figures of Speech In a chart like the one below, record your interpretations of the figures of speech in this poem.

Figure of Speech	Interpretation
Simile: "Cuba . . . appears as a sad and silent widow"	Cuba is bereft of her beloved patriots who suffer in exile.

Learning Objectives

For pages 1169–1172

In studying this text, you will focus on the following objectives:

Literary Study: Identifying juxtaposition.

Reading: Analyzing figures of speech.

Writing: Writing a reflection.

Vocabulary

majesty (maj′is tē) *n.* greatness or magnificence of quality or nature; splendor; p. 1171 *When we stood at the foot of the mountain, we truly appreciated its majesty.*

commence (kə mens′) *v.* to begin; p. 1171 *The luncheon commenced with the introduction of the guests of honor.*

hindrance (hin′drəns) *n.* a thing that presents a challenge, struggle, or delay to someone or something; obstacle; p. 1171 *Inexperience and lack of education were hindrances in his job search.*

flutter (flut′ər) *v.* move with uneven or trembling motion; p. 1171 *The first leaves fluttered to the ground, marking the beginning of fall.*

Tip: Word Usage Try answering a specific question to explore the meaning of a new word. For example, How can fear become a **hindrance** to success?

Two Countries

José Martí
Translated by Elinor Randall

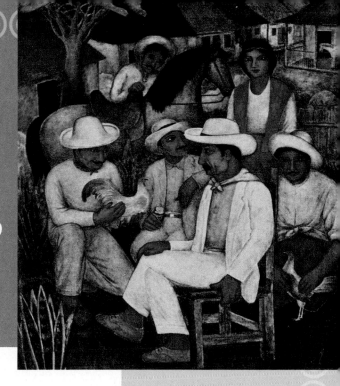

I have two countries: Cuba and the night.
Or are both one? No sooner does the sun
Withdraw its **majesty,** than Cuba,
With long veils and holding a carnation,
5   Appears as a sad and silent widow.
I know about that bloodstained carnation
That trembles in her hand! My breast
Is empty, destroyed and empty
Where the heart lay. Now is the time
10 To **commence** dying. Night is a good time
To say farewell. Light is a **hindrance**
As is the human word. The universe
Talks better than man.
                              Like a flag
That calls to battle, the candle's
15 Red flame **flutters.** I feel a closeness
And open windows. Crushing the carnation's
Petals silently, widowed Cuba passes by
Like a cloud that dims the heavens. . . .

Analyze Figures of Speech *Why does the speaker personify the universe?*

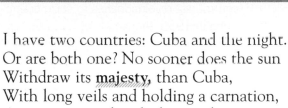

Vocabulary

majesty (maj′is tē) *n.* greatness or magnificence of quality or nature; splendor

commence (kə mens′) *v.* to begin

hindrance (hin′drəns) *n.* a thing that presents a challenge, struggle, or delay to someone or something; obstacle

flutter (flut′ər) *v.* move with uneven or trembling motion

After You Read

Respond and Think Critically

Respond and Interpret

1. Which line or passage in this poem made the strongest impression on you? Explain.

2. (a)According to the speaker, what happens when the sun sets? (b)How is this related to the speaker's emotions in lines 7–9?

3. (a)Do you think this poem is set in Cuba, or is the speaker somewhere else? Explain. (b)What point is the author making about Cuba?

Analyze and Evaluate

4. A **symbol** is an object or action that stands for something else in addition to itself. (a)What might the bloodstained carnation symbolize? (b)What does the crushing of the carnation's petals symbolize?

5. **Ellipsis points** are a mark of punctuation (. . .) indicating that words have been left out in a quotation. Outside a quotation, ellipsis points indicate an unfinished or implied thought. Why might Martí have chosen to end his poem with ellipsis points?

Connect

6. **Big Idea** **Transplanting Traditions** What vision of Cuba does Martí share in this poem?

7. **Connect to Today** After Fidel Castro led communist revolutionaries to seize control of Cuba in 1959, thousands of middle-class and professional Cubans fled to the United States. How might one of these modern Cuban exiles react to Martí's poem?

Literary Element Juxtaposition

By using **juxtaposition**, poets can create unexpected pairings and stunning contrasts.

1. In line 5, what effect does the poet create by juxtaposing the words *sad* and *silent*?

2. In line 8, what does the phrase "destroyed and empty" suggest about the speaker?

Reading Strategy Analyze Figures of Speech

A **simile** is a comparison, using the words *like* or *as,* of two things that have something in common. **Personification** is a figure of speech that gives human characteristics to nonhuman things.

1. (a)What does the simile in lines 13–15 suggest? (b)How does it support the poems' tone?

2. Identify two examples of personification.

LOG ON ▶ **Literature** Online

Selection Resources For Selection Quizzes, eFlash-cards, and Reading-Writing Connection activities, go to glencoe.com and enter QuickPass code GLW6053u6.

Vocabulary Practice

Practice with Usage Respond to these statements to help you explore the meanings of the vocabulary words from the poem.

1. Describe a time you witnessed a display of nature's **majesty.**

2. Explain how a typical weekday **commences** for you.

3. Give an example of an event that might prove to be a **hindrance** to a relationship.

4. List some animals that move by **fluttering.**

Writing

Write a Reflection Write a brief reflective essay in which you express what a particular place means to you. This could be the place where you now live, or another place you feel attached to. In your essay, use figures of speech to make your descriptions come alive. Refer to the chart you made on page 1170 for ideas.

Set a Purpose for Reading

Read to learn about the scientific and ethical debates that followed the discovery of an ancient skeleton.

Preview the Article

"Who Were the First Americans?" describes how new archaeological evidence is challenging conventional theories about the earliest humans in the Americas.

1. Read the **subheads,** or smaller headlines within the article. What controversies might this article address?

2. Briefly skim the entire article. What types of evidence do you think the authors will use to support their claims?

Reading Strategy
Determine Main Idea and Supporting Details

The **main idea** is the most important thought in a paragraph or a text. **Supporting details** are pieces of evidence that back up the main idea, including examples, reasons, facts, or descriptions. As you read, ask yourself, What are the main ideas and supporting details?

TIME

Who Were the First AMERICANS?

They may have been a lot like Kennewick Man, whose hotly disputed bones are helping rewrite our earliest history.

By MICHAEL D. LEMONICK and ANDREA DORFMAN

IT WAS CLEAR FROM THE MOMENT JIM CHATTERS FIRST SAW the partial skeleton that no crime had been committed—none recent enough to be prosecutable, anyway. Chatters, a forensic anthropologist, had been called in by the coroner of Benton County, Washington, to consult on some bones found by two college students on the banks of the Columbia River, near the town of Kennewick. The bones were obviously old, and when the coroner asked for an opinion, Chatters' first guess, based on the skull's superficially Caucasian-like features, was that they probably belonged to a settler from the late 1800s. Then a CT scan revealed a stone spear point set in the skeleton's pelvis, so Chatters sent a bit of finger bone off to the University of California at Riverside for radiocarbon dating. When the results came back, it was clear that his estimate was dramatically off the mark. The bones weren't 100 or even 1,000 years old. They belonged to a man who had walked the banks of the Columbia more than 9,000 years ago.

In short, the remains that came to be known as Kennewick Man were almost twice as old as the celebrated Iceman discovered in 1991 in an Alpine glacier, and among the oldest and most complete skeletons ever found in the Americas. Plenty of archaeological sites date back that far, or nearly so, but scientists have found only about 50 skeletons from such ancient times, most of them fragmentary. Any new find can thus add crucial insight into the ongoing mystery of who first colonized the New World—the last corner of the globe to be populated by humans. Kennewick Man could cast some much-needed light on the difficult questions of when that migration took place, where the first Americans originally came from and how they got here.

U.S. government researchers examined the bones, but it would take almost a decade for independent scientists to get a good look at the skeleton. Although it was found in the summer of 1996, the local Umatilla Indians and four other Columbia Basin tribes almost immediately claimed it as ancestral remains under the Native American Graves Protection and Repatriation Act, demanding that the skeleton be reburied without the violation of scientific study. A group of researchers sued, starting a legal tug-of-war and negotiations that ended in 2005, with the scientists getting their first extensive access to the bones. And now, for the first time, we know the results of that examination.

What the Bones Revealed

It was clearly worth the wait. The scientific team that examined the skeleton was led by forensic anthropologist Douglas Owsley of the Smithsonian Institution's National Museum of Natural History. (Forensic anthropologists analyze skeletal remains and help identify individuals who died in mass disasters, wars, or due to homicide, suicide, or accidental death.) Owsley has worked with thousands of historic and pre-historic skeletons, including those

of Jamestown colonists, Plains Indians and Civil War soldiers. He helped identify remains from the 9/11 attack on the Pentagon and mass graves in Croatia.

In this case, Owsley and his team were able to nail down or make strong guesses about Kennewick Man's physical attributes. He stood about 5' 9" tall and was fairly muscular. He was clearly right-handed: the bones of the right arm are markedly larger than those of the left. In fact, says Owsley, "the bones are so robust that they're bent," the result, he speculates, of muscles built up during a lifetime of hunting and spear fishing.

An examination of the joints showed that Kennewick Man had arthritis in the right elbow, both knees, and several vertebrae but that it wasn't severe enough to be crippling. He had suffered plenty

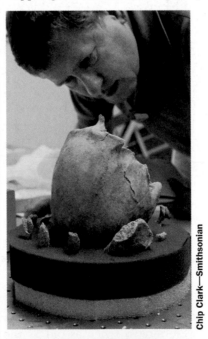

Forensic anthropologist Owsley takes one last look at the pieces of Kennewick Man's skull before having them scanned for posterity.

Chip Clark—Smithsonian

of trauma as well. "One rib was fractured and healed," says Owsley, "and there is a depression fracture on his forehead and a similar indentation on the left side of the head." None of those fractures were fatal, though, and neither was the spear jab. "The injury looks healed," says Owsley. Previous estimates had Kennewick Man's age as 45 to 55 when he died, but Owsley thinks he may have been as young as 38. Nothing in the bones reveals what caused his death.

But that's just the beginning of an impressive catalog of information that the scientists have added to what was already known—all the more impressive given the limitations placed on the team by the U.S. Army Corps of Engineers. The Corps is responsible for the skeleton because it has jurisdiction over the federal land on which it was found. The researchers had to do nearly all their work at the University of Washington's Burke Museum, where Kennewick Man has been housed in a locked room since 1998, under the watchful eyes of representatives of both the Corps and the museum. And they had to follow a strict schedule that had to be submitted in advance. "We only had 10 days to do everything we wanted to do," says Owsley. "It was like a choreographed dance."

Perhaps the most remarkable discovery: Kennewick Man had been buried deliberately. By looking at concentrations of calcium carbonate, a colorless or crystal-like compound, left behind as underground water collected on the underside of the bones and then evaporated, scientists can tell that he was lying on his back with his feet rolled slightly outward and his arms at his side, the palms facing down—a position that could hardly have come about by accident. And there was no evidence that animal scavengers had been at the body.

The researchers could also tell that Kennewick Man had been buried parallel to the Columbia, with his left side toward the water: the bones were ground down on that side by water that eroded the bank and eventually dumped him out. It probably happened no more than six months before he was discovered, says team member Thomas Stafford, a research geochemist based in Lafayette, Colorado. "It wouldn't have been as much as a year," he says. "The bones would have been more widely dispersed."

The deliberate burial makes it especially frustrating for scientists that the Corps in 1998 dumped hundreds of tons of boulders, dirt and sand on the discovery site— officially as part of a project to combat erosion along the Columbia River, although some scientists suspect it was also to avoid further conflict with the local tribes. Kennewick Man's actual burial pit had already been washed away by the time Stafford visited the site in December 1997, but a careful survey might have turned up objects that could have been buried with him. And if his was part of a larger burial plot, there's now no way for archaeologists to locate any contemporaries who might have been buried close by.

Still, the bones have more secrets to reveal. They were never

fossilized, and a careful analysis of their carbon and nitrogen makeup, yet to be performed, should reveal plenty about Kennewick Man's diet. Says Stafford: "We can tell if he ate nothing but plants, predominantly meat or a mixture of the two." The researchers may be able to determine whether he preferred meat or fish. It's even possible that DNA could be extracted and analyzed someday.

While the Corps insisted that most of the bones remain in the museum, it allowed the researchers to send the skull fragments and the right hip, along with its spear point, to a lab in Lincolnshire, Illinois, for ultrahigh-resolution CT scanning. The process produced virtual slices just 0.39 mm (about 0.02") thick—"much more detailed than the ones made of ancient Egypt's King Tut's mummy," says Owsley. The slices were then digitally recombined into 3-D computer images that were used to make exact copies out of plastic. The replica of the skull has already enabled scientists to clear up a popular misconception that dates back to the initial reports of the discovery.

Was Kennewick Man Caucasian?

Thanks to Chatters' mention of Caucasian-like features back in 1996, the myth that Kennewick Man might have been European never quite died out. The reconstructed skull confirms that he was not—and Chatters never seriously thought otherwise. "I tried my hardest to curtail that business about Caucasians in America early," he says. "I'm not talking about today's Caucasians.

Map of multiple human migrations.

I'm saying they had 'Caucasoid-like' characteristics. There's a big difference." Says Owsley: "[Kennewick Man] is not North American looking, and he's not tied in to Siberian or Northeast Asian populations (or groups of people). He looks more Polynesian or more like the Ainu [an ethnic group that is now found only in northern Japan but in prehistoric times lived throughout coastal areas of eastern Asia] or southern Asians."

That assessment will be tested more rigorously when researchers compare Kennewick Man's skull with databases of several thousand other skulls, both modern and ancient. But for the time being, at least, the evidence fits in with a revolutionary new picture that over the past decade has utterly transformed anthropologists' long-held theories about the colonization of the Americas.

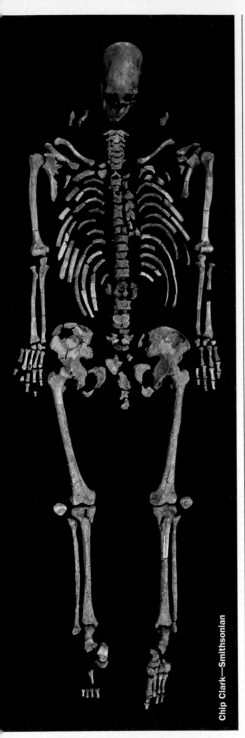

Skeleton of Kennewick Man

Chip Clark—Smithsonian

Who Really Discovered America?

The conventional answer to that question dates to the early 1930s, when stone projectile points—typically used as dart or arrow points—that were nearly identical began to turn up at sites across the American Southwest. They suggested a single cultural tradition that was christened Clovis, after an 11,000-year-old-plus site near Clovis, New Mexico. And because no older sites were known to exist in the Americas, scientists assumed that the Clovis people were the first to arrive. They came, according to the theory, no more than 12,000 years B.P. (before the present), walking across the dry land that connected modern Russia and Alaska at the end of the last ice age, when sea level was hundreds of feet lower than it is today. From there, the earliest immigrants would have made their way south through an ice-free corridor that geologists know cut through what are now the Yukon and Mackenzie river valleys. They then traveled along the eastern flank of the Canadian Rockies to the continental United States and on to Latin America.

That's the story textbooks told for decades—and it's almost certainly wrong. The first cracks in the theory began appearing in the 1980s, when archaeologists discovered sites in both North and South America that seemed to predate the Clovis culture. Then came genetic and linguistic analyses suggesting that Asian and Native American populations diverged not 12,000 years ago but

closer to 30,000 years ago. Studies of ancient skulls hinted that the earliest Americans in South America had different ancestors from those in the North. Finally, it began to be clear that artifacts from Northeast Asia dating from just before the Clovis period and South American artifacts of comparable age didn't have much in common with Clovis artifacts.

Those discoveries led to all sorts of competing theories, but few archaeologists or anthropologists took them seriously until 1997. In that year, a prestigious panel of researchers took a hard look at evidence presented by Tom Dillehay, then at the University of Kentucky, from a site he had been excavating in Monte Verde, Chile. After years of skepticism, the panel finally affirmed his claim that the site proved humans had lived there 12,500 years ago. "Monte Verde was the turning point," says David Meltzer, a professor of prehistory at Southern Methodist University in Dallas who was on the panel. "It broke the Clovis barrier."

Why? Because if people were living in southern Chile 12,500 years ago, they must have crossed over from Asia considerably earlier, and that means they couldn't have used the ice-free inland corridor; it didn't yet exist. "You could walk to Fairbanks," says Meltzer. "It was getting south from Fairbanks that was a problem." Instead, many scientists now believe, the earliest Americans traveled down the Pacific coast—possibly even using boats. The idea has been around for a long time, but few took it seriously before Monte Verde.

Multiple Migrations

Even if the earliest Americans traveled down the coast, that doesn't mean they couldn't have come through the interior as well. Could there have been many waves of migration along a variety of different routes? One way scientists have tried to get a handle on that question is through genetics. Their studies have focused on two different types of evidence extracted from the cells of modern Native Americans: mitochondrial DNA, which resides outside the nuclei of cells and is passed down only through the mother; and the Y chromosome, which is passed down only from father to son. Since DNA changes subtly over the generations, it serves as a sort of molecular clock, and by measuring differences between populations, you can gauge when they were part of the same group.

Or at least you can try. Those molecular clocks are still rather crude. "The mitochondrial DNA signals a migration up to 30,000 years ago," says research geneticist Michael Hammer of the University of Arizona. "But the Y suggests that it occurred within the last 20,000 years." That's quite a discrepancy. Nevertheless, Hammer believes that the evidence is consistent with a single, or primary pulse of migration.

Theodore Schurr, director of the University of Pennsylvania's Laboratory of Molecular Anthropology, thinks there could have been many migrations. "It looks like there may have been one primary migration, but certain genetic markers are more prevalent in North America than in South America," Schurr explains, suggesting secondary waves. At this point, there's no definitive proof of either idea, but the evidence and logic lean toward multiple migrations. "If one migration made it over," Dillehay, now at Vanderbilt University, asks rhetorically, "why not more?"

—With reporting by Dan Cray/Los Angeles
From TIME, Updated 2007

Respond and Think Critically

Respond and Interpret

1. Write a brief summary of the main ideas in this article before you answer the following questions. For help on writing a summary, see page 1147.

2. (a)How old are the remains of the Kennewick Man? (b)What are some physical characteristics of Kennewick Man?

3. (a)What restrictions did the U.S. Army Corps of Engineers place on scientific study of Kennewick Man's remains? (b)What did local Native American groups originally demand?

Analyze and Evaluate

4. (a)What "remarkable discovery" did the researchers make about Kennewick Man's burial? (b)What evidence led them to this discovery?

5. (a)Until the 1980s, what was the accepted theory about the origin of the first Americans? (b)How did archaeological evidence from Monte Verde, Chile, prove this theory wrong?

6. (a)Why might local Native American groups have considered scientific study of Kennewick Man's remains as a kind of "desecration"? (b)In your opinion, was it appropriate for scientists to study the remains? Explain.

Connect

7. How does the conflict between scientists and Native American groups described in this article relate to the conflicts you have read about in Unit 6, Part 1?

A Antigua, view of English Harbor and Nelson's Dockyard

B *Panama City, Evening.* Bauer Photography.

LOG ON ▶ **Literature** Online

Literature and Reading For more about the history and literature of this period, go to glencoe.com and enter QuickPass code GLW6053u6.

PART TWO

THE MODERN
AMERICAS

1800–PRESENT

Storyteller. Helen Cordero (b.1915). Ceramic. Fred Jones Jr. Museum of Art, University of Oklahoma.

Being There

The Americas have undergone great changes over the past two centuries. Between 1776 and 1867, most countries in the Americas won their independence from England, Spain, and Portugal. In their short histories, many of these countries have faced severe problems, including civil wars, dictatorships, poverty, and overpopulation. In recent times, people in the Americas have become increasingly concerned about the environment as portions of the tropical rain forests are destroyed and natural disasters have ravaged communities.

Looking Ahead

Authors in the Americas have responded to these sweeping changes by creating styles, such as magic realism, that fuse traditional and contemporary elements. Some authors of the region have drawn on local geography and folklore to explore the continuity of the past and present, while others have explored the contradictions of life in postcolonial society.

Keep the following questions in mind as you read:

- How did colonialism shape the modern Americas?
- What is the relationship between dreams and reality?
- How do geography and nature influence a community?

TIMELINE 1800–PRESENT

MODERN AMERICAN LITERATURE

1800

1830
Emily Dickinson is born in Amherst, Massachusetts

1839
Joaquim Maria Machado de Assis is born in Rio de Janeiro, Brazil

1850

1855
Walt Whitman publishes *Leaves of Grass*

1888 ▶
Rubén Darío publishes *Azul*, initiating the Modernismo movement

AMERICAN EVENTS

1800

1804
Haiti becomes first independent nation in the West Indies ▼

▲
1821
Mexico and Central America win independence from Spain; Peru proclaims independence from Spain

1822
Brazil declares independence from Portugal

1836
Texas declares independence from Mexico

1850

1861
Benito Juarez becomes President of Mexico

1865
American Civil War ends

1867
British establish the Dominion of Canada

1876
Porfirio Díaz takes power in Mexico

1888
Brazil abolishes slavery

WORLD EVENTS

1800

1821
Electric motor is developed in Great Britain

1837 ▶
Queen Victoria is crowned Queen of Great Britain

1845–1849
Potato famine strikes Ireland

1861
Italians establish a united kingdom

1877
Samurai revolt against abolition of feudalism in Japan

LOG ON ▶ **Literature** Online

Literature and Reading To explore the Interactive Timeline, go to glencoe.com and enter QuickPass code GLW6053u6.

1900

1900
José Enrique Rodó publishes *Ariel*

1924
Pablo Neruda publishes *Twenty Love Poems and a Song of Despair*

▲
1945
Gabriela Mistral becomes first Latin American to win the Nobel Prize in Literature

1950

1963
Martin Luther King Jr. writes his letter from Birmingham jail

1968
Alice Munro wins Canada's prestigious Governor General's Literary Award for fiction for the first time

2001
Trinidadian author Sir V. S. Naipaul wins the Nobel Prize in Literature

2003
Isabel Allende publishes *My Invented Country*
▼

1900

1910
Mexican Revolution begins

1912
European immigrants to Argentina surpass 300,000

1921
Diego Rivera begins work on his first mural in Mexico

1950

1959
Fidel Castro establishes communist government in Cuba

1969
Canada passes Official Languages Act

1970s
Major oil deposits are discovered in Gulf of Mexico

2005
Hurricane Katrina causes devastation in the United States' Gulf Coast

1900

1904
Russia completes the first Trans-Siberian Railroad

1914–1918
World War I

1931
Japan invades China

1936
First regular television broadcasts begin in Great Britain

1948
State of Israel is formed
▼

▲
1961
Yuri Gagarin, a Russian, becomes the first human to orbit Earth

1975
Vietnam War ends

1991
Soviet Union collapses

Reading Check

Analyze Graphic Information How long after Fidel Castro took power in Cuba did the Soviet Union collapse?

Learning Objectives

For pages 1178–1189

In studying this text, you will focus on the following objectives:

Literary Study: Analyzing literary periods.

Reading: Evaluating historical influences.
Connecting to the literature.

THE MODERN AMERICAS

1800–PRESENT

Historical, Social, and Cultural Forces

Diversity in the Americas

Modern societies in the Americas reflect a diversity of cultural traditions and ethnic heritages. This multiculturalism stems from the traditions of the native people who first inhabited the Americas as well as from colonialism, slavery, and immigration.

Politics in the Americas

As the nineteenth century began, the United States was adjusting to its newfound independence, while Canada and many Latin American countries remained under colonial rule. As the century continued, most of these countries gained their independence; however, power in many Latin American countries remained concentrated among elite landowners. In 1867, the British North American Act established Canada as a Dominion of Britain, though it was run primarily as an independent state. (The British Parliament's authority was transferred to the Canadian Parliament in 1982.) In Mexico, guerrilla armies waged war against the dictatorship of Porfirio Díaz in 1910 and 1920, finally establishing a constitutional republic. The new Mexican constitution became a model for many other countries in the region.

In 1959, Fidel Castro overthrew Cuba's dictator and installed a communist government. The United States took many steps to prevent similar uprisings in other Latin American countries, including giving support to military dictatorships throughout the region in the 1980s. The end of the twentieth century saw a return to democracy in some Latin American countries.

Effective vote - No Re-election (Sufragio effectivo - no reeleccion), **detail with marching peasants.**
Juan O'Gorman. Mural. Museo Nacional de Historia, Castillo de Chapultepec, Mexico City, D.F.

Checking Voting Rolls Alongside Hindu Deities

Human Rights

Human rights in the Americas have improved greatly since the beginning of the nineteenth century. At that time, slavery was still legal in the United States, and indigenous groups on both continents endured removal from their ancestral lands and the loss of their cultural identities. The human rights abuses against these groups continued well into the twentieth century, fueling the civil rights movement in the United States and a number of movements by indigenous peoples in other countries in the Americas.

In the twentieth century, Latin Americans also fought for freedom from abuse under military regimes, and similar human rights struggles continue today. Many people from Mexico and Central America have sought better opportunities in the United States. In 1962, Cesar Chavez, a former farmworker and the son of Mexican immigrants, founded the National Farm Workers Association to advocate for the rights of migrant workers. It became the first successful union of its kind in the country. As Hispanic immigration to the United States increases, Americans continue to confront related issues, such as questions about ethnic diversity and bilingual education in schools.

> "We are Europeans yet we are not Europeans. What are we then? It is difficult to define what we are, but our works speak for us."
>
> —Mexican author Octavio Paz, in his Nobel lecture

Globalization

Recent political and economic changes in the Americas reflect the increasingly interconnected global landscape of the twenty-first century. In 1994, Mexico joined Canada and the United States in the North American Free Trade Agreement (NAFTA), which removed trade barriers between countries in the region. Improvements in road transportation, literacy, and technology continue to decrease the isolation of rural Latin Americans. In an increasingly global culture, the people of the Americas continue to reinvent themselves while remaining connected to their diverse backgrounds and regional traditions.

Mexican Muralists

Murals have been an important form of Mexican art since the wall paintings of the ancient Maya. In the early 1900s, Mexican artists sought to synthesize the events of Mexico's present with indigenous styles of expression. Artists such as Diego Rivera, David Siqueiros, and José Orozco created murals depicting the Mexican Revolution on the walls of public buildings. These expressive paintings of workers, soldiers, peasants, and revolutionary leaders such as Emiliano Zapata captured the excitement and fervor of the time. An equally important artist of this era was Frida Kahlo, who married Rivera. In her vivid self-portraits, Kahlo used symbolic images to depict her physical and mental struggles.

> *"I never painted dreams. I painted my own reality."*
>
> —Frida Kahlo

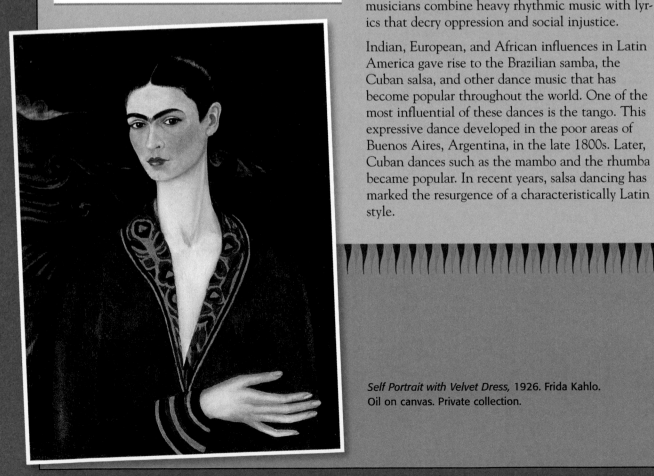

Self Portrait with Velvet Dress, 1926. Frida Kahlo. Oil on canvas. Private collection.

Music of the Americas

Tango dancers in Plaza Dorrego, San Telmo.

The Americas have produced some of the most famous musical styles in the world, including blues, jazz, salsa, rock and roll, and reggae. The influence of African musical traditions in North America has been especially notable, beginning with the slave songs of the nineteenth century. The call-and-response pattern common in many blues songs can be traced to African musical roots. Jazz, which developed at the beginning of the twentieth century, combines improvisation with African rhythms and European harmonies. Reggae—Jamaica's best known cultural export—originated there in the late 1960s, not long after Jamaica gained independence from Britain. Reggae musicians combine heavy rhythmic music with lyrics that decry oppression and social injustice.

Indian, European, and African influences in Latin America gave rise to the Brazilian samba, the Cuban salsa, and other dance music that has become popular throughout the world. One of the most influential of these dances is the tango. This expressive dance developed in the poor areas of Buenos Aires, Argentina, in the late 1800s. Later, Cuban dances such as the mambo and the rhumba became popular. In recent years, salsa dancing has marked the resurgence of a characteristically Latin style.

Carnival

On the West Indian island of Trinidad and in Rio de Janeiro, Brazil, internationally famous events called Carnival mark the beginning of Lent—the 40-day period of fasting and reflection before Easter that some Christians observe. In these two places, more than a million people join in the street festivities—singing, dancing, parading in fantastic costumes, and engaging in masquerade and band competitions. The origins of Carnival are obscure, but the celebration probably originated in pre-Christian nature festivals and was brought from Europe to the Americas by Catholics. Many of the musical instruments, rhythms, and dances of Carnival have influenced popular music worldwide. The steel drums and rhythmic calypso of Trinidad and the samba dances of Brazil were first heard and seen on the streets at Carnival.

Colorful costume from Parade of Bands during Carnival- Port of Spain, Trinidad.

PREVIEW **Big Ideas** of **The Modern Americas**

1 The Legacy of Colonialism	**2** Magic Realism	**3** Nature and the Imagination
Colonialism had both positive and negative consequences for the people of the Americas. Authors have responded to this legacy by exploring the injustices of colonial societies, the relationship between homeland and identity, and the multiculturalism produced by immigration.	One of the dominant literary styles in modern Latin American literature is magic realism, which features fantastic, supernatural events that occur in narratives with realistic elements. This literature meshes local folklore with Surrealist imagery to explore the relationship between perception and reality.	Nature remains a vital subject in literature from North and South America, where authors explore connections between the natural world and a range of social issues. Modern Latin and Native American poets create lush nature imagery that reflects the importance of geography and the power of sensory experience.
See page 1186	**See page 1187**	**See page 1188**

The Legacy of Colonialism

Almost every region in North and South America and the Caribbean has been influenced by European colonialism. In South America and the Caribbean, these years of oppression left wounds that were difficult to heal, even after countries had gained independence.

Colonial Ideology

The Spanish and Portuguese in South America had two goals: to increase the wealth of their home countries and to convert native peoples to Christianity. These settlers claimed huge plots of land for themselves, displacing indigenous peoples who had been there for generations. Native Americans were forced to work on colonial farms, and many died of European diseases.

Inspired by the American Revolution, Latin Americans successfully fought for independence in the early 1800s. But independence did not fundamentally change the colonial structure of Latin American societies. The region continued to export agricultural raw materials and import consumer goods as it had during colonial times, a practice that ensured continued economic dependence on Europe. As a result, power remained concentrated in the hands of elite estate owners. Vast inequality, reinforced by sharp class distinctions, persisted through much of the next century.

Latin American authors have addressed the legacy of colonialism in a variety of ways. In the nineteenth century, some authors reflected on the contrast between the European-based life of the elite and the rural cultures of Native Americans. These works sought to overthrow the racial ideology that supported colonialism in Latin America. Twentieth-century authors such as Rosario Castellanos (see pages 1199–1208) wrote about the class prejudices that remain embedded in society.

> "The colonial experience of my generation was almost wholly without violence . . . It was a terror of the mind."
>
> —George Lamming, West Indian novelist

Identity and Homeland

Many contemporary Latin American and Caribbean authors continue to explore the effects of colonialism on their homelands, often addressing issues such as discrimination, identity, and exile. Some, like Antiguan author Jamaica Kincaid (see pages 1277–1286), portray both the nurturing and restricting power of homeland. In her novel *Annie John*, Kincaid's protagonist struggles with ambivalent feelings as she leaves Antigua to pursue her dream in England.

Coffee, 1935. Candido Portinari. Oil on canvas. Museu Nacional Belas Artes, Rio de Janeiro, Brazil.

Reading Check

Analyze Cause-and-Effect Relationships What factors contributed to continuing social inequality in Latin America following independence?

Big Idea 2
Magic Realism

I n the mid-twentieth century, Latin American authors developed a unique form of expression called magic realism. Many Latin American authors believe this style best expresses the unique history and hopes of the Latin American people.

El secreto compartido, 1999. Alfredo Castañeda (b. 1938). Oil on canvas, 80 x 110 cm. Private collection.

> "*The fantastic is something that one must never say goodbye to lightly.*"
>
> —Julio Cortázar

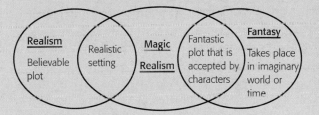

From Folklore to Surrealism

Works of magic realism include strong, realistic narratives that incorporate elements of local folklore and myth. Through this combination of styles, magic realist authors seek to mesh avant-garde literary trends, such as Surrealism, with their unique regional identities. In addition to exploring the world of dreams and fantasy, these authors also address social and political ills. In addition to fantastic elements, these works often include humor and exaggeration and present distorted views of time and identity.

The method of storytelling in works of magic realism focuses on the flexibility of reality when viewed from different perspectives. The most famous example of the genre is Gabriel García Márquez's (see pages 1243–1251) 1967 novel *One Hundred Years of Solitude.* The novel is set in the fictional town of Macondo, where local events slip back and forth between reality and fantasy. For example, villagers are unsurprised when a local priest rises into the air and floats. However, when these same villagers are introduced to magnets, telescopes, and magnifying glasses, they are dumbfounded by what they see as magic. Narratives such as this suggest that reality is subjective rather than objective.

The Latin American Boom

Argentine author Jorge Luis Borges and Cuban author Alejo Carpentier developed the magic realist style in the 1940s. In the decades that followed, a so-called boom of Latin American fiction brought international fame to authors such as Márquez, Julio Cortázar (see pages 1230–1241), Carlos Fuentes, and Mario Vargas Llosa. In the 1980s and 1990s, many female magic realist voices emerged, including the Chilean novelist Isabel Allende (see pages 1261–1263). Though many consider the style to be unique to Latin America, it has influenced literature around the world. Such diverse authors as American novelist Toni Morrison, German novelist Günter Grass, and Indian author Salman Rushdie have produced works containing elements of magic realism.

Reading Check

Compare and Contrast How are fantasy and magic realism alike, and how do they differ?

For centuries, people have been captivated by the rugged beauty of the Americas. Modern literature of the region often explores the beauty and power of nature and the tensions between nature and civilization.

Geography and Myth

Many contemporary Latin American poets explore the link between physical landscape and cultural identity. Octavio Paz (see pages 1220–1223) and Pablo Neruda (see pages 1210–1214), the foremost poets of the Latin American *vanguardia*, or avant-garde, movement sought to illuminate the past by exploring local geography. In poems such as "Hymn Among Ruins," Paz meditates on the passage of time by describing ancient architectural relics. His works draw from European traditions such as Surrealism and Romanticism as well as local folk traditions.

Neruda also found inspiration in the geography of his homeland. In "Heights of Machu Picchu," one of his most famous works, he evokes the glory of the ancient Incas in describing a majestic ruin. In his later poems, Neruda shifted his focus toward the simple and the commonplace. These poems seek to illuminate the richness beneath everyday items, such as an artichoke or a piece of wood.

Nature as Metaphor

The works of contemporary North American authors, such as the Native American poet Joy Harjo (see pages 1287–1291), often reflect an appreciation and understanding of nature. In many North American works, nature and natural elements serve as metaphors for events or problems. American and Canadian essayists, poets, and novelists have often explored the influence of regional landscapes on local communities. These authors—including Henry David Thoreau, Willa Cather, Eudora Welty, and Jack London—are connected in the national

Turtle Sounds, 1986. David Dawangyumptewa. Watercolor, 23 x 30 in. Coconino Center for the Arts, Flagstaff, AZ.

> *And we go on, keep giving birth*
> *and watch*
> *ourselves die, over and over.*
> *And the ground spinning beneath us*
> *goes on talking.*
>
> —Joy Harjo, from "For Alva Benson, and For Those Who Have Learned to Speak"

consciousness with the regional landscapes they depicted. In her richly detailed short stories, Canadian author Alice Munro (see pages 1264–1275) evokes the physical surroundings of her small-town Ontario characters as she explores the cultural values that both define and limit them.

Reading Check

Apply Background Knowledge Why might the ruins of the ancient Maya and Inca be so meaningful to Latin American poets?

WRAP-UP

Legacy of the Period

The cultural heritage of the Americas is very diverse, drawn from its indigenous peoples and the colonists, slaves, and immigrants who settled there. In the United States, literary movements such as Transcendentalism reflected European influences while expressing a distinctly American perspective. In Canada, the writings of immigrants such as Michael Ondaatje, from Sri Lanka, and Rohinton Mistry, from India, show the influence of their South Asian heritage.

Latin American authors have won five Nobel Prizes since 1945. Poets such as Pablo Neruda and novelists such as Isabel Allende have inspired readers throughout the world through their intriguing imagery and their use of magic realism.

Among Native Americans, the oral storytelling tradition remains vital in contemporary life. Leslie Marmon Silko has preserved the stories and cadences of Native American oral traditions. Silko, N. Scott Momaday, and Louise Erdrich have also explored the effects of white culture on Native American identity.

Four Mexican Musicians, Mexico.

Cultural Links

- Magic realism has influenced authors such as Salman Rushdie and Nobel Prize winners Toni Morrison and Günter Grass.

- Gabriel García Márquez and other Latin American novelists were inspired by American authors, including William Faulkner and Ernest Hemingway.

- Music from the Americas such as blues, jazz, hip-hop, and rock and roll has influenced musicians throughout the world, including The Rolling Stones and Led Zeppelin.

LOG ON ▶ **Literature** Online

Unit Resources For additional skills practice, go to glencoe.com and enter QuickPass code GLW6053u6.

Activities

Use what you have learned about the period to do one of these activities.

1. Follow Up Go back to the Looking Ahead on page 1179 and answer the questions.

2. Contrast Literary Periods Works of magic realism sometimes resemble Greek myths. In the myth of Echo and Narcissus, for example, an extraordinary transformation occurs. Select a Greek myth and write a short essay, comparing its elements with those of magic realism.

3. Speaking/Listening Research a contemporary issue in Latin America. Then create a radio or TV broadcast in which you take sides on the issue and present supporting evidence.

4. Take Notes Use this organizer to keep track of the Big Ideas in this part.

FOLDABLES Study Organizer

THREE-POCKET BOOK

Big Idea 1   Big Idea 2   Big Idea 3

Before You Read

A Canary's Ideas

Meet **Joaquim Maria Machado de Assis**

(1839–1908)

Joaquim Maria Machado de Assis once belonged to a liars' club. Everything said in the club had to be a lie. Because the best lies closely resemble the truth, this was no doubt excellent training for an author who would break new ground in the shadowy terrain between the real and the fantastic.

> "I myself am missing, and this lack is essential."
>
> —Machado des Assis

A Brazilian Sensation The grandchild of freed slaves, Machado de Assis—also known simply as Machado—was born to workers on an estate in Rio de Janeiro, Brazil, much like the one described in the final scene of "A Canary's Ideas." He had only an elementary formal education and was orphaned as a teenager. By the age of seventeen, he was making a living by working in a printing shop. In addition to all these challenges, Machado's problems with stuttering, vision, and epilepsy plagued him as an adult.

Machado began his writing career in the same way many authors do—by writing in the established ways or according to the popular conventions of their time. For Machado, that meant writing Romantic poetry. Most critics deemed his first poems genuinely awful; nevertheless, they were Machado's first steps on the path to finding his own voice. As he practiced his craft, he showed increasing aptitude for many forms, including essays, drama, and better poetry. His work gained him recognition and largely ceremonial government posts that enabled him to spend the majority of his time writing. He became a critical success and an important figure in the literary world of Rio de Janeiro and a national sensation in Brazil.

Early Magic Realist Today, Machado's fame rests on his short stories and his novels. These works helped lay the foundations of magic realism, one of the dominant literary styles of modern Latin American literature. Works of magic realism layer the fantastic and the surreal with otherwise realistic detail; they also embrace ambiguity. You can experience that ambiguity and absurdity in the quotation above, which is uttered by the narrator of Machado's novel *Dom Casmurro*. Notice how these words turn literary convention upside down by presenting the book's narrator missing in action. This quote also shows Machado's sense of humor.

Machado began to publish witty, although pessimistic, novels and short stories like *Dom Casmurro* after he turned 40. In a historical period dominated by the optimistic belief that humans were moving forward in the world, he explored the irrational nature of human behavior and the absurdity of life. Machado's work influenced many twentieth-century authors such as Jorge Luis Borges and Carlos Fuentes.

 Literature Online

Author Search For more about Joaquim Maria Machado de Assis, go to glencoe.com and enter QuickPass code GLW6053u6.

Literature and Reading Preview

Connect to the Story

How do you know what is real and what is imaginary? Discuss this question with a small group.

Build Background

In this story, Machado points his witty pessimism at science. The central character is Macedo, an ornithologist (a scientist who studies birds). Although his knowledge should surely dissuade him from leaping to the conclusion that a canary can talk and discuss philosophy, he eagerly initiates detailed observation and study of the bird in the hopes of astounding the world.

Set Purposes for Reading

Big Idea Magic Realism

As you read, ask yourself, How are fantastic events interwoven with realistic people, places, and things?

Literary Element Narrator

A **narrator** is the person who tells the events in a work of fiction. A narrator can be unreliable and offer a faulty or distorted vision of events. As you read, ask yourself, What does the narrator know and not know, and what shapes his view of reality?

Reading Strategy Synthesize

When you **synthesize,** you combine existing ideas to create something new. That is, you begin with information you read, but you examine and rearrange it to arrive at a richer, more complete understanding. As you read, ask yourself, What appears to be unusual, strange, or surprising?

Tip: Record Questions To navigate a work of magic realism and synthesize meaning from it, record questions about anything that strikes you as surreal, fantastic, contradictory, or ambiguous.

Text	My Questions
Paragraphs 1 and 2	• Why does the narrator say no one took Macedo seriously but then retell Macedo's narrative in a serious way? • Why does the narrator speak in the first person, as if he were Macedo?

Learning Objectives

For pages 1190–1198

In studying this text, you will focus on the following objectives:

Literary Study: Analyzing narrator.

Reading: Synthesizing.

Writing: Connecting to science.

Vocabulary

austere (ôs tēr´) *adj.* stern or severe in appearance or manner; p. 1192. *The austere greeting contained no hint of welcome.*

banal (bān´əl) *adj.* lacking originality; commonplace; p. 1193 *Keira's sonnet was just a banal repetition of the model poem, without any fresh images.*

phenomenon (fə nom´ə non´) *n.* an observable fact or subject of scientific study; a remarkable event or occurrence; p. 1194 *The spread of the beetle to higher elevations was a phenomenon several scientists had recorded.*

presumptuous (pri zump´choo əs) *adj.* excessively bold or arrogant; taking liberties; p. 1195 *Steven made the presumptuous move of entering the house before he was invited.*

cursory (kur´sə rē) *adj.* hasty and not thorough; superficial; p. 1196 *The woman disliked the artist's works, so she gave his new painting only a cursory glance.*

A Canary's Ideas

Joaquim Maria Machado de Assis
Translated by
Jack Schmitt and Lorie Ishimatsu

Reality, 1986. Andre Rouillard. Acrylic on canvas.

A man by the name of Macedo, who had a fancy for ornithology, related to some friends an incident so extraordinary that no one took him seriously. Some came to believe he had lost his mind. Here is a summary of his narration.

At the beginning of last month, as I was walking down the street, a carriage darted past me and nearly knocked me to the ground. I escaped by quickly side-stepping into a secondhand shop. Neither the racket of the horse and carriage nor my entrance stirred the proprietor, dozing in a folding chair at the back of the shop. He was a man of shabby appearance: his beard was the color of dirty straw, and his head was covered by a tattered cap which probably had not found a buyer. One could not guess that there was any story behind him, as there could have been behind some of the objects he sold, nor could one sense in him that **austere,** disillusioned sadness inherent in the objects which were remnants of past lives.

The shop was dark and crowded with the sort of old, bent, broken, tarnished, rusted articles ordinarily found in secondhand shops, and everything was in that state of semidisorder befitting such an establishment. This assortment of articles, though

---

banal, was interesting. Pots without lids, lids without pots, buttons, shoes, locks, a black shirt, straw hats, fur hats, picture frames, binoculars, dress coats, a fencing foil, a stuffed dog, a pair of slippers, gloves, nondescript vases, epaulets, a velvet satchel, two hatracks, a slingshot, a thermometer, chairs, a lithographed portrait by the late Sisson, a backgammon board, two wire masks for some future Carnival[1]—all this and more, which I either did not see or do not remember, filled the shop in the area around the door, propped up, hung, or displayed in glass cases as old as the objects inside them. Further inside the shop were many objects of similar appearance. Predominant were the large objects—chests of drawers, chairs, and beds—some of which were stacked on top of others which were lost in the darkness.

I was about to leave, when I saw a cage hanging in the doorway. It was as old as everything else in the shop, and I expected it to be empty so it would fit in with the general appearance of desolation. However, it wasn't empty. Inside, a canary was hopping about. The bird's color, liveliness, and charm added a note of life and youth to that heap of wreckage. It was the last passenger of some wrecked ship, who had arrived in the shop as complete and happy as it had originally been. As soon as I looked at the bird, it began to hop up and down, from perch to perch, as if it meant to tell me that a ray of sunshine was frolicking in the midst of that cemetery. I'm using this image to describe the canary only because I'm speaking to rhetorical people, but the truth is that the canary thought about neither cemetery nor sun, according to what it told me later. Along with the pleasure the sight of the bird brought me, I felt indignation regarding its destiny and softly murmured these bitter words:

"What detestable owner had the nerve to rid himself of this bird for a few cents? Or what indifferent soul, not wishing to keep his late master's pet, gave it away to some child, who sold it so he could make a bet on a soccer game?"

The canary, sitting on top of its perch, trilled this reply:

"Whoever you may be, you're certainly not in your right mind. I had no detestable owner, nor was I given to any child to sell. Those are the delusions of a sick person. Go and get yourself cured, my friend . . ."

"What?" I interrupted, not having had time to become astonished. "So your master didn't sell you to this shop? It wasn't misery or laziness that brought you, like a ray of sunshine, to this cemetery?"

"I don't know what you mean by 'sunshine' or 'cemetery.' If the canaries you've seen use the first of those names, so much the better, because it sounds pretty, but really, I'm sure you're confused."

"Excuse me, but you couldn't have come here by chance, all alone. Has your master always been that man sitting over there?"

"What master? That man over there is my servant. He gives me food and water every day, so regularly that if I were to pay him for his services, it would be no small sum, but canaries don't pay their servants.

---

1. *Carnival,* traditionally, is a festival held before Lent, the season of penitence observed by some Christian denominations. Carnivals include feasting, dances, and masquerades.

banal (bā′nəl) *adj.* lacking originality; commonplace

Magic Realism *What real and fantastic elements does Machado combine in this passage?*

In fact, since the world belongs to canaries, it would be extravagant for them to pay for what is already in the world."

Astonished by these answers, I didn't know what to marvel at more—the language or the ideas. The language, even though it entered my ears as human speech, was uttered by the bird in the form of charming trills. I looked all around me so I could determine if I were awake and saw that the street was the same, and the shop was the same dark, sad, musty place. The canary, moving from side to side, was waiting for me to speak. I then asked if it were lonely for the infinite blue space …

"But, my dear man," trilled the canary, "what does 'infinite blue space' mean?"

"But, pardon me, what do you think of this world? What is the world to you?"

"The world," retorted the canary, with a certain professorial air, "is a secondhand shop with a small rectangular bamboo cage hanging from a nail. The canary is lord of the cage it lives in and the shop that surrounds it. Beyond that, everything is illusion and deception."

With this, the old man woke up and approached me, dragging his feet. He asked me if I wanted to buy the canary. I asked if he had acquired it in the same way he had acquired the rest of the objects he sold and learned that he had bought it from a barber, along with a set of razors.

"The razors are in very good condition," he said.

"I only want the canary."

I paid for it, ordered a huge, circular cage of wood and wire, and had it placed on the veranda of my house so the bird could see the garden, the fountain, and a bit of blue sky.

It was my intention to do a lengthy study of this **phenomenon,** without saying anything to anyone until I could astound the world with my extraordinary discovery. I began by alphabetizing the canary's language in order to study its structure, its relation to music, the bird's appreciation of aesthetics,[2] its ideas and recollections. When this philological[3] and psychological analysis was done, I entered specifically into the study of canaries: their origin, their early history, the geology and flora of the Canary Islands, the bird's knowledge of navigation, and so forth. We conversed for hours while I took notes, and it waited, hopped about, and trilled.

As I have no family other than two servants, I ordered them not to interrupt me, even to deliver a letter or an urgent telegram or to inform me of an important visitor. Since they both knew about my scientific pursuits, they found my orders perfectly natural and did not suspect that the canary and I understood each other.

Needless to say, I slept little, woke up two or three times each night, wandered about aimlessly, and felt feverish. Finally, I returned to my work in order to reread, add, and emend.[4] I corrected more than one observation, either because I had misunderstood something or because the bird had not expressed it clearly. The definition of the

---

2. *Aesthetics* (es thet′iks) is a branch of philosophy dealing with the nature of beauty and art, as well as their creation and appreciation.
3. *Philological* (fil′ ə loj′ i kəl) means "of or relating to philology, the comparative study of languages, including their origins, developments, and interrelationships."
4. To *emend* is to correct a text.

Narrator *How trustworthy is the narrator?*

Vocabulary

phenomenon (fə nom′ə non′) *n.* an observable fact or subject of scientific study; a remarkable event or occurrence

---

Synthesize *What do the canary's comments here reveal about its worldview?*

Narrator *In this paragraph, what makes the narrator believable? What makes him suspect?*

Paisaje (Landscape). Juan Cárdenas (Columbian, b. 1939). Oil on linen, 50 x 65 cm. Private collection.

View the Art The figure in the painting may be Cárdenas, who often paints incidents from his own life. What kind of mood did he create in this painting? How does it remind you of the story?

world was one of these. Three weeks after the canary's entrance into my home, I asked it to repeat to me its definition of the world.

"The world," it answered, "is a sufficiently broad garden with a fountain in the middle, flowers, shrubbery, some grass, clear air, and a bit of blue up above. The canary, lord of the world, lives in a spacious cage, white and circular, from which it looks out on the rest of the world. Everything else is illusion and deception."

Synthesize *How do the similarities and differences between the canary's past and present worldview contribute to the sense of ambiguity or fantasy?*

The language of my treatise[5] also suffered some modifications, and I saw that certain conclusions which had seemed simple were actually **presumptuous.** I still could not write the paper I was to send to the National Museum, the Historical Institute, and the German universities, not due to a lack of material but because I first had to

5. A *treatise* (trē′tis) is a book or an essay that examines a topic thoroughly and systematically.

Vocabulary

presumptuous (pri zump′chŌŌ əs) *adj.* excessively bold or arrogant; taking liberties

put together all my observations and test their validity. During the last few days, I neither left the house, answered letters, nor wanted to hear from friends or relatives. The canary was everything to me. One of the servants had the job of cleaning the bird's cage and giving it food and water every morning. The bird said nothing to him, as if it knew the man was completely lacking in scientific background. Besides, the service was no more than **cursory,** as the servant was not a bird lover.

One Saturday I awoke ill, my head and back aching. The doctor ordered complete rest. I was suffering from an excess of studying and was not to read or even think, nor was I even to know what was going on in the city or the rest of the outside world. I remained in this condition for five days. On the sixth day I got up, and only then did I find out that the canary, while under the servant's care, had flown out of its cage. My first impulse was to strangle the servant—I was choking with indignation and collapsed into my chair, speechless and bewildered. The guilty man defended himself, swearing he had been careful, but the wily bird had nevertheless managed to escape.

"But didn't you search for it?"

"Yes, I did, sir. First it flew up to the roof, and I followed it. It flew to a tree, and then who knows where it hid itself? I've been asking around since yesterday. I asked the neighbors and the local farmers, but no one has seen the bird."

I suffered immensely. Fortunately, the fatigue left me within a few hours, and I was soon able to go out to the veranda and the garden. There was no sign of the canary. I ran everywhere, making inquiries and posting announcements, all to no avail. I had already gathered my notes together to write my paper, even though it would be disjointed and incomplete, when I happened to visit a friend who had one of the largest and most beautiful estates on the outskirts of town. We were taking a stroll before dinner when this question was trilled to me:

"Greetings, Senhor Macedo, where have you been since you disappeared?"

It was the canary, perched on the branch of a tree. You can imagine how I reacted and what I said to the bird. My friend presumed I was mad, but the opinions of friends are of no importance to me. I spoke tenderly to the canary and asked it to come home and continue our conversations in that world of ours, composed of a garden, a fountain, a veranda, and a white circular cage.

"What garden? What fountain?"

"The world, my dear bird."

"What world? I see you haven't lost any of your annoying professorial habits. The world," it solemnly concluded, "is an infinite blue space, with the sun up above."

Indignant, I replied that if I were to believe what it said, the world could be anything—it had even been a secondhand shop …

"A secondhand shop?" it trilled to its heart's content. "But is there really such a thing as a secondhand shop?" ❧

Vocabulary

cursory (kur′sə rē) *adj.* hasty and not thorough; superficial

Synthesize *Who appears to control reality?*

Magic Realism *What do the canary's final words suggest about reality?*

After You Read

Respond and Think Critically

Respond and Interpret

1. What questions do you have about the canary or about Macedo?

2. (a)Where does Macedo find the canary? (b)Why is he surprised to find it there?

3. (a)How does the canary initially define the world? (b)How does this idea conflict with Macedo's assumptions about the canary?

4. (a)What new idea of the world does the canary express in Macedo's home? (b)How is the canary's new idea consistent with its former idea?

Analyze and Evaluate

5. How does this story satirize or ridicule scientific observation?

6. (a)Does the canary regard itself as a master or a servant? Explain. (b)How does this relationship contribute to the contradiction or ambiguity in the story?

Connect

7. **Big Idea** **Magic Realism** How does the canary take over reality?

8. **Connect to Today** What message about science and reality might this story offer to a modern reader? Explain.

Literary Element Narrator

A **narrator** tells a story. Some narrators are **unreliable** because their account of events is faulty or distorted in some way. Some unreliable narrators intentionally mislead readers, while others fail to understand the true meaning of the events they describe. Many stories with unreliable narrators are written in the first person.

1. This story is a narration of a narration. Does that make the narrator unreliable? Explain.

2. Do you think first-person narration is a better choice for this story than third-person narration? Explain.

3. When Macedo becomes physically ill, how does his physical state reflect his ability to accurately and objectively retell and interpret events?

Review: Anthropomorphism

As you learned on page 39, **anthropomorphism** is the assignment of human characteristics to gods, animals, or inanimate objects.

Partner Activity Work with a classmate to find examples of anthropomorphism in the story and to identify the human qualities each conveys. Complete a chart like the one below. When you are done, decide how anthropomorphism is used in "A Canary's Ideas" to suggest a philosophy of human or animal life. Also consider what it contributes to the magic realism of the story.

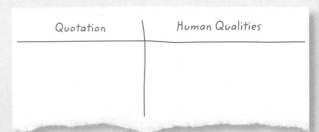

Quotation	Human Qualities

SAT Skills Practice

Unlike Macedo, the canary develops its ideas without regard for

(A) the scientific method

(B) firsthand observations

(C) individual instincts

(D) the natural environment

(E) the present moment

Vocabulary Practice

Practice with Denotation and Connotation
Denotation is the literal meaning of a word.
Connotation is its implied meaning. For example, the words *sad* and *despairing* have a similar denotation—"unhappy" —but *despairing* has a stronger connotation. Work with a partner to complete a graphic organizer like the one below for each vocabulary word. Include the vocabulary word in one box and a word that has a similar denotation in another. Explain which word has the stronger connotation.

austere   banal   phenomenon
presumptuous   cursory

EXAMPLE:

Academic Vocabulary

*Machado's story shows how, for the canary, reality is a matter of **individual** perception.*

Individual is an academic word. To further explore its meaning, describe a situation in which you saw a group of people combine their **individual** talents to achieve success.

For more on academic vocabulary, see pages 36–37 and R83–R85.

Connect to *Science*

Research and Report

Assignment In Machado's story, the canary concludes that the world "is an infinite blue space, with the sun up above." Research the cognition of birds and their ability to communicate, and create a multimedia presentation based on your findings.

Investigate Use print and online sources to research how and why birds communicate, as well as why only certain birds can "talk," or mimic human speech. To guide your research, create a K-W-L chart like the one below.

What I Know	What I Want to Know	What I Learned
Some birds can mimic human speech.	Can they actually comprehend the meaning of the words?	

As you take notes, be sure to annotate unfamiliar scientific terms, such as *ornithology* (the study of birds). Then synthesize the information in your K-W-L chart into a few general ideas you want to present. To review the synthesis process, consult the chart you made on page 1191.

Create Create a multimedia oral report that incorporates imagery, speech, and sound. You may wish to use presentation software or a slide projector to show images of birds as you speak. Alternately, you might present video or audio recordings of birds "talking." Remember that the media components you choose are meant to enhance, rather than replace, your presentation's oral component.

Report In your oral report, be sure to attribute information to the proper sources and clearly explain scientific terms. Rehearse your presentation several times to maximize the effectiveness of your multimedia aids and resolve any technical difficulties that might arise.

 Literature Online

Selection Resources For Selection Quizzes, eFlashcards, and Reading-Writing Connection activities, go to glencoe.com and enter QuickPass code GLW6053u6.

Before You Read

The Luck of Teodoro Méndez Acúbal

Meet **Rosario Castellanos**

(1925–1974)

Lola Alverez Bravo

Being born into a society that expected little more of its female members than to marry and have children can be a significant obstacle to any young woman who has other ambitions. Rosario Castellanos (rō sä′rē ō kä stä yä′nōs) overcame this obstacle and more to become one of the most important twentieth-century Mexican woman authors.

Growing Up in Chiapas Born into a wealthy family, Castellanos spent time with her native Maya nanny and other household workers on her father's plantations in the Chiapas region of southern Mexico. Her relationships with these people provided the warmth she never received from her parents, who preferred her younger brother. When he died suddenly, her devastated parents said the "wrong child" had died. During the late 1930s, agrarian reform affected Castellanos's family when the government seized its land and redistributed it among the peasants. This change in fortune led the family to move to Mexico City when Castellanos was sixteen. There, she completed her secondary education and enrolled in college. In 1948, her parents died within weeks of each other. This sudden loss put her in a state of crisis, but she recognized she was now free to pursue her own ambitions.

Spearheading Feminism In 1950, Castellanos received her master's degree in philosophy and published her thesis, "On Feminine Culture." This work is generally regarded as the starting point for the feminist movement in Mexico. In it, Castellanos criticized the patriarchal nature of Mexican society for the fact that women rarely participated in cultural activities. A year later, she returned to Chiapas where she studied the

> "Laughter is the most immediate form of freeing ourselves from that which oppresses us the most, of distancing ourselves from that which imprisons us!"
>
> —Rosario Castellanos

culture of the Maya Chamula group. In her later fiction, Castellanos often focused on relations between the Chamulas and the landowners. She believed that Mexican women and the Chamulas suffered from similar forms of oppression.

Later Years During the 1960s, Castellenos lectured at universities in the United States and Mexico. In 1971, she was appointed Mexico's ambassador to Israel. While carrying out her diplomatic responsibilities, she continued to write and teach. When she was only 49, she died in a household accident. She is buried in the Rotunda of Illustrious Men in Mexico City, one of only two women so honored.

 LOG ON ▶ **Literature** Online

Author Search For more about Rosario Castellanos, go to glencoe.com and enter QuickPass code GLW6053u6.

Literature and Reading Preview

Connect to the Story

How might the acquisition of a lot of money change someone? List the possible effects of suddenly coming into wealth.

Build Background

"The Luck of Teodoro Méndez Acúbal" is set in Chiapas, once a center of Mayan civilization. Many of its inhabitants are descended, either completely or partly, from the Maya. Over the centuries, conflicts have broken out between the Maya and landowners in Chiapas. Ethnic, class, and language barriers have made it difficult for many Maya to achieve an adequate standard of living.

Set Purposes for Reading

Big Idea The Legacy of Colonialism

As you read, ask yourself, How does the multicultural legacy of the area affect its poorest inhabitants?

Literary Element Plot

The **plot** is the sequence of events in a story. Most plots develop around a **conflict,** a struggle between opposing forces, and begin with **exposition,** which introduces the characters, setting, and situation. The **rising action** adds **complications** that culminate in the **climax,** the point of highest tension. The climax gives way rapidly to its logical result in the **falling action,** and finally to the **resolution,** in which the final outcome is revealed. As you read, ask yourself, Where does each plot element occur?

Reading Strategy Preview and Review

When you **preview** a literary work, you look at the title, the art, and the opening paragraph to get an idea of what the work is about. When you **review,** you reread sections of text. Before you read, ask yourself, How can the title, the art, and the first paragraph help me understand the story?

Tip: Scan the Text In a chart like the one below, note various text features and what each suggests.

Feature	What It Suggests
Title: "The Luck of Teodoro Méndez Acúbal"	Luck has a role—is it good luck or bad luck?
Opening art	

Learning Objectives

For pages 1199–1208

In studying this text, you will focus on the following objectives:

Literary Study: Analyzing plot.

Reading: Previewing and reviewing.

Listening and Speaking: Conducting an interview.

Vocabulary

irrevocable (i rev′ə kə bəl) *adj.* incapable of being brought back, undone, or changed; p. 1203 *After the house was sold, the decision to move was irrevocable.*

propriety (prə prī′ə tē) *n.* conformity to what is acceptable in conduct or speech; p. 1204 *Cara's sense of propriety prevented her from wearing shorts to the wedding.*

condescending (kon′ di sen′ ding) *adj.* characterized by an air of superiority or smugness; p. 1205 *Armando's condescending attitude made it unpleasant for Justine to be around him.*

disdain (dis dān′) *n.* an attitude of scorn or contempt for something considered inferior; p. 1205 *Her disdain for Harry prompted her to regard his comments as "silly and idiotic."*

diligence (dil′ə jəns) *n.* persistent hard work; p. 1206 *Erin's diligence was rewarded when she finally learned to play the piece flawlessly.*

The Luck of **Teodoro Méndez Acúbal**

Rosario Castellanos
Translated by Myralyn F. Allgood

Union (La union), July 1923-early 1924. Diego Rivera © Banco de Mexico Trust. Mural, 2.06 x 1.33 m. Secretaria de Educacion Publica, Mexico City, D.F.

Walking along the streets of Jobel (with his eyes cast downward as custom dictates for those of his humble station), Teodoro Méndez Acúbal spotted a coin. All but lost in the dust, caked with mud, worn from years of use, it had been ignored by the white *caxlanes*.[1] For the *caxlanes* walk with their heads held high. Moved by pride, they contemplate from afar the important matters that absorb them.

Teodoro stopped, more out of disbelief than greed. Kneeling as if to fasten one of his sandals, he waited until no one was looking to pick up what he had found. He hid it quickly in the folds of his sash.

He stood again, swaying, overcome by a kind of dizziness. Weak-kneed and dry-mouthed, his eyes blurred as he felt his heart pounding, pulsing between his eyebrows.

Staggering from side to side as if in a drunken stupor, Teodoro began to make his way down the street. From time to time the passersby had to push him aside to avoid bumping into him. But Teodoro's spirit was too troubled to be bothered by what was going on around him. The coin, hidden in his sash, had transformed him into another man—a stronger man than before, it is true. But also more fearful.

---

1. *Caxlanes* (käs lä ́nās) are the dominant socioeconomic class in Chiapas, which has a large Mayan population.

Preview and Review *Based on the title and this first paragraph, what can you predict about the story?*

The Legacy of Colonialism *What details here and earlier in the story suggest differences between the social classes?*

He stepped off the path that led to his village and sat down on a fallen log. Could this be all a dream? Pale with anxiety, Teodoro's hands felt his sash. Yes, there it was—firm and round—the precious coin. Teodoro unwrapped it, moistened it with his breath and saliva and rubbed it against his clothing. On the metal (it had to be silver, judging from its whitish color) the outline of a profile appeared. Majestic. And around the edge, letters, numbers, and signs. Calculating its weight, testing it with his teeth, listening to its ring, Teodoro was able—at last—to determine its value.

And so, with this stroke of fortune, he had become rich. Richer than the owner of great flocks of sheep or vast stretches of cornfields. He was as rich as . . . as a *caxlán*. And Teodoro was amazed that the color of his skin had not changed.

The images of the members of his family (his wife, his three children, his aging parents) struggled to invade Teodoro's reverie. But he dispelled them with an air of displeasure. He saw no reason to tell anyone about his discovery, much less share it. He worked to maintain his household. That's as it should be; it's the custom, an obligation. But as for this stroke of fortune, it was his. Exclusively his.

And so, when Teodoro arrived at his hut and sat down by the fire to eat, he did not speak. His own silence made him uncomfortable, as if being quiet were a way of mocking everyone else. To punish himself he allowed his feelings of loneliness to grow within him, along with his shame. Teodoro was a man set apart, stifled by his secret. Moreover, this anguish produced physical discomfort—a cramp in the pit of his stomach, a chill deep in the marrow of his bones. Why suffer all this, when with a word the pain would disappear? To keep himself from

Virgin of Guadalupe, c. 19th century. Artist Unknown. Mexico.
View the Art It is believed that the Virgin of Guadalupe appeared to Juan Diego in 1531, miraculously imprinting her image on his cape. What values do you think the Virgin of Guadalupe might represent?

uttering it, Teodoro grasped his sash and felt the lump there, made by the metal.

During the sleepless night, Teodoro talked to himself: what shall I buy? Before now he had never wanted things. So convinced was he that they were beyond his reach that he passed them by without a thought, without the slightest curiosity. And now he wasn't about to consider necessities—a blanket, a machete, a hat. No. These are things to be bought with wages. But Méndez Acúbal had not earned this coin. It was his luck, an outright gift. It was given to him so he could play with it, so he could waste it, so he could have something impractical and beautiful.

Teodoro had no idea about prices. On his next trip to Jobel, he began to notice the dealings of buyers and sellers. Both appeared to be calm. The one feigning lack of interest, the other the desire to please, they spoke of pesos and centavos,[2] of pounds and

---

Plot *What conflict is Teodoro experiencing?*

---

2. *Pesos and centavos* (sen tä ´ vōs) are coins used as currency in some Latin American countries. One hundred centavos equal one peso.

measures, of many other things that whirled about in Teodoro's head, making no sense at all.

Exhausted, Teodoro abandoned the struggle and took refuge in a delightful notion: with his silver coin he could buy anything he wanted.

Months went by before Teodoro made his **irrevocable** selection. It was a clay figurine, a small statue of the Virgin.[3] It was also a real find, because the figure lay in the midst of a clutter of objects that decorated the window of a store. From that time on, Teodoro hovered around it like a lover. Hours and hours went by. And always he was there, standing like a sentinel beside the window.

Don Agustín Velasco, the merchant, watched him with his tiny squinting eyes (eyes of a hawk, his mother would say) from inside the store.

Even before Teodoro acquired the custom of appearing in front of his establishment, the Indian's features had attracted the attention of Don Agustín. No Ladino[4] could help but notice a Chamula[5] walking on the sidewalks (reserved for the *caxlanes*), and less so when he walked as slowly as if out for a stroll. It was unusual for this to happen, and Don Agustín had not even considered it possible. But he now had to admit that things might go further: an

Indian was also capable of daring to stand before a window contemplating the display, not just with the assurance of one who can appreciate it, but with the bold insolence of one who comes to buy.

Don Agustín's thin, yellowish face grimaced in a gesture of scorn. For an Indian to go to Guadalupe Street to shop for candles for his saints, or whiskey for his festivals, or tools for his work is acceptable. The people who deal with them have neither illustrious lineage nor family names; they have no fortunes and therefore work at demeaning jobs. For an Indian to enter a pharmacy to ask for healing powders or liquid potions or miraculous ointments can be tolerated. After all, pharmacists belong to the middle-class families that wish to move upward and mingle with their betters, and that is why it's good for the Indians to humble them by frequenting their places of business.

But for an Indian to position himself so firmly in front of a jewelry store—no ordinary jewelry store at that, but the one belonging to Don Agustín Velasco, descendant of conquistadors, well received in the best circles, appreciated by his colleagues—was, at the very least, unfathomable. Unless . . .

A terrible thought began to gnaw at him. What if the boldness of this Chamula was based on the strength of his tribe? It wouldn't be the first time, the salesman admitted bitterly. Rumors . . . where had he heard rumors of revolt? Quickly Don Agustín tried to recall the places he had visited in the past few days: the Bishop's Palace, the Casino, the meeting at Doña Romelia Ochoa's house.

What foolishness! Don Agustín smiled, silently laughing at himself. How right

---

3. *Virgin* refers to Mary, the mother of Jesus.
4. *Ladino*, in the dialect of Chiapas, refers to an individual of mixed Mayan and Spanish heritage. Ladinos make up the middle class.
5. *Chamula* (chä mōō´lä) are a group of pure Mayan heritage, who make up the least privileged socioeconomic class.

The Legacy of Colonialism *How does this passage highlight the injustices and the racial prejudices that exist in this colonial society?*

Vocabulary

irrevocable (i rev´ə kə bəl) *adj.* incapable of being brought back, undone, or changed

Plot *Notice that the point of view has shifted from that of Teodoro to that of Don Agustín. Why do you think this shift has taken place, and how do you think it will affect the plot?*

Bishop Manuel Oropeza had been when he said that every sin has its punishment. And Don Agustín, who rigorously abstained from alcohol, tobacco, and women, was still a slave to one bad habit: gossip.

Slyly he made himself a part of conversations in doorways, in the market, even in the Cathedral. Don Agustín was the first to hear a rumor, to sniff out the scandals, and he longed for shared confidences, for secrets to guard and for intrigues to plot.

And at night, after supper (of thick chocolate provided by his anxious, worn-out mother), Don Agustín made a habit of attending a gathering of some sort. There they talked and entertained each other with stories. About love affairs, feuds over inheritances, sudden and unexplained fortunes, duels. For several nights the conversation had revolved around one topic: Indian uprisings. Everyone present had been witness, participant, victim, or victor in one or another. They recalled details of those they had seen. Terrible images that made Don Agustín tremble: fifteen thousand

Visual Vocabulary

In Latin America, a *hacienda* generally refers to a large ranch, farm, or plantation, especially to the main building or owner's residence.

Chamulas ready for war, besieging Ciudad Real.[6] Haciendas plundered, men killed, women (no, no, we must not think of these things), women . . . in the end, violated.

Victory always fell on the side of the *caxlanes* (anything else would have been inconceivable), but at such a price, such loss.

Is experience worth anything? Judging by the Indian standing at the window of his jewelry store, no. The inhabitants of Ciudad Real, caught up in their daily routines and interests, forgot the past, which should serve

as a lesson to them, and went about their business as if no danger threatened. Don Agustín was horrified by such an irresponsible attitude. The security of his life was so fragile that all it took was the face of a Chamula, seen through a glass, to shatter it completely.

Don Agustín looked out again into the street hoping to find the Indian no longer present. But Méndez Acúbal remained there still, motionless and attentive.

The passersby walked near him without any sign of surprise or alarm. This consoling fact (and the familiar sounds that came from the back of the house) restored Don Agustín's sense of tranquility. He could no longer justify his fears. Events like the one at Cancuc, like Pedro Díaz Cuscat's siege of Jobel, and Pajarito's threats[7]—those couldn't happen again. These were different times, more secure for decent people.

And besides, who was going to provide arms, who was going to lead the rebels? The Indian who was here, with his nose pressed against the window of the jewelry store, was alone. And if things got out of hand, no one was to blame but the townspeople themselves. No one was going to respect them if they themselves were not worthy of respect. Don Agustín disapproved of his fellow citizens' conduct, as if he had been betrayed by them.

They say that some—not many, thank God—even shake hands with the Indians. Indians—what a race of thieves!

The thought left a peculiarly painful taste in Don Agustín's mouth. Not only from a sense of **propriety,** as entrenched in him as in anyone else in his profession, but from a special circumstance.

---

6. *Ciudad Real* (sü däd´rä äl´) is a city in Chiapas.

7. *[Cancuc . . . Pajarito's threats]* are references to conflicts involving Maya and people of European descent.

Vocabulary

propriety (prə prī´ə tē) *n.* conformity to what is acceptable in conduct or speech

Ranchos Orilleros, 1932. José Cúneo. Oil on burlap, 24 1/4 x 36 in. Private collection.

Don Agustín did not have the courage to admit it, but what tormented him was the suspicion that he was himself insignificant. And to make matters worse, his mother confirmed his suspicions in many ways. Her attitude toward this, her only child (son of Saint Anne,[8] she used to say), born when he was more a bother than a comfort, was one of Christian resignation. The "boy"— his mother and the servants continued to call him that in spite of the fact that Don Agustín was past forty—was very shy, cowardly, and passive. How many business deals had slipped through his fingers! And how many of those he did make resulted in nothing but failure! The Velasco fortune had dwindled considerably since Don Agustín took charge of things. And as for the prestige of the firm, it was maintained with great difficulty, and only because of the respect his late father, still mourned by mother and son, instilled in everyone.

But what could one expect from a wimp, an "overgrown child"? Don Agustín's mother shook her head sighing. And she kept on with her wheedling, her prudery, her **condescending** comments, for this was her way of expressing **disdain.**

Instinctively, the shopkeeper knew that he had before him the opportunity to prove his courage to others and himself. His zeal, his keen insight, would be evident to everyone. One simple word—thief—had given him the clue: the man with his nose pressed against the glass of his jewelry store was a thief. No doubt about it. Besides, the case was not uncommon. Don Agustín

---

> **Preview and Review** *What information does the author provide here and earlier about Don Agustín?*

> **Vocabulary**
>
> **condescending** (kon´di sen´ding) *adj.* characterized by an air of superiority or smugness
> **disdain** (dis dān´) *n.* an attitude of scorn or contempt for something considered inferior

---

8. *Saint Anne* was the mother of Mary, mother of Jesus.

could think of countless anecdotes of robberies and even worse crimes attributed to the Indians.

Satisfied with his deductions, Don Agustín didn't settle for merely preparing a defense. His sense of racial, class, and professional solidarity obliged him to share his suspicions with the other merchants, and together they went to the police. The neighborhood was prepared, thanks to the **diligence** of Don Agustín.

But the person responsible for those precautions suddenly disappeared from sight. After a few weeks he appeared again in his customary spot and in the same posture: standing guard. Because Teodoro didn't dare go in. No Chamula had ever attempted such a bold act. If he were to risk being the first, surely they would throw him out into the street before his lice had a chance to escape into the establishment. But, if by remotest chance they didn't eject him, and if they allowed him to remain inside the store long enough to discuss the matter, Teodoro wouldn't know how to express his desires. He could neither understand nor speak Spanish. And so, to unclog his ears, to loosen his tongue, he had been drinking Indian whiskey. The liquor had instilled in him a sense of power. His blood flowed, hot and fast, through his veins. The ease with which he moved his muscles dictated his actions. As if in a dream, he crossed the threshold of the jewelry store. But the cool dampness and the still, musty air inside brought him abruptly back to reality with a shock of terror. From a jewelry case the flashing eye of a diamond stared at him threateningly.

"May I help you, Chamula? What would you like?"

By repeating such pleasantries, Don Agustín sought to gain time. At the same time his hands searched for the gun he kept in the counter drawer. The Indian's silence frightened him more than any threat. He dared not raise his eyes until he had the gun in his hand.

The look he encountered paralyzed him. A gaze of surprise, of reproach. Why was the Indian staring at him like that? Don Agustín wasn't the one at fault. He was an honest man, he had never harmed anyone. And it appeared that he would be the first victim of these Indians who had suddenly set themselves up as judges! Here was his executioner, coming toward him with his fingers searching the folds of his sash, soon to draw forth who knows what instrument of death.

Don Agustín clutched the gun but could not fire. He cried out to the police for help.

When Teodoro tried to get away, he couldn't, because a crowd had gathered in the doorway of the store blocking his path. Shouts, gestures, angry faces. The police seized the Indian, questioned him, searched him. When the silver coin appeared in the folds of his sash, a shout of triumph arose from the crowd. Don Agustín excitedly held up the coin for all to see. The shouting exhilarated him. "Thief, thief!"

Teodoro Méndez Acúbal was taken to jail. Since the charges against him were not unusual, no one was in a hurry to gather the facts of the case. His file grew yellow with age on the shelves of the police department. ❧

Plot *What part of the plot do these details represent?*

Vocabulary

diligence (dil′ ə jəns) *n.* persistent hard work

Plot *The climax is the moment of greatest tension, where the story can resolve itself in one or more ways. Identify the climax of this story.*

Preview and Review *Is this story ironic? Explain.*

After You Read

Respond and Think Critically

Respond and Interpret

1. (a)How did you react to the story's ending? (b)Why do you think you responded that way?

2. (a)According to the narrator, why does Teodoro find a coin that the *caxlanes* failed to notice? (b)What does this explanation suggest about relations between Chamulas and *caxlanes* in Jobel?

3. (a)What does Teodoro decide to purchase with the coin? (b)What does this decision suggest about him?

4. (a)Why does Don Agustín grow suspicious of Teodoro? (b)How does Don Agustín's family background influence his feelings regarding the Chamulas?

5. (a)What happens when Teodoro finally goes into the store? (b)How does Don Agustín misunderstand Teodoro's actions?

Analyze and Evaluate

6. What, if anything, did you find humorous in this story? Explain.

7. Do you think Teodoro is idealized in the story or portrayed realistically? Explain.

Connect

8. **Big Idea** **The Legacy of Colonialism** What do you think Castellanos is saying about colonial society in places like Jobel?

9. **Connect to Today** Do the social and justice systems in this story relate to modern-day class struggles in the United States? Explain.

Literary Element Plot

ACT Skills Practice

1. When does Don Agustín first begin to grow wary of Teodoro?

   A. Even before Teodoro begins to position himself in front of the shop.

   B. After Teodoro begins to position himself in front of the shop.

   C. After Teodoro enters the shop.

   D. After Teodoro reaches into his sash for the coin.

2. The resolution of the story occurs when Teodoro:

   F. finds the coin.

   G. decides to buy the clay figurine.

   H. enters the shop.

   J. goes to jail.

Review: Irony

As you learned on page 291, **irony** is a discrepancy between appearance and reality. **Dramatic irony** occurs when the reader or the audience of a literary work knows something a character does not know. It can be used for comic effect, to generate suspense, or to increase our sympathy for a character who is about to make a fateful error.

Partner Activity Meet with a classmate and discuss the dramatic irony in "The Luck of Teodoro Méndez Acúbal." Consider these questions in your discussion.

1. What dramatic irony develops from Don Agustín's fear of Teodoro?

2. (a)What dramatic irony occurs at the end of the story? (b)How does this irony affect your response to the ending? Explain.

Reading Strategy — Preview and Review

You can deepen your understanding and enjoyment of a work when you **preview** it before you begin reading and then **review** it after you have finished. Previewing includes considering the title, looking at the art and trying to guess its relationship to the text, and skimming the first paragraph or two. Later, reviewing the text is a way to verify the accuracy of the predictions you made during your preview.

1. How do the art on the opening page and the information in the first paragraph give you a clue as to what the story is about?

2. In reviewing the story, what seems ironic about the title and the opening art?

Vocabulary Practice

Practice with Synonyms With a partner, brainstorm three synonyms for each boldfaced vocabulary word below. Then discuss your choices with your classmates.

| irrevocable | propriety | condescending |
| disdain | diligence | |

EXAMPLE: complacent

Synonyms: contented, serene, happy

Sample explanation: Both serene and complacent mean "contented," though complacent has more negative connotations.

Academic Vocabulary

*The **structure** of the society in Castellanos's story consists of an upper class and a lower class.*

Structure is an academic word often used to refer to the relations or hierarchies between different groups in a society. To further explore the meaning of this word, complete the following sentence.

_____ could be one advantage of living in a society with a rigid structure.

For more on academic vocabulary, see pages 36–37 and R83–R85.

Listening and Speaking

 Interview

Assignment Imagine you are an international reporter who has come to Jobel to write an article about the incident at the jewelry store. With a partner, role-play a 750-word interview with Teodoro or Don Agustín about their encounter that day.

Prepare Review the graphic organizer you filled out on page 1200. Using that information as a starting point, discuss the interview subject's character traits and motivation with your partner. Also discuss what facts may have been overlooked in other reports of the incident. If you are the reporter, prepare a list of probing questions that would help you uncover the truth about the incident. Remember that your questions should reflect an objective stance.

If you are the interviewee, prepare to role-play by reviewing your character's behavior in the story. Think about what questions the reporter might ask and imagine how your character would respond.

Interview If you are the reporter, take careful notes on your subject's responses. Allow your subject to respond completely to each question, ask further questions to clarify information, and check to make sure you have recorded your subject's statements correctly. If you are the interviewee, remember to stay in your role, speaking as your character rather than expressing your own ideas and opinions.

Report Write a brief reflection on how role-playing helped you better understand the themes of the story. If you are the interviewee, you may wish to comment on what was frustrating about playing your character.

Evaluate Write a paragraph evaluating your partner's performance in the interview.

 Literature Online

Selection Resources For Selection Quizzes, eFlashcards, and Reading-Writing Connection activities, go to glencoe.com and enter QuickPass code GLW6053u6.

Comparing Literature

Across Time and Place

Compare Literature About Animals

The beauty and the mystery of animal life continue to inspire authors and readers in today's technological age. The following literary works by Pablo Neruda (pä´blō nā roo´dä), Rainer Maria Rilke (rī nər mä rē´ä ril´kə), Isak Dinesen (ē säk dē´nə sən), and Po Chü-i demonstrate how animals spark our imaginations and influence our lives.

Learning Objectives

For pages 1209–1219

In studying these texts, you will focus on the following objectives:

Literary Study: Analyzing alliteration.

Reading:
Evaluating figurative language.
Comparing cultural contexts.
Comparing themes.

Writing: Writing a poem.

COMPARE THE [Big Idea] Nature and the Imagination

Humans have drastically altered the earth's natural landscape in the process of developing their societies. This process of change provides the backdrop for these four literary works, each of which takes place in a region where plants and animals have been put in captivity or otherwise impacted by humans. As you read, ask yourself, How does each author show the relationship between people and animals?

COMPARE Portrayals of Animals

Wild or domestic, common or exotic, animals serve many purposes in literature. To some authors, animals are relatable figures with tendencies much like our own. To others, animals symbolize qualities that are frightening, inspiring, or even sublime. As you read, ask yourself, What do the animals in these works represent for the authors?

COMPARE Styles

An author's established style often shapes the subject of his or her work. Neruda, Rilke, Dinesen, and Po Chü-i have distinct styles that make comparing their work a productive way to see how a similar subject can be treated in a variety of ways. As you read, ask yourself, What are the similarities and differences between these authors' styles?

Horse and a Youth in Blue, 1905-1906. Pablo Picasso. Watercolour and gouache on paper, 49.8 x 32.1 cm. Tate Gallery, London. © ARS, NY.

Literature Online

Author Search For more about Pablo Neruda, Rainer Maria Rilke, Isak Dinesen, and Po Chü-i, go to glencoe.com and enter QuickPass code GLW6053u6.

Before You Read

Chile

Horses

Meet **Pablo Neruda**
(1904–1973)

A
s a shy, lonely boy growing up in southern Chile, Pablo Neruda immersed himself in literature and the natural world. "Nature there went to my head like a strong whiskey," he commented. "I was barely ten at the time, but already a poet." At age fifteen, Neruda began publishing his work, and by his early twenties, he was one of Chile's most popular authors.

Early Fame Neruda was born Neftalí Ricardo Reyes Basoalto. However, because his father disapproved of his literary aspirations, the poet published his first collection of poems using the pen name Pablo Neruda. Later, he changed his name legally. His second collection, *Twenty Love Poems and a Song of Despair*, achieved instant popularity when it was published in 1924; even so, Neruda was unable to earn a living by writing. To earn money, he entered Chile's diplomatic service, beginning a life of travel and adventure.

Travel, Politics, and Poetry Neruda took diplomatic positions in Asia, South America, and Europe, drawing poetic inspiration from the places he saw and the people he met. In 1933, he published the collection *Residence on Earth*, in which he moved beyond his earlier lyrical poems to a more experimental technique and a darker, surrealist vision. During his subsequent involvement with the Spanish Civil War, Neruda grew deeply committed to left-wing politics. In the poems in *Spain in My Heart* (1937), he expressed socialist ideals in impassioned verse.

In 1940, Neruda took a post as a consul in Mexico, where he studied that country's ancient civilizations. After returning to Chile, he joined

> "If you ask what my poetry is, I must confess that I don't know; but if you'll ask my poetry, it will tell you who I am."
>
> —Pablo Neruda

the Communist Party and won election to the Senate. After harshly criticizing the president, however, he was forced to move abroad. He left Chile on horseback, crossing the Andes mountains by night. For the next several years, Neruda traveled through the Soviet Union, Poland, Hungary, and Mexico.

The Voice of a Continent In 1952, Neruda returned to his beloved Chile. In 1971, he was awarded the Nobel Prize in Literature. When presenting the prize, Swedish Academy member Karl Ragnar Gierow emphasized that, while Neruda's body of work has universal appeal, it speaks particularly to the people of Latin America. "In [Neruda's] work," he commented, "a continent awakens to consciousness."

Literature and Reading Preview

Connect to the Poem

What qualities do you associate with horses? Discuss this question with a partner. Consider the size, strength, and appearance of real horses and horses you know from movies or books.

Build Background

Pablo Neruda wrote about 50 volumes of poetry in a career that spanned half a century. Some of his poems are dense, highly experimental works; others are simple and direct. Uniting the different phases of his career are his love for the people and the landscape of Chile, his exuberance, and the freshness of his imagery.

Set Purposes for Reading

Big Idea Nature and the Imagination

As you read, ask yourself, How does the natural world function as a source of meaning in the Latin American literary tradition?

Literary Element Alliteration

Alliteration is the repetition of consonant sounds at the beginnings of words. Poets often use alliteration to emphasize a particular line by making it more memorable, or to echo the mood or the action of a poem. As you read, ask yourself, Where and why does Neruda use alliteration?

Reading Strategy Evaluate Figurative Language

Figurative language is language used for descriptive effect to convey ideas or emotions. Metaphors, similes, and personification are figurative language. When you **evaluate figurative language,** you identify these expressions and judge how effective they are. As you read, ask yourself, How effective is Neruda's use of figurative language to evoke an idea or a feeling?

Tip: Use a Graphic Organizer As you read the poem, assess Neruda's figurative language using a diagram like this one.

Passage	Type of Figurative Language	Evaluation
"The air white like a moistened loaf."	Simile	Effective because it gives the reader the physical sensation of a damp, bleak winter day

Vocabulary

sheer (shēr) *adj.* unmixed; pure; p. 1213 *Alex felt sheer joy as he held his newborn daughter for the first time.*

disgruntled (dis grən′təld) *adj.* unhappy; grumpy; p. 1213 *After yet another customer treated him rudely, the disgruntled waiter announced he was quitting.*

unwitting (un wit′ing) *adj.* not knowing; unaware; p. 1213 *The vendor assured the unwitting tourist that the sunglasses he was selling were designer brands.*

obliterate (ə blit′e rāt′) *v.* to erase from memory; to destroy all traces of; p. 1213 *Maureen sought to obliterate her unsuccessful past by moving to another city and starting a new career.*

Tip: Word Usage When you encounter a new word, it might help you to answer specific questions about the word. For example, Do you know someone who is frequently **disgruntled**? How does this person behave?

Horses

Pablo Neruda
Translated by Alastair Reid

The Small Yellow Horses, 1912. Franz Marc. Germany Staatsgalerie, Stuttgart.

It was from the window I saw the horses.

I was in Berlin, in winter. The light
was without light, the sky skyless.

The air white like a moistened loaf.

5 From my window, I could see a deserted arena,
a circle bitten out by the teeth of winter.

All at once, led out by a man,
ten horses were stepping into the snow.
Emerging, they had scarcely rippled into existence
10 like flame, than they filled the whole world of my eyes,
empty till now. Faultless, flaming,
they stepped like ten gods on broad, clean hooves,
their manes recalling a dream of pure grace.

Their rumps were globes, were oranges.

15 Their color was amber and honey, was on fire.

Their necks were towers
carved from the stone of pride,
and in their furious eyes, **sheer** energy
showed itself, a prisoner inside them.

20 And there, in the silence, at the midpoint of the day, in a dirty, **disgruntled** winter,
the horses' intense presence was blood,
was rhythm, was the beckoning Grail° of being.

I saw, I saw, and, seeing, I came to life.
25 There was the **unwitting** fountain, the dance of gold,
the sky,
the fire that sprang to life in beautiful things.

I have **obliterated** that gloomy Berlin winter.

I shall not forget the light from these horses.

23 **Grail:** in legend, the cup used by Jesus at the Last Supper. It was sought by Arthurian knights during a long, difficult quest.

Evaluate Figurative Language *Does the poet's use of personification enhance your sense of the setting? Explain.*

Nature and the Imagination *What do the horses represent to the speaker?*

Alliteration *How does the use of alliteration contribute to the meaning of these lines?*

Vocabulary

sheer (shēr) *adj.* unmixed; pure
disgruntled (dis grən′təld) *adj.* unhappy; grumpy
unwitting (un wit′ing) *adj.* not knowing; unaware
obliterate (ə blit′e rāt′) *v.* to erase from memory; to destroy all traces of

After You Read

Respond and Think Critically

Respond and Interpret

1. What emotions did you feel as you finished reading this poem? Explain.

2. (a)Why do you think the horses are being led outside? (b)In your opinion, what do lines 22 and 23 of the poem mean?

3. (a)How do the horses affect the speaker? (b)What does the speaker mean by "I have obliterated that gloomy Berlin winter" (line 27)?

Analyze and Evaluate

4. (a)Why might Neruda have set this poem in a city rather than the countryside? (b)Why might Neruda have set this poem in winter?

5. (a)**Mood** is the overall feeling of a literary work. What mood is established early in the poem? Explain. (b)When does the mood change, and how does Neruda achieve this effect?

6. **Style** is an author's distinctive manner of expression—not *what* is said, but *how* it is said. (a)What aspects of Neruda's style stood out to you? (b)How effective is Neruda's style? Explain.

Connect

7. **Big Idea** **Nature and the Imagination** How is the speaker in this poem both separated from and connected to the natural world?

8. **Connect to Today** Is Neruda's message of the power of nature still relevant for readers today? Explain.

Literary Element Alliteration

Alliteration, the repetition of consonant sounds, can emphasize rhythm and convey emotion.

1. Explain the cumulative effect of the alliteration in lines 10 and 11.

2. Why do you think alliteration is used in lines 20–26?

Reading Strategy Evaluate Figurative Language

Evaluating figurative language means assessing an author's use of devices such as simile, metaphor, and personification.

Partner Activity With a partner, discuss how the use of personification in line 21 contributes to the poem.

Vocabulary Practice

Practice with Word Usage Respond to these statements to explore the vocabulary words.

1. Describe a moment when you felt **sheer** terror.

2. List things that might cause an employee to become **disgruntled**.

3. Explain an incident when someone was **unwitting**.

4. Name a natural phenomenon that could **obliterate** a city.

🚀 **Writing**

Write a Poem Write a poem describing an experience you have had with nature that reminds you of the speaker's experience. For example, you might write about an encounter with an animal. Use alliteration to enhance the emotional effects of your poem and figurative language to make it more vivid. For ideas, refer to the chart you filled out on page 1211.

Build Background

In 1902, Austrian-Czech author Rainer Maria Rilke (1875–1926) went to Paris, France, to write a book about French sculptor Auguste Rodin. The artist's ability to capture the essence of a being or an object impressed Rilke. In *dinggedichte* ("thing-poems"), Rilke attempted a similar focus and offered exacting descriptions of animals, landscapes, works of art, and physical objects. The speaker's feelings are usually left unstated, yet Rilke suggested them by focusing on the visible world. "The Panther" describes a caged animal in a Paris park.

The Panther

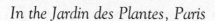

Rainer Maria Rilke
Translated by Stephen Mitchell

In the Jardin des Plantes, Paris

His vision, from the constantly passing bars
has grown so weary that it cannot hold
anything else. It seems to him there are
a thousand bars; and behind the bars, no
    world.

5   As he paces in cramped circles, over and
    over,
the movement of his powerful soft strides
is like a ritual dance around a center
in which a mighty will stands paralyzed.

Only at times, the curtain of the pupils
10 lifts, quietly—. An image enters in,
rushes down through the tensed, arrested
    muscles,
plunges into the heart and is gone.

Last Refuge. Yvonne Delvo. Oil on canvas. Private collection.

Quickwrite

The poet W. H. Auden wrote that Rilke conveys ideas with "physical rather than intellectual symbols . . . Rilke thinks of the human in terms of the nonhuman." What idea about humankind might Rilke be conveying through the image of the panther? Write a few paragraphs addressing this question.

Build Background

Before becoming an author, Isak Dinesen (1885–1962) studied painting; later she said this training taught her how to observe nature. Dinesen, whose legal name was Karen Blixen, was born into an upper-class Danish family and moved to Africa after her marriage. Seven years later, when her marriage had fallen apart, she stayed in Africa to run a large coffee plantation near Nairobi, Kenya. Her 1937 memoir, *Out of Africa*, portrays incidents that occurred on the plantation, her friendships with Africans and colonists, and her relationship with English hunter Denys Finch-Hatton. The book also reflects her deep love for Africa.

THE IGUANA

from Out of Africa   Isak Dinesen

In the Reserve I have sometimes come upon the Iguana, the big lizards, as they were sunning themselves upon a flat stone in a riverbed. They are not pretty in shape, but nothing can be imagined more beautiful than their coloring. They shine like a heap of precious stones or like a pane cut out of an old church window. When, as you approach, they swish away, there is a flash of azure, green and purple over the stones, the color seems to be standing behind them in the air, like a comet's luminous tail.

Guana, plate from *Brehms Tierleben Allgemeine Kunde des Tierreichs,* 1892. Colour lithograph. Private collection.

Once I shot an Iguana. I thought that I should be able to make some pretty things from his skin. A strange thing happened then, that I have never afterwards forgotten. As I went up to him, where he was lying dead upon his stone, and actually while I was walking the few steps, he faded and grew pale, all color died out of him as in one long sigh, and by the time that I touched him he was gray and dull like a lump of concrete. It was the live impetuous blood pulsating within the animal, which had radiated out all that glow and splendor. Now that the flame was put out, and the soul had flown, the Iguana was as dead as a sandbag.

Often since I have, in some sort, shot an Iguana, and I have remembered the one of the Reserve. Up at Meru I saw a young Native girl with a bracelet on, a leather strap two inches wide, and embroidered all over with very small turquoise-colored beads which varied a little in color and played in green, light blue and ultramarine. It was an extraordinarily live thing; it seemed to draw breath on her arm, so that I wanted it for myself, and made Farah buy it from her. No sooner had it come upon my own arm than it gave up the ghost.[1] It was nothing now, a small, cheap, purchased article of finery. It had been the play of colors, the duet between the turquoise and the "nègre,"—

So sad did it seem that I remembered the saying of the hero in a book that I had read as a child:"I have conquered them all, but I am standing amongst graves."

that quick, sweet, brownish black, like peat[2] and black pottery, of the Native's skin,—that had created the life of the bracelet.

In the Zoological Museum of Pietermaritzburg, I have seen, in a stuffed deep-water fish in a showcase, the same combination of coloring, which there had survived death; it made me wonder what life can well be like, on the bottom of the sea, to send up something so live and airy.

I stood in Meru and looked at my pale hand and at the dead bracelet, it was as if an injustice had been done to a noble thing, as if truth had been suppressed. So sad did it seem that I remembered the saying of the hero in a book that I had read as a child: "I have conquered them all, but I am standing amongst graves."

In a foreign country and with foreign species of life one should take measures to find out whether things will be keeping their value when dead. To the settlers of East Africa I give the advice: "For the sake of your own eyes and heart, shoot not the Iguana." ∾

---

1. In this context, *gave up the ghost* means "became lifeless."

2. *Peat* is a plant-based fuel source.

Discussion Starter

Dinesen compares the experience of shooting an iguana with that of buying a beaded bracelet from a young girl. Do you think this comparison is appropriate or effective? Explain. How does this comparison reflect the larger issue of European colonialism in Africa? Discuss these issues in a small group.

Build Background

Poet Po Chü-i (772–846) devoted his life to uniting literature with social protest. Born to a poor family in China's Henan province, Po began writing poems at the age of five. As an adult, he worked as a government official and became highly critical of the corrupt, decadent lifestyle of China's upper class. In 814, he was exiled for slandering members of the court. Po also became an outspoken critic of the courtly poetry that dominated Chinese literature at the time. For Po, the elegant nature poetry of the court only demonstrated that literature had become divorced from its moral and social functions. "The work of literature," he wrote, "must truthfully reflect the life of the people." To this end, Po wrote satirical and allegorical poems based on the forms of traditional folk ballads. In these poems, he criticized the greed of public officials and portrayed the hardships of China's oppressed peasant class.

THE *Red* COCKATOO

Po Chü-i
Translated by Arthur Waley

Birds of Asia. John Gould. Coloured lithograph. Christie's Images.

Sent as a present from Annam—
A red cockatoo.
Colored like the peach-tree blossom,
Speaking with the speech of men.
And they did to it what is always done
To the learned and eloquent.
They took a cage with stout bars
And shut it up inside.

Quickwrite

Po Chü-i wrote poems that were allegories of the problems he saw in courtly society. What problem is he responding to in this poem? How does he use the red cockatoo to address it? Do similar problems exist in contemporary society? Write a paragraph addressing these questions.

Wrap-Up: Comparing Literature

Across Time and Place

- *Horses* by Pablo Neruda

- *The Panther* by Rainer Maria Rilke

- *The Iguana from Out of Africa* by Isak Dinesen

- *The Red Cockatoo* by Po Chü-i

COMPARE THE [Big Idea] Nature and the Imagination

Visual Display The literary works by Neruda, Rilke, Dinesen, and Po Chü-i demonstrate the influence of setting on our lives. Using works of art from the authors' cultures (contemporary Latin America, early-twentieth-century Europe, late colonial Africa, and Tang dynasty China), create a collage that illustrates the relationship between the natural world and human society that these works suggest. Share your display with your classmates.

Black panther. Francois Pompon. Bronze. Private collection.

COMPARE Portrayals of Animals

Group Activity The authors here use animals for a variety of purposes. In a small group, discuss the following questions. Cite evidence from the texts to support your points.

1. In these literary works, animals function as rounded characters, objects of another character's reflections, and symbols. Which of these categories best applies to the animal(s) in each of the works? Explain.

2. Where is the speaker or the narrator located in relation to the animal(s) in each of the works? Does he or she take part in the action described?

3. Which portrayals of animals most resemble one another in these works? Explain.

COMPARE Styles

Writing Four distinct styles differentiate these works: "Horses" is written in free verse, "The Panther" is written in four quatrains of iambic pentameter, "The Iguana" is prose nonfiction, and "The Red Cockatoo" is written in the simple style of a folk ballad. Consider the elements that contribute to each author's style, such as diction and figurative language. Then write a brief essay in which you compare two of the authors' styles, reflecting on how each style reinforces a specific theme.

Literature Online

Selection Resources For Selection Quizzes, eFlashcards, and Reading-Writing Connection activities, go to glencoe.com and enter QuickPass code GLW6053u6.

Before You Read

Fable

Meet **Octavio Paz**
(1914–1998)

Opposites, conflicts, contraries: these ideas and images, which so often trouble readers, were the building blocks of Octavio Paz's work. In apparent contradictions, such as Paz's favorite image of "burnt water," the poet saw a kind of transcendent union, or what he called "a higher synthesis." This sense of opposites is present in the following lines from one of Paz's most well-known poems, "Between What I See and What I Say . . .":

> "*poetry*
> *comes and goes*
> *between what is*
> *and what is not.*
> *It weaves*
> *and unweaves reflections.*"
>
> —Octavio Paz

Politics Meets Poetry Born in 1914 in Mexico City, Paz was immediately influenced by politics. His father had been active in the revolution of 1911, and Paz's family had to flee briefly to Los Angeles, California. Home again in Mexico City, Paz composed poetry and short stories at an early age; his first volume of poetry was published when he was nineteen. He attended law school for a brief period and maintained a lifelong interest in politics. He supported the leftists in the Spanish Civil War in their fight against the Fascists, and when he returned home to Mexico, he brought the cause with him.

At the same time that he wrote volumes of prose and poetry, he worked as a Mexican diplomat in Europe, India, the United States, and Japan, and spoke out about causes around the world. In fact, his diplomatic career ended when he protested the Mexican government's crackdown on student demonstrators in Mexico City.

Turning to the Maya Paz's concern with politics was not limited to contemporary issues or conflicts. Deeply influenced by a journey he took as a young man to study the Mayan ruins of the Yucatán, Paz became concerned with the indigenous cultures of Mexico and the period of the Spanish Conquest, a time that stood out for him as a fundamental moment in Mexico's history. Some readers interpret "Fable" as an expression of that fateful moment when the conquistadors displaced the great civilization of the Maya. Others see one or more of Paz's three great subjects in the poem: time, history, and the political reality in which we all live.

During his lifetime, Paz was a leading figure in the careers of other authors, whom he nurtured and showcased in his many literary journals and reviews. Influential and respected for decades, Paz received many honors, including the Nobel Prize in Literature in 1990.

 Literature Online

Author Search For more about Octavio Paz, go to glencoe.com and enter QuickPass code GLW6053u6.

Literature and Reading Preview

Connect to the Poem

Have you ever had a dream in which impossibly strange things happened, things that could never happen in your real life? Write a journal entry that describes this dream and its significance.

Build Background

As a young writer, Paz was deeply attracted to a new movement in literature and the visual arts called Surrealism. This movement, which developed in Europe in the 1920s, sought to reveal the unconscious mind in dreamlike images. It relied on fantastic images and combined things in irrational ways. For example, a tree growing out of a hand is surreal. That is, it could happen only in a dream or a dreamlike vision, or it is an image created by the subconscious mind.

Set Purposes for Reading

Big Idea Nature and the Imagination

As you read the poem, ask yourself, How does the speaker transform images from nature into something different?

Literary Element Style

Style is the author's choice and arrangement of words and sentences in a literary work. Style can reveal an author's purpose in writing and his or her attitude toward a subject or audience. As you read "Fable," ask yourself, How does the poet's style reveal information about the poem's central message?

Reading Strategy Interpret Imagery

When you **interpret imagery**, you come up with associations, suggestions, and meanings for the sensory details in a literary work. You might also decide how a particular image affects you as a reader.

....

Tip: Record Reactions Because Surrealist imagery is irrational, a good starting point for interpreting it is by deciding how it makes you feel. As you read "Fable," ask yourself, Does each image strike you as positive, negative, or neutral? Record your reactions in a chart like this one.

Positive	Negative	Neutral
youth of water	broken mirrors	fire and air

Learning Objectives

For pages 1220–1223

In studying this text, you will focus on the following objectives:

Literary Study: Analyzing style.

Reading: Interpreting imagery.

Writing: Writing an essay.

Imaginary Flowers, 1944. Juan O'Gorman. Christies, London.

FABLE

Octavio Paz

Translated by Eliot Weinberger

El pollito (The Chick), 1945.
Frida Kahlo. Oil on masonite,
28 x 20 cm. Fundacion
Dolores Olmedo, Mexico City.

Ages of fire and of air
Youth of water
From green to yellow
           From yellow to red
From dream to watching
           From desire to act
5   It was only one step and you took it so lightly
Insects were living jewels
The heat rested by the side of the pond
Rain was a willow with unpinned hair
A tree grew in the palm of your hand
10 And that tree laughed, sang, prophesied
Its divinations[1] filled the air with wings
There were simple miracles called birds
Everything was for everyone
             Everyone was everything
There was only one huge word with no back to it
15 A word like a sun
One day it broke into tiny pieces
They were the words of the language we now speak
Pieces that will never come together
Broken mirrors where the world sees itself shattered

---

1. *Divinations* are prophecies or premonitions of future events that are
   arrived at by supernatural means.

Style *What does the repetition of the words* from *and to* in these lines
suggest? Explain.

Interpret Imagery *What kind of change do the broken mirrors
suggest? Explain.*

After You Read

Respond and Think Critically

Respond and Interpret

1. Which line or lines do you find most difficult to understand in this poem? Explain.

2. (a)Which lines in the poem are about beginnings? (b)What is the speaker's attitude toward these beginnings?

3. (a)How does line 5 signal that a change is taking place? (b)Up to this point, what is the speaker's attitude toward the change?

4. (a)Which line suggests harmony between all people and all things? (b)To what single idea, image, or concept is this harmony related?

5. (a)To what does the speaker compare the word? (b)What does the comparison suggest?

Analyze and Evaluate

6. What kind of event does this poem describe? Cite evidence from the poem to support your answer.

7. This fable has no talking animals nor a stated lesson (both common features of fables). Why do you think the poet called the poem "Fable"?

Connect

8. **Big Idea** **Nature and the Imagination** How does the poem personify nature?

9. **Connect to the Author** Paz was interested in his country's history. How might this poem be read as a fable about the Spanish conquest of the native peoples of the Yucatán?

Literary Element Style

Although Paz avoids traditional rhyme and meter in "Fable," he nevertheless uses poetic devices.

1. Do you think the free verse form of the poem is effective? Explain.

2. (a)Identify examples of repetition and parallelism in the poem. (b)What is their effect?

Reading Strategy Interpret Imagery

Examine the chart you created on page 1221 of positive, negative, and neutral reactions to the imagery in the poem. Use this information to interpret the poem.

1. Explain how the imagery changes throughout the poem from positive to neutral to negative.

2. Look back at the color imagery in lines 3–4. What kind of shift might it suggest?

LOG ON ▶ **Literature** Online

Selection Resources For Selection Quizzes, eFlashcards, and Reading-Writing Connection activities, go to glencoe.com and enter QuickPass code GLW6053u6.

Academic Vocabulary

*Paz's poem describes a **transformation**: the world goes from having only one "word" to having many languages and realities.*

Transformation is an academic word. In an everyday setting, a person who dramatically altered his or her appearance might be said to have gone through a physical **transformation**. To further explore the meaning of this word, answer the following question. What is a story you have read in which a person undergoes a dramatic inner **transformation**?

For more on academic vocabulary, see pages 36–37 and R83–R85.

Writing

Write an Essay Scholar Jason Wilson suggests that the lack of punctuation in "Fable" supports Paz's portrayal of paradise as a place where "everybody belong[s] to the world and . . . all flows." Do you agree with this interpretation? Write an expository essay presenting your opinion, citing quotations from the poem to support it.

Before You Read

When Greek Meets Greek

Meet **Samuel Selvon**
(1923–1994)

Born in Trinidad to an Indian father and an Indian-Scottish mother, Samuel Selvon experienced life under colonialism firsthand. He served as a radio operator for the British Royal Naval Reserve during World War II and moved to London after the war. Within a few years, he was writing full-time. Using his own experiences and observations, he exposed racial prejudices in England and Trinidad. Known for his use of Trinidadian dialect, vibrant descriptions, and informal tone, Selvon makes serious issues accessible.

Island Setting Selvon published his first novel, *A Brighter Sun*, in 1952. The story focuses on a young East Indian couple who struggle to survive World War II and search to find their place in Trinidad's racially segregated colonial society. Several other works, including *I Hear Thunder* and *An Island Is a World*, are also set in Trinidad and focus on the world Selvon and so many West Indians tried to escape—only to find they weren't accepted in Britain either. Selvon regarded *An Island Is a World* as his favorite and most personal work.

London Setting After living in London for six years and witnessing the prejudice and poverty immigrants faced, Selvon published *The Lonely Londoners*. The novel deals with racial misconceptions, including the belief in white supremacy and blacks' inability to succeed. Like *A Brighter Sun*, *The Lonely Londoners* was critically acclaimed. Reviewer Whitney Balliett called *The Lonely Londoners* "a nearly perfect work of its kind . . . This is the blessedly balanced realism that skirts completely the depressing passion of the naturalist novelist—the romance of total misery."

Market Scene. Jean-Pierre (1914-1979). Private collection.

> "If I have anything significant to say on an issue it is to be found inside my novels and short stories."
>
> —Samuel Selvon

Selvon found both humor and sympathy for his fellow man. Unlike some authors, he was more concerned with "the translation of emotions, feelings, and situations," rather than creating an "epic or saga," claiming "there is more than enough history and drama here for others to do more comprehensive and detailed studies." He published ten novels, two collections of short stories, nearly twenty radio plays, and numerous articles for the BBC and weekly and monthly newspapers including *London Magazine*, *New Statesman*, *Nation*, and *The Sunday Times*. His work greatly contributed to the growth of West Indian fiction, and critics claim that even if he had only written *A Brighter Sun* and *The Lonely Londoners*, he would still be considered an important and extremely influential author.

LOG ON ▶ **Literature** Online

Author Search For more about Samuel Selvon, go to glencoe.com and enter QuickPass code GLW6053u6.

Literature and Reading Preview

Connect to the Story

If you moved to another country, would you seek other Americans or try to meet others? Discuss this in a small group.

Build Background

After World War II many people from the West Indies, Africa, and Asia moved to Britain in search of a better life. By the mid-1950s, more than 25,000 West Indians were arriving in Britain every year. They often settled and formed communities in particular neighborhoods, and their increasing numbers aroused hostility from some British people. Parliament's efforts to control immigration had little effect.

Set Purposes for Reading

Big Idea The Legacy of Colonialism

As you read, ask yourself, How does Selvon use humor to expose the racial tensions between the British and the West Indians?

Literary Element Dialect

Dialect is the version of a language spoken by members of a regional or social group. Dialects may differ from the standard form of a language in vocabulary, pronunciation, or grammatical form. Much of "When Greek Meets Greek" is written in a Caribbean-English dialect. As you read, ask yourself, How does Selvon use dialect to make his story more realistic?

Reading Strategy Make Inferences About Characters

When you **make inferences about characters,** you draw conclusions about them based on their traits, beliefs, actions, and motivations. Making inferences helps you look more deeply at the characters and leads you toward the story's theme. Look for clues about the characters in descriptions, dialogue, events, and relationships. As you read, ask yourself, What can I infer about the characters from Selvon's use of dialogue and details?

....

Tip: Take Notes Use a chart like the one below to track details and dialogue that reveal information about each character. Then use that information to make an inference about the characters.

Character	Details	Dialogue
Ram	"most of the time his eyes colliding up with <u>No Colors, Please,</u> or <u>Sorry, No Kolors.</u>"	

Learning Objectives

For pages 1224–1229

In studying this text, you will focus on the following objectives:

Literary Study: Analyzing dialect.

Reading: Making inferences about characters.

Writing: Writing a story.

Vocabulary

collide (kə līd′) *v.* to run into accidentally; to come together with direct impact; p. 1226 *Not paying attention to where she was going, the woman collided with me and nearly knocked me over.*

menace (men′is) *n.* a person or thing that is a threat or danger; p. 1228 *That aggressive dog is a menace to the neighborhood.*

perusal (pə rōō′zəl) *n.* the act of reading in detail or examining carefully; examination p. 1228 *After my lawyer's perusal of the lease, I signed it and wrote the landlord a check.*

....

Tip: Analogies Analogies are comparisons based on relationships between words and ideas. In the analogy *menace : threat :: animosity : hostility,* both pairs of words are synonyms.

Alegría-Alegría! Antonio Seguí (Argentina, b. 1934). Oil on canvas, 65.4 x 81.3 cm. Private collection.

When Greek Meets Greek

Samuel Selvon

One morning Ramkilawansingh (after this, we calling this man Ram) was making a study of the notice boards along Westbourne Grove what does advertise rooms to let. Every now and then he writing down an address or a telephone number, though most of the time his eyes **colliding** up with *No Colors, Please,* or *Sorry, No Kolors.*

"Red, white and blue, all out but you," Ram was humming a little ditty what children say when they playing whoop. Just as he get down by Bradley's Corner he met Fraser.

"You look like a man who looking for a place to live," Fraser say.

"You look like a man who could tell me the right place to go," Ram say.

Dialect *What do you notice about the way the characters talk?*

"You try down by Ladbroke Grove?" Fraser ask.

"I don't want to go down in that criminal area," Ram say, "at least, not until they find the man who kill Kelso."

"Then you will never live in the Grove," Fraser say.

"You are a contact man,"[1] Ram say, "which part you think I could get a room, boy?"

Fraser scratch his head. "I know of a landlord up the road who vow that he ain't ever taking anybody who come from the West Indies. But he don't mind taking Indians. He wouldn't know the difference when he see you is a Indian . . . them English people so foolish they believe every Indian come from India."

"You think I stand a chance?" Ram ask.

"Sure, you stand a chance. All you have to do is put on a turban."

"I never wear a turban in my life; I am a born Trinidadian, a real Creole. All the same, you best hads give me the address, I will pass around there later."

So Fraser give him the address, and Ram went on reading a few more boards, but he got discourage after a while and went to see the landlord.

The first thing the landlord ask him was: "What part of the world do you come from?"

"I am an Untouchable[2] from the heart of India," Ram say. "I am looking for a single room. I dwelt on the banks of the Ganges. Not too expensive."

"But you are not in your national garments," the landlord say.

"When you are in Rome," Ram say, making it sound like an original statement, "do as the Romans do."

Visual Vocabulary
The *Ganges* (gan′jēz) is India's major river. It is sacred to followers of the Hindu religion.

While the landlord sizing up Ram, an Indian tenant come up the steps to go inside. This fellar was Chandrilaboodoo (after this, we calling this man Chan) and he had a big beard with a hair net over it, and he was wearing a turban. When he see Ram, he clasp his hands with the palms touching across his chest by way of greeting.

The old Ram catch on quick and do the same thing.

"*Acha, Hindustani,*"[3] Chan say.

"*Acha, pilau, papadom, chickenvindaloo,*"[4] Ram say desperately, hoping for the best.

Chan nod his head, say good morning to the landlord and went inside.

"That was a narrow shave," Ram thought, "I have to watch out for that man."

"That was Mr. Chan," the landlord say, "he is the only other Indian tenant I have at the moment. I have a single room for two pounds. Are you a student?"

"Who is not a student?" Ram say, getting into the mood of the thing. "Man is for ever studying ways and means until he passes into the hands of Allah."

Well, to cut a long story short, Ram get a room on the first floor, right next door to Chan, and he move in that same evening.

---

1. A *contact man* is someone who has useful information that is not common knowledge.
2. An *Untouchable* is a member of the lowest caste (hereditary social group) in India.

Make Inferences About Characters *What can you infer about Ram's attitude toward his heritage from this description?*

The Legacy of Colonialism *Why is this the first thing the landlord asks? What can you infer about the relationship between West Indians and the British?*

---

3. *Acha Hindustani* (ä′chä hin′dōō stä′nē) is a traditional greeting.
4. *Pilau* (pi′lou), *papadom* (pä′pä dom), and *chicken vindaloo* (vin′də lōō) are three traditional Indian foods.

But as the days going by, Ram had to live like cat-and-mouse with Chan. Every time he see Chan, he have to hide in case this man start up this Hindustani talk again, or start to ask him questions about Mother India. In fact, it begin to get on Ram nerves, and he decide that he had to do something.

"This house too small for the two of we," Ram say to himself, "one will have to go."

So Ram went down in the basement to see the landlord.

"I have the powers of the Occult,"[5] Ram say, "and I have come to warn you of this man Chan. He is not a good tenant. He keeps the bathroom dirty, he does not tidy up his room at all, and he is always chanting and saying his prayers loudly and disturbing the other tenants."

"I have had no complaints," the landlord say.

"But I am living next door to him," Ram say, "and if I concentrate my powers I can see through the wall. That man is a **menace**, and the best thing you can do is to give him notice. You have a good house here and it would be a pity to let one man spoil it for the other tenants."

"I will have a word with him about it," the landlord say.

Well, the next evening Ram was in his room when he hear a knock at the door. He run in the corner quick and stand upon his head, and say, "Come in."

The landlord come in.

"I am just practicing my yogurt," Ram say.

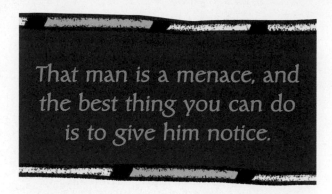

That man is a menace, and the best thing you can do is to give him notice.

"I have had a word with Mr. Chan," the landlord say, "and I have reason to suspect that you have deceived me. You are not from India, you are from the West Indies."

Ram turn right-side up. "I am a citizen of the world," he say.

"You are flying false colors,"[6] the landlord say. "You do not burn incense like Mr. Chan, you do not dress like Mr. Chan, and you do not talk like Mr. Chan."

"Give me a break, old man," Ram say, falling back on the good old West Indian dialect.

"It is too late. You have already started to make trouble. You must go."

Well, the very next week find Ram out scouting again, giving the boards a **perusal**, and who he should chance to meet but Fraser.

He start to tell Fraser how life hard, how he had to keep dodging from this Chan fellar all the time, and it was pure torture.

"Listen," Fraser say, "you don't mean a big fellar with a beard, and he always wearing a turban?"

"That sound like him," Ram say. "You know him?"

"Know him!" Fraser say. "Man, that is a fellar from Jamaica who I send to that house to get a room!" ◡

---

5. *Powers of the Occult* are supernatural abilities to reveal secret knowledge.

The Legacy of Colonialism *Ram's mispronunciation of yoga is an example of humor. Why do you think Selvon uses humor here?*

Vocabulary

menace (men′is) *n.* a person or thing that is a threat or danger

---

6. *Flying false colors* means engaging in deception.

Make Inferences About Characters *What conclusions can you draw about Chan? Why do you think he acts and dresses like he's from India?*

Vocabulary

perusal (pə roo′zəl) *n.* the act of reading in detail or examining carefully; examination

After You Read

Respond and Think Critically

Respond and Interpret

1. Were you surprised by the ending? Explain.

2. (a)Why has Ram had difficulty finding a place to live? (b)What advice does Fraser offer Ram? (c)How does Ram respond to this advice?

3. (a)What happens when Ram meets Chan? (b)Why does Ram feel threatened by Chan?

4. (a)Why does Ram try to get Chan kicked out of the house? (b)Does Ram's plan work? Explain.

Analyze and Evaluate

5. Did you find Ram to be a sympathetic character? Explain.

6. **Situational irony** exists when the outcome of a situation is unexpected. Identify an example of situational irony and explain why it is ironic.

7. **Tone** is the attitude a narrator takes toward the reader, a subject, or a character. How would you describe the narrator's tone?

Connect

8. **Big Idea** **The Legacy of Colonialism** How does the story's theme relate to the legacy of colonialism?

9. **Connect to Today** What kinds of prejudice and ignorance exist in the United States today? How do people use humor to deal with them?

Literary Element Dialect

Dialects often differ in pronunciation, vocabulary, and grammar. The dialect in the story often uses nonstandard progressive forms—"We calling this man Ram" instead of "We will call this man Ram."

1. Identify an example of dialect in the story that differs in grammar from Standard English.

2. (a)Why might Selvon have chosen to use dialect in this story? (b)What is its effect?

Reading Strategy Make Inferences About Characters

When you **make inferences about characters,** you use clues from the text and your own experiences to determine what the author implies about characters. Consult your chart from page 1225.

1. Why do you think Ram feels compelled to play a "cat-and-mouse" game with Chan?

2. Based on the landlord's actions and dialogue, what can you infer about his beliefs?

Vocabulary Practice

Practice with Analogies Choose the word that best completes the relationship expressed in the original pair of words.

1. collide : crash :: sprint :
  a. trickle   **c.** stroll
  b. dash   **d.** pause

2. menace : threat :: conclusion :
  a. finale   **c.** start
  b. assumption   **d.** draft

3. perusal : examination :: difference :
  a. distinction   **c.** variety
  b. similarity   **d.** occasion

Writing

Write a Story Think of a familiar setting in which a case of mistaken identity could occur. Write a story about this situation, choosing whether to make your readers aware of the mistake early or reveal it in a surprise ending. Use **dialect** in either your dialogue or narration. If your character is hiding his or her identity, show his or her motivations.

Before You Read

The Night Face Up

Meet Julio Cortázar
(1914–1984)

Julio Cortázar (hōō´lē ō kôr tä´sär) was born in Brussels, Belgium, when his Argentine parents were there on a business trip shortly before World War I. They waited out the war in Europe, returning to Argentina in 1918. A short time later, his father abandoned the family, and Cortázar and his younger sister were raised by their mother, aunt, and grandmother in a suburb of Buenos Aires. He later described his early years as a time of great sadness that he escaped by reading fantasy and poetry.

A Varied Career Early in Cortázar's career, he taught school and—although he had to leave college for financial reasons—continued his studies on his own, reading foreign literature and writing poetry. In 1944 and 1945, he taught French literature at the university level but resigned in 1946 after being briefly imprisoned for political demonstrations against Juan Perón, the president of Argentina. Cortázar left the country in 1951 to move to Paris, France, where he resided the rest of his life. He worked as a United Nations translator a few months a year and wrote and traveled the rest of the year.

Cortázar published his first collection of short stories the year he left Argentina. He soon won acclaim as a novelist as well as a short story writer. Cortázar loved using experimental literary techniques. His narratives often shift back

> *"No one can retell the plot of a Cortázar story; each one consists of determined words in a determined order. If we try to summarize them, we realize that something precious has been lost."*
>
> —Jorge Luis Borges

and forth through time and space, challenging the laws of nature and logic.

The Anti-Novel *Hopscotch*, which Cortázar published in 1963, is one of the most important modern Latin American novels. Described as an open-ended anti-novel, it is divided into three sections: 36 chapters set in Paris, twenty chapters set in Buenos Aires, and 99 short pieces called "Expendable Chapters." The reader is invited to rearrange the material in an activity resembling hopscotch, jumping back and forth through the volume. This experimental technique is not exclusive to *Hopscotch*; Cortázar played with time sequences and the perception of reality in many other works.

A True Humanitarian Cortázar was passionately involved in the political issues of his day. Throughout the 1970s and up to the time of his death, he was committed to the cause of justice in Latin America. He campaigned tirelessly in favor of human rights and against the atrocities of the military regime in Argentina. He died in Paris of leukemia.

LOG ON **Literature** Online

Author Search For more about Julio Cortázar, go to glencoe.com and enter QuickPass code GLW6053u6.

Literature and Reading Preview

Connect to the Story

Have you ever had a dream that felt like it was really happening? Write a journal entry in which you describe the details of the dream.

Build Background

In "The Night Face Up," Cortázar explores a frightening aspect of the Aztec culture. When the Aztecs dominated what is now central and southern Mexico, their religion included the ritual sacrifice of humans. In one form of sacrifice, priests cut out the beating hearts of victims on temple altars. Most of the sacrificial victims were prisoners of war or from groups the Aztecs had conquered.

Set Purposes for Reading

Big Idea Magic Realism

As you read, ask yourself, When do realistic elements mesh with fantastic, unbelievable events?

Literary Element Point of View

Point of view is the perspective from which a story is told. In **third-person limited** point of view, the narrator reveals the thoughts of one character. In **third-person omniscient** point of view, the narrator knows what all characters are thinking. As you read the story, ask yourself, How does the author use point of view to offer different perspectives?

Reading Strategy Identify Sequence

When you **identify sequence,** you look for clues that will help you determine the order in which events occur. Such clues might include sequence words such as *first, next,* and *then.* They might also include references to the time of day, indications of light and darkness, and terms that refer to time, such as *now, three days,* and *twenty minutes later.* As you read, ask yourself, Where does each event fit in the timeline of events?

Tip: Use Matrices Use a matrix like this one to keep track of the sequence of events. In your matrix, compare both settings.

	Reality?	Dream?
First	Accident	Battle
Second	Taken by ambulance to hospital	Taken by Aztec captors to temple

Learning Objectives

For pages 1230–1240

In studying this text, you will focus on the following objectives:

Literary Study: Analyzing point of view.

Reading: Identifying sequence.

Vocabulary

solace (sol′is) *n.* a source of relief; mental or spiritual comfort; p. 1233 *For solace in his time of grief, he turned to the music they had both enjoyed.*

lucid (lo͞o′sid) *adj.* having full use of one's mental abilities; clearheaded; p. 1233 *His senile father often has lucid intervals.*

supplication (sup′lə ka′shən) *n.* a humble entreaty; a prayer of request; p. 1235 *The governor pardoned the prisoner after hearing the inmate's mother give her supplication.*

beneficent (bə nef′ə sənt) *adj.* doing or producing good; p. 1235 *The beneficent work of Mother Teresa improved the lives of many people.*

Tip: Antonyms Words that have opposite meanings are antonyms. For example, *lucid* and *confused* are antonyms. Like synonyms, antonyms are always the same part of speech.

The Night Face Up

Fire and Destruction, 1985. Juri Palm. Oil on canvas.
Art Museum of Estonia, Tallinn.

Julio Cortázar
Translated by Paul Blackburn

H alfway down the long hotel vestibule,[1] he thought that probably he
was going to be late, and hurried on
into the street to get out his motorcycle
from the corner where the next-door super-
intendent let him keep it. On the jewelry
store at the corner he read that it was ten
to nine; he had time to spare. The sun filtered through the tall downtown buildings,
and he—because for himself, for just going
along thinking, he did not have a name—
he swung onto the machine, savoring the
idea of the ride. The motor whirred

between his legs, and a cool wind whipped
his pants legs.

He let the ministries[2] zip past (the pink,
the white), and a series of stores on the
main street, their windows flashing. Now
he was beginning the most pleasant part of
the run, the real ride: a long street bordered
with trees, very little traffic, with spacious
villas[3] whose gardens rambled all the way
down to the sidewalks, which were barely
indicated by low hedges. A bit inattentive
perhaps, but tooling along on the right side
of the street, he allowed himself to be carried away by the freshness, by the weightless contraction of this hardly begun day.

---

1. A *vestibule* (ves′ tə būl′) is a small passage or hall
   between the outer door and the interior of a building.

Point of View *What point of view does Cortázar use here?*

2. *Ministries,* here, are government office buildings.
3. *Villas* are urban homes with a yard and garden space.

This involuntary relaxation, possibly, kept him from preventing the accident. When he saw that the woman standing on the corner had rushed into the crosswalk while he still had the green light, it was already somewhat too late for a simple solution. He braked hard with foot and hand, wrenching himself to the left; he heard the woman scream, and at the collision his vision went. It was like falling asleep all at once.

He came to abruptly. Four or five young men were getting him out from under the cycle. He felt the taste of salt and blood, one knee hurt, and when they hoisted him up he yelped, he couldn't bear the pressure on his right arm. Voices which did not seem to belong to the faces hanging above him encouraged him cheerfully with jokes and assurances. His single **solace** was to hear someone else confirm that the lights indeed had been in his favor. He asked about the woman, trying to keep down the nausea which was edging up into his throat. While they carried him face up to a nearby pharmacy, he learned that the cause of the accident had gotten only a few scrapes on the legs. "Nah, you barely got her at all, but when ya hit, the impact made the machine jump and flop on its side . . ." Opinions, recollections of other smashups, take it easy, work him in shoulders first, there, that's fine, and someone in a dustcoat giving him a swallow of something soothing in the shadowy interior of the small local pharmacy.

Within five minutes the police ambulance arrived, and they lifted him onto a cushioned stretcher. It was a relief for him to be able to lie out flat. Completely **lucid,** but realizing that he was suffering the effects of a terrible shock, he gave his information to the officer riding in the ambulance with him. The arm almost didn't hurt; blood dripped down from a cut over the eyebrow all over his face. He licked his lips once or twice to drink it. He felt pretty good, it had been an accident, tough luck; stay quiet a few weeks, nothing worse. The guard said that the motorcycle didn't seem badly racked up. "Why should it," he replied. "It all landed on top of me." They both laughed, and when they got to the hospital, the guard shook his hand and wished him luck. Now the nausea was coming back little by little; meanwhile they were pushing him on a wheeled stretcher toward a pavilion[4] further back, rolling along under trees full of birds, he shut his eyes and wished he were asleep or chloroformed.[5] But they kept him for a good while in a room with that hospital smell, filling out a form, getting his clothes off, and dressing him in a stiff, grayish smock. They moved his arm carefully, it didn't hurt him. The nurses were constantly making wisecracks, and if it hadn't been for the stomach contractions he would have felt fine, almost happy.

They got him over to X ray, and twenty minutes later, with the still-damp negative lying on his chest like a black tombstone, they pushed him into surgery. Someone tall and thin in white came over and began to look at the X rays. A woman's hands were arranging his head, he felt that they were moving him from one stretcher to another.

---

4. A *pavilion*, here, is an extension of a main building, such as a hospital.
5. *Chloroformed* (klôr′ə fôrmd) means "rendered unconscious through the use of chloroform, a sweet-smelling, colorless liquid."

Point of View *In this passage, how does the narrator reveal the character's thoughts?*

Identify Sequence *List the events that have occurred in the story so far in chronological order.*

Vocabulary

solace (sol′is) *n.* a source of relief; mental or spiritual comfort

lucid (lōō′sid) *adj.* having full use of one's mental abilities; clearheaded

The man in white came over to him again, smiling, something gleamed in his right hand. He patted his cheek and made a sign to someone stationed behind.

It was unusual as a dream because it was full of smells, and he never dreamed smells. First a marshy smell, there to the left of the trail the swamps began already, the quaking bogs from which no one ever returned. But the reek lifted, and instead there came a dark, fresh composite fragrance, like the night under which he moved, in flight from the Aztecs. And it was all so natural, he had to run from the Aztecs who had set out on their manhunt, and his sole chance was to find a place to hide in the deepest part of the forest, taking care not to lose the narrow trail which only they, the Motecas,[6] knew.

What tormented him the most was the odor, as though, notwithstanding the absolute acceptance of the dream, there was something which resisted that which was not habitual, which until that point had not participated in the game. "It smells of war," he thought, his hand going instinctively to the stone knife which was tucked at an angle into his girdle of woven wool. An unexpected sound made him crouch suddenly stock-still and shaking. To be afraid was nothing strange, there was plenty of fear in his dreams. He waited, covered by the branches of a shrub and the starless night. Far off, probably on the other side of the big lake, they'd be lighting the bivouac[7] fires; that part of the sky had a reddish glare. The sound was not repeated. It had been like a broken limb. Maybe an animal that, like himself, was escaping from the smell of war. He stood erect slowly, sniffing the air. Not a sound could be heard, but the fear was still following, as was the smell, that cloying[8] incense of the war of the blossom. He had to press forward, to stay out of the bogs and get to the heart of the forest. Groping uncertainly through the dark, stooping every other moment to touch the packed earth of the trail, he took a few steps. He would have liked to have broken into a run, but the gurgling fens lapped on either side of him. On the path and in darkness, he took his bearings. Then he caught a horrible blast of that foul smell he was most afraid of, and leaped forward desperately.

"You're going to fall off the bed," said the patient next to him. "Stop bouncing around, old buddy."

He opened his eyes and it was afternoon, the sun already low in the oversized windows of the long ward. While trying to smile at his neighbor, he detached himself almost physically from the final scene of the nightmare. His arm, in a plaster cast, hung suspended from an apparatus with weights and pulleys. He felt thirsty, as though he'd been running for miles, but they didn't want to give him much water, barely enough to moisten his lips and make a mouthful. The fever was winning slowly and he would have been able to sleep again, but he was enjoying the pleasure of keeping awake, eyes half-closed, listening to the other patients' conversation, answering a question from time to time. He saw a little white pushcart come up beside the bed, a blond nurse rubbed the front of his thigh with alcohol and stuck him with a fat needle connected to a tube which ran up to a bottle filled with a milky, opalescent[9] liquid.

---

6. *Motecas* are another Native American culture of central Mexico.

7. A *bivouac* (biv′ ⊙⊙ ak′) is a temporary military encampment.

Identify Sequence *What shift in time and place seems to have taken place in this section?*

8. *Cloying* means "causing weariness by too much of anything pleasant."

9. *Opalescent* means "having a play of colors like that of an opal, a translucent gemstone."

Jungle with Branches (Selva con rama). María Eugenia Terrazas. Watercolor, 70 x 60 cm. Private collection.

A young intern arrived with some metal and leather apparatus which he adjusted to fit onto the good arm to check something or other. Night fell, and the fever went along dragging him down softly to a state in which things seemed embossed as through opera glasses,[10] they were real and soft and, at the same time, vaguely distasteful; like sitting in a boring movie and thinking that, well, still, it'd be worse out in the street, and staying.

A cup of a marvelous golden broth came, smelling of leeks, celery and parsley. A small hunk of bread, more precious than a whole banquet, found itself crumbling little by little. His arm hardly hurt him at all, and only in the eyebrow where they'd taken stitches a quick, hot pain sizzled occasionally. When the big windows across the way turned to smudges of dark blue, he thought it would not be difficult for him to sleep. Still on his back so a little uncomfortable, running his tongue out over his hot, too-dry lips, he tasted the broth still, and with a sigh of bliss, he let himself drift off.

10. *Opera glasses* are small, lightweight binoculars.

First there was a confusion, as of one drawing all his sensations, for that moment blunted or muddled, into himself. He realized that he was running in pitch darkness, although, above, the sky crisscrossed with treetops was less black than the rest. "The trail," he thought, "I've gotten off the trail." His feet sank into a bed of leaves and mud, and then he couldn't take a step that the branches of shrubs did not whiplash against his ribs and legs. Out of breath, knowing despite the darkness and silence that he was surrounded, he crouched down to listen. Maybe the trail was very near, with the first daylight he would be able to see it again. Nothing now could help him to find it. The hand that had unconsciously gripped the haft[11] of the dagger climbed like a fen scorpion up to his neck where the protecting amulet[12] hung. Barely moving his lips, he mumbled the **supplication** of the corn which brings about the **beneficent** moons, and the prayer to Her Very Highness,[13] to the distributor of all Motecan possessions. At the same time he felt his ankles sinking deeper into the mud, and the waiting in the darkness of the obscure grove of live oak grew intolerable to him. The war of the blossom had started at the beginning of the moon and had been going on for three days and three nights now. If he managed to hide in the depths of the forest, getting off the trail further up

11. The *haft* of a dagger is its handle.
12. An *amulet* is an object worn to bring good fortune or to protect against disease or misfortune.
13. *Her Very Highness* is an apparent reference to a Motecan deity.

Point of View *How does the point of view contribute to the confused and fearful mood of the story?*

Vocabulary

supplication (sup´lə kā´shən) *n.* a humble entreaty; a prayer of request

beneficent (bə nef´ə sənt) *adj.* doing or producing good

Detail from Aztec Codex, early 16th century AD. Manuscript on paper, 39 x 40 cm. Bibliotheque de l'Assemblee Nationale, Paris.

past the marsh country, perhaps the warriors wouldn't follow his track. He thought of the many prisoners they'd already taken. But the number didn't count, only the consecrated period. The hunt would continue until the priests gave the sign to return. Everything had its number and its limit, and it was within the sacred period, and he on the other side from the hunters.

He heard the cries and leaped up, knife in hand. As if the sky were aflame on the horizon, he saw torches moving among the branches, very near him. The smell of war was unbearable, and when the first enemy jumped him, leaped at his throat, he felt an almost-pleasure in sinking the stone blade flat to the haft into his chest. The lights were already around him, the happy cries. He managed to cut the air once or twice, then a rope snared him from behind.

Identify Sequence *How does the image of the knife help connect the events? What other elements link the sequence of events?*

"It's the fever," the man in the next bed said. "The same thing happened to me when they operated on my duodenum.[14] Take some water, you'll see, you'll sleep all right."

Laid next to the night from which he came back, the tepid[15] shadow of the ward seemed delicious to him. A violet lamp kept watch high on the far wall like a guardian eye. You could hear coughing, deep breathing, once in a while a conversation in whispers. Everything was pleasant and secure, without the chase, no . . . But he didn't want to go on thinking about the nightmare. There were lots of things to amuse himself with. He began to look at the cast on his arm, and the pulleys that held it so comfortably in the air. They'd left a bottle of mineral water on the night table beside him. He put the neck of the bottle to his mouth and drank it like a precious liqueur. He could now make out the different shapes in the ward, the thirty beds, the closets with glass doors. He guessed that his fever was down, his face felt cool. The cut over the eyebrow barely hurt at all, like a recollection. He saw himself leaving the hotel again, wheeling out the cycle. Who'd have thought that it would end like this? He tried to fix the moment of the accident exactly, and it got him very angry to notice that there was a void there, an emptiness he could not manage to fill. Between the impact and the moment that they picked him up off the pavement, the passing out or what went on, there was nothing he could see. And at the same time he had the feeling that this void, this nothingness, had lasted an eternity. No, not even time, more as if, in this void, he had passed across something, or

14. The *duodenum* (dōō´ə dē´nəm) is part of the small intestine.
15. *Tepid* means "moderately or slightly warm."

had run back immense distances. The shock, the brutal dashing against the pavement. Anyway, he had felt an immense relief in coming out of the black pit while the people were lifting him off the ground. With pain in the broken arm, blood from the split eyebrow, contusion on the knee; with all that, a relief in returning to daylight, to the day, and to feel sustained and attended. That was weird. Someday he'd ask the doctor at the office about that. Now sleep began to take over again, to pull him slowly down. The pillow was so soft, and the coolness of the mineral water in his fevered throat. The violet light of the lamp up there was beginning to get dimmer and dimmer.

As he was sleeping on his back, the position in which he came to did not surprise him, but on the other hand the damp smell, the smell of oozing rock, blocked his throat and forced him to understand. Open the eyes and look in all directions, hopeless. He was surrounded by an absolute darkness. Tried to get up and felt ropes pinning his wrists and ankles. He was staked to the ground on a floor of dank, icy stone slabs. The cold bit into his naked back, his legs. Dully, he tried to touch the amulet with his chin and found they had stripped him of it. Now he was lost, no prayer could save him from the final . . . From afar off, as though filtering through the rock of the dungeon, he heard the great kettledrums of the feast. They had carried him to the temple, he was in the underground cells of Teocalli itself, awaiting his turn.

He heard a yell, a hoarse yell that rocked off the walls. Another yell, ending in a moan. It was he

Visual Vocabulary
Teocalli was the chief temple in Tenochtitlán, the Aztec capital.

who was screaming in the darkness, he was screaming because he was alive, his whole body with that cry fended off what was coming, the inevitable end. He thought of his friends filling up the other dungeons, and of those already walking up the stairs of the sacrifice. He uttered another choked cry, he could barely open his mouth, his jaws were twisted back as if with a rope and a stick, and once in a while they would open slowly with an endless exertion, as if they were made of rubber. The creaking of the wooden latches jolted him like a whip. Rent, writhing, he fought to rid himself of the cords sinking into his flesh. His right arm, the strongest, strained until the pain became unbearable and he had to give up. He watched the double door open, and the smell of the torches reached him before the light did. Barely girdled by the ceremonial loincloths, the priests' acolytes[16] moved in his direction, looking at him with contempt. Lights reflected off the sweaty torsos and off the black hair dressed with feathers. The cords went slack, and in their place the grappling of hot hands, hard as bronze; he felt himself lifted, still face up, and jerked along by the four acolytes who carried him down the passageway. The torchbearers went ahead, indistinctly lighting up the corridor with its dripping walls and a ceiling so low that the acolytes had to duck their heads. Now they were taking

---

16. *Acolytes* (ak′ə līts′) are individuals who assist a priest at religious services.

Magic Realism *What details in this passage emphasize the overlap of the two worlds the narrator experiences?*

him out, taking him out, it was the end. Face up, under a mile of living rock which, for a succession of moments, was lit up by a glimmer of torchlight. When the stars came out up there instead of the roof and the great terraced steps rose before him, on fire with cries and dances, it would be the end. The passage was never going to end, but now it was beginning to end, he would see suddenly the open sky full of stars, but not yet, they trundled him along endlessly in the reddish shadow, hauling him roughly along and he did not want that, but how to stop it if they had torn off the amulet, his real heart, the life-center.

In a single jump he came out into the hospital night, to the high, gentle, bare ceiling, to the soft shadow wrapping him round. He thought he must have cried out, but his neighbors were peacefully snoring. The water in the bottle on the night table was somewhat bubbly, a translucent shape against the dark azure shadow of the windows. He panted, looking for some relief for his lungs, oblivion for those images still glued to his eyelids. Each time he shut his eyes he saw them take shape instantly, and he sat up, completely wrung out, but savoring at the same time the surety that now he was awake, that the night nurse would answer if he rang, that soon it would be daybreak, with the good, deep sleep he usually had at that hour, no images, no nothing . . . It was difficult to keep his eyes open, the drowsiness was more powerful than he. He made one last effort, he sketched a gesture toward the bottle of water with his good hand and did not manage to reach it, his fingers closed again on a black emptiness, and the passageway went on endlessly, rock after rock, with momentary ruddy flares, and face up he choked out a dull moan because the roof was about to end, it rose, was opening like a mouth of shadow, and the acolytes straightened up,

and from on high a waning[17] moon fell on a face whose eyes wanted not to see it, were closing and opening desperately, trying to pass to the other side, to find again the bare, protecting ceiling of the ward. And every time they opened, it was night and the moon, while they climbed the great terraced steps, his head hanging down backward now, and up at the top were the bonfires, red columns of perfumed smoke, and suddenly he saw the red stone, shiny with the blood dripping off it, and the spinning arcs cut by the feet of the victim whom they pulled off to throw him rolling down the north steps. With a last hope he shut his lids tightly, moaning to wake up. For a second he thought he had gotten there, because once more he was immobile in the bed, except that his head was hanging down off it, swinging. But he smelled death, and when he opened his eyes he saw the blood-soaked figure of the executioner-priest coming toward him with the stone knife in his hand. He managed to close his eyelids again, although he knew now he was not going to wake up, that he was awake, that the marvelous dream had been the other, absurd as all dreams are—a dream in which he was going through the strange avenues of an astonishing city, with green and red lights that burned without fire or smoke, on an enormous metal insect that whirred away between his legs. In the infinite lie of the dream, they had also picked him up off the ground, someone had approached him also with a knife in his hand, approached him who was lying face up, face up with his eyes closed between the bonfires on the steps. ❧

---

17. *Waning* means "diminishing in size, strength, or brightness."

Point of View *What does this passage reveal about the narrator's perception of the events at the beginning of the story?*

After You Read

Respond and Think Critically

Respond and Interpret

1. Which images in this story linger in your mind? Explain.

2. (a)Describe the motorcycle accident. (b)Which symptoms resulting from the accident may affect the rider's perception of reality?

3. (a)What happens to the rider after the accident? (b)What is the rider's impression of the hospital? Use details from the story to support your response.

4. (a)What are the two settings of the story? (b)What parallels exist between these two settings?

5. (a)Why is the Moteca man running through the forest? (b)Until the last paragraph, what does the narrator lead us to believe about the scenes involving the Moteca man?

Analyze and Evaluate

6. (a)What plot twist occurs at the end of the story? (b)Do you think the ending can be explained logically? Why or why not?

7. (a)**Irony** is a contrast between what is expected or believed to be true and what actually occurs or exists. Describe the most important irony of the story. (b)Were you satisfied with the ending? Explain.

8. (a)How would you explain the title of the story? (b)Do you think the title is effective? Explain.

Connect

9. **Big Idea** **Magic Realism** (a)What details does Cortázar use to convey the sensation of waking from a dream? (b)How do these details contribute to the sense that perception and reality are often two different things?

10. **Connect to Today** What kinds of books, movies, or television shows do you know that blur the line between fantasy and reality?

Primary Visual Artifact

Aztec Customs

Aztec religion emphasized the god of the sun, who died each evening and was born anew the next morning. At dawn, he began his struggle, driving away the stars and the moon with a shaft of light. The Aztecs believed the sun god needed human nourishment to maintain his strength for this important task. The Aztecs viewed war, therefore, as a religious endeavor that provided victims for sacrifice.

The knife shown here, with a mosaic handle and a stone blade, was made for use in those ceremonial sacrifices.

Group Activity Discuss the following questions with your classmates. Refer to the art and cite evidence from "The Night Face Up" to support your answers.

1. Explain the connection between the art and various descriptions in "The Night Face Up."

2. Notice the intricate detail of the mosaic on the handle of the knife. What might this level of artistry suggest about Aztec culture?

From which point of view is "The Night Face Up" told?

A. First person.

B. Second person.

C. Third-person omniscient.

D. Third-person limited.

Review: Style

As you learned on page 1221, **style** is the expressive qualities that distinguish an author's work. Elements of style include sentence length and variety, diction, organization, and use of figurative language, dialect, or rhythmic devices.

Partner Activity With a classmate, discuss how Cortázar plays with sentence structure conventions. Consider the fact that poets and fiction writers frequently violate the rules of sentence structure to create specific literary effects. In "The Night Face Up," Cortázar uses both sentence fragments and comma splices (clauses joined by commas, often in combination with fragments). Work with your partner to complete a chart like the one below. Then consider this question: How does Cortázar's use of sentence fragments and comma splices convey a sense of confusion and rapid action?

Sentence Type	Examples
Fragment	The shock, the brutal dashing against the pavement.
Comma splice	They had carried him to the temple, he was in the underground cells of Teocalli itself, awaiting his turn.

In "The Night Face Up," the author jumps back and forth in time. Yet within each time frame, the sequence of events is clear. If you **identify sequence** as you read, you can keep the events organized in your mind. Consult your chart from page 1231 and then answer the following questions.

1. (a)Which event in the city sequence corresponds to the narrator's realization that he's "gotten off the trail" in the Aztec sequence? (b)Which city event matches the narrator's being captured and taken to the temple?

2. How does the movement from one sequence to another add to the mystery of the story?

Practice with Antonyms Antonyms are words that have opposite meanings. With a partner, brainstorm three antonyms for each boldfaced vocabulary word below. Then discuss your choices with your classmates. Be prepared to explain why you chose your words.

solace   lucid   supplication   beneficent

EXAMPLE: zealous
Antonyms: indifferent, apathetic, uninterested
Sample explanation: A zealous person would show great enthusiasm, but an apathetic person would not.

In "The Night Face Up," Cortázar creates an **analogous** relationship between the sensations experienced when dreaming and those experienced when awake.

Analogous is an academic word. For example, one might say that the relationship between the body and the brain is analogous to the relationship between a car and driver. To further explore this word, complete the following sentence.

The feeling Cortázar's protagonist has when riding his motorcycle is analogous to the feeling I have when _____.

For more on academic vocabulary, see pages 36–37 and R83–R85.

Respond Through Writing

Review

Learning Objectives

In this assignment, you will focus on the following objectives:

Writing: Writing a review.

Grammar: Understanding how to use transitional phrases.

Convince an Audience When deciding whether to read a book, people often consult reviews. Write a 500-word critical review of Cortázar's story. Include your opinions about both the effectiveness of the point of view and the sequence of events. Your audience is a group of peers who like literature.

Understand the Task In a **review,** a writer presents his or her well-supported opinions about a work of literature or nonfiction.

Prewrite Read book and film reviews for ideas on how to express your own opinions and format your review. Pay attention to the language these critics use, and think about how to use similar words and phrases.

Next, reread the story and determine your controlling idea. To help you plan your review, fill out a pro-and-con chart like the one below.

"The Night Face Up"	
Pros	Cons
Alternating between two stories keeps the reader interested	The story is frustratingly inconclusive

Draft As you draft your review, make sure you back up your points with evidence from the story. Make sure you cite all quotations correctly. Try to anticipate disagreements your audience might have and address these in your paper. You can make your analysis more convincing by using rhetorical strategies that professional reviewers use, such as

- **Glittering generalities**—emotionally charged words, such as *heroism* or *love,* that are associated with deeply valued concepts

- **Rhetorical questions**—questions posed to prove a point rather than to get an answer

Revise After you have drafted your review, check it for logic. Do your examples support your opinion? Exchange with a partner and review each other's work. Incorporate your partner's comments in your draft.

Edit and Proofread Proofread your paper, correcting any errors in spelling, grammar, and punctuation. Use the word-count feature on your computer to make sure your review is 500 words. Review the Grammar Tip in the side column to help you with transitional phrases.

▶ **Grammar Tip**

Transitional Phrases

Transitional phrases clarify the relationship between two ideas. They often include transitional words such as *however, next,* and *therefore.* Transitional words express relationships based on sequence (*when, before, soon, first, second*), space (*beyond, farther, in front of*), and importance (*in fact, especially, above all*). Look at the following sentence:

"The Night Face Up" is an entertaining read. More important, it is a story that challenges readers' beliefs about reality.

More important is a transitional phrase. It makes the relationship between the two sentences clearer.

Multiple-meaning Words

A **multiple-meaning word** is a word that has several related definitions listed in a single dictionary entry.

Test-Taking Tip

To determine the intended use of a multiple-meaning word, look for context clues.

Vocabulary Workshop

Multiple-Meaning Words

Literature Connection In the following sentence from Julio Cortázar's "The Night Face Up," *right* means "situated to the side of the body that is east when one is facing north."

> "*A bit inattentive perhaps, but tooling along on the right side of the street, he allowed himself to be carried away by the freshness, by the weightless contraction of this hardly begun day.*"

Right can also mean "correct," "appropriate," and "having its axis perpendicular to the base." *Right* is a **multiple-meaning word,** or a word that has several related definitions listed within a single dictionary entry. Multiple-meaning words are different from homographs, which are words that are spelled alike but different in meaning or derivation or pronunciation. Homographs have separate dictionary entries that are usually designated by superscript numerals.

Here are two groups of sentences in which multiple-meaning words are used differently according to context.

The test results came back <u>positive</u>.
She always had a <u>positive</u> attitude.
I'm <u>positive</u> I saw him in the store.

He is the <u>object</u> of my affection.
That is an oddly shaped <u>object</u>.
The <u>object</u> of this class is to learn about world literature.

Practice Read each of the sentences below. On a separate piece of paper, write the letter of the best definition for the underlined word. Use a dictionary if you need help.

1. I put little <u>stock</u> in his word because he's been wrong before.

   a. a portion of financial capital in a corporation

   b. confidence or faith

   c. the descendants of one individual

2. Studying for the test will be the <u>key</u> to success.

   a. an instrument by which the bolt of a lock is turned

   b. something that provides a solution

   c. one of the levers of a keyboard instrument

Before You Read

The Handsomest Drowned Man in the World

Meet **Gabriel García Márquez**

(born 1928)

Born to a poor family in Aracataca, Colombia, Gabriel García Márquez spent the first eight years of his life living with his grandparents "in an enormous house, full of ghosts." Later, García Márquez would model many of his characters on his grandparents "because I knew how they talked, how they behaved." His grandmother shared local legends with the boy, while his grandfather, a retired colonel, told him stories of the fierce civil war that Colombians call the War of a Thousand Days (1899–1902).

The Fantastic Epicenter García Márquez's childhood home, near the Caribbean coast of Colombia, is the epicenter of his fictional universe. Many of his early novels and stories are set in Macondo, a fictional version of his hometown. His native region provided him with material for his writing and a way of viewing the world that included a taste for the fantastic.

García Márquez was a gifted student and serious about his studies—until he enrolled in college to study law, as his parents wished. García Márquez wanted to be a writer instead. He focused on writing nonfiction during his college years but also began to write fiction. He became a journalist and soon abandoned the study of law to devote himself to writing full time.

One Hundred Years of Solitude The novel that catapulted García Márquez to fame was published in 1967. *One Hundred Years of Solitude* placed characters in Macondo, where anything, it seemed, was possible. International acclaim followed; so, too, did a new respect for the style of writing known as magic realism. Although García Márquez was not the first author to

"*In the Caribbean, we are capable of believing anything.*"

—Gabriel García Márquez

employ this style, he was the author, more than any other, who validated the style and made it an international sensation.

García Márquez has continued to write rich literary works, including *The Autumn of the Patriarch*, a political work about a dictator; and *Love in the Time of Cholera*, a fictional remembrance of love. In 1982, García Márquez received the Nobel Prize in Literature. Since then, he has continued to publish novels, short stories, and some works of nonfiction.

LOG ON **Literature** Online

Author Search For more about Gabriel García Márquez, go to glencoe.com and enter QuickPass code GLW6053u6.

Literature and Reading Preview

Connect to the Story

What motivates people to make a new start? Discuss this question with a partner. Consider both positive and negative events that could serve as motivation.

Build Background

García Márquez has explained that he knows the art of "saying incredible things with a completely undisturbed face." Authors who use magic realism often blur the lines between reality and fantasy by treating extraordinary events as typical occurrences. The settings in these stories are usually realistic locations, but the characters and events take on a bizarre quality. Some critics have explained this dual nature as an outgrowth of colonialism. Countries composed of multiple cultures, such as Latin American countries, must make sense of more than one reality at a time. Magic realism allows space for the reality of the conquerors and the conquered, as well as the everyday and the fantastic.

Set Purposes for Reading

Big Idea **Magic Realism**

As you read the story, ask yourself, What is real and what is fantastic?

Literary Element **Hyperbole**

Hyperbole is a figure of speech that uses exaggeration to express strong emotion, make a point, or evoke humor. As you read the story, ask yourself, Why does the author use hyperbole?

Reading Strategy Question

When you **question,** you participate actively in your reading by investigating the story. As you read, ask yourself questions such as: What is going on here? What does this mean? or Why did the character say, do, or think that? Then find details in the story that might answer your questions.

....

Tip: Take Notes Use a chart to keep track of your questions and answers.

My Question	My Answer
How big could he possibly be? How small are the villagers' homes?	He could be bloated by having been in the sea; the villagers might live in tiny homes. The villagers may be small people; the man might be a giant only by comparison.

Learning Objectives

For pages 1243–1251

In studying this text, you will focus on the following objectives:

Literary Study: Analyzing hyperbole.

Reading: Questioning.

Writing: Applying hyperbole.

Vocabulary

haggard (hag′ərd) *adj.* worn or wasted, as from hunger; p. 1246 *Leah was haggard after having spent two days lost on Mount Spenser.*

frivolity (fri vol′ə tē) *n.* silliness; p. 1247 *The adults, who had work to do, could not take part in their children's frivolity.*

improvise (im′prə vīz′) *v.* to create to meet an unexpected need; p. 1247 *Chuck did not have packing tape, so he had to improvise in order to seal the package.*

....

Tip: Context Clues When you come across an unfamiliar term, pay close attention to its context. For example, you can figure out that *improvise* means "to create to meet an unexpected need" in the sentence above because the clue "did not have packing tape" lets you know Chuck has to seal the package in another way.

The Handsomest Drowned Man in the World

Gabriel García Márquez

Translated by Gregory Rabassa and J. S. Bernstein

Regreso del lunauta (Return of the Astronaut), 1969. Raquel Forner. Oil on canvas, 160 x 120 cm. National Air and Space Museum, Smithsonian Institution, Washington, DC.

The first children who saw the dark and slinky bulge approaching through the sea let themselves think it was an enemy ship. Then they saw it had no flags or masts and they thought it was a whale. But when it was washed up on the beach, they removed the clumps of seaweed, the jellyfish tentacles, and the remains of fish and flotsam,[1] and only then did they see that it was a drowned man.

They had been playing with him all afternoon, burying him in the sand and digging him up again, when someone chanced to see them and spread the alarm in the village. The men who carried him to the nearest house noticed that he weighed more than any dead man they had ever known, almost as much as a horse, and they said to each other that maybe he'd been floating too long and the water had got into his bones. When they laid him on the floor they said he'd been taller than all other men because there was barely enough room for him in the house,

but they thought that maybe the ability to keep on growing after death was part of the nature of certain drowned men. He had the smell of the sea about him and only his shape gave one to suppose that it was the corpse of a human being, because the skin was covered with a crust of mud and scales.

They did not even have to clean off his face to know that the dead man was a stranger. The village was made up of only twenty-odd wooden houses that had stone courtyards with no flowers and which were spread about on the end of a desertlike cape. There was so little land that mothers always went about with the fear that the wind would carry off their children and the few dead that the years had caused among them had to be thrown off the cliffs. But the sea was calm and bountiful and all the men fit into seven boats. So when they found the drowned man they simply had to look at one another to see that they were all there.

---

1. *Flotsam* is the floating wreckage of a ship or its cargo.

Magic Realism *What does this detail tell you about the villagers and their beliefs?*

That night they did not go out to work at sea. While the men went to find out if anyone was missing in neighboring villages, the women stayed behind to care for the drowned man. They took the mud off with grass swabs, they removed the underwater stones entangled in his hair, and they scraped the crust off with tools used for scaling fish. As they were doing that they noticed that the vegetation on him came from faraway oceans and deep water and that his clothes were in tatters, as if he had sailed through labyrinths of coral.[2] They noticed too that he bore his death with pride, for he did not have the lonely look of other drowned men who came out of the sea or that **haggard,** needy look of men who drowned in rivers. But only when they finished cleaning him off did they become aware of the kind of man he was and it left them breathless. Not only was he the tallest, strongest, most virile, and best built man they had ever seen, but even though they were looking at him there was no room for him in their imagination.

They could not find a bed in the village large enough to lay him on nor was there a table solid enough to use for his wake. The tallest men's holiday pants would not fit him, not the fattest ones' Sunday shirts, nor the shoes of the one with the biggest feet. Fascinated by his huge size and his beauty, the women then decided to make him some pants from a large piece of sail and a shirt from some bridal brabant[3] linen so that he could continue through his death with dignity. As they sewed, sitting

in a circle and gazing at the corpse between stitches, it seemed to them that the wind had never been so steady nor the sea so restless as on that night and they supposed that the change had something to do with the dead man. They thought that if that magnificent man had lived in the village, his house would have had the widest doors, the highest ceiling, and the strongest floor, his bedstead would have been made from a midship frame held together by iron bolts, and his wife would have been the happiest woman. They thought that he would have had so much authority that he could have drawn fish out of the sea simply by calling their names and that he would have put so much work into his land that springs would have burst forth from among the rocks so that he would have been able to plant flowers on the cliffs. They secretly compared him to their own men, thinking that for all their lives theirs were incapable of doing what he could do in one night, and they ended up dismissing them deep in their hearts as the weakest, meanest, and most useless creatures on earth. They were wandering through that maze of fantasy when the oldest woman, who as the oldest had looked upon the drowned man with more compassion than passion, sighed:

"He has the face of someone called Esteban."[4]

It was true. Most of them had only to take another look at him to see that he could not have any other name. The more stubborn among them, who were the youngest, still lived for a few hours with the illusion that when they put his clothes on and he lay among the flowers in patent

---

2. *Coral,* formed from the skeletal deposits of marine animals, can form reefs that extend for hundreds of miles.
3. *Brabant* is a region in western Europe known for its textiles. Here, the word is used as an adjective.

Hyperbole *Why is this an example of hyperbole?*

Question *What question might you ask about these details that describe the man's burial clothing?*

---

4. *Esteban* is the Spanish equivalent of Steven, which derives from the Greek for "crown."

Vocabulary

haggard (hag′ərd) *adj.* worn or wasted, as from hunger

leather shoes his name might be Lautaro.[5] But it was a vain illusion. There had not been enough canvas, the poorly cut and worse sewn pants were too tight, and the hidden strength of his heart popped the buttons on his shirt. After midnight the whistling of the wind died down and the sea fell into its Wednesday drowsiness. The silence put an end to any last doubts: he was Esteban. The women who had dressed him, who had combed his hair, had cut his nails and shaved him were unable to hold back a shudder of pity when they had to resign themselves to his being dragged along the ground. It was then that they understood how unhappy he must have been with that huge body since it bothered him even after death. They could see him in life, condemned to going through doors sideways, cracking his head on crossbeams, remaining on his feet during visits, not knowing what to do with his soft, pink, sea lion hands while the lady of the house looked for her most resistant chair and begged him, frightened to death, sit here, Esteban, please, and he, leaning against the wall, smiling, don't bother, ma'am, I'm fine where I am, his heels raw and his back roasted from having done the same thing so many times whenever he paid a visit, don't bother, ma'am, I'm fine where I am, just to avoid the embarrassment of breaking up the chair, and never knowing perhaps that the ones who said don't go, Esteban, at least wait till the coffee's ready, were the ones who later on would whisper the big boob finally left, how nice, the handsome fool has gone. That was what the women were thinking beside the body a little before dawn. Later, when they covered his face with a handkerchief so that the light would not bother him, he looked so forever dead, so defenseless, so much like their men that

the first furrows of tears opened in their hearts. It was one of the younger ones who began the weeping. The others, coming to, went from sighs to wails, and the more they sobbed the more they felt like weeping, because the drowned man was becoming all the more Esteban for them, and so they wept so much, for he was the most destitute, most peaceful, and most obliging man on earth, poor Esteban. So when the men returned with the news that the drowned man was not from the neighboring villages either, the women felt an opening of jubilation in the midst of their tears.

"Praise the Lord," they sighed, "he's ours!"

The men thought the fuss was only womanish **frivolity.** Fatigued because of the difficult nighttime inquiries, all they wanted was to get rid of the bother of the newcomer once and for all before the sun grew strong on that arid, windless day. They **improvised** a litter with the remains of foremasts and gaffs,[6] tying it together with rigging so that it would bear the weight of the body until they reached the cliffs. They wanted to tie the anchor from a cargo ship to him so that he would sink easily into the deepest waves, where fish are blind and divers' die of nostalgia,[7] and bad currents would not bring him back to shore, as had happened with other bodies. But the more they hurried, the more the women thought of ways to waste time. They walked about like startled hens,

---

5. *Lautaro* is an allusion to a native South American hero who fought against the Spanish.

6. *Gaffs* are hooks for lifting heavy fish.
7. Here, *nostalgia* refers to the effects that changes in atmospheric pressure may have on deep-sea divers; symptoms include depression and disorientation.

Question *What question might you ask about this detail, or any of the other details in this paragraph?*

Vocabulary

frivolity (fri vol′ə tē) *n.* silliness
improvise (im′prə vīz′) *v.* to create to meet an unexpected need

pecking with the sea charms on their breasts, some interfering on one side to put a scapular of the good wind on the drowned man, some on the other side to put a wrist compass on him, and after a great deal of *get away from there, woman, stay out of the way, look, you almost made me fall on top of the dead man*, the men began to feel mistrust in their livers and started grumbling about why so many main-altar decorations for a stranger, because no matter how many nails and holy-water jars he had on him, the sharks would chew him all the same, but the women kept piling on their junk relics, running back and forth, stumbling, while they released in sighs what they did not in tears, so that the men finally exploded with *since when has there ever been such a fuss over a drifting corpse, a drowned nobody, a piece of cold Wednesday meat*. One of the women, mortified by so much lack of care, then removed the handkerchief from the dead man's face and the men were left breathless too.

He was Esteban. It was not necessary to repeat it for them to recognize him. If they had been told Sir Walter Raleigh,[8] even they might have been impressed with his gringo accent, the macaw on his shoulder, his cannibal-killing blunderbuss,[9] but there could be only one Esteban in the world and there he was, stretched out like a sperm whale, shoeless, wearing the pants of an undersized child, and with those stony nails

that had to be cut with a knife. They only had to take the handkerchief off his face to see that he was ashamed, that it was not his fault that he was so big or so heavy or so handsome, and if he had known that this was going to happen, he would have looked for a more discreet place to drown in, seriously, I even would have tied the anchor off a galleon[10] around my neck and staggered off a cliff like someone who doesn't like things in order not to be upsetting people now with this Wednesday dead body, as you people say, in order not to be bothering anyone with this filthy piece of cold meat that doesn't have anything to do with me. There was so much truth in his manner that even the most mistrustful men, the ones who felt the bitterness of endless nights at sea fearing that their women would tire of dreaming about them and begin to dream of drowned men, even they and others who were harder still shuddered in the marrow of their bones at Esteban's sincerity.

That was how they came to hold the most splendid funeral they could conceive of for an abandoned drowned man. Some women who had gone to get flowers in the neighboring villages returned with other women who could not believe what they had been told, and those women went back for more flowers when they saw the dead man, and they brought more and more until there were so many flowers and so many people that it was hard to walk about. At the final moment it pained them to return him to the waters as an orphan and they chose a father and mother from among the best people, and aunts and uncles and cousins, so that through him all the inhabitants of the village became kinsmen.

---

8. *Sir Walter Raleigh* was a British sailor who explored South America in the sixteenth century.
9. A *blunderbuss* is a short rifle with a broad muzzle.

---

10. A *galleon* is a large sailing ship.

Magic Realism *What do these lines show about the men's changing view of the drowned man?*

Some sailors who heard the weeping from a distance went off course and people heard of one who had himself tied to the mainmast, remembering ancient fables about sirens.[11] While they fought for the privilege of carrying him on their shoulders along the steep escarpment[12] by the cliffs, men and women became aware for the first time of the desolation of their streets, the dryness of their courtyards, the narrowness of their dreams as they faced the splendor and beauty of their drowned man. They let him go without an anchor so that he could come back if he wished and whenever he wished, and they all held their breath for the fraction of centuries the body took to fall into the abyss. They did not need to look at one another to realize that they were no longer all present, that they would never be. But they also knew that everything would be different from then on, that their houses would have wider doors, higher ceilings, and stronger floors so that Esteban's memory could go everywhere without bumping into beams and so that no one in the future would dare whisper the big boob finally died, too bad, the handsome fool has finally died, because they were going to paint their house fronts gay colors to make Esteban's memory eternal and they were going to

Women in Procession from For Complete Social Security of All Mexicans. David Alfaro Siqueiros. Mural. Hospital de la Raza, Mexico City © Estate of David Alfraro Siqueiros. ©ARS, NY.

View the Art Siqueiros's murals are known for their force and energy. How do these women remind you of the women in the story?

break their backs digging for springs among the stones and planting flowers on the cliffs so that in future years at dawn the passengers on great liners would awaken, suffocated by the smell of gardens on the high seas, and the captain would have to come down from the bridge in his dress uniform, with his astrolabe,[13] his pole star, and his row of war medals and, pointing to the promontory of roses on the horizon, he would say in fourteen languages, look there, where the wind is so peaceful now that it's gone to sleep beneath the beds, over there, where the sun's so bright that the sunflowers don't know which way to turn, yes, over there, that's Esteban's village. ✨

11. *[Tied . . . sirens]* refers to the *Odyssey,* in which Odysseus has himself tied to the mast so he can navigate safely past the Sirens (mythical enchantresses whose singing charmed sailors into jumping overboard).
12. An *escarpment* is a steep slope.

Hyperbole *Explain the hyperbole in this passage.*

13. An *astrolabe* (as´trə lāb´) is a device used to observe and calculate the position of celestial bodies.

Question *Ask a question about how the drowned man has affected the villagers.*

After You Read

Respond and Think Critically

Respond and Interpret

1. Did you find this story to be humorous or serious? Explain.

2. (a)What do the children think when they first notice Esteban's body? (b)How is the children's reaction to Esteban different from the adults' reaction?

3. (a)What is unusual about Esteban's appearance? (b)Is the description of Esteban's face and body realistic or fantastic? Explain.

4. (a)What do the women think about as they sew Esteban's clothes? (b)What do the women's thoughts suggest about them?

5. (a)What changes do the villagers want to make in honor of Esteban? (b)Have the villagers actually changed as a result of their experience with Esteban? Explain.

Analyze and Evaluate

6. An **allusion** is a reference to a well-known person, place, or event from history, literature, or religion. Identify an allusion in the story and explain what it suggests to you.

7. Why might García Márquez have decided not to name the village and its inhabitants?

Connect

8. **Big Idea** **Magic Realism** Does the author's creation of fantasy tend to mock the characters and their world or to celebrate them? Explain.

9. **Connect to Today** If this story were to occur in a village or a city in the United States, how might people react?

Literary Element **Hyperbole**

ACT Skills Practice

1. Which of the following is *not* an example of hyperbole?

   A. Some sailors who heard the weeping of the villagers went off course.

   B. The women thought Esteban could have called fish out of the sea.

   C. The strength of Esteban's heart popped the buttons on his shirt.

   D. The women thought that the drowned man's name must be Esteban.

2. Which of the following passages offers the strongest example of hyperbole?

   F. "he would have put so much work into his land that springs would have burst forth from among the rocks"

   G. "They only had to take the handkerchief off his face to see that he was ashamed"

   H. "The tallest men's holiday pants would not fit him"

   J. "mothers always went about with the fear that the wind would carry off their children"

Review: Theme

As you learned on page 927, a **theme** is the central message about life in a literary work. Most works, like this one, have an implied theme.

Partner Activity Meet with a classmate to discuss the theme that is implied in the description of the changes that will be made in the village. Then discuss the theme that is implied when the villagers return the drowned man's body to the sea.

Review the chart of questions you made on page 1244. As you answer the questions below, consider what you know and what you do not from the details presented in the story.

1. What is the best answer you can give to the question of who the drowned man is? Cite details from the story to support your answer.

2. List two other questions that the story does not answer fully.

Vocabulary Practice

Practice with Context Clues Look back at the story to find context clues for the boldfaced vocabulary words below. Record your findings in a graphic organizer like the one shown.

haggard   frivolity   improvise

EXAMPLE:

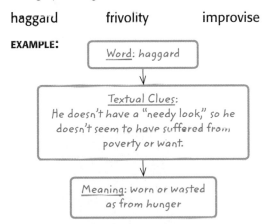

Word: haggard

Textual Clues:
He doesn't have a "needy look," so he doesn't seem to have suffered from poverty or want.

Meaning: worn or wasted as from hunger

Academic Vocabulary

In Marquez's story, the villagers **channel** *their need for a hero into the elaborate myth they create about the drowned man.*

Channel is an academic word. The word is also used in many everyday contexts. For example, an executive might **channel** information to employees by having those directly below her pass information on to those below them. To explore the meaning of the word further, answer the following question: When might you send a complaint through official **channels**?

For more on academic vocabulary, see pages 36–37 and R83–R85.

Write with Style

 Apply Hyperbole

Assignment The use of hyperbole in "The Handsomest Drowned Man in the World" contributes to the story's magic realism. In nonfiction writing, such as a persuasive essay, exaggeration can also be employed in a variety of ways. Write a persuasive essay of 750 words in which you use hyperbole to stimulate interest or appeal to emotion.

Get Ideas Generate ideas for your persuasive essay from multiple sources, including brainstorming, journals, and print and electronic media. To help determine whether there is sufficient difference of opinion on a potential issue to make it an interesting subject, use a chart to diagram arguments for and against the issue. You should be able to support each side with two or three reasons. If the balance leans too heavily one way or the other, it's likely that most people have already made up their minds on the issue.

Give It Structure One of the most effective ways to organize a persuasive essay is by order of importance, presenting your arguments and evidence from the most important to the least important. As you draft your essay, decide how to introduce hyperbole effectively. One way is to make an exaggerated statement in your introduction to add a touch of humor or to hook your audience. Another is to use hyperbole as an emotional appeal to motivate your audience to take action on an issue.

Look at Language Be judicious in your use of hyperbole: a little exaggeration goes a long way. Unwisely used, hyperbole can weaken the effect of the arguments and the evidence that are the foundation of your case.

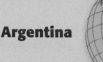

Before You Read

Bishop Berkeley or Mariana of the Universe

Meet **Liliana Heker**

(born 1943)

Many of Liliana Heker's (hāk′ ər) protagonists are young women trying to find their place in the world. In the story you are about to read, at least one of the two female main characters seems far too young to argue as intelligently and articulately as she does. This character trait is just one of the ways Heker challenges your perception of reality.

At Home in Argentina Heker grew up in Buenos Aires, Argentina. She began writing professionally at the age of seventeen with the help of Abelardo Castillo, a writer and an editor of a literary magazine. When Heker was 23, she published her first collection of short stories, *Those Who Beheld the Burning Bush*. The book established Heker as one of the most promising Argentinean writers of her generation. Soon afterward, she became chief editor of the literary journal *El escarabajo de oro (The Golden Scarab)*. In 1977, she cofounded *El Ornitorrinco (The Platypus)*, a literary magazine that published the work of local and foreign writers and provided an important leftist forum. Through directorship of these journals, she influenced literary ideas in her country for more than twenty years.

When Argentina fell under a military dictatorship in 1966, Heker decided not to follow other authors into exile. Instead, she remained in her country and continued to write. Over the years, Heker published more short stories, including *The Stolen Party: And Other Stories* and *The Edges of the Real*. Heker also went on to publish novels, the first of which won a major literary prize. More recently, she has published several essays, including the collection *Las hermanas de Shakespeare (Shakespeare's Sisters)*, a study of women authors.

Realism Without Magic In the 1970s, political life in Argentina grew more volatile, a military junta seized power, and the process of national reorganization—popularly known as the Dirty War—began. During these years, as the world gradually came to realize later, people were imprisoned, tortured, and finally "disappeared." Not surprisingly, much of Heker's work from this period took a political turn, and she has continued to write in a political vein since then. Her most well-known novel is *El fin de la historia (The End of History)*, published in 1996. It portrays the cruel realities of 1970s Argentina. Yet it remains a work of fiction, one in which Heker says she "tried to blur the border between documentation and fiction."

In 1980, Heker published a collection of interviews with famous people on the topic of life and death. More than twenty years later, she enlarged and reissued the work. The volume offers countless insights, big and small, including some of Heker's own, such as this one:

"In the end, no artist, and no human being, wants to disappear without leaving footprints."

—Liliana Heker

 Literature Online

Author Search For more about Liliana Heker, go to glencoe.com and enter QuickPass code GLW6053u6.

Literature and Reading Preview

Connect to the Story

What is the loneliest situation you can imagine? Discuss this question in a small group.

Build Background

The title of Heker's story refers to the eighteenth-century philosopher George Berkeley (bär′ klē). He argued that the existence of physical things is dependent on perception. A chair, for example, consists of a group of qualities such as shape, color, and weight. In Berkeley's view, these qualities are ideas. Since ideas must exist in the mind, the chair exists only if it can be perceived. Berkeley realized that his theory could be misinterpreted to support views opposed to common sense. Such misinterpretation is at the heart of Heker's story.

Set Purposes for Reading

Big Idea Magic Realism

In this story, the lines between theory and reality seem to blur. As you read, ask yourself, How does one character manipulate the other's sense of reality?

Literary Element Allusion

An **allusion** is a reference in a work of literature to a character, a place, or a situation from history, literature, music, or art. As you read, ask yourself, Why does the title of this story allude to Bishop Berkeley?

Reading Strategy Analyze Conflict

The basis of a story's plot is conflict—a struggle between opposing forces. An **external conflict** exists when a character struggles against some outside force, such as another character, a force of nature, or society. An **internal conflict** is a struggle within a character. When a character struggles to make a difficult decision, for example, he or she is experiencing internal conflict. Stories often involve more than one kind of conflict. As you read, ask yourself, What kinds of conflicts do the characters experience?

Tip: Sort Information Record and classify the conflicts in a chart like this one.

Internal Conflict	External Conflict
Mariana has conflicting visions of Lucia.	

Learning Objectives

For pages 1252–1260

In studying this text, you will focus on the following objectives:

Literary Study: Analyzing allusion.

Reading: Analyzing conflict.

Listening and Speaking: Participating in a literature group.

Vocabulary

pounce (pouns) v. to swoop down on and quickly seize upon or take advantage of something; p. 1255 *Amit would pounce on any error his opponent made and turn it to his advantage.*

mediocre (mē′ dē ō′ kər) adj. of moderate or low quality; undistinguished; p. 1255 *Although Diego was talented, he viewed his latest work as only mediocre and did not want others to see it.*

resignation (rez′ ig nā′ shən) n. unresisting acceptance; p. 1256 *Some workers responded to the news of the factory closing with anger; others, however, accepted the news with resignation.*

gravely (grāv′ lē) adv. in a serious or dignified manner; p. 1256 *Mr. Watkins spoke gravely as he described the damage done by the storm.*

Bishop Berkeley or Mariana of the Universe

Liliana Heker

Translated by
Alberto Manguel

La nina con mascara de la muerte (Girl with a Death Mask), 1938 Frida Kahlo. Oil on tin, 14.9 x 11 cm. Private collection.

"How much longer till Mom comes home?"

It's the fourth time Mariana has asked that same question. The first time, her sister Lucia answered that she'd be back real soon; the second, how the heck was she to know when Mom would be back; the third time she didn't answer, she just raised her eyebrows and stared at Mariana. That was when Mariana decided that things weren't going all that well and that the best thing to do was not to ask any more questions.

Anyhow, she asked herself, *Why do I want Mom to come back, if I'm here with Lucia . . . ?* She corrected herself: *Why do I want Mom to come back, if I'm here with my big sister?* She blinked, deeply moved by the thought. *Big sisters look after little sisters,* she told herself as if she were reciting a poem. *How lucky to have a big sister.* Lucia, with large guardian-angel wings, hovered for a second over Mariana's head. But in a flash the winged image was replaced by another, one which returned every time their mother left them on their own: Lucia, eyes bulging out of their sockets, hair in a furious tangle, was pointing a gun at her. Sometimes there was no gun. Lucia would **pounce** on her, trying to rip Mariana's eyes out with her nails. Or strangle her. The reason was always the same: Lucia had gone mad.

It is a well-known fact that mad people kill normal people, which meant that if Lucia went mad when they were alone together, she'd kill Mariana. That was obvious. Therefore Mariana decides to abandon her good intentions and asks again, for the fourth time, "How much longer till Mom comes home?"

Lucia stops reading and sighs.

"What I'd like to know," she says (and Mariana thinks, *She said "I'd like to know"; does one say "I would like to know" or "I should like to know"?*) "What I'd like to know is why in God's name do you always need Mom around?"

"No." *Now she'll ask me, "No what?" She always manages to make things difficult.* But Lucia says nothing, and Mariana continues, "I was just curious, that's all."

"At twelve."

"What do you mean, at twelve!" Mariana cries. "But it's only ten to nine now!"

"I mean at twelve, six and six," Lucia says.

Analyze Conflict *What kind of conflict is expressed in the opening paragraphs?*

Magic Realism *How does the author manipulate time or reality in these first three paragraphs?*

Vocabulary

pounce (pouns) *v.* to swoop down on and quickly seize upon or take advantage of something

---

Mariana howls with laughter at the joke; she laughs so hard that for a moment she thinks she'll die laughing. To tell the truth, she can't imagine anyone else on earth could be as funny as her sister. *She's the funniest, nicest person in the world, and she'll never go mad. Why should she go mad, she, who's so absolutely terrific?*

"Lu," she says adoringly, "Let's play something, okay? Let's, okay?"

"I'm reading."

"Reading what?"

"**Mediocre** Man."

"Ah." *I bet now she'll ask me if I know what mediocre man means, and I won't know, and she'll say then, "Why do you say 'Ah,' you idiot?"* Quickly she asks, "Lu, I can't remember, what does Mediocre Man mean?"

"The Mediocre Man is the man who has no ideals in life."

"Ah." This lays her mind at rest, because she certainly has ideals in life. She always imagines herself already grown up, all her problems over, everyone understands her, things turn out fine, and the world is wonderful. That's having ideals in life.

"Lu," she says, "we, I mean, you and I, we're not mediocre, are we?"

"A pest," Lucia says, "That's what you are."

"Lucia, why is it that you're so unpleasant to everyone, eh?"

"Listen, Mariana. Do you mind just letting me read in peace?"

"You're unpleasant to everyone. That's terrible, Lucia. You fight with Mom, you fight with Dad. With *everyone*." Mariana

Vocabulary

mediocre (mē′ dē ō′ kər) *adj.* of moderate or low quality; undistinguished

lets out a deep sigh. "You give your parents nothing but trouble, Lucia."

"Mariana, I wish you'd just drop dead, okay?"

"You're horrible, Lucia, horrible! You don't say to anyone that you wish they would drop dead, not to your worst enemy, and certainly not to your own sister."

"That's it, now start to cry, so that afterwards they will scream at me and say that I torture you."

"Afterwards? When afterwards? Do you know exactly *when* Mom will be back?"

"Just afterwards." Lucia has gone back to reading *Mediocre Man*. "Afterwards is afterwards." She lifts her eyes and frowns as if she were meditating on something very important. "The future, I mean."

"What future? You said Mom would be back very soon."

Lucia shakes her head in **resignation** and goes back to her book.

"Yes, of course, she'll be back very soon."

"No. Yes, of course, no. Is she coming back very soon or isn't she coming back very soon?"

Lucia glares at Mariana; then she seems to remember something and smiles briefly.

"And anyway what does it matter?" She shrugs her shoulders.

"What do you mean, what does it matter? You don't know what you're saying, do you? If someone comes home very soon, it means she comes home very soon, doesn't it?"

"*If* someone comes home, yes."

"What?"

"I just said that *if* someone comes home, then yes. Will you please let me read?"

"You're a cow, that's what you are! What you really want is for Mom never to come home again!"

Lucia closes the book and lays it down on the bed. She sighs.

"It has nothing to do with my wanting it or not," she explains. "What I'm saying is that it simply doesn't matter if Mom is here or there."

"What do you mean, there?"

"Just there; anywhere; it's all the same."

"Why the same?"

Lucia rests her chin on both her hands and stares **gravely** at Mariana.

"Listen, Mariana," she says, "I've got something to tell you. Mom doesn't exist."

Mariana jumps.

"Don't be stupid, okay?" she says, trying to look calm. "You know Mom doesn't like you saying stupid things like that."

"They're not stupid things. Anyway, who cares what Mom says, if Mom doesn't exist?"

"Lu, I'm telling you for the last time: I-don't-like-you-say-ing-stu-pid-things, okay?"

"Look, Mariana," Lucia says in a tired tone of voice. "I'm not making it up; there's a whole theory about it, a book."

"What does it say, the book?"

"What I just said. That nothing really exists. That we imagine the world."

"*What* do we imagine about the world?"

"Everything."

"You just want to frighten me, Lucia. Books don't say things like that. What does it say, eh? For real."

"I've told you a thousand times. The desk, see? There isn't really a desk there, you just imagine there's a desk. Understand? You, now, this very minute, imagine that you're inside a room, sitting

Vocabulary

resignation (rez´ig nā´shən) *n.* unresisting acceptance

Vocabulary

gravely (grāv´lē) *adv.* in a serious or dignified manner

on the bed, talking to me, and you imagine that somewhere else, far away, is Mom. That's why you want Mom to come back. But those places don't really exist, there is no here or far away. It's all inside your head. You are imagining it all."

"And you?"

"I what?"

"There's you, see?" Mariana says with sudden joy. "You can't imagine the desk in the same exact place that I imagine it, can you?"

"You've got it all wrong, Mariana sweetheart. You just don't understand, as usual. It's not that both of us imagine that the desk is in the same place: it's that *you imagine* that both of us imagine that the desk is in the same place."

"No, no, no, no. *You got* it all wrong. Each of us doesn't imagine things on our own, and one can't guess what the other is imagining. You *talk* about what you imagine. I say to you: how many pictures are there in this room? And I say to myself: there are three pictures in this room. And at exactly the same time you tell me that there are three pictures in this room. That means that the three pictures are here, that we see them, not that we imagine them. Because two people can't imagine the same thing at the same time."

"Two can't, that's true."

"What do you mean?"

"I'm saying that *two* people can't."

"I don't understand what you're saying."

"I'm saying that you are also imagining *me*, Mariana."

"You're lying, you're lying! You're the biggest liar in the whole world! I hate you, Lucia. Don't you see? If I'm imagining you, how come you know I'm imagining you?"

Hace mucho tiempo (Having Too Much Time), 1995. Alicia Carletti. Oil on canvas, 100 x 80 cm, Zurbaran Galeria, Buenos Aires, Argentina.

View the Art Like magic realist authors, Alicia Carletti combines the everyday and the bizarre in her art. What character in the story does this girl remind you of? Explain.

"I *don't* know, I don't *anything*. You are just making me up, Mariana. You've made up a person called Lucia, who's your sister, and who knows you've made her up. That's all."

"No, come on, Lu. Say it's not true. What about the book?"

"What book?"

"The book that talks about all this."

"That talks about what?"

"About things not really existing."

"Ah, the book . . . The book is also imagined by you."

"That's a lie, Lucia, a lie! I could never imagine a book like that. I never know

Analyze Conflict *Describe the conflict between Mariana and Lucia.*

Magic Realism *In this passage, how does the author play with the nature of reality?*

about things like that, don't you understand, Lu? I could never imagine something
as complicated as that."

"But my poor Mariana, that book is
nothing compared to the other things
you've imagined. Think of History and the
Law of Gravity and Maths and all the
books ever written in the world and
Aspirins, and the telegraph and planes. Do
you realize what you've done?"

"No, Lucia, no, please. Everyone knows
about those things. Look. If I bring a lot of
people into this room, and I say when I
count up to three, we all point to the radio
at the same time, then you'll see. We'll all
point in the same direction. Let's play at
that, Lu, please, come on; let's play at pointing at things. Please."

"But are you stupid or what? I'm telling
you that *you* are the one who's imagining
all the people in the world."

"I don't believe you. You say that just to
frighten me. I can't imagine all the people
in the world. What about Mom? What
about Dad?"

"Them too."

"Then I'm all alone, Lu!"

"Absolutely. All alone."

"That's a lie, that's a lie! Say that you're
lying! You're just saying that to frighten
me, right? Sure. Because everything's here.
The beds, the desk, the chairs. I can see
them, I can touch them if I want to. Say
yes, Lu. So that everything's like before."

"But why do you want me to say yes, if
anyway it will be *you* imagining that *I* am
saying yes?"

"Always me? So there's no one but *me* in
the world?"

"Right."

"And you?"

"As I said, you're imagining me."

"I don't want to imagine any more, Lu.
I'm afraid. I'm really frightened, Lu. How
much longer till Mom comes home?"

Mariana leans out of the window. Mom,
come back soon, she begs. But she no longer knows to whom she's begging, or why.
She shuts her eyes and the world disap-
pears; she opens them, and it appears again.
Everything, everything, everything. If she
can't think about her mother, she won't
have a mother any more. And if she can't
think about the sky, the sky . . . And dogs
and clouds and God. Too many things to
think about all at once, all on her own.
And why she, alone? Why *she* alone in the
universe? When you know about it, it's so
difficult. Suddenly she might forget about
the sun or her house or Lucia. Or worse,
she might remember Lucia, but a mad
Lucia coming to kill her with a gun in her
hand. And now she realizes at least how
dangerous all this is. Because if she can't
stop herself thinking about it, then Lucia
will really be like that, crazy, and kill her.
And then there won't be anyone left to
imagine all those things. The trees will disappear and the desk and thunderstorms.
The color red will disappear and all the
countries in the world. And the blue sky
and the sky at night and the sparrows and
the lions in Africa and the earth itself and
singing songs. And no one will ever know
that, once, a girl called Mariana invented
a very complicated place to which she gave
the name of Universe. ꝏ

Analyze Conflict *What is the connection between
Mariana's reaction to Lucia's philosophical theory and her
conflicting attitudes toward her older sister?*

Magic Realism *What is Mariana's state of mind at the
end of the story?*

After You Read

Respond and Think Critically

Respond and Interpret

1. What would you like to say to Mariana? What would you like to say to Lucia?

2. (a)What question does Mariana keep asking Lucia? (b)Why do you think the author gives Mariana this piece of dialogue?

3. (a)How does Lucia react to Mariana's question? (b)What motivates Lucia to react this way?

4. (a)In what two ways does Mariana imagine Lucia in her mind? (b)What do these images suggest about Mariana's attitude toward her older sister?

5. (a)What theory does Lucia present about the girls' mother? (b)How does Mariana respond to Lucia's theory?

Analyze and Evaluate

6. (a)How old do Lucia and Mariana seem to you? Cite evidence from the story to support your answer. (b)Why do you think the reader learns almost nothing about the characters that goes beyond the present event?

7. Do you think Lucia is really trying to offer an accurate version of Berkeley's ideas about existence? Explain.

8. How well does the title reflect the content of the story?

Connect

9. **Big Idea** **Magic Realism** How is this story an example of magic realism?

10. **Connect to the Author** Heker remained in Argentina during one of the country's most oppressive periods—a time when civilians were kidnapped from their homes, tortured, and killed. How might these experiences have affected her desire to play with the nature of reality in this short story?

Literary Element **Allusion**

SAT Skills Practice

The author of this story alludes to Bishop Berkeley's philosophy in order to

(A) logically disprove it

(B) push it to an absurd extreme

(C) praise its genius

(D) show a contrast between the ideas of children and adults

(E) highlight a difference between old and new ways of thinking

Review: Dialogue

As you learned on page 1026, **dialogue** is conversation between characters in a literary work. Dialogue helps reveal characters, suggest the theme, and advance the plot.

1. Does "Bishop Berkeley or Mariana of the Universe" depend more on narration or dialogue to advance the plot? Explain.

2. How does dialogue function as the device for presenting the philosophical idea that underpins the story?

3. What makes the dialogue an ideal device for exposing and intensifying the main external conflict?

Reading Strategy — Analyze Conflict

In this story the central conflict between the sisters is transformed into a conflict of ideas. Review the chart you made on page 1253 and then respond to the following items.

1. Describe an external conflict in "Bishop Berkeley or Mariana of the Universe."

2. Describe an internal conflict in the story.

Vocabulary Practice

Practice with Denotation and Connotation

Denotation is the literal, or dictionary, meaning of a word. **Connotation** is the implied, or cultural, meaning of a word.

Next to each vocabulary word below is a word that has a similar denotation. Choose the word that has the more negative connotation.

1. **pounce**   leap

2. **mediocre**   moderate

3. **resignation** submissiveness

4. **gravely**   seriously

Academic Vocabulary

*Lucia makes the **qualitative** observation that people imagine their own realities.*

Qualitative is an academic word. In making a diagnosis, a doctor would assess **qualitative** data, such as a patient's description of his or her symptoms, along with quantitative (numerical) data, such as the patient's temperature and blood pressure. To study this word further, answer the following question: What types of **qualitative** data might be collected by a person taking a census?

For more on academic vocabulary, see pages 36–37 and R83–R85.

Listening and Speaking

 Literature Groups

Assignment With a small group, discuss whether you believe "reality" is real or imagined. Consider the gray areas that emerge in the distinction between reality and the imagination. Use specific arguments to back up your points.

Prepare To prepare for the discussion, review the information on page 1187, noting the philosophical assumptions that underpin magic realist works. Make charts like the one below to organize arguments from the story and your own opinions.

Argument	Evaluation
<u>Passage</u>: "…two people can't imagine the same thing at the same time." <u>Meaning</u>: Things must exist outside of our imaginations. <u>Logic, Reasons, or Evidence</u>: Both Mariana and Lucia would see three pictures in the room without consulting one another, so the pictures must be real.	<u>Response</u>: I don't agree, though the argument seemed convincing at first. <u>Counterargument</u>: As Lucia says, Mariana is forgetting that she might also be imagining the existence of other people.

Discuss During the discussion, listen carefully to your peers and build off their ideas. Take notes on what is said. When you want to introduce a different idea, try using a transitional statement like the one below.

So far, we have been talking about _____. But I think the real issue is _____.

Report Use your notes to create a short oral report on your discussion and the consensus—if any—that your group reached. Conclude the report by synthesizing ideas from the discussion into a few remaining questions. Create a visual aid such as a flowchart to illustrate the progression of ideas in your discussion.

Evaluate Write a paragraph in which you assess the effectiveness of your discussion.

Literary Perspective
on Magic Realism

from
My Invented Country

Isabel Allende
Translated by
Margaret Sayers Peden

Learning Objectives

For pages 1261–1263

In studying this text, you will focus on the following objectives:

Reading: Analyzing philosophical assumptions. Making connections across literature. Analyzing informational text.

Set a Purpose for Reading

Read to understand how one author's experiences and beliefs shaped her magic realist fiction.

Build Background

In 1973, Isabel Allende's cousin, the president of Chile, was assassinated in a brutal coup. Allende and her family soon found life too dangerous in Chile and moved to Caracas, Venezuela, where Allende began her first novel, *The House of the Spirits.* Allende wrote the novel in a magic realist style, endowing each of the characters with magical qualities and including spirits of the dead who speak to the living. In the following excerpt from her memoir, Allende reflects on the role her imagination has played in shaping her memories and her writing.

Reading Strategy Analyze Philosophical Assumptions

When you **analyze philosophical assumptions,** you look for clues to what an author believes. Assumptions may be stated directly or may be implied in the conclusions the author draws. As you read, take notes on Allende's beliefs about subjectivity, reality, and the imagination.

From the instant I crossed the cordillera[1] of the Andes one rainy winter morning, I unconsciously began the process of inventing a country. I have flown over those mountains many times since, and I am always deeply moved because the memory of that morning assaults me full-force as I look down on the magnificent spectacle of the mountains. The infinite solitude of those white peaks, those dizzying abysses, the blue depths of the sky, symbolizes my farewell to Chile. I never imagined I would be gone for so long. Like all Chileans—except the military—I was convinced that given our tradition, the soldiers would soon return to their barracks, there would be a new election, and we would have a democratic government again. I must have intuited something in regard to the future, however, because I spent my first night in Caracas crying inconsolably in a borrowed bed. Deep down, I sensed that something had ended forever, and that my life was taking a new direction. I have felt the pangs of nostalgia ever since that first night, and they did not lessen for many

---

1. A *cordillera* is a system of mountain ranges.

Andrea wrote a composition for school in which she said that she liked her "grandmother's imagination." I asked her what she was referring to, and without hesitation she replied, "You remember things that never happened." Don't we all do that? I have read that the mental process of imagining and that of remembering are so much alike that they are nearly indistinguishable. Who can define reality? Isn't everything subjective? If you and I witness the same event, we will recall it and recount it differently. Comparing the versions of our childhood that my brothers tell, it's as if each of us had been on a different planet. Memory is conditioned by emotion; we remember better, and more fully, things that move us, such as the joy of a birth, the pleasure of a night of love, the pain of a loved one's death, the trauma of a wound. When we call up the past, we choose intense moments—good or bad—and omit the enormous gray area of daily life.

years—until the dictatorship fell and I again stood on the soil of my country. Through the intervening years, I lived with my eyes turned south, listening to the news, waiting for the moment I could go back, as I selected my memories, altered some events, exaggerated or ignored others, refined my emotions, and so gradually constructed the imaginary country in which I have sunk my roots.

I have constructed an idea of my country the way you fit together a jigsaw puzzle, by selecting pieces that fit my design and ignoring the others. My Chile is poetic and poor, which is why I discard the evidence of a modern, materialistic society in which a person's value is measured by wealth, fairly acquired or otherwise, and insist on seeing signs everywhere of my country of old. I have also created a version of myself that has no nationality, or, more accurately, many nationalities. I don't belong to one land, but to several, or perhaps only to the ambit[2] of the fiction I write. I can't pretend to know what part of my memory is reliable and how much I've invented, because the job of defining the line between them is beyond my ability. My granddaughter

If I had never traveled, if I had stayed on, safe and secure in the bosom of my family, if I had accepted my grandfather's vision and his rules, it would have been impossible for me to recreate or embellish my own existence, because it would have been defined by others and I would merely be one link more in a long family chain. Moving about has forced me, time after time, to readjust my story, and I have done that in a daze, almost without noticing, because I have been too preoccupied with the task of surviving. Most of our lives are similar, and can be told in the tone used to read the telephone directory—unless we decide to give it a little oomph, a little

---

2. *Ambit* means "bounds" or "scope."

color. In my case, I have tried to polish the details and create my private legend, so that when I am in a nursing home awaiting death I will have something to entertain the other senile old folks with.

I wrote my first book by letting my fingers run over the typewriter keys, just as I am writing this, without a plan. I needed very little research because I had it all inside, not in my head but in that place in my chest where I felt a perpetual knot. I told about Santiago in the time of my grandfather's youth, just as if I'd been born then; I knew exactly how a gas lamp was lit before electricity was installed in the city, just as I knew the fate of hundreds of prisoners in Chile during that same period. I wrote in a trance, as if someone was dictating to me, and I have always attributed that favor to the ghost of my grandmother, who was whispering into my ear. Only one other time have I been gifted with a book dictated from that other dimension, and that was when I wrote my memoir *Paula* in 1993. I have no doubt that in writing that book I received help from the benign spirit of my daughter.[3]

---

3. Allende named the memoir *Paula* after her daughter, who died in 1992 at the age of 28. The book focuses on her daughter's illness and death.

Who, really, are these and the other spirits who live with me? I haven't seen them floating around the hallways of my home, wrapped in white sheets, nothing as interesting as that. They are simply memories that come to me and that from being caressed so often gradually acquire flesh. That happens with people, and also with Chile, that mythic country that from being missed so profoundly has replaced the real country. That country inside my head, as my grandchildren describe it, is a stage on which I place and remove objects, characters, and situations at my whim. Only the landscape remains true and immutable; I am not a foreigner to the majestic landscape of Chile. My tendency to transform reality, to invent memory, disturbs me, I have no idea how far it may lead me. Does the same thing happen with people? If, for example, I saw my grandparents or my daughter for an instant, would I recognize them? Probably not, because in looking so hard for a way to keep them alive, remembering them in the most minimal details, I have been changing them, adorning them with qualities they may not have had. I have given them a destiny much more complex than the ones they lived. ∾

Respond and Think Critically

Respond and Interpret

1. Write a brief summary of the main ideas in this excerpt before you answer the following questions. For help in writing a summary, see page 1147.

2. (a)What is the meaning of the title of Allende's memoir? (b)What facts about Chile does she say she chooses to ignore?

3. (a)How does Allende say she would be different if she had not left Chile? (b)In what way does she say her exile has influenced her writing?

Analyze and Evaluate

4. (a)What assumption does Allende make about subjectivity? (b)Do you agree with this assumption? Explain.

5. (a)What does Allende believe about the nature of memory? (b)Do her beliefs about memory seem to distress her? Explain.

Connect

6. What insights into magic realism did you gain from reading this excerpt?

Before You Read

Day of the Butterfly

Meet **Alice Munro**

(born 1931)

> *"I'm not an intellectual writer. I'm very, very excited by what you might call the surface of life."*
>
> —Alice Munro

Most of Alice Munro's short stories are set among the Scotch-Irish settlers of southern Ontario, and she gained international recognition for her finely drawn depictions of these rural and small-town Canadians.

A Farmer's Daughter The eldest of three children, she was born Alice Laidlaw in the small farming community of Wingham, Ontario. Her father was a poultry farmer who for a time raised silver foxes for fur; her mother was a schoolteacher who was ambitious for her daughter. Munro began writing in her teens, hiding in a locked schoolroom to do so because writing was considered an "odd" activity. She left home in 1949 to attend the University of Western Ontario, where she helped support herself with various odd jobs and began writing in earnest. She published her first short story while she was at school.

A Wife and a Mother She left the university after two years to marry James Munro. The couple moved to British Columbia, where they opened a bookstore and raised three children. She found, however, that her literary ambitions often conflicted with family responsibilities. During this time she led, she says, "two completely different lives—the real and absolutely solitary life and the life of appearances." Although she went through periods of depression, her "incredible stubbornness" allowed her to continue writing. Her first collection of stories, *Dance of the Happy Shades*, was published in 1968, winning the Governor General's Literary Award, Canada's highest literary prize—one of three such awards she

would win. Her marriage to Munro broke up in 1972, and she moved back to Ontario, where she later remarried. She lives with her second husband on a farm twenty miles from Wingham.

A Regional Author Although Munro's stories are rooted in a rural setting, she achieves universality through her telling details of characters and setting. "I love the landscape so much— more than love it. It's something I know so thoroughly I don't want to detach from it." Known for her realistic descriptions, Munro believes it is important "to get at the exact tone or texture of how things are." Many of her stories are about misfits or people who feel isolated in some way. Several of her short stories have been adapted as radio and television dramas. In 1990, she won the Canada Council Molson prize for her "outstanding lifetime contribution to the cultural and intellectual life of Canada."

LOG ON ▶ **Literature** Online

Author Search For more about Alice Munro, go to glencoe.com and enter QuickPass code GLW6053u6.

Literature and Reading Preview

Connect to the Story

What are the most important factors that have influenced your choice of friends? Discuss this question with a partner.

Build Background

Most of Alice Munro's stories are set in the rolling farmland of southern Ontario—where her family has lived since the 1840s. She remembers the residents of Wingham as practical people who considered reading a waste of time. Even now, Munro says, many of her relatives generally consider her writing "a very meaningless, useless type of work."

Set Purposes for Reading

Big Idea Nature and the Imagination

As you read, ask yourself, How does the setting influence the attitudes and the actions of the characters?

Literary Element Dialect and Idiom

A **dialect** is a variation of a language spoken in a particular region or by a particular class. Dialects may differ from the standard forms of a language in vocabulary, pronunciation, or grammatical form. An **idiom** is an expression whose meaning differs from its literal meaning. For example, a character in this story says Myra has to *look after* her little brother, meaning she must take care of him. If you see unusual language as you read, ask yourself, Is this an example of dialect or an idiom?

Reading Strategy Analyze Characterization

Characterization refers to the methods an author uses to reveal a character's personality. Describing personality traits—for example, stating that a character is lazy—is **direct characterization**. **Indirect characterization** lets readers draw their own conclusions about characters—based on such things as the characters' words, thoughts, and actions.

....

Tip: Compile Details Use a chart like the one below to record details of characterization, both direct and indirect.

Character	Detail	Type
Gladys	"Oh she [Myra] washes it in cod-liver oil . . ."	indirect
Myra	cryptically uncommunicative	direct

Learning Objectives

For pages 1264–1275

In studying this text, you will focus on the following objectives:

Literary Study: Analyzing dialect and idiom.

Reading: Analyzing characterization.

Listening and Speaking: Reporting on literary criticism.

Vocabulary

cryptically (krip′tik lē) *adv.* secretly or mysteriously; p. 1267 *"The proof of a pudding is in the eating," Mother said cryptically.*

self-possessed (self′ pə zest′) *adj.* in control of oneself; p. 1268 *She was a very self-possessed young woman and refused to be rattled by the comments of the construction workers.*

supplementary (sup′lə men′tər ē) *adj.* extra or additional; p. 1271 *The supplementary income Mark brought home from his second job helped his family a great deal.*

....

Tip: Word Usage When you encounter a new word, try asking yourself a question about it to help you remember its meaning. For example, What is the difference between someone who is **self-possessed** and someone who is **insecure**?

Day of the Butterfly

Alice Munro

I do not remember when Myra Sayla came to town, though she must have been in our class at school for two or three years. I start remembering her in the last year, when her little brother Jimmy Sayla was in Grade One. Jimmy Sayla was not used to going to the bathroom by himself and he would have to come to the Grade Six door and ask for Myra and she would take him downstairs. Quite often he would not get to Myra in time and there would be a big dark stain on his little button-on cotton pants. Then Myra had to come and ask the teacher: "Please may I take my brother home, he has wet himself?"

That was what she said the first time and everybody in the front seats heard her—though Myra's voice was the lightest singsong—and there was a muted giggling which alerted the rest of the class.

Our teacher, a cold gentle girl who wore glasses with thin gold rims and in the stiff solicitude of certain poses resembled a giraffe, wrote something on a piece of paper and showed it to Myra. And Myra recited uncertainly: "My brother has had an accident, please, teacher."

Everybody knew of Jimmy Sayla's shame and at recess (if he was not being kept in, as he often was, for doing something he shouldn't in school) he did not dare go out on the school grounds, where the other little boys, and some bigger ones, were waiting to chase him and corner him against the back fence and thrash him with tree branches. He had to stay with Myra. But at

---

Analyze Characterization *Is this an example of direct or indirect characterization? Explain.*

Dialect and Idiom *Why does the teacher insist that Myra use this phrase instead of her own words?*

our school there were the two sides, the Boys' Side and the Girls' Side, and it was believed that if you so much as stepped on the side that was not your own you might easily get the strap. Jimmy could not go out on the Girls' Side and Myra could not go out on the Boys' Side, and no one was allowed to stay in the school unless it was raining or snowing. So Myra and Jimmy spent every recess standing in the little back porch between the two sides. Perhaps they watched the baseball games, the tag and skipping and building of leaf houses in the fall and snow forts in the winter; perhaps they did not watch at all. Whenever you happened to look at them their heads were slightly bent, their narrow bodies hunched in, quite still. They had long smooth oval faces, melancholy and discreet—dark, oily, shining hair. The little boy's was long, clipped at home, and Myra's was worn in heavy braids coiled on top of her head so that she looked, from a distance, as if she was wearing a turban too big for her. Over their dark eyes the lids were never fully raised; they had a weary look. But it was more than that. They were like children in a medieval painting, they were like small figures carved of wood, for worship or magic, with faces smooth and aged, and meekly, **cryptically** uncommunicative.

Most of the teachers at our school had been teaching for a long time and at recess they would disappear into the teachers' room and not bother us. But our own teacher, the young woman of the fragile gold-rimmed glasses, was apt to watch us from a window and sometimes come out, looking brisk and uncomfortable, to stop a fight among the little girls or start a running game among the big ones, who had been huddled together

Still Closer, 1995. Daniel Nevins. Oil, acrylic, collage on wood, 51 x 39 in. Private collection.

View the Art Nevins has said that he strives to convey stories through his paintings. What scene or characters from this story does this painting remind you of?

playing Truth or Secrets. One day she came out and called, "Girls in Grade Six, I want to talk to you!" She smiled persuasively, earnestly, and with dreadful unease, showing fine gold rims around her teeth. She said, "There is a girl in Grade Six called Myra Sayla. She *is* in your grade, isn't she?"

We mumbled. But there was a coo from Gladys Healey. "Yes, Miss Darling!"

"Well, why is she never playing with the rest of you? Every day I see her standing in the back porch, never playing. Do you think she looks very happy standing back

Vocabulary

cryptically (krip′tik lē) *adv.* secretly or mysteriously there? Do you think you would be very happy, if *you* were left back there?"

Nobody answered; we faced Miss Darling, all respectful, **self-possessed,** and bored with the unreality of her question. Then Gladys said, "Myra can't come out with us, Miss Darling. Myra has to look after her little brother!"

"Oh," said Miss Darling dubiously. "Well you ought to try to be nicer to her anyway. Don't you think so? Don't you? You will try to be nicer, won't you? I *know* you will." Poor Miss Darling! Her campaigns were soon confused, her persuasions turned to bleating and uncertain pleas.

When she had gone Gladys Healey said softly, "You will try to be nicer, won't you? I *know* you will!" and then drawing her lip back over her big teeth she yelled exuberantly, "I don't care if it rains or freezes." She went through the whole verse and ended it with a spectacular twirl of her Royal Stuart tartan skirt. Mr. Healey ran a Dry Goods and Ladies' Wear, and his daughter's leadership in our class was partly due to her flashing plaid skirts and organdy blouses and velvet jackets with brass buttons, but also to her early-maturing bust and the fine brutal force of her personality. Now we all began to imitate Miss Darling.

Visual Vocabulary
Tartan is a plaid wool cloth woven in the particular pattern of a Scottish clan.

Analyze Characterization *What does Gladys's action suggest about her character?*

Vocabulary

self-possessed (self′ pə zest′) *adj.* in control of oneself

We had not paid much attention to Myra before this. But now a game was developed; it started with saying, "Let's be nice to Myra!" Then we would walk up to her in formal groups of three or four and at a signal, say together, "Hel-lo Myra, Hello My-ra!" and follow up with something like, "What do you wash your hair in, Myra, it's so nice and shiny, My-ra." "Oh she washes it in cod-liver oil, don't you, Myra, she washes it in cod-liver oil, can't you smell it?"

And to tell the truth there was a smell about Myra, but it was a rotten-sweetish smell as of bad fruit. That was what the Saylas did, kept a little fruit store. Her father sat all day on a stool by the window, with his shirt open over his swelling stomach and tufts of black hair showing around his belly button; he chewed garlic. But if you went into the store it was Mrs. Sayla who came to wait on you, appearing silently between the limp print curtains hung across the back of the store. Her hair was crimped in black waves and she smiled with her full lips held together, stretched as far as they would go; she told you the price in a little rapping voice, daring you to challenge her and, when you did not, handed you the bag of fruit with open mockery in her eyes.

One morning in the winter I was walking up the school hill very early; a neighbor had given me a ride into town. I lived about half a mile out of town, on a farm, and I should not have been going to the town school at all, but to a country school nearby where there were half a dozen pupils and a teacher a little demented since her change of life. But my mother, who was an ambitious woman, had prevailed on the town trustees to accept me and my father to pay the extra tuition, and I went to

---

Nature and the Imagination *How does this natural setting influence the actions of the characters?*

school in town. I was the only one in the class who carried a lunch pail and ate peanut-butter sandwiches in the high, bare, mustard-colored cloakroom, the only one who had to wear rubber boots in the spring, when the roads were heavy with mud. I felt a little danger, on account of this; but I could not tell exactly what it was.

> *A role was shaping up for me that I could not resist playing. I felt a great pleasurable rush of self-conscious benevolence. . . .*

I saw Myra and Jimmy ahead of me on the hill; they always went to school very early—sometimes so early that they had to stand outside waiting for the janitor to open the door. They were walking slowly, and now and then Myra half turned around. I had often loitered in that way, wanting to walk with some important girl who was behind me, and not quite daring to stop and wait. Now it occurred to me that Myra might be doing this with me. I did not know what to do. I could not afford to be seen walking with her, and I did not even want to—but, on the other hand, the flattery of those humble, hopeful turnings was not lost on me. A role was shaping for me that I could not resist playing. I felt a great pleasurable rush of self-conscious benevolence; before I thought what I was doing I called, "Myra! Hey, Myra, wait up, I got some Cracker Jack!" and I quickened my pace as she stopped.

Myra waited, but she did not look at me; she waited in the withdrawn and rigid attitude with which she always met us. Perhaps she thought I was playing a trick on her, perhaps she expected me to run past and throw an empty Cracker Jack box in her face. And I opened the box and held it out to her. She took a little. Jimmy ducked behind her coat and would not take any when I offered the box to him.

"He's shy," I said reassuringly. "A lot of little kids are shy like that. He'll probably grow out of it."

"Yes," said Myra.

"I have a brother four," I said. "He's awfully shy." He wasn't. "Have some more Cracker Jack," I said. "I used to eat Cracker Jack all the time but I don't any more. I think it's bad for your complexion."

There was a silence.

"Do you like Art?" said Myra faintly.

"No. I like Social Studies and Spelling and Health."

"I like Art and Arithmetic." Myra could add and multiply in her head faster than anyone else in the class.

"I wish I was as good as you. In Arithmetic," I said, and felt magnanimous.

"But I am no good at Spelling," said Myra. "I make the most mistakes, I'll fail maybe." She did not sound unhappy about this, but pleased to have such a thing to say. She kept her head turned away from me staring at the dirty snowbanks along Victoria Street, and as she talked she made a sound as if she was wetting her lips with her tongue.

"You won't fail," I said. "You are too good in Arithmetic. What are you going to be when you grow up?"

She looked bewildered. "I will help my mother," she said. "And work in the store."

"Well I am going to be an airplane hostess," I said. "But don't mention it to anybody. I haven't told many people."

Analyze Characterization *What does this admission reveal about the narrator's character?*

Dialect and Idiom *What does the narrator mean by this?*

Vegetation. Tamas Galambos. Oil on canvas. Private collection.

"No, I won't," said Myra. "Do you read Steve Canyon in the paper?"

"Yes." It was queer to think that Myra, too, read the comics, or that she did anything at all, apart from her role at the school. "Do you read Rip Kirby?"

"Do you read Orphan Annie?"

"Do you read Betsy and the Boys?"

"You haven't had hardly any Cracker Jack," I said. "Have some. Take a whole handful."

Myra looked into the box. "There's a prize in there," she said. She pulled it out. It was a brooch,[1] a little tin butterfly, painted gold with bits of colored glass stuck onto it to look like jewels. She held it in her brown hand, smiling slightly.

I said, "Do you like that?"

Myra said, "I like them blue stones. Blue stones are sapphires."

"I know. My birthstone is sapphire. What is your birthstone?"

"I don't know."

"When is your birthday?"

"July."

"Then yours is ruby."

"I like sapphire better," said Myra. "I like yours." She handed me the brooch.

"You keep it," I said. "Finders keepers."

Myra kept holding it out, as if she did not know what I meant. "Finders keepers," I said.

"It was your Cracker Jack," said Myra, scared and solemn. "You bought it."

"Well you found it."

"No—" said Myra.

"Go on!" I said. "Here, I'll *give* it to you." I took the brooch from her and pushed it back into her hand.

---

1. A *brooch* (brōch) is an ornamental pin.

Dialect and Idiom *Is this phrase an example of dialect or idiom? What does it mean?*

We were both surprised. We looked at each other; I flushed but Myra did not. I realized the pledge as our fingers touched; I was panicky, but *all right*. I thought, I can come early and walk with her other mornings. I can go and talk to her at recess. Why not? *Why not?*

Myra put the brooch in her pocket. She said, "I can wear it on my good dress. My good dress is blue."

I knew it would be. Myra wore out her good dresses at school. Even in midwinter among the plaid wool skirts and serge tunics, she glimmered sadly in sky-blue taffeta, in dusty turquoise crepe, a grown woman's dress made over, weighted by a big bow at the v of the neck and folding empty over Myra's narrow chest.

And I was glad she had not put it on. If someone asked her where she got it, and she told them, what would I say?

It was the day after this, or the week after, that Myra did not come to school. Often she was kept at home to help. But this time she did not come back. For a week, then two weeks, her desk was empty. Then we had a moving day at school and Myra's books were taken out of her desk and put on a shelf in the closet. Miss Darling said, "We'll find a seat when she comes back." And she stopped calling Myra's name when she took attendance.

Jimmy Sayla did not come to school either, having no one to take him to the bathroom.

In the fourth week or the fifth, that Myra had been away, Gladys Healey came to school and said, "Do you know what— Myra Sayla is sick in the hospital."

It was true. Gladys Healey had an aunt who was a nurse. Gladys put up her hand in the middle of Spelling and told Miss Darling. "I thought you might like to know," she said. "Oh yes," said Miss Darling. "I do know."

"What has she got?" we said to Gladys. And Gladys said, "Akemia,[2] or something. And she has blood transfusions." She said to Miss Darling, "My aunt is a nurse."

So Miss Darling had the whole class write Myra a letter, in which everybody said, "Dear Myra, We are all writing you a letter. We hope you will soon be better and be back to school, Yours truly. . . ." And Miss Darling said, "I've thought of something. Who would like to go up to the hospital and visit Myra on the twentieth of March, for a birthday party?"

I said, "Her birthday's in July."

"I know," said Miss Darling. "It's the twentieth of July. So this year she could have it on the twentieth of March, because she's sick."

"But her *birthday* is in July."

"Because she's sick," said Miss Darling, with a warning shrillness. "The cook at the hospital would make a cake and you could all give a little present, twenty-five cents or so. It would have to be between two and four, because that's visiting hours. And we couldn't all go, it'd be too many. So who wants to go and who wants to stay here and do **supplementary** reading?"

We all put up our hands. Miss Darling got out the spelling records and picked out the first fifteen, twelve girls and three boys. Then the three boys did not want to go so

2. *Akemia* is a mispronunciation of *leukemia,* which is a form of cancer that affects the blood.

she picked out the next three girls. And I do not know when it was, but I think it was probably at this moment that the birthday party of Myra Sayla became fashionable.

Perhaps it was because Gladys Healey had an aunt who was a nurse, perhaps it was the excitement of sickness and hospitals, or simply the fact that Myra was so entirely, impressively set free of all the rules and conditions of our lives. We began to talk of her as if she were something we owned, and her party became a cause; with womanly heaviness we discussed it at recess, and decided that twenty-five cents was too low.

We all went up to the hospital on a sunny afternoon when the snow was melting, carrying our presents, and a nurse led us upstairs, single file, and down a hall past half-closed doors and dim conversations. She and Miss Darling kept saying, "Sh-sh," but we were going on tiptoe anyway; our hospital demeanor was perfect.

At this small country hospital there was no children's ward, and Myra was not really a child; they had put her in with two gray old women. A nurse was putting screens around them as we came in.

Myra was sitting up in bed, in a bulky stiff hospital gown. Her hair was down, the long braids falling over her shoulders and down the coverlet. But her face was the same, always the same.

She had been told something about the party, Miss Darling said, so the surprise would not upset her; but it seemed she had not believed, or had not understood what it was. She watched us as she used to watch in the school grounds when we played.

"Well, here we are!" said Miss Darling. "Here we are!"

And we said, "Happy birthday, Myra! Hello, Myra, happy birthday!" Myra said, "My birthday is in July." Her voice was lighter than ever, drifting, expressionless.

"Never mind when it is, really," said Miss Darling. "Pretend it's now! How old are you, Myra?"

"Eleven," Myra said. "In July."

Then we all took off our coats and emerged in our party dresses, and laid our presents, in their pale flowery wrappings, on Myra's bed. Some of our mothers had made immense, complicated bows of fine satin ribbon, some of them had even taped on little bouquets of imitation roses and lilies of the valley. "Here Myra," we said, "here Myra, happy birthday." Myra did not look at us, but at the ribbons, pink and blue and speckled with silver, and the miniature bouquets; they pleased her, as the butterfly had done. An innocent look came into her face, a partial, private smile.

"Open them, Myra," said Miss Darling. "They're for you!"

Myra gathered the presents around her, fingering them, with this smile, and a cautious realization, an unexpected pride. She said, "Saturday I'm going to London[3] to St. Joseph's Hospital."

"That's where my mother was at," somebody said. "We went and saw her. They've got all nuns there."

"My father's sister is a nun," said Myra calmly.

She began to unwrap the presents, with an air that not even Gladys could have bettered, folding the tissue paper and the ribbons, and drawing out books and puzzles and cutouts as if they were all prizes she had won. Miss Darling said that maybe she should say thank you, and the person's name with every gift she opened, to make sure she knew whom it was from, and so Myra said, "Thank you, Mary Louise, thank

---

3. *London* is a city in southern Ontario, Canada.

Nature and the Imagination *Do you think Myra realizes how dangerously ill she is? Explain.*

you, Carol," and when she came to mine she said, "Thank you, Helen." Everyone explained their presents to her and there was talking and excitement and a little gaiety, which Myra presided over, though she was not gay. A cake was brought in with *Happy Birthday Myra* written on it, pink on white, and eleven candles. Miss Darling lit the candles and we all sang Happy Birthday to You, and cried, "Make a wish, Myra, make a wish—" and Myra blew them out. Then we all had cake and strawberry ice cream.

Myra said, "I got too many things. You take something."

At four o'clock a buzzer sounded and the nurse took out what was left of the cake, and the dirty dishes, and we put on our coats to go home. Everybody said, "Good-bye, Myra," and Myra sat in the bed watching us go, her back straight, not supported by any pillow, her hands resting on the gifts. But at the door I heard her call; she called, "Helen!" Only a couple of the others heard; Miss Darling did not hear, she had gone out ahead. I went back to the bed.

Myra said, "I got too many things. You take something."

"What?" I said. "It's for your birthday. You always get a lot at a birthday."

"Well you take something," Myra said. She picked up a leatherette case with a mirror in it, a comb and a nail file and a natural lipstick and a small handkerchief edged with gold thread. I had noticed it before. "You take that," she said.

"Don't you want it?"

"You take it." She put it into my hand. Our fingers touched again.

"When I come back from London," Myra said, "you can come and play at my place after school."

"Okay," I said. Outside the hospital window there was a clear carrying sound of somebody playing in the street, maybe chasing with the last snowballs of the year. This sound made Myra, her triumph and her bounty, and most of all her future in which she had found this place for me, turn shadowy, turn dark. All the presents on the bed, the folded paper and ribbons, those guilt-tinged offerings, had passed into this shadow, they were no longer innocent objects to be touched, exchanged, accepted without danger. I didn't want to take the case now but I could not think how to get out of it, what lie to tell. I'll give it away, I thought, I won't ever play with it. I would let my little brother pull it apart.

The nurse came back, carrying a glass of chocolate milk.

"What's the matter, didn't you hear the buzzer?"

So I was released, set free by the barriers which now closed about Myra, her unknown, exalted, ether-smelling hospital world, and by the treachery of my own heart. "Well thank you," I said. "Thank you for the thing. Good-bye."

Did Myra ever say good-bye? Not likely. She sat in her high bed, her delicate brown neck, rising out of a hospital gown too big for her, her brown carved face immune to treachery, her offering perhaps already forgotten, prepared to be set apart for legendary uses, as she was even in the back porch at school. ❧

Analyze Characterization *What does this gesture reveal about Myra's character?*

Dialect and Idiom *What does Helen want here? Why?*

After You Read

Respond and Think Critically

Respond and Interpret

1. Did your feelings for the narrator, Helen, change during the story? Explain.

2. (a)Why is Myra unpopular with the other girls at school? (b)Why do Myra's classmates begin to tease her after ignoring her for so long?

3. (a)Why does Helen start a conversation with Myra on the way to school? (b)Why might Helen be more sympathetic toward Myra than the other girls?

4. (a)What gift does Helen give to Myra? (b)Do you think Helen has decided to become Myra's friend when she gives her the gift? Why or why not?

5. (a)How does Myra's reputation in class change after she goes into the hospital? (b)Why do you think Miss Darling makes up an excuse for the students to visit Myra in the hospital?

Analyze and Evaluate

6. **Irony** is a contrast between what is believed or expected and what actually exists or occurs. Identify an example of irony in the story.

7. (a)From what **point of view** is the story told? (b)What effect does this point of view have on your impression of the characters?

Connect

8. **Big Idea** Nature and the Imagination How do nature and the cycle of life influence the characters in the story?

9. **Connect to the Author** Many of Munro's characters are isolated people or misfits. Which characters in this story, if any, fit that description?

Literary Element Dialect and Idiom

A **dialect** is a language variation spoken in a particular part of a country or by a particular class. An **idiom** is an expression whose meaning differs from its literal meaning. Idioms are often specific to members of a particular society or culture and may not be understood by outsiders. What do these idiomatic expressions from "Day of the Butterfly" mean?

1. "get the strap" (p. 1267)

2. to "wait on" a person (p. 1268)

3. "wait up" (p. 1269)

4. "grow out of it" (p. 1269)

Review: Symbol

As you learned on page 791, a **symbol** is a person, a place, or a thing that has meaning in itself and also stands for something beyond itself. One way to recognize a symbol is by noting that something is especially important to one or more characters. In this story, the title calls attention to a possible symbol.

Partner Activity Meet with a classmate to discuss these questions.

1. What does the butterfly pin seem to symbolize to Myra?

2. What does the butterfly seem to symbolize to Helen?

3. How is Myra like a butterfly?

Reading Strategy Analyze Characterization

SAT Skills Practice

Myra's calm acceptance of the gifts from her classmates (page 1272) serves primarily to suggest that

(A) she is not an emotional person

(B) she does not value material objects

(C) she does not understand that she is ill

(D) she fears her classmates

(E) she has changed since her classmates last saw her

Vocabulary Practice

Practice with Word Usage Respond to these questions to help you explore the meanings of the vocabulary words from the story.

1. If someone said something to you **cryptically**, would it be easy to understand? Explain.

2. How might someone who is **self-possessed** behave?

3. If you are given **supplementary** information about something, what type of information is it?

Academic Vocabulary

*Helen's perspective **shifts** from the beginning of the story to the end: she begins to see Myra as "legendary" rather than pitiable.*

Shift is an academic word. In more casual conversation, someone might say that moving an automobile from one gear to another is called *shifting gears*. To further explore the meaning of this word, answer this question: What accounts for the sudden **shift** in Helen's behavior on the day she gives Myra the tin butterfly?

For more on academic vocabulary, see pages 36–37 and R83–R85.

Research and Report

 Literary Criticism

Assignment Munro has said "I'm very, very excited by what you might call the surface of life." What lies beneath the surface in her writing? Search for literary criticism about Munro's work and give an oral presentation in which you evaluate how various critics describe her work.

Prepare Scholar Coral Ann Howells points out that in Munro's early stories, there is "always the sense of ordinary surfaces covering over some secret or scandal which threatens to collapse them." Look for more criticism in books about Munro, anthologies of criticism, scholarly journals, and online databases. Write down statements from the critics and find details from the story that support them.

Review the graphic organizer on page 1265 and think about how the details you recorded fit the critics' comments. When you find critical statements you disagree with, cite examples from the story that disprove them. Be sure to define unfamiliar terms you come across. Remember also to rehearse your report so it flows naturally.

Report When you give your report, make eye contact, speak loudly and clearly, and maintain good posture. Modify your tone of voice and use a variety of gestures to help convey your opinions.

Evaluate Use a chart like the one below to evaluate your research and delivery.

	Research	Delivery
Strength	Used criticism from a wide variety of sources	Used logical organization
Weakness	Didn't use evidence to support my disagreements with critics	Didn't vary my tone or gestures

Grammar Workshop

Semicolons

Literature Connection In this sentence from "Day of the Butterfly," Alice Munro uses a semicolon to link related ideas.

> *"Perhaps they watched the baseball games, the tag and skipping and building of leaf houses in the fall and snow forts in the winter; perhaps they did not watch at all."*

A **semicolon** can connect two or more main, or independent, clauses into one sentence. For example, you can connect the closely related clauses "Jimmy Sayla was not used to going to the bathroom by himself" and "He would have to come to the Grade Six door and ask Myra to take him" with a semicolon to form the following sentence: "Jimmy Sayla was not used to going to the bathroom by himself; he would have to come to the Grade Six door and ask Myra to take him."

SITUATION To replace a comma and a coordinating conjunction in a compound sentence

Myra and Jimmy went to school very early, and the janitor was the only one there.

Myra and Jimmy went to school very early; the janitor was the only one there.

SITUATION To use a semicolon before a conjunctive adverb in a compound sentence

The students thought Myra smelled of cod-liver oil, however, she smelled like her father's fruit market.

The students thought Myra smelled of cod-liver oil; however, she smelled like her father's fruit market.

Conjunctions and Conjunctive Adjectives

A **conjunction** is a word, such as *and, or,* or *but,* that joins single words or groups of words. A **conjunctive adjective** is used to clarify the relationship between clauses of a compound sentence. Some examples include the words *therefore, however, consequently,* and *furthermore.*

Tip

When deciding whether to use a semicolon, first determine if the sentence has at least two clauses that express complete thoughts.

Language Handbook

For more about semicolons, see Language Handbook, p. R40.

Revise Rewrite the following sentences using a semicolon.

1. Alice Munro is a Canadian author, and she took twelve years to write her first volume of short stories.
2. Her story, "Day of the Butterfly," is entertaining, however, it focuses on a young girl with leukemia.
3. The story is told through a first-person narrator. She is Myra's classmate.

Before You Read

A Walk to the Jetty

Meet Jamaica Kincaid
(born 1949)

"Everyone thought I had a way with words," Jamaica Kincaid once wrote, "but it came out as a sharp tongue. No one expected anything from me at all." Smart and rebellious, Kincaid didn't let others' expectations stand in her way. She turned her way with words into a thriving career.

A Young Troublemaker
Born Elaine Potter Richardson, Kincaid grew up on the Caribbean island of Antigua. When she was nine years old, the first of her three brothers was born, causing her to feel estranged from her mother. As a result, she became an avid reader, often ducking out of family and social obligations to spend more time reading. Once, when she was supposed to be babysitting, she instead sneaked off by herself to read. Her mother became so irate over the incident that she doused all of Kincaid's books with kerosene and set them ablaze.

> "I think life is difficult. I am interested in pursuing a truth, and the truth often seems to be not happiness but its opposite."
>
> —Jamaica Kincaid

Possessed of both a sharp mind and a sharp tongue, Kincaid was often dubbed a troublemaker by her teachers. However, they also recognized her extraordinary intellectual abilities and at one point suggested she was worthy of a scholarship to further her education. Despite this encouragement, Kincaid's mother insisted her young daughter was needed at home. As years went by, Kincaid felt more and more trapped by the vast sea that surrounded Antigua. But her troubled early years on the island provided a rich cultural backdrop—one to which she would return over and over in her writing.

Breaking into Magazines When Kincaid was seventeen, her family's financial situation took a turn for the worse, and she was sent to New York to work as a nanny. She was determined to write, however, and she applied repeatedly to various fashion magazines published in New York City. Finally, she wrote an article that was published in *Ingenue* magazine. The article was so successful that the magazine hired Kincaid to write a series. Her confidence grew as one literary success followed another. Kincaid eventually became first a staff writer for and then a regular contributor to the prestigious *New Yorker* magazine.

Kincaid writes with great emotion and insight about family and culture. From her lonely and difficult childhood, she has charted her own course to become an internationally renowned author.

Literature and Reading Preview

Connect to the Story

How do you think you would feel if you were about to leave home forever? Respond to this question in your journal.

Build Background

The work you are about to read is from the last chapter of *Annie John,* a coming-of-age novel about a girl growing up on the small (108 square miles) eastern Caribbean island of Antigua. After she turns seventeen, Annie decides to move to England and study for a career in nursing. In "A Walk to the Jetty" (a *jetty* is a landing pier), Kincaid portrays Annie's confused feelings about her departure.

Set Purposes for Reading

Big Idea The Legacy of Colonialism

The island of Antigua was a British colony. As you read, ask yourself, How would you describe the relationship between homeland and identity experienced by the protagonist?

Literary Element Foreshadowing and Flashback

Authors use **foreshadowing** to present clues about events that will occur later in a story. In a **flashback,** the narrator interrupts the action of a literary work to present a scene that took place at an earlier time. As you read the story, ask yourself, What are examples of foreshadowing and flashback?

Reading Strategy Make and Verify Predictions

One way to get the most from your reading is to **make predictions,** or educated guesses, about what will happen later in a work. Base your predictions on details the author provides about time, place, situation, and characters. You then **verify predictions** by looking for evidence that confirms their accuracy. As you read, ask yourself, What predictions can I make about events and their outcomes?

Tip: Take Notes Use a chart like the one below to make and verify predictions.

Passage	Notes	Prediction
"My mother had arranged with a stevedore to take my trunk to the jetty."	The narrator's mother is sending a trunk ahead. The narrator will take a trip.	This story may be about a person leaving home.

Learning Objectives

For pages 1277–1286

In studying this text, you will focus on the following objectives:

Literary Study: Analyzing foreshadowing and flashback.

Reading: Making and verifying predictions.

Writing: Applying flashback.

Vocabulary

loom (lo͞om) *v.* to come into sight in enlarged or distorted form; p. 1279 *In the carnival's haunted house, a face loomed out of the darkness.*

guffaw (gu fô′) *n.* a loud or boisterous burst of laughter; p. 1283 *The comedian made each person break into a guffaw.*

shrivel (shriv′əl) *v.* to become wrinkled as a result of lack of moisture; p. 1283 *If a grape shrivels, it becomes a raisin.*

stupor (sto͞o′pər) *n.* a dulled mental state, often as a result of shock or stress; a daze; p. 1284 *The young man sat in a stupor after the car accident.*

Tip: Connotation and Denotation
A word's denotation is its literal, or dictionary, meaning. Each word, however, has a different connotation, the feeling or the impression it suggests. For example, *scorn* and *dislike* have similar denotations, but the connotation of *scorn* is more negative and hostile.

Village Life. Victor Collector. Oil on canvas. Private collection.

A Walk to the Jetty *from* Annie John

Jamaica Kincaid

My mother had arranged with a stevedore[1] to take my trunk to the jetty ahead of me. At ten o'clock on the dot, I was dressed, and we set off for the jetty. An hour after that, I would board a launch that would take me out to sea, where I then would board the ship. Starting out, as if for old time's sake and without giving it a thought, we lined up in the old way: I walking between my mother and my father. I **loomed** way above

my father and could see the top of his head. We must have made a strange sight: a grown girl all dressed up in the middle of a morning, in the middle of the week, walking in step in the middle between her two parents, for people we didn't know stared at us. It was all of half an hour's walk from our house to the jetty, but I was passing through most of the years of my life. We passed by the house where Miss Dulcie, the seamstress that I had been apprenticed to for a time, lived, and just as I was passing by, a wave of bad feeling for her came over me, because I suddenly remembered that

---

1. A *stevedore* (ste′vǝ dôr′) is one who works at or is responsible for loading and unloading ships in port.

Vocabulary

loom (lo͞om) *v.* to come into sight in enlarged or distorted form

Make and Verify Predictions *Based on this sentence, what do you predict will be the focus of this story?*

the months I spent with her all she had me do was sweep the floor, which was always full of threads and pins and needles, and I never seemed to sweep it clean enough to please her. Then she would send me to the store to buy buttons or thread, though I was only allowed to do this if I was given a sample of the button or thread, and then she would find fault even though they were an exact match of the samples she had given me. And all the while she said to me, "A girl like you will never learn to sew properly, you know." At the time, I don't suppose I minded it, because it was customary to treat the first-year apprentice with such scorn, but now I placed on the dustheap of my life Miss Dulcie and everything that I had had to do with her.

We were soon on the road that I had taken to school, to church, to Sunday school, to choir practice, to Brownie meetings, to Girl Guide meetings, to meet a friend. I was five years old when I first walked on this road unaccompanied by someone to hold my hand. My mother had placed three pennies in my little basket, which was a duplicate of her bigger basket, and sent me to the chemist's shop[2] to buy a pennyworth of senna leaves, a pennyworth of eucalyptus leaves, and a pennyworth of camphor.[3] She then instructed me on what side of the road to walk, where to make a turn, where to cross, how to look carefully before I crossed, and if I met anyone that I knew to politely pass greetings and keep on my way. I was wearing a freshly ironed yellow dress that had printed on it scenes of

acrobats flying through the air and swinging on a trapeze. I had just had a bath, and after it, instead of powdering me with my baby-smelling talcum powder, my mother had, as a special favor, let me use her own talcum powder, which smelled quite perfumy and came in a can that had painted on it people going out to dinner in nineteenth-century London and was called Mazie. How it pleased me to walk out the door and bend my head down to sniff at myself and see that I smelled just like my mother. I went to the chemist's shop, and he had to come from behind the counter and bend down to hear what it was that I wanted to buy, my voice was so little and timid then. I went back just the way I had come, and when I walked into the yard and presented my basket with its three packages to my mother, her eyes filled with tears and she swooped me up and held me high in the air and said that I was wonderful and good and that there would never be anybody better. If I had just conquered Persia,[4] she couldn't have been more proud of me.

We passed by our church—the church in which I had been christened and received and had sung in the junior choir. We passed by a house in which a girl I used to like and was sure I couldn't live without had lived. Once, when she had mumps, I went to visit her against my mother's wishes, and we sat on her bed and ate the cure of roasted, buttered sweet potatoes that had been placed on her swollen jaws, held there by a piece of white cloth. I don't know how, but my mother

---

2. A *chemist's* shop is a pharmacy, in British usage.
3. *Senna leaves, eucalyptus* (ū kə lip′təs) *leaves* and *camphor* are plant products used for medicinal purposes.

Foreshadowing and Flashback *This is just one in a series of flashbacks. What other flashback has occurred in the story so far?*

---

4. The phase *conquered Persia* means " accomplished an extraordinary feat." The allusion is to Alexander the Great, who vanquished the Persian Empire in the fourth century B.C.

Make and Verify Predictions *Have your predictions of what the story would be about been verified so far? If so, explain why. If not, how does the story differ?*

found out about it, and I don't know how, but she put an end to our friendship. Shortly after, the girl moved with her family across the sea to somewhere else. We passed the doll store, where I would go with my mother when I was little and point out the doll I wanted that year for Christmas. We passed the store where I bought the much-fought-over shoes I wore to church to be received in. We passed the bank. On my sixth birthday, I was given, among other things, the present of a sixpence. My mother and I then went to this bank, and with the sixpence I opened my own savings account. I was given a little gray book with my name in big letters on it, and in the balance column it said "6d." Every Saturday morning after that, I was given a sixpence—later a shilling, and later a two-and-sixpence piece—and I would take it to the bank for deposit. I had never been allowed to withdraw even a farthing[5] from my bank account until just a few weeks before I was to leave; then the whole account was closed out, and I received from the bank the sum of six pounds ten shillings and two and a half pence.

We passed the office of the doctor who told my mother three times that I did not need glasses, that if my eyes were feeling weak a glass of carrot juice a day would make them strong again. This happened when I was eight. And so every day at recess I would run to my school gate and meet my mother, who was waiting for me with a glass of juice from carrots she had

Tartane, Martinique. Claude Salez. Oil on canvas. Private collection.

just grated and then squeezed, and I would drink it and then run back to meet my chums. I knew there was nothing at all wrong with my eyes, but I had recently read a story in *The Schoolgirl's Own Annual* in which the heroine, a girl a few years older than I was then, cut such a figure to my mind with the way she was always adjusting her small, round, horn-rimmed glasses that I felt I must have a pair exactly like them. When it became clear that I didn't need glasses, I began to complain about the glare of the sun being too much for my eyes, and I walked around with my hands shielding them—especially in my mother's presence. My mother then bought for me a pair of sunglasses with the exact horn-rimmed frames I wanted, and how I enjoyed the gestures of blowing on the lenses, wiping them with the hem of my uniform, adjusting the glasses when they slipped down my nose, and just removing them from their case and putting them on. In three weeks, I grew tired of them and they found a nice resting place in a drawer, along with some other things that at one time or another I couldn't live without.

---

5. A *sixpence,* a *shilling,* and a *farthing* are former monetary units in various British Commonwealth countries. A shilling was worth twelve pence (pennies) or one-twentieth of a pound; a farthing was worth one-fourth of a penny.

Foreshadowing and Flashback *You may note that, so far, almost all the events in this story take place in the past. What do you think the author is building up to?*

We passed the store that sold only grooming aids, all imported from England. This store had in it a large porcelain dog— white, with black spots all over and a red ribbon of satin tied around its neck. The dog sat in front of a white porcelain bowl that was always filled with fresh water, and it sat in such a way that it looked as if it had just taken a long drink. When I was a small child, I would ask my mother, if ever we were near this store, to please take me to see the dog, and I would stand in front of it, bent over slightly, my hands resting on my knees, and stare at it and stare at it. I thought this dog more beautiful and more real than any actual dog I had ever seen or any actual dog I would ever see. I must have outgrown my interest in the dog, for when it disappeared I never asked what became of it. We passed the library, and if there was anything on this walk that I might have wept over leaving, this most surely would have been the thing. My mother had been a member of the library long before I was born. And since she took me everywhere with her when I was quite little, when she went to the library she took me along there, too. I would sit in her lap very quietly as she read books that she did not want to take home with her. I could not read the words yet, but just the way they looked on the page was interesting to me. Once, a book she was reading had a large picture of a man in it, and when I asked her who he was she told me that he was Louis Pasteur[6] and that the book was about his life. It stuck in my mind, because she said it was because of him that she boiled my milk to purify it before I was allowed to drink it, that it was his idea, and that that was why the process was called pasteurization. One of the things

I had put away in my mother's old trunk in which she kept all my childhood things was my library card. At that moment, I owed sevenpence in overdue fees.

As I passed by all these places, it was as if I were in a dream, for I didn't notice the people coming and going in and out of them, I didn't feel my feet touch ground, I didn't even feel my own body—I just saw these places as if they were hanging in the air, not having top or bottom, and as if I had gone in and out of them all in the same moment. The sun was bright; the sky was blue and just above my head. We then arrived at the jetty.

My heart now beat fast, and no matter how hard I tried, I couldn't keep my mouth from falling open and my nostrils from spreading to the ends of my face. My old fear of slipping between the boards of the jetty and falling into the dark-green water where the dark-green eels lived came over me. When my father's stomach started to go bad, the doctor had recommended a walk every evening right after he ate his dinner. Sometimes he would take me with him. When he took me with him, we usually went to the jetty, and there he would sit and talk to the night watchman about cricket or some other thing that didn't interest me, because it was not personal; they didn't talk about their wives, or their children, or their parents, or about any of their likes and dislikes. They talked about things

Visual Vocabulary
Cricket is a bat-and-ball game popular throughout the West Indies.

---

6. *Louis Pasteur* was a nineteenth-century French chemist who invented the process known as pasteurization.

Make and Verify Predictions *What prediction can you make about Annie's state of mind based on her description of her dreamlike state?*

in such a strange way, and I didn't see what they found funny, but sometimes they made each other laugh so much that their **guffaws** would bound out to sea and send back an echo. I was always sorry when we got to the jetty and saw that the night watchman on duty was the one he enjoyed speaking to; it was like being locked up in a book filled with numbers and diagrams and what-ifs. For the thing about not being able to understand and enjoy what they were saying was I had nothing to take my mind off my fear of slipping in between the boards of the jetty.

Now, too, I had nothing to take my mind off what was happening to me. My mother and my father—I was leaving them forever. My home on an island—I was leaving it forever. What to make of everything? I felt a familiar hollow space inside. I felt I was being held down against my will. I felt I was burning up from head to toe. I felt that someone was tearing me up into little pieces and soon I would be able to see all the little pieces as they floated out into nothing in the deep blue sea. I didn't know whether to laugh or cry. I could see that it would be better not to think too clearly about any one thing. The launch was being made ready to take me, along with some other passengers, out to the ship that was anchored in the sea. My father paid our fares, and we joined a line of people waiting to board. My mother checked my bag to make sure that I had my passport, the money she had given me, and a sheet of paper placed between some pages in my Bible on which were written the names of the relatives—people I had not known existed—with whom I would live in England. Across from the jetty was a wharf, and some stevedores were loading and unloading barges. I don't know why seeing that struck me so, but suddenly a wave of strong feeling came over me, and my heart swelled with a great gladness as the words "I shall never see this again" spilled out inside me. But then, just as quickly, my heart **shriveled** up and the words "I shall never see this again" stabbed at me. I don't know what stopped me from falling in a heap at my parents' feet.

When we were all on board, the launch headed out to sea. Away from the jetty, the water became the customary blue, and the launch left a wide path in it that looked like a road. I passed by sounds and smells that were so familiar that I had long ago stopped paying any attention to them. But now here they were, and the ever-present "I shall never see this again" bobbed up and down inside me. There was the sound of the seagull diving down into the water and coming up with something silverish in its mouth. There was the smell of the sea and the sight of small pieces of rubbish floating around in it. There were boats filled with fishermen coming in early. There was the sound of their voices as they shouted greetings to each other. There was the hot sun, there was the blue sea, there was the blue sky. Not very far away, there was the white sand of the shore, with the run-down houses all crowded in next to each other, for in some places only poor people lived near the shore. I was seated in the launch between

---

Make and Verify Predictions *Do you think Annie will get on the boat, given her reservations about leaving? Explain.*

Vocabulary

guffaw (gu fô´) *n.* a loud or boisterous burst of laughter

The Legacy of Colonialism *What internal conflict does Annie experience about leaving her homeland?*

Vocabulary

shrivel (shriv´əl) *v.* to become wrinkled as a result of lack of moisture

my parents, and when I realized that I was gripping their hands tightly I glanced quickly to see if they were looking at me with scorn, for I felt sure that they must have known of my never-see-this-again feelings. But instead my father kissed me on the forehead and my mother kissed me on the mouth, and they both gave over their hands to me, so that I could grip them as much as I wanted. I was on the verge of feeling that it had all been a mistake, but I remembered that I wasn't a child anymore, and that now when I made up my mind about something I had to see it through. At that moment, we came to the ship, and that was that.

The good-byes had to be quick, the captain said. My mother introduced herself to him and then introduced me. She told him to keep an eye on me, for I had never gone this far away from home on my own. She gave him a letter to pass on to the captain of the next ship that I would board in Barbados.[7] They walked me to my cabin, a small space that I would share with someone else—a woman I did not know. I had never before slept in a room with someone I did not know. My father kissed me good-bye and told me to be good and to write home often. After he said this, he looked at me, then looked at the floor and swung his left foot, then looked at me again. I could see that he wanted to say something else, something that he had never said to me before, but then he just turned and walked away. My mother said, "Well," and then she threw her arms around me. Big tears streamed down her face, and it must have been that—for I could not bear to see my mother cry—which started me crying, too. She then tightened her arms around me

and held me to her close, so that I felt that I couldn't breathe. With that, my tears dried up and I was suddenly on my guard. "What does she want now?" I said to myself. Still holding me close to her, she said, in a voice that raked across my skin, "It doesn't matter what you do or where you go, I'll always be your mother and this will always be your home."

I dragged myself away from her and backed off a little, and then I shook myself, as if to wake myself out of a **stupor.** We looked at each other for a long time with smiles on our faces, but I know the opposite of that was in my heart. As if responding to some invisible cue, we both said, at the very same moment, "Well." Then my mother turned around and walked out the cabin door. I stood there for I don't know how long, and then I remembered that it was customary to stand on deck and wave to your relatives who were returning to shore. From the deck, I could not see my father, but I could see my mother facing the ship, her eyes searching to pick me out. I removed from my bag a red cotton handkerchief that she had earlier given me for this purpose, and I waved it wildly in the air. Recognizing me immediately, she waved back just as wildly, and we continued to do this until she became just a dot in the matchbox-size launch swallowed up in the big blue sea.

I went back to my cabin and lay down on my berth. Everything trembled as if it had a spring at its very center. I could hear the small waves lap-lapping around the ship. They made an unexpected sound, as if a vessel filled with liquid had been placed on its side and now was slowly emptying out. ❧

---

7. *Barbados* (bär bā′dōz) is the easternmost island of the West Indies in the Caribbean Sea.

Make and Verify Predictions *How do you think Annie will handle her departure?*

Vocabulary

stupor (stō̅o′pər) n. a dulled mental state, often as a result of shock or stress; a daze

After You Read

Respond and Think Critically

Respond and Interpret

1. What memories of yours were stirred as you read this story?

2. (a)How have Annie's feelings about Miss Dulcie changed since she was her apprentice? (b)What does this change in her feelings suggest about Annie?

3. (a)What happened when Annie returned from her first unaccompanied walk on the road? (b)From Annie's description of that walk, how would you describe the relationship between Annie and her mother when Annie was little?

4. (a)What does Annie recall about her walks to the jetty as a child? (b)What parallel does Annie draw between her trips to the jetty as a child and the present moment?

Analyze and Evaluate

5. Why do you think Annie notices things she had long ignored as she rides on the launch? Support your answer with details from the story.

6. (a)Why does Annie think her parents might be looking at her with scorn on the launch? (b)What conflicting emotions does Annie experience on the launch?

7. (a)Why does Annie become wary of her mother when they are saying good-bye? (b)What does this tell you about the nature of their relationship?

Connect

8. **Big Idea** **The Legacy of Colonialism** In an analysis of *Annie John,* scholar Laura Niesen de Abruna suggests that the daughter's relationship with the mother is similar to the daughter's relationship with her "motherland," or homeland. Do you agree? Explain.

9. **Connect to the Author** Kincaid left Antigua for the United States when she was seventeen. Do you think this experience influenced *Annie John*? Explain.

Literary Element Foreshadowing and Flashback

ACT Skills Practice

Kincaid includes the flashback that describes Annie's walks to the jetty with her father (page 1282) primarily to:

A. clarify the tensions between Annie and her father.

B. provide an enjoyable diversion from the main action.

C. draw a parallel between Annie's childhood fear of falling and her fear of leaving home.

D. illustrate Annie's desire for independence from her family.

Review: Conflict

As you learned on page 754, an **internal conflict** is a struggle within the mind of a character torn between opposing feelings, desires, or goals.

Partner Activity With a partner, create a chart like the one below to identify internal conflicts in "A Walk to the Jetty."

Text	Conflict
"I could see that he wanted to say something else, something that he had never said to me before, but then he just turned and walked away."	Internal conflict of Annie's father: he wants to tell his daughter something but cannot find the words to do so.

Make and Verify Predictions

Have you ever read or watched a detective story, decided who committed the crime, and then changed your mind as more clues emerged? You were adjusting your prediction. Did you exclaim, "I knew it!" when the murderer was revealed? You were verifying your prediction. Review the chart you made on page 1278 and then answer the following questions.

1. How did Annie's memories of her past help you make predictions about the present events in the story?

2. (a)What did you predict about the narrator's emotional response at the end of the story? (b)Could you verify this prediction? Explain.

Vocabulary Practice

Practice with Denotation and Connotation
Denotation is the literal, or dictionary, meaning of a word. **Connotation** is the implied, or cultural, meaning of a word. For example, the words *amusing* and *hilarious* have a similar denotation, "funny," but they have different connotations:

Weaker *Stronger*
amusing   hilarious

Work with a partner to complete a graphic organizer like the one below for each bold-faced vocabulary word. Include the vocabulary word in one box and a word that has a similar denotation in another. Then explain which word has the stronger connotation.

loom   **guffaw**   **shrivel**   **stupor**

EXAMPLE:

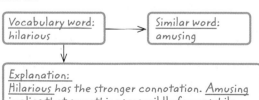

Write with Style

 ## Apply Flashback

Assignment In this excerpt from Kincaid's novel, Annie recalls a number of details from her life as she walks toward a ship bound for her new life across the Atlantic Ocean. Write a short story in which you use flashbacks to illuminate the significance of the present, as Kincaid does.

Get Ideas You will most likely need to go through several drafts to integrate the flashbacks smoothly into your story. Once you have come up with some ideas, think about the complexity of the task and then make a schedule for yourself. Working backward from the assignment's due date, set deadlines for yourself that will allow you enough time to take a break between each stage of drafting and revising.

Give It Structure Remember that you will need to use logical transitions to show how the flashbacks relate to the main action. Come up with details in the present that would trigger memories for the characters. Then brainstorm transitional sentences that could guide readers back into the present at the end of the flashbacks. Organize your ideas in a diagram like the one below.

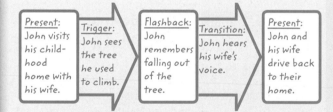

Look at Language As you revise, replace vague adjectives with more precise, vivid ones. Work to establish a distinctive voice and a personal style. If you use a thesaurus, be aware of the different shades of meaning contained within the different synonyms you find. Use a variety of sentence patterns to maintain the reader's interest.

LOG ON ▶ **Literature** Online

Selection Resources For Selection Quizzes, eFlashcards, and Reading-Writing Connection activities, go to glencoe.com and enter QuickPass code GLW6053u6.

Before You Read

Fishing

Meet **Joy Harjo**
(born 1951)

Born into the Muskogee (Creek) Indian tribe, Joy Harjo knew at an early age she was going to be an artist. Since her childhood in Tulsa, Oklahoma, she has immersed herself in painting, theater, music, film, and the written word.

Native American Roots The daughter of a Cherokee-French mother and a Creek father, Harjo is descended from a long line of tribal leaders and orators. She describes this heritage as the foundation of her writing: "I know when I write that there is an old Creek within me that often participates."

Harjo studied painting and theater at the Institute of American Indian Arts in Santa Fe, New Mexico, and the University of New Mexico in Albuquerque. In 1970, she adopted her paternal grandmother's surname and became known as Joy Harjo.

Making Magic from Words At the age of 22, Harjo heard Simon Ortiz's work at a poetry reading. His poems, steeped in the mood and the voice of the familiar Southwest, inspired her. She studied Native American, African American, and Latino authors and soon began to write her own poems. She switched her major to poetry, claiming that her own poetry was "taking on more magical qualities than my painting. I could say more when I wrote." Besides Ortiz, her influences came to include Leslie Marmon Silko, James Wright, Pablo Neruda, and Meridel Le Sueur. After finishing her bachelor's degree, she went on to receive her master of fine arts in creative writing from the University of Iowa in 1978. She has taught at a number of educational institutions, includ-

> "*Writing helped me give voice to turn around a terrible silence that was killing me.*"
>
> —Joy Harjo

ing the Institute of American Indian Arts, the University of Colorado, the University of Arizona, the University of New Mexico, and the University of California, Los Angeles.

Much of Harjo's poetry—as well as the song lyrics she writes for her band—focuses on the history and contemporary problems of Native Americans. Although she does not identify herself as a political author, she has worked tirelessly to use her art as a means to spread awareness about Native American culture. Her poems often reflect her strong ties to the landscape and the people of the American Southwest. Harjo has escaped her "terrible silence" to become a compelling literary voice in the United States and beyond.

Fish too anticipate the game of fishing. Their ancestors perfected the moves, sent down stories that appear as electrical impulses when sunlight hits water. The hook carries great symbology in the coming of age, and is crucial to the making of warriors. The greatest warriors are those who dangle a human for hours on a string, break sacred water for the profanity of air, then snap fiercely back into pearly molecules that describe fishness.

They smell me as I walk the banks with fishing pole, night crawlers[2] and a promise I made to that old friend Louis to fish with him this summer. This is the only place I can keep that promise, inside a poem as familiar to him as the banks of his favorite fishing place. I try not to let the fish see me see them as they look for his tracks on the soft earth made of fossils and ashes. I hear the burble of fish talk: *When is that old Creek coming back? He was the one we loved to tease most, we liked his songs and once in a while he gave us a good run.*

Last night I dreamed I tried to die. I was going to look for Louis. It was rather comical. I worked hard to **muster** my last breath, then lay down in the summer, along the banks of the last mythic river, my pole and tackle box next to me. What I thought was my last breath floated off as a cloud making an umbrella of grief over my relatives. How embarrassing when the next breath came, and then the next. I reeled in one after another, as if I'd caught a bucket of suckers[3] instead of bass. I guess it wasn't my time, I explained, and went fishing anyway as a liar and I know most fishers to be liars most of the time. Even Louis when it came to fishing, or even dying.

The leap between the sacred and **profane** is as thin as fishing line, and is part of the mystery on this river of life, as is the way our people continue to make warriors in the strangest of times. I save this part of the poem for the fish camp next to the oldest spirits whose dogs bark to greet visitors. It's near Louis's favorite spot, where the wisest and fattest fish laze. I'll meet him there.

A few weeks before he died I wrote my friend the Muscogee poet, Louis Oliver, a promise that I would go fishing with him in Oklahoma that summer. Fishing to Louis was holy communion.

The struggle of the universe is exemplified in the sport. Yet it's possible to find the answer to every question with the right pole, the right place on the river.

As I mailed the letter I had a strange feeling the letter would never reach him. That cloud of illogic hovered over me for a few days.

When I was informed of his death I knew I had to keep that promise.

This is how I kept it.

---

2. *Night crawlers* are large earthworms found on the soil surface after dark. They are prized as fish bait.

Summarize *In this sentence, which key words would you underline to remember in a summary?*

Vocabulary

muster (mus′tər) *v.* to cause to gather

---

3. *Suckers* are a group of toothless freshwater fish, not valued by fishers.

Nature and the Imagination *What imagery does the author use to support ideas about the relationship between fishing and life?*

Vocabulary

profane (prō fān′) *adj.* not concerned with religious purposes

After You Read

Respond and Think Critically

Respond and Interpret

1. What insights did you gain from reading this poem? Write a few sentences in your journal to answer this question. Then share your response with a classmate.

2. (a)What has the speaker promised Louis? (b)Why does the speaker have to write a poem to keep this promise?

3. (a)Why did the speaker try to die in her dream? (b)What makes the dream comical?

Analyze and Evaluate

4. (a)Is the poem set in a real or an imaginary place? (b)What does the river symbolize in this poem?

5. (a)In your opinion, could this poem stand on its own, without the italicized sentences that explain the background? Explain. (b)How does the italicized ending affect the emotional quality of the poem?

Connect

6. **Big Idea** **Nature and the Imagination** According to Harjo, the fisher's hook plays a role in the coming of age of the fish. What do you think the hook might symbolize in terms of the life and the coming of age of a human?

7. **Connect to the Author** Harjo's poem is a personal message to her friend, yet she connects his death to the "river" of life. Why do you think she puts this single event into a larger context?

Literary Element Voice

Harjo uses metaphor and personification to create a tribute to an old friend in her moving prose poem "Fishing."

1. What does the description of the dream reveal about the speaker's personality?

2. Why do you think the speaker believes that the fish enjoyed Louis's visits?

Reading Strategy Summarize

Underlining key words and phrases or taking notes can test your recall before you write a summary.

Partner Activity With a partner, discuss the main idea of each section and decide which key words and phrases you would use in a summary. Consult the chart you made on page 1288. Summarize each section, then summarize the whole poem.

LOG ON ▶ **Literature** Online

Selection Resources For Selection Quizzes, eFlash-cards, and Reading-Writing Connection activities, go to glencoe.com and enter QuickPass code GLW6053u6.

Vocabulary Practice

Practice with Antonyms With a partner, brainstorm three antonyms for each boldfaced vocabulary word below. Then discuss your choices with your classmates. Be prepared to explain your choices.

relentless   muster   profane

EXAMPLE: thwart
Antonyms: aid, help, assist
Sample explanation: A person who thwarts something prevents it from happening; a person who aids something helps it happen.

Writing

Write a Letter In "Fishing," the speaker writes that she sent a letter to her friend Louis Oliver just before he died, though she "had a strange feeling the letter would never reach him." What do you imagine she wrote in this letter? Write a letter to Louis Oliver, pretending you are the speaker. Do your best to imitate her voice throughout.

Literary Analysis

Literature Connection As evidenced in the following sentence, Julio Cortázar uses vivid sensory details to create suspense and terror in "The Night Face Up."

> "But he smelled death, and when he opened his eyes he saw the blood-soaked figure of the executioner-priest coming toward him with the stone knife in his hand."

A **literary analysis** is a type of essay in which you examine specific literary or stylistic elements, such as imagery, in a story or a poem in order to better understand the work as a whole. Literary analysis fits under the larger category of **literary criticism,** which involves the study, the interpretation, and the evaluation of literature. To write an effective literary analysis, you will need to become familiar with the goals and the strategies listed below.

Writing Process

At any stage of a writing process, you may think of new ideas. Feel free to return to earlier stages as you write.

Prewrite

Draft

Revise

Focus Lesson:
Sentence Openers

Edit and Proofread

Focus Lesson:
Run-on Sentences

Present

Rubric

Goals	Strategies
To present a concise explanation of the meaning of a work	☑ In your introduction, present a thesis that states your interpretation of the work's meaning. ☑ In your conclusion, restate your thesis and summarize your main points.
To analyze specific literary elements of the work	☑ Show how elements such as plot, tone, style, and figurative language contribute to the work's meaning.
To support your analysis with evidence	☑ Present direct quotations and concrete examples from the work. ☑ Draw your own conclusions about the meaning of these examples. ☑ Explain how your evidence relates to your thesis.
To present your ideas in a logical order	☑ Include a clear introduction and conclusion. ☑ Use each body paragraph to develop one main idea. ☑ Use transitions between ideas and sections of your essay.

Writing and Research For prewriting, drafting, and revising tools, go to glencoe.com and enter QuickPass code GLW6053u6.

Assignment: Analyze a Short Story

Write an analysis of a short story, using evidence to support your thesis. As you move through the stages of writing, keep your audience and purpose in mind.

Audience: peers, classmates, and teachers who are familiar with the story

Purpose: to present an interpretation of the story's meaning and an analysis of the effects that create that meaning

Analyze a Professional Model

In the following essay on Gabriel García Márquez's story "The Handsomest Drowned Man in the World," scholar Rena Korb argues that the reason the drowned man in the story has such a profound effect on the villagers is that they are willing to accept fantastic events in their daily lives. As you read, pay close attention to the comments in the margin. They point out features you might want to include in your own literary analysis.

An Analysis of "The Handsomest Drowned Man in the World" by Rena Korb

In addition to *One Hundred Years of Solitude*, García Márquez's short story "The Handsomest Drowned Man in the World" highlights his talents at using magic realism to draw the reader into a world unlike one in which most people dwell . . . In the story, García Márquez presents a tiny coastal town filled with people who seem unremarkable in any way except for their ability to accept the fantastic and thus enrich their own lives. . . .

Because the villagers naturally accept the fantastic, an enormous drowned man who washes upon their shore does not frighten them nor do they reject him. Instead of being freakish for his size, he is "the tallest, strongest, most virile and best built man they had ever seen." The drowned man, whom they come to call Esteban, has more ideal qualities than just the physical. He is compassionate,

Introduction

In your introduction, mention the title of the work and the author, and capture your reader's attention.

Thesis

Summarize your interpretation in one sentence.

Main Points

Begin each body paragraph with a main point that relates to your thesis.

recognizing the anxiety that his size causes and possessing the artful knowledge that "the lady of the house looked for her most resistant chair and begged him, frightened to death, sit here" . . .

Evidence

Support your main points with direct quotations from the text.

Because the villagers do not spend their time wondering how Esteban came to exist, they can concentrate on what is important: the man. Looking in his face they see that "he did not have the lonely look of other drowned men who came out of the sea or that haggard, needy look of men who drowned in rivers." When they realize that he will have to be dragged to his funeral (no one can carry him), they understand the shame and awkwardness his size caused him in life. Not only do they understand how Esteban feels, but they begin to understand a bit more about their own lives. As the women sit up all night, sewing an outfit for Esteban, "it seemed to them that the wind had never been so steady nor the sea so restless . . . and they supposed that the change had something to do with the dead man." Already their lives, fed by the "calm and bountiful" sea, are changing. . . .

Analysis

Explain how your textual evidence supports your thesis.

Literary Elements

Focus on specific literary elements and explain how these elements contribute to the story's meaning.

The use of another element of magic realism helps justify the monumental effect Esteban had: the mythic. In the personage of Esteban are shades of heroes from different cultures and time periods. His very name, Spanish for Stephen, invokes St. Stephen, the first Christian martyr. Esteban also may recall Estevanico (a diminutive form of the name), an African slave who explored Florida and the Southwest United States in the 1500s. He was the first African many Indians had ever seen, and they thought he might be a god and gave him many gifts. As with Esteban, his appearance led him to be revered as something more than an ordinary man; just as the villagers would strive "to make Esteban's memory eternal," legends were passed down for generations, right until the present day, about Estevanico. . . .

Context

Explain allusions or context to help the reader better understand the text.

The story may best be seen as presenting the multiple realities that are inherent to magic realism. Just as the villagers have to be open to possibilities in order to reap the benefits of Esteban's visit, so must readers suspend their disbelief.

Conclusion

Restate your thesis and include a few final, thought-provoking comments.

Reading-Writing Connection Think about the writing techniques you just encountered and try them in your literary analysis.

Prewrite

Explore a Story What short story from Unit 6 was particularly interesting to you? Carefully reread the story, writing down passages that embody the author's themes and writing style.

Choose a Focus After you have reread the story, look over your notes. Consider which literary elements and stylistic devices contribute to the story's meaning. Then choose a particular aspect as your focus. For example, you could focus on how an author uses figurative language to develop a story's theme.

Analyze the Elements Make a chart like the one below to examine how the author uses specific literary and stylistic elements.

Julio Cortázar's "The Night Face Up"		
Element	Passages	Effect
Sensory Details	"the damp smell, the smell of oozing rock"	Lends reality and immediacy
Transitions	"'You're going to fall off the bed,' said the patient next to him."	Creates a jarring feeling

Develop a Working Thesis Review your chart and think about what your details say about the story as a whole. Then write a one-sentence working thesis that explains how the author uses literary devices to develop the story's meaning.

Create a Structure Think about the main points you want to make in your essay and the order in which you will make them. Then create an outline for each of your body paragraphs, including quotations and ideas from your analysis chart as support. Use the format below to organize each of your body paragraphs.

Main Point: Cortázar presents the ancient setting of the dream as a self-contained world with its own rituals and customs.	→	Evidence: The protagonist takes note of the "quaking bogs from which no one ever returned"; later, he refers to "the supplication of the corn which brings about the beneficent moons."	→	Analysis: These are details specific to the Moteca world, which the contemporary protagonist could not know; however, they are presented in such a matter-of-fact manner that readers accept them.

Persuasion Versus Analysis

Remember that the goal of a literary analysis is different from that of a persuasive essay. Although you want your audience to agree with your interpretation of the text, your goal in a literary analysis is to explain *how* the author achieves certain effects rather than to offer your opinion about the merit of the work.

Avoid Plagiarism

Give credit to all of your sources, even if your only source is your short story. If you paraphrase sections of the story or include a direct quote, refer to the relevant page number. If you quote directly from the story, make sure you write the quote accurately.

Draft

Stay in the Present Draft your essay from start to finish, using the present tense (also known as the literary present) when referring to events in the text.

Analyze a Workshop Model

Here is a final draft of a literary analysis. Read the essay and answer the questions in the margin. Use the answers to these questions to guide you as you write.

Writing Frames

As you read the workshop model, think about the writer's use of the following literary analysis frames.

- Having finished the story, some readers may wonder _____; however, _____.

- By presenting _____ Cortázar leads readers to _____.

Try using these kinds of frames to present your analysis to readers.

Introduction

Why does the writer include this information at the beginning of the introduction?

Thesis

How does the writer's thesis connect the literary elements to the text's broader meaning?

Competing Realities: Julio Cortázar's "The Night Face Up"

The protagonist in Julio Cortázar's "The Night Face Up" moves fluidly between two realities. Lying in a hospital bed after a motorcycle accident, he has a recurring dream in which he is a Moteca Indian escaping from Aztecs who want to offer him as a sacrifice. This dream becomes increasingly vivid until the narrator reveals that it is real, and that the contemporary setting has been the dream. The author uses a fluid style, sensory details, and a jarring plot structure to draw readers into both the contemporary setting and the ancient one, refusing to present either as more "real" than the other. This creates a disorienting effect that challenges readers' assumptions about fiction and reality.

Cortázar narrates in such a matter-of-fact style that it is easy to accept both the dream and the contemporary setting on their own terms. One example comes at the beginning of the story, when Cortázar's unnamed protagonist is "late" for some event, but there is no sense of urgency. Instead, the protagonist enjoys a motorcycle ride through an environment that seems familiar to him. Cortázar uses long sentences to describe this scene: buildings "zip past (the pink, the white)," and the protagonist calmly "allow[s] himself to be carried away by the freshness, by the weightless contraction of the hardly begun day." Cortázar's calm tone and flowing style make the setting seem natural and believable.

Similarly, Cortázar presents the ancient setting of the dream as a self-contained world with its own rituals and customs. The protagonist takes note of the "quaking bogs from which no one ever returned"; later, he refers to "the supplication of the corn which brings about the beneficent moons." These are details specific to the Moteca world, which the contemporary protagonist could not know; however, they are presented in such a matter-of-fact manner that readers accept them. Cortázar also employs vivid imagery to lend a sense of reality to details in both settings. For example, there is a "damp smell, the smell of oozing rock"; similarly, in the hospital, a "blond nurse rub[s] the front of [the protagonist's] thigh with alcohol." Such sensory details suggest a knowledge of both time periods, so it is difficult to dismiss either setting as fantasy.

Because both settings seem so thoroughly real, the transitions between them create jarring interruptions. For instance, Cortázar shifts from the first two dream sequences by inserting abrupt comments from the patient in the hospital bed next to the protagonist. This creates a jolting effect; readers must reorient themselves to the new setting after each shift. Readers can no better understand what is "real" than the protagonist can.

In the end, Cortázar chooses the opposite of the comfortable, expected conclusion, which would state that the ancient Moteca sequences were "only a dream." Instead, he forces readers to see something far more disturbing: that the "dream" in the story is every bit as real as the "reality," and that both are in fact "absurd as all dreams are." By presenting two equally convincing worlds, Cortázar leads readers to recognize their reliance on literary conventions and their willingness to accept fiction at face value. Like other magic realist authors, he draws attention to the fine line between reality and fantasy by presenting the simultaneous existence of two different realities in a natural way. His story shows how easily the illusion of reality can be created or pulled away.

Exposition

Literary Elements

How does the writer's discussion of sensory details help support the thesis?

Evidence

Why does the writer include both of these quotations in the same sentence?

Conclusion

What makes this conclusion effective?

Revise

When you have finished writing, use the checklist below to evaluate your literary analysis.

Checklist

☑ Do you provide a concise thesis statement that includes your interpretation of the theme or the effect to be analyzed?

☑ Do you show how specific literary elements in the story contribute to its overall meaning?

☑ Do you present quotations from the story along with analysis that supports your main points?

☑ Do you present your points in a logical, effective order?

> **Focus Lesson**

Sentence Openers

To improve the flow of your paragraphs, open your sentences with different words. Avoid beginning every sentence with a pronoun, a noun, or the word *the*. Instead, try starting some sentences with a transitional or descriptive word (such as *therefore* or *finally*), a phrase (such as *after the accident* or *during the dream*), or a clause (such as *before the man arrives* or *because he is frightened*).

Draft:

He is lying in a hospital bed after a motorcycle accident when he has a recurring dream in which he is a Moteca Indian escaping from Aztecs who want to offer him as a sacrifice.

Revision:

Lying in a hospital bed after a motorcycle accident,[1] he has a recurring dream in which he is a Moteca Indian escaping from Aztecs who want to offer him as a sacrifice.

1: Opens with a clause

Traits of Strong Writing

Follow these traits of strong writing to express your ideas effectively.

Ideas

Organization

Voice

Word Choice

Sentence Fluency

Conventions

Presentation

For more information on using the Traits of Strong Writing, see pages R28–R30.

Word Choice

This academic vocabulary word appears in the Workshop model.

environment (in vī′rən mənt) *n.* the circumstances, the objects, or the conditions by which one is surrounded; *Instead, the protagonist enjoys a motorcycle ride through an environment that seems familiar to him.*

Using academic vocabulary may help strengthen your writing. Try to use one or two academic vocabulary words in your essay. See the complete list on pages R83–R85.

Edit and Proofread

Get It Right When you have completed the final draft of your literary analysis, proofread it for errors in grammar, usage, mechanics, and spelling. Refer to the Language Handbook, pages R40–R59, as a guide.

> **Focus Lesson**

Run-on Sentences

A run-on sentence joins two independent clauses (groups of words that could stand alone as sentences) using a comma or no punctuation. Below is an example of a run-on sentence from an early draft of the Workshop model, along with two possible corrections.

Original: The following is a run-on sentence. Two independent clauses (highlighted) are separated by a comma.

This creates a jolting effect, readers must reorient themselves to the new setting after each shift.

Improved: Use a semicolon to separate the two independent clauses.

This creates a jolting effect; readers must reorient themselves to the new setting after each shift.

Improved: Use a comma and a coordinating conjunction to join the independent clauses.

This creates a jolting effect, and readers must reorient themselves to the new setting after each shift.

Present/Publish

Follow Conventions Once you have finished reviewing your work, read through it again to make sure you have included quotation marks around any text quoted directly from the story. Then check to see that you have written the titles of works in the proper format. Short story titles should be in quotation marks, while book titles should be italicized or underlined. Check that your essay meets any length requirements and is neatly presented in handwriting or typed form.

Peer Review Tips

As you revise, ask a partner to point out places where you could add transitional words and phrases—such as *first, second, finally, more important,* and *moreover*— to show the logical progression of ideas within and between paragraphs. Transitional words and phrases strengthen your points by showing a clear line of thinking.

Word-Processing Tip

Type your analysis on a computer and adjust your spacing, margins, and font size so that it is easy to read.

Writer's Portfolio

Place a clean copy of your literary analysis in your portfolio to review later.

Literature Online

Writing and Research For editing and publishing tools, go to glencoe.com and enter QuickPass code GLW6053u6.

Writing Frames

As you prepare your review, think about using some of the following frames to get started.

- My own view is that _____, because _____.

- Of course, some might disagree with my claim and say that _____.

Speaking, Listening, and Viewing Workshop

Critical Review

Literature Connection Literary analyses are often published in scholarly journals geared toward specialized audiences. A more widely read form of literary criticism is the **critical review.** Critical reviews feature thoughtful analysis, but they also take a firm stand on the merits of a work—often praising or panning it.

> **Assignment** Plan and orally deliver a critical review of a literary work from the unit.

Develop Your Opinion

In a critical review, you present your opinion of a work and back it up with evidence. Follow these steps to plan the content of your presentation.

- Use a chart like the one in the Unit 6 Writing Workshop (see page 1295) to examine significant passages from the text. If you review the same story you analyzed for the Writing Workshop, you will have already examined the literary elements, and you probably have an opinion of the work.

- Think about how the passages you analyze contribute to the work as a whole. Does the author achieve the desired literary effects? How convincingly does the author develop the theme?

- Write a one- or two-sentence summary of your opinion. This will serve as your thesis. It should include descriptive words about the work, along with a statement of the effectiveness of the author's use of literary and stylistic devices. This thesis can be more subjective than one for an analytical essay.

- Write down your supporting arguments and quotations. Choose vivid, attention-grabbing quotations that will be memorable.

Thesis: Cortázar's "The Night Face Up" is the strangest story I've ever read.

Prepare Your Presentation

Once you have formed your opinion of the work, follow these steps to plan your oral presentation:

- Listen to the language used by book and film critics on television. They often deliver their opinions in a colloquial, casual style but use formal, analytical language to back up their ideas.

- As you listen to these samples, think of words and phrases that you could use to spice up your own main points. Replace dry language with colorful, descriptive phrases wherever possible.

- Create a visual aid that will help reinforce your evaluation of the work. One possibility is to write out quotations in large lettering on a piece of poster board so that you can refer to them as you speak.

Rehearse

Rehearse your presentation for a friend or a family member. Ask this person to comment on how well you analyze evidence to support your opinion of the work. Also ask for feedback on the language and the style of your presentation, and have your partner evaluate your use of the following techniques.

Techniques for Delivering an Oral Presentation

Verbal Techniques	Nonverbal Techniques
☑ **Pace** Pause after important ideas.	☑ **Gestures** Make natural hand gestures that emphasize your points.
☑ **Tone** Adjust your tone to emphasize important points.	☑ **Eye Contact** Look at your audience.
☑ **Pronunciation** Speak each word clearly.	☑ **Display** Point to your visual aids when appropriate.
☑ **Volume** Speak loudly enough so that everyone can hear you.	☑ **Posture** Stand tall and be proud of your work.

Use the First Person

Unlike a literary analysis, a critical review includes your personal response to a literary work. In a critical review, it is appropriate to use the word *I* and to discuss your opinion about the work.

Presentation Tips

Use the following checklist to evaluate your presentation.

- Did you vary your tone and use natural gestures?
- Did you make eye contact with the audience?
- Did you face the audience and not the visuals?

Independent Reading

Literature of the Region

THE EUROPEAN COLONIZATION OF THE AMERICAS LED TO FIERCE CULTURAL CONFLICTS AND THE blending of traditions. This legacy is evident in a variety of works from the region, which often combine local mythology with European styles. In their works, modern authors of the Americas frequently explore the effects of contemporary political struggles, the power of memory and personal experience, and the importance of love and community.

True History of the Conquest of New Spain

Bernal Díaz del Castillo

Combining elements of autobiography, history, and fiction, *True History of the Conquest of New Spain* describes Díaz's firsthand experience as a soldier and conquistador during the Spanish settlement of the Americas. Frustrated by other Spanish accounts of discovery, which he felt were biased and incomplete, Díaz set out to tell the story of the foot soldiers who risked their lives in the conquest. Díaz's narrative is notable for its colloquial writing style; its intricate, realistic portrayals of his comrades; and its relative sympathy toward the indigenous peoples of the Americas.

A Gabriela Mistral Reader

Gabriela Mistral

This collection by the first Latin American author to receive the Nobel Prize in literature contains poems and other works of love, pain, and hope. Much of Mistral's poetic inspiration stemmed from the tragic death of her fiancé at a young age, and her works are frequently infused with a sense of loss and spiritual struggle. For more poetry by Mistral, look for *Selected Poems of Gabriela Mistral*, translated by American author Doris Dana, who was awarded Chile's Order of Merit (the country's highest honor) for her work.

Barrio Boy

Ernesto Galarza

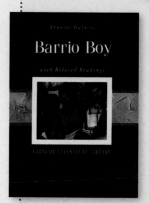

Caught between opposing forces of the Mexican Revolution, a family sets out from a small mountain village hoping to find safety and a new life in Sacramento, California.

. . . And the Earth Did Not Devour Him

Tomás Rivera

This compilation of short stories and vignettes follows one year's painful events for a boy in a community of migrant workers in the United States.

The Bridge of San Luis Rey

Thornton Wilder

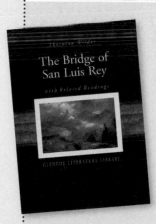

The collapse of Peru's most famous bridge in 1714 is the catalyst for this Pulitzer Prize-winning novel, which explores the workings of fate and divine intervention.

CRITICS' CORNER

"As best exemplified by One Hundred Years of Solitude, *García Márquez's ingenious mixture of realism and fantasy has resulted in the creation of a total fictional universe in which the commonplace takes on an aura of magic and the impossible is made believable. His penetrating insights into the ambiguities of human nature are enhanced by a rich vein of anecdotes and leitmotifs [recurring themes] he taps from his private mythology."*

—George R. McMurray

One Hundred Years of Solitude

Gabriel García Márquez

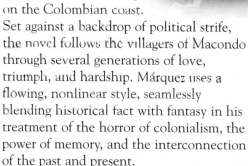

Considered to be García Márquez's masterpiece, this novel tells the story of the fictional town of Macondo, a small village on the Colombian coast. Set against a backdrop of political strife, the novel follows the villagers of Macondo through several generations of love, triumph, and hardship. Márquez uses a flowing, nonlinear style, seamlessly blending historical fact with fantasy in his treatment of the horror of colonialism, the power of memory, and the interconnection of the past and present.

Hold a Panel Discussion

Read one of the books listed here and form a group with students who have read other books on the list. Hold a panel discussion in which you compare the books' treatments of a common subject, such as colonialism, tradition, or love.

Assessment

English–Language Arts

Reading: Fiction and Informational Text

Carefully read the following passage. Use context clues to help you define any words with which you are unfamiliar. Pay close attention to the author's **tone** and use of **characterization**. Then, on a separate sheet of paper, answer questions 1–5 on page 1306.

from *The House of the Spirits* by Isabel Allende
Translated by Magda Bogin

That was Marcos's longest trip. He returned with a shipment of enormous boxes that were piled in the far courtyard, between the chicken coop and the woodshed, until the winter was over. Marcos spent two weeks assembling the contents according to an instruction manual written in English, which he was
5 able to decipher thanks to his invincible imagination and a small dictionary. When the job was finished, it turned out to be a bird of prehistoric dimensions, with the face of a furious eagle, wings that moved, and a propeller on its back. It caused an uproar. The police, on horseback and carrying lances, had trouble keeping the crowds far enough away from the center of the park, where Marcos
10 waited dressed in mechanic's overalls, with huge racer's goggles and an explorer's helmet. He was also equipped with a compass, a telescope, and several strange maps that he had traced himself based on various theories of Leonardo da Vinci and on the polar knowledge of the Incas. Against all logic, on the second try the bird lifted off without mishap and with a certain elegance, accompa-
15 nied by the creaking of its skeleton and the roar of its motor. It rose flapping its wings and disappeared into the clouds, to a send-off of applause, whistlings, handkerchiefs, drumrolls, and the sprinkling of holy water. All that remained on earth were the comments of the amazed crowd below and a multitude of experts, who attempted to provide a reasonable explanation of the miracle. Clara
20 continued to stare at the sky long after her uncle had become invisible. She thought she saw him ten minutes later, but it was only a migrating sparrow. After three days the initial euphoria that had accompanied the first airplane flight in the country died down and no one gave the episode another thought, except for Clara, who continued to peer at the horizon.
25 After a week with no word from the flying uncle, people began to speculate that he had gone so high that he had disappeared into outer space, and the ignorant suggested he would reach the moon. With a mixture of sadness and relief, Severo decided that his brother-in-law and his machine must have fallen into some hidden crevice of the cordillera, where they would never be found.
30 Nívea wept disconsolately and lit candles to San Antonio, patron of lost objects.

Severo opposed the idea of having masses said, because he did not believe in them as a way of getting into heaven, much less of returning to earth, and he maintained that masses and religious vows, like the selling of indulgences, images, and scapulars, were a dishonest business. Because of his attitude, Nívea
35 and Nana had the children say the rosary behind their father's back for nine days. Meanwhile, groups of volunteer explorers and mountain climbers tirelessly searched peaks and passes, combing every accessible stretch of land until they finally returned in triumph to hand the family the mortal remains of the deceased in a sealed black coffin. The intrepid traveler was laid to rest in a gran-
40 diose funeral. His death made him a hero and his name was on the front page of all the papers for several days. The same multitude that had gathered to see him off the day he flew away in his bird paraded past his coffin. The entire family wept as befit the occasion, except for Clara, who continued to watch the sky with the patience of an astronomer. One week after he had been buried, Uncle
45 Marcos, a bright smile playing behind his pirate's mustache, appeared in person in the doorway of Nívea and Severo del Valle's house. Thanks to the surreptitious prayers of the women and children, as he himself admitted, he was alive and well and in full possession of his faculties, including his sense of humor. Despite the noble lineage of his aerial maps, the flight had been a failure. He
50 had lost his airplane and had to return on foot, but he had not broken any bones and his adventurous spirit was intact. This confirmed the family's eternal devotion to San Antonio, but was not taken as a warning by future generations, who also tried to fly, although by different means.

Informational Reading Carefully read the following announcement, playing close attention to details and specific instructions. Then answer questions 6–8 on page 1306.

Recall Alert

Product: Joe's Airplanes Company has announced a recall of 2,000 rechargeable battery packs for toy airplanes. The recall affects battery packs included with Intrepid III toy airplanes sold worldwide between June 1, 2005 and February 1, 2007. The code MARCOS857 is printed near the top of affected battery packs.
5 Battery packs imprinted with DELVALLES858 are not affected by the recall.
Problem: The battery cells may overheat and pose a fire hazard.
What to do: All consumers should stop using the battery packs immediately and email recall@joesairplanes.com (U.S. consumers) or intcustserv@joesairplanes.com (international consumers) for information about obtaining free
10 replacement battery packs.

Items 1–5 apply to the passage from *The House of the Spirits*.

1. Which of the following can you infer about the relationship between Severo and Nívea del Valle?
   A. They are casual acquaintances.
   B. They are brother and sister.
   C. They are husband and wife.
   D. They are mother and son.

2. What is the main source of the tension between Severo and Nívea del Valle?
   F. a disagreement over religious practices
   G. a disagreement over the whereabouts of the missing Marcos
   H. a long-standing disagreement over child-rearing methods
   J. a disagreement over how to dispose of the remains of the dead

3. At what point does Nívea weep disconsolately and light candles to San Antonio?
   A. during Marcos's funeral
   B. after the groups of volunteers return the mortal remains of the deceased
   C. before Marcos takes off on his adventure
   D. after a week with no word from Marcos

4. As it is used in lines 47–48, the word *surreptitious* most nearly means:
   F. persistent
   G. obvious
   H. stealthy
   J. insincere

5. From information in the passage, which of the following best describes the character of Marcos?
   A. He is outgoing and universally loved.
   B. He is cautious.
   C. He is adventurous and imaginative.
   D. He has trouble making decisions.

Items 6–8 apply to "Recall Alert."

6. Where should consumers look for the code MARCOS857?
   F. on the Web site joesairplanes.com
   G. on the side of Intrepid III toy airplanes
   H. near the top of their battery packs
   J. in an e-mail sent to consumers by Joe's Airplanes Company

7. What action does Joe's Airplanes Company plan to take to assist consumers affected by the recall?
   A. reclaim all affected Intrepid III toy airplanes
   B. sell replacement battery packs at a reduced rate
   C. provide refunds on purchases of the Intrepid III
   D. provide free replacement battery packs

8. What action should be taken by a consumer who lives in Mexico and possesses a battery pack with the code MARCOS857 that she purchased in 2006?
   F. She should e-mail recall@joesairplanes.com.
   G. She should e-mail intcustserv@joesairplanes.com.
   H. She should contact Joe's Airplanes Company by phone.
   J. She should take no action.

Vocabulary Skills: Sentence Completion

For each item in the Vocabulary Skills section, choose the word or words that best complete the sentence. Write your answers on a separate sheet of paper.

1. Racial and class barriers are often a _____ to the many Maya who wish to achieve a higher standard of living.
   A. conception
   B. ploy
   C. solace
   D. hindrance

2. Pablo Neruda _____ from traditional subject matter in his odes, writing about ordinary, rather than _____, objects.
   F. strays...exalted
   G. improvises...haggard
   H. veers...lucid
   J. collides...mediocre

3. Despite their commonplace subject matter, Neruda's odes avoid _____ by revealing the great beauty and majesty of everyday objects.
   A. supplication
   B. frivolity
   C. resignation
   D. haste

4. In Neruda's poem "Horses," the vibrant presence of the horses helps _____ the effects of a monotonous winter day.
   F. revive
   G. improvise
   H. mitigate
   J. muster

5. Many consecrated Native American religious sites have sustained _____ damage by development.
   A. irrevocable
   B. austere
   C. banal
   D. fallacious

6. Magic realist authors often combine two distinct elements: precise realism and _____ fantasy.
   F. sheer
   G. haggard
   H. supplementary
   J. unwitting

7. Corn was the primary source of _____ for the prehistoric peoples who _____ the Mississippi region of North America.
   A. sustenance...inhabited
   B. coercion...commenced
   C. humility...fluttered
   D. diligence...pounced

8. In the early years of European settlement, deadly _____ claimed the lives of Native Americans, who lacked immunity to European diseases.
   F. stragglers
   G. epidemics
   H. guffaws
   J. stupors

9. Christopher Columbus often presented a/an _____ and demeaning view of native peoples he encountered.
   A. irrevocable
   B. condescending
   C. tedious
   D. edible

10. In Alice Munro's "Day of the Butterfly," the students' attempts to "be nice" to Myra are _____ because the students are actually mocking her.
    F. fallacious
    G. edible
    H. relentless
    J. presumptuous

Grammar and Writing Skills: Paragraph Improvement

In the following excerpt from a student's first draft of a persuasive essay, numbers appear beneath underlined parts. The numbers correspond to items below that provide options for replacing or ask questions about the underlined parts. Numbers that appear in boxes within the essay refer to questions about specific paragraphs or about the essay as a whole. On a separate sheet of paper, record the letter of the best option in each item. If you think the original should not be changed, choose "NO CHANGE." Read the passage through once before you begin to answer the questions. As you read, pay close attention to the writer's use of **commas, verb tenses,** and **quotations.**

[1]

In Pablo Neruda's poem "Horses," the speaker described a transition from a deadened emotional state to one of renewed hope. The poem is written in highly irregular free verse, which could trick a reader into believe that Neruda gave little thought to poetic forms or conventions. This is not the case. The poem's formal characteristics, on the contrary, are essential to its meaning. Specifically, Neruda uses irregular stanzas enjambment and sound devices to reinforce the poem's theme of emotional transformation.

[2]

Neruda's short, irregular stanzas add to the poem's meaning in several ways. First, they create dramatic pauses during which the reader can fully absorb the poem's images. For example, Neruda includes a two-line stanza in lines 2–3: "I was in Berlin in winter. The light / was without light, the sky skyless." This is followed by a vivid one-line stanza: "The air white like a moistened loaf (line 3)." The pauses after each of these stanzas reinforces the silence and

emptiness of the scene. The short stanzas also echo the natural movement of the speaker's thoughts, readers are able to follow the speaker's observations as though they were experiencing the scene themselves.

[3]

Irregular enjambment also proves essential to the emotional power of "Horses." Using line breaks to create dramatic pauses in his sentences Neruda gives the poem a vigorous rhythm. In lines 20–21, Neruda inserts a line break in the middle of the word *midpoint*, added unexpected energy and drama to its words. This formal move echoes the vitality of the horses in the poem. Neruda also uses rich personification in the poem. **10**

1. **A.** NO CHANGE
   B. the speaker describing a transition
   C. the speaker describes a transition
   D. the speaker in describing a transition

2. **F.** NO CHANGE
   G. trick a reader into believing that
   H. trick a reader believing that
   J. trick a believing reader that

3. **A.** NO CHANGE
   B. irregular stanzas enjambment, and sound devices
   C. irregular stanzas, enjambment, and sound devices
   D. irregular stanzas: enjambment and sound devices

4. **F.** NO CHANGE
   G. "The air white like a moistened loaf (line 3)".
   H. "The air white like a moistened loaf," line 3.
   J. "The air white like a moistened loaf" (line 3).

5. **A.** NO CHANGE
   B. The pauses after each of these stanzas reinforce the silence
   C. The pauses after each of these stanzas, reinforce the silence
   D. The pauses after each of these stanzas reinforced the silence

6. **F.** NO CHANGE
   G. thoughts, readers are able to follow. The speaker's observations as though
   H. thoughts, so readers are able to follow the speaker's observations as though
   J. thoughts, readers are able to follow the speaker's observations, as though

7. **A.** NO CHANGE
   B. in his sentences, Neruda
   C. in his sentences. Neruda
   D. in his sentences

8. **F.** NO CHANGE
   G. adds
   H. adding
   J. had been adding

9. **A.** NO CHANGE
   B. our
   C. his
   D. those

10. Which sentence should be deleted from the final paragraph?
    F. the second sentence
    G. the third sentence
    H. the fourth sentence
    J. the fifth sentence

Essay

Write an essay comparing and contrasting the styles of two short stories from this unit. Discuss how stylistic elements such as figurative language, tone, and imagery contribute to the meaning of each story. Be sure to include specific examples from the texts in your essay. As you write, keep in mind that your essay will be evaluated for **ideas, organization, voice, word choice, sentence fluency,** and **grammar and spelling conventions.**

LOG ON ▶ **Literature** Online

Assessment For additional test practice, go to glencoe.com and enter QuickPass code GLW6053u6.

Reference Section

Literary Terms Handbook

A

Absurd, Theater of the See *THEATER OF THE ABSURD.*

Act A major unit of a drama or play. Modern dramas generally have one, two, or three acts. Older dramas typically have five acts. Acts may be divided into one or more scenes.

See also *DRAMA, SCENE.*

Allegory The use of events, actions, objects, and persons in a narrative to represent moral qualities, universal struggles, or abstract ideas such as love, fear, or virtue. An allegory may be as brief as a metaphor, or it may be the basis for an entire novel. Virgil's *Aeneid* contains a number of allegorical episodes.

See pages 93 and 899.

See also *METAPHOR.*

Alliteration The repetition of consonant sounds at the beginnings of words. For example, in line 13 of Léopold Sédar Senghor's "Night of Sine," the *s* sound is repeated:

> What do they **s**ay **s**o **s**ecretly to the stars?

See page 1211.

See also *SOUND DEVICES.*

Allusion A reference to a well-known person, place, or event from history, literature, or religion. Allusions enrich the reading experience by adding another dimension of meaning. *Lautaro,* one of the names suggested for the drowned man in Gabriel García Márquez's "The Handsomest Drowned Man in the World," is an allusion to a great native South American hero who fought against the Spanish.

See page 1253.

Ambiguity The state of having more than one meaning. The richness of literary language lies in its ability to evoke multiple layers of meaning. The red glow in Khalida Asghar's "The Wagon" is an intentionally ambiguous detail.

Analogy A comparison that shows similarities between two things that are otherwise dissimilar. An analogy often explains something unfamiliar or abstract by comparing it with something familiar or concrete. In "Jade Flower Palace," Tu Fu draws an analogy between the inevitable effect of time on the palace and its effect on human life.

See page 620.

Anecdote A brief story giving an amusing, insightful look at a single incident or event.

Antagonist In a literary work, the person or force opposing the protagonist, or central character. The antagonist may be an individual, a group of people, a force of nature, or a social force such as racial or class prejudice. The reader is generally not meant to sympathize with the antagonist. In Bessie Head's story, "The Prisoner Who Wore Glasses," Warden Hannetjie is the antagonist.

See pages 820 and 977.

See also *PROTAGONIST.*

Anthropomorphism The assignment of human characteristics to gods, animals, or inanimate objects. It is a key element in fables and folktales, in which the main characters are often animals. Coyote in "Coyote Finishes his Work," as retold by Barry Lopez, is an example of anthropomorphism.

See page 39.

See also *FABLE, FAIRY TALE, FOLKLORE, FOLKTALE.*

Antithesis The balanced contrast of two phrases or ideas. Through antithesis, authors help emphasize important ideas, as in "Creation Hymn" from the Rig-Veda:

> Their cord was extended across. Was there below?
>
> Was there above? There were seed-placers;
>
> there were powers. There was impulse beneath; there was giving-forth above.

See page 492.

Archetype A symbol, character, image, or story pattern that is common to human experience across cultures and throughout the world and evokes strong responses, often based on unconscious memory. In their purest form, archetypes occur in the oral tradition, but they also appear in written works of literature. The story of an ancient divine ruler such as Osiris, who teaches his people the essential skills of civilization, is an example of the archetype of the culture hero. Archetypes can be divided into the following categories:

> **Character archetype: Includes familiar individuals such as the wise leader, the rebel, the damsel in distress, and the traitor.**

> **Image archetype: Objects or places that have a universal symbolism. For example, a lily can be a symbol of purity.**

> **Plot pattern archetype: Stories that occur in many cultures. Making the long journey home, completing the "impossible" task, and outwitting the formidable enemy are all archetypal plots.**

> **Theme archetype: Ideas that occur wherever people tell stories. The ideas that good can overcome evil, that people can redeem themselves, and that an underworld exists are all archetypal themes.**

See page 17.
See also *FOLKLORE, MYTH, ORAL TRADITION, STOCK CHARACTER, SYMBOL.*

Argument A type of persuasive writing in which logic and reason are used to try to influence a reader's ideas or actions. In Sophocles' *Oedipus the King,* Creon's speech in which he defends himself against accusations of treason is an example of argument.
See page 321.
See also *RHETORICAL DEVICES.*

Aphorism See *MAXIM.*

Aside In a play, a comment that a character makes to the audience that other characters onstage do not hear. The speaker turns to one side—or "aside"—

away from the action onstage. Asides, which are rare in modern drama, reveal what a character is thinking or feeling.
See also *DRAMA, DRAMATIC CONVENTION, SOLILOQUY.*

Assonance The repetition of similar vowel sounds, especially in a line of poetry. The repeated *a* sound in "the flash of a hand" from Czesław Miłosz's poem "Encounter" is an example of assonance.
See also *SOUND DEVICES.*

Atmosphere The dominant emotional feeling of a literary work that contributes to the mood. Authors create atmosphere primarily through details of setting such as time, place, and weather.
See also *MOOD, SETTING.*

Author's purpose An author's reasons for creating a literary work. These may include a desire to entertain, inform, or explain, or to express feelings, impressions, and opinions. The author's purpose in the Egyptian poem "The Immortality of Writers" is to emphasize the lasting importance of literature.
See page 402.

Autobiography The story of a person's life written by that person. Since autobiographies generally stress the author's personal views, they are often not as objective as other forms of nonfiction, such as history books. Some fictional works, such as Jamaica Kincaid's "A Walk to the Jetty," are partially autobiographical.
See pages 626 and 1033.
See also *BIOGRAPHY, DIARY, JOURNAL, MEMOIR, NONFICTION.*

B

Bias An inclination toward a certain opinion or position on a topic.

Biography A nonfiction narrative of a person's life written by someone other than that person. Colette's "Two Memories of Sido" is a memoir but contains elements of biography.
See also *MEMOIR.*

C

Cadence The rhythmic rise and fall of language when it is spoken or read aloud.
See also *FREE VERSE, METER.*

Caesura A pause in a line of poetry, usually near the middle of a line, with two stressed syllables before and two after, creating a strong rhythm. A caesura is used to produce variations in meter and to draw attention to certain words. Some pauses are indicated by punctuation, others by phrasing or meaning.

Canto From the Italian word for song, a subdivision in a long poem such as Dante's *Divine Comedy.*

Carpe diem A Latin phrase meaning "seize the day"; in other words, "make the most of each moment." In *carpe diem* poems, the speaker emphasizes the shortness of life—usually to persuade a young woman to yield to love while she still has her youth and beauty.

Character A person, an animal, or a presence in a literary work. Characters may be major or minor depending on their importance to the work. Characters can be described as flat or round. A flat character reveals only one personality trait, whereas a round character shows varied and sometimes contradictory traits. In Bessie Head's "The Prisoner Who Wore Glasses," Brille is a round character; his children are flat characters. Characters may also be classified as static or dynamic. A static character remains the same throughout the story. A dynamic character changes. In Head's story, Martha is a static character; Hannetjie is a dynamic character.
See pages 125 and 1002.

Characterization The methods an author uses to develop the personality of a character. With direct characterization, the author makes direct statements about a character's personality, simply stating that a character is, for example, shy or selfish. Indirect characterization requires that readers draw their own conclusions about a character based on evidence from the story. This evidence might include the character's appearance, words, thoughts, or actions, and other

characters' thoughts and comments on that character.
See page 608.

Chorus A performer or group of performers whose function is to comment on the action that has just occurred in a drama and to sing and dance between scenes. The chorus serves as a bridge between the actors and the audience. Often an element in ancient Greek drama, the chorus is also found in other dramatic traditions, such as Japanese Noh drama.
See page 251.
See also *NOH.*

Climax The point of greatest interest or emotional intensity in a literary work. Also called the turning point, the climax usually comes near the end of a story or drama. For example, the climax of Rosario Castellanos's "The Luck of Teodoro Méndez Acúbal" occurs when Teodoro reaches into his sash for the coin and Don Augustín pulls a gun on him.
See also *DRAMATIC STRUCTURE, PLOT.*

Colloquialism Informal language used in everyday conversation, but not in formal writing or speech. In Alice Munro's "Day of the Butterfly," a child, speaking colloquially, says, "That's where my mother was at . . . They've got all nuns there."
See also *DIALECT, VERNACULAR.*

Comedy A type of drama or story that is humorous and often has a happy ending. Miguel de Cervantes's *Don Quixote* is a comedy. Comedy can be divided into two categories: high and low. High comedy makes fun of human behavior in a witty, sophisticated manner. Low comedy involves physical humor and simple, often vulgar, wordplay.
See also *DRAMA, HUMOR, PARODY, SATIRE, WIT.*

Conflict A struggle between two opposing forces in the plot of a story. An external conflict exists when a character struggles against an outside force, such as another person, nature, society, or fate. An internal conflict occurs within the mind of a character who is torn between opposing feelings or goals. Many characters experience both external and internal conflicts.
See pages 583 and 754.

Connotation The unspoken or unwritten meanings associated with a word beyond its literal definition, or denotation. Paying attention to the connotations of words is often helpful in understanding literature that deals with abstract concepts or includes many abstract words. Words such as *peered* and *blood-red* in Khalida Asghar's "The Wagon" have an eerie and foreboding connotation.

See also *DENOTATION.*

Consonance The repetition of consonant sounds within or at the ends of nonrhyming words. For example, notice the *l* sounds in this line of Horace's "Better to Live, Licinius":

> to take in sai<u>l</u> when it swe<u>ll</u>s in a wind
> that's a litt<u>l</u>e too kind

See also *SOUND DEVICES.*

Couplet Two consecutive rhymed lines of poetry that follow the same rhythmic pattern.

D

Denotation The literal, or dictionary, meaning of a word.

See also *CONNOTATION.*

Description Writing that creates a clear image of an appearance, feeling, or action. Good descriptive writing appeals to the senses through imagery. The use of figurative language and precise verbs, adjectives, and adverbs can also help make a description vivid.

See pages 150 and 871.

See also *IMAGERY, SENSORY DETAILS.*

Dialect A version of a language spoken by people in a particular region or social group. For example, Cockney is an English dialect spoken by working-class residents of East London. Dialects of the same language may differ from one another in pronunciation, vocabulary, and grammar.

See page 1225.

Dialogue Written conversation between characters in a literary work. Dialogue brings characters to life by revealing their personalities and by showing what they are thinking and feeling as they interact with other characters. Dialogue can also create mood, advance the plot, and develop theme. Plays are composed almost completely of dialogue.

See pages 1026 and 1265.

See also *MOOD, PLOT, THEME.*

Diary A work in which a person keeps an informal record of events in his or her life. Unlike a journal, a diary is most often a simple, spontaneous account of daily life. Sei Shōnagon's *The Pillow Book* is a diary.

See page 717.

See also *AUTOBIOGRAPHY, JOURNAL, MEMOIR, NONFICTION.*

Diction An author's choice of words and the way they are arranged; an important element in the author's voice or style. Diction can be described in any number of ways, such as formal or informal, old-fashioned or modern, friendly or detached, plain or ornate, depending on vocabulary and style. Skilled authors choose their words carefully to convey a particular meaning or feeling.

See page 525.

See also *AUTHOR'S PURPOSE, CONNOTATION, STYLE, TONE, VOICE.*

Drama A story intended to be acted out in front of an audience, also called a play or stage play. The script of a dramatic work often includes the author's instructions to the actors and the director, known as stage directions. A drama may be divided into acts, which may also be broken up into scenes, indicating changes in location or the passage of time. Sophocles' *Oedipus the King* is a drama.

See pages 248 and 736..

See also *ACT, DRAMATIC CONVENTION, DRAMATIC STRUCTURE, NOH, PROP, SCENE, STAGE DIRECTIONS, TRAGEDY.*

Dramatic convention An unrealistic device that a playwright uses to present a story on stage, which the audience accepts as realistic. For example, audiences at Noh plays accept the convention of male actors playing female roles. They also accept unrealistic shifts in time.

Dramatic structure The way information is presented in a play. Common elements in dramatic structure are exposition, or revelation of important background information; rising action, which adds complications to the plot; climax (also called turning point or crisis), the moment of greatest emotional intensity or suspense; falling action, which unravels the complications; and resolution, which resolves them or brings them to a close.

See also *CLIMAX, EXPOSITION, FALLING ACTION,*

E

Elegy A poem dealing with loss, sadness, or human mortality and the emotional consequences. Nāzik al-Malā'ikah's "Elegy for a Woman of No Importance" is a modern example of this ancient poetic form.

End rhyme The repetition of sounds in the syllables at the ends of lines that appear close to one another in a poem. The following lines from Oodgeroo of the tribe Noonuccal's "Municipal Gum" contain end rhyme.

> In the cool world of leafy forest <u>halls</u>
>
> And wild bird <u>calls</u>.

See page 807.
See also *RHYME.*

End-stopped line A line of poetry that contains a complete thought and is thus punctuated at the end. The following example from the Egyptian poem "So small are the flowers of Seamu" is an end-stopped line:

> Your voice gives life, like nectar.

See also *ENJAMBMENT.*

Enjambment The continuation of a sentence from one line of a poem to the next, also called a run-on line. Enjambment enables poets to express a thought or image within the structure of the line, as well as to extend it to the next line(s), while still maintaining unity of thought. Enjambment occurs in the following lines from Heinrich Heine's "The Lorelei."

> The wonderful melody reaches
>
> A boat, as it sails along.

See page 521.
See also *END-STOPPED LINE, RUN-ON LINE.*

Enlightenment A European philosophical and literary movement characterized by faith in human reason and skepticism toward traditional religion. This movement is sometimes referred to as "The Age of Reason" or Rationalism, a related movement. The Enlightenment worldview stimulated an outburst of scientific inquiry and intellectual freedom, which laid the foundation for a modern worldview based on rationalism, secularism, and the rights of the individual. These ideas shook established ways of seeing the world; the arguments of such Enlightenment thinkers as John Locke and Jean-Jacques Rousseau helped shape the ideals of the American Revolution and the Declaration of Independence.

Epic A long narrative poem about a larger-than-life hero who embodies the values of his or her people. Many early epics, such as *Gilgamesh,* were composed orally and preserved by storytellers before being written down. Such oral epics, or folk epics, may be developed in different versions as they are passed along from generation to generation. Literary epics, such as Virgil's *Aeneid,* are composed as written texts, although they are often modeled on oral epic poetry. Many epics share standard characteristics known as epic conventions. These include an invocation, or formal plea to a deity for inspiration; epithets, something like nicknames, such as "the swift runner Achilles"; epic similes, which are longer and more elaborate than typical similes; and a set rhythm or metrical structure.

See page 58 and 879.

See also *EPIC HERO, EPITHET, FOLKLORE, FOLKTALE, MYTH, ORAL TRADITION.*

Epic hero A legendary, larger-than-life figure whose adventures form the core of an epic.

See pages 193, 449, and 564.

See also *EPIC, EPITHET, FOLKLORE, FOLKTALE, MYTH, ORAL TRADITION.*

Epigram See *MAXIM*.

Epigraph A quotation from another work or source that occurs at the beginning of a literary work and highlights a theme or main idea of the work at hand. "The Lion-Makers" from the *Panchatantra* begins with an epigraph.

Epiphany A sudden, unexpected moment of insight. A key element of many modern short stories, epiphany is often employed in the stories of Katherine Mansfield, author of "The Doll's House."

Epithet A word or brief phrase used to characterize a person, place, or thing. In the *Iliad,* for instance, the epithet "breaker of horses" is used to identify Hector.
See also *EPIC*.

Essay A short piece of literary nonfiction devoted to a single topic from a limited viewpoint. Essays may be classified as formal or informal. Formal essays include expository essays, which offer information about a topic, and persuasive essays, which promote a specific opinion or position. Informal essays include personal essays, such as the memoir or the reflective essay, which explores the meaning and effect of a personal observation or experience from the author's life.
See also *NONFICTION*.

Exaggeration An overstatement for the purpose of emphasis.
See also *HYPERBOLE*.

Existentialism A philosophy that seeks the meaning of existence itself. Existentialists believe that life is empty of any purpose or value other than that which individuals give to their own lives. Existentialism developed as a pragmatic response to the alienation and confusion that many people believed defined contemporary life. Many Existentialists came to the conclusion that life was essentially meaningless and absurd. Along with the French philosopher Jean-Paul Sartre, Albert Camus emerged as a spokesman for these complex responses to the world. However, rather than describing a world of bottomless despair, Camus argued that when people can see the underlying meaninglessness in the world, they can begin to make choices that give meaning to their lives.
See also *THEATER OF THE ABSURD*.

Exposition An author's introduction of the characters, setting, and conflict at the beginning of a story, novel, or play.
See also *PLOT*.

Extended metaphor A metaphor that compares two unlike things in various ways throughout a paragraph, stanza, or an entire literary work.
See also *METAPHOR*.

F

Fable A brief folktale, often featuring animals or inanimate objects as characters, told to teach a specific lesson or moral. In some fables, such as those of Aesop, the lesson or moral is stated explicitly. In other fables, the reader must infer the lesson based on what happens in the story.
See also *ANTHROPOMORPHISM*.

Fairy tale A type of folktale that features supernatural elements, such as spirits, talking animals, and magic.
See also *ANTHROPOMORPHISM, FABLE, FOLKLORE, FOLKTALE, LEGEND, MYTH*.

Falling action The action that follows the climax in a play or story. The falling action may show the results of the climax. It may also include the denouement, a French word meaning "unknotting." The denouement, or resolution, explains the plot or unravels the mystery.
See also *CLIMAX, DRAMATIC STRUCTURE, PLOT*.

Fantasy A story that takes place in an unreal world and features incredible characters and events.

Farce A type of comedy with stereotyped characters in ridiculous situations. Anton Chekhov often wrote farces.
See also *COMEDY, HUMOR, PARODY, SATIRE*.

Fiction A narrative written in prose in which the situations and characters are invented by the writer. Novels, short stories, folktales, fairy tales, fables, and other forms of made-up stories are types of fiction.
See also *FABLE, FAIRY TALE, FOLKTALE, NOVEL, SHORT STORY*.

Figurative language Language used for descriptive effect in order to convey ideas or emotions. Figurative expressions, while not literally descriptive, express an aspect of the subject beyond the literal level.

See page 749.

See also *FIGURES OF SPEECH.*

Figures of speech Language that uses expressions that are not literally true, but express some truth beyond the literal level. Types of figures of speech include hyperbole, metaphor, personification, simile, and understatement. Pablo Neruda's poem "Horses" contains several figures of speech. "The air white like a moistened loaf" is a simile, "they filled the whole world of my eyes" is a metaphor, and the reference to "the teeth of winter" is personification.

See also *HYPERBOLE, IMAGERY, METAPHOR, OXYMORON, PERSONIFICATION, SIMILE, SYMBOL, UNDERSTATEMENT.*

Flashback An interruption in the chronological order of a narrative to relate a scene from an earlier time. An author may use this device to give the reader background information or to create tension or contrast. In "A Walk to the Jetty," the narrator has many flashbacks while walking with her mother to the jetty, including memories of her apprenticeship as a seamstress and her friend's case of the mumps.

See pages 815 and 1278.

Flat character See *CHARACTER.*

Foil A character whose personality traits are unlike, and best understood in contrast to, another character's. Often a foil is a minor character who serves, through contrast, to emphasize the distinctive characteristics of the main character. Through the use of a foil, a writer calls attention to the strengths or weaknesses of a character. In Alice Munro's "Day of the Butterfly," Gladys Healey, the prime antagonist, is a foil for Helen, the narrator.

Folklore The traditional beliefs, customs, stories, songs, and dances of a culture. Folklore is based on the concerns of ordinary people and is passed down through oral traditions.

See also *EPIC, FABLE, FAIRY TALE, FOLKTALE, LEGEND, MYTH, ORAL TRADITION.*

Folktale A story that has been passed down from one generation to the next by word of mouth. Folktales do not have a known author, although they are often retold by authors for audiences of different times and cultures. They generally reflect the values of the societies that preserve them. Most folktales are simple narratives told for entertainment, although they might also teach moral values. Folktales include animal stories, trickster stories, fairy tales, myths, legends, and tall tales. "Coyote Finishes His Work" is a Native American folktale.

See also *EPIC, FABLE, FAIRY TALE, FOLKLORE, LEGEND, MYTH, ORAL TRADITION.*

Foot The basic unit in the measurement of rhythm in poetry. A foot usually contains one stressed syllable and one or more unstressed syllables.

See also *METER, RHYTHM, SCANSION.*

Foreshadowing The use of clues by the author to prepare readers for events that will happen later in a story. Foreshadowing helps build suspense and draws the reader into the plot. In Leo Tolstoy's story "How Much Land Does a Man Need?", Pakhom's dream foreshadows the danger in his accepting the Bashkir chief's deal.

See page 1278.

Form The arrangement of words and lines in a poem. Many modern authors use loosely structured forms instead of following traditional or formal patterns. These poets vary the lengths of lines and stanzas, relying on emphasis, rhythm, pattern, and the placement of words and phrases to convey meaning. *Form* can also be used as a synonym for *genre.*

See pages 739 and 830.

Formal speech A speech whose main purpose is to persuade, although it may also inform and entertain. There are four main types of formal speech: legal, political, ceremonial, and religious.

See page 335.

Frame story A plot structure that includes the telling of a story within a story. The frame is the outer story, which usually precedes and follows the inner, more important story. This technique is common in both ancient and modern writing. Some literary works, such as Giovanni Boccaccio's *Decameron,* have frames that bind together many different stories.

Free verse Poetry that does not follow a regular meter or rhyme scheme. Although poets who write free verse ignore traditional rules, they use techniques such as sound devices and cadence to create musical patterns in their poems.

See page 1050.

See also *CADENCE, SOUND DEVICES.*

G

Genre A category or type of literature. Examples of genres include poetry, drama, short story, essay, and epic. The term also refers to subcategories of literature. For example, fantasy, magic realism, mystery, romance, and science fiction are subgenres of fiction.

H

Haiku A Japanese poetry form consisting of seventeen syllables arranged in three lines. The first and third lines have five syllables each, and the middle line has seven. Because they are so short, haiku rely heavily on the power of suggestion. Words in haiku are chosen for the associations they create in the reader's mind. Usually about nature, a traditional haiku uses striking and often contrasting imagery to evoke an insight or capture a mood. The haiku existed originally as a subset of a type of poetry called the renga, but was developed into its own form by the Japanese haiku master Bashō and his contemporaries.

See also *TANKA.*

Hero The chief character in a literary work, typically one whose qualities or deeds arouse admiration. For example, Gilgamesh is the hero of *Gilgamesh.* Although the word *hero* is applied only to males in traditional usage—*heroine* being the term used for females—modern usage applies the term to either gender.

See also *EPIC HERO.*

Historical context The time and place in which a literary work was written, including the traditions, customs, beliefs, and values of that time and place. Miguel de Cervantes's *Don Quixote,* for example, is set in sixteenth-century Spain and contrasts the chivalry idealized in literature with the reality of that time.

Historical fiction Fiction that sets characters against a backdrop of events from a past time period that actually existed. Some works of historical fiction include actual historical figures along with fictitious characters.

History A factual account of real events that occurred in the past. Typically, a history is arranged chronologically and seeks to provide an objective description of what took place.

Humor The quality of a literary work intended to be funny or amusing, although it can also be an important tool of persuasion. There are three basic types of humor. Humor of situation develops from the plot of a literary work, which may contain exaggerated or unexpected events. Humor of character uses exaggerated personalities to make us laugh at the flaws of human nature. Humor of language may include wordplay, verbal irony, exaggeration, or sarcasm. Humorous writing can be equally effective in fiction and nonfiction.

See also *PARODY, SARCASM, SATIRE, WIT.*

Hymn A lyric poem or song addressed to a divine being. The term is also applied to a section of a longer religious poem. The excerpt in this book from the Maya text the *Popol Vuh* is a hymn.

Hyperbole A figure of speech that uses intentional exaggeration to express strong emotion, make a point, or create humor. Notice the hyperbole in this line from "The Handsomest Drowned Man in the World".

> the hidden strength of his heart popped
> the buttons on his shirt.

See page 1244.

See also *EXAGGERATION, FIGURES OF SPEECH.*

I

Idiom An expression whose meaning is different from its literal meaning. Phrases such as "catch his eye," "turn the tables," and "over the hill" are idiomatic expressions in English. Idioms can add realism to dialogue in a story and contribute to characterization.

See page 1265.

See also *DIALECT.*

Imagery Descriptive language that appeals to one or more of the five senses: sight, hearing, touch, taste, and smell. The use of sensory details helps create an emotional response in the reader. Most imagery is visual, but imagery can also help readers hear sounds, feel textures, taste foods, and smell aromas (as in this portion of Aleksandr Solzhenitsyn's "Freedom to Breathe").

> No food on earth, no wine, not even a woman's kiss is sweeter to me than this air steeped in the fragrance of flowers, of moisture and freshness.

See pages 30, 121, 242, 377, 704, and 787.

Implied comparison A comparison that is suggested rather than directly stated. An implied comparison is conveyed by connecting images in a new or unexpected way rather than by indicating that the one image *is* the other (metaphor) or is *like* the other (simile). For instance, in his haiku, Kobayashi Issa links the image of melting snow to that of children.

In medias res Latin phrase meaning "in the middle of things." A work of literature is said to start in medias res when the story begins in the middle of the action. A work of literature that starts in medias res skips the exposition and moves directly to the rising action.

Inversion The reversal of the usual word order in a prose sentence or a line of poetry. Writers use inversion to maintain rhyme scheme or meter, to vary sentence structure, or to emphasize certain words or phrases. In this passage from Li Po's "The River-Merchant's Wife: A Letter," the verb (*played*) comes before the subject (*I*), a reversal of the usual order.

> While my hair was still cut straight across my forehead
>
> <u>Played</u> <u>I</u> about the front gate, pulling flowers.

Irony A contrast or discrepancy between expectation and reality, or between what is expected and what actually happens. Dramatic irony occurs when the reader or audience knows something that a character does not know. For instance, in "The Story of Pyramus and Thisbe" by Ovid, the reader knows that Thisbe is merely hiding when Pyramus believes that she is dead. Situational irony occurs when what actually happens is the opposite of what is expected or appropriate. In Giovanni Boccaccio's "Federigo's Falcon," the hero serves his prized falcon to the lady as a meal, not knowing she has come to ask for it as a gift for her son. Verbal irony occurs when a writer or speaker says one thing but really means the opposite. It might occur when a person responds to a disappointment with an expression such as "That's great."

See pages 52 and 291.

J

Journal A personal record of experiences, ideas, and reflections that is kept on a regular basis. A journal is often begun with the intention of keeping a record of a significant time or series of events. Like letters, journals are a form of autobiographical or personal writing, but are usually less intimate than a diary and emphasize events rather than emotions.

See page 1137.

See also *AUTOBIOGRAPHY, DIARY, MEMOIR, NONFICTION.*

Juxtaposition The placement of two or more distinct things side by side in order to contrast or compare them. It is commonly used to evoke an emotional response in the reader.

See page 1170.

K

Kabuki A theater created for the common people that arose around 1600, eventually replacing Noh as Japan's most popular dramatic form. A group of female performers originated the style. However, the government viewed Kabuki as excessively provocative and banned women from performing it in 1629. Today, Kabuki, like Noh, exists as an all-male art form. Unlike Noh plays, Kabuki plays are extravagant and unrestrained. They usually have a historical or domestic focus, and feature lower-class heroes who resist oppression by the nobility. Like Noh, Kabuki makes use of dance, music, and stylized gestures. However, Kabuki performers wear no masks and constantly interact with their audience.

See page 736.

See also *NOH.*

L

Legend A traditional story handed down from past generations and believed to be based on historical fact. Legends usually celebrate the heroic qualities of a national or cultural leader. Because legends are the stories of the people, they are often expressions of the values or character of a nation.

See also *EPIC, FABLE, FOLKLORE, HERO, MYTH, ORAL TRADITION.*

Legendary heroes Idealized figures, sometimes based on real people, who embody qualities admired by the cultural group to which they belong. The adventures and accomplishments of these heroes are preserved in legends or tales that are handed down from generation to generation. Achilles is a legendary hero.

See also *EPIC HERO, HERO, LEGEND, MYTH.*

Line The basic unit of poetry. A line consists of a word or a row of words. In metered poems, lines are measured by the number of feet they contain.

See also *FOOT, STANZA.*

Lyric poetry Poetry in which the speaker expresses personal thoughts and feelings. Lyric poems are usually short and musical. While the subject of a lyric poem might be an object, a person, or an event, the emphasis of the poem is on the experience of emotion rather than telling a story.

See also *ELEGY, ODE, POETRY, SONNET.*

M

Magic realism A prose fiction style that originated in Europe and is now especially associated with Latin American authors, such as Gabriel García Márquez, Julio Cortázar, and Liliana Heker. In a magic realist work, figures from history, mythology, literature, and dreams may appear and play a part in everyday life. The rules of everyday life itself change: characters may suddenly travel great distances in space or time. Magic realism differs from surrealism in its emphasis on the intrusion of fantastic elements into normal life.

Maxim A short saying that contains a general truth or gives practical advice. Philosophers have often used maxims to share advice, particularly about mortality and behavior, as Lao-tzu does in the *Tao Te Ching.* A maxim is also known as an adage or aphorism.

See pages 512 and 685.

Memoir A type of narrative nonfiction that presents the story of a period in the author's life and is usually written from the first-person point of view. A memoir often emphasizes the author's thoughts and feelings, his or her relationships with other people, or the impact of significant historical events on his or her life. Isak Dinesen's *Out of Africa* is a memoir.

See page 1064.

See also *AUTOBIOGRAPHY, DIARY, JOURNAL.*

Metaphor A figure of speech that makes a comparison between two seemingly unlike things without using the words *as* or *like.* An extended metaphor compares two unlike things point by point throughout a paragraph, a stanza, or an entire piece of writing.

See pages 767 and 1165.

See also *FIGURES OF SPEECH, SIMILE.*

Meter or **Metrical structure** A regular pattern of stressed and unstressed syllables that gives a line of poetry a predictable rhythm. The unit of meter within the line is the foot. A particular meter is named for the type of foot and the number of feet per line.

See page 803.

See also *FOOT, RHYTHM.*

Metonymy A figure of speech in which a word or phrase is substituted for another thing that is related. For example, the executive branch of the British government is often referred to as "Downing Street," where the prime minister lives in London.

See also *SYNECHDOCHE.*

Modernism A literary style developed in the late nineteenth century that reflected a break with existing tradition. In addition to technical experimentation, Modernist authors and artists in the first half of the twentieth century were interested in the irrational or inexplicable, as well as in the workings of the unconscious mind. Liliana Heker's "Bishop Berkeley or Mariana of the Universe" displays Modernist characteristics.

Monologue A long speech or written expression of thoughts by a character in a literary work.

Mood The overall feeling or emotional quality that a work of literature creates for readers. An author's choice of language, subject matter, setting, diction, and tone, as well as sound devices such as rhyme, rhythm, and meter, can help create mood. Mood is a broader term than tone, which refers specifically to the attitude of the speaker or narrator. It also differs from atmosphere, which is concerned mainly with the physical qualities that contribute to mood, such as time, place, and weather.

See page 713.

See also *ATMOSPHERE, TONE.*

Moral A practical lesson about right and wrong conduct, often found in an instructive story such as a fable or parable. "The Lion-Makers" from the *Panchatantra* has a moral at the end.

See page 596.

See also *FABLE.*

Motif A significant word, phrase, character, image, metaphor, idea, or other element that recurs throughout a work or several works of literature and is related to the theme.

See page 1132.

Motivation The reason or reasons behind a character's actions. A character's motivation may be stated directly, or the reader may have to infer motivation from details in the story. Characters are often motivated by a combination of factors that can include external circumstances, internal morals, or emotional impulses.

See page 93.

Myth A traditional story that explains some aspect of human life or the natural world. Myths reflect the religious beliefs of a particular people. They often depict the actions of gods or heroes. Ovid's *Metamorphoses* retells a number of Greek and Roman myths. Creation myths explain the origin of the world and its inhabitants.

See page 1121.

See also *FOLKLORE, FOLKTALE, LEGEND, ORAL TRADITION.*

N

Narrative Any writing or speech that tells a story. Narratives may be fiction or nonfiction, prose or poetry. Driven by a conflict or problem, a narrative unfolds event by event and leads to a resolution. The story is narrated, or told, by a narrator and can take the form of a novel, an essay, a poem, or a short story.

See also *AUTOBIOGRAPHY, BIOGRAPHY, ESSAY, MEMOIR.*

Narrative poetry Verse that tells a story. Narrative poems are usually contrasted with lyric poems. Ballads, epics, and romances are all types of narrative poetry. Ovid's "The Story of Pyramus and Thisbe" is an example of a narrative poem. Epics, such as Homer's *Iliad* and Virgil's *Aeneid,* are long narrative poems that recount the deeds of an epic hero.

See page 369.

See also *EPIC, LYRIC POETRY, NARRATIVE.*

Narrator The character who tells a story. The narrator may be a character in the story, as in "A Walk to the Jetty" by Jamaica Kincaid, or outside the story, as in "The Night Face Up" by Julio Cortázar. Narrators are not always truthful; a narrator in a work of literature may be reliable or unreliable. Some unreliable narrators intentionally mislead readers. Others fail to understand the true meaning of the events they describe. Most stories with unreliable narrators are written in the first person.

See pages 637 and 1191.

See also *NARRATIVE, POINT OF VIEW, SPEAKER.*

Noh A highly stylized form of Japanese drama that originated in the Middle Ages, growing out of Zen Buddhist religious festivals. The traditional theater of the nobility, Noh developed its permanent form in the fourteenth century. It retains a strong spiritual element, using powerful gestures and meditative silences to tell stories. A Noh play (also spelled *No*) usually tells the tale of a restless ghost and typically has only three or four roles, all performed by men. The stage is small and bare. The actors, in contrast, wear elaborate costumes and masks. Throughout the play, a chorus echoes the words of the main characters, who dance and gesture to the music of a flute player and drummers. Most action in a Noh play is symbolic. For example, a character may take only a few steps to indicate that he is on a long journey.

See page 736.

See also *CHORUS, KABUKI.*

Nonfiction Literature about real people, places, and events. The broadest category of literature, nonfiction includes autobiographies, biographies, journals, memoirs, diaries, essays, letters, speeches, travelogues, news articles, reports, and many other types of writing.

Novel A long fictional prose narrative containing a plot, or ordered sequence of events that takes place in a specific setting and is concerned with character development and statement of theme, or message. Miguel de Cervantes's *Don Quixote* is generally considered the first modern novel in European literature.

O

Ode A lengthy lyric poem with an elevated style and an exalted or enthusiastic tone. Some odes follow the form's original intent of glorifying a public figure or commemorating an important event, but the Roman poet Horace developed an ode that was more personal and meditative. Odes are traditionally written in three stanzas and include rhyme.

See page 364.

See also *LYRIC POETRY.*

Onomatopoeia The use of a word or phrase that imitates or suggests the sound of what it describes, for example *hiss, swoosh,* or *crackle.*

See also *SOUND DEVICES.*

Oral tradition The passing of literature by word of mouth from one generation to the next. Oral literature was a way of recording the past, glorifying leaders, and teaching morals and traditions to young people. Literature in most of the world began in this way. In West Africa the *griot*—or professional storyteller—committed stories and family histories to memory and recited verses to music, acting out dramatic parts.

See also *EPIC, FABLE, FOLKLORE, FOLKTALE.*

Oratory The art of effective public speaking, or the use of persuasive skills when speaking. Oratory is common in politics, law, and religion. Today, oratory is usually called "public speaking."

Oxymoron A term made of two words that contradict each other, for example, *jumbo shrimp.*

P

Parable A simple story that teaches a moral or religious lesson. It differs from a fable in that the characters are people instead of animals. The New Testament of the Bible contains many of Jesus' parables.

See pages 487 and 731.

See also *FABLE.*

Paradox A situation or statement that appears to be contradictory but is actually true, either in fact or in a figurative sense. For example, one of Catullus's poems contains this paradox:

> I couldn't like you if you were the best of women,
>
> or stop loving you, no matter what you do.

See page 559.

Parallelism The use of a series of words, phrases, or lines that have similar grammatical form. Authors employ this technique to emphasize an idea or emotion, to create a sense of unity or balance in a literary work, or for musical effect. Lao-tzu uses parallelism in the following lines from the *Tao Te Ching:*

> There is a time for being ahead,
>
> a time for being behind;
>
> a time for being in motion,
>
> a time for being at rest;

See pages 477 and 690.

Parody The humorous imitation of a particular writing style or literary work, often intended as a criticism but sometimes done simply for humor. *Don Quixote* is a parody of chivalry and stories about knight-errantry.

See page 936.

See also *HUMOR, SARCASM, SATIRE, WIT.*

Persona The character created by the author to tell the story. Whether the story is told by an omniscient narrator or by one of the characters, the author of the work often adopts a persona—a personality different from his or her real one. The attitudes and beliefs of the persona may differ from those of the author.

See also *NARRATOR, POINT OF VIEW, SPEAKER, VOICE.*

Personification A figure of speech in which human qualities are attributed to an animal. Poets use this device to highlight an idea or to create striking descriptions. In "Two Countries," José Martí uses personification to describe Cuba:

> . . . Cuba,
>
> With long veils and holding a carnation,
>
> Appears as a sad and silent widow.

See pages 134 and 517.

Persuasion Writing, usually nonfiction, which attempts to convince readers to think or act in a certain way. Philosophical essays sometimes appeal to the reader's intellect through logic and evidence and—as in Confucius's *Analects*—sometimes by giving rules and examples. Political speeches and advertisements may rely more on emotional appeals.

See page 1057.

See also *ARGUMENT, RHETORICAL DEVICES.*

Petrarchan sonnet A sonnet, also called an Italian sonnet, divided into a group of eight lines, called the octave, and a group of six lines, called the sestet. The rhyme scheme of the octave is *abba, abba.* The sestet may follow a number of different rhyme schemes. Among the most common patterns are *cde cde, cde dcd,* and *cdc dee.* The octave usually presents a single theme, or main idea, and the sestet expands, contradicts, or develops it.

See page 920.

See also *SONNET.*

Plot The sequence of events in a narrative work. Most plots develop around a conflict, a struggle between opposing forces. Exposition introduces the story's characters, setting, and conflict. Rising action develops the conflict with complications. The climax is the emotional high point of the story. Falling action shows what happens after the climax. The resolution shows how the conflict is resolved.

See pages 84 and 1200.

Poetry A form of literary expression that differs from prose in emphasizing the line, rather than the sentence, as the unit of composition. The traditional characteristics of poetry include emotional, imaginative language; employment of figures of speech; division into stanzas; and the use of rhyme and regular meter.

See also *FIGURATIVE LANGUAGE, PROSE, RHYME, STANZA.*

Point of view The perspective from which a story is told. In a story with first-person point of view, the narrator is a character in the story and uses the words *I* and *me* to tell the story, as in Jamaica Kincaid's "A Walk to the Jetty." In a story with third-person point of view, the narrator is someone who stands outside the story and describes the characters and action. In a story with third-person limited point of view, the narrator reveals the thoughts, feelings, and observations of only one character, to referred to in the third person. Julio Cortázar's "The Night Face Up" is told from a third-person limited point of view. In a story with third-person omniscient point of view, the narrator knows everything that goes on—including the thoughts and feelings of every character, as in Rosario Castellanos's story, "The Luck of Teodoro Méndez Acúbal."

See pages 497 and 1231.

See also *NARRATOR, PERSONA, SPEAKER.*

Postmodernism A broad contemporary movement in art, music, film, literature, and other cultural areas that is viewed as growing out of or replacing Modernism. Many of the characteristic features of Postmodernist literature extend or exaggerate tendencies of Modernism. For example, Modernist writers turned away from the apparent objectivity of Realism; Postmodernists go further, introducing a frankly artificial, self-conscious playfulness into their works.

See also *MODERNISM.*

Propaganda Written or spoken material designed to bring about a change or damage a cause through the use of emotionally charged words, name-calling, or other techniques.

Props A theater term (a shortened form of *properties*) for the objects and elements of the scenery used in a stage play, movie, or television show.

See also *DRAMA, STAGE DIRECTIONS.*

Prose Literature that is written in sentences and paragraphs (as distinguished from poetry, which is arranged in lines and stanzas). Essays, short stories, novels, magazine articles, and most plays are examples of prose.

Prose poem A short prose composition that uses rhythm, imagery, and other poetic devices to express an idea or emotion. Unlike metrical and free verse, prose poetry does not have line breaks; instead, the sentences appear in standard paragraph form. A prose poem allows the writer to express a poetic idea without following the usual rules of poetic form. "Fishing" by Joy Harjo is a prose poem.

See page 1073.

See also *POETRY, PROSE.*

Protagonist The central character in a literary work around whom the main conflict revolves. Generally, the reader or audience is meant to sympathize with the protagonist. Brille is the protagonist of Bessie Head's "The Prisoner Who Wore Glasses."

See page 820.

See also *ANTAGONIST, CHARACTER, CONFLICT, HERO, TRAGEDY*

R

Realism A literary movement of late-nineteenth- and early-twentieth-century authors that sought to re-create the texture of everyday life and address the problems of ordinary people. The Realists sought to depict life objectively as it is really lived, without sentimentality or idealization; they usually focused on the problems of middle- and lower-class people. Their work is often filled with details based on careful observation of everyday life. Anton Chekhov and Leo Tolstoy are considered Realists.

Repetition The recurrence of sounds, words, phrases, lines, or stanzas in a literary work. Authors may use repetition to help unify their work, to create a musical or rhythmic effect, or to emphasize an idea. Rhyme, parallelism, and alliteration are types of repetition. Note the repetition in this passage from Léopold Sédar Senghor's "Night of Sine":

> <u>Listen</u> to its song, <u>listen</u> to our dark blood beat, <u>listen</u>
>
> To the deep pulse of Africa beating in the mist of forgotten villages.

See page 79.

See also *SOUND DEVICES.*

Resolution See *DRAMATIC STRUCTURE, PLOT.*

Rhetorical devices Persuasive techniques used by public speakers and authors of literary works, especially those written to persuade. Rhetorical devices include repetition, parallelism, analogy, logic, and the skillful use of connotation and anecdote. Effective rhetoric often appeals to logic, emotion, morality, or authority. A rhetorical question is a question to which no answer is expected or the answer is obvious.

See also *ANALOGY, ANECDOTE, ARGUMENT, CONNOTATION, PARALLELISM, PERSUASION, REPETITION.*

Rhyme The repetition of sounds in words that appear close to each other in a poem. Words rhyme when their accented vowels and all the letters that follow sound the same. For example, the word *borrow* rhymes with *tomorrow,* and the word *sincere* rhymes with *fear.* Internal rhyme occurs within lines of poetry. End rhyme occurs at the ends of lines. When words sound similar but do not rhyme exactly (like *pain* and *again*), they are called half rhymes or slant rhymes.

See page 973.

See also *RHYME SCHEME.*

Rhyme scheme The pattern of end rhyme, designated by letters. A different letter of the alphabet signals each new rhyme (for example *aabbcc* or *ababcdcd*). Notice the rhyme scheme (*aaba*) in the following lines from Omar Khayyám's *Rubáiyát:*

> Awake! for Morning in the Bowl of <u>Night</u>
>
> Has flung the Stone that puts the Stars to <u>Flight</u>:
>
> And Lo! the Hunter of the East has <u>caught</u>
>
> The Sultán's Turret in a Noose of <u>Light.</u>

See pages 506 and 1022.

See also *FORM, RHYME.*

Rhythm The pattern of beats created by the arrangement of stressed and unstressed syllables in a line, especially in poetry. Rhythm gives poetry a musical quality and can add emphasis to certain words or ideas to help convey meaning. Rhythm can be regular or irregular. Meter is a regular pattern of stressed and unstressed syllables that sets the overall rhythm of certain poems. The basic unit in measuring rhythm is the foot, which usually contains one stressed syllable and one or more unstressed syllables. Free verse, which does not have a regular meter, often follows the rhythm of natural speech.

See page 803.

Romanticism An artistic movement that began in Europe in the 1800s and emphasized imagination, nature, passion, and feeling over intellect and reason. The works of William Wordsworth, Samuel Taylor Coleridge, Lord Byron, and John Keats represent the height of Romantic poetry.

Ruba'i A Persian word meaning "quatrain," or four-line verse.

Run-on line See *ENJAMBMENT.*

S

Sacred Text Writings such as the Tanakh, the Qur'an, or the Rig-Veda that are revered as holy or are closely linked to religion or religious rituals. These texts, which are sometimes called scriptures, are often regarded as divine revelations, directly communicated from God to human beings on a specific occasion.

See page 456.

Sarcasm The use of bitter or caustic language to point out shortcomings or flaws.

See also *IRONY, SATIRE.*

Satire Writing that uses humor to comment on human flaws, ideas, social customs, or institutions in order to change them. The purpose of satire is to persuade, although satires can only be effective if they are also entertaining. In order to get his or her point across, a satirist might use such literary techniques as irony, exaggeration, parody, and understatement. For example, Cervantes's *Don Quixote* satirizes stories that idealize chivalry.

See pages 142 and 961.

Scansion The analysis of the meter of a line of verse. To scan a line of poetry means to note the stressed and unstressed syllables and to divide the line into its feet, or rhythmic units.

See also *FOOT, METER, RHYTHM*

Scene A subdivision of an act in a play.

Sensory details Evocative words or phrases that convey sensory experiences—seeing, hearing, tasting, touching, and smelling. Sensory details make writing come alive by helping readers imagine what is being described.

See also *IMAGERY*.

Setting The time and place in which the events of a literary work occur. The elements of setting may include geographical location, historical period, season of the year, time of day, and the beliefs and customs of a society. Setting can help establish the atmosphere and mood of a story. It can also influence the way characters think and behave.

See pages 108 and 1149.

See also *ATMOSPHERE, HISTORICAL CONTEXT, MOOD*.

Short story A short, fictional prose narrative that generally includes the following major elements: setting, characters, plot, point of view, and theme.

See also *FICTION, NOVEL, PLOT*.

Simile A figure of speech that uses the words *like* or *as* to compare two seemingly unlike things. R.K. Narayan's "Like the Sun" contains the following simile:

> Truth, Sekhar reflected, is like the sun. I suppose no human being can ever look it straight in the face without blinking or being dazed.

An epic simile is a long, elaborate comparison that continues for several lines. It is a feature of epic poems, but is found in other poems as well.

See pages 210, 529, and 763.

See also *ANALOGY, FIGURES OF SPEECH, METAPHOR*.

Soliloquy In drama, a long speech by a character who is alone on the stage. A soliloquy reveals the private thoughts and emotions of that character.

Sonnet A fourteen-line lyric poem developed in Italy during the Renaissance. A Shakespearean sonnet, sometimes called an English sonnet, has three quatrains (groups of four lines), which are followed by a rhymed couplet of two lines. The rhyme scheme is as follows: *abab, cdcd, efef, gg*. A Shakespearean sonnet retains the break in thought between octave and sestet, but forcefully states the theme, or sometimes inverts the theme, in the concluding couplet. A Petrarchan sonnet has an eight-line octave and a six-line sestet.

See also *PETRARCHAN SONNET and RHYME SCHEME*.

Sound devices Techniques used to emphasize particular sounds in writing. Authors use sound devices, such as alliteration, consonance, assonance, and onomatopoeia, to underscore the meaning of certain words, enhance the rhythm of a piece, or add a musical quality to the work.

See page 1042.

See also *ALLITERATION, ASSONANCE, CONSONANCE, ONOMATOPOEIA, RHYME, RHYTHM*.

Speaker The voice that communicates with the reader of a poem, similar to the narrator in a work of prose. Sometimes the speaker's voice is that of the poet, but in some poems the speaker has a distinct identity, perhaps of a fictional person or even an inanimate object, so one should never assume that the speaker and the poet are identical. A speaker who is clearly different from the writer, as in Li Po's "The River-Merchant's Wife: A Letter," is called a persona.

See pages 359 and 811.

See also *NARRATOR, PERSONA*.

Stage directions Notes in the text of a play that describe the appearance and movements of the characters, as well as the sets, costumes, and lighting. Stage directions serve primarily as instructions for the cast and crew of a theatrical production, but they also help readers imagine the action of the play.

Stanza A group of lines forming a unit in a poem or song. A stanza in a poem is similar to a paragraph in prose. Typically, stanzas are separated in a poem by a line of space.

See also *LINE.*

Stereotype A generalization about a group of people that is made without regard for individual differences. In literature, this term is often used to describe a conventional or flat character who conforms to an expected, fixed pattern of behavior. Stereotypes are used to make or reflect broad generalizations about a group of people.

See also *STOCK CHARACTER.*

Stock character A character who represents a type that is recognizable as belonging to a particular genre. For example, cruel stepmothers or charming princes are often found in fairy tales. Valiant knights and heroes are found in legends and myths. The hard-boiled detective is found in detective stories. Stock characters have conventional traits and mannerisms shared by all members of their type.

See also *ARCHETYPE, CHARACTER, STEREOTYPE.*

Structure The particular order or pattern an author uses to present ideas. Narratives commonly follow a chronological order, while the structure of persuasive or expository writing may vary. Listing detailed information, using cause and effect, or describing a problem and offering a solution are some other ways an author can structure a text. Poetic structure—more commonly known as form—refers to the organization of words, lines, and images as well as ideas.

See page 984.

See also *FORM, PLOT.*

Style The expressive qualities that distinguish an author's work, including word choice and the length and arrangement of sentences, as well as the use of figurative language and imagery. Style can reveal an author's attitude and purpose in writing.

See page 1221.

See also *AUTHOR'S PURPOSE, FIGURATIVE LANGUAGE, IMAGERY, TONE.*

Subject The topic of a literary work.

Surprise ending An unexpected plot twist at the end of a story. The ending might surprise readers because the author provides ambiguous clues or withholds important information. A surprise ending is most effective when it adds to the meaning of a story rather than merely overturns the reader's expectation.

Surrealism A literary and artistic style that originated in Europe in the 1920s. Typically, surrealist works feature ordinary people and objects brought together in strange and unexpected ways, or bizarre and impossible events treated as if they were normal, as in Naguib Mahfouz's "Half a Day." Surrealism differs from magic realism in its emphasis on what surrealists see as the strangeness in everyday life.

Suspense The tension or excitement that a reader feels about what will happen next in a story. Authors often create suspense by raising questions in the reader's mind about the outcome of a plot. Suspense is especially important in the plot of an adventure or mystery story.

See page 887.

See also *FORESHADOWING.*

Symbol A person, place, or thing that exists on a literal level but represents something else on a figurative level. Some literary symbols have meanings that are widely understood. A rushing river, for example, often symbolizes the passing of time, just as sunrise often symbolizes rebirth or hope. In "Fishing," Joy Harjo uses fishing as a symbol for the struggle of the universe.

See pages 533 and 791.

Symbolist poetry A kind of poetry that emphasizes suggestion and inward experience instead of explicit description. Symbolist poets such as Arthur Rimbaud, Paul Verlaine, and Stéphane Mallarmé influenced twentieth-century authors such as T.S. Eliot and Ezra Pound.

See also *MODERNISM.*

Synecdoche A figure of speech in which a part is used for the whole or a whole is used for a part. In this line from the book of Revelation in the Bible, "All nations, and kindreds, and people, and tongues," *tongues* (a part) is used for the whole (languages).

See also *FIGURATIVE LANGUAGE, METONYMY.*

T

Tanka An unrhymed Japanese verse form that consists of five lines. The first and third lines have five syllables each; the other lines have seven syllables each.

See also *HAIKU.*

Theater of the Absurd Drama that does not tell a story but instead presents a series of scenes in which the characters, confused and anxious, seem to exist in a meaningless world. The movement, spearheaded by Thomas Beckett, flourished in the 1950s and 1960s.

See also *DRAMA.*

Theme The main idea or message about life that a poem, story, novel, or play conveys. All the details of a literary work point to the theme, which is usually an insight into human experience. Sometimes a theme is directly stated, either by a narrator or by another character. More often, a theme is implied or suggested. The reader must figure out the theme from the work's details. Themes and subjects are different. The subject of a work might be love; the theme would be what the author says about love—for example, love is cruel, love is wonderful, or love is fleeting. Many literary works have more than one theme.

See pages 471 and 927.

See also *AUTHOR'S PURPOSE, MORAL.*

Thesis The main idea of an essay or other work of nonfiction. The thesis may be implied but is usually stated directly.

See also *ESSAY, NONFICTION.*

Tone The attitude that an author takes toward the audience, a subject, or a character. Tone is conveyed through elements such as word choice, punctuation, sentence structure, and figures of speech. An author's tone may convey a variety of attitudes, such as sympathy, seriousness, irony, sadness, bitterness, or humor.

See pages 25, 695, and 1015.

See also *ATMOSPHERE, AUTHOR'S PURPOSE, DICTION, MOOD, NARRATOR, SPEAKER, STYLE, VOICE.*

Tragedy A play in which the main character, or tragic hero, is brought to ruin or suffers a great sorrow as a result of a fatal character flaw, errors in judgment, or forces beyond human control, such as fate. Traditionally, the tragic hero is a person of high rank who, out of an exaggerated sense of power and pride, violates a human, natural, or divine law. By breaking the law, the hero poses a threat to society and causes the suffering or death of family members, friends, and associates. In the last act of a traditional Greek tragedy, these wrongs are set right when the tragic hero is punished or dies and order is restored. According to the Greek philosopher Aristotle, the purpose of tragedy is to arouse pity (through identification with the main character) and fear (through dread at the possibility of sharing the main character's tragic flaw) in the audience as the tragic hero's terrible fate unfolds. Oedipus is the tragic hero of Sophocles' *Oedipus the King.*

See page 274.

See also *DRAMA.*

Tragic hero See *TRAGEDY.*

Trickster figures Characters that represent that part of human nature that wants to break rules and cause trouble. Tricksters try to outwit people, animals, and even gods. Although they are generally self-centered, we may admire them for their cunning and ability to overcome obstacles. Trickster figures are most commonly depicted in animal form. Almost every folklore tradition has its own trickster figures, such as West Africa's Anansi.

See also *ANTHROPOMORPHISM, ARCHETYPES, FOLKLORE.*

Turning point See *DRAMATIC STRUCTURE.*

U

Understatement Language that emphasizes the importance of something by treating it as unimportant.

See also *HYPERBOLE.*

Unreliable narrator See *NARRATOR.*

V

Vernacular Ordinary speech of a particular country or region. Vernacular is more casual than cultivated, formal speech. Slang, dialect, and idiom are commonly included as part of vernacular. Authors often employ vernacular to enhance the realism of their narrative or dialogue.

See also *DIALECT, IDIOM.*

Voice The distinctive use of language that conveys the author's or narrator's personality to the reader. Voice is determined by elements of style such as word choice and tone.

See page 1287.

See also *DICTION, NARRATOR, PERSONA, SPEAKER, STYLE, TONE.*

Verse paragraph A group of lines in a poem that form a unit. Unlike a stanza, a verse paragraph does not have a fixed number of lines. Many contemporary poems are made up of verse paragraphs. Verse paragraphs help to organize a poem into thoughts, as paragraphs help to organize prose.

See also *FREE VERSE, PROSE POEM, STANZA.*

Wit A type of humor that relies on cleverness, especially on innovative observation and deft wordplay.

See also *COMEDY, HUMOR, PARODY, SARCASM, SATIRE.*

Word choice See *DICTION.*

Reading and Thinking with Foldables®

by Dinah Zike, M.Ed., Creator of Foldables®

Using Foldables® Makes Learning Easy and Enjoyable

Anyone who has paper, scissors, and maybe a stapler or some glue can use Foldables in the classroom. Just follow the illustrated step-by-step directions. Check out the following samples:

 Reading Objective: to understand how one character's actions affect other characters in a short story

Use this Foldable to keep track of what the main character does and how his or her actions affect the other characters.

 Step ❶ Place a sheet of paper in front of you so that the short side is at the top. Fold the paper in half from top to bottom.

 Step ❷ Fold in half again, from side to side, to divide the paper into two columns. Unfold the paper so that the two columns show.

 Step ❸ Draw a line along the column crease. Then, through the top layer of paper, cut along the line you drew, forming two tabs.

Step ❹ Label the tabs *Main character's actions* and *Effects on others.*

| Main character's actions | Effects on others |

Step ❺ As you read, record the main character's actions under the first tab. Record how each of those actions affects other characters under the second tab.

Short Story

Reading Objective: to analyze a short story on the basis of its literary elements

As you read, use the following Foldable to keep track of five literary elements in the short story.

 Step ❶ Stack three sheets of paper with their top edges about a half-inch apart. Be sure to keep the side edges straight.

 Step ❷ Fold up the bottom edges of the paper to form six tabs, five of which will be the same size.

 Step ❸ Crease the paper to hold the tabs in place and staple the sheets together along the crease.

Story Title
Setting
Characters
Plot
Point of View
Theme

Step ❹ Turn the sheets so that the stapled side is at the top. Write the title of the story on the top tab. Label the five remaining tabs *Setting, Characters, Plot, Point of View,* and *Theme.*

Step ❺ Use your Foldable as you read the short story. Under each labeled tab, jot down notes about the story in terms of that element.

You may adapt this simple Foldable in several ways.
- Use it with dramas, longer works of fiction, and some narrative poems—wherever five literary elements are present in the story.
- Change the labels to focus on something different. For example, if a story or a play has several settings, characters, acts, or scenes, you could devote a tab to each one.

Drama

Reading Objective: to understand conflict and plot in a drama

As you read the drama, use the following Foldable to keep track of conflicts that arise and ways that those conflicts are resolved.

 Step ❶ Place a sheet of paper in front of you so that the short side is at the top. Fold the paper in half from side to side.

 Step ❷ Fold the paper again, one inch from the top as shown here.

 Step ❸ Unfold the paper and draw lines along all of the folds. This will be your chart.

Step ❹ At the top, label the left column *Conflicts* and the right column *Resolutions.*

Step ❺ As you read, record in the left column the various conflicts that arise in the drama. In the right column, explain how each conflict is resolved by the end of the drama.

You may adapt this simple Foldable in several ways.
- Use it with short stories, longer works of fiction, and many poems—wherever conflicts and their resolutions are important.
- Change the labels to focus on something different. For example, you could record the actions of two characters, or you could record the thoughts and feelings of a character before and after the story's climax.

 Lyric Poem

Reading Objective: to interpret the poet's message by understanding the speaker's thoughts and feelings

As you read the poem, use the following Foldable to help you distinguish between what the speaker *says* and what the poet *means.*

 Step ❶ Place a sheet of paper in front of you so that the short side is at the top. Fold the paper in half from top to bottom.

 Step ❷ Fold the paper in half again from left to right.

 Step ❸ Unfold and cut through the top layer of paper along the fold line. This will make two tabs.

 Step ❹ Label the left tab *Speaker's Words.* Label the right tab *Poet's Meaning.*

Step ❺ Use your Foldable to jot down notes on as you read the poem. Under the left tab, write down key things the speaker says. Under the right tab, write down what you think the poet means by having the speaker say those things.

You may adapt this simple Foldable in several ways.
- Use it to help you visualize the images in a poem. Just replace *Speaker's Words* with *Imagery* and replace *Poet's Meaning* with *What I See.*
- Replace the label *Speaker's Words* with *Speaker's Tone* and under the tab write adjectives that describe the tone of the speaker's words.
- If the poem you are reading has two stanzas, you might devote each tab to notes about one stanza.

Functional Documents

Functional documents are specialized forms of expository writing that serve specifc purposes. Functional documents are an everyday part of business, school, and even home life. They must be clear, concise, accurate, and correct in style and usage.

Letter of Application

A letter of application is a form of business writing. It can be used when applying for a job, an internship, or a scholarship. In most cases, the letter is intended to accompany a résumé or an application. Because detailed information is usually included in the accompanying form, a letter of application should provide a general overview of your qualifications and the reasons you are submitting an application. A letter of application should be concise. You should clearly state which position you are applying for and then explain why you are interested and what makes you qualified. The accompanying material should speak for itself.

❶ The optional subject line indicates the topic of the letter.

❷ In a business letter, the greeting is followed by a colon.

❸ The writer states her purpose directly and immediately.

❹ The writer comments briefly on her qualifications.

❺ The writer makes reference to the accompanying material.

32 South Street
Austin, Texas 78746
May 6, 2009

Melissa Reyes
City Life Magazine
2301 Davis Avenue
Austin, Texas 78764

❶ Re: Internship

❷ Dear Ms. Reyes:

I am a junior at City High School and editor of the City High Herald. I am **❸** writing to apply for your summer internship at City Life magazine. As a journalism student and a longtime fan of your magazine, I feel that an internship with your magazine would provide me with valuable experience in the field of journalism. I believe that my role with the City High Herald has **❹** given me the skills necessary to be a useful contributor to your magazine this summer. In addition, my enclosed application shows that I am also a **❺** diligent worker.

I thank you for considering my application for your summer internship, and I hope to be working with you in the coming months.

Sincerely,
Anne Moris
Anne Moris

Activity

Choose a local business where you might like to work. Write a letter of application for an internship at that business. Assume that you will be submitting this letter along with a résumé or an internship application that details your experience and qualifications.

Résumé

The purpose of a résumé is to provide the employer with a comprehensive record of your background information, related experience, and qualifications. Although a résumé is intended to provide a great deal of information, the format is designed to provide this information in the most efficient way possible.

❶ Jane Wiley
909 West Main Street, Apt. #1
Urbana, Illinois 61802
(217) 555-0489 • jane@internet.edu

Goal
Seeking position in television news production

❷ Education
Junior standing in the College of Communications at the University of
    Illinois, Urbana-Champaign
2005 Graduate of City High School

Honors
Member of National Honor Society

Activities
❸ Member, Asian American Association: 2005–Present
Environmental Committee Chairperson, Asian American Association:
    August 2006–May 2007

Work Experience
❹ Radio Reporter, WPGU, 107.1 FM, Champaign, Illinois: May 2007–Present
❺ • Rewrote and read stories for afternoon newscasts
• Served as field reporter for general assignments

Cashier, Del's Restaurant, Champaign, Illinois: May 2006–August 2006
• Responsible for taking phone orders
• Cashier for pickup orders

Assistant Secretary, Office of Dr. George Wright, Woodstock, Illinois:
May 2005–August 2005
• Answered phones
• Made appointments

❶ The header includes all important contact information.

❷ All important education background is included.

❸ Related dates are included for all listed activities.

❹ The job title is included along with the place of employment.

❺ Job responsibilities are briefly listed, with a parallel structure used in each bulleted item.

Activity
Create an outline that lists the information that you would want to include in a résumé. Use a word processor to help format your outline.

Job Application

When applying for a job, you usually need to fill out a job application. When you fill out the application, read the instructions carefully. Examine the entire form before beginning to fill it out. If you fill out the form by hand, make sure that your handwriting is neat and legible. Fill out the form completely, providing all information directly and honestly. If a question does not apply to you, indicate that by writing *n/a,* short for "not applicable." Keep in mind that you will have the opportunity to provide additional information in your résumé, in your letter of application, or during the interview process.

❶ **Please type or print neatly in blue or black ink.**

❷ **Name:** _____ **Today's date:** _____
Address: _____
Phone #: _____ **Birth date:** _____ **Sex:** __ **Soc. Sec. #:** ____

* *

❸ **Job History** (List each job held, starting with the most recent job.)

1. Employer: _____ Phone #:_____
Dates of employment: _____
Position held: _____
❹ Duties: _____

2. Employer: _____ Phone #:_____
Dates of employment: _____
Position held: _____
Duties: _____

* *

Education (List the most recent level of education completed.)

_____

* *

Personal References:

1. Name: _____ Phone #:_____
Relationship: _____

2. Name: _____ Phone #:_____
Relationship: _____

❶ The application provides specific instructions.

❷ All of the information requested should be provided in its entirety.

❸ The information should be provided legibly and succinctly.

❹ Experience should be stated accurately and without embellishment.

Activity

Pick up a job application from a local business or use the sample application shown. Complete the application thoroughly. Fill out the application as if you were actually applying for the job. Be sure to pay close attention to the guidelines mentioned above.

Memos

A memorandum (memo) conveys precise information to another person or a group of people. A memo begins with a leading block. It is followed by the text of the message. A memo does not have a formal closing.

TO: All Employees
FROM: Jordan Tyne, Human Resources Manager
❶ SUBJECT: New Human Resources Assistant Director
DATE: November 3, 2009

❷ Please join me in congratulating Daphne Rudy on her appointment as assistant director in the Human Resources Department. Daphne comes to our company with five years of experience in the field. Daphne begins
❸ work on Monday, November 10. All future general human resource inquiries should be directed to Daphne.

Please welcome Daphne when she arrives next week.

❶ The topic of the memo is stated clearly in the subject line.

❷ The announcement is made in the first sentence.

❸ All of the important information is included briefly in the memo.

Business E-mail

E-mail is quickly becoming the most common form of business communication. While e-mail may be the least formal and most conversational method of business writing, it shouldn't be written carelessly or too casually. The conventions of business writing—clarity, attention to your audience, proper grammar, and the inclusion of relevant information—apply to e-mail.

An accurate subject line should state your purpose briefly and directly. Use concise language and avoid rambling sentences.

To: LiamS@internet.com
From: LisaB@internet.com
CC: EricC@internet.com
Date: January 7, 8:13 a.m.
❶ Subject: New Product Conference Call

Liam,

❷ I just wanted to make sure that arrangements have been made for next week's conference call to discuss our new product. The East Coast sales team has already scheduled three sales meetings at the end of the month with potential buyers, so it's important that our sales team is prepared to talk about the product. Please schedule the call when the manufacturing director
❸ is available, since he will have important information for the sales team.

Lisa

❶ Subject line clearly states the topic.

❷ The purpose is stated immediately and in a conversational tone.

❸ Important details are included in a brief, direct fashion.

Activity
Write an e-mail to your coworkers. Inform them of a change in company procedure that will affect them.

Travel Directions

When planning an event or a social occasion, it is often necessary to provide people with detailed directions to the location. These directions must be clear enough to enable those who are unfamiliar with the surrounding area to easily find their way. Creating a map that shows the route with clearly labeled streets can also be a great help.

Directions to Darien High School's Graduation Ceremony

From I-95 North, take Exit 11. **❶**

Turn Left onto Post Road (Route 1).

At the first light, turn Left onto Samuel Avenue. Travel 2.5 miles. **❷**

Turn Right onto Cherry Hill Road.

Turn Left onto High School Lane. **❸**

Follow signs to Visitor Parking.

❶ Begins at a point from which most people will be coming

❷ Offers travel distances to help travelers locate streets

❸ Gives the name of each street along the route

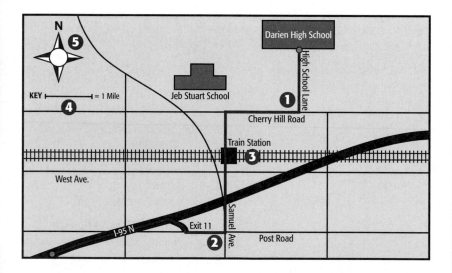

❶ Clearly labels all streets to be traveled

❷ Labels major cross streets so the traveler can keep better track of his or her progress

❸ Includes landmarks to help identify the area

❹ Includes legend to show scale

❺ Includes compass rose to help orient the traveler

Activity

Write directions and draw an accompanying map to a location in your town. Be sure to include enough details and give clear enough directions to enable even someone who is unfamiliar with the area to find the destination.

Technical Writing

Technical writing involves the use of very specific vocabulary and a special attention to detail. The purpose of technical writing is to describe a process clearly enough so that the reader can perform the steps and reach the intended goal, such as installing software, connecting a piece of equipment, or programming a device.

Instructions for Connecting DVD Player to HDTV

❶ Your DVD player can be connected to an HDTV using RCA cables or, for best picture quality, an HDMI cable.

Connecting with RCA Cables:

❷ **Step 1:** Insert the ends of the red, white, and yellow cables into the jacks labeled "AUDIO/VIDEO OUT." Be sure to match the colors of the cable with the colors of the jack.

Step 2: Insert the other ends of the RCA cables into the jacks labeled "AUDIO/VIDEO IN" on your HDTV. These are usually located on the side or the back of the television. Again, be sure to match the colors of the cables with the colors of the jacks.

Connecting with HDMI Cable:

Step 1: Insert one end of the HDMI cable into the HDMI port located on the back of the DVD player.

Step 2: Insert the other end of the HDMI cable into the HDMI port on your HDTV.

❸ **Note:** Your HDTV may have more than one HDMI port. If so, be sure that you set your HDTV to the correct input when viewing.

❶ Uses specific language to clearly describe the process

❷ Lists each step individually

❸ Directs attention to possible variations the reader may encounter

Activity

Choose a device that you own or have access to, such as an MP3 player or a cell phone. Write brief step-by-step directions on how to perform a specific function on the device, so that someone else can follow your instructions and perform the function successfully.

Writing Handbook

Using the Traits of Strong Writing

What are some basic terms you can use to discuss your writing with your teacher or classmates? What should you focus on as you revise and edit your compositions? Check out the following terms, or traits, that describe the qualities of strong writing. Learn the meaning of each trait and find out how using the traits can improve your writing.

Ideas

The message or the theme and the details that develop it

Writing is clear when readers can grasp the meaning of your ideas right away. Check to see whether you're getting your message across.

☑ Does the title suggest the theme of the composition?

☑ Does the composition focus on a single narrow topic?

☑ Is the thesis—the main point or central idea—clearly stated?

☑ Do well-chosen details elaborate your main point?

Organization

The arrangement of main ideas and supporting details

An effective plan of organization points your readers in the right direction and guides them easily through your composition from start to finish. Find a structure, or order, that best suits your topic and writing purpose. Check to see whether you've ordered your key ideas and details in a way that keeps your readers on track.

☑ Are the beginning, middle, and end clearly linked?

☑ Is the internal order of ideas easy to follow?

☑ Does the introduction capture your readers' attention?

☑ Do sentences and paragraphs flow from one to the next in a way that makes sense?

☑ Does the conclusion wrap up the composition?

Voice

A writer's unique way of using tone and style

Your writing voice comes through when your readers sense that a real person is communicating with them. Readers will respond to the **tone** (or attitude) that you express toward a topic and to the **style** (the way that you use language and shape your sentences). Read your work aloud to see whether your writing voice comes through.

☑ Does your writing sound interesting?

☑ Does your writing reveal your attitude toward your topic?

☑ Does your writing sound like you—or does it sound like you're imitating someone else?

Word Choice

The vocabulary a writer uses to convey meaning

Words work hard. They carry the weight of your meaning, so make sure you choose them carefully. Check to see whether the words you choose are doing their jobs well.

☑ Do you use lively verbs to show action?

☑ Do you use vivid words to create word pictures in your readers' minds?

☑ Do you use precise words to explain your ideas simply and clearly?

Sentence Fluency

The smooth rhythm and flow of sentences that vary in length and style

The best writing is made up of sentences that flow smoothly from one sentence to the next. Writing that is graceful also sounds musical—rhythmical rather than choppy. Check for sentence fluency by reading your writing aloud.

☑ Do your sentences vary in length and structure?

☑ Do transition words and phrases show connections between ideas and sentences?

☑ Does parallelism help balance and unify related ideas?

Conventions

Correct spelling, grammar, usage, and mechanics

A composition free of errors makes a good impression on your readers. Mistakes can be distracting, and they can blur your message. Try working with a partner to spot errors and correct them. Use this checklist to help you.

☑ Are all words spelled correctly?

☑ Are all proper nouns—as well as the first word of every sentence—capitalized?

☑ Is your composition free of sentence fragments?

☑ Is your composition free of run-on sentences?

☑ Are punctuation marks—such as apostrophes, commas, and end marks—inserted in the right places?

Presenting and Publishing

The formatting of writing for various purposes

For many writers, the writing process is not complete until they present their work to an audience. This can mean submitting your writing for publication in a school paper or a national magazine, or it can simply mean preparing your writing in a neat and presentable format. For readers to fully appreciate your writing, it is very important that you present it neatly, effectively, and according to professional standards.

Format

- The standard typeface setting for most writing submissions is Courier 12 point.

- Double-space your work so that it is easy to read.

- Leave one-inch margins on all sides of every page.

- Italicize titles or when using terms from other languages. You may also italicize words to add emphasis, but do this only when it is necessary to make your point clear. (If you are submitting your writing to a professional publication, underline words that should appear in italics.)

- Most word processing programs make it easy to set the page number to appear in the upper right-hand corner of each page. Include your last name before each page number after the first page.

- If you are including charts, graphs, maps, or other visual aids, consider setting them on their own page. This will allow you to show the graphic at a full size that is easy to read.

Organization

- On a separate sheet of paper, center your name under the title of your work. If you are submitting your writing for publication, include the total number of words in the upper right-hand corner, and your name and address in the upper left-hand corner.

- The body of your work follows immediately.

- End your presentation with your list of works cited.

Research Paper Writing

More than any other types of papers, research papers are the product of a search—a search for data, for facts, for informed opinions, for insights, and for new information.

Selecting a topic

- If a specific topic is not assigned, choose a topic. Begin with the assigned subject or a subject that interests you. Read general sources of information about that subject and narrow your focus to some aspect of it that interests you. Good places to start are encyclopedia articles and the tables of contents of books on the subject. A computerized library catalog will also display many subheads related to general topics. Find out if sufficient information about your topic is available.

- As you read about the topic, develop your paper's central idea, which is the purpose of your research. Even though this idea might change as you do more research, it can begin to guide your efforts. For example, if you were assigned the subject of the Civil War, you might find that you're interested in women's roles during that war. As you read, you might narrow your topic down to women who went to war, women who served as nurses for the Union, or women who took over farms and plantations in the South.

Conducting a broad search for information

- Generate a series of researchable questions about your chosen topic. Then research to find answers to your questions.

- Among the many sources you might use are the card catalog, the computer catalog, the *Readers' Guide to Periodical Literature* (or an electronic equivalent), newspaper indexes, and specialized references such as biographical encyclopedias.

- If possible, use primary sources as well as secondary sources. A **primary source** is a firsthand account of an event—for example, the diary of a woman who served in the army in the Civil War is a primary source. **Secondary sources** are sources written by people who did not experience or influence the event. Locate specific information efficiently by using the table of contents, indexes, chapter headings, and graphic aids.

Developing a working bibliography

If a work seems useful, write a **bibliography card** for it. On an index card, write down the author, title, city of publication, publisher, date of publication, and any other information you will need to identify the source. Number your cards in the upper right-hand corner so you can keep them in order.

Following are model bibliography, or source, cards.

Book

❶ Settle, Mary Lee   **❷** 6

   ❸ <u>All the Brave Promises.</u>

   ❹ Columbia: University of

     South Carolina Press,

   ❺ 1995.

   ❻ Evanston Public Library   **❼** D810.W754

❶ Author
❷ Source number
❸ Title
❹ City of publication/ Publisher
❺ Date of publication
❻ Location of source
❼ Library call number

Periodical

> **❶** Chelminski, R.   **❷** 2
> **❸** "The Maginot Line"
> **❹** *Smithsonian*, June 1997: 90–99

❶ Author

❷ Source number

❸ Title

❹ Title of magazine/date/page number(s)

Online Source

> **❶** "Job Hunting Resources"   **❷** 6
> **❸** The Career Building Network
> **❹** CareerBuilder
> **❺** 14 Feb. 2002
> **❻** http://www.careerbuilder.com

❶ Title   **❹** Sponsoring organization

❷ Source number   **❺** Date of access

❸ Title of database   **❻** URL

Evaluating your sources

Your sources should be **a**uthoritative, **r**eliable, **t**imely, and **s**uitable **(arts)**.

- The source should be **authoritative.** The author should be well-known in the field. An author who has written several books or articles about a subject or who is frequently quoted may be considered an authority. You might also consult *Book Review Index* and *Book Review Digest* to find out how other experts in the field have evaluated a book or an article.

- The source should be **reliable.** If possible, avoid material from popular magazines in favor of that from more scholarly journals. Be especially careful to evaluate material from online sources. For example, the Web site of a well-known university is more reliable than that of an individual. (You might also consult a librarian or your instructor for guidance in selecting reliable online sources.)

- The source should be **timely.** Use the most recent material available, particularly for subjects of current importance. Check the publication date of books as well as the month and year of periodicals.

- The source should be **suitable,** or **appropriate.** Consider only material that is relevant to the purpose of your paper. Do not waste time on books or articles that have little bearing on your topic. If you are writing on a controversial topic, you should include material that represents more than one point of view.

Compiling and organizing note cards

Careful notes will help you to organize the material for your paper.

- As you reread and study sources, write useful information on index cards. Be sure that each note card identifies the source (use the number of the bibliography card that corresponds to each source).

- In the lower right-hand corner of the card, write the page number on which you found the information. If one card contains several notes, write the page number in parentheses after the relevant material.

- Three helpful ways to take notes are paraphrasing, summarizing, and quoting directly.

  1. **Paraphrase** important details that you want to remember; that is, use your own words to restate specific information.

  2. **Summarize** main ideas that an author presents. When you summarize several pages, be sure to note the page on which the material begins and the page on which it ends—for example, 213–221.

  3. **Quote** the exact words of an author only when the actual wording is important. Be careful about placing the author's words in quotation marks.

- Identify the subject of each note card with a short phrase written in the upper left.

See the sample note card below, which includes information about careers and goals from three pages.

Careers and goals   12
Many people "crave work that will
spark . . . excitement and energy." (5)
Sher recognizes that a career does
not necessarily satisfy a person's aim
in life. (24) She also offers tips on how
to overcome obstacles that people
experience in defining their goals. (101)

- Organize your note cards to develop a **working outline.** Begin by sorting them into piles of related cards. Try putting the piles together in different ways that suggest an organizational pattern. (If, at this point, you discover that you do not have enough information, go back and do further research.) Many methods of organization are possible. You might also combine methods of organization.

Developing a thesis statement
A thesis statement tells what your topic is and what you intend to say about it—for example, "World War II changed the lives of African Americans and contributed to the rise of the civil rights movement."

- Start by examining your central idea.
- Refine it to reflect the information that you gathered in your research.
- Next, consider your approach to the topic. What is the purpose of your research? Are you proving or disproving something? illustrating a cause-and-effect relationship? offering a solution to a problem? examining one aspect of the topic thoroughly? predicting an outcome?
- Revise your central idea to reflect your approach.
- Be prepared to revise your thesis statement if necessary.

Drafting your paper
Consult your working outline and your notes as you start to draft your paper.

- Concentrate on getting your ideas down in a complete and logical order.
- Write an introduction and a conclusion. An effective introduction creates interest, perhaps by beginning with a question or a controversial quotation; it should also contain your thesis statement. An effective conclusion will summarize main points, restate your thesis, explain how the research points to important new questions to explore, and bring closure to the paper.

Avoiding plagiarism
Plagiarism is the act of presenting an author's words or ideas as if they were your own. This is not only illegal, but also unethical. You must credit the source not only for material directly quoted but also for any facts or ideas obtained from the source.

Consider this example:

From the original SparkNotes study guide by Melissa and Stephanie Martin

Throughout the novel, Twain depicts the society that surrounds Huck as little more than a collection of degraded rules and precepts that defy logic. This faulty logic appears early in the novel, when the new judge in town allows Pap to keep custody of Huck.

Plagiarized usage

Twain's depiction of society is as a collection of illogical rules and principles. A good example of this is when Pap is awarded custody of Huck.

Simply rewording the original passage is not enough. In order to legally and ethically use the words or ideas of another writer you must credit the writer of the original or rework the original into your own new idea.

Using material without plagiarizing

1. **Quote the original directly and credit the author.**

   As Melissa and Stephanie Martin note in their SparkNotes study guide, Huck lives in a society that is "little more than a collection of degraded rules and precepts that defy logic." They offer the example of Pap being awarded custody of Huck.

2. **Paraphrase the original and credit the author.**

   In their SparkNotes study guide, Melissa and Stephanie Martin note that Twain depicts society as a collection of illogical rules and principles. A good example of this is when Pap is awarded custody of Huck.

3. **Use the information in the original to create your own idea.**

   It is hard to blame Huck for wanting to escape from a world where he is forced to follow arbitrary rules, and where he is forced to live with an abusive father.

Crediting your source is not only fair to the writer of the original source; it is also the law. Plagiarism is a serious offense and can result in failing grades, expulsion, and even legal action.

- In addition to citing books and periodicals from which you take information, cite song lyrics, letters, and excerpts from literature.

- Also credit original ideas that are expressed graphically in tables, charts, and diagrams, as well as the sources of any visual aids you may include, such as photographs.

- You do not need to cite the source of any information that is common knowledge, such as "John F. Kennedy was assassinated in 1963 in Dallas, Texas."

In-text citations The most common method of crediting sources is with parenthetical documentation within the text. Generally a reference to the source and page number is included in parentheses at the end of each quotation, paraphrase, or summary of information borrowed from a source. An in-text citation points readers to a corresponding entry in your **works-cited list**—a list of all your sources, complete with publication information, that will appear as the final page of your paper. The Modern Language Association (MLA) recommends the following guidelines for crediting sources in text. You may wish to refer to the *MLA Handbook for Writers of Research Papers* by Joseph Gibaldi for more information and examples.

- Put in parentheses the author's last name and the page number where you found the information: An art historian has noted, "In Wood's idyllic farmscapes, man lives in complete harmony with Nature; he is the earth's caretaker" (Corn 90).

- If the author's name is mentioned in the sentence, put only the page number in parentheses: Art historian Wanda Corn has noted, "In Wood's idyllic farmscapes, man lives in complete harmony with Nature; he is the earth's caretaker" (90).

- If no author is listed, put the title or a shortened version of the title in parentheses. Include a page number if you have one: Some critics believe that Grant Wood's famous painting *American Gothic* pokes fun at small-town life and traditional American values ("Gothic").

Compiling a list of works cited

At the end of your text, provide an alphabetized list of published works or other sources cited.

- Include complete publishing information for each source.

- For magazine and newspaper articles, include the page numbers. If an article is continued on a different page, use + after the first page number.

- For online sources, include the date accessed.

- Cite only those sources from which you actually use information.

- Arrange entries in alphabetical order according to the author's last name. Write the last name first. If no author is given, alphabetize by title.

- For long entries, indent five spaces every line after the first.

How to cite sources

On the next three pages, you'll find sample style sheets that can help you prepare your list of sources—the final page of the research paper. Use the one your teacher prefers.

MLA Style

MLA style is most often used in English and social studies classes. Center the title *Works Cited* at the top of your list.

Source	Style
Book with one author	Isaacson, Walter. *Einstein: His Life and Universe.* New York: Simon & Schuster, 2007.
Book with two or three authors	Mortenson, Greg, and Relin, David Oliver. *Three Cups of Tea: One Man's Mission to Promote Peace…One School at a Time.* New York: Penguin Books, 2006. [If a book has more than three authors, name only the first author and then write "et al." (Latin abbreviation for "and others").]
Book with editor(s)	Lehman, David, and McHugh, Heather, eds. *The Best American Poetry 2007.* New York: Scribner, 2007.
Book with an organization or a group as author or editor	Adobe Creative Team. *Adobe Photoshop CS3 Classroom in a Book.* Berkeley: Adobe Press, 2007.
Work from an anthology	Kilmer, Joyce. "Trees." *The Poetry Anthology, 1912–2002.* Ed. Joseph Parisi. Chicago: Ivan R. Dee, 2004. 7
Introduction in a published book	Jackson, Peter. Introduction. *The Making of* Star Wars*: The Definitive Story Behind the Original Film.* By J. W. Rinzler. New York: Del Rey, 2007. iii.
Encyclopedia article	"Jazz." *Encyclopedia Britannica.* 15th ed. 2007.
Weekly magazine article	Sacks, Oliver. "A Bolt from the Blue." *The New Yorker.* 23 July 2007: 38–42.
Monthly magazine article	Plotnikoff, David. "Hungry Man." *Saveur.* July 2007: 35–36.
Newspaper article	Long, Ray, and Meitrodt, Jeffrey. "Some Budget Progress Made." *Chicago Tribune.* 26 July 2007: B3. [If no author is named, begin the entry with the title of the article.]
Internet	"Americans Embracing 'Green' Cleaning." *ABC News.* 30 January 2006. ABC News Internet Ventures. 1 August 2007 <http://abcnews.go.com/Technology/Business/story?id=1544322>.
Online magazine article	Parks, Bob. "Robot Buses Pull In to San Diego's Fastest Lane." *Wired Magazine.*15.08 (July 2007). 25. Oct. 2007 <http://www.wired.com/cars/futuretransport/magazine/15-08/st_robot>.
Radio or TV program	"Jungles." *Planet Earth.* Animal Planet. Discovery Channel. 25 July 2007.
Videotape or DVD	Guggenheim, David, dir. *An Inconvenient Truth.* DVD. Paramount, 2006. [For a videotape (VHS) version, replace "DVD" with "Videocassette."]
Interview	Campeche, Tanya. E-mail interview. 25 Feb. 2004. [If an interview takes place in person, replace "E-mail" with "Personal"; if it takes place on the telephone, use "Telephone."]

CMS Style

CMS style was created by the University of Chicago Press to meet its publishing needs. This style, which is detailed in *The Chicago Manual of Style* (CMS), is used in a number of subject areas. Center the title *Bibliography* at the top of your list.

Source	Style
Book with one author	Isaacson, Walter. *Einstein: His Life and Universe.* New York: Simon & Schuster, 2007.
Book with two or three authors	Mortenson, Greg, and David Oliver Relin. *Three Cups of Tea: One Man's Mission to Promote Peace…One School at a Time.* New York: Penguin Books, 2006. [If a book has more than ten authors, name only the first seven and then write "et al." (Latin abbreviation for "and others").]
Book with editor(s)	Lehman, David, and Heather McHugh, eds. *The Best American Poetry 2007.* New York: Scribner, 2007.
Book with an organization or a group as author or editor	Adobe Creative Team. *Adobe Photoshop CS3 Classroom in a Book.* Berkeley: Adobe Press, 2007.
Work from an anthology	Kilmer, Joyce. "Trees." *The Poetry Anthology, 1912–2002.* Ed. Joseph Parisi, 7. Chicago: Ivan R. Dee, 2004.
Introduction in a published book	Rinzler, J. W. *The Making of* Star Wars: *The Definitive Story Behind the Original Film.* Introduction by Peter Jackson. New York: Del Rey, 2007.
Encyclopedia article	[Credit for encyclopedia articles goes in your text, not in your bibliography.]
Weekly magazine article	Sacks, Oliver. "A Bolt from the Blue." *The New Yorker,* July 23, 2007, 38–42.
Monthly magazine article	Plotnikoff, David. "Hungry Man." *Saveur,* July 2007, 35–36.
Newspaper article	Long, Ray and Jeffrey Meitrodt. "Some Budget Progress Made." *Chicago Tribune.* July 26, 2007, B3. [Credit for unsigned newspaper articles goes in your text, not in your bibliography.]
Internet	ABC News Internet Ventures. "Americans Embracing 'Green' Cleaning." *ABC News,* 2006, http://abcnews.go.com/Technology/Business/story?id=1544322.
Online magazine article	Parks, Bob. "Robot Buses Pull In to San Diego's Fastest Lane." *Wired Magazine.* 15.08 (July 2007). http://www.wired.com/cars/futuretransport/magazine/15-08/st_robot.
Radio or TV program	[Credit for radio and TV programs goes in your text, not in your bibliography.]
Videotape or DVD	Guggenheim, David, dir. *An Inconvenient Truth.* Paramount, 2006. DVD. [For a videotape (VHS) version, replace "DVD" with "Videocassette."]
Interview	[Credit for interviews goes in your text, not in your bibliography.]

APA Style

The American Psychological Association (APA) style is commonly used in the sciences. Center the title *References* at the top of your list.

Source	Style
Book with one author	Isaacson, Walter. (2007). *Einstein: His life and universe.* New York: Simon & Schuster.
Book with two or three authors	Mortenson, Greg and Relin, David Oliver. *Three cups of tea: One man's mission to promote peace...One school at a time.* New York: Penguin Books, 2006. [If a book has more than ten authors, name only the first seven and then write "et al." (Latin abbreviation for "and others").]
Book with editor(s)	Lehman, David and McHugh, Heather. (Eds.). (2007). *The best American poetry 2007.* New York: Scribner.
Book with an organization or a group as author or editor	Adobe Creative Team. (2007). *Adobe Photoshop CS3 Classroom in a Book.* Berkeley: Adobe Press.
Work from an anthology	Kilmer, Joyce. "Trees." *The Poetry Anthology, 1912–2002.* Ed. Joseph Parisi, 7. Chicago: Ivan R. Dee, 2004.
Introduction in a published book	[Credit for introductions goes in your text, not in your references.]
Encyclopedia article	Jazz. (2007). In *Encyclopedia Britannica.* (Vol. 6, pp. 519). Chicago: Encyclopedia Britannica.
Weekly magazine article	Sacks, Oliver. (2007, July 23). A bolt from the blue. *The New Yorker,* 38–42.
Monthly magazine article	Plotnikoff, David. (2007, July). Hungry man. *Saveur,* 103, 35–36.
Newspaper article	Long, Ray and Meitrodt, Jeffrey. (2007, July 26). Some budget progress made. *Chicago Tribune,* p. B3. [If no author is named, begin the entry with the title of the article.]
Internet	ABC News Internet Ventures. (2006, January 30). *ABC News.* "Americans Embracing 'Green' Cleaning." Retrieved August 1, 2007, from http://abcnews.go.com/Technology/Business/story?id=1544322.
Online magazine article	Parks, Bob. (2007, July). Robot buses pull in to San Diego's fastest lane." *Wired Magazine.* 15.08. Retreived July 25, 2007, from http://www.wired.com/cars/futuretransport/magazine/15-08/st_robot.
Radio or TV program	Jungles. (2007, July 25). *Planet Earth* [Television series episode]. Animal Planet. Silver Spring, MD: Discovery Channel.
Videotape or DVD	Guggenheim, David (Director). (2006). *An inconvenient truth.* DVD. Paramount, 2006. [For a videotape (VHS) version, replace "DVD" with "Videocassette."]
Interview	[Credit for interviews goes in your text, not in your bibliography.]

Reading Handbook

Reading Handbook

Being an active reader is a crucial part of being a lifelong learner. It is also an ongoing task. Good reading skills are recursive; that is, they build on each other, providing the tools you'll need to understand text, to interpret ideas and themes, and to read critically.

Understanding Text Structure

To follow the logic and message of a selection and to remember it, analyze the **text structure,** or organization of ideas, within a writer's work. Recognizing the pattern of organization can help you discover the writer's purpose and will focus your attention on important ideas in the selection. **Look for signal words** to point you to the structure.

- **Spatial sequence** uses words or phrases such as *nearby, to the left, above,* and *behind* to show the physical arrangement of people and objects in an area.

- **Order of importance** will use words such as *most important* and *least necessary* to compare the importance of things or ideas.

- **Chronological order** often uses such words as *first, then, after, later,* and *finally* to show a sequence of events in time.

- **Cause-and-effect order** discusses chains of events using words or phrases such as *therefore, because, subsequently,* or *as a result.*

- **Comparison-contrast order** may use words or phrases such as *similarly, in contrast, likewise,* or *on the other hand.*

- **Problem-solution order** presents a problem and then offers one or more solutions. A problem-solution structure may incorporate other structures such as order of importance, chronological order, or comparison-contrast order.

Comprehension Strategies

Because understanding is the most critical reading task, lifelong learners use a wide variety of reading strategies before, during, and after reading to ensure their comprehension.

Determining the Main Idea

The **main idea** of a selection is the writer's purpose in writing the selection. As you read, it will be helpful to determine the main idea not only of the entire piece, but also of each paragraph. After identifying the important details in each paragraph, pause and ask yourself

- What is the main point of this selection?
- What do these details add up to?
- What is the writer trying to communicate?

Summarizing

A summary is a short restatement of the main ideas and important details of a selection. Summarizing what you have read is an excellent tool for understanding and remembering a passage. To summarize a selection:

- Identify the **main ideas.**
- Determine the essential **supporting details.**
- Relate all the main ideas and essential details in a **logical sequence.**
- **Paraphrase**—that is, restate the selection in your own words.
- Answer **who, what, where, when,** and **why** questions.

The best summaries can easily be understood by someone who has not read the selection. If you're not sure whether an idea is a main idea or a supporting detail, try taking it out of your summary. Does your summary still sound complete?

Distinguishing between fact and opinion

It is always important to be able to tell whether the ideas in a selection are facts or the writer's opinions.

- **Facts** can be proven or measured; you can verify them in reference materials. Sometimes you can observe or test them yourself.

  Example: Chicago is about 800 miles from New York City.

- **Opinions** are often open to interpretation and contain phrases such as "I believe" or "from my point of view."

  Example: Chicago to New York is too far to drive.

As you read a selection, evaluate any facts as well as any opinions you find. Ask yourself:

- Are the facts relevant? Are they actually true?
- Are the opinions well informed and based on verifiable facts? Are they persuasive?

Drawing inferences and supporting them

An **inference** involves using your reason and experience to come up with an idea based on what a writer implies or suggests but does not directly state.

- **Drawing a conclusion** is making a general statement you can explain with reason or with supporting details from the text.

- **Making a generalization** is generating a statement that can apply to more than one item or group.

What is most important when inferring is to be sure that you have accurately based your thoughts on supporting details from the text as well as on your own knowledge.

Making a prediction

A **prediction** is an educated guess as to what a text will be about, based on initial clues a writer provides. You can also make predictions about what will happen next in a story as you read.

- Take breaks during your reading and **ask yourself questions** about what will happen next, such as, "How will this character react to this news?"

- **Answer these questions for yourself,** supporting your answers with evidence from the text. For example, "Sam will be jealous when he hears the news, because he is in love with Antonia."

- As you continue reading, **verify** your predictions.

Reading silently for sustained periods

When you read for long periods of time, your task is to avoid distractions. Check your comprehension regularly by summarizing what you've read so far. Using study guides or graphic organizers can help you get through difficult passages. Take regular breaks when you need them and vary your reading rate with the demands of the task.

Keep in mind:

Whichever strategies you choose to use while reading, it will always be helpful to:

- Read slowly and carefully.
- Reread difficult passages.
- Take careful notes.

Also, when reading more difficult material, consider these steps to modify or change your reading strategies when you don't understand what you've read.

- Reread the passage.
- Consult other sources, including text resources, teachers, and other students.
- Write comments or questions on another piece of paper for later review or discussion.

Language Handbook

Grammar Glossary

This glossary will help you quickly locate information on parts of speech and sentence structure.

A

Absolute phrase. *See* Phrase.

Abstract noun. *See* Noun chart.

Action verb. *See* Verb.

Active voice. *See* Voice.

Adjective A word that modifies a noun or pronoun by limiting its meaning. Adjectives appear in various positions in a sentence. (The *gray* cat purred. The cat is *gray*.)

Many adjectives have different forms to indicate degree of comparison. (**short, shorter, shortest**)

The positive degree is the simple form of the adjective. (**easy, interesting, good**)

The comparative degree compares two persons, places, things, or ideas. (**easier, more interesting, better**)

The superlative degree compares more than two persons, places, things, or ideas. (**easiest, most interesting, best**)

A predicate adjective follows a linking verb and further identifies or describes the subject. (**The child is happy.**)

A proper adjective is formed from a proper noun and begins with a capital letter. Many proper adjectives are created by adding these suffixes: *-an, -ian, -n, -ese,* and *-ish.* (**Chinese, African**)

Adjective clause. *See* Clause chart.

Adverb A word that modifies a verb, an adjective, or another adverb by making its meaning more specific. When modifying a verb, an adverb may appear in various positions in a sentence. (**Cats *generally* eat less than dogs. *Generally,* cats eat less than dogs.**) When modifying an adjective or another adverb, an adverb appears directly before the modified word. (**I was *quite* pleased that they got along so well.**) The word *not* and the contraction

-n't are adverbs. (**Mike *wasn't* ready for the test today.**) Certain adverbs of time, place, and degree also have a negative meaning. (**He's *never* ready.**)

Some adverbs have different forms to indicate degree of comparison. (**soon, sooner, soonest**)

The comparative degree compares two actions. (**better, more quickly**)

The superlative degree compares three or more actions. (**fastest, most patiently, least rapidly**)

Adverb clause. *See* Clause chart.

Antecedent. *See* Pronoun.

Appositive A noun or a pronoun that further identifies another noun or pronoun. (**My friend *Julie* lives next door.**)

Appositive phrase. *See* Phrase.

Article The adjective *a, an,* or *the.*

Indefinite articles (*a* and *an*) refer to one of a general group of persons, places, or things. (**I eat *an* apple *a* day.**)

The definite article (**the**) indicates that the noun is a specific person, place, or thing. (***The* alarm woke me up.**)

Auxiliary verb. *See* Verb.

B

Base form. *See* Verb tense.

C

Clause A group of words that has a subject and a predicate and that is used as part of a sentence. Clauses fall into two categories: *main clauses,* which are also called *independent clauses,* and *subordinate clauses,* which are also called *dependent clauses.*

A main clause can stand alone as a sentence.

Types of Subordinate Clauses			
Clause	Function	Example	Begins with . . .
Adjective clause	Modifies a noun or a pronoun	Songs *that have a strong beat* make me want to dance.	A relative pronoun such as *which, who, whom, whose,* or *that*
Adverb clause	Modifies a verb, an adjective, or an adverb	*Whenever Al calls me,* he asks to borrow my bike.	A subordinating conjunction such as *after, although, because, if, since, when,* or *where*
Noun clause	Serves as a subject, an object, or a predicate nominative	*What Philip did* surprised us.	A word such as *how, that, what, whatever, when, where, which, who, whom, whoever, whose,* or *why*

There must be at least one main clause in every sentence. (*The rooster crowed,* and *the dog barked.*)

A subordinate clause cannot stand alone as a sentence. A subordinate clause needs a main clause to complete its meaning. Many subordinate clauses begin with subordinating conjunctions or relative pronouns. (*When Geri sang her solo,* the audience became quiet.) The chart on this page shows the main types of subordinate clauses.

Collective noun. *See* Noun chart.

Common noun. *See* Noun chart.

Comparative degree. *See* Adjective; Adverb.

Complement A word or phrase that completes the meaning of a verb. The four basic kinds of complements are *direct objects, indirect objects, object complements,* and *subject complements.*

A direct object answers the question *What?* or *Whom?* after an action verb. (**Kari found a** *dollar.* **Larry saw** *Denise.*)

An indirect object answers the question *To whom? For whom? To what?* or *For what?* after an action verb. (**Do** *me* **a favor. She gave the** *child* **a toy.**)

An object complement answers the question *What?* after a direct object. An object complement is a noun, a pronoun, or an adjective that completes the meaning of a direct object by identifying or describing it. (**The director made me the** *understudy* **for the role. The little girl called the puppy** *hers.***)**

A subject complement follows a subject and a linking verb. It identifies or describes a subject. The two kinds of subject complements are *predicate nominatives* and *predicate adjectives.*

A predicate nominative is a noun or pronoun that follows a linking verb and tells more about the subject. (**The author of "The Raven" is** *Poe.*)

A predicate adjective is an adjective that follows a linking verb and gives more information about the subject. (**Ian became** *angry* **at the bully.**)

Complex sentence. *See* Sentence.

Compound preposition. *See* Preposition.

Compound sentence. *See* Sentence.

Compound-complex sentence. *See* Sentence.

Conjunction A word that joins single words or groups of words.

A coordinating conjunction (*and, but, or, nor, for, yet, so*) joins words or groups of words that are equal in grammatical importance. (**David** *and* **Ruth are twins. I was bored,** *so* **I left.**)

Correlative conjunctions (*both . . . and, just as . . . so, not only . . . but also, either . . . or, neither . . . nor, whether . . . or*) work in pairs to join words and groups of words of equal importance. (**Choose** *either* **the muffin** *or* **the bagel.**)

(Choose *either* the muffin *or* the bagel.)

A subordinating conjunction *(after, although, as if, because, before, if, since, so that, than, though, until, when, while)* joins a dependent idea or clause to a main clause. **(Beth acted *as if* she felt ill.)**

Conjunctive adverb An adverb used to clarify the relationship between clauses of equal weight in a sentence. Conjunctive adverbs are used to replace *and (also, besides, furthermore, moreover)*; to replace *but (however, nevertheless, still)*; to state a result *(consequently, therefore, so, thus)*; or to state equality *(equally, likewise, similarly).* **(Ana was determined to get an A; *therefore,* she studied often.)**

Coordinating conjunction. *See* Conjunction.

Correlative conjunction. *See* Conjunction.

D

Declarative sentence. *See* Sentence.

Definite article. *See* Article.

Demonstrative pronoun. *See* Pronoun.

Direct object. *See* Complement.

E

Emphatic form. *See* Verb tense.

F

Future tense. *See* Verb tense.

G

Gerund A verb form that ends in *-ing* and is used as a noun. A gerund may function as a subject, the object of a verb, or the object of a preposition. **(*Smiling* uses fewer muscles than *frowning.* Marie enjoys *walking.*)**

Gerund phrase. *See* Phrase.

I

Imperative mood. *See* Mood of verb.

Imperative sentence. *See* Sentence chart.

Indicative mood. *See* Mood of verb.

Indirect object. *See* Complement.

Infinitive A verb form that begins with the word *to* and functions as a noun, an adjective, or an adverb. **(No one wanted *to answer.*)** Note: When *to* precedes a verb, it is not a preposition but instead signals an infinitive.

Infinitive phrase. *See* Phrase.

Intensive pronoun. *See* Pronoun.

Interjection A word or phrase that expresses emotion or exclamation. An interjection has no grammatical connection to other words. Commas follow mild ones; exclamation points follow stronger ones. **(*Well,* have a good day. *Wow!*)**

Interrogative pronoun. *See* Pronoun.

Intransitive verb. *See* Verb.

Inverted order In a sentence written in *inverted order,* the predicate comes before the subject. Some sentences are written in inverted order for variety or special emphasis. **(Up the beanstalk *scampered Jack.*)** The subject also generally follows the predicate in a sentence that begins with *here* or *there.* **(*Here* was the solution to his problem.)** Questions, or interrogative sentences, are generally written in inverted order. In many questions, an auxiliary verb precedes the subject, and the main verb follows it. **(*Has* anyone *seen* Susan?)** Questions that begin with *who* or *what* follow normal word order.

Irregular verb. *See* Verb tense.

L

Linking verb. *See* Verb.

M

Main clause. *See* Clause.

Mood of verb A verb expresses one of three moods: indicative, imperative, or subjunctive.

The indicative mood is the most common. It makes a statement or asks a question. **(We *are* out of bread. *Will* you *buy* it?)**

The imperative mood expresses a command or makes a request. **(*Stop* acting like a child! Please *return* my sweater.)**

Types of Nouns		
Noun	Function	Examples
Abstract noun	Names an idea, a quality, or a characteristic	capitalism, terror
Collective noun	Names a group of things or persons	herd, troop
Common noun	Names a general type of person, place, thing, or idea	city, building
Compound noun	Is made up of two or more words	checkerboard, globe-trotter
Noun of direct addrress	Identifies the person or persons being spoken to	*Maria,* please stand.
Possessive noun	Shows possession, ownership, or the relationship between two nouns	my *sister's* room
Proper noun	Names a particular person, place, thing, or idea	Cleopatra, Italy, Christianity

The subjunctive mood is used to express, indirectly, a demand, suggestion, or statement of necessity **(I demand that he *stop* acting like a child. It's necessary that she *buy* more bread.)** The subjunctive is also used to state a condition or wish that is contrary to fact. This use of the subjunctive requires the past tense. **(If you *were* a nice person, you *would return* my sweater.)**

N

Nominative pronoun. *See* Pronoun.

Noun A word that names a person, a place, a thing, or an idea. The chart on this page shows the main types of nouns.

Noun clause. *See* Clause chart.

Noun of direct address. *See* Noun chart.

Number A noun, pronoun, or verb is *singular* in number if it refers to one; *plural* if it refers to more than one.

O

Object. *See* Complement.

P

Participle A verb form that can function as an adjective. Present participles always end in *-ing.* **(The** woman comforted the *crying* child.) Many past participles end in *-ed.* **(We bought the beautifully *painted* chair.)** However, irregular verbs form their past participles in some other way. **(Cato was Caesar's *sworn* enemy.)**

Passive voice. *See* Voice.

Past tense. *See* Verb tense.

Perfect tense. *See* Verb tense.

Personal pronoun. *See* Pronoun; Pronoun chart.

Phrase A group of words that acts in a sentence as a single part of speech.

An absolute phrase consists of a noun or pronoun that is modified by a participle or participial phrase but has no grammatical relation to the complete subject or predicate. **(*The vegetables being done,* we finally sat down to eat dinner.)**

An appositive phrase is an appositive along with any modifiers. If not essential to the meaning of the sentence, an appositive phrase is set off by commas. **(Jack plans to go to the jazz concert, *an important musical event.*)**

A gerund phrase includes a gerund plus its complements and modifiers. **(*Playing the flute* is her hobby.)**

An infinitive phrase contains the infinitive plus its complements and modifiers. **(It is time *to leave for school.*)**

A participial phrase contains a participle and any modifiers necessary to complete its meaning. **(The woman *sitting over there* is my grandmother.)**

A prepositional phrase consists of a preposition, its object, and any modifiers of the object. A prepositional phrase can function as an adjective, modifying a noun or a pronoun. **(The dog *in the yard* is very gentle.)** A prepositional phrase may also function as an adverb when it modifies a verb, an adverb, or an adjective. **(The baby slept *on my lap*.)**

A verb phrase consists of one or more auxiliary verbs followed by a main verb. **(The job *will have been completed* by noon tomorrow.)**

Positive degree. *See* Adjective.

Possessive noun. *See* Noun chart.

Predicate The verb or verb phrase and any objects, complements, or modifiers that express the essential thought about the subject of a sentence.

A simple predicate is a verb or verb phrase that tells something about the subject. **(We *ran*.)**

A complete predicate includes the simple predicate and any words that modify or complete it. **(We *solved the problem in a short time*.)**

A compound predicate has two or more verbs or verb phrases that are joined by a conjunction and share the same subject. **(We *ran to the park and began to play baseball*.)**

Predicate adjective. *See* Adjective; Complement.

Predicate nominative. *See* Complement.

Preposition A word that shows the relationship of a noun or pronoun to some other word in the sentence. Prepositions include *about, above, across, among, as, behind, below, beyond, but, by, down, during, except, for, from, into, like, near, of, on, outside, over, since, through, to, under, until, with.* **(I usually eat breakfast *before* school.)**

A compound preposition is made up of more than one word. **(according to, ahead of, as to, because of, by means of, in addition to, in spite of, on account of)** **(We played the game *in spite of* the snow.)**

Prepositional phrase. *See* Phrase.

Present tense. *See* Verb tense.

Progressive form. *See* Verb tense.

Pronoun A word that takes the place of a noun, a group of words acting as a noun, or another pronoun. The word or group of words that a pronoun refers to is called its antecedent. **(In the following sentence, *Mari* is the antecedent of *she*. *Mari likes Mexican food, but she doesn't like Italian food*.)**

A demonstrative pronoun points out specific persons, places, things, or ideas. *(this, that, these, those)*

An indefinite pronoun refers to persons, places, or things in a more general way than a noun does. *(all, another, any, both, each, either, enough, everything, few, many, most, much, neither, nobody, none, one, other, others, plenty, several, some)*

An intensive pronoun adds emphasis to another noun or pronoun. If an intensive pronoun is omitted, the meaning of the sentence will be the same. **(Rebecca *herself* decided to look for a part-time job.)**

An interrogative pronoun is used to form questions. *(who? whom? whose? what? which?)*

A personal pronoun refers to a specific person or thing. Personal pronouns have three cases: nominative, possessive, and objective. The case depends upon the function of the pronoun in a sentence. The first chart on the next page shows the nominative and objective forms.

A reflexive pronoun reflects back to a noun or pronoun used earlier in the sentence, indicating that the same person or thing is involved. **(We told *ourselves* to be patient.)**

A relative pronoun is used to begin a subordinate clause. *(who, whose, that, what, whom, whoever, whomever, whichever, whatever)*

Proper adjective. *See* Adjective.

Proper noun. *See* Noun chart.

R

Reflexive pronoun. *See* Pronoun.

Relative pronoun. *See* Pronoun.

S

Sentence A group of words expressing a complete thought. Every sentence has a subject and a predicate. Sentences can be classified by function or by structure. The second chart on this page shows the categories by function; the following subentries describe the categories by structure. *See also* Subject; Predicate; Clause.

A simple sentence has only one main clause and no subordinate clauses. *(Alan found an old violin.)* A simple sentence may contain a compound subject or a compound predicate or both. *(Alan and Teri found an old violin. Alan found an old violin and tried to play it. Alan and Teri found an old violin and tried to play it.)* The subject and the predicate can be expanded with adjectives, adverbs, prepositional phrases, appositives, and verbal phrases. As long as the sentence has only one main clause, however, it remains a simple sentence. *(Alan, rummaging in the attic, found an old violin.)*

A compound sentence has two or more main clauses. Each main clause has its own subject and predicate, and these main clauses are usually joined by a comma and a coordinating conjunction. *(Cats meow, and dogs bark, but ducks quack.)* Semicolons may also be used to join the main clauses in a compound sentence. *(The helicopter landed; the pilot had saved four passengers.)*

A complex sentence has one main clause and one or more subordinate clauses. *(Since the movie starts at eight, we should leave here by seven-thirty.)*

A compound-complex sentence has two or more main clauses and at least one subordinate clause. *(If we leave any later, we may miss the previews, and I want to see them.)*

Simple predicate. *See* Predicate.

Simple subject. *See* Subject.

Subject The part of a sentence that tells what the sentence is about.

A simple subject is the main noun or pronoun in the subject. *(Babies crawl.)*

A complete subject includes the simple subject and any words that modify it. *(The man from New Jersey won the race.)* In some sentences, the simple subject and the complete subject are the same. *(Birds fly.)*

Personal Pronouns			
Case	Singular Pronouns	Plural Pronouns	Function in Sentence
Nominative	I, you, she, he, it	we, you, they	subject or predicate nominative
Objective	me, you, her, him, it	us, you, them	direct object, indirect object, or object of a preposition

Types of Sentences			
Sentence Type	Function	Ends with . . .	Examples
Declarative sentence	Makes a statement	A period	I did not enjoy the movie.
Exclamatory sentence	Expresses strong emotion	An exclamation point	What a good writer Consuela is!
Imperative sentence	Makes a request or gives a command	A period or an exclamation point	Please come to the party. Stop!
Interrogative sentence	Asks a question	A question mark	Is the composition due?

A compound subject has two or more simple subjects joined by a conjunction. The subjects share the same verb. (*Firefighters* and *police officers* protect the community.)

Subjunctive mood. *See* Mood of verb.

Subordinate clause. *See* Clause.

Subordinating conjunction. *See* Conjunction.

Superlative degree. *See* Adjective; Adverb.

T

Tense. *See* Verb tense.

Transitive verb. *See* Verb.

V

Verb A word that expresses action or a state of being. *(cooks, seem, laughed)*

An action verb tells what someone or something does. Action verbs can express either physical or mental action. (Crystal *decided* to *change* the tire herself.)

A transitive verb is an action verb that is followed by a word or words that answer the question *What?* or *Whom?* (I *held* the baby.)

An intransitive verb is an action verb that is not followed by a word that answers the question *What?* or *Whom?* (The baby *laughed.*)

A linking verb expresses a state of being by linking the subject of a sentence with a word or an expression that identifies or describes the subject. (The lemonade *tastes* sweet. He *is* our new principal.) The most commonly used linking verb is *be* in all its forms *(am, is, are, was, were, will be, been, being).* Other linking verbs include *appear, become, feel, grow, look, remain, seem, sound, smell, stay, taste.*

An auxiliary verb, or helping verb, is a verb that accompanies the main verb to form a verb phrase. (I *have been* swimming.) The forms of *be* and *have* are the most common auxiliary verbs: *(am, is, are, was, were, being, been; has, have, had, having).* Other auxiliaries include *can, could, do, does, did, may, might, must, shall, should, will, would.*

Verbal A verb form that functions in a sentence as a noun, an adjective, or an adverb. The three kinds of verbals are gerunds, infinitives, and participles. *See* Gerund; Infinitive; Participle.

Verb tense The tense of a verb indicates when the action or state of being occurs. All the verb tenses are formed from the four principal parts of a verb: a base form *(talk)*, a present participle *(talking)*, a simple past form *(talked)*, and a past participle *(talked)*. A regular verb forms its simple past and past participle by adding *-ed* to the base form. *(climb, climbed)* An irregular verb forms its past and past participle in some other way. *(get, got, gotten)*

In addition to present, past, and future tenses, there are three perfect tenses.

The present perfect tense expresses an action or a condition that occurred at some indefinite time in the past. This tense also shows an action or a condition that began in the past and continues into the present. (She *has played* the piano for four years.)

The past perfect tense indicates that one past action or condition began *and* ended before another past action started. (Andy *had finished* his homework before I even began mine.)

The future perfect tense indicates that one future action or condition will begin *and* end before another future event starts. Use *will have* or *shall have* with the past participle of a verb. (By tomorrow, I *will have finished* my homework, too.)

The progressive form of a verb expresses a continuing action with any of the six tenses. To make the progressive forms, use the appropriate tense of the verb *be* with the present participle of the main verb. (She *is swimming.* She *has been swimming.*)

The emphatic form adds special force, or emphasis, to the present and past tense of a verb. For the emphatic form, use *do, does,* or *did* with the base form. (Toshi *did want* that camera.)

Voice The voice of a verb shows whether the subject performs the action or receives the action of the verb.

A verb is in the active voice if the subject of the sentence performs the action. (The referee *blew* the whistle.)

A verb is in the passive voice if the subject of the sentence receives the action of the verb. (The whistle *was blown* by the referee.)

Troubleshooter

The Troubleshooter will help you recognize and correct errors that you might make in your writing.

Sentence Fragment

Problem: A fragment that lacks a subject
The grass is wet. Can't be mowed now.

Solution: Add a subject to the fragment to make it a complete sentence.
The grass is wet. It can't be mowed now.

Problem: A fragment that lacks a complete verb
We enjoyed our dinner. Beans, rice, and salad.
The storm was fierce. The wind blowing hard.

Solution A: Add either a complete verb or a helping verb to make the sentence complete.
We enjoyed our dinner. Beans, rice, and salad make a good meal.
The storm was fierce. The wind was blowing hard.

Solution B: Combine the fragment with another sentence.
We enjoyed our dinner of beans, rice, and salad.
The storm was fierce with the wind blowing hard.

Problem: A fragment that is a subordinate clause
We went to the park. Where we had often gone before.
Jan won the swimming medal. Which she gave to her parents.

Solution A: Combine the fragment with another sentence.
We went to the park, where we had often gone before.
Jan won the swimming medal, which she gave to her parents.

Solution B: Rewrite the fragment as a complete sentence, eliminating the subordinating conjunction or the relative pronoun and adding a subject or other words necessary to make a complete thought.
We went to the park. We had often gone there before.
Jan won the swimming medal. She gave it to her parents.

Problem: A fragment that lacks both a subject and a verb
The birds woke us with their songs. At six in the morning.

Solution: Combine the fragment with another sentence.
The birds woke us with their songs at six in the morning.

Rule of Thumb: Sentence fragments can make your writing hard to understand. Make sure every sentence has a subject and a verb.

Note: In almost all of the writing you do, especially for school, you should avoid sentence fragments. However, sentence fragments can be used to create special effects, such as adding emphasis or conveying realistic dialogue.
"Not again!" she cried.
The pizza was gone. All of it.

Run-On Sentence

Problem: Comma splice—two main clauses separated only by a comma
The sky is pitch black, there is no moon.

Solution A: Replace the comma with an end mark of punctuation, such as a period or a question mark, and begin the new sentence with a capital letter.
The sky is pitch black. There is no moon.

Solution B: Place a semicolon between the two main clauses.
The sky is pitch black; there is no moon.

Solution C: Add a coordinating conjunction after the comma.
The sky is pitch black, and there is no moon.

Problem: Two main clauses with no punctuation between them
We picked the apples then we made pies.

Solution A: Separate the main clauses with an end mark of punctuation, such as a period or question mark, and begin the second sentence with a capital letter.
We picked the apples. Then we made pies.

Solution B: Separate the main clauses with a semicolon.
We picked the apples; then we made pies.

Solution C: Add a comma and a coordinating conjunction between the main clauses.
We picked the apples, and then we made pies.

Problem: Two main clauses with no comma before the coordinating conjunction
Elephants still live in the wild but they are endangered.

Solution: Add a comma before the coordinating conjunction to separate the two main clauses.
Elephants still live in the wild, but they are endangered.

Rule of Thumb: It often helps to have someone else read your longer sentences to see if they are clear. Since you know what the sentences are supposed to mean, you might miss the need for punctuation.

Lack of Subject-Verb Agreement

Problem: A subject that is separated from the verb by an intervening prepositional phrase
Ten pieces of the puzzle is on the floor.
The shoe department in each of our stores are closing.

Solution: Make the verb agree with the subject, which is never the object of a preposition.
Ten pieces of the puzzle are on the floor.
The shoe department in each of our stores is closing.

Problem: A predicate nominative that differs in number from the subject
Hamburgers is tonight's dinner.
Tonight's dinner are hamburgers.

Solution: Ignore the predicate nominative, and make the verb agree with the subject of the sentence.
Hamburgers are tonight's dinner.
Tonight's dinner is hamburgers.

Problem: A subject that follows the verb
On my desk is two letters from my dad.
Here is my answers to them both.

Solution: In an inverted sentence look for the subject after the verb. Then make sure the verb agrees with the subject.
On my desk are two letters from my dad.
Here are my answers to them both.

Rule of Thumb: Reversing the order of an inverted sentence may help you decide on the verb form to use: "My answers to them both are here."

Problem: A collective noun as the subject
The cross country team are in first place.
The team gathers at the captain's house after each meet.

Solution A: If the collective noun refers to a group as a whole, use a singular verb.
The cross country team is in first place.

Solution B: If the collective noun refers to each member of a group individually, use a plural verb.
The team gather at the captain's house after each meet.

Problem: A noun of amount as the subject
Five bushels are a great many tomatoes.
Three marbles is in my pocket.

Solution: Determine whether the noun of amount refers to one unit and is therefore singular or whether it refers to a number of individual units and is therefore plural.
Five bushels is a great many tomatoes.
Three marbles are in my pocket.

Problem: A compound subject that is joined by *and*
The hill and the lake makes a lovely setting for a picnic.
Spaghetti and meatballs are her favorite dinner.

Solution A: If the parts of the compound subject do not belong to one unit or if they refer to different people or things, use a plural verb.
The hill and the lake make a lovely setting for a picnic.

Solution B: If the parts of the compound subject belong to one unit or if both parts refer to the same person or thing, use a singular verb.
Spaghetti and meatballs is her favorite dinner.

Problem: A compound subject that is joined by *or* or *nor*
Neither those trees nor that shrub are healthy.

Solution: Make the verb agree with the subject that is closer to it.
Neither those trees nor that shrub is healthy.

Problem: A compound subject that is preceded *by many a, every,* or *each*
Many a dog and cat ends up in an animal shelter or a pound.

Solution: When *many a, every,* or *each* precedes a compound subject, the subject is considered singular. Use a singular verb.
Many a dog and cat end up in an animal shelter or a pound.

Problem: A subject that is separated from the verb by an intervening expression
That issue, as well as several others, are bothering me.

Solution: Certain expressions, such as those beginning with *as well as, in addition to,* and *together with,* do not change the number of the subject. Ignore an intervening expression between a subject and its verb, and make the verb agree with the subject.
That issue, along with several others, is bothering me.

Problem: An indefinite pronoun as the subject
Neither of the boys are on time.

Solution: Determine whether the indefinite pronoun is singular or plural, and make the verb agree. Some indefinite pronouns are singular—*another, anyone, everyone, one, each, either, neither, anything, everything, something,* and *somebody.* Some are plural—*both, many, few, several,* and *others.* Some can be singular or plural—*some, all, any, more, most,* and *none.* In these cases, find the noun to which the pronoun refers to determine which verb form to use.
Neither of the boys is on time.

Lack of Pronoun-Antecedent Agreement

Problem: A singular antecedent that can be either male or female.
A climber must check his equipment carefully.

Solution A: Traditionally, a masculine pronoun has been used to refer to an antecedent that may be either male or female. This usage ignores or excludes females. Reword the sentence to use *he or she, him or her,* and so on.
A climber must check his or her equipment carefully.

Solution B: Reword the sentence so that both the antecedent and the pronoun are plural.
Climbers must check their equipment carefully.

Solution C: Reword the sentence to eliminate the pronoun.
A climber must check the equipment carefully.

Rule of Thumb: Although you may see the masculine forms used exclusively in older literature, they are not acceptable in contemporary writing.

Problem: A second-person pronoun that refers to a third-person antecedent
Juan likes sitcoms that make you think as well as laugh.

Solution A: Use the appropriate third-person pronoun.
Juan likes sitcoms that make him think as well as laugh.

Solution B: Use an appropriate noun instead of a pronoun.
Juan likes sitcoms that make people think as well as laugh.

Problem: A singular indefinite pronoun as an antecedent
Each of the volumes has their own index.

Solution: *Each, every, either, neither,* and *one* are singular and therefore require singular personal pronouns even when followed by a prepositional phrase that contains a plural noun.
Each of the volumes has its own index.

Rule of Thumb: To help you remember that *each, either,* and *neither* are singular, think *each one, either one,* and *neither one.*

Lack of Clear Pronoun Reference [Unclear Antecedent]

Problem: A pronoun reference that is weak or vague
We spent several weeks at the farm this summer, and it was exciting.
The label says to shake it before pouring a serving.

Solution A: Rewrite the sentence, adding a clear antecedent for the pronoun.
We spent our vacation at the farm this summer, and it was exciting.

Solution B: Rewrite the sentence, substituting a noun for the pronoun.
The label says to shake the bottle of salad dressing before pouring a serving.

Problem: A pronoun that could refer to more than one antecedent
Lauren and Abby wrote six songs, and she recorded them all.
Don't buy a car from that dealership; it will let you down.

Solution A: Rewrite the sentence, substituting a noun for the pronoun.
Lauren and Abby wrote six songs, and Abby recorded them all.

Solution B: Rewrite the sentence, making the antecedent of the pronoun clear.
A car from that dealership will let you down; don't buy one there.

Problem: The indefinite use of *you* or *they*
You just have to laugh at that scene in the movie.
They say the weather will be clear tomorrow.

Solution A: Rewrite the sentence, substituting a noun for the pronoun.
The audience just has to laugh at that scene in the movie.

Solution B: Rewrite the sentence, eliminating the pronoun entirely.
According to the forecast, the weather will be clear tomorrow.

Shift in Pronoun

Problem: An incorrect shift in person between two pronouns
Lynn likes the front seat, where you are most comfortable.
The Chins planted a maple on the south side of the house, where you need shade the most.

Solution A: Replace the incorrect pronoun with a pronoun that agrees with its antecedent.
Lynn likes the front seat, where she is most comfortable.

Solution B: Replace the incorrect pronoun with an appropriate noun.
The Chins plants a maple on the south side of the house, where the house needs shade the most.

Shift in Verb Tense

Problem: An unnecessary shift in tense.
The children will give their mother flowers, and they kiss her.
After the party ended, we go home.

Solution: When two or more events occur at the same time, be sure to use the same verb tense to describe each event.
The children will give their mother flowers, and they will kiss her.
After the party ended, we went home.

Problem: A lack of correct shift in tenses to show that one event precedes or follows another
By the time the concert ended, we sat for four hours.

Solution: When two past events being described have occurred at different times, shift from the past tense to the past perfect tense to indicate that one action began and ended before another past action began. Use the past perfect tense for the earlier of the two actions.
By the time the concert ended, we had sat for four hours.

Rule of Thumb: When you need to use several verb tenses in your writing, it may help to first jot down the sequence of events you're writing about. Be clear in your mind what happened first, next, last.

Incorrect Verb Tense or Form

Problem: An incorrect or missing verb ending
When I began taking lessons, I learn about quarter, half, and whole notes.
I had start the lessons two months ago.

Solution: Add *–ed* to a regular verb to form the past tense and the past participle.
When I began taking lessons, I learned about quarter, half, and whole notes.
I had started the lessons two months ago.

Problem: An improperly formed irregular verb
James brung the book back to the library.
Catherine has writed six pages on that topic.

Solution: Irregular verbs form their past and past participles in some way other than by adding *–ed*. Memorize these forms, or look them up.
James brought the book back to the library.
Catherine has written six pages on that topic.

Problem: Confusion between the past form and the past participle
We have ate too many apples.
She had swam the Chesapeake last July.

Solution: Use the past participle form of an irregular verb, not the past form, when you use the auxiliary verb *have*.
We have eaten too many apples.
She had swum the Chesapeake last July.

Problem: Improper use of the past participle
The catcher thrown several runners out.
The DiCaprios done a fine job rearing those children.

Solution A: The past participle of an irregular verb cannot stand alone as a verb. Add a form of the auxiliary verb *have* to the past participle to form a complete verb.
The catcher had thrown several runners out.
The DiCaprios have done a fine job rearing those children.

Solution B: Replace the past participle with the past form of the verb.
The catcher threw several runners out.
The DiCaprios did a fine job rearing those children.

Misplaced or Dangling Modifier

Problem: A misplaced modifier
The children were swimming in the photograph.
Swooping down on a fish, I spotted the gull.
I saw a man at the movies eating popcorn.

Solution: Modifiers that modify the wrong word or seem to modify more than one word in a sentence are called misplaced modifiers. Move the misplaced phrase as close as possible to the word or words it modifies.
The children in the photograph were swimming.
I spotted the gull swooping down on a fish.
I saw a man eating popcorn at the movies.

Problem: Incorrect placement of the adverb *only*
Tricia only has enough money to buy a pencil.

Solution: Place the adverb *only* immediately before the word or group of words it modifies.
Only Tricia has enough money to buy a pencil.
Tricia has enough money to buy only a pencil.
Tricia has only enough money to buy a pencil.

Rule of Thumb: Note that each time *only* is moved,

the meaning of the sentence changes. Check to be sure your sentence says what you mean.

Problem: A dangling modifier
Croaking loudly, I listened to the sounds of the frogs in the bog.
Stealing home, the game was won for the Pirates.

Solution: Dangling modifiers do not seem to logically modify any word in the sentence. Rewrite the sentence, adding a noun to which the dangling phrase clearly refers. Often you will have to add other words too.
I listened to the sounds of the frogs croaking loudly in the bog.
Stealing home, Layla won the game for the Pirates.

Missing or Misplaced Possessive Apostrophe

Problem: Singular nouns
The womans child loved the circus trapeze artists.

Solution: Use an apostrophe and *–s* to form the possessive of a singular noun, even one that ends in *s*.
The woman's child loved the circus's trapeze artists.

Problem: Plural nouns ending in *– s*
The hikers cars were parked at the base of the trail.

Solution: Use an apostrophe alone to form the possessive of a plural noun that ends in *–s*.
The hikers' cars were parked at the base of the trail.

Problem: Plural nouns not ending in *–s*
Did Brian join the mens group?

Solution: Use an apostrophe and *–s* to form the possessive of a plural noun that does not end in *–s*.
Did Brian join the men's group?

Problem: Pronouns
Everyones contribution helps.
These pencils are your's, and those pencils are their's.

Solution A: Use an apostrophe and *–s* to form the possessive of a singular indefinite pronoun.
Everyone's contribution helps.

Solution B: Do not use an apostrophe with any of the possessive personal pronouns.
These pencils are yours, and those pencils are theirs.

Problem: Confusion between *its* and *it's*
Will you tell me when its ten o'clock?
The cat licked it's fur.

Solution: Do not use an apostrophe to form the possessive of *it.* Use an apostrophe to form the contraction of *it is.*
Will you tell me when it's ten o'clock?
The cat licked its fur.

Missing Commas with Nonessential Element

Problem: Missing commas with nonessential participles, infinitives, and their phrases
Pounding hard on the roof the rain awakened me.
The whole set of cups chipped from many years of use was discarded.
To answer your question this software package is worth the price.

Solution: Determine whether the participle, infinitive, or phrase is essential to the meaning of the sentence. If it is not essential, set off the phrase with commas.
Pounding hard on the roof, the rain awakened me.
The whole set of cups, chipped from many years of use, was discarded.
To answer your question, this software package is worth the price.

Problem: Missing commas with nonessential adjective clauses
My mother who is a very generous woman gave us investment tips.

Solution: Determine whether the clause is essential to the meaning of the sentence. If it is not essential, set off the clause with commas.
My mother, who is a very generous woman, gave us investment tips.

Problem: Missing comas with nonessential appositives
John the lead-off batter singled on a line drive

Solution: Determine whether the appositive is essential to the meaning of the sentence. If it is not essential, set off the appositive with commas.
John, the lead-off batter, singled on a line drive.

Rule of Thumb: To determine whether a word or phrase is essential, try reading the sentence without it.

Problem: Missing commas with interjections and parenthetical expressions
Wow what a great cat that is!
On Saturdays as a rule we sleep late.

Solution: Set off the interjection or parenthetical expression with commas.
Wow, what a great cat that is!
On Saturdays, as a rule, we sleep late.

Missing Commas in a Series

Problem: Missing commas in a series of words, phrases, or clauses
Alicia Nirupam and Matt made the honor roll.
Mark made the dough kneaded it and left it to rise.
The firefighter carries the child out of the apartment down the stairs and into the arms of her mother.
Joe pitched the tent Meg gathered firewood and Bud unloaded the truck.

Solution: When there are three or more elements in a series, use a comma after each element that precedes the conjunction.
Alicia, Nirupam, and Matt made the honor roll.
Mark made the dough, kneaded it, and left it to rise.
The firefighter carries the child out of the apartment, down the stairs, and into the arms of her mother.
Joe pitched the tent, Meg gathered firewood, and Bud unloaded the truck.

Rule of Thumb: When you're having difficulty with a rule of usage, try rewriting the rule in your own words. Then check with your teacher to be sure you have grasped the concept.

Mechanics

This section will help you use correct capitalization, punctuation, and abbreviations in your writing.

Capitalization

This section will help you recognize and use correct capitalization in sentences.

Rule: Capitalize the first word in any sentence, including direct quotations and sentences in parentheses unless they are included in another sentence.

Example: *She said, "Come back soon."*

Example: *Emily Dickinson became famous only after her death. (She published only six poems during her lifetime.)*

Rule: Always capitalize the pronoun *I* no matter where it appears in the sentence.

Example: *Some of my relatives think that I should become a doctor.*

Rule: Capitalize proper nouns, including

a. names of individuals, and titles used in direct address that precede a name or describing a relationship.
Example: *George Washington; Dr. Morgan; Aunt Margaret*

b. names of ethnic groups, national groups, political parties and their members, and languages.
Example: *Italian Americans; Aztec; the Republican Party; a Democrat; Spanish*

c. names of organizations, institutions, firms, monuments, bridges, buildings, and other structures.
Example: *Red Cross; Stanford University; General Electric; Lincoln Memorial; Tappan Zee Bridge; Chrysler Building; Museum of Natural History*

d. trade names and names of documents, awards, and laws.
Example: *Microsoft; Declaration of Independence; Pulitzer Prize; Sixteenth Amendment*

e. geographical terms and regions or localities.
Example: *Hudson River; Pennsylvania Avenue; Grand Canyon; Texas; the Midwest*

f. names of planets and other heavenly bodies.
Example: *Venus; Earth; the Milky Way*

g. names of ships, planes, trains, and spacecraft.
Example: *USS Constitution; Spirit of St. Louis; Apollo 11*

h. names of most historical events, eras, calendar items, and religious names and items.
Example: *World War II; Age of Enlightenment; June; Christianity; Buddhists; Bible; Easter; God*

i. titles of literary works, works of art, and musical compositions.
Example: *"Why I Live at the P.O."; The Starry Night; Rhapsody in Blue*

j. names of specific school courses.
Example: *Advanced Physics; American History*

Rule: Capitalize proper adjectives (adjectives formed from proper nouns).

Example: *Christmas tree; Hanukkah candles; Freudian psychology; American flag*

Punctuation

This section will help you use these elements of punctuation correctly.

Rule: Use a period at the end of a declarative sentence or a polite command.

Example: *I'm thirsty.*
Example: *Please bring me a glass of water.*

Rule: Use an exclamation point to show strong feeling or after a forceful command.

Example: *I can't believe my eyes!*
Example: *Watch your step!*

Rule: Use a question mark to indicate a direct question.

Example: *Who is in charge here?*

Rule: Use a colon

a. to introduce a list (especially after words such as *these*, *the following*, or *as follows*) and to introduce material that explains, restates, or illustrates previous material.

Example: *The following states voted for the amendment: Texas, California, Georgia, and Florida.*
Example: *The sunset was colorful: purple, orange, and red lit up the sky.*

b. to introduce a long or formal quotation.
Example: *It was Mark Twain who stated the following proverb: "Man is the only animal that blushes. Or needs to."*

c. in precise time measurements, biblical chapter and verse references, and business letter salutations.
Example: 3:35 P.M.   7:50 A.M.
         Gen. 1:10–11   *Matt. 2:23*
         Dear Ms. Samuels: *Dear Sir:*

Rule: Use a semicolon
a. to separate main clauses that are not joined by a coordinating conjunction.
Example: *There were two speakers at Gettysburg that day; only Lincoln's speech is remembered.*

b. to separate main clauses joined by a conjunctive adverb or by *for example* or *that is.*
Example: *Because of the ice storm, most students could not get to school; consequently, the principal canceled all classes for the day.*

c. to separate the items in a series when these items contain commas.
Example: *The students at the rally came from Senn High School, in Chicago, Illinois; Niles Township High School, in Skokie, Illinois; and Evanston Township High School, in Evanston, Illinois.*

d. to separate two main clauses joined by a coordinating conjunction when such clauses already contain several commas.
Example: *The designer combined the blue silk, brown linen, and beige cotton into a suit; but she decided to use the yellow chiffon, yellow silk, and white lace for an evening gown.*

Rule: Use a comma
a. between the main clauses of a compound sentence.
Example: *Ryan was late getting to study hall, and his footsteps echoed in the empty corridor.*

b. to separate three or more words, phrases, or clauses in a series.
Example: *Mel bought carrots, beans, pears, and onions.*

c. between coordinate modifiers.

Example: *That is a lyrical, moving poem.*

d. to set off parenthetical expressions, interjections, and conjunctive adverbs.
Example: *Well, we missed the bus again.*
Example: *The weather is beautiful today; however, it is supposed to rain this weekend.*

e. to set off nonessential words, clauses, and phrases, such as:
  —adverbial clauses
Example: *Since Ellen is so tall, the coach assumed she would be a good basketball player.*

  —adjective clauses
Example: *Scott, who had been sleeping, finally woke up.*

  —participles and participial phrases
Example: *Having found what he was looking for, he left.*

  —prepositional phrases
Example: *On Saturdays during the fall, I rake leaves.*

  —infinitive phrases
Example: *To be honest, I'd like to stay a while longer.*

  —appositives and appositive phrases
Example: *Ms. Kwan, a soft-spoken woman, ran into the street to hail a cab.*

f. to set off direct quotations.
Example: *"My concert," Molly replied, "is tonight."*

g. to set off an antithetical phrase.
Example: *Unlike Tom, Rob enjoys skiing.*

h. to set off a title after a person's name.
Example: *Margaret Thomas, Ph.D., was the guest speaker.*

i. to separate the various parts of an address, a geographical term, or a date.
Example: *My new address is 324 Indian School Road, Albuquerque, New Mexico 85350.*

Example: *I moved on March 13, 1998.*

j. after the salutation of an informal letter and after the closing of all letters.
Example: *Dear Helen,   Sincerely,*

k. to set off parts of a reference that direct the reader to the exact source.
Example: *You can find the article in the* Washington Post, *April 4, 1997, pages 33–34.*

l. to set off words or names used in direct address and in tag questions.
Example: *Yuri, will you bring me my calculator?*
Lottie became a lawyer, didn't she?

Rule: Use a dash to signal a change in thought or to emphasize parenthetical material.

Example: *During the play, Maureen—and she'd be the first to admit it—forgot her lines.*

Example: *There are only two juniors attending—Mike Ramos and Ron Kim.*

Rule: Use parentheses to set off supplemental material. Punctuate within the parentheses only if the punctuation is part of the parenthetical expression.

Example: *If you like jazz (and I assume you do), you will like this CD. (The soloist is Miles Davis.)*
Example: *The upper Midwest (which states does that include?) was hit by terrible floods last year.*

Rule: Use brackets to enclose information that you insert into a quotation for clarity or to enclose a parenthetical phrase that already appears within parentheses.

Example: *"He serves his [political] party best who serves the country best."—Rutherford B. Hayes*
Example: *The staircase (which was designed by a famous architect [Frank Lloyd Wright]) was inlaid with ceramic tile.*

Rule: Use ellipsis points to indicate the omission of material from a quotation.

Example: *". . . Neither an individual nor a nation can commit the least act of injustice against the obscurest individual. . . ." —Henry David Thoreau*

Rule: Use quotation marks
a. to enclose a direct quotation, as follows:
Example: *"Hurry up!" shouted Lisa.*

When a quotation is interrupted, use two sets of quotation marks.

Example: *"A cynic," wrote Oscar Wilde, "is someone who knows the price of everything and the value of nothing."*

Use single quotation marks for a quotation within a quotation.

Example: *"Did you say 'turn left' or 'turn right'?" asked Leon.*

In writing dialogue, begin a new paragraph and use a new set of quotation marks every time the speaker changes.

Example: *"Do you really think the spaceship can take off?" asked the first officer.*
"Our engineer assures me that we have enough power," the captain replied.

b. to enclose titles of short works, such as stories, poems, essays, articles, chapters, and songs.
Example: *"The Lottery"* [short story]
"Provide, Provide" [poem]
"Civil Disobedience" [essay]

c. to enclose unfamiliar slang terms and unusual expressions.
Example: *The man called his grandson a "rapscallion."*

d. to enclose a definition that is stated directly.
Example: *Gauche is a French word meaning "left."*

Rule: Use italics
a. for titles of books, lengthy poems, plays, films, television series, paintings and sculptures, long musical compositions, court cases, names of newspapers and magazines, ships, trains, airplanes, and spacecraft. Italicize and capitalize articles *(a, an, the)* at the beginning of a title only when they are part of the title.
Example: *E.T.* [film]; *The Piano Lesson* [play]
The Starry Night [painting]
the *New Yorker* [magazine]
Challenger [spacecraft]
The Great Gatsby [book]
the *Chicago Tribune* [newspaper]

b. for foreign words and expressions that are not used frequently in English.
Example: *Luciano waved good-bye, saying, "Arrivederci."*

c. for words, letters, and numerals used to represent themselves.
Example: *There is no Q on the telephone keypad.*
Example: *Number your paper from 1 through 10.*

Rule: Use an apostrophe

a. for a possessive form, as follows:

Add an apostrophe and *s* to all singular nouns, plural nouns not ending in *s,* singular indefinite pronouns, and compound nouns. Add only an apostrophe to a plural noun that ends in *s.*

Example: *the tree's leaves*
the man's belt
the bus's tires
the children's pets
everyone's favorite
my mother-in-law's job
the attorney general's decision
the baseball player's error
the cats' bowls

If two or more persons possess something jointly, use the possessive form for the last person named. If they possess something individually, use the possessive form for each one's name.

Example: *Ted and Harriet's family*
Ted's and Harriet's bosses
Lewis and Clark's expedition
Lewis's and Clark's clothes

b. to express amounts of money or time that modify a noun.

Example: *two cents' worth*

Example: *three days' drive (You can use a hyphenated adjective instead: a three-day drive.)*

c. in place of omitted letters or numerals.

Example: *haven't [have not]   the winter of '95*

d. to form the plural of letters, numerals, symbols, and words used to represent themselves. Use an apostrophe and *s.*

Example: You wrote two *5's* instead of one.

Example: How many *s's* are there in Mississippi?

Example: Why did he use three *!'s* at the end of the sentence?

Rule: Use a hyphen

a. after any prefix joined to a proper noun or proper adjective.

Example: *all-American   pre-Columbian*

b. after the prefixes *all-, ex-,* and *self-* joined to any noun or adjective; after the prefix *anti-* when it joins a word beginning with *i;* after the prefix *vice-* (except in some instances, such as *vice president*); and to avoid confusion between words that begin with *re-* and look like another word.

Example: *ex-president*
self-important
anti-inflammatory
vice-principal
re-creation of the event
recreation time
re-pair the socks
repair the computer

c. in a compound adjective that precedes a noun.

Example: *a bitter-tasting liquid*

d. in any spelled-out cardinal or ordinal numbers up to *ninety-nine* or *ninety-ninth,* and with a fraction used as an adjective.

Example: *twenty-three   eighty-fifth*
one-half cup

e. to divide a word at the end of a line, between syllables.

Example: *air-port   scis-sors*
fill-ing   fin-est

Abbreviations

Abbreviations are shortened forms of words.

Rule: Use only one period if an abbreviation occurs at the end of a sentence. If the sentence ends with a question mark or an exclamation point, use the period and the second mark of punctuation.

Example: *We didn't get home until 3:30 A.M.*

Example: *Did you get home before 4:00 A.M.?*

Example: *I can't believe you didn't get home until 3:30 A.M.!*

Rule: Capitalize abbreviations of proper nouns and abbreviations related to historical dates.

Example: *John Kennedy Jr.   P.O. Box 333*
800 B.C.   A.D. 456   1066 C.E.

Use all capital letters and no periods for most abbreviations of organizations and government agencies.

Example: *CBS   CIA   FBI*
IBM   NFL
MADD   GE

Spelling

The following basic rules, examples, and exceptions will help you master the spellings of many words.

Forming plurals

English words form plurals in many ways. Most nouns simply add *s*. The following chart shows other ways of forming plural nouns and some common exceptions to the pattern.

General Rules for Forming Plurals		
If the word ends in	**Rule**	**Example**
ch, s, sh, x, z	add *es*	glass, glasses
a consonant + *y*	change *y* to *i* and add *es*	caddy, caddies
a vowel + *y* or *o*	add only *s*	cameo, cameos monkey, monkeys
a consonant + *o* common exceptions	generally add *es* but sometimes add only *s*	potato, potatoes cello, cellos
f or *ff* common exceptions	add *s* change *f* to *v* and add *es*	cliff, cliffs hoof, hooves
lf	change *f* to *v* and add *es*	half, halves

A few plurals are exceptions to the rules in the previous chart, but they are easy to remember. The following chart lists these plurals and some examples.

Special Rules for Forming Plurals	
Rule	**Example**
To form the plural of most proper names and one-word compound nouns, follow the general rules for plurals.	Cruz, Cruzes Mancuso, Mancusos crossroad, crossroads
To form the plural of hyphenated compound nouns or compound nouns of more than one word, make the most important word plural.	sister-in-law, sisters-in-law motion picture, motion pictures
Some nouns have unusual plural forms.	goose, geese child, children
Some nouns have the same singular and plural forms.	moose scissors pants

Adding prefixes

When adding a prefix to a word, keep the original spelling of the word. Use a hyphen only when the original word is capitalized or with prefixes such as *all-*, *ex-*, and *self-* joined to a noun or an adjective.

co + operative = cooperative
inter + change = interchange
pro + African = pro-African
ex + partner = ex-partner

Suffixes and the silent *e*

Many English words end in a silent letter *e*. Sometimes the *e* is dropped when a suffix is added. When adding a suffix that begins with a consonant to a word that ends in silent *e*, keep the *e*.

like + ness = likeness sure + ly = surely
COMMON EXCEPTIONS awe + ful = awful;
judge + ment = judgment

When adding a suffix that begins with a vowel to a word that ends in silent *e*, usually drop the *e*.

believe + able = believable
expense + ive = expensive
COMMON EXCEPTION mile + age = mileage

When adding a suffix that begins with *a* or *o* to a word that ends in *ce* or *ge*, keep the *e* so the word will retain the soft *c* or *g* sound.

notice + able = noticeable
courage + ous = courageous

When adding a suffix that begins with a vowel to a word that ends in *ee* or *oe*, keep the final *e*.

see + ing = seeing   toe + ing = toeing

Drop the final silent *e* after the letters *u* or *w*.

argue + ment = argument
owe + ing = owing

Keep the final silent *e* before the suffix *-ing* when necessary to avoid ambiguity.

singe + ing = singeing

Suffixes and the final *y*

When adding a suffix to a word that ends in a consonant + *y*, change the *y* to *i* unless the suffix begins with *i*. Keep the *y* in a word that ends in a vowel + *y*.

try + ed = tried   fry + ed = fried
stay + ing = staying   display + ed = displayed
copy + ing = copying joy + ous = joyous

Adding *ly* and *ness*

When adding *ly* to a word that ends in a single *l*, keep the *l*, but when the word ends in a double *l*, drop one *l*. When the word ends in a consonant + *le*, drop the *le*. When adding *-ness* to a word that ends in *n*, keep the *n*.

casual + ly = casually
practical + ly = practically
dull + ly = dully
probable + ly = probably
open + ness = openness
mean + ness = meanness

Doubling the final consonant

Double the final consonant in words that end in a consonant preceded by a single vowel if the word is one syllable, if it has an accent on the last syllable that remains there even after the suffix is added, or if it is a word made up of a prefix and a one-syllable word.

stop + ing = stopping
admit + ed = admitted
replan + ed = replanned

Do not double the final consonant if the accent is not on the last syllable, or if the accent shifts when the suffix is added. Also do not double the final consonant if the final consonant is *x* or *w*. If the word ends in a consonant and the suffix begins with a consonant, do not double the final consonant.

benefit + ed = benefited
similar + ly = similarly
raw + er = rawer
box + like = boxlike
friend + less = friendless
rest + ful = restful

Forming Compound Words

When joining a word that ends in a consonant to a word that begins with a consonant, keep both consonants.

out + line = outline
after + noon = afternoon
post + card = postcard
pepper + mint = peppermint

ie and *ei*

Learning this rhyme can save you many misspellings: "Write *i* before *e* except after *c*, or when sounded like *a* as in *neighbor* and *weigh*." There are many exceptions to this rule, including *seize, scizure, lei-sure, weird, height, either, neither, forfeit.*

-cede, -ceed, and *-sede*

Because of the relatively few words with *sēd* sounds, these words are worth memorizing.

These words use *-cede:* **accede, precede, secede.**
One word uses *-sede:* **supersede.**
Three words use *-ceed:* **exceed, proceed, succeed.**

Logic and Persuasion Handbook

Persuasion

Propositions

One of the main reasons people write and talk is to persuade each other. Persuasive writing and speaking attempts to convince someone of the truth of a **proposition,** that is, a statement or claim. There are four basic types of proposition:

- A proposition of **fact** is a claim that certain information is correct.
  Candidate Wilkins comes from Illinois.

- A proposition of **value** is a statement that a feeling or judgment is valid.
  Candidate Wilkins is a friendly woman.

- A proposition about a **problem** combines fact and judgment.
  Candidate Wilkins is not qualified to run.

- A proposition of **policy** is a claim that someone should do something.
  Everyone should vote for candidate Wilkins.

A proposition may be **true** or **false.** In evaluating persuasive speaking and writing, you need to know which type of proposition is being made so that you can decide whether it is true or false.

Evidence and Arguments

Persuasive writing and speaking usually includes **evidence,** that is, reasons why someone should accept a proposition. Together, a proposition and a reason for accepting it make up an **argument.**

Everyone should vote for candidate Wilkins, because she is the most qualified.

An argument may be **valid** or **invalid,** that is, reasonable or unreasonable.

Appeals

Arguments are meant to appeal to certain beliefs, values, or feelings belonging to the reader or listener. Most reasons given in support of a proposition make at least one of four types of **appeal:**

- An **appeal to logic** is a claim based on fact and reason.
  Wilkins is unqualified, because she does not meet the age requirement.

- An **appeal to ethics or values** is a claim based on shared values or judgments.
  Wilkins is best, because she is the most honest and caring.

- An **appeal to authority** is a claim based on sources believed to be reliable.
  Wilkins is best, because the Metropolitan Bar Association supports her.

- An **appeal to emotion** is a claim based on shared feelings.
  Wilkins is best, because she has overcome hardship.

In evaluating arguments, you need to know which type of appeal is being made so that you can decide whether it is valid or invalid. Note that an argument may involve more than one type of appeal.

Exercise: Analyzing an Argument

Read the following statements. For each statement, identify the type of proposition made and the type of appeal used to support it..

1. If we want clean beaches, then we need to provide trash cans and arrange for garbage removal in the summer.

2. It is our responsibility as human beings to keep ocean ecosystems healthy by polluting them as little as possible or not at all.

3. According to eminent marine biologists, we have a lot to learn about the animals that live in the ocean depths.

4. Restricting owners of beachfront property from building wherever they want to on their property is highly unfair.

Statement	Proposition	Appeal
1	about a problem	
2		
3		
4		to ethics or values

Logic

Inductive Reasoning

Inductive reasoning involves putting facts together to come up with a generalized statement as a conclusion.

Specific facts:

Fact 1. *Star Wars* is the second-biggest money-maker of all time.

Fact 2. The number one movie at the box office in 2004 was *Shrek 2*.

Fact 3. *Spider-Man* broke many box office records in 2002.

Generalization: Science fiction and fantasy films do very well at the box office.

Errors In Inductive Reasoning

To avoid errors in inductive reasoning, be sure you use a large enough sample of specific facts, and of course, make sure your facts are accurate. Assuming you have a large enough sample of accurate facts, make sure that your generalization is logical.

For example, it would be illogical to conclude from the facts above that movies whose titles begin with the letter *S* do well at the box office.

Deductive Reasoning

Deductive reasoning is essentially the opposite of inductive reasoning. With deductive reasoning you start with a generalization to come to a conclusion about a specific case.

Generalization: Paul can only eat vegetarian food.
Specific fact: The Glory Diner offers vegetarian food.
Conclusion: Paul can eat at the Glory Diner.

Syllogisms

A syllogism is a formal statement of a deductive argument. It consists of a **major premise,** or general statement; a **minor premise,** or related fact; and a **conclusion** based on the two.

Major premise: People who travel between countries need a passport.
Minor premise: Jody is flying from the United States to Spain.
Conclusion: Jody needs a passport.

Errors In Deductive Reasoning

Errors in deductive reasoning result from faulty construction of the argument. Make sure the major premise is a universal statement, that both premises are true, and that the conclusion follows logically from the premises.

Note: A syllogism is *valid* if it follows the rules of deductive reasoning. A syllogism is *true* if the statements are factually accurate. Therefore, a perfectly valid syllogism can be untrue. For example:

Major premise: All voters are good citizens. [There is more to good citizenship than voting.]
Minor premise: My parents are voters.
Conclusion: Therefore, my parents are good citizens.

This conclusion is valid according to the premises; however, it isn't necessarily true because the major premise is flawed.

Exercise: Analyzing Logical Reasoning

For each argument below, identify whether inductive or deductive reasoning is used. Evaluate whether the conclusion is valid or invalid and explain your evaluation.

1. An epic poem is a serious, long narrative poem centered on the life of a cultural or national hero or heroine. *El Cid* is an epic poem. In more than 30,000 lines, it celebrates the life and accomplishments of a Spanish military and political leader who lived in the eleventh century.

2. If a computer can play compact discs, the computer must have been built before 1985. This computer can play CDs. This computer must have been built before 1985.

3. Many humorists use puns. Mark Twain used puns in his writing and his speeches. Ogden Nash used puns in his poems. Woody Allen uses puns in his movies.

Exercise: Using Logical Reasoning

Write a short essay arguing a proposition. In your argument, use at least two examples each of valid inductive and deductive reasoning.

Logical Fallacies

A **logical fallacy** is a particular type of faulty reasoning. Fallacies often seem reasonable at face value, so they are often used, both intentionally and unintentionally. Some fallacies are so common that they have names.

To identify fallacies in the writing and speaking of others and to avoid them in your own persuasive communication, you need to be able to identify fallacies and to understand why they are illogical.

- ### Ad Hominem

  Don't listen to what Smyth says about the election; he spent time in prison.

  An ad hominem argument (literally, an argument "against the person") implies that a defect in a person's character or behavior is evidence that what he says is unreliable. Note that the ad hominem fallacy contains a hidden premise: *People who have spent time in prison cannot have valid opinions.* Because this premise is untrue, the argument about Smyth is untrue also.

- ### Non Sequitur or False Causality

  This shirt is unlucky: every time I wear it, something bad happens.

  Non sequitur literally means "it doesn't follow." Just because two events occur together, it doesn't follow logically that one caused the other.

- ### Glittering Generalities

  If you love freedom, vote for Jack.

  Glittering generalities are words with overwhelmingly positive connotations, used to make it seem impossible to disagree with an idea. How can you argue against the idea of freedom? A listener's initial reaction to this statement might be, "Freedom is a good thing, so I must vote for Jack."

- ### Overgeneralization and Stereotype

  Tall people make excellent basketball players.

  An overgeneralization is any conclusion that may be accurate about a small group, but is inaccurate when applied to a much larger group. An overgeneralization about a group of people is called a stereotype.

- ### Argument from Authority and Celebrity Endorsement

  Four out of five doctors recommend Pumpidox for most heart conditions.

  Argument from authority is the quoting of an alleged expert on a certain topic. As a logical fallacy, arguments from authority rely solely on the mention of the word "expert," and give no clear facts from the expert. Companies often hire celebrities to appear in commercials for their products in the hope that audiences will respond to the likability of the famous person, even if that person has no real expert knowledge about the product.

- ### The Bandwagon Effect

  Choose America's favorite toothpaste!

  The term "jumping on the bandwagon" means doing or thinking something because everyone else is doing it or thinking it. This type of reasoning provides no evidence to support a decision or viewpoint.

- ### Card Stacking

  Senator Porter voted against childcare laws and recycling programs. It's time for new leadership!

  Card stacking involves piling on evidence that supports one side of an argument while ignoring or suppressing valid evidence supporting the other side. Saying that a politician voted against positive-sounding programs does not mean that he or she didn't have good reason to, or that the opposition has a better record.

Ethical Reasoning and Propaganda

Propaganda

Propaganda is the process of persuading by deliberately misleading or confusing an audience. Through the use of combinations of logical fallacies, propaganda can appeal to ethics or values, authority, or emotion, but they do so in a way that is unsupported or inappropriate.

Political propaganda

A vote for Marmelard is a vote for the enemy!

America: You're with us or against us!

Advertising

Be the best parent you can be: Serve your kids Super Goody cereal.

The most successful people shop at Blorland's Department Store.

Ethical Reasoning

Reasoning that persuades by helping its intended audience make informed decisions is called **ethical reasoning.** As a writer or speaker, you have the responsibility to use ethical reasoning and avoid propaganda. This means that you must gather complete information about a topic, check your facts for accuracy, and make sure that your reasoning includes no errors in logic or false conclusions. You should address opposing evidence with clear and accurate argumentation. Using ethical reasoning in your persuasive writing or speeches will strengthen your positions as your audience sees that you have logically addressed all sides of an idea.

Identifying Unethical Persuasive Techniques

The following essay contains several examples of faulty reasoning. Read through the entire text once, then go back and look for logical fallacies, invalid arguments, and manipulative appeals. For each example you find, make an entry in a chart like the one shown. Then write a paragraph evaluating the essay's argument.

Passage	Type(s) of Appeals	Why Invalid
"Principal Spaly"	Appeal to logic	Card stacking

Don't Take Away Our Freedom

The school board recently announced plans to remove all vending machines from our schools' cafeterias. They say that candy, snacks, and cola are bad for students. But is starvation good for students? Is taking away freedom to choose good for students?

Every expert on nutrition agrees that it is not healthy for kids to go for hours between meals without some sort of snack in between to tide them over. If the school board has its way, students will be passing out at their desks from hunger and dehydration. Principal Spaly claims that students are more likely to pass out from a "sugar crash." This is the same Principal Spaly who recently showed what he thought of students when he denied sophomores the right to park at the high school.

We are taught in these very schools that America is a land of democracy, freedom, and liberty. It is clear that the school board has forgotten this. Any student who loves his or her school will write to the school board and let them know how we feel.

Glossary/Glosario

This glossary lists the vocabulary words found in the selections in this book. The definition given is for the word as it is used in the selection; you may wish to consult a dictionary for other meanings of these words. The key below is a guide to the pronunciation symbols used in each entry.

	Pronunciation Key				
a	**a**t	ō	h**o**pe	ng	si**ng**
ā	**a**pe	ô	f**o**rk, **a**ll	th	**th**in
ä	f**a**ther	oo	w**oo**d, p**u**t	th	**th**is
e	**e**nd	ōō	f**oo**l	zh	trea**s**ure
ē	m**e**	oi	**oi**l	ə	**a**go, tak**e**n, pen**ci**l,
i	**i**t	ou	**ou**t		lem**o**n, cir**cu**s
ī	**i**ce	u	**u**p	´	primary stress
o	h**o**t	ū	**u**se	´	secondary stress

English

A

abate (ə bāt´) *v.* to lessen or reduce in force or intensity; **p. 474**

abhor (ab hôr´) *v.* to detest; **p. 494**

abstinence (ab´ stə nəns) *n.* the act of doing without food, drink, or other pleasures; **p. 937**

accomplice (ə kom´ plice) *n.* a participant in a crime or wrongdoing; **p. 824**

acquittal (ə kwit´ əl) *n.* setting free from a criminal charge by verdict, sentence, or other legal process; **p. 336**

acrid (ak´ rid) *adj.* strong, bitter, and often unpleasant in smell or taste; **p. 81**

affront (ə frunt´) *n.* a deliberate insult; **p. 61**

aggravate (ag´ rə vāt´) *v.* to make something worse; **p. 122**

anguish (ang´ gwish) *n.* severe physical or mental pain; suffering; **p. 902**

Español

A

abate/amainar *v.* bajar o disminuir; **p. 474**

abhor/aborrecer *v.* detestar; **p. 494**

abstinence/abstinencia *s.* vivir sin comida, bebida u otros placeres; **p. 937**

accomplice/cómplice *s.* participante en un delito o crimen; **p. 824**

acquittal/absolución *s.* liberación de una acusación criminal mediante veredicto, sentencia u otro proceso legal; **p. 336**

acrid/acre: *adj.* sabor o olor fuerte, amargo y a menudo desagradable; **p. 81**

affront/afrenta *s.* insulto hecho a propósito; **p. 61**

aggravate/agravar *v.* empeorar o hacer peor; **p. 122**

anguish/angustia *s.* fuerte dolor físico o mental; sufrimiento; **p. 902**

animosity (an´ ə mos´ i tē) *n.* ill will or resentment; **p. 135**

anticipate (an tis´ ə pāt´) *v.* expect; consider in advance; **p. 734**

antidote (an´ ti dōt´) *n.* something that relieves, prevents, or counteracts; **p. 462**

appease (ə pēz´) *v.* to make peace with concessions; to satisfy insistent demands; **p. 193**

arable (ar´ ə bəl) *adj.* fit for growing crops; **p. 984**

arid (ar´ id) *adj.* excessively dry; **p. 608**

artifice (är´ tə fis) *n.* ingenious deception; **p. 1166**

assailant (ə sā´ lənt) *n.* attacker; **p. 54**

assertion (ɔ sur´ shən) *n.* a forceful or confident statement of fact or belief; **p. 514**

assertive (ə sur´ tiv) *adj.* bold; forceful in a confident way; **p. 127**

assiduously (ə sij´ wəs lē) *adv.* attentively or busily; **p. 758**

asunder (ə sun´ dər) *adv.* into parts; into different pieces; **p. 873**

attainment (ə tān´ mənt) *n.* accomplishment; **p. 597**

austere (ôs tēr´) *adj.* stern or cold in appearance or manner; **p. 1192**

austerity (ôs ter´ ə lē) *n.* a morally strict act; **p. 566**

avail (ə vāl´) *n.* use or advantage; **p. 86**

avarice (av´ ər is) *n.* greed; **p. 569**

B

banal (bə nal´) *adj.* lacking originality, freshness, or novelty; **p. 1193**

banish (ban´ ish) *v.* to drive away or remove by authority; **p. 721**

banquet (bang´ kwit) *n.* an elaborate, ceremonial meal; **p. 19**

barbaric (bär bar´ ik) *adj.* crude; wild in taste, style, or manner; **p. 222**

bedlam (bed´ ləm) *n.* a state of uproar or confusion; **p. 128**

animosity/animosidad *s.* mala voluntad o resentimiento; **p. 135**

anticipate/anticipar *v.* esperar o consider con antelación; **p. 734**

antidote/antídoto *s.* algo que alivia, impide o contrarresta; **p. 462**

appease/apaciguar *v.* hacer paz con concesiones; satisfacer exigencias; **p. 193**

arable/arable *adj.* capaz de ser cultivado; **p. 984**

arid/árido *adj.* excesivamente seco; **p. 608**

artifice/artificio *s.* decepción ingeniosa; **p. 1166**

assailant/agresor *n.* atacante **p. 54**

assertion/afirmación *s.* declaración de hecho o creencia con firmeza o confianza; **p. 514**

assertive/autoritario *adj.* audaz; fuerte pero con confianza; **p. 127**

assiduously/diligentemente *adv.* atenta o aplicadamente; **p. 758**

asunder/partido *adv.* dividido violentamente por la mitad o en dos; **p. 873**

attainment/consecución *s.* logro; **p. 597**

austere/austero *adj.* severo o frío en apariencia o forma; **p. 1192**

austerity/austeridad *s.* un acto moralmente restringido; **p. 566**

avail/provecho *s.* uso o ventaja; **p. 87**

avarice/avaricia *s.* codicia; **p. 569**

B

banal/banal *adj.* carente de originalidad, frescura o novedad; **p. 1193**

banish/desterrar *v.* hacer exiliar o salir por autoridad; **p. 721**

banquet/banquete *s.* comida ceremonial elaborada; **p. 19**

barbaric/bárbaro *adj.* rudimentario; salvaje en sabor, estilo o forma; **p. 222**

bedlam/manicomio *s.* un estado de confusión o ánimo; locura; **p. 128**

beneficent (bə nef′ ə sənt) *adj.* doing or producing good; **p. 1235**

bereft (bi reft′) *adj.* deprived or robbed; **p. 213**

C

candor (kan′ dər) *n.* honesty or frankness; openness; **p. 963**

censure (sen′ shər) *v.* to find fault with and criticize; **p. 338**

chaste (chāst) *adj.* innocent; pure; **p. 929**

chastise (chas tīz′) *v.* to punish, reprimand, or discipline severely; **p. 721**

chide (chīd) *v.* to scold; **p. 494**

clandestine (klan des′ tin) *adj.* kept secret for an illicit reason; **p. 534**

clemency (klem′ ən sē) *n.* mercy; leniency, especially toward an enemy; **p. 966**

coax (kōks) *v.* to persuade by means of gentle urging or flattery; **p. 112**

coercion (kō ur′ shən) *n.* force; repression; **p. 1140**

coincide (kō′ in sīd′) *v.* to occupy the same place in space or time; **p. 151**

collide (kə līd′) *v.* to run into accidentally; to come together with direct impact; **p. 1226**

commandeer (kom′ ən dēr′) *v.* to take arbitrary or forceful possession of; **p. 198**

commence (kə mens′) *v.* to begin; **p. 1171**

commiserate (kə miz′ ə rāt′) *v.* sympathize with; pity; **p. 329**

compassion (kəm pash′ ən) *n.* sympathetic awareness of another's distress; **p. 522**

compulsory (kəm pul′ sər ē) *adj.* mandatory; enforced; **p. 1004**

conception (kən sep′ shən) *n.* thought; idea; design; plan; **p. 1123**

condescending (kon′ di sen′ ding) *adj.* characterized by an air of superiority or smugness; **p. 1205**

beneficent/beneficioso *adj.* hacer o producir bien; **p. 1235**

bereft/desprovisto *adj.* deprivado o robado de algo; **p. 213**

C

candor/franqueza *s.* honestidad o transpariencia; **p. 963**

censure/censurar *v.* criticar y reprobar; **p. 338**

chaste/casto *adj.* inocente; puro; **p. 929**

chastise/reprender *v.* castigar o disciplinar; **p. 721**

chide/reprobar *v.* reprender o castigar; **p. 494**

clandestine/clandestino *adj.* mantener en secreto por razones ilícitas; **p. 534**

clemency/clemencia *s.* merced; indulgencia, especialmente hacia un enemigo; **p. 966**

coax/engatusar *v.* persuadir con halagos o exhortación suave; **p. 112**

coercion/coacción *s.* fuerza, represión; **p. 1140**

coincide/coincidir *v.* ocupar el mismo lugar en espacio o tiempo; **p. 151**

collide/colisionar *v.* chocar con por accidente o con impacto directo; **p. 1226**

commandeer/requisar *v.* apropriarse con fuerza o de modo arbitrario; **p. 198**

commence/comenzar *v.* empezar; **p. 1171**

commiserate/compadecer *v.* simpatizar con; sentir lástima; **p. 329**

compassion/compasión *s.* conciencia simpática del dolor de otro; **p. 522**

compulsory/obligatorio *adj.* mandatorio, forzoso; **p. 1004**

conception/concepción *s.* pensamiento, idea; diseño, plan; **p. 1123**

condescending/condescendiente *adj.* caracterizado por un aire de superioridad o arrogancia; **p. 1205**

confound (kən found´) v. to confuse or bewilder; **p. 499**

congealed (kən jēld´) adj. thickened; changed from a liquid to a solid state; **p. 793**

consecrate (kon´ sə krāt´) v. to elevate into a sacred position through a religious rite; **p. 110**

considerably (kən sid´ ər ə blē) adv. greatly; by a large amount; **p. 526**

console (kən sōl´) v. to alleviate a person's grief, sense of loss, or trouble; to comfort; **p. 1028**

conspire (kən spīr´) v. to join in agreement; to plot; **p. 508**

consternation (kon´ stər nā´ shən) n. great fear or shock; upset; **p. 964**

constituency (kən stich´ ōō ən se) n. voters in a district; a group of supporters; **p. 95**

consummation (kon´ sə mā´ shən) n. end; completion; **p. 327**

contrary (kon´ trer ē) adj. unfavorable; **p. 931**

corrupt (kə rupt´) adj. morally unsound; evil; **p. 472**

covenant (kuv´ ə nənt) n. an agreement; a pact **p. 473**

crucial (krōō´ shəl) adj. essential; decisive; **p. 287**

cryptically (krip´ tik lē) adv. secretly or mysteriously; **p. 1267**

cunningly (kun´ ing lē) adv. cleverly; sneakily; **p. 130**

cursory (kur´ sə rē) adj. hasty and not thorough; superficial; **p. 1196**

D

decay (di kā´) v. to rot or decompose; **p. 31**

decipher (di sī´ fər) v. to translate; figure out; **p. 938**

deem (dēm) v. to regard in a certain way; **p. 514**

defiance (di fī´ əns) n. a refusal to recognize or obey someone or something; **p. 97**

confound/confundir v. desconcertar o frustrar; **p. 499**

congealed/cuajado adj. espesado, cambiado de un estado líquido a sólido; **p. 793**

consecrate/consecrar v. elevar a una posición sagrada mediante un rito religioso; **p. 110**

considerably/considerablemente adv. bastante; por una cantidad enorme; **p. 526**

console/consolar v. aliviar el dolor, sentido de pérdida o problema de una persona; confortar; **p. 1028**

conspire/conspirar v. tramar; acordarse; **p. 508**

consternation/consternación s. gran miedo o choque; upset; **p. 964**

constituency/electores s. votantes potenciales en un distrito electoral; grupo de partidarios; **p. 95**

consummation/consumación s. finalización, terminación; **p. 327**

contrary/contrario adj. desfavorable; **p. 931**

corrupt/corrupto adj. malo; moralmente impuro; **p. 472**

covenant/alianza s. cláusula, pacto o promesa; **p. 473**

crucial/crucial adj. esencial; decisivo; **p. 287**

cryptically/ocultamente adv. enigmática o misteriosamente; secretamente; **p. 1267**

cunningly/astutamente adv. ingeniosamente; disimuladamente; **p. 130**

cursory/somero adj. rápido y superficial, **p. 1196**

D

decay/decaer v. pudrirse o descomponer; **p. 31**

decipher/descifrar v. traducir; deducir; **p. 938**

deem/estimar v. creer or percibir de cierta manera; **p. 514**

defiance/desafío s. cuando se niega a reconocer o obeír a alguien o algo; **p. 97**

defile (di fīl´) v. to make unclean; **p. 386**

demolition (dem´ ə lish´ ən) n. an act of tearing down or breaking to pieces; destruction; **p. 405**

demonstrate (dem´ ən strāt´) v. to participate in a public display of group opinion; to rally or march; **p. 539**

demur (di mur´) n. a hesitation or an objection; **p. 611**

denizen (den´ ə zən) n. an inhabitant; **p. 114**

denounce (di nouns´) v. to inform against; accuse publicly; **p. 262**

depraved (di prāvd´) adj. marked by evil; **p. 406**

derisively (di rī´ siv lē) adv. using ridicule or scorn to show contempt; **p. 61**

desist (di zist´) v. to cease; to stop; **p. 136**

detect (di tekt´) v. discover or determine something; **p. 370**

detest (di test´) v. dislike intensely; hate; **p. 691**

detractor (di trak´ tər) n. one who speaks ill of someone or something; **p. 336**

devoted (di vō´ tid) adj. dedicated; feeling strong attachment; **p. 536**

dictates (dik´ tāts) n. principles that must be followed; **p. 687**

dignity (dig´ nə tē) n. worthiness; the quality of being worthy of honor; **p. 254**

diligence (dil´ ə jəns) n. persistent hard work; alertness; **p. 1206**

dimension (di men´ shən) n. a measure of physical form or proportion; **p. 1051**

dire (dīr) adj. terrible; bad enough to arouse dread; **p. 265**

discord (dis´ kôrd) n. angry or quarrelsome disagreement; lack of harmony; **p. 986**

discourteous (dis kur´ tē əs) adj. impolite; **p. 942**

discreetly (dis krēt´ lē) adv. unnoticeably; **p. 61**

disdain (dis dān´) n. an attitude of scorn or contempt for those considered inferior; **p. 1205**

defile/defilar v. ensuciar; **p. 386**

demolition/demolición s. acto de derrumbar o romper en trozos; destrucción; **p. 405**

demonstrate/manifestarse v. participar en una exhibición pública de opinión colectiva; reunirse y andar; **p. 539**

demur/reparo s. vacilación u obyección; **p. 611**

denizen/morador s. habitante; **p. 114**

denounce/denunciar v. acusar públicamente; informar en contra; **p. 262**

depraved/depravado adj. marcado por el malo; **p. 406**

derisively/de burla adv. usando ridículo o desdén para mostrar menosprecio; **p. 61**

desist/desistir v. cesar, abstenerse, parar; **p. 136**

detect/detectar v. descubrir o notar algo; **p. 370**

detest/detestar v. caerle intensamente mal; odiar; **p. 691**

detractor/detractor s. uno que habla mal de algo o de alguien; **p. 336**

devoted/devoto adj. dedicado, unido, vinculado fuertemente; **p. 536**

dictates/dictámenes s. principios que deben ser seguidos; **p. 687**

dignity/dignidad s. valor; la qualidad de ser digno de honor; **p. 254**

diligence/diligencia s. trabajo persistente; estado de alerta; **p. 1206**

dimension/dimensión s. medida de forma física o proporción; **p. 1051**

dire/funesto adj. terrible; nefasto; suficientement malo para incitar miedo; **p. 265**

discord/discordia s. falta de armonía; desacuerdo antipático o peleador; **p. 986**

discourteous/descortés adj. falta de cortesía, maleducado; **p. 942**

discreetly/discretamente adv. sin percibir; **p. 61**

disdain/desdén s. una actitud de menosprecio para los que se consideran inferiores; **p. 1205**

disgruntled (dis grən′ təld) *adj.* unhappy; grumpy; **p. 1213**

disillusion (dis′ i lōō′ zhən) *n.* the state of being freed from misleading images or naïve trust; **p. 1029**

disparage (dis par′ ij) *v.* speak badly of; **p. 985**

dispel (dis pel′) *v.* to drive off; **p. 27**

disperse (dis purs′) *v.* scatter or spread in many directions; **p. 993**

dissension (di sen′ shən) *n.* disagreement; discord; **p. 54**

distinguishing (dis ting′ gwish ing) *adj.* marking as different; characterizing; **p. 560**

distorted (dis tôr′ tid) *adj.* twisted out of normal or original shape or condition; **p. 1029**

distressed (dis tres′ d) *adj.* anxious; anguished; upset; **p. 1018**

diversified (di vur′ sə fīd) *adj.* varied; **p. 19**

docile (dos′ əl) *adj.* easily taught; obedient; **p. 687**

dolorous (dō′ lər əs) *adj.* expressing sadness or causing pain; **p. 808**

dreary (drēr′ ē) *adj.* dull or sorrowful; **p. 921**

droves (drōvz) *n.* large numbers of animals or people, moving along together; crowds; **p. 195**

dubious (dōō′ bē əs) *adj.* of a questionable nature; **p. 122**

dupe (dōōp) *v.* to deceive or delude; **p. 381**

E

edible (ed′ ə bəl) *adj.* fit to eat; **p. 1126**

elasticity (i las′ tis′ ə tē) *n.* the quality of being easily adaptable or adjustable, so as to fit changes or new circumstances; **p. 1035**

elude (ē lōō′d) *v.* to avoid or escape; **p. 1067**

emaciated (i mā′ shē āt id) *adj.* thin and feeble; **p. 1006**

disgruntled/contrariado *adj.* infeliz, descontento; **p. 1231**

disillusion/desilusión *s.* estado de liberación de imágenes engañosas o confianza ingénua; **p. 1029**

disparage/menospreciar *v.* hablar mal de; **p. 985**

dispel/disipar *v.* hacer desparecer o desvanecer; **p. 27**

disperse/dispersar *v.* esparcir o tirar en muchas direcciones; **p. 993**

dissension/disensión *s.* desacuerdo; discordia; **p. 54**

distinguishing/distintivo *adj.* característico, marcando una diferencia; **p. 560**

distorted/distorsionado *adj.* retorcido en contraste con su forma o condición natural o normal; **p. 1029**

distressed/afligido *adj.* ansioso; angustiado; descontento; **p. 1018**

diversified/diversificado *adj.* variado; **p. 19**

docile/dócil *adj.* fácilmente instruido; obediente; **p. 687**

dolorous/doloroso *adj.* expresando tristeza o causando dolor; **p. 808**

dreary/lóbrego *adj.* deprimente o sombrío; **p. 921**

droves/hordas *s.* un número grande de animales o personas, moviendo en grupo; muchedumbre o manada; **p. 195**

dubious/dudoso *adj.* de una naturaleza discutible o sospechosa; **p. 122**

dupe/embaucar *v.* engañar o deludir; **p. 381**

E

edible/comestible *adj.* apto para ser comido; **p. 1126**

elasticity/elasticidad *s.* la qualidad de ser flexible y adaptarse a cambios o nuevas circunstancias; **p. 1035**

elude/eludir *v.* evitar o escapar; **p. 1067**

emaciated/emaciado *adj.* delgado y débil; **p. 1006**

endorse (en dôrs′) *v.* to inscribe with one's signature to show legal or official approval; **p. 145**

endure (en door′) *v.* continue to exist; last; **p. 692**

enlist (en list′) *v.* to join or give help; convince (someone) to join or to give help; **p. 203**

enmity (en′ mə tē) *n.* hatred or ill will; **p. 944**

epidemic (ep′ ə dem′ ik) *n.* rapid spread of disease affecting many people; **p. 1157**

ethereal (i thēr′ ē əl) *adj.* otherworldly; **p. 1007**

extent (iks tent′) *n.* amount or distance; **p. 687**

exult (ig zult′) *v.* to rejoice greatly; **p. 881**

F

fallacious (fə lā′ shəs) *adj.* erroneous; **p. 1166**

fasten (fas′ ən) *v.* to attach firmly; **p. 245**

fatuous (fach′ o͞o əs) *adj.* silly; foolish; **p. 569**

feign (fān) *v.* to make a false show of; pretend; **p. 882**

fettered (fe′ tərd) *adj.* chained; tied up; **p. 613**

fidelity (fi del′ ə tē) *n.* faithfulness; **p. 1060**

flag (flag) *v.* to decline in interest or attraction; **p. 796**

flout (flout) *v.* to treat with disdain or contempt; scoff at; **p. 137**

flutter (flut′ ər) *v.* move with uneven or trembling motion; **p. 1171**

forage (fôr′ ij) *v.* to hunt or search for food; **p. 804**

foreboding (fôr bō′ ding) *n.* a feeling that something bad or harmful will happen; **p. 285**

formidable (fôr′ mi də bəl) *adj.* tending to inspire awe, wonder, or alarm; **p. 612**

frail (frāl) *adj.* easily broken or damaged; fragile; **p. 832**

frantically (fran′ tik lē) *adv.* in a manner marked by fast and nervous activity; **p. 823**

frivolity (fri vol′ ə tē) *n.* silliness; **p. 1247**

endorse/endosar *v.* firmar para aprobar legal o oficialmente; **p. 145**

endure/perdurar *v.* continuar existiendo; durar; **p. 692**

enlist/alistar *v.* unirse para ayudar; reclutar; convencerle a alguien a aliarse; **p. 203**

enmity/enemistad *s.* odio o mala voluntad; **p. 944**

epidemic/epidemia *s.* diseminación rápida de enfermedad que afecta a mucha gente; **p. 1157**

ethereal/etéreo *adj.* de otro mundo; **p. 1007**

extent/extensión *s.* amplitud; alcance; distancia; **p. 687**

exult/exultarse *v.* regocijarse enormemente; **p. 881**

F

fallacious/falaz *adj.* erróneo; **p. 1166**

fasten/sujetar *v.* atar o abrochar firmemente; **p. 245**

fatuous/fátuo *adj.* tonto; ridículo; **p. 569**

feign/fingir *v.* hacer una impresión falsa; disimular; **p. 882**

fettered/encadenado *adj.* atado, puesto en grillos; **p. 613**

fidelity/fidelidad *s.* sentido de fe; lealtad; **p. 1060**

flag/decaer *v.* perder o disminuir en interés o atracción; **p. 796**

flout/desacatar *v.* desobedecer; tratar con desdén y menosprecio; **p. 137**

flutter/revolotear *v.* mover tremblando o con gestos irregulares o discontinuos; **p. 1171**

forage/forrajear *v.* buscar comida; **p. 804**

foreboding/aprensión *s.* sentimiento o premonición que algo malo o dañoso occurirá; **p. 285**

formidable/formidable *adj.* lo que inspira asombro, preocupación o maravilla.; **p. 612**

frail/endeble *adj.* fácilmente roto o dañido; frágil; **p. 832**

frantically/fránticamente *adv.* marcado por actividad rápida y nerviosa; **p. 823**

frivolity/frivolidad *s.* tontería; **p. 1247**

fruitless (frōōt′ lis) *adj.* unproductive; useless; sure to end in failure; **p. 499**

fumble (fum′ bəl) *v.* to grope or handle clumsily; **p. 147**

furrows (fur′ ōs) *n.* grooves or tracks cut in the earth by a plow; wrinkles; **p. 1018**

furtively (fər′ tiv lē) *adv.* in a secret manner; **p. 755**

futile (fū′ til) *adj.* useless; worthless; ineffectual; **p. 371**

G

gauge (gāj) *v.* to estimate; judge; **p. 286**

gesticulate (jes tik′ yə lāt′) *v.* to make gestures, especially when speaking; **p. 719**

glean (glēn) *v.* gather after reapers; gather slowly, bit by bit; discover or find out slowly; **p. 479**

glistening (glis′ən′ ing) *adj.* glittering; twinkling; **p. 216**

glittering (glit′ ər ing) *adj.* marked by a sparkling quality or brilliance; **p. 751**

gloat (glōt) *v.* to regard with malignant satisfaction; **p. 224**

graceful (grās′ fəl) *adj.* showing effortless beauty or movement; **p. 831**

gratitude (grat′ ə tōōd′) *n.* thankfulness; **p. 95**

gravely (grāv′ lē) *adv.* in a serious or dignified manner; **p. 1252**

grudge (gruj) *n.* a feeling of hatred or resentment; **p. 894**

guffaw (gu fô′) *n.* loud or boisterous burst of laughter; **p. 1283**

H

haggard (hag′ ərd) *adj.* worn or wasted, as from hunger; **p. 1246**

haste (hāst) *n.* quickness of action or movement; hurry; **p. 1151**

fruitless/infructuoso *adj.* inútil; no productivo; lo que acabará en fracaso; **p. 499**

fumble/buscar a tientas *v.* hurgar o revolver torpemente; **p. 147**

furrows/surcos *s.* vías o ranuras abiertas en la tierra por un arado; arrugas; **p. 1018**

furtively/furtivamente *adv.* de manera secreta; **p. 755**

futile/inútil *adj.* sin valor, incapaz; **p. 371**

G

gauge/calcular *v.* evaluar, medir; **p. 286**

gesticulate/gesticular *v.* hacer gestos, especialmente mientras habla; **p. 719**

glean/cosechar *v.* recoger después de la cosecha; recoger lentamente, poco a poco, o descubrir lentamente; **p. 479**

glistening/centelleante *adj.* brillante, relumbrante; **p. 216**

glittering/resplandesciente *adj.* marcado por una qualidad de luz o brillo; **p. 751**

gloat/regodearse *v.* ver con satisfacción maligna; **p. 224**

graceful/grácil *adj.* mostrando belleza o movimiento sin esfuerzo; **p. 831**

gratitude/gratitud *s.* sentido de agradecimiento; **p. 95**

gravely/gravemente *adv.* de manera seria o digna; **p. 1252**

grudge/rencilla *s.* un sentido de odio o resentimiento; **p. 894**

guffaw/carcajada *s.* una risa alta y ruidosa; **p. 1283**

H

haggard/demacrado *adj.* cansado o emaciado, como de hambre; **p. 1246**

haste/apuro *s.* prisa; rapidez de acción o movimiento; **p. 1151**

heedless (hēd′ lis) *adj.* inconsiderate; thoughtless; **p. 62**

hindrance (hin′ drəns) *n.* a thing that presents a challenge, struggle, or delay to someone or something; obstacle; **p. 1171**

homage (hom′ ij) *n.* the honor or respect that is shown to another person; **p. 687**

horde (hôrd) *n.* a teeming crowd or throng; **p. 87**

horrendous (hô ren′dəs) *adj.* horrible; frightful; **p. 310**

hover (huv′ ər) *v.* to hang in the air; **p. 26**

humane (hū mān′) *adj.* marked by compassion, sympathy, or consideration for humans or animals; **p. 1003**

humility (hū mil′ ə tē) *n.* modesty; meekness; **p. 1152**

I

ignominious (ig′ nə min′ ē əs) *adj.* marked or characterized by disgrace or shame; **p. 205**

impartial (im pär′ shəl) *adj.* treating everyone or everything in an equal way; **p. 122**

impel (im pel′) *v.* to urge forward as if through moral pressure; **p. 384**

impervious (im pur′ vē əs) *adj.* not easily affected or disturbed; **p. 639**

imploring (im plôr′ ing) *adj.* begging or beseeching; **p. 798**

improvise (im′ prə vīz′) *v.* to create to meet an unexpected need; **p. 1247**

impulse (im′ puls) *n.* a sudden desire or feeling that makes one want to act; **p. 560**

incessant (in ses′ ənt) *adj.* continuing without interruption; **p. 139**

incomprehensible (in′ kom pri hen′ sə bəl) *adj.* unintelligible; indiscernible; not understood; **p. 629**

incredulous (in krej′ ə ləs) *adj.* doubting; skeptical; **p. 323**

heedless/hecho caso omiso *adj.* sin prestar atención o pensar; **p. 62**

hindrance/estorbo *s.* obstáculo; algo que presenta un desafío, pelea o demora; **p. 1171**

homage/homenaje *s.* el honor o respeto dado a otro; **p. 687**

horde/horda *s.* una multitud animada o muchedumbre; **p. 87**

horrendous/horrendo *adj.* horrible, miedoso; **p. 310**

hover/cernerse *v.* sostenerse en el aire; **p. 26**

humane/humanitario *adj.* marcado por compasión, simpatía o consideración para humanos o animales; **p. 1003**

humility/humildad *s.* modestia; docilidad; **p. 1152**

I

ignominious/ignominioso *adj.* marcado o caracterizado por desgracia o vergüenza; **p. 205**

impartial/imparcial *adj.* tratar a todo y a todo el mundo de manera igual; **p. 122**

impel/impeler *v.* pedirle a alguien con insistencia y con presión moral; **p. 384**

impervious/impermeable *adj.* no influido o perturbado fácilmente; **p. 639**

imploring/implorante *adj.* rogante o suplicante; **p. 798**

improvise/improvisar *v.* crear para responder a una necesidad no anticipada; **p. 1247**

impulse/impulso *s.* un deseo o sentimiento repentino que inspira a uno a actuar; **p. 560**

incessant/incesante *adj.* continuar sin cesar o interrumpir; **p. 139**

incomprehensible/incomprensible *adj.* no comprendido; imperceptible; ininteligible; **p. 629**

incredulous/incrédulo *adj.* dudoso; escéptico; **p. 323**

increment (ing´ krə mənt) *n.* something gained or added in a series, usually at regular intervals; **p. 623**

incur (in kur´) *v.* to bring upon oneself; **p. 494**

indiscriminately (in´ dis krim´ ə nit lē) *adv.* randomly; haphazardly; **p. 1006**

inexorable (i nek´ sər ə bəl) *adj.* relentless; unyielding; **p. 639**

inflict (in flikt´) *v.* to give or cause; **p. 305**

inhabit (in hab´ it) *adj.* to reside or live in; **p. 1133**

inordinate (in ôr´ də nit) *adj.* excessive; **p. 568**

inquisitive (in kwiz´ ə tiv) *adj.* curious about the world or the affairs of others; **p. 720**

insular (in´ sə lər) *adj.* isolated; narrow-minded; **p. 628**

intermittently (in´ tər mit´ ənt lē) *adv.* on and off again; coming at intervals; **p. 588**

intersection (in´ tər sek´ shən) *n.* a place where roads cross one another; **p. 731**

intimation (in tə mā´ shən) *n.* an indirect suggestion; **p. 338**

intransigence (in tran´ sə jənts) *n.* the state of being uncompromising; **p. 757**

irrevocable (i rev´ ə kə bəl) *adj.* incapable of being brought back, undone, or changed; **p. 1203**

J

jubilant (jōō´ bə lənt) *adj.* joyful, rejoicing; **p. 817**

L

lament (lə ment´) *v.* to mourn or express grief for; **p. 19**

listless (list´ lis) *adj.* showing disinterest; spiritless; **p. 808**

loom (lōōm) *v.* to come into sight in enlarged or distorted form; **p. 1279**

lucid (lōō´ sid) *adj.* having full use of one's faculties; clear-headed; **p. 1233**

increment/incremento *s.* algo ganado o añadido en una serie, generalmente por entregas; **p. 623**

incur/incurrir en *v.* provocar o buscarse algo; **p. 494**

indiscriminately/indiscriminadamente *adv.* hecho caprichosamente o al azar; **p. 1006**

inexorable/inexorable *adj.* sin rendir; **p. 639**

inflict/afligir *v.* dar o causar; **p. 305**

inhabit/habitar *adj.* vivir o residir en; **p. 1133**

inordinate/exorbitante *adj.* excesivo; **p. 568**

inquisitive/inquisitivo *adj.* curioso sobre el mundo o los asuntos de otros; **p. 720**

insular/insular *adj.* aislado; cerrado mentalmente; **p. 628**

intermittently/intermitente *adv.* llegando por intérvalos irregulares; **p. 588**

intersection/intersección *s.* un lugar donde los caminos se entrecruzan; **p. 731**

intimation/indicio *s.* una sugestión indirecta; **p. 338**

intransigence/intransigencia *s.* estado de no comprometerse; **p. 757**

irrevocable/irrevocable *adj.* incapaz de ser recuperado, cambiado o deshecho; **p. 1203**

J

jubilant/de júbilo *adj.* exultante, feliz; **p. 817**

L

lament/lamentar *v.* expresar pena por o llorar la pérdida de alguien; **p. 19**

listless/apático *adj.* mostrando desinterés; lánguido; **p. 808**

loom/avecinarse *v.* acercarse o aparecer en forma distorsionada o ampliada; **p. 1279**

lucid/lúcido *adj.* estado de tener uso completo de las facultades; mentalidad clara; **p. 1233**

lush (lush) *adj.* luxuriant; thick with vegetation; **p. 816**

M

magnitude (mag′ nə tōōd′) *n.* great size or importance; **p. 585**

majesty (maj′ is tē) *n.* greatness or magnificence of quality or nature; splendor; **p. 1171**

malicious (mə lish′ əs) *adj.* marked by a desire to cause pain, injury, or distress to another; **p. 522**

marvelous (marv′ ə ləs) *adj.* extraordinary; causing wonder; **p. 793**

mediocre (mē′ dē ō′ kər) *adj.* of moderate or low quality; undistinguished; **p. 1251**

menace (men′ is) *n.* a person or thing that is a threat or danger; **p. 1228**

mere (mēr) *adj.* being nothing more or less than; **p. 1052**

mesmerize (mez′ mə rīz′) *v.* to hypnotize; spellbind; **p. 97**

misery (miz′ ər ē) *n.* unhappy state of mind; great distress; wretchedness; **p. 873**

mitigate (mi′ tə gāt′) *v.* to lessen; **p. 1166**

moderation (mod′ ə rā′ shən) *n.* avoiding or limiting excesses or extremes; self-control; **p. 365**

modest (mod′ ist) *adj.* unassuming; plain; simple; **p. 1017**

monotony (mə not′ ən ē) *n.* tiresome sameness; **p. 768**

munificence (mū nif′ ə səns) *v.* great generosity; **p. 406**

murmur (mər′ mər) *v.* to say something in an indistinct voice; to say something quietly and cautiously; **p. 518**

muster (mus′ tər) *v.* to cause to gather; **p. 1290**

mutter (mut′ ər) *v.* to speak in a low voice or indistinctly with lips partially closed; **p. 804**

myriad (mir′ ē əd) *adj.* countless; of a very great number of persons or things; **p. 1060**

lush/exuberante *adj.* lleno de vegetación; abundante; **p. 816**

M

magnitude/magnitud *s.* gran tamaño o importancia; **p. 585**

majesty/majestad *s.* esplendor; magnificencia de calidad o naturaleza; **p. 1171**

malicious/malicioso *adj.* marcado por el deseo de causar dolor o herir a otro; **p. 522**

marvelous/maravilloso *adj.* extraordinario; causando asombro; **p. 793**

mediocre/mediocre *adj.* de calidad moderada o baja; sin distinguir; **p. 1251**

menace/amenaza *s.* una persona o cosa que es un peligro; **p. 1228**

mere/mero *adj.* ser nada más o menos que; **p. 1052**

mesmerize/cautivar *v.* hipnotizar; fascinar; **p. 97**

misery/miseria *s.* un estado mental infeliz; gran angustia; desgracia; **p. 873**

mitigate/mitigar *v.* disminuir; **p. 1166**

moderation/moderación *s.* evitar o limitar lo excesivo o lo extremo; control sobre sí mismo; **p. 365**

modest/modesto *adj.* sin pretensión; simple; sencillo; **p. 1017**

monotony/monotonía *s.* repetición tediosa; **p. 768**

munificence/munificencia *v.* gran generosidad; **p. 406**

murmur/murmurar *v.* decir algo en una voz suave; decir algo calladamente con prudencia; **p. 518**

muster/llamar a asambea *v.* reunir; lograr a formar; **p. 1290**

mutter/refunfuñar *v.* hablar en una voz baja o indistinta o hablar entre dientes; **p. 804**

myriad/millar de *adj.* de un gran número de personas o cosas; **p. 1060**

N

nautical (nô′ ti kəl) *adj.* of or relating to sailors or ships; **p. 1052**

negate (ni gāt′) *v.* to make ineffectual or powerless; **p. 1060**

nimble (nim′ bəl) *adj.* sure-footed; light and quick; **p. 909**

nonentity (non en′ tə tē) *n.* a person or a thing of little or no importance; **p. 95**

nullity (nul′ ə tē) *n.* a mere nothing; something insignificant; **p. 598**

O

obliterate (ə blit′ e rāt′) *v.* to erase from memory; to destroy all traces of; **p. 1213**

oblivion (ə bliv′ ē ən) *n.* state of having been forgotten; **p. 304**

obscure (əb skyoor′) *v.* to hide from view; **p. 126**

obsessed (əb sesd′) *adj.* having an excessive concern; **p. 979**

obsolete (ob′ sə lēt′) *adj.* outdated; no longer in use; **p. 817**

P

pensive (pen′ siv) *adj.* thoughtful; **p. 964**

penuriously (pi noor′ ē əs lē) *adv.* marked by severe poverty; **p. 929**

perish (per′ ish) *v.* to die or cease to exist; **p. 31**

perpetual (pər pech′ oo əl) *adj.* everlasting; eternal; **p. 804**

perusal (pə roo′ zəl) *n.* the act of reading in detail or examining carefully; examination; **p. 1228**

pester (pes′ tər) *v.* to harass or annoy with petty irritations; **p. 145**

phenomenon (fə nom′ ə non′) *n.* an observable fact or subject of scientific study; a remarkable event or occurrence; **p. 1194**

pity (pit′ ē) *n.* sympathy for another's suffering; **p. 921**

N

nautical/náutico *adj.* relacionado con marineros o barcos; **p. 1052**

negate/negar *v.* hacer ineficaz o rendir sin poder; **p. 1060**

nimble/hábil *adj.* ligero y rápido; de pie firme; **p. 909**

nonentity/don nadie *s.* persona insignificante o cosa de poca importancia; **p. 95**

nullity/nulidad *s.* una cosa trivial; algo insignificante; **p. 598**

O

obliterate/arrasar *v.* destruir todos los rastros de; borrar de la memoria; **p. 1213**

oblivion/olvido *s.* estado de haber sido olvidado; **p. 304**

obscure/ocultar *v.* esconder de la vista; **p. 126**

obsessed/obsesionado *adj.* preocupado excesivamente; **p. 979**

obsolete/obsoleto *adj.* anticuado; ya no usado; **p. 817**

P

pensive/meditabundo *adj.* pensativo; **p. 964**

penuriously/penuriamente *adv.* marcado por pobreza severa; **p. 929**

perish/perecer *v.* morir o cesar a existir; **p. 31**

perpetual/perpétuo *adj.* eterno; imperecedero; **p. 804**

perusal/examinación *s.* el actor de leer cuidadosa o detenidamente; **p. 1228**

pester/importunar *v.* molestar o fastidiar con irritaciones triviales; **p. 145**

phenomenon/fenómeno *s.* hecho o tema de estudio científico que se puede observar; evento o acontecimiento notable; **p. 1194**

pity/lástima *s.* simpatía por el sufrimiento de otro; **p. 921**

plaintively (plān′ tiv lē) *adv.* in a manner expressing suffering or woe; **p. 758**

plausible (plô′ zə bəl) *adj.* appearing worthy of belief; **p. 824**

plight (plīt) *n.* a situation that is hard to manage or resolve; **p. 122**

ploy (ploi) *n.* a trick or tactic; **p. 1166**

poignancy (poin′ yən sē) *n.* the quality of painfully affecting one′s feelings; **p. 567**

pounce (pouns) *v.* to swoop down on and quickly seize upon or take advantage of something; **p. 1251**

precipitous (pri sip′ ə təs) *adj.* having very steep sides; **p. 405**

prelude (prel′ ūd) *n.* an event preceding and preparing for a more important matter; **p. 823**

presumption (pri zump′ shən) *n.* attitude or conduct that oversteps the bounds of propriety or courtesy; **p. 931**

presumptuous (pri zump′ choo əs) *adj.* excessively bold or arrogant; taking liberties; **p. 1195**

prevail (pri vāl′) *v.* to gain ascendancy through strength or superiority; to triumph; **p. 459**

primordial (prī môr′ dē əl) *adj.* original; existing from the beginning; **p. 589**

pristine (pris′ tēn ′) *adj.* pure; unspoiled; **p. 590**

proclaim (prə klām′) *v.* to announce publicly; to make known; to declare; **p. 561**

profane (prō fān′) *adj.* not concerned with religious purposes; **p. 1290**

prolong (prə lông′) *v.* lengthen in time or space; draw out; **p. 1017**

propriety (prə prī′ ə tē) *n.* conformity to what is acceptable in conduct or speech; **p. 1204**

prosperity (pros per′ ə tē) *n.* the state of being successful; **p. 514**

provincial (prə vin′ shəl) *adj.* belonging or peculiar to a particular province; local; lacking sophistication or polish; **p. 628**

plaintively/lastimeramente *adv.* en una manera que expresa lástima o pena; **p. 758**

plausible/verosímil *adj.* lo que aparenta ser creíble; **p. 824**

plight/apuro *s.* situación difícil de resolver o negociar; **p. 122**

ploy/treta *s.* un engaño o táctica; **p. 1166**

poignancy/lo conmovido *s.* la calidad de afectar dolorosamente las emociones de uno; **p. 567**

pounce/saltar *v.* lanzarse sobre algo para captarlo o aprovecharse; **p. 1251**

precipitous/precípito *adj.* con lados empinados; **p. 405**

prelude/preludio *s.* un evento que precede y que prepara para un evento importante; **p. 823**

presumption/presunción *s.* actitud o conducta que va más allá de las fronteras de la cortesía o del decoro; **p. 931**

presumptuous/presuntuoso *adj.* excesivamente audaz o arrogante; tendencia a tomarse libertades; **p. 1195**

prevail/prevalecer *v.* ascender mediante fuerza o superioridad; triunfar; **p. 459**

primordial/primordial *adj.* original; que existe desde del comienzo; **p. 589**

pristine/inmaculado *adj.* puro; impoluto; **p. 590**

proclaim/proclamar *v.* anunicar públicamente; hacerlo saber; declarar; **p. 561**

profane/profano *adj.* no relacionado con propósitos religiosos; **p. 1290**

prolong/prolongar *v.* extender en tiempo o espacio; alargar; **p. 1017**

propriety/decoro *s.* conformidad con lo que se acepta en conducta o habla; **p. 1204**

prosperity/prosperidad *s.* el estado de tener éxito; **p. 514**

provincial/provincial *adj.* perteneciente a o particular de una provincia específica; local; carente de sofisticación o pulcro; **p. 628**

prudent (prōōd′ ənt) *adj.* sensible; sound in judgment; **p. 1058**

pungent (pun′ jənt) *adj.* having a sharp or stinging quality, especially affecting the sense of taste or smell; **p. 643**

R

radiant (rā′ dē ənt) *adj.* glowing; beaming; **p. 26**

random (ran′ dəm) *n.* lack of careful choice or plan; **p. 294**

range (rānj) *n.* the full extent over which something moves or is seen, heard, effective, etc.; scope; **p. 526**

rare (rār) *adj.* distinctive or seldom seen; **p. 522**

rational (rash′ ən əl) *adj.* able to reason; **p. 892**

ravaged (rav′ ijd) *adj.* devastated; ruined; **p. 454**

rebuke (ri būk′) *v.* to criticize sharply; **p. 110**

redeem (ri dēm′) *v.* buy back, as with property; **p. 482**

reel (rel) *v.* stand or move unsteadily; sway from a blow or shock; **p. 905**

refuge (ref′ ūj) *n.* shelter or protection from danger; **p. 879**

refuse (ref′ ūs) *n.* trash; garbage; **p. 87**

relentless (ri lent′ lis) *adj.* showing or promising no lessening of severity or intensity; **p. 1289**

renown (ri noun′) *n.* a state of being widely acclaimed; **p. 939**

reprisal (ri prī′ zəl) *n.* the act of using force in retaliation for damage or loss suffered; **p. 750**

resignation (rez′ ig nā′ shən) *n.* unresisting acceptance; **p. 1252**

respites (res′ pits) *n.* periods of temporary relief, rest, or delay; **p. 1036**

retaliation (ri tal′ ē ā′ shən) *n.* revenge; **p. 116**

retort (ri tôrt′) *v.* to reply in kind, especially with anger or with a witty or an insulting response; **p. 54**

prudent/prudente *adj.* sensible; sensato en los juicios; **p. 1058**

pungent/acre *adj.* tener un qualidad fuerte o mordaz, que afecta especialmente el sentido de sabor o olfato; **p. 643**

R

radiant/radiante *adj.* resplandeciente; brillante; **p. 26**

random/al azar *s.* falta de selección o plan meticuloso; **p. 294**

range/ámbito *s.* la esfera entera por la que algo se mueve, es oído o tiene alcance; campo; **p. 526**

rare/raro *adj.* distinto o poco visto; **p. 522**

rational/racional *adj.* capaz de razonar; **p. 892**

ravaged/asolado *adj.* devastado; arruinado; **p. 454**

rebuke/reprender *v.* criticar fuertemente; **p. 110**

redeem/desempeñar *v.* comprar de nuevo, como con propiedad; **p. 482**

reel/tambalearse *v.* estar de pie o moverse inestablemente; moverse en respuesta a un golpe o choque; **p. 905**

refuge/refugio *s.* sanctuario o protección de peligro; **p. 879**

refuse/desperdicios *s.* residuos; basura; **p. 87**

relentless/incesante *adj.* lo que aparenta o promete no disminuir en severidad o intensidad; **p. 1289**

renown/renombre *s.* estado de ser ampliamente aclamado; **p. 939**

reprisal/represalia *s.* el acto de usar fuerza en venganza por daño sufrido; **p. 750**

resignation/resignación *s.* aprobación o aceptación sin resistencia; **p. 1252**

respites/respiros *s.* periodos breves de descanso, alivio o demora; **p. 1036**

retaliation/represalias *s.* venganza; **p. 116**

retort/réplica *v.* responder con ira o con contestación humorosa o ofensiva; **p. 54**

retract (ri trakt´) *v.* take back or deny; **p. 287**

revered (ri vērd´) *adj.* regarded as worthy of great honor; **p. 929**

revive (ri vīv´) *v.* to recover; to come back to life; **p. 1134**

rivet (riv´ it) *v.* fixed firmly; completely engrossed; **p. 1068**

ruddy (rud´ ē) *adj.* having a rosy or reddish complexion; **p. 816**

rustle (rus´ əl) *v.* to make a succession of soft crackling sounds; **p. 80**

S

savage (sav´ ij) *adj.* wild; untamed, and often fierce; **p. 888**

scholarship (skol´ ər ship´) *n.* academic achievement or knowledge; **p. 597**

scorn (skôrn) *v.* disrespect; show contempt for; **p. 1059**

scrutinize (skro͞ot´ ən īz´) *v.* to examine with close attention to detail; **p. 623**

seclusion (si klo͞o´ zhən) *n.* solitude; privacy; isolation; **p. 1017**

sedately (si dāt´ lē) *adv.* in a dignified or serious manner; calmly; solemnly; **p. 631**

seldom (sel´ dəm) *adv.* rarely; **p. 734**

self-possessed (self´ pə zest´) *adj.* in control of oneself; **p. 1268**

sever (sev´ ər) *v.* cut or break apart; separate; divide; **p. 873**

sheer (shēr) *adj.* unmixed; pure; **p. 1213**

shirk (shurk) *v.* to evade or avoid one's duty; **p. 622**

shrill (shrill) *adj.* high-pitched; **p. 518**

shrivel (shriv´ əl) *v.* to become wrinkled as a result of lack of moisture; **p. 1283**

retract/retirar *v.* negar o retractarse; **p. 287**

revered/venerado *adj.* visto como digno de gran honor; **p. 929**

revive/resucitar *v.* recubrir, reanimarse; **p. 1134**

rivet/remachar *v.* atado firmemente; completamente fascinado; **p. 1068**

ruddy/rubicundo *adj.* tener una complexión rosada; **p. 816**

rustle/susurrar *v.* hacer una sucesión de sonidos suaves o crujientes; **p. 80**

S

savage/salvaje *adj.* feroz, sin domar, agreste; **p. 888**

scholarship/investigación *s.* estudio o conocimiento académico; **p. 597**

scorn/desdén *v.* falta de respeto; menospreciar; **p. 1059**

scrutinize/escudriñar *v.* examinar detenidamente; **p. 623**

seclusion/reclusión *s.* soledad; privacidad; aislamiento; **p. 1017**

sedately/reposadamente *adv.* tranquilamente; solemnemente; de manera dignificada o seria; **p. 631**

seldom/pocas veces *adv.* rara vez, raramente; **p. 734**

self-possessed/sereno *adj.* dueño de sí mismo; **p. 1268**

sever/cercenar *v.* cortar o romper; separar; dividir; **p. 873**

sheer/puro *adj.* sin mezclar con otra cosa; **p. 1213**

shirk/rehuir *v.* evitar o eludir la responsabilidad; **p. 622**

shrill/estridente *adj.* agudo; **p. 518**

shrivel/marchitarse *v.* encogerse y arrugarse por falta de humedad; **p. 1283**

sinister (sin´ is tər) *adj.* singularly evil; menacing; **p. 406**

sly (slī) *adj.* clever; wily; secretive; **p. 371**

sojourn (sō´ jurn) *v.* stay or reside temporarily; **p. 478**

solace (sol´ is) *n.* a source of relief; mental or spiritual comfort; **p. 1233**

solemn (sol´ əm) *adj.* serious; gravely important; **p. 1140**

solitary (sol´ ə ter´ ē) *adj.* characterized by loneliness or lack of companions; lonely; **p. 526**

solitude (sol´ ə tōōd´) *n.* state of being alone; isolation; **p. 979**

sordid (sôr´ did) *adj.* dirty; squalid; wretched; **p. 614**

splendid (splen´ did) *adj.* grand; magnificent; **p. 19**

stern (sturn) *adj.* harsh or severe in manner; firm or unyielding; **p. 365**

stifled (stī´ fəld) *adj.* muffled or repressed; **p. 153**

straggler (strag´ lər) *n.* one who lags behind or strays from a group; **p. 1156**

stray (strā) *v.* to wander away; to go off course; **p. 1138**

strut (strut) *v.* to walk in a proud manner; **p. 882**

stupefied (stōō´ pə fīd) *adj.* stupid, groggy, or insensible; **p. 623**

stupor (stōō´ pər) *n.* a dulled mental state, often as a result of shock or stress; a daze; **p. 1284**

submerge (səb murj´) *v.* to go under water; **p. 153**

subtle (sut´ əl) *adj.* hard to detect; **p. 243**

sullen (sul´ ən) *adj.* showing resentment and ill humor by sulky withdrawal; **p. 280**

supplementary (sup´ lə men´ tər ē) *adj.* extra or additional; **p. 1271**

sinister/siniestro *adj.* singularmente malo; amenazante; **p. 406**

sly/ladino *adj.* listo, astuto, secreto; **p. 371**

sojourn/residir por una temporada *v.* quedar provisionalmente o durante una estadía breve; **p. 478**

solace/solaz *s.* una fuente de alivio mental o espíritual; **p. 1233**

solemn/solemne *adj.* serio; gravemente importante; **p. 1140**

solitary/solitario *adj.* caracterizado por soledad o falta de compañeros; solo; **p. 526**

solitude/soledad *s.* estado de estar solo; aislamiento; **p. 979**

sordid/sórdido *adj.* sucio; esquálido; desdichado; **p. 614**

splendid/espléndido *adj.* grandioso; magnífico; **p. 19**

stern/severo *adj.* agresivo o duro en actitud; firme o sin rendir; **p. 365**

stifled/sofocar *adj.* reprimido o ahogado; **p. 153**

straggler/rezagado *s.* uno que se queda atrás o se aparta de un grupo; **p. 1156**

stray/extraviarse *v.* apartarse; alejarse del camino; **p. 1138**

strut/pavonearse *v.* caminar de modo orgulloso; **p. 882**

stupefied/estupefacto *adj.* estúpido, insensible o atontado; **p. 623**

stupor/estupor *s.* un estado mental atontado muchas veces como resultado de choque o estrés; **p. 1284**

submerge/sumergir *v.* descender bajo agua; **p. 153**

subtle/sútil *adj.* difícil de detectar; **p. 243**

sullen/hosco *adj.* mostrando resentimiento al retirarse malhumorado; **p. 280**

supplementary/suplementario *adj.* extra o adicional; **p. 1271**

suppliant (sə´ plē´ ənt) *n.* one who asks humbly and earnestly; **p. 386**

supplication (sup´ lə kā´ shən) *n.* humble entreaty; prayer of request; **p. 1235**

suppress (sə pres´) *v.* keep in or hold back; **p. 370**

surge (surj) *n.* a strong, sudden increase or flow; **p. 648**

surpass (sər pas´) *v.* to exceed; **p. 244**

sustenance (sus´ tə nəns) *n.* food; nourishment; means of support; **p. 1157**

swell (swel) *v.* to increase in size or volume; expand; **p. 365**

T

taint (tānt) *v.* to contaminate morally; to corrupt; **p. 825**

tamper (tam´ pər) *v.* meddle improperly; **p. 692**

tangible (tan´ jə bəl) *adj.* real; actual; definite; **p. 326**

taut (tôt) *adj.* having no give or slack; tightly drawn; **p. 152**

tedious (tē´ dē əs) *adj.* tiresome because of length or dullness; boring; **p. 1144**

tempo (tem´ pō) *n.* pattern or rate of movement; **p. 768**

tepid (tep´ id) *adj.* lukewarm; halfhearted; **p. 631**

thicket (thik´ it) *n.* a dense growth of shrubs, underbrush, or small trees; **p. 498**

throng (throng) *n.* a crowd of many people; **p. 86**

titter (ti´ tər) *v.* to laugh nervously; **p. 796**

toil (toil) *n.* fatiguing work or effort; **p. 54**

torment (tôr´ ment) *n.* great pain or suffering; **p. 879**

torrent (tôr´ ənt) *n.* a powerful flood or outpouring; **p. 81**

suppliant/suplicante *s.* uno que pide con humildad y seriedad; **p. 386**

supplication/súplica *s.* ruego humilde; oración de petición; **p. 1235**

suppress/suprimir *v.* guardar o retener; **p. 370**

surge/subida *s.* un aumento o flujo repentino y fuerte; **p. 648**

surpass/superar *v.* exceder; **p. 244**

sustenance/sustento *s.* comida, alimento; apoyo; **p. 1157**

swell/hincharse *v.* aumentar en tamaño o volumen; expandir; **p. 365**

T

taint/mancillar *v.* contaminar moralmente; corrumpir; **p. 825**

tamper/alterar *v.* tocar o cambiar incorrectamente; **p. 692**

tangible/tangible *v.* real; definido; palpable; **p. 326**

taut/tirante *adj.* no ser flojo; tenso; **p. 152**

tedious/tedio *adj.* cansado debido a la extensión o falta de interés; aburrido; **p. 1144**

tempo/tempo *s.* pauta o ritmo de movimiento; **p. 768**

tepid/tibio *adj.* poco cálido; poco entusiasta; **p. 631**

thicket/matorral *s.* crecimiento denso de plantas, arbustos o árboles pequeños; **p. 498**

throng/muchedumbre *s.* multitud de muchas personas; **p. 86**

titter/reírse disimuladamente *v.* reírse nerviosamente con risitas ahogadas; **p. 796**

toil/labor *s.* gran esfuerzo o trabajo duro; **p. 54**

torment/tormento *s.* gran dolor o sufrimiento; **p. 879**

torrent/torrente *s.* gran flujo o desahogo; **p. 81**

trample (tram′ pəl) *v.* to walk upon and damage by crushing or bruising; to stomp; **p. 750**

tranquil (trang′ kwəl) *adj.* calm; peaceful; **p. 32**

treacherous (trech′ ər əs) *adj.* hazardous; dangerous; **p. 458**

trespass (tres′ pəs) *v.* illegally enter property; **p. 987**

trivial (triv′ ē əl) *adj.* commonplace; of little importance; **p. 720**

tumult (too′ məlt) *n.* commotion or noisy confusion; **p. 501**

U

undaunted (un dôn′ tid) *adj.* courageously firm or resolute, especially in the face of danger or difficulty; not discouraged; **p. 1036**

undulant (un′ jə lənt) *adj.* having a wavy form or motion; **p. 750**

unwitting (un wit′ ing) *adj.* not knowing; unaware; **p. 1213**

V

vague (vāg) *adj.* unclear; without form; indistinct; **p. 518**

veer (vēr) *v.* to change direction or course; **p. 1144**

vengeance (ven′ jəns) *n.* revenge; the return of a harmful deed for a harmful deed; **p. 255**

verdict (vur′ dikt) *n.* decision; judgment; **p. 901**

versatility (vər′ sə ti′ lə tē) *n.* ability to do many things well; **p. 326**

vigorously (vig′ ər əs lē) *adv.* energetically; **p. 143**

vivacity (vi vas′ ə tē′) *n.* liveliness; animation; **p. 964**

vulnerable (vul′ nər ə bəl) *adj.* weak; unable to defend oneself; **p. 314**

trample/pisotear *v.* caminar por encima y hacer daño aplastando; **p. 750**

tranquil/tranquilo *adj.* calmado; pacífico; **p. 32**

treacherous/traicionero *adj.* peligroso, arriesgado; **p. 458**

trespass/traspasar *v.* entrar en propiedad ajena ilegalmente; **p. 987**

trivial/trivial *adj.* común; de poca importancia; **p. 720**

tumult/tumulto *s.* conmoción o confusión ruidosa; **p. 501**

U

undaunted/impertérrito *adj.* firme o resoluto con coraje, especialmente ante peligro o dificultad; difícil de desanimar; **p. 1036**

undulant/ondulante *adj.* con forma de olas o que hace movimientos en forma de olas; **p. 750**

unwitting/involuntario *adj.* sin saber; inconsciente; **p. 1213**

V

vague/vago *adj.* poco claro; sin forma; indistinto; **p. 518**

veer/virar *v.* cambiar rumbo o sentido; **p. 1144**

vengeance/venganza *s.* hacer una hazaña dañina a cambio de otra hazaña dañina; **p. 255**

verdict/veredicto *s.* decisión; juicio; **p. 901**

versatility/versatilidad *s.* capacidad de hacer muchas cosas; **p. 326**

vigorously/vigurosamente *adv.* con mucha energía; **p. 143**

vivacity/vivacidad *s.* entusiasmo; animación; **p. 964**

vulnerable/vulnerable *adj.* débil; incapaz de defenderse; **p. 314**

W

waive (wāv) *v.* to reject, decline, or give up; p. 507

winnow (win′ ō) *v.* to remove by exposing to air currents; free from lighter particles; to sift; to separate; p. 480

writhe (rīth) *v.* twist the body violently; contort; p. 873

Y

yearn (yurn) *v.* to desire or long; p. 816

W

waive/renunciar *v.* rechazar, no exigir, rehusar; p. 507

winnow/aventar *v.* echar en el aire para esparcir; separar; diseminar en partículos; tamizar; p. 480

writhe/retorcerse *v.* mover el cuerpo violentamente, contorsionarse; p. 873

Y

yearn/anhelar *v.* desear o ansiar; p. 816

Academic Word List

To succeed academically in high school and prepare for college, it is important to know academic vocabulary—special terms used in classroom discussion, assignments, and tests. These words are also used in the workplace and among friends to share information, exchange ideas, make decisions, and build relationships. Research has shown that the words listed below, compiled by Averil Coxhead in 2000, are the ones most commonly used in these ways. You will encounter many of them in the Glencoe Language Arts program. You will also focus on specific terms in connection with particular reading selections.

Note: The lists are ordered by frequency of use from most frequent to least frequent.

List One

analysis
approach
area
assessment
assume
authority
available
benefit
concept
consistent
constitutional
context
contract
create
data
definition
derived
distribution
economic
environment
established
estimate
evidence
export
factors
financial
formula
function
identified
income
indicate
individual
interpretation
involved
issues
labor
legal
legislation
major
method
occur
percent
period
policy
principle
procedure
process
required
research
response
role
section
sector
significant
similar
source
specific
structure
theory
variables

List Two

achieve
acquisition
administration
affect
appropriate
aspects
assistance
categories
chapter
commission
community
complex
computer
conclusion
conduct
consequences
construction
consumer
credit
cultural
design
distinction
elements
equation
evaluation
features
final
focus
impact
injury
institute
investment
items
journal
maintenance
normal
obtained
participation
perceived
positive
potential
previous
primary
purchase
range
region
regulations
relevant
resident
resources
restricted
security
select
site
sought
strategies
survey
text
traditional
transfer

List Three

alternative
circumstances
comments
compensation
components
consent
considerable
constant
constraints
contribution
convention
coordination
core
corporate
corresponding
criteria
deduction
demonstrate
document
dominant
emphasis
ensure
excluded
framework
funds
illustrated
immigration
implies
initial

instance
interaction
justification
layer
link
location
maximum
minorities
negative
outcomes
partnership
philosophy
physical
proportion
published
reaction
registered
reliance
removed
scheme
sequence
sex
shift
specified
sufficient
task
technical
techniques
technology
validity
volume

List Four

access
adequate
annual
apparent
approximated
attitudes
attributed
civil
code
commitment
communication

concentration
conference
contrast
cycle
debate
despite
dimensions
domestic
emerged
error
ethnic
goals
granted
hence
hypothesis
implementation
implications
imposed
integration
internal
investigation
job
label
mechanism
obvious
occupational
option
output
overall
parallel
parameters
phase
predicted
principal
prior
professional
project
promote
regime
resolution
retained
series
statistics
status

stress
subsequent
sum
summary
undertaken

List Five

academic
adjustment
alter
amendment
aware
capacity
challenge
clause
compounds
conflict
consultation
contact
decline
discretion
draft
enable
energy
enforcement
entities
equivalent
evolution
expansion
exposure
external
facilitate
fundamental
generated
generation
image
liberal
license
logic
marginal
medical
mental
modified
monitoring

network
notion
objective
orientation
perspective
precise
prime
psychology
pursue
ratio
rejected
revenue
stability
styles
substitution
sustainable
symbolic
target
transition
trend
version
welfare
whereas

List Six

abstract
accurate
acknowledged
aggregate
allocation
assigned
attached
author
bond
brief
capable
cited
cooperative
discrimination
display
diversity
domain
edition
enhanced

estate
exceed
expert
explicit
federal
fees
flexibility
furthermore
gender
ignored
incentive
incidence
incorporated
index
inhibition
initiatives
input
instructions
intelligence
interval
lecture
migration
minimum
ministry
motivation
neutral
nevertheless
overseas
preceding
presumption
rational
recovery
revealed
scope
subsidiary
tapes
trace
transformation
transport
underlying
utility

List Seven

adaptation
adults
advocate
aid
channel
chemical
classical
comprehensive
comprise
confirmed
contrary
converted
couple
decades
definite
deny
differentiation
disposal
dynamic
eliminate
empirical
equipment
extract
file
finite
foundation
global
grade
guarantee
hierarchical
identical
ideology
inferred
innovation
insert
intervention
isolated
media
mode
paradigm
phenomenon
priority
prohibited

publication
quotation
release
reverse
simulation
solely
somewhat
submitted
successive
survive
thesis
topic
transmission
ultimately
unique
visible
voluntary

List Eight

abandon
accompanied
accumulation
ambiguous
appendix
appreciation
arbitrary
automatically
bias
chart
clarity
commodity
complement
conformity
contemporary
contradiction
crucial
currency
denote
detected
deviation
displacement
dramatic
eventually
exhibit

exploitation
fluctuations
guidelines
highlighted
implicit
induced
inevitably
infrastructure
inspection
intensity
manipulation
minimized
nuclear
offset
paragraph
plus
practitioners
predominantly
prospect
radical
random
reinforced
restore
revision
schedule
tension
termination
theme
thereby
uniform
vehicle
via
virtually
visual
widespread

List Nine

accommodation
analogous
anticipated
assurance
attained
behalf
bulk

ceases
coherence
coincide
commenced
concurrent
confined
controversy
conversely
device
devoted
diminished
distorted
duration
erosion
ethical
format
founded
incompatible
inherent
insights
integral
intermediate
manual
mature
mediation
medium
military
minimal
mutual
norms
overlap
passive
portion
preliminary
protocol
qualitative
refine
relaxed
restraints
revolution
rigid
route
scenario
sphere

subordinate
supplementary
suspended
team
temporary
trigger
unified
violation
vision

List Ten

adjacent
albeit
assembly
collapse
colleagues
compiled
conceived
convinced
depression
encountered
enormous
forthcoming
inclination
integrity
intrinsic
invoked
levy
likewise
nonetheless
notwithstanding
odd
ongoing
panel
persistent
posed
reluctant
so-called
straightforward
undergo
whereby

Index of Skills

References beginning with **R** refer to handbook pages.

Literary Concepts

Reading and Critical Thinking

Vocabulary

Research, Test-Taking, and Study Skills

Interdisciplinary Activities

Index of Authors and Titles

Acknowledgments

Unit 1

From "the Harper's Song for Inherkhawy" from *Ancient Egyptian Literature: An Anthology,* translated by John L. Foster. Copyright © 2001. By permission of the University of Texas Press.

"Pleasant Songs: Part II" ("So Small Are the Flowers of Seamu") edited by Ezra Pound, translated by Noel Stock, from *Love Poems of Ancient Egypt,* copyright © 1962 by Noel Stock. Reprinted by permission of New Directions Publishing Corp.

"Coyote Steals Fire" from *American Indian Trickster Tales* by Richard Erdoes and Alphonso Ortiz, copyright © 1998 by Richard Erdoes & The Estate of Alphonso Ortiz. Used by permission of Viking Penguin, a division of Penguin Group (USA) Inc.

"Master Cat Or Puss in Boots" by Charles Perrault, translated by Maria Tatar, from *The Annotated Classic Fairy Tales,* edited by Maria Tatar. Copyright © 2002 by Maria Tatar. Used by permission of W.W. Norton & Company, Inc.

"Edju and the Two Friends" from Radin, Paul; *African Folktales.* Copyright © by Bollingen Foundation, Inc., New York, NY, revised 1964. First Princeton/Bollingen Paperback printing, 1970. Reprinted by permission of Princeton University Press.

"The Lion's Awakening" from *Sundiata: An Epic of Old Mali, 2nd Edition,* by D.T. Niane. Copyright © 1965 by Longmans, Green & co. Reprinted by permission of Pearson Education Limited.

"Half a Day", translated by Denys Johnson-Davis, copyright © 1991 by American University in Cairo Press, from *The Time and the Place & Other Stories* by Naguib Mahfouz. Used by permission of Doubleday, a division of Random House, Inc.

"The Voter" from *Girls at War and Other Stories* by Chinua Achebe, copyright © 1972, 1973 by Chinua Achebe. Used by permission of Doubleday, a division of Random House, Inc.

From *No Future Without Forgiveness* by Desmond Tutu, copyright © 1999 by Desmond Tutu. Used by permission of Doubleday, a division of Random House, Inc.

"The Prisoner Who Wore Glasses," copyright © Bessie Head, from *Tales of Tenderness and Power,* Ad. Donker, 1989.

From *Things Fall Apart* by Chinua Achebe. Copyright © 1959 by Chinua Achebe. Reprinted by permission of Harcourt Education.

From *Ake: The Years of Childhood* by Wole Soyinka, copyright © 1981 by Wole Soyinka. Used by permission of Random House, Inc.

Unit 2

"The Death of Hector," by Homer, "The Rage of Achilles," by Homer from *The Iliad* by Homer, translated by Robert Fagles, copyright © 1990 by Robert Fagles. Used by permission of Viking Penguin, a division of Penguin Group (USA) Inc.

From "Echoes of the Heroic Age" by Caroline Alexander, *National Geographic,* December 1999. Copyright © 1999 The National Geographic society. Reprinted by permission.

Excerpt from *Sappho: Poems and Fragments,* translated by Stanley Lombardo. Copyright © 2002 by Hackett Publishing Company. Reprinted by permission of Hackett Publishing Company, Inc. All rights reserved.

"Oedipus the King," by Sophocles, from *Three Theban Plays* by Sophocles, translated by Robert Fagles, copyright © 1982 by Robert Fagles. Used by permission of Viking Penguin, a division of Penguin Group (USA) Inc.

From *The History of the Peloponnesian War* by Thucydides, translated by Rex Warner, with an introduction and notes by M.I. Finley (Penguin Classics 1954, Revised Edition 1972). Translation copyright © Rex Warner, 1954. Introduction and Appendices copyright © M.I. Finley, 1972. Reprinted by permission.

From *The Dialogues of Plato* by William Chase Greene, editor, from the translation of Benjamin Jowett. Copyright 1927 by Horace Liveright, Inc., renewed 1954 by Liveright Publishing Corporation. Used by permission of Liveright publishing Corporation.

"Better to Live, Licinius" from *Odes and Epodes of Horace: A Modern English Verse Translation,* by Joseph P. Clancy. Copyright © 1960 by The University of Chicago. Reprinted by permission.

"The Story of Piramus and Thisbe" from *Metamorphoses* by Ovid, translated by Rolfe Humphries. Copyright © 1955 Indiana University Press. Reprinted by permission of Indiana University Press.

"Book Two: The Final Hours of Troy" from *Virgil: The Aeneid* by Virgil, translated by Robert Fagles, copyright © 2006 by Robert Fagles. Used by permission of Viking Penguin, a division of Penguin Group (USA) Inc.

From *The Annals of Imperial Rome* by Tacitus, translated with an introduction by Michael Grant (Penguin Classics 1956, Sixth revised edition 1989). Copyright © Michael Grant Publications Ltd, 1956, 1959, 1971, 1973, 1975, 1977, 1989.

Excerpt from *The Bells of Nagasaki* by Takashi Nagai, translated by William Johnston. Copyright © 1984 by Kodansha International Ltd. Reprinted by permission.

From *The Lives of the Twelve Caesars* by Suetonius, translated by Joseph Garvorse, copyright 1931 and renewed 1959 and 1967 by Modern Library, a division of Random House, Inc. Used by permission of Modern Library, a division of Random House, Inc.

Unit 3

Reprinted and edited with the permission of The Free Press, a division of Simon & Schuster Adult Publishing Group, from *Gilgamesh: A New English Version* by Stephen Mitchell. Copyright © 2004 by Stephen Mitchell. All rights reserved.

Reprinted with the permission of Simon & Schuster Adult Publishing Group from *The Bible Designed To Be Read As Living Literature: the Old and New Testaments in the King James Version,* edited by Ernest Sutherland Bates. Copyright 1936 by Simon & Schuster, Inc. Copyright renewed © 1964 by Simon & Schuster Inc.

"The Exordium" and "Daylight" from *The Koran,* translated by N.J. Dawood (Penguin Classics 1956, Fifth revised edition 1990). Copyright © N.J. Dawood, 1956, 1959, 1966, 1968, 1974, 1990, 1993, 1997, 1999, 2003. Reprinted by permission of Penguin Group (UK)

"The Second Voyage of Sinbad the Sailor" from *Tales from the Thousand and One Nights,* translated by N.J. Dawood, wood engravings by William Harvey (Penguin Classics 1954, Revised edition 1973). Translation copyright © N.J. Dawood, 1954, 1973.

"The Counsels of the Bird" reprinted with permission from *Teachings of Rumi: The Masnavi* (Octagon Press Ltd., London).

From "Love Song for Words" by Nazik Al-Malaika, translated by Matthew

Sorenson and Christopher Middleton, from *Modern Arabic Poetry,* copyright © 1991 Columbia University Press. Reprinted by permission.

"The Sound of Birds at Noon" by Dahlia Ravikovitch, translated by Chana Bloch and Ariel Bloch, from *The Window.* Reprinted by permission of Chana Bloch.

"The Diameter of the Bomb" from *The Selected Poetry of Yehuda Amichai,* by Yehuda Amichai, edited and translated by Chana Bloch and Stephen Mitchell. Copyright © 1966 The Regents of the University of California. Published by the University of California Press. Reprinted by permission.

"Butterflies" by Fawziyya Abu Khalid, from *The Literature of Modern Arabia,* copyright © 1988 by the King Saud University. Reprinted by permission of Kegan Paul International.

"Poem" by Fawziyya Abu Khalid, translated by Salwa Jabsheh and John Heath-Stubbs, from from *Modern Arabic Poetry,* copyright © 1991 Columbia University Press. Reprinted by permission.

"The Letter" translated by Mattias Ripa & Blake Ferris, from *Persepolis: The Story of a Childhood,* by Marjane Satrapi, translated by Mattias Ripa & Blake Ferris, copyright © 2003 by L'Associaiton, Paris, France. Used by permission of Pantheon Books, a division of Random House, Inc.

"Creation Hymn" from *The Rig Veda: An Anthology of One Hundred and Eight Hymns,* selected, translated and annotated by Wendy Doniger O'Flaherty (Penguin Classics 1981). Copyright © Wendy Doniger O'Flaherty, 1981.

"Hundred Questions" from *The Mahabharata* by R.K. Narayan. Copyright © 1978 by R.K Narayan. Used by permission of the Wallace Literary Agency, Inc.

From "Homer in India" by William Dalrymple, copyright William Dalrymple, 2006. Reprinted by permission of David Goodwin Associates on behalf of the author.

"Rama and Ravana in Battle" from *The Ramayana* by R.K. Narayan, copyright © 1972 by R.K. Narayan. Used by permission of Viking Penguin, a division of Penguin Group (USA) Inc.

"The Lion-Makers" from *The Panchatantra,* translated from the Sanskrit by Arthur W. Ryder. Copyright © 1956 by Mary E. and Winifred Ryder. Reprinted by permission of The University of Chicago Press.

"The Oak and the Reed" from *La Fontaine: Selected Fables,* translated by James Michie, introduction by Geoffrey Grigson (Allen Lane 1979, Penguin Classics, 1982). Translation copyright © James Michie, 1979. Introduction copyright © Geoffrey Grigson, 1979.

"The Elephant Who Changed the World" from *Fables for Our Time,* copyright © 1956 by James Thurber. Copyright © renewed 1984 by Rosemary A. Thurber. Reprinted by arrangement with Rosemary A. Thurber and The Barbara Hogenson Agency, Inc.

"Like the Sun" by R.K. Narayan, from *Under the Banyan Tree* by R.K. Narayan, copyright © 1985 by R.K. Narayan. Used by permission of Viking Penguin, a division of Penguin Group (USA) Inc.

"By Any Other Name" from *Gifts of Passage* by Santha Rama Rau. Copyright 1951 by Santha Rama Rau. Copyright renewed © 1979 by Santha Rama Rau. Reprinted by permission of HarperCollins Publishers. "By Any Other Name" originally appeared in The New Yorker.

"The Taj Mahal" from *Step Across This Line* by Salman Rushdie, copyright © 2002 by Salman Rushdie. Used by permission of Random House, Inc.

Unit 4

Reprinted with the permission of Scribner, an imprint of Simon & Schuster Adult Publishing Group, from *The Analects of Confucius,* by Arthur Waley, translator. Copyright © 1938 by George Allen & Unwin Ltd. All rights reserved.

29, 31, 33 from *Tao Te Ching by Lao Tzu, A New English Version, with Foreward and Notes* by Stephen Mitchell. Translation copyright © 1988 by Stephen Mitchell. Reprinted by permission of HarperCollins Publishers.

"The River-Merchant's Wife: A Letter" by Ezra Pound, from *Personae,* copyright © 1926 by Ezra Pound. Reprinted by permission of New Directions Publishing Corp.

Excerpts from "The Southern Emperor Rules the Land" and "Homage to the Trung Queens" from *Heritage of Vietnamese Poetry,* edited and translated by Huynh Sanh Thong. Repritned by permission of Yale University Press.

"Jade Flower Palace" by Tu Fu, translated by Kenneth Rexroth, from *One Hundred Poems from the Chinese,* copyright © 1971 by Kenneth Rexroth. Reprinted by permission of New Directions Publishing Corp.

"Huzun," translated by Maureen Freely, from *Istanbul: Memories and the City* by Orhan Pamuk, translated by Maureen Freely, copyright © 2004 by Alfred A. Knopf, a division of Random House, Inc. Used by permission of Alfred A. Knopf, a division of Random House, Inc.

Excerpts from *The Pillow Book of Sei Shōnagon,* translated by Ivan Morris. Copyright © 1991 Columbia University Press. Reprinted by permission.

"Four Views of Spring Rain" by Yosa Buson, from *The Penguin Book of Japanese Verse,* translated by Geoffrey Bownas and Anthony Thwaite (Penguin Books, 1964). Reprinted by permission.

"A World of Dew and Melting Snow" by Kobayashi Issa, from *The Penguin Book of Japanese Verse,* translated by Geoffrey Bownas and Anthony Thwaite (Penguin Books, 1964). Reprinted by permission.

"Poverty's Child" and "The Sun's Way" by Basho, from An Introduction to Haiku by Harold G. Henderson, copyright © 1958 by Harold G. Henderson. Used by permission of Doubleday, a division of Random House, Inc.

Three haiku from Introduction (p. xi) by Bashō, Buson and Issa, from *The Essential Haiku: Versions of Bashō, Buson & Issa, Edited and With an Introduction* by Robert Hass. Introduction and selection copyright © 1994 by Robert Hass. Unless otherwise noted, all translations copyright © 1994 by Robert Hass. Reprinted by permission of HarperCollins Publishers.

"Rainforest" and "River Bend" from *A Human Pattern: Selected Poems* by Judith Wright. (ETT Imprint, Sydney, 1996) Reprinted by permission.

"Municipal Gum" by Oodgeroo of the tribe Noonuccal, from *My People, 3rd Edition,* The Jacaranda Press, 1990, reproduced by permission of John Wiley & Sons Australia.

"Clouds on the Sea" by Ruth Dallas, from *Fire in the Sea,* edited by Sue Cowing. Copyright © 1996 University of Hawaii Press. Reprinted by permission of the University of Hawaii Press.

From Pin Yathay: *Stay Alive, My Son.* Copyright © 1987, 2000 by Pin Yathay. Used by permission of the publisher, Cornell University Press.

"Moana" by Kauraka Kauraka, from *Fire in the Sea,* edited by Sue Cowing. Copyright © 1996 University of Hawaii Press. Reprinted by permission of the University of Hawaii Press.

"Island" by Albert Wendt, from *Fire in the Sea,* edited by Sue Cowing. Copyright © 1996 University of Hawaii Press. Reprinted by permission of the University of Hawaii Press.

From *The Selected Poems of T-ao Ch'ien,* translation copyright © 1993 by David Hinton. Reprinted by permission of Copper Canyon Press.

Unit 5

From *The Prose Edda: Tales from Norse Mythology,* by Snorri Sturluson, translated by Jean I. Young, copyright © 1964 by The Regents of the University of Califonia. Repritned by permission of the University of California Press.

From *The Song of Roland,* translated by Frederick Goldin. Copyright © 1978 by W.W. Norton & Company, Inc. Used by permission of W.W. Norton & Company, Inc.

From *The Divine Comedy* by Dante Alighieri, translated by John Ciardi. Copyright 1954, 1957, 1959, 1960, 1961, 1965, 1967, 1970 by the Ciardi Family Publishing Trust. Used by permission of W.W. Norton & Company, Inc.

"The Divine Comedy" by Jorges Luis Borges, translated by Eliot Weinberger, from *Seven Nights,* copyright © 1984 by Eliot Weinberger. Reprinted by permission of New Directions Publishing Corp.

"33" ("Secretly I am building in the heart…") from *Homecoming.* Copyright © 1984, 1996 by Julia Alvarez. Published by Plume, an imprint of Penguin Group (USA); originally published by Grove Press. Reprinted by permission of Susan Bergholz Literary Services, New York. All rights reserved.

"Federigo's Falcon- 9th Tale" from *The Decameron,* translated by Richard Aldington. Copyright © Estate of Richard Aldington, 1957, 1985. Reprinted by permission of Rosica Colin Limited.

Excerpts from *Don Quixote* by Miguel de Cervantes, a new translation by Edith Grossman. Introduction by Harold Bloom. Translation copyright © 2003 by Edith Grossman; introduction copyright © 2003 by Harold Bloom. Reprinted by permission of HarperCollins Publishers.

"The Lorelei" from *Poetry and Prose of Heinrich Heine,* by Heinrich Heine, edited by Frederic Ewen. Copyright © 1948, 1976 by Citadel Press. All rights reserved. Reprinted by arrangement with Citadel Press/ Kensington Publishing Corp. www.kensingtonbooks.com.

"My Bohemia" translated by Wyatt Mason, from *Rimbaud Complete* by Arthur Rimbaud, translated by Wyatt Mason, copyright © 2002 by Wyatt Mason. Used by permission of Modern Library, a division of Random House, Inc.

"First Sorrow" from *The Penal Colony* by Franz Kafka, translated by Edwin & Willa Muir, copyright 1948 and renewed 1976 by Schocken Books. Used by permission of Schocken Books, a division of Random House, Inc.

"Lot's Wife," translation by Richard Wilbur, from *Walking to Sleep: New Poems and Translations,* copyright © 1969 and renewed 1997 by Richard Wilbur, reprinted by permission of Harcourt, Inc.

"War" from *The Medals and Other Stories* by Luigi Pirandello. Copyright © 1939 by E.P. Dutton & Co. Reprinted by permission of the Pirandello Estate and Toby Cole, agent.

"The Guitar" from *Lorca and Jimenez: Selected Poems,* copyright © 1973, 1997 by Robert Bly. Reprinted by permission.

"Encounter" from *Bells in Winter* by Czeslaw Milosz. Copyright © 1974, 1977, 1978 by Czeslaw Milosz. Reprinted by permission of HarperCollins Publishers.

"The World, My Friends, My Enemies, You and the Earth" from *Poems of Nazim Hikmet,* translated by Randy Blasing and Mutlu Konuk. Translation copyright © 2994, 2002 by Randy Blasing and Mutlu Konuk. Reprinted by permission of Persea Books, Inc. (New York).

Excerpt from *Crime and Punishment* by Feodor Dostoevsky, translated and edited by Jessie Coulson. Reprinted by permission of Oxford University Press.

Unit 6

Reprinted with the permission of Simon & Schuster Adult Publishing Group from *Popol Vuh* by Dennis Tedlock. Copyright © 1985, 1996 by Dennis Tedlock.

From *The Broken Spears* by Miguel Leon-Portilla. Copyright © 1962, 1990 by Miguel Leon-Portilla. Expanded and Updated edition © 1992 by Miguel Leon-Portilla. Reprinted by permission of Beacon Press, Boston.

"Sonnet 145" reprinted by permission of the publisher from *Sor Juana* by Octavio Paz, translated by Margaret Sayers Peden, p. 299, Cambridge, Mass: The Belknap Press of Harvard University Press, copyright © 1988 by the President and Fellows of Harvard College.

"A Canary's Ideas" from *The Devil's Church and Other Stories* by Joaquim Maria Machado de Assis, translated by Jack Schmitt and Lori Ishimatsu, copyright © 1977. By permission of the University of Texas Press.

"The Luck of Teodoro Mendez Acubal" from *Another Way to Be: Selected Works of Rosario Castellanos,* by Rosario Castellanos, foreword by Edward D. Terry. Copyright © 1990 by The University of Georgia Press. Reprinted by permission.

"Horses" from *A New Decade,* by Pablo Neruda. English translation copyright © 1969 by Alistair Reid. Used by permission of Grove/ Atlantic, Inc.

"The Panther," copyright © 1982 by Stephen Mitchell, from *The Selected Poetry of Rainer Maria Rilke* by Rainer Maria Rilke, translated by Stephen Mitchell. Used by permission of Random House, Inc.

"The Iguana" from *Out of Africa* by Isak Dinesen, copyright 1937 by Random House, Inc. and renewed 1965 by Rungstedlundfonden. Used by permission of Random House, Inc.

"The Red Cockatoo," by Po Chu-yi, from *Anthology of Chinese Literature,* edited by Cyril Birch. Copyright © 1995 by Grove Press, Inc. Used by permission of Grove/Atlantic, Inc.

"Fable" by Octavio Paz, translated by Muriel Rukeyser, from *Early Poems 1935-1955,* copyright © 1973 by Octavio Paz and Muriel Rukeyser. Reprinted by permission of New Directions Publishing Corp.

From "Between What I See and What I Say…" by Octavio Paz, translated by Eliot Weinberger, from *Collected Poems 1957-1987,* copyright © 1986 by Octavio Paz and Eliot Weinberger. Reprinted by permission of New directions Publishing Corp.

"The Handsomest Drowned Man in the World" from *Leaf Storm and Other Stories* by Gabriel García Márquez. Copyright © 1971 by Gabriel García Márquez. Reprinted by permission of HarperCollins Publishers.

"Bishop Berkley or Mariana of the Universe" by Liliana Heker is reprinted with permission from the publisher of *Short Stories by Latin American Women,* edited by Celia Correas de Zapata (© 1990 Arte Publico Press-University of Houston).

From *My Invented Country: A Nostalgic Journey Through Chile* by Isabel Allende. Translated by Margaret Sayers Peden. Copyright © 2003 by Isabel Allende. Translation copyright © 2003 by HarperCollins Publishers Inc. Reprinted by permission of HarperCollins Publishers.

"Fishing" from *The Woman Who Fell From the Sky* by Joy Harjo. Copyright © 1994 by Joy Harjo. Used by permission of W.W. Norton & Company, Inc.

From "For Alva Benson, and for Those Who Have Learned to Speak" by Joy Harjo. Reprtined by permission of the author.

From Rena Korb's article on Gabriel García Márquez, from *Short Stories for Students, Presenting Analysis, Context and Criticism on Commonly Studied Short Stories* by Kathleen Wilson. Reprinted with permission of Thomson Learning: www.thomsonrights.com. FAX: 800-730-2215.

From *House of the Spirits* by Isabel Allende, translated by Magda Bogin, copyright © 1985 by Alfred A. Knopf, A Division of Random House Inc. Used by permission of Alfred A. Knopf, a division of Random House, Inc.

Photography

Cover Erich Lessing/Art Resource, NY (bkgd) Farinaz Taghavi/Getty Images 2 Bridgeman Art Library/Getty Images; **4** (t)Digital Vision/PunchStock; (b)Michel Gounot/Godong/CORBIS; **5** Christie's Images; **6** (tl)HIP/Art Resource, NY; (tr)Boltin Picture Library/Bridgeman Art Library; (c)Erich Lessing/Art Resource, NY; (b)The Art Archive/Museo Capitolino Rome/Alfredo Dagli Ort; **7** (tl)Werner Forman/Art Resource, NY; (tr)British Library, London/Bridgeman Art Library; (cl)Museo Nacional de Antropologia, Mexico City/Giraudon/Bridgeman Art Library; (cr)Martin Gray/National Geographic Image Collection; (b)HIP/Art Resource, NY; **8** The Art Archive/Bibliothèque Musée du Louvre/Gianni Dagli Orti; **9** Boltin Picture Library/Bridgeman Art Library; **10** (l)Glen Allison/Getty Images; (r)Horniman Museum, London/Heini Schneebeli/Bridgeman Art Library; **11** Werner Forman/CORBIS; **12** The Art Archive/Ragab Papyrus Institute Cairo/Gianni Dagli Orti; **13** Private Collection/Heini Schneebeli/Bridgeman Art Library; **14** Private Collection, Paul Freeman/Bridgeman Art Library; **15** Scala/Art Resource, NY; **18** HIP/Art Resource, NY; **20** Erich Lessing/Art Resource, NY; **21** Comstock/PunchStock; **24** Erich Lessing/Art Resource, NY; **26** Gianni Dagli Orti/CORBIS; **28** Bildarchiv Preussischer Kulturbesitz/Art Resource, NY; **31** Valley of the Kings, Thebes, Egypt, Held Collection/Bridgeman Art Library; **32** Werner Forman/Art Resource, NY; **34** British Museum, London/Bridgeman Art Library; **35** The Art Archive/Dagli Orti; **38** The Metropolitan Museum of Art/Art Resource, NY; **39** Private Collection, Photo ©Bonhams, London, UK/Bridgeman Art Library; **40** Private Collection, Photo ©Boltin Picture Library/Bridgeman Art Library; **42** Private Collection, Photo ©Heini Schneebeli/Bridgeman Art Library; **44** Museo Nacional de Antropologia, Mexico City/Michel Zabe/AZA/Bridgeman Art Library; **47** Private Collection, Roger Perrin/Bridgeman Art Library; **48** Private Collection/Bridgeman Art Library; **51 53** C.A.A.C - The Pigozzi Collection, Geneva; **56–57** (t)Authors Image/Alamy Images; Jason Lauré; **60** Musee Barbier-Mueller, Geneva/Heini Schneebeli/Bridgeman Art Library; **61** Andy Crawford/Getty Images; **62** Brooklyn Museum/CORBIS; **64** (t)Private Collection/Bridgeman Art Library; (b)Joseph Van Os/Stone/Getty Images; **67** Indianapolis Museum of Art, IN, Gift of Mr and Mrs Harrison Eiteljorg/Bridgeman Art Library; **68** (t)Mary Evans/The Womens Library; (c)Private Collection/Michael Graham-Stewart/Bridgeman Art Library; (bl)Imperial War Museum, London/Bridgeman Art Library; (br)Private Collection/Bridgeman Art Library; **69** (t)Ulf Andersen/Getty Images; (c)AP Images; (b)AFP/Getty Images; **70** Private Collection/Michael Graham-Stewart/Bridgeman Art Library; **71** Alain DeJean/Sygma/CORBIS; **72** (l)Rick D'Elia/CORBIS; (r)Atlantide Phototravel/CORBIS; **73** Lindsay Hebberd/CORBIS; **74** The Newark Museum/Art Resource, NY; **75** Bernard Bisson/CORBIS SYGMA; **76** Louise Gubb/CORBIS SABA; **77** Schomburg Center/Art Resource, NY; **78** Felix Man/Stringer/Getty Images; **80** Held Collection/Bridgeman Art Library; **83** Reza; Webstan/CORBIS; **85** David A. Land/Jupiter Images; **87** Robert Harding Picture Library Ltd/Alamy Images; **92** AFP/Getty Images; **94** Private Collection/Bridgeman Art Library; **96** J.Garcia/photocuisine/CORBIS; **98** Contemporary African Art Collection Limited/CORBIS; **103 105** David Turnley/CORBIS; **107** John Newcomb/SuperStock; **109** Private Collection/Bridgeman Art Library; **113** (t)Christie's Images; (b)Frans Lemmens/Alamy Images; **115** Wendy L. Goldberg-Hammon/Stock

Illustration RF/Getty Images; **117** (l c)Getty Images; **120** Ulf Andersen/Getty mages; **122** Ariadne Van Zandbergen/Alamy Images; **124** George Hallett; **126** Photodisc/PunchStock; **128** Private Collection/Michael Graham-Stewart/Bridgeman Art Library; **129** Heini Schneebeli/Bridgeman Art Library; **133** Graham Jepson/Writer Pictures; **135** Jeffrey L. Rotman/CORBIS; **137** Bettmann/CORBIS; **138** C.A.A.C. - The Pigozzi Collection, Geneva; **141** Private Collection/Bridgeman Art Library; **146** Angelo Cavalli/Getty Images; **149** Private Collection, Curwen Gallery/Bridgeman Art Library; **151** Collection of HM King Hussein of Jordan/Bridgeman Art Library; **152** Brand X Pictures/JupiterImages; **156** Khali Mazraawl/AFP/GETTY; **159** Darren Greenwood/Design Pics/CORBIS; **163** Stockbyte/PunchStock; **168** (l)Lindsey Gable/The McGraw-Hill Companies; (r)Grey Villet/Time & Life Pictures/Getty Images; **169** (l)The McGraw-Hill Companies; Eliot Elisofon/Time & Life Pictures/Getty Images; Jacques Langevin/CORBIS SYGMA; **178** (t)Reed Kaestner/CORBIS; (b)Schmitz-Söhnigen/zefa/CORBIS; **179** Erich Lessing/Art Resource, NY; **180** (tl)Nationalmuseet, Copenhagen/Bridgeman Art Library; (tr)Nimatallah/Art Resource, NY; (cl)Scala/Art Resource, NY; (cr)Erich Lessing/Art Resource, NY; (b)Snark/Art Resource, NY; **181** (tr tl)Scala/Art Resource, NY; (bl)Borromeo/Art Resource, NY; (bc br)Erich Lessing/Art Resource, NY; **182** Réunion des Musées Nationaux/Art Resource, NY; **183** British Museum, London/Bridgeman Art Library; **184** (t)Scala/Art Resource, NY; (b)Erich Lessing/Art Resource, NY; **185** (t)Bettmann/CORBIS; (b)Bridgeman Art Library; **186** Erich Lessing/Art Resource, NY; **187** Bildarchiv Preussischer Kulturbesitz/Art Resource, NY; **188** Scala/Art Resource, NY; **189** Mike Blake/Reuters/CORBIS; **190** The Metropolitan Museum of Art/Art Resource, NY; **191** Ashmolean Museum, University of Oxford/Bridgeman Art Library; **192** The Art Archive/Museo Capitolino Rome/Alfredo Dagli Orti; **194** Giraudon/Art Resource, NY; **197** Scala/Art Resource, NY; **199** Christie's Images; **204 206 211** Scala/Art Resource, NY; **214** Erich Lessing/Art Resource, NY; **219** Philip Harrington/The National Museum, Athens/National Geographic Society; **220** Giraudon/Art Resource, NY; **222** Museum of Fine Arts, Boston, Massachusetts, William Francis Warden Fund/Bridgeman Art Library; **226** Fitzwilliam Museum, University of Cambridge,/Bridgeman Art Library; **228** Christie's Images; **229** Getty Images; **232** (b)Galleria degli Uffizi, Florence, Italy/Bridgeman Art Library; **232–233** (t)Claudio H. Artman/Alamy Images; **233** (b)akg London; **234** The Art Archive/National Archaeological Museum Athens/Gianni Dagli Orti; **234** Victoria & Albert Museum, London/Bridgeman Art Library; **236** National Geographic; **237** Erich Lessing/Art Resource, NY; **238** The Art Archive/Archaeological Museum Delphi/Gianni Dagli Orti; **239** National Geographic; **241** Scala/Art Resource, NY; **244** Victoria & Albert Museum, London/Bridgeman Art Library; **248** Sheridan/Ancient Art & Architecture Collection; **249** Paul A. Souders/CORBIS, **250** Gianni Dagli Orti/CORBIS; **252** The Israel Museum, Jerusalem, ©DACS/Vera & Arturo Schwarz Collection of Dada and Surrealist Art/Bridgeman Art Library; **255** ©1998 Kate Rothko-Prizel & Christopher Rothko/Artists Rights Society, New York/Art Resource, NY; **256** Staatliche Museen, Berlin/Bridgeman Art Library; **261** Arte & Immagini srl/CORBIS; **262** C. M Dixon/Ancient Art & Architecture Collection Ltd; **267** Tate Gallery, London/Art Resource, NY; **272** Christie's Images; **281** SuperStock; **288** Erich Lessing/Art Resource, NY; **295** Christie's Images; **300** Donald Cooper/Photostage; **305 315** Erich Lessing/Art Resource, NY; **316** (l c)Getty Images; **316** (b)The Art Archive/Museo Nazionale Taranto/Gianni Dagli Orti; **320 322** Erich Lessing/Art Resource, NY; **327** INTERFOTO Pressebildagentur/Alamy Images; **328** The Detroit Institute of Arts, Founders Society Purchase/Bridgeman Art Library; **329** Vanni/Art Resource, NY; **334** Réunion des Musées Nationaux/Art Resource, NY; **337** Alinari/Art Resource, NY; **343** Karen Moskowitz; **344** HIP/Art Resource, NY; **346** (t)Anthony Cassidy/JAI/CORBIS; (b)Alessandro Saffo/Grand Tour/CORBIS; **347** Bildarchiv Preussischer Kulturbesitz/Art Resource, NY; Giraudon/Art Resource, NY; **348** (tl)Musee National du Bardo, Le Bardo, Tunisia/Giraudon/Bridgeman Art Library; (tr cl cr br)Scala/Art Resource, NY; (bl)Liu Liqun/CORBIS; **349** (tl)Louvre, Paris/Bridgeman Art Library; (bl)Metropolitan Museum of Art, New York/

Bridgeman Art Library; (br)Werner Forman/Art Resource, NY; **350** Bibliotheque Nationale, Paris/Bridgeman Art Library; **351** Private Collection, Alinari/Bridgeman Art Library; **352** (l)British Museum, London/Bridgeman Art Library; (r)Atlantide Phototravel/CORBIS; **353** Scala/Art Resource, NY; **354** The Art Archive/Musée Archéologique Naples/Alfredo Dagli Orti; **355** Scala/Art Resource, NY; **356** Gianni Dagli Orti/CORBIS; **357** Mitchell Gerber/CORBIS; **358** The Granger Collection; **359** Scala/Art Resource, NY; **360** Bradford City Art Gallery and Museum, England/SuperStock; **363** Scala/Art Resource, NY; **365** Museo della Civilta Romana, Rome, Italy/Bridgeman Art Library; **368** Scala/Art Resource, NY; **373** De Morgan Foundation, London/SuperStock; **376** Roger Wood/CORBIS; **378** National Gallery, London/SuperStock; **381** The De Morgan Centre, London/Bridgeman Art Library; **385** San Diego Museum of Art/Bridgeman Art Library; **393** Christie's Images; **396** (tl tc)Getty Images; (b)Bildarchiv Preussischer Kulturbesitz/Art Resource, NY; 400 Ashmolean Museum, University of Oxford, UK/Bridgeman Art Library; **401** akg-images; **403** Buddy Mays/CORBIS; **404** Giraudon/Art Resource, NY; **405** Royalty-Free/CORBIS; **410** Underwood & Underwood/CORBIS; **412** Bettmann/CORBIS; **413** Private Collection, England & Co. Gallery, London/Bridgeman Art Library; **415** Bettmann/CORBIS; **418** Boltin Picture Library/Bridgeman Art Library; **421** Held Collection/Bridgeman Art Library; **424** Ancient Art and Architecture Collection Ltd./Bridgeman Art Library; **426** (l)Time & Life Pictures/Getty Images; (r)Museo Capitolino, Rome, Italy/Bridgeman Art Library; **427** (l)The McGraw-Hill Companies; (c)Lindsey Gable/The McGraw-Hill Companies; (r)Museo Archeologico Nazionale, Naples/Bridgeman Art Library; **436** (t)Jose Fuste Raga/CORBIS; (t)Peter Horree/Alamy Images; (c)Gary J. Antonetti, Ortelius Design, Inc.; (b)Gary Braasch/CORBIS; **438** (c)Gianni Dagli Orti/CORBIS; (bl)Bettmann/CORBIS; (br)Museum of Fine Arts, Houston, TX, Museum purchase funded by 'One Great Night in November 1988'/Bridgeman Art Library; **439** (t)The Trustees of the Chester Beatty Library, Dublin/Bridgeman Art Library; (c)Sandro Vannini/CORBIS; (c)West Semitic Research/Dead Sea Scrolls Foundation/CORBIS; **440** Kazuyoshi Nomachi/CORBIS; **441** Louvre, Paris/Bridgeman Art Library; **442** (l)Ashmolean Museum, University of Oxford, UK/Bridgeman Art Library; (r)Hans Georg Roth/CORBIS; **443** Murat Taner/zefa/CORBIS; **444** Instituto da Biblioteca Nacional, Lisbon, Portugal/Bridgeman Art Library; **445** Victoria & Albert Museum, London/Art Resource, NY; **446** Israel Museum, Jerusalem/Bridgeman Art Library; **447** Private Collection, ©DACS /Roger Perrin/Bridgeman Art Library; **448** Erich Lessing/Art Resource, NY; **450** Louvre, Paris, France, Peter Willi/Bridgeman Art Library; **452** Michael Holford; **455** Mary Evans Picture Library; **456** Victoria & Albert Museum, London/Art Resource, NY; **457** akg-images; **461** Museo Archeologico Prenestino, Palestrina, Italy, Roger-Viollet, Paris/Bridgeman Art Library; **462** Erich Lessing/Art Resource, NY; **464** (l c)Getty Images; (b)Reuters/CORBIS; **467** HIP/Art Resource, NY; **469** Victoria & Albert Museum, London/Art Resource, NY; **470** The Jewish Museum, NY/Art Resource, NY; **472** San Marco, Venice, Italy, Lauros/Giraudon/Bridgeman Art Library; **481** Southampton City Art Gallery, Hampshire, UK/Bridgeman Art Library; **483** (l c)Getty Images; (b)Scala/Art Resource, NY; **486** British Library Board. All Rights Reserved/Bridgeman Art Library; **487** Cameraphoto Arte, Venice/Art Resource, NY; **489** Erich Lessing/Art Resource, NY; **491** Bibliotheque Nationale, Paris/Bridgeman Art Library; **493 494** Giraudon/Art Resource, NY; **496** Private Collection, Roger Perrin/Bridgeman Art Library; **498** Freer Gallery of Art, Smithsonian Institution, Washington D.C.; **499** Goodshoot/Fotosearch; **500 502** Freer Gallery of Art, Smithsonian Institution, Washington D.C.; **505** The Fine Art Society, London/Bridgeman Art Library; **507** Chehel Sotun, or 'The 40 Columns', Isfahan, Iran, Giraudon/Bridgeman Art Library; **508** Bonhams, London/Bridgeman Art Library; **511** akg London; **513** Art Resource, NY; **518** Private Collection/Bridgeman Art Library; **520** Haaratz/Writer Pictures; **522** Martin Harvey; Gallo Images/CORBIS; **524** peitschphoto.com/Writer Pictures; **526 528** Private Collection/Bridgeman Art Library; **529** age_fotostock/SuperStock; **530** Private Collection/Bridgeman Art Library; **532** Eric Robert/VIP Production/

CORBIS; **534–540** Marjane Satrapi; **543** Khalil Mazraawi/AFP/Getty Images; **544** ©2002 Tom Stoddart; **546** (t)Ric Ergenbright/CORBIS; (c)Gary J. Antonetti, Ortelius Design, Inc.; (b)Sheldan Collins/CORBIS; **547** Jason Horowitz/zefa/CORBIS; **548** (tl)Bibliotheque Nationale, Paris, Archives Charmet/Bridgeman Art Library; (tr)Redlink/CORBIS; (c)Victoria & Albert Museum, London/Bridgeman Art Library; (b)The Granger Collection, New York; **549** (t)CORBIS SYGMA; (cr)Hulton-Deutsch Collection/CORBIS; (cr)Private Collection, The Stapleton Collection/Bridgeman Art Library; (b)Musee Conde, Chantilly, France/Bridgeman Art Library; (ct)Stapleton Collection/CORBIS; **550** National Museum of Karachi, Pakistan/Bridgeman Art Library; **551** Ashmolean Museum, University of Oxford, UK/Bridgeman Art Library; **552** (l)Horniman Museum, London/Photo ©Heini Schneebeli/Bridgeman Art Library; (r)Stapleton Collection, UK/Bridgeman Art Library; **553** Dinodia Photo Library/Brand X/CORBIS; **554** Victoria & Albert Museum, London,The Stapleton Collection/Bridgeman Art Library; **555** Reuters/CORBIS; **556** Thierry Prat/Sygma/CORBIS; **557** Robbie Jack/CORBIS; **558** Freud Museum, London/Bridgeman Art Library; **560** National Museum of India, New Delhi/Bridgeman Art Library; **561** Werner Forman/Art Resource, NY; **563** National Museum of India, New Delhi/Bridgeman Art Library; **565** Réunion des Musées Nationaux/Art Resource, NY; **567** Private Collection, The Stapleton Collection/Bridgeman Art Library; **568** Surya Temple, Somnath, Mumbai, India, Dinodia/Bridgeman Art Library; **570** The Pierpont Morgan Library/Art Resource, NY; **571** Getty Images; **574** Free Agents Limited/CORBIS; **574–575** (t) Iconotec/Alamy Images; **575** (b)Owen Franken/CORBIS; **576** ©Raghu Rai/Magnum Photos; **579** The Metropolitan Museum of Art/Art Resource, NY; **580** Jeffrey L. Rotman/CORBIS; **582** ©British Museum/Art Resource, NY; **584** Erich Lessing/Art Resource, NY; **587** HIP/Art Resource, NY; **588** Photodisc/PunchStock; **591** Private Collection, Archives Charmet/Bridgeman Art Library; **594** The Pierpont Morgan Library/Art Resource, NY; **595** Giraudon/Art Resource, NY; **597** The Metropolitan Museum of Art/Art Resource, NY; **598** Christie's Images/Bridgeman Art Library; **601** akg-images; **603** Bridgeman Art Library/SuperStock; **606** Private Collection, Archives Charmet/Bridgeman Art Library; **607** E.O. Hoppé/CORBIS; **609** Private Collection/Bridgeman Art Library; **611** Author's Image; **613** BananaStock/PunchStock; **615** Bradford Art Galleries and Museums, West Yorkshire, UK/Bridgeman Art Library; **616** (l c)Getty Images; (b)Alinari Archives/CORBIS; **621** Fry Art Gallery, Saffron Walden, Essex/Bridgeman Art Library; **623** Private Collection/Bridgeman Art Library; **625** Hulton Archive/Getty Images; **627** Private Collection/Bridgeman Art Library; **629** arabianEye FZ LLC/Alamy Images; **630** Private Collection/Bridgeman Art Library; **636** Neil McAllister/Alamy Images; **638** Ignacio Auzike/ArtBox Images/Getty Images; **640** Edward North/Alamy Images; **641** Private Collection/Bridgeman Art Library; **643** Arts Council Collection, Hayward Gallery, London/Bridgeman Art Library; **644** Private Collection, Will's Art Warehouse, London/Bridgeman Art Library; **647** Bill Lyons Photography; **649** Chris Rainier/CORBIS; **653** Will & Deni McIntyre/CORBIS; **656** Dan Guravich/CORBIS; **660 661** Bob Sciarrino/Star Ledger/CORBIS; **662** (l)Royal Asiatic Society, London/Bridgeman Art Library; (r)The McGraw-Hill Companies; **663** (t c b)The McGraw-Hill Companies; **672** (t)Bruno Levy/zefa/CORBIS; **672** (b)Keren Su/Getty Images; **673** Tomb of Qin shi Huang Di, Xianyang, China/Bridgeman Art Library; **674** (t)Lee & Lee Communications/Alamy Images; (cl)Asian Art & Archaeology, Inc./CORBIS; (cr)Tomb of Qin shi Huang Di, Xianyang, China/Bridgeman Art Library; (b)Danny Lehman/CORBIS; **675** (tl)The Art Archive; (tr)Micheline Pelletier/CORBIS; (cl)Werner Forman/Art Resource, NY; (cr)Hans Gedda/Sygma/CORBIS; (b)Private Collection, ©Michael Graham-Stewart/Bridgeman Art Library; **676** Scala/Art Resource, NY; **677** Private Collection/Bridgeman Art Library; **678** (t)Stapleton Collection, UK/Bridgeman Art Library; (b)Marc Garanger/CORBIS; **679** Frank Leather; Eye Ubiquitous/CORBIS; **680** Oriental Museum, Durham University, UK/Bridgeman Art Library; **681** HIP/Art Resource, NY; **682** British Library, London/©British Library Board. All Rights Reserved/Bridgeman Art Library; **683** Brooklyn Museum of Art, New

York, USA/Bridgeman Art Library; **684** Vanni/Art Resource, NY; **685** Bibliotheque Nationale, Paris/Bridgeman Art Library; **689** Bibliotheque Nationale, Paris, Archives Charmet/Bridgeman Art Library; **690** Erich Lessing/Art Resource, NY; **691** Art Institute of Chicago; **694** Erich Lessing/Art Resource, NY; **695** Brooklyn Museum of Art, New York, Gift of Anna Ferris /Bridgeman Art Library; **696** The Cleveland Museum of Art; **699** HIP/Art Resource, NY; **700–701** (t)Photodisc/PunchStock; (b)Private Collection, Photo ©Christie's Images/Bridgeman Art Library; **702** David Forbert/SuperStock; **704** Private Collection, Giraudon/ Bridgeman Art Library; **705** Christie's Images; **707** Roger Wood/ CORBIS; **709** Underwood & Underwood/CORBIS; **711** Dave Bartruff/ CORBIS; **712** Victoria & Albert Museum, London/Art Resource, NY; **713** UCL Art Collections, University College London/Bridgeman Art Library; **714** Katsushika Hokusai/Bridgeman Art Library/Getty Images; **716** Musee des Beaux-Arts, Angers, Giraudon/Bridgeman Art Library; **719** British Library Board. All Rights Reserved/Bridgeman Art Library; **721** Private Collection/Bridgeman Art Library; **723** Dean Conger/CORBIS; **725** The Stapleton Collection/Bridgeman Art Library; **726** Asian Art & Archaeology, Inc./CORBIS; **726** Getty Images; **730** Artkey/CORBIS; **733** Mary Evans Picture Library; **736** Guthrie/Art Resource, NY; **737** Reuters/CORBIS; **738** Snark/Art Resource, NY; **739** Victoria & Albert Museum, London/Bridgeman Art Library; **740** The Art Institute of Chicago; **742** The Trustees of the Chester Beatty Library, Dublin/ Bridgeman Art Library; **745** Brooklyn Museum of Art, New York, Frank L. Babbott Fund/Bridgeman Art Library; **746** The Trustees of the Chester Beatty Library, Dublin/Bridgeman Art Library; **748** Ann Arbor/Writer Pictures; **751** Jacques Langevin/CORBIS SYGMA; **753** AGIP RA/ Lebrecht Music & Arts; **755** The Art Insititue of Chicago; **757** Leeds Museums and Art Galleries (City Museum) UK/Bridgeman Art Library; **759** (t)Getty Images; (b)Private Collection, Paul Freeman/Bridgeman Art Library; **762** AGIP RA/Lebrecht Music & Arts; **763** Gahoe Museum, Jongno-gu, South Korea/Bridgeman Art Library; **764** Victoria & Albert Museum, London/Art Resource, NY; **766** ChinaStock; **768** China Photos/Getty Images; **771** Greg Davis/OnAsia Images; **772** Tetsuya Miura, **774** (t)Douglas Pearson/CORBIS; **774** (b)Private Collection, ©Agnew's, London/Bridgeman Art Library; **775** Erich Lessing/Art Resource, NY; **776** (t)LonelyPlanetImages; (b)Wolfgang Kaehler/ CORBIS; (bl)The Art Archive/Mireille Vautier; **777** (tl)Private Collection/ Bridgeman Art Library; (tr)David Van Der Veen/epa/CORBIS; (c)Commonwealth Institute, London/Bridgeman Art Library; (b)Ray Moreton/Hulton Archive/GettyImages; **778** Jose Fuste Raga/CORBIS; **779** The Art Archive/Private Collection/Marc Charmet; **780** (l)Bob Krist/CORBIS; (r)Gian Berto Vanni/CORBIS; **781** Christine Osborne/ CORBIS; **782** Jacques Pavlovsky/Sygma/CORBIS; **783** Stuart Westmorland/CORBIS; **784** The Art Archive; **785** Bettmann/CORBIS; **786** ©The Metropolitan Museum of Art/Art Resource, NY; **787** Private Collection, Photo ©Boltin Picture Library/Bridgeman Art Library; **788** SuperStock; **790** Bettmann/CORBIS; **792** Private Collection, ©DACS/ Bridgeman Art Library; **794** Photodisc/PunchStock; **797** Pushkin Museum, Moscow/©DACS/Bridgeman Art Library; **799** (l c)Getty Images; (b)Victoria & Albert Museum, London/Art Resource, NY; **802** NLA/Writer Pictures; **804** Digital Vision/PunchStock; **806** Oliver Strewe/CORBIS; **808** Penny Tweedie/CORBIS; **810** Courtesy of The Otago Daily Times; **811** Werner Forman/Art Resource, NY; **814** Private Collection/Bridgeman Art Library; **817** Indochina Arts Partnership; **819** Sophie Bassouls/CORBIS SYGMA; **821 825** Courtesy of Monirith Chhea; **829** Courtesy of Albert Wendt; **831** TIMOTCA, Laguna Beach, CA; **832** Art Wolfe; **836** Bettmann/CORBIS; **838** Lisa Pines/ GettyImages; **843** Bruce Laurance/GettyImages; **844** Ryan Pyle/None/ CORBIS; **846** Private Collection/Bridgeman Art Library; **848** (l)Ulla Montan/Writer Pictures; (r)R.S. Criddle/Cover: Jeanne K. Pietrzak; **849** (t b)The McGraw-Hill Companies; (r)Courtesy Penguin Books; **856** Photothèque R. Magritte-ADAGP/Art Resource, NY; **858** (t)Herbert Spichtinger/zefa/CORBIS; (b)Victoria & Albert Museum, London/Art Resource, NY; **859** Germanisches Nationalmuseum, Nuremberg/ Bridgeman Art Library; **860** (tl b)Werner Forman/Art Resource, NY; (tr)Private Collection, Lauros/Giraudon/Bridgeman Art Library; (cl cr)Erich Lessing/Art Resource, NY; **861** (t)Palazzo Vecchio (Palazzo della Signoria) Florence/Bridgeman Art Library; (cl)Erich Lessing/Art Resource, NY; (cr)Tokyo Fuji Art Museum, Japan/Bridgeman Art Library; (b)British Library, London/Bridgeman Art Library; **862** SuperStock; **863** Sotheby's Picture Library, London/Bridgeman Art Library; **864** SuperStock; **865** (l)Scala/Art Resource, NY; (r)Erich Lessing/Art Resource, NY; **866** HIP/Art Resource, NY; **867** Erich Lessing/Art Resource, NY; **868 869** Scala/Art Resource, NY; **872** Arni Magnusson Institute, Reykjavik/Bridgeman Art Library; **877** Giraudon/Art Resource, NY; **879** Scala/Art Resource, NY; **881** Germanisches Nationalmuseum, Nuremberg/Bridgeman Art Library; **884** akg-Images; **886** Writer Pictures; **888** SuperStock; **891** Huntington Library/SuperStock; **894** Bibliotheque Nationale, Paris/Bridgeman Art Library; **896** Bibliotheque des Arts Decoratifs, Paris, Archives Charmet/Bridgeman Art Library; **900** British Museum, London/Bridgeman Art Library; **905** Christie's Images; **906** SuperStock; **912** (t)Getty Images; (b)The Art Archive/Biblioteca Nazionale Marciana Venice/Alfredo Dagli Orti; **915** HIP/Art Resource, NY; **918** Alte Pinakothek, Munich, Giraudon/Bridgeman Art Library; **919** Alinari/Art Resource, NY; **921** Kunsthistorisches Museum, Vienna/ Bridgeman Art Library; **923** The Maas Gallery, London/Bridgeman Art Library; **924** Collection of Gustau Camps, Barcelona/Bridgeman Art Library; **925** Art Resource, NY; **926** Erich Lessing/Art Resource, NY; **928** SuperStock; **930** Pushkin Museum of Fine Arts, Moscow/ SuperStock; **932** The Pierpont Morgan Library/Art Resource, NY; **934** Giraudon/Art Resource, NY; **935** Private Collection, Ken Welsh/ Bridgeman Art Library; **937** akg-Images; **940** Harris Museum and Art Gallery, Preston, Lancashire/Bridgeman Art Library; **943** Bonhams, London/Bridgeman Art Library; **945** Getty Images; **948** (b)Paul Almasy/CORBIS; (t)Jose Fuste Raga/CORBIS; **949** Tate, London/Art Resource, NY; **950** (t)The Art Archive/Musée du Louvre Paris/Gianni Dagli Orti; (c)Timothy McCarthy/Art Resource, NY; (b)Pennsylvania Academy of the Fine Arts/Bridgeman Art Library; **951** (t)SOPHIE BASSOULS/CORBIS SYGMA; (cl)HIP/Art Resource, NY; (c)Snark/Art Resource, NY; (cr)Stephen Ferry/Getty Images; (b)Bettmann/CORBIS; (br)Philippe Wojazer/Reuters/CORBIS; **952** Musee d'Orsay, Paris, Giraudon/Bridgeman Art Library; **953** Bettmann/CORBIS; **954** (l)Stapleton Collection, UK/Bridgeman Art Library; (r)Geoffrey Clements/CORBIS; **955** Philadelphia Museum of Art, Pennsylvania, PA©DACS/Bridgeman Art Library; **956** Hamburger Kunsthalle, Hamburg/Bridgeman Art Library; **957** Erich Lessing/Art Resource, NY; **958** THE GRANGER COLLECTION; **959** Metropolitan Museum of Art, New York ©DACS/Bridgeman Art Library; **960** Bridgeman-Giraudon/Art Resource, NY; **966** Pushkin Museum, Moscow, Giraudon/Bridgeman Art Library; **967** (b)Bildarchiv Preussischer Kulturbesitz/Art Resource, NY; (t)Getty Images; **970** Wallace Collection, London/Bridgeman Art Library; **971** Bibliotheque de l'Opera Garnier, Paris, Joseph Martin/ Bridgeman Art Library; **972** Bildarchiv Preussischer Kulturbesitz/Art Resource, NY; **973** nagelestock.com/Alamy Images; **974** Russell-Cotes Art Gallery and Museum, Bournemouth/Bridgeman Art Library; **976** Stapleton Collection/CORBIS; **978** Sotheby's Picture Library, London; **980** akg-images; **983** Adoc-photos/Art Resource, NY; **985** State Russian Museum, Moscow/Scala/Art Resource, NY; **987** Chris Hammond/Alamy Images; **988** akg-images; **992** Christie's Images; **997** (b)CORBIS; (t)Getty Images; **1001** Bettmann/CORBIS; **1003** Nationalmuseum, Stockholm ©DACS/Bridgeman Art Library; **1005** State Russian Museum, St. Petersburg, Russia/Bridgeman Art Library; **1009** (l c)Getty Images; (b)Underwood & Underwood/CORBIS; **1012** Bettmann/CORBIS; **1013** Musee d'Orsay, Paris, Lauros/Giraudon/ Bridgeman Art Library; **1014** Private Collection, Archives Charmet/ Bridgeman Art Library; **1016** The Fine Art Society, London/Bridgeman Art Library; **1019** Musee de la Ville de Paris, Musee Carnavalet, Paris, Archives Charmet/Bridgeman Art Library; **1021** The State Russian Museum/CORBIS; **1022** The Detroit Institute of Arts, Founders Society Purchase, R.H. Tannahill Foundation fund/Bridgeman Art Library; **1023** Rafael Valls Gallery, London/Bridgeman Art Library; **1025** Bettmann/ CORBIS; **1027** Fry Art Gallery, Saffron Walden, Essex, UK/Bridgeman Art Library; **1032** Musee d'Art Moderne Richard Anacreon, Granville,

France, Archives Charmet/Bridgeman Art Library; **1035** (l)CNAC/ MNAM/Dist. Réunion des Musées Nationaux/Art Resource, NY; **1035** (r)Photodisc/GettyImages; **1036** Sotheby's Picture Library, London; 1038 (t)Getty Images; (b)Private Collection, Archives Charmet/ Bridgeman Art Library; **1041** Geraint Lewis/Writer Pictures; **1042** The Museum of Modern Art/Licensed by SCALA/Art Resource, NY; **1043** Isabella Stewart Gardner Museum, Boston/Bridgeman Art Library; **1045** Sophie Bassouls/CORBIS SYGMA; **1046** National Museum in Cracow, Poland/Bridgeman Art Library; 1046 Sotheby's Picture Library, London; **1049** Courtesy Persea Books; **1051** Hardware Gallery, London/Bridgeman Art Library; **1054** DigitalVision/Getty Images; **1054–1055** Iconotec/Alamy Images; **1055** Swim Ink 2, LLC/CORBIS; **1056** Roger Viollet/Getty Images; **1058** (l)Getty Images; (r)Erich Lessing/Art Resource, NY; **1063** Eddie Adams/Sygma/CORBIS; **1065** Courtesy Alfred Tibor; **1067** Digital Image ©The Museum of Modern Art/Licensed by SCALA/Art Resource, NY; **1072** Tim Brakemeier/dpa/ CORBIS; **1073** ©1999 Artists Rights Society (ARS)/ADAGP, Paris/ Sotheby's Picture Library, London; **1074** State Russian Museum, St. Petersburg/Bridgeman Art Library; **1077** Bettmann/CORBIS; **1078** Reuters/CORBIS; **1079** Lynn Goldsmith/CORBIS; **1080** Jim Sugar/ CORBIS; **1085** Newport Museum and Art Gallery, South Wales/ Bridgeman Art Library; **1087** Royalty-Free/CORBIS; **1095** (l)Archivo Iconografico, S.A./CORBIS; (r)Lindsey Gable/The McGraw-Hill Companies; **1096** (l)Réunion des Musées Nationaux/Art Resource, NY; (r)Hulton-Deutsch Collection/CORBIS; **1097** (t cl b)The McGraw-Hill Companies; (cr)AGIP RA/Lebrecht Music & Arts; **1104** Schalkwijk/Art Resource, NY; **1106** (t)Wolfgang Kaehler Photography; (b)Charles & Josette Lenars/CORBIS; (c)Gary J. Antonetti, Ortelius Design, Inc.; **1107** British Museum, London/Bridgeman Art Library; **1108** (t)The Art Archive/Antochiw Collection Mexico/Mireille Vautier; (b)The Art Archive/British Museum/Harper Collins Publishers; **1109** (t)Museo Nacional de Historia, Mexico City/Bridgeman Art Library; (cl)The Art Archive/Manuel Cohen; (c)The Art Archive/Monastery of the Rabida, Palos, Spain/Gianni Dagli Orti; (cr)The Art Archive/American Museum Madrid; (bl)Private Collection, Photo ©Heini Schneebeli/Bridgeman Art Library; (br)Bettmann/CORBIS; **1110** Bettmann/CORBIS; **1111** Archivo Iconografico, S.A./CORBIS; **1112** (t)Charles & Josette Lenars/ CORBIS; (b)Erich Lessing/Art Resource, NY; **1113** Lindsay Hebberd/ CORBIS; **1114** Michel Zabe/Art Resource, NY; **1115** Giraudon/Art Resource, NY; **1116** Erich Lessing/Art Resource, NY; **1117** Hugh Sitton/zefa/CORBIS; **1118** (c)Jami Woy/The McGraw-Hill Companies; **1118–1119** (t)brianlatino/Alamy Images; **1119** Jami Woy/The McGraw-Hill Companies; **1120** Private Collection/Bridgeman Art Library; **1122** Museo Casa Diego Rivera (INBA), Guanajuato, Mexico, Index/he Bridgeman Art Library; **1123** (r)Erich Lessing/Art Resource, NY; (l)Kevin Schafer/Getty Images; **1124** Private Collection, Photo ©Boltin Picture Library/Bridgeman Art Library; **1126** British Museum/ Werner Forman Archive/Topham/The Image Works; **1131** Galen Rowell/CORBIS; **1133** Jerry Jacka Photography; **1136** SuperStock; **1138** Adam Woolfitt/CORBIS; **1139** ©1999 Artists Rights Society (ARS)/ADAGP, Paris/Christie's Images; **1140** Mary Evans Picture Library; **1141** The Newark Museum/Art Resource, NY; **1145** Getty Images; **1148** Bildarchiv Preussischer Kulturbesitz/Art Resource, NY; **1150** Museum fur Volkerkunde, Vienna/Bridgeman Art Library; **1153** Michel Zabe/Art Resource, NY; **1154** SuperStock/Alamy Images; **1155** Private Collection, Photo ©Boltin Picture Library/Bridgeman Art Library; **1162** Biblioteca Medicea-Laurenziana, Florence/Bridgeman Art Library; **1163** The Art Archive/Museo Ciudad Mexico/Alfredo Dagli Orti; **1164** Erich Lessing/Art Resource, NY; **1166** Philadelphia Museum of Art/ CORBIS; **1169** Bettmann/CORBIS; **1171** Snark/Art Resource, NY; **1174** CHIP CLARK-SMITHSONIAN; **1175** Time Inc.; **1176** CHIP CLARK-SMITHSONIAN; **1178** (t)Wolfgang Kaehler Photography; (b)Bauer Photography ©2007; **1179** Fred Jones Jr. Museum of Art, University of Oklahoma, USA, Gift of Dr. and Mrs. R. E. Mansfield, 2003/Bridgeman Art Library; **1180** (tl)Private Collection, Photo ©Boltin Picture Library/Bridgeman Art Library; (tr)Nik Wheeler/CORBIS; (c)Jean Pierre Amet/CORBIS SYGMA; (b)Private Collection/Bridgeman Art

Library; **1181** (t)Time & Life Pictures/Getty Images; (cl)Chihuahua City Museum, Mexico, Sean Sprague/Mexicolore/Bridgeman Art Library; (c)Rykoff Collection/CORBIS; (cr)Penni Gladstone/CORBIS; (b)Atlantide Phototravel/CORBIS; **1182** Schalkwijk/Art Resource, NY; **1183** Steve Raymer/CORBIS; **1184** (t)Jon Hicks/CORBIS; (b)Private Collection/Photo: Jorge Contreras Chacel/Bridgeman Art Library; **1185** Wolfgang Kaehler Photography; **1186** Museu Nacional Belas Artes, Rio de Janeiro, Giraudon/Bridgeman Art Library; **1187** Christie's Images; **1188** Jerry Jacka Photography; **1189** Hugh Sitton/zefa/CORBIS; **1190** Nettie Lee Benson Latin American Collection, University of Texas at Austin; **1193** JUPITERIMAGES/Comstock Images/Alamy Images; **1195** Christie's Images; **1199** Lola Alverez Bravo/Writer Pictures; **1201** Schalkwijk/Art Resource, NY; **1202** SuperStock; **1204** Chlaus Lotscher/ Peter Arnold; **1205** Christie's Images/SuperStock; **1209** Tate, London/ Art Resource, NY; **1210** SuperStock, Inc./SuperStock; **1212** Erich Lessing/Art Resource, NY; **1215–1216** Private Collection/Bridgeman Art Library; **1218** Christie's Images/Bridgeman Art Library; **1219** Private Collection, ©DACS/Bridgeman Art Library; **1220** Time & Life Pictures/ Getty Images; **1221** Christie's Images/CORBIS; **1222** INBA/Schalkwijk/ Art Resource, NY; **1224** Private Collection/Bridgeman Art Library; **1226** Christie's Images; **1227** Mark Downey/Getty Images; **1230** Ulla Montan/Writer Pictures; **1232** Art Museum of Estonia, Tallinn/ Bridgeman Art Library; **1235** Kactus Foto, Santiago/SuperStock; **1236** Bridgeman-Giraudon/Art Resource, NY; **1237** (l)Bridgeman-Giraudon/ Art Resource, NY; (r)Historical Picture Archive/CORBIS; **1239** (tl tc)Getty Images; (b)©British Museum/Art Resource, NY; **1243** Colita/ CORBIS; **1245** National Air and Space Museum, Smithsonian Institution. NASM 5008, CAT NO 1975-0095.; **1249** Schalkwijk/Art Resource, NY; **1252** Emiliano Lasalvia/Eniefoto/Writer Pictures; **1254** INBA/Christie's Images; **1257** Zurbaran Galeria, Buenos Aires/ SuperStock; **1261** William J Hebert/Getty Images; **1262** TongRo Image Stock/Alamy Images; **1264** Paul Hawthorne/AP Images; **1267** Daniel Nevins/SuperStock; **1268** colinspics/Alamy Images; **1270** Bridgeman Art Library/SuperStock; **1277** Jeremy Bembaron/CORBIS SYGMA; **1279 1281** Private Collection/Bridgeman Art Library; **1282** ImageSource/PunchStock; **1287** Paul Abdoo/Writer Pictures; **1289** Jerry Jacka Photography; **1293** Carl & Ann Purcell/CORBIS; **1297** Werner Forman/Art Resource, NY; **1300** Michael Newman/PhotoEdit; **1302** Bettmann/CORBIS; **1303** (t c b)The McGraw-Hill Companies; (cl)Colita/CORBIS; **ix** Brooklyn Museum/CORBIS; **vi** Brooklyn Museum of Art, New York, USA, Frank L. Babbott Fund /Bridgeman Art Library; **vii** Christie's Images; **viii** Erich Lessing/Art Resource, NY; **x** Photodisc/ PunchStock; **xi** (tl)Scala/Art Resource, NY; (br)Reed Kaestner/CORBIS; **xii** (t)Scala/Art Resource, NY; (b)Christie's Images; **xiii** Gianni Dagli Orti/CORBIS; **xiv** akg London; **xix** (tl)Erich Lessing/Art Resource, NY; (br)Indochina Arts Partnership; **xv** Jason Horowitz/zefa/CORBIS; **xvi** Private Collection/Bridgeman Art Library; **xvii** Tomb of Qin shi Huang Di, Xianyang, China/Bridgeman Art Library; **xviii** China Photos/Getty Images; **xx** Germanisches Nationalmuseum, Nuremberg/Bridgeman Art Library; **xxi** SuperStock; **xxii** (t)The Art Archive/Musée du Louvre Paris/Gianni Dagli Orti; **xxiii** Digital Image ©The Museum of Modern Art/Licensed by SCALA/Art Resource, NY; **xxiv** (t)British Museum, London/Bridgeman Art Library; (b)Museum fur Volkerkunde, Vienna/ Bridgeman Art Library; **xxv** Private Collection, Photo ©Boltin Picture Library/Bridgeman Art Library; **xxvi** Art Museum of Estonia, Tallinn/ Bridgeman Art Library.